Managerial Economics and Organizational Architecture

The McGraw-Hill Series in Economics

Managerial Economics and Organizational Architecture

Sixth Edition

JAMES A. BRICKLEY

CLIFFORD W. SMITH

JEROLD L. ZIMMERMAN

*William E. Simon Graduate School
of Business Administration*

University of Rochester

Mc
Graw
Hill
Education

MANAGERIAL ECONOMICS AND ORGANIZATIONAL ARCHITECTURE, SIXTH EDITION

Published by McGraw-Hill Education, 2 Penn Plaza, New York, NY 10121.

Some ancillaries, including electronic and print components, may not be
available to customers outside the United States.

This book is printed on acid-free paper.

1 2 3 4 5 6 7 8 9 0 QVS/QVS 1 0 9 8 7 6 5

ISBN 978-0-07-352314-9
MHID 0-07-352314-3

Senior Vice President, Products & Markets:
  Kurt L. Strand
Vice President, General Manager, Products &
  Markets: Marty Lange
Vice President, Content Design & Delivery:
  Kimberly Meriwether David
Managing Director: James Heine
Director, Product Development: Rose Koos
Senior Brand Manager: Katie Hoenicke
Lead Product Developer: Michele Janicek
Senior Product Developer: Christina Kouvelis
Director of Digital Content Development:
  Doug Ruby

Director, Content Design & Delivery:
  Linda Avenarius
Executive Manager: Faye M. Herrig
Content Project Managers: Mary Jane
  Lampe, Sandra Schnee
Buyer: Carol A. Bielski
Cover Design: Studio Montage
Content Licensing Specialist:
  Rita Hingtgen
Cover Image: © Corbis / Glow Images
Compositor: MPS Limited
Typeface: 10.75/12 Adobe Garamond
Printer: Quad/Graphics

Library of Congress Cataloging-in-Publication Data

Brickley, James A.
    Managerial economics and organizational architecture / James A. Brickley, Clifford
W. Smith, Jerold L. Zimmerman, William E. Simon, Graduate School of Business
Administration, University of Rochester.—Sixth edition.
        pages cm.—(The McGraw-Hill series in economics)
    ISBN 978-0-07-352314-9 (alk. paper)
1. Managerial economics. 2. Organizational effectiveness. I. Title.
    HD30.22.B729 2015
    658—dc23
                            2014043202

www.mhhe.com

Dedicated to our children—

London, Nic, Alexander, Taylor, Morgan, Daneille, and Amy.

PREFACE

The past few decades have witnessed spectacular business failures and scandals. In 2001 and 2002, Enron, WorldCom, Arthur Andersen, as well as other prominent companies imploded in dramatic fashion. Internationally, scandals emerged at companies such as Parmalat, Royal Dutch Shell, Samsung, and Royal Ahold. In 2007 and 2008, prominent financial institutions around the world shocked financial markets by reporting staggering losses from subprime mortgages. Société Générale, the large French bank, reported over $7 billion in losses due to potentially fraudulent securities trading by one of its traders. JPMorgan Chase bailed out Bear Stearns, a top-tier investment bank, following their massive subprime losses. Washington Mutual and Lehman Brothers were added to the list of "top business failures of all time."

Due to these cases and others, executives now face a more skeptical investment community, additional government regulations, and stiffer penalties for misleading public disclosures. A common perception is that bad people caused many of these problems. Others argue that the sheer complexity of today's world has made it virtually impossible to be a "good" manager. These views have raised the cry for increased government regulation, which is argued to be a necessary step in averting future business problems.

We disagree with this view. We suggest that many business problems result from poorly structured organizational architectures. The blueprints for many of these prominent business scandals were designed into the firms' "organizational DNA." This book, in addition to covering traditional managerial economic topics, examines how firms can structure organizations that channel managers' incentives into actions that create, rather than destroy, firm value. This topic is critical to anyone who works in or seeks to manage organizations—whether for-profit or not-for-profit.

New Demands: Relevant Yet Rigorous Education

Thirty years ago, teaching managerial economics to business students was truly a "dismal science." Many students dismissed standard economic tools of marginal analysis, production theory, and market structure as too esoteric to have any real relevance to the business problems they anticipated encountering. Few students expected they would be responsible for their prospective employers' pricing decisions. Most sought positions in large firms, eventually hoping to manage finance, operations, marketing, or information systems staffs. Traditional managerial economics courses offered few insights that obviously were relevant for such careers. But a new generation of economists began applying traditional economic tools to problems involving corporate governance, mergers and acquisitions, incentive conflicts, and executive compensation. Their analysis focused on the internal structure of the firm—not on the firm's external markets. In this book, we draw heavily from this research and apply it to how organizations can create value through improved organizational design. In addition, we present traditional economic topics—such as demand, supply, markets, and strategy—in a manner that emphasizes their managerial relevance within today's business environment.

Today's students must understand more than just how markets work and the principles of supply and demand. They also must understand how self-interested parties within organizations interact, and how corporate governance mechanisms can control these interactions. Consequently, today's managerial economics course must cover a broader menu of topics that are now more relevant than ever to aspiring managers facing this post-Enron world. Yet, to best serve our students, offering relevant material must not come at the expense of rigor. Students must learn how to think logically about both markets and organizations. The basic tools of economics offer students the skill set necessary for rigorous analysis of business problems they likely will encounter throughout their careers.

Besides the heightened interest in corporate governance, global competition and rapid technological change are prompting firms to undertake major organizational restructurings as well as to produce fundamental industry realignments. Firms now attack problems with focused, cross-functional teams. Many firms are shifting from functional organizational structures (manufacturing, marketing, and distribution) to flatter, more process-oriented organizations organized around product or region. Moreover, this pace of change shows no sign of slowing. Today's students recognize these issues; they want to develop skills that will make them effective executives and prepare them to manage organizational change.

Business school programs are evolving in response to these changes. Narrow technical expertise within a single functional area—whether operations, accounting, finance, information systems, or marketing—is no longer sufficient. Effective managers within this environment require cross-functional skills. To meet these challenges, business schools are becoming more integrated. Problems faced by managers are not just finance problems, operations problems, or marketing problems. Rather, most business problems involve facets that cut across traditional functional areas. For that reason, the curriculum must encourage students to apply concepts they have mastered across a variety of courses.

This book provides a multidisciplinary, cross-functional approach to managerial and organizational economics. We believe that this is its critical strength. Our interests span economics, finance, accounting, information systems, and financial institutions; this allows us to draw examples from a number of functional areas to demonstrate the power of this underlying economic framework to analyze a variety of problems managers face regularly.

We have been extremely gratified by the reception afforded the first five editions of *Managerial Economics and Organizational Architecture.* Adopters report that the earlier editions helped them transform their courses into one of the most popular courses within their curriculum. This book has been adopted in microeconomics, human resources, and strategy courses in addition to courses that focus specifically on organizational economics. The prior editions were founded on powerful economic tools of analysis that examine how managers can design organizations that motivate self-interested individuals to make choices that increase firm value. Our sixth edition continues to focus on the fundamental importance of markets and organizational design. We use the failures of Enron (Chapter 1), Société Générale (Chapter 1), Arthur Andersen (Chapter 22), and Adelphia (Chapter 10) as case studies to illustrate how poorly designed organizational architectures can be catastrophic. Other books provide little coverage of such managerially critical topics as developing effective organizational architectures, including performance-evaluation systems and compensation plans; assigning decision-making authority among employees; and managing transfer-pricing disputes among divisions. Given the increased importance of corporate governance, this omission has been both significant and problematic. Our primary objective in writing this book is to provide current and aspiring managers with a rigorous, systematic, comprehensive framework for addressing such organizational problems. To that end, we have endeavored to write the underlying theoretical concepts in simple, intuitive terms and illustrate them with numerous examples—most drawn from actual company practice.

The Conceptual Framework

Although the popular press and existing literature on organizations are replete with jargon—TQM, reengineering, outsourcing, teaming, venturing, empowerment, and corporate culture—they fail to provide managers with a systematic, comprehensive framework for examining organizational problems. This book uses economic analysis to develop such a framework and then employs that framework to organize and integrate the important organizational problems, thereby making the topics more accessible.

Throughout the text, readers will gain an understanding of the basic tools of economics and how to apply them to solve important business problems. While the book covers the standard managerial economics problems of pricing and production, it pays special attention to organizational issues. In particular, the book will help readers understand:

- How the business environment (technology, regulation, and competition in input and output markets) drives the firm's choice of strategy.

- How strategy and the business environment affect the firm's choice of organizational design—what we call *organizational architecture*.

- How the firm's organizational architecture is like its DNA; it plays a key role in determining a firm's ultimate success or failure, since it affects how people in the organization will behave in terms of creating or destroying firm value.

- How corporate policies such as strategy, financing, accounting, marketing, information systems, operations, compensation, and human resources are interrelated and thus why it is critically important that they be coordinated.

- How the three key features of organizational architecture—the assignment of decision-making authority, the reward system, and the performance-evaluation system—can be structured to help managers to achieve their desired results.

These three components of organizational architecture are like three legs of the accompanying stool. Firms must coordinate each leg with the other two so that the stool remains functional. Moreover, each firm's architecture must match its strategy; a balanced stool in the wrong setting is dysfunctional: Although milking stools are quite productive in a barn, tavern owners purchase taller stools.

Performance Evaluation (What are the key performance measures used to evaluate managers and employees?)

Decision-Rights Assignment (Who gets to make what decisions?)

Rewards (How are people rewarded for meeting performance goals?)

The components of organizational architecture are like three legs of a stool. It is important that all three legs be designed so that the stool is *balanced*. Changing one leg without the careful consideration of the other two is typically a mistake.

Reasons for Adopting Our Approach

This book focuses on topics that we believe are most relevant to managers. For instance, it provides an in-depth treatment of traditional microeconomic topics (demand, supply, pricing, and game theory) in addition to corporate governance topics (assigning decision-making authority, centralization versus decentralization, measuring and rewarding performance, outsourcing, and transfer pricing). We believe these topics are more valuable to prospective managers than topics typically covered in economics texts such as public-policy aspects of minimum-wage legislation, antitrust policy, and income redistribution. A number of other important features differentiate this book from others currently available, such as:

- Our book provides a comprehensive, cross-functional framework for analyzing organizational problems. We do this by first describing and integrating important research findings published across several functional areas, then demonstrating how to apply the framework to specific organizational problems.

- This text integrates the topics of strategy and organizational architecture. Students learn how elements of the business environment (technology, competition, and regulation) drive the firm's choice of strategy as well as the interaction of strategy choice and organizational architecture.

- Reviewers, instructors, and students found the prior editions accessible and engaging. The text uses intuitive descriptions and simple examples; more technical material is provided in appendices for those who wish to pursue it.

- Numerous examples drawn from the business press and our experiences illustrate the theoretical concepts. For example, the effect of the 9/11 terrorist attacks on demand curves is described in Chapter 4 and how one devastated company located in the World Trade Center responded is discussed in Chapter 14. These illustrations, many highlighted in boxes, reinforce the underlying principles and help the reader visualize the application of more abstract ideas. Each chapter begins with a specific case history that is used throughout the chapter to unify the material and aid the reader in recalling and applying the main constructs.

- Nontraditional economics topics dealing with strategy, outsourcing, leadership, organizational form, corporate ethics, and the implementation of management innovations are examined. Business school curricula often are criticized for being slow in covering topics of current interest to business, such as corporate governance. The last six chapters examine recent management trends and demonstrate how the book's framework can be used to analyze and understand topical issues.

- Problems, both within and at the end of chapter, are drawn from real organizational experience—from the business press as well as our contact with executive MBA students and consulting engagements. We have structured exercises that provide readers with a broad array of opportunities to apply the framework to problems like ones they will encounter as managers.

Organization of the Book

- **Part 1: Basic Concepts** lays the groundwork for the book. Chapter 2 summarizes the economic view of behavior, stressing its management implications. Chapter 3 presents an overview of markets, provides a rationale for the existence of organizations, and stresses the critical role of the distribution of knowledge within the organization.

- **Part 2: Managerial Economics** applies the basic tools of economic theory to the firm. Chapters 4 through 7 cover the traditional managerial-economics topics of demand, production and cost, market structure, and pricing. These four chapters provide the reader with a fundamental set of microeconomic tools and use these tools to analyze basic operational policies such as input, output, and product pricing decisions. Chapters 8 and 9 focus on corporate strategy—the former on creating and capturing values and the latter on employing game theory methods to examine the interaction between the firm and its competitors, suppliers, as well as other parties. These chapters also provide important background material for the subsequent chapters on organizations: A robust understanding of the market environment is important for making sound organizational decisions. Chapter 10 examines conflicts of interest that exist within firms and how contracts can be structured to reduce or control these conflicts.

- **Part 3: Designing Organizational Architecture** develops the core framework of the book. Chapter 11 provides a basic overview of the organizational-design problem. Chapters 12 and 13 focus on two aspects of the assignment of decision rights within the firm—the level of decentralization chosen for various decisions followed by the bundling of various tasks into jobs and then jobs into subunits. Chapters 14 and 15 examine compensation policy. First we focus on the level of compensation necessary to attract and retain an appropriate group of employees. We then discuss the composition of the compensation package, examining how the mix of salary, fringe benefits, and incentive compensation affects the value of the firm. In Chapters 16 and 17, we analyze individual and divisional performance evaluation. Part 3 concludes with a capstone case on Arthur Andersen.
- **Part 4: Applications of Organizational Architecture** uses the framework that we have developed to provide insights into contemporary management issues. Chapters 18 through 23 discuss the legal form of organization, outsourcing, leadership, regulation, ethics, and management innovations.

Fitting the Text into the Business Curriculum

Our book is an effective tool for a variety of classes at the MBA, executive MBA, and undergraduate level. Although this text grew out of an MBA elective course in the economics of organizations at the University of Rochester, the book's modular design allows its use in a variety of courses. We have been encouraged by the creativity instructors have shown in the diversity of courses adopting this text. Besides the introductory microeconomics course, this book also is used in elective courses on corporate governance, strategy, the economics of organizations, and human resources management. The basic material on managerial economics is presented in the first 10 chapters. The tools necessary for understanding and applying the organizational framework we develop within this text have been selected for their managerial relevance. In our experience, these economics tools are invaluable for those students with extensive work experience, and for those who didn't major in economics as an undergraduate. Those with an economics background may choose to forgo components of this material. We have structured our discussions of demand, production/cost, market structure, pricing, and strategy to be optional. Thus, readers who do not require a review of these tools can skip Chapters 4 through 9 without loss of continuity.

We strongly recommend that all readers cover Chapters 1 through 3 and 10; these chapters introduce the underlying tools and framework for the text. Chapters 4 through 9, as we noted above, cover the basic managerial-economics topics of demand, costs, production, market structure, pricing, and strategy. Chapters 11 through 17 develop the organizational architecture framework; we recommend that these be covered in sequence. Finally, Chapters 18 through 23 cover special managerial topics: outsourcing, leadership, regulation, ethics, and the process of management innovation and managing organizational change. They are capstone chapters—chapters that apply and illustrate the framework. Instructors can assign them based on their specific interests and available time.

Sixth Edition

This book is noted for using economics to analyze real-world management problems. The sixth edition maintains and extends this focus. Changes from the fifth edition include:

- Learning objectives have been added to focus on the core concepts of the chapter to aid in the assessment of learning outcomes.

- Extended and more in-depth coverage of important managerial economics concepts, including supply and demand analysis, comparative advantage, constant versus increasing cost industries, price competition with differentiated products, inter-temporal decisions (Fisher Separation Theorem) and behavioral economics.

- Managerial applications, examples, exhibits, and other boxed materials have been updated.

- Key managerial insights from important recent research in organizational economics have been added.

- Data has been updated, where appropriate.

- We have responded in various ways to reader feedback from earlier editions.

Supplements

The following ancillaries are available for quick download and convenient access via the Instructor Library material available through McGraw-Hill Connect®.

- **PowerPoint Presentations:** Fully updated for the sixth edition, each chapter's PowerPoint slides are closely tied to the book material and are enhanced by animated graphs. You can edit, print, or rearrange the slides to fit the needs of your course.

- **Test Bank:** The test bank offers hundreds of questions categorized by level of difficulty, AACSB learning categories, Bloom's taxonomy, and topic.

- **Computerized Test Bank:** McGraw-Hill's EZ Test is a flexible and easy-to-use electronic resting program that allows you to create tests from book-specific items. It accommodates a wide range of question types and you can add your own questions. Multiple versions of the test can be created and any test can be exported for use with course management systems. EZ Test Online gives you a place to administer your EZ Test-created exams and quizzes online. Additionally, you can access the test bank through McGraw-Hill *Connect*®.

- **Instructor's Manual:** The instructor's Manual provides chapter overviews, teaching tips, and suggested answers to the end-of-chapter Self-Evaluation Problems and Review Questions.

Digital Solutions

McGraw-Hill Connect® Economics

connect |ECONOMICS **Less Managing. More Teaching. Greater Learning.**

McGraw-Hill's *Connect® Economics* is an online assessment solution that connects students with the tools and resources they'll need to achieve success.

McGraw-Hill's *Connect Economics* Features

Connect Economics allows faculty to create and deliver exams easily with selectable test bank items. Instructors can also build their own questions into the system for homework or practice. Other features include:

Instructor Library The *Connect Economics* Instructor Library is your repository for additional resources to improve student engagement in and out of class. You can select and use any asset that enhances your lecture. The *Connect Economics* Instructor Library includes all of the instructor supplements for this text.

Student Resources Any supplemental resources that align with the text for student use will be available through Connect.

Student Progress Tracking *Connect Economics* keeps instructors informed about how each student, section, and class is performing, allowing for more productive use of lecture and office hours. The progress-tracking function enables you to:

- View scored work immediately and track individual or group performance with assignment and grade reports.

- Access an instant view of student or class performance relative to learning objectives.

- Collect data and generate reports required by many accreditation organizations, such as AACSB.

- Connect Insight is a powerful data analytics tool that allows instructors to leverage aggregated information about their courses and students to provide a more personalized teaching and learning experience.

Diagnostic and Adaptive Learning of Concepts: LearnSmart and SmartBook offer the first and only adaptive reading experience designed to change the way students read and learn.

LEARNSMART® Students want to make the best use of their study time. The LearnSmart adaptive self-study technology within *Connect Economics* provides students with a seamless combination of practice, assessment, and remediation for every concept in the textbook. LearnSmart's intelligent software adapts to every student response and automatically delivers concepts that advance students' understanding while reducing time devoted to the concepts already mastered. The result for every student is the fastest path to mastery of the chapter concepts. LearnSmart:

- Applies an intelligent concept engine to identify the relationships between concepts and to serve new concepts to each student only when he or she is ready.

- Adapts automatically to each student, so students spend less time on the topics they understand and practice more those they have yet to master.

- Provides continual reinforcement and remediation, but gives only as much guidance as students need.

- Integrates diagnostics as part of the learning experience.

- Enables you to assess which concepts students have efficiently learned on their own, thus freeing class time for more applications and discussion.

SMARTBOOK® Smartbook is an extension of LearnSmart—an adaptive eBook that helps students focus their study time more effectively. As students read, Smartbook assesses comprehension and dynamically highlights where they need to study more.

For more information about Connect, go to **http://connect.mheducation.com**, or contact your local McGraw-Hill sales representative.

McGraw-Hill's Customer Experience Group

We understand that getting the most from your new technology can be challenging. That's why our services don't stop after you purchase our products. You can e-mail our Product Specialists 24 hours a day to get product-training online. Or you can search our knowledge bank of Frequently Asked Questions on our support website. For Customer Support, call **800-331-5094**, or visit **www.mhhe.com/support**.

Create

create™ McGraw-Hill Create™ is a self-service website that allows you to create customized course materials using McGraw-Hill's comprehensive, cross-disciplinary content and digital products. You can even access third party content such as readings, articles, cases, videos, and more. Arrange the content you've selected to match the scope and sequence of your course. Personalize your book with a cover design and choose the best format for your students—eBook, color print, or black-and-white print. And, when you are done, you'll receive a PDF review copy in just minutes!

CourseSmart

VitalSource CourseSmart® Go paperless with eTextbooks from CourseSmart and move light years beyond traditional print textbooks. Read online or offline anytime, anywhere. Access your eTextbook on multiple devices with or without an Internet connection. CourseSmart eBooks include convenient, built-in tools that let you search topics quickly, add notes and highlights, copy/paste passages, and print any page.

ACKNOWLEDGMENTS

No textbook springs from virgin soil. This book has its intellectual roots firmly planted in the work of dozens who have toiled to develop, test, and apply organization theory. As we detailed in the preface to the first edition, the genesis of this book was a course William Meckling and Michael Jensen taught on the economics of organizations at the University of Rochester in the 1970s. Bill's and Mike's research and teaching stimulated our interest in the economics of organizations, prompted much of our research focused on organizational issues, and had a profound effect on this text. No amount of citation or acknowledgments can adequately reflect the encouragement and stimulation that they provided, both personally and through their writings.

Bill and Mike emphasized three critical features of organizational design: (1) the assignment of decision rights within the organization, (2) the reward system, and (3) the performance-evaluation system. These three elements, which we call *organizational architecture,* serve as an important organizing device for this book. As readers will discover, this structure offers a rich body of knowledge useful for managerial decision making.

Important contributions to the literature on the economics of organizations have been made by a host of scholars. Through the work of these individuals, we have learned a tremendous amount. A number of our colleagues at Rochester also contributed to the development of the book. Ray Ball, Rajiv Dewan, Shane Heitzman, Scott Keating, Stacey Kole, Andy Leone, Glenn MacDonald, Larry Matteson, David Mayers, Kevin Murphy, Michael Raith, Mike Ryall, Greg Schaffer, Ronald Schmidt, Larry Van Horn, Karen Van Nuys, Ross Watts, Gerald Wedig, Michael Weisbach, and Ron Yeaple offered thoughtful comments and suggestions that helped to clarify our thinking on key issues. Don Chew, editor of the *Journal of Applied Corporate Finance,* provided invaluable assistance in publishing a series of articles based on the book; his assistance in writing these articles improved the exposition of this book enormously. Our collaboration with Janice Willett on *Designing Organizations to Create Value: From Strategy to Structure* (McGraw-Hill, 2003) enriched our understanding and exposition of many important topics.

This project also has benefited from an extensive development effort. In addition to generations of Simon School students, dozens of colleagues both in the United States and overseas formally reviewed the manuscript and gave us detailed feedback, for which we are very grateful. We offer our sincere thanks to following reviewers, for their thorough and thoughtful suggestions:

Avner Ben-Ner, *University of Minnesota*
Arnab Biswas, *University of West Florida*
Ben Campbell, *The Ohio State University*
Xiujian Chen, *Binghampton University*
Kwang Soo Cheong, *John Hopkins University*
Abbas Grammy, *California State University—Bakersfield*
Charles Gray, *University of Saint Thomas*
Folke Kafka, *University of Pittsburgh*
Brian Kench, *University of Tampa*
Tom Lee, *California State University—Northridge*
Matthew Metzgar, *University of North Carolina*
Ronald Necoechea, *Roberts Wesleyan College*
Harlan Platt, *Northeastern University*

Farhad Rassekh, *University of Hartford*
Amit Sen, *Xavier University*
Richard Smith, *University of California—Riverside*
Neil Younkin, *Saint Xavier University*

We owe special thanks to Henry Butler, Luke Froeb, Mel Gray, and Chris James; each provided insightful comments on the material. In addition, we are grateful for feedback from over 500 individuals who completed various surveys. Their thoughts served to guide our refinement of this work. We appreciate the efforts of Kathleen DeFazio who provided secretarial support. Finally, we wish to thank our colleagues at McGraw-Hill/Irwin—especially Mike Junior—for their encouragement to pursue this project. Through their vision and publishing expertise, they provided us with insights and feedback to help expand our audience while adhering to our mission.

This book represents the current state of the art. Nonetheless, development is ongoing as the research evolves and as we continue to learn. *Managerial Economics and Organizational Architecture* covers an exciting, dynamic area. We hope that a small portion of that excitement is communicated through this text. Reviewers, instructors, and students frequently mention the relevance of material to the business community, the accessibility of the text, and the logical flow within the text's framework. However, in the final analysis, it is instructors and their students who will determine the true value of our efforts.

We appreciate the extensive feedback we have received from many readers; their generous comments have improved this edition substantially. Although we had a definite objective in mind as we wrote this book, it is important to be open to suggestions and willing to learn from others who are traveling a similar yet distinct path. Although we are unlikely to please everyone, we will continue to evaluate suggestions critically and to be responsive where consistent with our mission. If readers would like to share their thoughts on this work or their classroom experiences, please feel free to contact any of us at the University of Rochester. Many thanks in advance for the assistance.

jim.brickley@simon.rochester.edu
cliff.smith@simon.rochester.edu
jerry.zimmerman@simon.rochester.edu

Contents in Brief

*These Web chapters and the Glossary can be found online via the Instructor Library material available through McGraw-Hill *Connect*®.

Contents

Part 1: Basic Concepts

Part 2: Managerial Economics

Part 3: Designing Organizational Architecture

Part 4: Applications of Organizational Architecture

Introduction

LEARNING OBJECTIVES

1. Define organizational architecture and discuss how economics can be used to help managers solve organizational problems and structure more effective organizational architectures.

2. Define Economic Darwinism and discuss its implications related to the benchmarking of business practices.

Enron Corporation was created in 1985 by the merger of two gas pipeline companies. Convinced that impending deregulation of the energy business would create opportunities for firms with the vision to recognize and the willingness to exploit them, Enron moved aggressively to build and implement an innovative business model. It was a pioneer in the trading of derivative securities tied to assets like natural gas, electricity, and coal. In its transformation from a traditional, capital-intensive gas pipeline company, it established a dramatically smaller reliance on hard assets, a flatter management structure, and an entrepreneurial, risk-taking environment—one that was quite open to creative and unconventional products and practices. It garnered tremendous recognition for these accomplishments; for six years in a row, it was named "Most Innovative" among *Fortune*'s Most Admired Companies list.

By 2000, Enron operated in several different business segments: *transportation and distribution,* supplying gas and electric transmission services; *wholesale services,* providing energy services and other products to energy suppliers and other firms; *retail services,* offering business customers energy products and services; *broadband services,* providing various service providers with access to a fiber-optic cable network; and *other businesses,* including water resources and wind energy. In 1990, 80 percent of Enron's revenues came from its regulated gas pipeline business, but by 2000, over 90 percent of revenues came from its wholesale energy operations and services segment. Enron's management argued that vertically integrated giants—like ExxonMobil, whose balance sheet was awash with oil reserves, gas stations, refineries, and other hard assets—were dinosaurs. "In the old days, people worked for the assets," said CEO Jeffrey Skilling. "We've turned it around—what we've said is the assets work for the people."

To finance this rapidly expanding array of businesses Enron relied on its bright young CFO, Andrew Fastow. In addition to tapping traditional sources of debt and equity capital, Fastow made extensive use of sophisticated partnerships whose financing details were kept off Enron's balance sheet.[1] For example, to finance its water business, Enron formed Azurix Corporation and raised $695 million by selling one-third of the company to public investors. Enron also formed a partnership called the Atlantic Water Trust in which it held a 50 percent stake. Enron's partner was Marlin Water Trust, which was marketed to institutional investors. To help attract lenders, Enron guaranteed the debt with its own stock: If Enron's credit rating fell below investment grade and the stock fell below a stipulated price, Enron itself would be responsible for the partnership's $915 million debt.

So long as Enron prospered, these guarantees appeared to cost the company little. But several of Enron's business segments began to experience significant problems. In late summer of 2000, a power shortage in California resulted in blackouts. Enron (along with other energy companies) was blamed by state politicians: California launched an investigation into price gouging by Enron and other power marketers. Enron's investment in water concessions in Brazil and England ran into political obstacles. For instance, British regulators cut the rates that it was allowed to charge its customers. Enron had a 65 percent stake in a $3 billion power project in India. But the power plant became embroiled in a dispute with its largest customer, who refused to pay for electricity. Following the September 11, 2001, terrorist attacks, the precipitous fall in oil prices generated losses for Enron's trading operations, and technology changes produced a glut of broadband services.

After reaching a peak of nearly $70 billion in August 2000, Enron's market value collapsed. Its bankruptcy filing in December 2001 is one of the most spectacular business failures ever seen.[2] November 2004 saw it emerge from one of the most complex bankruptcies in U.S. history. After 2006 Enron existed as an assetless shell corporation.

What went wrong? According to *BusinessWeek,*

> *Enron didn't fail just because of improper accounting or alleged corruption at the top. . . . The unrelenting emphasis on earnings growth and individual initiative, coupled with a shocking absence of the usual corporate checks and balances, tipped the culture from one that rewarded aggressive strategy to one that increasingly relied on unethical corner cutting. In the end, too much leeway was given to young, inexperienced managers without the necessary controls to minimize failures. This was a company that simply placed a lot of bad bets on businesses that weren't so promising to begin with.*

Thus, *BusinessWeek* suggests, Enron's problems were rooted in a fundamentally flawed organizational design. At fault were three key aspects of the company's corporate structure. First, in the course of flattening its management structure, Enron delegated an extraordinary level of decision-making authority to lower-level employees without retaining an appropriate degree of oversight. Second, performance was evaluated largely on near-term earnings growth and success in closing deals. Third, the company offered enormous compensation to its top performers, which encouraged excessive risk taking. Enron's internal risk management group was charged with reviewing deals, but the performance appraisals of the 180 employees within the group were based in part on the recommendations of the very people who

---

[1] It should be noted that Fastow was recognized by *CFO Magazine* in October 1999 with their CFO Excellence Award for Capital Structure Management.

[2] While the largest U.S. corporate bankruptcy at the time, Enron is now far from the largest. Lehman Brothers ($691 billion in 2008), Washington Mutual ($327 billion in 2008), WorldCom ($103.9 billion in 2002), General Motors ($91 billion in 2009 and CIT Group ($80.4 billion in 2009) were all greater in size.

generated the deals. Enron's problems appear to stem, at least in part, from its organizational design.

Managerial Economics and Organizational Architecture

Standard managerial economics books address a number of questions that are important for organizational success:

- Which markets will the firm enter?
- How differentiated will the firm's products be?
- What mix of inputs should the firm use in its production?
- How should the firm price its products?
- Who are the firm's competitors, and how are they likely to respond to the firm's product offerings?

Addressing these questions is certainly important—and in this book, we do—yet this tale of Enron's implosion suggests that this list is woefully incomplete. It is also important to address questions about the internal organization of the firm. A poorly designed organization can result in lost profits and even in the failure of the institution.

With the benefit of hindsight, it seems easy to identify elements of Enron's organization that, if changed, might have reduced the likelihood of its collapse. But the critical managerial question is whether before the fact one reasonably could be expected to identify the potential problems and to structure more productive organizations. We believe the answer to this fundamental managerial question is a resounding yes. To examine these issues, a rich framework that can be applied consistently is required.

We are not, of course, the first to recognize the importance of corporate organization or to offer analysis of how to improve it. The business section of any good bookstore displays a virtually endless array of prescriptions: *benchmarking, empowerment, total quality management, reengineering, outsourcing, teaming, corporate culture, venturing, matrix organizations, just-in-time production, and downsizing.* The authors of all these books would strongly agree that the firm's organization and the associated policies, adopted by management, can have profound effects on performance and firm value; and all buttress their recommendations with selected stories of firms that followed their advice and realized fabulous successes.

The problem with such approaches, however, is that each tends to focus on a particular facet of the organization—whether it be quality control, or worker empowerment, or the compensation system—to the virtual exclusion of all others. As a consequence, the suggestions offered by the business press are regularly myopic. These publications tend to offer little guidance as to which tools are most appropriate in which circumstances. The implicit assumption of most is that their technique can be successfully adopted by all companies. This presumption, however, is invariably wrong. Ultimately, this literature fails to provide managers with a productive framework for identifying and resolving organizational problems.

Organizational Architecture

In contrast to the approach of most business best sellers, we seek to provide a systematic framework for analyzing such issues—one that can be applied consistently in addressing organizational problems and structuring more effective organizations.

In this book, we offer a framework that identifies three critical aspects of corporate organization:

- The assignment of decision rights within the company
- The methods of rewarding individuals
- The structure of systems to evaluate the performance of both individuals and business units

Not coincidentally, these are the same three aspects of the organization we identified in the Enron case.

We introduce the term *organizational architecture* to refer specifically to these three key aspects of the firm. We hesitate to simply use "organization" to refer to these three corporate features because common usage of that term refers only to the organization's hierarchical structure—that is, decision-right assignments and reporting relationships—while it generally ignores the performance-evaluation and reward systems. We thus use organizational architecture to help focus specific attention on all three of these critical aspects of the organization.

Stated as briefly as possible, our argument is that successful firms assign decision rights in ways that effectively link decision-making authority with the relevant information for making good decisions. When assigning decision rights, however, senior leadership—including both management and the company's Board of Directors—must also ensure that the company's reward and performance-evaluation systems provide decision makers with appropriate incentives to make value-increasing decisions.

Depending on its specific circumstances, the firm will assign decision-making authority differently (some will decentralize particular decisions but centralize others) and will tailor its reward and performance-evaluation systems. Even though no two firms might adopt precisely the same architecture, successful firms ensure that these three critical aspects of organizational architecture are coordinated.

Our approach is integrative in the sense that it draws on a number of disciplines: accounting, finance, information systems, marketing, management, operations, political science, and strategy. But what also distinguishes our approach most clearly from that of the best sellers is our central reliance on the basic principles of economics.

Economic Analysis

Economics long has been applied to questions of pricing policy—for example, "how would raising the price of the firm's products affect sales and firm value?" We address standard managerial-economics questions involving pricing, advertising, scale, and the choice of inputs to employ in production. In addition, we apply these same tools to examine questions of organizational architecture. For example, "how would changing a division from a cost center to a profit center change incentives, alter employee decisions, and impact firm value?"

In essence, economics provides a theory to explain the way individuals make choices. For example, in designing organizations, it is important to keep in mind that individuals respond to incentives. Managers and employees can be incredibly resourceful in devising methods to exploit the opportunities they face. This also means, however, that when their incentives are structured inappropriately, they can act in ways that reduce the firm's value. In choosing corporate policies, it is critical that managers anticipate potential responses by customers, suppliers, or employees that might produce undesirable outcomes. Neglecting to do so invites individuals to "game" the system and can result in utter failure of well-intentioned policies.

R&D and Executive Turnover

Suppose a firm links the CEO's bonus to earnings and the CEO plans to retire in two years. The CEO might reduce the firm's research and development budget to boost earnings this year and next. Five years down the road, earnings will suffer with no new products coming on stream. By then, however, this CEO will be long gone. In fact, research suggests that this can be a problem for some R&D-intensive firms.

Source: P. Dechow and R. Sloan (1991), "Executive Incentives and the Horizon Problem," *Journal of Accounting and Economics* 14, 51–89.

We use economics to examine how managers can design organizations that motivate individuals to make choices that will increase a firm's value. For example, the evidence suggests that the problem highlighted in the accompanying box on chief executive officers slashing R&D budgets prior to their retirement is not widespread.[3] The research suggests that these perverse incentives can be controlled by basing the CEO's incentive compensation on stock prices and by managing CEO succession, so that decision rights are gradually transferred to the successor over the years prior to the final departure. Moreover, CEOs' postretirement opportunities for election to board seats appear linked to performance over the final years of their tenure.[4]

Standard economic analysis generally characterizes the firm simply as a "black box" that transforms inputs (labor, capital, and raw materials) into outputs. Little consideration traditionally has been given to the internal architecture of the firm.[5] In recent years, economists have focused more on questions of organizational architecture.[6] But little effort has been devoted to synthesizing the material in an accessible form that emphasizes the managerial implications of the analysis. We apply the basic tools of economics to examine the likely effect on a firm's value of decisions such as centralization versus decentralization, the bundling of tasks into specific jobs and jobs into business units within the firm, the use of objective versus subjective performance measures, compensating employees through fixed versus variable (or "incentive") compensation, and retaining activities within the firm versus outsourcing. In sum, we examine how managers can structure organizational architecture to motivate individuals to make choices that increase the firm's value.

[3]K. Murphy and J. Zimmerman (1993), "Financial Performance Surrounding CEO Turnover," *Journal of Accounting and Economics* 16, 273–315.

[4]J. Brickley, J. Linck, and J. Coles (1999), "What Happens to CEOs after They Retire? New Evidence on Career Concerns, Horizon Problems, and CEO Incentives," *Journal of Financial Economics* 52, 341–378.

[5]Of course, there are several notable exceptions: F. Knight (1921), *Risk, Uncertainty, and Profit* (London School of Economics: London); R. Coase (1937), "The Nature of the Firm," *Economica* 4, 386–405; and F. Hayek (1945), "The Use of Knowledge in Society," *American Economic Review* 35, 519–530.

[6]For example, R. Coase (1960), "The Problem of Social Cost," *Journal of Law and Economics* 3, 1–44; S. Cheung (1969), "Transaction Costs, Risk Aversion, and the Choice of Contractual Arrangements," *Journal of Law and Economics* 12, 23–42; A. Alchian and H. Demsetz (1972), "Production, Information Costs, and Economic Organization," *American Economic Review* 62, 777–795; K. Arrow (1974), *The Limits of Organization* (W. W. Norton: New York); M. Jensen and W. Meckling (1976), "Theory of the Firm: Managerial Behavior, Agency Costs and Ownership Structure," *Journal of Financial Economics* 3, 305–360; Y. Barzel (1982), "Measurement Costs and the Organization of Markets," *Journal of Law and Economics* 25, 27–48; O. Williamson (1985), *The Economic Institutions of Capitalism: Firms, Markets, Rational Contracting* (Free Press: New York); and B. Holmstrom and J. Tirole (1989), "The Theory of the Firm," in R. Schmalensee and R. Willig (Eds.), *Handbook of Industrial Economics* (North-Holland: New York).

MANAGERIAL APPLICATIONS

Economic Incentives and the Subprime Mortgage Crisis

"Subprime mortgages" are made to borrowers who do not qualify for standard market interest rates because of problems with their credit histories or inability to prove that they have enough income to support the monthly payments. In March 2007, the value of U.S. subprime mortgages was estimated at $1.3 trillion with over 7.5 million mortgages outstanding. During the second half of 2007, investors in subprime mortgages such as banks, mortgage lenders, real estate investment trusts, and hedge funds reported losses of close to $100 billion as a result of subprime mortgage defaults and devaluations. The stock market fell and became quite volatile as more details about the mortgage crisis were revealed over time.

One important factor that contributed to this crisis was the incentives of the mortgage brokers that originated the loans. Mortgage brokers, who originated nearly 70 percent of residential mortgages in recent years, don't lend their own money. They are paid for originating loans, which are sold to other investors who bear the primary risk. In many cases, the more loans they originate, the higher their compensation.

The financial incentives for originating mortgages motivated financial companies to offer products that made it easier for borrowers to qualify for the loans. For example, companies began offering "stated income loans" that required no proof of income. Consistent with the theory in this book, some borrowers overstated their incomes. In a recent review of 100 of these so-called liar loans, almost 60 percent of the stated amounts were exaggerated by over 50 percent. For example, in Atlanta a borrower received a $1.8 million loan by stating that he and his wife were top executives at a marketing firm who earned more than $600,000 per year with personal assets totaling $3 million. In reality, he was a phone company technician who earned $105,000 per year with savings of only $35,000.

The financial incentives and associated lack of controls produced not only risky loans but also billions of dollars of fraud. Rings of fraudulent borrowers would (1) recruit people with good credit to apply for very large loans using false income and asset statements, (2) find home appraisers to significantly inflate the values of the underlying properties, (3) pay the much lower asking prices to the sellers, and (4) pocket the difference, splitting the proceeds among the members of the ring. The houses then would go into foreclosure as the loans were not repaid.

Banking executives subsequently testified that they did not foresee this problem—"fraud was not really a consideration in our world." The premise of this book is that a careful analysis of the underlying organizational architecture (incentives and decision-right assignments) can help managers anticipate these types of problems and develop mechanisms to reduce their severity.

Source: M. Corkery (2007), "Fraud Seen as a Driver in Wave of Foreclosures," *The Wall Street Journal* (December 21), A1.

In this analysis, ideas of equilibrium—the interplay of supply and demand in product, labor, and capital markets—represent important constraints on managerial decisions. Understanding how prices and quantities change in response to changes in costs, product characteristics, or the terms of sale is a critical managerial skill. For example, the more than five-fold increase in crude oil prices from below $12 per barrel in 1999 to over $135 in 2008 prompted oil companies to

---

MANAGERIAL APPLICATIONS

Creative Responses to a Poorly Designed Incentive System

A manager at a software company wanted to find and fix software bugs more quickly. He devised an incentive plan that paid $20 for each bug the Quality Assurance people found and $20 for each bug the programmers fixed. Since the programmers who created the bugs were also in charge of fixing them, they responded to the plan by creating bugs in software programs. This action increased their payoffs under the plan—there were more bugs to detect and fix. The plan was canceled within a single week after one employee netted $1,700 under the new program.

Source: S. Adams (1995), "Manager's Journal: The Dilbert Principle," *The Wall Street Journal* (May 22), A12.

increase production, encouraged petrochemical companies to alter their input mix to economize on a now-more-expensive input, made salespeople reevaluate their decisions about contacting potential customers by phone rather than in person, and encouraged auto producers to focus more on gas economy in the design of new models. Yet these incentives to change depend on the structure of the organization. For instance, a salesperson is less likely to switch to greater reliance on telephone and mail when the firm reimburses all selling expenses than when salespeople are responsible for the costs of contacting potential customers.

Economic Darwinism

Survival of the Fittest[7]

The collapse of Enron, Charles Darwin might have noted, is an example of how competition tends to weed out the less fit. As described in *The Origin of Species,* natural history illustrates the principle of "survival of the fittest." In industry, we see *economic Darwinism* in operation as competition weeds out ill-designed organizations that fail to adapt. Competition in the marketplace provides strong pressures for efficient decisions—including organizational decisions. Competition among firms dictates that those firms with low costs are more likely to survive. If firms adopt inefficient, high-cost policies—including their organizational architecture—competition will place strong pressures on these firms to either adapt or close.

Fama and Jensen suggest that "the form of organization that survives in an activity is the one that delivers the product demanded by customers at the lowest price while covering costs." This survival criterion helps highlight that while a well-crafted organizational architecture can contribute to a firm's success, it is not sufficient for success. The firm must have a business strategy that includes products for which the prices customers are willing to pay exceed costs. The potential for value creation by a company that manufactures only buggy whips is quite limited no matter how well structured the firm's organizational architecture.

Nonetheless, given a firm's business strategy (including its product mix), its choice of organizational architecture can have an important impact on profitability and value. An appropriate architecture can lower costs by promoting efficient production; it also can boost the prices customers are willing to pay by helping to ensure high-quality production, reliable delivery, and responsive service.

Economic Darwinism and Benchmarking

In the biological systems that Darwin analyzed, the major forces at work were random mutations in organisms and shocks from the external environment (for instance, from changes in weather). But in the economic systems on which we focus, purposeful voluntary changes occur. For instance, in order to compete more effectively with Coke, Pepsi copied many of Coke's practices. Pepsi spun off its fast-food chains

---

[7]This section draws on A. Alchian (1950), "Uncertainty, Evolution, and Economic Theory," *Journal of Political Economy* 58, 211–221; G. Stigler (1951), "The Economics of Scale," *Journal of Law and Economics* 1, 54–71; and E. Fama and M. Jensen (1983), "Separation of Ownership and Control," *Journal of Law and Economics* 26, 301–325.

MANAGERIAL APPLICATIONS

Economic Darwinism: The Growth in Lead Directors

The collapse of Enron in December 2001 and subsequent scandals at Adelphia, Tyco, WorldCom, and other companies in 2002 shook public confidence in corporate governance. In July 2002, the United States enacted the Sarbanes–Oxley Act, which mandated substantial changes in corporate accounting and governance practices. Additional scandals and failures during the 2007–2008 financial crisis raised additional concerns about corporate governance and motivated additional legislation and regulation.

These events altered the basic business environment for publicly traded corporations. Over the past decade, investors, regulators, stock exchanges, the media and the general public have placed increased pressure on corporate boards of directors to become more independent and diligent in their monitoring of CEOs. One important trend in corporate governance has been the large increase in presiding and lead directors. Presiding directors are independent directors (a director with no other direct ties to the company or corporate management) who chair executive sessions of outside directors. Lead directors are more powerful, taking on additional responsibilities (such as serving as the principal liaison between the independent directors and the CEI and taking the lead role in overseeing formal evaluations of board members and the CEO). In 2003, only 36 percent of S&P 500 firms had presiding or lead directors, compared to 90 percent in 2013. Over 60 percent of the S&P 500 firms with presiding or lead directors in 2013 employed the more powerful position of lead director.

If you were to benchmark the current governance practices of large publicly traded corporations, you would find the appointment of a lead director is a dominant surviving practice in the current business environment. "One size," however, is unlikely to fit all firms. Managers should not simply adopt the prevailing organizational practices of other firms. More careful analysis is required.

Source: Spencer Stuart (2013), "Spencer Stuart Board Index 2013," www.spencerstuart.com.

(Taco Bell, KFC, and Pizza Hut) to focus on its core business—just as Coca Cola had done. Also, Pepsi changed its network of bottlers. One analyst remarked, "Pepsi is starting to look a lot more like Coke."[8] In fact, this practice has been formalized in the process of *benchmarking*.

Benchmarking generally means looking at those companies that are doing something best and learning how they do it in order to emulate them. But this process also occurs in less formal ways. As Armen Alchian argued, "Whenever successful enterprises are observed, the elements common to those observed successes will be associated with success and copied by others in their pursuit of profits or success."[9] For example, if the cover article in the next *Fortune* reports an innovative inventory control system at Toyota, managers across the country—indeed, around the globe—will read it and ask, *Would that work in my company, too?* Undoubtedly, the managers with the strongest interest in trying it will be those within firms currently suffering inventory problems.[10] Some will achieve success, but others may experience disastrous results caused by unintended though largely predictable organizational "side effects" (like Fastow's unchecked incentive for risk taking).

---

[8]N. Harris (1997), "If You Can't Beat 'Em, Copy 'Em," *BusinessWeek* (November), 50.

[9]A. Alchian. "Uncertainty, Evolution, and Economic Theory," *The Journal of Political Economy*, Vol. 58, No. 3 (Jun., 1950), p. 218.

[10]This raises the question of why any firm with an innovative idea would voluntarily disclose it. Perhaps the free publicity outweighs the lost competitive advantage.

MANAGERIAL APPLICATIONS

Organizing Xerox Service Center

Xerox has developed an expert system to assist employees who answer the company service center's 800 number to help callers who have problems with their photocopy machines. The system is designed to lead the employee through a set of questions to diagnose and fix the problem. If the machine operator cannot fix the problem with the assistance of the input from the service center employee, a service representative is dispatched to make a service call. This expert system is designed to evolve more effective prompts as experience accumulates. This will be accomplished by having service representatives call the service center after a service call. The nature of the problem and the actions taken are to be entered into the system. Xerox bases pay for the individuals who answer the 800 number on the number of service calls they handle; it bases compensation for service representatives on the number of service calls they make. Discuss the incentives these compensation practices create.

Although competition tends to produce efficiently organized firms over the longer run, uncritical experimentation with the organizational innovation *du jour* can expose the firm to an uncomfortably high risk of failure. Organizational change is expensive. Moreover, successful organizations are not just a collection of "good ideas." The elements of a successful organization must be carefully coordinated: The different elements of the firm's architecture must be structured to work together to achieve the firm's goals. For this reason, it is important to be able to analyze the likely consequences of a contemplated organizational change and forecast its impact on the entire firm.

This concept of economic Darwinism thus has important managerial implications. First, existing architectures are not random; there are sound economic explanations for the dominant organization of firms in most industries. Second, surviving architectures at any point in time are optimal in a *relative* rather than an *absolute* sense; that is, they are the best among the competition—not necessarily the best possible. Third, if the environment in which the firm operates changes—if technology, competition, or regulation change—then the appropriate organizational architecture normally changes as well. These three observations together suggest that although improvements in architecture are certainly always possible, a manager should resist condemning prevailing structures without careful analysis. Before undertaking major changes, executives should have a good understanding of how the firm arrived at its existing architecture and, more generally, develop a broader perspective of why specific types of organizations work well in particular settings. Finally, an executive should be particularly skeptical of claimed benefits of proposed organizational changes if the environment has been relatively stable.

Purpose of the Book

The primary thrust of this book is to provide a solid conceptual framework for analyzing organizational problems and structuring an effective organizational architecture. The book also provides basic material on managerial economics and discusses how it can be used for making operational decisions—for example, input, output, and pricing decisions. This material additionally supplies a set of tools and an understanding of markets, that is, important for making good organizational decisions.

MANAGERIAL APPLICATIONS

Transfers of Organizational Architecture across the Global Economy

In 1996, Tianjin Optical & Electrical Communication Group was typical of a Chinese state-owned company. Although the electronics manufacturer boasted skilled technicians, mismanagement left the company at the brink of bankruptcy. Motorola, Inc., changed that. It offered to take Tianjin Optical as a supplier, but only if Tianjin adopted the U.S. telecommunications company's quality-control and management practices. By 1999, Tianjin Optical was selling a third of its production to Motorola and reported a small profit. "Now, we think we can survive," says Zhang Bingjun, Tianjin Optical's chairman.

Each Tianjin employee receives an average of two weeks a year in classroom instruction stressing modern management practices. That effort has paid off: The Tianjin assembly lines produce a slim cellular phone every $2\frac{1}{2}$ seconds with virtually the same defect rate as in Motorola's U.S. plants. Motorola also provides training for more than 100 outside suppliers to boost the quality of their output. Motorola budgets about $2 million annually to "show [potential suppliers] Western management practices and create a mindset where they understand what we're doing and why," says a training director, Ying Shea.

This assistance in establishing a more effective organizational architecture and internal operating policies provided by a U.S. multinational corporation to its Chinese partners is but one example of the vital role that foreign businesses play within the Chinese business sector. Since China opened itself to foreign investment three decades ago, foreign companies have become an important conduit for economic reform. They have introduced not just modern production technology but also more efficient organizational architecture to the Chinese business community. Some estimates suggest that including these collateral benefits, foreign firms and their joint ventures account for as much as a fifth of China's trillion-dollar economy.

Source: E. Guyot (1999), "Foreign Companies Bring China More Than Jobs," *The Wall Street Journal* (September 15), A26.

Our Approach to Organizations

We begin with two basic notions: People act in their own self-interest, and individuals do not all share the same information. As we have indicated, this framework suggests that the three critical elements of organizational architecture are the assignment of decision rights, the reward system, and the performance-evaluation system. Successful organizations assign decision rights in a manner that effectively links decision-making authority with the relevant information to make good decisions. Correspondingly, successful organizations develop reward and performance-evaluation systems that provide self-interested decision makers with appropriate incentives to make decisions that increase the values of their organizations.

It is also important to note that modern organizations are extremely complex and that developing an understanding of how people within them behave is difficult. As in any book that addresses this set of topics, we face difficult trade-offs between adding more institutional richness to infuse more texture of the actual environment versus omitting details to keep the analysis more focused and manageable. At certain points (especially where little prior formal analysis of the problem exists), we take quite complex problems and discuss them in terms of simplified examples. Nonetheless, our experience suggests that in these cases, we derive important managerial insights to these topics through our admittedly simple examples.

Finally, we believe that a powerful feature of this economic framework is that it can be extended readily to incorporate a broad array of other managerial policies such as finance, accounting, information systems, human relations, operations, and marketing. In this sense, this book can play an important integrating role across the entire business curriculum. Such integration is becoming increasingly important with the expanded use of cross-functional teams within the business community.

ANALYZING MANAGERIAL DECISIONS: *Société Générale*

Société Générale was founded in the 1860s and in 2013 was France's third largest bank. Beginning in the mid-1980s, it pioneered some of the most complex instruments in international finance and became a global powerhouse in trading derivatives like futures and options. Through its trading activities, the bank earned billions of dollars and gained the respect of bankers throughout the world. In January 2008, *Risk,* a monthly magazine about risk management, named Société Générale its "Equity Derivatives House of the Year."

In late January 2008, Société Générale announced that it had discovered fraudulent securities trading by one of its low-level traders, Jérôme Kerviel. The bank reported that it expected the fraud to cost it a staggering $7.14 billion, making it one of the largest financial frauds in history. The announcement shocked the financial markets and made front-page headlines around the world. Observers questioned whether the bank could ever regain its former reputation and whether it could continue to exist without merging with another bank.

Société's CEO Daniel Bouton asserted that the fraud was the result of one employee's illegal activities, did not involve other employees at the bank, and represented the aberrant and unexplainable actions of one "rogue trader." He characterized Kerviel's actions as "irrational" since the trades were made on behalf of the bank "netting the trader no personal gains." Bouton emphasized that Kerviel was a low-level employee who had an annual salary and bonus for 2007 of less than $145,700.

In principle Kerviel engaged in a quite simple operation: arbitrage-trading on small differences between various stock market indexes such as the CAC in France and the DAX in Germany. Kerviel should have been able to lock in a virtually riskless profit by selling a security on the exchange with the higher price, while simultaneously buying an equivalent instrument on the exchange with the lower price. And although price differences are typically small, such arbitrage can produce a substantial profit if done in sufficient volume. In this arbitrage business, although Société Générale might accumulate large positions on both exchanges, those securities

that it bought and those it sold should balance. The bank was supposed to face little net exposure to price changes.

What the bank discovered was that Kerviel had bought securities on both markets. In effect, he had made enormous bets that European stock prices would increase. But they had fallen, and as a result the bank incurred a substantial loss.

The subsequent investigation revealed that Kerviel had been placing huge unhedged bets on European stocks for over a year. Prior to becoming a trader he had worked in the bank's trading accounting office. His knowledge of the bank's risk-management system allowed him to conceal the trades and bypass the firm's control system. He knew the timing of the nightly reconciliation of the day's trades and would delete and then re enter his unauthorized transactions without being caught. Bank managers, however, had apparently dismissed several warning signs about Kerviel's transactions. For example, the surveillance office at Eurex, one of Europe's biggest exchanges, alerted a compliance officer at the bank that for seven months a trader named Kerviel had engaged in "several transactions" that raised red flags. Kerviel's supervisors accepted his explanations for these trades apparently without much investigation.

Various bank officials, investigators, and traders who worked with Kerviel have concluded that Société Générale "allowed a culture of risk to flourish, creating major flaws in its operations" that enabled Kerviel's actions to proceed. Several current and former employees interviewed by the *New York Times,* indicated that Société Générale traders were rewarded for making risky investments with the bank's money and that it was not uncommon for traders briefly to exceed limits imposed on their trading, despite controls meant to prohibit this activity. Risk taking apparently was "embraced, as long as it made money for the bank." Top executives and other managers at the bank had received large bonuses because of the bank's successful trading operations.

Kerviel told investigators that all he wanted was to be respected and to earn a large bonus. He had come from a modest background and did not have the educational pedigree of many of his coworkers who had advanced degrees in math or engineering from the prestigious Grandes Ecoles—the MITs of France. He was noted for working very long hours and had worked his way up in the bank from being a clerk to a trader. One of his primary goals was to have his supervisors recognize his "financial genius."

1. Do you agree with Société Générale's CEO that Kerviel's actions were "irrational"?

2. Discuss how the bank's organizational architecture contributed to the problem.
3. What lessons might you learn from this case if you were an executive at another bank?

Source: This application is based on a series of articles from the *New York Times* published in early 2008. In particular see N. D. Schwartz and K. Bennhold, 2008, "A Trader's Secrets, a Bank's Missteps," *nytimes.com* (February 5).

Suggested Readings

A. Alchian (1950), "Uncertainty, Evolution, and Economic Theory," *Journal of Political Economy* 58, 211–221.

M. Jensen (1983), "Organization Theory and Methodology," *The Accounting Review* 58, 319–339.

M. Jensen and W. Meckling (1992), "Specific and General Knowledge, and Organizational Structure," *Journal of Applied Corporate Finance* 8:2, 4–18.

Self-Evaluation Problems

1–1. Briefly describe *Economic Darwinism.*

1–2. *The Wall Street Journal*[11] reports that

Franchisees, who pay fees and royalties in exchange for using franchisers' business formats, have become much more militant in recent years about what they see as mistreatment by franchisers. In general, Ms. Kezios is seeking federal and state laws to give franchisees more power in franchise arrangements. Among her goals: creating legally protected exclusive territories for franchisees.

How would you expect existing franchisees to react to this proposed regulation? How would you expect a potential new franchisee to react to this proposed regulation?

Solutions to Self-Evaluation Problems

1–1. *Economic Darwinism* is the economic counterpart of natural selection in biology. Competition in the marketplace weeds out those organizations that are less efficient and fail to adapt to the environment. The result is survival of the fittest.

1–2. Reducing the likelihood of encroachment by the franchiser benefits the existing franchisees to the extent that it shifts future profits from the franchiser to the franchisee. Thus, existing franchisees are likely to favor the proposed regulation. Potential new franchisees are less likely to favor the proposal. Presumably, they will have to pay a higher price for a new franchise if the franchiser has to grant the franchisee an exclusive territory. The potential franchisee might prefer to have a nonexclusive territory at a lower price. In any case, the franchiser is unlikely to favor the proposal; if it were efficient to convey exclusive territories, the original contract could have been structured that way.

Review Questions

1–1. What are the three aspects of *organizational architecture?*

1–2. In the process of benchmarking, a colleague of yours notes that Lincoln Electric, a producer of electric arc welders, has much higher productivity than does your company. Unlike your

[11]J. A. Tannenbaum (1995), "Focus on Franchising: Franchisee Gains," *The Wall Street Journal* (June 19), B2.

firm, Lincoln has an extensive piece-rate compensation system; much of its employees' total compensation is simply the number of units produced times the piece rate for that type unit. Your colleague recommends that your company adopt a piece-rate compensation system to boost productivity. What do you advise?

1–3. In the life insurance industry, we see two major ownership structures—common stock insurers and mutual insurers. In a common stock company, the owners—its stockholders—are a separate group from its customers—the policyholders. In a mutual, the policyholders are also the owners of the company. It has been argued that mutual insurance companies are dinosaurs—they are large, slow, bureaucratic, and inefficient. How would you respond to such an argument?

Economists' View of Behavior

LEARNING OBJECTIVES

1. Describe the economic model of behavior.
2. Define and apply marginal analysis in managerial decisions.
3. Define and apply the concept of opportunity costs.
4. Use graphs to explain, predict, and affect behavior in a wide range of applications.
5. Contrast the implications of the economic model with those from other behavioral models used by some managers.
6. Identify the key concepts that are used to mitigate risk when making decisions under uncertainty.

In May 2002, Merrill Lynch agreed to pay $100 million to settle charges that its analysts had recommended stocks to clients that they privately thought were poor investments. Internal e-mails provided strong support for this claim leveled by the New York State attorney general. For example, InfoSpace, an Internet services company, was rated highly in analysts' reports distributed to clients, yet privately the analysts suggested that it was a "powder keg" and a "piece of junk." Although InfoSpace's share price dropped from $261 to $14, Merrill analysts never recommended selling the stock. Merrill analysts rated Excite@Home "accumulate or buy," while privately the investment team called it a "piece of crap."

This episode at Merrill sent shock waves through other major investment houses—indeed through the entire investment community. Other investment firms publicly stated that they were taking strong steps to make sure that the situation at Merrill would not be repeated within their organizations. *Fortune* magazine ran a cover story entitled, "In Search of the Last Honest Analyst."[1] The scandal generated significant concerns throughout the world among both the general public and government regulators. For example, the New York attorney general began a sweeping investigation of analysts at Salomon Smith Barney and other investment firms that had recommended WorldCom to investors. In July 2002, WorldCom became the biggest company ever to file for bankruptcy in U.S. history. In December 2002, the nation's 10 top investment banks agreed to a $1.2 billion settlement with regulators aimed at "protecting investors from brokerages' conflicts of interest."

[1]June 10, 2002, issue.

Managers at Merrill, Salomon Smith Barney, and other investment companies had to act quickly to address this potential problem. As a first step, management had to understand what motivated the Merrill analysts to mislead their investment clients. Only then could they choose a policy to redress the situation. If management thought this problem was caused by a few dishonest employees, the appropriate response would have been to try to identify and fire those employees. If, instead, management believed the problem was caused by disgruntled employees taking out their frustrations on customers, a potential response would have been to adopt a job-enrichment program to increase employee satisfaction and, it would be hoped, analyst honesty. Alternatively, Merrill Lynch might have created incentives through its compensation plan that caused its analysts to issue misleading investment reports. If so, the appropriate response would be to restructure its compensation plan. Many other assumptions and responses are possible.

The example of Merrill Lynch illustrates a general point: Managers' responses to problems are likely to depend on their understanding of people's motives and their forecast of people's reactions—their responses thus depend on their underlying model of behavior. Most managerial actions attempt to change the behavior of individuals, such as employees, customers, union officials, or subcontractors. Managers with different understandings (or models) of what motivates behavior are likely to make different decisions and take different actions.

We begin this chapter by briefly summarizing the general framework economists use to examine individual behavior. Selected graphical tools are introduced to aid our analysis. Next, we use this economic framework to analyze the problem at Merrill Lynch. The managerial implications of this analysis are discussed. We contrast this economic view of behavior with alternative views and explore why the economic framework is particularly useful in managerial decision making. Finally, we analyze decision making under uncertainty. In Appendix A, we analyze the problem of consumer choice in more detail and in Appendix B, we illustrate how the graphical framework we present in this chapter can be used for analyzing inter-temporal choices.

Economic Behavior: An Overview

Individuals have unlimited wants. People generally want greater wealth, more attentive service, larger houses, more luxurious cars, and additional personal material items. They want more time for leisure activities. Most also want to improve the plight of others—starving children, the homeless, and disaster victims. People are concerned about vitality, religion, integrity, and gaining the respect and affection of others.

In contrast to wants, resources are limited. Households face limited incomes that preclude all the purchases and expenditures that household members might like to make. The available amount of land, trees, and other natural resources is finite. There are only 24 hours in a day. People become ill; death is inevitable.

Economic Choice

Economic analysis is based on the notion that individuals assign priorities to their wants and choose their most preferred options from the available alternatives. If Kathy Measer is confronted with a choice between a laptop or a desktop computer, she can tell you whether she prefers one over the other or whether she is indifferent between the two. Depending on the relative prices of the two products, she purchases her preferred alternative. If Kathy has a weekly budget of $1,000, she considers the many ways she might spend the money and then chooses the package of goods and services that will maximize her personal happiness. She cannot make all desired purchases on her limited budget. However, this choice is optimal for Kathy, given her limited resources.

Economists do not assert that people are selfish in the sense that they care only about their own personal consumption. Within the economic paradigm, people also care about such things as charity, family, religion, and society. For instance, Kathy will donate $100 to her church, as long as the donation provides greater satisfaction than alternative uses of the money.

Economists, however, often assume for modeling purposes that people care only about their own wealth to simplify the analysis. While wealth is not the only thing that people care about, it is very important to most people. Economic models based on this simplifying assumption often perform quite well relative to more complicated models that add unnecessary complexity to the analysis. Some situations, however, can require models that are based on different assumptions.

Economists do not contend that individuals are supercomputers that make infallible decisions. Individuals are not endowed with perfect knowledge and foresight, nor is additional information costless to acquire and process.[2] For example, Kathy might order an item from a restaurant menu only to find that she dislikes what she is served. Within this economic paradigm, she simply does the best she can in the face of her imperfect knowledge. But she learns from her experience and does not repeat the same mistakes in judgment time after time.[3]

Marginal Analysis

Marginal costs and benefits are the incremental costs and benefits that are associated with making a decision.[4] It is the marginal costs and benefits that are important in economic decision making. An action should be taken whenever the incremental benefits of that action exceed its incremental costs. Mary O'Dwyer has a contract to help sell products for an office supply company. She is paid $50 for every sales call that she makes to customers. Thus, Mary's marginal benefit for making each additional sales call is $50. Mary enjoys playing tennis more than selling. If she places a marginal value of more than $50 on the tennis that she would forgo by making an

---

[2]Economists sometimes use the idea of *bounded rationality*. Under this concept, individuals act in a purposeful and *intendedly rational* manner. However, they have cognitive limitations in storing, processing, and communicating information. It is these limitations which make the question of how to organize economic activity particularly interesting. H. Simon (1957), *Models of Man* (John Wiley & Sons: New York).

[3]At least this learning appears to occur outside the comics. For decades, Charlie Brown from *Peanuts* continued to try to kick the football held by Lucy van Pelt. Yet Lucy always pulled the ball at the last second. Few individuals are as incurably optimistic as Charlie Brown—they learn.

[4]Technical note: *Marginal* costs and benefits are typically defined as changes in costs and benefits associated with very *small changes* in a decision variable. For instance, the marginal costs of production are the additional costs from producing a small additional amount of the product (for instance, one more unit). Often decisions involve discrete choices, such as whether or not to build a new plant. In these cases, it is not possible to define a small change in the decision variable. *Incremental* costs and benefits are those costs and benefits which vary with such a decision. For our present discussion, the technical distinction between marginal and incremental is not important.

MANAGERIAL APPLICATIONS

Marginal Analysis of Customer Profitability

Banks often provide multiple products and services to the same customer (checking and savings accounts, mortgages, lines of credits, business loans, credit cards, international banking services, insurance, and so on). In the 1980s, most banks did not consolidate this information, and so it was difficult to determine if serving a given customer was profitable or not. Today many banks use "profitability software" to consolidate information on each customer. Many banks have found to their surprise that the incremental costs for serving many of their customers are larger than the incremental revenues. Fleet Bank, for example, found that as many as one-half of their customers were unprofitable. Armed with this information, banks work hard to maintain high-profit customers, while they either eliminate or alter services to unprofitable customers. For example, at many banks profitable customers are given special designations, such as "Gold Customer Status," and the banks extend special services to them. Preferred customers are frequently given special toll free lines; branch managers are furnished with their names and are instructed to meet and greet them when they visit a branch. They are assigned personal bankers, who call and introduce themselves. Customers are assigned profitability codes, for example, so employees can know whether they are dealing with a 5, 4, 3, 2, or 1 type customer (five being most profitable). When the loans for unprofitable customers come up for renewal, they are renewed at a higher rate, to try to nudge them into profitability, or possibly to get the customers to take their business elsewhere. In contrast, loan applications by customers in the 4 and 5 categories are quickly processed and given special attention. Banks provide but one example of how firms are making increased use of information technology to do more sophisticated marginal analysis—devoting their efforts to customers and products where the incremental revenues are greater than the incremental costs and eliminating and avoiding unprofitable activities.

Source: A. Hughes (2014), "How Banks Use Profitability Analysis," *Database Marketing Institute*, www.dbmarketing.com/articles/Art195.htm.

---

extra call, she should not make any more sales calls that day—the marginal costs would have exceeded the marginal benefits. She continues to make additional sales calls as long as the reduction in tennis playing is valued at less than $50.[5]

Marginal analysis is a cornerstone of modern economic analysis. In economic decision making, "bygones are forever bygones." Costs and benefits that have already been incurred are *sunk* (assuming they are nonrecoverable) and hence are irrelevant to the current economic decision. Mary paid $5,000 to join a tennis club last month. This fee does not affect her current decision of whether to play tennis or make an extra sales call. That expenditure is ancient history and does not affect Mary's current trade-offs.

As another example, consider Ludger Hellweg who owns a company that installs wood floors. He is offered $20,000 to install a new floor. The cost of his labor and other operating expenses (excluding the wood) are $15,000. He has wood for the job in inventory. It originally cost him $2,000. Price increases have raised the market value of the wood to $6,000, and this value is not expected to change in the near future. Should he accept the contract?

He should compare the incremental costs and benefits from the project. The marginal benefit is $20,000. The marginal cost is $21,000—$15,000 for the labor and operating expenses and $6,000 for the wood. The historic cost for the wood of $2,000 is not relevant to the decision. To replace the wood used on this job costs

---

[5]To keep this example simple, we abstract from several issues. We ignore any pleasure Mary receives from the process of selling. Also, selling effort today is likely to have some effect on her future professional progress. Finally, if Mary values a tennis game at 9 A.M. and one at 7 P.M. equally, she will sell during the business day and postpone tennis to the evening.

$6,000. Since the marginal costs exceed the marginal benefits, Ludger would be better off rejecting the contract than accepting it. This example illustrates that in calculating marginal costs, it is important to use the opportunity cost of the incremental resources, not their historic (accounting) cost.

Opportunity Costs

Because resources are constrained, individuals face *trade-offs*. Using limited resources for one purpose precludes their use for something else. For example, if Larry Matteson takes four hours to play golf, he cannot use that same four hours to paint his house. The *opportunity cost* of using a resource for a given purpose is its value in its best alternative use. The opportunity cost of using four hours to play golf is the value of using the four hours in Larry's next best alternative use.

Marginal analysis frequently involves a careful consideration of the relevant opportunity costs. If Larry starts a new pizza parlor and hires a manager at $30,000 per year, the $30,000 is an *explicit* cost (a direct dollar expenditure). Is he better off managing the restaurant himself, since he can avoid the explicit cost of $30,000 by not paying himself a salary? The answer to this question depends (at least in part) on the opportunity cost of his time. If he can earn exactly $30,000 in his best alternative job, the *implicit* cost of self-management is the same as the explicit cost of hiring an outside manager: He forgoes $30,000 worth of income if he manages the parlor himself. Both explicit and implicit costs are opportunity costs that should be considered in the analysis. Suppose that Larry's gross profit from the pizza parlor, before paying the manager a salary, is $35,000 and that he can earn $40,000 in an outside job. Hiring a manager for $30,000 yields a net profit of $5,000 from the pizza parlor. He also earns $40,000 from the outside job, for total earnings of $45,000. If he manages the pizza parlor himself, he earns only $35,000. In this example, it is better for him to work at the outside job and hire a manager to run the restaurant.[6]

Creativity of Individuals[7]

Within this economic framework, individuals maximize their personal satisfaction given resource constraints. Indeed, people are quite creative and resourceful in minimizing the effects of constraints. For instance, when the government adopts new

---

[6]Again, to keep the example simple, we assume there is no difference in personal satisfaction between Larry's outside job and managing the pizza parlor. We also postpone the discussion of consequences for the success of the pizza parlor from hiring a manager versus self-management until Chapter 10.

[7]This section draws on W. Meckling (1976), "Values and the Choice of the Model of the Individual in the Social Sciences," *Schweizerische Zeitschrift für Volkswirtschaft und Statistik* 112, 545–560.

ANALYZING MANAGERIAL DECISIONS: *Marginal Analysis*

You own a business that services trucks. A customer would like to rent a truck from you for one week, while you service his truck. You must decide whether or not to do this.

You have an extra truck that you will not use for any other purpose during this week. This truck is leased for a full year from another company for $300/week plus $.50 for every mile driven. You also have paid an annual insurance premium, which costs $50/week to insure the truck. The truck has a full 100-gallon fuel tank.

The customer has offered you $600 to rent the truck for a week. This price includes the 100 gallons of fuel that is in the tank. It also includes up to 500 miles of driving. The customer will pay $.50 for each additional mile that he drives above the 500 miles. You anticipate that the customer will

bring back the truck with an empty fuel tank and will have driven more than 500 miles. You sell fuel to truckers at a retail price of $4.00/gallon. Any fuel you sell or use can be replaced at a wholesale price of $3.25/gallon.

The customer will rent a truck from another company if you do not accept the proposed deal. In either case, you will service his truck. You know the customer and are confident that he will pay all charges incurred under the agreement.

1. Should you accept or reject the proposed deal?
2. Would your answer change if your fuel supplier limited the amount of fuel that you could purchase from him at the wholesale price? Explain.

taxes, almost immediately accountants and financial planners begin developing clever ways to reduce their impact. Some self-employed individuals were able to reduce the impact of recent tax increases by changing their status from a proprietorship to a corporation.

As another example, a 33-year-old Brazilian farm hand recently retired with full social security benefits after he satisfied social security auditors that he had been

MANAGERIAL APPLICATIONS

Creative Gaming of the System

The U.S. Government in 2009 promoted the sales of presidential and Native American $1 coins by offering free shipping on any order made to the U.S. Mint (which sold the coins at face value). Enthusiasts of frequent-flyer mileage programs saw a creative way to "game" the government's offer. Many credit cards are tied to the frequent-flyer programs of major airlines—for every dollar charged on the card, a mile is credited to the relevant frequent-flyer program. Several hundred "mile-junkies" responded by purchasing thousands of dollars worth of coins from the U.S. Mint using their credit cards. Once they received the coins, they deposited the money in their bank accounts to pay off their credit card charges before any interest costs were incurred. For example, Patricia Hansen, a San Diego retiree who loves to travel, ordered $10,000 in coins earning 10,000 miles toward free and upgraded travel. Her husband took the coins to the bank, as soon as they arrived, so that their credit card bill could be paid. The U.S. Mint eventually figured out what was going on and stopped the program that had resulted in increased costs for them, credit card companies, banks, and airlines. This example illustrates an important general point. *People often respond to economic incentives in creative ways.* Managers and government officials need to craft incentives thoughtfully.

Source: S. McCartney (2009), "Miles for Nothing: How the Government Helped Frequent Fliers Make a Mint," *The Wall Street Journal* (December 7), A1.

working since he was three years old. Because Brazil doesn't specify a minimum retirement age, the average Brazilian retires at age 49.[8]

Similarly, when hackers and corporate spies continue to develop more sophisticated schemes to steal information from Web sites or networks, software tools that detect break-ins also have grown in popularity and sophistication. This intrusion-detection software was about a $100 million industry in 1999 and is now estimated at over $2 billion.[9]

Understanding this creative nature of individuals has important managerial implications that we discuss later in this chapter, as well as throughout the book.

Graphical Tools

Economists often employ a set of graphical tools to illustrate how individuals make choices. These tools distinguish between the preferences (level of satisfaction) that the individual associates with each potential opportunity and the set of feasible opportunities that an individual faces. We use these tools throughout this book. They also are used in other courses within the typical business school curriculum, such as in finance, human relations, and marketing courses. Our intent is to introduce these tools so that the reader is comfortable using them in basic business applications. We subsequently apply the tools to analyze the problems at Merrill Lynch. Appendix A provides a more detailed development of the economic theory of individual choice (commonly called the "Theory of Consumer Choice").

Individual Objectives

Goods are things that people value. Goods include standard products like food and clothing, services like haircuts and education, as well as less tangible emotions such as love of family and charity. The economic model of behavior posits that people acquire goods that maximize their personal satisfaction, given their resource constraints (such as a limited income). Economists traditionally use the term *utility* in referring to personal satisfaction.

To provide a more detailed analysis of how people make choices, economists represent an individual's preferences by a *utility function*. This function expresses the relation between total utility and the level of goods consumed. The individual's objective is to maximize this function, given the resource constraints.[10] This concept can be illustrated most conveniently through a simple example where an individual cares about only two goods. The insights from this two-good analysis can be extended readily to the case of additional goods such as food, housing, clothing, respect, and charity.

Suppose that Dominique Lalisse values only food and clothing. In general form, his utility function can be written as follows:

$$\overset{+}{} \qquad \overset{+}{}$$
$$\text{Utility} = F(\text{Food, Clothing}) \qquad\qquad (2.1)$$

[8]P. Fritsch (1999), "In Brazil Retirement Has Become a Benefit Nearly All Can Enjoy," *The Wall Street Journal* (September 9), A1.

[9]J. D'Allegro (1999), "Intrusion Detection Matures," *National Underwriter* (March 8), 9; and Frost and Sullivan (2007), "World Intrusion Detection and Prevention Markets," www.frost.com

[10]Clearly, most individuals do not actually consider maximizing a mathematical function when they make these choices. However, this formulation can provide useful insights into actual behavior to the extent that it *approximates* how individuals make choices. Mathematicians have shown that if an individual's behavior is consistent with some basic "axioms of choice" (comparability, transitivity, nonsatiation, and willingness to substitute), the individual will make choices *as if* he or she were trying to maximize a mathematical function.

Figure 2.1 Indifference Curves

These indifference curves picture all combinations of food and clothing that yield the same amount of utility. The specific utility function in this example is $U = F^{1/2} \times C^{1/2}$, where F is food and C is clothing. Northeast movements are utility-increasing. Indifference curve 2 represents all combinations of food and clothing that yield 20 units of utility, whereas curve 1 pictures all combinations that yield 8 units of utility. Other indifference curves could be drawn for different levels of utility.

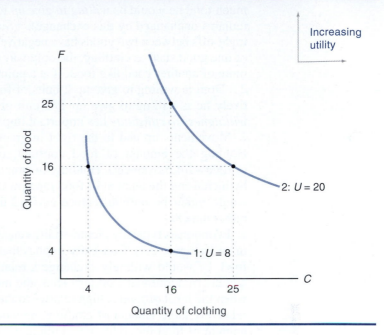

Dom prefers more of each good—thus, his utility rises with both food and clothing. In Dom's case, his specific utility function is

$$\text{Utility} = \text{Food}^{1/2} \times \text{Clothing}^{1/2} \tag{2.2}$$

For instance, if Dom has 16 units of food and 25 units of clothing, his total utility is 20 (that is, utility $= 16^{1/2} \times 25^{1/2} = 4 \times 5 = 20$). Dom is better off with 25 units of both food and clothing. Here, his utility is 25 (utility $= 25^{1/2} \times 25^{1/2} = 5 \times 5 = 25$).

Utility functions rank alternative bundles of food and clothing in the *order* of most preferred to least preferred, but they do not indicate how much one bundle is preferred to another. If the utility index is 100 for one combination of food and clothing and 200 for another, Dom will prefer the second combination. The second bundle does not necessarily make him twice as well off as the first bundle.[11] Neither does this formulation allow one person's utility of a bundle to be compared to another person's utility.

Indifference Curves

Preferences implied by the utility function can be illustrated graphically through *indifference curves*. An indifference curve pictures all combinations of goods that yield the same utility. Given his utility function in Equation (2.2), Dom is indifferent between either 16 units of food and 25 units of clothing or 25 units of food and 16 units of clothing. Both combinations yield 20 units of utility, and hence are on the same indifference curve. Figure 2.1 shows two of Dom's indifference curves. For example, if given a choice between any two points on curve 1, Dom would say that he does not care which one is selected—in either case, he obtains 8 units of utility.

---

[11]This is like rankings on a test—an individual who scores in the 80th percentile is not twice as smart as one from the 40th.

The slope at any point along one of Dom's indifference curves indicates how much food he would be *willing to give up* for a small increase in clothing (his utility remains unchanged by this exchange).[12] Standard indifference curves that illustrate trade-offs between two goods have negative slopes. If Dom obtains a smaller amount of one good such as clothing, the only way he can be equally as well off is to obtain more of another good like food. If at a point along an indifference curve the slope is 22, Dom is willing to give up 2 units of food to obtain 1 unit of clothing. Alternatively he is willing to give up 1/2 unit of clothing to obtain 1 unit of food. This *willingness to substitute* has important implications, which we discuss later.

Movements up and to the right in graphs like Figure 2.1 are utility-increasing. Holding the amount of food constant, utility increases by increasing clothing (a rightward movement). Holding the amount of clothing constant, utility increases by increasing the amount of food (an upward movement). Thus, in Figure 2.1, Dom would rather be on indifference curve 2 than on 1. He obtains 20 units of utility rather than 8.

Economists typically picture indifference curves as convex to the origin (they bow in, as in Figure 2.1). Convexity implies that if Dom has a relatively large amount of food, he would willingly exchange a relatively large quantity of food for a small amount of additional clothing. Thus, the indifference curves in Figure 2.1 are steep when the level of food is high relative to the level of clothing. In contrast, if he has a relatively large amount of clothing, he would be willing to substitute only a small amount of food for additional clothing. Correspondingly, the indifference curves in Figure 2.1 flatten as Dom has less food and more clothing. The behavior implied by the convexity of indifference curves is consistent with the observed behavior of many individuals—most people purchase balanced combinations of food and clothing.

Opportunities and Constraints

Dom would like more of both food and clothing. Unfortunately, he faces a budget constraint that limits his purchases. Suppose that he has an income of I and the prices per unit of food and clothing are P_f and P_c, respectively. In this single period analysis, we assume that Dom spends all his income on food and clothing. In a multiperiod context, Dom might want to save part of his income or borrow against future income. We examine these possibilities in Appendix B at the end of this chapter. Since he cannot spend more than *I*, his consumption opportunities are limited by the following constraint:

$$I \geq P_f F + P_c C \tag{2.3}$$

where *F* and *C* represent the units of food and clothing purchased. This budget constraint indicates that only combinations of food and clothing that cost no more than *I* are feasible. Rearranging terms, this constraint can be written as

$$F \leq I/P_f - (P_c/P_f)C \tag{2.4}$$

---

[12]Recall that the slope of a line is a measure of steepness, defined as the increase or decrease in height per unit of distance along the horizontal axis. Slopes of curves are found geometrically by drawing a line tangent to the curve at the point of interest and determining the slope of this tangent line. The slope at a point along one of Dom's indifference curves indicates how the quantity of food changes for small changes in the amount of clothing in order to hold utility constant. Since by definition Dom is indifferent to this exchange (he remains on the same indifference curve), he is *willing* to make the exchange.

Figure 2.2 Opportunities and Constraints

The constraint reflects the feasible combinations of food and clothing that are attainable given the person's income (I). The vertical and horizontal intercepts, respectively, show the amounts of food and clothing that can be purchased if no income is spent on the other good. The slope of the constraint is equal to -1 times the ratio of the prices of the two goods. For instance, if the price of clothing is $8 and the price of food is $2, the slope will be -4. This slope implies that 4 units of food must be given up for 1 unit of clothing. If both goods have the same price, the slope will be -1.

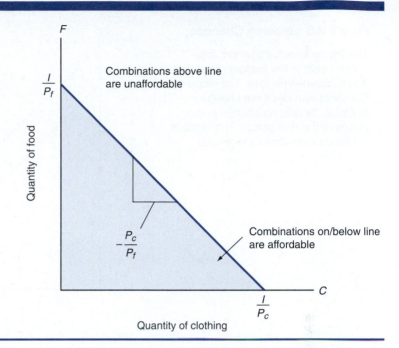

Figure 2.2 depicts these consumption opportunities—frequently called a *budget line*. All combinations of food and clothing on or below the line are attainable. Combinations above the line are infeasible given an income of I. The F intercept (on the vertical axis) of the line I/P_f indicates how much food Dom can purchase if his entire income is spent on food (no clothing is purchased). The C intercept is correspondingly I/P_c. The slope of the line $-P_c/P_f$ is -1 times the ratio of the two prices. The ratio P_c/P_f is the *relative price* of clothing in terms of food. It represents how many units of food he must forgo to acquire a unit of clothing: It is the opportunity cost of clothing. For example, if the price of clothing is $8 and the price of food is $2, the relative price of clothing is 4. To keep total expenditures constant, 4 units of food must be given up for every unit of clothing purchased. The relative price of food is P_f/P_c (in this example, 0.25); 1/4 unit of clothing must be given up for each unit of food purchased.

The constraint changes with changes in Dom's income and the relative prices of the two goods. As shown in Figure 2.3, changes in income result in parallel shifts of the constraint: Its slope is unaffected. An increase in income shifts the constraint outward (up and to the right), while a decrease in income shifts the constraint inward. The slope of the constraint changes with the relative prices of the two goods. As shown in Figure 2.4, if the price of clothing increases relative to the price of food, the constraint becomes steeper. If the price of clothing falls relative to the price of food, the constraint becomes flatter.

Individual Choice

Within this economic framework, Dom's goal is to maximize utility given his opportunities. Utility is maximized at the point of tangency between the constraint and

Figure 2.3 Income Changes

This figure shows that there is a parallel shift in the budget constraint when income changes. The slope of the constraint does not change because there is no change in the prices of the two goods. The slope is −1 times the ratio of the prices.

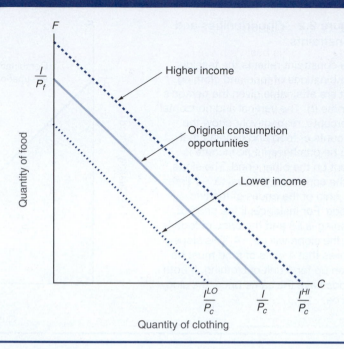

an indifference curve.[13] Figure 2.5 portrays the optimal choice. Dom could choose points like *b* and *c* on indifference curve 1. However, point *a* on curve 2 yields greater satisfaction (utility) and thus is preferred. Dom would prefer to be at any point on curve 3. Yet, these points are unattainable given his income.

Figure 2.4 Price Changes

This figure shows how his consumption opportunities change with changes in the price of clothing. The slope of the line is $-(P_c/P_f)$. Thus, an increase in the price of clothing (from P_c to P_c^{HI}) produces a steeper line, while a decrease (from P_c to P_c^{LO}) produces a flatter line. Changes in the price of food also affect the slope of the line.

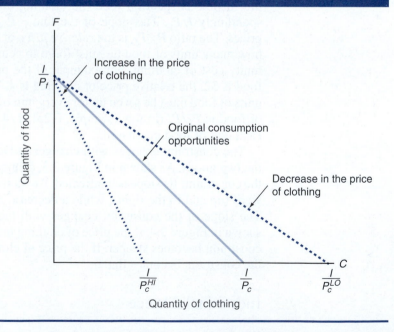

[13]For simplicity, we ignore the possibility of corner solutions—the points where the budget constraint intersects the axes. With corner solutions, the individual spends all income on only one good.

Figure 2.5   Optimal Choice

The individual is best off by choosing point *a* where the constraint is tangent to indifference curve 2. This optimal combination of food and clothing, *F** and *C**, yields higher level of satisfaction (utility) than other feasible alternatives (e.g., points *b* and *c*). The individual would prefer points on indifference curve 3, but these points are infeasible given his consumption opportunities.

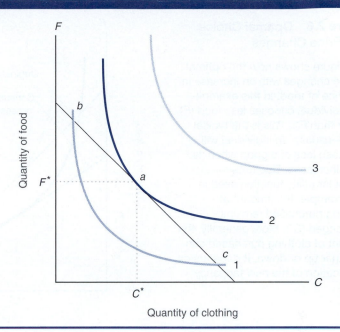

This graphical solution to Dom's choice problem has a simple intuitive interpretation. At the point of tangency, the indifference curve and the constraint have equal slopes. Recall that the slope of the indifference curve represents Dom's willingness to trade food for clothing, whereas the slope of the constraint represents the terms of trade available in the marketplace. At the optimal choice, the *willingness and ability to trade are equal.* At other feasible combinations of food and clothing, Dom's utility could be increased by making substitutions. For instance, if Dom were at a point where he was willing to trade 5 units of food for 1 unit of clothing and if the relative price of clothing were 4 units (the slope of the indifference curve is steeper than the constraint), Dom would be better off purchasing less food and more clothing. (He is willing to trade 5 units of food for 1 unit of clothing, but only must forgo 4 units of food to obtain 1 unit of clothing in the marketplace.) Alternatively, if Dom were at a point where he was only willing to forgo 1 unit of food for 1 unit of clothing (the slope of the indifference curve is flatter than the constraint), he would be better off purchasing more food and less clothing—since he receives 5 units of food for each unit of clothing forgone.

Earlier in this chapter, we discussed how marginal analysis is the cornerstone of modern economics. It is important to understand that the graphical tools presented in this section depict marginal analysis. In marginal analysis, individuals take actions as long as their incremental benefits are greater than their incremental costs. Our graphical analysis of individual choice corresponds to this decision rule. The relative price ratio, P_C/P_F, is the marginal cost of a unit of clothing, expressed as units of food—the units of food that are forgone is the opportunity cost of an additional unit of clothing. Similarly, the opportunity cost of an additional unit of food is P_F/P_C units of clothing. The slope of the indifference curve reflects the marginal benefit of an additional unit of clothing expressed as units of food. For example, if Dom is willing to trade 5 units of food for 1 unit of clothing (slope of the indifference curve = −5), his marginal benefit of one additional unit of clothing must equal the utility

Figure 2.6 Optimal Choice and Price Changes

This figure shows how the optimal choice changes with an increase in the price of food. In this example, the individual chooses less food (F_1^* rather than F_0^*). This is the typical case—usually, an individual will purchase less of a good when its price increases. Due to the particular utility function used in this example, the amount of clothing purchased remains unchanged (C^*). More generally, the amount of clothing purchased can go either up or down. It depends on the location of the new tangency point.

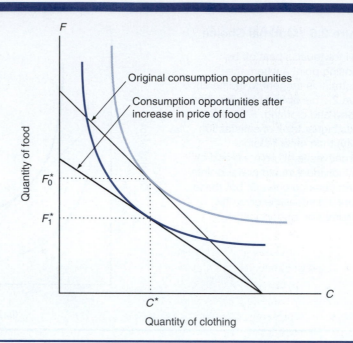

from 5 units of food. Similarly, his marginal benefit of a unit of food is equivalent to .2 units (1/5) of clothing. If Dom is not at the point of tangency between the indifference curve and the budget line, the marginal benefit of trading one good for the other must be greater than the marginal cost. Suppose Dom is willing to trade 5 units of food for 1 unit of clothing, but only has to trade 2 units of food for 1 unit of clothing in the marketplace. In this case, Dom should trade food for clothing since the marginal (incremental) benefit is greater than the marginal (incremental) cost. At the optimum (point of tangency) the marginal benefit of consuming 1 more unit of either good is equal to the marginal cost and there is no reason to make additional trades.

Changes in Choice

Dom's consumption opportunities will change whenever prices or income change. Consequently, he will make different choices. Recall that changes in relative prices alter the slope of the constraint. When the relative price of a good increases, individuals typically choose less of that good.[14] Figure 2.6 shows how Dom will purchase less food as its relative price increases—food is more expensive and so less attractive than it was at a lower price. Generally, the amount of clothing purchased can go either up or down; it depends on the location of the new tangency point. (Given the particular utility function assumed in this example, the amount of clothing purchased remains unchanged.) Even though the price of clothing is relatively more attractive, the increase in food prices can limit available income so as to reduce the amount purchased of both goods. Changes in Dom's income cause parallel shifts in the

[14]Although in principle some individuals might purchase more of a good if its price increases, this outcome is rarely observed.

ANALYZING MANAGERIAL DECISIONS: *Consumer Choice and Graphical Tools*

You are a manager for a company that bottles and sells wine in two different countries. You charge the same price for a bottle of wine in both countries. Yet, your wine sales are much higher in one country than the other. Your boss asks you to develop an explanation for the differences in wine sales between the two countries and to develop a plan to sell more wine in the country with low wine consumption.

Population sizes and family incomes in the two countries are very similar. You also know that each country imposes a *per bottle* tax on wine.

Begin by providing a plausible *economic* explanation (focusing on constraints) for the differences in wine sales in the two countries. Illustrate your explanation by using indifference curves and budget lines for representative consumers from the two countries. What data would you want to determine

if your explanation is likely to be correct? Are there other plausible explanations for the differences in wine consumption? Are there ways to determine which of these explanations is most likely to be driving the differences in consumption?

1. Suppose that your economic explanation is likely to be correct and that your company will not allow you to lower the price per liter that you charge for wine in the two countries. Discuss at least two potential actions that you might take to sell more wine in the country with low demand.

2. Now provide a potential *preference-based* explanation for the differences in wine sales. Suppose that this explanation is correct. Discuss whether there are likely to be feasible policies that you could use to increase wine sales in the country with the low demand.

constraint and will change his optimal choice. In Chapter 4, we examine in more detail how changes in income and prices affect consumption choices. Appendix A contains a more detailed analysis of the effects of price changes on individual choice and illustrates how this basic graphical analysis can be used to study inter-temporal choices, such as the choice between current consumption and savings.

Choices also change if preferences change. Now changes in preferences undoubtedly occur. (Do you really believe that Toys 'R' Us will have any difficulty satisfying the demands for toys that were highly popular in past years, such as Teenage Mutant Ninja Turtle action figures, Tomaguchi virtual pets, Tickle-Me-Elmo dolls, or Pokemon Cards next Christmas?) Yet, economists rarely focus on such explanations. Economics has little theory to explain what might cause preferences to change. And since a large premium is placed on operationalism in managerial economics, preference-based explanations generally are appealed to only after other potential explanations are exhausted. In a sense, these preference-based explanations are too easy—they work too well. Virtually any observed behavior could be explained by appealing to preferences: Why did the consumption of frozen yogurt increase relative to that of ice cream? People's preferences changed so that more frozen yogurt and less ice cream was demanded. But an observed reduction in consumption could have been "explained" just as readily. Without a deeper understanding of why preferences change, one is left "explaining" everything but with an analysis that allows you to predict nothing.

Ultimately, the managerial usefulness of this analysis comes from its power to identify policy instruments that have a predictable impact on the problems at hand. Across a broad array of problems, assuming that underlying preferences are reasonably stable and analyzing the impact of changes in opportunities and constraints regularly will yield important managerial insights and identify productive managerial tools.

Motivating Honesty at Merrill Lynch

Often, economists focus on consumption goods such as food and clothing. This focus is natural given the interests economists have in understanding consumer behavior. Yet this analysis can be extended easily to consider other goods that people care about, such as love and respect.[15] Such an extension can be used to analyze the problem at Merrill Lynch.

Suppose that Susan Chen, like other analysts at Merrill Lynch, values two goods—money and integrity. Her utility function is

$$\overset{+}{\text{Utility}} = F(\overset{+}{\text{Money}}, \overset{+}{\text{Integrity}}) \tag{2.5}$$

Money is meant to symbolize general purchasing power; it allows the purchase of goods such as food, clothing, and housing. Integrity is something Sue values for its own sake—being honest in her dealings with other people provides Sue with satisfaction and she values it for that reason.

Suppose that integrity can be measured on a numerical scale with Sue preferring higher values. For example, 5 units of integrity provide more utility than 4 units of integrity. (In actuality, measuring a good like integrity on a numerical scale might be quite difficult. Yet this complication does not limit the qualitative insights that we can derive from the analysis.)

Merrill paid its stock analysts an annual bonus that was based partly on the analyst's contribution to the investment banking side of the business (e.g., the firm's underwriting activities). If Sue were completely honest and rated a company as a poor investment, the management of that company might take its investment banking business to another firm. The resulting loss in Merrill's investment banking revenue would reduce Sue's annual bonus. This bonus scheme thus confronts Sue with a trade-off. She can be honest and derive satisfaction from maintaining her integrity, or she can be dishonest in her rating of the stock and obtain a higher bonus. (She also might consider the future effects on her income from developing a good or bad reputation as an investment analyst. However, the analysis in this chapter is framed in a simple one-period context and does not consider monetary returns from developing a good reputation. In subsequent chapters we extend the analysis and consider such multiperiod effects.)

Figure 2.7 depicts Sue's implied opportunities. This constraint shows the maximum combinations of income and integrity that are feasible given the compensation plan and conditions at the company.[16] If Sue sacrifices all integrity, she earns $\$_{\text{max}}$ a year. If she is scrupulously honest in her investment recommendations, she earns less (there is a positive floor on her income, $\$_{\text{min}}$, since her base salary does depend on the amount of investment banking business and her analysis undoubtedly will suggest recommending some of Merrill's clients' stocks). Intermediate options along the constraint are possible. While Sue would like to earn more than $\$_{\text{max}}$, higher income is not feasible in this job.

---

[15]G. Becker (1993), "Nobel Lecture: The Economic Way of Looking at Behavior," *Journal of Political Economy* 101, 385–409.

[16]For simplicity, we draw the constraint as linear. Linearity is not necessary for our analysis. Also, we want to emphasize that we put dollars on the vertical axis only because it is a convenient general indication of value, not because money is more important than other things. We could illustrate Sue's willingness to trade integrity against anything else Sue values, such as Big Macs, pianos, or pairs of jeans.

Figure 2.7 Nature of Opportunities Facing an Analyst at Merrill Lynch

The constraint depicts the maximum amounts of money and integrity that are possible for the analyst given the bonus plan and conditions at the company. If the analyst sacrifices all integrity and recommends stocks even if they are poor investments, the employee earns a maximum of $\$_{max}$ a year. Investment banking business is lost if the analyst gives objective advice and rates certain stocks as poor investments (selects a higher level of integrity). Income is lower since the analyst is paid a bonus based on investment banking revenues. I_c represents complete honesty.

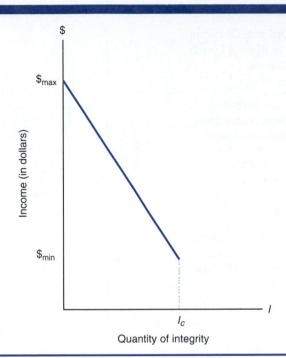

Sue chooses the combination of integrity and income that places her on the highest attainable indifference curve. This choice occurs at the point of tangency between her indifference curve and the constraint. Sue ends up selecting relatively low amounts of integrity because the bonus plan adopted by Merrill's management has made integrity expensive. If Sue were to choose more integrity, she would forfeit a relatively large amount of income.

Management can alter the opportunities Sue and her colleagues face by changing its compensation plan. In the Merrill case, reducing the emphasis of investment banking revenue in determining the annual bonus reduces the gains from dishonest advice and thus flattens the constraint. Changes in the slope of the constraint result in a different tangency point and hence a different choice. Figure 2.8 shows how Sue's optimal choice changes when the emphasis on investment banking revenue is decreased.[17] The result is more honest behavior. In essence, Sue "purchases" more integrity because it now is less expensive. Consistent with this analysis, Merrill, in its settlement with the State of New York, agreed to change the way it evaluated and compensated its analysts. Bonuses now are based on the quality of investment advice—not tied to its investment banking business.

[17]We have altered the compensation scheme in a manner that places Sue on the same indifference curve. Our rationale for doing this is as follows: Merrill Lynch must provide Sue with sufficient job satisfaction (utility) to retain her at the firm. Below this level of utility, Sue will quit and work elsewhere. Merrill Lynch is unlikely to want to pay Sue more than this minimum utility because it reduces firm profits. Thus, Merrill Lynch has an incentive to adjust compensation in a manner that keeps her on the same indifference curve. Sue's indifference curve in Figure 2.8 can be viewed as this "reservation" utility. These issues are covered in more detail in Chapter 14.

Figure 2.8 Optimal Choices of an Analyst at Merrill Lynch under Two Different Compensation Plans

Case 1 reflects the original compensation plan. In this case, compensation includes a high bonus based on investment banking revenues and the constraint is relatively steep. In Case 2, the firm reduces the emphasis on investment banking revenues in compensating analysts. The slope of the constraint is flatter. The result is that the individual chooses a higher level of integrity in Case 2 than in Case 1.

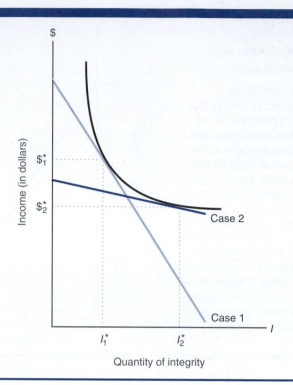

Managerial Implications

This analysis illustrates how the economic framework can be used to analyze and address management problems. Managers are interested in affecting the behavior of individuals such as employees, customers, union leaders, or subcontractors. Understanding what motivates individuals is critical. The economic approach views individual actions as the outcomes of maximizing personal utility. People are willing to make substitutions (e.g., less leisure time for more income) so long as the terms of trade are advantageous. Managers can affect behavior by appropriately designing the opportunities facing individuals. The design of the opportunities affects the trade-offs that individuals face and hence their choices. For example, management can motivate employees through the structure of compensation plans or customers through pricing decisions.

The outcome of individuals making economic choices is a function of both opportunities and preferences. Individuals try to achieve their highest level of satisfaction given the constraints they face. Our discussion of management implications, however, intentionally focuses on opportunities and constraints, not preferences. As a management tool, the usefulness of focusing on personal preferences often is limited. It is difficult to change what a person likes or does not like. Moreover, preferences rarely are observable, and (as we noted earlier) virtually any observed change in choice can be "explained" as simply a matter of a change in personal tastes. For instance, a preference-based explanation as to why employees were dishonest at Merrill Lynch is that these employees gained personal satisfaction from being dishonest (or compared to employees at other firms, Merrill Lynch employees were willing to trade large amounts of personal integrity for small financial rewards). This

MANAGERIAL APPLICATIONS

More to Life than Money

Should you hire a housekeeper or clean your house yourself? Should you mow your own lawn or hire the kid next door? People confront these types of questions everyday. Spending money on housekeepers, gardeners, etc. provides extra time to use for other activities, but it comes at the cost of having less money to purchase other things. People vary in their attitudes when it comes to time versus money. In a recent survey conducted by LearnVest and Chase Blueprint, 54 percent said they would like more money rather than more time, while 46 percent they want more free time relative to more money. It is not uncommon to see people in well paid positions retiring early to spend more time with family or to pursue other personal interests. For example, Kelly Malson was the CFO of World Acceptance Corp. and had an annual pay package valued at $4.8 million in 2013. During the summer of 2013, one of her college friends died of Lou Gehrig's disease at 46. Kelly, who was only 43, decided to quit her job to pursue her dreams while she still could, which included traveling to all 50 U.S. states and pursuing a graduate degree. Kelly, as well as most other people, clearly value things other than just money and regularly make choices that trade off money for other things that they value.

Source: C. Oakley (2013), "Would You Rather Have More Time or More Money?" *Forbes* (12/20) and M. Murphy (2013), "More CFOs Choose to Retire Early," *The Wall Street Journal* (December 10).

explanation is not very helpful in giving management guidance on how to address the problem. It suggests that Merrill Lynch might try to fire dishonest employees and replace them with employees who care more about personal integrity. But the difficulty of observing personal preferences limits the feasibility of this approach. It would be difficult for Merrill Lynch to know if, as a group, its new hires would be any less dishonest than the old employees. You cannot just ask applicants if they are honest—if they are not, they will have no qualms about claiming that they are.

The fact that individuals are clever and creative in limiting the effects of constraints greatly complicates management problems. Changing incentives will affect employee behavior, though sometimes in a perverse and unintended manner. Consider two of the Soviet Union's early attempts to adopt incentive compensation to motivate employees. To discourage taxi drivers from simply parking their cabs, they were rewarded for total miles traveled; to encourage additional production, chandelier manufacturers were rewarded on total volume of production—measured in kilograms. In response to these incentive plans, Moscow taxi drivers began driving empty cabs at high speeds on highways outside the city and chandelier manufacturers started producing such massive fixtures that they literally would collapse ceilings. (It is less costly to make one 100-kilo chandelier than five 20-kilo chandeliers; manufacturers also substituted lead for lighter-weight inputs.) Merrill Lynch initially adopted bonuses to motivate analysts to work harder and cooperate across business units. The deceitful behavior was a side effect that potentially was unanticipated when the plan was adopted.

In summary, the economic approach to behavior has important managerial implications. The framework suggests that a manager can motivate desired actions by establishing appropriate incentives. However, managers must be careful because setting improper incentives can motivate perverse behavior.

It is worth noting that economic analysis is limited in its ability to forecast the precise choices of a given individual because individual preferences are largely unobservable. The focus is on aggregate behavior or on what the typical person tends to do. For example, an economist might not be very good at predicting the responses of individual employees to a new incentive plan. An economist will be successful in

---

MANAGERIAL APPLICATIONS

Medicare Creates Perverse Incentives for Doctors

Doctors do not care about money but are motivated by concerns about providing the best care for patients—right? Apparently many doctors and the major drug company employees do not think so. Perverse incentives among physicians arguably have contributed to the problem of spiraling health care costs in the United States.

For years, Medicare (federal health program for the elderly) reimbursement policies allowed individual doctors to make hundreds of thousands of dollars a year in extra profits from the drugs they administered to patients in their offices (the doctors would buy the drugs themselves and bill Medicare, rather than having the patients get them directly from pharmacies). For example, many cancer doctors earned over $1 million per year on drug sales alone. Because the profits on different drugs varied enormously, doctors had incentives to prescribe medications with the highest profit margins. Some physicians have acknowledged that they performed treatments that got them the best reimbursements, "whether or not the treatments benefited patients."

Drug companies were well aware of the Medicare policies and calculated the profits that doctors received from prescribing specific drugs "down to the penny." For example, in 1998 Schering-Plough told its sales representatives that its drug for the treatment of bladder cancer could produce a profit for a physician of $2,373.84 per patient. Sales representatives in turn made sure that doctors were well aware when their drugs were in the high-profit category. For instance, a sales representative for AstraZeneca wrote in a letter to Arizona urologists, "DO THE MATH."

Medicare changed its reimbursement policies in 2005 and reduced the profits that physicians could make on drug sales. At least some physicians have responded by shifting from drug intensive treatments to other treatments that have higher profit margins. To quote one doctor, "People go where the money is, and you'd like to believe it's different in medicine, but it's really no different . . . as long as oncologists continue to be paid by the procedure instead of spending time with patients, they will find ways to game the system."

Source: A. Berensen (2007), "Incentives to Limit Any Savings in Treating Cancer," *nytimes.com* (June 12).

---

predicting that the typical employee will work harder—and thus output for the group will rise—when compensation is tied to output, than when a fixed salary independent of performance is paid. Managers typically are interested in structuring an organizational architecture that will work well and does not depend on specific people filling particular jobs. Individuals come and go, and the manager wants an organization that will work well as these changes occur. In this context, the economic framework is likely to be useful. To solve management problems where the characteristics of a specific individual are more important, other frameworks may be more valuable. For example, if the board is interviewing a potential new CEO, insights into that individual's behavior derived from psychology might be extremely useful.

Alternative Models of Behavior[18]

We have shown how the economic view of behavior can be used in managerial decision making. We now discuss four other models that are commonly used by managers (either explicitly or implicitly) to explain behavior. Our discussion of each of these models is simplified. The intent, however, is to capture the essence of a few of the more prominent views that managers have about behavior and to illustrate how managerial decision making is affected by the particular view. We contrast these

---

[18]This section draws on W. Meckling (1976).

MANAGERIAL APPLICATIONS

Happy Is Productive versus Economic Incentives—The Affordable Care Act

The Affordable Care Act, better known, as "ObamaCare," has generated significant controversy since it was signed into law in 2010. The Congressional Budget Office (CBO) conducts economic analysis for Congress and is "widely revered by both Democrats and Republicans alike as the gold standard for economic analysis." In 2014, the CBO reported that it expected the equivalent of 2.5 million Americans, who were otherwise willing and able to work before ObamaCare, to work less or not at all as a result of the law by 2024. The projection contrasts dramatically with earlier forecasts made by proponents of ObamaCare, who projected a resulting increase in employment. These positive forecasts were based in part on an implicit assumption of the Happy is Productive Model of Behavior. The logic is as follows. Most people want to work because being productive leads to greater happiness. Bad health, however, can prevent people from working. ObamaCare by promoting a healthier population will increase the number of employed people. This argument, however, ignores economic incentives. ObamaCare imposes a stiff economic cost on unemployed people who take jobs—they lose all or part of their government subsidies for purchasing health insurance. Economist Casey Mulligan sums up the economic incentives created by ObamaCare succinctly, "when you pay people for being low income, you are going to have more low-income people." While this is but one effect in evaluating the merits of ObamaCare, it would appear to be a potentially important one.

Source: J. Rago (2014), "The Weekend Interview with Casey Mulligan," *The Wall Street Journal* (February 8), A15.

---

alternative views with the economic view and argue why the economic framework is a particularly useful tool for managers.

Only-Money-Matters Model

Some people believe that the only important component of the job is the level of monetary compensation. But as we have already suggested, people have an incredibly broad range of interests, extending substantially beyond money. And these interests are reflected in a diverse array of activities. As examples, much of the work through the Red Cross is undertaken by unpaid volunteers; people frequently choose early retirement, forgoing a regular paycheck to enjoy additional leisure time; riskier occupations command higher pay in order to attract people into those jobs.

Some of this confusion can result from a misinterpretation of standard economic analysis. Central to economics is the study of trade-offs (recall our discussion of indifference curves illustrating trade-offs between food and clothing). Economists frequently use money as one of the goods being considered. But in these cases, money is merely a convenient unit of value: It simply represents general purchasing power. Its use does not suggest that only money matters.

Happy-Is-Productive Model

Managers sometimes assert that happy employees are more productive than unhappy employees. Managers following this happy-is-productive model see as their goal the designing of work environments that satisfy employees. Psychological theories, such as Maslow's and Herzberg's, are frequently used as guides in efforts to increase job satisfaction.[19]

---

[19]F. Herzberg, B. Mausner, and B. Snyderman (1959), *The Motivation to Work* (John Wiley & Sons: New York); and A. Maslow (1970), *Motivation and Personality* (Harper & Row: New York).

MANAGERIAL APPLICATIONS

Culture and Behavior

In Tokyo, lost cell phones, umbrellas, and cash regularly find their way to the Tokyo Metropolitan Police Lost and Found Center—the Japanese are scrupulous about turning in found articles. In 2002 the center handled $23 million in cash and 330,000 umbrellas. Scrupulous behavior of this type is far less common in New York City and many other cities around the world. What accounts for this "cultural difference?" The historic and current behavior of the Japanese can be explained at least in part by economic incentives.

The system traces its roots to a code written in 718. Lost goods, animals, and servants had to be handed over to a government official within five days of being found. Not handing over found objects was severely punished. In 1733 two officials who kept a parcel of clothing were led around town and executed. Current law gives the finder seven days to turn in found goods. If the item is reclaimed, the finder is entitled to a reward (5 to 20 percent). If the item is not reclaimed within six months, the finder can claim it.

The most commonly reclaimed item is a cell phone—about 75 percent are returned. The least reclaimed are umbrellas at 0.3 percent.

Source: N. Onishi (2004), "Never Lost, but Found Daily," *New York Times* (January 8), A1.

A manager adhering to the happy-is-productive model might suggest that the problem at Merrill Lynch was motivated by disgruntled employees who took out their frustrations on customers. This view implies that Merrill Lynch could reduce the problem by promoting employee satisfaction through such actions as designing more interesting jobs, increasing the rates of pay, and improving the work environment. Happier employees would be expected to provide customers with better investment advice.

The economic and happy-is-productive models do not differ based on what people care about. The economic model allows individuals to value love, esteem, interesting work, and pleasant work environments, as well as more standard economic goods such as food, clothing, and shelter. The primary difference in the models is what motivates individual actions. In the happy-is-productive model, employees exert high effort when they are happy. In the economic model, employees exert effort because of the rewards.

To contrast the two models, consider offering an employee guaranteed lifetime employment plus a large salary, which will be paid independent of performance. The happy-is-productive model suggests that the employee will be more productive, because the high salary and job security are likely to increase job satisfaction. The economic model suggests that the employee would exert less effort—since the employee receives no additional rewards for working harder and will not be fired for exerting low effort.

Good-Citizen Model

Some managers subscribe to the good-citizen model. The basic assumption is that employees have a strong personal desire to do a good job; they take pride in their work and want to excel. Under this view, managers have three primary roles. First, they need to communicate the goals and objectives of the organization to employees. Second, they must help employees discover how to achieve these goals and objectives. Finally, managers should provide feedback on performance so that employees can continue to improve their efforts. There is no reason to have incentive pay, since individuals are interested intrinsically in doing a good job.

This view suggests that the problems at Merrill Lynch occurred because employees misunderstood what was good for the company. Employees might have thought that increasing investment banking revenues was in the company's best interests, even if it required a certain amount of dishonesty. Under the good-citizen view, the management of Merrill Lynch could motivate employee honesty by clearly communicating to its analysts that Merrill Lynch would be better off in the long run if they did not deceive their customers. Managers might be instructed to hold a series of analyst meetings to stress the value of honesty and objective investment advice.

In the good-citizen model, employees place the interests of the company first. There is never a conflict between an employee's personal interest and the interest of the company. In contrast, the economic model posits that employees maximize their own utility. Potential conflicts of interest often arise. The economic view predicts that pleas from Merrill Lynch management that analysts be more honest would have little effect on behavior unless they also changed the reward system to make it in the interests of analysts to be more honest.

Product-of-the-Environment Model

The product-of-the-environment model argues that the behaviors of individuals are largely determined by their upbringings. Some cultures and households encourage positive values in individuals, such as industry and integrity, whereas others promote negative traits, such as laziness and dishonesty. This model suggests that Merrill Lynch had dishonest analysts. A response would have been to fire these employees and replace them with honest analysts from better backgrounds.

Which Model Should Managers Use?

Behavior is a complex topic. No behavioral model is likely to be useful in all contexts. For example, the economic model is unlikely to be helpful in predicting whether a given individual will prefer a red shirt to a blue shirt (selling at the same price). But our focus is on managerial decision making. In this context, there are reasons to believe that the economic model is particularly useful.

Managers are frequently interested in fostering *changes* in behavior. For example, managers want consumers to buy more of their products, employees to exert more effort, and labor unions to accept smaller wage increases. In contrast to other models, the economic framework provides managers with concrete guidance on how to alter behavior. Desired behavior can be encouraged by changing the feasible opportunities facing the decision maker. For example, incentive compensation can be used to motivate employees, and price changes can be used to affect consumer behavior.

There is ample evidence to support the hypothesis that this economic framework is useful in explaining changes in behavior. The most common example is that consumers tend to buy less of a product at higher prices. The evidence suggests that the model is also useful in explaining aspects of behavior in many other contexts, including voting; the formation, dissolution, and structure of families; drug addiction; and the incidence of crime.[20]

[20]G. Becker (1993).

The Economic Framework and Criminal Behavior

Criminals often are viewed as psychologically disturbed. Evidence, however, suggests that criminal behavior can be explained, at least in part, by the economic framework. This framework predicts that a criminal will consider the marginal costs and benefits of a crime and will commit the crime only when the benefits exceed the costs. Under this view, increasing the likelihood of detection and/or the severity of punishment will reduce crimes. In a pioneering study, Issac Ehrlich examined whether the incidence of major felonies varied across states with the expected punishment. He found that the incidence of robberies decreased about 1.3 percent in response to each 1 percent increase in the proportionate likelihood of punishment. The incidence of crime also decreased with the severity of the punishment. Since Ehrlich's study, scholars have conducted extensive research on this topic. In general, the results support the conclusion that the economic model plays a useful role in explaining criminal activity.

Source: I. Ehrlich (1973), "Participation in Illegitimate Activities: A Theoretical and Empirical Investigation," *Journal of Political Economy* 81, 521–565.

The good-citizen model appears less successful in predicting behavior in business settings. Management would be an easy task if employees would work harder and produce higher-quality products simply on request. The happy-is-productive model also has material limitations. Most importantly, the existing evidence suggests that there is little relation between job satisfaction and performance (see Scott's "Criticisms of the Happy-Is-Productive Model" in the accompanying box). Happy employees are not necessarily more productive. Sometimes, managers might want to follow the implications of the product-of-the-environment model and fire employees with undesirable traits. Yet, this approach is of limited use in solving most managerial problems. Also, given laws that limit discrimination, this approach can subject the firm to potentially serious legal sanctions.

Criticisms of the Happy-Is-Productive Model

W. Richard Scott summarizes some of the major concerns about the happy-is-productive model (sometimes referred to as the human-relations movement):

> Virtually all of these applications of the human-relations movement have come under severe criticism on both ideological and empirical grounds. Paradoxically, the human-relations movement, ostensibly developed to humanize the cold and calculating rationality of the factory and shop, rapidly came under attack on the grounds that it represented simply a more subtle and refined form of exploitation. Critics charged that workers' legitimate economic interests were being inappropriately deemphasized; actual conflicts of interest were denied and "therapeutically" managed; and the roles attributed to managers represented a new brand of elitism. The entire movement was branded as "cow sociology" just as contented cows were alleged to produce more milk, satisfied workers were expected to produce more output.

> The ideological criticisms were the first to erupt, but reservations raised by researchers on the basis of empirical evidence may in the long run prove to be more devastating. Several decades of research have documented no clear relation between worker satisfaction and productivity.

Source: W. R. Scott (1981), *Organizations: Rational, Natural and Open Systems* (Prentice Hall: Englewood Cliffs), 89–90.

ANALYZING MANAGERIAL DECISIONS: *Interwest Healthcare Corp.*

Interwest Healthcare is a nonprofit organization that owns 10 hospitals located in three western states. Cynthia Manzoni is Interwest's CEO. Vijay Singh, Interwest's CFO, and the administrators of the 10 hospitals report to Manzoni.

Singh is deeply concerned because the hospital staffs are not being careful when entering data into the firm's management information system. This data involves information on patient intake, treatment, and release. The information system is used to compile management reports such as those relating to the costs of various treatments. Also, the system is used to compile reports that are required by the federal government under various grant programs. Singh reasons that without good information, the management and government reports are less useful and potentially misleading. Moreover, the federal government periodically audits Interwest and might discontinue aid if the reports are deemed inaccurate. Thus, Singh is worried about the managerial implications and the potential loss of federal funds.

Singh has convinced Manzoni that a problem exists. She also realizes the importance of an accurate system for both management planning and maintaining federal aid. Six months ago, she invited the hospital administrators and staff members from the corporate financial office to a retreat at a resort. The purpose was to communicate to the hospital administrators the problems with the data entry and to stress the importance of doing a better job. The meeting was acrimonious. The hospital people accused Singh of being a bureaucrat who did not care about patient services. Singh accused the hospital staffs of not understanding the importance of accurate reporting. By the end of the meeting, Manzoni thought that she had a commitment by the hospital administrators to increase the accuracy of data entry at their hospitals. However, six months later, Singh claims that the problem is as bad as ever.

Manzoni has hired you as a consultant to analyze the problem and to make recommendations that might improve the situation.

1. What are the potential sources of the problem?
2. What information would you want to analyze?
3. What actions might you recommend to increase the accuracy of the data entry?
4. How does your view of behavior affect how you might address this consulting assignment?

Behavioral Economics

The traditional economic model of behavior assumes that individuals are *rational,* in that they employ marginal analysis in decision making—they balance the incremental costs and benefits to arrive at choices that maximize their personal happiness. One, however, does not have to look far to observe people making choices that by this definition appear economically irrational. For example, how many of us have eaten all the food served on a plate, even when we are not hungry and want to lose weight? Do we have some vague notion that we are not wasting food by eating more than we really need or want? How many of us might volunteer to help a distressed person change a flat tire for free, but feel insulted if they offered to pay us for the work?

Simple behavioral observations, as well as more formal evidence from experiments, suggest that people do not always behave rationally. A somewhat new field called *Behavioral Economics* has emerged that covers a wide range of attempts to extend the standard economics framework to account for potentially relevant features of human behavior that are not included in standard analysis[21]. While

---

[21]See *Behavioral Economics and Its Application* (2007), edited by P. Diamond and H. Vartiainen (Princeton University Press, Princeton and Oxford) for a collection of papers that summarize behavioral research on a variety of economic topics.

behavioral economists do not argue that economic incentives are unimportant, they tend to focus more on the cognitive, emotional, and social factors that affect individuals in making economic decisions. The ultimate objective of this research is to provide a better understanding of both aggregate market and individual economic behavior than we can get from the standard analysis alone.

The assumptions used in any type of scientific modeling, however, are never entirely realistic. Indeed, the purpose of a model is to simplify the analysis to make it tractable. For instance, a physical scientist might assume "unrealistically" that there is a perfect vacuum to derive a scientific formula. The test of her model, however, should not be based on the realism of her assumptions, but on how well the model helps us to predict or understand real-world phenomena. By this criterion, standard economic analysis has stood the test of time. For many decades, it has proven useful in helping managers to understand their competitive environments better and for improving their decision making and performance. This book presents the standard economic framework and focuses on the many managerial insights that it provides. A detailed study of Behavioral Economics, while potentially interesting, is beyond the scope of this book.

The need for more "realistic" assumptions in a model depends in part on the purpose of the model. For example, suppose that your boss has to go to Chicago for a business meeting and wants you to provide directions on how to drive to the specific location. You have at least two choices: (1) you might download a satellite photograph of the Chicago area or (2) you might get a map. Although the satellite photo would certainly include more realism, for this purpose, the map would be more useful. Most of the additional realism in the photograph is extraneous for your particular purpose. The map abstracts from these unimportant aspects of the area to highlight those facets that are important. It is precisely this sense in which within this book, we employ models that abstract from an array of aspects of reality to highlight those things that are important for the particular issue at hand. On a few occasions, particularly in the chapters on organizational architecture, we analyze issues for which behavioral economics provides particularly relevant insights for managers. In these cases, we present both the standard economic analysis of the problem, as well as discussion of the implications from the behavior research.

Decision Making under Uncertainty

Throughout this chapter, we have considered cases where the decision maker has complete certainty about the items of choice. For instance, Dom Lalisse knew the exact prices of food and clothing, and Sue Chen knew the precise trade-off between integrity and compensation at Merrill Lynch. Decision makers, however, often face uncertainty. For instance, in choosing among risky investment alternatives (such as stocks and bonds), an individual must forecast the likely payoffs. Even so, there can be significant uncertainty about the eventual outcomes. The analysis presented in this chapter can be extended readily to incorporate decision making under uncertainty.[22] A detailed analysis of decision making under uncertainty is beyond the scope of this book. This section introduces a few key concepts that we will use later in this book.

---

[22]For example, E. Fama and M. Miller (1972), *The Theory of Finance* (Dryden Press: New York), Chapter 5.

Expected Value

Taylor McClure sells real estate for RealCo. He receives a sales commission from his employer. For simplicity, suppose that Taylor has three possible incomes for the year. In a good year, he sells many houses and earns $200,000, whereas in a bad year he earns nothing. In other years, he receives $100,000. Probability refers to the likelihood that an outcome will occur. In this example, each outcome is equally likely, and thus has a probability of $1/3$ of occurring. The *expected value* of an uncertain payoff is defined as the weighted average of all possible outcomes, where the probability of each outcome is used as the weights. The expected value is a measure of central tendency—the payoff that will occur on average. In our example, the expected value is[23]

$$\text{Expected value} = (1/3 \times 0) + (1/3 \times 100,000) + (1/3 \times 200,000) \quad (2.6)$$
$$= \$100,000$$

Variability

Although Taylor can expect average earnings of $100,000, his income is not certain. The *variance* is a measure of the variability of the payoff. It is defined as the expected value of the squared difference between each possible payoff and the expected value. In this example, the variance is

$$\text{Variance} = 1/3(0 - 100,000)^2 + 1/3(100,000 - 100,000)^2 \quad (2.7)$$
$$+ 1/3(200,000 - 100,000)^2$$
$$= 6.7 \text{ billion}$$

The *standard deviation* is the square root of the variance:

$$\text{Standard deviation} = (6.7 \text{ billion})^{1/2} = \$81,650 \quad (2.8)$$

Variances and standard deviations are used as measures of risk. It does not really matter which we use, since one is a simple transformation of the other (higher standard deviations correspond to higher variances). In this example, we focus on the standard deviation—in part because the standard deviation is expressed in the same units as the mean, dollars (the units for the variance would be dollars squared). Higher standard deviations reflect more risk. An event with a definite outcome has a standard deviation of zero.

Risk Aversion

Like most people, Taylor is *risk-averse:* Holding the expected payoff fixed, he prefers a lower standard deviation. He, therefore, gains utility from an increase in expected value, but he experiences a reduction in utility from increases in standard deviation. Figure 2.9 shows three of Taylor's indifference curves. Each curve shows all combinations of expected value and standard deviation that give Taylor equal

---

[23]Note that the expected value need not equal one of the possible outcomes. As a weighted average, it can be a value between outcomes. In this example, it happens to correspond to one of the possible outcomes, $100,000.

Figure 2.9   Indifference Curves for Expected Value and Standard Deviation

This figure displays three indifference curves for a *risk-averse* individual. The individual prefers higher expected value but lower standard deviation. Standard deviation is a measure of risk. Since risk is a "bad," the indifference curves are positively sloped. Upward and leftward moves are utility-increasing. Currently, the individual has a compensation package that has an expected value of $100,000 and a standard deviation of $81,650. The *certainty equivalent* of this package is $80,000. The *risk premium* is $20,000.

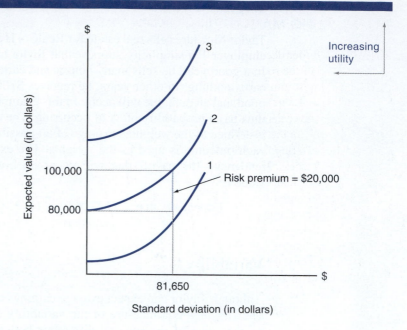

utility. In contrast to our previous analysis, here one of the objects of choice is a "bad"—Taylor dislikes risk. Thus, in this figure, the indifference curves have positive slopes, and upward and leftward movements are utility-increasing (recall in the standard analysis that the curves have negative slopes, and upward and rightward movements are utility-increasing). The slopes of the indifference curves indicate Taylor's degree of risk aversion. Steeper slopes translate into higher risk aversion. (If the slopes of the indifference curves are steep, Taylor must receive a relatively large increase in expected value for each additional unit of risk to maintain a constant level of utility.) If his indifference curves were totally flat, he would be *risk-neutral.* A risk-neutral person cares only about expected value and is indifferent to the amount of risk. Indifference curve 3 is associated with the highest level of utility, whereas curve 1 is associated with the lowest utility. Taylor is currently on curve 2. Given a choice among compensation plans with different expected payoffs and risk, Taylor will choose the combination that places him on the highest attainable indifference curve.

Certainty Equivalent and Risk Premium

Figure 2.9 indicates that Taylor is indifferent between the risky commission scheme, which has an expected payoff of $100,000, and a certain income of $80,000. The $80,000 is Taylor's *certainty equivalent* for the risky income stream—he is willing to trade the uncertain income of $100,000 for a certain income of $80,000. The difference between the expected value of the risky income stream and the certainty equivalent is called the *risk premium.* This $20,000 premium, which comes in the form of a higher expected payoff, must be paid to keep Taylor indifferent between the risky income stream and his certainty equivalent.

ANALYZING MANAGERIAL DECISIONS: *Risk Aversion versus Risk Taking*

Lauren Arbittier decides to bet $2,000 on number 35 of the roulette wheel in a Las Vegas casino. Almost immediately she starts to question her decision. Lauren normally is a risk avoider who hardly ever gambles. But she works at Trilogy Software where the CEO understands that taking risks and suffering the consequences are critical to the firm's success. The CEO wants to develop people who take chances. "You don't win points . . . for trying." Lauren is participating in Trilogy's three-month training program for all new recruits. It educates employees about, among other things, how to evaluate risky projects, not just to immediately accept or reject the project because it is risky. The program also suggests to employees that they will not be rewarded at Trilogy unless they take

risks. Thus, although Lauren does not like taking risks, working for Trilogy, she has economic incentives to do so.

There are at least three ways in which the Trilogy training program might be effective: (1) It changes employees' preferences regarding risk bearing. (2) It more effectively identifies individuals with the risk tolerances that Trilogy desires. (3) It better communicates the consequences to Trilogy employees of undertaking risky ventures. Discuss the likely importance of these three mechanisms.

SOURCE: E. Ramstad (1998), "High Rollers, How Trilogy Software Trains Its Raw Recruits to Be Risk Takers," *The Wall Street Journal* (September 21), A1.

Suppose that Taylor receives a job offer from a competing real estate company that would pay him a fixed salary of $90,000 per year. Taylor considers the new job to be the same as his current job in all dimensions other than the compensation plan. Taylor's current compensation plan will not be sufficient to motivate him to continue to work for RealCo. Even though his current plan has a higher expected payoff, he would prefer the certain $90,000 to RealCo's risky commission plan. If RealCo wants to retain Taylor, it must offer him a compensation package that provides the same level of utility as the $90,000 for certain.

Risk Aversion and Compensation

Diversified shareholders, who invest in portfolios of companies, own much of the stock of large firms. Managers are often ill-diversified, having much of their human and financial capital invested in one firm. As we will discuss later in this book, this difference in diversification can lead to managers being overly risk averse in their investment decisions relative to those shareholders would prefer. Shareholders can induce managers to undertake more risky investment by adopting compensation plans that reward good outcomes, but that do not penalize bad outcomes heavily. The top management of Enron (see Chapter 1) arguably went too far in this direction, inducing their managers to take too much risk (effectively transforming their behavior from risk averse to "risk loving").[24] We expand on this issue later in the book.

[24]Most managers have risk-averse preferences (utility functions). Managerial actions, however, are a function of both preferences and constraints. Thus risk-averse preferences can be offset or reinforced by the design of the compensation plan. Compensation plans that limit the upside potential but not the downside induce less risky choices, whereas plans that limit the downside but not the upside induce more risky choices.

Summary

In this chapter we summarize the way economists view behavior. In the economic model, individuals are seen as having unlimited wants but limited resources. They rank alternative uses of limited resources in terms of preference and choose the most preferred alternative. Individuals are clever in figuring out ways of maximizing their satisfaction (utility) in the face of resource constraints. Individuals are not necessarily selfish in the sense that they care only about their personal wealth: They also care about charity, family, religion, and society. They are not infallible supercomputers.

The *opportunity cost* of using a resource is the value of the resource in its best alternative use. For example, the cost of having a manager use five hours to work on a project is the value of the manager's time in working on the next best alternative project. Economic decision making requires careful consideration of the relevant opportunity costs.

Marginal costs and benefits are the incremental costs and benefits that are associated with a decision. In calculating marginal costs, it is important to incorporate the opportunity costs of the incremental resources. For example, in deciding whether to purchase a new laptop computer, the marginal cost is its price and the marginal benefit is the value that the person places on the new computer. It is the marginal costs and benefits that are important in economic decision making. Action should be taken when the marginal benefits are greater than the marginal costs. *Sunk costs* that are not affected by the decision (e.g., unrecoverable funds previously spent on computers) are not relevant.

A *utility function* is a mathematical function that relates total utility to the amounts that an individual has of whatever items the individual cares about (*goods*). Preferences implied by a utility function are pictured graphically by *indifference curves*. Indifference curves depict all combinations of goods that yield the same level of utility. Individual choice involves maximizing utility given resource *constraints*. Graphically, the constraint depicts all combinations of goods that are feasible to acquire; it defines the feasible consumption opportunities. The optimal choice is where the indifference curve is tangent to the constraint. At this point, the individual is at the highest level of utility possible given the feasible opportunities.

Changes in opportunities result in changes in the optimal choice. An important implication is that managers can affect behavior by affecting constraints and opportunities. Managers, however, have to be careful. Individuals are clever at maximizing their utility, and establishing disfunctional incentives can have perverse consequences.

We contrast the economic model with other models of human behavior that managers often use. We argue that the economic model is often more useful than alternative models in managerial decision making.

The analysis in this chapter can be extended to the case where the decision maker faces uncertainty about the items of choice. An example of decision making under uncertainty is choosing among risky investment alternatives. One concept on which we will rely later in this book is *risk aversion*. When confronted with both a risky and a certain alternative having the same expected (or average) payoffs, a risk-averse person always will choose the certain outcome. A *risk premium* must be offered to entice the person to choose the risky alternative.

Throughout this chapter, we focus primarily on how managers might use this economic view to analyze and influence the behavior of employees. As we will see, the economic view is quite powerful and useful in explaining behavior in a variety of different contexts.

Suggested Readings

G. Becker (1993), "Nobel Lecture: The Economic Way of Looking at Behavior," *Journal of Political Economy* 101, 385–409.

M. Jensen and W. Meckling (1994), "The Nature of Man," *Journal of Applied Corporate Finance* 7, 4–19.

Self-Evaluation Problems

2–1. Suppose there are only two goods that Bob cares about—(1) material welfare and (2) leisure time that he "buys" from the outside world at $40 per unit and $20 per hour, respectively. He currently lives and works in Atlanta, has a budget totaling $1,000 per week for these two goods, and consumes 11 units of material welfare and 28 hours of leisure time.

   a. Show Bob's consumption choice on a graph using the actual budget line and a hypothetical indifference curve. (Label the axes and show the x and y intercepts.)

   b. How will Bob's optimal consumption choice change if the government imposes a $10/unit tax on the material welfare good?

   c. Suppose Bob has a chance to move (at zero cost) to Saint Louis where material welfare and leisure time cost $50 and $10, respectively. His budget remains the same as before and the government has decided not to impose a tax on the material good. Would Bob move to Saint Louis? Why or why not? Explain.

2–2. Amiko is an investor in the stock market. She cares about both the expected value and standard deviation of her investment. Currently she is invested in a security that has an expected value of $25,000 and a standard deviation of $10,000. This places her on an indifference curve with the following formula: Expected Value = $15,000 + Standard Deviation

   a. Is Amiko risk-averse? Explain.

   b. What is Amiko's "certainty equivalent" for her current investment? What does this mean?

   c. What is the risk premium on Amiko's current investment?

2–3. You have won a free ticket to see an Eric Clapton concert (which has no resale value). Bob Dylan is performing on the same night and is your next best alternative activity. Tickets to see Dylan cost $40. On any given day, you would be willing to pay up to $50 to see Dylan. Assume there are no other costs of seeing either performer. Based on this information, what is the opportunity cost of seeing Eric Clapton? (a) $0, (b) $10, (c) $40, or (d) $50[25]

Solutions to Self-Evaluation Problems

2–1. Individual Choice

   a.

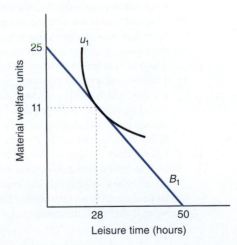

   b. The $10 tax increases the price of material welfare from $40 to $50. Refer to Figure 2.6 to see the effects of a price increase on optimal consumption (replace food with material

[25]Suggested by R. Frank (2005), "The Opportunity Costs of Economics Education," *New York Times* (September 1), C2.

welfare on the vertical axis and clothing with leisure time on the horizontal axis). Bob is likely to reduce his consumption of material welfare due to the price increase. His consumption of leisure time could either go up, down, or stay the same depending on the exact nature of his adjustment. The change in relative prices (reflected in the flatter budget line) will work in the direction of motivating Bob to substitute units of material welfare for more leisure time. However, Bob's new budget line will not allow him to stay on the same indifference curve as before (it rotates inward). His consumption of leisure time will depend on the exact location of the new tangency point on a lower indifference curve in the graph. Bob was spending $560 to purchase 28 hours of leisure time. Whether Bob consumes more or less leisure time after the price increase depends on how much money he has left over after buying fewer units of material welfare at the new higher price. For example, if he only reduces his consumption of material welfare from 11 to 10 units, he will have less money to spend on leisure time than before ($500 versus $560). Alternatively, if he reduces his consumption of material welfare to 8 or fewer units he will have more money than he had before to spend on leisure time. Which option he chooses depends on his specific utility function.

c. Bob would want to move to Saint Louis. In Saint Louis, his current consumption bundle only costs $830. This leaves $170 to spend on other goods. Since more is better than less, he can always do better in Saint Louis than he is currently doing in Atlanta.

2–2. Decision Making Under Uncertainty

a. Yes, Amiko is risk-averse. She is willing to take on more risk only if it is associated with a sufficiently higher expected return.

b. Amiko's certainty equivalent is $15,000. She would be willing to accept a certain return of $15,000 (the vertical intercept of her indifference curve) in lieu of her current risky investment that has an expected return of $25,000 and a standard deviation of $10,000.

c. The risk premium on Amiko's current investment is $10,000. This is the difference in the expected return of her risky investment and the risk-free investment (certainty equivalent). The $10,000 risk premium is what it takes in expected return to make her indifferent between the risk and risk-free investments.

2–3. Opportunity cost is a subtle concept that requires careful analysis to implement. Even trained economists can make mistakes if they are not careful to include all relevant costs in the analysis. Two researchers from Georgia State University (P. Ferraro and L. Taylor) posed the question to 200 professional economists at an annual meeting.

A careful application of the definition of opportunity costs yields a clear answer—$10. The next best alternative use of your time, going to the Bob Dylan concert, produces a net benefit of $10 (the $50 value you place on the Dylan concert minus the $40 to purchase the ticket). Marginal analysis implies that you should go to the Clapton concert as long as you obtain at least $10 worth of happiness from the concert. For example, if you value the Clapton concert at $15, you are $5 better off going to the Clapton concert than the Dylan concert, which yields only $10 of net value. Interestingly, only 21.6 percent of the professional economists surveyed chose the correct answer, a smaller percentage than if they had chosen randomly. Additional surveys revealed that the incorrect answers were driven by faulty analysis and not by the specific wording of the question. College students who had taken a course in economics did even worse.

The lesson is that managers, students, and even economists should be careful to include all of the relevant explicit and implicit opportunity costs in their analyses. Missing a hypothetical question on opportunity costs is inconsequential. Managers can destroy significant value if they make mistakes in evaluating opportunity costs in their decision making.

Review Questions

2–1. Which costs are pertinent to economic decision making? Which costs are *not* relevant?

2–2. A noted economist was asked what he did with his "free time." He responded by saying that "time is not free." Explain this response.

2–3. The Solace Company has an inventory of steel that it originally purchased for $20,000. It currently has an offer to sell the steel for $30,000. Should Solace's management agree to sell? Explain.

2–4. Suppose that you have $900 and want to invest the money for one year. There are three existing options.
   a. The city of Rochester is selling bonds at $90 per unit. The bonds pay $100 at the end of one year when they mature (no other cash flows).
   b. Put the money under your mattress.
   c. The one-year interest rate of saving in the Chase Bank is 7 percent.

   Which one will you choose? What is the opportunity cost of your choice? Explain.

2–5. Suppose Juan's utility function is given by $U = FC$, where F and C are the two goods available for purchase: food and clothing.
   a. Graph Juan's indifference curves for the following levels of utility: 100, 200, and 300.
   b. Are these curves convex or concave to the origin? What does this shape imply about Juan's willingness to trade food for clothing?
   c. Suppose Juan's budget is $100 and the prices of F and C are both $5. Graph the budget constraint.
   d. How many units of food and clothing will Juan purchase at these prices and income? Show graphically. What is his corresponding level of utility?
   e. The Johnson Company is the sole producer of clothing. What can the company do to induce Juan to purchase more clothing? Show graphically. (The graph does not have to be exact.)

2–6. Suppose that Bob's indifference curves are straight lines (as opposed to being convex to the origin). What does this imply about Bob's willingness to trade one good for the other? Give examples of goods where this type of behavior might be expected?

2–7. Suppose that Bob's indifference curves are perfectly L-shaped with the right angle occurring when Bob has equal amounts of both goods. What does this imply about Bob's willingness to trade one good for the other? Give examples of goods where this type of behavior might be expected?

2–8. a. Briefly describe the five models of behavior presented in this chapter.
   b. What are the implications of these models for managers attempting to influence their employees' behavior?

2–9. Employees in a plant in Minnesota are observed to be industrious and very productive. Employees in a similar plant in southern California are observed to be lazy and unproductive. Discuss how alternative views of human behavior and motivation might suggest different explanations for this observed behavior.

2–10. Employees at a department store are observed engaging in the following behavior: (a) they hide items that are on sale from the customers, and (b) they exert little effort in designing merchandise displays. They are also uncooperative with one another. What do you think might be causing this behavior, and what might you do to improve the situation?

2–11. One of the main tenets of economic analysis is that people act in their own narrow self-interest. Why then do people leave tips in restaurants? If a study were to compare the size of tips earned by servers in restaurants on interstate highways with those in restaurants near residential neighborhoods, what would you expect to find? Why?

2–12. Several school districts have attempted to increase teacher productivity by paying teachers based on the scores their students achieve on standardized tests (administered by outside testing agencies). The goal is to produce higher-quality classroom instruction. Do you think that this type of compensation scheme will produce the desired outcome? Explain.

2–13. A company recently raised the pay of employees by 20 percent. Employee productivity remained the same. The CEO of the company was quoted as saying, "It just goes to show that money does not motivate people." Provide a critical evaluation of this statement.

2–14. One physician who worked for a large health maintenance organization was quoted as saying:

> *One day I was listening to a patient's heart and realized there was an abnormal rhythm. My first thought was that I hoped that I did not have to refer the patient to a specialist.*

Indeed, HMO physicians have been criticized for not making referrals when they are warranted. How do you think the physician was compensated by the HMO? Explain.

2–15. Insurance companies have to generate enough revenue to cover their costs and make a normal profit—otherwise, they will go out of business. This implies that the premiums charged for insurance policies must be greater than the expected payouts to the policyholders. Why would a person ever buy insurance, knowing that the price is greater than the expected payout?

2–16. Critically evaluate the following statement: "Risk-averse people never take gambles."

2–17. Suppose that an investment can yield three possible cash flows: \$5,000; \$1,000; or \$0. The probability of each outcome is 1/3.
   a. What is the expected value and standard deviation of the investment?
   b. How much would a risk-neutral person be willing to pay for the investment?
   c. How much would a risk-averse person be willing to pay for the investment?

2–18. In order to spur consumer spending in 1998, the Japanese government considered an \$85 billion voucher system whereby every Japanese consumer would receive a shopping voucher that could be used to purchase Japanese products. For simplicity, assume the following: Each consumer has wealth of 1 million yen, consumers must allocate this wealth between consumption now (c_1) and consumption later (c_2), the interest rate is zero, the voucher is worth 100,000 yen, and it can be spent only in the current period. If it is not spent, it is lost.
   a. Plot a budget line for a representative consumer both before and after the voucher program (c_1 and c_2 are on the axes).
   b. Do you expect that current consumption of a typical consumer will increase by the full 100,000 yen of the voucher? Explain.
   c. How does the impact of this 100,000-yen voucher differ from simply giving the individual 100,000 yen?

2–19. People give to charity.
   a. Is this action consistent with the "economic view of behavior"? Explain.
   b. Suppose there is a big drop in charitable giving. At the same time there has been no decline in per capita income or total employment. Using the economic model, what potential factors might have led to this decline in giving?
   c. How might the decline in giving be explained by the product-of-the environment model?

2–20. The Japanese are very good at returning lost property to local police stations. If you lose a wallet filled with cash in Japan it is likely to be turned into the police. This is true even though the person finding it could keep it without anyone else knowing. This behavior is not what you would find in New York City.
   a. Does this observation about Japan imply that the economic model does not explain behavior in Japan? Explain.
   b. Police stations in Japan are filled with lost umbrellas. It used to be that the typical Japanese would make a trip to the local police station to search for a lost umbrella. Now they don't. Explain this behavior using the Economic Model.
   c. Do you think that the typical Japanese is more likely to come to a police station to find a lost cell phone or a lost umbrella? Explain using the Economic Model.

2–21. Some states in the United States allow citizens to carry handguns. Citizens can protect themselves in the case of robberies by using these guns. Other states do not allow citizens to carry handguns. Criminals, however, tend to have handguns in all states. *Use economic analysis* to predict the effects of handgun laws on the behavior of the typical criminal. In particular:
   (1) Do you think criminals will commit more or fewer robberies in the states with the laws?
   (2) How do you think the laws will affect the *types of robberies* criminals commit? Be sure to explain your *economic reasoning*.

2–22. Discuss the following statement: "Sunk costs matter. People who pay \$20,000 to join a golf club play golf more frequently than people who play on public golf courses."

2–23. Jenny is an investor in the stock market. She cares about both the expected value and standard deviation of her investment. Currently she is invested in a security that has an expected value of $15,000 and a standard deviation of $5,000. This places her on an indifference curve with the following formula: Expected Value = $10,000 + Standard Deviation.

    a. Is Jenny risk averse? Explain.

    b. What is Jenny's "certainty equivalent" for her current investment? What does this mean?

    c. What is the risk premium on her current investment?

2–24. Accounting problems at Enron ultimately led to the collapse of the large accounting firm Arthur Andersen. When the Enron scandal first became public, Andersen's top management blamed one "rogue partner" in the Houston office who they claimed was less honest than other partners at the firm. They fired the partner and asked that people not hold the remaining partners accountable for "one bad apple." What model of behavior was Andersen's management using when it analyzed the source of the problem? According to the economic view of behavior, what was the more likely cause of the problem?

2–25. According to a recent article in *The Atlanta Journal-Constitution* (January 29, 2004), "materialism, not necessity, gave birth to dual-income families." In supporting the argument, the author cites the following figures from the Department of Commerce: In 1970 the average wage per job was $6,900, which in 2001 dollars (adjusting for inflation) amounts to $31,500. In 2001, the average wage per job was $35,500. The main thesis of the article is that dual-income families are a result of a shift in consumer preferences toward consumption as opposed to leisure time/time spent with the family.

    a. Assume the average person worked 250 days during a year both in 1970 and 2001, and that, as reported in the article, only one person worked in the average family in 1970, while both parents did in 2001. Provide a graphical analysis of the typical family's choice between family income and combined parent leisure time that supports the author's argument, relying on the tools presented in class. Be careful in labeling your graph(s), and provide a clear and concise explanation for your graph(s). Note that there are 365 days in a year so that the total parent leisure time that is possible is 730 days (assuming neither spouse works). Assume it is possible for each family member to work anywhere from 0 to 365 days a year (at the going salary rate) if they choose to do so.

    b. Assume that in 1971 the average single person worked 220 days per year, while the same person worked 260 days per year in 2001. Moreover, suppose the average daily wage in 2001 dollars was $125 in 1970 and $140 in 2001. Show graphically how the author's argument would not necessarily apply to the average single person (i.e., assume preferences are unchanged). Explain clearly and concisely why the average worker may be choosing to work more in 2001 and carefully label your graph.

2-26. Russell and Joe have hired Maria to help cook in their restaurant. Maria had previously owned her own breakfast business. Her speed in cooking was well-known. Russell and Joe have been surprised that her productivity has fallen significantly since she became their paid employee. Use the economic view of behavior and marginal analysis to provide a potential explanation for Maria's reduced productivity.

2-27. Michael is a fan of the Rhinos—the local professional soccer team. At the beginning of the season, he purchased nonrefundable season tickets to their 10 home games for a total of $100. Michael places equal value on each of the home games. His value for any given game is independent of how many other games he attended during the year. Michael would be willing to stay at home, which he derives no benefit from, and miss an individual game, if he could sell the ticket for one game for $20 or more.

Michael has attended three out of the last five home games. The sixth home game of the season is tomorrow night. Michael's friend Fred has offered to sell him an extra ticket to a sold-out concert for $50 that happens to be on the same night as the game. Normally, Michael would be willing to pay $70 to attend the concert. There is no way that Michael can attend both the Rhinos' game and the concert. Looking online, Michael finds that he can sell his ticket for tomorrow night's Rhinos' game for $5.

    a. What type/types of cost is the $100 that Michael paid for the season tickets? Explain why.

    b. Which event will Michael decide to attend? Explain why.

c. How much would Fred have to charge Michael for the concert ticket in order to make Michael not care which event he attended? Explain why.

2-28. An entrepreneur quits his job as a banker and invests $100,000 of his savings in a new business venture that he will manage. Discuss the two most obvious opportunity costs that he will incur from this decision.

2-29. In one hour, John can assemble either 20 telephones or 10 answering machines. It takes Sally two hours to assemble either 20 telephones or 10 answering machines. Does either person have an absolute advantage in assembling either product? What about a competitive advantage? Explain (make sure you define absolute and competitive advantage and provide the opportunity costs for each person). Draw the combined production possibilities curve for the two people assuming that they work eight hours. Put answering machines on the horizontal axis.

2-30. You are trying to decide whether to fly or drive from Rochester to Boston during your summer visit. The trip is approximately 400 miles. You can purchase a round-trip nonstop flight for $230. The duration of each flight is 3.5 hours (seven hours in total). If you drive, it will take you approximately seven hours each way (14 hours in total). Your car gets 32 miles to the gallon and you expect gas will cost $3/gal. Tolls are $15 each way. You value your time at $15 per hour.
   a. Calculate the total cost of driving to Boston and back.
   b. Under these conditions, will you drive or fly?
   c. What if you value your time at $20, rather than $15, per hour?
   d. You are offered a deal for $180 total airfare if you take a flight with a one hour layover in NYC (total flying time does not change). Do you take the deal? Will this change your flying versus driving decision? (Use the $15 per hour value of time in the calculation.)
   e. What are some other costs you may want to consider in this analysis?
   f. If you were expecting a snow storm, how might this change your analysis? What are some other costs you may want to take into consideration?

2-31. The school is having a happy hour on Friday. If you go, you will get two free drink tickets and snacks, for which you would normally pay $15. However, you will have to pay $10 for the cab fare home. You also have a free student ticket to the local profession team's soccer game. There is no resale value, as free tickets are still available.
   a. What is the opportunity cost of going to the soccer game?
   b. If you would not normally pay to go to the soccer game, which will you choose?

2-32. Bill and Chris produce balls and bats. In one hour, Bill can produce two bats or four balls, while Chris can produce one bat or three balls. They each work 10 hours a day.
   a. Which of the following, if any, is true? Explain why.
      1. Chris has an absolute advantage producing balls and a comparative advantage producing balls.
      2. Chris has an absolute advantage producing balls and Bill has a comparative advantage producing balls.
      3. Bill has an absolute advantage producing balls and a comparative advantage producing balls.
      4. Bill has an absolute advantage producing balls and Chris has a comparative advantage producing balls.
   b. If Chris and Bill each split their time evenly between producing balls and producing bats, what is the total number of bats and balls that will be produced in one day?
   c. Can the combined production of balls be increased while holding the number of bats produced constant? How?
   d. Graph the combined production possibilities frontier for Bill and Chris. Place Bats on the vertical axis and Balls on the horizontal axis. [The graph would show the maximum combined amount of bats that could be produced by Bill and Chris for each feasible combined amount of balls that could be produced.]

Appendix A: Consumer Choice

The main text of this chapter provided a simple graphical analysis of individual choice. It introduced utility functions, indifference curves, and budget lines. It depicted the optimal choice as the tangency between an indifference curve and the budget line where the willingness and ability to trade are equal. This simple analysis explained how the optimal choice changes with changes in relative prices or income. This economic framework has important implications since managers often want to influence and/or predict the behavior of individuals, such as customers and employees.

This appendix extends the economic framework of individual choice (commonly called *consumer choice*). Its intent is to provide a deeper and richer understanding of this important model of behavior. This appendix also discusses how this model relates to an important topic that is covered in more detail later in this book—demand functions.

Marginal Utility

A utility function expresses the relation between a person's total utility and the level of goods consumed. Utility functions can take many forms. For illustration, suppose that Tom Morrell values only food and clothing and that his utility function is

$$U = FC \tag{2.9}$$

where F is the units of food and C is the units of clothing that Tom consumes within the period. Notice, this simple utility function is multiplicative in both food and clothing. If Tom has no clothing, then no matter how much food he has, he has utility of zero. Likewise, if he has no food, then no matter has much clothing he has, his utility again is zero. If Tom's consumption bundle consists of 20 units of both food and clothing his utility is 400, while his utility is only 100 if he has 10 units of both goods. Tom prefers the first bundle, but he is not necessarily four times happier when he has 20 units, rather than 10 units, of each good. The utility function provides an *ordinal ranking* of consumption bundles—not a *cardinal ranking* where "absolute" comparisons can be made.

Marginal utility measures the additional utility that is obtained by consuming one additional unit of a good, while holding all other goods constant. Marginal utility is an important concept in economic analysis since optimizing individuals focus on the marginal (incremental) benefits and costs in making consumption choices. Figure 2.10 graphs Tom's utility as a function of food, while holding clothing constant at 10 units. The equation for this graph is

$$U = 10F \tag{2.10}$$

The marginal utility of food in this example is 10—for each additional unit of food that Tom consumes he receives 10 additional units of utility. More generally for any given quantity of clothing, C, the marginal utility of food is C (given Tom's utility function). Similar logic implies that the marginal utility of clothing is F.[26] We denote the marginal utilities for food and clothing by MU_F and MU_C, respectively.

---

[26]Note for the mathematically inclined: The marginal utility of any good X is equal to the partial derivative of the utility function with respect to X. In this example, the partial derivative with respect to F is C, and with respect to C is F. In this example, the marginal utility of each good is constant. More realistically, the marginal utility of a good will eventually decline as the consumer continues to receive more of the good. We employ this utility function only to simplify the presentation.

Figure 2.10   Tom's Utility as a Function of Food with Clothing Held Constant at 10 Units ($U = 10F$)

This figure displays Tom's utility as a function of food with clothing held constant at 10 units. *Marginal utility* measures the additional utility that is obtained by consuming one additional unit of a good, while holding all other goods constant. The marginal utility of F in this example is 10 (the slope of the line)—for each additional unit of F that Tom consumes he receives 10 additional units of utility.

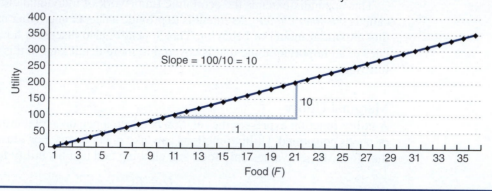

Slope of an Indifference Curve

Now that we have defined marginal utility, we can derive the slope of an indifference curve. Consider Tom's indifference curve for $U = 100$. The equation for this indifference curve, which is pictured in Figure 2.11, is $F = 100/C$.[27] Because all points on the indifference curve generate 100 units of utility, the total gain in utility

Figure 2.11   Slope of One of Tom's Indifference Curves: $-(MU_C/MU_F)$

This figure displays an indifference curve for 100 units of utility from Tom's utility function: $U = FC$. The equation for the indifference curve is $F = 100/C$. The slope of an indifference curve at any point is $-(MU_C/MU_F)$. The slope at a point is defined as the slope of the tangency line at that point. The tangency lines at points A and C are two examples. In this example, the slope at any point is $-(F/C)$. The absolute value of the slope, which is called the *Marginal Rate of Substitution (MRS)*, declines continuously along the curve. This property implies that Tom becomes less willing to trade F for C as C increases relative to F.

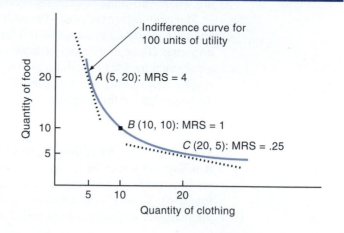

----

[27]The decision to place food on the *y*-axis is arbitrary. If we had placed clothing on the *y*-axis the equation for the indifference curve would be $C = 100/F$.

associated with an increase in C must be balanced by an offsetting decline in utility from reduced consumption of F (as Tom moves along the curve):

$$MU_C(\Delta C) + MU_F(\Delta F) = 0 \qquad (2.11)$$

where ΔF and ΔC represent the changes in food and clothing. The first term in Equation (2.11) represents the change in utility from changing the amount of clothing, while the second term represents the change in utility from changing the amount of food. These terms are equal in magnitude and of opposite sign along an indifference curve, and so total utility remains unchanged.

The slope of the indifference curve for a small change in C is given by $(\Delta F/\Delta C)$. Rearranging Equation (2.11):

$$(\Delta F/\Delta C) = -(MU_C/MU_F) \qquad (2.12)$$
$$\text{Slope of the indifference curve} = -(MU_C/MU_F)$$

In the example where $U = FC$, the slope of the indifference curve is $-(F/C)$ since $MU_C = F$ and $MU_F = C$. For example, at the point where $F = 5$ and $C = 20$ the slope is $-.25$. The intuition for this result is as follows: If a marginal unit of clothing yields five units of utility, while a marginal unit of food yields 20 units of utility, food can be traded for clothing at a rate of .25 units for one unit, and utility will remain the same (for small changes in the two goods).

The absolute value of the slope of an indifference curve is called the *Marginal Rate of Substitution (MRS)*. The MRS reflects the individual's willingness to trade at a point on an indifference curve (in this example, trading food for clothing). Consider Tom's willingness to trade when he has a consumption bundle of 10 units of both goods. The slope at this point is $-(10/10) = -1$. The MRS, which is equal to one, implies that Tom is willing to give up a small quantity of food to receive an equal number of units of clothing. (If Tom were to increase his consumption of C by 1 unit he would have to reduce his consumption of F by approximately 1 unit to keep his utility the same.) The MRS declines along the convex curve indicating that Tom becomes less willing to trade food for clothing as the amount of clothing increases relative to food.[28]

Individual Choice

Recall that the equation for the budget line is

$$F = (I/P_F) - (P_C/P_F)C \qquad (2.13)$$

The absolute value of the slope, (P_C/P_F), reflects the consumer's *ability to trade* in the market place. For example, when the price of clothing is $2/unit and the price of food is $1/unit, two units of food must be given up to consume one additional unit of clothing $(P_C/P_F = 2)$. The intercept (I/P_F) indicates how many units of food could be purchased if the entire budget is spent on food.

At the optimal consumption bundle the budget line is tangent to an indifference curve (which is the highest attainable indifference curve given the budget constraint).

---

[28]The slope of a curve is defined at a point on a curve and the slope changes along the curve. The slope of -1 at the point [10,10] reflects Tom's willingness to trade for very small changes in C. For a full unit change in C, the decline in F is only *approximately* (as we reduce the size of the exchange—.1 unit of food or .01 unit of food—the change in utility approaches zero) equal to one. A one unit increase in C and a one unit decrease in F produce a consumption bundle with 99 units of utility. This value is approximately equal to the starting point of 100.

This condition implies that the MRS is equal to the ratio of the prices at the optimum. Since the MRS is equal to the ratio of the marginal utilities for the two goods:

$$\text{MU}_C/\text{MU}_F = P_C/P_F \qquad (2.14)$$

The left side of Equation (2.14) represents the willingness to trade, while the right side reflects the ability to trade. At the point where the consumer is maximizing his utility (the optimum), the two are equal.

We can rearrange Equation (2.14) as follows:

$$\text{MU}_C/P_C = \text{MU}_F/P_F \qquad (2.15)$$

Equation (2.15) is an important and familiar result in consumer theory. It says that the consumer's utility is maximized when the budget is allocated among goods so that the *marginal utility per dollar of expenditure is the same for each good*. At any combination where this condition does not hold, the consumer can be made better off by making feasible changes in the consumption bundle. For example, suppose Tom has an initial bundle where the marginal utility per dollar for clothing is 10 and for food is 20. Since he is getting more utility per dollar from food, he should spend less money on clothing and more on food. As he trades clothing for food, his marginal utility of clothing increases while his marginal utility of food decreases. Tom will eventually reach the optimal consumption bundle where the marginal utility-to-price ratios are equal. Equation (2.15) reflects a condition known as the *equal marginal principle*—the marginal utility per dollar is the same for all goods at the optimum.[29] This principle reappears in various forms in the economic analysis of both consumer and producer behavior.

Solving for the Optimal Consumption Bundle

Suppose that Tom has a budget of $100 and the prices of food and clothing are $1 and $2, respectively. How much of each good will he buy? This problem is straightforward since it involves two unknown variables (*F* and *C*) and two independent equations. One equation is the optimality condition Equation (2.14); the second is the budget line Equation (2.13).

At Tom's optimal choice, the MRS must equal the price ratio (i.e., $\text{MU}_C/\text{MU}_F = P_C/P_F$). Substituting the values for Tom's marginal utilities yields

$$F/C = 2 \qquad (2.16)$$
$$C = F/2$$

Tom must also satisfy his budget constraint:

$$F = 100 - 2C \qquad (2.17)$$

We can solve for the amount of food that Tom will purchase by substituting Equation (2.16) into Equation (2.17):

$$F = 100 - 2\,(F/2)$$
$$F^* = 50$$

$C^* = 25$ is found by substituting $F^* = 50$ into Equation (2.16).

At the optimal consumption bundle, Tom obtains 1,250 units of utility (25×50). He can increase his consumption of clothing by purchasing 26 units of clothing and

---

[29]This condition is also referred to as the "equimarginal principle."

48 units of food (26 × \$2 + 48 × \$1 = \$100). However, this bundle would yield only 1,248 units of utility (26 × 48). Alternatively, he could decrease his consumption of clothing by one unit and increase his consumption of food by two units ($C = 24$; $F = 52$). This bundle also would produce only 1,248 units of utility. Indeed any feasible alternative bundle would yield less than 1,250 units of utility.

The equal marginal principle holds at Tom's optimal consumption bundle—the marginal utility per dollar of expenditure (MU_i/P_i) is 25 for both goods. This condition implies that Tom has no incentive to shift expenditures from one good to the other since both goods yield the same marginal utility per dollar of spending.

The *marginal utility of income* is defined as the additional utility that the consumer receives from one additional dollar of income. It can be shown that at the optimum, the marginal utility-to-price ratio for all goods is equal to the marginal utility of income. For example, if Tom's income increases by \$1, he could increase his utility by 25 units by purchasing additional quantities of either good.

Demand Functions

A *demand function* expresses the mathematical relation between the quantity demanded for a product (how many units consumers will purchase) and the factors that determine consumer choice (such as prices and income). In a more general setting than our simple example, the demand for clothing is likely to be affected by the price of clothing, consumer income, the prices of other products, and other variables (such as advertising expenditures). Managers care about consumer choice since a good understanding of the demands for their products is important for making productive investment, pricing, advertising, and other decisions. In subsequent chapters, we focus on aggregate demand for a product (total demand across all consumers in the market) without directly tying the analysis back to individual consumer behavior as analyzed in this chapter. Nevertheless, it is useful to recognize that aggregate demand for a given product can conceptually be derived from the framework presented in this appendix.

The derivation of Tom's demand function for either food or clothing is particularly easy (given his utility function). Tom's optimal consumption bundle is where his MRS equals the price ratio. In Tom's case, this condition is

$$F/C = P_C/P_F \qquad (2.18)$$

Tom's total expenditures on either food or clothing is equal to the quantity purchased of the good times its price. By cross-multiplying Equation (2.18) we see that Tom's expenditures on food and clothing are always equal:

$$(F \times P_F) = (C \times P_C) \qquad (2.19)$$

Equation (2.19) implies that Tom will always spend half his income on each good (this result is driven by his particular utility function). It follows that Tom's total expenditures on clothing are $(C \times P_C) = I/2$. Solving for C produces Tom's demand function for clothing:

$$C = I/(2P_C) \qquad (2.20)$$

This demand function implies that Tom will purchase more clothing as his income rises and less clothing as his income falls. His clothing purchases vary inversely with the price of clothing.

In our example, Tom had an income of \$100 and $P_C = \$2$/unit. Consistent with Equation (2.20), we found that he consumed 25 units of clothing. The demand function implies that if Tom's income were to increase to \$200 (holding price constant) he would purchase 50 units of clothing. In contrast, his clothing purchases would fall to 12.5 units if P_C increased to \$4 (holding income constant at \$100). Tom is only one consumer who purchases clothing. The total (aggregate) quantity demanded for clothing at a given price is equal to the sum of the purchases made by all consumers in the market.

Since Tom always spends half his income on clothing, the amount of clothing that he purchases is not affected by the price of food. This is a special case, which does not hold for many other utility functions. Consider Anne George whose utility function is $U = C^{.5} + F^{.5}$. Anne's demand for clothing is $C = I/[(P_C^2/P_F) + P_C]$.[30] This function indicates that Anne's clothing purchases increase with income and the price of food, but decrease with the price of clothing. For example, at the initial prices and income ($P_F = \$1$, $P_C = \$2$, and $I = \$100$) Anne purchases 16.67 units of clothing. If the price of food were to increase from \$1 to \$2, her demand for clothing increases to 25 units. When the prices for food and clothing are equal she spends half her income on each good. As relative prices change, Anne spends a higher percentage of her income on the relatively less-expensive good.

Income and Substitution Effects

Equation (2.20) indicates that Tom's demand for clothing decreases with the price of clothing. Figure 2.12 displays the example where the price of clothing increases from \$2 to \$4 (holding income constant at \$100 and the price of food at \$1). Remember, Tom's utility function is $U = CF$. The price increase causes the budget line to rotate inward. The new budget line, B_2 is steeper than the original line, B_1 (slopes of -4 and -2, respectively).

The inward shift of the budget line implies that Tom has less purchasing power than he had prior to the price increase. The area between the two budget lines contains consumption bundles that he could have purchased when $P_C = \$2$ that he can no longer afford. The reduced consumption possibilities imply that Tom has effectively less purchasing power than he had prior to the price increase. Thus, an increase in the price of clothing has two effects. One is to increase the price of clothing relative to the price of food (i.e., P_C/P_F increases); the other is to reduce Tom's effective income (purchasing power). As we will see, both effects influence Tom's response to the price increase.

Tom purchased 25 units of clothing and 50 units of food when $P_C = \$2$, $P_F = 1$, and $I = \$100$. This choice, which is at the point of tangency between the original indifference curve, I_1, and budget line, B_1, is labeled as t_1 in Figure 2.12. His optimal consumption bundle following the price increase, consisting of 12.5 units of clothing and 50 units of food, is pictured by the point of tangency, t_2, between the indifference curve, I_2, and the new budget line, B_2. The decline in the quantity demanded for clothing from 25 units to 12.5 units represents the *total effect* of the price change (a decrease of 12.5 units). The total effect can be decomposed into a substitution effect and an income effect.

The *substitution effect* is the change in the quantity demanded of a good when its price changes, holding the prices of other goods and utility constant. To hold utility constant, Tom must be *compensated* for the price increase by receiving enough additional income to maintain his previous level of utility of 1,250 units ($U = FC = 25 \times 50 = 1,250$). Without this increase in income, he could not afford any of the bundles

---

[30]For practice, derive the demand function from Anne's utility function (for this utility function: $MU_C = .5C^{(-.5)}$ and $MU_F = .5F^{(-.5)}$).

Figure 2.12   Income and Substitution Effects

This figure illustrates income and substitution effects. Tom's original budget line and indifference curve are denoted by B_1 and I_1; here he chooses 25 units of clothing and 50 units of food as denoted by t_1. An increase in the price of clothing from \$2 to \$4 causes the budget line to rotate inward as pictured by B_2. At the new optimum, t_2, Tom purchases 12.5 units of clothing and 50 units of food. The 12.5 unit decline in the demand for clothing is the *total effect* of the price change, which is the sum of the substitution and income effects. The substitution effect is 7.3 units. It is pictured by Tom's optimal choice, t', which assumes that Tom has received additional income to keep him on the original indifference curve. The income effect of 5.2 units is the additional decline in demand due to the fact that Tom does not actually receive the hypothetical increase in income. The hypothetical increase is used to isolate the "pure price effect" from the effect of reduced purchasing power due to the price increase.

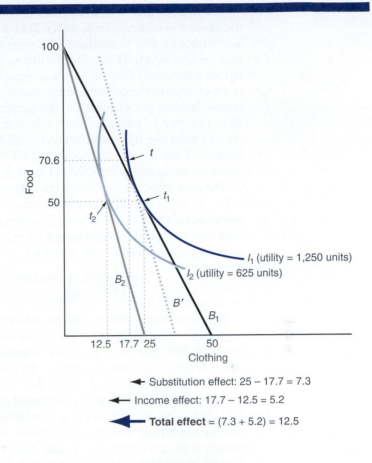

Substitution effect: $25 - 17.7 = 7.3$
Income effect: $17.7 - 12.5 = 5.2$
Total effect $= (7.3 + 5.2) = 12.5$

on the original indifference curve at the new prices. To focus on the effect of changes in relative prices (versus changes in effective income), we examine what Tom would do if he actually received this hypothetical income increase. This hypothetical situation is depicted by an imaginary budget line, B' in Figure 2.12—which is parallel to the new budget line, B_2, and tangent to the original indifference curve, I_1, at t'. The resulting combination of 70.6 units of food and 17.7 units of clothing is the least expensive bundle that Tom can purchase at the new prices that yields 1,250 units of utility.[31] Since the cost is \$141.40, Tom's income would have to increase by \$41.40 to afford this combination. Thus, if he were to receive enough additional income to compensate for the price increase, he would respond by purchasing 7.3 units less of clothing and 20.6 units more of food than when the price of clothing was only \$2. This substitution between clothing and food occurs because clothing is relatively more expensive. Figure 2.12 depicts the 7.3 unit decline in Tom's clothing purchases with an arrow labeled "substitution effect." The convexity of the indifference curves implies that the substitution effect is positive.

[31]This consumption bundle is found by solving two equations simultaneously. One equation is for the indifference curve containing bundles that yield 1,250 units of utility ($F = 1{,}250/C$); the second equation is that the slope of the indifference curve and the new budget line are equal at the point of tangency ($F/C = 4$).

The hypothetical $41.40 increase in income is used to isolate the "pure effect" of the change in relative prices. Since Tom does not actually receive this extra income, he will not be able to purchase 70.6 units of food and 17.7 units of clothing (his actual income is still $100). The decline in purchasing power from the price increase has an additional effect on Tom's demands for clothing and food. The *income effect* is the change in the quantity demanded of a good because of a change in purchasing power, holding prices constant. The parallel shift in the budget constraint from B' to B_2 in Figure 2.12 captures Tom's effective decrease in income. As Tom's budget decreases from the hypothetical level of $141.40 to the actual level of $100, he consumes 5.2 fewer units of clothing ($17.7 - 12.5 = 5.2$). The 5.2 unit reduction in quantity demanded is depicted in Figure 2.12 with an arrow labeled "income effect."

The total effect is that Tom's quantity demanded for clothing drops by 12.5 units ($25 - 12.5 = 12.5$) due to the price increase. The total effect, which is the sum of the substitution and income effects, is pictured by an arrow labeled "total effect." The final result is that Tom purchases 12.5 units of clothing and 50 units of food and obtains 625 units of utility (50×12.5):

$$\text{Total Effect} = \text{Substitution Effect} + \text{Income Effect}$$
$$12.5 \quad = \quad 7.3 \quad + \quad 5.2$$

The substitution effect is always positive—changes in relative prices motivate substitutions toward the relatively less-expensive good. The income effect for a *normal good* is also positive. As income decreases (increases) total consumption must decrease (increase); thus, on average the demand for goods must move in the same direction as the income change. Nonetheless, for some goods the income effect is negative. For example, in contrast to a normal good the demand for canned meat products is likely to vary inversely with income (wealthy people are likely to shun canned meat and purchase fresh meat, such as steak). We call goods with demands that vary inversely with income *inferior goods*. A positive income effect reinforces the substitution effect and increases the magnitude of the response, while a negative income effect mitigates the substitution effect and reduces the magnitude of the response. In Tom's case the 7.3 unit substitution effect is reinforced by the 5.2 unit income effect. For most goods, the income effect is small relative to the substitution effect, and thus the total effect usually is in the same direction as the substitution effect.

The income effect in Tom's case is relatively large (42 percent of the total effect). This is due to the assumption that Tom can only purchase two goods. Since Tom spends half his budget on clothing, he experiences a large drop in purchasing power when the price of clothing doubles. In contrast to this simple example, most consumers purchase many goods and spend a relatively small percentage of their budgets on any one good (e.g., salt, toothpaste, apples, and so on). Thus, a change in the prices of the typical good does not have an important effect on the purchasing power of the consumer. This observation implies that for many products the substitution effect is much more important than the income effect. For example, suppose that your nearby grocery store raises the price of cucumbers by $1/pound. Conceptually, your income (purchasing power) is lower than it was before since you can no longer purchase as many potential consumption bundles. This small decline in effective income, however, is not likely to be the driving force behind your response to the price change. The relative increase in the price of cucumbers might motivate you to use more tomatoes and fewer cucumbers in your next salad. However, this decision is driven by the change in relative prices of cucumbers and tomatoes—not by the small change in your purchasing power.

Figure 2.13 Income Effects in the Supply of Labor

This figure displays Ralph Kramden's choice between work and leisure. Ralph has a total of 100 hours per week that he divides between work and leisure activities (the remaining hours are used for sleeping, etc.). At a wage rate of $10/hr., Ralph works 60 hours/week and has a total income of $600. At a wage rate of $20/hr., he chooses to work fewer hours (40) and to consume more leisure time (60 hours). While the increase in the wage rate increases the opportunity cost of leisure time, the income effect is larger than the substitution effect. At the higher income level ($800), Ralph places greater value on leisure time and works 20 fewer hours than when the wage rate was $10/hr.

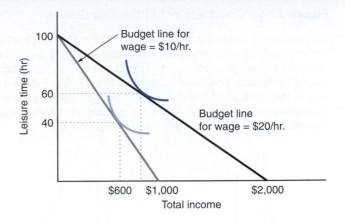

Some goods, such as housing or transportation, constitute a relatively large proportion of the typical consumer's budget. For these goods, income effects can be more important. Since these goods are the exception rather than the rule, we can safely ignore income effects in many applications. Correspondingly, we tend to concentrate on substitution effects in analyzing the effects of changes in relative prices. The reader, however, should be aware that other applications exist where income effects are important.

One prominent case where income effects can be important is the supply of labor. Figure 2.13 depicts Ralph Kramden who is choosing between work and leisure time. Ralph is a bus driver whose employer allows him to choose the number of hours he works each week. Ralph has a total of 100 hours per week that he divides between work and leisure activities (the remaining hours are used for sleeping, etc.). At a wage rate of $10 per hour, Ralph chooses to work 60 hours per week and has a total income of $600; the other 40 hours are used for leisure activities. The budget line rotates outward when the wage rate is increased to $20/hr. The new budget line is flatter than the original line (slope is 1/20 versus 1/10). The reduced slope captures the increase in the opportunity cost of leisure—leisure now costs Ralph $20/hr. The substitution effect works in the direction of motivating Ralph to reduce his leisure time and to work more hours. The substitution effect in this example, however, is outweighed by the income effect. At the higher wage rate, Ralph chooses to work only 40 hours per week; his total income is $800, which is $200 more than he made working 60 hours at $10/hr. At an income level of $800, Ralph values an additional hour of leisure time at more than the $20 he could make from using the hour for work. At the lower level of income ($600) he placed a smaller value on an extra hour of leisure time (he had to work more hours to provide basic support for his family).

Magnitude of the Substitution Effect

Economists typically assume that indifference curves are convex to the origin. Convexity is consistent with the behavioral observation that a person's willingness to

Figure 2.14   Convexity of Indifference Curves

This figure compares the typical indifference curve with the two extremes. The first extreme is the case of *perfect complements* where the indifference curve is shaped as a right angle. In this case, the two goods are used in fixed proportions. An individual receives no additional utility from receiving more units of just one of the goods. The other extreme case is *perfect substitutes*, where the indifference curve is a straight line. In this case, the MRS does not change as the person receives more of one good relative to the other. The substitution effect in response to a change in relative prices is larger when the two goods are close substitutes than when they are close complements.

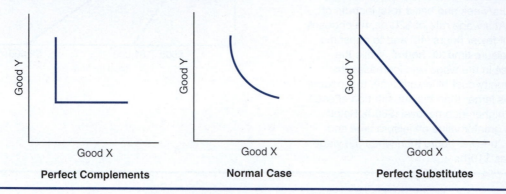

Good Y / Good X	Good Y / Good X	Good Y / Good X
Perfect Complements	**Normal Case**	**Perfect Substitutes**

trade one good for the other generally declines as the relative amount of the second good increases (i.e., the MRS declines as the good on the horizontal axis increases). While Tom is willing to trade a large amount of food for a unit of clothing when he has lots of food and little clothing, his willingness to trade food for clothing declines as he reduces his food stock relative to his supply of clothing.

The substitution effect is always positive with convex indifference curves. An increase in the relative price of one good motivates substitution away from that good toward other goods (holding utility constant). The magnitude of the substitution effect, however, varies depending on the convexity (curvature) of the indifference curve.

Figure 2.14 compares the typical indifference curve with the two extremes. The first extreme is the case of *perfect complements* where the indifference curve is shaped as a right angle. In this case, the two goods are used in fixed proportions. An individual receives no additional utility from receiving more units of just one of the goods. For utility to increase, the quantity of both goods must increase. An example is shoes. The typical individual requires both a left and right shoe. Utility is not increased if the individual receives a right shoe unless it is matched with a left shoe.

The other extreme is *perfect substitutes,* where the indifference curve is a straight line. In this case, the MRS does not change as the person receives more of one good relative to the other. For example, a person's willingness to trade $10 bills for $20 bills remains at 2 for 1 regardless of the relative supply of the two goods.

While most goods are neither perfect complements nor perfect substitutes, the convexity of indifference curves varies among products. Some indifference curves have significant curvature (tend to be closer to right angles), while others are relatively straight. The substitution effect is smaller when the indifference curve is more convex (closer to perfect complements). For example, a small increase in the price of left shoes will not motivate consumers to purchase fewer left shoes and more right shoes. In contrast, a small price change can motivate large shifts from one good to another when they are close substitutes. For instance, a small price change can motivate a consumer to switch from one brand of orange juice to another if the consumer is largely indifferent between the two brands (i.e., they are viewed as close substitutes). Geometrically, as the convexity of an indifference curve increases, the consumer does not have to move as far from the initial optimum to reach the new optimum as relative prices change (higher convexity implies that the slope of the indifference curve is changing more rapidly along the curve).

Additional Considerations

Our analysis has focused exclusively on *interior solutions* where the consumer optimally purchases positive quantities of both goods. This focus is justified because it is the usual case with convex indifference curves. Nevertheless, there are special cases where it is optimal for the consumer to spend the entire income on only one of the goods. This outcome is known as a *corner solution*. For example, in the case of perfect substitutes it is optimal for the consumer to purchase only one of the goods unless the budget line and straight-line indifference curve have the same slopes, in which case the consumer is indifferent between purchasing either of the two goods (and thus might purchase positive quantities of both goods). For instance, you might be relatively indifferent between holding your cash as $5 bills or $10 bills at an exchange rate of two for one. However, you will hold only one type of bill at other exchange rates. If you have the ability to trade one $10 bill in the marketplace for three $5 bills you should clearly do so. Similarly, while you might be indifferent between purchasing two similar brands of orange juice when they sell for identical prices, you will quickly shift to buying only one brand if that one goes on sale.

For simplicity we have focused on an example based on only two goods. When there are more than two goods in the marketplace, an increase in the price of one good can motivate a reduction in the demand for other complementary goods. For example, an increase in the price for playing golf can reduce the demand for golf equipment. The substitution effect constitutes movement away from golf-related goods to other goods, which are now relatively less expensive. We examine complementarity and substitutability of products in greater detail in Chapter 4.

Calculus Derivation of Equal Marginal Principle

The equal marginal principle states that the marginal utility to price ratio is equal for all goods at the consumer's optimal consumption bundle. At any combination where this condition does not hold, the consumer can be made better off by making feasible changes in the consumption bundle. This section provides a calculus-based derivation of this principle.

The utility function for the two-good case takes the following general form:

$$U = f(x_i, x_j) \tag{2.21}$$

To find the slope of an indifference curve, we totally differentiate Equation (2.21). We set this differential equal to zero, since utility does not change along an indifference curve:

$$dU = [\partial U/\partial x_i dx_i] + [\partial U/\partial x_j dx_j] = 0 \tag{2.22}$$

The slope of the indifference curve is defined by dx_i/dx_j (when good i is placed on the y-axis). Thus the

$$\text{slope of the indifference curve} = -(\partial U/\partial x_j)/(\partial U/\partial x_i) \tag{2.23}$$
$$= -MU_j/MU_i \tag{2.24}$$

ANALYZING MANAGERIAL DECISIONS: *Consumer Choice*

1. Define the following terms: *marginal utility, ordinal utility, marginal rate of substitution, equal marginal principle, demand function, substitution effect, income effect, normal good, inferior good, perfect complement,* and *perfect substitute.*

2. Susan Pettit's preferences for coffee (by the pound) and doughnuts (by the dozen) can be characterized as follows:

$$MU_{coffee} = MU_x = y^2$$
$$MU_{doughnuts} = MU_y = 2xy$$

   a. If the ratio of relative prices is $(P_x/P_y) = 6/3 = 2$, and Susan's income is $90 per period, what combination of pounds of coffee and dozens of doughnuts will she choose?

   b. Now let the ratio of coffee to doughnut prices decline to unity $(=1)$, holding the price of doughnuts constant. How does Susan respond to the reduction in the relative price of coffee?

   c. Redo parts (a) and (b) for the case of income of $60 per period.

   d. Derive Susan's demand function for coffee.

   e. Is coffee a normal or inferior good for this consumer?

   f. Does Susan consider coffee and doughnuts to be either perfect complements or perfect substitutes? Explain.

3. Susan's demand function for coffee in the previous problem includes only the price of coffee and income. Thus, changes in the price of doughnuts do not affect the demand for coffee. Does this imply that there is no *substitution effect* between the two goods? Explain.

4. (More challenging problem) Mario Casali is a TV newscaster who gets an annual clothing allowance to buy suits that he must wear during his televised forecasts. He allocates the allowance each year between expensive Italian suits and cheap American suits. Mario's utility function for suits is $SA^{.5}$ where S is the number of Italian suits bought and A is the number of American suits bought. Last year, Mario bought two Italian suits and four American suits. [Note: $MU_S = A^{.5}$ and $MU_A = .5SA^{(-.5)}$]

   a. If Mario was maximizing his utility last year, what was the ratio of the price of an Italian suit to the price of an American suit (P_S/P_A)?

   b. What was Mario's clothing allowance last year if the price of an Italian suit was $1,000?

   c. If Mario has the same allowance this year as last year, and American suit prices have not changed, how high would the price of Italian suits have to rise in order for Mario to want to buy exactly one Italian suit this year?

This expression has a straightforward interpretation. For illustration, assume that at some fixed combination of x_i and x_j, the marginal utility of good i is 1 and the marginal utility of good j is 2. This means that 2 units of i can be given up for 1 unit of j and utility will stay the same. This is true by definition, since j has twice the marginal utility of i.

At a consumer's optimum the slope of the budget line $(-P_j/P_i)$ is equal to the slope of the indifference curve:

$$-MU_j/MU_i = -P_j/P_i \qquad (2.25)$$

Rearranging this expression yields the Equal Marginal Principle:

$$MU_j/P_j = MU_i/P_i \qquad (2.26)$$

This principle immediately generalizes to utility functions with more than two goods.

Appendix B: Inter-Temporal Decisions and the Fisher Separation Theorem

Introductory economics generally concentrates on single-period problems. For example, how does a consumer choose to spend her income within a single period? How much should a firm produce in a single period to maximize its profits? What prices should it charge for this output?

The frameworks introduced in this book, however, also are used to analyze multiperiod problems. Indeed, this is what the modern study of finance is largely about. How does an individual choose between consumption today versus saving for the future? How does a firm choose between paying cash dividends now versus investing to earn higher future profits?

This appendix provides a simple example of how the consumer choice framework presented in this chapter can be used to analyze inter-temporal consumption decisions. It also provides a brief introduction to the important problem of a firm deciding on whether to pay higher cash dividends now or to invest the cash to earn higher profits in the future. In so doing, we introduce an important concept that is the starting point of the modern study of finance—the *Fisher Separation Theorem.*

Simple Example of Inter-temporal Choice

Mary Donaldson graduated from college five years ago and has been working as an entry-level employee at a bank. She has taken leave from her job to enter a one-year, full-time MBA program, which begins today. The bank has paid for her tuition, books, and basic room and board. It has also promised to promote her when she completes the program. While Mary earns no salary from the bank while she is in the program, the bank has promised to pay her $75,000 per year in her new position. Mary currently has $25,000 in savings.

Mary can borrow money from a bank at a 5 percent interest rate if she wants to consume more while she is in school than she can buy with her $25,000. For example, she might want to rent a better apartment than the one she has been provided. She also might want to travel internationally on her school breaks or to upgrade her music system or automobile. Alternatively, Mary might want to save all or part of her $25,000 so that she can consume more in the future. She knows that she will likely want to buy a house once she starts her new job. She will also have moving and other expenses that will not be covered by her company. She earns 5 percent interest on her savings.

Mary's problem is to decide how much to consume today versus how much to consume in the future given her current savings, future income, and the market interest rate. The key insights that arise from analyzing this problem can be illustrated most conveniently by assuming that Mary cares only about consumption at two points in time: today and one year from today. (This simplification is similar to our earlier focus on only two goods—food and clothing.) To simplify the analysis further, we assume that there is no uncertainty about Mary's future income of $75,000 and that she pays no taxes on her interest or job income.

If Mary saves all $25,000 over the next year, she will have $(1.05 \times \$25,000) =$ $26,250 at the end of the year in her account. Added to her $75,000 salary, the maximum sum she could have to spend next year is $101,250. Mary, however, might want to increase her current consumption at the cost of not being able to consume as much next year. If Mary wants to spend more than $25,000 today, she will have to borrow to do it. The bank will not loan Mary more money than she is able to pay back (with interest) given her future income of $75,000. The maximum ($B$) that she can borrow is

$$(1.05) \, B = \$75,000$$
$$B = \$75,000/1.05 = \$71,428$$

Adding the maximum borrowing of $71,428 to the initial $25,000 gives Mary a maximum of $96,428 to consume today, assuming she consumes nothing next year.

Mary is highly unlikely to want to consume all of her funds in just one period. Rather she is likely to want consume at least something in each period. We refer to her $25,000 in current savings and the $75,000 she will receive next year in income as her *endowment*. One option is for Mary to consume her endowment at the time it is received. In this way, she neither saves nor borrows. Depending on her preferences, however, Mary might want to borrow something from the bank to consume more today or to save part of her $25,000 to consume more in the future.

The solution to Mary's decision problem can be pictured using the graphical framework introduced in this chapter. Figure 2.15 displays Mary's inter-temporal budget line. The variable on the y-axis is Mary's consumption next year (c_2); the

---

Figure 2.15   Mary's Inter-Temporal Consumption Choice

Mary's initial endowment consists of $25,000 in current savings and $75,000 in future income. The interest rate for borrowing and lending is 5 percent. The inter-temporal budget line shows all feasible combinations of consumption today and consumption next year, given Mary's endowment and the interest rate. Mary's optimal choice is where the budget line is tangent to an indifference curve. The figure depicts two possible optima that assume different preferences for Mary. The one on the left is the case where she is a net saver. She saves part of her initial $25,000 so that she can increase her consumption in the second period. The one on the right shows the case where she borrows against her future income to increase her current consumption. The actual outcome depends on Mary's particular preferences.

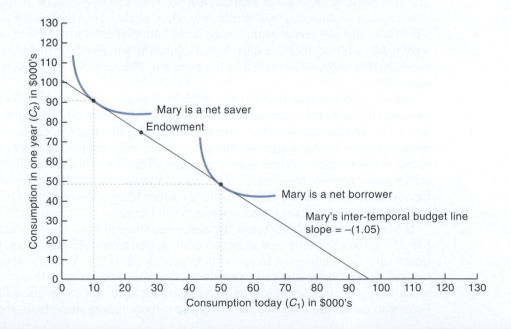

variable on the x-axis is her consumption today (c_1). The budget line goes through her endowment and shows all the feasible alternatives that Mary has, given her endowment and the 5 percent interest rate. The y-intercept of $101,250 is the maximum amount she can consume next year if she chooses to consume nothing today. The x-intercept of $96,428 is the maximum she can consume today if she chooses to consume nothing next year. The slope of the budget line is -1.05, which more generally can be expressed as $-(1 + r)$, where r is the interest rate. Note that a change in the interest rate will change the slope of the budget line. An increase would make the line steeper, while a decrease would make it flatter. In all cases the line would include the endowment point.

Mary's preferences can be pictured with standard indifference curves. All combinations of c_1 and c_2 along a given indifference yield the same level of utility. Mary's optimal consumption choice occurs at the point of tangency between her budget line and an indifference curve (assuming an interior solution). Mary would like to be on an even higher indifference curve, but this is the best she can do, given her endowment and the interest rate of 5 percent. Whether Mary decides to borrow or save depends on her preferences. Figure 2.15 depicts two possibilities. The tangency on the left occurs at a point where Mary is a net saver (she saves part of her $25,000 to increase next year's consumption); the tangency on the right shows the case where Mary is a net borrower (she borrows to consume more today at the cost of not being able to consume as much next year). Which of these, if either, that she will choose depends on Mary's particular preferences for inter-temporal consumption.

Exercise for the Reader. As previously noted, a change in the interest rate will change the slope of the budget line. This, in turn, will change Mary's optimal choice. Use the standard choice diagram depicted in Figure 2.15 to demonstrate each of the following: If Mary is a borrower when the interest rate is 5 percent, she will also be a borrower if the interest rate falls to 3 percent. However, if Mary is a borrower at 5 percent and interest rate rises to 7 percent, she may still be a borrower, but she might decide to switch to being a lender. Now suppose that Mary is a lender at the initial 5 percent rate. What will she do if interest rates rise? What if they fall?

Terminology. The maximum that Mary can borrow, given her future income of $75,000, is $71,428 at the 5 percent interest rate. In the business world, the $71,428 is referred to as the *present value* of the $75,000 future cash flow. It is the amount that Mary would need today to obtain $75,000 in one year investing at the market interest rate of 5 percent. The ability to earn 5 percent on her savings implies that Mary would be indifferent between receiving $71,428 today or $75,000 one year from now (since she could reproduce the $75,000 future cash flow with $71,428 today). The process of transforming future cash flows into present values is called *discounting*. The present value in this example was obtained by dividing the $75,000 by 1.05. More generally the present value of a cash flow, C, occurring one year in the future is $C/(1 + r)$, where r is the annual interest rate.[32] The $75,000 cash flow in this example is the *future value* of the $71,428.

---

[32]Calculating present vales is a bit more complicated when expected future cash flows occur at multiple dates in the future and when they vary in their riskiness. However, the basic concept is the same. A dollar today is worth more than a dollar in the future (since you could obtain the same dollar in the future by investing a smaller amount today).

Fisher Separation Theorem

Now consider an inter-temporal investment decision by a firm. Deon and Ramona each own 50 percent of the firm. The firm has $100,000 in cash that it could distribute to the owners as cash dividends. This would give Deon and Ramona additional cash today. Alternatively the firm could use the funds to invest in a project that would allow it to pay higher future dividends to its owners.

Our previous example suggests that individuals can differ in their inter-temporal consumption preferences (some might want to save for the future, while others might want to spend more on current consumption). An important question is whether the managers of the firm should consider Deon and Ramona's time preferences in deciding whether to invest in the project. The somewhat surprising answer is that under certain assumptions the answer is no.

Modern finance courses typically start with the assumption *of perfect capital markets*, which are characterized by zero transaction costs, no taxes, and perfect information. In a perfect market, Deon and Ramona will unanimously agree that the firm should invest in the project if it increases the present value of the firm's cash flows, even if they have quite different time preferences. This important result is one part of what is known as the *Fisher Separation Theorem*—named after the economist Irving Fisher. The other implication, which focuses on how the project is financed, will be addressed later in this appendix.

The basic logic for why the firm's investment decision can be separated from its owners' preferences is as follows. If the firm invests the $100,000 today it will receive $110,000 as a cash inflow in one year. For simplicity, assume the firm makes this investment, then (1) the investment is riskless (the firm will receive the $110,000 for sure) and (2) the firm will discontinue operations at the end of the year and distribute $55,000 each to Deon and Ramona. Alternatively, the firm might forgo the investment, discontinue operations and pay $50,000 to each of the owners in cash dividends today. We assume for this analysis that the firm, Deon, and Ramona can all borrow or lend at a market interest rate of 5 percent (subject to having the funds to pay back loans with interest).

If the firm decides to liquidate and pay $100,000 in cash dividends, the present value of the firm's cash flows is by definition $100,000 (since the cash flows occur at the present time). The present value of $110,000 received in one year is $110,000/1.05 = $104,762. According to the Fisher Separation Theorem, both Deon and Ramona will want the firm to invest regardless of their inter-temporal preferences for consumption since it increases the present value of the firm's cash flows.

To see why, suppose that Deon wants to consume all he can today, while Ramona wants to save all she can today to consume more in the future. If the firm invests in the project, it will be able to pay $55,000 to each owner in one year. Deon can borrow $52,381 from a bank using his future $55,000 as collateral ($52,381 × 1.05 = $55,000). In contrast if the firm does not make the investment, Deon will only have the current dividend of $50,000 to consume today—a loss of $2,381 in current consumption. Ramona, in turn, could borrow nothing today and have $55,000 to spend next year if the firm decides to invest. If instead the firm discontinues operations today, she will only have (1.05) × $50,000 = $52,500 to consume next year—a loss of $2,500 in future value. The difference is due to the fact that the firm can earn 10 percent on its investment, compared to the 5 percent that Ramona earns from personal savings. The conclusion is that Deon and Ramona will both want the firm to invest even though they have dramatically different time preferences.

Large corporations often have thousands of shareholders. The basic result illustrated in this simple two-person example, however, readily extends to many joint owners. In a perfect capital market, all owners will unanimously agree that the firm should invest in any project that will increase the present value of its cash flows. The owners, in turn, can use their own borrowing and lending in capital markets to meet their individual inter-temporal preferences.

Financing Decision. The second part of the Fisher Separation Theorem focuses on the firm's financing decision. According to the Fisher Separation Theorem, the financing decision does not affect value in a perfect capital market and is therefore irrelevant. In other words, the firm's financing decision can be separated from its investment decisions. The investment decision should be based on present value, while the financing decision is irrelevant in a perfect market. In our current example, this implies that it would not matter whether the firm forgoes its current dividend and uses the $100,000 to finance the investment (as analyzed above) or pays the $100,000 in current dividends and borrows $100,000 to finance the investment.

The logic for this result can be illustrated by comparing how Deon and Ramona would fare if the firm were to borrow to finance the investment in the case analyzed earlier, where the project was financed by forgoing current dividends. If the firm pays the $100,000 it has on hand in current dividends and borrows $100,000 to fund the investment, it will have to pay $105,000 back to the lender in a year. Since its cash flow from the project is $110,000, it will have $5,000 leftover to distribute to Deon and Ramona in one year as dividends. If Ramona invests the initial $50,000 cash dividend at 5 percent, she will have $52,500 at the end of the year in savings plus the $2,500 dividend that she will receive at that time. The total of $55,000 is exactly the same as when the firm paid no dividends and used its own cash to fund the project. Thus, Ramona is indifferent as to how the project is financed. Similarly under the second option, Deon could borrow $2,500/(1.05) = $2,381 to finance current consumption (using his future dividend of $2,500 as collateral). Added to the $50,000 current cash dividend, he will have $52,381 to spend today—the same amount that he would have if the firm financed the investment with cash and paid no current dividends. Deon is also indifferent as to which of the two financing options the firm chooses.

Modern finance theory starts with this perfect capital market analysis. The assumptions of zero transaction costs and perfect information are then relaxed to examine under what circumstances the Fisher Separation Theorem breaks down. The analysis focuses on whether there are "real-world" circumstances where the owners of the firm can disagree on a firm's investment decisions or where the financing decision affects firm value? The answer to these questions is yes, but answering them is beyond the scope of this book.

Exchange and Markets

LEARNING OBJECTIVES

1. Illustrate the concept of Pareto efficiency.

2. Explain the role of alienable private property rights in markets and why voluntary trade takes place.

3. Define and apply the concept of comparative advantage.

4. Explain the difference between demand and supply functions versus demand and supply curves.

5. Distinguish between movements along supply and demand curves and shifts in the curves.

6. Explain the forces that move prices and quantities toward their equilibrium levels in a competitive market.

7. Explain why long-run demand and supply curves are generally more elastic than short-run curves.

8. Predict (qualitatively) the relative changes in price versus quantity when demand or supply changes in applied settings.

9. Define and interpret consumer and producer surplus; define and interpret deadweight loss in terms of the value of foregone gains from trade.

10. Explain the effects of price controls both within the supply and demand model and in real-world terms.

Much of the world's economic activity occurs within "free markets" where individual decisions are coordinated through the price mechanism. For example, four of the countries with the largest gross domestic products (GDPs) in 2012 (the United States, Japan, Germany, and France) all have developed market systems. China with the second largest GDP has made increased use of markets since the 1990s. Prior to that time it had been a centrally planned economy with an extremely low per capita GDP.

On closer inspection, however, it is evident that a substantial amount if not most of the production in modern economies takes place inside firms, where multimillion dollar resource allocation decisions (e.g., on what to produce and how to produce it) are made by managers without the use of market transactions. The monetary size of the world's largest firms exceeds that of many economies. For instance, the 2012 GDPs of Peru, Kenya, and Portugal were $205 billion, $41 billion, and $212 billion, respectively; the 2012 net sales of ExxonMobil, Walmart, and Chevron were $453 billion, $447 billion, and $246 billion, respectively.

To be effective, managers must have a working understanding of both markets and firms. In this chapter, we contribute to this understanding by examining five important questions: Why do most people actively participate in market exchanges? How do market systems work? What is supply and demand analysis and how can it be used by managers? What are the relevant advantages of using market systems compared to central planning in large economies? Why do we observe so much economic activity conducted within firms in market economies?

Answers to these questions are particularly important to managers for two reasons. First, an understanding of how markets work helps managers make appropriate strategic and operational decisions (e.g., input, output, and pricing decisions). The supply and demand analysis that we introduce in this chapter is especially useful in many management applications. Second, understanding the relative advantages and disadvantages of markets, central planning, and firms is directly relevant to understanding firm-level issues such as which decision rights to be decentralized to employees and whether to make or buy each of the firm's inputs. The basic tools and concepts introduced in this chapter are used to analyze these specific management decisions in more depth in subsequent chapters.

Goals of Economic Systems

Every economic entity—be it a national economy, firm, or household—is confronted with three basic issues:

- What to produce
- How to produce it
- How to allocate the final output

Economic entities can be organized in alternative ways to address these issues. For instance, national economies can rely on either central planning or free markets. Similarly, firms and households can use centralized decision making, where the CEO or head of household makes all major decisions. Alternatively, other people in the firm or household can be granted substantial decision-making authority.

Given the alternatives, what is the best way to organize economic activities? To answer this question, we need some criterion for comparing alternative systems. Unfortunately, uniform agreement over such a criterion is unlikely. For instance, you might argue that an ideal system would produce your preferred mix of products and give them all to you—although your neighbor would certainly disagree. Given these differences in opinion, economists generally focus on a relatively uncontroversial but narrow criterion for comparing the effectiveness of economic systems: Pareto efficiency.[1] The production and distribution of goods and services in an economy is said to be Pareto-efficient if there exists no alternative that keeps all individuals at least as well off but makes even one person better off. If an economic system is not producing or distributing goods efficiently, it is conceptually possible to make its members better off by adopting Pareto-improving changes (thus benefiting some members without hurting others).

To illustrate the concept of Pareto efficiency, suppose that an economy can produce two goods: desktop and tablet computers. Currently the economy is producing

---

[1]The term is named after Vilfredo Pareto, 1848–1923, an Italian economist and sociologist.

1,000 desktops and 2,000 tablets. The two goods are being produced efficiently only if it is impossible to increase the production of one of the goods without decreasing the production of the other (given existing technology and resources). In contrast, suppose that some of the firms that are currently producing desktops are wasting raw materials due to suboptimal production methods (e.g., the firms could be scrapping more metal than necessary because of the way they cut metal sheets into final parts). In this case, the firms could increase their production of desktop computers by choosing more effective production methods without having any effect on the number of tablets that are being produced. Doing so would be a Pareto improvement. The distribution of desktops and tablets (once they are produced) among consumers in this economy is Pareto efficient if there is no alternative distribution that keeps all individuals at least as well off but makes even one person better off.

As example of inefficient distribution, suppose that John owns a tablet but prefers a desktop, while Gunter owns a desktop and is indifferent between owning a tablet or a desktop. The current allocation is not Pareto efficient since John would be made better off if he and Gunter were to exchange the two products, while Gunter would be no worse off. The trade would be Pareto improving. If a change in the allocation of the two goods in the economy adversely affects even one person, the move would not be Pareto-improving and an economist would have little formal basis to conclude whether the move would be good or bad for society at large.[2]

Within centrally planned economies, government officials decide what to produce, how to produce it, and who obtains the final output. In free markets, these decisions are decentralized to individuals within the economy. At least in concept, a central planner could order any feasible production and distribution of goods. Thus, any allocation of resources that could be achieved by a market economy also could be achieved by a centrally planned economy—at least in principle. We begin by discussing how market systems work and how they can produce a Pareto-efficient allocation of resources. We then discuss why in large economies a market is more likely to produce an efficient resource allocation than central planning.

Property Rights and Exchange in a Market Economy

A *property right* is a legally enforced right to select the uses of an economic good. A property right is *private* when it is assigned to a specific person. Private property rights are *alienable* in that they can be transferred (sold or given) to another individual. For example, if Valerie Fong owns an automobile, she can use the automobile as she sees fit (within limits set by traffic laws). Valerie can restrict others from using her vehicle. She also can sell the automobile (transfer to another person whatever property rights her ownership confers in the vehicle). The government maintains police and a court system to help enforce these property rights.

An important feature of a market economy is the use of private property rights. Owners of land and other resources have the legal rights to decide how to use these resources and frequently trade these rights to other individuals. They are free to start new

---

[2]Therefore, economics does not address the question of which of the many possible efficient resource allocations is best for a society. Producing your preferred set of products and giving them all to you is efficient (the allocation cannot be changed without making you worse off). However, others will argue that the allocation is not fair or equitable. Economists have no special training in resolving these fairness or equity issues. Thus, we focus our attention on efficiency, which most people will agree is a laudable objective— given limited resources it is good not to waste them.

MANAGERIAL APPLICATIONS

Patent for Priceline.com

Government-enforced patents better define property rights in new inventions. Patents in the United States are awarded for processes, machines, manufacturers, or compositions of matter that are considered useful, novel, and not obvious. Patents protect the intellectual property rights of the inventor and thus protect the common good by providing incentives to innovate novel and not obvious inventions.

Priceline.com received a patent for the world's first buyer-driven e-commerce system where users can go to the Internet to name their price for goods and services. Expedia.com challenged whether Priceline.com's process is really novel and not obvious. In 2001, the parties settled. Internet businesses where consumers can name their own price have to pay Priceline.com a royalty. This royalty is a tax on all Internet consumers. Awarding a patent for something that is obvious lowers incentives for future innovations that use this process.

Source: J. Gurley (1999), "The Trouble with Internet Patents," *Fortune* (July 19), 118; L. Flynn (2002), "The Web World Watches Closely as British Telecommunications Stakes a Patent Claim on a Now-Ubiquitous Function: Hyperlinking," *New York Times* (March 11).

---

businesses and to close existing businesses. In contrast, in centrally planned economies, property tends to be owned by the state; government officials decide how to use these resources.

Dimensions of Property Rights

Ownership involves two general dimensions: *use rights* and *alienability rights*. These aspects of ownership are not always bundled together. You own your body in the sense that you can decide what activities to pursue. Yet, there are significant legal restrictions on alienability. For instance, you cannot enter a legally enforceable contract to sell one of your kidneys, despite the fact that you have two, can live comfortably with one, and might value your second kidney much less than a wealthy individual who is dying from kidney failure. This restriction eliminates the possibility of a free market in kidneys. In some transactions, it is possible to sell use rights while retaining alienability rights. For instance, in a rental contract, the renter obtains the rights to use an apartment, but does not own or have the right to sell the unit. Conversely, the landlord has the right to sell the apartment, but does not have the right to use it during the term of the lease. (Rental, lease, and franchise agreements separate alienability and use rights; we examine these contracts in a later chapter.)

MANAGERIAL APPLICATIONS

Property Rights Insecurity in Colombia

Colombia has a continuing stream of impoverished farmers who are leaving the countryside and migrating to cities. They live in shantytowns that breed crime and violence. Yet Colombia has substantial arable land—an area equivalent in size to North Dakota. And only about 20 percent is used for agriculture. These seemingly inconsistent facts are both by-products of Colombia's more than four decades long conflict between the government and a paramilitary force that is deeply involved in drugs. The resulting violence induces many to flee. But others are forced off their land or intimidated into selling at bargain-basement prices.

Source: J. Forero (2004), "Colombia's Landed Gentry: Coca Lords and Other Bullies," *New York Times* (January 21), A4.

MANAGERIAL APPLICATIONS

While Animosity between the Governments of Venezuela and the United States Grows, So Does Trade

Former Venezuelan President Hugo Chavez predicted that "capitalism will lead to the destruction of humanity." In turn he worked hard to redirect his nation's trade away from the United States to what he considered "more like-minded nations," such as China and Iran. Washington has also taken steps to limit trade with Venezuela, such as halting American weapon sales to Venezuela.

The potential gains from trade between Venezuela and the United States, however, are large. For example, Venezuela is a leading producer of oil that is in high demand in the United States, while U.S. manufacturers produce automobiles and other products that are in high demand in Venezuela. Meanwhile many Venezuelans place lower value on an array of products produced by the like-minded nations, such as Chinese cars.

Despite the acrimony between the Venezuelan and U.S. governments, trade between the two countries continues to soar. Venezuela is the fourth largest oil supplier to the United States, while non-oil exports to the United States increased 116 percent during the first three months of 2006. Meanwhile, General Motors and Ford have been striving to meet soaring demand in Venezuela, with automobile sales up over 28 percent between July 2005 and 2006. General Motors, as Venezuela's largest car manufacturer, indicated that it planned to invest $20 million to expand its output in the country by 30 percent, adding 600 new workers.

Trading partners are made better off through exchange. There are strong incentives to engage in trade. This example illustrates that these incentives are not easily thwarted by political rhetoric. Trade continues to thrive even though companies and individuals face potential government actions that could affect their trading relationships and corresponding investments.

Source: S. Romero (2006), "For Venezuela, as Distaste for U.S. Grows So Does Trade," *nytimes.com* (August 16).

Gains from Trade

To understand how a market economy works, we must understand the motives for trading property rights. Why do people buy and sell? The basic answer is to make themselves better off.

Within the economic framework, people order their preferences and take actions that maximize their level of satisfaction (utility). Trade takes place because the buyer places a higher value on the item than the seller. The corresponding *gains from trade* make both parties better off—voluntary trade is *mutually advantageous*. For example, if José Coronas is willing to pay up to $26,000 for a particular automobile and Rochester Motors is willing to sell the automobile for as little as $20,000, the potential gains from trade are $6,000 ($26,000 − $20,000). If the automobile trades at $23,000, both parties are $3,000 better off. José gives up $23,000 to buy something that he values at $26,000, while Rochester Motors obtains $23,000 for something it values at only $20,000. At other prices between $20,000 and $26,000, the total gains are still $6,000 but they are not split evenly. For example, at a price of $25,000, José gains $1,000 in value, while Rochester Motors gains $5,000.[3]

From where do these gains from trade come? One source is differences in preferences. The buyer and seller simply may place different values on the traded item. For

[3]Sometimes, individuals regret a trade after the fact. For instance, José might be unhappy after he purchased a particular automobile from Rochester Motors. But given the information he had at the time of the transaction, he must have expected it to be advantageous to purchase the automobile or else he would not have done so (at least from Rochester Motors). José's ability to say no limits the extent to which he can be exploited in any voluntary trade.

A. Time it takes for Donna and Mario to produce meat and beer

	Meat (1 lb)	Beer (1 quart)
Donna	1 hour	2 hours
Mario	6 hours	3 hours

B. Allocation of time (30 hours per week) and output prior to specialization and trading

	Meat	Beer
Donna	18 hours; 18 lbs	12 hours; 6 quarts
Mario	18 hours; 3 lbs	12 hours; 4 quarts
Total production	**21 lbs**	**10 quarts**

C. Production with specialization

	Meat (lbs)	Beer (quarts)
Donna	30	0
Mario	0	10
Total production	**30 lbs**	**10 quarts**

D. One possible allocation after trading

	Meat (lbs)	Beer (quarts)
Donna	23	6
Mario	7	4

Table 3.1   Comparative Advantage

This table provides an example of comparative advantage. Panel A shows how many hours it takes for Donna and Mario to produce 1 pound of meat and 1 quart of beer. Donna and Mario each work 30 hours per week. Panel B shows their allocation of time and resulting output prior to meeting and trading. While Mario is less productive than Donna in an absolute sense for both goods, he has a comparative advantage in making beer (opportunity cost of ½ pound of meat for 1 quart of beer compared to Donna's opportunity cost of 2 pounds of meat). Donna has a comparative advantage in producing meat. Panel C illustrates how total production can be increased by having both people specialize in the activity where they have a comparative advantage. Panel D displays a possible final allocation after Donna and Mario trade. Specializing and trading produce real gains for both people.

example, some people value new automobiles more than other people do. Another important source of gains is that the seller may be able to produce the item more cheaply than the buyer and thus has a *comparative advantage* in its production. In advanced economies, individuals specialize in producing goods where they have a comparative advantage; they then trade to acquire other goods. Specialization greatly enhances the standard of living of a society. Imagine that you had to be completely self-sufficient, making your own clothing, growing your own food, building your own house, and producing your own vehicles for transportation. Your overall standard of living would be dramatically lower than it is living in a modern, specialized economy.

Table 3.1 presents a numerical example of comparative advantage. Donna Meyers and Mario Santini each produce their own food and drink through hunting and brewing beer. Panel A shows how many hours it takes for them to produce 1 pound of meat and 1 quart of beer. Panel B shows their allocation of time and resulting output working independently prior to their meeting and trading. Both work 30 hours per week.

Donna spends 18 hours per week hunting and 12 hours per week making beer, producing a total of 18 pounds of meat and 6 quarts of beer. Mario spends 18 hours hunting and 12 hours making beer, producing a total of 3 pounds of meat and 4 quarts of beer. Their total production prior to meeting is 21 pounds of meat (18 + 3) and 10 quarts of beer (6 + 4).

Donna has an *absolute advantage* over Mario in making both goods—it takes her fewer hours to produce either a pound of meat or a quart of beer. Mario, however, has a *comparative advantage* (lower opportunity cost) for producing beer. Mario's opportunity cost for producing 1 quart of beer is ½ pound of meat (he could have produced ½ pound of meat with the 3 hours he uses to produce a quart of beer), while Donna's opportunity cost is 2 pounds of meat. Conversely, Donna has a comparative advantage in hunting. Donna's opportunity cost for producing 1 pound of meat is ½ quart of beer, while Mario forgoes 2 quarts of beer to produce a pound of meat.

Panel C shows how total production can be increased by having each person specialize in producing the product for which they have a comparative advantage. Donna can produce 30 pounds of meat by spending all 30 hours on hunting, while Mario can produce 10 quarts of beer by focusing exclusively on beer production. This specialization maintains total beer production at 10 quarts and increases the production of meat by 9 pounds.[4] By specializing and trading, both parties can be made better off—there are gains from trade. The final allocation depends on the specific bargain reached by Donna and Mario. One possible outcome is presented in Panel D, where both parties have the same amount of beer as before but more meat. Specializing and trading results in a Pareto improvement relative to working in isolation.

[4]In this example, Donna and Mario completely specialize and produce only one product. More generally, at least one of the two people will specialize in producing one product. The other person might allocate some time to producing the same product (the one for which he does not have a comparative advantage) if additional gains are derived from producing more of the product than can be produced by the first person.

Figure 3.1 Comparative Advantage

This figure displays the example of comparative advantage presented in Table 3.1 graphically. Donna and Mario's Production Possibilities Frontiers (PPFs) show the combinations of the two products that each can produce individually, working 30 hours per week with no trade. The absolute value of the slope of Mario's PPF, ½ lb. meat/qt. beer, is his opportunity cost for producing beer. The absolute value of the slope of Donna's PPF, 2 lb. meat/qt. beer, is her opportunity cost for producing beer. Mario's lower opportunity cost implies that he has a comparative advantage in beer production. The combined PPF shows combinations of meat and beer production that are possible if they divide the work based on comparative advantage. Any point on the combined PPF is efficient in the sense that the output of one good cannot be increased without decreasing the output of the other good, given their productive capacities. The *y*-intercept of 35 is the maximum meat that can be produced if they produce no beer. Moving from there, the slope of the PPF is initially −1/2, which assumes Mario will produce the beer because of his comparative advantage. The kink in the PPF occurs where Mario reaches his maximum production of 10 beers. Donna must produce any desired beers beyond that point, and she has a higher opportunity. The combined and individual gains from specialization and trade are also pictured.

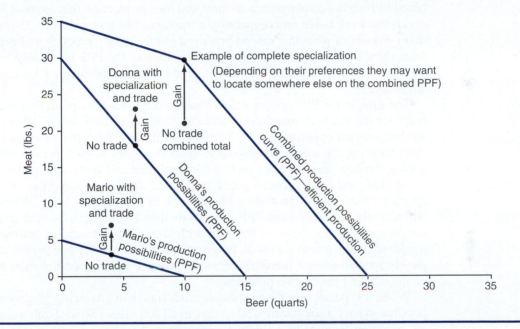

Figure 3.1 provides a graphical analysis of Mario and Donna's gains from specialization and trade. A Production Possibilities Frontier (PPF) shows all combinations of the two goods that can be produced with efficient production. Recall, with efficient production it is not possible to increase the production of one good without decreasing the production of the other. The figure pictures Mario and Donna's individual PPFs, as well as their combined PPF that assumes appropriate specialization. The individual PPF's picture Donna and Mario production choices when each work independently with no trade. As drawn, Donna can produce both more beer and more meat than Mario if there is no trade.

The absolute value of the slope of Mario's PPF, ½ lb. meat/qt. beer, is his opportunity cost for producing beer. The absolute value of the slope of Donna's PPF,

Gains from Trade

In 1880, the United States was about to become the world's most efficient economy. Yet labor productivity varied substantially among states. North Carolina, the least productive state, was only 18 percent of Nevada, the most productive. (In 1880, Nevada's productivity was high because many had migrated there to work in the mines.) In 2002, New Mexico, the poorest state, had a per capita income that was almost 60 percent of Connecticut, the richest state. As a giant free-trade zone, incomes in the United States have converged to similar standards. Although there are still differences, those differences have fallen substantially—and not at the expense of the rich states.

Source: V. Postrel (2004), "A Case Study in Free Trade: American Incomes Converge, but Not at the Bottom," *New York Times* (February 24), C2.

2 lb. meat/qt. beer, is her opportunity cost for producing beer. Mario's lower opportunity cost implies that he has a comparative advantage in beer production. The initial production choices with no trade are pictured on the respective PPFs. The combined PPF shows combinations of meat and beer production that are possible if they divide the work based on comparative advantage. The y-intercept of 35 is the maximum amount of meat that can be produced jointly if they produce no beer. Moving from there to positive beer production, the slope of the PPF is initially $-\frac{1}{2}$, which assumes Mario is assigned the task of producing beer because of his comparative advantage.

The kink in the PPF occurs where Mario reaches his maximum production of 10 beers for the week. Donna must produce any additional beers beyond that point, and she has a higher opportunity cost. The slope of the PPF from that point on is -2. Arrows showing the increased amount of meat that goes to each person (without reducing the beer they receive) picture the combined and individual gains from specialization and trade. These gains are based on the assumption of complete specialization and Donna trading Mario 7 lbs. of meat for six beers. Where the two will actually produce on the PPF depends on their preferences for beer and meat. In simple two good examples of this type with linear PPFs, it is never optimal for both people to produce both goods. It, however, can be optimal for one person to be completely specialized and the other person to produce some of both goods, depending on the demand for the two products.

While it is possible to have an absolute advantage in producing all goods, it is impossible to have a comparative advantage in all activities.[5] Specialization and trading are common features in economies throughout the world. Comparative advantage also arises in many management situations. For example, while a top-level manager might be able to perform many activities more effectively and in less time than a lower-level employee, the manager should not try to do all activities himself (make sales calls, work on the manufacturing line, change lightbulbs, answer phones, and so on). More value will be created if managers concentrate on activities for which they have a comparative advantage.

---

[5]Note for the mathematically inclined: Donna's opportunity cost for producing 1 pound of meat is $\frac{1}{2}$ quart of beer (1 qt. beer/hr.)/(2 lb. meat/hr.) = $\frac{1}{2}$ qt. beer/lb. meat. The reciprocal of this ratio, 2 lb. meat/qt. beer, is Donna's opportunity cost for producing beer expressed in pounds of meat. If Donna's ratio is smaller than Mario's ratio for one product, the reciprocal of Mario's ratio must be smaller than the reciprocal of Donna's ratio. Thus Donna has a comparative advantage in producing the first product, while Mario has a comparative advantage in producing the second product. It is a mathematical impossibility for one person to have a comparative advantage in producing all products.

ANALYZING MANAGERIAL DECISIONS: *Comparative Advantage in the Workplace*

You are a manager of a division of a company that is responsible for the final assembly of two computer products, modems and keyboards. You manage two employees, Julio and Chenyu, who each work 8 hours per day. Currently you have assigned both Julio and Chenyu to spend the first 7 hours of the day assembling keyboards and the last hour assembling modems. Julio can assemble 2 modems per hour and 14 keyboards per hour. Chenyu is more highly skilled in both activities. She averages 3 modems per hour and 15 keyboards per hour.

1. How many modems and keyboards are being assembled under the current work assignments?

2. What are Julio's opportunity costs for assembling modems and keyboards? What are Chenyu's? Does either employee have a comparative advantage in assembling one of the products?

3. Devise a way of reassigning the work activities between the two employees that keeps the number of modems being assembled the same as before but increases the number of keyboards.

4. What are potential reasons why you might not want to change the work assignments (assume that more assembly of either or both products is desirable)?

A common misconception is that trade takes place because people have too much of some goods—people sell to others what they cannot use themselves. This view, however, does not explain why individuals sell houses, cars, jewelry, land, and other resources that they value highly and have in short supply. The economic explanation for trade argues that trade takes place not because people have too little or too much of a good. Rather, trade takes place because a person is willing to pay a higher price for a good than it is worth to its current owner. While you might love your new sports car, you would still sell it if someone offered you a high-enough price. And winning bidders of collectibles auctioned on eBay are frequently individuals with collections of related items.

It is important to recognize that trade is an important form of value creation. Trading produces value that makes individuals better off. Gains from trade also provide important incentives to move resources to more productive uses. If George Nichols can make the most productive use of a piece of land, he will be willing to pay a higher price for the land than other potential users. The current owner, Jody Crowe, has the incentive to sell the land to George, because she gets to keep the proceeds from the sale. It is these incentives that help to promote a Pareto-efficient allocation of resources in a market economy. After all mutually advantageous trades are completed, it is impossible to change this allocation without making someone worse off.

Basics of Supply and Demand

Gains from trade explain why individuals buy and sell. But what coordinates the separate decisions of millions of individuals in a market economy to prevent chaos? Why are there not massive surpluses of some goods and huge shortages of other goods? What restricts the amounts demanded by the public to the amounts supplied? Answers to these questions come from an understanding of the market price system.

The Price Mechanism

The basic economics of a price system can be illustrated through standard supply and demand diagrams. Figure 3.2 displays a supply and demand diagram for a particular model of personal computer—for example, a Pentium dual-core machine with standard quality and features. The vertical axis on the graph shows the price for a PC, and the horizontal axis shows the total quantity of PCs demanded and supplied in the market for the period (e.g., a month).

The market includes all potential buyers and sellers of this type of PC. Suppose that in this market there are many buyers and sellers and that individual transactions are so small in relation to the overall market that the price is unaffected by any single sale or purchase. In this case, no buyer or seller has market power: All trades are made at the going market price. We label this type of market as *competitive*.

The *demand curve* depicts how many total PCs consumers are willing to buy at each price (holding all other factors constant). The demand curve slopes downward because consumers typically buy more if the price is lower. For example, consumers are likely to buy more PCs if the price is P^{LO} (say, $900) than if the price is P^{HI} (say, $1,500).

The *supply curve* depicts how many PCs producers are willing to sell at each price (holding all other factors constant). The curve slopes upward: At higher prices, producers are able and willing to produce and sell more units. For example, at a price of $900, many potential producers cannot cover their costs, and thus they refrain from entering production. At a price of $1,500, more units are manufactured and brought to market.

Figure 3.2   Supply and Demand in the PC Industry

The demand curve shows the number of PCs that consumers want to purchase at each price. The supply curve shows the number of PCs that producers want to sell at each price. Equilibrium occurs where the two curves intersect. Here, the quantity supplied equals the quantity demanded. If the price is above the market-clearing price of P^*, say at P^{HI}, there is a surplus of PCs. Producers supply more PCs than consumers want to purchase, and inventories build. If the price is below the market-clearing price, say at P^{LO}, there is a shortage. Producers supply fewer PCs than consumers want to purchase and inventories shrink. Surpluses and shortages put pressure on prices and quantities to move to equilibrium levels of P^*.

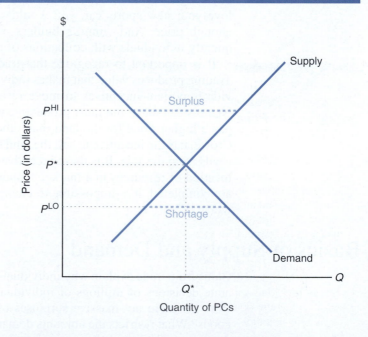

The two curves cross at the *market-clearing price P** and *quantity Q**. At the market-clearing price, the quantity of PCs demanded exactly equals the quantity supplied. Here, at a price of $1,200, the market is said to be in *equilibrium.*

There are strong pressures within markets that push prices and quantities toward their equilibrium levels. To see why, suppose that the market price is above the equilibrium price, such as P^{HI} in Figure 3.2. At this higher price, there is a *surplus* of PCs—suppliers produce more PCs than consumers are willing to purchase. As inventories of unsold PCs build, this surplus places downward pressure on prices as suppliers compete to try to sell their products. As prices fall, fewer PCs will be produced and more will be demanded, thus reducing the surplus. In contrast, if the price is below the market-clearing price, such as P^{LO} in Figure 3.2, inventories dwindle and back orders accumulate—there is a *shortage* of computers. Here, consumers will bid up the price of PCs as they compete for the limited supply. As prices rise, producers increase their output and consumers demand fewer PCs, thus reducing the shortage. When the market is in equilibrium, there is no pressure on prices and quantities—the quantity demanded exactly equals the quantity supplied. Inventories are stable at their desired levels, and the market price is stable at this point.

Supply and demand diagrams like that in Figure 3.2 are snapshots at a point in time. As time passes, both the supply and the demand curves are likely to change. Figure 3.3 shows the effects of a shift in the demand curve in the PC market. The left panel depicts an increase in demand. Here, there is a shift in the demand curve to the right, since at each price, consumers demand more PCs. Demand for PCs might increase for a variety of reasons, including an increase in the purchasing power of consumers or a decline in the prices of supporting software. These types of changes motivate consumers to purchase more PCs at any given price. After the demand shift at the old equilibrium price, inventories shrink and there is a shortage of PCs. This shortage places upward pressure on prices; higher prices in turn stimulate more production. The end result is a higher equilibrium price and quantity. The right panel shows that the opposite effect occurs with a reduction in demand. This shift to the left in the demand curve also can be caused by a variety of factors (e.g., a recession that causes businesses to reduce their purchases of PCs or an increase in personal tax rates that reduces consumers' purchasing power).

Figure 3.3 The Effects of a Shift in Demand on the Equilibrium Price and Quantity of PCs

The initial equilibrium is where the demand curve, labeled D_0, intersects the supply curve, labeled S_0. The left panel shows the effects of an increase in demand. The result is a higher equilibrium price and quantity. The right panel shows the effects of a decrease in demand. The result is a lower equilibrium price and quantity.

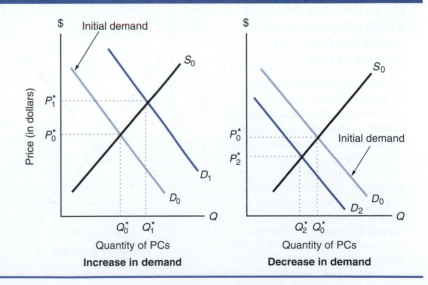

Increase in demand

Decrease in demand

MANAGERIAL APPLICATIONS

Shifts in Demand, Quantity, and Price at the PGA Tournament

The PGA Tournament features competition among the world's top golfers. In 2013, the PGA was held at Oak Hill Country Club in Rochester, New York. The event attracted over 30,000 spectators a day. Many of these spectators were from outside the Rochester area.

A significant number of these visitors were avid golfers who wanted to play while they were in Rochester. Rochester has several courses that are open to the public. However, many courses in the area are private (only members and their guests can play). Facing this dramatic temporary increase in the demand for public golf courses, several of the private courses decided to become public during the week of the PGA. These courses charged high fees ranging from $150 to $350 per round (their normal guest fees were approximately $75). This example highlights that shifts in demand motivate increases in the quantity supplied and the price of a product (in this case, golf times).

Figure 3.4 depicts the effects of a shift in supply in the PC market. The left panel displays a shift in the supply curve to the right. A rightward shift implies an increase in supply, because at each price producers make and offer more PCs. Many factors might cause an increase in supply. For example, a decline in the prices of labor and other inputs used for manufacturing PCs will make PC production more profitable and increase supply. Supply also might increase because of changes in technology that allow for less expensive, more efficient production. After the supply shift at the old equilibrium price, inventories accumulate and there is a surplus of PCs. This surplus places downward pressure on prices, which in turn increases the quantity of PCs demanded. The end result is a lower equilibrium price and higher equilibrium quantity. The right panel shows that the opposite effect occurs when supply shifts to the left.

Figure 3.4   The Effects of a Shift in Supply on the Equilibrium Price and Quantity of PCs

The initial equilibrium is where the demand curve, labeled D_0, intersects the supply curve, labeled S_0. The left panel shows the effects of an increase in supply. The result is a lower equilibrium price and an increase in equilibrium quantity. The right panel shows the effects of a decrease in supply. The result is a higher equilibrium price and a lower equilibrium quantity.

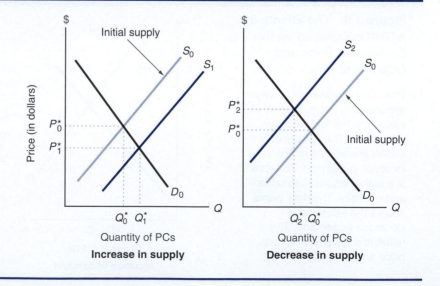

Shifts in Curves versus Movements along Curves

Demand and supply curves depict the quantities that will be demanded and supplied at each possible price, holding all other relevant variables constant. The price observed in the market determines the specific quantity demanded and quantity supplied in the marketplace (i.e., the price determines the relevant points on the two curves).

We have provided examples of how a change in an important non price variable can cause either the demand and/or supply curve to shift. It is common to refer to a rightward shift in the demand curve as an *increase in demand* and a leftward shift as a *decrease in demand*. Similarly, a rightward shift in the supply curve is referred to as an *increase in supply* (higher quantity is supplied at any given price) and a leftward shift as a *decrease in supply*.

A movement along a given demand or supply curve is caused by a change in price (holding other variables constant). The change in price is said to result in a change in the *quantity demanded or quantity supplied*.

It is important to be able to distinguish between shifts in demand and supply curves (changes in demand or supply) and movements along a given curve (changes in quantity demanded or quantity supplied). For example, reconsider the increase in supply pictured on the left in Figure 3.4. As we have discussed, this increase would have been motivated by a change in some relevant variable other than the price of the product, such as a decline in the hourly wage paid to labor. The rightward shift in supply indicates that producers will supply more of the product at *any* given price. The demand curve has not changed, so there is no change in demand. However, there is a change in the quantity demanded when supply increases—at the lower equilibrium price consumers purchase more of the product.

Note that a change in supply or demand is motivated by a change in a relevant variable other than the price of the good. On the other hand, a change in the quantity demanded or quantity supplied is caused by a change in the price of the good, induced by a shift in the other curve, holding all other variables that affect the position of the curve constant.

Using Supply and Demand Analysis for Qualitative Forecasts

Consulting firms, large companies, and governmental agencies use formal statistical analysis to develop quantitative estimates of demand and supply to use in analyzing specific markets. Managers, analysts, the media, and others, however, often use supply and demand analysis on a much less formal basis simply to forecast the direction of changes in prices and quantities in the marketplace.

For example, suppose that Mr. Fan owns a restaurant chain in the United States that features a menu of specialty beef dishes. Fan has just read in his morning newspaper that there have been newly reported cases of "Mad Cow Disease" in the United States. Several people who ate contaminated beef died recently from the disease. Fan recalls that Japan, South Korea, and other countries immediately stopped importing American beef when the first case of Mad Cow disease was reported in the United States a number of years ago. Among other things, Fan wants to know what effect the scare will have on the price that he will have to pay for beef over the upcoming months.

Fan can use supply and demand analysis to forecast the directional effect that the Mad Cow scare will have on beef prices. First, he needs to consider whether it will affect the demand for beef, the supply of beef or both. He is fairly confident that the scare will cause demand to decrease. As pictured in Figure 3.3, a decrease in demand is expected to result in a lower price for beef. However, Fan should not forget supply. For example, what if the government immediately ordered the slaughter and disposal of 90 percent of all cows in the United States to protect consumers from the disease? He needs to take both effects into account, unless he has good reason to assume that one of the effects is not likely to be important.

For practice, suppose that you are Fan and use supply and demand analysis to forecast the directional change in the price beef. Start by drawing a standard supply and demand diagram, as pictured in Figure 3.2 to depict the beef market prior to the scare. Draw the projected shifts in supply and demand caused by the scare. Note that the shifts in both curves have the same directional effect in reducing the equilibrium quantity. The effects on price, however, are in opposite directions. In such cases, you need to ask yourself, which effect is likely to be larger? Sometimes it is hard to forecast. Suppose in this case, Fan is relatively confident that the short-term supply of beef will not change very much. The government is unlikely to order the mass destruction of cows due to a few reported cases of the disease. If so, he might assume that the demand effect is likely to dominate and the near-term effect is likely to be a decline in beef prices. In the longer run, the cost of cattle ranching and beef processing could increase due to new government regulations, additional testing for Mad Cow disease, and so on. Thus the longer run effects are harder to forecast. For additional practice, what affect do you think the scare will have on the price of chicken products?

Fan is also likely to be interested in how the scare will affect customer demand for his beef dishes. Demand for products is the subject of the next chapter.

Linear Supply and Demand

Throughout this book we use linear demand and supply curves (as pictured in Figures 3.2 to 3.4). Linearity simplifies the analysis and is often a reasonable approximation in actual applications (at least over the range of actions being considered). This section provides a numerical example of supply and demand analysis using linear supply and demand curves.

Suppose that the supply function for apples is

$$Q_s = 30 + 0.2P_a - 3W \tag{3.1}$$

where Q_s is the quantity supplied of apples in millions of pounds, P_a is the market price for apples in cents, and W is the hourly wage rate paid to agricultural workers. The supply function indicates that farmers will produce more apples as either the market price of apples rises or the wage rate for workers falls. Farmers produce more apples when the wage rate falls since production costs are lower. Currently the wage rate is $10. Substituting this value in Equation (3.1) and solving for P_a produces the current supply curve[6]:

$$P_a = 5Q_s \tag{3.2}$$

---

[6]Recall that when graphing the supply and demand curves, the convention is to place price on the vertical axis.

ANALYZING MANAGERIAL DECISIONS: *Ethanol and Pork Prices*

Over the past decade, the federal government has taken significant steps to encourage the development of ethanol and other fuels made from plants as a partial replacement for gasoline. These actions have been undertaken by politicians in the midst of public concerns about the dependence on foreign oil, war in the Middle East, and global warming. The primary input for ethanol production is corn. In 2011, the 13.9 billion gallons of ethanol produced in the United States consumed over 20 percent of the domestic corn supply.

Suppose that the government has just passed new legislation mandating increased annual production of corn ethanol. You manage the Hog Heaven restaurant chain. Your restaurant chain, which has about 300 outlets throughout the United States, specializes in barbecue pork dishes but also offers chicken, beef, and vegetarian meals. Currently about 80 percent of your revenue comes from your pork dishes. The price of pork has a major impact on your costs. You are concerned that the federal promotion of ethanol might have an impact on pork prices and the profitability of your restaurant chain. Feed cost is typically about 50 to 60 percent of the total cost of production of pork producers. About 80 percent of the feed that hogs consume is corn.

1. Use basic supply and demand analysis to illustrate the likely effect of the government's mandated increase of ethanol production on (1) corn prices and (2) pork prices.
2. What actions might you consider given the results of your analysis?

Supply curves show the relation between price and quantity supplied holding all other factors constant (in this case the wage rate for agricultural workers).

Suppose that the demand function for apples is

$$Q_d = 20 - 1/3P_a + 0.002I \tag{3.3}$$

where I = per capita income. The demand function indicates that consumers will purchase more apples as the price falls and/or as income increases. Currently income is \$10,000. Substituting this value into the demand function and solving for P_a produces the current demand curve:

$$P_a = 120 - 3Q_d \tag{3.4}$$

In equilibrium, the quantity supplied equals the quantity demanded: $Q_s = Q_d = Q^*$ where Q^* denotes the equilibrium quantity. Substituting Q^* into the supply and demand curves (Equations [3.2] and [3.4]) and setting them equal (since there is one equilibrium price) allows us to find the equilibrium quantity, Q^*:

$$5Q^* = 120 - 3Q^* \tag{3.5}$$
$$Q^* = 15$$

The equilibrium price of 75 cents is found by substituting the equilibrium quantity of 15 into either the demand or supply curve Equations ([3.2] or [3.4]).[7]

---

[7]We could have found the equilibrium price by setting the demand and supply functions (Equations [3.1] and [3.3]) equal after substituting for the current values of W and I. The equilibrium quantity then could be found by substituting the equilibrium price into either Equation (3.1) or (3.3). We took the extra steps of solving for the demand and supply curves to illustrate how they are derived from the underlying demand and supply functions. We elaborate on this derivation in the case of the demand curve in the next chapter.

Note that changes in the wage rate shift the supply curve, while changes in income shift the demand curve. See if you can find the new equilibrium price and quantity if income increases to $20,000. Answer the problem before looking in this footnote for the answer.[8]

Determining the equilibrium in simple numerical supply and demand problems can be summarized as follows. Begin by inserting the current values for variables other than price into the supply and demand functions and solve the functions for P to get the demand and supply curves. Equate the supply and demand curves and solve for the equilibrium quantity, Q^*. Put Q^* into either the supply or demand curve equations and solve for the equilibrium price, P^*.

To consider the effect of a change in a non price variable, replace the original value with the new value and repeat the above steps to obtain the new equilibrium. It is a good idea to graph these kinds of problems on a standard supply and demand diagram, which shows the original equilibrium, as well as the shift in the relevant curve and the new equilibrium. Graphical analysis can often provide a more intuitive understanding of a problem. It also can be helpful as a check for arithmetic errors that can arise in purely algebraic solutions to the problem.

Supply and Demand—Extended Analysis

This section uses supply-and-demand framework to analyze other issues of managerial interest. It begins by considering whether a change in supply or demand is likely to have a greater impact on the equilibrium price or quantity. This analysis is followed by a related discussion of short-run versus long-run responses to changes in the marketplace. The section ends by considering under what circumstances a per-unit cost increase in an industry can be passed on to consumers through higher prices.

Price versus Quantity Adjustments

We have seen that the equilibrium price and quantity typically change when either the demand or supply curves shifts. Forecasting the direction of price and quantity changes in a market can be very useful to managers. However, it is even more useful to be able to forecast whether most of the impact of the change will be on price or quantity.

To analyze this question, we need to introduce the concept of demand and supply elasticities. Elasticities, which are defined more precisely later in this book, measure the sensitivity of quantity demanded and supplied to price changes.[9] The left panel of Figure 3.5 depicts two extreme demand curves—one is vertical and the

---

[8]An increase in income in this example shifts the demand curve to the right, resulting in both a higher equilibrium price and quantity (see Figure 3.2). More specifically, shifting the income from $10,000 to $20,000 results in an equilibrium quantity of 22.5 million pounds and an equilibrium price of $1.125 (112.5 cents).

[9]The responsiveness of consumption and production decisions to price changes varies across products. For example, consumers tend to be relatively responsive to price changes when it comes to restaurant meals but pay little attention to changes in the price of toothpaste. Similarly, the supply decisions of producers can be greatly affected by price in some cases and vary little in others (in the latter case consider a farmer who has grown a fixed quantity of a highly perishable commodity that must be sold before rots).

Figure 3.5 Perfectly Inelastic and Elastic Demand and Supply

This figure displays perfectly inelastic and elastic demand and supply curves. When demand (supply) is perfectly inelastic the quantity demanded (supplied) does not change with price. With perfectly elastic demand (supply), a small increase (decrease) in price relative to $5 in this figure will reduce the quantity demanded (supplied) to zero.

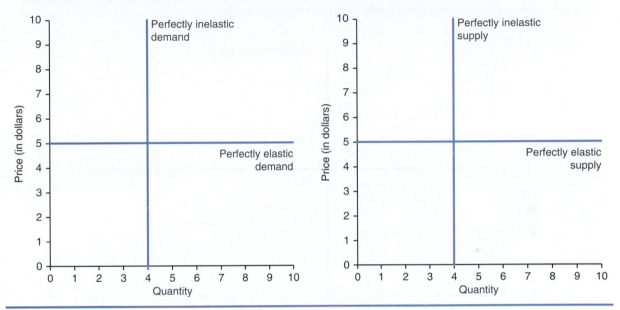

other is horizontal. The right panel displays similarly sloped supply curves. A vertical curve indicates that the quantity demanded or quantity supplied is the same regardless of price. Vertical supply and demand curves are referred to as *perfectly inelastic*. The horizontal curves depict the extreme opposite case where no quantity is demanded at prices above P^*, and no quantity is supplied at lower prices. Horizontal supply and demand curves are referred to as *perfectly elastic*. Typically industry demand curves and supply curves are less extreme—industry demand curves typically slope downward, while industry supply curves typically slope upward. At a given price and quantity, demand and supply curves with more vertical slopes are referred to as *relatively more inelastic* (since the relative change in quantity to a price change is small), while flatter curves are termed *relatively more elastic*.

In extreme cases, a change in demand or supply will result in only a price or quantity change—the other variable will remain unchanged. Figure 3.6 depicts these cases for an increase in demand. When supply is completely inelastic, an increase in demand increases price, but has no effect on quantity. For example, consider land in central New York City. Its supply is inelastic and the price for the land is determined by demand. The higher the demand, the higher will be the price. In contrast, when supply is perfectly elastic the increase in demand will cause an increase in quantity but no increase in price. Later in this book, we will discuss why horizontal long-run supply curves are reasonably common in certain types of industries.

Figure 3.6   Increase in Demand with Perfectly Inelastic or Elastic Supply

This figure displays the effect of a demand increase on the equilibrium price and quantity when supply is either perfectly inelastic or elastic. The original equilibrium price and quantity are $5 and 4 units respectively. When demand increases, only the equilibrium price changes when supply is perfectly inelastic (from $5 to $7). With perfectly elastic supply, only the equilibrium quantity changes (from 4 to 6). If demand were to decrease back to D1, the same general effects would happen in reverse.

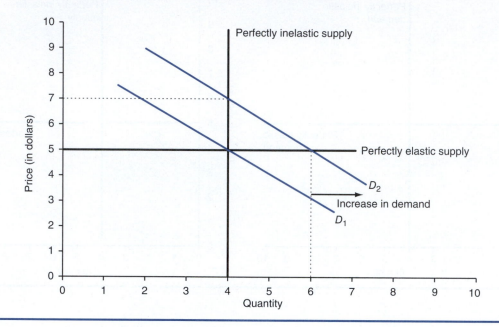

Figure 3.7 depicts the two extreme cases for an increase in supply. The effects are similar to what we saw for the increase in demand. An increase in supply will be fully reflected in price when demand is perfectly elastic and fully in quantity when demand is perfectly elastic. In the next chapter, we will examine in more detail the determinants of demand elasticities.

We have focused on increases in demand and supply. The effects are the same but in the opposite direction for decreases in supply and demand. While we have focused our attention on the extremes, the results generalize to more common in-between cases. If the supply curve is relatively inelastic, a change in demand will primarily affect the price of the product. In contrast, if the supply curve is relatively elastic a change in demand will primarily affect the quantity. Similarly, if the demand curve is relatively inelastic a shift in supply will be reflected primarily in price; if the demand curve is relatively elastic it will primarily affect the quantity.

Short-Run versus Long-Run Effects

Supply and demand curves tend to be relatively more inelastic in the short run than the long run. To see why, consider how consumers might respond to a large increase in the price of gasoline. Consumption of gasoline might not change very much in the

Figure 3.7 Increase in Supply with Perfectly Inelastic or Elastic Demand

This figure displays the effect of a supply increase on the equilibrium price and quantity when demand is either perfectly inelastic or elastic. The original equilibrium price and quantity are $5 and 4 units respectively. When supply increases, only the equilibrium price changes when demand is perfectly inelastic (from $5 to $3). With perfectly elastic demand, only the equilibrium quantity changes (from 4 to 6). If supply were to decrease back to S1, the same general effects would happen in reverse.

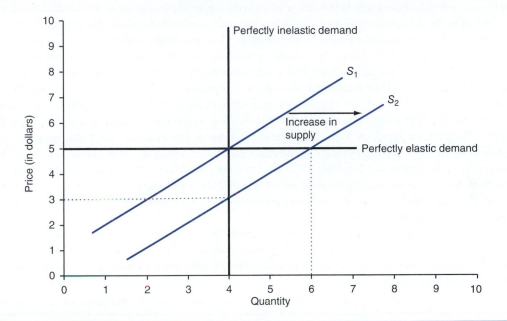

first weeks after the price increase. People have to get to work, school, and other places. The locations of people's homes and the types of automobiles they drive are largely fixed in the short run. All of these factors make the short-run demand relatively inelastic. With more time to adjust, however, consumers can reduce their consumption of gasoline by forming car pools with others to commute to work, purchasing vehicles that get better gas mileage, and so on. In the even longer run, they can relocate moving closer to their jobs, change jobs to work at locations closer to home, and so on. A similar analysis holds on the supply side of the market. Supply curves tend to be relatively more inelastic in the short run than the long run because suppliers have more flexibility to make changes over the longer run. Figure 3.8 depicts supply curves and demand curves for the so-called short run, medium run, and long run. Focus on the intersection point of the three curves as the initial starting price and quantity. Notice how a change in price is met with a greater change in quantity in the longer run, since the curves are more elastic.

We previously discussed how a shift in demand or supply will have a greater effect on price when the other curve is relatively inelastic and a greater effect on quantity when it is relatively elastic. Because demand and supply curves are likely to be more inelastic in the short run than the long run, shifts in demand and supply will tend to be reflected in price changes in the short run and in quantity changes in the long run.

MANAGERIAL APPLICATIONS

Decrease in Supply of Pilots Results in Reduction of Flights and Small Increases in Pilot Wages

In August 2013, the Federal Government increased the minimum experience required for commercial airline pilots from 250 hours to 1,500 hours. This reduced the supply of entry-level pilots materially. The primary employer of entry-level commercial pilots are the smaller regional airlines. Before this change, the starting salary paid at 14 U.S regional carriers averaged about $22,400 per year.

Supply and demand analysis suggests that this decrease in the supply of pilots would either decrease the number of pilots employed by the airlines, increase pilot wages, or some combination of both. Many of the routes flown by the regional airlines were only marginally profitable, and the airlines had only limited power to increase ticket prices to cover the increased costs for hiring pilots. These conditions imply that their demand for pilots would have been relatively elastic. The supply and demand framework predicts that the primary effect of a decrease in supply with relatively elastic demand would be a decline in the number of flights by these smaller regional airlines. Consistent with this forecast, many of the regional airlines cut their number of flights and hired fewer pilots, rather than raising wages of entry-level pilots. In the first quarter of 2014. Silver Airways announced that it was cutting its flights by 13 percent. Republic Airways, one of the nation's largest regional carriers announced due to the limited lumber of qualified commercial pilots, it was removing 27 of their 243 aircraft from operation. Great Lakes Aviation Ltd. stated that it was reducing the number of pilots from 300 in 2013 to about 100. However this reduction in the supply of qualified pilots, also resulted in small increases in pilot wages by 2014. For example, Silver Airways, a Florida-based airline with 35 planes, offered its current pilots salary increases of 5 to 10 percent and promised a $6,000 bonus if they continued to work for the company for one year.

Consistent with the economic view of behavior, some regional airlines responded "creatively." Because the new federal rules only required 250 hours of experience for commercial pilots flying planes with fewer than 10 seats they could hire pilots with this lower level of experience by removing 10 seats from a 19-seat airplane. Since these pilots were more plentiful, they were less expensive to hire.

Source: J. Nicas and S. Carey (2014), "What Can New Pilots Make? Near Minimum Wage" *The Wall Street Journal* (February 12).

Prices communicate important information to consumers and suppliers. For example, price increases signal to consumers to reduce their consumption of a product and to producers to figure out how to supply more of it. Ultimately, these responses translate into less extreme price changes and greater quantity changes in the longer run. In a sense, the large price changes in the short run help to motivate the output and consumption changes in the long run.

Industry Cost Increases and Price Adjustments

John MacDonald manages a company in a competitive industry that bottles and sells healthy juices to consumers. The current market price for juices in his industry is $5 per bottle. The government has just announced a new $2 per bottle tax that it is going to impose on suppliers in this industry. John wants to know whether he will be able to pass this cost increase on to consumers, for example, by charging $7 per bottle. Since his firm operates in a competitive industry he has no power to set the price. His hope is that the market price will increase to $7 to offset the cost increase. The question is will it? It turns out that the answer depends on the relative elasticities of supply and demand curves in the industry.

Figure 3.9 displays a graphical analysis of this example where the absolute values of the slopes of the demand and supply curves are roughly the same. The $2 per unit

Figure 3.8 Short, Medium, and Long Run

This figure displays the typical pattern observed for supply and demand curves in the short, medium, and long run. Both demand and supply tend to be more elastic in the longer run than the short run because consumers and producers have more time to make adjustments in quantities when price changes.

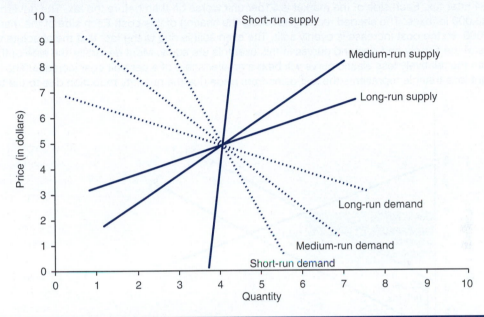

cost increase causes the supply curve to shift upward by $2. Suppliers have to pay $2 per unit to the government and thus require $2 more per unit to induce them to bring any specific quantity to the market, relative to the original supply curve. For example, suppliers were willing to bring 6,000 units to market at a price of $5. Now they require $7 to induce them to produce the same quantity. Note that the decrease in supply (upward/leftward shift in the curve) causes the price to increase to $6. Thus, suppliers are able to pass on half the cost to consumers. John and the other producers collect $6 for each unit sold. However, they only net $4 after paying the tax to the government. Each side of the market is $1 per unit worse off.[10]

More generally the sharing of a per-unit cost increase depends on the relative elasticities of the demand and supply curves. In the previous example, the supply and demand elasticities were about the same, so each side of the market bore about one-half the cost. When the two elasticities are not the same, the side of the market with the less elastic curve bears the larger share of the cost increase. Figure 3.10 depicts the two extreme cases for the demand curve. If the demand curve is perfectly inelastic, quantity remains unchanged and the price increases by the full amount of the cost

[10]Aside from paying the increase costs on units transacted, consumers and producers also experience lost gains from trade due to the reduction in quantity transacted. Their combined loss due to the reduction in trade is pictured by the deadweight loss (DWL) triangle in the graph. The tax does not only transfer money from consumers and producers to the government, but also causes a reduction in quantity and gains from trade. These losses are not offset by gains to others and so are commonly referred to as "deadweight losses."

Figure 3.9   Passing on Part of a Cost Increase to Consumers

This figure displays an example where suppliers face a new $2 per unit tax. The original equilibrium price and quantity were $5 and 6,000, respectively. The tax causes the supply curve to shift upward by $2. The new equilibrium price and quantity are $6 and 4,000 units, respectively. Consumers pay $6, but producers only net $4 after tax. Each side of the market is $1 per unit worse off than before the tax. The government collects $8,000 in taxes. The shaded rectangles reflect the sharing of this cost. Each side of the market bears $4,000, so the cost increase is evenly split. The even split is due to the fact that the absolute values of the slopes of the supply and demand curves in this example are equal. More generally, the side of the market with the relatively less elastic curve will bear a greater share of a per unit cost increase. The deadweight loss triangle represents the lost gains from trade due the quantity reduction due to the tax.

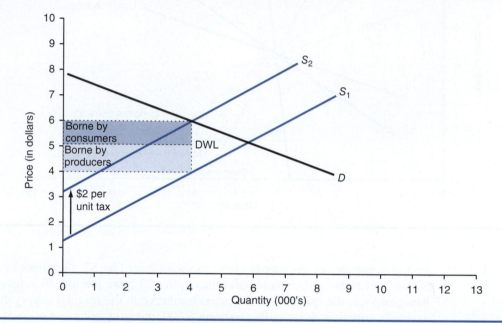

increase. Here the entire cost increase is passed on to consumers. In contrast, when demand is perfectly elastic the price remains the same and the quantity adjusts. In this case, none of the cost increase is passed on to consumers. Similarly, it can be shown that if supply is perfectly inelastic, producers bear all the costs. If supply is perfectly elastic all the cost is passed on to consumers. When neither side of the

MANAGERIAL APPLICATIONS

Supply of Online Résumés Bogs Down Employers

The Internet has reduced significantly the cost of submitting résumés to would-be employers. Job seekers no longer must print their résumés on high-quality paper, address, stamp, and mail an envelope. A click of the mouse and the résumé is gone. Some companies have thousands of résumés dumped into their e-mail boxes each day. During 1999 there were almost 5 million résumés on the Internet—200 times more than in 1994. When the cost of producing a good (like submitting a résumé) falls, its supply increases.

Source: S. Armour (1999), "Online Résumés Bogging Down Employers," *Democrat and Chronicle* (July 19), 1F.

Figure 3.10 Sharing of a Cost Increases at the Extremes

This figure shows the effects of a $2 per unit cost increase with perfectly inelastic and perfectly elastic demand. When demand is perfectly inelastic, the entire cost increase is passed on to consumers through a higher price and quantity does not change. With perfectly elastic demand the entire cost is borne by suppliers (none can be passed on). Price does not change and quantity falls.

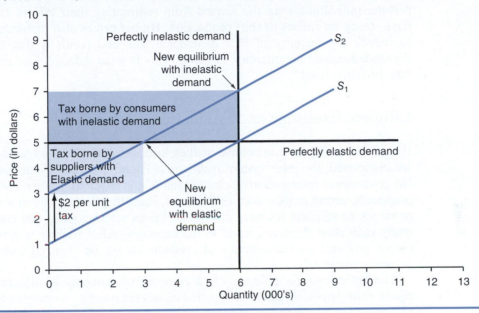

market is at one of the extremes, the cost is split. The side of the market with the relatively more elastic curve bears a smaller share of the cost.

Sometimes a cost increase is imposed on consumers, rather than on suppliers. For example, some states impose taxes on consumers when they purchase bottles of liquor at a store. While we do not do so here, it is relatively easy to show that the sharing of a cost increase does not depend on which side of the market initially incurs it. When a cost increase is imposed on consumers, the demand curve shifts downward, while the supply curve stays the same. The resulting price change results in the same net outcome for both parties as when the tax is imposed on suppliers. What matters in both cases are the relative elasticities of the supply and demand curves.

MANAGERIAL APPLICATIONS

Elastic Demand Limits Steelmakers' Abilities to Pass through Cost Increases

Higher prices for inputs, such as iron ore and coking coal, were expected to force up steel prices during 2011. Analysts, however, predicted that steelmakers would be unlikely to be able to raise steel prices enough to pass on the full increase in costs. Theory suggests that the ability of producers to pass through cost increases depends on the elasticity of demand. Analysts argued that weaker demand from the construction industry and the expectation that China might tighten its monetary policy due to concerns about rising inflation implied that steel makers would have difficulty in maintaining higher prices throughout the year. A UBS analyst summarized the basic economics of the situation as follows, "While mills can easily pass through higher input costs when demand is strong, unfortunately the current environment is less supportive."

Source. D. Maylie (2010), "Steelmakers Grapple with Price-Increase Pressures," *The Wall Street Journal* (December 28)

Prices as Social Coordinators

The equilibrium of supply and demand highlights the crucial role that prices play in coordinating the consumption and production decisions of individuals. For example, if too few PCs are being produced, inventories will shrink and dealers will raise prices. High-prices signal would-be producers to shift from producing lower-valued products to producing computers. Because property rights are private, individuals reap the reward from redirecting their efforts and therefore have strong incentives to shift production. Higher prices also motivate consumers to reduce the quantity of PCs demanded. The end result is that the quantity demanded equals the quantity supplied. This is what Adam Smith referred to as "the invisible hand."

Efficient Exchange and Production

If everyone trades in a competitive marketplace and all mutually advantageous trades are completed, the price system results in a Pareto-efficient resource allocation.[11] No government intervention or central planning is required. Rather, consumers and producers, acting in their own self-interest, react to price signals in a manner that produces an efficient resource allocation. Prices act to control and coordinate the many individual decisions made in the economy. After trading is completed, the output mix and final distribution of products cannot be changed without making someone worse off.

The basic logic for efficiency in a competitive economy is straightforward. At equilibrium prices, the quantity supplied equals the quantity demanded for all goods and there are no shortages or surpluses. Everyone who wants to make trades has done so, and all gains from trade have been exhausted. In making supply decisions, firms have strong private incentives to adopt the most efficient production methods and the value-maximizing output mix (these production choices maximize their profits). No changes in either production or distribution can be made without making someone worse off.

Measuring the Gains from Trade

In some applications it is useful to have measures of the gains from trade that are in units, such as dollars, that are independent of individuals' subjective utilities. Consumer surplus and producer surplus display this property and are commonly used to measure the gains from trade and the effects of specific actions and events on consumers, producers, and society as a whole.[12]

Figure 3.11 displays supply and demand curves for a market in which the equilibrium price and quantity are $10 and 10 units. The demand curve indicates that some

---

[11]These conditions will be met in a competitive market when trading costs are sufficiently low. Later, we will discuss factors that can motivate inefficiency in a market economy.

[12]Technically, consumers must have a specific type of utility function for consumer surplus to be an exact measure of their gains from trade in a market. However, it is generally a good approximation whenever consumers allocate their expenditures across many goods, which most do. The measure is widely used and accepted by most economists.

Figure 3.11 Consumer and Producer Surplus

In this figure, consumers pay $100 to obtain 10 units of the product ($10 × 10 units). They would have been willing to pay an additional $50 to obtain the 10 units. This $50 (Triangle A) represents the gains from trade to consumers and is called *consumer surplus*. Producers receive $100 of revenue, but would have been willing to supply the product if they had covered their incremental production costs of $50 (Triangle C). The extra $50 (Triangle B) is the gains from trade to producers and is called *producer surplus*.

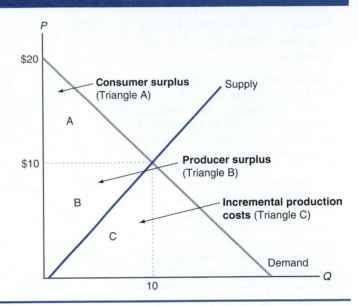

consumer would be willing to pay $19 to obtain the first unit of the product; however, the consumer only has to pay the market price of $10. The $9 "surplus" is a measure of the consumer's gains from trade from purchasing the first unit. The sum of the surplus at all points along the demand curve up to the equilibrium quantity of 10 units represents the aggregate difference between what consumers would be willing to pay for the product and what they have to pay given the market price. We call this difference, *consumer surplus* and display it graphically in Figure 3.11 by Triangle A. In this example, the consumer surplus is $50 (1/2 × 10 × 10). Note that in the aggregate, consumers would be willing to pay up to $150 dollars to obtain the 10 units (Triangle A + Triangle B + Triangle C), but only have to pay $100 (Triangle B + Triangle C). Their gains from trade from participating in this market are $50.

The same idea is used for measuring the net gains to producers. Later in this book, we show that the area under the supply curve represents the incremental costs that producers incur to produce the output. In this example, the incremental costs are $50 (Triangle C). Producers are willing to supply 10 units as long as the incremental revenue is at least equal to the incremental costs of $50. Producers, however, receive $100 (Triangle B + Triangle C). The extra $50 (Triangle B) represents the gains to trade for producers and is called *producer surplus*.

The total gains from trade produced in the market are measured by the sum of consumer and producer surplus. In this example, the total gains from trade (surplus) are $100 (Triangle A + Triangle B). We use the concepts of producer, consumer, and total surplus in several places in this book to measure the effects of various actions on consumers, producers, and "social welfare."

Government Intervention

We have discussed how a well-functioning price system can produce an efficient allocation of resources without government intervention or central planning. Nonetheless, governments sometimes intervene to establish caps or floors on

Figure 3.12 Economic Effects of a Government Price Cap on Gasoline

The free market equilibrium price in this figure is $3 per gallon. The government does not allow stations to charge more than $2 per gallon. At the $2 price, the quantity demanded is greater than the quantity supplied—there is a *shortage* of gasoline. The excess demand implies that gasoline must be allocated through nonprice mechanisms, such as waiting in line. Triangles A and B represent the lost gains from trade to consumers and producers (consumer and producer surpluses), respectively, induced by the price cap. Rectangle C represents a transfer of surplus from producers to consumers (ignoring other costs imposed on consumers). The price cap can also distort incentives of consumers to reduce consumption of gasoline, for example, by moving closer to work or buying smaller automobiles.

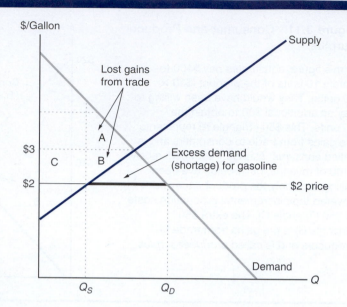

prices. This section examines the economic effects of these actions (in an otherwise well-functioning market).

Price Controls

The average retail price for gasoline in the United States was about $1.15 per gallon in 2003. Gasoline prices increased dramatically over the period 2004–2008 due to factors such as the increased demand for oil in China and India, the war in Iraq, and Hurricane Katrina. Gasoline prices, which averaged $1.60 per gallon in 2004, broke the $2.00 per gallon barrier in July of 2005. In August 2005, gasoline supply was disrupted by Katrina, the devastating storm that hit the Gulf Coast. Gasoline prices surged to over $3.00 per gallon. In subsequent months gasoline prices were volatile, rising from a low of $2.10 per gallon in November 2005 to a high of $3.20 per gallon in May 2007. In 2008 the price was above $4.00 per gallon. Consumers expressed fear and outrage over the high gasoline prices. Some groups asked the U.S. government to implement price controls to protect consumers from "unfair" gasoline prices.

Figure 3.12 displays the economic effects of a cap on the price of gasoline. The free market equilibrium price is $3.00 per gallon. However, suppose that the government passes a law that does not allow stations to charge more than $2.00 per gallon. At the $2.00 price, the quantity demanded, Q_D, is greater than the quantity supplied, Q_S—there is a *shortage* of gasoline. The excess demand implies that gasoline must be allocated through nonprice mechanisms. One mechanism is to serve customers in the order that they arrive until the supply is exhausted. This mechanism is likely to produce long lines and waits for gasoline. Also, customers who place the highest value on the gasoline (e.g., due to the importance of their travel) do not necessarily receive the product. The quantity supplied falls as a result of the price cap, resulting in lost gains from trade (total surplus). The reduction in consumer surplus and producer surplus is pictured by Triangles A and B, respectively. The consumers who obtain the gasoline for $2.00 potentially benefit from the cap at the expense of the gasoline dealers, the gasoline distributors, the gasoline refiners, and the individuals who own the mineral rights and receive a lower price for the quantity sold (unless the gains are offset by costs such as having to wait in line). Rectangle C pictures the transfer from producers to consumers (ignoring other costs).

During the 1970s, there was a severe shortage of gasoline in the United States due to an oil embargo and price controls. People still remember the long gas lines and substantial inconveniences experienced during that period. Some gas stations served customers based on their license plate numbers—odd numbers one day and even numbers the next. Customers also were limited in the number of gallons that they could purchase. These inconveniences have rarely been observed since the elimination of price controls in the early 1980s.

Consumers responded to higher gasoline prices during the 2004–2007 period in a variety of ways. Some reduced their travel plans, while others shifted to less expensive forms of transportation (e.g., carpooling, buses, and bikes). Some moved closer to work, while others purchased more fuel-efficient automobiles. Price controls not only produce shortages, but also distort incentives to take actions that reduce the consumption of the product.

Price Floors

A prominent example of a price floor is a *minimum wage law*. In the United States, the Fair Labor Standards Act (FLSA) requires employers to pay employees at least a minimum wage (in 2014, $7.25 per hour) for all hours they work. If a state has a minimum wage that is higher than the federal minimum, employers are obligated to pay the higher rate to employees working in that state. For example, the minimum wage in the State of Washington was $9.32 per hour in early 2014.

Figure 3.13 displays the economic effects of a minimum wage law. The market clearing price for unskilled labor in this example is $6.00 per hour. However, employers are not allowed to pay wages below $7.25 per hour. At $7.25, the quantity supplied of labor, Q_S, is greater than the quantity demanded, Q_D—there is unemployment. Firms would hire more workers at $6.00 and fewer people would enter the labor market; at $6.00, the quantity supplied equals the quantity demanded, Q^*, and there is no unemployment.[13]

The Q_D people who are employed at the minimum wage of $7.25 benefit from the law at the expense of their employers who have to pay higher wages (unless the employees incur offsetting costs to obtain and keep their jobs). Rectangle C pictures the transfer of surplus from employers to employed workers. In contrast, the people between Q_D and Q^* are hurt by the law. These people are willing to work for as little as $6.00 per hour and would obtain jobs in a free market. However, they are unemployed due to the minimum wage law. Overall, there is a reduction in the total gains from trade in the labor market. The lost surpluses for firms and labor are

---

[13]In reality, measured unemployment would not be zero absent minimum wage regulation. There are always going to be individuals changing jobs or searching for better jobs. We abstract from these considerations in this example.

Figure 3.13   Economic Effects of Minimum Wage Laws

This figure displays the supply and demand for unskilled labor. The free market equilibrium is a $6.00 wage rate and Q* people being hired. The government has imposed a minimum wage of $7.25 that results in an excess supply of labor (unemployment). The Q_D people who are employed at the minimum wage of $7.25 benefit from the law (unless they incur offsetting costs to obtain and keep their jobs). Rectangle C represents the transfer of surplus from employers to employed workers. In contrast, the people between Q_D and Q* are hurt by the law. These people are willing to work for as little as $6.00 per hour and would obtain jobs in a free market. However, they are unemployed due to the minimum wage law. Overall there is a reduction in the total gains from trade in the labor market. The lost surpluses from reduced trade for firms and labor are pictured by Triangles A and B, respectively.

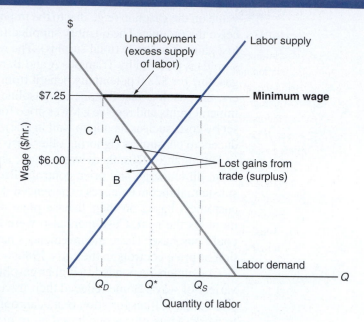

pictured by Triangles A and B, respectively. These triangles depict the lost surplus from not allowing companies and unemployed workers to enter into mutually beneficial employment relations below the minimum wage. In January 2014, the unemployment rate among teenagers in the United States was 22.6 percent compared to 6.8 percent for adults. One potential reason for the high unemployment rate among teenagers is the minimum wage.[14]

Minimum wage laws can also affect how people are paid. For example, suppose that prior to a new minimum wage law unskilled workers are paid $6.00 per hour plus health benefits. One likely effect of forcing employers to pay higher cash wages is a reduction in health benefits. Employees who prefer the health benefits to higher cash wages are worse off after the law.

---

[14]The U.S. government has tried to reduce the effects of the minimum wage law on teenagers by exempting them from the law for their first 90 days of employment. During this period, teenagers must be paid at least $4.25 per hour. Note that the amount of unemployment caused by the minimum wage laws depends on the slopes of the supply and demand curves (see Figure 3.13). Although most economists would agree with the direction of the effect, there is disagreement as to its magnitude. Many economists believe this effect is large, but some disagree. For example, D. Card and A. Krueger (1995), *Myth and Measurement: The New Economics of the Minimum Wage* (Princeton University Press: New Jersey).

CBO Estimates Effects of Proposed Increase in the Federal Minimum Wage

The Federal Minimum wage was $7.25 per hour in 2014. The President and various members of Congress supported proposed legislation that would have increased it to $10.10 per hour. They argued that $7.25 was not a "living wage" and that raising the minimum wage would lift many out of poverty. Opponents argued that by decreasing the number of jobs and thus increasing unemployment, such an increase would hurt many of the people who it was designed to help.

Economic theory argues that a binding minimum wage will decrease the number of jobs and increase unemployment. It also predicts that the people who find jobs at the higher rate will potentially be better off (it depends in part on how costly it was for them to find employment). The Congressional Budget Office (CBO) is a highly respected agency that conducts bipartisan economic analysis for Congress. In February 2014, the CBO issued a report projecting the impact of the proposed increase in the minimum wage. Consistent with economic theory, they predicted that the proposed hike would cause a loss of about $\frac{1}{2}$ million jobs. They further predicted that 16.5 million workers would experience wage increases. About 900,000 of them would be lifted out of poverty.

The higher wages paid to workers will have to be paid by someone—there is no "free lunch." As discussed in this chapter, the ultimate payers are not necessarily the companies that are required to pay higher wages. At least some of this cost increase is likely to be passed to consumers in the form of higher prices. Moreover, many employees currently hired at the minimum wage are entry-level workers with limited work experience and education. The increase in the quantity of labor supplied at the higher wage rate is likely to include suburban middle-class teenagers and others who have some more prior work experience. Given the limited number of jobs openings relative to people seeking work at the higher wage rate, the prospects of a minority, high-school dropout finding work could be even more bleak.

Source: E. Morath, D. Paletta, and C. Lee (2014), "Wage-Rise Report Sees Fewer Jobs, Less Poverty" *The Wall Street Journal* (February 20).

Externalities and the Coase Theorem[15]

Externalities exist when the actions of one party affect the well-being or production possibilities of another party outside an exchange relationship. Externalities can prevent a free market from being efficient. If a firm emits pollution into the air, it can adversely affect the welfare of the firm's neighbors. If the firm does not bear these

The Coase Theorem and the "Fable of the Bees"

A prominently discussed case of externalities is the so-called "Fable of the Bees." Beekeepers provide pollination services for the surrounding fruit growers, and the growers, in turn, provide nectar for the bees. Many economists would consider this to be a classic case of externalities. If beekeepers and growers do not receive compensation for the benefits they bestow on other parties, they will underinvest in their activities (from a social standpoint).

The Coase Theorem suggests that beekeepers and growers can privately negotiate to overcome this externality problem. This is exactly what is done. Beekeepers and growers often enter into contracts. Fruit growers hire beekeepers to supply hives of bees for pollination of those trees that give little suitable nectar, while the beekeepers pay growers for the privilege of "grazing" their bees on high nectar-producing trees. Given these payments, beekeepers and growers have incentives to consider the effects on the other party when they make their investment decisions. Through this process, beekeepers and growers can reach efficient levels of investment without help from the government.

Source: S. Cheung (1973), "The Fable of the Bees: An Economic Investigation," *Journal of Law and Economics* 16, 11–34.

[15]This section draws on R. Coase (1960), "The Problem of Social Cost," *Journal of Law and Economics* 3, 1–44.

costs, it is likely to select an inefficient level of pollution (i.e., to overpollute). In choosing how much to invest in pollution control equipment, the firm's managers will consider only its own costs and benefits. Efficient investment would require them also to consider costs and benefits imposed on neighbors (the efficient level of investment is where the total marginal costs of additional investment equal the total marginal benefits—not just those incurred privately by the firm).

Economists used to think that externalities surely would prevent a market system from producing an efficient allocation of resources. Government intervention seemed to be required to enhance efficiency. For example, the traditional recommendation was to tax firms based on their levels of pollution. Such a tax would give firms incentives to reduce pollution.

In 1960, Nobel Prize winner Ronald Coase presented a compelling argument that exchange in a free market is more powerful in producing efficient results than had been thought previously. As long as property rights can be traded, there is an incentive to rearrange these rights to enhance economic efficiency. The often-recommended government intervention might be unnecessary and in many cases undesirable. Suppose that a firm has the legal right to pollute as much as it wants. Its neighbors always can offer to pay the firm to reduce its pollution level. Thus, the firm faces a cost for polluting (if the firm pollutes, there is an opportunity cost of not receiving compensation from its neighbors). The firm will pollute only if the pollution is more valuable to the firm than the costs it imposes on its neighbors. This efficient solution is obtained without a pollution tax. The same level of pollution can occur even if the neighbors have the legal right to stop the firm from emitting any pollution as opposed to the firm's having the legal right to pollute as much as it wants. In this case, the firm can pay its neighbors for the right to pollute. Regardless of whether the firm or the neighbors have the legal right, the gains from trade are exhausted when the marginal benefit to the firm of polluting is equal to the sum of the marginal costs imposed on its neighbors plus those that the firm bears.

Coase's argument convinced most economists that externalities were less of a problem than previously thought. It also implied that the distribution of property (legal) rights might have less of an effect on the ultimate use of resources than it has on the distribution of income—as long as these rights can be exchanged. In our example, the firm might emit the same amount of pollution regardless of who initially is assigned the property right. However, the party with the property right obtains more wealth (since it is the one receiving or avoiding payments).

Nonetheless, as Coase points out, market exchange will not always solve the problem of externalities. The transactions that are necessary to overcome this problem are not free: There are *contracting costs*. These costs include search and information costs, bargaining and decision costs, and drafting, policing, and enforcement costs.[16] These costs can prevent a preferred outcome from occurring. In our example, the firm might limit its pollution for a payment that is far lower than the collective damage imposed on its neighbors. Nonetheless, the costs of bargaining with the firm and the costs of reaching agreement on how the neighbors should split the payment can prevent this mutually beneficial agreement from being reached. Generally, the costs of reaching an agreement increase with the number of bargainers. In our example,

> **The Coase Theorem**
> The ultimate resource allocation will be efficient, regardless of the initial assignment of property rights, as long as contracting costs are sufficiently low and the property rights are assigned clearly, are well enforced, and can be exchanged readily.

---

[16]C. Dahlman (1979), "The Problem of Externality," *The Journal of Law and Economics* 22, 148–162.

the likelihood of reaching an efficient agreement is highest if the firm only has to bargain with a single neighbor who owns all the surrounding property.

It also is important that property rights be clearly assigned, enforced, and exchangeable. Suppose there were no legal system to enforce property rights. Neighbors would be reluctant to pay a firm not to pollute—they do not obtain an enforceable property right to prevent the firm from polluting. After collecting the payment, the firm could renege on its promise to reduce pollution and the neighbors would have no recourse.

This discussion suggests that market economies will tend to produce an efficient resource allocation whenever property rights are clearly assigned and contracting costs of exchanging them are sufficiently low. When these conditions are met, efficiency will occur regardless of the initial distribution of property rights. This general principle is often referred to as the *Coase Theorem*.

The driving force behind the Coase Theorem is gains from trade: Individuals have incentives to search out and undertake mutually advantageous trades. This principle has important managerial implications. Even if a manager does not have all the property rights necessary to undertake a particular project, it does not mean that the project cannot be undertaken. If the proposed project creates enough value, the manager often can acquire the necessary property rights from their current owners. Suppose the Watts Construction Company can create substantial value by developing a shopping center on a site that currently is zoned for residential housing. Surrounding property owners might support a change in the zoning requirement, as long as they share in the value creation. Watts might be able to increase this support by offering to develop a new neighborhood park near the shopping mall.

MANAGERIAL APPLICATIONS

Property Rights Help Make Niger Greener

Niger in northern Africa historically has been known for being a barren, dust-choked country with many starving citizens. Most observers saw no hope in Niger's continued battle against desertification. The end result would be increased poverty and starvation.

Recent studies of vegetation patterns, however, show that Niger recently has added millions of new trees and is far greener than it was 30 years ago. Interestingly some of the vegetation is densest in some of the most densely populated regions of the country. This finding runs counter to the conventional claim that population growth leads to the loss of trees and accelerates land degradation.

One important factor for why Niger has become greener is a change in property rights. From colonial times, all trees in Niger were property of the state. State ownership gave farmers little incentive to grow and protect trees. Trees were cut down by residents for construction and chopped for firewood with little regard for the environmental costs. Government foresters were supposed to foster the growth of trees and to protect them from illegal destruction, but there were not enough foresters for an area nearly twice the size of Texas. Now the government allows individuals to own trees—there is private rather than public ownership. Farmers make money from their trees by selling branches, pods, fruits, and bark. Because these sales are more lucrative over time than cutting trees for firewood, the farmers preserve and protect them.

Niger remains in a fragile position since it is located in a drought-prone area. Recently acquired private property rights, however, have helped to foster the growth and protection of trees. According to experts, "more trees will help Niger's people to withstand whatever changes the climate might bring." Observers note that the improved situation in Niger was accomplished without having to spend a "lot of money."

Source: L. Polgreen (2007), "In Niger, Trees and Crops Turn Back the Desert," *nytimes.com* (February 11).

The Coase Theorem also suggests that contracting costs are central to the study of organizations. In the absence of contracting costs, efficient outcomes will occur independent of the way decision rights are assigned. From an efficiency standpoint, it does not matter whether decision rights are centralized or decentralized. It is contracting costs that make these organizational considerations important. We elaborate on this issue in the section that follows.

Markets versus Central Planning

History suggests that the price system is more efficient at controlling and coordinating production and consumption decisions in large economies than is central planning. Without the aid of government planners, market economies have produced products that are highly valued by consumers while avoiding large shortages or surpluses. In planned economies such as the former Soviet Union, shortages, surpluses, and other production mistakes are common.

There are at least two reasons why markets have been more successful than central planning in large economies. First, the price system motivates better use of knowledge and information in economic decisions. Second, it provides stronger incentives for individuals to make productive decisions. As we will discuss later, an understanding of these advantages can be useful for managers in making firm-level decisions, such as what decision-making authority to delegate to employees and whether to make or buy a firm's inputs.

General versus Specific Knowledge[17]

Figure 3.14 shows how the costs of transferring knowledge can be displayed on a continuum. At one end of this continuum is *general knowledge*. General knowledge is virtually free to transfer. Examples of general knowledge are prices and quantities—a storekeeper easily can tell you that the price of sugar is $1 per pound. As the costs of information transfer increase, the information is said to become more *specific*. We use the term *specific knowledge* to denote knowledge that is relatively high on this scale: It is expensive to transfer.

Figure 3.14   The Cost of Transferring Knowledge

The costs of transferring knowledge can be displayed on a continuum. At one end is *general knowledge*, which essentially is free to transfer. As the costs of information transfer increase, the information is said to become more *specific*. We use the term *specific knowledge* to denote knowledge that is relatively expensive to transfer.

---

[17]This section draws on M. Jensen and W. Meckling (1995), "Specific and General Knowledge, and Organizational Structure," *Journal of Applied Corporate Finance* 8:2, 4–18.

MANAGERIAL APPLICATIONS

Topic-Specific Search Engines

GlobalSpec.com is competing with Yahoo and Google—and winning. Its search engine for engineers has 3.5 million users and adds 20,000 more each week. "They own that market," says Charlene Li of Forrester. GlobalSpec has a well-defined customer base and detailed understanding of its users; this sets it apart from the generalist search engines. These features allow its "vertical site" to provide search results from a select group of topic-specific Web sites and precisely target advertising at particular audiences.

Source: (2007) "Specific Knowledge about Your Customer," *The Economist* (July 14), 75.

At least three factors influence the costs of transferring information. First are the characteristics of the sender and receiver. Generally, it is less expensive for people of similar training, language, and culture to communicate than for people from different backgrounds. Second is the technology available for communication. For example, the development of electronic mail (e-mail) has lowered the costs of transferring information. Third is the nature of the knowledge itself. Some knowledge is difficult to summarize, comprehend, or transfer in a timely fashion. Depending on the exact setting, the following types of knowledge often are specific in nature:

- **Idiosyncratic knowledge of particular circumstances.** The employee on the spot is most likely to know if a particular truck has room for additional cargo or if a certain customer wants to purchase a specific product. If this information is not used immediately, it may become useless. For example, by the time the information about the truck is transferred to another person (such as a central scheduler), the opportunity to load the truck with additional cargo can be lost (for instance, if the truck has departed).
- **Scientific knowledge.** Knowledge of how recombinant DNA works is not easily transferred to nonscientists.
- **Assembled knowledge.** An accountant who has completed a client's tax returns for several years is likely to have assembled important knowledge about the relevant parts of the tax code and the idiosyncrasies of the individual's

MANAGERIAL APPLICATIONS

The Dynamic Nature of Specific Knowledge

Historically, economies of scale have motivated firms in retailing to concentrate on standardized production and distribution. Knowledge about the idiosyncratic demands of people in particular neighborhoods tended to be ignored in stocking individual stores within a large retail chain: The information simply was too expensive to collect and process. This limited their ability to compete with small local stores that catered to the specific demands of local customers.

But the development of computers and electronic scanners has made information about idiosyncratic demands of individuals less specific. As a result, retail companies have begun to engage in more micromarketing. For instance, the Sears outlet in the North Hollywood section of Los Angeles is tailor-made to suit the neighborhood's Hispanic population. Signs are in Spanish. The store is stocked with ethnic items, such as a broad selection of compact discs and tapes by Latin American artists. A few hundred miles to the north, the Sears store in San Jose offers a large number of clothing items in extra-small sizes to attract the area's Asian population. On the other hand, Sears stores in Florida carry large, roomy clothes that appeal to the large population of elderly residents.

Source: (1995) "Customers on Target," *Financial Times* (August 18).

income and deductions. Another example is learning to operate a complex machine. In neither case is this information easily transferred to others.

Specific knowledge is critical in properly allocating resources. Many economic opportunities are short-lived and must be acted on quickly by the person on the spot (who has the specific information of the opportunity) or lost. Not incorporating the proper scientific or assembled knowledge into economic decisions can have costly implications. For an economic system to be successful, it must promote the use of relevant specific knowledge in economic decisions.

Knowledge Creation

It is important to realize that knowledge is dynamic. There are at least two factors that can motivate changes in the costs of transferring knowledge. The first is technology: Improved communications and computer technology have greatly lowered the costs of transferring certain types of information, making it more general. Second, individuals can take actions to convert specific knowledge to more general knowledge, for example, by drafting an operating manual.

Nonaka and Takeuchi argue that converting hunches, perceptions, mental models, beliefs, experiences, and other types of specific knowledge into a form that can be communicated and transmitted in formal and systematic language is a key aspect of successful new product innovation.[18] As one example, consider Matsushita's development of an automated fresh bread maker in the 1980s. Specific knowledge of how to knead dough to produce tasty bread was held by master bakers. This knowledge was not easily transferred to others, and past attempts to produce fully automated bread makers had failed because they produced poor-quality bread. Yet specific knowledge about how to manufacture automated bread machines was held by engineers. To produce a successful bread machine, relevant specific knowledge had to be transferred between bakers and engineers. To accomplish this transfer, managers from Matsushita took bread-making lessons from a master baker at an Osaka hotel. Eventually, the managers discovered that the key to good bread making is to twist and stretch the dough during the kneading process. This concept was general knowledge that could be passed along to design engineers. Matsushita's "Home Baker" was the first fully automatic bread-making machine for home use and has become a quite successful product.

In 1778, economist–clergyman Thomas Malthus predicted that population would grow more rapidly than the food supply resulting in mass starvation.[19] His argument was straightforward: Because land and other natural resources are finite, the growth in population (fueled by the "passion of the sexes") would eventually exceed the available food supply. But this prediction—which prompted economics to be labeled the "dismal science"—has not come to pass. For instance, population in the United States increased from 76 million in 1900 to 296 million in 2005 (an increase of nearly 300 percent), yet the amount of land and the number of workers devoted to

---

[18]I. Nonaka and H. Takeuchi (1995), *The Knowledge-Creating Company* (Oxford University Press: New York).

[19]T. Malthus (1778), "An Essay on the Principle of Population" (printed for J. Johnson, in St. Paul's Church Yard, London).

MANAGERIAL APPLICATIONS

Converting IT Wetware into Software

Charles Belford, president of the Canadian-based management consulting firm Managements Smarts, Inc., advises clients to get more value out of their existing information technology (IT) without buying new software or hardware. He argues that firms should revise their current delegation of authority, governance, and planning and management practices to identify low-cost, low-risk IT enhancements. Managers should be given incentives to ensure that successful pilot tests are properly identified and then disseminated throughout the organization. He encourages clients to reorganize so that a senior manager has enterprise-wide oversight to exploit IT packages to ensure their full potential for the company. For an example, Mr. Belford says, "By revising the current delegation of authority for managing Web site content in your company, you may be able to turn your obese Web site or your bulimic internal intranet network into healthy assets that actually serve their respective constituencies."

Mr. Belford maintains that the only way to convert IT wetware (successful local IT applications) into recipes or software and then leverage this newly created software throughout the firm is by changing the company's organizational architecture.

Source: C. Belford, "Add Value to Tech Assets without Breaking the Bank," *The Globe and Mail* (March 28, 2002), B16.

---

agricultural production over the same period fell dramatically. Today less than 3 percent of the U.S. population works in agriculture, while the per capita food supply is at an all-time high. And this increase in the food supply is not just a U.S. phenomenon. From 1951 to 1992, world food production per capita increased 34 percent.[20] So why was Malthus wrong?

Malthus, as well as more recent pessimists, has underestimated the importance of improvements in technology—figuring out better ways to use existing resources.[21] For example, today's computers are far more powerful than those of a decade ago, yet they take fewer resources to produce. Moreover, computer designers have discovered ways to make the materials used in computers more recyclable. This process of discovering better ways to use existing resources occurs not only in manufacturing but also in service-related industries as well. For example, consider the implications of McDonald's innovations in the 1950s in the delivery of "fast food."

Economist Paul Romer argues that the opportunities for this type of discovery and growth essentially are unlimited.[22] People are constantly taking ideas and knowledge that are in their "wetware" (brains) and converting them into "software" (recipes and formulas) that can be employed to produce new products and services. Matsushita's conversion of the specific knowledge held by the master baker into more general knowledge that could be used by engineers is a good example. As we will discuss in Chapter 8, good managers understand this mechanism for creating knowledge and value and foster it within their firms.

---

[20]J. Perloff (2001), *Microeconomics* (Addison Wesley: Boston), 154.

[21]For a more recent example of concern about the implications of finite resources, see D. Meadows New York (1977), *Limits to Growth: A Report for the Club of Rome's Project on the Predicament of Mankind* (New York American Library).

[22]For nontechnical discussions of Romer's theory of economic growth, see P. Romer (1993), "Economic Growth," *Fortune Encyclopedia of Economics* (Time Warner Books: New York); P. Romer (1995), "Beyond the Knowledge Worker," World Link, (January/February), 55–60.

Specific Knowledge and the Economic System[23]

Nobel Prize–winner Friedrich Hayek offered a compelling argument that market economies are more likely than centrally planned economies to incorporate relevant specific knowledge in economic decision making. He argued that the relevant specific knowledge for economic decision making is not given to any one individual; instead, it is distributed among many people in the economy. This knowledge, by definition, does not lend itself to statistical aggregation; it is costly to transfer. A central planner invariably lacks the mental or computing ability to process large volumes of this sort of information. Hayek thus concluded that central planners often ignore important specific knowledge in economic decisions.

In contrast, economic decisions in a market system are decentralized to individuals who are likely to have the relevant specific knowledge. Technical and marketing geniuses, like William Gates at Microsoft and Michael Dell at Dell Computer, are free to start new businesses and to market products of their choosing. The information that motivates these decisions does not have to be transferred to some central office in Washington where centralized production decisions are made. Thus, the information is more likely to be used effectively.

The activities of decentralized decision makers are coordinated by prices. For instance, an increase in market-determined wage rates (the price of labor) signals to producers that labor is in short supply and should be conserved. Higher wages, in turn, motivate producers to conserve labor. An important advantage of the price system that is stressed by Hayek is that prices economize on the costs of transferring information to coordinate decisions. Companies normally do not have to know all the details of why labor costs have increased. The simple fact that wages have increased tells them most of the things they need to know to make value-maximizing decisions.[24]

Incentives in Markets

Private property rights are critical for making a market economy work because they provide strong incentives for decentralized decision makers to act on their specific information—the wealth effects of economic decisions are borne directly by the resource owners. If Alice Chan owns a piece of property, she has incentives to use the land productively because she gets to keep any profits. If Jamal Hammoud can make more productive use of the land, Alice will sell the land to Jamal (there are gains from trade). Property rights are rearranged so that decision rights over resources are linked with the relevant specific knowledge.

In contrast, decision makers in centrally planned economies have limited incentives to make productive use of information (even if they have it) since they do not own the resources under their control. Further, lower-level bureaucrats have limited incentives to carry out decisions made by the central authority. The best use of a particular automobile might be to transport tourists from a local airport. A central planner, however, might give the car to his brother because he is more concerned about making his brother happy than about making the economy more productive. After all, he does not keep the profits from transporting tourists—they go to the state.

---

[23]This section draws on F. Hayek (1945), "The Use of Knowledge in Society," *American Economic Review* 35, 519–530.

[24]Producers also might want to know the expected future prices of labor. For instance, if the price increase is expected to be transitory, the company might want to avoid making layoffs.

ANALYZING MANAGERIAL DECISIONS: *Nobel Prize–Winner F. A. Hayek on the "Miracle" of the Price System*

It is worth contemplating for a moment a very simple and commonplace instance of the action of the price system to see what precisely it accomplishes. Assume that somewhere in the world a new opportunity for the use of some raw material, say, tin, has arisen, or that one of the sources of supply of tin has been eliminated. It does not matter for our purpose—and it is significant that it does not matter—which of these two causes has made tin more scarce. All that the users of tin need to know is that some of the tin they used to consume is now more profitably employed elsewhere and that, in consequence, they must economize tin. There is no need for the great majority of them even to know where the more urgent need has arisen, or in favor of what other needs they ought to husband the supply. If only some of them know directly of the new demand and switch resources over to it, and if the people who are aware of the new gap thus created in turn fill it from still other sources, the effect will rapidly spread throughout the entire economic system. This influences not only all the uses of tin but also those of its substitutes and the substitutes of these substitutes, the supply of all things made of

tin, and their substitutes, and so on. All this takes place without the great majority of those instrumental in bringing about these substitutions knowing anything at all about the original cause of these changes. The whole acts as one market, not because any of its members surveys the whole field, but because their limited individual fields of vision sufficiently overlap so that through many intermediaries the relevant information is communicated to all. The mere fact that there is one price for any commodity—or rather that local prices are connected in a manner determined by the cost of transport, etc.—brings about the solution which (if conceptually possible) might have been arrived at by one single mind possessing all the information which is in fact dispersed among all the people involved in the process.

Some people (e.g., Hayek) argue that decentralization of economic decisions in the economy leads to an efficient resource allocation. What differences exist within the firm that make the link between decentralization and efficiency less clear?

Source: F. Hayek (1945), "The Use of Knowledge in Society," *American Economic Review* 35, 519–530.

Contracting Costs and Existence of Firms

Hayek's argument suggests that markets are better than central planning. Why, then, is so much activity conducted within firms, where resource allocation decisions are made by managers in a manner that is closely akin to central planning?[25] Conceptually, firms do not have to exist. All production and exchange could be carried out through market transactions. In the case of the PC, each consumer could buy all the parts that make up the PC in separate market transactions and then pay someone to assemble them. In reality, of course, most computers are made by firms and only the final products are sold to the consumer.

Ronald Coase provides an answer to the question as to why resources are allocated by both markets and firms.[26] His basic argument is that economic transactions involve contracting costs, including search and information costs, bargaining and decision costs, and policing and enforcement costs. There is also an opportunity

---

[25]Within a firm, resources often are transferred from one division to another by an administrative order from management. For example, managers often are transferred among divisions by administrative decisions. Prices are not used to make these decisions—the divisions typically do not bid for the managers.

[26]R. Coase (1937), *Economica*, "The Nature of the Firm," New Series, IV, 386–405.

cost if the transaction results in an inefficient resource allocation (we discuss this in detail in Chapter 10). The optimal method of organizing a given economic transaction is the one that minimizes contracting costs.[27] In some cases, the method will be market exchange. In other cases, the method will involve firms.

Contracting Costs in Markets

A primary set of costs of using markets for exchange involves the discovery and negotiation of prices.[28] For example, firms have the following two potential advantages:

- **Fewer transactions.** If there are N customers and M factors of production, a firm can hire the M factors and sell to the N customers. The total transactions are $N + M$. In contrast, if each customer contracts separately with each factor of production, there are $N \times M$ transactions. For example, 10 workers might be required to assemble a computer. If there are 1,000 customers and each customer negotiates with each worker, there are a total of 10,000 transactions. If a firm hires the 10 workers and sells computers to the 1,000 customers, there are 1,010 transactions.

- **Informational specialization.** Think of buying a PC. How much do you know about buying each separate part? PC producers, on the other hand, specialize in this knowledge. The consumer buying from a firm only has to be concerned with the quality of the end product.

In Chapter 19, we shall elaborate on one particularly important set of contracting costs that motivates the existence of firms, those associated with *specific assets*. Assets are specific when they are worth more in their current use than in alternative uses. An extreme example is a machine that is used to produce parts that can be used only by one particular producer. The machine is valuable in producing parts for the particular buyer but is essentially worthless in alternative uses. In this case, independent suppliers are reluctant to purchase the machine since they do not want to be at the mercy of a single buyer. For instance, suppliers might worry that the buyer will try to force a reduction in future prices, make unreasonable quality or quantity demands, or curtail purchases. It is these concerns that make simple market transactions between buyers and sellers unlikely when the relevant assets are highly specific. A potential response to this problem is for the producer to own the machine and make the input parts within a single larger firm.

Another potential advantage of firms is that in some cases they can reduce contracting costs through established reputations. Individuals are likely to have confidence in trading with parties who are expected to continue to participate in the marketplace over a long time. They understand that these parties have incentives to be honorable in order to enhance their reputation and future business opportunities.

---

[27]It is not always possible to separate contracting costs from the basic costs of production. The optimal method of production can depend on the way the transaction is organized. Therefore, it is more precise to say that the optimal method of organization is the one that minimizes total costs (production and contracting costs). The basic arguments are easier to explain if we focus on contracting costs.

[28]Economists generally agree that contracting costs motivate the existence of firms. There is disagreement concerning which contracting costs are most important. Our intent in this chapter is to give the reader a general sampling of the kinds of costs that can be important.

Herbert Simon on Organizations and Markets

The United States often is referred to as a market economy. In reality, much of the economic activity in the United States, as well as in other market economies, is conducted within firms. To quote Herbert Simon, a former Nobel Prize winner,

> Suppose a visitor from Mars approaches the earth from space, equipped with a telescope that reveals social structures. The firms reveal themselves, say, as solid green areas with faint interior contours marking out divisions and departments. Market contracting costs show as red lines connecting firms, forming a network in the spaces between them. Within the firms the approaching visitor also sees pale blue lines, the lines of authority connecting bosses with various levels of workers. . . . No matter whether the visitor approached the United States or the Soviet Union, urban China or the European Community, the greater part of the space below would be within the green areas, for almost all the inhabitants would be employees, within firm boundaries. Organizations would be the dominant feature on the landscape. A message sent back home, describing the scene, would speak of "large green areas interconnected by red lines." It would not likely speak of a "network of red lines connecting green spots."

Source: H. Simon (1991), "Organizations and Markets," *Journal of Economic Perspectives* 5, 25–44.

Organizations tend to have longer lives than individuals and thus might be expected to be more likely to honor agreements than unknown individuals (some major corporations date back to the nineteenth century). This increased trust can motivate lower expenditures on negotiating and policing agreements.

Government regulation also helps explain the existence of some firms. Sometimes firms can produce more cheaply because they avoid taxes at intermediate stages of production compared to market transactions.

Contracting Costs within Firms

We have discussed several contracting costs that can motivate the existence of firms. Given these costs, why isn't the economy just one big firm? The answer is that resource allocation by firms also involves contracting costs. For example, as firms become larger, it becomes increasingly difficult for managers to make efficient and timely decisions. They are more likely to make errors and to be less responsive to changing circumstances. As a firm grows, important decisions must be delegated to employees who are not owners of the firm, thereby generating costs to motivate these nonowners to work in the interests of the owners.

Corporate Focus and Stock Returns

Ronald Coase argues that the use of markets involves contracting costs and that sometimes these costs can be reduced by including transactions within firms. However, firms also involve contracting costs. In the 1990s, many companies concluded that they had become too large and diversified. These companies, in turn, decided to refocus on their core businesses and to shed unrelated activities (e.g., through asset sales). Evidence suggests that on average, these firms increased their stock market values by increasing their focus on core activities.

Source: R. Comment and G. Jarrell (1995), "Corporate Focus and Stock Returns," *Journal of Financial Economics* 37, 67–87.

Efficient Organization

Individuals involved in trade and production have incentives to implement cost-reducing methods of organization because there are greater gains to be shared. For example, at a given price, more profits can be generated if costs are reduced.[29] In competitive markets, individuals will constantly search for new and better ways to reduce costs to improve their competitive advantage and profits. The bottom line is that firms will be used to organize economic activities whenever their cost is lower than that of using markets, and vice versa. Also, as we will see, this same process has important implications for the internal design of organizations.

Managerial Objectives

Our discussion to this point has treated decision makers within firms as owners. Owners have a strong interest in increasing the profits of the firm, since they get to keep the proceeds. In public corporations managers are rarely major owners of the firm. Nonetheless, in Chapters 4 to 9 the book, we assume that managers strive to maximize firm profits—or more precisely firm value, the present value of the firm's profit stream: They make input, output, and pricing decisions with value maximization as their sole objective.[30] This perspective is a reasonable starting point because if firms fail to make profits over time, they cease to exist. Most managers are under constant pressure to create value. There also are other mechanisms, such as incentive compensation, that can be structured to align the interests of managers and owners. These mechanisms help make profit maximization a reasonable first approximation of the managers' objective function. Profit maximization is the basic premise used in most economics textbooks. Starting in Chapter 10, however, we shall present a richer characterization of the firm and analyze management/owner conflicts in greater detail. The appendix to this chapter provides a more detailed discussion of managerial objectives, focusing on the topics of shareholder value and stock-market efficiency.

Managerial Decisions

We began this chapter with an overview of how market economies operate. An understanding of this topic is critical if managers are to make productive economic decisions. It is important to understand how a shift in either supply or demand affects

---

ACADEMIC APPLICATIONS

CEO Turnover and Firm Profits

A standard assumption in microeconomics is that managers strive to maximize profits. One reason that managers are likely to be concerned about profits is that poor profits and stock price performance increase the likelihood that they will be fired. For instance, research suggests that the worst performing firms are about 1.5 times as likely to have a management change as the best performers.

Source: For a review of this evidence, see J. Brickley (2003), "Empirical Research on CEO Turnover and Firm Performance: A Discussion," *Journal of Accounting and Economics* 36, 227–233.

---

[29]A firm's profit (II) is the difference between its total revenues (TR) and total costs (TC): II = TR − TC. If a company has sales of \$1 million and costs of \$750,000, it earns a profit of \$250,000.

[30]Much of our basic analysis focuses on maximizing profit in a single period. This approach yields useful managerial insights without overly complicating the analysis.

ACADEMIC APPLICATIONS

Firms versus Markets: When Markets Ruled

Economic theory argues that activities are organized within firms when the cost is lower than using markets, and vice versa. Today, much of the economic activity in the world is conducted within firms. It is hard to envision a world where large firms do not play an important role in the production and distribution of products. The importance of firms, however, is a relatively recent phenomenon. Prior to the middle of the nineteenth century, there were virtually no large firms. Most production was conducted by small, owner-managed operations. The activities of these operations were coordinated almost entirely through market transactions and prices. To quote Alfred Chandler in describing business organization before 1850,

> The traditional American business was a single-unit business enterprise. In such an enterprise an individual or a small number of owners operated a shop, factory, bank, or transportation line out of a single office. Normally this type of firm handled only a single economic function, dealt in a single product line, and operated in one geographic area. Before the rise of the modern firm, the activities of one of these small, personally owned and managed enterprises were coordinated and monitored by market and price mechanisms.

The large firm became feasible only with the development of improved energy sources, transportation, communications, and legal/court systems. Coal-fired steam power generators provided a source of energy that made it possible for the factory to replace artisans and small mill owners, and railroads enabled firms to ship production in large quantities to newly emerging urban centers. The telegraph allowed firms to coordinate activities of workers over larger geographic areas. These developments tended to make it less expensive to coordinate production and distribution using administrative controls, rather than to rely on numerous market transactions among all the intermediaries in the system.

Source: A. Chandler (1977), *The Visible Hand: The Managerial Revolution in American Business* (Harvard University Press: Cambridge, MA).

product prices. (In Chapters 4 to 9, we shall extend this analysis and examine in more detail how managers might make optimal input, output, and pricing decisions.)

We also discussed the role of knowledge and incentives in determining the effectiveness of alternative economic systems and the importance of contracting costs in determining whether or not economic transactions are conducted within

ANALYZING MANAGERIAL DECISIONS: *Labor Unions and a Proposed Tax on Luxury Goods*

You work as a stock analyst. You specialize in analyzing markets for "high-end" manufactured products. The President has recommended that Congress impose a tax of $20,000 on every person who purchases a new yacht. He argues that rich people who can afford to purchase yachts (they cost around $2,000,000 each) should pay higher taxes. The money raised would be used to provide additional benefits to returning war veterans.

You are writing a research report on the firms that manufacture yachts. You want to include a statement in the report about whether you think the proposal is likely to pass Congress and become law. You have analyzed the proposal and the voting records of members of Congress. You have decided that the proposal will not obtain enough votes to pass Congress, unless the major labor unions representing employees in this industry support it. You know that many of the yacht-producing firms hire veterans who could benefit from the programs funded by the tax.

a. Draw a standard supply and demand diagram depicting the market for yachts prior to the tax.

b. Analyze the effects of imposing a $25,000 per yacht tax on consumers (on a qualitative basis).

c. Based on this analysis, do you think that the labor unions will support the proposed tax? Explain. What does it depend upon?

markets or organizations. Although we have focused our discussion at the economic-system level, these issues are directly relevant to understanding firm-level decisions on organizational architecture. If firms are to be productive, they must be structured in ways that promote the use of the relevant specific knowledge and economize on the costs of organization. They also must establish appropriate incentives, so that their employees act in a productive manner. Starting in Chapter 10, we shall extend the concepts introduced in this chapter to questions of organizational architecture.

Summary

There are many different ways of organizing economic activities. Economists focus on *Pareto efficiency* in evaluating the effectiveness of alternative economic systems. An allocation is Pareto-efficient if there is no alternative that keeps all individuals at least as well off but makes at least one person better off. Pareto-improving changes in a resource allocation are viewed as welfare-increasing.

An important feature of a market economy is the use of *private property rights*. A property right is a legally enforced right to select the uses of an economic good. A property right is private when it is assigned to a specific person. Private property rights are *alienable* in that they can be transferred (sold or gifted) to other individuals.

In free markets, property rights frequently are exchanged. Trade occurs because it is mutually advantageous. The buyer values the good more than the seller, and there are *gains from trade*. Trade is an important form of value creation. Trading produces value that makes individuals better off. Gains from trade also motivate the movement of resources to more productive users. Total output and standards of living often increase when individuals specialize in production activities for which they have a *comparative advantage* (lower opportunity costs).

Prices coordinate the individual actions in a market economy. If too little of a good is being produced, inventories will shrink, prices will rise, and producers will have incentives to increase output to exploit the profit opportunity. If too much of a good is being produced, prices will fall, inventories will build, and producers will have incentives to cut production. The market is in *equilibrium* when the quantity supplied of a product equals the quantity demanded. There are strong pressures in competitive economies that move the market toward equilibrium. In equilibrium, there are no *shortages* or *surpluses* and inventories are stable at their desired levels. Equilibrium prices and quantities change with changes in the supply and demand for products.

Consumer surplus and *producer surplus* are measures of the gains from trade to consumers and producers from participating in a market. Government-imposed price caps or floors result in market imbalances and lost surplus (in an otherwise well-functioning market).

Externalities exist when the actions of one party affect the consumption or production possibilities of another party outside an exchange relationship. Externalities can cause markets to fail to produce an efficient resource allocation. Competitive markets will produce a Pareto-efficient allocation of resources if the costs of making mutually advantageous trades are sufficiently low. The *Coase Theorem* indicates that the ultimate resource allocation will be efficient, regardless of the initial assignment of property rights, as long as *contracting costs* are sufficiently low and property rights are clearly assigned, well enforced, and readily exchangeable.

General knowledge is inexpensive to transfer, whereas *specific knowledge* is expensive to transfer. Specific knowledge is quite important in economic decisions.

Central planning often fails because important specific knowledge is not incorporated in the planning process. Within market systems, economic decisions are decentralized to individuals with the relevant specific knowledge. Prices convey general knowledge that coordinates the decisions of individuals. Private property rights provide important incentives to individuals to act productively, since they bear the wealth effects of their decisions.

In principle, all economic activity could be conducted through market transactions. However, even in market economies, much economic activity occurs within firms, where administrative decisions rather than market prices are used to allocate resources. Firms exist because of the contracting costs of using markets. However, organizing transactions within firms also involves costs. Individuals have incentives to organize transactions in the most efficient manner—to increase the gains from trade. Economic activities tend to be organized within firms when the cost is lower than that of using markets, and vice versa.

This chapter provides important background information on both markets and organizations. In Chapters 4 to 9, we shall extend the analysis of markets and study important managerial decisions such as output, inputs, pricing, and strategy. In these next six chapters, we assume that managers strive to maximize firm profits. In the remainder of the book, we shall extend the analysis of organizations and cover a variety of important topics about organizational design. A reader interested primarily in organizational design can move directly to Chapter 10 without loss of continuity.

Suggested Readings	R. Coase (1988), *The Firm, the Market, and the Law* (The University of Chicago Press: Chicago). J. Earwell, M. Milgate, and P. Newman (1989a), *Allocation, Information, and Markets* (W.W. Norton: New York). ———— (1989b), *The Invisible Hand* (W.W. Norton: New York). F. Hayek (1945), "The Use of Knowledge in Society," *American Economic Review* 35, 519–530. M. Jensen and W. Meckling (1995), "Specific and General Knowledge, and Organizational Structure," *Journal of Applied Corporate Finance* 8:2, 4–18. O. Williamson (1985), *The Economic Institutions of Capitalism* (Free Press: New York).

Self-Evaluation Problems

3–1. Two men, Tom Hanks and Forest Gump, have been marooned separately on the same deserted island. There are two activities each man can undertake to obtain food: fishing and gathering coconuts. Tom can catch 40 fish per hour or gather 10 coconuts per hour. Forest can catch 10 fish per hour or gather 8 coconuts per hour. Answer the following questions:

a. Does Tom have a comparative advantage in producing both products? Explain.

b. Tom and Forest have not yet met. Tom is working 2 hours a day and producing (and consuming) 48 fish and 8 coconuts (*Note:* the fish are very small). Forest is also working 2 hours a day, but he is producing and consuming 15 fish and 4 coconuts. Now assume that Tom and Forest meet and develop a trading relationship. Come up with a production and trading scheme such that they can each work the same amount per day as before, but each is better off than before. Provide specific numbers to show how they are better off.

3–2. a. Suppose sugar has the demand curve $P = 50 - 5Q$ and the supply curve $P = 5Q$. Compute the equilibrium price and quantity and show graphically. Calculate the consumer surplus and producer surplus associated with this outcome.

b. What factors might cause the equilibrium price and quantity of sugar to change?

Solutions to Self-Evaluation Problems

3-1. a. No, while Tom has an absolute advantage in producing both products, he only has a comparative advantage in fishing. Forest has a comparative advantage in gathering coconuts. His marginal cost for gathering one coconut is 1.25 fish (10/8), while Tom has a marginal cost of 4 fish (40/10).

   b. One specific example is as follows: Say Tom produces only fish and Forest produces only coconuts. There will be a total of 80 fish and 16 coconuts. Now suppose they set a price of 2 fish per coconut and Tom buys 10 coconuts (for a price equal to 20 fish). Then Tom consumes 60 fish and 10 coconuts and Forest consumes 20 fish and 6 coconuts. They each consume more of both commodities, so they are each better off even though they are working the same amount as before. Many other examples could be constructed.

3-2. a. Set demand equal to supply: $50 - 5Q = 5Q$ and solve for the equilibrium quantity, $Q^* = 5$. Place Q^* into either the supply or demand equation and solve for the equilibrium price, $P^* = \$25$. Graphically, the picture is

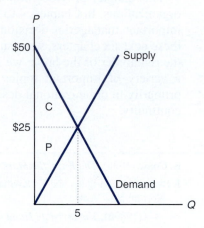

Triangle C pictures the consumer surplus. The area of a triangle is $.5(\text{Base} \times \text{Height})$. Therefore the consumer surplus is $.5(5 \times 25) = \$62.5$. The producer surplus pictured by Triangle P is also $\$62.5$.

   b. Changes in the equilibrium price and quantity are induced by shifts in either the supply or demand curves. Factors that affect demand include such things as consumer income and the prices of other goods. For example, if an increase in consumer income caused the demand curve for sugar to shift to the right (an increase in demand) both the equilibrium price and quantity would increase. Factors that affect supply of sugar include such things as the prices of inputs used in the production process (e.g., land, labor, and fuel prices). If an increase in the price of labor caused the supply curve to shift to the left (a decrease in supply), the equilibrium price of sugar would increase and the equilibrium quantity would decrease.

Review Questions

3-1. What is Pareto efficiency? Why do economists use this criterion for comparing alternative economic systems?

3-2. What is a property right? What role do property rights play in a market economy?

3-3. Twin brothers, Tom and Bill, constantly fight over toys. For instance, Tom will argue it is his turn to play with a toy, while Bill argues it is his turn. Their parents frequently have to intervene in these disputes. Their mom has conceived an idea that might reduce these conflicts. In particular, every toy in the house would be "owned" by one of the boys. The owner would have complete authority over the use of the toy. The mom reasons that ownership would cut down on disputes. Any time there is an argument over a toy, the owner gets the final and immediate say. The boys' dad is concerned that this idea will prevent the boys from learning to "share." He envisions that under the new system, Tom will not allow Bill to play with his toys and Bill will not allow Tom to play with his toys. The old system forces them to figure out a way to share the toys. Do you think that their dad's concerns are valid? Explain.

3–4. Many economists favor free trade between nations. They argue that free trade will increase total world output and make people of trading nations better off. Discuss how this argument relates to concepts presented in the chapter.

3–5. What do you think will happen to the price and quantity of DVD players if
   a. The availability of good movies to play on DVD players increases?
   b. Personal income increases?
   c. The price of inputs used to produce DVD players decreases?
   d. Ticket prices at local movie theaters decline substantially?

3–6. Suppose that the U.S. government caps the price of milk at $1 per gallon. Prior to the cap milk sold for $1 per gallon. Picture the effects of the price cap using a supply and demand graph. Explain how the cap affects consumers and producers.

3–7. **a.** What is an externality?
   b. Why might externalities lead a firm to discharge too much pollution into a river?
   c. Congress has passed a law that limits the level of cotton dust within textile factories. Why might a textile firm allow too much cotton dust within its workplace?

3–8. What is the difference between general and specific knowledge? How can specific knowledge motivate the use of decentralized decision making?

3–9. Evaluate the following statement:

   Using free markets and the price system always results in a more efficient resource allocation than central planning. Just look at what happened in Eastern Europe.

3–10. **a.** What are contracting costs?
   b. Give a few examples of contracting costs.
   c. What effect does the existence of contracting costs have on market economies?

3–11. If markets are so wonderful, why do firms exist?

3–12. In certain professional sports, team owners "own" the players. Owners can sell or trade players to another team. However, players are not free to negotiate with other team owners on their own behalf. The team owners initially obtain the rights to players through an annual draft that is used to allocate new players among the teams in the league. They also can obtain the rights to players by purchasing them from another team. Players do not like this process and often argue that they should be free to negotiate with all teams in the sporting league. In this case, they would be free to play for the team that offers the most desirable contract. Owners argue that this change in rights would have a negative effect on the distribution of talent across teams. In particular, they argue that all the good players would end up on rich, media-center teams such as New York or Los Angeles (because these teams could afford to pay higher salaries). The inequity of players across teams would make the sport less interesting to fans and thus destroy the league. Do you think the owners' argument is correct? Explain.

3–13. The guide at the Washington Monument tells your 10-year-old nephew, "Enjoy the monument. As a citizen, you are one of its owners." Your nephew asks you if that is true. What do you say?

3–14. Locust Hill Golf Club is a private country club. It charges an initiation fee of $23,000. When members quit the club, they receive no refund on their initiation fees. They simply lose their membership. Salt Lake Country Club is also a private golf course. At this club, members join by buying a membership certificate from a member who is leaving the club. The price of the membership is determined by supply and demand. Suppose that both clubs are considering installing a watering system. In each case, the watering system is expected to enhance the quality of the golf course significantly. To finance these systems, members would pay a special assessment of $2,000 per year for the next three years. The proposals will be voted on by the memberships. Do you think that the membership is more likely to vote in favor of the proposal at Locust Hill or for the one at Salt Lake Country Club? Explain.

3–15. Critically evaluate the advice of the Providence Consulting Group, which recommended to your company,

> *That you analyze all the business divisions in your company. Rank them on growth potential. Sell all the low-growth units and invest the money in the high-growth units. Make sure not to sell the high-growth units.*

3–16. Suppose that the U.S. government begins charging a $1 sales tax to all consumers for each dress shirt they buy.
   a. What is likely to happen to the price (not including the tax) and quantity demanded of dress shirts? Show using supply and demand graphs.
   b. What is likely to happen to the demand for sport shirts (not taxed) and undershirts (which are worn primarily with dress shirts)? Explain.

3–17. Title-loan firms offer high-interest loans (the interest rate can exceed 200 percent per year) to high-risk customers. The title of a car often is used as collateral. If the borrower defaults on the loan, the company can repossess the car. Recently, the financial press has reported stories of poor people who have had their cars repossessed by title lending companies. Legislation is being proposed in some states to make this lending practice illegal. A proponent of the law made the following argument. "The market for loans is very competitive given all of the banks, savings and loans, and finance companies. Outlawing title lending will make poor people better off. It will motivate the lending companies to provide loans with less onerous terms. Thus, low income people and people with bad credit histories will be able to obtain credit on more favorable terms." Do you agree with this argument? Explain.

3–18. Suppose that annual demand in the U.S. market for ice cream cones can be expressed as $Q_D = 800 + 0.2I - 100P$, where Q_D is the number of cones demanded in millions of cones, I equals average monthly income in dollars, and P is price in dollars per cone. Supply can be expressed as $Q_S = 200 + 150P$ (with the same units for quantity and price).
   a. Graph the demand and supply curves for ice cream cones, assuming that average monthly income is $2,000, and solve for the equilibrium price and quantity.
   b. Now assume that average monthly income drops to $750 and supply is unchanged. Draw the new demand curve on the same graph as used in (*a*) above and solve for the new equilibrium price and quantity. How would you describe the shift in demand *intuitively*?

3–19. The rent control agency of Rochester has found that aggregate demand is $P = 500 - 5Q_D$. Quantity, Q_D, is measured in thousands of apartments. Price, P, equals the monthly rental rate in dollars. The city's board of realtors acknowledges that this is a good demand estimate and has shown that supply can be expressed as $P = 5Q_S$.
   a. If the agency and the board are right about demand and supply, respectively, what is the free-market price? How many apartments are rented?
   b. If we assume an average of three persons per apartment, what is the expected change in city population if the agency sets a maximum average monthly rent of $100 and all those who cannot find an apartment leave the city?

3–20. Assume that before the ice storm of 2003, the weekly demand and supply for ice in the Rochester Metro Area was given by the following equations:

$$D_{pre}: P = 100 - Q$$
$$S_{pre}: S = 5 + 0.5Q$$

   a. Draw a graph representing the Rochester ice market before the storm and label it carefully. What was the equilibrium price for the Rochester ice market before the storm? And the total quantity of ice traded?
   b. As a result of the ice storm, electricity went out in the Rochester area. The demand for ice increased due to the lack of electricity to power refrigerators. The lack of power also

caused the supply to decrease. Ice producers were still able to produce some ice using electric generators. Other ice had to be imported from other areas with power. The relevant post-storm equations are the following:

$$D_{post}: P = 110 - Q$$
$$S_{post}: P = 10 + 2Q$$

Draw a graph representing the Rochester ice market after the storm and label it carefully. What is the new equilibrium price? What is the quantity?

c. An open-ad in a local newspaper, commenting on the dramatic increase in price of ice following the storm, stated:

> *Obviously, avarice and greed won out over decency and morality as ice-vendors took advantage of the ice storm to increase prices and gouge their loyal customers.*

Do you agree with this statement? Explain.

3–21. Suppose the supply and demand for wheat is given by:

$$\text{Supply: } Q_s = 1,800 + 240P$$
$$\text{Demand: } Q_d = 2,550 + 10I - 266P$$

Where P = the price per bushel of wheat and I = income. The current value of I is 100.

a. Find the current equilibrium price and quantity of wheat sold in the marketplace.

b. Find the equilibrium price and quantity if income increases to 150.

c. Show the change in equilibrium using a standard supply and demand graph. Make sure to label the axes and the curves. The graph does not need to be to scale. Just illustrate in a general way what is going on.

3–22. Assume that the demand curve for sporting guns is described by $Q^D = 100 - 2p$ and the supply is described by $Q^S = -20 + p$ (Q^D and Q^S are in millions, p is in $).

a. Compute the competitive equilibrium price and quantity. Draw a graph of a supply and demand curve and label it correctly. Compute the total value created in the market for sporting guns (*Hint:* total value = consumer surplus + producer surplus).

b. Suppose that the government views sporting guns as a luxury product and taxes the consumers $6 for each sporting gun they buy. Solve the new competitive equilibrium. What losses do consumers of sporting guns incur as a result of the tax? What losses, if any, do the producers of sporting guns incur?

3–23. Suppose there has been a storm in Nebraska that has destroyed part of the corn crop in the field. The demand curve for corn has not changed. As a result, the market clearing prices and quantities before and after the storm are: $P_b = 50$, $Q_b = 2,000$; $P_a = 100$, $Q_a = 1,500$. (The subscripts a and b refer to "after the storm" and "before the storm.")

a. Assume a linear demand curve for corn; that is $P = \alpha + \beta Q$. Calculate α, β with the provided information, and draw the demand curve with P on the y-axis and Q on the x-axis. Label the intercept and the slope on the graph.

b. The supply curve for the period after the storm is $P = (1/15)Q$, and it is parallel to the supply curve before the storm. Is the supply curve before the storm above or below that after the storm? Calculate the slope and the intercept of the supply curve before the storm. Draw both supply curves on a new graph with P on the y-axis and Q on the x-axis. Add the demand curve (calculated in part a) to the graph.

c. Suppose consumers care only about corn consumption and apple consumption (they live in a two-good world). How would the change in the price of corn affect the budget constraint of the typical consumer? Show graphically. How would the change in relative prices affect the typical consumer's consumption of corn versus apples? Is this result consistent with your observation from the demand and supply framework (i.e., an increase in the price of corn is associated with a decrease in the equilibrium quantity)? Explain.

3-24. Suppose that the demand function for wheat is $Q_D = 1.1 - .25P + .1I$, where P = the price of wheat and I = per capita income. The supply function for wheat is $Q_S = 4.3 + .5P - .04P_o$, where P_o = the price of oil. Currently, $I = 20$ and $P_o = 50$.

    a. Plot the supply curve and demand curve on the standard supply and demand graph.

    b. Find the equilibrium price and quantity and depict it on your graph.

    c. Calculate the resulting consumer surplus and producer surplus.

    d. What would happen to the equilibrium price and quantity if income were to increase (holding other factors constant)? Give a brief economic explanation for why this would occur.

    e. What would happen to the equilibrium price and quantity if the price of oil were to increase (holding other factors constant)? Give a brief economic explanation for why this would occur.

    f. What would happen to the equilibrium price and quantity if income and the price of oil were both to increase at the same time? Give a brief economic explanation for why this would occur.

3-25. Input cost increases have caused the industry supply curve for golf balls to shift. The equilibrium quantity changed, but the price did not. Can you say anything about the elasticity of either the demand or supply curves from observing these effects? Will consumer expenditures on golf balls increase or decrease? Explain.

3-26. Suppose the demand function for a product is $P = 100 - (1/6)Q + 2I$, where I is income and the supply function is $P = (1/3)Q$. Currently $I = 25$.

    a. Find the current equilibrium price and quantity.

    b. Suppose the government imposes a $5 per unit excise tax on the product (charged to the supplier). Find the new equilibrium price and quantity.

    c. Draw a graph that shows the equilibriums before and after the tax. Show the areas of the graph that represent the tax borne by consumers and the tax borne by suppliers (together they add up to the total tax collected). Also depict the deadweight loss imposed by the tax.

    d. Explain in words what the deadweight loss represents.

    e. What happens if the $5 per unit tax is imposed on consumers rather than suppliers?

3-27. In 1990, Congress adopted a new tax on luxury goods, such as yachts, private airplanes, and jewelry. Assume this was charged as a per unit tax to the consumer. Was this a good way to accomplish the objective of taxing rich people? Explain.

3-28. Your firm operates in a competitive industry. All firms in the industry have experienced an increase in the cost of raw materials. Do you think that the firms in your industry will be able to pass the cost increase on to consumers through higher prices? Explain.

3-29. Suppose that the Swiss government wants to encourage good grooming by Thun citizens. To "encourage" better grooming it places a 15 CHF price cap on haircuts (no company can charge more than 15 CHF for a haircut). The government official who sponsored the new regulation argued (1) more people will want to get haircuts at a lower price and (2) thus more people will get haircuts. Do you agree with the economic reasoning of this official? Explain.

3-30. Suppose that the demand curve for wheat is $P = 100 - Q$ and the supply curve is $P = Q$. Find the equilibrium price and quantity. Calculate consumer and producer surplus. Suppose that the government imposes a price cap of 30. Show the effect graphically and calculate the resulting consumer surplus, producer surplus and deadweight loss.

**Appendix:
Shareholder
Value and
Market
Efficiency**

In the United States, top managers (officers and directors) have a fiduciary duty to act in the interests of the corporation and its shareholders. Consistent with this legal obligation, executives constantly profess to the media, stock analysts, and other constituencies a fundamental allegiance to increasing shareholder value, as reflected by the price of the common stock. Some critics, however, contend that managers ignore their legal duty and make decisions that benefit themselves at the expense of shareholders. We have little doubt that abstract legal principles, like fiduciary duty, are insufficient to induce corporate leaders to maximize shareholder value. However, theory and evidence suggests that there are a variety of internal and external control mechanisms that provide additional incentives to managers to be concerned about shareholder value. We examine these mechanisms beginning in Chapter 10.

Analyzing managerial decisions based on the assumption of shareholder wealth maximization has two benefits. First, it suggests what managers should do to meet their fiduciary responsibilities. Second, it describes what good managers actually do when they have sufficient incentives to focus on shareholder value.

Finance courses analyze investment and financing decisions where it is crucial to consider intertemporal tradeoffs among cash flows. For example, should a manager invest $1,000,000 to build a plant today that has the potential to yield $100,000 per year profit in the future? In contrast, managerial economics largely focuses on operational decisions where intertemporal tradeoffs in cash flows are relatively less important. For example, what current price should the manager charge to maximize profits? These decisions can be analyzed under the simplifying assumption that managers seek to maximize single-period profits. Little is gained from the added complexity of assuming that managers seek to maximize shareholder wealth, which involves the valuation of multiperiod cash flows.[31]

In Chapters 4 to 7, we present an economic analysis of demand, production, cost, market structure, and pricing. Here we follow the standard approach in managerial economics and assume that managers strive to maximize single-period profits. In subsequent chapters, where intertemporal considerations are more important, we assume that mangers seek to maximize shareholder wealth.

The main text does not require a detailed understanding of stock market valuation. It is sufficient simply to understand that share price incorporates the effects of managerial actions on both current and future profits—appropriately adjusted for the timing and risk of the cash flows. In this appendix we go beyond what is necessary for the main text by providing a more detailed analysis of shareholder value. We begin by introducing the concept of present value and deriving an expression for the current value of a share of common stock. We then discuss the concept of stock market efficiency and its resulting managerial implications.

Present Value

Is it better to receive a dollar today or a dollar a year from now? The obvious answer is that it is better to receive the dollar today, since it can be invested to yield more than a dollar in the future. Suppose that you invest a dollar in a risk-free asset (such as a U.S. Treasury security) with a 5 percent interest rate. At the end of one year, your investment will be worth $1.05. The investment, which promises $1.05 for certain in one year, and a dollar today have equivalent value since the dollar can be invested to produce the same future cash flow.[32] The *future value* of a dollar invested in the risk-free asset for one year is $1 \times (1.05) = \$1.05$. Conversely, the *present value* of $1.05 received for certain in one year is $\$1.05/1.05 = \$1$.

---

[31]In stationary settings where the same action is optimal in each period, the two objective functions are equivalent.

[32]This equivalence of the risk-free investment and the dollar today holds even if the investor wants to consume a dollar today as long the investment can be sold in the marketplace for its present value.

The concept of present value extends to multiple periods. One dollar invested at 5 percent for n periods is worth $\$(1.05)^n$ at the end of the nth period. The present value of this future value is $\$(1.05)^n/(1.05)^n = \$1.00$. More generally the present value of W dollars received for certain at the end of n periods is $W/(1 + r)^n$, where r is the risk-free interest rate. For example, suppose that a risk-free investment promises a cash flow of \$1.50 in five years and the annual interest rate is 5 percent. The present value of the investment is $\$1.50/(1.05)^5 = \$1.175$ (investing \$1.175 for five years at 5 percent yields a terminal value of \$1.50, assuming any intermediate cash flows are reinvested).

Investments often generate multiple cash flows over time. For example, a 10-year U.S. Treasury bond pays a fixed rate of interest every 6 months until the security matures at which time a final principal payment is made along with the final interest payment (20 total payments). The present value of a stream of cash flows is equal to the sum of the present values of the cash flows for each period. The general formula for the present value of a risk-free investment is

$$\text{Present Value} = \Sigma CF_t/(1 + r)^t \tag{3.6}$$

where CF_t is the cash flow that occurs in period t ($t = 1$ to n, the terminal period). For example, the present value of a 3-year bond that pays \$100 at the end of each year and a principal payment of \$1,000 at maturity is: $100/(1.05) + 100/(1.05)^2 + 1,100/(1.05)^3 = \$1,136.16$ (assuming a 5 percent risk-free rate).

The concept of present value is extremely useful when comparing alternative investments with different time-series patterns of cash flows. Present value allows an "apples-to-apples" comparison of the alternatives since all are expressed in a common dimension—their present values. The best investment is the one with the highest net present value—the difference between the present value of its benefits and costs.

Share Value

Our analysis of present value has focused on risk-free investments, where promised future cash flows were known with certainty and correspondingly *discounted* by the risk-free rate to obtain present values. Common stocks, however, are risky investments—the ultimate payouts to shareholders are not certain, but depend on the fortunes of the firm. While a firm might be expected to pay a given stream of dividends over time, investors might receive higher or lower payments depending on the fortunes of the firm.

The values of stocks and other risky investments are determined by discounting *expected cash flows* by *risk-adjusted discount rates*. The discount rate used for valuing an investment increases with the risk of the expected cash flows. (Finance courses teach that the relevant risk from the perspective of a shareholder who holds this firm's stock in a well-diversified portfolio is its systematic risk, that which cannot be eliminated through holding a diversified portfolio of investments.)

The intuition of stock valuation can be illustrated using a simple example. Suppose that a stock has the potential to pay a liquidating dividend to shareholders of either \$50 or \$150 at the end of the year. Each outcome has a probability of .5, and thus the expected cash flow is $(.5 \times \$50) + (.5 \times \$150) = \$100$. If we discount the \$100 expected cash flow at the risk-free rate of 5 percent we obtain $\$100/(1.05) = \$95.24$. Purchasing the stock at a price of \$95.24 by definition yields an expected return of 5 percent $((100 - 95.24)/95.24)$. Risk averse investors, however, will not purchase the stock at this price since they can earn the same return for certain by investing the \$95.24 in a risk-free asset. For the stock to appeal to a risk-averse investor, it must sell for a lower price and thus offering a higher expected return.

Suppose investors would purchase this stock if it yielded an expected rate of return of 10 percent. The resulting price of $90.91 is found by discounting the expected cash flow of $100 by the risk-adjusted discount rate of 10 percent ($100/1.10 = $90.91).

More generally, companies are expected to last more than one period and may pay dividends in multiple periods. The value of a stock is equal to the sum of the present values of each of the expected future dividends. Expressed in equation form, the current value of a share of stock, P_0, is

$$P_0 = D_1/(1 + k) + D_2/(1 + k)^2 \cdots + D_\infty/(1 + k)^\infty \qquad (3.7)$$

where D_t is the expected dividend paid to the investor at each time t, and k is the risk-adjusted discount rate (expected return).[33] Cash flows that are expected to occur further into the future have less impact on the valuation due to this discounting process. Thus, analysts generally exert most of their effort predicting cash flows over the first 5 to 10 years of the investment. Simplifying assumptions typically are used for estimating the present value of the remaining cash flows.

In special cases, Equation (3.7) reduces to simple expressions. One prominent example is the *constant growth model*. This model assumes that investors expect the firm's dividends will grow each period at a constant rate $g < k$, and that the firm will last forever. It is easy to show that Equation (3.7) reduces in this case to

$$P = D_1/(k - g) \qquad (3.8)$$

Suppose that investors expect that the HG Corporation will pay a $5 dividend at the end of the year and that the dividend will grow at 5 percent annually forever. The price of the stock at the beginning of the year, assuming a risk-adjusted discount rate of .10 percent, is $P_0 = \$5/(.10 - .05) = \$100$.

Equation (3.8) illustrates that the value of the stock is not determined by the current dividend alone. Growth firms often pay few dividends in their early years so that internally generated cash can be reinvested in the business. Nonetheless, they can sell at high prices if the market anticipates that they will make large payouts after their growth slows. Consider Microsoft Corporation as its growth rate slowed in 2004. In July 2004, Microsoft announced that it would double its annual dividend to shareholders by $3.5 billion per year, pay a one-time special dividend of $32 billion, and repurchase $30 billion of company stock over the following four years. The special dividend payment was the largest in S&P 500 history and quickly turned Microsoft from a small dividend payer to the tenth highest on the S&P 500 Index.

Stock Market Efficiency

Investments with identical cash flows and risk sell for the same price in a well-functioning stock market.[34] Since rational investors always will purchase the lower-priced of two identical securities, identical securities must sell for the same price for the market to clear (quantity supplied equal to quantity demanded for each security). In equilibrium the expected returns on identical securities are equal.

[33]Most investors receive part of their returns in the form of capital losses or gains when they sell the stock. This observation does not invalidate Equation (3.7) since the price of the stock at the time of the sale reflects the discounted value of the remaining expected cash flows. Also, the equation holds even when some shareholders receive payouts in the form of share repurchases.

[34]Other characteristics such as liquidity and tax implications can be valued by the market. For simplicity we concentrate on risk. The same principle holds in the more general case; investments with identical characteristics that are valued by the market should sell at the same price.

ANALYZING MANAGERIAL DECISIONS: *Shareholder Value and Market Efficiency*

1. Suppose that you purchase a newly issued 10-year U.S. Treasury bond for $10,000. The bond has a promised interest rate of 5 percent ($250 every six months). The stated interest rate of 5 percent (annual payment of $500 divided by the initial face value of $10,000) does not change over the life of the bond. Do you expect that the market value of the bond will be constant or variable over the life of the bond? Explain.
2. Calculate the present value of an investment with the following expected cash flows at a discount rate of 10 percent: year 1 = $500, year 2 = $600, and year 3 = $650. Recalculate the present value at discount rates of 15 percent and 5 percent.
3. Is the discount rate used by investors to value a given stock necessarily constant over time? Explain.
4. Find an event reported in today's business press that is likely to have an important effect on the cash flows for a given firm. Use Yahoo's finance Web site to produce a chart of the company's stock price around the time or day of the announcement of the event (http://www.finance.yahoo.com). Explain why the market reacted the way it did.

A stock market is *efficient* if it responds quickly and rationally to new information (i.e., share prices fully reflect available information; each stock is priced to yield a competitive return given its risk; stocks are not systematically under- or overvalued). In an efficient capital market, the market values of securities reflect the present values of the expected future net cash flows to shareholders, including expected cash flows from future investments. If an event occurs that changes expected cash flows or risk of a firm, the share price will adjust quickly to reflect the new information. As a result, investors should expect to receive competitive returns from purchasing stocks at current prices (i.e., the market-determined expected return for securities with similar characteristics). Depending on the fortunes of the firm, investors may end up earning more or less than the expected return. However, they should not expect to "beat the market" on a systematic basis.

The efficient markets hypothesis is perhaps the most extensively tested hypothesis in all the social sciences. The evidence is consistent with the view that stock markets are at least reasonably efficient with respect to public information. Major stock markets react quickly to new information, and investors generally can expect that they will not earn abnormal returns from trading stocks based on publicly available information.

The research on efficient markets has important implications for corporate managers. First, there is no ambiguity about the firm's objective function—managers should maximize the current market value of the firm. Hence, management does not have to choose between maximizing the firm's current value or its future value, and there is no reason for management to have a time horizon that is too short. Second, management decisions that increase reported earnings, but do not affect current or future cash flows, represent wasted effort. Third, if new securities are issued at market prices, which reflect an unbiased assessment of future payoffs, then concern about dilution or the sharing of positive net present value projects with new security holders is eliminated. Fourth, security returns are meaningful measures of firm performance. This allows scholars, management, and analysts to use security returns to estimate the effects of various corporate policies and events on the market value of the corporation.

For example, soon after Hurricane Katrina wreaked havoc on the Gulf Coast in summer 2005, the stocks of property insurance companies fell dramatically, while the stocks of companies such as Home Depot (which sells lumber and other building supplies) increased. According to the efficient markets hypothesis these reactions reflect the stock market's unbiased estimate of the valuation effects of the storm. The evidence that security returns are a meaningful measure of firm performance also provides support for using equity-based compensation to provide incentives to top management.

chapter

4

Demand

LEARNING OBJECTIVES

1. Define and mathematically express a demand function.
2. Explain the Law of Demand and the connection between declining marginal value and downward sloping demand curves.
3. Explain price elasticity and its relation to total revenue.
4. Define marginal revenue and discuss its relation to the demand curve, total revenue, and price elasticity.
5. Interpret and explain income and cross elasticities.
6. Identify differences between industry and firm demand.
7. Discuss network effects.
8. Derive and graph demand curve, marginal revenue, total revenue, and price elasticity when given a linear demand function.

The Players Theater Company is a regional repertory theater in the Midwest. Each year, it produces six plays, ranging from Shakespeare to contemporary musicals. PTC has priced its tickets at $30. On a typical night, approximately 200 of the theater's 500 seats are filled. The PTC board met recently to discuss a possible price decrease to $25 for next season. Advocates of the proposal argued that the decrease in ticket prices would increase the theater's customer base, the number of tickets sold, and revenues for the company.

At the meeting, the PTC board engaged in a heated debate over the proposal. It soon became evident that the board had insufficient information to make a sound decision. For instance, nearby restaurants, which serve PTC customers, have indicated that they are planning to implement substantial price increases before the beginning of the next season. Would this increase affect the demand faced by PTC and thus the appropriate ticket price? Although customers might buy more tickets at lower prices, would total revenue or profits necessarily increase? Would it be better to attract additional customers by lowering price or by improving the quality of PTC plays? After a lively discussion, the proposed decrease in price was tabled for further study.

This discussion at the PTC board meeting highlights the fact that managers require a detailed understanding of product demand to make sound pricing decisions. Understanding product demand also is important for decisions on advertising, production levels, new product development, and capital investment projects.

Chapter 3 offered an introduction to supply and demand analysis. In that chapter, we introduced the notion of a demand curve and discussed some of the factors that can cause a demand curve to shift. In this analysis, we focused on the aggregate demand curve for all the firms in the industry. In this chapter we provide a more extensive analysis of demand at the firm level. Important topics include demand functions, demand curves, factors affecting demand, industry versus firm-level demand, network effects, demand for product attributes, product life cycles, and demand estimation. In the technical appendix to this chapter, we derive point elasticities, analyze marginal revenue for a linear demand curve, and examine a special (log-linear) demand function. Most of the analysis in this chapter (e.g., the relation between price and revenue changes) applies to both industry-level and firm-level demand curves. We focus on firm level demand because of its particular importance to managers.[1]

Demand Functions

Managers require a fundamental knowledge of the factors that affect the demand for their product. Only by understanding these factors can they make sound decisions on pricing, output, capital expenditures, and other strategic issues. In fact, poor pricing decisions can destroy firm value and damage executive careers. Kraft Foods demoted the head of its North American business unit, Betsy Holden, after she raised prices and Kraft lost market share. Over this period Kraft's stock price fell 20 percent while other food companies' stock prices rose 9 percent.[2]

A *demand function* is a mathematical representation of the relation between the quantity demanded of a product and all factors that influence this demand. In its most general form, a demand function can be written as

$$Q = f(X_1, X_2, \ldots X_n) \tag{4.1}$$

where the X_is are those factors that affect the demand for this product.

The quantity demanded Q is the dependent variable in the demand function, since its value depends on the variables on the right-hand side of the equation. The X_is are the independent variables. In this chapter, we focus on three particularly important independent variables: the price of the product, the prices of related products, and the incomes of potential customers. This analysis can be extended to include other variables, such as advertising expenditures, tastes and preferences, and consumer expectations (e.g., about future prices).

For concreteness, we continue to focus on PTC as an example. We assume that PTC faces a demand function for tickets on any given night that can be expressed by the following function:[3]

$$Q = 117 - 6.6P + 1.66P_s - 3.3P_r + 0.0066I \tag{4.2}$$

---

[1]The supply and demand analysis in Chapter 3 implicitly assumes that the market is "perfectly competitive." As explained later in this book, firm-level demand curves are horizontal in perfectly competitive industries. The firm-level demand curves in this chapter are downward sloping, which implies that the firm has at least some "market power." Most firms have at least a small degree of market power, for example, due to locational or other advantages in serving a subset of customers.

[2]S. Ellison and V. O'Connell (2003), "Kraft Removes Holden as Co-Chief," *The Wall Street Journal* (December 17), A3 and A8; E. Herman (2005), "Former Co-CEO Holden Leaves Kraft," *Chicago Sun-Times* (June 25).

[3]Note that this function assumes that PTC can sell fractional tickets. This assumption does not have a material effect on our analysis. However, it allows us to draw continuous demand curves. One way to think of quantity in this example is as the *average* number of tickets sold for a performance. In this case, fractional tickets are possible. Note also that we assume that demand is constant for each performance by PTC. PTC performances are all scheduled for Friday and Saturday nights. If they expand their schedule to include weeknights or matinees, it is likely that demand conditions for these performances will differ and hence so should prices. These issues are discussed in Chapter 7.

Figure 4.1   Demand Curves

The left panel shows the demand curve for the Players Theater Company tickets. By convention, price is placed on the vertical axis, while quantity is placed on the horizontal axis. The equation for PTC's demand curve is: $P = 60 - 0.15Q$. The curve indicates that, for example, 200 tickets are purchased at $30 and 133 tickets are purchased at $40. The right panel indicates that the demand curve shifts to the right as income increases from $50,000 to $51,000—at each price, consumers buy more tickets. Movements along a demand curve are motivated by changes in price and are called *changes in the quantity demanded.* Movements of the entire demand curve are motivated by other factors, such as changes in income, and are referred to as *changes in demand.*

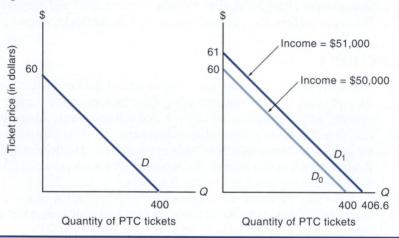

where P is the price of PTC tickets, P_s is the ticket price at a nearby symphony hall, P_r is the average meal price at nearby restaurants, and I is the average household income of area residents.

As our starting point, we assume PTC tickets are currently priced at $30; symphony tickets and meals are priced at $50 and $40, respectively; income is $50,000. Given these values, the demand function implies that PTC sells 200 tickets per night. We now examine each of the independent variables in this demand function in more detail.

Demand Curves

The price of the product is particularly important in demand analysis for two reasons: First, prices are among the most important variables that customers consider in making purchasing decisions. Second, managers choose the price of their products; variables such as the prices of other products and income levels largely are beyond their control. Given its special importance, economic analysis traditionally singles out the effects of price from other independent variables in the demand function.

A *demand curve* for a product displays for a particular period of time how many units will be purchased at each possible price, holding all other factors fixed.[4] The left panel of Figure 4.1 depicts the demand curve for PTC tickets. By convention,

---

[4]Technical note: We derive an individual's demand curve from the indifference curve/budget line analysis in the appendix to Chapter 2. The price of one good—say, food—is varied, holding the price of other goods and income fixed. The person's optimal choices are recorded. The individual's demand curve simply plots the optimal choices of the good (in this case, food) against the associated prices. The firm-level demand curve, in turn, is the sum of the demands of all individuals at each price.

MANAGERIAL APPLICATIONS

Learning the Law of Demand the Hard Way

Trillions of dollars of products are now sold online. It is not uncommon for companies to make mistakes in posting online prices. For example, in 2012 United Airlines posted a price of $43 for first-class airline tickets from New York to Hong Kong—the normal price is around $11,000. In 2013, Walmart accidently posted an $8.85 price for computer monitors, digital projectors, and other products that normally sell for hundreds of dollars. Consistent with the law of demand these types of errors typically motivate a rapid and large increase in the number of orders placed by customers. Online pricing errors are particularly problematic, since potential customers throughout the country or around the globe view the posted prices. Placing a wrong price tag on an item in a store is typically much less consequential. In extreme cases, such as the United Airline and Walmart errors, companies often tell customers the price was a mistake and cancel the orders. However, this action understandably upsets potential customers, who might be less likely to purchase from the company in the future. Also the legality of canceling orders can be unclear. Companies frequently honor small pricing errors to avoid upsetting customers.

Source: S. Kim (2013), "Why Walmart Canceled Mispriced Item Orders," *ABC News* (November 7); and T. Hume (2012) "Too Good to be True: New York to Hong Kong for $43," *CNN Travel* (July 23).

price is placed on the vertical axis, while quantity is placed on the horizontal axis.[5] The equation for PTC's demand curve is

$$P = 60 - 0.15Q \qquad (4.3)$$

This expression is obtained by substituting the current values of the other variables into Equation (4.2) and solving for P. The equation indicates that, for example, 200 tickets are purchased at $30 and 133 tickets are purchased at $40.[6]

Demand curves hold other factors fixed. Changes in income or the prices of symphony tickets or restaurant meals will cause shifts in the position of the demand curve (the intercept changes). For instance, the right panel of Figure 4.1 indicates that the demand curve shifts to the right as income increases from $50,000 to $51,000—at each price, patrons purchase 6.6 more tickets. Movements along a demand curve reflect changes in price and conventionally are called *changes in the quantity demanded*. Movements of the entire demand curve are caused by other factors (such as this change in income) and are referred to as *changes in demand*.

Law of Demand

Demand curves generally slope downward—individuals purchase less (or certainly no more) of a product as the price increases. PTC's demand curve has a slope of -0.15. Although it is conceptually possible that individuals might purchase more of a product as the price rises, as a practical consideration, managers are quite safe in assuming that the quantity demanded for their products varies inversely with price.[7] It would be foolish for PTC board members to think that they would sell more tickets if they raised the price. The negative slope of demand curves has become known as the *law of demand*.

[5] In subsequent chapters, we consider costs which are a function of quantity produced. Placing P on the vertical axis allows us to display both demand (revenue) and costs on the same graph in a convenient fashion.

[6] Rounded to the nearest dollar.

[7] Goods for which the income effect swamps the substitution effect so that consumers purchase more at higher prices are called *Giffin Goods*. We ignore this possibility throughout the rest of this book.

ANALYZING MANAGERIAL DECISIONS: *Setting Tuition and Financial Aid*

The Board of Ursinus College in Pennsylvania raised its tuition and fees 17.6 percent to $23,460 in 2000. It subsequently received 200 more applications than the year before. The president of the college surmised that "applicants had apparently concluded that if the college cost more, it must be better." Other colleges that raised tuition to match rival colleges in recent years include University of Notre Dame, Bryn Mawr College, Rice University, and the University of Richmond. They also experienced an increase in applications. In contrast, North Carolina Wesleyan College lowered their tuition and fees about 10 years ago by 22 percent and attracted fewer students. The college president concluded that "it didn't work out the way it had been hoped. People don't want cheap."

You are hired as a consultant to a President of a liberal arts college in the East. You are asked to evaluate a recommendation by the college's Admissions Director, Susan Hansen, to increase tuition and to reduce financial aid to students. Susan argues that the data from competing colleges suggest that the demand curves for colleges slope upward—the quantity demanded increases with price. Susan projects that the increase in tuition and reduction in financial aid will solve the school's financial problems. Last year, the college enrolled 400 new students who each paid an effective tuition of $15,000 (after financial aid), totaling $6,000,000. She projects that with the increased demand from charging an effective tuition of $25,000, the college will be able to enroll 600 new students (of equal or better quality), totaling $15,000,000. Evaluate Susan's analysis and recommendation.

Source: J. D. Glater and A. Finder (2006), "In Twist on Tuition Game, Popularity Rises with Price," *nytimes.com* (December 12).

Elasticity of Demand

Demand curves vary in their sensitivity of quantity demanded to price. In some cases, a small change in price leads to a big change in quantity demanded, whereas in other cases a big price change leads to only a small change in quantity demanded. Information on this sensitivity is critically important for managerial decision making. For instance, the board would not want to lower ticket prices to $25 if it could fill the theater by reducing prices only to $28.

One measure of the responsiveness of quantity demanded to price is simply the slope of the demand curve. But this measure is of limited usefulness, in part because it depends on the particular dimensions in which quantities are quoted. For instance, if the slope of a demand curve is -2 when the quantity is expressed in tons, it is only -0.001 when the quantity is stated in pounds. Using the magnitude of the slope coefficient to derive insights into the sensitivity of quantity demanded to price requires additional computation. Economists more frequently use a dimensionless measure of this sensitivity known as the *price elasticity of demand, η.* (Frequently, this elasticity is simply referred to as the *elasticity of demand.*)

Demand elasticity measures the *percentage change in quantity demanded given a percentage change in its price.* The law of demand indicates that price elasticities are negative; convention, however, dictates that we state this elasticity as a positive number. Higher price elasticities mean greater price sensitivity. The elasticity of demand, η, thus is given by

$$\eta = -(\% \text{ change in } Q)/(\% \text{ change in } P) \tag{4.4}$$

MANAGERIAL APPLICATIONS

Walmart Supercenters and Demand Elasticities for Grocery Products

Price elasticities usually increase with available substitutes. Over the last 25 years, the price elasticity for grocery products has increased substantially in many markets where Walmart built supercenters—a substitute for traditional supermarkets and other grocery stores. Unlike traditional supermarkets, supercenters offer a wide range of products at substantially discounted prices (e.g., groceries, clothing, home furnishings and electronic equipment). Supercenters are very large relative to most grocery stores, averaging about 179,000 square feet in 2014. Walmart began establishing supercenters in the South and Southwest regions of the United States in the late 1980s. It is now the largest grocery market chain in the country with supercenters in 48 of the 50 states. Researchers have found that the prices for groceries at supercenters are more than 25 percent lower than at traditional supermarkets prior a Walmart entry. As a result, Walmart entry into a market motivates competing stores to lower their prices. Walmart supercenters benefit some consumers directly by selling groceries to them at much lower prices than they paid historically. Consumers, who continue to shop at traditional supermarkets, benefit indirectly from lower prices at these stores. Not surprisingly, traditional supermarkets oppose Walmart supercenters. Labor unions also oppose them because the increased competition makes it difficult for traditional grocery stores to continue to pay the historic level of wages to organized labor. Zoning restrictions and other regulations, which are endorsed by traditional supermarkets and labor, have blocked Walmart entry in some markets. Consumers in these markets continue to pay relatively high prices for their grocery products.

Source: J.Hausman and E. Leibtag (2007), "Consumer Benefits from Increased Competition in Shopping Outlets: Measuring the Effect of Walmart," *Journal of Applied Econometrics* and *Form 10-K Walmart Stores, Inc.*, for fiscal year ended January 31, 2014.

Calculating Price Elasticities

This elasticity can be approximated between any two points using the concept of *arc elasticity*.[8] The formula for an arc elasticity is

$$\eta = -[\Delta Q /(Q_1 + Q_2)/2] \div [\Delta P/(P_1 + P_2)/2] \qquad (4.5)$$

where Δ represents the change between the two points.[9] Figure 4.2 displays two points on PTC's demand curve for theater tickets. As shown in the figure, the arc elasticity between these two points is 1.4. Hence, over this region, for every 1 percent increase in price, patrons reduce the quantity of tickets purchased by approximately 1.4 percent.

Price elasticities lie between zero and infinity. If the price elasticity is zero, quantity demanded is unaffected by price. In this case, as depicted in the left panel of Figure 4.3, the demand curve is vertical. If the price elasticity is infinite, a small increase in price will lead customers to purchase none of the product. In this case, as displayed in the right panel of Figure 4.3, the demand curve is a horizontal line. For instance, a small farmer might not be able to sell any soybeans if they were priced above the prevailing market price. Demand is elastic if the price elasticity is greater than one, unitary if equal to one, and inelastic if less than one.

Elasticity varies along most demand curves. For instance, with a linear demand curve, elasticity will be high when quantities are low and approach zero as the

---

[8]Price elasticity can be measured at a point on the demand curve. The concept of *point elasticity* requires elementary knowledge of calculus and, more importantly, a smooth mathematical demand curve. While our example assumes such a curve, data on demand often is available for only a few price-quantity combinations. We show how to calculate point elasticities in the appendix to this chapter.

[9]Equation (4.4) can be expressed as $\eta = -\Delta Q /Q \div \Delta P/P$. When calculating the elasticity between two points, the question arises as to which Q and P to use in this expression, the starting or ending values. Equation (4.5) uses the average of these two values—the initial plus the ending values divided by 2.

Figure 4.2 Arc Elasticity

This figure displays two points on PTC's demand curve for theater tickets. As displayed in the figure, the arc elasticity between these two points is 1.4. Thus, over this range, for every 1 percent increase in price there is approximately a 1.4 percent reduction in the quantity of tickets purchased.

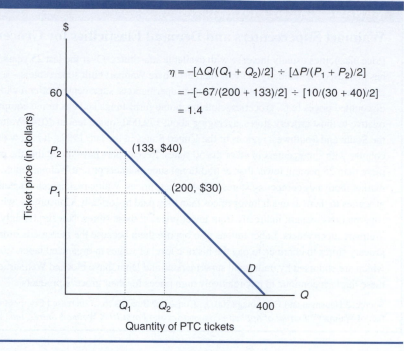

$$\eta = -[\Delta Q/(Q_1 + Q_2)/2] \div [\Delta P/(P_1 + P_2)/2]$$
$$= -[-67/(200 + 133)/2] \div [10/(30 + 40)/2]$$
$$= 1.4$$

quantities become large. (Try calculating some arc elasticities along PTC's demand curve.) We discuss this topic in greater detail later. (In the appendix to this chapter, we present a special demand curve that has constant elasticity—it does not vary along the curve.)

Figure 4.3 Range of Price Elasticities

Price elasticities lie between zero and infinity. If the price elasticity is zero, quantity demanded is unaffected by price. In this case, as depicted in the left panel of the figure, the demand curve is vertical. If the price elasticity is infinite, as in the right panel, a small increase in price will cause people to purchase none of the product, and the demand curve is a horizontal line.

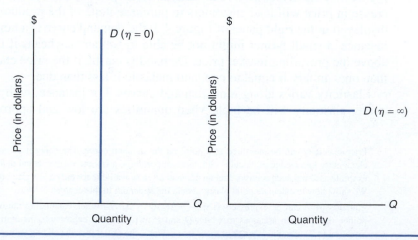

Figure 4.4 Price Elasticities, Price Changes, and Total Revenue

How total expenditures on a product change with price depends directly on the price elasticity. This figure displays the relation between small price changes, total revenue, and price elasticities.

Inelastic demand ($\eta < 1$)
 $\uparrow P \Rightarrow \uparrow$ Total revenue
 $\downarrow P \Rightarrow \downarrow$ Total revenue

Unitary elasticity ($\eta = 1$)
 $\Delta P \Rightarrow$ No change in total revenue

Elastic demand ($\eta > 1$)
 $\uparrow P \Rightarrow \downarrow$ Total revenue
 $\downarrow P \Rightarrow \uparrow$ Total revenue

Price Changes and Total Revenue

One of the board's concerns is how total revenue changes if it lowers ticket prices. We now demonstrate that the relation between revenue and price depends on the demand elasticity. Total revenue is calculated by multiplying the quantity purchased times the price (i.e., $P \times Q$). If price elasticity is *inelastic* (less than one), then the quantity demanded is less responsive to a change in price; a 1 percent increase in price results in less than a 1 percent decrease in quantity. Thus total revenue increases. Conversely, a price decrease results in a decrease in revenue. In contrast, if demand elasticity is *unitary* (equal to one), a 1 percent change in price results in an offsetting 1 percent change in quantity and hence total revenue is unchanged. Finally, if demand is *elastic* (value greater than one), a small increase in price results in a decline in revenue, whereas a small decrease in price results in an increase in revenue. These relations are summarized in Figure 4.4. We discuss these relations in greater detail below.

Determinants of Price Elasticities

The elasticity of demand tends to be high when there are good substitutes for the product. For instance, if a flight is overbooked airlines have little trouble finding

MANAGERIAL APPLICATIONS

Price Elasticities

Economists have estimated the price elasticities of various products, such as

Sugar	= 0.31
Potatoes	= 0.31
Tires	= 1.20
Electricity	= 1.20
Haddock	= 2.20
Movies	= 3.70

These estimates indicate that sugar and potatoes have relatively low-price elasticities. This might be expected given that these products represent a small portion of most people's budgets. Also, sugar has few close substitutes. Haddock and movies have high elasticities. Haddock is a narrowly defined product (as opposed to fish) and has many close substitutes. Movies are a luxury item for many people; higher prices cause individuals to consume other forms of entertainment.
Source: E. Mansfield and G. Yohe (2004), *Microeconomics* (W.W. Norton: New York), 135.

MANAGERIAL APPLICATIONS

Demand Elasticities and Airline Pricing

Round-trip airfares are substantially lower if the traveler stays over a Saturday night. Airline companies offer this discount to increase revenues (and profits). The typical traveler who stays over a Saturday night is a tourist. Tourists have relatively high price elasticities for air travel. Lowering the price from the standard fare correspondingly increases revenue: The price decrease is more than offset by the increase in tickets sold. Airline companies do not offer comparable discounts to travelers who complete the round-trip midweek. These customers are primarily business travelers who have relatively inelastic demands. Lowering price would decrease revenue because the decrease in price would not be offset by an increase in tickets sold. Airline companies also offer fewer discounts during peak periods, such as the period around the Thanksgiving holiday. During these periods, demand is relatively inelastic and they can fill the planes without offering substantial discounts.

volunteers to surrender their seats when alternate flights are available that involve no material delay in arrival. Conversely, if the overbooked flight is the last of the day, to elicit volunteers might require several free tickets.

The elasticity of demand for PTC tickets is likely to increase with the number of competing events in the city. With many entertainment options, a small increase in the price of PTC tickets might be sufficient to induce a substantial number of potential consumers to attend other events. When alternatives are more limited, additional customers will decide to pay the higher price for PTC tickets rather than just stay at home.

Demand elasticities also can depend on the importance of the goods within consumers' budgets. Goods such as salt and pepper, which consume a relatively small proportion of a person's income, tend to be relatively price-insensitive, or inelastic. On the other hand, goods such as major appliances and automobiles represent more substantial purchases. Customers are more likely to comparison-shop to collect product information and thus are more likely to be price-sensitive.

A third determinant of price elasticity is the length of the period to which the demand curve pertains. Demand tends to be more elastic or responsive to price changes over a longer period than within a shorter period. An increase in PTC ticket prices is likely to result in an immediate decline in tickets sold. Long-run effects will be even larger as consumers identify other entertainment options or fail to renew season tickets (these effects will cause the demand curve to shift to the left). Similarly, a large increase in the price of oil will result in a near-term decline in the quantity of oil demanded—people will set their thermostats to a lower temperature and drive less. Over time, the effect will be larger as consumers insulate their homes better, buy smaller, more fuel-efficient cars, and shift to alternative energy sources.

Other factors that can affect price elasticities include the degree of brand loyalty and whether consumers view the product as a "necessity" or "luxury good." Branded products with high customer loyalty and products that are viewed as necessities will generally be less price elastic than unbranded products and luxury goods. Consumers vary in what they consider to be necessities versus luxuries. Many people consider sail boats to be a luxury good, but for people who race them for a living, they are more likely to be viewed as a necessity. Differences in the demands for products across potential customers will be explored in more detail in a later chapter.

Linear Demand Curves

The PTC board's decision on whether or not to lower prices depends on the relation between price and total revenue and thus its demand elasticity: It would make little sense for the board to lower prices if a price reduction would lower total revenue. We now provide a more in-depth analysis of the relation between price and revenue and discuss the PTC board's optimal pricing policy. Through this analysis, we illustrate the properties of linear demand curves. Knowing these properties is useful for understanding the subsequent analysis in this book.[10]

Total Revenue

PTC's total revenue (TR) for any given performance is equal to the quantity of tickets sold times the price. Price is given by the demand curve in Equation (4.3). Thus, total revenue can be expressed as

$$\begin{aligned} \text{TR} &= P \times Q \\ &= (60 - 0.15Q)Q \\ &= 60Q - 0.15Q^2 \end{aligned} \qquad (4.6)$$

Figure 4.5 displays PTC's demand and total revenue curves. Total revenue increases as price decreases up to the midpoint of the demand curve. Over this range, demand is elastic: The percentage decline in price is smaller than the percentage increase in quantity demanded. The elasticity is unitary at the midpoint. Past the midpoint, price declines result in reduced total revenue; thus, demand is inelastic over this range. These are general properties of linear demand curves.

Marginal Revenue

An important concept in economics is *marginal revenue,* which is defined as the *change in total revenue given a one-unit change in quantity.* Intuitively, marginal revenue for the first unit is just its price. Thus, the intercepts of the demand and marginal revenue curves are the same. As quantity increases, marginal revenue is below price—to sell an extra unit, the price charged for all units must decrease. Marginal revenue is positive up to the midpoint of the demand curve (total revenue is increasing over this interval). At the midpoint, demand elasticity is unitary and marginal revenue is zero. Beyond the midpoint, marginal revenue is negative—the increase in revenue from selling another unit is less than the decline in revenue from lowering price (see the appendix). Hence, marginal revenue (MR) for a linear demand curve is a line with the same intercept as the demand curve but with twice the negative slope (see Figure 4.5). The equation for PTC's marginal revenue is

$$\text{MR} = 60 - 0.3Q \qquad (4.7)$$

Profit Maximization

All of PTC's costs are fixed and do not depend on the quantity of tickets sold on a given evening—actors and utilities have to be paid regardless of how many people attend the performance. Thus, the PTC board's objective is to maximize total revenue (for PTC, with costs fixed, maximizing total revenue is equivalent to

---

[10]Technical note: This result also can be applied to nonlinear demand curves. At a specific point, construct the tangent to the demand curve. Now, if the tangency point is at the midpoint of the tangent, the elasticity is unitary, and so forth.

Figure 4.5   Demand, Total Revenue, and Marginal Revenue for Linear Demand Curves

This figure displays PTC's demand and total revenue curves in the upper and lower panels. Total revenue increases as price decreases up to the midpoint of the demand curve. Thus, over this range, demand is elastic: The percentage decline in price is smaller than the percentage increase in quantity demanded. The elasticity is unitary at the midpoint. Past the midpoint, price declines result in reduced total revenue; and thus, demand is inelastic over this range. An important concept in economics is *marginal revenue,* which is defined as the *change in total revenue given a unitary change in quantity.* In the appendix, we show that marginal revenue (MR) for a linear demand curve is a line with the same intercept as the demand curve but with twice the negative slope. The marginal revenue curve for PTC is pictured in the figure.

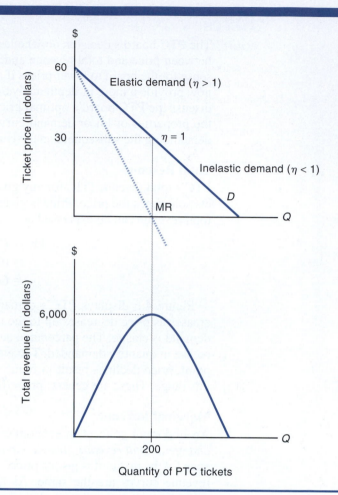

ANALYZING MANAGERIAL DECISIONS: *Demand Curve for an Electronics Product*

You work for a company in India that manufactures and exports batteries and other charge storage devices. You are the sales manager for a DC-DC converter that is used to step up or step down the voltage in various industrial applications. You currently price the product at 4,000 Indian Rupees (INR) and sell 100,000 units. You estimate that if you priced the product at 3,000 INR you would sell 150,000 units.

You think it is reasonable to assume that your demand curve is linear.

1. Derive the equation for your demand curve from the two price and sales points.
2. Are you currently operating in the elastic or inelastic portion of your demand curve?
3. You are paid a sales commission based on your total sales. What price would you charge to maximize your bonus?
4. Is this price likely to be optimal from your firm's standpoint, which has profit maximization as a goal?

Complementarity between Computer Hardware and Software

Over the past 25 years there has been a dramatic decrease in the price of personal computers. Not only has the price of PCs decreased, but their quality and computing power have improved substantially as well. This decrease in the price of personal computers has increased the quantity of PCs demanded enormously. In addition, it also has increased the demand for software products. Today, some of the largest companies in the world (e.g., the Microsoft Corporation) specialize in writing of software for PCs. Computer hardware and software are complements and thus have negative cross elasticities.

maximizing total profit). Figure 4.5 indicates that revenues are maximized at a price of $30. Hence under current conditions, the PTC board should not lower the ticket price to $25. Currently, the company is collecting $30 × 200 = $6,000 in revenue per night. If the price is decreased to $25, total revenue would be $25 × 233 = $5,825 per night.[11] (The upcoming increase in restaurant prices will change the optimal pricing policy. A practice problem at the end of this chapter explores this policy change.)

Note that, in contrast to this example, most firms do not want to maximize total revenue. PTC, with only fixed costs, is a special case. In most firms, both costs and revenues vary with output. A profit-maximizing firm must consider both effects. We discuss these considerations in greater detail in Chapters 5 through 7.

Other Factors That Influence Demand

In addition to a product's own price, the prices of related products and incomes of potential customers are among the more important factors that influence product demand.

Prices of Related Products

Complements versus Substitutes

The demand for a product can be affected by the prices of related products. For instance, if the local symphony raises its ticket prices, arts patrons will be less likely to attend the symphony and more likely to attend the PTC. Thus, there is a positive relation in Equation (4.3) between the demand for PTC tickets and the price of symphony tickets. Goods that compete with each other in this manner are referred to as *substitutes*. In contrast, if local restaurants raise their prices, the demand for PTC tickets falls (note the negative sign in the demand function). For instance, some potential PTC customers will choose to stay home because the total cost of an evening on the town has increased. Products like theater tickets and meals at restaurants, which tend to be consumed together, are *complements*. Another example of complements is digital video disk players and DVD movies. Between 1997 and 1999, the price of DVD players fell from $600 to $299. Sales of DVD players rose from under 50,000 to 600,000 over these two years. And as consumers experience the better sound quality and video, they also are buying bigger TVs and better sound systems. Big-screen TVs were up 12 percent and audio sales 11 percent. "The

---

[11]From the demand curve: $25 = 60 - 0.15Q$. Therefore, $Q = 233$.

MANAGERIAL APPLICATIONS

Derived Demand

Some products are demanded, not because individuals receive pleasure from consuming them, but rather because they are useful in the consumption of other products. Demands for these products are derived from the demands from other products. Take motor oil, for example. Few people derive satisfaction from purchasing oil for their automobiles. Rather, it is a derived demand from consuming transportation services provided by their cars. Procter & Gamble (P&G) discovered that spraying a bit of their Clean Shower bathroom cleaning product on a razor each day can extend the razor's life three or four times. They are formulating a product targeted to this use. Thus, this new product's demand is derived from the demand for razor blades.

biggest market driver is DVD," said Terry Shimek, owner of Shimek's Audio Video in Anchorage, Alaska. Moreover, the demand for DVD movies increased as well. Initially caught flat-footed, Hollywood started making more movies available on DVD. The number jumped from 1,800 in 1988 to 5,000 in 1999. (That is compared to 18,000 on VHS tape.)[12]

Cross Elasticities

One frequently used measure of substitution between two products is the *cross elasticity of demand.* Cross elasticity is defined as the *percentage change in the quantity demanded of a good, given a percentage change in the price of some other good.* Cross elasticities between any two goods, *X* and *Y*, can be calculated using a formula that is analogous to Equation (4.5):

$$\eta_{xy} = [\Delta Q_x/(Q_{x1} + Q_{x2})/2] \div [\Delta P_y/(P_{y1} + P_{y2})/2] \qquad (4.8)$$

Unlike price elasticities, which are invariably positive (at least when you multiply them by −1), cross elasticities can be either positive or negative—substitutes have positive cross elasticities whereas complements have negative cross elasticities. Whether a commodity has strong substitutes or complements depends, in part, on how finely the commodity is defined. Pepsi and Coke might have relatively large cross elasticities. The cross elasticities between colas, more broadly defined, and other soft drinks are likely to be smaller.[13]

Cross elasticities are useful because managers frequently want to forecast what will happen to their own sales as other companies change their prices. The PTC board is concerned about the effects that a forthcoming increase in restaurant prices would have on its ticket demand. If meals in local restaurants and theater tickets are strong complements, a substantial increase in restaurant prices would cause a serious decline in the demand for PTC tickets. In this case, the PTC board might want to offset this shift in demand by lowering ticket prices or advertising more heavily. In contrast, if meals and tickets are weak complements, the increase in meal prices would have little effect on ticket demand. In our example, a $10 increase in meal prices will result in 33 fewer ticket sales per night. Using the formula in Equation (4.8), the corresponding cross elasticity between these two points [(200, $40); (167, $50)] is

---

[12]E. Ramsted (1999), "As Prices Tumble, Sales of DVD Players Explode for the Holidays," *The Wall Street Journal* (December 9), 31.

[13]Next, we extend this discussion to show how cross elasticities can be used by managers to define a firm's industry.

MANAGERIAL APPLICATIONS

Estimates of Cross Elasticities

Economists have estimated the cross elasticities for various commodities. Below are a few of these estimates:

$$
\begin{array}{ll}
\text{Electricity and natural gas} = 0.20 \\
\text{Beef and pork} \qquad\quad\ = 0.28 \\
\text{Natural gas and fuel oil} \quad = 0.44 \\
\text{Margarine and butter} \quad\ = 0.81
\end{array}
$$

All the pairs of commodities listed above are substitutes. Complements such as DVD players and DVD movies have negative cross elasticities. Natural gas apparently is not a very strong substitute for electricity. Although people can use either gas or electricity for heating, natural gas is not generally used for lighting. On the other hand, natural gas and fuel oil are closer substitutes (both tend to be used for heating). Margarine and butter are strong substitutes. Note that the cross elasticities for some goods depend on how much time consumers have to adjust to changes in relative prices. For example, the cross elasticity between natural gas and fuel oil is likely to be much higher in the long run, since it takes time to replace old furnaces and other equipment with newer equipment powered by the less-expensive fuel source. In contrast, customers can adjust to a relative change in the prices of margarine and butter on their next trips to the grocery store.

Source: E. Mansfield and G. Yohe (2004), *Microeconomics* (W. W. Norton: New York), 135.

-0.81: For every 1 percent increase in meal prices over this range there is, on average, a 0.81 percent decline in ticket sales. This elasticity suggests that PTC tickets and restaurant meals are rather strong complements.

Income

Normal versus Inferior Goods

Another factor that frequently affects the demand for a product is the income of potential buyers. As a person's income increases, more products are purchased, and the combined expenditures across all products rise. The demand for specific products,

---

MANAGERIAL APPLICATIONS

Cross Elasticity and Pfizer's Lost Profits in Japan

Pfizer, the world's largest pharmaceutical company, produces the leading drug to help people quit smoking. It is marketed under the brand name of Chantix in the United States and Champix in Japan. According to the *Wall Street Journal*, Pfizer lost millions of dollars of potential sales by underestimating the cross elasticity of demand between Champix and cigarettes. On October 1, 2011 the price of cigarettes increased significantly in Japan due to a government tax. Tens of thousands of people, who wanted to quit smoking, went to their doctors for prescriptions of Champix. Unfortunately, Pfizer had produced far too little of the drug to meet the demand. Clinic directors were upset and argued, "they should have predicted something like this." After all, Pfizer had known about the planned tax increase for over a year. A Pfizer spokesman responded to these complaints by stating, "we expected more demand, but not to this extent." Whether or not Pfizer could have predicted the very large cross elasticity between Champix and cigarettes with available data and information remains an open question. But had they done so, they would have increased their revenues and profits by potentially millions of Yen.

Source: H. Tabuchi (2011), "In Japan, Pfizer is Short of Drug to Help Smokers, *The Wall Street Journal* (January 3).

however, can either rise or fall as income increases. The demand for goods such as gourmet foods or jewelry would be expected to increase with income, whereas the demand for other goods like canned processed meat or cabbage might decline. Goods for which demand increases with income are called *normal goods.* PTC tickets are normal goods. Goods for which demand declines with income are called *inferior goods.*

Income Elasticities

The sensitivity of demand to income is measured by their *income elasticity.* The income elasticity is defined as the *percentage change in the demand for a good, given a percentage change in income (I).* Income elasticities can be calculated using the following formula.

$$\eta_I = [\Delta Q / (Q_1 + Q_2)/2] \div [\Delta I / (I_1 + I_2)/2] \tag{4.9}$$

The income elasticity is positive for normal goods and negative for inferior goods.

The income elasticity of a firm's product has important implications. Firms producing products with high income elasticities are more affected by cyclical fluctuations; they tend to grow more rapidly in expanding economies but contract more sharply in depressed economies. Managers must anticipate these fluctuations in managing cash flows and hiring decisions. Demands for products with small income elasticities are more stable over economic cycles. Studies indicate that goods like domestic servants, medical care, education for children, and restaurant meals tend to have relatively large income elasticities, whereas goods such as most food products, gasoline, oil, and liquor have relatively small (in absolute value) income elasticities.

Income elasticities also can influence location decisions. For instance, PTC has a relatively high-income elasticity (above 1.6). This elasticity was one of the factors that motivated the founders to locate their theater in a community with a high per capita income. They anticipated that they would have fewer customers if they located in a less affluent area.

MANAGERIAL APPLICATIONS

Estimates of Income Elasticities

Economists have estimated the income elasticities for various products. Below are a few of these estimates:

Flour	= −0.36
Margarine	= −0.20
Milk	= 0.07
Meat	= 0.35
Dentist services	= 1.41
Restaurant consumption	= 1.48

According to these estimates, flour and margarine are inferior goods. People spend less on these goods as their incomes rise. The other goods are normal goods (expenditures on the products rise with income). Dentist services and restaurant consumption are particularly sensitive to income changes.

Source: E. Mansfield and G. Yohe (2004), *Microeconomics* (W. W. Norton: New York), 135.

A Pampered Dog Loses His Stylist

Even wealthy consumers are affected by changes in income. Consider Betsy Illium, a marketing consultant to medical practices, who owns four Manhattan apartments (three are investment properties). In early 2008, Illium became concerned that her income would decline given forecasts of a looming economic recession. "It's frightening," she said, with much of her wealth being tied up in real estate. In response she decided to replace her dog Dobbin's regular groomer, who charged $130, with one from Petco, which charged only $65. She also decided to send her dirty sheets and towels to a laundry service rather than to a higher priced dry cleaner. In her case, high-priced dog groomers and dry cleaning are normal goods (her demands for these products increase with income), while laundry services and low-priced dog groomers are inferior goods (her demands for these products decreased with income). Illium became "appalled when she calculated that Dobbin's grooming, her own weekly hair, nail and massage appointments, gourmet groceries, restaurant meals and Starbuck's coffee cost nearly $2,000 a month." She realized that she would have to "tighten her alligator belt" due to the threat of recession.

Source: S. Rosenbloom (2008), "Tightening the Alligator Belt," *nytimes.com* (January 27).

Other Variables

We have concentrated on three of the more important independent variables in most demand functions—the product's own price, prices of related products, and income. Other variables, such as advertising expenditures, also can be important. In all cases, the analysis is similar. Demand responds to a change in some other variable. Sensitivity can be measured by the appropriate elasticity—for instance, an advertising elasticity. Obviously, managers do not have the time to consider all the conceivable variables that might have trivial impacts on the demand for their products. Good decision making requires that managers understand the effects of the more important factors, which usually include the product's own price, the prices of close substitutes and important complements, and incomes.

Industry versus Firm Demand

Industry Demand Curves

Although we have concentrated our analysis on firm-level demand, demand functions and demand curves can be defined for entire industries. For instance, a demand function could be specified for the entertainment industry in PTC's market area. Such a function would relate the total ticket sales for all entertainment events to factors that affect this demand. Managers often are interested in total industry demand because it provides important information on the size of their potential markets and trends that affect them. For instance, a company's executives might judge the performance of a store manager that reports flat sales quite differently if market demand is shrinking and the store is increasing market share versus a case where market demand is increasing but the store is losing market share. Moreover, estimates of industry demand sometimes can be obtained at modest cost from outside analysts or business publications.

Firms within an industry compete directly and their products are likely to be relatively strong substitutes. The overall industry, on the other hand, is less likely to have strong substitutes. A person wanting to go to an entertainment event might

MANAGERIAL APPLICATIONS

9/11 Causes Massive Shifts in Demand Curves

The 9/11 terrorist attacks on the World Trade Center and Pentagon caused the demand curves for numerous goods and services to shift. Consider the following examples of industries whose demand curves shifted left:

- Hotels lowered room rates by 30 to 40 percent. Marriott Hotels put a third of its hourly employees on part-time schedules.

- Disney trimmed the hours at its theme parks and reduced the hours of 40,000 part-time workers.

- The U.S. airline industry estimated that 9/11 caused it to lose about $7 billion and saw its revenues drop by 40 percent. Following 9/11 many planes flew at less than 50 percent capacity and airlines laid off 20 percent of their workforce. The U.S. government provided $15 billion of loan guarantees to the airline industry.

- Spot prices for crude oil plummeted to a two-year low of $20 per barrel.

But not all firms saw the demand for their goods and services adversely affected by 9/11. The following firms saw their demand curves shift to the right:

- Sales of American flags skyrocketed. Annin & Co., a 675-employee flag maker and market leader, increased output of its most popular 3-by-5-foot U.S. flags from 30,000 to 100,000 a week by October 2001. Its five plants added shifts, but dealers still had to wait 15 weeks for delivery of popular-size flags.

- The demand for biometric systems increased. Biometric systems identify people using digital face, iris, or fingerprint scans. The biometric trade association doubled its worldwide revenue growth forecasts following 9/11. The three largest publicly traded biometric firms' stock prices rose on average 70 percent when the stock markets reopened on 9/17.

- InVision Technologies, which makes bomb-detection systems for airports that cost between $750,000 and $1.5 million each, saw its stock price increase 165 percent on the first trading session after the markets reopened.

- The U.S. government increased the defense department's budget by $10 to $15 billion. A significant percentage of those funds were expected to be spent on intelligence technologies, such as those produced by software companies like Narus, which track and sort data and e-mail on the Internet to identify potential terrorists.

On average, publicly traded companies suffered significant reductions in demand. For instance, the stock market suffered its worst one-week loss since the Great Depression; following 9/11 stocks lost $1.2 trillion in market value. Nonetheless, there were winners scattered among the larger population of losers.

Source: E. Brown (2001), "Heartbreak Hotel?" *Fortune* (November 26), 161–163; M. Gunther (2001), "The Wary World of Disney," *Fortune* (October 15), 104; K. Marron (2002), "Systems That Use Physical Traits to Control Access to Sensitive Data Are Catching On in Post-Sept. 11 Era," *The Globe and Mail* (March 28), B16; B. O'Keefe (2001), "Securing the Air, One Bag at a Time," *Fortune* (October 15), 244; B. Powell (2001), "The Economy under Siege," *Fortune* (October 15), 87–108; J. Simons (2001), "Greed Meets Terror," *Fortune* (October 29), 145–146; S. Tully (2001), "From Bad to Worse," *Fortune* (October 15), 118–128; D. Voreacos (2001), "As Country Wraps Itself in Flags, Company Strains to Make Them," *Houston Chronicle* (October 7), 10; M. Warner (2001), "Web Warriors," *Fortune* (October 15), 148.

choose among several options based on price. Entertainment events more broadly defined have fewer alternatives. Thus, demands facing individual firms within an industry tend to be more price-elastic than those for the entire industry.

Defining Industry and Market Area

We have indicated that managers can gain important insights by analyzing industry-level demand. One problem that managers face in conducting this type of analysis is defining the relevant industry and market area. Is PTC competing in the live theater industry or in a more broadly defined entertainment industry? Cross elasticities provide important information to answer these types of questions. The cross elasticity between PTC tickets and symphony tickets is 0.4. This relatively high value (see the box titled Estimates of Cross Elasticities presented earlier in this chapter) suggests that PTC competes against companies in a broader entertainment industry than just live theater.[14] The managers at PTC also must define the relevant geographic area of their marketplace. If PTC raises its prices, will its customers shift to theaters in other nearby cities? If so, these cities should be included in the definition of PTC's market area.

Network Effects

For some products, demand increases with the number of users. For example, fax machines and telephones are not particularly useful unless there is a *network* of users. This consideration is quite important for many of today's communication and information products. For instance, consumers were reluctant to buy new products, such as 3-D television sets, Blu-ray players, and new word processing programs, until they became convinced that the products had the potential for widespread use. Consumers understand that if a product does not garner sufficient demand, important complementary products, such as Blu-ray movies, will not be produced in high volumes or at attractive prices. Also they worry that it will be difficult to acquire reliable, inexpensive service for the new product. They may learn to use a new technology only to find that it is discontinued because of insufficient demand. For example, despite vigorous efforts by Sony to promote its Betamax technology for video recording, the technology was displaced completely by the VHS format. VHS suffered a similar fate from DVDs and Blu-ray.

Products where these network concerns are important often have relatively elastic demands. When price is lowered, there are two effects. One is the standard price

---

MANAGERIAL APPLICATIONS

Store Layout Affects Demand

Paco Underhill calls himself a "retail anthropologist." His consulting firm videotapes consumers as they shop at his clients' stores such as Sears, The Gap, and McDonald's. He then offers recommendations for store layout. For example, most North Americans turn right after entering a store while most British and Australian customers turn left. Consumers tend to avoid narrow aisles; they apparently dislike being jostled from behind (what he calls the "butt-brush factor"). Junk food should be placed on low or middle shelves so kids can reach them. After finding that women spend only half the time in the store when accompanied by a man, he recommends placing numerous chairs around stores so men can sit comfortably while the women shop.

Source: K. Labich (1999), "Attention Shoppers: This Man Is Watching You," *Fortune* (July 19), 131–133.

---

[14]Cross elasticities also are used as evidence in antitrust cases. Antitrust cases generally focus on whether or not a company has significant market power within an industry. Thus, the definition of the industry is quite important. A company might have a significant market share (and thus apparent power) in a narrowly defined industry, but a small market share in a more broadly defined market. For instance, the government suggested that the ReaLemon Company had monopolized the reconstituted concentrated lemon juice market—supplying over 90 percent of that market. The company responded that the appropriate market definition was broader: They faced vigorous competition from reconstituted natural-strength lemon juice, fresh lemons, frozen lemonade, lime juice, and so on.

---

effect: Consumers purchase more of the product because it is being sold at a more attractive price. The second is the *network effect:* Demand for the product increases even more because more people are using the product. When a new consumer purchases the product, there is an externality for other users; because there is an additional user of the product, the product becomes more attractive for other current and potential users.

Network effects have important implications not only on product pricing, but on product design as well. For instance, when software manufacturers are designing software upgrades, they have to decide whether to make the new product compatible with prior versions of the software and with competing products on the market. Making a new product compatible with competing products can reduce the uniqueness of the product. However, the net effect can be to increase overall demand for the product because of network effects. For example, a consumer might be more willing to buy an Apple computer if it is compatible with Windows computers because of the enhanced ability to interact with Windows users.

Product Attributes

Thus far, we have taken the *attributes* of the product as given. Our analysis of the demand for PTC tickets is based on the existing quality and selection of plays, their starting times, the quality of seating, and so on. Given these characteristics, we examined how price and other factors affect the demand for PTC tickets.

Understanding consumer demand also plays an important role in the design of the product. For instance, do local patrons prefer Shakespeare or more contemporary

---

MANAGERIAL APPLICATIONS

Understanding What Consumers Want

Innovative companies strive to develop new products that will be demanded by customers. Managers, however, vary in their beliefs about the best way to discover consumer demand. Steve Jobs, former CEO of Apple Inc., thought that consumer surveys and other market research were relatively useless, since consumers often don't know whether they will purchase a new product until they see it. Many industry "experts" were highly skeptical about the potential demand for iPads when the product was first announced. They criticized Jobs for not conducing market research prior to the launch. Jobs, however, strongly believed that consumers would want to purchase the product once they experienced it, and he was right. Henry Ford, the founder of Ford Motor expressed this same belief about market research when he famously said, "If I had asked people what they wanted, the would have said faster horses." Jim Goodnight, one of the founders and long–time CEO of SAS, strongly believed that it is critical for his company to obtain ideas and suggestions from customers about potential new software products. SAS has successfully developed an expanding range of new and upgraded software products for nearly four decades. In 2013, it employed 13,764 people and had sales of over $3 billion. While these CEOs differ in their beliefs about the value of market research, all three were highly successful in managing their companies and in introducing new products that were highly demanded by customers.

Source: W. Isaacson (2011), *Steve Jobs* (Simon & Schuster) and *SAS Overview and Annual Report 2013.*

plays? Do they prefer mysteries or musicals? Do they value comfortable seating with additional leg room or seating that is closer to the stage? Can the anticipated decrease in demand from increased restaurant prices be offset by changing the starting time of the plays? (Delaying the starting time by 30 minutes might give people more time to eat at home before going to the play.)

Answers to these types of questions are important in managerial decision making and establishing corporate strategy. Indeed, when managers speak of the importance of understanding consumer demand, they often are referring to understanding the specific product attributes that are important to customers. Marketing managers are responsible for understanding the broad range of product attributes that affect demand. These include price, product design, packaging, promotion and advertising, and distribution channels.[15] This broad focus on demand has played an especially important role in management innovations like total quality management programs (see Web Chapter 23, available via Connect).

An important problem facing most firms is how to incorporate information that may be held by many people throughout a firm—for example, about such matters as consumer demand—into the decision making process for product design. We defer discussions of this problem until the last half of this book. These sections provide insights into how to design the firm's organizational architecture to help ensure that relevant information is incorporated in the decision making process.

Product Life Cycles

Our discussion of product attributes suggests that managers constantly seek to develop new and better ways to identify and respond to consumer demands. This activity leads to the introduction of new products. Managers generally recognize that market demand for a new product is unlikely to remain stable over time. Often, the

---

[15]For a more formal economic analysis of the demand for product attributes, see K. Lancaster (1966), "A New Approach to Consumer Theory," *Journal of Political Economy* 74, 132–157.

Figure 4.6   Product Life Cycle

The product-life-cycle hypothesis suggests that the industry demand for a new product goes through four main phases: *introduction, growth, maturity,* and *decline.*

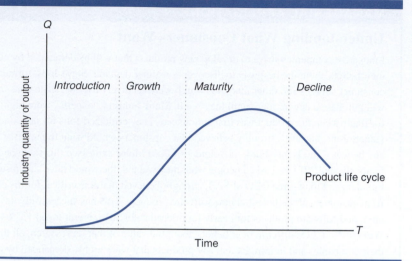

industry demand curve for a new product shifts outward as the product becomes more widely known. Eventually, however, the demand is likely to shift inward as consumers shift toward other new and improved products. This pattern in the demand for new products is known as the *product life cycle.*

As depicted in Figure 4.6, the product-life-cycle hypothesis suggests that the demand for a product can be categorized into four main phases: introduction, growth, maturity, and decline. In the growth phase, the industry-level demand increases rapidly. In the maturity phase, the demand continues to increase and then begins to decrease. In the decline phase, the demand continues to fall. Eventually, the product is withdrawn from the market. Managers should recognize these trends in new-product planning, as well as in entry, exit, and pricing decisions for given products.

The increase in demand during the growth phase encourages new firms to enter the industry. For instance, the growth in the demand for personal computers (PCs) during the 1990s prompted many firms to begin production. Given the entry of new firms, original firms typically lose market share. If industry demand grows at a faster rate than the number of firms, existing firms realize sales growth, even though their market

MANAGERIAL APPLICATIONS

Demand for Prostitutes Declines in the United States Over Time

The demand for goods and services frequently changes over time. Popular media opinion is that the demand for prostitutes, "the world's oldest profession," is booming in the United States. The evidence, however, suggests otherwise. The sexual mores are much more liberal today than they were a century ago. It is generally much easier for men to find premarital "hookups." The increased supply of noncommercial sex appears to have reduced the demand for prostitutes. In 1948, 69 percent of men surveyed indicated that they had paid for sex at least once, while in 2006 the percentage was only 15. Consistent with basic supply and demand analysis, the decline in demand has been accompanied by a decrease in the price paid to street prostitutes. The average annual income for prostitutes is estimated to have declined from $25,000 per year to $18,000 per year (both in 2007 dollars) over the period 1911–2007.

Source: (2014) "Sex, Lies and Statistics," *The Economist* (March 22).

share falls. If the number of new firms grows faster than industry demand, existing firms will experience a reduction in demand, depressing prices and firm profits.

This discussion suggests that the first firms to introduce a successful product sometimes can have "first-mover advantages." In this case, they enjoy high profits until competitive entry occurs. They also can develop a customer base and have a longer time period to learn how to produce the product efficiently. These advantages explain why firms frequently strive to be the first to develop and launch new products. However, in attempting to exploit an innovative product, managers must anticipate the impact that their policies are likely to have on entry decisions by potential rivals.

The analysis also suggests that managers should be careful in evaluating whether to enter an industry during its growth phase. Competition during this phase can be intense; moreover, the demand they face is expected to decline at some point in the future. To prosper in such an environment, a new firm must have some type of *competitive advantage* over its rivals (e.g., being a low-cost producer).

Demand Estimation[16]

In our PTC example, we know the demand function. Most managers are not so lucky: They must estimate their demand functions. Sometimes it is easy to estimate demand, at least for the very near term. Other times it is quite difficult. Some companies employ statistical techniques to provide numerical estimates of demand functions. Other companies use more qualitative approaches.

Demand estimation is a complex topic that is largely beyond the scope of this book. Here, we simply provide a brief discussion of three general techniques used in estimating demand: *interviews, price experimentation,* and *statistical analysis*. Our intent is to provide insights into the basic costs and benefits of each approach. These insights make managers more informed consumers of demand estimates and offer guidance as to the type of demand analysis to employ in a given situation. Although each approach has its limitations, the approaches are not mutually exclusive. Because the limitations differ, many managers employ several methods and aggregate the estimates to increase their understanding of demand.

Interviews

Interview approaches attempt to estimate demand through customer surveys, questionnaires, and focus groups. Perhaps the most naive version of this approach is simply to ask consumers what they would purchase if faced with different prices. The answers to these questions can be remarkably unreliable. First, people have incentives to be less than completely truthful since customers would like the firm to offer lower prices. Second, even if they try to be truthful, they might have difficulty forecasting what they would actually purchase given the array of alternatives available in the marketplace.

More sophisticated approaches to customer interviews are possible. For example, an individual might be asked about the difference in price between two competing products. Now if you found that individuals had purchased one of the products but

---

[16]This section draws on W. Baumol (1977), *Economic Theory and Operations Analysis* (Prentice Hall: Englewood Cliffs, NJ), 234–236.

did not know the price of the other, you might conclude that customers were relatively insensitive to price.

Sometimes companies use a *simulated market* where people are given play money and asked to simulate purchase decisions. These experiments can yield useful insights. Again, however, the decisions people make with play money need not mirror the decisions they would make with their own money.

Consumer surveys play a particularly important role in providing information about the attributes that are valued by customers. Many businesses request that buyers fill out customer-service and complaint forms. Businesses often follow up sales or service with telephone calls to customers to ask about product and service quality and customer satisfaction. Among the most important sources of information about customer preferences are the direct contacts that salespeople and other company representatives have with their customers.

All the interview approaches, however, can produce remarkably inaccurate information if the sample is not representative of the population of the firm's customers. For instance, if you are interested in estimating demand for a good with a negative income elasticity, distributing surveys at an upscale mall might be a poor way to proceed. More subtle problems with eliciting interview information also can arise. One team of researchers cautions, "The curious, the exhibitionistic, and the succorant are likely to overpopulate any sample of volunteers. How secure a base can volunteers be with such groups over-represented and the shy, suspicious, and inhibited under-represented?"[17]

Price Experimentation

A second approach is to undertake price experiments. For instance, the board might decrease PTC's ticket price to $25 and carefully track changes in ticket sales. However as part of the company's marketing strategy, PTC prints brochures that detail the season's plays, costs, dates, and ticket prices. Thus, experimenting with their ticket prices would require reprinting their brochures. This raises the cost to PTC of this type of price experimentation. Some other types of firms incur few costs in changing prices; for instance, it is particularly easy for companies that market through the Internet to experiment with their prices.

Many firms are unlike PTC in that they operate at multiple locations. If a firm has the flexibility to vary prices across different geographic markets, it has the potential to gain more information than if it is limited to experimenting at a single location. But care must be exercised. Ideally, the local markets are separated geographically and have their own media outlets. Thus advertising lower prices in one market will not shift demand from the firm's other locations.

There are at least three limitations in the use of price experimentation. First, demand can differ, depending on whether customers anticipate that a price change will be permanent or temporary. It can be difficult to identify customers' expectations about future prices. Second, direct-market tests are not controlled experiments; several changes might be occurring simultaneously. For instance, the board might lower PTC's ticket prices at the same time that the symphony changes its prices. The observed change in demand would reflect both effects. Third, some managers worry

---

[17]E. Webb, D. Campbell, R. Schwartz, and L. Schrest (1966), *Unobtrusive Measures* (Rand McNally College Publishing Company: Chicago).

ACADEMIC APPLICATIONS

On Estimating Demand Curves for Common Stocks

There has been a long-running debate over the demand elasticities of common stocks of individual firms. Many economists argue that these demand curves are perfectly elastic, since there are numerous stocks with similar risk-return characteristics available in the market. In this case, the demand curves for individual stocks are horizontal. Others argue that each stock is unique and has very few substitutes. Here, the individual demand curves would be downward-sloping.

Managers care about the slopes of the demand curves for their common stock since these slopes affect the price at which they can sell new securities. If demand curves slope downward, price must be decreased below the current market price to sell new securities. If demand curves are horizontal, new securities can be issued at the current market price. Managers, of course, want to sell new stock at the highest possible price.

The existing empirical evidence suggests that stock prices decline by about 3 percent when firms announce new issues of common stock. This finding seems to suggest that the demand curves for common stocks are downward-sloping. This finding, however, is subject to alternative interpretations. If investors think that managers tend to issue new stock when they believe it is overvalued, an announcement of a new issue will cause the entire demand curve to shift down and price will decline (since investors infer from the announcement that the firm is overvalued). The observation that price declines when new stock is issued is not sufficient to allow us to identify the price elasticity of a firm's common stock—the price decrease might be due to either a shift in demand or a shift in quantity demanded.

This example illustrates that it is not always easy to estimate demand curves, even when extensive data on prices and quantities are readily available. Indeed, the data on prices and volumes for publicly traded securities are among the best available in the world.

Source: C. Smith (1986), "Investment Banking and the Capital Acquisition Process," *Journal of Financial Economics* 15, 3–29.

that price experimentation is risky. They are concerned that customers lost as a result of a price increase might be difficult to regain even if subsequently the price were lowered. Alternatively, it might be difficult to raise the price once a firm had lowered it (customers might be annoyed and purchase from rivals).

Statistical Analysis

Often, companies use statistical techniques such as regression analysis to estimate demand functions. Computers and large databases on sales, prices, and other relevant factors have increased the usefulness of this approach materially. By using statistical techniques, the effects of specific factors often can be isolated. It is possible to analyze large samples of actual market data to obtain more reliable results.

Even though statistical approaches can provide managers with important information on demand, they must recognize that there are potential problems. Just because a researcher can produce reams of computer output formatted into tables and multicolored graphs implies neither that the analysis is well done nor that the results are reliable. Below, we briefly discuss three types of problems that managers encounter regularly in statistical approaches to estimating demand.

Omission of Important Variables

The problem of *omitted variables* can be illustrated by an example. Assume that the actual demand function for a company is

$$\text{Sales} = 120 - 2P + 8A + 0.04I \tag{4.10}$$

	2006	2007	2008
Income (*I*)	$3,000	$4,000	$3,500
Advertising (*A*)	2	3	2.5
Price (*P*)	10	10	10
Sales (*S*)	236	284	260
True demand	$S = 120 - 2P + 8A + 0.04I$		
Estimated demand	$S = 140 + 48A$		

Table 4.1   An Example of the Omitted-Variables Problem

The true demand curve of the company in this example is Sales $= 120 - 2P + 8A + 0.04I$. The data for 2006 to 2008 are presented in the table. If the analyst omits income and uses statistical techniques to estimate a relation between advertising and sales, the analyst will obtain the following equation: Sales $= 140 + 48A$. The model predicts sales perfectly (based on the data in the table). The estimated equation, however, significantly overstates the influence of advertising. The omitted-variables problem is present whenever important variables are left out of the analysis that are correlated with the explanatory variables that are included in the analysis.

where   *P* is the price of the product
        A is advertising expenditures
        I is income

Table 4.1 presents the data for 2006, 2007, and 2008. While this data is potentially available to the marketing manager, Brendis Isaccsdottir, who wants to estimate demand, does not necessarily know that both advertising and income are important determinants of demand. Suppose that Brendis ignores income and uses statistical techniques to estimate a relation between sales and advertising.[18] Standard regression techniques would yield the following equation:

$$\text{Sales} = 140 + 48A \tag{4.11}$$

The model appears to predict sales perfectly (based on the data in the table). The equation, however, materially overstates the true influence of advertising and can lead to spectacular mistakes in decision making. Based on this analysis, Brendis might budget far too much for advertising. This omitted-variables problem is present whenever important excluded variables are correlated with explanatory variables that are included in the statistical analysis.[19] Including unimportant variables does not bias estimated coefficients for the other variables (however, including irrelevant variables reduces the precision of the various estimates).

Multicollinearity

If the factors that affect demand are highly correlated (tend to move together), it might be impossible to estimate their individual effects with much precision. For instance, two important variables in the demand function might be income and education. If in the data set to be analyzed high income is always associated with high education, it might be impossible to separate the two effects.

---

[18]The manager does not have to worry about controlling for price, since it was constant over the period ($10).

[19]The problem does not always result in overstated coefficients on the explanatory variables. Depending on the nature of the correlation among the explanatory variables, the coefficients can be either overstated or understated. The estimated coefficient in this example is overstated because advertising and income are positively correlated.

Figure 4.7 An Example of the Identification Problem

An analyst has collected data on past prices and sales for her firm's industry. The demand and supply curves have shifted over the three years. Connecting the three price-quantity points provides a poor estimate of the current industry demand curve (labeled D_3 in the graph). The three points are *equilibrium* points, given all conditions that affect the demand and supply of the product at each point in time. They are not three points along the same demand (or supply) curve.

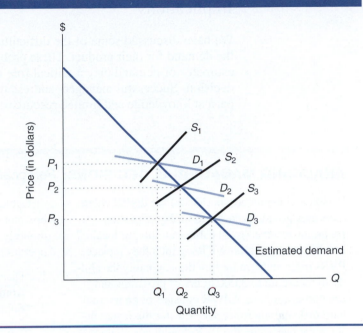

Identification Problem

Another potentially important problem that can confront Brendis is the *identification problem*. This problem also can be illustrated by example. Suppose the marketing manager has collected data on past prices and sales for a given industry with the aim of estimating an industry demand curve. In the past three years, the following sales and price combinations have been observed: (10, $10), (12, $8), and (14, $6). Is it valid for Brendis to connect these three points as an estimate of the demand curve? Because of the identification problem, the answer is generally no.

Each data combination reflects the intersection of the demand curve and supply curve for the industry for each year. If the demand curve has shifted over the three years due to changes in factors such as personal income, the points come from three different demand curves. Connecting the points does not provide an estimate of the current demand curve. In fact, if supply considerations have been stable while demand has shifted, it will trace out the industry's supply curve. Suppose in our example that both the demand and supply curves have shifted in each year. As shown in Figure 4.7, the resulting combinations of price and quantity are observed *equilibrium* points, given the conditions during the relevant time periods. Connecting these points provides a poor estimate of the current demand curve D_3.

Sometimes, Brendis will not have enough information to solve the identification problem and is better off using consumer interviews or market experiments to estimate demand. Other times, she has enough information to identify the demand function (she needs to be able to specify factors that influence demand, but not supply, and vice versa). One special case in which Brendis does not have to worry about the identification problem is when the *demand curve is stable*. Suppose the demand curve did not shift over the three years and all the different sales-price combinations were caused by changes in supply. In this case, she can obtain a reasonable estimate of the demand curve simply by connecting the observed sales-price combinations.

Implications

We have discussed some of the difficulties that managers face in trying to estimate the demand for their product. These problems can be difficult to solve. Nonetheless, estimates of demand play a critical role in decision making—especially the pricing decision. Successful managers address these problems the best they can, given imperfect knowledge and limited resources.

ANALYZING MANAGERIAL DECISIONS: *Personal Video Recorders*

Personal video recorders (PVRs) are digital video recorders used to record and replay television programs received from cable, satellite, or local broadcasts. But unlike VCRs, which they replace, PVRs offer many more functions, notably the ability to record up to 3,000 hours of programs and easy programming. A PVR consists of an internal hard disk and microprocessor. After the owner installs the hardware, the PVR downloads all upcoming TV schedules to the hardware via a phone or cable connection. Users merely enter the name of the show(s) they want recorded and the system finds the time and channel of the show and automatically records it. Users must subscribe to a cable or satellite system if they wish to record programs off these channels.

Besides ease of programming and much larger recording capacity than videotape, PVRs allow the user to watch a prerecorded show while the unit is recording up to five new programs, pause watching live programs (e.g., if the phone rings) and then resume watching the rest of the live broadcast, view instant replays and slow motion of live programs, and skip commercials. In effect, PVRs, like older VCRs, allow viewers to control when they watch broadcast programs (called "time shifting"). However, PVRs provide much sharper pictures and are much simpler to operate than VCRs, and PVRs allow the user to download the television schedule for the next week.

Two companies that begin selling PVRs and subscription services were: TiVo and ReplayTV. Both firms started in 1997. As of 2013 TiVo had about one million subscribers and ReplayTV had been purchased by DirectTV. Companies are developing new technologies that make it even easier for users to "snip" commercials.

Cable companies now offer a combined cable box and PVR in one unit for a small additional monthly charge. This further simplifies setup and operation, and the user gets a single bill.

1. Discuss how PVRs will affect the demand from advertisers?

2. Suppose you are in charge of setting the price for commercial advertisements shown during *Enemies,* a top network television show. There is a 60-minute slot for the show. However, the running time for the show itself is only 30 minutes. The rest of the time can be sold to other companies to advertise their products or donated for public service announcements. Demand for advertising is given by:

$$Q_d = 30 - 0.0002P + 26V$$

where Q_d = quantity demanded for advertising on the show (minutes), P = the price per minute that you charge for advertising, and V is the number of viewers expected to watch the advertisements (in millions).

a. All your costs are fixed and your goal is to maximize the total revenue received from selling advertising. Suppose that the expected number of viewers is one million people. What price should you charge? How many minutes of advertising will you sell? What is total revenue?

b. Suppose price is held constant at the value from part (a). What will happen to the quantity demanded if due to PVRs the number of expected viewers falls to 0.5 million? Calculate the "viewer elasticity" based on the two points. Explain in words what this value means.

3. As more viewers begin using PVRs, what happens to the revenues of the major networks (CBS, NBC, ABC, and FOX)?
4. Discuss the long-run effects if a significant proportion of the viewers begin adopting these "advertising snipping" systems.
5. What advice would you give the major commercial networks and producers of programming for these networks as more consumers adopt PVRs?

Source: J. Gudmundsen (2002), "Video Gizmos Change the Rules," *Democrat and Chronicle* (August), 5E and 8E; B. Fisher (2003), "TiVo and Replay TV Have Features to Satisfy Any TV Junkie," *Detroit News* (June 24); R. Reilly (2003), "Great Invention Period," *Sports Illustrated* (December 22).

Summary

Understanding product demand is critical for many managerial decisions such as pricing, setting production levels, undertaking capital investment, and establishing an advertising budget. This chapter provides a basic analysis of demand.

A *demand function* is a mathematical representation of the relations among the quantity demanded of a product over a specified time period and the various factors that influence this quantity. We focus on three independent variables in the demand function: the price of the product, the prices of related products, and customers' incomes.

A *demand curve* for a product displays how many units will be purchased over a given period at each price holding all other factors fixed. Movements along a demand curve reflect changes in price and are called *changes in the quantity demanded.* Movements of the entire demand curve are caused by other factors, such as changes in income, and are referred to as *changes in demand.*

Demand curves generally slope downward to the right: Quantity demanded varies inversely with price. This relation often is referred to as the *law of demand.* Demand curves vary in their sensitivities of the quantity demanded to price. *Price elasticity* is defined as the percentage change in quantity demanded from a percentage change in price (expressed as a positive number). The price elasticity tends to be high when there are close substitutes for the product and when the good represents a significant expenditure for the consumer. Demand tends to be more elastic over the long run than over the short run. How total revenue from a product changes with price depends on the price elasticity. A small price increase results in an increase in expenditures when demand is *inelastic* and a decrease in expenditures when demand is *elastic.* Total expenditures remain unchanged when the demand elasticity is *unitary.*

An important concept in economics is *marginal revenue,* which is defined as the *change in total revenue given a one-unit change in quantity.* Marginal revenue for a linear demand curve is given by the line with the same intercept as the demand curve but with twice the negative slope. Total revenue increases with quantity when marginal revenue is positive and decreases with quantity when marginal revenue is negative.

The price of related products can affect the demand for a product. Goods that compete with each other are referred to as *substitutes.* Products that tend to be consumed together are *complements.* One frequently used measure of substitution between two products is the *cross elasticity of demand.* The cross elasticity is positive for substitutes and negative for complements.

Another factor that can affect the demand for a product is the income of potential buyers. The sensitivity of demand to income is measured by the *income elasticity.* The income elasticity is positive for *normal goods,* and negative for *inferior goods.*

Demand curves can be defined for individual firms or entire industries. The price elasticities for individual firms within an industry are generally higher than for the industry as a whole. Cross elasticities can be helpful in defining the appropriate industry.

For some products, demand increases with the number of users. For example, telephones are not very useful unless there is a *network* of users. Products where these network concerns are important often have relatively elastic demands. When price is lowered, there is both a *standard price effect* and a *network effect.*

The standard economic analysis of demand takes the *attributes* of the product as given. Information about consumer demand, however, is also important in the initial design of products. In Chapters 11–23 of this book, we provide important insights into how to design the firm's organizational architecture to help ensure that this type of information is incorporated in the decision making process.

Managers use three basic approaches to estimate demand: *interviews, price experimentation,* and *statistical analysis.* All three approaches can suffer from potentially serious problems. Managers have to do the best they can given imperfect information and limited resources. Knowledge of the potential pitfalls can make managers more intelligent producers and users of demand estimates.

Suggested Reading

G. Stigler (1987), *The Theory of Price* (Macmillan: New York), Chapter 3.

Self-Evaluation Problems

4–1. Suppose Product A has the demand function $Q_A = 10 - 5P_A + 2P_B + 0.01I$. The initial values of the variables are $Q_A = 15$, $P_A = \$4$, $P_B = \$2.5$ and $I = \$2,000$.
   a. When P_A moves to $\$3.4$, keeping other variables at their initial values, Q_A becomes 18. What is the corresponding own-price arc elasticity of demand?
   b. If income, I, increases to $\$2,250$ per period with all other variables held at their initial values, Q_A becomes 17.5. What is the corresponding income arc elasticity of demand?
   c. If P_B increases to $\$3$ with all other variables held at their initial values, Q_A becomes 16. What is the corresponding cross-price arc elasticity of demand?
   d. Is Product A an inferior or normal good? Are Product A and Product B substitutes or complements? Explain.
   e. Is the firm charging the revenue maximizing price for Product A at the initial values? Explain.
   f. Compute the MR at the initial values.

4–2. Suppose your firm faces a demand curve of $P = 90 - .30Q$. Find the revenue maximizing output and price. Calculate the total revenue. Is this outcome on the elastic, inelastic, or unitary elastic part of the demand curve? Is this price the optimal price for your firm to charge? Display this choice graphically (showing the demand and marginal revenue curves).

4–3. The BJC Company has the following demand function:

$$Q = 300 - 30(\text{price}) + 0.01(\text{income})$$

Currently, price is $\$5$ and income is $\$20,000$.
   a. Calculate the point elasticities for price and income.
   b. Is the product a normal or an inferior good?

4–4. Last year, Americans bought 5,000 Ferraris. The average retail price of a Ferrari was
$100,000. Statistical studies have shown that the price elasticity of demand is 0.4. Assume
the demand curve is linear. Estimate it using the above information.
  a. Is demand elastic or inelastic?
  b. What will happen to revenue if the company raises its price?

Solutions to Self-Evaluation Problems

4–1. a. $\eta_{P_A}^{Q_A} = Absolute\ Value \dfrac{-(18-15)}{(3.4-4)} \times \dfrac{3.7}{16.5} = \dfrac{3}{0.6} \times \dfrac{3.7}{16.5} = 1.12$

  b. $\eta_I^{Q_A} = \dfrac{(17.5-15)}{(2250-2000)} \times \dfrac{2125}{16.25} = \dfrac{2.5}{250} \times \dfrac{2125}{16.25} = 1.307$

  c. $\eta_{P_B}^{Q_A} = \dfrac{(16-15)}{(3-2.5)} \times \dfrac{2.75}{15.5} = \dfrac{1}{0.5} \times \dfrac{2.75}{15.5} = 0.354$

  d. Product A is normal because an increase in income leads to an increase in demand for the
  product. Products A and B are substitutes because the cross-price elasticity is positive.
  Consumers substitute away from B and purchase more A when the price of B increases.

  e. No, the firm is not charging the revenue maximizing price for Product A. Revenue maximization occurs at the price/quantity where MR = 0 and the corresponding own-price
  elasticity is one. But here we see that $\eta_{P_A}^{Q_A} = 1.12 > 1$. Therefore, the current price is
  higher than the revenue maximizing price, while the current quantity is lower than the
  revenue maximizing quantity.

  f. Start with the original demand function, $Q_A = 10 - 5P_A + 2P_B + 0.01I$ and insert the
  initial values for P_B and I. Solve for P_A. This produces the demand curve for Product A:
  $P_A = 7 - .2Q$. The MR function has the same intercept at the demand curve, but twice
  the negative slope: MR = 7 − .4Q. At the initial quantity of 15, MR = $1. Producing an
  additional unit increases revenue by $1.

4–2. The demand curve is given by $P = 90 - .30Q$. The marginal revenue curve is MR = 90 −
.60Q. Revenue maximization occurs where MR = 0. Thus the revenue maximizing quantity, Q^*, is

$$90 - .60Q^* = 0$$
$$Q^* = 150.$$

The revenue maximizing price is found by inserting Q^* into the demand function:

$$P^* = 90 - (.3 \times 150) = \$45.$$

Revenue maximization occurs at the midpoint of the demand curve, where the price elasticity is equal to one (unitary elasticity). The goal of the firm is to maximize profits, not revenue. Thus the firm is not at the optimal price unless the marginal cost of production = $0.
  Graphically the analysis is pictured as follows:

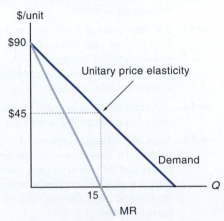

4–3. a. The current quantity demanded is 350. Thus, the price elasticity is 30(5/350) = .429. The income elasticity is .01($20,000/350) = .571.

      b. The product is a normal good (income elasticity is positive).

4–4. If the demand curve is linear, it must take the form $P = a - bQ$. To estimate a and b we use the information provided. The elasticity of demand can be expressed as:

$$\eta = abs\,[(-1/b) \times (P/Q)]$$

We are told that at $P = 100,000$ and $Q = 5,000$, the elasticity of demand equals 0.4. Substituting the known values, solve for b:

$$0.4 = (1/b) \times (100,000/5,000)$$
$$b = 50$$

$$100,000 = a - 50 \times 5,000$$
$$a = 350,000$$

Review Questions

4–1. What is the difference between a demand function and a demand curve?

4–2. How will each of the following affect the position of the demand curve for DVD players?
    a. An increase in the price of DVD movies.
    b. A decrease in the price of DVD players.
    c. An increase in per capita income.
    d. A decrease in the price of movie tickets.

4–3. If the demand for a product is inelastic, what will happen to total revenue if price is increased? Explain.

4–4. What are the signs of cross elasticities for substitute products? Explain.

4–5. Distinguish between normal and inferior goods.

4–6. Is it true that a normal good must have an income elasticity that is more than one? Explain.

4–7. Suppose that the price of Product A falls from $20 to $15. In response, the quantity demanded of A increases from 100 to 120 units. The quantity demanded for Product B increases from 200 to 300. Calculate the arc cross elasticity between Product B and Product A. Is B a substitute or complement for A? Explain. Does Product A follow the "law of demand"? Explain.

4–8. How can cross elasticities be used to help define the relevant firms in an industry?

4–9. Suppose the price of heating oil increases significantly. Discuss the likely short-run and long-run effects.

4–10. The Alexander Machine Tool Company faces a linear demand curve. Currently, it is selling at a price and quantity where its demand elasticity is 1.5. Consultants have suggested that the company expand output because it is facing an elastic demand curve. Do you agree with this recommendation?

4–11. For three years in a row, income among consumers has increased. Alexander Machine Tool has had sales increases in each of these three years. Does Alexander Machine Tool produce inferior or normal goods? Forecasts predict that income will continue to rise in the future. Should Alexander Machine Tool anticipate that demand for its products will continue to rise? Explain.

4–12. The cross elasticity between Product A and Product B is 10. Do you think that Product A is likely to face an elastic or inelastic demand curve? Explain.

4–13. Vijay Bhattacharya is interested in estimating the industry demand curve for a particular product. He has gathered data on historical prices and quantities sold in the industry. He knows that the industry supply curve has been stable over the entire period. He is considering estimating a regression between price and quantity and using the result as an estimate of the demand curve. Do you think this technique will result in a good estimate of the demand curve? Explain.

4–14. Maria Tejada, a civil engineer, uses data on population trends to forecast the use of a particular highway. Her forecasts indicate severe road congestion by the year 2010. She suggests building a new road. Comment on this approach.

4–15. Alexander Machine Tool faces the demand curve $P = \$70 - 0.001Q$. What price and quantity maximize total revenue? What is the price elasticity at this point?

4–16. Studies indicate that the income elasticity of demand for servants in the United States exceeds 1. Nevertheless, the number of servants has been decreasing during the last 75 years, while incomes have risen significantly. How can these facts be reconciled?

4–17. Prior to a price increase, the price and quantity demanded for a product were $10 and 100, respectively. After the price increase, they were $12 and 90.
   a. Calculate the arc elasticity of demand.
   b. Is the demand elastic or inelastic over this region?
   c. What happened to total revenue?

4–18. Define marginal revenue. Explain why marginal revenue is less than price when demand curves slope downward.

4–19. In 1991, Rochester, New York, had a serious ice storm. Electric power was out in houses for days. The demand for power generators increased dramatically. Yet the local merchants did not increase their prices, even though they could have sold the units for substantially higher prices. Why do you think the merchants adopted this policy?

4–20. Seven teenagers, four boys and three girls, were given $200 each to go on a shopping spree. An advertising agency, which specializes in youth markets, gave the teens the money. An account executive accompanied the teens while they were shopping. The agency wanted to learn not only what they bought, but also what they talked about to see what was on their minds. "It's not so much to stay in tune with trends, because trends are elusive. It's more what's really happening with teens and what's important to them."[20]
   a. Discuss the trade-offs between sample size (7 teens), cost, and reliability of what is learned from this experiment.
   b. An agent accompanied the teens while they were shopping. Why didn't the ad agency avoid this expense and just look at what the teens bought?

4–21. Southwest Airlines estimates the short-run price elasticity of business air travel to be 2 and the long-run elasticity to be 5. Is ticket demand more elastic in the short run or long run? Does this seem reasonable? Explain.

4–22. Gasoline prices increased substantially in 2004 and 2005. What adjustments did people make to minimize the long-term effects of this price increase?

4–23. Assume that demand for product A can be expressed as $Q_A = 500 - 5P_A + 3P_B$ and demand for product B can be expressed as $Q_B = 300 - 2P_B + P_A$. Currently, market prices and quantities for these goods are $P_A = 5$, $P_B = 2$, $Q_A = 481$, and $Q_B = 301$.
   a. Suppose the price of product B increases to 3. What happens to the quantity demanded of both products?
   b. Calculate the arc cross-elasticity between product A and product B using prices for product B of 2 and 3.
   c. Are these goods substitutes or complements?

4–24. The Zenvox Television Company faces a demand function for its products that can be expressed as $Q = 4,000 - P + 0.5I$, where Q is the number of televisions, P is the price per television, and I is average monthly income. Average monthly income is currently equal to $2,000. Answer the following questions.
   a. Graph the demand curve (sometimes called the "inverse" demand curve) faced by Zenvox at the current income level. Be sure to label this and all graphs you draw carefully. On the same graph, depict marginal revenue. At what price and quantity is Zenvox's total revenue maximized? What is the marginal revenue at this point? Show the calculation.

[20]"Teens Track Retail Trends for Ad Agency (1999)," *Democrat and Chronicle* (September 5), 1E.

b. What is the price elasticity of Zenvox's demand function at the price and quantity derived in part (*a*)? Explain what this value means in words.

c. Why might Zenvox choose to produce at a price and quantity different than that derived in part (*a*)?

4–25. According to an article in *Forbes* (March 2001) teen cigarette smoking declined significantly between 1975 and 2000. The most dramatic decline occurred in the years 1975–1981. Since then teen smoking has increased in some years and declined in others. Between 1975 and 1981 there was a slight decrease in the price of cigarettes. Thus the dramatic decline in smoking is not attributable to an increase in cigarette prices. One theory is that the significant increase in gasoline prices over this period motivated many teens not to smoke.

a. Discuss how a rise in gasoline prices might affect the demand for cigarettes among teens.

b. Suppose there are two goods in the world, cigarettes and gasoline. Draw a figure that shows how an increase in gasoline prices can result in a decline in both gasoline and cigarette consumption. Use the standard consumer behavior graph with budget lines and indifference curves. Be sure to label your figure appropriately.

c. In the late 1990s the price of cigarettes increased from $2.50 per pack to $3.25 per pack. In one community during this time period, the number of packs of cigarettes consumed by teenagers fell from 10,000 to 9,000. Assume that everything except cigarette prices remained the same. Calculate the arc price elasticity among teens between these price points.

d. Calculate the total expenditures on cigarettes by the teens in part (*c*) both before and after the price increase. Did total revenue increase or fall? Discuss how this answer is implied by the arc elasticity that you calculated in part (*c*).

4–26. In an article appearing in the Dow Jones News Service on February 5, 2004, the agency cites Saudi Arabia's concern about the overproduction of oil by the OPEC cartel.

Assume the current daily demand for OPEC's oil is given by the following equation:

$$P = 50 - 0.001Q$$

where P is the price per barrel (ppb) and Q is the quantity of barrels sold daily (in thousands). *Moreover, suppose the marginal cost of producing a barrel is constant at zero.*

a. Would it surprise you to learn that OPEC's declared objective is to sell 25 million barrels a day for an average price of $25 per barrel? Why or why not? Explain. You may use a graph to support your argument.

b. Assume that after OPEC's meeting this week, the new demand for OPEC oil will be given by $P = 40 - .001Q$. Would OPEC's stated objective (25 million barrels at an overall price of $25) be attainable after this change? Explain. Assume OPEC ignores the demand shift. What's the maximum price per barrel they can charge if they decide to keep producing 25 million barrels per day? What is the profit in this case?

c. Now suppose that OPEC recognizes that demand has changed (as in [*b*]) and wants to maximize profits. What is the daily quantity they should supply? At what price? What is the profit in this case? What is the price elasticity of demand at this price/quantity combination? Explain.

4–27. As a result of strikes in Canada the world price of nickel rose by 20 percent in December. Over the same period, the quantity demanded of nickel decreased from 10,000,000 to 8,500,000 pounds worldwide. The world price of nickel was 70 cents per pound before the strikes.

a. Show graphically the effect of Canadian strikes on the market for nickel.

b. Given the information above, what's the price elasticity of the world demand for nickel over the relevant price range?

c. Did the total expenditure for nickel increase, decrease, or remain constant after the strikes? How is this consistent with your answers to parts (*a*) and (*b*)? Explain clearly and concisely.

4–28. Assume the demand curve for gasoline is given by the equation

$$P = 10 - 0.0005Q,$$

where P is the price per gallon and Q is the quantity of gasoline in gallons. Assume that the only supplier of gasoline in the region is General Gasoline Co. and that the marginal cost of production is constant at zero.

a. If the company is currently charging $4 a gallon, is it maximizing profit? If so, prove it. If not, find out the price that maximizes its profit, and compare the profits at the two prices.

b. Discuss the likely effect of the introduction of a fuel-efficient car in the region; that is, what would happen to the equilibrium quantity. Show the changes on a graph that displays (you don't need to show actual numbers) General Gasoline's pricing solution and explain.

4–29. The accompanying chart presents data on the price of fuel oil, the quantity demanded of fuel oil, and the quantity demanded for insulation.

	Fuel Oil	Insulation
Price per Gallon	Quantity Demanded (millions of gallons)	Quantity Demanded (millions of tons)
$3	100	30
$5	90	35
$7	60	40

a. Calculate the price elasticity (arc elasticity) of demand for fuel oil as its price rises from 30 to 50 cents; from 50 to 70 cents. Calculate the change in total revenue in the two cases. Explain how the changes in revenue relate to your estimated elasticities.

b. Calculate the arc cross elasticity of demand for insulation as the price of fuel oil rises from 50 to 70 cents. Are fuel oil and insulation substitutes or complements? Explain.

4–30. Japan has 4,350 miles of expressway—all toll roads. In fact, the tolls are so high that many drivers avoid using expressways. A typical 3-hour expressway trip can cost $47. A new $12 billion bridge over Tokyo Bay that takes 10 minutes and costs $25 rarely is busy. One driver prefers snaking along Tokyo's city streets for hours to save $32 in tolls.[21] Assume that the daily demand curve for a particular stretch of expressway is:

$$P = 800 \text{ yen} - .16Q$$

a. At what price-quantity point does this demand curve have a price elasticity of one?

b. Assume the government wishes to maximize its revenues from the expressway, what price should it set? And how much revenue does it generate at this price?

c. Suppose that traffic engineers have determined that the efficient utilization of this particular toll road is 4,000 cars per day. This traffic level represents an optimum tradeoff between congestion (with its associated reduction in speeds and increase in accidents) between expressways and surface roads. If 4,000 cars per day is the socially efficient utilization of the toll road, what price should be set on the toll road? And how much revenue is collected by the government?

d. Which price, the one in part (*b*), or the one in part (*a*) would you expect the government to set?

[21]J. Singer (2003), "Lonesome Highways: In Japan, Big Tolls Drive Cars Away," *The Wall Street Journal* (September 15), A1 and A15.

Appendix: Demand[22]

In the chapter, we presented formulas for arc elasticities that estimate elasticities between two points on the demand curve. This appendix shows how to calculate elasticities at single points on the demand curve. It also derives the equation for marginal revenue for a linear demand curve and discusses a special (log-linear) demand function.

Point Elasticities

Elasticities measure the percentage change in quantity demanded for a percentage change in some other variable. There are several ways to express the formula for an elasticity. One way, using price elasticity as an example, follows:

$$\eta = -(\Delta Q/Q)/(\Delta P/P) \tag{4.12}$$
$$= -(\Delta Q/\Delta P) \times (P/Q)$$

By definition, as the change in P goes to zero, the limit of the first term $(\Delta Q/\Delta P)$ is the partial derivative of Q with respect to P. At a particular point on the demand curve, the elasticity of demand for small changes in P is given by

$$\eta = -(\partial Q/\partial P) \times (P/Q) \tag{4.13}$$

As an example, consider the demand function for PTC theater tickets:

$$Q = 117 - 6.6P + 1.66P_S - 3.3P_R + 0.0066I \tag{4.14}$$

The point elasticity at the current price-quantity combination of $30 and 200 tickets is

$$\eta = -(-6.6) \times (30/200) = 1 \tag{4.15}$$

Recall that this is the value that we derived graphically in the text (see Figure 4.5).

Other point elasticities—for example, point cross elasticities—can be calculated in a similar fashion. Simply substitute the appropriate variable (e.g., the price of another product) for P in Equation (4.13).

Marginal Revenue for Linear Demand Curves

Marginal Revenue (MR) is the change in total revenue for an additional unit of quantity. As the change in quantity becomes very small, the limit of this definition is the partial derivative of total revenue with respect to Q.

Linear demand curves take the following form:

$$P = a - bQ \tag{4.16}$$

Thus, total revenue, $P \times Q$ can be written as:

$$\mathrm{TR} = (a - bQ) \times Q \tag{4.17}$$
$$= aQ - bQ^2$$

Marginal revenue is

$$\mathrm{MR} = \partial \mathrm{TR}/\partial Q = a - 2bQ \tag{4.18}$$

---

[22]This appendix requires elementary knowledge of calculus.

This formula is a line that has the same intercept as the demand curve, but with twice the negative slope.

Marginal Revenue and Demand Elasticity

In this section, we derive the relation between marginal revenue and demand elasticity. This relation is useful in a number of contexts. For example, it underlies a formula that we use in Chapter 7 to analyze how a firm's optimal price markup over cost relates to the product's demand elasticity.

By definition:

$$\text{TR} = PQ \tag{4.19}$$
$$\text{MR} = \partial\text{TR}/\partial Q = (\partial/\partial Q \times Q) + P$$

Multiply the quantity in parentheses by P/P:

$$\text{MR} = (\partial P/\partial Q \times Q) \times (P/P) + P \tag{4.20}$$
$$= (\partial P/\partial Q \times Q/P) \times P + P$$
$$= P \times [1 - 1/\eta]$$

Equation (4.20) indicates that marginal revenue is equal to price when demand is perfectly elastic. In this case, the firm can sell one more unit at the market price without having to lower the price. MR falls as the elasticity decreases and is negative when demand is inelastic ($\eta < 1$).

Log-Linear Demand Functions

The following demand function is frequently used in empirical demand estimation:

$$Q = \lambda P^{\alpha} I^{\gamma} \tag{4.21}$$

where Q is the quantity demanded
          P is price
          I is income

(Other variables such as advertising and the price of other goods are commonly included as other explanatory variables.) An important property of this demand function is that the *price and income elasticities are constant* (they do not vary along the demand function) and are equal to $-\alpha$ and γ, respectively. In particular:

$$\eta = -(\partial Q/\partial P) \times (P/Q) \tag{4.22}$$
$$= -(\lambda\alpha P^{\alpha-1}I^{\gamma}) \times (P/\lambda P^{\alpha}I^{\gamma})$$
$$= -\alpha$$

Similarly, γ is the income elasticity.

Taking the natural logarithm of the demand function in Equation (4.21) yields

$$\ln Q = \ln\lambda + \alpha\ln P + \gamma\ln I \tag{4.23}$$

This equation is linear in the logarithms; it thus can be estimated by standard regression analysis using data on Q, P, and I. The estimated coefficients α and γ are estimates of the price and income elasticities. Other types of elasticities—for example, cross elasticities—can be estimated by including other variables in the demand equation.

Production and Cost

LEARNING OBJECTIVES

1. Explain what is meant by a production function.
2. Distinguish between returns to scale and returns to a factor.
3. Create a graphical analysis of the cost-minimizing input mix and explain how it is affected by changes in relative prices of inputs.
4. Define and describe the relationship among total, marginal, and average costs.
5. Describe the connection between production and cost functions.
6. Distinguish between short- and long-run costs curves.
7. Define fixed and variable costs and their role in decision making.
8. Explain long-run costs, sources of economies and diseconomies of scale and scope, and the notion of minimum efficient scale.
9. Explain why MR = MC at the profit maximizing output.
10. Understand how many units of a factor (such as labor) a firm should purchase at different factor prices.

The global demand for steel has increased in recent years due in part to major construction projects in countries such as China and India. Construction crews were particularly busy in China on projects related to the 2008 Beijing Olympics, the 2010 Shanghai World Exposition, and new housing. While the world production of steel also has increased, the net result has been an increase in steel prices from their historic levels. In the early 1990s, steel sold for under $100 per ton. In July 2014, the price was $740 per ton. This more than sevenfold increase in the price of steel far exceeds the rate of inflation, which was about 70 percent over the same period. Steel prices not only increased over this period but also displayed high volatility. In spring 2002 the price was as low as $222, but by fall 2004 it had increased to above $700. It subsequently retreated to under $500 in late 2005, but by mid-2008 exceeded $1,200.[1]

Automobile manufacturers are a major user of steel. High steel prices provide strong incentives to these companies to find ways to mitigate the price increase, for example, by substituting away from steel toward relatively less expensive production materials. Consider their actions during the 1990s when steel prices began their recent assent. In 1994, domestic steel

[1]Steel prices are from steelbenchmarker.com.

prices increased as the U.S. economy recovered from a recession.[2] Indeed, the steel market was the strongest it had been in 20 years: Specifically, steel prices had risen from below $90 to over $135 per ton between 1992 and 1994. After significant price increases earlier in the year, domestic steel companies were planning to increase sheet-steel prices by another 10 percent at year's end. In the tight electrogalvanized markets, price increases as high as 20 percent were expected. (In fact, in 1995, prices exceeded $142 per ton.)

To counter the effects of the increase in domestic steel prices, U.S. auto companies actively pursued new overseas suppliers. For instance, in July 1994, General Motors invited bids for sheet steel from foreign companies such as Sidmar, Solldac, Thyssen, and Klockner. The increases in steel prices affected both companies' pricing and output decisions. The increases in steel prices also placed pressure on U.S. automakers to use other raw materials in the production process. For example, auto companies increased their use of aluminum in engines, transmissions, body components, heating and cooling systems, and suspension systems in 1995.[3] (Aluminum prices had been relatively stable; they were $.534 per pound at the beginning of 1992 and $.533 in January 1994.) Potential applications focused on replacing cast iron or steel with aluminum. In addition, auto companies increased research on new ways to use plastics, magnesium, and recyclable materials in their production process.

This example raises a number of questions that are of interest to managers. First, how do firms choose among substitutable inputs in the production process? How does the optimal input mix change with changes in the input prices? How do changes in input prices affect the ultimate cost of production and the output choices of firms? In this chapter we address these and related questions. Major topics include production functions, choice of inputs, costs, profit maximization, cost estimation, and factor demand curves. In the appendix, we derive the factor-balance equation.

Production Functions

A *production function* is a descriptive relation that links inputs with output. It specifies the *maximum* feasible output that can be produced for given amounts of inputs. Production functions are determined by the available technology. Production functions can be expressed mathematically. For instance, given current technology, an automobile supplier is able to transform inputs like steel, aluminum, plastics, and labor into finished auto parts. In its most general form, the production function is expressed as

$$Q = f(x_1, x_2, \ldots x_n) \tag{5.1}$$

where Q is the quantity produced and $x_1, x_2, \ldots x_n$ are the various inputs used in the production process.

---

[2]Details of this example are from "General Motors Eyes Imports to Counter Price Increases," *Metal Bulletin* (July 11, 1994), 21.

[3]A. Wrigley (1994), "Automotive Aluminum Use Climbing in 1995's Models: Automotive Applications Will Use Some 120 Million Lbs. in 1995," *American Metal Market* (August 9), 1.

MANAGERIAL APPLICATIONS

Increasing Returns to Scale Motivates Amazon to Invest in Large Warehouses

The *Law of Increased Dimensions* (the "Container Principle") implies that the doubling of the height and width of a container leads to more than a proportionate increase in cubic capacity (volume). The corresponding increasing returns to scale have led Amazon.com to invest in huge warehouses that are capable of storing hundreds of thousands of items. As of 2014, Amazon owned or leased over 84 million square feet of space for housing its fulfillment and data centers. Its largest fulfillment centers are over 1.2 million square feet in size. These large centers are located near major airports, which are used in the shipping of orders. The resulting cost efficiencies deriving from the size and location of these centers have contributed to Amazon's performance.

Source: Amazon.com (2014), *Form 10-K for Fiscal Year Ended December 31, 2013* (January 31)

To simplify the exposition, suppose that the auto part in this example is produced from just two inputs—steel and aluminum. An example of a specific production function[4] in this context is

$$Q = S^{1/2}A^{1/2} \tag{5.2}$$

where S is pounds of steel, A is pounds of aluminum, and Q is the number of auto parts produced.

With this production function, 100 pounds of steel and 100 pounds of aluminum will produce 100 auto parts over the relevant time period, 400 pounds of steel and 100 pounds of aluminum will produce 200 auto parts, and so on.[5]

Returns to Scale

The term *returns to scale* refers to the relation between output and the *proportional variation of all inputs* taken together. With *constant returns to scale,* a 1 percent change in all inputs results in a 1 percent change in output. For example, Equation (5.2) presents a production function with constant returns to scale. If the firm uses 100 pounds of each input, it produces 100 auto parts. If the firm increases both inputs by 1 percent to 101 pounds, it produces 101 auto parts.[6]

With *increasing returns to scale,* a 1 percent change in all inputs results in a greater than 1 percent change in output. An example of such a production function is

$$Q = S A \tag{5.3}$$

Here, 100 pounds of steel and 100 pounds of aluminum produce 10,000 auto parts, while 101 pounds of steel and aluminum produce 10,201 auto parts (a 2 percent increase in output). Firms often experience increasing returns to scale over at least some range of output. One major reason is that a firm operating on a larger scale can engage in more extensive specialization. For instance, if an automobile company has only three employees and three machines, each employee and each machine has to

---

[4]This production function is an example of a Cobb-Douglas production function, which takes the general form $Q = \lambda S^{\alpha}A^{\gamma}$. Cobb-Douglas production functions are used frequently in empirical estimation. Not all firms, however, have production processes that are well described by this particular type of production function.

[5]$100^{1/2} \times 100^{1/2} = 10 \times 10 = 100$, and $400^{1/2} \times 100^{1/2} = 20 \times 10 = 200$.

[6]$[(100 \times 1.01)^{1/2}] \times [(100 \times 1.01)^{1/2}] = 101$.

perform a myriad of tasks for the company to produce automobiles. Given the broad array of tasks that each worker and machine has to perform, efficiency is likely to be low. In contrast, a large firm employing thousands of workers and machines can engage in much greater specialization. (As noted in Chapter 3, specialization often produces efficiency gains.)

With *decreasing returns to scale,* a 1 percent change in all inputs results in a less than 1 percent change in output. An example is

$$Q = S^{1/3}A^{1/3} \tag{5.4}$$

The likelihood that a firm will choose to operate where it experiences decreasing returns to scale is open to debate. Some economists argue that firms should seldom display decreasing returns to scale. If a facility of a given size can produce a given output, why can't the firm simply replicate that facility and produce twice the output with twice the inputs? Indeed, most empirical studies on the subject suggest that the typical firm initially experiences increasing returns to scale, followed by constant returns to scale over a quite broad range of output. On the other hand, several empirical studies indicate that some firms probably do experience decreasing returns to scale.[7] Also, casual observation suggests that some larger firms suffer from inefficiencies to a greater extent than do smaller firms—for example, coordination and control problems become more severe as a firm becomes larger.

In our examples, the returns to scale are the same over all ranges of output. For instance, Equation (5.2) always displays constant returns to scale, while Equation (5.4) always displays decreasing returns. Most production functions vary in returns to scale over the range of output. Most frequently, production functions have increasing returns to scale when output is relatively low, followed by constant returns to scale as output continues to increase, and possibly decreasing returns to scale when output is high. Other combinations are possible.

Returns to a Factor

Returns to a factor refers to the relation between output and the variation in a single input, *holding other inputs fixed.* Returns to a factor can be expressed as total, marginal, or average quantities. The *total product* of an input is the schedule of output obtained as that input increases, holding other inputs fixed. The *marginal product* of an input is the change in total output associated with a one-unit change in the input, holding other inputs fixed. Finally, the *average product* is the total product divided by the number of units of the input employed.

To illustrate these concepts, consider the production function in Equation (5.2): $Q = S^{1/2}A^{1/2}$. Table 5.1 presents the total, marginal, and average product of S, holding A fixed at 9.[8] For this production function, total product increases as S increases; marginal product, however, declines. This means that although total product increases with S, it does so at a decreasing rate. Average product also decreases over the entire range.

[7]For example, E. Berndt, A. Friedlaender, and J. Chiang (1990), "Interdependent Pricing and Markup Behavior: An Empirical Analysis of GM, Ford, and Chrysler," working paper, National Bureau of Economic Research, Cambridge, MA.

[8]The production function assumes that production does not have to take place in discrete units. For instance, output might be expressed in tons; clearly production in fractions of tons is possible.

Units of S	Units of A	Total Product of S	Marginal Product of S	Average Product of S
1	9	3.00	3.00	3.00
2	9	4.24	1.24	2.12
3	9	5.20	0.96	1.73
4	9	6.00	0.80	1.50
5	9	6.70	0.70	1.34

Table 5.1   Returns to a Factor

This table shows the total, marginal, and average products of steel for the production function $Q = S^{1/2} A^{1/2}$. Aluminum is held fixed at 9 units. The total product of S is the total output for each level of S; the marginal product of S is the incremental output from one additional unit of S; and the average product of S is output divided by the total units of S.

More generally, marginal and average products do not have to decline over the entire range of output. Indeed, many production functions display increasing marginal and average products over some ranges. However, most production functions reach a point after which the marginal product of an input declines. This observation often is called the *law of diminishing returns* (or law of diminishing marginal product), which states that the marginal product of a variable factor eventually will decline as its use is increased. To illustrate this principle, consider the classic example of farming a plot of land. Land is fixed at 1 acre, and no output can be harvested without any workers. If 10 bushels of grain can be produced by one worker, the marginal product of the first unit of labor is 10 bushels. The change in output might be even greater as the firm moves from one to two workers. For instance, two workers might be able to produce 25 bushels of grain by working together and specializing in various tasks. The marginal product of labor is 15 bushels and thus, over this range, marginal

MANAGERIAL APPLICATIONS

Studying for an Exam—the Law of Diminishing Returns

Your performance on the CPA exam depends on both your effort and aptitude in the subject. Your aptitude is largely a fixed input (e.g., it is hard to increase your basic IQ). Effort on the other hand is something you can control and vary. For example, if you are preparing for the CPA exam, you could spend many or few hours reading books and working problems. The choice is yours. If you exert no effort, you are unlikely to do well on the exam and easily could fail. If you study, your performance is likely to improve. Initially, as you begin to allocate additional hours to studying for the exam, your rate of improvement might be quite large. For instance, you might expect to increase your exam score by 20 points if you study one versus no hours. As you continue to spend more time on studying for the exam, your rate of improvement (marginal product of effort) is likely to decline—you will reach a point of diminishing returns. Indeed at some point your exam score could decline with additional effort as you become too tired to take the exam—the marginal product of effort becomes negative. Basic economics says that you should study for an exam up to the point where the incremental benefits of studying additional time are equal to the incremental costs. The law of diminishing returns implies that the incremental benefits will eventually become smaller and possibly negative. The incremental costs of studying an additional hour depend on your opportunity cost of time—for what else could you use the time? It is unlikely to be optimal for you to spend additional time studying for the CPA exam if that causes you to neglect your other professional responsibilities.

Figure 5.1 Returns to a Factor: A Common Case

This figure illustrates a common pattern for total product, marginal product, and returns to a factor. In the lower panel, marginal product rises, then falls, and eventually becomes negative. When marginal product is rising (between zero and S_1), total product increases at an increasing rate (the curve is convex) in the lower panel. When marginal product is falling but positive (between S_1 and S_2), total product continues to increase but does so at a decreasing rate. Beyond S_2, marginal product is negative and total product falls with additional output. Average product is rising where it is below marginal product and is falling where it is above marginal product. Average and marginal products are equal where average product is at a maximum.

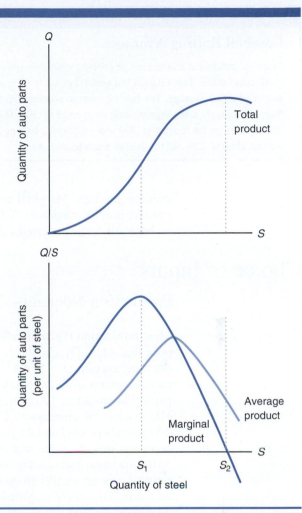

product is increasing. Eventually, as the firm continues to add more workers, while holding land fixed, output will grow at a slower rate. At some point, total output might actually decline with additional workers because of coordination or congestion problems. In this case, the marginal product is negative.

Figure 5.1 illustrates returns to a factor in this common case. The upper panel displays total product, and the lower panel displays marginal and average products. As the use of input S goes from zero to S_1, marginal product rises. Over this range total product is convex—total product increases at an increasing rate.[9] At S_1, diminishing returns set in and the marginal product begins to fall. Between S_1 and S_2, marginal product is positive and so total product continues to increase. However, it does so at a decreasing rate (the curve is concave). Beyond S_2, marginal product is negative, hence total output falls with increases in S. Average product is rising where marginal product is above average product and is falling where marginal product is below

[9]Technical note: The marginal product at a point is equal to the slope of the total product curve at that point ($MP = \partial TP/\partial S$). Thus, marginal product is decreasing when the total cost curve is concave and increasing when it is convex.

MANAGERIAL APPLICATIONS

Baseball Batting Averages

Marginal product is above average product when average product is rising and below average product when average product is falling. This relation is a general property of marginals and averages. A useful illustration is a baseball player's batting average. The batting average is defined as the number of hits divided by the number of times at bat. Suppose a player starts a game with an average of .300. If the player gets two hits with four at bats, the marginal batting average for the day is .500 and the player's batting average must rise. If the player gets one hit with four at bats, the marginal is .250 and the overall average must drop.

---

average product. Marginal product and average product are equal where average product is at its maximum.[10] This relation is a general rule.[11] The accompanying box on baseball batting averages illustrates the intuition behind this relation.

Choice of Inputs

Production Isoquants

Most production functions allow some substitution among inputs. For example, suppose that Alexi Dyachenko is chief operating officer, managing a firm with the production function $Q = S^{1/2}A^{1/2}$, and he wants to produce 100 auto parts. In this case, there are many different combinations of steel and aluminum that will yield 100 auto parts. For instance, 100 auto parts can be produced using 100 pounds of steel and 100 pounds of aluminum, 25 pounds of steel and 400 pounds of aluminum, or 400 pounds of steel and 25 pounds of aluminum. Figure 5.2 displays all the possible combinations of inputs that can be used to produce exactly 100 auto parts. Obviously, 100 auto parts also could be produced with more inputs—points above or to the right of a point on this isoquant—but those points represent inefficient production methods. This curve is called an *isoquant* (*iso,* meaning the same, and *quant* from quantity). An isoquant shows all input combinations that produce the same quantity assuming efficient production. There is a different isoquant for each possible level of production. Figure 5.2 shows the isoquants for 100, 200, and 300 auto parts.

Production functions vary in terms of how easily inputs can be substituted one for another. In some cases, no substitution is possible. Suppose that in order to produce 100 auto parts you must have 100 pounds of aluminum and 100 pounds of steel, to produce 200 auto parts you must have 200 pounds of aluminum and 200 pounds of steel, and so on. Having extra steel or aluminum without the other metal yields no additional output—they must be used in *fixed proportions.* As shown in Figure 5.3, isoquants from fixed-proportion production functions are shaped as right angles. At the other extreme are *perfect* substitutes: The inputs can be substituted freely one for another. Suppose that one auto part always can be produced using either 2 pounds of steel or 2 pounds of aluminum. In this case, the firm can produce 100 auto parts by using either 200 pounds of aluminum or 200 pounds of steel, or any combination in

---

[10]Graphically, marginal product is the slope of a line drawn tangent to the total product curve of that level of output; average product is the slope of the line connecting a point on the total product curve with the origin.

[11]Averages and marginals also are equal when the average is at a minimum.

Figure 5.2 Isoquants

An *isoquant* displays all possible ways to produce a given quantity. There is a different isoquant for each possible level of production. This figure shows the isoquants for 100, 200, and 300 auto parts for the production function $Q = S^{1/2}A^{1/2}$.

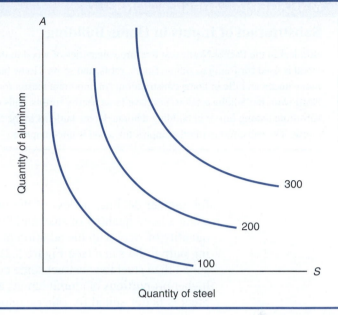

between. As shown in Figure 5.3, the corresponding isoquant is a straight line. Most production technologies imply isoquants that are between these two extremes. As depicted in Figure 5.3, typical isoquants have curvature, but are not right angles. The degree of substitutability of the inputs is reflected in the curvature: The closer the isoquant is to a right angle (the more convex), the lower the degree of substitutability.

Generally, isoquants are convex to the origin (as pictured in the center panel in Figure 5.3—the typical case). Convexity implies that the substitutability of one input

Figure 5.3 Isoquants for Fixed Proportion Production Functions, Perfect Substitutes, and the Normal Case

Production functions vary in terms of how easily inputs can be substituted for one another. In some cases, inputs must be used in *fixed proportions* and no substitution is possible. Here, isoquants take the shape of right angles. At the other extreme are *perfect substitutes,* where the inputs can be freely substituted for one another. Here, isoquants are straight lines. Most production functions have isoquants that are between the two extremes. The isoquants in the normal case have curvature but are not right angles.

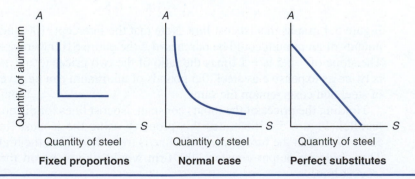

for another declines as less of the first input is used. In our example, if the firm is using a large quantity of steel and little aluminum, it can eliminate a relatively large quantity of steel with the addition of only a small quantity of aluminum while keeping output the same (see Figure 5.2). In this case, aluminum would be much better suited than steel to construct some components of the auto part. But as the firm uses higher proportions of aluminum, its ability to substitute aluminum for steel declines: Steel is better suited for other components. Most production processes display this property.

Isocost Lines

Given that there are many ways to produce a given level of output, how does Alexi choose the most efficient input mix? The answer depends on the costs of the inputs. Suppose that the firm faces competitive input markets and can buy as much of each input as it wants at prevailing market prices. The price of steel is denoted P_s, whereas the price of aluminum is denoted P_a. Total cost (TC) is equal to the sum of the quantities of each input used in the production process times their respective prices. Thus,

$$\text{TC} = P_s S + P_a A \tag{5.5}$$

Isocost lines display all combinations of S and A with the same cost. Suppose $P_s = \$.50$ per pound and $P_a = \$1$ per pound, and the given cost level is $100. In this case,

$$\$100 = \$.50S + \$A \tag{5.6}$$

or equivalently,

$$A = 100 - 0.5S \tag{5.7}$$

Figure 5.4 graphs this isocost line. Note that the intercept, 100, indicates how many pounds of aluminum could be purchased if the entire $100 were spent on aluminum. The slope of -0.5 is -1 times the ratio of the two prices (P_s/P_a): Since aluminum is twice as expensive as steel, 0.5 pounds of aluminum can be given up for 1 pound of steel and costs remain the same.

Holding the prices of the inputs constant, isocost lines for different cost levels are parallel. Figure 5.4 illustrates this property using the isocost lines for $100 and $200. Note that the further away the line is from the origin, the higher the total cost. Thus, holding output constant, the firm would like to be on the lowest possible isocost line.

Figure 5.4 Isocost Curves

Isocost lines display all combinations of inputs that cost the same. In this example, P_s = $.50 per pound and P_a = $1 per pound. The figure shows isocost lines for $100 and $200 of expenditures. The slope of an isocost line is −1 times the ratio of the input prices—in this example, −0.5. Isocost lines for different expenditure levels are parallel.

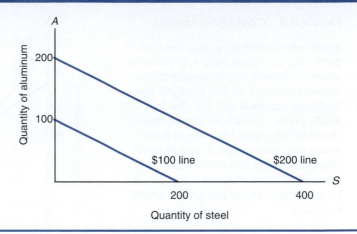

The slope of an isocost line changes with changes in the ratio of the input prices. As depicted in Figure 5.5, if the price of steel increases to $1, the line becomes steeper (slope of −1). Here, the firm must give up 1 pound of aluminum to obtain 1 pound of steel. Alternatively, if the price of steel falls to $.25 (not depicted in the figure), the line becomes flatter (slope of −0.25). In this case, the firm has to give up only 0.25 pound of aluminum for every pound of steel. Similarly, the slope of the line also changes with changes in the price of aluminum. What determines the slope of the line are the *relative prices* (recall the slope is $-P_s/P_a$).

Cost Minimization

For any given level of output, Q^*, Alexi will want to choose the input mix that minimizes total costs. As shown in Figure 5.6, the cost-minimizing mix (S^*, A^*) occurs at the point of tangency between the isoquant for Q^* with the isocost line. Alexi

Figure 5.5 Isocost Lines and Changes in Input Prices

This figure depicts the effect of changes in input prices on the slopes of isocost lines. The solid line shows the isocost line when the price of aluminum is $1 and the price of steel is $.50. The dotted line shows the isocost line where the prices of both inputs are $1. Total cost in each case is $100.

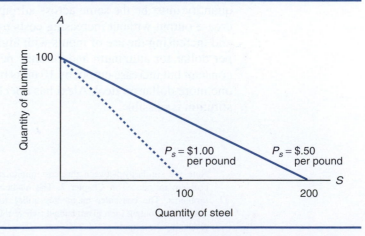

Figure 5.6 Cost Minimization

The input mix that minimizes the cost of producing any given output, Q^*, occurs where an isocost line is tangent to the relevant isoquant. In this example, the tangency occurs at (S^*, A^*). The firm would prefer to be on an isocost line closer to the origin. However, the firm would not have sufficient resources to produce Q^*. The firm could produce Q^* using other input mixes, such as (S', A'). However, the cost of production would increase.

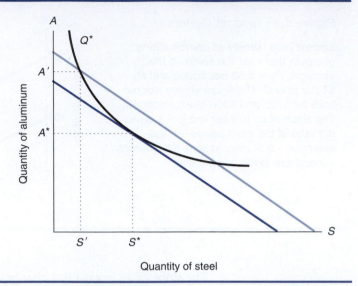

Quantity of steel

would like to produce the output less expensively (using an isocost line closer to the origin). However, lower-cost production is not feasible. Alexi could select other input mixes to produce Q^*.[12] But any other input mix would place the firm on a higher isocost line. Consider the combination (S', A') in Figure 5.6. This combination of inputs also produces Q^* units of output. Yet this output can be produced at a lower cost by using less aluminum and more steel.

In the appendix to this chapter, we show that at the optimal input mix, the following condition holds

$$MP_s/P_s = MP_a/P_a \qquad (5.8)$$

where MP_i is the marginal product of input i. (Recall that the marginal product of an input is described in Table 5.1.) Condition (5.8) has a straightforward interpretation. The ratio of the marginal product to price indicates how much additional output can be obtained by spending an extra dollar on the input. At the optimal output mix this quantity must be the same across all inputs. Otherwise, it would be possible to increase output without increasing costs by reducing the use of inputs with low ratios and increasing the use of inputs with high ratios. For instance, if the ratio is 10 units per dollar for aluminum and 20 units per dollar for steel, the firm could hold costs constant but increase output by 10 units by spending one less dollar on aluminum and one more dollar on steel. Alexi has not chosen an optimal input mix when such substitution is possible.

---

[12]Note the similarity between this cost minimization problem and the consumer's utility maximization problem introduced in Chapter 2. The mathematics are the same—both are constrained optimization problems. The consumer maximizes utility for a given budget. Cost minimization is equivalent to maximizing output for a given budget (where the budget is that associated with the lowest-cost method of producing the output).

Figure 5.7 Optimal Input Mix and Changes in Input Prices

This figure illustrates how the optimal input mix for producing a given output, Q^*, changes as the price of an input increases. In this example, the price of steel increases and the firm uses less steel and more aluminum to produce the output. This effect is called the *substitution effect*. The strength of the substitution effect depends on the curvature of the isoquant. The greater the curvature, the less the firm will substitute between the two inputs.

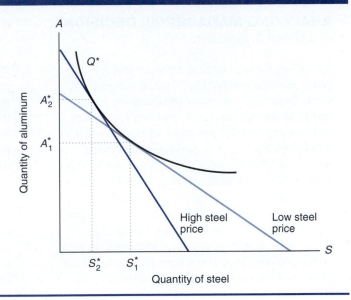

Changes in Input Prices

An increase in the relative price of an input will motivate Alexi to use less of that input and more of other inputs. Figure 5.7 illustrates how the optimal input mix for producing Q^* changes as the price of steel increases: Alexi chooses less steel and more aluminum to produce the output. This effect is called the *substitution effect*. The strength of the substitution effect depends on the curvature of the isoquant. The

MANAGERIAL APPLICATIONS

$15 per hour Minimum Wage Increases the Relative Cost of Labor at SeaTac Airport

The minimum wage for hotel and car services employees working near SeaTac Airport (Seattle Washington) increased to $15 per hour at the beginning of 2014, making it the highest in the country. The new minimum was more than twice the Federal minimum of $7.25 per hour.

Economic theory predicts that SeaTac hotels and car rental agencies will respond to the higher relative price of labor by substituting capital for labor. For example, a restaurant owner would have increased incentives to convert to having customers order food with tablet computers located at each table (an increasingly common practice), while a car rental agency would have increased incentives to use kiosks and other technologies for serving customers.

It is too early to assess all the effects this increase in the minimum wage will actually have on employment in the area. It depends in part on the ability of companies to substitute capital for labor. Some local hotel managers have stated that they are in a service industry and are highly unlikely to substitute capital for labor due to the higher wage rate. The Clarion Hotel, however, within six weeks of the new law, had closed their full-service restaurant and was considering replacing it with a less labor-intensive café.

Many people have been watching this "experiment" in increasing the minimum wage to such a high level. They will have to wait to observe the long-run effects, since it takes time for businesses to convert to more capital-intensive processes, such as using tablet computers for food ordering.

Source: A. Martinez (2014), "$15 Wage Floor Slowly Takes Hold in SeaTac," *Seattle Times* (February 13).

ANALYZING MANAGERIAL DECISIONS: *Choosing the Mix of People and Machines in a Retail Supercenter*

You manage a large retail supercenter that sells groceries and other products to 30,000 customers per week. Currently, you employ 80 check-out clerks and 10 automated check-out machines (customers scan and pay for their purchases without a clerk's assistance). Each clerk is paid wages and fringe benefits of $800 per week. It also costs you $800 per week to lease each machine (price includes installation, software support, and servicing). A vendor has offered to lease you additional machines at this price. You estimate that by leasing 10 more machines you can meet your service requirements with 30 fewer clerks. Should you lease the additional machines or continue to service your customers with your current input mix?

1. You conduct additional analysis and estimate that you can service the 30,000 customers with the following combinations of clerks and machines. Calculate the total costs for each of these combinations. What combination of inputs serves the customers at the lowest possible cost?

Clerks	Machines
80	10
50	20
30	30
22	40
15	50
12	60

2. Plot the input combinations in the table on a graph that contains clerks on the vertical axis and machines on the horizontal axis. Connect the points by lines to approximate an isoquant as pictured in Figure 5.6. Add the cost minimizing isocost curve to the graph (you can derive this line from the input prices and the total cost of the low-cost input combination). How do the slopes of the isocost curve and isoquant compare at the optimal input combination?

3. Suppose that the marginal product of clerks at the optimal input combination is 500. Explain in words what this means. What is the marginal product of machines at this point? Explain why.

4. Suppose that the cost of leasing a machine declines to $500 per week. What is your new optimal input mix? How does this affect your graph?

5. Are there any other factors that should be considered in making this decision on the optimal mix of machines and clerks Discuss briefly.

greater the curvature, the less Alexi will substitute between the two inputs for any given change in prices. The substitution effect helps explain the reactions of automobile companies to the 1994 increases in domestic steel prices. These companies increased their use of foreign steel. They also searched for additional ways to replace steel with other inputs such as aluminum.

Costs

We have analyzed how firms should choose their input mix to minimize costs of production. We now extend this analysis to focus more specifically on costs of producing different levels of output. Analysis of these costs plays an important role in output and pricing decisions.

Figure 5.8   Cost Curves

This figure displays the total, marginal, and average cost curves of a hypothetical firm. The upper panel pictures total cost. Total cost increases with output. Between zero and Q_1, total cost increases but at a decreasing rate (the curve is concave). As shown in the lower panel, over this range, marginal cost decreases. Past Q_1, total cost increases at an increasing rate (the curve is convex) and marginal cost increases. Average cost declines where marginal cost is below average cost and rises where marginal cost is above average cost. This relation is a general rule.

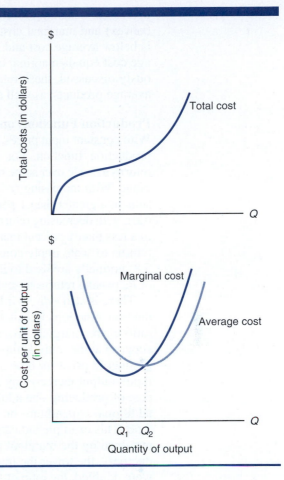

Cost Curves

The *total cost curve* depicts the relation between total costs and output. Conceptually, the total cost curve can be derived from the isoquant/isocost analysis discussed above. For each feasible level of output, there is a least-cost method of production—as depicted by the tangency between the isoquant and the isocost line. The total cost curve simply displays the cost of production associated with the isocost line and the corresponding output. For instance, if the least-cost method of producing 100 auto parts is $1,000, one point on the total cost curve is (100, $1,000). If the least-cost method of producing 200 parts is $1,500, another point is (200, $1,500). *Marginal cost* is the change in total costs associated with a one-unit change in output. *Average cost* is total cost divided by total output. Managers sometimes refer to marginal cost as incremental cost, whereas they use the term *unit cost* to refer to average cost.

Figure 5.8 displays the total, marginal, and average cost curves for a hypothetical firm. (This figure illustrates a common pattern for cost curves, although not all firms have cost curves with this same shape.) The upper panel indicates that total cost increases with output. Between zero and Q_1, total cost increases but at a decreasing rate (the curve is concave). As shown in the lower panel, over this range, marginal cost decreases.[13] Past Q_1, total cost increases at an increasing rate (the total cost curve is convex) and marginal cost increases. Average cost is declining where marginal cost is below average cost and is rising where marginal cost is above average cost. Average cost equals marginal cost where average cost is at its minimum point. As previously discussed, these relations are general rules: They apply to average costs and average products, as well as batting averages and GPAs.

Production Functions and Cost Curves

With constant input prices, the shapes of cost curves are determined by the underlying production function. For instance, if the production function displays increasing returns to scale over some range of output, long-run average cost must decline over that range. With increasing returns to scale, a 1 percent increase in input expenditures results in a greater than 1 percent increase in output and average cost must fall. In contrast, with decreasing returns to scale, a 1 percent increase in input expenditures results in a less than 1 percent increase in output and average cost must rise. Finally, constant returns to scale imply constant average cost. U-shaped curves (as pictured in Figure 5.8) normally are used to illustrate average costs. This slope suggests an initial region of increasing returns to scale, followed by decreasing returns to scale.[14]

There is also a direct link between the marginal cost curve and the underlying production function. Recall from Equation (5.8) that cost minimization requires the ratio of the marginal product to price to be equal across all inputs. For illustration, suppose at the optimal input mix to produce 100 auto parts, the ratio of the marginal product to price for both steel and aluminum is 2. By expending $1 more on either input, output increases by 2 units. The reciprocal of this ratio $(1/2)$ is their marginal cost of producing one additional unit of output—if 2 units are produced with $1 of additional expenditure on inputs, the marginal cost of producing one extra unit is $.50. This example indicates that, holding input prices constant, marginal cost is determined by the marginal productivity of the inputs: The higher their marginal productivity, the lower the marginal cost. If the marginal productivities in our example were doubled, the ratio of the marginal product to price would be 4 and the marginal cost would be $.25. The inverse relation between marginal productivity and marginal cost makes intuitive sense. If with a given increase in inputs more output can be produced, the marginal cost of producing that output is lower.

Input prices also can affect the shapes of the cost curves. For instance, a declining average cost can be motivated by discounts on large volume purchases. Similarly, a machine that produces 20,000 units might not be twice as expensive as a machine that produces only 10,000 units. Alternatively, if the firm bids up the price of inputs with large purchases, average cost can rise with increased output. Thus, the long-run average cost curve can slope upward even if the firm does not experience decreasing returns to scale.

---

[13]Technical note: The marginal cost at a point is the derivative of total cost (MC $= \partial TC/\partial Q$). Graphically, it is equal to the slope of the total cost curve at that point. Thus, marginal cost decreases when the total cost curve is concave and increases when it is convex. The average cost curve is the slope of the line connecting a point on the total cost curve with the origin.

[14]Some economists argue that the typical long-run average cost curve is flat to the right of its minimum efficient scale. Once that output is reached, additional output can be produced at a constant average cost by simply replicating the process (the production function does not experience decreasing returns to scale). But this argument presumes that organizational costs do not increase disproportionally with firm size. See P. McAfee and J. McMillan (1995), "Organizational Diseconomies of Scale," *Journal of Economics and Management Strategy* 4:3, 399–426.

MANAGERIAL APPLICATIONS

Industry Responds to Higher Metals Prices

Metals prices rose substantially between 2003 and 2004; for instance, the price of hot rolled steel increased by more than 80 percent. Manufacturing firms limited the impact of these higher raw materials prices through improved productivity and switching to less expensive substitutes. For example, some stainless steel makers began to use more chromium and manganese and less nickel. Craig Yarde of Yarde Metals in Southington, CT, said that the run-up in prices had benefited his company by increasing the market value of the 40 million pounds of metals in its inventory, mostly aluminum and stainless steel.

Source: B. Simmon (2004), "Surge in Cost of Metal Squeezes Pricing and Profits," *New York Times* (February 26), C1.

Opportunity Costs

Managers must be careful to use the correct set of input prices in constructing cost curves. In Chapter 2, we defined *opportunity cost* as the value of a resource in its next best alternative use. Current market prices for inputs more accurately reflect opportunity costs than *historical costs*. For instance, if an auto supplier purchases 1,000 pounds of aluminum for $600 and subsequently the market price increases to $900, the opportunity cost of using the aluminum is $900. If the company uses the aluminum, its replacement cost is $900. Alternatively, the current inventory could be sold to another firm for $900. In either case, the firm forgoes $900 if it uses the aluminum in its production process.

The *relevant costs* for managerial decision making are opportunity costs. It is important to include the opportunity costs of all inputs whether or not they have actually been purchased in the marketplace. For instance, if an owner spends time working in the firm, the opportunity cost is the value of the owner's time in its next best alternative use.

Short Run versus Long Run

Cost curves can be depicted for both the *short run* and the *long run*. The short run is the operating period during which at least one input (typically capital) is fixed in supply. For instance, in the short run it might be infeasible to change plant size or change the number of machines. In the long run, the firm has complete flexibility—no inputs are fixed.

The definitions of short run and long run are not based on calendar time. The length of each period depends on how long it takes the firm to vary all inputs. For a cleaning-services firm operating out of rented office space, the short run is a relatively brief period—perhaps only a few days. For a large manufacturing firm with heavy investments in long-lived specialized plant and equipment, the short run might be a relatively long time period—it might be a matter of years.

Short-run cost curves sometimes are called *operating curves* because they are used in making near-term production and pricing decisions. For these decisions, it often is appropriate to take the plant size and certain other factors as given (since these factors are beyond the control of the managers in the short term). Long-run cost curves frequently are referred to as *planning curves,* since they play a key role in longer-run planning decisions relating to plant size and equipment acquisitions.

Fixed and Variable Costs

In the short run, some costs are fixed and do not vary with output. These *fixed costs* are incurred even if the firm produces no output. For instance, the firm has to pay managers' salaries, interest on borrowed capital, lease payments, insurance premiums, and property taxes whether or not it produces any output. *Variable costs* change with the level of output. These costs include items like raw material, fuel, and certain labor costs. In the long run, all costs are variable.

Short-Run Cost Curves

Figure 5.9 displays the short-run cost curves for the TAM Corporation. For this firm, suppose that the basic plant size is fixed and that all other inputs are variable. The upper panel depicts total cost. Total cost is the sum of the fixed cost (FC) and total variable cost (TVC). The shape of the total cost curve is completely determined by the shape of the total variable cost curve. Fixed costs simply shift up the location of the curve. Between 0 and Q_1, the total cost curve is concave. Over this range, the marginal productivity of variable factors increases (assuming fixed input prices). Past Q_1, the total cost curve is convex and the marginal productivity of variable factors decreases. This type of pattern is expected given the law of diminishing returns. At low output levels, fixed inputs are not efficiently utilized. Increasing the variable

Figure 5.9 Short-Run Cost Curves

This figure displays the short-run cost curves of a hypothetical firm. The upper panel depicts total cost (TC) and total variable cost (TVC). Fixed costs simply shift the position of the variable cost curve. The lower panel depicts marginal and average costs. Average fixed cost declines with output since the fixed cost is being spread over more units. Marginal cost (MC) declines to Q_1 and then increases beyond that point due to diminishing returns. Marginal cost depends only on the variable input factors and is *completely independent of the fixed cost.* Average total cost (ATC) and AVC decline as long as marginal cost is lower than the average cost and increase beyond that point. Marginal cost is equal to both ATC and AVC at their respective minimum points. Average total cost is always larger than AVC, since ATC = AFC + AVC. However, this difference becomes smaller as output increases and AFC declines.

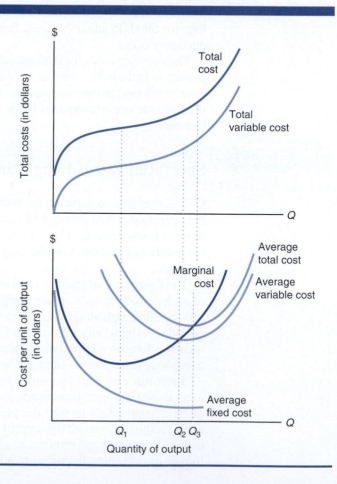

Drugstore Chains "Play Doctor" Due to Increased Demand and Low Variable Costs

Large chains, such as CVS, Walgreens, Target and Kroger, operate thousands of retail pharmacies at locations throughout the United States. In recent years, a growing number of these pharmacies have begun to offer walk-in clinics for basic medical services, such as vaccinations, diabetes screening, earwax removal, and treatments for sore throats and the flu. The number of retail pharmacies with medical clinics (as well as the services they provide) is expected to increase substantially due to expanded insurance coverage under the Affordable Care Act. CVS, currently the market leader with 800 locations, has plans to open another 150 facilities in 2014.

Many of the costs for providing medical services at these retail locations are fixed. For example, the costs for leasing the building, electricity, security guards, and much of the staffing would largely be the same whether or not additional medical services are provided at the given retail location. To be profitable, the chains only have to cover their variable costs for providing the new service, such as hiring additional nurse practitioners and the direct or opportunity costs for providing space and seating for waiting patients. CVS charges prices between $79 and $99 for most of its services. The relatively low prices, relatively quick service, convenient hours, and opportunities to shop while waiting have proven attractive to many customers.

Not surprisingly, some physician groups have objected to these clinics which compete with them for patients. They argue that the quality of medical services is inferior at the clinics. Some researchers, however, have found that the quality of care at these retail clinics is on par with traditional medical offices for certain medical services.

Source: S. Reddy (2014), "Drug Stores Play Doctor: Physicals, Flu Diagnosis, and More," *wsj.com* (April 7).

inputs increases output materially. Over this range, total cost increases—but does so at a decreasing rate. Eventually, the marginal productivity of the variable inputs declines and it becomes increasingly expensive to produce extra units of output.

The lower panel depicts marginal and average costs. Average fixed cost (AFC) is total fixed cost divided by output. Average fixed cost declines with output since the fixed cost is spread over more units. Marginal cost (MC) declines up to Q_1 and then

Small Airport in "Big Trouble"

The difficulties of competing with plant sizes significantly below minimum efficient scale are highlighted by the problems facing small U.S. airports. Commercial airline companies have cut many flights in recent years at these airports due to the lack of profitability. It is estimated that U.S. airlines reduced the number of flights by 14 percent from 2007 through 2012 with midsize and small airports being the hardest hit. As examples, Des Moines, Iowa and Burlington, Vermont lost 22 and 24 percent of their flights, respectively over this period.

The low volume of passengers and limited number of flights increase the average costs of providing services to customers at these smaller airports. Airlines that continue to offer flights at these airports have increased their fares substantially. For example, the small airport at Huntsville, Alabama had the highest average domestic fares among the tracked airports in the fall of 2013, averaging $559 for a round trip fare compared to the national average of $390. Yet the economic viability of continuing to offer flights at these many of these smaller airports remains questionable.

Local officials argue that the airports in their smaller communities are good for business and hope that the convenience to local customers more than offsets the higher ticket prices. Many local fliers, however, opt to drive to larger airports where the ticket prices are less expensive, the planes larger and the flight options more extensive. Some local communities have opted to provide financial incentives and subsidies to airline companies to offset their lack of profitability at their smaller airports. The economic and political viability of these programs, however, remains unclear.

Source: S. Carey (2014), "Why Small Airports are in Big Trouble," *wsj.com* (April 7).

increases beyond that point due to diminishing returns. Note that marginal cost depends only on the variable input factors and is *completely independent of the fixed cost*. Average variable costs (AVCs) are total variable costs divided by output. Both average total cost (ATC) and average variable cost decline as long as marginal cost is lower than average cost; they increase beyond that point. Marginal cost is equal to both average total cost and average variable cost at their respective minimum points. Average total cost is always larger than average variable cost, since ATC = AFC + AVC. However, this difference becomes smaller as average fixed cost declines with higher output.

Long-Run Cost Curves

In the short run, firms are unable to adjust their plant sizes. In the long run, however, if a firm wants to produce more output, it can build a larger, more efficient plant. In the long run, the average cost (LRAC) of production is less than or equal to the short-run average cost of production. Indeed, the LRAC curve can be thought of as an *envelope* of the short-run average cost curves. Figure 5.10 illustrates this concept. The figure shows four potential plant sizes. Each of the four plants provides the low-cost method of production over some range of output, assuming that only these four plant sizes are feasible. For instance, the smallest plant provides the lowest-cost method of producing any output from zero to Q_1, while the next largest plant provides the low-cost method of producing outputs from Q_1 to Q_2, and so on. The heavy portion of each curve indicates the minimum long-run average cost for producing each level of output.

Figure 5.10   Long-Run Average Costs as an Envelope of Short-Run Average Cost Curves

In the long run, the average cost (LRAC) of production is less than or equal to the short-run average cost (SRAC) of production. The LRAC curve can be thought of as an *envelope* of the short-run average cost curves. The figure shows four potential plant sizes. Each of the four plants provides the low-cost method of production over some range of output. For instance, the smallest plant provides the lowest-cost method of producing any output from zero to Q_1, while the next largest plant provides the low-cost method of producing output from Q_1 to Q_2, and so on. The heavy portion of each curve indicates the minimum long-run average cost for producing each level of output, assuming that there are only these four possible plant sizes.

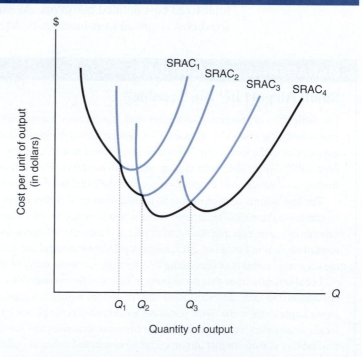

Public Utilities

The production of electric power typically is associated with large economies of scale: The average cost of producing electricity decreases with the quantity produced. This production characteristic implies that it is generally more efficient to have one large plant that produces power for an area than several smaller plants. A problem with having one producer of electric power in an area, however, is that the firm has the potential to overcharge consumers for electricity since there are limited alternative sources of supply. Concerns about this problem provide one motivation for the formation of public utility commissions that regulate the prices that utility companies can charge consumers.

If we extend this analysis by assuming there are many different feasible plant sizes that vary only slightly in size, the resulting LRAC curve will be relatively smooth, as pictured in Figure 5.11. This figure also pictures the long-run marginal cost curve (LRMC). As we have discussed, the marginal cost is below average cost where average cost is falling and above average cost where it is rising. The two are equal at the minimum average cost.

Minimum Efficient Scale

Minimum efficient scale is defined as that plant size at which long-run average cost first reaches its minimum point. In Figure 5.11, this minimum occurs at Q^*. The minimum efficient scale affects both the optimal plant size and the level of potential competition.

Average production cost is minimized at the minimum efficient scale. As we discuss in the next chapter, competition provides incentives for firms to adopt this plant size. If firms build plants that depart materially from minimum efficient scale, they will be at a competitive disadvantage and could be forced out of business. One complicating factor is transportation costs. If transportation costs are high, cost

Figure 5.11 Long-Run Average and Marginal Cost Curves

If there are many different plant sizes that vary only slightly in size, the resulting long-run average cost (LRAC) curve is relatively smooth, as pictured in this figure. The long-run marginal cost (LRMC) is below average cost where average cost is falling and above average cost where it is rising. The two are equal at the minimum average cost. The minimum efficient scale is defined as the plant size at which LRACs are first minimized (Q^* in this example).

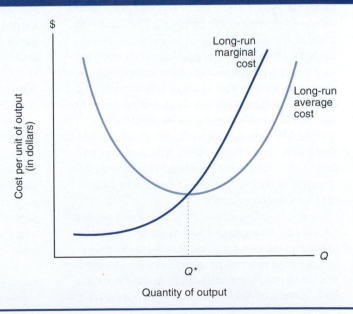

Size Doesn't Always Matter

Regis Corporation has 10,000 beauty salons, buys shampoo by the train load, spends millions on advertising, and uses sophisticated technology to track performance at each salon. Nonetheless, the 300,000 independent salons in the United States still compete quite effectively with Regis chains like Supercuts. Paul Finkelstein, Regis CEO says. "We don't run a big business. We run ten thousand $300,000 businesses." He says it's salon location first, and quality of stylists second that make the business go. Those are factors that an independent salon also can offer.

Source: F. Bailey (2003), "In Some Businesses, Size Is Irrelevant to Success," *The Wall Street Journal* (November 11), B13.

disadvantages of smaller regional plants can be more than offset by cost savings in transporting the product to customers. In this case, when total production and distribution costs are considered, firms with plants that are smaller than the minimum efficient scale can survive in a competitive marketplace.

Generally, the number of competitors will be large and competition more vigorous when the minimum efficient scale is small relative to total industry demand. For instance, suppose that Kate Polk is evaluating the possibility of entering an industry where she sees established firms reporting substantial profits. If her firm would have to produce 10 percent of the market's output to be cost-efficient, Kate should be concerned that her entry is likely to drive the price down and thus she would be less likely to enter the market than if she needed to produce only 1 percent of the market's output for efficient production.

ANALYZING MANAGERIAL DECISIONS: *Developing Economies of Scale for Malaysia's Proton Holdings*

Proton Holdings Bhd is a national carmaker in Malaysia. In late 2007, the Malaysian government owned 43 percent of the company. The remaining stock of the company traded on public stock exchanges. Proton was among Malaysia's worst performing companies in 2005, after competition from foreign carmakers and a lack of new models cost the firm significant market share and profits. It has since hired a new chief executive, sold its loss-making MV Agusta motorbike firm, and pledged to find a new technology partner. The company has been under substantial pressure, with its share of domestic sales falling from 75 percent to 44 percent over the past decade.

Analysts polled in late 2007 noted that the company's new management had made several moves to revamp the company and that these efforts were bearing fruit in terms of increased sales volume and market share. New models such as the *Persona*, a sport edition of *Savvy*, and *Satria Neo* were relative

successes. The management also implemented stringent cost controls. Nonetheless, analysts concluded that Proton's long-run ability to survive depends on whether it can achieve increased production volume and economies of scale. Without sufficient scale it is unlikely that the company will survive the intense local and worldwide competition. The analysts assert that by itself, Proton would find it hard to achieve economies of scale and to develop new technologies.

Suppose that you are hired as a consultant to advise Proton's management. What do the analysts mean when they say that Proton needs to achieve economies of scale to be competitive? Discuss at a general level the types of actions that the company might want to consider to achieve the necessary scale.

Source: K. Fong (2007), "No Economies of Scale for Proton without Global Partner," *StarBiz*, thestar online (November 21).

Figure 5.12   Learning Curve

A learning curve displays the relation between average cost for a given output period, Q^*, and cumulative past production. In this example, there are significant learning effects in the early stages of production. These effects become minimal as the firm continues to produce the product.

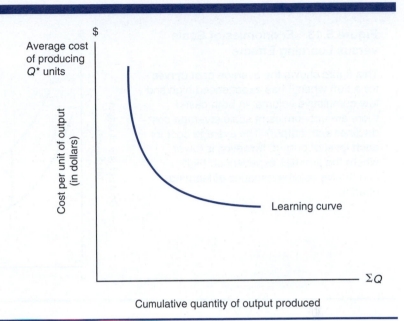

Cumulative quantity of output produced

Industries where average cost declines over a broad range of output are characterized as having *economies of scale*. Significant economies of scale limit the number of firms in the industry. For instance, if the minimum efficient scale is 25 percent of total industry sales, there is room for only four firms to produce at that volume. The level of competition among existing firms can vary significantly, even if there are only a few firms in the industry. However, threat of entry is less pressing than in industries where scale economies are low. The threat of potential new competitors is often an important consideration in a firm's strategic planning. In subsequent chapters, we examine how a firm's market structure affects managerial decision making.

Learning Curves

For some firms, the long-run average cost of producing a given level of output declines as the firm gains production experience. For example, with more output, employees might gain important information on how to improve production processes. They also become more proficient as they gain experience on the job.[15] A *learning curve* displays the relation between average cost and cumulative production volume. Cumulative production is the total amount of the product produced by the firm across all previous production periods. Figure 5.12 presents an example where there are significant learning effects in the early stages of production. Eventually, however, these effects frequently become minimal as the firm continues to produce the product.

---

[15] A. Alchian (1959), "Costs and Outputs," in *The Allocation of Economic Resources*, by M. Abramovitz and others (Stanford University Press: Palo Alto, CA), 23–40.

Figure 5.13 Economies of Scale versus Learning Effects

This figure shows the average cost curves for a firm when it has experienced high and low cumulative volume. In both cases, there are economies of scale (average cost declines with output). The average cost for each level of output, however, is lower where the firm has experienced high cumulative volume because of learning effects.

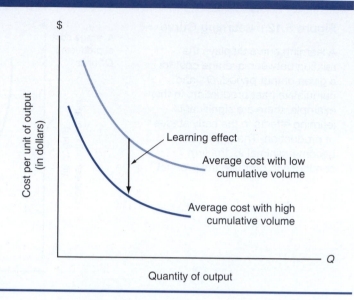

Figure 5.13 illustrates the difference between economies of scale and learning effects. Economies of scale imply reductions in average cost as the quantity being produced within the production period increases. Learning effects imply a shift in the entire average cost curve: The average cost for producing a given quantity in a production period decreases with cumulative volume. Learning effects sometimes can provide existing firms in an industry a competitive advantage over potential entrants; it depends on the nature of the information (Chapter 3) and the distribution of that information across employees. We discuss this issue in more detail in Chapter 8.

Economies of Scope

Thus far, we have focused on the production of a single product. Most firms, however, produce multiple products. *Economies of scope* exist when the cost of producing a set of products jointly within one firm is less than the cost of producing the products separately across independent firms. Joint production can produce cost savings for a vari-

---

ACADEMIC APPLICATIONS

Economies of Scale and Learning Effects in the Chemical Processing Industry

Marvin Lieberman studied economies of scale and learning effects in the chemical processing industry. He found that for each doubling in plant size, average production costs fell by about 11 percent. For each doubling of cumulative volume, the average cost of production fell by about 27 percent. Thus, there is evidence of both economies of scale and learning effects in the chemical processing industry. The size of the estimates suggests that learning effects are more important than economies of scale in explaining the observed decline in costs within the industry from the 1950s to the 1970s.

Source: M. Lieberman (1984), "The Learning Curve and Pricing in the Chemical Processing Industries," *Rand Journal* 15, 213–288.

MANAGERIAL APPLICATIONS

Jimmy Beans Wool—Economies of Scope Fail to Materialize

Jimmy Beans Wool is an online yarn and fabric seller with a store in Reno, Nevada. The company was founded in 2002 and by 2013 had sales of over $7 million dollars. The company initially focused exclusively on selling yarn. It grew "organically" at an annual rate of around 50 percent over the period 2007–2012 and earned a national reputation for its high rate of growth. The owners envisioned that Jimmy Beans could be a $100 million business within a few years. The owners invested to expand their product line by selling fabrics to grow sales. They made significant investments in inventory, building remodeling, and marketing. Unfortunately, sales did not grow, and the company suffered a significant financial setback.

The owners say that they "fell into the trap of thinking if we can sell yarn, we can sell anything." This is an all too common managerial misconception that has led to other unsuccessful expansions and mergers. Good managers avoid this kind of hubris and are careful not to overestimate economies of scope. Economies of scope are most likely to exist in closely related products where there are true synergies in either production or distribution. The assumption that economies are produced by a manager who can "manage anything" quite often proves false.

Source: A. Gardella (2014), "Seeking Even Faster Growth, An E-Commerce Company Stumbles," *New York Times* (April 2).

ety of reasons. Efficiencies can result from common use of production facilities, coordinated marketing programs, and sharing management systems. Also, the production of some products provides unavoidable by-products that are valuable to the firm. For instance, a sheep rancher jointly produces both mutton and wool.

Economies of scope help explain why firms produce multiple products. For instance, PepsiCo is a major producer of soft drinks; yet it also produces a wide range of snack foods (e.g., corn chips and cookies). These multiple products allow PepsiCo to leverage its product development, distribution, and marketing systems.

Economies of scope and economies of scale are different concepts. Economies of scope involve cost savings that result from joint production, whereas economies of scale involve efficiencies from producing higher volumes of a given product. It is possible to have economies of scope without having economies of scale and vice versa.

Profit Maximization

Thus far, we have focused on the costs of producing different levels of output. However, what output level should a manager choose to maximize firm profits? To answer this question, we return to the concept of *marginal analysis* that we initially introduced in Chapter 2.

Marginal costs and benefits are the incremental costs and benefits that are associated with a particular decision. It is these incremental costs and benefits that are important in economic decision making. An action should be taken whenever the incremental benefits of that action exceed its incremental costs. In deciding whether or not to produce one more unit of a product, the incremental benefit is marginal revenue (see Chapter 4), while the incremental cost is equal to marginal production cost (including any distribution costs)—fixed costs do not affect the decision. Therefore, the firm should produce extra units so long as marginal revenue exceeds marginal cost; the firm should not produce extra units if marginal revenue

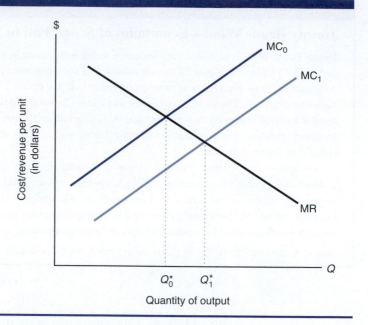

Figure 5.14   Changes in Marginal Cost and Optimal Output

This figure illustrates that a decrease in marginal cost (from MC_0 to MC_1) raises the optimal output of the firm (from Q_0^* to Q_1^*).

is less than marginal cost. At the *profit-maximizing level of production,* the following condition holds:[16]

$$MR = MC \qquad (5.9)$$

As we saw in Chapter 4, marginal revenue depends on the demand curve for the product. The effective demand curve that the firm faces will be affected by the degree of competition in the product market. In Chapter 6, we examine how the output decisions of firms vary across different market settings.

The changes in metal prices throughout the 1990s changed the total cost of automobile manufacturing. Typically, such changes are accompanied by changes in the *marginal cost* of production. For example, a reduction in steel prices would mean not only a substitution toward steel from other inputs but also an increase in output. Figure 5.14 illustrates this effect. Note that this analysis holds other factors constant. If the demand for automobiles is falling at the same time (thus shifting marginal revenue downward), the net effect could be an increase in output. However, the increase in output would be less than if steel prices were constant.

Factor Demand Curves

In discussing the optimal input mix, we noted that the following condition must hold for efficient production:

$$MP_i/P_i = MP_j/P_j \qquad (5.10)$$

---

[16]Technical note: Since profits equal total revenues minus total costs, Equation (5.9) is the first-order condition for profit maximization. This condition holds at both minimum and maximum profits. At the maximum, the marginal cost curve cuts the marginal revenue curve from below—the second-order condition.

for all inputs i and j. The ratios of marginal product to price reflect the incremental output from an input associated with an additional dollar expenditure on that input. The reciprocals of these ratios reflect the dollar cost for incremental output or the marginal cost:

$$P_i/MP_i = P_j/MP_j = MC \qquad (5.11)$$

At the profit-maximizing output level, MR = MC. Therefore, at the optimal output level the following condition must hold

$$P_i/MP_i = MR \qquad (5.12)$$

MANAGERIAL APPLICATIONS

China Becomes the "World's Smokestack"

This chapter focuses on how firms choose among alternative input mixes. Another important production decision is where to locate the plant. Costs can vary dramatically across locations due to differences in the prices for labor, land, transportation and other inputs, taxes, environmental and safety regulations, threat of terrorism, and political risk. The steel industry provides a good example of how changes in costs can motivate significant changes in the location of production.

During the 1950s the Ruhr Valley in Germany had the world's highest growth rate in steel production. In its heyday, Germany produced 10 percent of the world's steel supply. In 2006, Germany produced only 3.8 percent of the world's supply, ranking seventh behind China, Japan, the United States, Russia, India, and South Korea. China, which has displayed meteoric growth in steel production, supplied 34 percent.

German steel production slowed in the 1960s as miners had to dig deeper for coal and taxes and labor costs continued to increase. Another important factor was new environmental regulation. The emissions from steel plants had made the Ruhr Valley one of the most polluted places in the world. The air was dark and grimy. The residents suffered from an inordinate incidence of lung and other pollution-related diseases. The white shirts that men wore to church on Sunday turned to grey by the time they came home. In an effort to "green the country," the government imposed costly pollution control requirements on the steel companies.

Differences in labor costs and environmental standards motivated a shift in steel production from Germany to China as "smoke-spewing plants" were disassembled in the Ruhr Valley and moved 5,000 miles away to China. The Phoenix steel mills in Dortmund had been among Germany's largest since before World War II. In the late 1990s, they were slated for closure and were likely headed for the scrap heap. The Chinese realized that they could buy a relatively sophisticated German blast furnace for a small fraction of what a new one would cost. A Chinese company sent workers to Dortmund who labeled every part of the seven-story blast furnace, disassembled it, and packed it into wooden crates for the voyage to China. They worked day and night to accomplish this task in a much shorter time than it would have taken German workers, who were governed by strict union and government work rules.

The Hebei Province is "China's new Ruhr Valley." Its air is heavily polluted and its citizens suffer from a variety of associated health problems. Meanwhile, the Ruhr Valley's pollution level has substantially improved. This improvement, however, has come at a cost. Dortmund, which in 1960 had 30,000 residents working in the steel industry, now has less than 3,000. While Dortmund continues to have high unemployment, the decline in steel jobs has been offset to some extent by new jobs in other less-polluting industries.

The willingness to pay for clean air generally increases with a country's income. In March 2014, Chinese Premier Li Keqiang stated in a speech before the Chinese legislature, "we will declare a war on pollution and fight with the same determination we battled poverty." Government officials have pledged a series of pollution reforms targeted at energy-intensive industries, such as steel, aluminum, cement, and coal. Economics, however, teaches us "there is no free lunch." Analysts predict that the proposed reforms will increase production cost and potentially force some of the factories to close.

Source: J. Kahn and M. Landler (2007), "China Grabs West's Smoke-Spewing Factories," *nytimes.com* (December 21); and W. Ma and C.-W. Yap (2014), "China Needs Industry to Enlist a War on Poverty," *Dow Jones Reprints* (March 6).

Figure 5.15   Factor Demand Curve

The demand curve for a factor of production is the *marginal revenue product curve* (MRP) for the input. The marginal revenue product is defined as the marginal product of the input times the marginal revenue. It represents the additional revenue that comes from using one more unit of input. The firm maximizes profits where it purchases inputs up to the point where the price of the input equals its marginal revenue product.

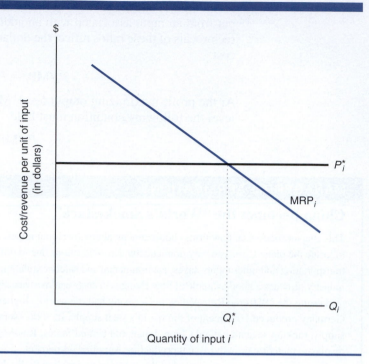

or equivalently,

$$P_i = \text{MR} \times \text{MP}_i \tag{5.13}$$

Equation (5.13) is the firm's demand curve for input i.[17] It has a straightforward interpretation. The right-hand side of the equation represents the incremental revenue that the firm obtains from employing one more unit of the input (the incremental output times the incremental revenue). We call this incremental revenue the *marginal revenue product* (MRP$_i$) of input i. Figure 5.15 illustrates the demand curve for an input.[18] At the current input price of P_i^*, the firm optimally uses Q_i^* units of the input. The firm optimally employs additional units of the input up to the point where the marginal cost of the input (its price with constant input prices) is equal to the marginal revenue product of the input. Intuitively, if the marginal revenue product is greater than the input price, the firm increases its profitability by using more of the input. If the marginal revenue product is less than the price of the input, the firm increases profitability by reducing the use of the input. Profits are maximized when the two are equal.

Our discussion of the profit-maximizing output level and the optimal use of an input might appear to suggest that these decisions are two distinct choices. The two decisions, however, are linked directly. Once the firm chooses the quantities of inputs,

[17]Technical note: The marginal product of input i can depend on the levels of other inputs used in the production process. Thus, the demand curve for an input must allow other inputs to adjust to their optimal levels as the price of input i changes. This adjustment is not important if the marginal product of input i is not affected by the levels of the other inputs.

[18]Technical note: The second-order condition for maximum profits ensures that the demand curve for the input is the *downward-sloping* portion of the marginal revenue product curve. Thus, Figure 5.15 displays only the downward-sloping portion of the curve.

MANAGERIAL APPLICATIONS

Hog Producers React to Increase in Corn Prices

Pork is the most widely eaten meat in the world, providing about 38 percent of daily meat protein worldwide (despite the fact that it is not consumed by some people due to religious restrictions). The United States Department of Agriculture reports that in 2006 the per capita consumption of pork was 43.9 kg, 40 kg, and 29 kg in China, Europe, and the United States, respectively. Ironically in China's "Year of the Pig" (2007), there was a crisis that increased pork prices by 50 percent. The dramatic price increase caused both social unrest and government intervention to "help keep pork affordable."

Feed cost is typically about 50–60 percent of the total cost of producing pork. In the United States, corn accounts for about 80 percent of the typical hog feed. Rising fuel prices and government policies promoting the use of corn-based ethanol as an alternative to gasoline caused U.S. corn prices nearly to double in the summer and fall of 2006. This price change significantly increased the cost of feeding hogs. U.S. hog producers were able to lessen the effects of the increase in corn prices by switching to feed mixes that use less corn and more dried distilled grain and solubles (DDGS). DDGS is a by-product of the corn-based ethanol production process. Scientists found that DDGS could be substituted for corn at a 10 percent inclusion rate without having a significant effect on the efficiency, growth, or carcass traits of the hogs. Corn and DDGS, however, are not perfect substitutes in the hog production process. Feed mixes with higher DDGS inclusion rates (e.g., 20 percent and 30 percent) produced smaller pigs that offset the advantages of lower feed costs.

This example highlights a general point about production costs. Increases in input prices increase production costs. The effect of the price increase often can be mitigated by shifting the input mix toward relatively less expensive inputs. The ability to reduce costs in this manner depends on the degree of substitutability among the inputs.

Source: J. Lawrence (2006), "Impact on Hog Feed Cost of Corn and DDGS Prices," *Iowa Farm Outlook* (November 15), 1–4.

output is determined by the production function. Thus, profit-maximizing firms choose the output where marginal revenue equals marginal cost and produce that output so that the price of each input is equal to its marginal revenue product. In our auto example, an increase in steel prices would be expected to motivate *simultaneous* adjustments in both the number of automobiles produced and the methods used to produce them.

MANAGERIAL APPLICATIONS

Demand for Labor Falls Following 9/11 Terrorist Attacks

Organized labor was particularly hard hit by the terrorist attacks following 9/11. Of the 760,000 job cuts in the three months following the attack, roughly 50 percent were union members—nearly four times organized labor's 13.5 percent of the U.S. workforce. The reason for this higher-than-average job loss is because unions are disproportionately represented in the hard-hit travel and tourism industries. Unions representing public employees also are seeing large job cuts as state and local budgets are cut. September 11 significantly shifted consumers' demand for travel and tourism services to the left. When demand shifts to the left, so does the firm's marginal revenue curve. Hence, labor's marginal revenue product—the product of marginal revenue and the factor's marginal product (holding constant labor's marginal product)—also shifts to the left.

Source: A. Bernstein (2001), "A Sock in the Eye for Labor," *BusinessWeek* (December 17), 44.

Cost Estimation

Our discussion indicates that a detailed knowledge of costs is important for managerial decision making. Short-run costs play an extremely important role in operating decisions. For instance, when the marginal revenue from increased output is above the short-run marginal cost of production, profits increase by expanding production. Alternatively, if marginal revenue is below short-run marginal cost, reducing output increases profits. Long-run costs, in turn, provide important information for decisions on optimal plant size and location. For instance, if economies of scale are important, one large plant is more likely optimal with the product transported to regional markets. Alternatively, if scale economies are small, smaller regional plants, which reduce transportation costs, are more likely optimal.

If managers are to incorporate costs in their analyses in this manner, they must have accurate estimates of how short-run and long-run costs are related to various factors both within and beyond the control of the firm.[19] Among the most commonly used statistical techniques for estimating cost curves is regression analysis. A regression estimates the relation between costs and output (possibly controlling for other factors, such as the product mix or the weather, which affect costs). The data for this analysis can be either time-series data on costs, output, and other variables, or cross-sectional data, which includes observations on variables across firms or plants at a point in time. For instance, in many applications, it is assumed that short-run total costs are approximately linear[20]

$$\text{VC} = a + bQ \tag{5.14}$$

where VC is total variable costs for the period and Q is the quantity of output produced.

A detailed discussion of cost estimation is beyond the scope of this book. Suffice it to say that similar problems arise in cost estimation as arise in the case of demand estimation (e.g., omitted-variables problems). Among the most common problems in cost estimation are difficulties in obtaining data on relevant costs. Cost estimates often are based on accounting reports, which record historical costs. As we have indicated, these historical costs do not necessarily reflect the opportunity costs of using resources. Moreover, there is the issue of choosing the appropriate functional form. Equation (5.14) presumes a linear model. However, cost curves need not be linear. For instance, it might be appropriate to use a quadratic model, which would include an additional Q^2 term.

One of the more serious problems complicating cost estimation is the fact that most plants produce multiple products. Multiple products are produced in the same plant because there are economies of scope. Rather than produce two different types of cereals in two separate plants, it typically is cheaper to produce them in one plant; fixed resources can be used more efficiently. If a plant produces multiple products, total and average costs for each product can be calculated only by allocating fixed

---

[19]In addition, some firms estimate cost curves to obtain insights into their underlying production functions. Recall that the shapes of cost curves depend on the underlying production functions. Thus, it often is possible to infer the characteristics of a production function from the shape of the corresponding cost curves. Typically, the data for estimating cost curves is more readily available than the necessary data for estimating production functions.

[20]Variable costs are normally estimated with an intercept. Although variable costs undoubtedly are zero when output is zero, most cost curves are nonlinear. Forcing the intercept to be zero yields a less precise estimate of this slope—the change in costs associated with a change in output.

ANALYZING MANAGERIAL DECISIONS: *Rich Manufacturing*

Gina Picaretto is production manager at the Rich Manufacturing Company. Each year her unit buys up to 100,000 machine parts from Bhagat Incorporated. The contract specifies that Rich will pay Bhagat its production costs plus a $5 markup (*cost-plus pricing*). Currently, Bhagat's costs per part are $10 for labor and $10 for other costs. Thus the current price is $25 per part. The contract provides an option to Rich to buy up to 100,000 parts at this price. It must purchase a minimum volume of 50,000 parts.

Bhagat's workforce is heavily unionized. During recent contract negotiations, Bhagat agreed to a 30 percent raise for workers. In this labor contract, wages and benefits are specified. However, Bhagat is free to choose the quantity of labor it employs.

Bhagat has announced a $3 price increase for its machine parts. This figure represents the projected $3 increase in labor costs due to its new union contract. It is Gina's responsibility to evaluate this announcement.

1. Why do many firms use cost-plus pricing for supply contracts?
2. What potential problems do you envision with cost-plus pricing?
3. Should Gina contest the price increase? Explain.
4. Is the increase more likely to be justified in the short run or the long run? Explain.
5. How will a $3 increase in the price of machine parts affect Gina's own production decisions?

costs across the products. This allocation often is arbitrary and complicated further by the existence of joint costs. Cost accountants use accounting records to track costs of individual products. Fixed and variable resources used by each product are recorded. These product costs, calculated by the cost accountants, typically are used to estimate short-run and long-run average and marginal costs.

Despite these estimation problems, cost curves play an important role in managerial decision making. Nonetheless, it is important that managers maintain a healthy skepticism when using these estimates. For instance, in making major decisions, it generally is instructive for managers to examine whether a proposed decision is still attractive with reasonable variation in the estimated parameters of the cost function—that is, to conduct *sensitivity analysis*.

Summary

A *production function* is a descriptive relation that connects inputs with outputs. It specifies the *maximum* possible output that can be produced for given amounts of inputs. *Returns to scale* refers to the relation between output and a proportional variation in *all inputs* taken together. A production function displays *constant returns to scale* when a 1 percent change in all inputs results in a 1 percent change in output. With *increasing returns to scale,* a 1 percent change in all inputs results in a greater than 1 percent change in output. Finally, with *decreasing returns to scale,* a 1 percent change in all inputs results in a less than 1 percent change in output. *Returns to a factor* refers to the relation between output and the variation in only one input, *holding other inputs fixed*. Returns to a factor can be expressed as total, marginal, or average quantities. The *law of diminishing returns* states that the marginal product of a variable factor will eventually decline as the use of the input is increased.

Most production functions allow some substitution of inputs. An *isoquant* displays all combinations of inputs that produce the same quantity of output. The optimal input mix to produce any given output depends on the costs of the inputs. An *isocost line* displays all combinations of inputs that cost the same. *Cost minimization* for a given output occurs where the isoquant is tangent to the isocost line. Changes in input prices change the slope of the isocost line and the point of tangency. When the price of an input increases, the firm will reduce its use of this input and increase its use of other inputs (*substitution effect*).

Cost curves can be derived from the isoquant/isocost analysis. The *total cost curve* depicts the relation between total costs and output. *Marginal cost* is the change in total cost associated with a one-unit change in output. *Average cost* is total cost divided by total output. Average cost falls when marginal cost is below average cost; average cost rises when marginal cost is above average cost. Average and marginal costs are equal when average cost is at a minimum. There is a direct link between the production function and cost curves. Holding input prices constant, the slopes of cost curves are determined by the underlying production technology.

Opportunity cost is the value of a resource in its next best alternative use. Current market prices more closely reflect the opportunity costs of inputs than *historical costs*. The *relevant costs* for managerial decision making are the opportunity costs.

Cost curves can be depicted for both the *short run* and the *long run*. The short run is the operating period during which at least one input (typically capital) is fixed in supply. During this period, *fixed costs* can be incurred even if the firm produces no output. In the long run, there are no fixed costs—all inputs and costs are *variable*. Short-run cost curves are sometimes called *operating curves* because they are used in making near-term production and pricing decisions. Fixed costs are irrelevant for these decisions. Long-run cost curves are referred to as *planning curves,* since they play a key role in longer-run planning decisions relating to plant size and equipment acquisitions.

The *minimum efficient scale* is defined as that plant size at which long-run average cost is first minimized. The minimum efficient scale affects both the optimal plant size and the level of potential competition. Industries where the average cost declines over a broad range of output are characterized as having *economies of scale.*

A *learning curve* displays the relation between average cost and the cumulative volume of production. For some firms, the long-run average cost for producing a given level of output declines as the firm gains experience from producing the output (i.e., there are significant learning effects).

Economies of scope exist when the cost of producing a joint set of products in one firm is less than the cost of producing the products separately across independent firms. Economies of scope help explain why firms often produce multiple products.

The profit-maximizing output level occurs at the point where *marginal revenue equals marginal cost.* At this point, the marginal benefits of increasing output are offset exactly by the marginal costs.

The *marginal revenue product* of input i (MRP_i) equals the marginal product of the input times marginal revenue. Profit-maximizing firms use an input up to the point where the MRP of the input equals the input price. At this point, the marginal benefit of employing more of the input is offset exactly by its marginal cost.

Managers often use estimates of cost curves in decision making. A common statistical tool for estimating these curves is regression analysis. One common problem in statistical estimation is the difficulty of obtaining good information on the opportunity costs of resources. Another problem with estimating cost curves involves allocating fixed costs in a multiproduct plant. Cost accountants track the costs and estimate product costs.

Suggested Reading

G. Stigler (1987), *The Theory of Price* (Macmillan: New York), Chapters 6–10.

Self-Evaluation Problems

5–1. The Zimmerman Company digs ditches. It faces the production function, $Q = L^{1/2}K$, where Q is the number of ditches dug, L is hours of labor, and K is the number of digging tools.

a. Complete the following table:

	K = 0	K = 1	K = 2	K = 3
L = 0				
L = 1				
L = 2				
L = 3				

b. Does the production function display increasing, decreasing, or constant returns to scale? Explain.

c. Are the marginal products of K and L increasing, decreasing, or constant? Explain.

d. Assume constant input prices. Draw the *general shapes* of the following: (1) long-run average cost; (2) short-run marginal cost, assuming L is fixed; (3) short-run marginal cost, assuming K is fixed.

5–2.[21] A product is produced using two inputs x_1 and x_2 costing $w_1 = \$10$ and $w_2 = \$5$ per unit, respectively. The production function is $y = 5x_1^{1.5}x_2^2$ where y is the quantity of output, and x_1, x_2 are the quantities of the two inputs. The marginal products of inputs 1 and 2 for this production function are:

$$MP_1 = 7.5 \times x_1^{0.5} \times x_2^2$$
$$MP_2 = 10 \times x_1^{1.5} \times x_2$$

a. What input quantities (x_1^*, x_2^*) minimize the cost of producing 10,000 units of output?

b. What is the total cost of producing the 10,000 units?

Solutions to Self-Evaluation Problems

5–1. a.

	K = 0	K = 1	K = 2	K = 3
L = 0	0	0	0	0
L = 1	0	1	2	3
L = 2	0	1.41	2.83	4.24
L = 3	0	1.73	3.46	5.19

b. The production function shows increasing returns to scale. As you increase both inputs by the same proportion, output goes up by a higher proportion (e.g., if you double both inputs output goes up by more than double). This can be seen along the diagonal of the table.

c. The marginal product of K is constant. If you hold L fixed and increase K, the marginal increase in output is constant as you add more and more K. You can see this along the

[21]This problem requires slightly higher skills in algebra than most of the other problems in the book. Readers who cannot work the problem on their own should study the general approach used in the solution to obtain a better understanding of the conditions for cost minimization.

rows of the table. The marginal product of L is decreasing. If you hold K fixed and increase L, the marginal increase in output declines as you add more and more L. This can be seen along the columns of the table.

d. Increasing returns to scale implies that LRAC declines as output is increased (there are economies of scale). The marginal product of K is constant. Thus SRMC is constant when K is the variable input. For example, when $L = 1$, each additional unit of K produces one extra unit of output (see the second row of the table). In this case, SRMC (the cost of producing an additional unit of output) is simply the price of K. The marginal product of L is decreasing. Thus SRMC is increasing when L is the variable input. The general shapes of the graphs are:

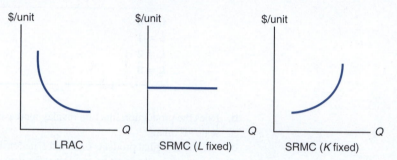

LRAC   SRMC (L fixed)   SRMC (K fixed)

5-2. a. The cost-minimizing combination of inputs is found by equating their marginal product to price ratios: $MP_1/P_1 = MP_2/P_2$. This condition can be expressed as:

$$\frac{MP_1}{MP_2} = \frac{w_1}{w_2}$$

So, we get

$$\frac{MP_1}{MP_2} = \frac{w_1}{w_2} \Longrightarrow \frac{7.5 \times x_1^{0.5} \times x_2^2}{10 \times x_1^{1.5} \times x_2} = \frac{10}{5}$$

$$\Longrightarrow \frac{3}{4} x_1^{-1} x_2 = 2 \Longrightarrow \frac{x_2}{x_1} = \frac{8}{3}$$

Thus:

$$x_1 = (3/8)\, x_2 \qquad\qquad (i)$$

Use the relation in equation (i) to express the production function for $y = 10{,}000$ units as a function of only x_2. You now have a solvable equation with one unknown variable, x_2:

$$y = 5 x_1^{1.5} x_2^2 \Longrightarrow 10{,}000 = 5\left(\frac{3x_2}{8}\right)^{1.5}(x_2)^2 = 5\left(\frac{3}{8}\right)^{1.5} x_2^{3.5}$$

Solving for x_2 and obtaining x_1 from equation (i):

$$x_2^* = 13.357$$
$$x_1^* = 5.01$$

b. The total cost of producing the 10,000 units is simply the sum of the expenditures made to acquire each of the inputs:

$$TC = w_1 x_1 + w_2 x_2 = 10 \times 5.01 + 5 \times 13.357 = \$116.87$$

Review Questions

5-1. Distinguish between returns to scale and returns to a factor.

5-2. Your company currently uses steel and aluminum in a production process. Steel costs $.50 per pound, and aluminum costs $1.00 per pound. Suppose the government imposes a tax of

$.25 per pound on all metals. What affect will this have on your optimal input mix? Show using isoquants and isocost lines.

5–3. Your company currently uses steel and aluminum in a production process. Steel costs $.50 per pound, and aluminum costs $1.00 per pound. Suppose that inflation doubles the price of both inputs. What affect will this have on your optimal input mix? Show using isoquants and isocost lines.

5–4. Is the "long run" the same calendar time for all firms? Explain.

5–5. You want to estimate the cost of materials used to produce a particular product. According to accounting reports, you initially paid $50 for the materials that are necessary to produce each unit. Is $50 a good estimate of your current production costs? Explain.

5–6. Suppose that average cost is minimized at 50 units and equals $1. What is marginal cost at this output level?

5–7. What is the difference between economies of scale and economies of scope?

5–8. What is the difference between economies of scale and learning effects?

5–9. Suppose that you can sell as much of a product as you want at $100 per unit. Your marginal cost is: MC = 2Q. Your fixed cost is $50. What is the optimal output level? What is the optimal output, if your fixed cost is $60?

5–10. Discuss two problems that arise in estimating cost curves.

5–11. Suppose that the marginal product of labor is: MP = 100 − L, where L is the number of workers hired. You can sell the product in the marketplace for $50 per unit, and the wage rate for labor is $100. How many workers should you hire?

5–12. Textbook authors typically receive a simple percentage of total revenue generated from book sales. The publisher bears all the production costs and chooses the output level. Suppose the retail price of a book is fixed at $50. The author receives $10 per copy, and the firm receives $40 per copy. The firm is interested in maximizing its own profits. Will the author be happy with the book company's output choice? Does the selected output maximize the joint profits (for both the author and company) from the book?

5–13. Suppose your company produces one product and that you are currently at an output level where your price elasticity is 0.5. Are you at the optimal output level for profit maximization? How can you tell?

5–14. Semiconductor chips are used to store information in electronic products, such as personal computers. One of the early leaders in the production of these chips was Texas Instruments (TI). During the early period in the development of this industry, TI made the decision to price its semiconductors substantially below its production costs. This decision increased sales, but resulted in near-term reductions in profits. Explain why TI might have made this decision.

5–15. The AFL-CIO has been a steadfast proponent of increasing the minimum wage. Offer at least two reasons why they might lobby for such increases.

5–16. Mountain Springs Water Company produces bottled water. Internal consultants estimate the company's production function to be $Q = 300L^2K$, where Q is the number of bottles of water produced each week, L is the hours of labor per week, and K is the number of machine hours per week. Each machine can operate 100 hours a week. Labor costs $20 per hour, and each machine costs $1,000 per week.
  a. Suppose the firm has 20 machines and is producing its current output using an optimal K/L ratio. How many people does Mountain Springs employ? Assume each person works 40 hours a week.
  b. Recent technological advancements have caused machine prices to drop. Mountain Springs can now lease each machine for $800 a week. How will this affect the optimal K/L ratio (i.e., will the optimal K/L ratio be smaller or larger)? Show why.

5–17. The Workerbee Company employs 100 high school graduates and 50 college graduates at respective wages of $10 and $20. The total product for high school graduates is 1,000 +

$100Q_H$, whereas the total product for college graduates is $5{,}000 + 50Q_C$. Q_H = the number of high school graduates, while Q_C = the number of college graduates. Is the company hiring the optimal amount of each type of worker? If not, has it hired too many high school or too many college graduates? Explain.

5–18.

Q	TC	TFC	TVC	MC	AC	AFC	AVC
0							
1	500			80			
2				60			
3				50			
4				60			
5				75			
6				95			
7				120			
8				150			
9				185			

   a. Complete the above table.
   b. Graph TC, TFC, TVC, MC, AC, AFC, and AVC against Q.

5–19. Suppose the Jones Manufacturing Company produces a single product. At its current input mix the marginal product of labor is 10 and the marginal product of capital is 20. The per unit price of labor and capital are $5 and $10, respectively. Is the Jones Company using an optimal mix of labor and capital to produce its current output? If not, should it use more capital or labor? Explain.

5–20. Suppose the production function of PowerGuns Co. is given by

$$Q = 25LK$$

where Q is the quantity of guns produced in the month, L is the number of workers employed, and K is the number of machines used in the production. The monthly wage rate is $3,000 per worker and the monthly rental rate for a machine is $6,000. Currently PowerGuns Co. employs 25 workers and 40 machines. Assume perfect divisibility of labor and machines.
   a. What is the current average product of labor for PowerGuns Co.? What is the current marginal product of machines? (Assume 1 unit increase in machines.)
   b. Does PowerGuns' production function display increasing, decreasing, or constant returns to scale? Explain.
   c. What is the total cost of the current production of PowerGuns in a month? What is the average cost to produce a shooting gun? Assuming the number of machines does not change, what is the marginal cost of producing one additional gun?
   d. What is the law of diminishing returns? Does this production display this characteristic? Explain.

5–21. Assume Canon's production function for digital cameras is given by $Q = 100(L^{0.7}K^{0.3})$, where L and K are the number of workers and machines employed in a month, respectively, and Q is the monthly output. Moreover, assume the monthly wage per worker is $3,000 and the monthly rental rate per machine is $2,000. (*Note*: Given the production function, the marginal product functions are $MP_L = 70(L^{-0.3}K^{0.3})$ and $MP_K = 30(L^{0.7}K^{-0.7})$).
   a. If Canon needs to supply 60,000 units of cameras per month, how many workers and machines should it optimally employ?
   b. What are the total cost and average cost of producing the quantity given in (*a*)?

5–22. For simplicity, throughout this problem, assume labor (L), capital (K), and quantity produced (Q) can be infinitely divided—that is, it is fine to hire 3.3 workers, rent 4.7 machines, and/or produce 134.2 units. Answer the following questions, assuming the production function for DurableTires Corp. is $Q = L^{1/3}K^{1/2}$, where Q is the quantity of tires produced, L is the number of workers employed, and K is the number of machines rented.

a. What is the quantity of tires produced when the company employs 64 workers and 36 machines?

b. What are the average product of labor (L) and the average product of machines (K) when the input mix is the one given above? Clearly and concisely, please explain how you would interpret these numbers.

c. Continue to assume the input mix given above: What is the marginal product of labor (L), if the number of workers is increased by 1 unit? What is the marginal product of capital (K), if the number of machines is increased by 1 unit, instead? Clearly and concisely, explain how you would interpret these numbers.

d. Does DurableTires' production function display increasing, decreasing, or constant returns to scale? Explain. Would your answer change, if the production function were $Q = L^{1/2}K^{1/2}$? How? Explain.

e. Does DurableTires' production function display increasing, decreasing, or constant returns to labor? Explain. Would your answer change, if the production function were $Q = L^{1/2}K^{1/2}$? How? Explain.

5–23. Answer the following questions, continuing to assume the production function for DurableTires Corp. is $Q = L^{1/3}K^{1/2}$, where Q is the quantity of tires produced, L is the number of workers employed, and K is the number of machines rented. Moreover, assume the wage per unit of labor (W_L) is $50 and the rental price per machine is $200 ($W_K$).

a. What is the total cost of producing the quantity of tires you found in your answer to question 5–23(a)? And the average cost? Assuming the number of machines rented does not change, what is the marginal cost of producing one additional tire?

b. Given the production function above, the marginal product of labor and the marginal product of capital are $MP_L = 1/3(L^{-2/3}K^{1/2})$ and $MP_K = 1/2(L^{1/3}K^{-1/2})$, respectively. Given the wage and rental rate above, is DurableTires Corp. adopting an optimal input mix to produce the quantity of tires found in question 5–23(a)? If yes, why? If not, why not, and how could DurableTires Corp. save money producing that same quantity of tires? Explain.

c. What happens to the optimal input mix you found in question 5–23, if the government introduces a tax that raises the cost of labor to $150 per worker? Explain.

5–24. Assume DurableTires Corp. faces the following demand curve, $P = 250 - 0.1Q$. If DurableTires' marginal cost is constant at $35, how many tires should it produce in order to maximize its profits? What's DurableTires' profit in this case? Should the elasticity of demand be greater, equal, or less than 1 at the profit-maximizing price and quantity? Explain (*Hint:* you may use a graph to support your argument).

Appendix: The Factor-Balance Equation[22]

This appendix derives the factor-balance equation—Equation (5.9) in the text:

$$MP_i/P_i = MP_j/P_j \qquad (5.15)$$

This condition must hold if the firm is producing output in a manner that minimizes costs (assuming an interior solution).

Recall that at the cost-minimizing method of production, the isoquant curve and isocost line are tangent. Thus, they must have equal slopes. The factor-balance equation is found by setting the slope of the isoquant equal to the slope of the isocost line and rearranging the expression. In the text, we showed that the slope of the isocost line is $-P_j/P_i$. We now derive the slope of an isoquant.

---

[22]This appendix requires a basic knowledge of calculus.

Slope of an Isoquant

The production function in the two-input case takes the following general form:

$$Q = f(x_i, x_j) \qquad (5.16)$$

To find the slope of an isoquant, we totally differentiate Equation (5.16). We set this differential equal to zero, since quantity does not change along an isoquant:

$$dQ = [\partial Q/\partial x_i \, dx_i] + [\partial Q/\partial x_j \, dx_j] = 0 \qquad (5.17)$$

The slope of the isoquant is defined by dx_i/dx_j. Thus,

$$\text{Slope of an isoquant} = -(\partial Q/\partial x_j)/(\partial Q/\partial x_i) \qquad (5.18)$$
$$= -\text{MP}_j/\text{MP}_i \qquad (5.19)$$

This expression has a straightforward interpretation. For illustration, assume that at some fixed combination of x_i and x_j, the marginal product of i is 1 and the marginal product of j is 2. At this point, the slope of the isoquant is -2. This means that 2 units of i can be given up for 1 unit of j and output will stay the same. This is true by definition since j has twice the marginal product of i.

Factor-Balance Equation

When employing the cost-minimizing production method, the slope of the isoquant is the same as the slope of the isocost line:

$$-\text{MP}_j/\text{MP}_i = -P_j/P_i \qquad (5.20)$$

Rearranging this expression gives us the factor-balance equation:

$$\text{MP}_i/P_i = \text{MP}_j/P_j \qquad (5.21)$$

This expression immediately generalizes to production functions with more than two inputs.

Market Structure

LEARNING OBJECTIVES

1. List the basic characteristics of market structure.
2. Explain why perfect competition is a useful benchmark model.
3. Explain a firm's short-run supply decision and firm and industry supply curves.
4. Explain shutdown and exit decisions.
5. Explain graphically and intuitively long-run equilibrium and how changes in a market affect the equilibrium in the short and long run.
6. Explain the difference between a constant cost and increasing cost industry.
7. List potential barriers to entry in an industry.
8. Contrast the monopolistic and competitive market outcomes.
9. Define oligopoly and Nash equilibrium.
10. Describe standard economic models of oligopolies focusing on output and price competition, respectively.
11. Describe the "prisoner's dilemma" and discuss how it relates to cartel incentives.

The market for cable television has grown tremendously since Home Box Office (a subsidiary of Time Inc.) began broadcasting in 1975.[1] Today millions of subscribers purchase multichannel packages from cable companies. Historically consumers in most local markets had but one choice—purchase cable TV from the one local provider or watch the locally broadcast "free" channels. Subject to regulatory constraints, local cable companies could set their prices without fear that they would be undercut by the competition. Correspondingly, annual price increases for cable TV often exceeded the rate of inflation. According to the Federal Communications Commission, the average monthly price for cable TV rose by more than 90 percent between 1995 and 2005.

In 1994, DirecTV began providing an alternative to cable TV—satellite TV. Initially, customers had to shell out up to $850 for installation and dish equipment, and pay ongoing fees to acquire satellite TV. Many consumers did not consider satellite TV to be a viable alternative because of the price. Fledgling satellite companies were able to attract some customers because

[1] Some of the details for this example are from P. Grant (2002), "The Cable Guy Cuts His Rates," *The Wall Street Journal* (September 25); Reuters Limited (2002), "FCC: Cable Prices Rose 7.5% over 12 Months" (April 4); C. Wexler (2006), "Ask Yourself Why . . . Cable Rates Got So High," *Common Cause* (October).

they offered more channels and a clearer digital picture than the typical cable company; they were most successful in locations not served by cable companies.

By 2002, the market had changed significantly. Local cable companies were offering more channels and higher quality reception, while satellite companies had lowered their prices and hookup fees substantially. To many consumers, satellite TV and cable TV had become relatively close substitutes. Thus the decision between these two services began to depend more on their relative prices. One consumer who switched from paying $80 per month for Mediacom's cable service to DirecTV's satellite service priced at $50 per month summed it up when he said, "I feel like I got everything I had with digital cable but at a lot cheaper price."

In response to the increased competition, cable company managers initiated several major policy changes. First, they became more competitive in the pricing of cable TV services. Charter Communications, with over 4 million residential subscribers in 2014, is one example of a cable company that altered its pricing policies in response to competitive pressures. In St. Louis, for instance, its basic service of 125+ channels for $59.99 per month competed with Dish Network's service of 120+ channels for $29.99 per month and DirectTV's basic package of 150+ channels for $29.99 per month. In addition, Charter faced increased competition from Internet video providers, such as Netflix and Amazon Instant Video. In explaining an earlier price freeze in that market, Charter's CEO stated, "We've got to think twice about rate increases." Second, cable companies began offering new price/channel packages to cater to various consumer groups with different price/channel sensitivities. For example, AT&T introduced a premium package of 150 channels for $50 per month and an economy package of 100 channels for $40 per month. Previously they only had offered a 125-channel package for $43 month. Third, increased competition also affected the companies' advertising strategies. For example, companies began promoting the relative benefits of cable TV (such as access to local channels, reduced "rain fade," not having satellite equipment detract from the appearance of the home, and so on).

The example of cable TV illustrates how policy choices—such as pricing, product design, and advertising—are influenced critically by the market environment. Policies that work within a protected market environment often have to be amended materially when facing a more competitive environment. It is important that managers understand the firm's market environment and how this set of market circumstances affects decision making. Our purpose in this chapter is to enhance that understanding by exploring the implications of alternative market structures. Our primary focus is on output and basic pricing decisions within different market structures. In subsequent chapters, we examine more complex pricing policies and how other policies, such as aspects of the firm's strategy and organizational architecture, depend on the market environment.

We begin by discussing markets and market structure in greater detail. We then provide an analysis of competitive industries. Perfect competition is at one end of a continuum based on the environment in which prices are determined within the industry. Competitive markets provide important managerial implications for firms operating within a broad class of market settings. Next, we discuss barriers to entry that can limit competition within an industry. This section is followed by an analysis of the market structure at the other end of the continuum: monopoly. In a monopolistic industry, there is but one firm. In contrast to firms in competitive industries, a monopolist has substantial discretion in setting prices. After a brief discussion of a relatively common hybrid structure—monopolistic competition—we consider the case of oligopoly, where a small number of rival firms constitute the industry.

Markets

A *market* consists of all firms and individuals who are willing and able to buy or sell a particular product.[2] These parties include those currently engaged in buying and selling the product, as well as potential entrants. *Potential entrants* are all individuals and firms that pose a sufficiently credible threat of market entry to affect the pricing and output decisions of incumbent firms.

Market structure refers to the basic characteristics of the market environment, including (1) the number and size of buyers, sellers, and potential entrants; (2) the degree of product differentiation; (3) the amount and cost of information about product price and quality; and (4) the conditions for entry and exit. We begin our analysis of alternative market structures by examining competitive markets.

Competitive Markets

Economists generally characterize competitive markets by four basic conditions:

- A large number of potential buyers and sellers
- Product homogeneity
- Rapid dissemination of accurate information at low cost
- Free entry into and exit from the market

Although few markets are perfectly competitive, many markets closely approximate this description. Moreover, competition establishes a benchmark that yields useful insights into other market settings. An example of a market that comfortably satisfies the conditions for a competitive market is the market for soybeans. In this market, a relatively large number of farmers grow soybeans, and a large number of firms and individuals purchase soybeans. Soybeans are a relatively homogeneous commodity; the product varies little across producers. There are limited informational disparities, and entry as well as exit are essentially costless.

In competitive markets, individual buyers and sellers take the market price for the product as given—no single participant has any real control over price. If a seller charges more than the market price, buyers simply will purchase the product from other suppliers. And firms always can sell their output at the market price; thus they have no reason to offer discounts to attract buyers. In this setting, firms view their demand curves as horizontal—a firm can sell any feasible output at the market price, $P*$—but sells no output at a price above $P*$. Figure 6.1 illustrates a horizontal demand curve. With a horizontal demand curve, both marginal revenue (MR) and average revenue (AR) equal price.

Firm Supply

Short-Run Supply Decisions

In the last chapter, we saw that a firm's profit is maximized at the output where marginal revenue equals marginal cost. The intuition of this result is straightforward—it makes sense to expand output as long as incremental revenue is greater than

---

[2]The specific characteristics of a product often vary across firms. Knowing which firms and individuals to group together as a market, therefore, is not always straightforward. As discussed in Chapter 4, cross elasticities are helpful in defining markets. Products with high cross elasticities can be considered in the same market because they are "close substitutes."

Figure 6.1   Firm Demand Curve in Perfect Competition

In competitive markets, firms take the market price of the product as given. The demand curve is horizontal. Both marginal revenue and average revenue are equal to the market price.

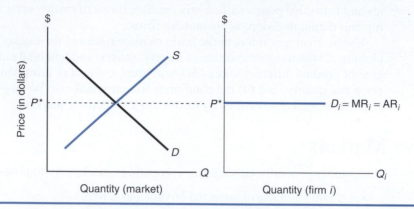

incremental cost. Past this point, profits decline with additional output since incremental revenue is less than incremental cost. In a competitive market, marginal revenue is equal to price (P). In the short run, the firm takes its plant size (and possibly other inputs) as given. The relevant cost is *short-run marginal cost* (SRMC). The condition for short-run profit maximization in a competitive industry is

$$P^* = \text{SRMC} \tag{6.1}$$

This condition—one of the more important propositions in economics—indicates that at any price, a competitive firm should produce the output where price equals short-run marginal cost. The firm, however, has the additional option of producing no output at all. When the price of the product is insufficient to cover its *average variable cost* (AVC), the firm is better off if it ceases production. With no output, the firm loses money since it generates no revenue to cover its fixed costs. However, this loss is smaller than the one it would incur if the firm produced any other level of output (since revenue from sales would be lower than its variable production costs). Hence the *shutdown condition for the short run* is

$$P^* < \text{AVC} \tag{6.2}$$

A firm's supply curve depicts the quantity that the firm will produce at each price. Therefore the firm's short-run supply curve is that portion of its short-run marginal cost curve above average variable cost. Figure 6.2 highlights this supply curve.

Long-Run Supply Decisions

Firms can lose money in the short run yet still find it optimal to stay in business. In the long run, however, a firm must be profitable or it is better to exit this market. Price must equal or exceed *long-run average cost* (LRAC). Thus, the *shutdown condition for the long run* is

$$P^* < \text{LRAC} \tag{6.3}$$

Figure 6.2 The Firm's Short-Run Supply Curve

The firm's short-run supply curve is the portion of the short-run marginal cost (SRMC) curve that is above average variable cost (AVC). At prices below average variable cost, the firm is better off not producing any output.

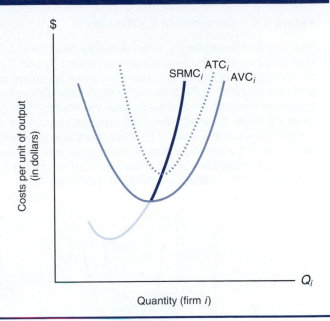

In the long run, a firm can adjust its plant size. The long-run supply decision of a firm is based on *long-run marginal costs* (LRMC). The long-run supply curve of a firm is that portion of its long-run marginal cost curve above long-run average cost. This supply curve is depicted in Figure 6.3.[3]

Figure 6.3 The Firm's Long-Run Supply Curve

The long-run supply curve for firm *i* is the portion of the long-run marginal cost (LRMC) curve that is above long-run average cost (LRAC). If price is below LRAC, the firm should go out of business.

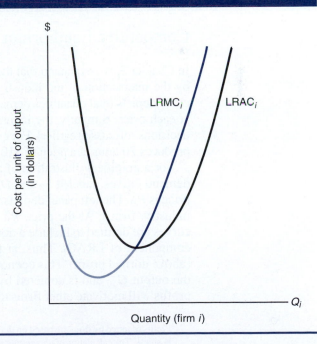

[3]There is no inconsistency between short-run and long-run profit maximization. The LRMC at any given output is equal to the SRMC, given that the firm has the optimal plant size for the output. Hence, the firm simultaneously can choose an output where $P* = \text{SRMC} = \text{LRMC}$.

Figure 6.4 Competitive Equilibrium

The left panel illustrates the long-run supply decision of firm i, a representative firm in the industry. In the right panel, supply and demand curves (labeled S_0 and D_0) determine the market price, P_0^*. At the price, P_0^*, the firm produces Q_{i0}^*. At the price P_0^*, the firm is earning an *economic profit*. This economic profit is the profit per unit ($P_0^* - LRAC_i$) times the total output Q_{i0}^* and is depicted by the shaded rectangle. Economic profits will motivate other firms to enter the industry. This entry will shift the supply curve to the right and lower the price. Additional entry will occur up to the point where there are no economic profits. This condition occurs at a price of P_1^*. Here, there are no incentives for firms to enter or leave the industry (incumbents are earning a normal rate of profit and inventories are stable at their desired levels), and the market is in *equilibrium*. In a competitive equilibrium, firms produce output at the low point on their average cost curves ($P_1^* = LRMC_i = LRAC_i$). Thus, the equilibrium is associated with efficient production.

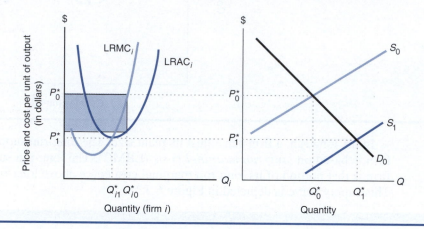

Competitive Equilibrium

In Chapter 3, we explained that the market price in a competitive market is determined by the intersection of the industry demand and supply curves. The industry demand curve depicts total quantities demanded aggregated across all buyers in the marketplace at each price. Similarly, the industry supply curve is the sum of all individual supply decisions (discussed earlier). For example, if there are 100 firms in the industry and each produces 20 units at a price of $10, the industry supply at that price will be 2,000 units.

For a graphical illustration of a competitive equilibrium, consider the supply and demand curves, labeled S_0 and D_0 in the right panel of Figure 6.4. Here, the market price is P_0^*. The left panel depicts the long-run supply decision of a typical firm in the industry, firm i. At the price P_0^*, firm i produces the quantity of output Q_{i0}^*. Cost curves are defined to include a normal rate of profit (a normal return on capital is one component of LRAC). Thus, at the price P_0^*, firm i is earning an *economic profit* (above normal profit). This economic profit is the profit per unit ($P_0^* - LRAC$) times the output Q_{i0}^* and is depicted by the shaded rectangle. The existence of economic profits will motivate other firms to enter the industry.[4] This entry will shift the supply

---

[4]Profits reported by firms are based on the accounting definition: Sales revenue minus the explicit costs of doing business. The calculation of *accounting profits,* therefore, does not include the opportunity cost of the owner's entrepreneurial effort or equity capital. Economic profits include these costs. Positive economic profits attract entry because the returns are higher than the returns in the alternative activities. Positive accounting profits do not always invite entry—the returns do not always cover the opportunity costs of the owners.

curve to the right; inventories will build above their desired levels because of the increased production; hence firms will lower price. Additional entry will occur up to the point where there are no longer economic profits. This condition is pictured in Figure 6.4 at a price of P_1^*. Here, there are no incentives for firms to enter or leave the industry (incumbents are earning a normal rate of profit); inventories are stable at their desired levels and the market is in *equilibrium*. In a competitive equilibrium, firms produce output at the minimum point on their average cost curves ($P^* =$ LRMC = LRAC). Thus, this equilibrium is associated with efficient production.

Constant versus Increasing Cost Industries

Standard supply and demand graphs, such as Figures 6.1 and 6.4, usually picture industry supply curves as upward sloping. While short-run industry supply curves typically slope upward, long-run industry curves in many industries are essentially horizontal (flat)—supply is perfectly elastic. Whether the long-run industry supply curve is horizontal or upward sloping depends on the incremental costs of expanding industry output.

In the *short run*, firms have some fixed inputs and entry or exit of firms have not had time to occur. The *Law of Diminishing Marginal Returns* states that the marginal products of variable inputs will eventually decline as output increases. A firm's short-run marginal costs will increase once this output level is reached (since the variable inputs are less productive, but cost the same). Upward sloping short-run marginal cost curves imply that both firm and industry supply curves will generally slope upward in the short run (as pictured in the standard graphs). An increase in demand for the product will cause the short-run equilibrium price to increase, and existing firms will earn economic profits in the near term. Economic profits, in turn, will induce entry and a resulting long-run fall in price.

Whether the long-run industry supply curve is flat or upward sloping depends on whether the firm is a *constant-cost* or *increasing cost* industry. In a constant-cost industry, all existing firms and potential entrants face the same average costs of production independent of the number of firms in the industry. For instance, they might all have identical cost curves to those pictured for the representative firm in the left panel of Figure 6.4. As an example, consider fast-food restaurants in a large market area. A new restaurant entering this market will likely incur nearly identical costs to existing firms for retail-building space, labor, wholesale food products, and other inputs required for operation. In addition, wage rates and the prices of other inputs are unlikely to be affected with more or fewer restaurants. Thus, the average cost of producing meals is likely to be independent of the number of restaurants in the market area. With

---

MANAGERIAL APPLICATIONS

Entry in Low-Carb Food

An estimated 32 million Americans are following the Atkins Diet and spending $2.5 billion a year on low-carb foods. Atkins Nutritionals sells 120 products and has licensed its name to dozens of companies. "There's not much growth in the food industry and Atkins is getting most of it," says John McMillin of Prudential Securities. But food giants from Kraft to General Mills are beginning to offer competing products. For instance, Heinz is introducing its One Carb ketchup. "Competition is inevitable," says Atkins President, Scott Kabak.

Source: B. Grow (2003), "The Low-Carb Food Fight Ahead," *BusinessWeek* (December 22), 48.

constant costs, the long-run industry supply curve is horizontal at a price equal to the common minimum long-run average cost for firms in the industry (P_1^* in Figure 6.4). At higher prices, existing firms earn economic profits, which promotes entry and downward pressure on price. At lower prices, firms do not cover average costs and thus are unprofitable. Some will exit the industry putting upward pressure on price.

With a horizontal (perfectly elastic) long-run supply curve, the long-run market price does not change as demand for the product increases or decreases (price is determined by costs, not demand). Rather a change in demand affects only the quantity produced and the number of firms in the industry. For example, if the minimum average cost for firms in a constant-cost industry is $50, the long-run equilibrium price will be $50. This is the only price where no firms have incentives either to exit or to enter the industry. If demand increases or decreases, the price will stay at $50 but the equilibrium quantity will adjust (draw a horizontal supply curve at $50 and view what happens as the demand curve shifts). Our analysis in Chapter 3 describes the ability of suppliers to pass on a per-unit cost increase depends on the relative elasticities of supply and demand curves. Perfectly elastic long-run supply curves imply that a cost increase, such as a government excise tax, will ultimately be borne by consumers in the form of higher prices.

In increasing cost industries, the costs of production increase as the number of firms in the industry increases. For example, in many agricultural markets additional output must be produced on less productive farmland, which implies higher per-unit costs. In such an industry, price must increase to induce additional production (since the current price is below the incremental cost of producing additional output). In this case, the long-run supply curve is upward sloping. Here a change in demand will affect both the equilibrium quantity and price.

As we will discuss in more detail in Chapter 8, existing firms in an increasing cost industry often do not earn economic profits when the product price increases due to an increase in demand. Rather, the prices of the inputs that made the initial low-cost production possible (e.g., a particularly productive piece of farmland will sell for a higher price than less-productive farmland) are likely to increase, so that in equilibrium no firm has a cost advantage or economic profits. If the product and

ACADEMIC APPLICATIONS

Phantom Freight

Most plywood in the United States is produced in the Pacific Northwest. Due to this dominance, plywood prices throughout the country are essentially the Northwest price plus shipping. If this condition did not hold, Northwest suppliers would curtail shipping plywood to cities with low prices and increase shipping to cities with high prices. The changes in supply would affect the prices in the cities until, in equilibrium, the prices across cities would differ only by transportation costs.

In a U.S. court case, Southeast timber producers were sued for charging customers Northwest's price plus shipping and then delivering locally produced plywood. It was ruled that these companies were making unjust profits because they did not actually incur the shipping costs. The jury awarded billions of dollars to the customers. Were these companies really making economic profits? The answer is probably not. The local production in the Southeast had a shipping advantage to Southeast customers. The factor that made this advantage possible was scarce timber land in the Southeast. Presumably, the price of this scarce timber land was bid up to the point where plywood producers were making only a normal profit given the prevailing price for plywood in the Southeast (which was the Northwest price plus shipping).

Source: A. Alchian and W. Allen (1983), *Exchange and Production: Competition, Coordination and Control* (Wadsworth Publishing: Belmont), 228–231.

ANALYZING MANAGERIAL DECISIONS: *United Airlines*

The *WSJ* recently presented data suggesting that United Airlines was not covering its costs on flights from San Francisco to Washington D.C. The article quoted analysts saying that United should discontinue this service. The costs per flight (presented in the article) included the costs of fuel, pilots, flight attendants, food, etc. used on the flight. They also included a share of the costs associated with running the hubs at the two airports, such as ticket agents, building charges, baggage handlers, gate charges, etc. Suppose that the revenue collected on the typical United flight from San Francisco to Washington does not cover these costs. Does this fact imply that United should discontinue these flights? Explain.

all the relevant input markets are perfectly competitive, generally no firm in the industry will be able to make economic profits over the long run. It is important for managers to consider this likely reality when they make investment and other strategic decisions.

Strategic Considerations

Although few markets exactly match economists' idealized conditions for perfect competition, many markets approximate this structure. In most industries, there are strong competitive forces that reduce economic profits over time. These forces imply that many strategic advantages (e.g., being the first in a new market) are likely to be short-lived. If the conditions in the market resemble the competitive model, it is important to move quickly to take advantage of transitory opportunities. In addition, potential entrants should realize that observed economic profits in an industry are likely to be bid away as time passes. This consideration can affect both long-range capital spending and entry decisions. For instance, given the increased competition, cable TV companies increased the level of scrutiny they applied to internal investment proposals. In a competitive market, firms must strive for efficiency and cost control; inefficient firms lose money and are forced out of the market.

Barriers to Entry[5]

Although the competitive model is a reasonable approximation in many markets, there are other industries where firms have notable market power—output decisions of individual firms have a noticeable impact on prices. A necessary condition for market power to exist is that there are effective *barriers to entry* into the industry.

To understand what constitutes an effective entry barrier, it is useful to consider the decisions of individual firms to enter an industry. Firms consider entering a new market when they observe extant firms reporting large profits. For instance, if Wen Ho observes a firm such as a cable TV company reporting large profits, his firm (like a number of other firms) is likely to consider entering the industry. Entry decisions depend on three important factors: First, Wen will be concerned about whether his entry will affect product prices. This depends, at least in part, on how existing firms are likely to respond to a new entrant. For example, are they likely to cut prices? Second, Wen will be concerned about incumbent advantages. Do existing firms have

---

[5]This section provides a brief summary of the literature in economics on barriers to entry; it draws on S. M. Oster (1994), *Modern Competitive Analysis* (Oxford Press: New York).

advantages that an entering firm will have difficulty duplicating—ones that make it unlikely that the new firm will enjoy similar profits? Third, Wen will be concerned about costs of exit. How much will it cost to leave the industry if this incursion fails? We discuss each of these factors in turn.

Incumbent Reactions

Specific Assets

Specific assets are assets that have more value in their current use than in their next best alternative use. Consider the case of the Alaskan Pipeline. It has a high value in its current use. Yet it is completely specialized for transporting oil from the North Slope to Prudoe Bay—it has virtually no other use. Moreover, it could be moved only at enormous expense. If existing firms in an industry have invested heavily in assets quite specialized to that market, they are likely to fight harder to maintain their positions than if their assets are less specific and can be shifted at low cost to alternative activities.

Scale Economies

Industries with significant economies of scale have minimum efficient scales that occur at high output levels. In such industries, a new entrant must produce at high volume to be cost-effective. Large-scale production is more likely to have a material effect on price. For example, if the minimum efficient scale is 30 percent of total market demand, price certainly will decline if a new entrant tries to capture such a large share of the market—its entry undoubtedly would trigger vigorous price competition from incumbents. Note that the absolute size of the minimum efficient scale is not as important as is this scale relative to the size of the total market. Minimum efficient scale varies enormously across industries. In one study, estimates of minimum efficient scale, as a percentage of industry capacity, ranged from 0.5 percent (fruit/vegetable canning) to 33 percent (gypsum products).[6] Globalization of markets increases effective market size, thereby reducing this entry barrier—for example, consider the size of American versus global automobile markets.

Reputation Effects

Potential entrants can be influenced by the reputations of existing firms in the industry for reactions to new entrants. In certain circumstances, it can pay for an existing firm to react more aggressively than would be implied by considering only its immediate interests. For example, facing a new rival, the firm might engage in extensive price cutting to establish a reputation as a formidable competitor. Note, however, that threats by firms to cut prices if entry occurs sometimes lack credibility. If new firms actually enter, existing firms might not follow through with their threats because they would be harmed by their own price cuts. Thus, it can be reasonable for a potential entrant to ignore threats—if the entrant believes that incumbents are bluffing. We examine these considerations in greater detail in Chapter 9.

Excess Capacity

If firms with excess capacity cut production, they can be confronted with much higher average costs (depending on the slopes of their average cost curves). Also, firms with excess capacity are better able to satisfy the demands of new customers

---

[6]K. Lancaster and R. Dulaney (1979), *Modern Economics: Principles and Policy* (Rand McNally: New York), 211.

Excess Capacity at Alcoa

In 1940, Alcoa Aluminum lost an important antitrust case involving its production strategy of maintaining excess capacity. The judge ruled that he could think of no better "effective" deterrent to entry.

should they lower price and force a rival out of business. Potential competitors, therefore, may be less likely to enter when there is excess capacity in the industry because they anticipate more aggressive reactions on the part of incumbents.[7] Excess capacity frequently exists for completely innocuous reasons. For example, a firm facing cyclical production or anticipating growth has excess capacity over some time spans because it has invested in additional capacity to satisfy peak demands better. In other cases, excess capacity may be chosen specifically to deter entry.

Incumbent Advantages

Precommitment Contracts

Existing firms often have long-term contracts for raw materials, distribution outlets, shelf space, and delivery of the final product. These contracts can serve as a deterrent to entry, since they limit the opportunities for customers and suppliers to switch from incumbent firms to new entrants.

Licenses and Patents

Sometimes, entry is limited through government restrictions such as licensing requirements and patents. For instance, the number of doctors is limited effectively by state medical licensing requirements. This restriction allows doctors to charge higher prices than if entry were unrestricted. Regulators and licensed physicians justify such restrictions with arguments based on consumer protection. Yet, whether or not consumers benefit from stringent licensing is debatable—given that they pay higher prices.

Normal patent life is 17 years. Over this period, other firms are prohibited from copying the innovation; thus a patent provides a firm with potential market power. Patents also provide important incentives to innovate. From a practical standpoint, the effectiveness of a patent in blocking entry varies dramatically (some patents can be circumvented by clever design, e.g.).

Learning-Curve Effects

In Chapter 5, we discussed how average costs are reduced in some industries through production experience. As production experience accumulates, the firm learns how to lower unit costs. Learning-curve effects can result in new rivals having a cost disadvantage relative to existing firms. Whether these effects are important depends on whether the new entrants simply can copy the techniques learned by existing firms through their experience.

Pioneering Brand Advantages

Sometimes, a firm benefits from being first in an industry. In some industries—over-the-counter drugs, for example—a satisfied customer might be reluctant to switch

[7]Excess capacity can occur because of significant declines in industry demand. In this case, profits are likely to be low and entry will not be attractive. Our current discussion focuses on cases where incumbents are making economic profits and have excess capacity. These economic profits might not induce entry because of the fear of price cutting by incumbents.

Entry in Consumer Electronics

Since its founding two decades ago, Xoceco Inc. has evolved from producing low-cost color TVs for the Chinese market to producing flat-screen TVs. They plan to market in the United States by supplying companies like Dell or Hewlett-Packard. Rather than spending lavishly in chips and software to power their products, they buy the components, assemble the gadgets, and undercut the industry leaders' prices. Thus, consumer electronics leaders like Sony and Matsushita are threatened the way IBM was by the rise of the PC clone.

Source: E. Ramstad and P. Dvorak (2003), "Off-the-Shelf Parts Create New Order in TVs, Electronics," *The Wall Street Journal* (December 16), A1.

---

brands even if the price of a competing product is substantially lower. This tendency is likely to be strongest in *experience goods,* which have to be tried by the customer to ascertain quality. For instance, customers might hesitate to try a new pain reliever because they fear that it might not be as effective as their regular brand. Where quality can be judged by inspection prior to purchase, this advantage of incumbents is lower. Sometimes the incumbent's advantage with an experienced good can be overcome by a new entrant through free samples, endorsements, or government certification. Each of these methods entails additional costs—these costs of overcoming incumbent advantages deter entry.

Exit Costs

Another important entry consideration centers on the costs of exit. In some industries, it is possible to "hit and run." For instance, forming a new company to seal asphalt driveways requires little investment in specialized equipment or training. A new firm can enter quickly when the profit potential is high and exit at low cost if profits decline. In other industries, especially those with specific assets, exit costs can be high. In such industries firms bear significant costs, such as moving employees to new locations and liquidating plants and other assets when they decide to exit. High exit costs deter initial entry.

Monopoly

Effective barriers to entry limit the threat of competition and give incumbent firms market power. Although competitive markets are at one end of the spectrum, at the other end is *monopoly*—where there is but a single firm in the industry. Here, industry and firm demand curves are one and the same.

Government Restrictions on Exit

Some regulators want to restrict companies from closing plants. These regulators appear motivated by concerns over people who lose their jobs when a company closes a plant. Restrictions on plant closings, however, are likely to reduce the desirability of entry into an industry—firms will be reluctant to enter an industry if they cannot exit easily when they are losing money. Thus, potential effects of government restrictions on exit are less vigorous competition in the affected industries, higher consumer prices, and lower levels of employment.

Profit Maximization

Suppose that a monopolist charges the same price to all customers. (As discussed shortly, such a pricing policy might be motivated by either government regulation or the inability to prevent resale among customers; in Chapter 7, we relax this restriction.) The firm's objective is to choose the price–quantity combination along the demand curve that maximizes profits. This combination occurs where marginal revenue equals marginal cost.

For purposes of illustration, consider the following linear demand curve:

$$P = 200 - Q \qquad (6.4)$$

(Assume that marginal cost is constant at $10.) Recall that the marginal revenue curve for a linear demand curve is a line with the same intercept and twice the negative slope. Figure 6.5 displays the demand curve, marginal revenue curve, and marginal cost curve in this example. Optimal output occurs at 95 units—where MR = MC. To sell this output, the firm charges a price of $105. The firm makes $95 profit per unit ($105 − $10) for a total profit of $9,025 ($95 × $95); this is indicated by the shaded rectangle *abcd*.

As opposed to pure competition, monopolistic suppliers charge customers more than the marginal and average costs of production and distribution; the firm thus earns an economic profit. Monopolies restrict output compared to competitive industries. In our example, if the industry were competitive, the market price would be $10 (marginal cost) and total quantity sold would be 190 units.

Unexploited Gains from Trade

Given the monopolist's output and pricing choices, some consumers are willing to pay more than the marginal cost of production and distribution, yet do not purchase the product. Thus, not all gains from trade are exhausted. The associated loss in

---

Figure 6.5   Monopoly

This figure illustrates the price and output decisions of a monopolist. In the example, demand is $P = 200 - Q$. Marginal costs are $10. The profit-maximizing output occurs at 95 units, where MR = MC. To sell this output, the firm charges a price of $105. The firm makes $95 per unit profit ($105 − $10) for a total profit of $9,025 ($95 × 95), as indicated by the shaded rectangle *abcd*. Some consumers are willing to pay more than the marginal cost of production, yet do not receive the product. The associated loss in potential gains from trade is pictured by the shaded triangle *cde*. The firm does not lower the price to sell to these consumers because it does not want to lower the price for other customers.

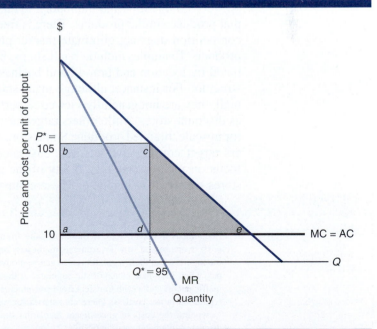

ANALYZING MANAGERIAL DECISIONS: *Pricing and Investment Decisions*

You work for a drug manufacturing company that holds a patent on Hair Grow, the world's most effective drug for restoring hair. Your job is to analyze the pricing and investment decisions facing the firm. Your marketing group estimates that Hair Grow has the following demand curve:

$$P = 101 - .00002Q$$

1.   Your marginal cost for producing a Hair Grow pill is $1. What is the profit-maximizing price and quantity? What is your profit?

2.   Suppose that your production facility can only produce 1,000,000 pills. What is your optimal price and quantity given the production constraint? What are your profits?

3.   Suppose that you could increase the capacity of your plant to 3,000,000 pills within a two-year period for a cost of $30,000,000. Should you undertake the investment (for simplicity, assume you can borrow the funds for the expansion at a 0 percent interest rate)?

potential gains from trade is pictured by the shaded triangle *cde* in Figure 6.5. Consumers along this segment of the demand curve value the product at more than $10 but less than $105. The firm does not lower the price to sell to these consumers because it does not want to lower the price for other customers (recall that in this chapter we presume the firm charges the same price to all customers). From the firm's standpoint, any gain from selling to additional customers would be more than offset by the loss from lowering its price to all its customers.[8]

Monopolistic Competition

As the name implies, *monopolistic competition* is a market structure that is a hybrid between competition and monopoly. In this market structure, there are multiple firms that produce similar products. There is free exit from and entry into the industry. Yet competition does not eliminate market power because the firms sell differentiated products. Examples include retail shops, books, movies, gasoline stations (differentiated by location and brand), and business schools. It is the most common market structure. For instance, although many shoe stores compete for customers at a large mall, they are not generally viewed as perfect substitutes. Some position themselves as discount stores, while others target customers who are willing to pay high prices for upscale, branded products. Some stores focus on selling athletic shoes, while others target conservative business customers. Some focus on women, while others focus on men or children. If any of the existing stores are highly profitable, new stores can enter to compete. These companies thus have some market power. New

[8]Economists frequently refer to these lost gains from trade as a *deadweight loss*. This inefficiency (or *social cost*) is one reason why governments might pass regulations like antitrust laws to restrict the formation of monopolies. But these regulations also can be motivated by concerns about the higher prices that consumers pay when they face monopolistic suppliers. Although government regulation has the potential to reduce inefficiencies and wealth transfers from consumers to firms, it is important to keep in mind that government regulation is not costless. There are salaries for regulators and court costs, for instance. From a societal viewpoint, the costs of government regulation should be weighed against the benefits. These issues are discussed in greater detail in Chapter 21.

MANAGERIAL APPLICATIONS

Monopolistic Competition in Golf Balls

There are many brands of golf balls. Some golfers view the balls as perfect substitutes and simply purchase the lowest-priced brand. Other golfers prefer one brand to another. For instance, they might believe one brand of ball flies farther or provides greater control than competing brands. These golfers are willing to pay a higher price for their favorite ball than for competing balls. However, they often will substitute if the price difference is more than a few dollars a dozen. Also, if a company develops some popular feature, like a larger number of dimples on the ball, the feature is typically copied by other companies within a short time period. Since a golf equipment company has a *monopoly* in producing its own brand, it has some market power. However, this power is limited given the *competition* in the industry.

stores are likely to enter the industry if the existing firms report large profits—there are no significant barriers to entry.

Monopolistic competition is similar to monopoly in that firms under both market structures face downward-sloping demand curves: A toothpaste company can raise its price without losing all sales. Given that the firms face downward-sloping demand curves, each strives to select the price–quantity combination that maximizes its profits. The output decision is based on the same analysis as for the pure monopolist—choose that output where MC = MR.

The difference between monopoly and monopolistic competition is that in monopolistic competition, economic profits invite entry and imitation. If a shoe store earns high profit from carrying a new product line, others will have an incentive to compete by offering that product line or a very similar line. Entry and imitation will shift the original firm's demand curve to the left and reduce profits. Zero economic profits exist when the demand curve is shifted to the point where average cost equals price. Figure 6.6 shows this condition.

Figure 6.6 Monopolistic Competition

In monopolistic competition, firms sell differentiated products. This figure shows the demand curve for firm i in such an industry. The curve is downward-sloping. Similar to monopoly pricing, the firm selects the output where marginal revenue equals marginal cost. Monopolistic competition differs from monopoly in that abnormal profits will invite entry. Entry shifts the demand curve for the firm to the left (as some of the customers buy from the new firms). The firm makes no economic profits when price is equal to average cost. This condition occurs at price P_i^* and quantity Q_i^*.

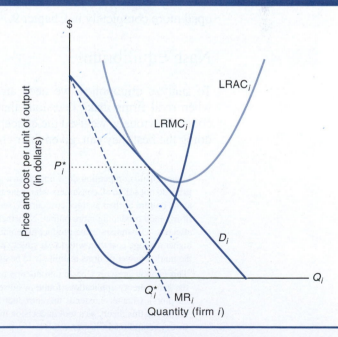

These competitive responses will tend to force profits to zero. Yet some brands continue to be more distinctive than others. Also, costs can vary because of differences in production techniques and inputs. It is possible for some firms to earn economic profits in monopolistic competition.[9]

Oligopoly

Within *oligopolistic markets,* only a few firms produce most of the output. Examples of oligopolistic industries include automobiles and steel during the 1950s. These industries had important scale economies and other substantial entry barriers. In 1995, the top four cereal makers in the United States produced about 90 percent of industry output, while the top eight accounted for virtually all production. Products may or may not be differentiated. Firms can earn substantial profits. These profits are not reduced through new entry because of effective entry barriers. Yet as we shall see, economic profits sometimes can be eliminated in oligopolistic industries through competition among the existing firms.

In our analysis of other market structures, we assume that firms take the prices of their competitors as given. A firm was not expected to respond to announcements of changes in prices by rival firms. This assumption certainly is reasonable in the case of competitive markets with many small firms, as well as in the case of monopoly with only one large firm. But this assumption rarely is valid within oligopolistic industries. For instance, when American Airlines considers lowering its prices on particular routes, it obviously must be concerned about whether United Airlines and its other competitors will follow suit. In fact, firms in oligopolistic industries ordinarily will be quite concerned about how their rivals will react to most major policy decisions, be they advertising campaigns or product design decisions. Decision making within these industries requires *strategic thinking*. Decision makers must realize that competitors are rational parties operating in their own self-interest. Thus, it is important for decision makers to place themselves in their rivals' positions and consider how they might react. (This basic principle, which we now examine briefly, is developed more completely in Chapter 9.)[10]

Nash Equilibrium

To analyze oligopolies, we need an underlying principle to define an equilibrium when rival firms make decisions that explicitly take each other's behavior into account. Previously, we used the concept that a market is in equilibrium when firms are doing the best they can, given their circumstances and have no reason to change price

---

[9]Monopolistic competition does not exhaust all gains from trade for two reasons. First, as in monopoly, the firms do not sell to all consumers who value the product at above marginal cost. Second, firms do not operate at the bottom of their average cost curves (see Figure 6.6). Lower average cost would be obtained with fewer firms, each producing more output. Nonetheless, regulation to address these inefficiencies is unlikely to be effective. Consumers value product differentiation and are arguably better off with more variety at slightly higher average cost than with lower variety produced at lower average cost. Second, with few entry barriers, the market power of firms is unlikely to be great.

[10]This chapter presents a basic introduction to game theory. The material provides sufficient background for the game theory applications found in subsequent parts of the book (these are in the appendices of several chapters). Chapter 9 extends this introduction of game theory and discusses in more detail how managers might use this theory as a tool in decision making. Readers interested in a more detailed treatment of game theory should read Chapter 9.

Figure 6.7 Nash Equilibrium

In this example, there are two firms in an industry—WonCo and TuInc. Each independently chooses a price for an identical product. The firms choose either a high price or a low price. The payoffs are given in the table (the upper-left entry in a cell displays the profits for WonCo, the lower right shows the profits for TuInc). The equilibrium is for WonCo to charge a high price and TuInc to charge a low price—the shaded cell. Any other combination is unstable: That is, given the action of one of the firms, the other firm has the incentive to deviate. This equilibrium is called a *Nash equilibrium*.

or output. For example, in a competitive equilibrium, there is no reason for entry or exit (existing firms are making "normal" profits). No existing firm has any reason to change its output level (all are producing where MC = MR = P^* and inventories are stable at their desired levels).

We can apply this same basic idea to oligopolistic markets with minor modification. In the following analysis, a firm does the best it can, given what its rivals are doing. In doing so, the firm anticipates that other firms will respond to any action it takes by doing the best they can as well. Actions are *noncooperative* in that each firm makes decisions that maximize its profits, given the actions of the other firms. The firms do not collude to maximize joint profits. An equilibrium exists when each firm is doing the best it can, given the actions of its rivals. Economists call this a *Nash equilibrium* for Nobel laureate John Nash who first developed these general concepts.

To illustrate this approach, assume a simple setting: There are two firms in an industry—a *duopoly*. Each independently chooses a price for an identical product. The firms choose either a high price or a low price. The payoffs are given in Figure 6.7. (The entry on the upper left in each cell is for WonCo, while the entry on the lower right is for TuInc.) For example, if both firms charge a high price, WonCo's profits are $400 and TuInc's profits are $200.[11]

The equilibrium is for WonCo to charge a high price and TuInc to charge a low price. Any other combination is unstable: Given the action of one of the firms, the other firm has the incentive to change its price. For instance, if both firms charge a high price, it is in the interests of TuInc to lower its price—its profits go from $200 to $250. The other combinations of WonCo charging a low price and TuInc a high price and both firms charging a low price are similarly unstable: Each firm has an incentive to alter its price given the other firm's choice. A Nash equilibrium is self-enforcing. If WonCo charges a high price, it is optimal for TuInc to charge a low price. Similarly, if TuInc charges a low price, it is optimal for WonCo to charge a high price. Given the choice of one firm, there is no reason for the other to alter its strategy.

---

[11]The profits differ due to differences in the underlying production costs.

In this example, the Nash equilibrium is not the outcome that maximizes the joint profits of the two companies. Combined profits would be higher if both firms charged a high price. Conceptually, the combined profits under this pricing policy could be split in a manner that would make both firms better off than in the Nash equilibrium. For instance, the combined profits of $600 could be split, with each firm receiving $300. As this example illustrates, noncooperative equilibria do not necessarily maximize the joint value of the firms. (Since the potential gains from trade are not exhausted, it is often the case that one or more firms can be made better off, without making other firms worse off, by changing the joint decisions.)

Output Competition

The first major analysis of oligopoly was published by Augustine Cournot in 1838. To illustrate his model, suppose again that there are only two firms in the industry and that they produce identical products. In the *Cournot model,* each firm treats the *output* level of its competitor as fixed and then decides how much to produce. In equilibrium, neither firm has an incentive to change its output level, given the other firm's choice. (Thus, this is a Nash equilibrium.)

Suppose the duopolists face the following total industry demand:

$$P = 100 - Q \tag{6.5}$$

where $Q = Q_A + Q_B$. For simplicity, assume that both firms have marginal costs of zero: $MC_A = MC_B = 0$. Each firm takes the other firm's output as fixed. Thus, the anticipated demand curve for firm i ($i = $ A or B) is

$$P_i = (100 - \overline{Q}_j) - Q_i \tag{6.6}$$

where $\overline{Q}_j = $ expected output of the other firm. The marginal revenue for firm i is[12]

$$MR_i = (100 - \overline{Q}_j) - 2Q_i \tag{6.7}$$

Firm i's profits are maximized by setting marginal revenue equal to marginal cost (in this case, zero). Doing so, and rearranging the expression, yields the following *reaction curve:*

$$Q_i = 50 - 0.5Q_j \tag{6.8}$$

The reaction curve indicates firm i's optimal output given the output choice of firm j. Both firms have the same reaction curve in this example, except that the subscripts are reversed.

Equilibrium occurs where the two curves cross. At these output levels, each firm is maximizing profit given the other firm's output choice. Neither firm has an incentive to alter its output. The equilibrium is pictured in Figure 6.8. In equilibrium, each firm produces 33 units for a total output of 66 units; the price is $33.34. This output level is lower than in a competitive market. With competition, total output would be 100 units and the price would be zero (where $P^* = MC$). In the Cournot equilibrium, firms make economic profits: Price is $33.34; average costs are zero. Each firm thus reports profits of $1,110.89. This profit is lower than the two firms could obtain if they directly colluded and jointly produced the monopolistic output of 50 units (e.g., 25 units per firm). With effective collusion, joint profits would be $2,500 rather than $2,221.78. Figure 6.9

---

[12]Recall that marginal revenue for a linear demand curve is a line with the same intercept, but twice the negative slope.

Figure 6.8 Cournot Equilibrium

The duopolists in this example face the total industry demand curve, $P = 100 - Q$, where Q is the sum of the two outputs. Both firms face a marginal cost of zero. The figure shows the reaction curves for each firm. The reaction curve indicates firm i's optimal output given the output choice of firm j (i, j = A or B). The Cournot equilibrium occurs where the two reaction curves cross. Each firm produces 33.33 units. The market price is $33.34. The output for the firms is lower and the profits are greater than in the competitive equilibrium. The output for the firms is greater and the profits are lower than in the collusive (monopoly) equilibrium.

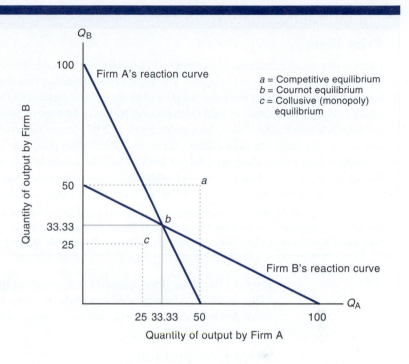

Figure 6.9 Comparison of Prices and Outputs among Collusive, Cournot, and Competitive Equilibria

In this example, the total industry demand curve is $P = 100 - Q$. Marginal cost is zero. The figure shows the price–quantity outputs for the industry under collusive, Cournot, and competitive equilibria. The output is smallest and the price is highest for the collusive equilibrium. The output is largest and the price is smallest for the competitive equilibrium.

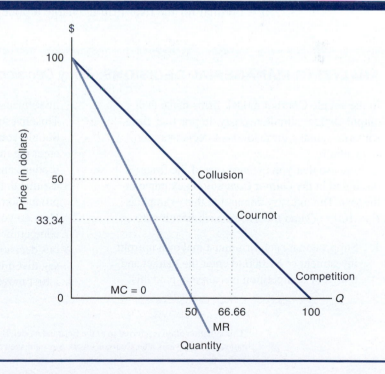

MANAGERIAL APPLICATIONS

Price Wars

Firms in oligopolistic industries sometimes engage in intense price competition to their mutual detriment. Examples include the airline and wireless industries. The major airlines, including American, United, Delta, and Northwest, periodically enter fare wars that lower the price of air travel for consumers and lower the combined profits of the airline industry. For instance, in 2005 Delta lowered its fares in the hope of gaining new passengers. This price reduction was matched by other airlines within hours. In 2002 wireless carriers such as Sprint PCS, AT&T Wireless, and Verizon stole each other's customers offering look-alike calling plans and rock-bottom prices. As soon as one company offered a new calling plan, the rest followed suit. Outside analysts generally agree that the firms lose profits through these price cuts. Financial analysts following the stocks of wireless service companies recommended to their clients that they reduce the amount invested in this sector because intense price competition was lowering profits.

Source: S. Mehta (2001), "First That Old Sinking Feeling," *Fortune* (December 10), 34–35; and M. Rollins (2002), "Wireless Services Second Quarter Preview: Less Than a Zero Sum Game," *Solomon Smith Barney Industry Note* (July 8); J. Horwich (2005), "Northwest Matches Delta's Fare War . . . Reluctantly," Minnesota Public Radio (January 5).

displays the three price–quantity outcomes using the original industry demand curve. (This model can be extended readily to more than two firms. The same general results hold: As the number of firms grows, outcomes approach those of a competitive market.)

Price Competition

In the Cournot model, firms focus on choosing output levels. An alternative possibility is that firms might focus on choosing product price.[13] Here, the Nash equilibrium is for both firms to choose a price equal to marginal cost—the competitive outcome. To see why, suppose one of the firms chooses a price, $P' > $ MC. In this case, it is optimal for the rival firm to charge a price just below P' to capture all industry

ANALYZING MANAGERIAL DECISIONS: *Entry Decision*

In the simple Cournot model, firms make their output choices simultaneously. In practice, firms sometimes make these kinds of decisions sequentially.

Suppose that you manage one of the firms discussed in the *Output Competition* example in the text. The industry demand in this example is $P = 100 - Q$ and the MC of each firm is zero.

1. Suppose that each firm must make an upfront investment of $1,000 to enter the market and that your competition has already paid this investment and chosen to produce 50 units. This investment is nonrecoverable (sunk). Should you make the $1,000 investment and enter the market? If so, how much should you produce and what are your profits? Continue to assume that your firm will survive for only one production period.

2. How do your profits and those of your competitor compare to the case of simultaneous decisions discussed in the text? Would you say that this example of output competition has a first mover advantage or disadvantage?

[13]This situation often is referred to as the Bertrand model. Bertrand was a French economist who wrote a short note almost 50 years after Cournot's work was published arguing that in some markets, producers set prices rather than quantities.

sales. (Since we assume the firms' products are identical, customers buy the product from the firm that offers the lower price.) Given that the second firm charges a price just below P', it is now optimal for the first firm to charge a slightly lower price. This process continues; only when price equals marginal cost does neither firm have an incentive to lower price. (Lowering price further would result in selling below cost, thus generating a loss.) Of course, both firms would like to devise a way of avoiding competition and capturing higher profits. Yet as we discuss below, fostering cooperation can be difficult—and in certain cases, illegal.

Empirical Evidence

There are various economic models of oligopoly. We have presented but two of them simply to illustrate that economic theory does not make unambiguous predictions about what to expect within such industries. Some models yield outcomes close to pure competition—firms sell at marginal cost and make no economic profits. Other models yield outcomes closer to pure monopoly. What actually occurs in oligopolistic markets depends on the specific market and competing firms (there is no one model that fits all situations). It is ultimately an empirical issue. Available evidence

ACADEMIC APPLICATIONS

Price Competition with Differentiated Products

We demonstrated in the main text how price competition could lead to zero economic profits in an oligopolistic industry. The analysis focused on two firms producing *homogenous* (identical) products. Often competing firms produce differentiated products. Products are *horizontally differentiated* when at the same price some consumers buy one and some buy the other. For example, Ford and General Motors (GM) engage in price competition in most segments of the car market, but consumers do not view their products as perfect substitutes. At the same price, some would buy a Ford, while others would buy a Chevy (produced by GM). A given customer, however, might be induced to purchase her less-preferred product with a sufficient price discount. Ford and GM are likely to consider this possibility when they price their products. Economists refer to price competition in this setting as *Bertrand Competition with Differentiated Products.*

The basic economic model of this competition considers two firms, producing horizontally differentiated products. The degree of differentiation ranges from $D = 0$ (all customers view the products as homogenous and thus perfect substitutes) to $D = 1$ (complete differentiation, where a given customer does not substitute from one product to the other based on price). Depending on the degree of differentiation, it is possible for both firms to earn long-run economic profits in this setting, even if they compete on price. Both firms earn zero economic profits when they are viewed as perfect substitutes ($D = 0$)—the case analyzed in the text. Profit increases with the degree of differentiation. With complete differentiation ($D = 1$), each firm can simply price as a monopolist to the set of customers who prefer its product (since customers do not view the products as substitutes). Profits fall with the degree of substitution since the firms have increased incentives to lower price to attract additional customers from the other firm. In equilibrium, price competition makes each firm worse off than if they had been able to collude on price.

Managers invest in marketing, advertising, packaging, and new product design to differentiate their products from competitors. Interestingly, successful differentiation can benefit not only the investing firm, but also the competing firms (there is a positive externality). The investing firm gains by having increased pricing power to extract profits from customers who prefer its products. However, by definition the other firm is also more differentiated, which allows it to extract additional profits from the customers who prefer its products. For example, suppose a firm is successful in promoting its clothing line among teenagers. While teenagers would be more likely to buy the product, more conservative adults might be more likely to buy the other.

suggests that oligopolies typically result in less output than competitive markets and that firms earn economic profits—at least in some industries.[14] Firms sometimes compete on price, to each other's detriment, and normally earn less in aggregate than a monopolist could.

Cooperation and the Prisoners' Dilemma

As we have discussed, in oligopolistic industries it is in the private interests of firms to find ways to cooperate and capture more profits than through competition. In principle, firms are most profitable if they effectively collude and act as a monopolist in jointly setting price and output for the industry. Collusion maximizes joint profits, which then can be divided among the firms in the industry. Many governments understand these incentives and have passed a variety of antitrust laws to limit firms' ability to engage in fixing prices. These laws are designed to lower the prices consumers pay for products. Some of the more restrictive of these laws have been adopted in the United States. Internationally, firms tend to have more latitude in forming cooperative agreements in attempting to increase profits—for example, consider the OPEC cartel.[15]

Prisoners' Dilemma

Even when free to cooperate, firms find that cooperation is not always easy to achieve. Individual firms have incentives to "cheat" and not adhere to output and price agreements. This incentive can be illustrated by the well-known *prisoners' dilemma*. In the original prisoners' dilemma, there are two suspects; hence, suppose the SEC has been investigating an insider trading scheme and their investigation is focused on two securities brokers, Avi Wasserman and Bea Haefner, who are arrested and charged with a crime. Police have insufficient evidence to convict them for insider trading violations unless one of them confesses. The police place Avi and Bea in separate rooms and try to get them to confess. If neither confesses, they are convicted of less serious crimes associated with their trading activities and are sentenced to only 2 months in jail. If both confess, they spend 12 months in jail. However, if one confesses but the other does not, the confessor is released under a plea bargain in return for testifying while the other is sentenced to 18 months in jail—12 for the crime and 6 for obstructing justice. The payoffs in terms of jail time faced by each individual are displayed in Figure 6.10.

The Nash equilibrium is for both suspects to confess. Given these payoffs, it is always in the *individual interests* of each suspect to confess, taking the action of the other party as given. If Avi does not confess, Bea is set free by confessing. Alternatively, if Avi confesses, Bea reduces her jail sentence from 18 to 12 months by also confessing. Either way, it is in Bea's interests to confess—confessing is a *dominant strategy*. Since the payoffs are symmetrical, it also is optimal for Avi to confess. Although it is in the individual interests of each party to confess, it is clearly in their *joint interests* not to confess. By not confessing, each only serves 2 months in jail,

---

[14]D. Carlton and J. Perloff (1990), *Modern Industrial Organization* (HarperCollins: New York), Chapter 10, discusses some of the relevant empirical literature.

[15]In smaller countries, much of the local production of key products is exported. In this case, it can be in the countries' interests to allow the formation of cartels. Ultimately, consumers pay higher prices and there are inefficiencies. However, many of these costs are imposed on people in other countries.

Figure 6.10 Prisoners' Dilemma

In the prisoners' dilemma, there are two suspects: Suppose the SEC has been investigating an insider trading scheme and their investigation is focused on two securities brokers, Avi Wasserman and Bea Haefner, who are arrested and charged with a crime. The police do not have sufficient evidence to convict them for insider trading unless one of them confesses. The police place the suspects in separate rooms and ask them to confess. If neither confesses, they are convicted of minor violations uncovered by the investigation of their trading activities and are sentenced to 2 months. If both confess, they spend 12 months in jail. However, if one confesses and the other does not, the confessor is released under a plea bargain in return for testifying but the other is sentenced to 18 months in jail—12 for the crime and 6 for obstructing justice. The payoffs in terms of jail time faced by each individual are displayed. Each entry in the table lists the jail sentences for Avi and Bea, respectively. The Nash equilibrium is for both suspects to confess—the shaded cell. Given the payoffs, it is always in the *individual interests* of each suspect to confess (taking the action of the other party as given).

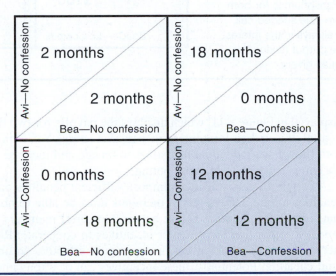

compared to 12 months if both confess. The prisoners' dilemma suggests that any agreement for neither to confess is likely to break down when they make their individual choices unless there is some mechanism to enforce their joint commitment not to confess. (For particular crimes one such mechanism might be the Mob: Both suspects have incentives not to confess if they expect to be executed for providing evidence to the police.)

Cartels

Cartels consist of formal agreements to cooperate in setting price and output levels. (These activities are generally illegal in the United States.) Firms trying to maintain cartels can face a problem like the prisoners' dilemma—we might call it the *cartel's dilemma.* Members can agree to restrict output to increase joint profits. However, individual firms have incentives to cheat. If all other firms restrict output, prices will not be affected significantly by the extra output of one firm. However, that firm's profits will increase from selling additional output at the cartel-maintained high price. But if all firms react to these incentives by increasing output, the cartel breaks down. Actual cartels often unravel because of such incentives. This outcome is

Figure 6.11   Cartel's Dilemma

Two firms, AVInc and BeaCo, attempt to form a cartel. If both firms restrict output, prices are high and each firm's profit is $500. If both cheat on the cartel and increase output, price will be low and each firm's profit is $200. If one firm expands output while the other restricts output, the market price will be at an intermediate level; the firm with the high output will make $600 (because of the increased sales), but the other firm will only make $150 (because of the lower price). These payoffs are displayed. The Nash equilibrium is for both firms to increase output—the shaded cell. Given the payoffs, it is always in the interest of each firm to increase output (taking the output of the other firm as given).

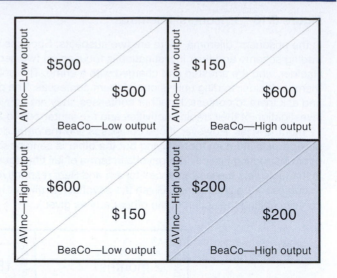

displayed in Figure 6.11, which displays the payoffs for two firms attempting to form a cartel. It is in their joint interests to restrict output. Yet, as in the prisoners' dilemma, both firms have individual incentives to renege and increase output. The Nash equilibrium is for each to increase output.

A cartel can persist if it can impose sufficient penalties on cheaters. But for these penalties to be effective, cartel members must be able to observe (or reliably infer) that a firm has cheated. To the extent that cartel members expect to interact on a *repeated basis,* there are greater incentives to cooperate. Repeated interaction also increases incentives to invest in developing effective enforcement mechanisms to limit cheating. Potentially, these incentives can be strong enough to resolve the cartel's dilemma. In general, cooperation is easier to enforce if the number of firms in the industry is small: It is easier to identify and punish cheaters.

Even when firms are not permitted to form cartels, there may be ways of cooperating to increase profits. For example, over time, a firm might become known as a price leader. Such a firm changes prices in the face of new demand or cost conditions in a way that approximates what a cartel would do. Other firms follow the price changes, thus acting like members of a cartel. Individually, firms still can have short-run incentives to cheat (e.g., reducing price to get more sales). However, firms might resist this short-run temptation to foster cooperation in the long run and hence obtain higher long-run profits.[16]

Another potential mechanism to foster cooperation is the structure of contracts with buyers employed by firms in the industry. *Most-favored-nation clauses* provide buyers with guarantees that the seller will not sell to another buyer at a lower price. These clauses reduce incentives of sellers to lower the price for one buyer because that same price concession would have to be offered to other buyers as well. *Meeting-the-*

---

[16]Indeed, economists have shown that within any long-term relationship, with no specified ending date, cooperation is a *possible equilibrium*—the parties need not succumb to the cartel's dilemma. We discuss this issue in more detail in Chapter 9 and in the appendix to Chapter 10.

MANAGERIAL APPLICATIONS

Collusion in the Lysine Industry

In 2009, Warner Brothers produced a feature film named the "Informant!" that focused on price fixing (based on the book by K. Eichenwald). Matt Damon portrayed Mark Whitacre, a high-ranking executive at Archer Daniels Midland Company (ADM). He reported to FBI agents in the 1990s that his employer was engaged in illegal price fixing and helped them collect evidence by secretly recording company executives negotiating pricing agreements with Japanese competitors. In 1996, ADM pleaded guilty to price fixing and paid a $100 million fine.

Lysine is an amino acid derived from corn used in swine and poultry feed to promote growth. ADM entered the lysine market in 1991. Prior to that time, the market had been dominated by two Japanese companies. ADM quickly gained market share. However, with the competition, the price of lysine fell from about $1.30 per pound to $.60 per pound. According to Whitacre, ADM executives began discussions in 1992 with their Japanese competitors about how it would be in their mutual self-interest to collude and fix prices. Collectively, the competitors were forgoing millions of dollars of profit per month because of the competition among the three companies. Whitacre indicates that a favorite saying at ADM was (a prominent line in the movie): *"The competitor is our friend, and the customer is our enemy."*

Whitacre lost his whistle-blower immunity when the FBI discovered that he had committed a multimillion dollar fraud against ADM. He was sentenced to 10 years in jail and was released from prison in December 2006 after serving 8.5 years. In recent years, he had been employed as the Chief Operating Officer and President of Operations of the biotech company, Cypress Systems.

Source: Warner Brothers (2009), "The Informant!" (movie).

---

competition clauses guarantee that a seller will meet the price of a competitor. Such a clause makes it difficult for firms to cheat on an agreement not to lower price since price concessions are more likely to be brought to each other's attention by customers.

Our discussion of these strategic interactions among rivals in output markets is meant only to provide a basic introduction to these issues.

Summary

A *market* consists of all firms and individuals who are willing and able to buy or sell a particular product. These parties include those currently engaged in buying and selling the product, as well as *potential entrants. Market structure* refers to the basic characteristics of the market environment, including (1) the number and size of buyers, sellers, and potential entrants; (2) the degree of product differentiation; (3) the amount and cost of information about product price and quality; and (4) the conditions for entry and exit.

Competitive markets are characterized by four basic conditions: A large number of potential buyers and sellers; product homogeneity; rapid, low-cost dissemination of information; and free entry into and exit from the market. In competitive markets, individual buyers and sellers take the market price of the product as given: They have no control over price. Firms thus view their demand curves as horizontal. The firm's short-run supply curve is that portion of its short-run marginal cost curve above short-run average variable cost. The long-run supply curve is that portion of its long-run marginal cost curve above long-run average cost. In a competitive equilibrium, firms make no economic profits. Production is efficient in that firms produce at their minimum long-run average cost. Firms in competitive industries must move rapidly to take advantage of transitory opportunities. They also must strive for efficient production in order to survive. Some firms in the industry can employ resources that give them a competitive advantage (e.g., an extremely talented manager). Yet in such cases, any excess returns often go to the factor of production responsible for the particular advantage, rather than to the firm's owners.

Although the competitive model provides a useful description of the interaction between buyers and sellers for many industries, there are others where firms have substantial market power—prices are affected materially by the output decisions of individual firms. Market power can exist when there are substantial *barriers to entry* into the industry. Expectations about incumbent reactions, incumbent advantages, and exit costs all can serve as entry barriers.

The extreme case of a firm with market power is *monopoly*, where the industry consists of only one firm. Here, industry and firm demand curves are one and the same. In contrast to competitive markets, consumers pay more than marginal cost and the firm earns economic profits. Output is restricted from competitive levels. With a monopoly, not all the potential gains from trade are exhausted.

Monopolistic competition is a hybrid between competition and monopoly. It is like monopoly in that firms under both market structures face downward-sloping demand curves. Market power comes from differentiated products. Examples include retail shops at malls, gas stations (that differ in location and brand), books, movies, and business schools. The analyses of output and pricing policies are similar in the two cases. The difference between monopoly and monopolistic competition is that in monopolistic competition, economic profits invite entry that limits profits.

In *oligopolistic markets*, only a few firms account for most production. Products may or may not be differentiated. Firms can earn substantial profits. However, these profits can be eliminated through competition among existing firms in the industry. To analyze output and pricing decisions in oligopolistic industries, we use the concept of a *Nash equilibrium:* A *Nash equilibrium* exists when each firm is doing the best it can given the actions of its rivals. In the *Cournot model,* each firm treats the *output* level of its competitor as fixed and then decides how much to produce. In equilibrium, firms make economic profits. However, these profits are not as large as would be made if the firms effectively colluded and posted the monopoly price. Other models of oligopoly yield different equilibria. For instance, one model based on *price competition* yields the competitive solution in the case of homogeneous products: Price equals marginal cost with no economic profits. Economic theory makes no clear-cut prediction about the behavior of firms in oligopolistic industries. Economic models must be crafted to fit the specific details of the industry and the nature of the competition. Available evidence suggests that in some oligopolistic industries, firms restrict output from competitive levels and hence capture some economic profits.

It is in the economic interests of firms in oligopolistic industries to find ways to cooperate, thereby capturing higher profits. An ostensible motive for antitrust laws is to limit the dead-weight social costs that occur when firms collude on price. Even when firms are free to cooperate, effective cooperation is not always easy to achieve. Individual firms have incentives to deviate from agreed-on outputs and prices. This incentive is illustrated by the *prisoners' dilemma.* This model highlights incentives that can cause cartels to be unstable. However, firms sometimes can cooperate successfully when they can impose penalties on noncooperative firms. Cooperation also can be sustained through the incentives provided by long-run, *repeated relationships.*

While short-run economic profits are possible in all market structures, the overall analysis suggests that most firms will not earn economic profits over the longer run. Firms do not earn long-run economic profits in perfect competition or in the more common structure of monopolistic competition. Absent government fiat, competition, and technological change makes it hard to maintain monopolies and oligopolistic market power over time. Increases in international trade also can reduce the market power of domestic firms. An important bottom line is that managers should consider potential competition in making decisions in all market structures.

Suggested Readings	A. Dixit and B. Nalebuff (1991), *Thinking Strategically* (Norton: New York). G. Stigler (1987), *The Theory of Price* (Macmillan: New York), Chapter 3. R. Pindyck and D. Rubinfeld (1992), *Microeconomics* (Macmillan: New York), Chapters 8–13.

Self-Evaluation Problems

6–1. The total and marginal cost of producing Product A are

$$TC = \$1,000 + 2Q^2$$
$$MC = 4Q$$

The $1,000 is a fixed cost in the short run, but can be avoided in the long run by shutting down (going out of business). There is only one possible plant size for this operation; thus SRMC = LRMC = $4Q$ in this problem. Derive and graph the firm's short-run and long-run supply curves (on separate graphs).

6–2. Suppose your firm faces a demand curve of $P = 90 - .30Q$ and the marginal cost of production is $10 per unit. Find the profit-maximizing output and price. Display this choice graphically (showing the demand, marginal revenue, and marginal cost curves). Is this outcome on the elastic, inelastic, or unitary elastic part of the demand curve? What are your profits?

6–3. Genesee and Natural Light are the two sole competitors in the ultra low-end beer market in the Rochester metro area. Both firms have marginal costs of 0 and fixed costs of 200. The industry demand curve is $P = 100 - 0.1Q$, where $Q = Q_1 + Q_2$

    a. Assume the firms compete on quantity (Cournot competition). What is the equilibrium price and total production in the market? How much profit will each firm make?

    b. If firms compete on price (rather than quantity), is the answer in Part A a Nash equilibrium? Explain.

    c. Now assume that Genesee acquires Natural Light's Rochester operations and has a total regional monopoly on ultra low-end beer. What price will they charge? How much profit will the combined firm make? Is this more or less than in Part A? Explain briefly why you found what you did.

    d. Now suppose that neither firm has entered the Rochester market and that it costs $10,000 to build a plant. Suppose that Genesee spends $10,000 to build a plant and starts producing 400 units. Will Natural Light want to spend $10,000 to enter the market? Show why. Assume that there is only one production period to consider.

Solutions to Self-Evaluation Problems

6–1. The firm's short-run supply curve is the portion of its short-run marginal cost curve that lies above average variable cost (AVC). AVC is $VC/Q = 2Q^2/Q = 2Q$. SRMC, which is $4Q$, is everywhere above $2Q$. Therefore the firm's short-run supply curve is $P = 4Q$:

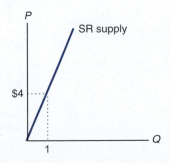

The firm's long-run supply curve is the portion of its long-run marginal cost curve that lies above long-run average total cost (LRAC). LRAC in this problem is

$$\text{LRAC} = \text{TC}/Q = \$1{,}000/Q + 2Q$$

Recall that LRAC falls when LRMC is below it and rises when LRMC is above it. LRAC is minimized when it equals marginal cost. This is the point where positive supply begins (the firm stays in business), since its LRMC is above LRAC at every quantity beyond this point. The point can be found by setting LRAC = LRMC and solving for Q and LRMC:

$$\$1{,}000/Q + 2Q = 4Q$$
$$\$500 = Q^2$$
$$Q = 22.36 \text{ units}$$

At this quantity LRMC = LRAC = \$89.44. At this price the firm breaks even (TR = TC). At lower prices the firm loses money and in the long run it is optimal to shut down. Thus the firm's long-run supply is 0 up to a price of \$89.44 and is $P = 4Q$ at higher prices:

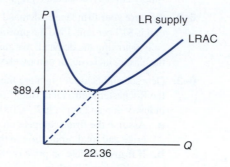

6–2. Profit maximization occurs where MR = MC. The MR function has the same intercept as the linear demand curve but twice the negative slope. Therefore the profit-maximizing condition is

$$90 = .60Q = 10.$$

Solving this equation produces the profit-maximizing quantity, $Q^* = 133.33$ units. The optimal price (from the demand curve) is \$50. The firm makes a profit of \$40 per unit for a total profit of \$5,333.20. The outcome is on the elastic portion of the demand curve (above the midpoint on the linear curve). It is never optimal for a firm to produce on the inelastic portion of its demand curve since revenue is increased and costs reduced by lowering output. The graph for this problem is

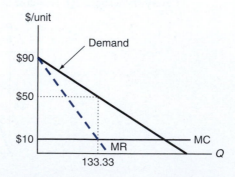

6–3. **a.** In Cournot competition, each firm maximizes its own profits taking the other firm's output as given. In the equilibrium, both of the firm's expectations about the other firm's output are realized. The profit-maximizing conditions for the two firms are

$$MR_1 = (100 - .1Q_2^*) - .2Q_1 = 0 \text{ (optimal condition firm 1)}$$
$$MR_2 = (100 - .1Q_1^*) - .2Q_2 = 0 \text{ (optimal condition firm 2)}$$

The equilibrium occurs at quantities that jointly satisfy these two equations. In this problem, both firms are identical. Thus in equilibrium $Q_1^* = Q_2^*$. Substitute this relation into either of the two equations to produce a single equation with one unknown variable. Using the first equation:

$$(100 - .1Q_1^*) - .2Q_1^* = 0$$
$$Q_1^* = 333.33 \text{ units} = Q_2^*$$

Total production $(Q_1^* + Q_2^*) = 666.66$ units. The equilibrium price from the industry demand curve is $33.34. Each firm makes profits of ($33.34 $\times$ 333.33) − $200 = $10,913.22.

b. No, the solution in Part A is not a Nash equilibrium if the firms compete on price. In a Nash equilibrium, each firm is choosing optimally given the choice of the other firm. If one firm chooses a price of $33.34, the other firm would do better by undercutting the price and capturing the entire market. For example, if firm 1 cuts its price by $1 to $32.34 it will sell 676.6 units (assuming the other firm does not match the price decrease) and make a profit of $21,674.48 (greater than the $10,913.22 in Part A). The Nash equilibrium with price competition and homogenous products is for both firms to price at MC ($0 in this problem).

c. After the merger, Genesee is a monopolist. Its demand curve is the industry demand curve. It will maximize profits by setting its MR, $100 - 0.2Q = 0$. $Q^* = 500$ units and P^* from the demand curve is $50. The firm makes a profit of ($50 $\times$ 500) − $200 = $24,800. This profit is higher than the combined profit in Part A ($21,826.44). As a monopoly, the firm can charge the price (and produce the corresponding quantity) that maximizes total profits for the industry. Firms make economic profits in the Cournot equilibrium but their competition (noncollusion) produces an outcome with lower profits than monopoly.

d. No, Natural Light will not enter. If Genesee is producing 400 units, Natural Light's demand curve is $P = (100 - .1 \times 400) - .1Q_2$. Its optimal production (setting its MR = 0) is 300 units and the resulting price will be $30 (given 700 total units are being produced). Natural Light's profits are (300 $\times$ $30) − 200 = $8,800, which are less than the $10,000 entry fee.

Review Questions

6–1. What four basic conditions characterize a competitive market?

6–2. The short-run marginal cost of the Ohio Bag Company is $2Q$. Price is $100. The company operates in a competitive industry. Currently, the company is producing 40 units per period. What is the optimal short-run output? Calculate the profits that Ohio Bag is losing through suboptimal output.

6–3. Should a company ever produce an output if the managers know it will lose money over the period? Explain.

6–4. What are economic profits? Does a firm in a competitive industry earn long-run economic profits? Explain.

6–5. The Johnson Oil Company has just hired the best manager in the industry. Should the owners of the company anticipate economic profits? Explain.

6–6. A Michigan court ruled in the 1990s that General Motors did not have the right to close a particular Michigan plant and lay people off. Do you think this ruling benefited the people of Michigan? Explain.

6–7. The Suji Corporation has a monopoly in a particular chemical market. The industry demand curve is $P = 1,000 - 5Q$. Marginal cost is $3Q$. What is Suji's profit-maximizing output and price? Calculate the corresponding profits.

6–8. Assume the industry demand for a product is $P = 1,000 - 20Q$. Assume that the marginal cost of product is $10 per unit.

   a. What price and output will occur under pure competition? What price and output will occur under pure monopoly (assume one price is charged to all customers)?

   b. Draw a graph that shows the lost gains from trade that result from having a monopoly.

6–9. In 1981, the United States negotiated an agreement with the Japanese. The agreement called for Japanese auto firms to limit exports to the United States. The Japanese government was charged with helping make sure the agreement was met by Japanese firms. Were the Japanese firms necessarily hurt by this limited ability to export? Explain.

6–10. Compare the industry output and price in a Cournot versus a competitive equilibrium. Do firms earn economic profits in the Cournot model? Does economic theory predict that firms always earn economic profits in oligopolistic industries? Explain. What does the empirical evidence indicate?

6–11. What is a Nash equilibrium? Explain why a joint confession is the Nash equilibrium in the prisoners' dilemma.

6–12. Candak Corporation produces professional quality digital cameras. The market for professional digital cameras is monopolistically competitive. Assume that the inverse demand curve faced by Candak (given its competitors' prices) can be expressed as $P = 5,000 - 0.2Q$ and Candak's total costs can be expressed as $TC = 20,000,000 + 0.05Q^2$. Answer the following questions.

   a. What price and quantity will Candak choose?

   b. Is this likely to be a long-run equilibrium for Candak Corporation? Why or why not? If not, what is likely to happen in the market for professional digital cameras, and how will it affect Candak?

6–13. Will a monopolist ever choose to produce on the inelastic portion of its demand curve? Explain.

Pricing with Market Power

LEARNING OBJECTIVES

1. Explain a profit-maximizing firm's basic pricing objective.
2. Explain how block pricing and two-part tariffs can sometimes be used to increase profits when facing homogenous consumers.
3. Define price discrimination and explain how it can sometimes be used to increase profits relative to the benchmark case of a single per-unit price.
4. Develop both cost and valuation-related explanations for real-world examples of apparently similar goods sold at different prices.
5. Explain "personalized pricing" (first-degree price discrimination) and provide examples; discuss the social cost implications.
6. Explain "group pricing" (third-degree price discrimination) and provide examples.
7. Explain "menu pricing" (second-degree priced discrimination) and provide examples.
8. Understand how coupons and rebates are sometimes used to price discriminate.
9. Discuss how product bundling might increase profits and provide examples.

Intuit began as a small software company in 1983 with its new program *Quicken*—a personal finance program that addressed the common household problem of balancing the family's checkbook. By 2013, Intuit had grown to a company with over $4.1 billion in annual revenue and publicly traded stock on the Nasdaq Stock Market. Its flagship products in 2014 included *Quicken, QuickBooks,* and *TurboTax.*

A visit to Intuit's website in 2014 would have revealed many interesting pricing decisions. Consider the following examples: (1) Intuit offered five Windows versions of *Quicken* including its *Starter, Deluxe, Premier, Home & Business* and *Rental Property Manager* editions. The prices for these products ranged from the *Starter Edition* selling at $39.99 to the *Rental Property Manager Edition* selling at $164.99. (2) The four higher priced editions could read computer files produced by older versions of *Quicken,* but the low-priced *Starter Edition* could not. Thus existing users who wanted to update their software, but use existing data files, had to purchase one of the higher priced alternatives. (3) A Mac version of *Quicken* was priced at $49.99. (4) Customers who purchased *Quicken* were offered free shipping and a free mobile app. (5) Online customers could enter a "Special Offer Code" that gave discounts to customers with the code. (6) Intuit provided a

60-day unconditional money-back guarantee on all its *Quicken* products (essentially allowing consumers to try it out for free). (7) Packages of 50 standard checks were priced at $1.14 per check, while packages of 2,000 checks were priced at only 13 cents per check. (8) Customers could purchase check value packs that bundled checks, envelopes and deposit slips at prices that were up to $70 lower than if the products were purchased separately.

Pricing is a key managerial decision. These examples illustrate some of the complexities associated with product pricing. For example, how should managers set their basic prices? Why do firms use coupons and rebates? Why are some customers charged higher prices for the same product than others? Why do firms bundle products? Why do firms offer a line of similar products at different price points? Why would a firm ever give its products away? Why do some firms offer volume discounts?

In this chapter we present a basic analysis of pricing with market power and provide answers to these and related questions. We organize the remainder of the chapter as follows: First, we discuss the underlying objective of pricing decisions. Next, we analyze the benchmark case where the firm charges the same price to all customers. Subsequently, we consider more complex pricing policies. The chapter ends with a brief discussion of several other issues, including multiperiod considerations, strategic interactions, legal and implementation issues.

Pricing Objective

A firm has *market power* when it faces a downward-sloping demand curve. Firms with market power can raise price without losing all customers to competitors. The ultimate objective is to choose a pricing policy that maximizes the firm's value. We continue with the standard economic analysis in which managers seek to maximize profits over a single period. Although managers actually seek to maximize the present value of all future profits, if the business setting is expected to be stationary, these problems are equivalent. Later in this chapter, we discuss how concerns about future profits can affect the current pricing decision. Nonetheless, our single-period analysis is a productive place to begin for providing useful insights into pricing decisions.

Figure 7.1 depicts a firm's demand curve for and its marginal cost of producing the product. The demand curve reflects what consumers are willing to pay for the product. Only in quite special cases is it in the interests of the firm to sell the product at below marginal cost: It can do better by not producing the product. (Later in this chapter, we examine multiperiod considerations that might prompt firms to set current price below marginal cost.) Thus, the maximum potential gains from trade are given by the shaded triangle. If the firm were to sell the product at marginal cost, all the gains would go to consumers in the form of *consumer surplus* (assuming a constant marginal cost). Consumer surplus is defined as the difference between what the consumer is willing to pay for a product and what the consumer actually pays when buying it. Profit-maximizing managers try to devise pricing policies that capture as much of the available gains from trade as possible: The managerial ideal would be to capture all the potential consumer surplus as company profit.

We begin by reviewing the benchmark case where the firm charges all customers the same price. In this case (which was introduced in Chapters 4 and 6), the firm captures some, but not all, of the potential gains from trade. Subsequently, we consider more complex pricing policies.

Figure 7.1 **Pricing with Market Power**

The demand curve reflects what consumers are willing to pay for the product. It typically is not in the firm's interest to sell the product below marginal cost, since it can do better by not producing the product. Thus, the maximum potential gains from trade are given by the shaded triangle. The firm's objective is to select a pricing policy that maximizes its share of the gains from trade and thus firm profit.

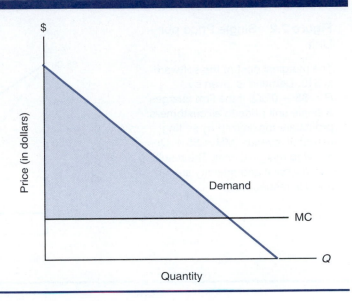

Benchmark Case: Single Price per Unit

Profit Maximization

Suppose that Intuit sells a software product called *Checkware*. It pays royalties of $10 per copy to the software developer and selects a retail price to post on the Internet. All customers buy at this price regardless of the quantity purchased. Intuit has no other incremental costs and faces the following demand curve:

$$P = 85 - 0.5Q \qquad (7.1)$$

where P is price and Q is quantity (in thousands of copies).

What price should Intuit select to maximize profits?

Chapter 6 shows that profits are maximized by selecting a price–output combination in which marginal revenue equals marginal cost. Marginal revenue is $85 - Q$, and marginal cost is $10 in this example.[1] Thus the optimal quantity and price are 75,000 and $47.50, respectively. Profits are $2,812,500. Figure 7.2 illustrates the solution graphically.

We focus on this example to offer a number of basic insights. It is important to note, however, that this analysis simplifies the pricing problem in at least four important ways. First, all consumers are charged the same unit price, regardless of the quantity purchased. Thus, more complicated pricing strategies are not considered. Second, the firm sells only one product; thus interactions among products are not considered. Third, the demand curve is for a single period. The analysis focuses on maximizing single-period profits and abstracts from longer-term considerations (e.g., how pricing this period might affect either demand or costs in future periods). Fourth, the demand curve assumes that the prices of competing products are constant no matter what price Intuit charges. In some markets, there is likely to be interaction

---

[1]For expositional simplicity, we assume marginal cost is constant; in the more general case, one also requires information about the marginal cost function.

Figure 7.2 Single Price per Unit

The marginal cost of the software is $10. Demand is given by $P = 85 - 0.5Q$. If the firm charges a single unit price to all customers, profits are maximized by setting marginal revenue (MR = $85 - Q$) equal to marginal cost. The resulting optimal price and quantity are $47.50 and 75, respectively.

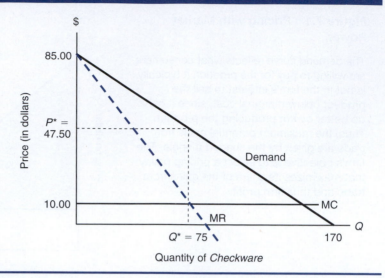

Quantity of *Checkware*

in the pricing decisions of firms within the industry. Later in this chapter, we consider the implications of relaxing these assumptions.

Relevant Costs

Managers maximize profits by setting marginal cost equal to marginal revenue. As emphasized throughout this book, sunk costs are irrelevant for the pricing–output decision—only *incremental costs* matter. Suppose that Intuit previously had spent $100,000 for developing and promoting its website. While Intuit hopes to generate enough profits to offset this initial investment, this expenditure is sunk and hence is irrelevant for its current pricing decisions.

Also as discussed earlier, it is important for managers to focus on *opportunity costs,* not accounting costs. For instance, suppose that Intuit has some *Checkware* packages in inventory for which it had paid $18 per copy in royalties (e.g., the contract with the developer could call for an $18 royalty per copy for the first 20,000 copies and $10 per copy thereafter). This historical cost is not relevant for the current pricing decision. Rather what is important is the current cost for replacing the inventory—$10.[2]

Price Sensitivity

Additional insights into a monopolist's pricing decision can be developed using the concept of price elasticity introduced in Chapter 4. Recall that the price elasticity η is a measure of price sensitivity. The higher the price elasticity, the more sensitive is the quantity demanded to price changes. With some algebra, it is easy to show that the monopolist's optimal pricing policy of setting marginal revenue equal to marginal cost can be rewritten as

$$P^* = MC^*/[1 - 1/\eta^*] \tag{7.2}$$

where P^* is the profit-maximizing price, $MC^* =$ marginal cost, and η^* is the elasticity of demand, all at the optimal output level.

[2]Suppose that a package was sold for $16 that originally costs $18. The company reports an accounting loss of $2. However, if the company has to pay $10 to replace the unit in inventory, it actually has an economic profit of $6. (When the wholesale price fell from $18 to $10, Intuit lost $8 for each unit in inventory.)

Figure 7.3 Price Sensitivity and Optimal Markup

The optimal price markup above marginal cost depends on the elasticity of demand. The optimal markup decreases with the elasticity of demand at the optimal price/quantity combination. The demand curve for *Checkware* on the left is less elastic than the demand curve for *Illustrator* on the right. Correspondingly, the optimal markup is higher for the demand curve on the left ($37.50 above cost versus $16.25 above cost). At the optimal price and quantities, the elasticity for the demand curve on the left is 1.27 versus 1.62 for the demand curve on the right.

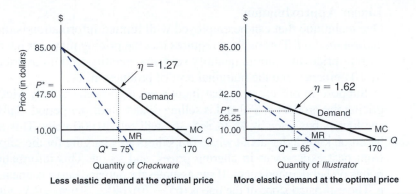

Recall that the elasticity of demand ranges between 0 (totally inelastic) and ∞ (infinitely elastic). Market power decreases as demand becomes more elastic at the optimal price.

No firm should operate on the inelastic portion of its demand curve ($\eta < 1$). To understand why, assume this conclusion is false—suppose the profit-maximizing price is on the inelastic portion of the demand curve. Now consider a price above this profit-maximizing price. With inelastic demand, total revenue increases with an increase in price. As price is increased, fewer units are sold and production costs fall. With an increase in revenue and a reduction in costs, profits must increase with price: Hence the maximum profit cannot lie on the inelastic portion of the demand curve. Thus, we are assured that $\eta^* > 1$, and the optimal price is greater than marginal cost.

If a firm has substantial market power, its demand will be less elastic at the optimal price and the markup over marginal cost will be high. In contrast, if the firm has limited market power (e.g., there are many good substitutes), elasticity will be high and the markup low.

In our *Checkware* example, the markup is $37.50 ($47.50 − $10). The elasticity at the optimal price–quantity combination is 1.27 (using the technique from the appendix of Chapter 4). Figure 7.3 compares this case with that of a more elastic demand curve for another software product—*Illustrator*:[3]

$$P = 42.50 - 0.25Q \tag{7.3}$$

With this demand curve, the optimal output and price are 65,000 and $26.25, respectively. The elasticity at this combination is 1.62 compared to 1.27 in the first example. Correspondingly, the markup is lower ($16.25 vs. $37.50).

[3]For both demand curves, the quantity sold is 170 when price is zero; however, quantity declines more rapidly with price increases in the second case.

Estimating the Profit-Maximizing Price

Economic theory suggests that managers should price so that marginal revenue equals marginal cost. One practical problem in applying this principle is that managers often do not have precise information about their demand curves and thus their marginal revenue. Thus, depending on the circumstances, policies like cost-plus or markup pricing (discussed below) can serve as useful approximations or rules of thumb in the absence of better information.

Linear Approximation

One technique that can be employed with limited information is the *linear approximation method.* This method requires that the pricing manager have estimates of the current price, the current quantity sold, the quantity sold if the price is changed (say by 10 percent), and the marginal cost of production.

Suppose in our example that Intuit's pricing manager, Sally McGraw, currently is pricing the product at \$70 and is selling 30,000 units per period. Sally estimates that if she lowers her price by \$5 to \$65, she will sell 40,000 units. This estimate might be based on knowledge about what competitors are charging for the same product, results from past experiences in altering prices, and so on. This information gives her two points on her demand curve. If she assumes the demand curve is linear, she can solve for it. The estimated slope of the line is $(65 - 70)/(40 - 30) = -0.5$ (with quantities measured in thousands of units). To solve for the intercept, she would substitute the current price and quantity into the equation for a line ($P = a + bQ$) with slope equal to -0.5:

$$\$70 = a - 0.5(30)$$

Solving for the intercept yields

$$a = 85$$

Hence, the estimated demand curve is

$$P = 85 - 0.5Q \tag{7.4}$$

Given this estimated demand curve and a marginal cost of \$10, Sally has enough information to solve for the "optimal" price. Whether or not this price is close to the true optimal price depends on the accuracy of her cost and sensitivity estimates and on whether the demand curve is close to being linear. Even if the demand curve is not linear, linearity may not be a bad approximation, especially if she begins at a price that is not too far from the optimal price.

In this example, Sally will lower the price from \$70 to \$47.50. The corresponding change in sales will provide her with additional information, which will be useful for future pricing decisions. For example, was the increase in sales close to what she predicted? If she worries that a \$23.50 price reduction is too drastic given her lack of confidence in her estimate of the demand curve, she might start with a smaller price reduction, followed by more reductions if additional experience warrants them. Alternatively, she might offer a \$23.50 rebate on the purchase price. If the price cut turns out to be a bad idea, she can simply eliminate the rebate (rebates are discussed in greater detail below).

Cost-Plus Pricing

One of the more common pricing methods used by firms is *cost-plus pricing.* Firms that use this technique calculate average total cost and then mark up the price to yield a target rate of return.

For example, suppose that Sally expects to sell 75,000 units and targets a 20 percent return on sales. Total costs include the $10 variable cost per unit and the $100,000 of up-front investment. To solve for the implied price, Sally begins by calculating a *unit cost*:

$$\text{Unit cost} = \text{variable cost} + (\text{fixed costs/unit sales}) \tag{7.5}$$

so in this case,

$$\text{Unit cost} = \$10 + (\$100,000/75,000) = \$11.33$$

The price that will yield the target rate of return is found using the following formula:

$$\text{Price} = \text{unit cost}/(1 - \text{target rate of return}) \tag{7.6}$$

In our example, this formula implies a price of $14.16 ($11.33/0.8); the return on sales is ($14.16 − $11.33)/$14.16 = 0.20.

We have stressed how profit-maximizing pricing considers only incremental costs and depends on the price sensitivity of customers. Cost-plus pricing appears to ignore both of these considerations. The cost-plus price marks up average total cost and seems to ignore the demand for the product—just because Sally targets a 20 percent return on sales does not mean that customers will necessarily buy the product in the required quantities at the implied price.

Firms that consistently use bad pricing policies will find themselves earning lower profits than they could with better pricing techniques and even may go out of business. But if cost-plus pricing is so unsound, why is it so widely used in the marketplace? One explanation is that managers implicitly consider market demand in choosing the target return and the target sales volume. If Sally knows that the product faces little competition, more units can be sold and a higher return will be chosen than when facing greater competition. Conceptually, there is always some target volume and return on total cost that produces the profit-maximizing price.

In our first example, the optimal price and quantity for *Checkware* are $47.50 and 75,000, respectively. The corresponding unit cost is $11.33. Using a target return of 76.15 percent in Equation (7.6) will produce the profit-maximizing price of $47.50. If Sally realizes that she has substantial market power with *Checkware,* she should select a high target return (in this case—76.15 percent). Correspondingly, for products where she has less market power, she *Checkware,* then Sally could choose a target return of 56.84 percent and the implied price would be $26.25.

The idea that managers choose target returns and volumes based on market power when they employ cost-plus pricing is supported empirically. Consider the price markups by a typical grocery store employing cost-plus pricing. Stable products such as bread, hamburger, milk, and soup are relatively price-sensitive and carry low margins (markups of under 10 percent above cost). Products with high margins tend to be those with relatively inelastic demand, such as spices, seasonal fresh fruit, and nonprescription drugs (markups as high as 50 percent or more). One experienced grocery store manager noted that "price sensitivity is the primary consideration in setting margins."[4] Cost-plus pricing is more useful when the rate of return that yields the profit-maximizing price on the product is relatively stable over the relevant range of cost variation for a given product and varies little across a set of related products.

---

[4]J. Pappas and M. Hirschey (1990), *Managerial Economics,* 6th edition (Chicago: Dryden Press).

Markup Pricing

Many managerial economics textbooks suggest a pricing rule-of-thumb based on Equation (7.2): $P^* = MC^*/[1 - 1/\eta^*]$. This method—typically referred to as *markup pricing*—consists of substituting an estimate of the current price elasticity and marginal cost into Equation (7.2) and solving for the optimal price.

Equation (7.2) is a condition that holds at the optimal price–quantity combination. But price elasticity generally varies along the demand curve. If Sally currently is at a suboptimal price–quantity combination, the current elasticity will differ from that at the optimal point. Using the current price elasticity in Equation (7.2) will yield a good estimate of the optimal price only when it is close to the elasticity at the optimal price and quantity.

On the Importance of Assumptions

In our *Checkware* example, the underlying demand curve is linear. Unsurprisingly, the linear approximation works well. In contrast, the markup pricing rule does not. If Sally begins at a price of $70 and a quantity of 30,000, then the demand curve ($P = 85 - 0.5Q$) implies that the elasticity is 4.66 (this can be derived using the technique from the appendix of Chapter 4). Plugging 4.66 into Equation (7.2) along with the marginal cost of $10 yields an "optimal" price of $12.73. But this is far from the optimal price of $47.50. This illustration highlights the importance of considering the underlying assumptions in choosing among alternative rules of thumb. It is easy to imagine other circumstances where the markup pricing rule yields a better estimate than the linear approximation.

MANAGERIAL APPLICATIONS

Parker Hannifin Increases Profits by Adopting an Economically Sound Pricing Policy

Parker Hannifin Corporation is a large industrial parts maker. Throughout much of its century-long history, the company used a simple cost-plus pricing policy for its 800,000 parts. It calculated how much it cost to make and deliver each product and added a flat percentage on top, usually 35 percent. This policy was inconsistent with basic economic theory, which indicates that prices should not be based on just costs. The customers' willingness to pay (price sensitivity) also should be considered.

Donald Washkewicz became Parker's CEO in early 2001. He quickly decided that Parker should "stop thinking like a widget maker and start thinking like a retailer, determining prices by what a customer is willing to pay rather than what a product costs to make." He reasoned that sports teams raise ticket prices if they're playing a well-known opponent. Why shouldn't Parker do the same?

In October 2001, Washkewicz unveiled a new plan, which involved creating a new senior position for pricing and bringing in outside consultants. In implementing this plan, Parker's analysts divided its many products into four basic categories (A, B, C, and D) based on their estimated demand sensitivities. They determined that about a third of Parker's products fell "into niches where there was little or no competition or where Parker offered some other unique value." Based on this analysis, Parker increased many of its product prices, while lowering the prices of other products where they faced stiff competition.

Parker's management believes that this new pricing strategy was a major reason why the company's operating income increased by $200 million between 2002 and 2006. From the end of 2002 to April 2007, Parker's stock price increased nearly 88 percent, compared to a 25 percent jump in the S&P 500. Parker's experience highlights how pricing decisions can have a major effect on profits and value.

Source: T. Aeppel (2007), "Seeking Perfect Prices, CEO Tears Up the Rules" *The Wall Street Journal* (March 27).

Figure 7.4 Potential for Higher Profits

If the firm charges a single unit price, profits are maximized at a price of *P** and a corresponding quantity of *Q**. The corresponding profits are shown by the shaded rectangle. Consumers receive surplus equal to triangle *abc*, and triangle *def* represents unrealized gains from trade (consumers who value the product at more than cost but who do not buy the product because of the high price). The firm can earn higher profits if it can devise a more complex pricing policy that allows it to capture some of the potential profits represented by these two triangles.

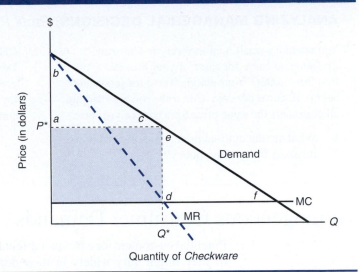

Potential for Higher Profits

In the benchmark case of a single unit price, the firm captures some, but not all, of the potential gains from trade. Figure 7.4 provides an illustration. Firm profits are displayed by the shaded rectangle, and the associated consumer surplus is the triangle labeled *abc*. The triangle, labeled *def*, shows additional potential gains from trade that would accrue from selling to customers who value the product above its marginal cost, but who do not buy the product at the higher unit price *P**. Below we discuss how a firm might increase profits through more complicated pricing strategies that allow it to capture some of the gains from trade displayed by these two triangles.

Microsoft's Market Power and Pricing

In 2001 Microsoft managed to boost sales of its Windows products by 16 percent while worldwide shipments of PCs fell 4 percent. Windows and Microsoft Office software continue to throw off amazing amounts of cash. Analysts agree that most customers really don't have a choice of desktop software. While analysts rarely describe Microsoft as a "monopoly," they frequently refer to Microsoft's "unique market position" or "huge installed base." Microsoft has found several ways to raise prices. Microsoft stopped requiring companies to buy individual copies of software for each employee. It now offers a multiyear site license where one copy of the software can be downloaded to individual PCs. With multiyear licenses, organizations pay an annual fee to Microsoft to use its software rather than buying individual copies. Alvin Parks, an analyst with the research firm Gartner Inc., argued that this new pricing policy "means a price increase for everybody, eventually." Walter Casey, an analyst at Banc One, says, "They're trying to force people to upgrade, [though] maybe they'd say 'encourage.'"

Source: R. Buckman (2002), "Microsoft Sprints On as Tech Sector Plods," *The Wall Street Journal* (August 8), C1–C3.

ANALYZING MANAGERIAL DECISIONS: *Profit Potential for a Microbrewery*

You operate a small microbrewery in Germany. The demand curve for cases of your beer is $P = 50 - .002Q$. Your marginal cost for producing beer is 10 euros per case. Currently you are charging all customers the same price for a case of your beer.

1. What are the optimal price, quantity, and profits under this pricing policy?

2. Calculate the surplus that goes to consumers.
3. Describe how you might capture additional profits using a more sophisticated pricing policy that does not involve capturing more of the consumer surplus. Explain.

Homogeneous Consumer Demands

Potential customers for a product might have quite similar individual demand curves, or they might vary widely in their demands for the product. For instance, in the *Checkware* example, all potential customers might be willing to pay the same maximum price for the product. Alternatively, some customers might be willing to pay a high price for the product, whereas others might be willing to buy the product only at a quite low price. We begin our discussion of more complicated pricing strategies by examining the case of homogeneous demands—in the limit they are identical. These same techniques are appropriate where the firm is dealing with a given individual customer and wants to extract maximum profit. Subsequently, we examine the case of heterogeneous demands.

Block Pricing

The overall demand curve for a product is the sum of individual customer demands at each price. For many products, individual customers are likely to consider purchasing multiple units (consider fruit, clothes, and so on). In the benchmark case, individuals pay the same price per unit independent of the number of units purchased. More generally, the company might charge a given customer different prices per unit, depending on the number of units purchased. Profits sometimes can be increased (even if all customers have similar demand curves) by basing the price per unit on the number of units purchased.[5]

Individuals have downward-sloping demand curves for products. This implies that the marginal value that a customer places on each additional unit declines as the quantity purchased increases. Conceptually, the firm could capture all the potential gains from trade with a customer by charging a price equal to the marginal value of each unit. Thus it might charge $100 for the first unit, $99 for the second unit, $98 for the third unit, and so on (where the prices represent the customer's marginal value of each additional unit). Practical considerations often will preclude such a pricing policy. However, the policy might be approximated by charging a high price for the first purchase block (e.g., up to 5 units) and declining prices for subsequent blocks. For example, the company might charge the customer $98 per unit up to the first five, $95 per unit for the next five, and so on. As discussed below, block pricing not only is used to extract

---

[5]Note that in the following discussion, we assume that a customer cannot buy a large quantity and then resell it to other customers (undercutting the prices that the company charges to other customers for small quantities). The importance of this assumption is discussed in more detail below.

Block Pricing at Best Buy

Best Buy priced Nintendo DS Games during July 2014 in the following manner. A given consumer was charged full price for the first game ($39.99 for the most popular games), but could purchase a second game at half price. Demand curves usually slope downward, and it is likely that the typical consumer's willingness to pay for additional games declines with the number purchased. Presumably Best Buy believed that by offering the discount for the second game, it would make higher profits than if it sold all games at full price. For example, if all games were priced at $39.99, Best Buy would sell only one game to consumers who value the second game at less than $39.99 but more than Best Buy's marginal cost (which is presumably less than half the listed price).

Whether half is the optimal discount depends on the typical consumer's willingness to pay for the second game. With heterogeneous consumers, Best Buy also should consider the additional profits obtained from selling the second game at half price to those customers who value it less than the first game versus the lost profits from consumers who would have been willing to pay full price for two games. This trade-off is not an issue in the case of homogenous consumers analyzed in this section of the main text. Another consideration, which goes beyond the scope of the simple analysis in this chapter, is whether giving a discount on a second game today reduces future sales at the full price. For example, consumers might be willing to buy only one game at full price today. However, after playing it for an extended time period, they might be willing to pay full price for another game in the future. Apparently, Best Buy believed that the additional profits from offering the second game at a substantially discounted price were larger than the lost profits from these additional concerns.

Source: Best Buy, www.bestbuy.com (2014).

additional profits from a homogeneous customer base, but also is used in certain circumstances to increase profits when customer demands are more heterogeneous.[6]

Another type of block pricing can occur in the choice of package size. Suppose a typical customer values a first T-shirt at $16 and a second at $10. If vendors sell the shirts individually, they have to charge $10 or less to get a customer to buy two. If they offer them in packs of two at a price of $26, customers will be willing to purchase the package and pay an average price of $13 per shirt.

Two-Part Tariffs

With a *two-part tariff,* the customer pays an up-front fee for the right to buy the product and then pays additional fees for each unit of the product consumed. A classic example is an amusement park, where a customer pays a fee to get in and then so much per ride (Disneyland used to price in this manner).[7] Golf and tennis clubs, computer information services, and telephone service providers are examples of companies that frequently use two-part tariffs.

The benchmark case of charging one price to all customers is a special case of a two-part tariff. The entry fee is zero and the additional units can be purchased at the quoted price. Making more general use of two-part pricing (charging a positive entry fee and a subsequent usage price) can sometimes increase profits substantially relative to the benchmark case. As we discuss below, this is most likely to be true when potential consumers have relatively homogeneous demands for the product.

---

[6]For expositional simplicity, we have assumed that marginal cost is constant. If production, packaging, or distribution costs decline with volume, price discounts would be offered, even without market power. With market power, the price reductions will exceed the cost reduction as volume increases.

[7]W. Oi (1971), "A Disneyland Dilemma: Two-Part Tariffs for a Mickey Mouse Monopoly," *Quarterly Journal of Economics* (February), 77–96.

Figure 7.5 Two-Part Tariff

In this example, all potential customers had identical demands. The figure displays a demand curve for a representative consumer, $P = 10 - Q$. The managerial cost of producing the product is $1. The potential consumer surplus that the firm could capture is $40.50, as shown by the shaded triangle. Maximum profits can be extracted by charging an up-front fee equal to all the consumer surplus (or slightly less) and then charging a price equal to marginal cost, $1. Under such a scheme, the consumer purchases 9 units.

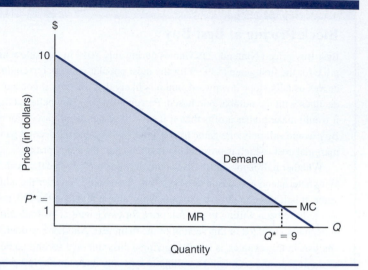

For illustration, consider an example where all consumers have identical demands for the product, $P = 10 - Q$. Figure 7.5 displays a demand curve for a representative consumer. The marginal cost of producing the product is $1. The potential gains from trade that the firm could capture are shown by the shaded triangle and are equal to $40.50 ($0.5 \times 9 \times 9$). Maximum profits can be extracted by charging an up-front fee equal to all the gains from trade (or slightly less) and then charging a price equal to marginal cost, $1. With this pricing strategy, the consumer purchases 9 units. In contrast, if the firm charged a single unit price, the best it could do would be a profit of $20.25 (by setting marginal revenue equal to marginal cost). In this case, the price is $5.50 per unit and the consumer purchases 4.5 units.

Two-part tariffs also can be used profitably when customers' demands are not identical, but this pricing strategy tends to be less effective the more consumers vary in their demands for the product. From a practical or legal standpoint, a company might have to offer the same two-part tariff to all potential customers. Charging a high entry fee allows the firm to extract more surplus from customers who have high demands for the product, but potential customers with lower demands will choose not to purchase. When customers' demands vary widely, it often is best to charge a low entry fee (possibly zero) and then charge a price above marginal cost for use. In this case, given the costs of implementing a two-part tariff (devising the pricing strategy, collecting the fees, and so on), the firm frequently is better off just charging a single price. However, in the next section, we discuss other pricing policies that can increase profits when facing more heterogeneous demands.

Price Discrimination—Heterogeneous Consumer Demands

Potential customers often vary materially in their willingness to pay for a product. In our benchmark case, the firm charges the same price to all potential customers. With a heterogeneous customer base, the company can make higher profits if it is able to charge different prices to customers, based on their willingness to pay.

Price discrimination occurs whenever a firm charges differential prices across customers (for a given quantity and quality) based on their willingness to pay—not on differences in production and distribution costs. With price discrimination, the markup or profit margin realized varies across customers. Two conditions are necessary for

Two-Part Pricing for Capital Goods

Frequently a consumer buys a capital good from a firm and then purchases another good to obtain the services of the capital good. For example, Gillette sells razors and razor blades, Hidden Fence installs pet containment systems that require special batteries sold only by Hidden Fence. This situation is like a two-part tariff. With homogeneous consumers, profits are maximized by setting the price of the capital good to extract all consumer surplus and pricing the consumable at marginal cost. With heterogeneous consumers it is typically optimal to charge a lower price for the capital good and a price above marginal cost for the consumable.

profitable price discrimination. First, customers must vary in their willingness to pay for a given quantity of the product (demand must be heterogeneous). Otherwise, there is no point in segmenting the market. Second, the firm must be able to identify submarkets and restrict transfers among consumers across different submarkets. Otherwise, any attempt to charge differential prices to customers will be undercut by resale across the submarkets. One group of consumers can buy at the low price, then resell to the other groups at a price below the firm's prices to these groups.

Sometimes managers have quite good information about individuals' product demands (which specific customers are willing to pay more for the product). For instance, if Andrew Leone has sold automobiles to the same customers on repeated occasions, he is likely to have relatively good information about each customer's price sensitivity. In other cases, managers have poor information about individual product demands. For example, early in his career Andy had less experience and accumulated information to differentiate among customers who came to the dealership. But he still might be able to engage in certain kinds of price discrimination with information only about the range or distribution of customer demands. We begin our

Supreme Court Rules in Favor of Selling Imports of Copyrighted Items

To price discriminate successfully, a firm must not only be able to identify submarkets with varying consumer demands, but also must be able to restrict trade among these submarkets. The ability of firms to do this is far from perfect. Tens of billions of dollars of so-called "gray market" sales occur annually, where genuine products are sold in the United States after being purchased abroad at lower prices. These sales undercut the higher prices charged by manufacturers in the United States. Walmart and Costco participate in this market by selling gray-market products at substantial discounts. Many gray-market sales are also made through eBay (the operator of the world's largest online marketplace). According to a 2009 Deloitte analysis, imports of gray-market products to the U.S. cost manufacturers as much as $63 billion in sales a year.

The willingness to pay for textbooks varies significantly across countries around the world. Publishers typically charge much higher prices for textbooks in the United States than abroad. In 2013, the U.S. Supreme Court considered an appeal of a $600,000 jury award against a graduate student who had imported John Wiley & Sons textbooks from his native Thailand, and sold them in the United States for a profit. The case was widely considered to be of great importance due to the size of the gray market.

The Court ruled in a 6-3 decision that manufacturers cannot block imports of copyrighted items made and sold abroad. The $600,00 jury award, which had been imposed on the graduate student, was overturned. This ruling makes it more difficult for publishers and other companies to price discriminate between United States and foreign customers, thus bolstering the multibillion dollar gray market for products produced by U.S firms.

Source: G. Stohr (2013), "Costco Scores Win Supreme Court Ruling on Imports of Copyrighted Items," *Seattle Times* (March 19)

MANAGERIAL APPLICATIONS

Tuition Pricing

Firms engaging in personalized pricing strive to extract the maximum willingness to pay from each customer. While colleges and universities do not engage in perfect personalized pricing, they effectively charge different prices to students for tuition through the use of financial aid packages. Stated tuition is the maximum price that any student is charged. Low-income students, who are likely to be relatively price-sensitive, typically are offered more financial aid than high-income students. In addition, top students who are likely to have numerous scholarship offers, and thus more options, are offered significant discounts. An average student from a high-income family typically pays much higher effective tuition than other students.

examination of price discrimination by considering the case where the manager has good information about individual demands. We then consider the case where the manager has information only about the distribution of demands.

Exploiting Information about Individual Demands

Personalized Pricing[8]

Suppose there are many potential customers. Each customer places a value on the product that signifies the maximum that that individual would pay for the product—their reservation price. For simplicity, suppose each customer purchases at most 1 unit. Personalized pricing (*first-degree price discrimination*) extracts the maximum amount each customer is willing to pay for the product. Each consumer is charged a price that makes that customer indifferent between purchasing and not purchasing the product. In this case, the firm extracts all the potential gains from trade. This extreme form of price discrimination is rare and typically is possible only when the number of customers is extremely small and resale is impossible. With personalized pricing, the firm sells to all customers who are willing to pay more than the marginal cost of production. All gains from trade are exhausted, and the outcome is efficient. All the gains from trade, however, go to the firm.

While perfect personalized pricing is rare, new technologies are making it easier for companies to customize quoted prices. For example, companies selling over the Internet can vary quoted prices based on past buying histories, demographic information obtained through electronic registration, clickstreams, and so on. Similarly, companies that sell through catalogs can—and often do—include personalized inserts, where the quoted prices vary depending on the customer's buying history and personal characteristics (e.g., zip code). This type of personalized pricing was more difficult under older printing technologies and before the existence of computerized databases that store customer information.[9] Salespeople might also vary product offerings and prices based on a customer's attire. For example, some wine stewards suggest more expensive wines (with higher price markups) to customers who wear expensive shoes and/or watches.

---

[8]Economists often categorize price discrimination as first-, second-, or third-degree. These terms were originated by A.C. Pigou (1950), *The Economics of Welfare* (Macmillan: London). Unfortunately, they are not very descriptive. Following C. Shapiro and H. Varian (1999), *Information Rules: A Strategic Guide to the Network Economy* (Harvard Business School Press: Boston), we use more descriptive terms like personalized pricing, menu pricing, and group pricing.

[9]Note, however, that the Internet also lowers information costs and that this makes market segmentation (a necessary aspect of effective price discrimination) more difficult (recall the earlier Managerial Application on made-for-export cigarettes).

Virtual Vineyards

Virtual Vineyards offers premium wines and specialty foods—such as El Serpis Anchovy Stuffed Olives and Fox's Fine Foods Killer Corn Relish—over the Internet. The company also offers advice, monthly wine programs, and a variety of other services at its Web site. Virtual Vineyards tracks the clickstream of each user and instantaneously makes special offers based on the behavior. In a similar vein, Amazon.com tracks the purchases of each consumer and recommends additional related books the next time the user logs on. The Internet has made possible many marketing opportunities not available through other media.

Source: C. Shapiro and H. Varian (1999), *Information Rules: A Strategic Guide to the Network Economy* (Harvard Business School Press: Boston).

Group Pricing

Managers sometimes can gauge an individual's price sensitivity by observing a characteristic of the individual such as age or country of residence. In these cases, the manager can have a fairly good idea of a specific individual's demand for the product, even if the manager never has interacted with the customer.

Group pricing (*third-degree price discrimination*) results when a firm separates its customers into several groups and sets a different price for each group, based on the willingness to pay of the typical group member. For example, utility companies charge different rates to individual versus commercial users, computer companies give educational discounts, and airlines charge different rates based on the amount of notice given for the reservation. Beyond.com charged government agencies and large companies lower prices than other customers. As illustrated in the following example, a firm that can segment its market maximizes profits by setting marginal revenue equal to marginal cost for each market segment.

Firms use a variety of characteristics to divide customers into groups. Three prominent examples are age, time of purchase, and income. For instance, movie

Pricing of Books

Firms divide customers into groups based on various characteristics. Different prices are charged to each group, depending on their elasticity of demand.

One characteristic used by book publishers to segment the market is time. When a new book comes to market, it usually is offered only in a hardcover edition for a relatively high price. Subsequently, it is offered in paperback at a substantially reduced price. Individuals who have a high demand for the book (and thus a low-price elasticity) do not want to wait for the paperback edition and thus pay a high price for the book. Those with lower demands wait for the cheaper edition. After the paperback edition comes to market, the publisher generally will continue to offer the hardcover edition. Hardcover books are likely to make better gifts than paperbacks. Also customers are likely to prefer hardcovers for their libraries. Thus there continues to be a market for both types of books. Continuing to offer multiple versions is an example of menu pricing (discussed below).

In 2014, Amazon.com offered several versions of *Harry Potter and the Deathly Hollows* by J. K. Rowling—Book 7 in the popular series. The hardcover version sold for $22.46, whereas the paperback sold for $9.81. In addition, there was a paperback, large-print edition for $10.31, an audio CD for $49.97, and a Kindle Edition for $9.99. The hardcover and paperback editions also could be purchased as part of specially boxed book sets. When each of the seven Harry Potter books was originally introduced, it was available only in relatively expensive hard-copy and audio editions.

theaters frequently give discounts to senior citizens and students, price lower for matinees than for evening performances, and vary prices across locations depending on the average income in the area. The objective is to charge a higher price to the groups who are willing to pay more for a given quantity of the product.

Consider the Snowfish Ski Resort, which can separate its demand into local skiers and out-of-town skiers. The marginal cost of servicing a skier of either type is $10. Suppose the resort faces the following demand curves:

$$\text{Out of town:} \qquad Q_0 = 500 - 10P \qquad\qquad (7.7)$$
$$\text{Local:} \qquad Q_1 = 500 - 20P \qquad\qquad (7.8)$$

Total demand at any one price is the sum of the demands for the two types of consumers:[10]

$$Q = 1,000 - 30P \qquad\qquad (7.9)$$

If the company sells all tickets at one price, profit maximization will occur at[11]

$$P^* = \$21.66; \quad Q^* = 350; \quad Q_0^* = 283; \quad Q_1^* = 67; \quad \text{Profit} = \$4,081$$

The company can make higher profits by charging different prices to the two sets of skiers. The optimal prices are found by setting the marginal revenue equal to the marginal cost in each of the two market segments. Under this pricing policy, the following prices, quantities, and profits are observed:

$$P_0^* = \$30; \quad Q_0^* = 200; \quad P_1^* = \$17.50; \quad Q_1^* = 150; \quad \text{Profit} = \$5,125$$

where P_0^* and P_1^* = prices charged to out-of-town and local skiers, respectively. The resort charges higher prices to the out-of-town skiers, who are less sensitive to ticket prices than local skiers.

Figure 7.6 displays the optimal pricing policy for each market segment. Snowfish treats the two markets as separate and charges the optimal monopolistic price to each segment. Consistent with Equation (7.2), the optimal markup is lower in the more price-sensitive local market. Using the point-elasticity formula developed in the appendix to Chapter 4, it can be shown that at the optimal prices, the elasticities for the local and out-of-town skier markets are 2.33 and 1.5, respectively. The respective markups above marginal cost are $7.50 and $20 (given the prices of $17.50 and $30).

There are a number of methods that Snowfish might use to charge the two groups different prices. Discount coupons might be sold at supermarkets away from major resort hotels. Presumably, most of the sales at these supermarkets will be to local customers. Alternatively, discount books of tickets (nontransferable) could be sold locally prior to the start of ski season. Ski resorts use both techniques. These policies are more profitable the more difficult it is for out-of-town skiers to buy the tickets at prices less than $30.

---

[10]This demand curve assumes that price is lower than or equal to $25. At higher prices, the local skiers purchase no tickets and the total demand curve is simply the demand curve for out-of-town skiers ($Q = 500 - 10P$).

[11]The reader should know by now that the solution to this problem is found by setting marginal revenue equal to marginal cost and solving for Q^*. Price can then be found from the equation for the demand curve. For instance, the total demand curve can be obtained by rearranging Equation (7.9): $P = 33.33 - 0.033Q$. When the tickets are sold at one price to all consumers, the marginal revenue is MR $= 33.33 - 0.067Q$. Since marginal cost is $10, the optimal quantity is 350; price is $21.66. The optimal prices and quantities for the individual market segments are found by completing similar calculations using Equations (7.7) and (7.8).

Figure 7.6 Optimal Pricing at Snowfish Ski Resort

Snowfish can segment its customers into two market segments, out-of-town skiers and local skiers. The marginal cost of serving either type of skier is $10. The optimal pricing policy is to set the monopoly price in each market segment. The markup is higher for out-of-town skiers because they have less elastic demands than local skiers. At the optimal prices ($30 and $17.50), the demand elasticities are 1.50 for out-of-town skiers and 2.33 for local skiers.

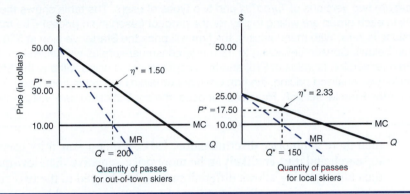

Using Information about the Distribution of Demands

In some settings, the manager does not have enough information to divide customers into meaningful groups. For instance, even if a retailer knows that low-income individuals are more price-sensitive than high-income individuals, the retailer may not be able to gauge the incomes of customers when they come to the store.[12] Nonetheless, the manager might have enough information about the range or distribution of individual demands to engage in profitable price discrimination. In this section we discuss two prominent methods that can be used in this setting. Both rely on the principle of *self-selection*. Consumers are provided with options. They then reveal information about their individual price sensitivities by their choices.

Menu Pricing

With menu pricing (*second-degree price discrimination*), all potential customers are offered the same menu of purchase options. The classic example involves block pricing, where the price per unit depends on the quantity purchased.[13] For instance, cellular phone companies typically give customers a choice among several rate plans, where the price per minute varies with the minimum number of minutes per month specified across each plan. Customers use their private information about likely usage to select the best rate plan for themselves. By carefully constructing the menu of options, the company makes more profits than if it simply offered the product at one price to all potential customers (e.g., offering phone service at $.10 per minute, independent of volume). If such quantity discounts are based solely on costs,

[12]Also it may be neither practical nor legal to charge customers different prices for the same products even if the retailer were to know each customer's income.

[13]Recall that block pricing can be used to increase profit either by extracting more profits from a given homogeneous customer population or by increasing profits through charging different prices to high- versus low-volume customers. In this section, we discuss the second use.

	Sophisticated User	Unsophisticated User
Starter edition	$45	$30
Premier edition	$100	$30

Table 7.1   Example of Menu Pricing

In this example, there are two versions of *TurboTax* and two types of users. The table shows the maximum price that customers in each group are willing to pay for the product (reservation prices). The marginal cost of producing both versions is zero. With menu pricing, the firm will price the Starter version at $30 and the Premier version at $85 (or just below). Consumers acting to maximize consumer surplus will self-select. Sophisticated users will buy the Premier version (surplus of $15) and the unsophisticated users will buy the Starter version (surplus of zero). Unlike personalized pricing, the firm does not obtain all the gains from trade. The firm would like to charge more for the Premier version. However, if it does, the sophisticated user will purchase the Starter version.

then there is no price discrimination. However, large-quantity users have incentives to search and thus are likely to be more price-sensitive than low-quantity users, and thus block pricing allows different rates to be charged to the two groups even if per-unit costs are similar. Public utilities frequently price in this manner.

A related pricing strategy is to offer potential customers a menu of price–quality combinations. For instance, *TurboTax* markets both a Premier and Starter version of its software. The Premier version contains additional features that are likely to appeal to sophisticated users. The marginal costs of producing and distributing both versions are virtually equal. However, the company marks up the Premier version more because the typical customer choosing this version is likely to be less price-sensitive than the typical customer choosing the Starter version.

Table 7.1 presents a numerical example of menu pricing. Here the market for *TurboTax* software is divided into two types of users, sophisticated and unsophisticated. The reservation prices (maximum willingness to pay) for the Premier and Starter versions are given for both types of users. The marginal cost of producing the software is assumed to be zero.

Ideally, the company would like to identify the two types of users prior to purchase. Assuming it could prevent reselling the software among consumers, the company would maximize profits by charging $100 to the sophisticated users, who would purchase the Premier version, and $30 to the unsophisticated users, who would purchase the Starter version. This pricing strategy is equivalent to personalized pricing.

Since the company cannot identify the type of user prior to purchase, it prices the Starter version at $30 and the Premier version at just below $85 (e.g., $84.99). The customers, who know their own type, choose the quality–price combination that maximizes their individual consumer surplus. Unsophisticated buyers purchase the Starter version (which yields no consumer surplus). Sophisticated users buy the Premier version and gain a surplus of just over $15 (the surplus they would enjoy if they purchased the Starter version). The potential for the sophisticated buyer to purchase the lower-quality product limits the price that can be charged for the Premier version. If the Premier version were priced above $85, sophisticated users would obtain greater consumer surplus by buying the Starter version at $30, and no Premier versions would be sold.

The end result is that the sophisticated user gains some consumer surplus and the company makes less profit than it would if it could engage in either personalized or group pricing. Nonetheless, it does better than if it offered only one version at a single

ANALYZING MANAGERIAL DECISIONS: *Cell Phone Pricing*

You are a pricing manager for a cell phone company. You have two types of customers with different demand curves for your service. The demand curves for an individual customer from each group for hours of talk time per month are

$$\text{Type A customer: } P = 10 - 2Q$$
$$\text{Type B customer: } P = 10 - Q$$

Your marginal cost for providing hours of phone service is zero (all your costs are fixed). There are 1,000 customers of each type.

You know the demand curves for the two types of customers. However, it is impossible for you to identify when a person purchases a plan whether the customer is from one group or the other.

1. Design a menu plan that extracts all of the consumer surplus from the Type A customers

and as much as possible from the Type B customers given that they have the option to purchase your first plan (it might help to graph the problem). Each of the plans on the menu must offer a maximum number of hours of talk time per month for a fixed monthly fee. (*Hint*: You can extract all the consumer surplus from the Type A customers using a two-part tariff. Such a plan can be expressed in terms of offering a fixed number of minutes at a fixed price.)

2. What are the total profits from offering the two plans?

3. What happens if you increase the monthly fee for the plan designed for the Type B customers? Explain.

---

price. For instance, the company could offer just the Premier version at a price of $100 and sell only to sophisticated users or offer the product at $20 and sell to both types of users. But it generally is more profitable to offer both quality-price combinations.[14]

Coupons and Rebates

Firms frequently use coupons in product pricing. For instance, most Sunday papers contain numerous coupons offering discounts to customers who use the coupons before their expiration dates. Coupons also are distributed through direct mailings, product packages, and magazines.

Firms also frequently offer rebates, where the customer using the rebate is refunded some portion of the purchase price. For instance, automobile manufacturers often offer significant rebates (e.g., $1,000) to customers who purchase cars during the rebate period. Software manufacturers and retailers (e.g., Microsoft and Intuit) frequently offer rebates for their products. Rebate offers regularly are attached to products sold at grocery stores.

Coupons and rebates give price discounts to customers. Price discounts in turn might be given to attract new customers (new first-time users or brand switchers) or to increase sales among current customers. Price discrimination is one primary reason why some firms use coupons and rebates to make price discounts rather than simply lowering the price.

Coupons have to be clipped and brought to the store, whereas rebates often require customers to complete and mail rebate forms to the manufacturer. Many customers do not use available coupons or rebates to purchase products because the money saved through using the coupon or rebate is less than the value of the time it

---

[14]If the number of sophisticated users is large relative to the number of unsophisticated users, it might be better to price the deluxe version at $100 and sell only to sophisticated users.

takes to search for and redeem the offer. The typical coupon/rebate user is likely to have a relatively low opportunity cost of time (e.g., the user might not work outside the home or have a low income); such consumers are likely to be more price-sensitive. Thus, issuing coupons and rebates is one way of lowering effective prices to potential customers with more elastic demands.[15]

In 2008 Intuit offered a $10 rebate to existing customers for the Windows version of *Quicken Deluxe* (along with a $20 price reduction). Customers who applied for the rebate paid a net price of $29.99, whereas a customer failing to use the rebate paid a price of $39.99. Customers failing to redeem a $10 rebate presumably place a high value on their time and are unlikely to be very price-sensitive.[16] Consistent with the principles of price discrimination, they pay a higher price for the product than the more price-sensitive rebate user.

Coupon/rebate programs can be expensive. For instance, there are the costs of designing the promotion, printing and circulating the offer, and handling the redemptions. These costs can be significant and should be compared with the benefits in choosing whether to offer the program. We have indicated that one of the potential benefits of these programs is increased profit through price discrimination. Another potential benefit is the increase in future profits from new customers who start using the product due to the sales promotion—if they like the product, they might purchase it in the future even if a coupon is not offered.[17] Coupons (e.g., in newspapers and magazines) sometimes can be viewed as a form of advertising that lowers information costs about the product.

Interestingly, some retail companies have offered rebates for the Windows version of a program while offering no rebate for the Mac version. Mac users typically have fewer software products to choose among than Windows users. Also, local software retailers are likely to carry a smaller inventory of Mac products than Windows products. The lack of available substitutes implies that the typical Mac customer is likely to be less price-sensitive than the typical Windows customer. Beyond.com thus offered coupons to Windows users with their higher price sensitivity, and no coupons to the less price-sensitive Mac users. Finally, if Macs are less likely to exist in the future than Windows-based machines, the benefits of attracting new customers for future sales are lower for Macs.

Bundling

To this point, we have considered the case where the firm sells a single product. This section extends the analysis by providing an introduction to the case of multiple products.[18]

---

[15]Price discrimination is unlikely to explain the use of large rebates or coupons. For instance, if an automobile company offers customers a $2,000 rebate, it reasonably can forecast that all customers will take advantage of this offer. Thus rebates are essentially equivalent to giving all customers a price reduction, for example, by having a sale. Rebates, however, often are offered by the manufacturer who does not have direct control over the retail price. For a more extensive discussion of coupons, rebates, and other sales promotions see R. Blattberg and S. Neslin (1990), *Sales Promotion: Concepts, Methods, and Strategies* (Prentice Hall: Englewood Cliffs).

[16]Alternatively, customers might be purchasing the product on the behalf of their companies. In this case, since the company is paying the bill, the customer might be less price-sensitive.

[17]Sometimes this benefit can be obtained simply by lowering the purchase price (e.g., by having a sale).

[18]The topic of pricing multiple products can be relatively complex. Our intent here is to provide a basic introduction to the idea of product bundling. For a more detailed analysis, see J. Long (1984), "Comments on 'Gaussian Demand and Commodity Bundling,'" *Journal of Business* 57, S235–S246.

	Microsoft Streets	Microsoft Trip Planner	Bundle
Consumer	$15	$25	$40
Professional	$30	$20	$50

Table 7.2 Product Bundling

In this example, there are two types of customers, professionals and ordinary consumers. The table shows the reservation prices for *Microsoft Streets* and *Microsoft Trip Planner.* The reservation price for the bundle for any consumer is the sum of the reservation prices for the individual products. If the firm wants to sell both products to both types of customers, it must price the products at $70 and $60, respectively (the minimum reservation prices for each product). It collects $130 from each customer. It can do better by selling the products in a bundle for a price of $150 (the minimum reservation price for the bundle). Bundling increases profits in this example because the two groups have opposite *relative valuations* of the two products. Professionals are willing to pay more for *Streets* than consumers, while the opposite holds for *Trip Planner.* Thus, the minimum reservation price for the bundle is greater than the sum of the minimum reservation prices for the separate products.

Companies frequently bundle products for sale. For example, in 2014 Microsoft offered *Microsoft Streets and Trips* as a bundle for $39.95.[19] This bundle combined leading street-mapping and trip-planning technologies into a single package. Other examples include retailers bundling free parking with a purchase at their store, newspapers selling advertising in both morning and afternoon editions at one price, season tickets for sporting events, and restaurants offering fixed-price complete dinners.

One reason for bundling products is to extract additional profits from a customer base with heterogeneous product demands.[20] For example, Table 7.2 presents two types of potential customers: consumers and professional users. The figure displays the maximum prices (reservation prices) that the individual customers within each group are willing to pay for *Microsoft Streets* and *Microsoft Trip Planner.* The marginal cost of producing either product is assumed to be zero (to simplify the discussion). Potential customers purchase a product only if their surplus is nonnegative.

Why would the company bundle the products, forcing customers to purchase both in order to obtain either? If the firm did not bundle, the most it could charge for *Streets* would be $15 and for *Planner* $20 if it wanted to sell to both groups of customers. Using this policy, it would collect $35 from each customer. The company,

MANAGERIAL APPLICATIONS

Bundling Videogames

Microsoft is in a battle with Sony Corp. over videogames. Microsoft is bundling a limited edition Xbox packaged with Microsoft's Halo (a shooting game) for $169. Halo is one of the most popular titles exclusive to the Xbox, and Microsoft expects that this offer will spur sales of the game machine itself.

Source: R. Guth (2004), "Game Gambit: Microsoft to Cut Xbox Price," *The Wall Street Journal* (March 19), B1.

[19]Microsoft has sold this product for many years but announced that it would be discontinued at the end of 2014.

[20]Products also might be bundled to reduce packaging costs or to reduce the costs to customers who want to buy the products together. For example, to the extent that most users want to utilize features of both street mapping and trip planning, the technologies might be combined to lower the costs to the customer of obtaining and integrating the two products.

MANAGERIAL APPLICATIONS

Harry Potter: An Example of Price Discrimination

In 2010, Sears.com offered a set of Harry Potter DVDs for around $55 plus shipping—approximately $10. A customer could obtain a rebate form online and mail it in for a rebate of the shipping costs. Why not simply sell the DVDs for $55? Wouldn't costs be avoided? For example, it is expensive to issue and mail checks and print posters and coupons.

   To illustrate the potential benefits of the policy, suppose that if the DVDs were sold at the same price to all customers, Sears.com would have priced them at $65. With this policy, Sears.com would lose the potential profit from selling to consumers who are willing to pay a price above Sears' production cost but less than $65. Sears' apparent objective was to find a way to sell to these consumers at a lower price without having to lower the price to other consumers. One way to accomplish this objective was through rebates. Presumably, those willing to purchase at $65 had higher opportunity costs for their time (on average). This made them less likely to fill out and mail in the coupons. Customers not using the rebates paid a price of $65, whereas the customers using the rebate coupons paid $55.

   There are a variety of issues to consider in deciding on such a rebate program. First, there is a trade-off between the costs of administering the program and the benefits of additional sales. Also, there is the loss of $65 sales to customers who would have purchased at $65 but now use the rebate coupons.

---

however, can bundle the products and sell to all customers at a price of $40 (the minimum reservation price for the bundle).

   In this example, the two groups have opposite *relative valuations* of the two products. Professional users are willing to pay more for *Streets* than consumers, whereas consumers are willing to pay more for *Planner* than professional users. This feature implies that the minimum bundle value is greater than the sum of the minimum reservation prices for each product. Thus, the firm makes more money selling the bundle than selling the products separately. If one group valued both products higher than the other group, there would be no gains from bundling (the minimum bundle value would be the same as the sum of the minimum individual reservation prices).

   Typically, products are not just sold in bundles. Often firms use a tactic of *optional* (*mixed*) bundling, where the products can be purchased separately or in a bundle at a price below the sum of the individual prices. Optional bundling can be more profitable than pure bundling when some customers value one product highly, but value the other product below the marginal cost of production. For these customers, the extra revenue the firm would earn from selling the bundle would be lower than the extra cost of producing it.

Other Concerns

Multiperiod Considerations

Future Demand

In 2008 Intuit offered a free edition of *TurboTax*. If the objective is to maximize single-period profits for a single product (as in the benchmark case), it is never optimal to set a price of zero.[21] Managers, however, are concerned with sales not only in the current period but in future periods as well. Giving the product away can attract

---

[21]Firms that sell multiple products can have incentives to price selected individual products below marginal cost. For example, McDonald's sometimes has promotions that sell hamburgers at below cost. The intent is to attract customers who buy other products, such as fries, at prices substantially above cost.

new customers; it lowers the full cost of consuming the good below that of competing products. If they like the product, they will purchase the product in the future at positive prices. This is a major reason why firms provide "free samples" of their products.

Offering a product at a price below marginal cost is a more effective pricing strategy if information costs are higher. If a customer takes the time to learn to use a new software product (such as *TurboTax*), the customer often will want to continue to use the program in the future, rather than take the time to learn to use a new product. Thus at similar prices, the customer is more likely to buy upgrades and future editions of the current software rather than switch to a competing product. This *lock-in effect* is a reason why some software firms give away their products (or charge low prices) in the early stages of development.

Firms sometimes charge lower prices than the optimal single-period price because they value maintaining customer goodwill. For example, a severe ice storm in March 1991 produced a major power outage in upstate New York. Electric generators were in high demand and could have been sold to customers at extremely high prices. But local stores did not raise the price of generators substantially. One concern apparently was that they would be seen as taking advantage of customers—that such a tactic would undermine the firm's reputation and reduce future demand. Drug companies face similar concerns when they price new drugs. These companies have an incentive to charge the profit-maximizing price for their products (to help reimburse them for their development and other costs). However, in setting prices these companies have to consider the reactions of "public-interest" groups and government regulators.

Future Costs

As discussed in Chapter 5, for some firms the long-run average cost of producing a given level of output declines as the firm gains experience in producing the product. For instance, employees can gain important information on how to improve the production process as they gain more experience. When these *learning effects* are important, it can be optimal for the firm to produce a high volume of the product initially to gain experience and thus a cost advantage over competing firms in subsequent periods. This high output is correspondingly sold at lower prices than if the firm produced the lower volume associated with optimizing single-period profits.

Many cost advantages, however, are short-lived because competing firms often can copy innovations. Thus managers should consider carefully whether it is appropriate to adopt such a high-volume, low-price strategy. Chapter 8 discusses this issue in more detail.

HISTORICAL APPLICATIONS

Early Use of the Free Sample

In 1870, after over 10 years of experimentation, Robert Chesebrough opened a factory in Brooklyn to produce petroleum jelly. But he initially sold not one bottle. He tried giving samples to doctors and druggists, but they failed to reorder. Finally, he decided he had to create a market for his salve, so he loaded a wagon full of 1-ounce bottles and drove around the state giving away samples. When people ran out, they went to their druggist, who then began to place orders. Chesebrough soon had a dozen wagons canvassing the countryside. As demand continued to expand, Vasoline made the persistent Chesebrough an extremely wealthy man.

Source: I. Flatow (1992), *They All Laughed* (Harper Perennial, New York).

MANAGERIAL APPLICATIONS

Apple Apologizes for Its Pricing of iPhones

Apple Computer provides a good example of how concerns about customer relations and long-term reputation can affect pricing decisions. In June 2007, Apple and AT&T launched the iPhone at a price of $599. Many iPod aficionados waited in line for hours to obtain the new, much-hyped phone. Within three months, Apple reduced the price by $200 to $399.

Customers who had purchased the phone at $599 were outraged. Many of these customers had been long-term users of Macs and iPods. They felt betrayed when "newer, less loyal customers" were able to buy the iPhone at a much lower price by waiting only a few months. Some of the iPhone purchasers said the timing of the price cut would discourage them from buying Apple products in the future. "This is like a slap in the face to early adopters," said John Keck, an executive at an advertising agency in Detroit. Apple received a flood of negative e-mails. The customers' strong reactions were featured prominently in media reports, including the major television networks and newspapers.

In response to this criticism, Apple's CEO Steve Jobs issued a rare public apology and offered a $100 credit to all customers who had paid the original price. In a letter posted on Apple's Web site Jobs' wrote, "Our early customers trusted us, and we must live up to that trust with our actions in moments like this."

If Apple expected to go out of business in the near future, there would be little economic reason to give the credit to people who had purchased products in the past. Jobs, however, presumably expected Apple to be around for the long term and that the company must maintain a reputation for being fair and honorable. He was concerned not only about the current year's profits, but about future years' profits as well.

Source: N. Wingfield (2007), "Steve Jobs Offers Rare Apology, Credit for iPhone," *The Wall Street Journal Online* (September 7), A1.

Storable Products

In a number of our examples, we have discussed products that can be stored. This means that sales of the product and consumption of the product are not the same. When you lower the price of a product, the quantity demanded rises for two reasons: First, as demand curves slope downward and as prices drop, there is more consumption; second, if the price reduction is temporary, the customer will purchase additional units to be consumed at future dates. Thus, for storable goods, the variation over time in sales is greater than the variation in consumption.

Strategic Interaction

The analysis in this chapter starts with a demand curve for the product. Managers choose a pricing strategy that maximizes profits given demand and its cost structure. This approach holds the price of substitute products constant (recall the definition of

MANAGERIAL APPLICATIONS

Market Segmentation

The European Commission is trying to forge a single market for drugs across the European union. Bayer, the German drug maker, was found guilty of striking agreements with French and Spanish wholesalers to dissuade them from exporting Adalat, a heart treatment, from Spain and France where the price is low, to Britain, where it is 40 percent higher. The European Court of Justice, Europe's highest court, ruled that the commission was wrong to fine Bayer for their actions. This ruling provides Bayer with more flexibility to segregate markets and offer the same product at different prices.

Source: P. Meller (2004), "Europe Effort to Control Pricing Is Set Back," *New York Times* (January 7), W1.

a demand curve). Thus, the reactions of competitors are not considered explicitly in this analysis. Although this approach serves as a useful starting point in many practical applications, it is not as useful in markets with only a few major competitors. In these markets, it often is foolish to ignore rival reactions in setting prices. For example, if United Airlines offers a major price reduction to customers, it is reasonably safe to assume that the other major airlines (e.g., American Airlines and Delta) will not hold their prices constant. In these situations, it is important for managers to consider explicitly the reactions of rival firms when they price their products. Chapter 9 provides a set of tools (derived from game theory), that is, useful for managers within these interactive settings.

Legal Issues

In addition to factors affecting supply and demand, laws and regulations sometimes limit the firm's ability to charge different prices to different customers in specific markets. For example, the Robinson–Patman Act limits the ability of firms in the United States to charge retailers different prices unless they can justify the price by showing differences in their costs. (Companies have had considerable difficulty sustaining a cost justification defense.) Laws in some countries also limit the maximum prices that can be charged for various products. Managers contemplating the pricing policies discussed in this chapter should check the legality of a proposed pricing policy given the laws they face within a particular jurisdiction.

Legal constraints can drive the firm's choice of pricing policy in a variety of ways. For example, prompted by complaints from local merchants in a college town, the city council passed a law to restrict street vendors from selling handcrafted items. But the law exempted flower vendors: There was a long-standing tradition of giving flowers to dates before ball games, and local ladies had long supplied the cut flowers. Undeterred, the craft vendors bought bouquets of flowers, placed a flower on each item, and sold the flower with the craft item bundled in for "free." Some manufacturers in the 1970s began offering rebates rather than cutting product price because when price controls were implemented by the U.S. government, rebates and price cuts were treated differentially.

Xerox originally leased copying machines with a requirement that the lessee buy Xerox paper; it set the paper price above marginal cost. IBM used a similar pricing plan for tabulation machines and IBM cards. The intent was to extract higher profits from higher-volume users. The government successfully charged

---

MANAGERIAL APPLICATIONS

Apple Settles Antitrust Case by Lowering iTune Prices in Britain

Many forms of price discrimination are legal in countries around the world. Companies, however, can face regulatory constraints in pricing. On January 9, 2008, Apple Computer settled an antitrust suit by agreeing to cut prices on iTunes digital music in Britain to align them with those in continental Europe. The European Commission had accused Apple in spring 2007 of unfairly charging British consumers more than their counterparts in the euro zone for tracks from iTunes. British consumers had been paying about $1.55 per song, while other European consumers were paying about $1.46 per song. Under the settlement, all the European customers will be charged the same price.

Source: E. Pfanner (2008), "Apple to Cut the Prices of iTunes in Britain." *nytimes.com* (January 10).

both companies with employing illegal tying arrangements. These companies could have achieved the same result with less legal exposure. Rather than sell paper and punch cards at prices above cost, they could have offered these items at marginal cost and rented the machines with a two-part price—a fixed amount per month plus so much per copy or card read.

Implementing a Pricing Strategy

In this chapter we have provided a basic introduction to product pricing. We have discussed the objective of pricing decisions, presented a basic economic analysis of product pricing, and provided a rationale for many observed pricing policies. We also have identified key features in the business environment (such as the nature of the customer base and the type of information, i.e., held by managers) that can affect pricing decisions.

Given our intent, we have kept the analysis relatively simple. The actual implementation of a pricing strategy is complicated by a number of important factors: First, the pricing policies presented in this chapter are not mutually exclusive. Many companies can and do use a combination of pricing policies (consider Beyond.com). Second, our analysis has focused primarily on pricing a single product, but most firms sell a variety of products. In many cases, it is important to consider the interactions of demands and costs of multiple products in developing a pricing strategy. Third, optimal pricing policies can change across time. Fourth, firms have to give more detailed consideration to the legal and strategic issues in formulating pricing strategies. Thus, to manage product pricing effectively, it is important to supplement the basic material presented in this chapter with industry experience and additional training in the economics of pricing.[22]

ANALYZING MANAGERIAL DECISIONS: *iTunes Music Pricing*[23]

Consumers have been able to purchase digital music and audiobooks over the Internet through Apple Computer's iTunes Music Store (Music Store) since April 2003. The Music Store is integrated with Apple's iTunes Software, which allows users to manage their digital music libraries and to interface with their iPods, iPhones, iPads, and other products.

Apple's stock price increased from $1 per share in April 2003 to over $95 per share in July 2014 (adjusted for stock splits). This 95-fold price increase compares to Microsoft's stock, which increased from about $18 per share to $42 per share over the same period. Apple's strong performance was fueled in part by the growth in its digital music business. In August 2005, Apple's market shares for downloaded music and MP3 players in the United States were approximately 75 percent and 80 percent respectively. In 2013, Apple's estimated market share for downloaded music was 63 percent.

---

[22]The high salaries paid to successful pricing managers highlight the complexity of pricing decisions in some industries. For instance, senior pricing managers are among the highest-paid professionals in major airline companies.

[23]This case is based on a number of articles and SEC filings in the public domain. Among the most important of these sources are J. Leeds (2005), "Apple, Digital Music's Angel, Earns Record Industry's Scorn," *New York Times* (nytimes.com, August 27); and J. Leeds (2008), "Free Song Promotion Is Expected from Amazon," *nytimes.com* (January 14).

Amazon, which introduced its online music store in 2008, was second with a market share of 22 percent.

From the inception of the Music Store until 2009, Apple priced all downloaded music at $.99 per song. About $.70 per song was paid to the major record companies that had the rights to the songs. The record companies were initially happy with this arrangement since it provided a way to collect at least some revenue from downloaded music. Prior to the development of iTunes, many consumers downloaded music through services such as Napster, with no royalties paid to the music companies or artists.

By August 2005, Music Store sales had become "big business" and two of the four major record companies expressed dissatisfaction with the $.99 price. Sony BMG Music Entertainment and Warner Music favored a more complex pricing scheme that would price songs by popularity. A popular new single, for example, might sell for $1.49, while a "golden oldie" might sell for substantially less than $.99. Executives from these two music companies argued that their revenue stream could be enhanced by flexible pricing. They complained that Apple had an incentive to sell downloaded music at too low a price to promote the sale of iPods. To quote one music company executive, "Mr. Jobs has got two revenue streams: one from our music and one from the sale of his iPods. I've got one revenue stream that it would require a medical professional to locate. It's not pretty."

Not all of the major record companies shared the same view. For example, as of August 2005, the Universal Music Group (a unit of Vivendi Universal—the industry's biggest company) supported Apple's desire to maintain the price of $.99 a track.

The difference in opinion among the four record companies reflected varying views on whether the rapidly expanding digital market was stable enough to bear a mix of prices— particularly a higher top-end price. Millions of consumers were still trading music free on unauthorized file-swapping networks and an increase in price would increase the incentives to engage in this practice. One music executive noted, "I don't think it's time yet. We need to convert a lot more people to the habit of buying music online. I don't think a way to convert more people is to raise the price."

In 2014, Apple priced most downloaded music at $1.29 per song. Adjusted for inflation, the 2014 price is very close to the 2003 price of 99 cents per song. Apple, however, sold a limited number of songs at 69 cents and 99 cents in 2014.

Over the years, Apple has had substantial power in negotiating with the record companies. No music company has tried to force Apple to change its pricing policies by withholding its music. Analysts, however, forecasted that Apple's leverage over the music companies could fall in the future due to increased competition, for example, from Amazon.com and major wireless companies who were likely to begin offering downloaded music services to cell phone customers.

1. Provide an argument for why a more variable pricing policy might increase the sales revenue from Apple's Music Store (compared to the flat pricing policy).
2. Why do you think Apple moved from one to three price points in 2009? What types of songs do you think Apple tends to sell at the lower prices?
3. Discuss other potential pricing policies that might increase the revenue from Music Store sales.
4. What are the risks and potential costs of implementing more sophisticated pricing schemes for the downloaded music?
5. Is Apple's pricing objective to maximize the revenue it receives from the sales of downloaded music? Is this the objective of the major record companies? Explain. (*Hint:* review the revenue/product data from Apple's 10-K— available online at www.sec.gov/cgi-bin/srch-edgar.)
6. Do you think that Apple's ability to control the pricing of downloaded music is likely to change in the future? Explain.

Summary

A firm has *market power* when it faces a downward-sloping demand curve. Firms with market power can raise price without losing all customers to competitors. The ultimate objective is to choose a pricing policy that maximizes the value of the firm.

Consumer surplus is defined as the difference between what the consumer is willing to pay for a product and what the consumer actually pays when buying it. Managers, in maximizing profits, try to devise a pricing policy that captures as much of the gains from trade as possible. Thus, they try to capture potential consumer surplus as company profit.

In the benchmark case, the firm chooses a single per-unit price for all customers. Profits are maximized at the price and output level where *marginal revenue equals marginal cost*. Fixed and sunk costs are irrelevant; only *incremental costs* matter in the pricing decision. The optimal price markup over marginal cost depends on the elasticity of demand at the optimal price/quantity combination. The optimal markup decreases as demand becomes more elastic: It is optimal to charge high prices when customers are not very price-sensitive.

Economic theory suggests that managers should price so that marginal revenue equals marginal cost. One practical problem in applying this principle is that managers often do not have precise information about their demand curves and thus their marginal revenue. The *linear approximation technique* can be used when the demand curve is roughly linear and the manager has basic information about current price-quantity, price sensitivity, and marginal cost. *Markup pricing* is a technique that managers can use when they have limited information and reason to believe that price elasticity varies little across the demand curve. One of the most common pricing methods used by firms is *cost-plus pricing*. Managers using this technique calculate average total cost and mark up the price to yield a desired rate of return. Cost-plus pricing appears inconsistent with profit maximization since it includes fixed and sunk costs and does not consider consumer demand explicitly. Managers, however, can consider consumer demand implicitly by choosing appropriate target returns (lower target returns are chosen when demand is more elastic). The widespread use of this pricing policy suggests that it can be a useful rule of thumb in some settings.

The benchmark policy charges the same price to all customers independent of the quantity purchased. Sometimes a firm can do better with more complicated pricing policies. With *block pricing* a high price is charged for the first block and declining prices for subsequent blocks. Block pricing either can be used to extract additional profits from a set of customers with similar demands or can be used to price-discriminate. With a *two-part tariff,* the customer pays an up-front fee for the right to buy the product and then pays additional fees for each unit of the product consumed. Two-part tariffs tend to work best when customer demand is relatively homogeneous.

Price discrimination occurs whenever a firm charges differential prices across customers based on their willingness to pay for a given quantity of the good (not based on differences in production and distribution costs). With price discrimination, the markup or profit margin realized varies across customers. Two conditions are necessary for profitable price discrimination. First, different demand must exist in various submarkets for the product (customers must be heterogeneous). Second, the firm must be able to identify submarkets and restrict transfers among consumers across different submarkets.

Personalized pricing extracts the maximum amount each customer is willing to pay for the product. Each consumer is charged a price that makes him or her indifferent between purchasing and not purchasing the product. *Group pricing* results when a firm separates its customers into several groups and sets a different price for each group. A firm that can segment its market maximizes profits by setting marginal revenue equal to marginal cost in each market segment (higher prices are charged to the less price-sensitive groups). Both personalized and group pricing require relatively good information about individual customer demands.

Even if the manager does not have detailed information about individual demands, price discrimination still is possible with sufficient information about the distribution of individual demands. With *menu pricing* all potential customers are given the same menu of options. The classic example involves block pricing, where the price per unit depends on the quantity purchased. Customers use their private information to select the best option for them. By carefully constructing the menu of options, the firm makes more profits than if it simply offered the product at one price to all potential customers.

Coupons and rebates offer price discounts to customers. Price discrimination is one reason why firms use coupons and rebates to make price discounts rather than simply lowering the price. Price-sensitive customers are more likely to use coupons and rebates—and thus are charged lower effective prices—than customers who are less price-sensitive. Similar to menu pricing, customers self-select, depending on private information about their personal characteristics. Coupon and rebate programs are expensive to administer. These costs have to be compared to the benefits in deciding whether to adopt such a program.

Firms frequently *bundle* products for sale. One reason for bundling products is to extract additional profits from a customer base with heterogeneous product demands. Bundling can be more profitable than selling the products separately when the *relative values* that the customers place on the individual products vary.

This chapter focuses on a single-period pricing problem, in which managers face a fixed demand curve and cost structure. The prices of competing products are held constant. In some situations, concerns about future demand and costs, as well as the reactions of competitors, can motivate managers to choose pricing policies that would not be appropriate in the simple single-period analysis. Chapter 9 addresses issues of strategic interaction in greater detail.

Suggested Readings

T. Nagel 1994, *The Strategy and Tactics of Pricing: A Guide to Profitable Decision Making,* 2nd edition (Prentice Hall: Englewood Cliffs).

C. Shapiro and H. Varian (1999), *Information Rules: A Strategic Guide to the Network Economy* (Harvard Business School Press: Boston).

Self-Evaluation Problems

7–1. ABC Software Solutions allows customers to access its software application remotely. Let P be the price charged to the customer each time the customer accesses the software. Customers are homogenous in their demands. The demand curve *for each customer* is $P = 20 - 0.1Q$, and ABC's total cost *for each customer* is $TC = 10 + 2Q$.

    a. If ABC charges a single price per access (and no up-front fee), what are the optimal P and Q per customer? Compute the profits per customer for ABC for this scenario.

    b. Suppose ABC charges a menu of two prices where each customer is charged one price per access for up to 90 uses and a lower price per access for additional uses. For simplicity, assume that ABC continues to charge the price determined in part a for the first 90 units. What is the optimal price to charge for additional units? Compute the profits per customer for this scenario.

    c. If ABC decides to levy a two-part tariff, what are the optimal up-front fee, P, and Q per customer? What is the profit per customer for this scenario?

7–2. Consider a firm with $MC = AC = 1$ trading with two buyers, whose demand functions are $Q_1 = 5 - 2P_1$ and $Q_2 = 7 - 3P_2$. The firm can distinguish the buyers and is able to price discriminate. Suppose the firm charges each buyer a single price per unit for the product. What is the optimal price-discrimination strategy? Calculate the firm's profits.

7–3. The Key Club is a bar that has two types of potential customers: Legal and underage drinkers. It is illegal to allow entry to underage drinkers, but there is no way to perfectly identify underage drinkers (fake IDs, etc.). Assume that Key Club's marginal cost is $3 per drink. The drink demand for a representative customer in each of the two groups is given by

$$P_L = 5 - Q_L \qquad \text{(legal drinkers)}$$
$$P_U = 3.5 - Q_U \qquad \text{(underage drinkers)}$$

Design a pricing policy that will extract *all* of the profit from the legal drinkers without appealing to underage drinkers at all.

7–4. Company XYZ supplies two products, DVD discs and DVD storage cases, to two different segments of customers (1 and 2). The following table summarizes the value that the typical customer in each segment assigns to the products offered by XYZ:

Customer Type	Discs	Cases
1	$6	$8
2	$7	$5

Assume that there are 10 customers of each type, that XYZ has no fixed costs, and that the marginal costs of producing discs and cases are both constant at zero.

a. What is the pricing strategy for XYZ if it prices the products individually? What is the corresponding profit?

b. If XYZ decides to offer discs and cases in a bundle, what price should it charge for the bundle? Is bundling a better strategy in this case? Why? Explain.

Solutions to Self-Evaluation Problems

7–1. Homogenous Consumer Demands

a. Profit maximization occurs when MR = MC: $20 - .2Q = 2$. Thus, $Q^* = 90$ and $P^* = \$11$. Profits/customer (TR − TC) = $800.

b. The problem assumes that ABC will continue to charge $11 for the first 90 uses. This leaves a residual demand curve of $P = 11 - .1Q$ (at a price of $11, no additional units are purchased; additional units are purchased as the firm lowers it price below $11 for the additional uses). Setting MR = MC for this curve: $11 - .2Q = 2$ yields and optimal price and quantity of $Q^{**} = 45$ and $P^{**} = \$6.50$. Each customer ends up purchasing 135 units, (the first 90 at the $11 price and 45 additional units at the $6.50 price). Total profits/customer for the two-price scheme: $(90 \times \$11) + (45 \times 6.50) - (10 + 270) = \$1,002.50$. Graphically the solution looks as follows:

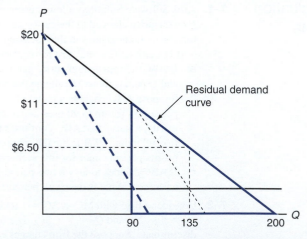

(*Note*: ABC could do slightly better if it solved for the two prices simultaneously. The problem held the first price constant to simplify the analysis.)

c. Under the profit-maximizing two-part tariff, ABC would charge MC = $2 for each access to its software. Each customer would access the software 180 times at this price (from the demand curve). Charging marginal cost maximizes the gains from trade (a customer accesses the software whenever he values it more than the cost to the company). ABC should charge an up-front fee that extracts all of these gains from trade as profit. Graphically the up-front fee is represented by the area of Triangle A in the following diagram. The area of a triangle is .5(base × height). Therefore the optimal up-front fee is .5(18 × 180) = $1,620. Total revenue from both the price/unit and the fee is $1,980. Total costs are [$10 + (2 × 180)] = $370. Thus the profit/customer from this scheme is $1,610. ABC obtains the maximum possible profits using the two-part tariff. It does worse with the quantity discount scheme and even worse with the single price scheme.

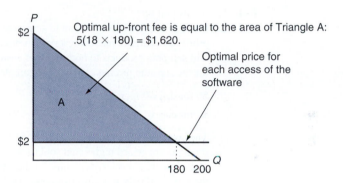

7–2. Group Pricing

Begin by solving the demand functions to obtain the two demand curves:

$$P_1 = 2.5 - .5Q_1$$
$$P_2 = (7/3) - 1/3\, Q_2$$

Set marginal revenue equal to marginal cost in both segments (the profit-maximizing conditions):

$$2.5 - Q_1 = 1$$
$$7/3 - 2/3\, Q_2 = 1$$

Next, solve for the equations to obtain the optimal quantities. Use these quantities and the demand curves to find the optimal prices: $Q_1^* = 1.5$ and $P_1^* = \$1.75$, and $Q_2^* = 2$ and $P_2^* = \$1.67$. Profits are equal to the sum of total revenue—total costs for the two segments: ($1.125 + $1.34) = $2.46.

7–3. Using Information about Distribution of Demands

A two-part tariff can be used to extract all the profit from the legal drinkers. Charge them $3.00 per drink (MC) and have a cover charge equal to their consumer surplus $(1/2 \times (.5 - .3) \times 2) = \$2.00$. The underage drinkers will not pay the cover charge to enter since their consumer surplus given a price of $3.00 per drink is less than the cover charge of $2.00. Their consumer surplus (before the cover charge) is $(1/2 \times (\$3.50 - 3.00) \times .5) = \$.125$. This pricing scheme motivates potential customers, who know their own types, to make choices that are consistent with the Club's objective of maximizing profits from legal drinkers without serving underage drinkers.

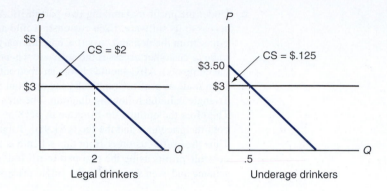

7–4. Product Bundling

a. Because marginal cost is equal to zero, maximizing revenue is the same as maximizing profit. By charging the low reservation price for each product (discs and cases), XYZ will sell both products to both types of customers. This is the profit-maximizing strategy for the separate pricing case in this example. Therefore, XYZ should charge:

$6 for discs

$5 for cases

The corresponding profit is $6 \times 20 + 5 \times 20 = \$220$. Profit is lower if either or both products are priced higher and sold to only one customer type. (*Note*: If the number of customers of each type changed, other strategies might be optimal. For example, if there were 100 Type 1 customers and one Type 2 customer, XYZ would be better off to price cases at $8 and sell them only to the Type 1 customers. The optimal solution could also be different with different assumptions about the marginal costs of producing the two products.)

b. A Type 1 customer has a reservation price of $14 (8 + 6) for the bundle, whereas a Type 2 customer has a reservation price of $12 (7 + 5). Given that there are an equal number of customers of each type, profits are maximized by charging $12 for the bundle. This is the highest price that ensures XYZ can sell the bundle to both types of customers. The corresponding profit is $12 \times 20 = \$240$.

Bundling results in higher profits than the individual product pricing strategy because the reservation prices for the two customer types are negatively correlated. Type 1 customers value cases more than Type 2 customers (8/5 > 1), whereas Type 2 customers value discs more than Type 1 customers (7/6 > 1). This negative correlation implies that the minimum reservation price for the bundle (= $12 for the Type 2 customers) is greater than the sum of the minimum reservation prices for the individual products ($11 = $5 + $6). Thus more revenue per customer is collected by selling the products in a bundle for $12, rather than pricing them separately at $5 and $6.

Review Questions

7–1. Macrosoft is a new producer of word processing software. Recently, it announced that it is giving away its product to the first 100,000 customers. Using the concepts from this chapter, explain why this might be an optimal policy.

7–2. The local space museum has hired you to assist them in setting admission prices. The museum's managers recognize that there are two distinct demand curves for admission. One demand curve applies to people ages 12 to 64, whereas the other is for children and senior citizens. The two demand curves are

$$P_A = 9.6 - 0.08Q_A$$
$$P_{CS} = 4 - 0.05Q_{CS}$$

where P_A is the adult price, P_{CS} is the child/senior citizen price, Q_A is the adult quantity, and Q_{CS} is the child/senior citizen quantity. Crowding is not a problem at the museum, and so managers consider marginal cost to be zero.

    a. What price should they charge to each group to maximize profits?

    b. How many adults will visit the museum? How many children and senior citizens?

    c. What are the museum's profits?

7–3. Textbook publishers have traditionally produced both United States and international editions of most leading textbooks. The United States version typically sells at a higher price than the international edition. (*a*) Discuss why publishers use this pricing plan. (*b*) Discuss how the Internet might affect the ability of companies to implement this type of policy.

7–4. Suppose in Table 7.2 (Product Bundling) that the professional user values *Microsoft Trip Planner* at $30 rather than $20. Keep all other valuations the same. Are there still obvious advantages from bundling the two products? Explain.

7–5. Explain why perfect personalized pricing is typically more profitable than menu pricing. Why then do companies use menu pricing?

7–6. In the example in this chapter, the linear approximation method produced the profit-maximizing price, whereas the markup pricing rule did not. Does this imply that the linear rule is always better than the markup rule? Explain.

7–7. Why do companies grant discounts to senior citizens and students?

7–8. You own a theater with 200 seats. The demand for seats is $Q = 300 - 100P$. You are charging $1.25 per ticket and selling tickets to 175 people. Your costs are fixed and do not depend on the number of people attending. Should you cut your price to fill the theater? Explain. What other pricing policies might you use to increase your profits?

7–9. The Snow City Ski Resort caters to both out-of-town skiers and local skiers. The demand for ski tickets for each market segment is independent of the other market segments. The marginal cost of servicing a skier of either type is $10. Suppose the demand curves for the two market segments are

$$\text{Out of town:} \quad Q_0 = 600 - 10P$$
$$\text{Local:} \qquad\quad Q_1 = 600 - 20P$$

    a. If the resort charges one price to all skiers, what is the profit-maximizing price? Calculate how many lift tickets will be sold to each group. What is the total profit?

    b. Which market segment has the highest price elasticity at this outcome?

    c. If the company sells tickets at different prices to the two market segments, what is the optimal price and quantity for each segment? What are the total profits for the resort?

    d. What techniques might the resort use to implement such a pricing policy? What must the resort guard against, if the pricing policy is to work effectively?

7–10. All consumers have identical demand for a product. Each person's demand curve is $P = 30 - 2Q$. The marginal cost of production is $2. Devise a two-part tariff that will exhaust all consumer surplus.

7–11. Xerox sells both copiers and a toner for their copiers. While customers are not required to buy Xerox toner, most do because specified machines use toner only for that machine. The Xerox toner and machines are closely designed and non-Xerox toner in Xerox machines produces inferior copies. Evaluate the statement: "Xerox makes 75 percent of its profits selling toner and 25 percent of its profits selling machines."

7–12. Some tennis clubs charge an up-front fee to join and a per-hour charge for court time. Others do not charge a membership fee but charge a higher per-hour fee for court time. Consider clubs in two different locations. One is located in a suburban area where the residents tend to be of similar age, income, and occupation. The other is in the city with a more diverse population. Which of the locations is more likely to charge a membership fee? Explain.

7–13. Consider three firms: a shoe store at the mall, an automobile dealership, and a house painting firm.

    a. Which firm would you expect to engage in the most price discrimination? Why?

    b. How has the Internet changed the pricing policies of these businesses?

7–14. Cellwave is a cellular phone company. Answer the following questions relating to its pricing policies:

    a. When Cellwave started, it sold to a group of homogeneous retail customers. Each person's monthly demand for cell phone minutes was given by $P = \$2 - 0.02Q$, where P = the price per minute and Q = the quantity of minutes purchased each month. Cellwave's marginal cost is 10 cents per minute. Suppose that Cellwave charges a single per minute price to all customers (independent of the number of minutes they use each month). What is the profit-maximizing price. Depict this choice on a graph. On a per customer basis, what are the company's profit, consumer surplus, and the deadweight loss?

    b. Suppose that Cellwave chooses to charge a two-part tariff (with a monthly fixed charge and a per minute rate) rather than a single per minute price. What two-part tariff extracts the entire consumer surplus? What are the company's profits (on a per customer basis)? How many minutes does each customer use per month? What is the deadweight loss?

    c. After several years of operation, Cellwave developed a new group of business customers (in addition to its old customer base). The business customers had homogeneous demands. Each of these customers' monthly demand for cell phone minutes was given by $P = \$2 - 0.004Q$. Graph the two demand curves for the two customer groups on the same figure along with the marginal cost. Suppose that Cellwave wants to menu price by offering two plans with different monthly fixed charges. Each plan would allow free calls up to some maximum limit of minutes per month. No calls are allowed beyond these maximums. Assume that Cellwave designs a plan that extracts all consumer surplus from the retail customers. Shade the area of the graph that shows how much consumer surplus must be given to each business customer to make the plan work. Explain why.

7–15. The Hewl-Pact Company produces a popular printer than prints over 100 pages per minute. It recently announced that it was introducing a lower priced model of the printer that can print 30 pages per minute. While not revealed to the public, it turns out that it costs the company more to produce the lower priced product. The two models are identical except for a $20 internal part for the low-priced model that slows the printer from 100 to 30 pages per minute. Provide an economic explanation for why the company decided to produce a new lower priced, but more costly, model of the printer.

Economics of Strategy: Creating and Capturing Value

LEARNING OBJECTIVES

1. Explain the general ways by which managers within an industry might increase value.
2. Discuss how competitive forces make it difficult for individual firms to capture value over the long term.
3. Explain why producer surplus is often captured as "rents" by superior assets.
4. List the conditions that must exist for a firm to make economic profits over the long run.
5. Summarize the economic costs and benefits of diversification (multiple businesses within the same firm).
6. Describe a general framework that can be used for strategic planning.
7. Show why it is impossible for some firms to capture value and why it is unlikely that any firm can capture value in perpetuity.

Over the past five decades, Walmart Stores rose from "humble beginnings" as a small discount retailer in Arkansas to become the world's largest retailer with more than $476 billion dollars in sales in 2014.[1] Its discount-variety stores, Sam's Clubs, supercenters (combined discount retail and bulk grocery stores) and smaller "neighborhood" and express stores are located throughout the United States, as well as in many other countries such as Mexico, Canada, Puerto Rico, Germany, Brazil, Argentina, China, Korea, and Indonesia. In 2014, Walmart operated over 11,000 retail units under 71 banners in 27 countries with e-commerce websites in 10 countries. It employed 2.2 million people around the world (1.3 million in the United States).

Since Sam Walton opened his first store in 1962, the overall financial performance of the company has been nothing less than phenomenal. To illustrate, suppose you had purchased $1,000 of the stock at the initial offering in 1970 and held it through 2008. This investment would have been worth more than $5 million (i.e., a 20 percent compound annual growth rate); in addition, you would have received cash dividends paid by the company over the period. This performance made Walmart one of the hottest stocks in the market.

---

[1]Details for this example are from Fortune 500 (2014), http://fortune.com/fortune500; Walmart—Our Story (2014), http://corporate.walmart.com/our-story; S. Foley (1994), "Wal-Mart Stores, Inc.," Harvard Business School Case 9-794-024; the financial press; company reports; and C. Loomis (2000), "Sam Would Be Proud," *Fortune* (April 17), 131–144.

While Walmart's performance has been spectacular, it has not been flawless. Following a large price drop in the second quarter of 1993 (over 20 percent during a period when the overall market was essentially flat), Walmart's stock price continued to decline modestly until 1997, even though the overall stock market was rising. In addition, sales growth at Walmart, which for a long period had outpaced the retail industry, fell to unremarkable levels.

In an attempt to increase performance during the 1990s, Walmart took a variety of actions; it opened new stores internationally, opened new supercenters, and logged on to the world of electronic commerce. In 1998, Walmart entered the traditional grocery store business in Arkansas where it opened three "experimental" 40,000-square-foot grocery stores (about the same size as traditional supermarkets). During the period from 1997 to 2005, Walmart stock again performed well relative to the general stock market and retail industry. Between 2006 and 2014, Walmart continued to perform somewhat better than the general stock market, but did substantially worse than Costco Wholesale Corporation. It, however, performed much better over this period than its rival, the Target Corporation. In July 2014, Walmart's new CEO announced a strategic shift from focusing on large supercenters to smaller stores and online sales.

All managers would like to outperform the general market as well as their specific industry over a sustained period. Examples like that of Walmart suggest that such performance is possible but raise at least five important questions:

- What accounts for the success of these firms?
- Should all properly managed firms expect sustained superior performance?
- What actions can managers take to generate superior performance?
- Can managers enhance financial returns through diversification (as Walmart was attempting to do by opening grocery stores)?
- Do all high-performing firms ultimately "fall back with the rest of the pack" as Walmart did in the mid-1990s?

This chapter applies the basic economic concepts developed in this book to address these and related questions.

Strategy

Strategy refers to the general policies that managers adopt to generate profits. For example, in what industries does the firm operate? What products and services does it offer and to which customers? In what basic ways does it compete or cooperate with other firms within its business environment? Rather than focusing on operational detail, a firm's strategy addresses broad, long-term issues facing the firm.[2] Typically, strategies do not remain constant but evolve through time. For example, Walmart's strategy in 2014 focuses on discount retailing and the related grocery industry, as well as online sales. It owns and operates five basic types of stores in the United States: discount-variety stores, Sam's Clubs, supercenters, neighborhood markets, and express stores. It offers a wide product assortment, "every-day low prices" (supported by a low-cost structure), limited advertising, and friendly, well-informed

---

[2]In the strategy literature, these questions are frequently divided: Corporate strategy refers to the choice of industries, whereas business strategy refers to the choice of how to compete within the chosen industries (e.g., whether to focus on cost or quality, or on some combination of the two).

"sales associates." Originally, its strategy focused on placing stores in the rural Southeast. Walmart now operates stores throughout the world. Ultimately, along with the *organizational architecture* of the firm, strategy is a key determinant of the success or failure of the enterprise.

The ultimate objective of strategic decision making is to realize sustained profits.[3] To achieve this objective, managers must devise ways both to *create and to capture value.* Earlier chapters focused on how value might be created and captured through input, output, and pricing policies. Those chapters also analyzed how competition constrains the ability of managers to capture value. But they (like most discussions in the traditional managerial economics literature) focused on a single product, taking the industry and product characteristics as given.

This chapter takes a broader look at how managers create and capture value. The next section presents an analysis of value creation within a given industry. Subsequent sections examine capturing value and the choice of industries. The final section offers a general framework for implementing the concepts in this chapter.

Firms often compete against a few identifiable rivals. For example, Boeing competes largely with Airbus in the production of commercial jet airplanes. It is particularly important for managers in such firms to consider likely responses of rivals when making strategic decisions about pricing, new investment, advertising, and so on. For example, it would be foolish if Boeing failed to consider likely responses by Airbus in setting the prices of its wide-body jets. In this chapter, we concentrate on the broader issues of how firms create and capture value; thus we abstract from how reactions by rivals might be incorporated explicitly in the analysis. In the next chapter we use game theory to provide an explicit analysis of reactions by rivals in the strategic decision-making process.

Value Creation

Figure 8.1 displays supply and demand curves for an industry. It differs from our previous supply and demand figures in one important respect: It explicitly displays both consumer-borne and producer-borne transaction costs. Consumer transaction costs include such things as the costs of searching for the product, learning product characteristics and quality, negotiating terms of sale with a supplier, and enforcing agreements. If these costs were lower, demanders would be willing to pay more for the product. For example, automatic teller machines increase the demand for banking services by reducing the amount of time customers spend in line and by providing basic banking services around the clock. The dotted demand curve indicates potential demand—what demand would be if consumer-borne transaction costs could be eliminated. The solid demand curve displays the effective demand given a per-unit consumer transaction cost of *a*. Similarly, producers bear costs in transacting with consumers and suppliers (e.g., negotiating terms with customers and paying attorneys to draft a supply agreement). The dotted supply curve indicates potential supply—the willingness of producers to supply the product if producer transaction costs were

---

[3]If stock market participants anticipate that a company is going to earn sustained abnormal profits, its stock price will be bid up so that in equilibrium investors will expect to earn only a normal rate of return by buying the stock. The fact that Walmart has generated both high profits and high stock returns over a long time period suggests that the company has repeatedly surprised the stock market with its earnings performance. In this book, we concentrate on the underlying profits of the company, not the stock market valuation of these profits. Stock market valuation is covered in finance classes and textbooks.

Figure 8.1   Ways to Create Value

This figure displays the supply and demand curves for an industry. It differs from previous diagrams by including producer and consumer transaction costs. [Per-unit consumer-borne (producer-borne) transaction cost is $a(b)$.] Consumers would demand more and producers would supply more if these costs were lower. Value consists of the sum of consumer and producer surplus. Managers can increase value by reducing transaction or production costs or by increasing the demand for the product—for example, by increasing the perceived quality of the product.

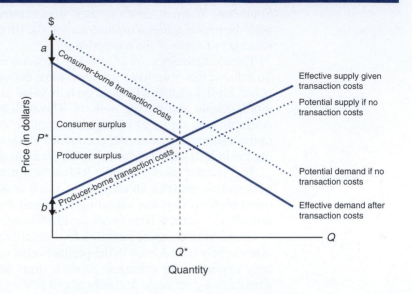

eliminated. The solid line shows the effective supply curve given a per-unit transaction cost of b.[4]

The area under the dotted demand curve (demand before transaction costs) and above the dotted supply curve (supply before transaction costs) up to Q^* is divided into four areas. First, there are the two parallelograms representing consumer and producer transaction costs. Next, there are the two triangles representing consumer and producer surpluses. *Total value* created by the industry is the sum of producer surplus and consumer surplus.

An important first step in making profits is discovering ways to create value. The second step, discussed below, devises ways to capture this value. Figure 8.1 suggests at least four general ways that managers within the industry might increase value.

- They can take actions to lower production costs or producer transaction costs, thus shifting the effective supply curve to the right.

- Managers can implement policies to reduce consumer transaction costs, thus shifting the effective demand curve to the right.

- They can take actions other than reducing consumer transaction costs to increase demand, shifting both the potential and effective demand curves to the right.

- Managers can devise new products or services—in essence creating a new figure.

We discuss each of these strategies in turn.[5]

[4]For expositional convenience, we assume that supply costs are separable into production and transaction costs. Admittedly, there are cases where they are joint or where the allocation is arbitrary.

[5]We depict demand and supply at the industry level because it facilitates our subsequent discussion on capturing value (which involves competition within the industry). The same four value-creating factors are important if we frame the problem using a firm's demand and costs.

MANAGERIAL APPLICATIONS

Creating Value: Reducing Consumer Waiting Time

Many firms undervalue their customer's waiting time. In 2000 the Oregon Public Utilities Commission ordered Qwest Communications to pay consumers $270 million to compensate them for installation delays. Cable companies require a four-hour window for appointments. Some doctors keep four busy patients waiting for every one that the doctor is seeing. If U.S. citizens value their time at $20 per hour, taxpayers spend $26 billion a year filing tax returns. Some companies recognize the value of their customers' time and build successful corporate strategies around reducing waiting time. Suppose a customer's after tax earnings are $100,000 and she works 2,000 hours; then her time is worth $50 per hour. If she decides to buy the latest $20 John Grisham novel at a bookstore, she might spend an hour driving to and from the store, parking, locating the book, and purchasing it. The total cost to purchase the book is $70. Compare that to spending six minutes buying the book online for $20 plus $4.50 shipping. The total cost of the online purchase is $29.50 (including the $5 for her time) for a saving of $40.50. In fact, most e-tailers' business strategy is to economize on customer time. The following companies have strategies aimed at conserving customer time. Wendy's serves up Big Bacon Classic within two-and-a-half minutes. Enterprise offers at-home pickup and return of rental cars. Virgin Atlantic Airlines picks up and checks in upper-class passengers from their chauffeured cars. J.C. Penney offers three-day delivery or in-store pickup of online orders.

Source: K. Barron (2000), "Hurry Up and Wait," *Forbes* (October 16), 158–164.

Production and Producer Transaction Costs

Chapter 5 discussed how managers should choose inputs to minimize production costs. Over time, managers can discover new technological opportunities to reduce these costs and increase value. They also can devise ways to lower the costs of transacting with customers and suppliers. For example, when personal computers first were developed, they were relatively expensive to produce. Over time, companies learned to reduce these production costs. As a result, the quantity of personal computers sold in the market has increased substantially—as has the total value (consumer plus producer surplus) created within this industry. Computer manufacturers also have devised ways to reduce their costs of transacting with suppliers and customers. For instance, large computer manufacturers have developed electronic connections with major software producers to lower the cost of ordering software programs. They also have developed computer links that reduce their costs of transacting with customers.

Walmart has shifted its effective supply curve to the right by developing new low-cost methods for producing and distributing retail services and products. For example, its extremely efficient hub-and-spoke distribution system has lowered the costs of stocking its stores. Walmart has reduced transaction costs through direct computer links with major suppliers, such as Procter and Gamble. These links have cut the costs of restocking products and essentially have eliminated writing paper checks to these vendors—they are paid through an electronic payment system.

Consumer Transaction Costs

Reducing consumer transaction costs also can increase value. For example, early Walmarts were established in small rural towns. One way that these stores added value was through reducing travel time for local residents, who previously had to

MANAGERIAL APPLICATIONS

The U.S. Government's Global Entry Program Reduces Consumer Transaction Costs

Since the terrorist attack on the World Trade Center in 2001, international fliers have been subjected to increased security checks when entering the United States. The associated increase in waiting times imposes transaction costs on international fliers and potentially decreases the demand for international travel.

The U.S. government's Global Entry program is designed to reduce the time it takes for "low-risk" fliers to enter the country. U.S. citizens (and certain others) can apply for a Global Entry pass online. After receiving preliminary approval, the applicant must complete an in-person interview with a U.S. customs agent at selected locations, during which the person is also photographed and fingerprinted.

Pass holders entering the United States from international flights head directly to a passport kiosk (at major airports) where they answer a few questions on a computer monitor. This process avoids having to wait in line for standard passport control agents. There are also special lines for pass holders to reduce the time they spend clearing customs.

A study released in July 2014, found that the use of Global Entry kiosks reduced average wait times by 33 percent at New York's JFK airport and more than 15 percent at New Jersey's Newark Liberty airport.

U.S. Customs and Border Protection spokeswoman Jennifer Evanitsky says the agency recognizes the importance of international travel to the nation's economy. The kiosks allow the agency's officers "to facilitate legitimate international travelers as quickly as possible while maintaining the highest standards of security," she says. This example, illustrates how technology often reduces consumer transaction costs.

Source: G. Stoller (2014), "Passport Kiosks Reduce Fliers Customers Wait Time," *USA Today* (July 16).

drive to urban centers to do a larger part of their shopping. Walmart also reduces consumer-borne transactions costs by the layout of their stores. For example, Walmart captures "market-basket data" from customer receipts at all its stores. By analyzing this data, Walmart can tell which products are likely to be purchased together. Walmart uses this knowledge to reduce customers' costs in navigating their stores by placing commonly purchased bundles of products together. Examples of such pairings include bananas with cereal, snack cakes with coffee, bug spray with hunting gear, tissues with cold medicine, measuring spoons with baking supplies, and flashlights with Halloween costumes.[6]

The entire industry that involves marketing over the Internet is another example of reducing consumers' transaction costs. For instance, when prospective customers use search engines to explore the Internet, they often are presented with a list of related books, which can be ordered electronically at a discount through companies such as Amazon.com. This service reduces consumer transaction/search costs by identifying books of potential interest and making it easier to place an order.

Other Ways to Increase Demand

The demand curve holds variables other than the price of the product constant. We already have discussed how managers can increase demand by reducing consumer transaction costs. They also can increase the effective demand for their products—and thus total value created through transactions—by affecting variables such as expected product quality, prices of complements, or prices of substitutes.

[6]E. Nelson (1998), "Why Wal-Mart Sings, 'Yes, We Have Bananas!'" *The Wall Street Journal* (October 6), B1.

Giving Away Razors to Increase Demand for Blades

King Gillette gave away free razors after he invented his famous double-edge disposable blade in 1885—United Cigar Store gave razors to customers who bought boxes of Cuban cigars—banks bought razors for pennies and gave them away as part of shave-and-save campaigns. These promotions were designed to get razors in the hands of consumers who would then buy a stream of future blades for the razors. In 2005 Gillette was acquired by P&G for $57 billion.

Source: (1999), "No Charge," *Attaché* (September), 14–16; and A. Coolidge (2005), "Gillette: P&G Not Our First Choice," *The Cincinnati Post* (March 16).

Product Quality

Actions that enhance perceived quality increase demand; total value also is raised unless these actions entail larger increases in production costs. For instance, the innovation of titanium golf clubs increased the demand for golf equipment, while the invention of parabolic skis increased the demand for skis and skiing. Another important dimension of product quality is delivery time. Most consumers prefer to receive products sooner rather than later. Amazon, in particular, recognizes this and strives to deliver its products to consumers faster than its competitors (even exploring the use of drones). The resulting increases in demand have been greater than the associated increases in production costs—thus, total value created within these industries has increased.

Price of Complements

Managers sometimes can act to reduce the price of complements, thus increasing the demand for their products. To illustrate, consider CompuInc, which produces personal computers, and PrintCo, which produces a complementary printer.[7] For simplicity, suppose that customers purchase either both products or neither product (they are quite strong complements), the price of CompuInc's personal computers is P_c, the price of PrintCo's printers is P_p, and the demand for each product is

$$Q = 12 - (P_c + P_p) \quad \text{when } P_c + P_p \text{ is 12 or less, 0, otherwise} \qquad (8.1)$$

Q (measured in thousands) is the number of computer–printer combinations sold, and the marginal cost of producing both products is 0.

If the two companies do not cooperate in setting prices, each will seek to maximize its individual profits, given its expectation of the other firm's price. In this case, CompuInc will view its demand curve as

$$P_c = (12 - \overline{P}_p) - Q \qquad (8.2)$$

while the PrintCo demand curve is

$$P_p = (12 - \overline{P}_c) - Q \qquad (8.3)$$

where $\overline{P}_p$ and $\overline{P}_c$ represent the expectations about the other firm's price.[8] Each firm's profit is maximized by setting MR = MC (0 in this example):

$$\text{CompuInc} \quad (12 - \overline{P}_p) - 2Q = 0 \qquad (8.4)$$

$$\text{PrintCo} \quad (12 - \overline{P}_c) - 2Q = 0 \qquad (8.5)$$

[7]See A. Brandenburger (1996), "Cheap Complements?" (mimeographed text, Harvard Business School).

[8]There is no reason to place a subscript on Q. By assumption it is the same for both firms.

Figure 8.2 Noncooperative Pricing for CompuInc and PrintCo

If the two companies price noncooperatively, each will try to maximize its individual profits given its expectation of the other firm's price. The equilibrium consists of prices P_p^* and P_c^*, which simultaneously solves these maximization problems. This figure displays the solution graphically. The figure displays the reaction curves for each firm. A given firm's reaction curve indicates its optimal price given the pricing decision of the other firm. In equilibrium (where the reaction curves cross), both firms choose a price of $4. A total of 4,000 units of each product is sold. The profits for each firm are $16,000. Combined profits are $32,000. (*Note:* If they cooperate and set each price at $3, combined profits will be $36,000.)

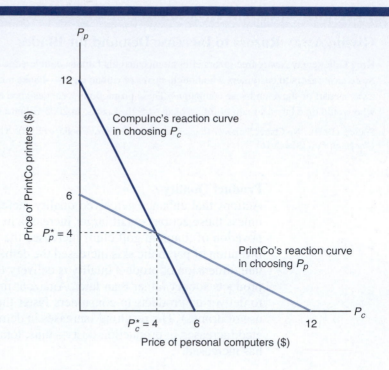

Substituting for Q from Equation (8.1) and rearranging the terms yield the following two reaction curves:

$$P_c = 6 - 0.5\overline{P}_p \tag{8.6}$$

$$P_p = 6 - 0.5\overline{P}_c \tag{8.7}$$

The equilibrium consists of prices P_p^* and P_c^* that simultaneously solve these two equations.[9] Figure 8.2 displays the solution graphically. In equilibrium, both firms choose a price of $4; thus, a total of 4 units of each product is sold. The profit for each firm is $16,000; combined profits are $32,000.

Now consider what happens if the firms were to coordinate the prices, for example, through a joint venture. To maximize the combined profits, the companies jointly set marginal revenue equal to marginal cost:[10]

$$12 - 2Q = 0 \tag{8.8}$$

They sell 6,000 units at a combined price of $6 (e.g., $P_c = P_p = \$3$). In this case, they make a combined profit of $36,000. This combined profit by pricing the products jointly is higher than the profit they would receive if they do not cooperate in setting prices. When the firms price independently, they do not consider the negative effect

---

[9]Recall from Chapter 6 that a Nash equilibrium is where each firm is doing the best it can, given the actions of its rivals.

[10]Note that the combined demand curve is $(P_c + P_p) = 12 - Q$; $MR = 12 - 2Q$.

MANAGERIAL APPLICATIONS

Technology and Value

During the later part of the 20th century there has been a massive change in information, communication, and production technologies. This technological change has provided important opportunities for increasing value. For example, the "business process reengineering" movement in the 1990s used computer and information technology to lower costs (for instance, by streamlining systems used to process orders, shipments, payables, and receivables). Flexible production technologies have allowed firms to custom-design certain products to fit specific customer demands better. Computer and information technologies have been used to reduce the costs of transacting with suppliers. Using technology to increase value is likely to remain a significant focus well into the 21st century.

---

that their higher prices have on the other's profit. Pricing cooperatively, they take this interaction into account. Note that in this case, consumers also would be better off because the prices of both products are lower and as a result, more product is purchased.

Prices of Substitutes

Low-priced substitutes reduce the demand for a product. Sometimes managers can affect the price of substitutes. For example, movie theaters frequently prohibit patrons from bringing food into the theater. These restrictions on lower-priced substitutes increase the demand for snacks offered by the theater.

New Products and Services

To this point, our discussion has focused on creating value by increasing demand or reducing the costs of producing existing products. Inventing new products and services also creates value. For example, consider the consumer electronics industry. Many of today's products that create significant value are relatively new developments: for instance, MP3 technology, digital cameras, and digital video displays (DVDs).[11]

Cooperating to Increase Value

Our example of computers and printers shows that firms sometimes can increase value through cooperating with each other, rather than competing. In this case, the companies were producers of complementary products. Opportunities to increase value through cooperation also can arise with customers, suppliers, and even competitors. For instance, cooperating with suppliers and customers in developing computer and information links can reduce supply costs and lead to the production of more valuable products—ones more tailor-made for the customer (recall the example of Dell Computers). One way competitors cooperate is in development projects to reduce joint costs. For example, major automobile manufacturers have participated jointly in the research and development of batteries for electric cars. Longer-lived batteries are essential for these companies to market electric cars on a wide-scale basis. If each company acts independently, development costs are expected to be higher. As another example, offshore drilling is quite expensive. Prior to soliciting

---

[11]Obviously, the classification of whether a product development constitutes a product improvement or a new product is somewhat arbitrary. For example, are Blu-ray players separate products or improvements over previously existing DVD players? This classification problem is not central to our focus. The basic point is that value often is created through the development/enhancement of products.

MANAGERIAL APPLICATIONS

Research and Development Joint Ventures

Firms can sometimes increase their values by cooperating with competing firms. One example is research and development (R&D) joint ventures. R&D costs are particularly high in the pharmaceutical industry. Pfizer CEO, Ian Read, predicted in 2013 that the number of joint ventures among rivals formed for developing drugs and expanding into different geographical markets would increase. Read believes the associated benefits from sharing costs, risks, and commercial benefits are large. In 2013, Pfizer participated in a joint venture with Johnson and Johnson to develop drugs for Alzheimer's patients and was contemplating additional ventures. Read cited vaccines, oncology, and neurodegenerative diseases as potential candidates for future partnerships with competitors, given the growing pressures to cut costs in drug development as healthcare systems demand increased savings.

Antitrust laws in many countries restrict competitors from collaborating to set prices. However, joint ventures to share development costs are frequently allowed under existing laws.

Source: A. Jack (2013), "Pfizer Chief Looks to Joint Ventures to Bolster Drug Development," *Financial Times* (June 6).

bids for offshore sites, the U.S. government allows the oil firms to conduct a survey of the area jointly; they share the data and divide the costs.

American antitrust laws generally make it illegal for rival firms to cooperate for the purpose of monopoly pricing. Nonetheless, many forms of cooperation are legal and increase the welfare of both producers and consumers (again consider our PC-printer example).

Converting Organizational Knowledge into Value

To create value, employees must convert their existing knowledge about production processes, transaction costs, customer demand, and so on, into ideas that can be implemented by the firm. In Chapter 3, we discussed the knowledge conversion process. In this section, we consider the strategic implications of this analysis. Recall that the resources within a firm can be divided into three general categories. First are its tangible assets, which include property, plant, and equipment. Second are its intangible assets, such as patents, trademarks, and brand-name recognition. These assets typically are not shown on the firm's balance sheet but can be significant in creating and capturing value—the firm's methods of doing business, its formulas and recipes, are a particularly important type of intangible asset. Third and perhaps most important are its human resources.

Firms in Silicon Valley frequently refer to these three types of resources as *hardware, software*, and *wetware*. Hardware consists of physical assets. Software is broadly used to describe the firm's "soft" assets, such as its formulas and recipes for creating value. Wetware refers to employee brainpower, that is, "wet computers."

A firm owns and thus can capture value from its hardware and software, but it only "rents" its wetware. Wetware is the private property of individual employees, who can take it with them to another firm if they so choose. To create and capture value, managers must find ways to convert the knowledge contained in employee wetware—even knowledge the employees may not realize they have—into software.

The evolution of the McDonald's Corporation provides a good example of how this process occurs. The first McDonald's unit was established in 1956. The company's hardware consisted of property and equipment. However, its most important asset was its software. McDonald's major source of value was its new formula for selling hamburgers, fries, and drinks to customers. This formula translated into a business approach that McDonald's was able to replicate in locations around the world. If McDonald's had stopped innovating in 1956, new companies that copied and improved on the original formula, such as Burger King, Wendy's, and Kentucky Fried Chicken, eventually would have forced McDonald's out of business. But McDonald's continually improved its formula for creating and capturing value by converting wetware into new software. Today McDonald's has a much wider product offering, more effective store designs, and better production processes than it had in 1956.

The development of the Filet-O-Fish Sandwich at McDonald's illustrates the conversion from wetware to software. Originally, the only food products McDonald's sold were hamburgers and fries. The product line intentionally was limited so that it could be produced efficiently and quickly, according to McDonald's formula for value creation. A franchisee in a Catholic neighborhood, however, was unable to sell many hamburgers on Fridays because Catholics were admonished from eating meat on Fridays. The franchisee worked hard to develop a tasty fish sandwich. At first, McDonald's would not let him sell the new sandwich because it was not consistent with the image as a hamburger company. It also would lead to inconsistency across units—something that a franchise company generally wants to avoid. Eventually, however, McDonald's saw the value that could be created and captured by offering a fish sandwich. Specialists at the corporate level devised ways to improve the sandwich and to lower production costs (e.g., by using a different type of fish that could be precut into a standard size). Ultimately, the Filet-O-Fish sandwich was introduced across all McDonald's units and has been a menu staple ever since.

The idea of a fish sandwich initially was contained in the wetware of the franchisee, while the ways to improve the product were in the wetware of specialists at the corporate level. At this stage, the ideas and knowledge were not creating value. But the wetware was eventually converted into software and is now part of the McDonald's formula for creating and capturing value. A similar story lies behind the "Big Mac," which was the brainchild of a franchisee in Pittsburgh who wanted a heftier sandwich to sell to steelworkers.

Software is different from hardware in that it is not a scarce resource. While a given machine can be used only at one location, software can be replicated to create value at locations throughout the world. For example, McDonald's currently has over 10,000 units operating under the same business format. (Of course, as we will discuss, software also can be copied by competing firms, thus reducing its profit potential.)

Whether or not a firm is likely to be successful in converting wetware into software depends critically on how decision rights are assigned within the firm and on how employees are evaluated and rewarded (the firm's organizational architecture). Chapters 11–17 provide a systematic analysis of these considerations.

Opportunities to Create Value

The discovery of better ways to use existing resources drives much of the value that firms create. Today's personal computers are far more powerful than the 1980s mainframes, yet they take significantly fewer resources to produce. The value created by improved computer technology has not come from the discovery of new raw

---

MANAGERIAL APPLICATIONS

Sonic Drive-Ins Convert Wetware to Software

Sonic Corp. is one of the largest fast-food chains in America with more than 3,500 restaurants in 44 states in 2014. Former CEO, Pattye Moore, stated in 2002 that she spent half her time visiting stores and eats at Sonic with her daughters three or four times a week. "We really get a lot of ideas that way. . . . We just go out and ask them what they're fixing for themselves. . . . We encourage our employees to play with their food."

Sonic employees at one store were bored with buns and started eating their burgers and chicken on thick, grilled toast. Sonic introduced "toaster sandwiches" that became popular with customers. One customer suggested sausage on a stick wrapped in a buttermilk pancake and deep fried. It is now a breakfast staple. One store manager created the grilled chicken wrap. All of these products were launched throughout the entire Sonic chain.

Notice how Sonic had encouraged people to experiment with new food dishes (enhancing their wetware) and then converts this wetware into software. Corporate management then chooses which of these ideas to pursue. The recipes are refined and codified. Sonic illustrates how one company had used its organizational architecture to convert wetware at one drive-in into literally new recipes (software) that are leveraged throughout the firm's other locations. Moreover, Sonic has a corporate culture that promotes experimentation, identifies potentially valuable wetware, and converts that wetware into software, which then is leveraged across the firm.

Source: http://corporate.sonic.drivenin.com (2014); and (200), "Required Eating Makes This Job Fun," *Democrat and Chronicle* (June 3), 7D.

---

materials or resources, but by using existing resources more efficiently. To quote growth theorist Paul Romer,[12]

> So it is not the raw materials or the mass of things on earth that really lies behind economic success and high standard of living, it is the process of rearrangement. And what underlies this process of rearrangement are instructions, formulas, recipes, and methods of doing things [software].

The possibilities for new value creation are immense. Consider Romer's simple example of a production process that involves just 20 steps. The order of the steps can be varied in an extremely large number of ways (approximately 2.4 followed by 17 zeros) and thereby affect the value created. In most production processes, of course, there is a natural ordering that precludes certain combinations of steps—it doesn't make sense to weld the body together after the car is painted. But given all the ways to rearrange the many resources on earth, the possibilities for continued value creation are enormous. This discussion suggests that firms face an essentially unlimited set of opportunities to create better "instructions, formulas, recipes, and methods" for making improved products at lower cost. New opportunities are likely to emerge as technology continues to evolve. For instance, the latter part of the 20th century saw a massive change in information, communication, and production technologies. This technological change has provided substantial opportunities for increasing value. The "business process reengineering" movement in the 1990s used computer and information technology to lower costs (for instance, by streamlining the systems used to process orders, shipments, payables, and receivables). Flexible production technologies have allowed firms to tailor the design of their products to fit specific customer demands. Computer and information technologies reduce the

---

[12]Paul Romer (1998), "Bank of America Roundtable on the Soft Revolution: Achieving Growth by Managing Intangibles," *Journal of Applied Corporate Finance* 11(2), 8–27.

Figure 8.3 Firm with Market Power versus a Firm in a Competitive Industry

The firm on the left has a downward-sloping demand curve and thus has market power. It can choose price–quantity combinations. Firms with market power often can capture economic profits. The other firm is in a competitive industry and thus faces a horizontal demand curve. Earning economic profits in this market setting is difficult. Firms along the dotted section on the supply curve (below the market clearing price of P^*) still would produce the product if demand and price fell. The shaded triangle represents producer surplus. This chapter discusses how a firm sometimes (but not always) can capture a portion of this producer surplus as an economic profit.

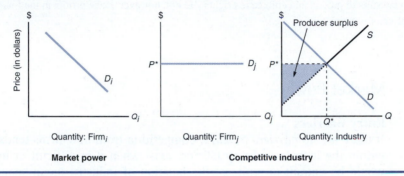

Capturing Value

Creating value is an essential first step in generating profits. But then it is necessary to capture this value. It does the firm little good to reduce transaction/production costs or to increase consumer demand (for instance, by creating new value-enhancing software) if rivals can copy these changes quickly and enter the market—such competition will eliminate the profits. (But of course, failure to innovate and keep up with the competition can lead to ruin.)

Figure 8.3 compares a firm in a competitive market to a firm with market power. In competitive markets, firms face horizontal demand curves and are price takers. With market power, firms choose price–quantity combinations. Chapters 6 and 7 indicated that firms often can capture value if they exploit their market power. Sometimes firms can capture value, even without market power, if they employ superior factors of production that allow them to be more productive than their rivals. In a competitive market, there typically are firms that would be willing to continue to produce the product even if demand and the market price fell. This production corresponds to the dashed section of the supply curve (below the market price P^*) in Figure 8.3. Also shown is the corresponding producer surplus. Sometimes (but not always) a firm can capture a portion of this producer surplus as economic profit. Next, we discuss the conditions under which market power and superior resources lead to economic profits.[13]

[13]A note on vocabulary: Economists say a firm is earning *rents* when it sells its product for a price higher than average total cost (which includes a "normal" rate of return). Positive rents imply that the firm is earning more than is necessary to motivate it to continue to produce the product over the long run (it is earning an economic profit). It is useful to distinguish between two types of rents: *Monopoly rents,* which correspond to our discussion of market power, and *Ricardian rents,* which correspond to our discussion of superior factors of production.

HISTORICAL APPLICATIONS

Creating but Not Capturing Value: Eli Whitney

A great problem in harvesting cotton during the 18th century was separating cotton from its seed. This laborious task was done by hand. It was so difficult that it took a worker a whole day to clean 1 pound of staple cotton. Eli Whitney, while visiting Georgia, was intrigued by this problem. Within a few weeks, he produced a machine he called a "cotton gin" (a shortened form of cotton engine). It greatly increased the amount of cotton that could be cleaned in a day and soon led to cotton becoming the chief crop in the South. Clearly, the invention of the cotton gin created significant value. Yet, before Whitney's invention was completed and patented, his first model had been widely copied. Virtually all his profits went into lawsuits to protect and enforce his rights. He did, however, make profits in the financial markets speculating on the price of cotton.

Market Power

Entry Barriers

If there are no *barriers to entry,* competition from new firms tends to erode profits within the industry.[14] Entry barriers exist when it is difficult or uneconomic for a would-be entrant to replicate the position of industry incumbents. These barriers include factors that make price cuts likely if a new firm enters (such as economies of scale), incumbent advantages (such as patents and brand names), and high costs of exit.

Numerous researchers have tested the theoretical link between entry barriers and profit potential.[15] Consistent with the theory, these studies generally confirm that price-cost margins tend to be lower in competitive industries. Researchers also have found a positive correlation between profit and specific entry barriers (such as economies of scale or advertising) as well as a positive correlation between profit and concentration (combined market share of the top few firms) across geographic markets *within* a given industry.[16]

While theory and evidence suggest that profit potential increases with entry barriers, the existence of such barriers is no guarantee of economic profits. There are at least four additional factors that are important. These include the degree of rivalry within the industry, threat of substitutes, buyer power, and supplier power.[17]

---

[14]As discussed in Chapter 6, a firm can have market power when there are limited entry barriers (in the case of differentiated products—monopolistic competition). Entry, however, often will eliminate or at least substantially limit economic profits.

[15]For a survey of some of the relevant studies, see R. Schmalensee (1989), "Studies of Structure and Performance," in R. Schmalensee and R. Willig (Eds.), *The Handbook of Industrial Organization* (North Holland: Amsterdam).

[16]In apparent contrast to the theory, researchers have failed to document a strong positive correlation between profits and concentration *across* industries. This is due in part to the difficulty of comparing accounting data across industries. Cross-industry differences in the treatment of depreciation and other accounting choices make interindustry comparisons problematic. Another difficulty is that industries can be concentrated for at least two quite different reasons. First, there can be actual barriers to entry. Second, there can be few firms in an industry because it lacks profit potential. If the sample contains both types of industries, it is not surprising that researchers find mixed results.

[17]M. Porter (1980), *Competitive Strategy* (Free Press: New York), labels these factors, along with the threat of entry, as the "five factors."

MANAGERIAL APPLICATIONS

Italian Textiles and Chinese Competition

For more than six centuries wool has been cleaned, dyed, and woven in Biella, Italy. Chinese manufacturers once competed primarily on price, offering low-quality textiles. But now the quality of Chinese textiles has improved markedly. This has exerted substantial pressure on prices and has led to layoffs and closings in the Italian cloth trade.

Source: C. Rhoades (2003), "Threat from China Starts to Unravel Italy's Cloth Trade," *The Wall Street Journal* (December 17), A1.

Degree of Rivalry

When the degree of rivalry is high, profits will be low even if there are entry barriers. Two factors that help determine the level of rivalry are the number and relative sizes of competitors. The fewer the number of competitors (the more concentrated the industry), the more likely that firms will recognize their mutual dependence and refrain from cutthroat competition. The presence of a large, dominant firm (as opposed to a comparable number of similarly sized firms) also can reduce rivalry because a dominant firm frequently takes the lead in setting prices and takes actions to sanction others that do not follow its lead (within the limits of antitrust constraints). The level of rivalry can change over time as basic conditions within the industry change. For example, if existing firms within an industry have excess capacity, they often will engage in price competition in an attempt to increase their individual outputs. In general, excess capacity, high fixed costs, lack of product differentiation, and slow growth all increase the degree of rivalry within the industry.

Threat of Substitutes

Even if entry is limited, firms within an industry are not immune to outside competition. There is the threat of substitutes. For instance, the large scale of investment potentially limits entry into the overnight delivery market (populated by firms such as FedEx and UPS). However, in recent years effective substitutes, such as e-mail and fax machines, have reduced the demand for delivery services (relative to what would have been without these technological developments). Similarly, banks face competition from money market accounts that offer customers the ability to write negotiable orders of withdrawal (usually restricted to amounts in excess of $100).

Buyer and Supplier Power

The final two factors that help determine a firm's market power are buyer and supplier power. If the industry has only a few large customers, profit is likely to be low since these customers will use their buying power to extract lower prices. Similarly, if the key suppliers to an industry are large, concentrated, or well organized (e.g., unionized), they will attempt to extract industry profits through high input prices. During the 1990s Intel and Microsoft were essentially sole suppliers of certain key inputs for the production of personal computers; hence they have been quite profitable.

Market Power and Strategy

Firms sometimes can increase economic profit by taking actions that promote entry barriers, reduce intra-industry rivalry, limit the availability of substitutes, or reduce buyer/supplier power. Examples of each type of activity are easy to find. For instance, American manufacturers frequently lobby for taxes or restrictions on imports to reduce entry by foreign firms. Firms in certain industries form cartels or other collusive

MANAGERIAL APPLICATIONS

Competition and the Number of Competitors

The degree of rivalry generally increases with the number of competitors. Depending on the nature of the industry, however, competition can be quite fierce even with only a few competitors. Coca-Cola had about 42 percent of domestic carbonated soft drink sales in 2014, while Pepsi had a market share of about 30 percent. Yet the battle between Coke and Pepsi has been intense for decades, with costly promotional contests and intense competition for distribution. Similarly, competition has been strong in the U.S. tobacco industry, although the three largest companies have had about 90 percent of the market. In detergents, two large companies, Procter and Gamble and Unilever, have conducted a global "soap war." To varying degrees, each of these industries is characterized by excess capacity, high fixed costs, lack of product differentiation, and slow growth—all factors that lead to greater rivalry.

agreements to reduce competition.[18] As we have discussed, organizations like the AMA act to limit the availability of substitute products or services (in their case new physicians, nurses, physician assistants, and midwives). Firms reduce buyer power by opposing buyer-cooperatives. Finally, firms thwart supplier power by opposing labor unions and expanding capacity in nonunionized locations—especially internationally.

Historically, many managers focused on capturing value through anticompetitive activities, such as erecting entry barriers. They have found that often it is difficult to limit competition—especially in a global marketplace. Also, as discussed in Chapter 21, regulators extract much of the producer surplus created through limits on competition, for example, through campaign contributions to encourage the adoption and enforcement of entry restrictions. Due to these considerations, much of the contemporary focus in strategy is on superior resources—the subject of the next section.[19]

ANALYZING MANAGERIAL DECISIONS: *Investing in a New Restaurant Concept*

For the last 10 years you have been working in the health food business. You have talked to many customers who have suggested a new restaurant concept. The restaurant would feature a variety of low calorie meals (under 500) made from healthy ingredients (e.g., organic fruits and vegetables and steroid/hormone free meat). The restaurant would include a bar with an extensive organic wine list and trendy decor. There would be an emphasis on high quality, friendly service, and colorful meal presentation. Your customers suggest that they would be willing to pay around $50 to eat a meal and have a glass of wine at this type of restaurant. They lament the fact that their community has no upscale restaurants that offer this type of fare.

You have conducted a detailed financial analysis of this potential business opportunity. You believe that you have good information on the costs of starting and operating the restaurant. You project that with a $50 meal price and anticipated demand you would earn a high profit and an excellent rate of return on your investment. You have the equity capital to start the business.

Several friends with MBAs argue that you would be crazy to start this business. They claim that there are few entry barriers to the restaurant industry and that "every person with business training knows that you can't make profits in a competitive industry." Should you drop the idea of opening the new business based on this argument? Explain.

---

[18]Managers must be careful undertaking these types of actions in the United States since many are illegal under American antitrust law.

[19]Examples of the contemporary focus in the strategy literature are D. Collis and C. Montgomery (1995), "Competing on Resources: Strategy in the 1990s," *Harvard Business Review,* 118–128; and J. Barney and W. Hesterly (2011), Strategic Management and Competitive Advantage: Concepts, 4th Edition (Prentice Hall: Boston).

Superior Factors of Production

Both human as well as physical assets vary in productivity. For example, Clayton Kershaw is a great baseball player, Steve Jobs of the Apple Inc. was a superb CEO, land in California's Imperial Valley is incredibly fertile, land adjacent to an expressway interchange offers customers quite convenient access, and so on. If an asset allows the firm to make a profit because of its superior productivity, other firms will compete for this resource and bid up its price. Thus, with well-functioning markets, the gains from superior productivity accrue to the responsible asset.

Producer Surplus Captured by Superior Assets

Figure 8.1 divides value into consumer surplus and producer surplus. Consumers receive the consumer surplus. Producer surplus goes to the owners of superior assets. As an example, consider Pete Irving, general manager of Speedy Modems. Last year, Speedy was just breaking even in producing modems at a price of $100. Demand for the particular type of modem increased, and the price rose to $150; Speedy began making a profit (producer surplus) of $50 per unit. This profit motivated other firms to produce the same type of modems. They were less productive than Speedy solely because they lacked a manager with Pete's talents. The rival firms began making job offers to Pete. To dissuade him from going to a rival firm, Speedy had to increase Pete's salary. Through this process, Pete's salary increased to the point where Speedy was making only a normal rate of profit—the same as the competing modem companies. The gains from his special talents went to Pete, not to the firm. This same process works for physical assets. For instance, if a firm rents a prime piece of land or a unique piece of equipment, rental rates will be bid up to reflect the asset's superior productivity. And if the firm owns the asset, its value (and thus the opportunity costs for continuing to use it) will be bid up—in effect, the firm pays the rent to itself for its continued use of the asset.

Figure 8.4 displays a graphical analysis of this general phenomenon. The illustration on the right depicts supply and demand in the marketplace. The initial price is P_0^*. A typical firm in the industry is depicted on the left and is making no economic profits—price equals long-run average cost (LRAC_0). The demand for the product increases and the market price goes up to P_1^*. The firm appears to have the potential to make an economic profit, since the price is above its initial long-run average cost. Competitors and new entrants, however, will bid for the special resources (such as a talented manager or a productive piece of land) that would allow the firm to produce the product at an average cost below price. In equilibrium, the firm's costs would

---

MANAGERIAL APPLICATIONS

Sugar Prices

The 2008 wholesale price for sugar in world markets was about $0.16 per pound. In contrast, the price in U.S. markets was over $0.26 per pound. The dramatic difference between the two prices is due largely to American tariffs on sugar imports. Foreign producers would be willing to sell to Americans at lower prices. Yet, they are not permitted to do so. This restriction benefits domestic sugar producers, who are able to sell their sugar at the higher price. Without entry restrictions, the U.S. price would be driven down to about $0.16 per pound. Such a domestic price decline would benefit American consumers but hurt American sugar producers.

Figure 8.4 **Producer Surplus Is Captured by Superior Assets**

The illustration below depicts supply and demand in the marketplace. The initial price is P_0^*. The typical firm in the industry is depicted on the left and is making no economic profits—price equals long-run average cost (LRAC$_0$). The demand for the product increases and the market price goes up to P_1^*. The firm appears to have the potential to make an economic profit, since the price is above its initial long-run average cost. Competitors and new entrants, however, will bid for the special resources (such as a talented manager or a piece of land) that would allow the firm to produce the product at an average cost below price. In equilibrium, the firm's cost would have increased to the point where its long-run average cost (LRAC$_1$) equals price. The additional producer surplus created by the increase in price (shaded area) goes to the scarce assets, which made lower-cost production possible at the initial price and output level.

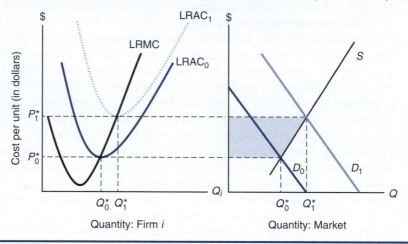

increase to the point where its long-run average cost (LRAC$_1$) again equals price.[20] The additional producer surplus created by the increase in price (shaded area) is reflected in the price or opportunity cost of the scarce assets, which made lower-cost production possible at the initial price and output level.

If the firm owns the scarce asset (e.g., a piece of land), the wealth of the firm's owners increases as the price of the asset is bid up. It is important, however, to realize that a firm does not have to use a superior asset to realize this value. In fact, the firm might be better off selling the assets to another firm. Managers sometimes overlook this alternative.

As an example, it has been argued that British Petroleum (BP) has a competitive advantage in producing retail gasoline because it owns productive oil fields in Alaska that it bought long ago at low prices.[21] Potential competitors are disadvantaged, it is argued, because they have to buy oil on the open market at a higher price than BP's current cost of extracting its oil. This argument is flawed because it fails to apply the concept of *opportunity costs* appropriately. If BP can sell its oil on the open market, the cost of using it internally is the revenue forgone from not selling it—and that is the current

---

[20]This analysis assumes that the asset is equally valuable to all firms. If this assumption does not hold, the firm's costs will not necessarily be bid up to the point where it makes no economic profits. Price will not be bid above the value to the next highest valued user. We discuss this issue next.

[21]This example is taken from a strategy textbook. Similar examples of faulty analysis are easy to find throughout the management literature.

		Accounting Profits	
Retail gasoline price		$4.00/gallon	$3.60/gallon
Retail sales		$4,000,000	$3,600,000
Extraction/refining costs		($400,000)	($400,000)
Station operating costs		($2,000,000)	($2,000,000)
Profits		**$1,600,000**	**$1,200,000**
		Economic Profits	
Retail gasoline price		$4.00/gallon	$3.60/gallon
Retail sales		$4,000,000	$3,600,000
Opportunity cost of gasoline		($2,000,000)	($2,000,000)
Station operating costs		($2,000,000)	($2,000,000)
Profits		**$0**	**($400,000)**

Table 8.1 BP Retail Gasoline Stations: Accounting versus Economic Profits

In this hypothetical example, BP's cost of extracting enough oil and refining it into a gallon of gasoline is $0.40. This gasoline can be sold on the wholesale market for $2.00. It costs $2 million to operate the retail stations (e.g. wages for station attendants). BP produces 1 million gallons of gasoline a month. There are no other relevant costs or revenues, except for the $2 million of other costs to operate the retail gasoline stations. The top panel shows BP's income statement using standard accounting techniques assuming gasoline prices of either $4.00 or $3.60 per gallon. Here the cost of gasoline is BP's cost of $0.40 per gallon for extracting oil and refining it into gasoline. BP reports positive profits at prices, $1,600,000 and $1,200,000, respectively. The bottom panel reproduces the income statements using the opportunity cost of the gasoline sold at the stations (its current spot market price). In the latter case, it is better for BP to get out of the retail market and to sell its gasoline (or possibly its land or gasoline) on the wholesale market. It nets $1,600,000 by selling the gasoline in the wholesale market compared to $1,200,000 by selling it through its own stations. BP is indifferent between the two alternatives when the price is $4.00 (in either case, BP nets $1,600,000). This example emphasizes the basic point made in Chapter 5: Managers should make business decisions using opportunity costs, not accounting costs.

spot market price of oil, not just BP's extraction cost. If other companies were more efficient in refining crude oil and producing gasoline for retail customers, BP would be more profitable if it sold the oil on the open market and did not compete in the production of gasoline. The wealth of BP shareholders is certainly greater because the company owns valuable oil rights in Alaska. But the critical question is how do managers best exploit this valuable asset. It might be best either to sell the land to another company, sell the oil from the land to another company, or refine the oil internally to produce and sell retail gasoline (or some other petroleum product). Its best course of action depends on the relative efficiency of BP versus its competitors in the extraction and distribution of oil or the production and distribution of gasoline. BP should not extract oil or produce retail gasoline simply because it owns its oil reserves.

Table 8.1 illustrates the difference between accounting and economic profits for BP's selling gasoline through its own retail gasoline stations. The following assumptions are used: (1) BP's cost of extracting enough oil and refining it into a gallon of gasoline is $0.40, (2) this gasoline can be sold on the wholesale market for $2.00, (3) station operating costs (e. g., wages for station attendants) are $2,000,000, (4) BP produces 1 million gallons of gasoline a month, and (5) there are no other relevant costs or revenues, except for $2 million of other retail gasoline operating costs. The top panel shows BP's income statement using standard accounting techniques assuming retail gasoline prices of either $4.00 or $3.60. Here the cost for gasoline is

BP's extraction and refining cost of $0.40 per gallon. BP reports positive profits at both prices—$1,600,000 and $1,200,000, respectively. Based on these accounting profits, it might appear that it is profitable for BP to operate its own retail stations. The bottom panel reproduces the income statements using the opportunity cost of the gasoline sold at the stations its market price. Using opportunity costs, BP breaks even when the price of gasoline is $4 but loses money when the price is $3.60. In the latter case, it is more profitable for BP to get out of the retail business and to sell gasoline in the wholesale market (or possibly the land or the mineral rights—this choice depends on BP's efficiency in extracting and refining the oil). BP makes $400,000 more in profits by selling the gasoline wholesale. BP is indifferent between selling gasoline wholesale or retail when the price is $4.00; either way, BP makes $1,600,000 over its production costs. This example illustrates a basic point: Managers should make business decisions using opportunity costs—not accounting costs.[22]

Second-Price Auctions

Competition tends to take a differentiated asset to its highest valued use, but at a price that reflects its *second-highest valued* use. In a competitive auction, no one has an incentive to bid more than the value they place on the asset. For example, if Lena Otis is the second-highest valued user of a piece of land, she will bid only up to her value, while José Ricardo, the highest valued user, can obtain the asset by bidding just slightly more. This principle implies that the producer surplus captured by the winning bidder is limited to the difference between the asset's first and second-highest valued uses; the rest of the value will be reflected in the price of the superior asset.

Team Production

Firms consist of collections of assets and explicit or implicit contracts with employees and other parties. For example, at Microsoft, their collection consists of CEO Tim Cook, all his senior managers and employees, the company's physical assets, brand name, and other intangible assets. Because of the interdependencies among workers and assets, the value of the inputs as a "team"[23] sometimes can be greater than the simple sum of the values if each worker and asset were employed at its next best use across other firms. Thus, it is possible that the overall firm will be more valuable than the sum of its parts. We characterize such a firm as having *team production capabilities*. A firm can capture value by maintaining team production advantages only if competing firms cannot assemble comparably productive teams. If rivals can, then in a competitive marketplace, the price of the product will be driven down so that the firm makes only a normal profit.

How do firms create team production capabilities that are difficult to duplicate? Part of the answer is a natural consequence of differences in the past histories of firms and the now-sunk choices by managers about goods produced, markets entered, individuals hired, and capital acquired. Due to these differences, firms acquire unique combinations of assets, organizational processes, communication channels, collective learning, and so on. As environments evolve, some firms find themselves—either

---

[22]In Chapter 17, we shall discuss how accounting costs can play an important role in helping to control incentive conflicts in organizations.

[23]The word *team* is used in a variety of contexts in the management literature (e.g., to refer specifically to small work groups of people). Here, we use the term in a broader sense to refer to a combination of assets (including human, physical, and organizational assets) used to produce a particular product or service.

MANAGERIAL APPLICATIONS

Team Capabilities at Sharp Corporation

During the 1970s, Sharp began marketing electronic calculators with liquid crystal displays. As the company developed expertise with LCD technology, Sharp began to apply it to other products, such as television sets. Through these actions, Sharp developed a set of resources and capabilities that other companies did not have. With the large growth in consumer electronics and computers during the 1980s and 1990s, potential applications for LCDs expanded rapidly. Sharp profited from this growth. Other companies could not immediately overcome Sharp's competitive advantage because of time constraints and their lack of Sharp's accumulated assets and experience. Companies such as Matsushita, NEC, and Canon entered the industry. Yet, Sharp was able to maintain its dominant position because of its special team capabilities. It continues as a leader in LCD technology; in 2007, Sharp negotiated a major deal with Toshiba to exchange its LCD sets for Toshiba TV chips. This advantage was not completely captured by its individual assets in their market values; individual assets would not have allowed other firms to copy Sharp's advantage. Thus part of this advantage went to Sharp's shareholders and was reflected in its stock price. No competitive advantage, however, lasts forever; in recent years Sharp has been out performed by some of its competitors, including the Samsung Electronics Company.

Source: D. Collis and C. Montgomery (1997), *Corporate Strategy* (Irwin: Chicago); and K. Hall (2007), "Sharp and Toshiba: Big TV Tieup," *BusinessWeek.com* (December 21).

---

through luck or foresight—to be in the enviable position of having developed team capabilities that are especially productive in these new circumstances, whereas others do not. For example, Walmart developed an efficient hub-and-spoke distribution network to serve its chain of successful rural stores. This system, along with its brand name and procurement advantages, also helped it compete successfully in larger urban areas.

Other firms can observe the team production capabilities of successful firms. Yet, duplicating these capabilities can be difficult because, from the outside, it is frequently difficult to pinpoint the exact source of synergies within the team: Many assets are combined in the typical firm. It also can be expensive to acquire the necessary assets (contracting/transaction costs), provide training to workers, and so on. In addition, implementing significant changes within an existing organization presents daunting challenges. That team capabilities often are expensive to duplicate is consistent with the observation that many firms enter a new business by buying an existing firm in the industry, rather than by developing the new business within the firm.

Team Capabilities and Organizational Architecture

A firm's architecture consists of its assignment of decision rights and its systems for evaluating and rewarding performance. Organizational architecture is important in contributing to team capabilities. For example, a decentralized firm can respond more quickly and effectively to a new opportunity that requires rapid "front-line" decision making (for instance, in competitive pricing to customers) than can a firm with a more centralized decision-making structure. Alternatively, other new opportunities that require detailed coordination of activities across several business units might favor the firm with the more centralized structure. As we shall discuss, it often is hard to copy another firm's architecture because multiple systems have to be changed in a coordinated manner. Implementing this type of major change within an organization can be surprisingly difficult.

Flexible Manufacturing and Team Capabilities

Economists argue that often it is appropriate to view managerial policies as a system of complements—each policy is more valuable when it is adopted along with other complementary policies. For example, a fall in the costs of flexible manufacturing equipment can favor the following simultaneous changes in a firm's strategy and organizational architecture: investment in more flexible manufacturing equipment, increased output, more frequent product innovations, more continuous product improvements, higher levels of training, additional investment in more efficient production design procedures (computer-aided design), greater autonomy of workers and hence better use of local information, more cross-training, greater use of teams, additional screening to identify prospective employees with greater potential, and increased horizontal communication.

Changing only a subset of these policies might be less productive than changing them all at once because of the complementarities: More value is created when there are reinforcing changes across this collection of policies. For example, employee training is likely to add less value if employees are not given increased autonomy to employ their new skills. Yet, making rapid changes in many elements of a firm's strategy and organizational architecture is expensive.

Firms in which more of these policies are already in place are more likely to take advantage of a reduction in the cost of flexible manufacturing than firms without these policies in place. Because of their team capabilities, these firms are likely to generate economic profits that will not be competed away in the near term.

In this example, the unexpected change in the environment is a fall in the cost of flexible manufacturing technology. This change benefits some firms but not others. If a different environmental change occurred, a different group of firms might benefit.

Source: J. Roberts (2007), *The Modern Firm: Organization Design for Performance and Growth* (Oxford Press: Oxford, UK).

A Partial Explanation for Walmart's Success

Sam Walton's initial strategy in the early 1960s was to establish stores in small towns (populations under 25,000) in rural Arkansas, Missouri, and Oklahoma. His intent was to place "good-sized stores in little one-horse towns, which everybody else was ignoring." As he increased the number of stores, he designed an extremely efficient distribution system—a hub-and-spoke system with regional distribution centers. He also cultivated key vendor relationships, a distinctive human resource management system, and a nonunionized workforce. As his network of stores increased, he opened additional stores in nearby states, eventually expanding throughout the country and internationally.

As Walmart continued to expand, its success became evident. Would-be competitors envied this success; yet, they did not have the capability to mimic Walmart's strategy. First, it did not make economic sense for companies to construct competing stores in the small rural communities where Walmart already operated. Surely, the resulting competition with Walmart would drive prices down in these "one-horse" towns. Walmart's first-mover advantage created an entry barrier and market power. Without a sufficient number of existing stores, it also did not make economic sense to copy Walmart's distribution system in the rural Southeast. As Walmart gained experience, it developed organizational processes and resources (team capabilities) that provided potential advantages over would-be competitors as it expanded into new geographic areas, such as the Pacific Northwest.

Walmart could have sold some of its resources, such as individual stores, yet potential buyers would have limited incentives to bid up the price of these assets

ANALYZING MANAGERIAL DECISIONS: *Leaving New York City for the Farmlands of Illinois*

You have worked as an investment banker in New York and Hong Kong for the last five years. You are tired of living in populated cities and yearn for a more peaceful environment.

The Wall Street Journal contained a story about the federal government's actions to increase corn-based ethanol as a substitute for gasoline in the United States. According to reports, new laws and regulations will result in the construction of hundreds of new ethanol factories over the next decade. Demand for corn to fuel the plants is expected to soar.

Based on a Web search, you found 80 acres of prime farmland for sale in Illinois at a price of $10,000 per acre. You have saved enough from your past bonuses to purchase the land. You are tempted to quit your job and purchase the land to farm corn.

Several colleagues have told you that it sounds like a good idea. They say that not only would it allow you to move to a less populated area, but it is a great business opportunity with little risk. Surely the price of farmland will increase dramatically over the next few years as the ethanol plants begin operation and the demand for corn skyrockets. Good farmland is limited, and you might reasonably expect its price to double or even triple over the next few years. You are smart and should be able to learn the farm business very quickly. In addition, you will have a cost advantage over farmers who wait to buy land at much higher prices. If you decide that you do not want to be a farmer, you can always sell the land at a "huge profit." Do you think your colleagues are giving you good advice? Explain.

unless they could have purchased them all together. For example, the value of an individual store is lower when it is not coupled with Walmart's distribution system.[24] Thus, although Walmart faced an opportunity cost from not selling its individual assets piecemeal to other firms, the value of keeping these assets together within the same firm was likely to be far higher than this opportunity cost. If Walmart were to construct an income statement based on its opportunity costs (as we did for BP in the bottom panel of Table 8.1), it would show a positive economic profit.[25]

Even though Walmart has had a competitive advantage in rural America, its advantage has been smaller in urban centers. Urban areas can support more than one discount store—thus promoting entry by Target, Kmart, and others. There also is more competition from nondiscount stores. Competing firms have copied many of Walmart's innovations in distribution, vendor relationships, and so on. Thus, in urban areas Walmart has had both less market power and a smaller productivity advantage. Walmart also has had problems at some of its international locations, such as Brazil. Internationally, Walmart's advantages from superior distribution and vendor relations are arguably smaller; also its brand name is less well-known than in the United States.

---

[24]A reader might wonder why Walmart couldn't sell the store to a buyer at a high price and contract with the buyer to allow it to use Walmart's distribution system. This issue is addressed in Chapter 19. That analysis suggests that given the nature of the assets, Walmart is better off owning them jointly.

[25]Recall that the opportunity costs of the individual resources are their next highest valued use outside of their current use.

MANAGERIAL APPLICATIONS

Economic Profits without Market Power—A Summary of the Key Concepts

Chapter 6 characterized competitive output markets in terms of four basic conditions: (1) many buyers and sellers, (2) product homogeneity, (3) rapid dissemination of accurate information at low cost, and (4) free entry into and exit from the product market. In this setting, firms have no market power and essentially are price takers in the output market: Firm demand curves are horizontal at the market price. The marginal firm sells the product at average cost and makes no abnormal profit.

In this chapter, we discuss how it is possible for some firms in a competitive market to make economic profits (produce at an average cost below the market price). Economists refer to these firms as being "inframarginal." To be inframarginal, two conditions must be met:

- Rivals cannot imitate the inframarginal firm and assemble teams of assets that produce the product at the same low cost—at least in the near term. If competitors can erode cost advantages through imitation, competition will drive the price down and eliminate above-normal profits (rents).

- The full value of the firm's superior productivity cannot be captured by selling its assets to other firms—unless they are sold together. Otherwise the opportunity cost of production will be the same as for their rivals (even if they can't assemble equally productive teams).

The fact that firms have different histories and paths can help explain the existence of team capabilities and inframarginal firms. Nonetheless, staying inframarginal is not easy. Potential competitors have strong incentives to discover ways to imitate successful firms or otherwise counteract their advantages. Also, to the extent that an advantage is based on an identifiable asset, such as a talented manager or a prime location, the opportunity cost of the resource is likely to rise from competitive pressures in factor markets. Thus, competitive pressures in both the product and factor markets make sustaining economic profits difficult.

All Good Things Must End

The business environment is constantly evolving with new technological innovations, changes in consumer tastes, new business concepts, new firms, and other developments. Given these changes, it is unlikely that any competitive advantage will last forever, unless the firm can find a succession of new value-increasing strategies.

MANAGERIAL APPLICATIONS

Nomura Securities Company: It Is Not Easy to Remake a Business

Japan's Nomura Securities Company—whose roots go back to the 19th century rice exchanges of Osaka—was one of the world's most profitable securities firms in the 1980s. In 1997 following a serious scandal involving payoffs to racketeers, the company almost collapsed. The company also was hurt because it strongly recommended a set of stocks to customers that then fell significantly in value. The new president, Junichi Ujiie, vowed to remake the company. He wanted to deemphasize the selling of individual stocks to customers and focus more on asset gathering and portfolio advice. His objective was to become more like Merrill Lynch or Morgan Stanley. By late 1999, Ujiie had failed to turn the company around. Indeed Nomura continued to lose out to smaller competitors in obtaining new business. Between 2000 and 2014, Nomura continued to struggle relative to competitors, such as Goldman Sachs. Its stock fell significantly during the 2007–2009 financial crisis and it largely failed to recover over the subsequent five-year period. Like many large companies, Nomura had trouble remaking itself to regain lost success and profitability.

Source: Yahoo Finance (2014), "Nomura Holdings," finance.yahoo.com; and B. Spindle (1999), "Nomura Restructuring Falters; Can Mr. Ujiie Still Remake the Firm?" *The Wall Street Journal* (September 3), A1.

MANAGERIAL APPLICATIONS

Walmart's Strategy Proves Timely during the 2007 Holiday Season

Walmart's experience in the fall of 2007 illustrates how differences in historic paths can give firms a competitive advantage of disadvantage as the economic environment changes.

The 2007 holiday shopping season was the weakest in five years. Consumer spending fell as consumers worried about oil prices that approached $100 per barrel and the prospect of economic recession. Relative to the previous year, same-store sales fell during the holiday season at Target (down 5 percent), Abercrombie & Fitch (2 percent), Gap (6 percent), Macy's (7.4 percent), Nordstrom (4 percent), JC Penney (7.5 percent), and Kohl's (11.4 percent). Walmart was one of the few retailers with strong performance, experiencing a 2.6 percent increase in same-store sales during the holiday season.

Throughout November and December of 2007, Walmart opened stores very early in the morning on multiple occasions enticing shoppers with big discounts on products such as high-definition DVRs. Thousands of consumers flooded Walmart stores in search of bargains. Its emphasis on low prices attracted consumers throughout the holiday season.

Other retail chains, such as Target, scrambled to adapt and offered similar promotions to attract price-focused customers. These efforts, however, were not as successful as Walmart's. Walmart was known among consumers for its historic focus on "everyday low prices." The historic business strategies of most of the other retailers focused on other dimensions. For example, Target had developed a reputation for "good design," while Nordstrom had developed a reputation for quality products and service. Historic strategies and reputations made it difficult for many of the chains to convince consumers that they were now focusing on low prices. Costco, which has historically focused on bulk merchandise and low prices, was one of the few other success stories with a same-store sales increase of 7 percent (4 percent excluding gasoline sales).

Source: M. Barbaro (2008), "Wal-Mart's Strategy Proved a Timely One," *nytimes.com* (January 11).

Just as the elements erode a mountain, persistent competition erodes firm profits over time. While entry may be limited, outside firms have strong incentives to devise methods of capturing profits from successful firms. Ultimately, one of these methods is likely to work. If one compares today's top firms with those of, say, 50 years ago, the lists are quite different. For example, today's top firms like Google, Microsoft, Walmart, and Apple did not exist 50 years ago, whereas many of the top firms from yesteryear have become less successful or gone out of existence.

Changing Fortunes

The fortunes of firms change over time. Due to competitive pressures, the top firms in one period are often not the top firms in subsequent periods. Below is a listing of the top 10 firms in terms of market value in 1970 and 2013. The lists are different, only General Electric is on both lists. (Standard Oil of NJ changed its name to Exxon in 1972 and merged with Mobil in 1999.)

Rank	1970	2013
1	IBM	Apple
2	AT&T	Exxon-Mobil
3	General Motors	Google
4	Standard Oil of NJ	Microsoft
5	Eastman Kodak	Berkshire Hathaway
6	Sears Roebuck	Johnson & Johnson
7	Texaco	Wells Fargo
8	General Electric	General Electric
9	Xerox	Walmart
10	Gulf Oil	JP Morgan Chase

Polaroid's Success and Ultimate Failure to Capture Value

From 1948, when Polaroid introduced its first instant camera, until 1972, when it unveiled its SX-70, the company continually improved its almost magical product. The first Polaroid camera produced sepia-toned prints, but over the years the company developed the ability to produce color photos that materialized right before one's eyes. In 1972, Polaroid's stock price was 90 times earnings, propelling the company into the Nifty Fifty (the top 50 companies in the *Fortune* 500). But the SX-70 was followed by a series of flops, including Polavision, a moving version of instant photography that was inferior to video. Moreover, the development of digital imaging provided an alternative method of viewing pictures immediately and precipitated Polaroid's Chapter 11 bankruptcy filing in October 2001. It stopped making cameras in 2007 and in 2009. The history of Polaroid illustrates two important points. First, successful firms develop new wetware that leads to innovative products, which satisfy customers' demands. Second, competition—often arising from new technologies—erodes the profitability of companies that, on a continuing basis, fail to innovate successfully.

Source: D. Whitford (2001), "Polaroid, R.I.P.," *Fortune* (November 12), 44; *http://en.wikipedia.org/wiki/Polaroid_Corporation*.

Consistent with this view, Walmart's growth slowed significantly during the first part of the 1990s. Although its performance improved during the late 1990s, economic theory and experience suggested that continued superior performance should not be expected over the long run.

Economics of Diversification

Although the New York Times Company, concentrate on a single major business, most large firms engage in numerous businesses: They are diversified. This raises the question: Is corporate diversification a productive strategy to create and capture value? *Economies of scope* are the primary reason that diversification might enhance value. In addition, combining businesses within the same firm can *promote complementary products*. But diversification also entails costs. Value maximization requires that firms consider both the benefits and the costs of diversification. In this section, we discuss these costs and benefits and analyze the circumstances under which diversification is most likely to create value. We also examine who is most likely to capture this value.

Benefits of Diversification

Economies of Scope

As discussed in Chapter 6, economies of scope exist when one firm could produce multiple products at lower cost than separate firms could produce the products. Economies of scope might occur anywhere along the vertical chain of production.[26] Consider the following examples: A diversified firm buys inputs at a discount reflecting its higher volume from using the same inputs in producing different products; a firm economizes on transportation costs because it delivers different

---

[26]The vertical chain of production consists of the various steps in taking raw materials and transforming them into consumer products. These steps include research and development, purchasing, production, outbound logistics, marketing, sales, service, support activities, and so on. See Chapter 19 for a more detailed discussion of this chain of activities.

MANAGERIAL APPLICATIONS

Walmart Diversifies into the Traditional Grocery Store Business

In 1998, Walmart opened three "experimental" 40,000-square-foot grocery stores in Arkansas. The potential benefits of this diversification derive from economies of scope. Walmart has a quite efficient distribution system that also can be used to stock the grocery stores. It has the potential to leverage its relationships with key vendors, which currently serve its discount stores and supercenters. Walmart's management has significant experience in managing stores in a related business. This experience is likely to be helpful in choosing store locations, establishing and running management systems, and so on.

---

products to the same customer; a firm uses salespeople more efficiently because they are able to offer customers an array of products; and a firm economizes on flotation costs because it raises capital to fund several businesses at once. Sometimes, producing one product unavoidably also produces others because of a jointness in the production process. For instance, if a firm produces beef by slaughtering cows, it also frequently makes economic sense to produce other products with the bones and hides.

Combining activities inside the same firm is not the only way to achieve these types of economies. There are alternative ways to organize that also accomplish this objective. For example, an independent wholesaler might offer retailers an array of products produced by separate manufacturers, centralize the billing of retailers, and provide a more efficient inventory and distribution system. Which method of organization is best depends on contracting costs. For example, negotiating and enforcing contracts among independent firms can be expensive, as can organizing activities within the same firm (see below). Sometimes integrating activities within the same firm is less expensive than contracting among firms. In this case, diversification creates value. We discuss the trade-offs in choosing among organizational forms in greater detail in Chapters 11–17 of this book.

Promoting Complements

Another potential reason for diversification is to promote the supply of complementary products. For example, Ford and General Motors entered the consumer credit business in 1919 and 1959, respectively.[27] One potential benefit of auto manufacturers' entering

---

MANAGERIAL APPLICATIONS

McFocus at McDonald's

McDonald's decided to shed at least some of its sideline ventures into pizza, fast-casual Mexican food, and takeout dining and concentrate on revitalizing its core hamburger business. McDonald's had gotten into Chipotle Mexican Grill, Donatos Pizza, and Boston Market to offer its best franchisees expansion opportunities and to find new growth vehicles. But neither goal has been achieved. "We cannot allow anything to distract our owner-operators, suppliers, and company people from maximizing the full potential of Brand McDonald's," said CEO Jim Cantalupo.

Source: R. Gibson (2003), "McDonald's May Exit from Ventures," *The Wall Street Journal* (November 10).

---

[27] See G. Stigler (1966), *The Theory of Price,* 3rd edition (Macmillan Press: London).

the financing business would be to increase the demand for automobiles by offering low-interest-rate loans to customers (recall Figure 8.1).[28] Contracting/transaction costs also were reduced because the consumer could fill out the loan application while purchasing the automobile. Today, communication systems, computers, and sophisticated credit-scoring systems make it easy to apply for a car loan from a lender over the phone or the Internet. This was true in neither 1919 nor 1959. Again there may have been other ways of organizing to achieve these economies (e.g., the automobile companies could have contracted to process loan applications for a bank). However, the costs of these organizational alternatives evidently were higher than combining the businesses within one company.

As another illustration, recall our example of PCs and printers. The companies benefited by coordinating the pricing of their products; another way of achieving this cooperation would be to merge the two firms.

Costs of Diversification

Although diversification has potential benefits, it also has potential costs. As firms grow, they often become bureaucratic and more expensive to manage. As we shall discuss in more detail in later chapters, it is difficult to devise compensation plans that motivate managers in large companies to behave like owners of smaller companies. Owners have a natural incentive to work hard and increase the value of their firms because they keep the profits of the firm, whereas salaried managers do not. If diversification occurs through the merger of two firms (as is often the case), it also can be quite expensive to develop common personnel, communication, information, and operating systems.

Management Implications

A Faulty Reason to Diversify

Some managers diversify to reduce earnings volatility. For example, the former CEO of Goodyear Tire justified diversification into the oil business because it was countercyclical to the tire industry. He reasoned that when gas prices were low, the company would do well in tires, since people would be driving more. When gas prices were high, the company might do poorly in tires but would do well in the oil business. Overall, earnings would be less volatile.

It is true that diversification can reduce earnings volatility. The problem with using this as a justification for diversification is that this reduction in volatility need not increase a firm's value. Shareholders (the owners of public companies) can diversify within their own investment portfolios at low cost. For example, it is easy for investors to purchase shares of both a tire company and an oil company. Through this diversification investors reduce return volatility on their overall portfolios. There is no reason

---

[28]Offering low-interest-rate loans benefited Ford and GM only if their cost of providing credit to customers was lower than the prevailing market price for credit (e.g., the loan market was noncompetitive or the auto company valued repossessed cars from bad loan customers more than other lenders). Otherwise, the companies could have obtained the same increase in sales by simply reducing the price of automobiles by the amount of the credit subsidy. (However, note that the credit subsidy might make it easier to price-discriminate between cash and credit customers. Low-interest rates might be used to hide price concessions to credit customers.) See S. Mian and C. Smith (1992), "Accounts Receivable Management Policy: Theory and Evidence," *Journal of Finance* 47, 169–200.

for investors to pay a premium for a company simply to reduce return volatility, since they can achieve this same objective by purchasing stock in the two separate companies.[29] At the same time the costs of integrating diverse businesses within the same firm can be significant.

When Does Diversification Create Value?

Related diversification occurs when the businesses serve common markets or use related technologies. For example, Disney Corporation operates theme parks, hotels, retail shops, and television stations. In each of these industries, Disney concentrates on employing its strong brand name to market family-oriented products. Their brand name reduces transaction costs to consumers in their search for quality products appropriate for children.

Net benefits are likely to be greater in related rather than unrelated diversification. If there is little interaction on either the production or demand side of the businesses, it is hard to envision where economies of scope might arise and by definition the two businesses would not produce complementary products.[30] An example of unrelated diversification is the decision by KinderCare Learning Centers, a day-care management firm, to enter the savings and loan business; it subsequently entered bankruptcy.

Value is increased only when the benefits of diversification are larger than the costs. There is a significant body of research on the value consequences of diversification.[31] For the most part, diversified firms have not performed well. Indeed, many of the large conglomerates during the 1980s, such as ITT and Tenneco, increased their values by divesting units (through sales and spinoffs) and refocusing on a more narrow line of businesses. Research documents that 55.7 percent of exchange-listed firms had a single business segment in 1988, compared to 38.1 percent in 1979. More importantly, the research shows that this increase in focus was associated with higher stock returns.[32] Diversification has been most effective in the case of related diversification where there are potential economies of scope and opportunities to promote complements.[33]

Who Captures the Gains from Diversification?

Even if diversification creates value, the owners of the diversified firm do not always capture this value. Again, it depends on whether the firm brings some special resource or team capability to the transaction. If it does not, the value is likely to be captured by another party due to competition. Consider the potential benefits of

---

[29]Although managers generally should be skeptical of the proposition that reductions in earnings volatility increase value, there are cases where the proposition is true, for example, if reducing earnings volatility reduces expected taxes or the costs associated with financial distress. See C. Smith and R. Stulz (1985), "The Determinants of Firms' Hedging Policies," *Journal of Financial and Quantitative Analysis* 20, 391–405.

[30]Some managers assert that their management skills are so good that they can create value in any business. Although this may be true, it is obvious that a given management team has limited capacity in the number of businesses the team can manage. Again, one might expect value to be maximized if the businesses are related.

[31]See J. Barney (1997), *Gaining and Sustaining a Competitive Advantage* (Addison-Wesley: Reading), 388–389, for a summary of this research. There are, however, examples of a few firms that appear to have created value through unrelated diversification.

[32]R. Comment and G. Jarrell (1995), "Corporate Focus and Stock Returns," *Journal of Financial Economics* 37, 67–87. This issue of the *Journal of Financial Economics* contains several other interesting articles on "corporate focus."

[33]There are some exceptions to this general finding. For example, General Electric is quite diversified and runs a variety of rather unrelated businesses. Nonetheless, it has performed extremely well.

MANAGERIAL APPLICATIONS

Diversification Problems at Xerox

During the 1980s Xerox diversified into financial services. The company had gained experience in finance through the leasing of its copy machines, and management believed that by acquiring firms in the financial sector, it could leverage this experience. In late 1982, Xerox purchased a property/casualty insurance company, Crum and Foster, for $1.6 billion. This acquisition was followed by other acquisitions in life insurance, real estate, and investment banking.

With minor exceptions, this diversification turned out to be a financial drain on Xerox. The economies of scope were not as great as had been hoped and problems in the financial businesses distracted top management from Xerox's main business—copiers. In the 1990s Xerox repositioned itself as the "document company" and sold its financial businesses to other companies. As of 2014, Xerox remained focused on providing business process and document solutions.

merging a television cable company with a long-distance telephone company. Suppose that there is one cable company with the rights to operate in a specific area, whereas there are several long-distance telephone companies. Competitive bidding among the telephone companies would imply that the phone company that valued it the most would get the cable company at a price equal to its value to the second-place phone company. This process would give most of the value gains to the owners of the cable company: They own the unique resource. Consistent with this example, substantial research documents many cases where target firms obtain most of the gains in corporate takeovers.[34]

Strategy Formulation

Developing and implementing strategies that increase a firm's value require an understanding of both the internal resources and capabilities of the firm and its external business environment.[35] Figure 8.5 displays these two factors.

Understanding Resources and Capabilities

An important first step in strategy development is understanding the firm's *resources and capabilities.* By resources and capabilities, we mean the firm's physical, human, and organizational capital. This includes the firm's hardware, software, and wetware; specifically, those activities which the firm can do better than other firms—its team production capabilities. It also is important to understand the opportunity costs of using these assets within the firm. For example, how much would they be worth if they were sold to other firms?

Understanding the Environment

As depicted in Figure 8.5, important factors in the business environment include the firm's *markets* (both input and output), *technology* (production, information, and

---

[34]See G. Jarrell, J. Brickley, and J. Netter (1988), "The Market for Corporate Control: The Empirical Evidence since 1980," *Journal of Economic Perspectives* 2, 49–68, for a summary of this research. Note, however, that it is more difficult to identify gains to acquiring firms than acquired firms: 1) Acquiring firms are generally much larger than acquired firms so even if merger gains were split evenly, they would be a much smaller percentage change in value of the acquirer, and 2) acquirers frequently have merger programs and are involved in a series of acquisitions, thus expected merger gains are capitalized into the acquiring firm's stock price.

[35]A variety of approaches to strategic management are discussed in the strategy literature. The framework outlined in this section is most consistent with the "strengths, weaknesses, opportunities, and threats" approach. See J. Barney (1997), *Gaining and Sustaining a Competitive Advantage* (Addison-Wesley: Reading).

Figure 8.5 Framework for Strategic Planning

Members of the management team should have a good understanding of their firm's internal resources and capabilities before they modify their strategies. They also should understand their external business environment. The objective is to use this knowledge to discover ways of creating and capturing value.

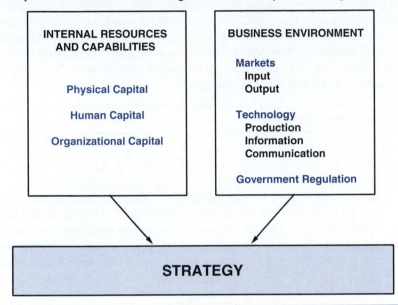

communications), and *government regulation.* Effective managers monitor the business environment to keep abreast of new developments in each of these areas.

Referring to Figure 8.1, managers *must* understand the business environment to identify opportunities for value creation. For example, what technological opportunities exist to reduce costs? It would be a poor decision to invest in an expensive technology to lower costs, if forecasted technological innovations are expected to make the investment obsolete soon. What opportunities exist to reduce consumer or producer transaction costs? Managers *must* have a detailed understanding of how transactions take place in the marketplace to discover ways of reducing transaction costs. What opportunities exist for improving consumer products? Are there ways of promoting complementary products? Are there potential industries in which the firm could leverage its resources and capabilities? Are there opportunities to create value through cooperating with other firms?

An understanding of the firm's environment also is important for identifying opportunities for, as well as threats to, capturing value. For example, what opportunities are there to block entry or the development of substitutes? What threats loom from potential substitutes, buyer power, supplier power, and industry rivalry?

Combining Environmental and Internal Analyses

Most resources and capabilities are finite—choices must be made. For example, firms have limited production capacity and human resources. Thus, they face trade-offs in deciding how to use these resources and in deciding whether it is worth the

---

MANAGERIAL APPLICATIONS

A Retail Success Story and Luck

IKEA, one of few retailers that has flourished on foreign soil, had 233 stores in 34 countries selling $14.8 billion a year worth of furniture in 2005. Its strategy is that well-designed furniture can be inexpensive without being ugly. IKEA entered international commerce by chance. Started in Sweden in the 1960s, local Swedish retailers pressured Swedish manufacturers to cut off supplies to the upstart IKEA. In response, IKEA turned to Poland for supplies and was surprised to find that it could buy well-crafted furniture more cheaply. This transformed IKEA into thinking about foreign suppliers and retail markets. The firm now has spread to Asia and North America. IKEA is a very patient firm. While trying to figure out how to please U.S. shoppers, IKEA absorbed losses for years. They "had to learn that Americans expected jumbo beds and didn't think in centimeters."

Source: J. Hagerty (1999), "How to Assemble a Retail Success Story," *The Wall Street Journal* (September 9), A24; K. Capell (2006), "IKEA's New Plan for Japan," *BusinessWeek* (April 26).

---

investment to supplement them. Also managers must decide whether it is best to use their marketable assets within the firm or whether to sell them to other firms. These strategic choices require managers to combine environmental and internal analyses: They must understand both their internal strengths and weaknesses, as well as the threats from and opportunities within their business environment. Typically, strategies do not remain constant, but evolve through time. It usually is important for managers to consider how other economic agents in the business environment will react to their strategic decisions (e.g., rival firms, suppliers, and buyers). In Chapter 9 we examine this issue in detail.

In deciding how best to use special resources and capabilities, it is important to be forward-looking. Sometimes it is more profitable to invest in complementary resources and capabilities that allow the firm to exploit its unique position better in the future. For example, it might have been profitable for Sharp to invest in acquiring complementary knowledge about computers and other technologies to supplement the firm's skills in LCDs.

Strategy and Organizational Architecture

To be successful, a company must have not only a good strategy, but also an appropriate architecture. Ultimately, both strategy and organizational architecture are key determinants of value. Chapters 11–17 of the book presume that the strategy of a firm has been determined and present a detailed analysis of how a firm's environment and strategy influence its organizational architecture. This approach is reasonable because the organizational design often is based on what the firm wants to do strategically. For example, if a firm adopts a strategy to react quickly to customer demands, it will probably have to design a decentralized decision system with accompanying performance evaluation and reward systems to motivate productive decisions. Figure 8.5, however, emphasizes that the effects are not all in one direction. A firm's architecture also can influence its strategy—it is an important part of the firm's internal resources. For example, if the firm has a well-functioning, decentralized decision-making system, it is more likely to enter markets for which this type of organizational design is well suited.

ANALYZING MANAGERIAL DECISIONS: *Walmart.com*

Conventional wisdom holds that to succeed in electronic commerce, you have to get in early. But in late 1999, Walmart decided to challenge that most sacred of web rules. After several years of tinkering with its website, watching while others broke new Internet ground, the retailing giant was ready to flex some cyber muscle. Up to that point, Walmart.com had realized modest success online, ranking 43rd among Internet shopping sites. It trailed web pioneers like eBay and Buy.com. In May 1999, Amazon.com greeted almost 10 million online visitors; Walmart.com saw only 801,000. For 1999, analysts expected Walmart's e-commerce activities to produce sales of less than $50 million out of the company's total sales of $157 billion.

Walmart faced increasing direct competition from Amazon.com. In July 1999, Amazon announced its expansion from books, music, and videos into toys and consumer electronics. Walmart already was a powerhouse in these product categories through its traditional stores. It announced that it would offer products from all 25 categories carried in a typical Walmart discount store. Moreover, it expected to offer a broader array of higher-priced items than its traditional stores—for instance, DVD players and digital cameras. It also enabled customers to return products ordered online to any of Walmart's 2,451 U.S. discount stores. Like Amazon, it planned to provide tailored online specials to match the shopping habits of its repeat customers.

The company announced plans to expand its online store offerings before the end of 1999 to match more closely the breadth of its traditional outlets. To facilitate this expansion, Walmart penned deals with Fingerhut Business Services and Books-a-Million. Both had expertise in distributing individual orders directly to customers' homes—quite a different set of skills from bulk shipments, which had been Walmart's forte.

Demographic shifts occurring in cyberspace offered the potential to help Walmart. Back in 1999 Jupiter Communication projected e-retailing to grow from approximately $12 billion in 1999 to an estimated $41 billion in 2002. Much of this expansion would be concentrated in Walmart's existing lower- and middle-class customer base. Jupiter analyst Kenneth R. Gasser noted, "Internet users are increasingly coming to resemble the population at large."

By 2005, Walmart.com had logged $1 billion of Internet sales. However, the world's largest retailer only ranked about 13th in Internet sales while Amazon.com had sales of over $10 billion. About 500 million total visitors clicked on Walmart.com in 2005, and the company predicted this to increase to 700 million in 2006. But, its online sales still only accounted for about 1 percent of Walmart's annual sales.

In January 2007, Walmart.com launched Soundcheck, an original series of musical performances that feature punk pop and rock bands to increase its digital music offerings. In March 2007, Walmart.com announced "Site to Store" where Walmart.com shoppers can purchase online and have orders delivered to their local store for free. By July, Site to Store sales more than doubled since its March rollout, and about 90 percent of participating stores had at least one Site to Store order within the first 48 hours of service activation. In January 2008, only 11 months after initiating its movie download service, Walmart.com quietly dropped this service because Hewlett-Packard Co. stopped providing the application that allowed shoppers to purchase and download videos such as movies and TV shows.

Placing yourself back in 1999, answer the following questions in a well-developed discussion:

1. What is the impact of Walmart.com on customer-borne transaction costs?
2. Do you think that Walmart.com is likely to create additional value?
3. Is it likely that Walmart will capture any value created by Walmart.com?
4. Should Walmart have pursued e-commerce more aggressively sooner?
5. What do you think the potential impact of Walmart.com will be on the company's efforts to expand internationally?

6. In November 2007, Walmart.com announced that it wants to be "the most visited, most valued online retail site." Suppose you were hired by an outside consulting firm to evaluate Walmart.com's potential to achieve this goal. Write a short report listing those factors that will enhance and those factors that will impede Walmart.com's ability to achieve the goal of "the most visited, most valued online retail site."

Source: W. Zellner (1999), "When Wal-Mart Flexes Its Cybermuscles," *BusinessWeek* (July 26), 82; S. Murphy (2007), "The Walmart.com Way," *Chain Store Age* (July), 80; www.internetretailer.com; and www.today.msnbc.msn.com/id/21940867.

Can All Firms Capture Value?

Consultants often suggest that any firm can develop a strategy that produces economic profits, even if it does not begin with unique resources or team capabilities. What is necessary is that the manager be a "visionary" and make sound investments in developing the skills and capabilities to compete successfully in the future. (Of course, for a fee these gurus would be happy to help the manager accomplish this objective.)

Basic economics suggests that these consultants are wrong. Even if a manager is exceptional at predicting the future and seeing what resources and capabilities are important, abnormal profits will not be earned on a systematic basis so long as there are other managers who follow the same strategy.[36] Competition will bid up prices of the required resources in the factor markets and bid down prices in the output markets. As in any competitive market in equilibrium, the expected outcome is a normal rate of return—not sustained abnormal performance.

Although some managers may be better at systematically predicting the future, luck plays a key role in the acquisition of valuable resources. Under this view, many firms invest in projects that before the fact are expected to yield normal returns. These firms take somewhat different paths in their investment strategies, development of internal processes, hiring decisions, and so on. As time passes and environments change, some firms find themselves with superior resources and team capabilities, whereas others do not. It takes managerial talent to identify whether or not the firm has valuable resources and capabilities and to decide how best to use them to maximize returns. Managers easily might think they have unique resources and capabilities when in fact they do not.[37]

Firms without special resources or capabilities at best can expect to earn a normal rate of return on their investment. Firms whose resources and capabilities do not fit the changed environment should not expect to earn a normal rate of return and might prepare to go out of business.[38] In a competitive environment, it can take significant managerial effort and talent (devoted to decisions like choosing products as well as producing and marketing them efficiently) just to earn a normal return.

[36]Even if no other manager were to have this skill, it still would not be clear that the firm would capture the gains: It is the manager who owns this unique resource.

[37]See M. Ryall (1998), "When Competencies Are Not Core: Self-Confirming Theories and the Destruction of Firm Value," working paper, University of Rochester.

[38]H. Kim and J. Schatzberg (1987), "Voluntary Corporate Liquidations," *Journal of Financial Economics* 19, 311–328. This article documents that, on average, shareholders incur significant financial gains around the announcements of voluntary liquidations. Apparently, the stock market is unsure that managers will make the tough decision to liquidate poorly performing firms and is happily surprised when liquidation announcements are made.

Summary

Strategy refers to the general policies that managers employ to generate value. Rather than focus on operational detail, a firm's strategy addresses broad, long-term issues facing the firm. Ultimately, along with its organizational architecture, strategy is a key determinant of the success or failure of the enterprise.

The ultimate objective of strategic decision making is to realize sustained profits. To achieve this objective, managers must devise ways to *create and capture value*. An essential first step in generating profits is discovering ways to create value. There are at least four general ways that managers can increase value: (1) They can take actions to lower production costs or producer transaction costs. (2) Managers can implement policies to reduce consumer transaction costs. (3) They can adopt strategies to increase demand. Demand might be increased by taking actions to increase perceived quality, lower the price of complements, or increase the price of substitutes. (4) They can devise new products or services. Sometimes more value is created by cooperating with firms than by competing against them. Successful firms find ways to convert ideas and knowledge in their employees' *wetware* into *software*—formulas and recipes for creating value.

The discovery of better ways to use existing resources drives much of the value that firms create. For example, the value created by improved computer technology has not come from the discovery of new raw materials or resources, but by using existing resources more efficiently. Firms face an essentially unlimited set of opportunities to create better "instructions, formulas, recipes, and methods" for making improved products at lower cost. New opportunities are likely to emerge as technology continues to evolve.

Creating value is a necessary first step in making profits. It is also necessary to capture value. A firm may have reduced its transaction/production costs or increased its consumer demand, but if other firms copy these changes quickly and enter the market, the competition will eliminate the profits. Chapter 6 indicates that the potential for firms to capture value increases with *market power*. Sometimes it also is possible to capture value without market power if the firm has *superior factors of production* that allow it to be more productive than competitors.

The existence of effective *entry barriers* is required for market power. Entry barriers exist when it is difficult or uneconomic for a would-be entrant to replicate the position of industry incumbents. The existence of barriers, however, is no guarantee of market power or economic profits. At least four other factors are important: The *degree of rivalry within the industry, threat of substitutes, buyer power,* and *supplier power.*

Both human as well as physical assets vary in productivity. If an asset allows the firm to make a profit because of its superior productivity, other firms will compete for this resource and bid up its price. Thus, in a well-functioning market, gains from superior productivity go to the responsible asset. For example, if a firm owns a unique piece of equipment, its price will be bid up to reflect its superior productivity. The firm itself does not always have to use such assets to realize its values. It might earn more profits by selling or leasing the assets to other firms.

Competition tends to take a differentiated asset to its highest valued use, but at a market price that reflects its *second-highest valued* use. Because of the interdependencies among employees and assets, the value of the inputs as a *team* sometimes can be greater than the sum of their values if each were employed at their next best uses across other firms. Thus, it is possible that the overall firm will be more valuable than the sum of its parts. We characterize such a firm as having *team production capabilities.* A firm can maintain team production advantages only when competing firms cannot assemble teams that are equally productive. Firms develop different team capabilities because they have different histories and development paths.

The business environment is constantly evolving with new technological developments, changes in consumer tastes, new business concepts, new firms, and so on. Given these changes, it is unlikely that any competitive advantage will last forever.

Some firms concentrate on a single major business, but many large firms engage in multiple businesses: They are at least partially diversified. *Economies of scope* provide the primary reason why diversification might enhance value. In addition, combining businesses in the same firm can *promote complementary products*. Although diversification has potential benefits, it also has potential costs. As firms grow, they often become bureaucratic and more costly to manage. If diversification occurs through the merger of two firms (as often is the case) it also can be quite expensive to develop common personnel, communication, information, and operating systems.

Some managers diversify to reduce earnings volatility. This often is a poor reason to diversify because shareholders can diversify on their own account simply by owning the shares of multiple companies. *Related diversification* occurs when the businesses use related technologies or serve common markets. The net benefits are likely to be greater in related rather than in unrelated diversification. For the most part, highly diversified firms have not performed well. Diversification has been most effective in the case of related diversification where there are potential economies of scope and opportunities to promote complements. Even if diversification creates value, the owners of the diversified firm do not always capture this value. Again, it depends on whether the firm brings some special resource or team capability to the transaction. Historically, most of the gains in corporate acquisitions go to the shareholders of target firms.

Developing and implementing strategies that increase a firm's value require an understanding of both the internal resources and capabilities of the firm and the external business environment. A firm's *resources and capabilities* include its physical, human, and organizational capital. Important factors in the business environment include the firm's *markets* (input and output), *technology* (production, information, and communications), and *government regulation*. Managers monitor the external environment to identify threats and opportunities for creating and capturing value.

Most resources and capabilities are finite—choices have to be made. To make optimal choices, managers must consider the firm's resources and capabilities jointly, as well as threats and opportunities within the external business environment. Ultimately, the firm's strategy, along with its organizational architecture, is a key determinant of a firm's value.

Strategy consultants often suggest that all firms can develop strategies that deliver systematic economic profits even if they do not begin with unique resources or team capabilities. Basic economics suggests that this claim is false. Even if a manager were good at predicting the future and seeing what resources and capabilities were important, abnormal profits would not be earned on a systematic basis so long as a sufficient number of other managers adopt the same strategies. If multiple managers adopt the same strategy, there will be competition in the output markets as well as in input markets to obtain the necessary resources and capabilities. As in any competitive market, the expected equilibrium outcome is a normal rate of return—not sustained abnormal performance. Firms whose resources and capabilities do not fit the changed environment will not expect to earn a normal rate of return; they should prepare to go out of business.

Suggested Readings	D. Besanko, D. Dranove, S. Schaefer and M. Shanley (2012), *Economics of Strategy* (Wiley: New York).

Suggested Readings

D. Besanko, D. Dranove, S. Schaefer and M. Shanley (2012), *Economics of Strategy* (Wiley: New York).

A. Brandenburger and B. Nalebuff (1996), *Co-opetition* (Doubleday: New York).

D. Collis and C. Montgomery (1995), "Competing on Resources: Strategy in the 1990s," *Harvard Business Review,* 118–128.

M. Porter (1980), *Competitive Strategy* (Free Press: New York).

P. Romer (1998), "Bank of America Roundtable on the Software Revolution: Achieving Growth by Managing Intangibles," *Journal of Applied Corporate Finance* 11(2): 8–27.

Self-Evaluation Problems

8-1. Racket Sports Inc. has invented a new long-lasting tennis ball, but only if the players use a new type of string in their rackets. The racket string is produced by the Strings and Things Company. The respective prices for the balls and strings are P_B and P_S. The marginal cost of producing either product is $5. Demand for each product is

$$Q = 20 - (P_B + P_S) \qquad \text{when } (P_B + P_S) \text{ less than 20 or less, 0, otherwise}$$

How will the two companies price the products if they do not cooperate? What are the resulting quantities and profits? What are the prices, quantities, and profits if the two companies price cooperatively? Explain why there is a difference.

8-2. Opportunity Cost and Competitive Advantage

The average price of jet fuel in March 2008 was $3.10 per gallon. In 2000 the price was only $0.87 per gallon. During this time period, Southwest Airlines hedged the price of fuel in financial markets. The hedge contracts helped "lock" Southwest Airlines into lower fuel prices—as the price of fuel increased, so did the value of their financial contracts. Roughly speaking, if the price of fuel increased at $1.00 per gallon, the financial contracts paid Southwest Airlines $1.00 per gallon, which effectively allowed them to purchase fuel at the price before the increase. Leading financial analysts argued that these hedges gave Southwest Airlines a competitive advantage over airline companies that had not hedged fuel prices. To quote one,

> *Southwest Airlines has a competitive advantage in the Texas market because of its fuel hedges. Its fuel costs only a $1.00 per gallon, while other airlines are paying $3.00. We do not see how these other airlines can continue to compete with Southwest on most of its routes.*

Do you agree with the analyst's statement? Explain.

Solutions to Self-Evaluation Problems

8-1. If the two companies do not cooperate in setting prices, each will seek to maximize its individual profits, given its expectation about the other firm's price. In this case, Racket Sports will view its demand curve as:

$$P_B = (20 - P_S^*) - Q$$

while Strings and Things will view its demand curve as:

$$P_S = (20 - P_B^*) - Q$$

where P_B^* and P_S^* represent the expectations about the other firm's price. Each firm will maximize its profits by setting MR = MC ($5 in this problem).

Racket Sports:	$(20 - P_S^*) - 2Q = 5$
Strings and Things:	$(20 - P_B^*) - 2Q = 5$

Substitute $Q = 20 - (P_B + P_S)$ and rearranging the terms yields the following two equations:

$$(20 - P_S^*) - 2[20 - (P_B + P_S)] = 5$$
$$(20 - P_B^*) - 2[20 - (P_B + P_S)] = 5$$

The equilibrium consists of the two prices that simultaneously solve these two equations. Note that in this problem the two firms face identical problems (they face the same expected demand curve and marginal cost). Thus in equilibrium, they will choose the same prices, $P_S^* = P_B^* = P^*$. Substituting and solving one of the equations:

$$(20 - P^*) - 2\,[20 - (P^* + P^*)] = 5$$
$$3P^* = 25$$
$$P^* = \$8.33$$

Each firm sells a total of $Q = 20 - (8.33 + 8.33) = 3.33$ units. The profit margin on each unit is $\$8.33 - \$5 = \$3.33$. The total profits per firm are $\$11.11$ ($9/3 \times 9/3$) and combined profits of $\$22.22$.

   If the two firms cooperate they will price the two products to maximize combined profits. To maximize combined profits, the companies will jointly set marginal revenue equal to marginal cost using the combined demand curve $P_C = 20 - Q$ and marginal cost $- \$10$, where $P_C =$ the combined price of $(P_B + P_S)$:

$$20 - 2Q = \$10$$

They sell 5 units at a combined price of $\$15$ (e.g., $P_S^* = P_B^* = \$7.50$) for a combined profit of $\$25 \,[= 5 \times (\$15 - \$10)]$. When the firms price independently, they do not consider the negative effect that their higher prices have on the other's profit. Pricing cooperatively, they take this interaction into account.

8–2.   The analyst's comment is not consistent with sound economic analysis. Southwest makes money on its financial contracts when fuel prices increase. This revenue helps to increase its profits relative to the profits of airline companies that do not have similar hedging contracts. However, Southwest still faces the same opportunity cost for fuel as other airlines—the market price. In deciding whether or not to fly a particular route, Southwest should consider the market price of fuel in its profit forecasts. It makes money on the financial contracts whether it flies the route or not. The marginal cost for fuel is the current market price. Either Southwest has to purchase additional fuel in the market to fly the route or use fuel that it has in inventory that could be sold to other airlines at the market price. Either way the opportunity cost of fuel is the current market price.

Review Questions

8–1.   Choose a company that markets computer products over the Internet (e.g., through a Web search). In what ways does the company create value? Is it likely to capture much of this value? Explain.

8–2.   Airbus and Boeing are two major producers of jumbo jets. Are these firms guaranteed to make high profits since there are only two large firms in the industry? Explain.

8–3.   The Watts Brewing Company owns valuable water rights that allow it to produce better beer than competitors. The company sells its beer at a premium and reports a large profit each year. Is this firm necessarily making economic profits? Explain.

8–4.   What are team capabilities? Give examples of firms that appear to have them.

8–5.   Sun Resorts has a hotel on a Caribbean Island. It recently spent money to lobby the government to build a better airport and expand air service. Why did they do this? Do you think that Sun Resorts cares about how many airlines will serve the island? Explain.

8–6.   Evaluate the following statement: "Business is war. Never consort with the enemy."

8–7.   The Long-Drive Golf Company manufactures a new line of golf clubs. The Cushion Bag Company makes a special golf bag that protects the delicate shafts on these clubs. The respective prices are P_c and P_b for the clubs and bags. The marginal cost for producing either product is 100. Demand for each product is

$$Q = 1{,}000 - (P_c + P_b) \qquad \text{when } P_c + P_b \text{ is 1,000 or less, 0, otherwise}$$

How will the two companies price the products if they do not cooperate? What are the resulting quantities and profits? What are the prices, quantities, and profits if the two companies price cooperatively? Explain why there is a difference.

8–8. One CEO justified the merger of his soft-drink company with a machine tool company in the following manner: "This is a great merger. First the products are unrelated. Thus our company's earnings volatility is likely to decrease. Second, our management team has proved that we are better managers than the former management team of the tool company, and thus we are likely to discover new ways to create and capture value within the tool company." Evaluate this rationale.

8–9. Pepsi produces Fritos and Lays potato chips in addition to its basic soft-drink products. Discuss potential ways that this business combination might increase value.

8–10. The Strippling Drug Company has just obtained an important patent for a new drug that increases male virility and cures male pattern baldness at the same time. Does this imply that Strippling has a competitive advantage in producing the drug? Explain.

chapter 9

Economics of Strategy: Game Theory

LEARNING OBJECTIVES

1. Define game theory.
2. Understand simple diagrams that depict games in strategic (normal) form.
3. Define dominant strategy.
4. Explain the economics of a prisoner's dilemma and provide examples of how these dilemmas can arise within firms.
5. Determine (pure strategy) Nash equilibria in simple two-person games.
6. Define mixed strategy and describe why managers might sometimes choose to use one.
7. Understand simple diagrams that depict sequential games in extensive form.
8. Apply backward induction to find the equilibrium in two-person sequential games.
9. Define first-mover advantage.
10. Describe the key managerial insights obtained from game theory.

The Boeing Company and Airbus Industrie (a consortium of four European firms) manufacture most of the world's large commercial jetliners.[1] In 2003 Airbus delivered more jetliners than Boeing for the first time in its 34-year history. With just two major companies in the market, one might expect that the firms would cooperate regularly, avoiding competition in order to increase prices and profits. In actuality, these companies frequently compete quite aggressively.

The choice between cooperation and aggressive competition is determined in part by the nature of the environment. For example, cooperation is more likely in circumstances where each firm is near capacity. But in 2001, Airbus orders had fallen by 28 percent and Boeing by 45 percent. These reductions mirrored the growing crisis in the airline industry. Airline losses were soaring in the face of declining demand for air travel in response to the combination of the slowdown in the global economy and the September 11, 2001, terrorist attacks. This was recognized in Morgan Stanley's August 12, 2002, research report on Boeing. It suggests "an already tough pricing environment gets

---

[1]Details for this example are from A. Bryant (1997), "The $1 Trillion Dogfight," *New York Times* (March 23), 3.1; M. Freudenheim and J. Tagliabue (1998), "Regulators Investigating Price Increases by Boeing and Airbus," *New York Times* (November 27), C.1; and D. Michaels (2004), "Airbus Zooms Past Boeing, but Strong Euro Poses a Threat," *The Wall Street Journal* (January 16), A9; and S. DuBois (2013), "Boeing vs. Airbus: Can't We All Just Get Along?" *Fortune Magazine* (March 19).

tougher if Airbus needs to fill slots available." Competition has continued to be intense in subsequent years. In 2013, Airbus and Boeing waged a "brutal price war to access emerging markets and to roll out new aircraft." In the 10-year period from 2004 to 2013, Boeing received 8,428 orders, while delivering, 4,458 planes, compared to Airbus that had 8,933 orders and 4,834 deliveries.

Many of the world's markets are like the commercial aircraft industry in that there are a few large firms who are the major players. Examples include soft drinks (Coke and Pepsi), U.S. domestic airlines (American, United, and Delta), copy machines (Canon and Xerox), candy (Hershey and Mars), and smartphones (Apple and Samsung). Even small firms often compete with an identifiable set of rivals and can act as the major players within a given market area. Consider two competing gasoline stations at an expressway interchange.

In this type of market, it generally is important for managers to consider rivals' responses when making major decisions. For example, part of Airbus' marketing plan in the late 1990s was to be overtly negative toward Boeing. One Airbus brochure depicted the Boeing 777 as an aging stretch limousine painted like a yellow taxicab, while the Airbus craft was pictured as a Mercedes luxury sedan. In another ad, Airbus pointed out that the Boeing 737 entered service in 1968, the same year Richard Nixon first was elected president of the United States. Perhaps not surprisingly, Boeing produced negative advertisements of its own. In choosing its advertising policy, Airbus presumably had to consider whether a negative campaign would be value-maximizing given Boeing's likely response. Similarly, Boeing had to consider Airbus' response in choosing its actions.

Game theory provides a useful set of tools for managers to use when considering rival responses in decision making. This chapter presents a more detailed discussion of the basic theory and shows how managers might use these tools in strategic decision making. This analysis also provides managers with a richer understanding of competition within different market settings. For example, it provides insights into why there is fierce competition in some concentrated industries (such as commercial aircraft), whereas in others the competition is more benign. Although we focus primarily on interactions among rival firms in product markets, these concepts also are useful to managers when dealing with other parties, such as suppliers, employees, or government officials.

Game Theory

Game theory is concerned with the general analysis of strategic interaction.[2] It focuses on optimal decision making when all decision agents are presumed to be rational, with each attempting to anticipate the likely actions and reactions of its

---

[2]The terms *strategy* and *strategic* are used in at least three related yet slightly different ways in the economics literature. In all three contexts, the decision maker is assumed to interact with others in the environment. Thus the optimal decision is affected by the actions of others. The focus of the analysis, however, varies among the three uses. First, the terms are employed to refer to the general policies that managers use to generate profits. The traditional strategy literature tends to use the terms within this context (e.g., what businesses should the firm be in and how should they compete?). Even though rival responses are in the background in this literature, they are not explicitly treated in the analysis. Second, the terms are used to refer more specifically to decision-making contexts where it is essential for managers to consider the behavior of identifiable rivals in choosing their policies (e.g., in setting prices in an industry with a few large firms). This is the primary use in this chapter. Third, they also are used in a more formal sense in game theory to describe the players' actions in a given game (e.g., to describe a player's "strategy" in playing a game). We introduce this usage and related concepts in this chapter.

ACADEMIC APPLICATIONS

Game Theorists Win the Nobel Prize

The Nobel Prize for Economics (or, more precisely, The Bank of Sweden Prize in Economic Sciences in Memory of Alfred Nobel) is the world's most prestigious award for contributions to the field of economics. It is awarded annually by the Royal Swedish Academy of Sciences. The prize consists of a gold medal, a diploma bearing a citation, and a sum of money—$1.3 million in recent years. It represents the ultimate recognition by one's peers.

In 1994, John Harsanyi, John Nash, and Reinhard Selten won the prize "for their pioneering analysis of the theory of noncooperative games." And again in 2005, game theorists Robert Aumann and Thomas Schelling received the prize. Their contributions have had an important impact not only on theoretical economics, but also on business practice. Firms hire game theorists as consultants in formulating strategic decisions (e.g., in government auctions, corporate takeovers, pricing, labor negotiations, and competitive positioning). Several best-selling business books have illustrated how game theory can be used in everyday business decisions. Game theory now is being taught within most major business schools. And for those who do not want to take a course or read a book, the movie *A Beautiful Mind*—based on Sylvia Nasser's award-winning biography of John Nash—won three Oscars in 2001, including Best Picture. (Note, however, that the movie's illustration of a Nash equilibrium is fundamentally flawed.)

rivals.[3] Although it began as a set of methods to analyze parlor games, this theory has evolved to the point where it is applied to study a wide variety of strategic interactions ranging from politics to competitive strategy. In this chapter, we introduce its basic elements and apply them in the context of managerial decision making.

Sound managerial decision making often requires "putting yourself behind your rivals' desk." Assuming rivals are rational and acting in their self-interest, what decisions are they likely to make and how are they likely to respond to your actions? A complicating factor is that rivals' optimal choices typically will depend on their expectations of what you will do; their expectations, in turn, depend on their assessments of your expectations about them. This type of circularity or recursive thinking might appear to make the overall problem completely intractable. Yet, this situation is precisely where game theory is most useful.

Strategic interactions can take a variety of forms and involve many players who choose among a variety of potential actions. In this chapter, we limit ourselves to simple two-player, two-action cases. This limitation allows us to depict strategic problems using convenient diagrams. The fundamental intuition and concepts developed in these basic cases readily extend to multiple players and multiple actions. Some problems involve simultaneous decisions by rivals, whereas others involve sequential choices. We begin by examining strategic problems involving simultaneous choices. Later, we consider sequential problems. In some cases, interaction is expected to be repeated; in others, it is not. Throughout most of this chapter, we focus on problems where the interaction is not expected to be repeated. Toward the end of the chapter—and in the appendix—we consider implications of repeated interaction.

---

[3]Game theory is divided into two branches. In *cooperative games,* players can negotiate binding contracts that allow them to plan and implement joint strategies. In this chapter, we focus on *noncooperative games,* where negotiation and enforcement of binding contracts is not possible. This type of game theory generally is more useful for analyzing managerial decision making.

Figure 9.1   Strategic Form

In this case, Boeing and Airbus individually choose and simultaneously submit a bid price for 10 planes. They can submit either a high price or a low price. If one company bids high and the other bids low, the order goes to the low bidder; if both companies submit the same bid, they split the order. This diagram presents the possible profits from the interaction in strategic form (normal form). Each cell presents the payoffs (in millions of dollars) of a pair of decisions. The entry on the lower right of each cell is the payoff for Airbus, whereas the entry on the upper left is for Boeing. Both firms have a dominant strategy (shaded cell)—submit a low price.

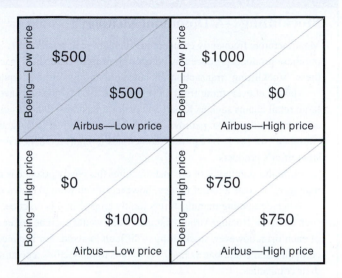

Simultaneous-Move, Nonrepeated Interaction

In strategic problems that involve *simultaneous moves,* rivals must make decisions without knowledge of the decisions made by their competitors. *Nonrepeated* means that the interaction is presumed to occur only once.[4] As an example, suppose that Boeing and Airbus are asked to submit sealed bids on the price of 10 jet airliners to a foreign national airline. Both companies doubt that they will compete in similar ways in the future. Both companies can submit either a high price or a low price. If one company bids high and the other bids low, the order goes to the low bidder; if both companies submit the same bid, they split the order. Each firm has the capacity to build all 10 airplanes.

Analyzing the Payoffs

Both companies privately submit their bids at the same time. The resulting payoffs (profits expressed in millions of dollars) depend on both firms' choices; they are displayed in Figure 9.1. This type of diagram presents the potential payoffs from the interaction in what is called *strategic form* (also called *normal form*). Each cell presents the payoffs in millions of dollars for a pair of decisions. The entry on the lower right of each cell is the profit for Airbus, and the entry on the upper left is for Boeing.[5]

---

[4]Many competitive situations have a logical sequencing of events (one company sets a price and others react) and repeat interaction. By starting with simple simultaneous, nonrepeated games, we can more easily explain the basic analytic tools used in game theory. The basic insights from this analysis can generally be extended to more complex situations.

[5]This diagram has two primary columns and two rows. Boeing is the row firm in the sense that its strategies vary between the two rows. Airbus is the column firm in that its strategies vary across columns. We place the payoff to the row firm at the upper left of the cell and the payoff to the column firm in the lower right. An alternative way to picture the payoffs is a simpler 2 × 2 table with each row representing one of Boeing's potential actions and each column representing one of Airbus' potential actions. The entries in each cell of the table would list the payoff to Boeing and to Airbus, respectively (e.g., 100, 0). Although this alternative is more common (possibly because it is easier to type), students seem to find diagrams like 9.1 easier to read. Both diagrams display the same information.

MANAGERIAL APPLICATIONS

Stocklifting—A Dominant Strategy?

Manufacturers frequently compete for shelf space in retail stores. Some spend hundreds of thousands of dollars to purchase products produced by competing firms to clear shelf space for their products. The merchandise, purchased in these "stocklifting" transactions, is later sold through product liquidators at large losses.

Makers of everything from bicycle chains to party napkins have lifted truckloads of competitors' products from large retail chains such as Kmart and major drugstores. Other stocklifting examples include cell phones, power adapters, leather cases, pet toys, humidifiers, flashlights, faucets, and glue. The stocklifted merchandise is subsequently "dumped" for resale by faraway (sometimes foreign) retailers. The purpose in each case is to clear shelf space for the stocklifter's products.

From the standpoint of the manufacturer this costly practice is a potentially dominant strategy. To quote one product manager, "It costs a ton of money; however, if you want to land a major retail account, you're going to have to do it."

When competing manufacturers jointly engage in this practice, they can find themselves in a "rivals' dilemma" such as in our Boeing/Airbus example: They would each be better off if no one stocklifted. Given the private incentives of each firm, however, stocklifting is difficult to avoid. For instance, after purchasing stocklifted products from a company, some liquidators make sales calls to the victims, encouraging them to "return the favor" by working with their companies.

Dominant Strategies

A *dominant strategy* exists when it is optimal for a firm to choose that strategy no matter what its rival does. In Figure 9.1, both firms have a dominant strategy—submit the low price. To illustrate, consider Boeing's position. If Airbus submits a high price (the right column), Boeing captures the entire order by submitting a low price. The resulting payoff of $1 billion is higher than the payoff of $750 million if both firms price high and split the order. If Airbus submits a low price (the left column), Boeing is clearly better off to price low and split the order. Its alternative is to price high and sell no planes. The same logic holds for Airbus. Given these strong incentives, the likely outcome is for both firms to submit a low price. Note that the firms would be better off if they jointly were to submit high prices. But this outcome is unlikely without repeated interactions. This problem has the same structure as the *prisoners' dilemma* introduced in Chapter 6—in this context, we might call it the *rivals' dilemma.* As we shall see, a "cooperative" outcome where both firms submit high prices without explicit collusion is more likely if their interaction is expected to be repeated.

This logic helps explain why Boeing and Airbus frequently compete aggressively on price. Airline orders frequently are measured in billions of dollars, so each sale is important. Further, customers (normally commercial airline companies) have economic incentives to deal with a single major supplier of aircraft since this policy reduces the required inventory of spare parts, technician training (maintenance personnel work only on one make of plane), and so on.[6] Thus if Boeing or Airbus lose an order, it implies the loss of potential future orders as well. Just as in Figure 9.1 the companies have strong economic incentives to submit low bids to capture orders.

Boeing and Airbus have particularly strong incentives to compete on price because each firm has the capacity to produce additional output. Boeing has stated that

---

[6]Given these considerations, our assumption that if the bids are the same, the order is split between Boeing and Airbus should be questioned. Yet, if the buyer flips a coin and gives all the order to the lucky bidder whenever the bids are equal, then the *expected* payoffs are the same as in Figure 9.1.

it wants to win two-thirds of all new orders (substantially above its current level), whereas Airbus wants to win about 50 percent (approximately equal to its current level). These conflicting goals promote price competition as each firm tries to take orders from the other. If the rivals faced tighter capacity constraints, to engage in aggressive price competition. For instance, in our simplified example, a firm clearly would not want to lower the price to capture the full order if it lacked the capacity to produce all 10 planes.

Nash Equilibrium Revisited

Firms do not always have dominant strategies. For instance, suppose in our example that the U.S. government places pressure on the foreign country to have its national airline purchase planes from Boeing (governments sometimes do this for their domestic producers). The airline still splits the order when the bids are the same and awards Boeing the entire order if Boeing is the low bidder. But due to this political pressure, if Boeing bids high and loses the bid, the airline will buy four planes from Boeing at the high price on a side deal after purchasing the 10 planes from Airbus at the low price. Figure 9.2 presents this new payoff structure. Submitting a low price is still a dominant strategy for Airbus. Boeing, however, does not have a dominant strategy. If Airbus submits a high price, it is optimal for Boeing to submits a low price to capture the entire order, whereas if Airbus submits a low price, it is better for Boeing to submit a high price and make the side deal.

Nash Equilibrium

When dominant strategies do not exist, the concept of a *Nash equilibrium* is useful in predicting the outcome. A Nash equilibrium is a set of strategies (or actions) in which each firm is doing the best it can, given the actions of its rival. In Figure 9.2, the combination of a low Airbus price and a high Boeing price is a Nash equilibrium. Neither firm would want to change its price given the price submitted by the other firm.

A particular problem might have multiple Nash equilibria. Nash equilibria are not necessarily the outcomes that maximize the joint payoff of the players. For instance, in Figure 9.1 the outcome where both firms submit low prices is a Nash equilibrium. Yet both firms would be better off if they were to collude and jointly submit high prices.

ACADEMIC APPLICATIONS

Are Nash Equilibria Likely?

Researchers have conducted many laboratory experiments on how people act in strategic situations. One particular question of interest is *Do they choose Nash equilibria?* The evidence suggests that the concept works relatively well in predicting behavior in simple single-move situations—especially if the individuals have prior experience interacting in similar ways with different partners in the past. It appears to work less well in more complex situations (e.g., situations that involve sophisticated mathematical calculations) and in repeated situations (we discuss implications of repetition later in this chapter). Also it often fails where coordination is required and there are multiple equilibria, unless there is a natural focal point.

Source: D. Davis and C. Holt (1993), *Experimental Economics* (Princeton University Press: Princeton).

Figure 9.2   Nash Equilibrium

Boeing and Airbus individually submit prices for 10 planes. They can submit either a high price or a low price. If one company bids high and the other bids low, the order goes to the low bidder; if both companies make the same bid, they split the order. If Boeing loses the bid, it sells four planes at the high price through a side deal. The circle technique provides a simple way to identify a Nash equilibrium. Start by assuming that Boeing will submit a low price (the top row). Circle the maximum payoff (in millions of dollars) that Airbus can achieve. This payoff (labeled #1) is in the cell where Airbus submits a low price (if the same payoff were to occur regardless of whether Airbus submits a high or low price, circle both cells). Second, move to the bottom row and assume that Boeing submits a high price; circle Airbus' higher payoff (#2). Third, assume Airbus will submit a low price (left column) and circle Boeing's higher payoff (#3). Fourth, move to the right column and assume Airbus submits a high price; circle Boeing's higher payoff (#4). If a Nash equilibrium exists, the payoffs in both halves of the cell will be circled. In this game, the Nash equilibrium is where Boeing submits a high price and Airbus submits a low price—shaded cell. (Note: Airbus has a dominant strategy—submit a low price—the low-price strategy is circled in both rows.)

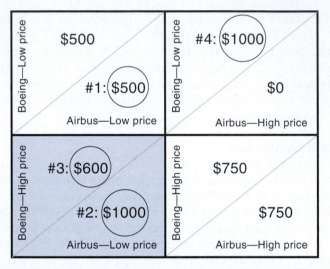

Identifying a Nash Equilibrium

The *circle technique* provides a simple way to identify a Nash equilibrium in such a problem. Consider the case in Figure 9.2. Start by assuming that Boeing will submit a low price (this is in the top row). Circle the maximum payoff that Airbus can achieve. This payoff (labeled #1) is in the cell where Airbus submits a low price (if the same payoff were to occur regardless of whether Airbus submits a high or low price, circle *both cells*). Second, move to the bottom row and assume that Boeing submits a high price; again circle Airbus' higher payoff (#2). Third, assume Airbus submits a low price (left column) and circle Boeing's higher payoff (#3). Finally, move to the right column and assume Airbus submits a high price; circle Boeing's higher payoff (#4). If a Nash equilibrium exists, the payoffs in both halves of the cell will be circled. In this problem, the Nash equilibrium is the shaded cell where Boeing submits a high price and Airbus submits a low price.

Dominant strategies also can be identified by this technique. If the firm has a dominant strategy, the strategy will be circled for all actions by the rival firm. In this example, submitting a low price is a dominant strategy for Airbus: For each of Boeing's possible actions submitting a low price is circled.

Management Implications

The power of a Nash equilibrium to predict the outcome in strategic situations stems from the fact that Nash equilibria are self-enforcing: They are stable outcomes. For instance, if Boeing can forecast Airbus' choice (perhaps because it understands that Airbus has a dominant strategy), it is optimal for Boeing to choose its equilibrium action, a high price. And Airbus has no incentive to avoid its equilibrium choice, a low price. Thus, even if both firms can accurately forecast the outcome, neither firm has an incentive to choose any other action.

Although the idea of a Nash equilibrium is quite useful, it is not as powerful in predicting the outcomes of strategic interactions as is the concept of a dominant strategy. When dominant strategies exist, there are strong private incentives to choose them, regardless of what the other player does. Thus, it is quite predictable that rivals will choose dominant strategies. With a Nash equilibrium, your best choice generally is contingent on what you expect your rival to do.

In many cases it is reasonable to expect that a Nash equilibrium will occur. This is more likely to be true when the rivals have more experience in similar strategic problems, have better information about each other, or when the Nash equilibrium is what is called a natural focal point.[7] For example, consider the problem in Figure 9.2. If Boeing has reasonable information about potential payoffs and Airbus' lack of political power within the specific country (it understands that there is a close working relationship between the local and U.S. governments), it will realize that Airbus has a dominant strategy to submit a low price. Boeing correspondingly will choose a high price—the Nash equilibrium. When rivals know little about the game or each other and when there is not a natural focal point, outcomes other than Nash equilibria (nonequilibrium outcomes) are more likely to occur.

Competition versus Coordination

To this point, we have analyzed competitive interaction. In each case, at least one of the firms has an incentive to submit a low bid to take sales from the other and garner additional profits. This potential gain comes at the expense of the other firm. Many strategic situations, however, involve coordination rather than competition.

Consider the problem in Figure 9.3, in which Boeing and Airbus make simultaneous choices of new communication systems for their planes.[8] Two technologies

---

[7]A focal point exists when there is a reasonable and obvious way to behave. To illustrate how a Nash equilibrium could be a focal point, consider a game where two strangers are asked to raise a hand. Both players receive a large payoff if they stick up the same hand (both left hands or both right hands) and nothing if they raise opposite hands. Two Nash equilibria exist: (1) both raising left hands, (2) both raising right hands. Nonequilibrium outcomes occur when the players raise opposite hands. The Nash equilibrium of both raising right hands is potentially a focal point. Most people are right-handed. If one player expects that the other is likely to raise his right hand because he is right-handed, she will have the incentive to raise her right hand as well. Reciprocally, it is reasonable for the other player to follow the same logic. Thus this outcome is potentially much more likely than either the nonequilibrium outcomes or the Nash equilibrium of two left hands.

[8]For example, suppose each company is working to introduce a new intermediate-capacity plane at next year's Paris Air Show and each views its choice of communication technology as a critical selling point for its model. Each will have to commit to a technology at the design phase, and each might be reluctant to discuss such features with its rival before the new model is unveiled.

ANALYZING MANAGERIAL DECISIONS: *Favoring a Government Ban on Advertising*

Cigarette manufacturers were among the first companies to advertise extensively on television. Older people today can still hum the heavily televised jingle, "Winston tastes good like a cigarette should," and recall the Old Gold Dancing Cigarette Pack—an oversized dancing cigarette package with shapely female legs. They can also remember beautiful women with black eyes as they testified that "Tareyton smokers would rather fight than switch." John Wayne and other movie stars appeared in commercials to endorse cigarettes. Cigarette companies were the major sponsors for many popular television shows. The companies also paid to have cigarettes included in the actual programs. In 1962, the cartoon characters Fred and Wilma Flintstone were shown smoking Winston cigarettes.

The U.S. federal Government banned television advertising of cigarettes starting in 1971. Interestingly the ban was supported by the leading cigarette

manufacturing companies even though they had advertised heavily on television since the 1940s.

1. Design a simple two-company game that illustrates why it might have been in the economic interests of the cigarette companies to support the ban. In designing the game, assume that there is no regulation and that the two firms simultaneously choose between advertising and not advertising. Display your hypothetical payoffs in strategic form (see Figure 9.1) and highlight the Nash equilibrium. Explain the intuition for why the firms in your example would favor regulation to ban advertising.

2. Can you conclude from your example that all firms in all industries will favor bans on television advertising? Explain. Can you ever envision a situation where one firm might favor the ban and a competing firm might be against it? Discuss.

exist: Alpha and Beta. Both firms benefit if they choose the same technology. A common technology standard allows producers to exploit scale economies and increases the likelihood that other companies will invest to develop new enhancements for the system because they can sell to both companies. Similarly, companies are more likely to develop service capabilities and stock larger inventories of

Figure 9.3   Coordination Game

Boeing and Airbus make simultaneous choices of new communication systems for their planes. Two technologies exist: Alpha and Beta (payoffs in millions of dollars). Both firms benefit if they choose the same technology. Applying the circle technique, we can see that there are two Nash equilibria: Alpha/Alpha and Beta/Beta (shaded cells).

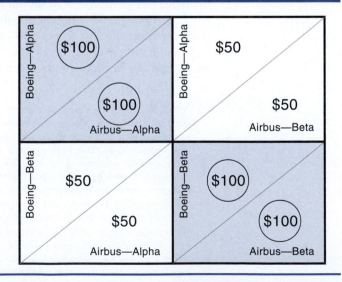

MANAGERIAL APPLICATIONS

Coordination Problems with High Definition Televisions

When combined with a good sound system, HDTV can provide a theater-like experience. The introduction of HDTV into the marketplace was slowed by coordination problems between television networks and manufacturers. Both groups thought that they would benefit by the development of this product. However, neither wanted to be the first to commit. Network executives were quoted as saying that they were reluctant to move forward with plans for new programming until the television manufacturers committed themselves to producing enough affordable sets to receive it. Yet manufacturers did not want to commit until the networks indicated that there would be enough digital programming for consumers to want to buy the sets. The situation was summed up in 1997 by a senior executive at CBS, "The networks are waiting to see what the TV makers are going to do, and the TV makers are waiting to see what the networks are going to do." In this situation, there are two Nash equilibria: Manufacturers and broadcasters both invest or neither invests. Due to coordination problems, firms may "get stuck" in the second equilibrium, even though both groups prefer the first. Although development of HDTV was slowed by coordination problems, it became a commercial reality by 1999. Manufacturers were selling the sets and broadcasting companies were providing more and more HDTV programming (the first equilibrium). Nonetheless, for HDTV to become a widely adopted product, available programming had to increase and set prices had to decline. Their initial prices for the sets ranged from about $5,000 to $10,000.

The coordination problems illustrated in this example arise frequently with new technologies. The overall value of a technology is usually higher when there are many users (there are network effects) and there is a common standard (e.g., consider how much less valuable DVDs would be if there were several different incompatible formats and only a small number of users of any one type). Adopting a uniform standard can be difficult when there are numerous players with somewhat conflicting interests. Sometimes governments, joint ventures among firms, and industry trade groups play a constructive role in promoting common standards, thereby helping to realize a preferred equilibrium. For example, in December 1996 the Federal Communications Commission set a timetable for stations and manufacturers converting to digital technology and, in October 2005, the Senate Commerce Committee set April 7, 2009, as the last date at which U.S. television stations can broadcast analog signals.

Source: J. Brinkley (1997), "Networks and Set Makers in Standoff over HDTV," *New York Times* (August 29), 5; and J. Kerr (2005), "Senate Looks to Spend $3B on Digital TV," *WashingtonPost.com* (October 20).

spare parts. The overall demand for planes also might be higher because airlines would have lower costs in learning a single system.

Applying the circle technique, we can see that there are two Nash equilibria: Alpha/Alpha and Beta/Beta. If precommitment communication is possible, it is quite likely that one of these equilibria will be reached. For instance, if both firms announce that they will choose Alpha, there is no private incentive to deviate from this choice. Coordination can prove more difficult in cases where precommitment communication is costly and/or there are many players.

Some strategic interactions involve elements of both competition and coordination. In the interactions problem in Figure 9.4, Boeing and Airbus benefit from choosing the same technology; again, there are two equilibria. But the companies are not indifferent between the two. Boeing prefers the Alpha technology, whereas Airbus prefers the Beta technology (the technologies are better matches for their particular aircraft design). Coordination in this setting can be more difficult than in pure coordination problems, since the firms want different outcomes. Nonetheless, if one of the firms is convinced of the choice the other firm is going to make, it has an economic incentive to follow suit and choose the same technology. Below we discuss ways that firms might be able to make credible statements regarding their upcoming choices.

Figure 9.4   Coordination/ Competition Game

Boeing and Airbus must make simultaneous choices of new communication systems for their planes. Two technologies exist: Alpha and Beta (payoffs in millions of dollars). Both firms benefit if they choose the same technology. Applying the circle technique, we can see that there are two Nash equilibria (shaded cells): Alpha/Alpha and Beta/Beta. Boeing prefers the Alpha/Alpha equilibrium, whereas Airbus prefers the Beta/Beta equilibrium.

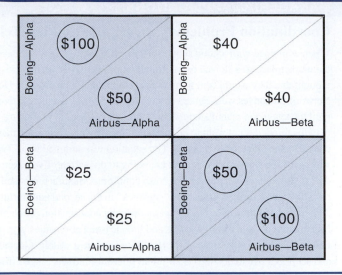

Mixed Strategies

In the strategic problems we have examined thus far, firms have chosen one specific action (e.g., a high or low price). This type of choice is known as a *pure strategy.* Sometimes it can pay to randomize; for example, choose a high price with probability p and a low price with probability $1 - p$. The benefit of this so-called *mixed strategy* derives from the element of surprise. For example, a football team does not want its opposing team to forecast its plays with 100 percent accuracy because it will field defenses specifically designed to stop the predicted plays. The team wants to mix up its plays and surprise the other team. This same logic can hold in business.

MANAGERIAL APPLICATIONS

Ice Cream Wars

The Indian frozen dessert market of $200 million a year is expected to grow 20 percent annually as Indians' inclination to snack is increasing. Two companies compete for the majority of India's ice cream market: Hindustan Lever, Ltd. (better known as HLL) and Amul. Between them they sell about 75 percent of the ice cream in most major markets. HLL is 51 percent owned by the British-Dutch giant Unilever, and Amul is owned by an Indian farmers' cooperative of 2 million farmers. Amul sells a no frills ice cream under the slogan "A taste of India" and spends less than 1 percent of their revenues on advertising; whereas HLL spends 10 to 15 percent. Amul sells its ice cream at about 12 percent less than HLL. Being a full-line dairy concern, Amul markets related products, thereby reducing its distribution costs. HLL claims they produce a higher quality product, but Amul counters that they have lower costs. HLL's executive director complains, "They rebuff attempts to form an ice cream trade body. How can we take them seriously?" But HLL is losing ground; their ice cream revenue was down in the first quarter of 2002, and they lost 2 percentage points of market share.

It appears as if Amul has a dominant strategy built around being the low-cost producer. Not only is Amul capturing market share from HLL, but also Amul has rejected HLL's attempt at a coordination game in the form of an "ice cream trade body."

Source: S. Rai (2002), "Battling to Satisfy India's Taste for Ice Cream," *New York Times* (August 20), W1.

Figure 9.5 Mixed Strategy

Boeing and Airbus simultaneously must commit to an advertising campaign. The advertising can focus on either the negatives of the other company's planes or the positive aspects of the company's own planes (payoffs in millions of dollars). Boeing is the market leader and benefits when both firms choose the same strategy. Airbus does better when it can differentiate itself by choosing a different strategy. The circle technique indicates that there is no equilibrium in pure strategies. There is a unique equilibrium in mixed strategies. In this equilibrium, each firm randomizes between the two campaigns (choosing each with a probability of .5).

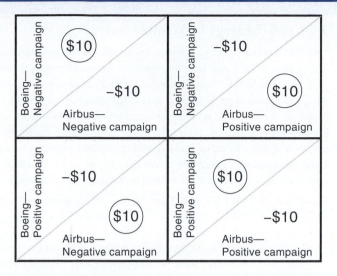

Consider the strategic problem in Figure 9.5 where Boeing and Airbus simultaneously must commit to an advertising campaign. The advertising might focus on either the negatives of the other company's planes or the positive aspects of the company's own planes. Boeing is the market leader and benefits more when both firms choose the same strategy. Airbus does better when it can differentiate itself by choosing a different strategy. The circle technique indicates that there is no equilibrium in pure strategies. If the campaigns match, Airbus wants to change. If the campaigns do not match, Boeing wants to change.

The problem has an equilibrium employing mixed strategies: Both firms randomize between the two actions with a probability of 0.5—they might base their actions on a coin flip. To understand why this is an equilibrium, consider the following logic.[9] This problem is what is called a zero-sum game: If Boeing gains $10 (million), Airbus loses $10 and *vice versa*. Thus if one company has a positive expected value in the game, the other must have a negative expected value. If Boeing selects one of the campaigns with a probability greater than 0.5, Airbus can choose the other campaign with a probability of 1 and gain more than half the time. For instance, suppose Boeing chooses a positive campaign with a probability of .6, Airbus would gain 60 percent of the time by always choosing a negative campaign. Its expected payoff would be $.6(10) + .4(-10) = 2 > 0$. Boeing's expected payoff would be $.6(-10) + .4(10) = -2 < 0$. The only way that Boeing can ensure an expected payoff of zero is by randomizing between the two actions with equal probabilities.[10] Symmetric

[9]All strategic interactions with a finite number of both players and actions have at least one Nash equilibrium in either pure or mixed strategies. In this chapter, we give examples of mixed strategies and discuss the general intuition behind the associated equilibria. More detailed discussion on how to solve for these equilibria can be found in Dixit and Nalebuff (1993), Chapter 7.

[10]If Boeing chooses each action with a probability of 0.5, the expected payoff is zero independent of Airbus' strategy. Suppose Airbus chooses the positive campaign with probability p. The probability of Boeing matching the positive campaign is $0.5p$ (the probability of two independent events is the product of the individual probabilities of the events). Similarly the probability of matching a negative campaign is $0.5(1 - p)$. Thus the likelihood of Boeing winning is $0.5p + 0.5(1 - p) = 0.5$. It correspondingly loses 0.5 of the time and has an expected payoff of zero. This is true independent of the p Airbus actually chooses.

ACADEMIC APPLICATIONS

A Mixed Strategy at Wimbledon

Tennis players can serve to either an opponent's backhand or forehand. The receiver can choose to move left or right in anticipation of the serve. Both the opponent and receiver want to mix their choices to catch the other off guard. For example, if the server always serves to the backhand, the receiver will know that it is best to favor that side. The server would then want to mix it up and serve to the opponent's forehand. In a mixed-strategy equilibrium, the expected payoff to a given player is the same regardless of which action he actually ends up taking. Thus, if the server is mixing between serving to the receiver's backhand and forehand, the likelihood of winning the point should be the same. To test whether the concept of a mixed-strategy equilibrium actually explains the behavior of top tennis players, researchers recorded the results of serves in 10 matches at Wimbledon. There, data supported the theory—the success rates with serves to either the forehand or backhand were the same.

Source: M. Walker and J. Wooders (2001), "Minimax Play at Wimbledon," *American Economic Review* 91, 1521–1538.

---

logic holds for Airbus. The outcome of both firms randomizing with a probability of 0.5 is a Nash equilibrium. Neither firm has an incentive to change its strategy given the strategy of the other firm.

In equilibrium, a firm receives the same expected payoff regardless of which of the campaigns it actually chooses. Thus if Boeing flips a coin that indicates it should choose a positive campaign, there is no reason to deviate and choose a negative campaign. In either case it gets the same expected payoff (zero). By definition, it would not be an equilibrium if either firm had an incentive to alter its choice.

Managerial Implications

Managers often make decisions in circumstances where the decision is not expected to be repeated and the payoff depends on the simultaneous decisions of other parties, be they rival firms, customers, suppliers, or employees. Potential examples include

---

MANAGERIAL APPLICATIONS

The Critical Importance of Considering Strategic Interactions—Borders Books

Borders liquidated its business in 2011. At the time, it was the nation's second largest bookstore chain. Nearly 11,000 employees lost their jobs when the company closed its hundreds of stores around the country.

Borders had been in business for 40 years, and along with Barnes and Noble had pioneered the large "brick-and-mortar" bookstore. The book-selling industry, however, changed dramatically in subsequent years with the Internet and the dramatic growth of Amazon.com and e-books.

Borders' management appeared largely to ignore Amazon's cost advantages in selling books online, as well as its incentives to undercut Borders' prices. Despite this competitive threat, Borders continued to invest in building and refurbishing stores with large inventories of books, CDs, and DVDs. In contrast to Barnes and Noble, they did not invest in developing online sales capacity. In the years leading up to its collapse, many shoppers visited Borders' stores to find or examine books, simply to purchase them from Amazon at a lower price.

The failure of Borders' management sufficiently to consider Amazon's competitive responses (as well as their typical customer's price sensitivity) contributed to their ultimate collapse. Managers generally will make better decisions if they incorporate the incentives and responses of competitors into their analysis.

Source: Y. Noguchi (2011), "Why Borders Failed While Barnes and Noble Survived," *npr.org* (July 19).

making a large investment decision to enter a new market or industry, pricing a new product, or making an acquisition bid for a firm.

To summarize the managerial implications of our analysis, consider Valerie Black, who must submit the bid for Boeing in our example. Val should perform the following calculations:

- Estimate the payoffs given each of her potential actions as well as those of her rival, Airbus.[11]
- Examine whether she has a dominant strategy—if so, she should employ it.
- Without a dominant strategy, she should make her best estimate of what Airbus will do and identify her corresponding best action (which might be a mixed strategy).
- Check whether the resulting outcome is a potential Nash equilibrium: Does the forecasted action of Airbus appear optimal from their viewpoint, given her proposed action? If so, her proposed action appears reasonable; if not, Val should reexamine the underlying assumptions of her initial forecast.

Her forecast probably should be revised if it is based on the implicit assumption that Airbus is either dumb or irrational (e.g., Airbus is unable to forecast a likely action on her part or does not know what is in its own best interests). In essence, Val should *place herself behind her rival's desk* and ask what she would do if she worked for Airbus. She should assume that Airbus undoubtedly is trying to forecast her actions, as well. Is there some reasonable set of beliefs that Airbus might have about her actions that would motivate the firm to choose the action in the initial forecast—can it be *rationalized?* If not, Val probably should revise the forecast. Since Val almost surely has less than perfect information about the factors affecting Airbus' choice, she may misforecast what Airbus actually does. Nonetheless, her goal is simply to do the best she can, given her imperfect information. Sometimes it will pay to collect additional information about a rival to make a better-informed choice (when the expected incremental benefits of the new information are larger than its incremental costs).

If Val is reasonably confident that Airbus will choose what appears to be a nonequilibrium strategy (e.g., Airbus has a track record of choosing a particular strategy in similar situations), she should reevaluate both her and her rival's available actions and their associated payoffs carefully. It is frequently the case that what appears to be a nonequilibrium move reflects an incomplete understanding of the alternatives. Ultimately, if she is quite confident that Airbus will choose a particular action, she should choose the action that maximizes her payoff, even if the outcome is not a Nash equilibrium.

If Val is extremely risk-averse and has little experience either dealing with this rival or managing in similar situations, one option is to choose a *secure strategy*—a strategy that guarantees the highest payoff given the worst possible case.[12] In other words, she forecasts the worst payoff that could arise for each of her potential actions and chooses the action that offers the highest payoff among the worst payoffs. But following such a strategy generally will not maximize the value of the firm (e.g., if the primary benefit is to guard against an unlikely outcome), and often she could do better with additional analysis and thought.

---

[11]If she has many potential actions, she may wish to simplify the problem by focusing on a few key possibilities. Sometimes it is not feasible to quantify the payoffs. In these cases, managers can go through the following steps on a more qualitative basis.

[12]Another name for this type of strategy is *maximin*.

Sequential Interactions

Thus far, we have limited our attention to simultaneous-move strategic problems. Yet in many business situations, managers make decisions sequentially. For example, consider the problem in Figure 9.4 where Boeing and Airbus simultaneously chose new communication technologies. Decisions of this type often are made sequentially. For example, Boeing might choose the technology in one year, while Airbus chooses it in the next. As we shall see, the equilibrium outcome of strategic interactions can vary, depending on whether they occur simultaneously or sequentially. For instance, in this technology choice problem, there are two possible equilibria given simultaneous choices, but only one given sequential choices.

Extensive Form

Figure 9.6 displays this strategic interaction in *extensive form* assuming that Boeing moves first (e.g., Boeing chooses the technology for the new model it introduces at this year's Paris Air Show, while Airbus will introduce its new model next year). The extensive form depicts the sequence of actions and the corresponding outcomes. A node indicates a point at which a firm must choose an action, while the branches leading from a node display possible choices at the node. At the first node (node 1) Boeing must choose between the Alpha and Beta technologies. Airbus makes the next move. Whether it is at node 2 or node 3 depends on Boeing's initial choice. At either node Airbus must choose whether to adopt the Alpha or Beta technology. The numbers at the end of the final branches indicate the ultimate payoffs to Boeing and Airbus, given the sequence of choices made by the two firms. (These payoffs are the same as in Figure 9.4.) If both firms choose the Alpha technology, the payoffs are 100

Figure 9.6 Extensive Form

In this sequential game, Boeing chooses the technology first and then Airbus makes a choice. This diagram shows the game in extensive form. A node indicates a point at which a firm must choose an action, whereas the branches leading from a node indicate the possible choices. The numbers at the end indicate the payoffs (in millions of dollars) for Boeing and Airbus, respectively. The game is solved by backward induction. Given the payoffs, Airbus will choose Alpha at node 2 and Beta at node 3. If Boeing forecasts these choices, it will choose Alpha at node 1. Bold lines indicate equilibrium choices.

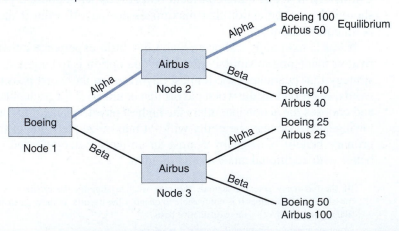

for Boeing and 50 for Airbus (as in the upper-left cell of Figure 9.4), while if they choose the Beta technology, the payoffs are reversed (as in the lower-right cell). Payoffs are lower for both firms when they choose different technologies.

Backward Induction

We analyze this extensive form using *backward induction*—looking forward to the final outcomes (decision nodes) and reasoning backward. To illustrate, continue with the example in Figure 9.6. Begin at the final two nodes (2 and 3). At node 2, Airbus has an incentive to choose Alpha because it prefers the payoff of 50 to 40. At node 3, Airbus chooses Beta. Now move to the initial node. If Boeing foresees how Airbus will act at the final nodes, Boeing will see that it is in its best interests to choose Alpha in the initial stage. If it chooses Alpha, Airbus will do so as well and Boeing will receive 100. By contrast if Boeing chooses Beta, Airbus will match that

---

ANALYZING MANAGERIAL DECISIONS: *Let's Make a Deal*

You work for a company that is frequently involved in negotiations to acquire companies from their current owners. You have been invited to be a guest on the popular television game show *Let's Make a Deal*. Your boss has agreed that you can participate on the game show during business hours because you might learn something that would be valuable in future business negotiations.

You are now on the game show. The following events have occurred to this point:

- The game show host showed you three doors, labeled Door #1, Door #2, and Door #3 and told you that behind one of the doors is the grand prize of $100,000. The other two doors contain smaller prizes of no more than $20,000. You assume that the host knows which door has the $100,000.

- You were told to choose one of the doors, and you randomly chose Door #1.

- The host subsequently opened Door #2 and showed you that it contains a smaller prize of $20,000.

- He has given you the following choice. You can keep what is behind Door #1 (your initial choice). You can trade it for the $20,000 behind Door #2, or you can trade it for the unknown contents behind Door #3.

- You want to go for the grand prize of $100,000. Thus you must decide whether to keep Door #1 or trade it for Door #3.

1. You initially selected Door #1. Prior to seeing the contents behind Door #2, what was the probability that Door #1 contained the grand prize? What was the probability that Door #1 did not contain the grand prize (i.e., the grand prize was behind one of the other two doors)?

2. The host subsequently showed you that Door #2 contained $20,000 and gave you the choice to keep what was behind Door #1 or to trade it for what was behind Door #3. What should you do or does it matter (assuming you want to go for the grand prize)? [*Hint:* "Put yourself behind the host's podium" and consider his choice to show you the contents behind one of the doors. It might be useful to view the situation as a sequential game where you choose the first door at Node 1 and the host subsequently chooses which of the remaining doors to show you at Node 2.]

3. Your boss let you participate in the game show because she thought you might learn something that would be of value to your company. Does your experience on the game show suggest any general principles that might be useful in managerial situations? Explain.

MANAGERIAL APPLICATIONS

First-Mover Advantage—Walmart

In Chapter 8, we discussed how Walmart was the first company to place large discount stores in many small towns in the southeastern region of the United States (for instance, in Arkansas). Even though Walmart has been quite profitable at these stores, other companies have been reluctant to place competing stores in the same towns. They realize that each town is big enough to support only one such store. If they did enter, they would have to compete with Walmart and both would lose money. Thus Walmart has a *first-mover advantage* in these communities.

---

choice and Boeing will receive a final payoff of 50. Thus, the equilibrium outcome is for Boeing to choose Alpha in the first stage with Airbus matching that choice in the second stage.

The *equilibrium strategy* of a firm given sequential strategic interaction consists of a sequence of its best actions, where the actions are taken at the corresponding nodes. In this problem, Boeing's equilibrium strategy is to choose Alpha in the first stage, whereas Airbus's equilibrium strategy is to choose Alpha in the second stage if Boeing chooses Alpha and Beta if Boeing chooses Beta. The strategies of the two firms are a Nash equilibrium: Neither firm wants to change its strategy given the other firm's strategy.

First-Mover Advantage

In this example, Boeing has a *first-mover advantage:* By moving first, Boeing makes higher profits than Airbus, who moves second. If Airbus moves first, the advantage is reversed. Knowing Boeing's incentive to match the technology in the second stage, Airbus would choose Beta in the first round and receive higher profits. This example illustrates that managers must consider carefully the order of moves in strategic situations. When Boeing and Airbus make simultaneous choices, there are two potential equilibria. In the sequential game there is only one. The outcome, however, depends on who moves first.

The first mover does not always have a strategic advantage. In some situations, the follower has the advantage. Consider a firm that cuts its development costs by copying product innovations by pioneering firms—after all, the second mouse gets the cheese.

Strategic Moves

Actions that are taken to influence the beliefs or actions of the rival in favorable ways are called *strategic moves.* Typically, they require individuals to restrict their own future actions. For example, prior to Boeing's choice, if Airbus could make a binding commitment to choose Beta no matter what Boeing did, it then would be in Boeing's interest to adopt the Beta technology in the first year.

Credibility

Can Airbus offset Boeing's first-mover advantage by simply announcing that it will adopt the Beta technology next year no matter what Boeing does this year? Boeing would be clearly better off to adopt the Beta technology if it really believed that Airbus would carry out its announced plan. Yet Boeing probably should ignore such a statement by Airbus unless it is *credible.* The statement would lack credibility if it would not be in Airbus' self-interest to carry out its announced plan were Boeing adopted the Alpha technology first. In that case,

Airbus would be foolish to adopt the Beta technology after Boeing chooses the Alpha technology given its low payoff.

For a strategic move to be credible, it must consist of a sufficient commitment to convince the rival to change its beliefs. Merely announcing a planned future action typically is not enough—*talk is cheap*. As an example of a potentially credible action, suppose that Airbus signs a contract with the manufacturer of the Beta technology to pay the supplier a large sum of money whether or not Airbus employs its technology in the following year. This contract is legally binding and expensive to renegotiate. Now Boeing has a substantive reason to believe that Airbus will carry through with its announced plan to adopt the Beta technology even if Boeing were to choose the Alpha system. If it does not, it still will have to pay a large sum of money to the supplier and thus would be worse off than if it were to match Boeing by choosing the Alpha technology. If Boeing decides this announcement is credible, Boeing should adopt the Beta system in the first year.[13]

Managerial Implications

Many strategic situations involve a sequence of actions by the rivals. Examples include management negotiations with a labor union and the dissemination of a new product within an industry.

To illustrate the management implications of our analysis of sequential strategic interactions, consider Helmut Mueller, the manager who must choose the communication technology for Airbus in the communication technology problem discussed earlier. Helmut should begin by defining carefully the sequence of moves. For example, he may have enough information to know that Boeing will choose a new technology this year, whereas Airbus' production schedule will not allow it to make a choice until the following year. He then should work backward to predict the likely outcome of their interaction. Starting at the end of the process, he will realize that he will have a strong incentive to match Boeing's choice in the second period. Moving to the first node, he should place himself behind a Boeing desk. He should realize that Boeing is likely to understand that Helmut will have strong incentives to match Boeing's technology in the second period. Given this belief, Boeing will adopt the Alpha technology. Airbus is less profitable with this outcome and thus would prefer the joint adoption of the Beta system. As a final step, he should analyze whether he could make any strategic moves that would influence the beliefs of Boeing managers and thus motivate them to adopt the Beta technology. He must realize that Boeing's management is unlikely to believe a simple announcement that Airbus will choose the Beta technology in the future. Helmut might conclude that a contract with the Beta manufacturer would provide sufficient commitment to alter Boeing's beliefs and choice. After entering this contract, it is important that Helmut make his action known to Boeing. For instance, Helmut might want to report the contract to the financial press.

[13]Note to the technically inclined: If Boeing actually believed Airbus's statement that it would choose Beta in the second round regardless of Boeing's first round choice, Boeing would logically choose Beta in the first round. The outcome Beta/Beta is *a second potential Nash equilibrium to this game*—neither party has an incentive to alter its choice of Beta given the other firm's action. However, this second potential equilibrium can be ruled out if we require that both parties expect each other to act rationally (in their own interest) at any node in the game (on or off the equilibrium path). Game theorists refer to this criterion for eliminating unlikely equilibria as "subgame perfection." We think this "selection criterion" is quite reasonable and should be employed by managers in their analysis of strategic situations. Using this criterion, there is only one economically reasonable equilibrium to this game, Alpha/Alpha (unless, as we discuss next, Airbus can make an economically credible commitment always to choose Beta in the second round).

MANAGERIAL APPLICATIONS

Strategic Behavior—NHL

Negotiations between management and labor unions can be viewed as a game. Both sides engage in strategic behavior, hoping to win more for their sides. Sometimes these strategic interactions result in labor strikes and lockouts that end up being costly to both parties.

Consider the labor dispute in the National Hockey League (NHL) during the 2012–2013 season. The failure of owners and the players to agree to a new contract before the old one expired resulted in a player lockout that lasted from September 15, 2012 to January 12, 2013. The regular season was reduced from 82 to 48 games and the annual All Star Game was cancelled.

As the September 2012 deadline approached, the owners and players exchanged a series of proposals and counter proposals. The union's last offer, prior to the deadline, continued to insist on a salary cap that was not linked to revenue and that would steadily increase over a five-year term. Owners refused to budge from their initial position of wanting to reduce the players' share of hockey-related revenues from 57 percent under the old contract to 46 percent. Both sides adopted "hard nose strategies" hoping the other side would cave into their demands prior to the deadline. They did not.

During the lockout, both sides presented a series of threats and counter threats. For example, various notable players, who had signed to play for European teams during the lockout, threatened not to return when the lockout ended. These threats, however, were not very credible and almost all players quickly returned to the NHL once the dispute was settled.

There is disagreement over which side came out better. The owners got a 50-50 split of revenues (a 7 percent reduction for the players from the previous contract), while the players got the better deal on the length of contracts, salary caps, and pension plan. What is clear is that the dispute was very costly to both sides. The NHL Commissioner estimated that the owners had combined losses of between $18 and $20 million per day during the lockout, while the players lost between $8 and $10 million in salaries. The dispute lasted 119 days.

Source: Tribune Company writers (2013), "Who Emerged As the Winner after the NHL Labor Dispute?", *Los Angeles Times Website* (January 7).

Repeated Strategic Interaction

Many strategic situations involve repeated interaction among rivals. For example, Boeing and Airbus have many opportunities to compete against each other to supply commercial jet aircraft. Indeed many, if not most, companies deal with the same competitors, suppliers, employees, and regulators over extended periods of time.

When interaction is expected to occur repeatedly, more equilibria frequently are possible. For instance, recall the situation illustrated in Figure 9.1. In this problem, Boeing and Airbus make bids to produce 10 airplanes. The dominant strategy is for

MANAGERIAL APPLICATIONS

It Pays to Think Sequentially

According to a story that frequently has circulated over the Internet, two college students drove to an out-of-town basketball game the day before an important exam. The students drank too much and were unprepared to take the test. Rather than flunk the exam, they decided to tell the teacher that a flat tire delayed their return. Being the understanding type, the professor said, "No problem; take the test tomorrow." The students arrived the next day to take the exam; they were put into separate rooms. The first question, worth 5 points, was quite easy. But confidence turned to apprehension as each student turned to the next question, worth 95 points, that simply asked, "Which tire?" If the students had thought ahead more carefully, they would have behaved differently.

MANAGERIAL APPLICATIONS

Price Fixing in the Auto-Parts Industry

A U.S. grand jury indicted three former executives of the Bridgestone Corporation in April 2014 for allegedly conspiring to fix automotive-part prices. The indictments were part of an ongoing investigation by the U.S. Department of Justice that had previously netted $2.29 billion in fines and 26 guilty pleas from automotive-part companies. The companies had admitted to taking part in explicit agreements among competitors to fix prices and rig bids in selling parts to automobile manufacturers.

Game theory implies that a cooperative equilibrium is possible given repeated interaction without explicit communication or collusion. One interpretation of joint price increases in an industry (above cost) is that the firms have moved from cutthroat competition where each firms was losing money to a more cooperative equilibrium. Experience suggests, however, that cooperative equilibria are not always easy to sustain. Consider the difficulties experienced by OPEC in trying to restrict output to maintain high oil prices or the American airline industry in avoiding price wars.

Source: L. Vellequette and P. Nussel (2014), "Bridgestone executives indicted for auto parts price fixing," *Automotive News* (April 16).

both to bid low, even though they would be better off if both bid high—a rivals' dilemma. With repeated interaction, the equilibrium still might consist of both firms' pricing low. However, other equilibria, such as both firms' pricing high, are possible. The basic idea is that with repeated interaction, there is more to consider than the short-run payoffs. The decision maker also has to consider the potential benefits of establishing a long-term cooperative relationship.

The appendix to this chapter contains an example of how rivals' dilemmas (such as in the Boeing/Airbus problem) sometimes can be overcome given repeated interaction.[14] The likelihood of a "cooperative" outcome increases if (1) the long-run gains from cooperating are larger relative to the short-run gains from not cooperating (assuming the other firm does), (2) it is easier for the firms to recognize whether or not cooperation has occurred, and (3) the expected length of the repeated relationship is longer. Discount rates also are important (higher discount rates imply that the decision maker cares more about present payoffs relative to future payoffs). The appendix emphasizes the managerial implications of this analysis. In Chapter 21, we revisit this topic by discussing how reputational concerns can motivate managers to behave with integrity in economic transactions.

While certain conditions increase the likelihood of cooperative outcomes in repeated settings, noncooperative outcomes can almost always still occur. Indeed, the so-called *Folk Theorem* tells us that there is generally a large set of potential Nash equilibria in repeated games.[15]

---

[14]Generally, it is important to have an uncertain ending date in the repeated relationship. If there is a finite ending date, both you and your rival are likely to realize that there is no incentive for either of you to cooperate in the last interaction. Then both of you will have an incentive not to cooperate in the next to the last interaction (since your reputation for cooperating will not matter in the last round). Yet if this is true, there is no incentive to cooperate in the interactions before. The final result can be no cooperation in the first interaction. If on the other hand the date of the final interaction is uncertain, there always can be some reason to cooperate.

[15]"Evolutionary Game Theory" argues that strategies with relatively efficient payoffs are more likely to "reproduce and survive" in a competitive environments. As in biological Darwinism, there is a tendency toward "survival of the fittest." The evolutionary approach has the potential to reduce the large number of possible equilibria in repeated games to a much smaller set of most plausible equilibria. See H. Gintis (2009), *Game Theory Evolving: A Problem-Centered Introduction to Modeling Strategic Interaction,* second edition (Princeton University Press: Princeton, NJ).

Figure 9.7 Incentive Game

The employee, Len Steenkamp, decides to work or shirk, and the manager, Kiana Ross, decides whether or not to monitor (payoffs in thousands of dollars). Len would prefer to shirk than to work, whereas it is costly for the manager to monitor. As the circle technique shows, there is no pure-strategy equilibrium. If the employee works, the manager does not want to monitor; if the manager does not monitor, the employee shirks. There is a mixed-strategy equilibrium where Len randomizes between working and shirking and Kiana randomizes between monitoring and not monitoring (all with a probability of .5).

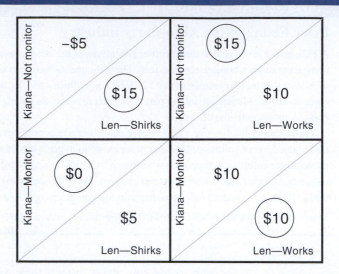

Strategic Interaction and Organizational Architecture

We have focused on competition between rival firms throughout this chapter, but the analysis of strategic interactions has much broader implications and can provide useful implications for managers when interacting with other parties within their own organization. Part 3 of this book examines organizational architecture. As an introductory example, consider the problem in Figure 9.7 between a manager, Kiana Ross, and a lower-level employee, Lenin Steenkamp. Len must decide whether to work or shirk. If he exerts effort, the value of his expected output is $25 (all numbers in this example are in thousands of dollars); if he shirks, the expected output is $5. Len does not like exerting effort and bears personal costs if he works that he values at $5, but no cost if he shirks. Kiana can monitor Len for a cost of $5 and can tell whether or not he has exerted effort.[16] The labor contract pays the employee $10, unless he is caught shirking—in which case, he is fired and receives no payment.

MANAGERIAL APPLICATIONS

Auditing—A Mixed-Strategy Equilibrium

Independent accountants commonly audit firms. One of the reasons audits exist is to help ensure that managers are not embezzling funds. Accountants do not verify all economic transactions when they audit a firm. Rather, they review most of the large transactions and draw a random sample of the smaller ones. If accountants reviewed every transaction, there would be little or no fraud (since managers would know they would get caught if they were fraudulent). However, given the correspondingly small chance of fraud, it would not make economic sense to bear the high costs of auditing every transaction. The result is a mixed-strategy equilibrium. Auditors randomly select accounts to audit and managers sometimes engage in fraud. In practice, auditors also audit accounts more intensely when available information (e.g., a suspicious account entry) increases the likelihood that fraud has occurred.

[16]Kiana cannot tell for sure if Len has worked from simply observing his output. Although the expected output is $25 or $5, depending on whether or not Len works, output is also affected by random factors beyond Len's control. Thus output can sometimes be high even if Len has not worked, and low even if he has.

ANALYZING MANAGERIAL DECISIONS: *Holland Sweetener versus Monsanto*

Aspartame is a low-calorie sweetener marketed by Monsanto under the name of NutraSweet. It was a major impetus to the rapid growth of Diet Coke and Diet Pepsi during the 1980s and 1990s. A scientist at the G. D. Searle & Co. first discovered aspartame in 1965; Searle received a patent for the product in 1970. U.S. regulators did not approve its use in soft drinks until 1983. In 1985, Monsanto acquired Searle—and with it a monopoly on aspartame. Monsanto's patents expired in 1987 and 1992 in Europe and the United States, respectively.

In 1986, Holland Sweetener was formed through a joint venture of Tosoh Corporation and Dutch State Mines. Its sole purpose was to challenge Monsanto in the aspartame market. It began by building a plant in the Netherlands to compete in the European market. The "big prize," however, was the U.S. soft-drink market, which was to open up at the end of 1992.

Initially, Holland Sweetener was quite optimistic about capturing a large share of the U.S. market. To quote their vice president of marketing and sales in referring to Coke and Pepsi, "Every manufacturer likes to have at least two sources of supply." To Holland Sweetener's surprise, they never became a big player in the U.S. market. In 1992, just before Monsanto's patent expired, Coke and Pepsi signed long-term contracts with Monsanto for the continued supply of NutraSweet. The big winners in this contract negotiation were Coke and Pepsi, who realized about $200 million a year in savings. Monsanto remained the major supplier to these companies, while Holland Sweetener was "left pretty much out in the cold." In 2006, Holland Sweetener announced it was exiting the aspartame business.

Envision a pricing problem between Monsanto and Holland Sweetener in 1992 that led to the Monsanto contract. Assume (1) the cost to Holland Sweetener of entering the U.S. market, $25 million, has been incurred; (2) Monsanto and Holland Sweetener simultaneously choose to quote either a high or low price to Pepsi and Coke for aspartame; (3) if both Monsanto and Holland Sweetener quote the same price, Pepsi and Coke contract with Monsanto because customers are familiar with the NutraSweet label—Holland Sweetener loses its initial investment; (4) if both firms submit a high price, Monsanto nets $300 million; (5) if both firms submit a low price, Monsanto nets $100 million; (6) if Monsanto prices high and Holland Sweetener prices low, Holland Sweetener nets $100 million (after the initial investment) and Monsanto nets $0.

1. Construct the strategic-form payoff matrix for this strategic pricing problem. Find the Nash equilibrium.
2. Now assume that the interaction is sequential where Holland Sweetener chooses to enter and if so they face the pricing problem in the second stage. Should Holland Sweetener enter?
3. Why do you think Holland Sweetener entered? Were they just dumb or were there other potential considerations?
4. Prior to Holland Sweetener's entry into the U.S. market, Pepsi and Coke began deemphasizing the NutraSweet label on their cans and bottles. Why do you think they did this?
5. Explain how Monsanto had a "first-mover's advantage."
6. Pepsi and Coke were the big winners in this case. Explain why.

Sources: A. Brandenburger and B. Nalebuff (1996), *Co-opetition* (Doubleday: Garden City; and DSM, Corporate Communications (2006), "DSM Press Release: Holland Sweetener Company to Exit from Aspartame Business," (March 30).

The circle technique indicates that there is no pure-strategy equilibrium. The reason is that if Len always works, Kiana has no incentive to monitor, whereas if Kiana were never to monitor, Len always would shirk. This problem has an equilibrium in mixed strategies, where Len works some of the time and shirks others, and Kiana monitors some of the time and not others.[17]

---

[17]In this equilibrium, both Kiana and Len randomize between their two actions, choosing each action .5 of the time.

Figure 9.7 indicates that the combined payoff is highest when Len always works and Kiana never monitors. Although this outcome is not a feasible equilibrium if the interaction is not repeated,[18] Kiana might be able to promote this equilibrium within an actual firm. For instance, one tool that Kiana has at her disposal is the structure of the labor contract. It might be possible to motivate Len to work in the absence of monitoring by paying him a share of total output, thus offering incentive compensation rather than a fixed salary. Altering the labor contract creates a new set of payoffs and potentially a more preferred equilibrium. Chapters 11–17 analyze, in detail, how managers can use compensation plans and other organizational arrangements to increase productivity and the firm's value.

This example is but one of many ways that managers might apply these methods to analyze business problems. The chapter appendix provides another example.

Summary

Game theory is concerned with the general analysis of strategic interaction. It focuses on optimal decision making when all decision makers are presumed to be rational, with each attempting to anticipate the likely actions and reactions of its rivals. These techniques can be employed to study a wide variety of phenomena ranging from parlor games to politics and competitive strategy. In this chapter, we introduce the basic elements of this theory in the context of managerial decision making.

In *simultaneous-move problems,* firms must make decisions without knowledge of the decisions made by their rivals. *Nonrepeated* means that the game is played only once. We diagram these interactions by showing the payoffs in *strategic (normal) form.*

A *dominant strategy* exists when it is optimal for the firm to choose a particular strategy no matter what its rival does. A firm should employ a dominant strategy if one exists.

Firms do not always have dominant strategies. When dominant strategies do not exist, we employ the concept of a *Nash equilibrium* to predict the outcome of the interaction. A Nash equilibrium is a set of strategies (or actions) in which each firm is doing the best it can, given the actions of its rival. A problem can have multiple Nash equilibria. Nash equilibria are not necessarily the outcomes that maximize the joint payoff of the firms. The *circle technique* provides a simple method to identify Nash equilibria.

The power of a Nash equilibrium to predict the outcomes of strategic interactions stems from the fact that Nash equilibria are self-enforcing—they are stable outcomes. In many cases it is reasonable to expect that a Nash equilibrium will occur. This is particularly true when the firms have experience with similar problems, when they have information about each other, or when the Nash equilibrium outcome is a natural "focal point."

Some interactions are *competitive*—at least one of the firms has an incentive to take actions that benefit them at the expense of their rival. Other strategic situations involve *coordination* rather than competition. Some interactions have elements of both.

When a firm chooses one specific strategy or action, it is called a *pure strategy.* Sometimes it can pay to randomize—to use a *mixed strategy.* The benefit of a mixed strategy comes from the element of surprise; sometimes a firm is at a disadvantage if it is too predictable.

---

[18]It is achieved one-quarter of the time in the mixed-strategy equilibrium (.5 × .5).

MANAGERIAL APPLICATIONS

Key Managerial Insights from Game Theory

Most business problems are more complex than the simple examples used in this chapter. Although technical challenges mount as the number of rivals and the range of potential actions increase, some of the basic insights from elementary game theory are quite robust. Some of the key insights are as follows:

- *Understand your business setting.* Identify the relevant set of rivals and the nature of their interaction. What are the potential actions? What information will they have when they choose their actions? What are the consequences of their various actions? Is similar interaction among these rivals likely to be repeated over time or across other markets?

- *Place yourself behind your rival's desk.* Consider the entire sequence of decisions that are likely to be made over the course of this interaction. Look forward to the ultimate set of potential outcomes and then reason backward to determine your best strategy. This process identifies critical choices that your rivals face and highlights why you should understand the basis for their choices.

- *With a first-mover advantage, move first.* If the business setting does not naturally permit you to implement your action first, consider whether you can credibly precommit to a particular action. Effective precommitment, by convincing your rivals of your future actions, can induce them to change their actions. This logic highlights the fact that maintaining flexibility undercuts your ability to precommit—in this sense, flexibility can be quite expensive.

- *With a second-move advantage, avoid moving first.* Delay implementation of actions where possible. Try to reduce the predictability of your actions. Finally, if you have to implement an action, maintain as much future flexibility to change your actions as possible.

- *Repetition facilitates cooperation.* Some productive form of cooperation is more likely when interaction is expected to be repeated either over time or across markets.

In many business situations, managers make decisions sequentially. Sequential interactions are pictured in *extensive form*. The extensive form displays the sequence of actions and corresponding outcomes. A node indicates a point at which a party must choose an action, and the branches leading from a node display the possible choices at the node. We solve the extensive form by *backward induction*—looking forward to the final decision nodes and reasoning backward.

In some interactions it is advantageous to move first: There is a *first-mover advantage*. In other cases it is better to move second.

Strategic moves are taken to influence the beliefs or actions of the rival in favorable ways. Typically, strategic moves involve a firm restricting its own future actions. For strategic moves to work, they must be *credible*. For a strategic move to be credible, it must include a commitment sufficient to convince its rival to change its beliefs.

Many strategic situations involve repeated interaction among rivals. When an interaction is expected to occur more than once, it is called *a repeated interaction*. Typically, more equilibria are possible with repeated interaction than in a nonrepeated problem. For instance, cooperation is a potential equilibrium in repeated rivals' dilemmas (see the appendix to this chapter for a more detailed analysis).

This chapter focuses primarily on competition between rival firms. The analysis of strategic interactions also provides managerial insights for interactions with other parties, such as suppliers and government regulators. It can be particularly useful in analyzing interactions with other employees within the firm.

Suggested Readings	A. Dixit and B. Nalebuff (1993), *Thinking Strategically* (W.W. Norton & Company: New York).
	J. McMillan (1996), *Games, Strategies, & Managers* (Oxford University Press: New York).

Self-Evaluation Problems

9–1. *Time Magazine* and *Newsweek* are two competing news magazines. Suppose that each company charges the same $5 price for their magazines. Each wants to maximize its sales given the $5 price. Each week, there are two potential cover stories. One is on politics. The other is on the economy. Sales of both companies are affected by the decisions on which story to place on their covers. The two magazines make this decision independently and at the same time. The resulting sales for the two companies are given in the following table:

Time Cover	*Newsweek* Cover	*Time* Sales ($000's)	*Newsweek* Sales ($000's)
Politics	Politics	400	150
Politics	Economy	700	200
Economy	Economy	200	150
Economy	Politics	300	700

    a. Construct a diagram that shows the payoffs to the two firms in *strategic (normal) form.*

    b. What is the *Nash equilibrium* in this game?

    c. Does either or both of the magazines have a *dominant strategy* in this game?

    d. Suppose that both magazines are owned by the same publishing company that maximizes the combined profits of the magazines. Will the company make the same choice as in the noncooperative game?

9–2. **a.** Suppose that *Newsweek* chooses and announces its cover story before *Time Magazine* chooses its cover. Construct a diagram that shows the payoffs of the game in *extensive form.*

    b. What is the *Nash equilibrium* in this game?

    c. Is there a *first-mover advantage* or *first-mover disadvantage* in this game?

Solutions to Self-Evaluation Problems

9–1. Simultaneous Moves, Nonreported Interaction

    a. Below is the *strategic form* of the game where the two magazines make simultaneous moves (note that the circles and shaded quadrant are for Part b of this problem).

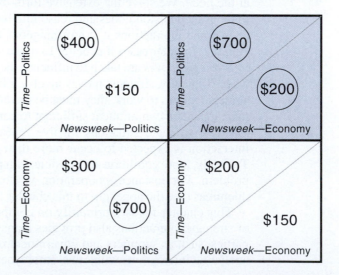

b. The *Nash equilibrium* can be found by the circle technique. When *Newsweek* chooses Politics (first column), *Time* does best by choosing Politics—circle the $400 payoff. When *Newsweek* chooses Economy (second column), *Time* does best by choosing Politics—circle the $700 payoff. When *Time* chooses Politics (first row), *Newsweek* does best by choosing Economy—circle the $200 payoff. When *Time* chooses Economy (second row), *Newsweek* does best by choosing Politics—circle the $700 payoff. The *Nash equilibrium* is for *Time* to choose Politics and *Newsweek* to choose Economy where both payoffs are circled. This is the shaded quadrant in the diagram.

c. *Time* has a dominant strategy in this game. It wants to choose Politics no matter what *Newsweek* does. *Newsweek* does not have a *dominant strategy*. Its optimal choice between Politics and Economy depends on what *Time* chooses to do.

d. The publishing company would place Economy on *Time*'s cover and Politics on *Newsweek*'s cover. The combined profits are $1,000 versus $900 in the noncooperative game.

9–2. Sequential Interaction

a. Below is the *extensive form* of the game, where *Newsweek* moves first.

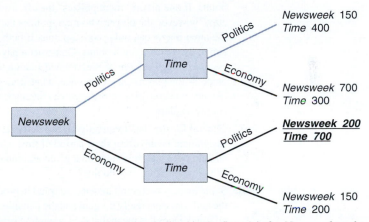

b. The *Nash equilibrium* (in bold and underlined in the figure) is for *Newsweek* to choose Economy and *Time* to choose Politics. This equilibrium is found as follows. *Newsweek* looks forward to *Time*'s choice and reasons backward. If *Newsweek* chooses Politics, *Time* will choose Politics and *Newsweek* will obtain 150 subscriptions. If it chooses Economy, *Time* will choose Politics and *Newsweek* obtains 200 subscriptions. Therefore it is in *Newsweek*'s interest to choose Economy. *Time* will subsequently choose Politics.

c. There is no *first-mover* or *second-mover advantage* in this game. *Time* has a *dominant strategy* always to choose Politics. Given this choice, *Newsweek* wants to choose Economy. Therefore the equilibriums in the simultaneous and sequential games are the same.

Review Questions

9–1. Some manufacturers that contract with the U.S. government have *most favored nation clauses* in their contracts. This provision makes the firm sell to the government at the lowest price it charges to any other customer. On the surface this provision seems to be advantageous to the government because it ensures them the lowest price charged to any customer. Others argue, however, that the clause gives manufacturers more power in bargaining with other buyers. Explain how this increased bargaining power might occur.

9–2. Suppose Microsoft can produce a new sophisticated software product. However, it wants to do so only if Intel produces high-speed microprocessors. Otherwise, the software will not sell. Intel, in turn, wants to produce high-speed microprocessors only if there is popular software on the market that requires high-speed processing. Is this a game of competition or coordination? What is the equilibrium?

9–3.   What is the relation between a dominant strategy and a Nash equilibrium?

9–4.   In this chapter we gave an example of coordination problems in the market for HDTVs. Show the game in strategic form using hypothetical payoffs of your choice. Use the arrow technique to identify the equilibria.

9–5.   Some foolish teenagers play "chicken" on Friday nights. Two teenagers drive their cars at each other at high speeds. The first to swerve to the side is the "chicken" and loses. If both swerve out of the way, they are both chickens and both lose. Neither of the drivers wants to get into an accident. It causes a significant loss in utility (possibly death). However, both do not want to be known as a chicken. This causes some loss in utility. What is the equilibrium of this game? Do you think the two drivers will necessarily produce an equilibrium outcome? Do you think the chances are better or worse for achieving an equilibrium outcome if the two players know each other? Explain. Do you think it matters whether the two players have played the game before? Explain.

9–6.   Two basketball players, Barbara and Juanita, are the best offensive players on the school's team. They know if they "cooperate" and work together offensively—feeding the ball to each other, providing screens for the other player, and the like—they can each score 12 points. If one player "monopolizes" the offensive game, while the other player "cooperates," however, the player who monopolizes the offensive game can score 18 points, while the other player can only score 2 points. If both players try to monopolize the offensive game, they each score 8 points. Construct a payoff matrix for the players that captures the essence of the decision of Barbara and Juanita to cooperate or monopolize the offensive game. If the players play only once, what strategy do you expect the players to adopt? If the players expect to play in many games together, what strategy do you expect the players to adopt? Explain.

9–7.   General Electric has frequently placed managers together to work on teams. Often the work assignment is only for a short period of time. General Electric makes sure that the quality of an employee's performance on a given assignment is recorded and shared with future teams. Why do you think they do this?

9–8.   Some managers commit undetected fraud in producing financial statements. Presumably, if the auditors were really diligent and the penalties for fraud were high enough, there would be no fraud. Does this mean that the accounting firms are not doing a good enough job in auditing? Explain.

9–9.   A labor leader has announced that her union will go on strike unless you grant the workers a significant pay raise. You realize that a strike will cost you more money than the pay raise. Should you concede to the wage increase? Explain.

9–10.   Suppose you are one of two producers of tennis balls. Both you and your competitor have zero marginal costs. Total demand for tennis balls is

$$P = 60 - Q$$

where Q = the sum of the outputs of you and your competitor.

   a.   Suppose you are in this situation only once. You and your competitor have to announce your individual outputs at the same time. You expect your competitor to choose the Nash equilibrium strategy. How much will you choose to produce and what is your expected profit?

   b.   Now suppose that you have to announce your output before your competitor does. How much will you choose to produce? What is your expected profit? Is it an advantage or a disadvantage to move first? Explain.

9–11.   You are considering placing a bid over the Internet in an eBay auction for a rare oriental rug. You are not a dealer in these rugs, and you do not have a precise estimate of its market value. You do not want to buy the rug for more than its market value. However, you would like to buy it if you can get it below the market value. You expect that many people will participate in the auction (including rug dealers). eBay asks that you give them the maximum bid you are willing to make. They will start low; whenever you are outbid, they will raise your bid just enough to lead the auction. eBay quits bidding on your behalf once your maximum price is reached. Your best guess at the market value is $1,000. What should you bid?

9–12. Formulate the following situation as an extensive form game (using a game tree) and solve it using backward induction. Bingo Corporation and Canal Corporation are the only competitors in the electronic organizer industry. Bingo Corporation is considering an R&D investment to improve its product. Bingo can choose from three levels of investment: High, Medium, and Low. Following Bingo's investment, Canal Corporation will have to choose between continuing to compete by selling its current product or undertaking an R&D project of its own. Canal can only choose one level of investment, so its choices are Invest or Not Invest. The net payoffs to Bingo if it invests High, Medium, or Low given that Canal chooses to Invest would be $50, $40, and $30, respectively, and the corresponding net payoffs to Canal would be $5, $10, and $15. On the other hand, the net payoffs to Bingo if it invests High, Medium, or Low given that Canal chooses to Not Invest would be $100, $80, and $60, respectively, and the corresponding net payoffs to Canal would be $0, $15, and $20. What will Bingo choose to do in equilibrium, and what will Canal's response be?

Appendix: Repeated Interaction and the Teammates' Dilemma[19]

Prisoners' dilemmas occur when it is in the joint interests of the parties to cooperate but individual incentives motivate an equilibrium where they fail to cooperate. Situations of this type occur frequently both between and within business firms. This appendix provides an example of how cooperation sometimes can be achieved when the decision makers are confronted with this same dilemma on a repeated basis. The example highlights the factors that are important in determining whether cooperation will be achieved in a repeated setting. Managerial implications are discussed.

Much of the analysis in this chapter has focused on interaction between rival firms. This example focuses on the interaction between two employees assigned to a team and is chosen to illustrate the wide applicability of the analysis of strategic interactions.

The Example

Anne van Gastel and Bert Dijkstra work on a production team. They want to agree to a "contract" that both will work hard so that they can earn a bonus. They face a problem in that the contract is not legally binding and effort is not contractible. This problem is similar to the prisoners' dilemma introduced in Chapter 6 as well as several examples in this chapter (e.g., the pricing problem between Boeing and Airbus).

Figure 9.8 displays the possible payoffs for this teammates' dilemma. If Anne and Bert both shirk, they receive salaries of $1,000. If both work hard, they receive a bonus. However, they experience disutility from the additional effort. The payoffs, net of this disutility, are $2,000 each. If Bert shirks and Anne works hard, they meet their production target and receive bonus payments. Bert, however, experiences no disutility from working hard and receives a payoff of $3,000. Anne also receives a cash bonus. However, being the only one to exert effort, she incurs a back injury. Her net payoff is $0. The opposite payoffs occur if Bert works and Anne shirks.

---

[19]This appendix modifies and extends an example in G. Miller (1992), *Managerial Dilemma: The Political Economy of Hierarchy* (Cambridge University Press: Cambridge), 184–186. It requires knowledge of basic statistics.

Figure 9.8 Payoffs to Two Members in a Single-Period Setting

The payoff on the upper left in each cell is the payoff for Anne, and the payoff on the lower right is for Bert. If Bert and Anne both shirk, they receive salaries of $1,000. If they both work hard, they receive a bonus. However, they experience disutility from working hard. The payoff, net of this disutility, is $2,000. If Bert shirks and Anne works hard, they meet their production target and receive a payoff of $3,000. Bert also receives a cash bonus. However, being the only one to exert effort, Anne incurs a back injury. Her net payoff is $0. The opposite payoff occurs if Bert works and Anne shirks. The Nash equilibrium in this single-period setting is for both to shirk (shaded cell). Given the payoffs, it is always in their individual interests to shirk.

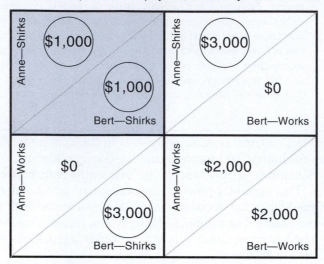

The Nash equilibrium in a single-period setting is for both to shirk. Given the pay-offs, it is always in their *individual interests* to shirk. If Anne works, Bert is better off shirking since he receives $3,000 rather than $2,000. Similarly, if Anne shirks, Bert would rather receive the $1,000 from shirking than the $0 payoff from working. This same logic holds for Anne. This equilibrium outcome is not efficient. Both Bert and Anne would prefer the outcome where they both work—there, payoffs are $2,000 instead of $1,000. The problem is that they can't observe each other's effort until after the work is complete.

Now suppose that Bert and Anne expect to work together in the future. In particular, suppose that in a given period there is a probability p that they will work together in the next period.[20] Thus, the probability that they will work together through n periods is p^{n-1}. Now suppose that Bert and Anne each consider only two options in choosing their effort levels. One is to follow the strategy of *always shirking* every period. If both Bert and Anne select this strategy, the expected sum of each person's future earnings will be[21]

$$E(\text{future earning}) = \$1,000 + \$1,000p + \$1,000p^2 \cdots \tag{9.1}$$

[20]In each period, Bert and Anne choose an effort level, observe output, and receive compensation from the firm.

[21]For simplicity, we ignore discounting future cash flows. Also, the formulation assumes that Bert and Anne have the possibility of living forever. Neither of these simplifications is crucial for our analysis.

Figure 9.9   Generalized Payoffs for Two Members in a Multiperiod Setting

Anne and Bert each consider two options in choosing their effort levels. One is to follow the strategy of always shirking every period. The other strategy, known as *tit-for-tat,* is to work hard for the first period and thereafter mimic their teammate's previous choice. For instance, if Bert works hard in the first period and Anne shirks, Bert will shirk in the second period. If one person shirks in the first period, then in all future periods both people shirk (the person who selects to shirk in the first period has chosen the strategy of always shirking). The upper-left payoff in each cell is Anne's, and the lower-right payoff is Bert's. In a given work period, there is a probability p that they will work together in the next period.

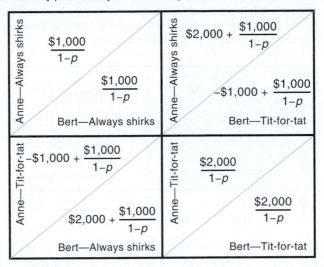

This expression is an infinite sum with a value of $\$1,000\,[1/(1-p)]$. The other strategy, known as *tit-for-tat,* is to work hard the first period and thereafter mimic their teammate's previous choice. For instance, if Bert works hard in the first period and Anne shirks, Bert will shirk in the second period. If one person shirks in the first period, then in all future periods both people shirk (the person who selects to shirk in the first period has chosen the strategy of *always shirking*).[22]

Both Bert and Anne want to maximize the expected sum of their individual future earnings from the working relationship. Figure 9.9 shows the generalized payoffs in the setting. Unlike the single-period case, it does not always pay a person to shirk. Clearly, if Anne expects Bert to shirk, she will shirk as well, since $\$1,000/(1-p)$ is always greater than $-\$1,000 + \$1,000/(1-p)$.[23] However, if Anne thinks that Bert is going to choose the tit-for-tat strategy, it *can be* in her interest to do so as well. Her expected payoff from selecting tit-for-tat is $\$2,000/(1-p)$. Thus, she will select tit-for-tat whenever p is greater than $1/2$—since $\$2,000/(1-p)$ is greater than $\$2,000 + \$1,000/(1-p)$. Symmetric logic holds for Bert's choice.

[22]Players adopting tit-for-tat strategies can get stuck in inefficient cycles of alternating honoring and cheating after a player makes a mistake, either in assessing the other player's choice or in choosing his own strategy in a single period (each player reacting to the other player's previous choice). Economists have suggested slight modifications that overcome this and several other conceptual problems with tit-for-tat. We concentrate on tit-for-tat since it is easy to explain and conveniently highlights the major factors that are likely to favor cooperative outcomes.

[23]The payoff from tit-for-tat is $[\$0 + (\$1,000p + \$1,000p^2 \cdots)] = [-\$1,000 + \$1,000 + (\$1,000p + \$1,000p^2 \cdots)] = -\$1,000 + \$1,000/(1-p)$.

Figure 9.10   Payoffs for Two Team Members of a Production Team When the Likelihood of Working Together in the Future Is Low (*p* = 1/3)

Bert and Anne each consider two options in choosing their effort levels. One is to follow the strategy of always shirking every period. The other strategy, known as *tit-for-tat*, is to work hard for the first period and thereafter mimic their teammate's previous choice. For instance, if Bert works hard in the first period and Anne shirks, Bert will shirk in the second period. If one person shirks in the first period, then in all future periods both people shirk (the person who selects to shirk in the first period has chosen the strategy of always shirking). The payoff on the lower left in each cell is Anne's payoff, while the payoff on the lower right is Bert's. In a given work period, there is a probability *p* that they will work together in the next period. In this example, the probability of working together in the future is relatively small (1/3). The circle technique indicates that the Nash equilibrium is for both to shirk (shaded cell).

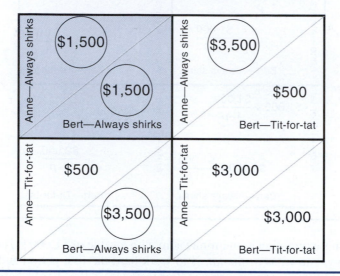

Figures 9.10 and 9.11 show the payoffs for Bert and Anne for the cases, where $p = 1/3$ and $p = 3/4$. When $p = 1/3$, the Nash equilibrium is for both to shirk—the probability of repeated interaction is not large enough to promote cooperation. This example illustrates the general point that reputational concerns are unlikely to promote cooperation when the relationship is expected to be short-term. In the second case, two equilibria are possible: mutual shirking or mutual cooperation.

The existence of multiple equilibria when $p = 3/4$ suggests that Bert's and Anne's initial expectations are important. For instance, if Bert expects Anne to shirk, he will shirk as well. However, if he expects her to choose tit-for-tat, it makes sense for him to select the same strategy. Anne has similar incentives. Thus, the efficient outcome—for both to work—will occur when there is a mutual expectation that both will work hard. This example suggests that businesses might promote cooperation by fostering particular expectations among employees. For instance, suppose the company publicizes in a credible manner that its employees have a long record of mutual cooperation. The firm might also invest in developing a reputation for hiring talented, motivated people who are unlikely to shirk. Given this "corporate culture," it is reasonable for Bert to expect that Anne will select tit-for-tat. Anne will have similar expectations. Both will select tit-for-tat, and the corporate culture is reinforced.

Figure 9.11 **Payoffs for Two Team Members of a Production Team When the Likelihood of Working Together in the Future Is High ($p = 3/4$).**

Bert and Anne each consider two options in choosing their effort levels. One is to follow the strategy of always shirking every period. The other strategy, known as *tit-for-tat,* is to work hard for the first period and thereafter mimic their teammate's previous choice. For instance, if Bert works hard in the first period and Anne shirks, Bert will shirk in the second period. If one person shirks in the first period, then in all future periods both people shirk (the person who selects to shirk in the first period has chosen the strategy of always shirking). The payoff on the lower left in each cell is Anne's payoff, and the payoff on the upper right is Bert's. In a given work period, there is a probability p that they will work together in the next period. In this example, the probability of working together in the future is relatively high (3/4). The arrow technique indicates that two Nash equilibria exist. One is mutual shirking; the other mutual tit-for-tat (both cells are shaded).

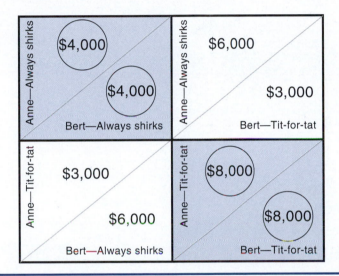

We have shown that the expected length of the relationship is important in determining the level of cooperation. So are the expected payoffs. For instance, if the payoffs from mutual shirking are increased to $1,500, the probability of working together in the next period must be 2/3 to promote cooperation. Alternatively, if the payoffs from mutual cooperation are $2,500, the required probability falls to 1/3. These examples illustrate the general principles that reputational concerns will work best at resolving incentive problems when the short-term gains from cheating are small and when the gains from continued cooperation are large.

Another factor that is important is the likelihood of being caught shirking. In this example, shirking is observed perfectly before the next period. If Bert and Anne do not know for certain that the other person has shirked, they might continue to cooperate even if the other person has shirked. In this case, the temptation to shirk will be greater.

Managerial Implications

Recently, managers have delegated more work assignments to teams. Problems like the one in this example can reduce team output and the firm's value. Managers can limit these problems and promote cooperation among team members by structuring rewards (e.g., bonuses) that are high if team members cooperate and low if they do not. Also, managers must be careful not to change team composition too frequently: Incentive problems are larger when team members do not expect to work together in the future.

Analyzing Managerial Decisions: Restructuring

The BQM Company frequently restructures. Employees regularly are transferred among departments and given different job assignments. Management argues that this action promotes a better trained and more responsive workforce. Do you see potential problems with this type of frequent restructuring? Does this mean that BQM is making a mistake? Explain.

Incentive Conflicts and Contracts

LEARNING OBJECTIVES

1. Define the firm as a focal point for a set of contracts.
2. Identify important owner-manager conflicts, as well as other potential stakeholder conflicts.
3. Explain how contracts can be used to help control incentive problems.
4. Explain how asymmetric information can increase the costs of contracting.
5. Differentiate between adverse selection problems and moral hazard problems.
6. List the components of agency costs.
7. Discuss how implicit contracts and reputational concerns can sometimes reduce incentive problems and contracting costs.
8. Explain why all the firm's stakeholders potentially have a common interest economizing on contracting costs.

A very large corporate takeover occurred in 1988—the purchase of RJR-Nabisco by Kohlberg, Kravis, Roberts & Company. Public accounts report lavish expenditures and decisions of questionable merit by RJR executives preceding the takeover. For example, Burrough and Helyar in their best seller *Barbarians at the Gate* write,

> *It was no lie. RJR executives lived like kings. The top 31 executives were paid a total of $14.2 million, or an average of $458,000. Some of them became legends at the Waverly for dispensing $100 tips to the shoeshine girl. [Ross] Johnson's two maids were on the company payroll. No expense was spared decorating the new headquarters, highlighted by the top-floor digs of the top executives. It was, literally, the sweet life. A candy cart came around twice a day dropping off bowls of bonbons at each floor's reception areas. Not Baby Ruths but fine French confections. The minimum perks for even lowly middle managers was one club membership and one company car, worth $28,000. The maximum, as nearly as anyone could tell, was Johnson's two dozen club memberships and John Martin's $105,000 Mercedes.*

In addition, it appears that major investment decisions at RJR often were driven by the preferences of managers rather than by value maximization. For instance, Ross Johnson, CEO of RJR, reportedly continued to invest millions of dollars in developing a smokeless cigarette long after it was obvious that the project would never be profitable.

More recently other executives have been charged with even more extreme examples of excessive behavior. For example, in July 2002, the U.S. Justice Department charged that John Rigas and his two sons "looted Adelphia on a massive scale" and used it as a "personal piggy bank." Over the past five decades Rigas had built a small cable company in rural Pennsylvania into Adelphia Communications—listed on Nasdaq and the sixth largest U.S. cable company. The government's complaint charged the Rigas family with using Adelphia's assets to buy company stock, timberland, New York condos, and a National Hockey League team; to build a golf course on family-owned property; to bankroll movies produced by a Rigas' daughter; and to pay for automobiles on behalf of a Rigas-owned dealership.[1] Rigas was subsequently convicted and sentenced to a 15-year jail term. He is scheduled to be released from prison in 2018.

The behavior of RJR and Adelphia executives raises at least four interesting issues:

- In previous chapters, we assumed that managers *always* maximize profits. Apparently, they do not. To understand management problems *within the firm,* we need a richer characterization of the firm and managerial decision making.

- Both RJR and Adelphia suggest that material conflicts of interest can exist between owners and managers: Shareholders are interested in the firm's value, whereas the managers are interested in their own utility. What other conflicts of interest exist within firms?

- These cases suggest that owner-manager conflicts can result in reduced productivity and waste. Unchecked, such conflicts of interest can destroy a firm. How do firms limit unproductive actions to enhance value and avoid failure?

- If techniques to limit unproductive actions exist, why did the owners (shareholders) at RJR and Adelphia allow the managers to engage in such dysfunctional behavior?

In this chapter, we examine these and related issues. We begin by enriching our understanding of the definition of a firm. We then use this more explicit understanding to discuss various conflicts of interest that exist within firms. Next, we examine how contracts help reduce or control these conflicts. We focus particular attention on the problems created by costly information. Finally, we discuss how reputational concerns can control incentive conflicts within firms.

Firms

In Chapter 3, we characterized the firm in terms of administrative decision making: Markets use prices to allocate resources; firms use managers. This prompted a discussion of the relative efficiency of firms and markets. Thus far in the book, we have treated the firm as if it had one central manager who acts to maximize the firm's value. This characterization is employed widely in economics and has proved quite useful in explaining production and pricing decisions.

[1]D. Lieberman and G. Farrell (2002), "Five Former Adelphia Arrested," *USA Today* (July 24); R. Grover (2002), "Adelphia vs. Deloitte in a Game of Blame," *BusinessWeek Online* (June 27); and R. Farzad (2005), "Jail Terms for 2 at Top of Adelphia," *New York Times* (June 21), C1.

Figure 10.1 The Firm as a Focal Point for a Set of Contracts

The firm is a creation of the legal system that has the standing of an individual in a court of law. The firm serves as one party to the many contracts that make up the firm.

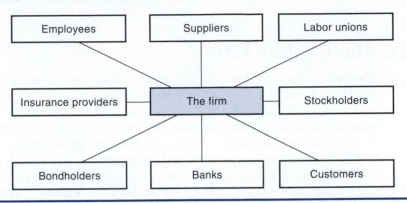

The actual decision-making process within firms, however, is extremely complex and differs from this simple characterization in at least three ways. First, there are many decision makers within firms. In large corporations, the board of directors makes major policy decisions including appointing the CEO. The CEO, in turn, retains certain important decision rights while delegating many operating decisions (for instance, pricing, production, and financing decisions) to lower-level managers. Even the lowest-paid employee in the firm usually has some decision-making authority. Second, the primary objective of most of these decision makers is not to maximize the value of the firm: The investment behavior of the RJR executives certainly suggests interests in things other than corporate value maximization. Third, firms often use internal pricing systems (transfer prices) to allocate internal resources.

Analyzing organizational issues *within the firm* requires a richer concept of the firm. Several useful definitions have been developed by economists.[2] We focus on one definition that is particularly useful for our purposes[3]: The firm is a focal point for a set of contracts. This definition focuses on the fact that the firm ultimately is a creation of the legal system; it has been granted the legal standing of an individual (it can enter contracts, sue, be sued, and so on). The term *focal point* indicates that the firm always is one of the parties to each of the many contracts that constitute the firm. Examples of these contracts are employee contracts, supplier contracts, customer warranties, stock, bonds, loans, leases, franchise agreements, and insurance contracts. This contract view of the firm is depicted in Figure 10.1.

Some contracts are explicit legal documents, whereas many others are implicit. And even within a relationship that has been formalized with an explicit contract,

> **Definition**
>
> The *firm* is a focal point for a set of contracts.

---

[2] O. Hart (1989), "An Economist's Perspective on the Theory of the Firm," *Columbia Law Review* 89, 1757–1774.

[3] M. Jensen and W. Meckling (1976), "Theory of the Firm: Managerial Behavior, Agency Costs and Ownership Structure," *Journal of Financial Economics* 3, 305–360.

there is a broad array of aspects of the relationship that are not spelled out within the written agreement—they are implicit. An example of an implicit contract is an employee's understanding that if a job is done well, it will result in a promotion. Implicit contracts are often difficult to enforce in a court of law. Later in this chapter, we discuss how reputational concerns can help ensure that individuals honor implicit contracts.

Incentive Conflicts within Firms[4]

Economic theory characterizes individuals as creative maximizers of their *own utility*. Thus, the collection of individuals that contract with the firm are not likely to have objectives that are automatically aligned. The owners of the firm have title to the residual profits (what is left over after other claimants are paid) and are likely to be interested in maximizing the present value of these profits. Other individuals within the firm do not share this goal necessarily. In this regard, the corporation is more like a market than a person. One sometimes hears statements like "GM would like to raise car prices." Although GM shareholders, managers, and other employees might favor higher automobile prices, GM's customers (including franchise dealers) undoubtedly would not. If someone stated that the wheat market favored higher prices, the statement would produce confusion. Suppliers in the wheat market would favor higher prices while demanders would not. Similarly, within firms the incentives of the contracting parties often conflict with one another. We now discuss some of the more important incentive conflicts that arise within firms. We then discuss how contracts can be used to reduce and control these conflicts.

Owner-Manager Conflicts

Owners often delegate the management of firms to professional managers. For instance, in large corporations, the residual profits are owned by shareholders who delegate significant decision authority to top executives. At least five sources of conflict arise between owners and managers:

- **Effort Choice.** Additional effort by managers generally increases the value of the firm, but since the managers expend the effort, additional effort reduces their utility.

- **Perquisite taking.** It is in the interests of owners to pay sufficient salaries and bonuses to attract and retain competent managers. However, owners do not want to overpay managers. In contrast, managers are likely to want not only higher salaries but also perquisites such as exclusive club memberships, lavish office furniture, luxurious automobiles, stimulating day care for children, and expensive French confections.

- **Differential risk exposure.** Managers typically have substantial levels of human capital and personal wealth invested in the firm. This large investment can make managers appear excessively risk-averse from the standpoint of the owners, who (at least in a large public corporation) typically invest only a

---

[4]This section draws on M. Jensen and C. Smith (1985), "Stockholder, Manager, and Creditor Interests: Applications of Agency Theory," in E. Altman and M. Subrahmanyam (Eds.), *Recent Advances in Corporate Finance* (Irwin Professional Publishers: Burr Ridge), 95–131.

The Spectrum of Organizations

The firm can be viewed as a focal point for a set of contracts. One, particularly, important feature of these contracts is the distribution of the residual profits. Organizations vary remarkably along this dimension. In a sole proprietorship like Esptein's Deli, the owner/manager is the residual claimant. In a partnership like the law firm of Nixon-Peabody, the claims are shared by the partners. In a large public corporation like Amazon.com, these claims often are held by thousands of shareholders who take little direct interest in managing the company. In a mutual like the Prudential Insurance Company, ownership and customer claims are merged. In a cooperative like Ocean Spray, supplier and ownership claims are merged. In an employee-owned firm like United Airlines, the claims are owned by the employees. Finally, in a not-for-profit institution like the American Red Cross there are no owners of the residual cash flows. In most of these large organizations, management authority is delegated to professional managers, who often have small or no ownership positions in the organization. According to Coase, individuals have incentives to select the form of organization that minimizes total contracting costs (see Chapter 3).

Our discussion of conflicts between owners and managers suggests that problems arise in public corporations because of the separation of ownership and control. These problems are costly to resolve. Given these costs, what are the offsetting benefits that promote the prominence of large corporations? One of the most significant benefits is that capital is raised from many investors who share in the risk of the company. Individual shareholders place only a small amount of their wealth in a given company, and thus avoid "placing all their eggs in one basket." This diversification makes risk-averse investors (see Chapter 2) willing to supply capital to corporations at a lower cost. This benefit, however, comes at the cost of having to control the incentive conflicts between managers and owners. Thus, in smaller operations, where raising large amounts of capital is less of an issue, one should expect to find sole proprietorships and small partnerships (where there is less separation of ownership and control). Indeed, this is what is observed.*

*There are also tax-related reasons that affect the choice of organizational form.

Source: M. Scholes, M. Wolfson, M. Erickson, and M. Hanlon (2014) *Taxes and Business Strategy* (Prentice-Hall: Englewood Cliffs).

small fraction of their wealth in any one firm.[5] Hence, managers might forgo projects that they anticipate would be profitable simply because they do not want to bear the risk that the project might fail and lead to a reduction in their compensation.

- **Differential horizons.** Managers' claims on the corporation generally are limited by their tenure with the firm. Therefore, managers have limited incentives to care about the cash flows that extend beyond their tenure. Owners, on the other hand, are interested in the value of the entire future stream of cash flows, since it determines the price at which they can sell their claims in the company.

- **Overinvestment.** Managers can be reluctant to reduce the size of a firm, even if it has exhausted available profitable investment projects; they prefer to empire build. Also, managers often are understandably reluctant to lay off colleagues and friends in divisions that are no longer profitable. Managers who fire their colleagues bear personal costs (disutility), whereas shareholders receive most of the benefits.

[5]To be more precise, we do not assume that the underlying preferences (utility functions) of owners and managers differ. Rather we focus on the fact that the risk of owners' claims on public firms can be managed more easily through diversification than can those of managers. The most valuable component of most managers' wealth is their human capital, and managers typically have but one job.

MANAGERIAL APPLICATIONS

Buyer-Supplier Conflicts

Immediately after the United States invaded Iraq, the U.S. military hired Halliburton to supply the U.S. troops in Iraq with supplies. One contract involved the provision of gasoline. The contract terms stated that Halliburton would be reimbursed for its costs plus receive a 1 percent profit margin. The problem with such cost-plus contracts is that they provide little incentive for the supplier to control costs, or to pick the most competitive subcontractors, since the higher the costs, the higher the profits to the supplier (Halliburton in this case). The Pentagon investigators charged that Halliburton purchased gasoline at almost double the market value after only receiving bids from two other gasoline suppliers. In 2005, the Defense Contract Audit Agency of the Pentagon and the U.S. Congress investigated the charges without coming to a definitive resolution.

Source: N. King, Jr. (2004), "Halliburton Says Two Employees Took Kickbacks for Iraq Contracts," *The Wall Street Journal* (January 23), A1, A5; and R. Klein (2005), "Audit Questions $1.4b in Halliburton Bills," *Boston Globe* (June 28), www.boston.com.

Other Conflicts

Similar types of incentive conflicts are likely to arise among most contracting parties in the firm. For example, top managers worry about effort and perquisite-taking problems with lower-level employees. The firm's creditors and shareholders can have disputes over the optimal dividend, financing, and investment policies of the firm. Firms can have incentives to default on warranties with customers. Managers often quarrel with labor unions. For example, Alcatel-Alsthom SA, a French conglomerate, was unable to divest any of its low-margin plants without engendering an uproar from its unions.[6]

Owners of firms would like to acquire high-quality inputs at low prices, whereas owners of supplying firms would like to provide inexpensive inputs at high prices. This tension produces conflicts between buyers and suppliers. Supplying firms worry about buying firms demanding price concessions, and buying firms worry that suppliers will either shirk on quality (to reduce cost) or raise prices.

Incentive conflicts also arise with joint ownership. For example, in a large accounting firm, the actions of each partner affect the profits of the organization, which are shared among the partners. This arrangement can motivate partners to *free-ride* on the efforts of others. Each partner hopes the other partners will work diligently to keep the firm profitable. However, each partner has an incentive to shirk: Individual partners gain the full benefit of their shirking but bear only part of the costs (their share of the reduced profits). Free-rider problems are common in most group activities and, if left unchecked, greatly reduce the output of teams. (We shall refer to such free-rider problems throughout the rest of this book.)

Controlling Incentive Problems through Contracts

What keeps these incentive conflicts from undermining cooperative undertakings and destroying all organizations? For example, might the fear that managers will use all company resources for their personal benefit dissuade owners from delegating

---

[6]D. Lavin (1998), "Union and Regulators Restrain Alcatel's Restructuring," *The Wall Street Journal* (August 7), A8.

MANAGERIAL APPLICATIONS

Experimental Evidence on Free-Rider Problems

Over a century ago a German scientist named Ringelmann asked workers to pull as hard as they could on a rope attached to a meter that measured the strength of their efforts. Subjects worked alone as well as in groups of two, three, and eight.

While the total amount of force on the rope increased as group size rose, the amount of effort by each person seemed to drop. While one person pulling alone exerted an average of 63 kg of force, this dropped to about 53 kg in groups of three and was reduced to about 31 kg in groups of eight. The greater the number of people performing the task, the less effort each one expended.

The impact of any social force directed toward a group from an outside source (e.g., a manager) is divided among its members. Thus, the more persons in the group, the less the impact such force will have upon each. Because they are working with others, each group member feels [that others] will take up any slack resulting from reduced effort on their part. And since all members tend to respond in this fashion, average output per person drops sharply.

Source: B. Kantowitz, H. Roediger and D. Elmer (2014), *Experimental Psychology,* 19th edition (Cengage Learning: Independence, KY).

operating authority to managers?[7] Fortunately, there are mechanisms that help control incentive conflicts. Among the most important are contracts.[8]

Contracts (both implicit and explicit) define the firm's organizational architecture—its decision right, performance evaluation, and reward systems. This architecture provides an important set of constraints and incentives that helps resolve incentive problems. For instance, if a contract specifies that Erin O'Malley, the firm's chief financial officer, will receive an annual salary of $200,000, she can be fired if she unilaterally pays herself more: She does not have the decision right to set her own compensation.[9] If Erin is evaluated on firm profits and rewarded with a large bonus for good performance, she has incentives to care about the firm's profits.

Costless Contracting

Under some circumstances, contracts can resolve incentive problems at low cost. As an example, consider Jerold Concannon, CEO of the Bagby Printing Company. Jerry gains utility U, from both his monetary compensation C and perquisites P such as company expenditures on luxury cars and club memberships:

$$U = f(C, P) \tag{10.1}$$

If the firm provides no perquisites to Jerry, it must pay him a salary S in cash compensation; otherwise, he will work for another firm. The owners of the firm are

---

[7]In fact, some authors suggest that this concern ultimately will cause the collapse of the public corporation. See A. Berle and G. Means (1932), *The Modern Corporation and Private Property* (Macmillan: New York).

[8]Other important mechanisms are the market for corporate control and the product market. Managers have incentives to increase a firm's profits because firms with inefficient managers can be taken over by other firms and the management team replaced. Indeed, this is what happened at RJR-Nabisco. Also, inefficient firms eventually go out of business in a competitive market.

[9]Restricting an agent's decision-making authority can reduce incentive problems. However, it also can mean that authority has not been granted to the individual with the best knowledge to make the decision. This tension is a fundamental concern in designing organizational architecture and is a central focus of Chapter 11.

MANAGERIAL APPLICATIONS

Incentive Conflicts Around the World

Incentive conflicts are not just an American business phenomenon, nor do they occur only in private firms. Rather, these conflicts exist in all types of organizations throughout the world.

In July 2013, the largest corporate governance scandal in Japanese history ended when the former chairman of the board and two other top executives of the Olympus Corporation, a multinational optical equipment manufacturer, pleaded guilty to charges of falsifying accounts to cover up losses of $1.7 billion. All three executives received prison sentences, ranging from 2.5 to 3 years.

The scandal surfaced in October 2011 when Michael Woodruff was ousted as CEO of Olympus. He had questioned the board of directors about large, irregular payments that they had authorized to financial advisors in corporate acquisitions. He wanted to have an accounting firm audit the transactions. The board responded by quickly firing him.

Woodruff did not leave the company quietly. He immediately left for London and provided the British Serious Fraud Office a file containing information on the transactions. He suggested that the potentially illegal payments were linked to the Board of Directors and the scandal continued to grow. Press coverage accelerated. Over the period from October 12 to November 12, 2011, Olympus' stock price fell from a price of 2,500 yen to 500 yen—an 80 percent decline. Olympus board members resigned in mass and the financial statements were ultimately restated. Criminal charges were filed against the former top executives/board members. The scandal raised investor concerns about corporate governance practices throughout Japan.

Source: BBC News Business (2013), "Olympus scandal: Former executives sentenced," www.bbc.com (July 3).

willing to pay Jerry S if he consumes no perquisites. However, as CEO, Jerry has numerous opportunities to consume company resources. These opportunities present an incentive problem: Jerry would like to spend company resources on himself, whereas the owners do not want Jerry to reduce the firm's value by consuming excessive perquisites. As we will see, some amount of perquisites actually increases value. But beyond this level of perquisite consumption, value falls.

Suppose for now that the owners of the firm have precise knowledge of the maximum potential profit of the firm, Π_M (if Jerry is paid S and consumes no perquisites). In this case, realized profits of the firm, Π_R (if he is paid S and consumes perquisites, P) are the difference between maximum profits and Jerry's excess perk consumption:

$$\Pi_R = \Pi_M - P \tag{10.2}$$

With this information, the owners can solve the potential incentive problem by offering Jerry the following compensation contract:

$$C = S - (\Pi_M - \Pi_R) \tag{10.3}$$

This contract, which reduces Jerry's salary by the difference between realized and maximum profits, is equivalent to charging Jerry the full cost of his perquisites—that is, $C = S - P$.

Figure 10.2 displays Jerry's choice of perquisites. His objective is to maximize his utility subject to the constraint that he is paid according to his compensation plan. Jerry chooses the combination (C^*, P^*), which occurs at the tangency point between his indifference curve and the compensation constraint. This combination

Figure 10.2   Optimal Perquisite Taking

The manager is paid a cash salary *S*, as long as the manager maximizes profits. If the manager fails to maximize profits by taking perquisites (e.g., too many club memberships, paying excessive salaries to top subordinates, or buying expensive company cars), the owners reduce the compensation by the amount of the lost profits. Given this compensation scheme, the manager chooses the combination (*C**, *P**). This choice is Pareto-efficient.

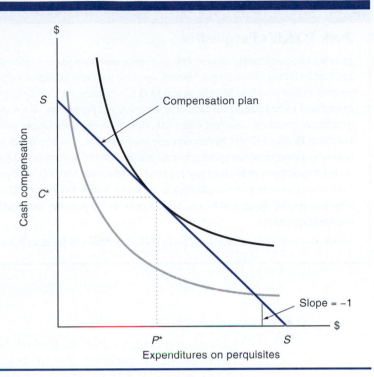

places Jerry on the highest indifference curve possible given the compensation plan. This choice is Pareto-efficient. The owners are indifferent to Jerry's choice: They always pay the equivalent of *S* (they pay him *S* − *P* in cash and *P* in perquisites). Jerry, however, is better off being able to choose the combination of salary and perks that he prefers. For example, Jerry had a back injury and prefers a more expensive, ergonomically designed desk chair to the company's standard office furniture, even though he knows that his compensation is reduced to reflect the additional expense. Also, Jerry might prefer a combination of salary and perquisites to a pure salary because perks frequently are untaxed.[10]

Note how the compensation plan aligns Jerry's and the owners' incentives. Jerry is given the decision right to choose how much the firm spends on his perquisites. The contract, however, charges Jerry the full cost of his perk consumption. In essence, he is rewarded for consuming fewer perquisites. This reward structure gives him private incentives to limit his perk consumption.

In this analysis the owners establish the firm's total compensation expense associated with Jerry's employment, *S*, Jerry chooses his optimal level of perk consumption, *P**, and this determines his cash compensation, *C** (= *S* − *P**). This

---

[10]This tax effect is reflected in Jerry's indifference curves. Over some range, Jerry is willing to trade more than a dollar of cash for a dollar's worth of perquisites because on an after-tax basis, he is better off. Over this range, the slope of the indifference curve has a slope with an absolute value greater than one. The optimal choice of salary and perks occurs at the point where the indifference curve's slope is −1.

mechanism probably seems far-fetched. Yet such an outcome can be approximated closely through negotiation. If at the beginning of the period Jerry negotiates for a perquisite level of P^*, the owners recognize that their total compensation expense will be the sum of his cash compensation plus his perk consumption. Thus, they will set his cash compensation at C^* ($= S - P^*$).

This example suggests that some perk taking by managers is likely to be efficient (from the standpoint of both the managers and the firm) because some perks increase productivity, as well as because of the differential tax treatment for perquisites and salary. Thus, the perk taking by RJR executives was not necessarily inconsistent with the shareholders' objective of value maximization. Without the perks, the shareholders might have had to pay higher salaries to attract and retain the management team. Evidence from the stock market, however, suggests that the behavior of RJR executives was excessive. The stock price of RJR went from about $55 per share at the beginning of the takeover contest in October 1988 to about $110 per share when the company was taken over. Furthermore, the management team subsequently was replaced. Thus, the old RJR management team does not appear to have been maximizing the firm's value.

Costly Contracting and Asymmetric Information

We have shown how, in some cases, well-designed contracts can resolve incentive problems at low cost. Yet the example of RJR suggests that contracts often are unsuccessful in accomplishing this objective.

Unlike our hypothetical example, contracts in practice are not costless to negotiate, write, administer, or enforce. For instance, suppose that the owners of Bagby Printing delegate executive compensation decisions to its board of directors. In this case, Jerry might be able to convince board members not to enforce his contract to reduce his salary for perk consumption. (Indeed, Ross Johnson

ANALYZING MANAGERIAL DECISIONS: *Opening a New Restaurant*

You are the owner of a small restaurant chain in the Portland, Oregon, area. All five of your restaurants employ the same basic business concept and have similar building designs, menus, and service formats. Each of the outlets has a head manager who has primary responsibility for the day-to-day operations at that location. All five of the outlets are within a 20-mile radius of your central office. You are actively involved in the business and frequently meet with your top management staff. You often spend time at the restaurants during business hours, visiting with customers and helping to manage the staff. You pay each of your managers $40,000 per year and provide them with a package of fringe benefits (e.g., paid vacation and insurance). Over the past three years you have also given each of the managers a $3,000 holiday bonus in December.

Several of your customers moved last year from Portland to Salt Lake City, Utah. They have e-mailed you suggesting that you open a restaurant in Salt Lake. They miss your food, service, and restaurant format. They believe the new restaurant would be successful. You have conducted market research and are thinking seriously about starting the new restaurant. One concern that you have is that Salt Lake is over 750 miles from Portland.

1. Discuss the incentive conflicts that are likely to arise between owners and managers of a restaurant.
2. You have been able to control these conflicts relatively well at your existing restaurants. Do you anticipate that the conflicts will be easier or harder to control at the new Salt Lake location?
3. Should you offer the new head manager at the Salt Lake location the same compensation contract that you are using for the five managers in Portland?

at RJR apparently attempted to keep board members loyal and supportive by paying them large retainers.) Board members participating in such collusion with senior managers can be replaced, but only at a cost. Legal fees alone can be substantial for writing and enforcing contracts (*Fortune 500* firms were estimated to have spent nearly $210 billion on legal fees in 2008—equal to about one-third of their profits.).[11]

A major factor limiting the ability of contracts to resolve incentive conflicts is costly information. In contrast to our example, it is unlikely that the owners of Bagby Printing actually would know the profit potential of the firm. Information is likely to be *asymmetric*: Jerry simply knows more than the owners about the firm's profit potential as well as his perk consumption. Given this distribution of information, controlling Jerry's perk taking by using a compensation contract that requires perfect information about the profit potential of the firm clearly is infeasible.

There are two general types of information problems that arise in contracting. The first problem is informational asymmetries before the contract is negotiated. The second is the problem of informational asymmetries during the implementation of the contract. Below, we elaborate on each of these problems. We begin with the postcontractual problems because of their importance in this text.

[11]J. Henry (2008), "Fortune 500: The Total Cost of Litigation Estimated at One-Third Profits," *elaw Forum* (February 1).

Postcontractual Information Problems

Agency Problems

An *agency relationship* consists of an agreement under which one party, the *principal,* engages another party, the *agent,* to perform some service on the principal's behalf. Many agency relationships exist within firms. Shareholders appoint boards of directors as their agents to oversee the management of firms. Boards delegate much of the operating authority to senior executives; they, in turn, assign tasks to lower-level employees. As we have discussed, there is good reason to believe that the incentives of principals and agents are not aligned automatically. There are *agency problems:* After the contract is set, agents have incentives to take actions that increase their well-being at the expense of the principals. For instance, as in the case of RJR, managers might shirk, consume perquisites, and choose investment and operating policies that reduce profits but increase the managers' expected well-being.

Asymmetric information typically precludes costless resolution of these contracting problems. Since the principal cannot observe the actions of the agent costlessly, the agent generally can engage in activities such as shirking and perk consumption without those activities invariably being detected by the principal. Nonetheless, the principal usually can limit such behavior by establishing appropriate incentives for the agent through the contract and by incurring *monitoring costs.* Also, agents might incur *bonding costs* to help guarantee that they will not take certain actions or to ensure that the principal will be compensated if they do (e.g., agents might bond themselves by purchasing insurance policies that pay the principal in the case of theft). The agent is willing to incur these expenses to increase the amount paid to the agent by the principal for the agent's services. If it is costly to control these contracting problems, then it generally will not pay for either party to incur sufficient costs to ensure that the agent will follow the wishes of the principal completely (at some point marginal cost exceeds the marginal benefits of additional expenditures to increase

---

MANAGERIAL APPLICATIONS

Technology to Reduce Monitoring Costs

Between 1997 and 2001 the percentage of companies recording and reviewing employee phone conversations has remained constant at around 10 percent. Those monitoring voice-mail messages have remained around 6 percent. But e-mail and Internet usage monitoring by employers has exploded from 15 percent to 46 percent of large U.S. companies. Firms are turning to monitoring employee use of e-mail and the Internet for good reason. Various surveys report that 90 percent of employees surf non-work-related Web sites at the office, 15 percent of employees spend over two hours a day surfing nonbusiness sites, and 10 percent receive 21 or more personal e-mails. Companies also fear expensive litigation resulting from an employee accessing sexually explicit material or circulating offensive e-mails.

Firms worried that employees are spending too much time on personal e-mails or surfing non-business-related sites are turning to technology to reduce the problems. One type of software blocks sites companies want to prevent employees from accessing, such as sex, gambling, shopping, and job search sites. Other software monitors how long each employee is online, the Web sites visited, and the time spent on each site. Managers look for unusual patterns and report them to the employee's supervisor, who usually talks to the employee and then blocks the sites. Blocking and usage monitoring software is relatively inexpensive, costing firms about $15 per employee per year.

Source: A. Cohen (2001), "Worker Watchers," *Fortune/CNET Technology Review* (Summer), 70–80.

compliance). The dollar equivalent of the loss in gains from trade that results from this divergence of interests within the agency relationship is known as the *residual loss. Total agency costs* are the sum of the *out-of-pocket costs* (monitoring and bonding costs) and the residual loss.

Example of Agency Costs

To illustrate the concepts of agency costs and asymmetric information, consider Good Tire Company and the Brown & Brown law firm. Good Tire wants outside legal counsel for contracting and litigation, as well as for general legal advice. Brown & Brown is capable of supplying these services.

Good Tire's marginal benefit, MB, for hours of legal services is

$$MB = \$200 - 2L \tag{10.4}$$

where L equals the hours per week of legal services provided to the firm. Good Tire faces some important legal issues, and thus the marginal benefits for legal services are quite high for the first few hours. But as these fundamental issues are resolved, the company receives advice on successively less important issues. Therefore, the marginal benefit of additional hours of legal services declines with the total number of hours provided.

Brown & Brown's marginal cost (MC) for providing additional hours of legal services is constant at $100 per hour:

$$MC = \$100 \tag{10.5}$$

Value is maximized—all potential gains from trade between Good Tire and Brown & Brown are realized—at the point where the marginal benefits of legal services equal their marginal costs:

$$MB = MC \tag{10.6}$$
$$200 - 2L = 100$$
$$L^* = 50 \text{ hours}$$

It is not optimal to provide more than 50 hours of legal services because the marginal benefits would be lower than the marginal costs. Correspondingly, it is suboptimal to provide fewer than 50 hours because the marginal costs of providing additional hours would be lower than the marginal benefits.

Assuming no contracting costs, an optimal contract simply might specify 50 hours per week of legal services. For example, Good Tire could agree to pay Brown & Brown $6,250 a week for 50 hours of legal work. This outcome is pictured in the left panel in Figure 10.3. The total gain from the exchange (surplus) is $2,500, as depicted by the triangle labeled *S*. At a price of $6,250 for legal services, the gains are split evenly between the two companies.[12] The fee covers Brown & Brown's costs of $5,000 (50 × $100) and provides it with a profit of $1,250. Good Tire receives gross benefits of $7,500. However, it pays a fee of $6,250, yielding net benefits of $1,250. If the two firms negotiate other prices for the 50 hours of legal services, the split in gains would be different. If the market for legal services is

---

[12]Recall that total benefits (TB) are equal to the area under the marginal benefit curve, while total costs (TC) are the area under the marginal cost curve. Thus, at 50 hours of legal service, the total surplus is $S = TB - TC$.

Figure 10.3   Agency Costs in Legal Contracting

The left panel shows the marginal benefit (MB) to Good Tire for hours of legal services (L) and the marginal cost (MC) to Brown & Brown for providing these services. Assuming no incentive problems, the optimal number of hours is 50. The total gains from trade, $2,500, are shown by the triangle labeled S. The right panel reflects the contracting costs between the two firms—Brown & Brown might bill for more hours than hours worked. The two firms spend $400 each for monitoring and bonding costs. These out-of-pocket costs are shown by the rectangle labeled O. Since it does not pay to resolve this incentive problem completely, we assume that Brown & Brown ends up providing only 40 hours of legal services. The triangle R represents the residual loss of $100. The original surplus S is reduced by the sum of the out-of-pocket costs and the residual loss. The resulting surplus, labeled S', is $1,600. How this surplus is split depends on the price charged for the legal services.

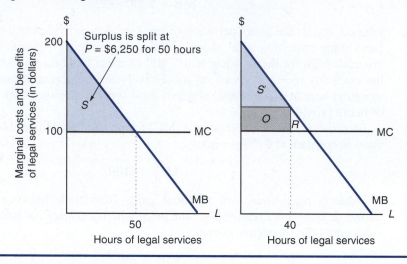

perfectly competitive, the price would be $5,000 ($100 per hour), and all gains would go to Good Tire. But as long as total hours are set at 50, the agreement is efficient and total surplus is $2,500.

A potential incentive problem can confound this relationship: It is costly for Good Tire to observe how many hours of legal work Brown & Brown actually provides to the firm (there is asymmetric information). Thus, Brown & Brown might work far fewer than 50 hours but still claim it worked the full amount. Indeed, the problem might be so severe that Good Tire does not hire Brown & Brown at all. In this case, the total potential gains from trade are lost. This contracting cost is a residual loss: The lost surplus that results because it is simply too costly to resolve this incentive problem.

More generally, the two firms might be able to promote a mutually advantageous exchange by controlling this incentive problem through expenditures on monitoring and bonding. For example, Good Tire might spend $400 per week to hire a manager specifically to oversee Brown & Brown's work, and Brown & Brown might spend $400 per week to document that it is actually conducting legal work for the firm. But it is unlikely that it will pay the two parties to expend sufficient resources to guarantee that Brown & Brown will do no overbilling. For example, the end result might be that, after the $800 expenditures on monitoring and bonding, Brown & Brown provides 40 hours of legal service (more hours than if there were no monitoring/bonding) and bills for 50 hours. Both parties anticipate this outcome and might negotiate a price of $5,200 for the legal service.[13] This price is lower than in the case where information is costless and there are no incentive problems: Good Tire is unwilling to pay as much for the anticipated 40 hours as it would if it were sure it would receive 50 hours of legal services.

The right panel in Figure 10.3 illustrates this outcome. The triangle, labeled *R*, is the residual loss of $100—the lost surplus that results because it is not efficient to resolve the incentive problem completely. In addition, the two companies pay $400 each for monitoring and bonding. These payments reduce the surplus by $800, as shown by the rectangle labeled *O*.[14] The remaining surplus is $1,600. This surplus is equal to the original surplus of $2,500 minus the total contracting costs of $900—the sum of the out-of-pocket costs (monitoring and bonding costs) and the residual loss. In the end, Brown & Brown earns a net profit of $800 [= $5,200 − (40 × 100) − 400]. Good Tire obtains net benefits of $800 [= $6,400 − $5,200 − $400].[15] Both firms are $450 per week worse off than in the case where there was neither asymmetric information nor incentive problems.

Precontractual Information Problems

Information normally is asymmetric at the time of contract negotiations, as well. For example, in negotiating a labor contract, the prospective employee typically has superior information on what wage is acceptable, whereas the employer knows more about what the firm is willing to pay. Precontractual informational asymmetries also generate contracting costs and can cause at least two major problems—bargaining failures and adverse selection.

Bargaining Failures

Asymmetric information can prevent parties from reaching an agreement even when in theory a contract could be constructed that would be mutually advantageous. Suppose that Sheri Merriman is willing to accept a job for as little as $2,500 per month and Jon Park, the human resources manager, is willing to pay as much as $3,000 per month. In principle, a mutually advantageous contract could be negotiated at any price between $2,500 and $3,000. Neither side, however, is likely to know the other side's reservation price (the highest price that Jon is willing to offer and the lowest price that Sheri is willing to accept). In an attempt to get the best price possible, both parties might overreach, resulting in a bargaining failure. In her initial interview, Sheri might ask for $3,500. Hearing this, Jon might discontinue negotiations because he doubts that he can hire Sheri for less than $3,000 (his reservation price). This phenomenon helps to explain the existence of labor strikes that end up hurting both labor

---

[13]Good Tire cannot observe the actual hours worked by Brown & Brown. Nonetheless, it can have *rational expectations* (an unbiased forecast given the information that it does have) that Brown & Brown will work 40 hours, yet bill for 50. Note that the $5,200 price is chosen somewhat arbitrarily in this example; as we will see, it is the price that splits the surplus.

[14]The placement of this rectangle is arbitrary. All that is important is that the area of the original surplus be reduced by the $800 out-of-pocket expenses.

[15]The $6,400 is the gross surplus for Good Tire. It is the area under the marginal benefit curve between zero and 40 hours.

MANAGERIAL APPLICATIONS

Incentive Problems between Homeowners and Real Estate Agents

Real estate agents perform an important economic function in connecting buyers and sellers of homes and in marketing the listed properties. The typical agent conducts an initial evaluation of the property, takes pictures to use in marketing materials, helps to set the price, writes ads, shows the house to prospective buyers, negotiates the offers, and sees the deals through to the end. The typical contract between the seller and the agent pays the agent a commission of 6 percent of the final selling price, which generally is split among agents involved in the sale.

While the sales commission helps to motivate the agent, it does not provide strong incentives for the agent to work hard to obtain a high price. As an example, suppose that a prospective buyer offers $300,000 to purchase a house and the opportunity cost of the agent is $2,000 per day. The agent believes that by working an extra day she can obtain a price of $320,000 for the home. The commission is $18,000 if the house is sold for $300,000 versus $19,200 if the house sells for $320,000. From the agent's perspective, it is not worth working a full day to obtain the higher commission. The $2,000 opportunity cost exceeds the extra $1,200 in commissions, which would likely be shared with other agents. The seller's and agent's incentives are not perfectly aligned.

If the agent owned the house, there would be no incentive conflict. The agent would have strong incentives to work an extra day to obtain a $20,000 higher price, since it would far exceed the opportunity cost of working to obtain it. A recent study of the sale of nearly 100,000 home sales in suburban Chicago identifies over 3,000 houses sold that were owned by agents. Using the data from the sales of those 100,000 Chicago homes, and controlling for other important variables—location, age and quality of the house, aesthetics, whether or not the property was an investment, and so on—it turns out that real-estate agents keep their own homes on the market for an average of 10 days longer and sell it for an extra 3-plus percent, or about $10,000 on a $300,000 house. When agents sell their own house, they hold out and work for a higher offer; in contrast, when they are acting as an agent, they encourage the sellers to take the first decent offer that comes along. While homeowners often benefit from holding out for a higher selling price, the agents want to make deals and make them fast. Why not? Their share of the 6 percent commission provides too puny of an incentive to encourage them to do otherwise. Homeowners potentially benefit if they understand these incentives and do not act blindly in accepting whatever advice an agent has to offer.

Source: S. Levitt and S. Dubner (2009), *Freakonomics: A Rogue Economist Explores the Hidden Side of Everything* (Harper Perennial): New York.

and the company. (Strikes result in lower productivity and sales; thus there are fewer profits to be divided between labor and the company.)

Adverse Selection

A second problem caused by precontractual informational asymmetries is *adverse selection*. Adverse selection refers to the tendency of an individual with private information about something that affects a potential trading partner's costs or benefits to extend an offer that would be detrimental to the trading partner.

As an example, consider the market for health insurance.[16] Table 10.1 displays three individuals and their expected medical costs for the year. Angela is the healthiest and expects to spend only $100 on medical expenses, whereas Cindy is the least healthy and expects to spend $900; Bruno is in the middle with expected expenditures of $500. The average expected expenditure for all three individuals is thus $500 per person.

It is likely that each individual knows more about his or her health than an insurance company does: Individuals know how they have been feeling and their health

---

[16]Managers often are involved in designing or modifying fringe-benefit policies. Understanding the following problem is important in this activity. We discuss this issue in greater detail in Chapter 11.

	Expected Annual Medical Expenditure
Angela Wilson	$100
Bruno Lopez	$500
Cindy Lo	$900
All three individuals	$500 per person

Table 10.1   Example of Adverse Selection in Insurance Markets

This table shows the expected annual medical expenditures for three individuals. If an insurance company sells insurance to all three at a price above $500 per year, it expects to make a profit. However, if the company prices insurance at $500, Angela is unlikely to purchase the insurance. Bruno and Cindy have average expected expenditures of $700 per person. Thus, if Bruno and Cindy are the sole purchasers, the company must sell the insurance at above $700 to break even. In this case, Bruno might not buy the insurance. The end result can be a market failure, where the company prices the insurance at $900 and sells only to Cindy.

habits, whereas an insurance company is likely to have information that is restricted to the typical expenditures for readily observed categories within the population (e.g., age and gender categories). In this spirit, suppose that each individual knows his or her expected expenditure whereas the insurance company knows only the expected expenditure for the three individuals as a group—$500 per person. If the company expects to make a profit, it must sell insurance policies at premiums that exceed the expected expenditures of the buyers.

The information structure in this example can dissuade some potential customers from transacting in the market, thereby reducing the gains from trade. For instance, assume that the insurance company tries to sell insurance at $510. If all three parties were to buy the insurance, the company would expect to make a profit. However, at this price, Angela might not want to purchase insurance. She expects to spend only $100 on medical expenses; from her perspective, the insurance appears extremely expensive.[17] At a premium of $510, if only Bruno and Cindy bought the insurance, the company on average would lose money: Expected losses would be $190 per policyholder since their expected expenses would be $700. The insurance company might anticipate that healthy individuals will not buy the insurance at $510 and quote a higher price. For example, if the insurer offered the policies to both Cindy and Bruno and they purchased at $710, it would make a profit. However, at this price Bruno is less likely to buy the insurance because the price is substantially above his expected expenditure of $500. In the end, the insurance company might price insurance at a cost above $900 and sell only to Cindy—the least healthy of the three.

The company might be able to sell insurance to all three parties by becoming better informed about the individual health status of each of its applicants so that it could quote more customized rates. For example, it might require a medical exam of all applicants, as well as access to their medical records. In this case, different rates could be charged, depending on the health of the individual. Collecting information, however, is costly, and thus there is an incentive to consider these costs in the design of the

---

[17]Since Angela is risk-averse, she would be willing to spend more than $100 for insurance (see Chapter 2). However, here we assume that she concludes that $510 is too expensive.

MANAGERIAL APPLICATIONS

Rising Health Care Costs Create Employee Conflicts

As health care costs rise, many employers are passing on these costs to their employees who are paying a larger fraction of the total health insurance premium. Since at most companies, 80 percent of the health care costs are generated by 20 percent of the employees, healthy workers resent having to pay more to finance the unhealthy habits of a few. David Jackson who works at Rockford Products Corp. points to a coworker driving a forklift truck. "Just look at that guy, his belly's almost touching the steering wheel. It's gross." The forklift driver weighs 340 pounds and has trouble walking because of pain in his ankles due to his weight. Because workers are bearing more of their health insurance costs, workers are starting to pay attention to their colleagues' eating and smoking behavior. Young workers are questioning how much they should pay for seniors, or why employees with one or two children should pay for employees with large families. While such behavior induced by increasing the percentage of health insurance paid by the employees is creating friction within companies, such peer pressure might actually lead to a healthier workforce.

Source: T. Aepel (2003), "Skyrocketing Health Costs Start to Pit Worker vs. Worker," *The Wall Street Journal* (June 17), A1, A6.

organization and its policies.[18] For instance, since the cost of the additional information is fixed, the insurer might require exams of applicants requesting broader coverage limits but not for those willing to accept narrower coverage.

In some cases, adverse-selection problems can be reduced by the clever design of contracts. An insurance company might be able to offer a menu of contracts with different deductibles, coinsurance requirements, and prices that would motivate these individuals to *self-select* based on their private information. For example, Angela might choose a low-priced insurance contract with a high deductible, whereas Cindy might choose a high-priced contract that provides full insurance. In this case, the company might be able to sell insurance to all three customers at a profit.

Sometimes, it is possible for individuals to communicate, or *signal,* their private information to other parties in a credible fashion. For example, Angela might be able to convince the insurance company that she is quite healthy and should be offered insurance at a low rate. (She might document that she participated in six marathon races during the year.) Angela's communication to the company will be convincing to the company only if the cost to Bruno and Cindy for sending the same signal is higher than Angela's (e.g., because they are not in excellent health, they are unable to participate in marathons). Otherwise, they could take the same action to claim they were healthy, and then there would be no reason for the company to believe any of their claims.

---

[18]The company also might overcome the problem by selling group insurance to a company that employs all three individuals. In this case, the individuals do not select whether or not to be covered. Thus, the insurance company can make a profit at a premium above $500 per person. Note that insurance regulations vary across countries. The *Affordable Care Act (ACA)* enacted in 2010, currently requires insurance companies in the United States to offer the same rates for health insurance regardless of preexisting conditions or sex. These restrictions potentially make it more costly for U.S. insurance companies to address adverse selection problems. The ACA requires all individuals who are not otherwise covered to purchase private coverage or pay a penalty. The intent of this provision is to reduce the adverse selection problem. It remains in question as to whether this will be effective, given that many of the young and healthy may choose to pay the penalty, rather than to purchase what for them are overpriced policies.

MANAGERIAL APPLICATIONS

Fraud in Small Firms

The nightly news often features stories about fraud and other scandals in large corporations. Fraud and other incentive conflicts, however, are not just large firm problems. They can and do occur in firms of all size.

In 2014, the office manager of a Florida medical office, Heart Care Centers of Central Florida, was arrested for embezzlement. According to the county sheriff, she had embezzled more than $650,000 over a two-year period, using the money to rent an upscale home, buy furniture, electronics, a 2014 Audi Q7, and an S7. She was booked on 128 felony charges, including money laundering, fraudulent use of a credit card, and forgery. According to reports,

> *She transferred money from the medical group to her companies ... opened credit cards and lines of credit, some under the medical group's name, some under doctors' name.*

The global losses of companies due to employee fraud are estimated to be $3.7 trillion annually. Small companies are among the most common victims. Fraud occurs in all regions throughout the world. While it is not practical to eliminate all possibilities of fraud, the problem can be reduced by various practices, such as requiring all employees in financial positions to take periodic vacations (where their functions are performed by other employees) and periodic review or audits of the accounts.

Source: A. Ford (2014), "BCSO: Titusville medical office manager embezzled thousands'" *Florida Today* (May 1).

Adverse-selection problems are not limited to insurance markets; they occur in many settings. Prospective employees are likely to know more about their talents and productivity than employers. Similarly, the seller of a used car knows more about the quality of the car than the buyer. Thus, at a given price, sellers are more likely to offer "lemons" than high-quality cars.[19] In these settings, traders often develop mechanisms that help reduce adverse-selection problems. Used-car dealers offer warranties that guarantee that if the car is a lemon, the dealer will repair or exchange it at the dealer's expense. Also, there are diagnostic mechanics that provide prospective buyers with a professional assessment of the quality of a car.

Implicit Contracts and Reputational Concerns

Implicit Contracts

Many of the contracts that constitute the firm are implicit: They consist of promises and understandings that are not formalized within legal documents. Examples include promises of promotions and salary increases for a job well done and informal understandings that suppliers will not shirk on quality. By definition, implicit contracts are difficult to enforce in court; they depend largely on private incentives of individuals to honor their terms. Given the incentive conflicts that we discuss in this chapter, why would individuals ever expect others to honor terms of implicit contracts? Specifically, why would an employee ever trust an unwritten promise by a manager to give the employee a raise for a job done well? Doesn't the manager always have incentives to abrogate the contract after the job is complete? After the task is complete, the benefits are sunk. Not granting the raise would appear to reduce costs, increase profits, and thereby increase the manager's bonus.

---

[19]G. Akerlof (1970), "The Market for Lemons: Quality Uncertainty and the Market Mechanism," *Quarterly Journal of Economics* 84, 488–500.

MANAGERIAL APPLICATIONS

Sony's Implicit Contract

Sony Corporation has a valuable brand name and an implicit contract with customers for providing consistent high-quality products and services. Violations of this implicit contract are likely to diminish customers' trust in the company and reduce the value of the Sony brand name.

In 2011, hackers infiltrated the Sony PlayStation network and stole data on more than 77 million users. Just a few days later, the hackers struck again by infiltrating an older database, containing sensitive customer information including names, addresses, birth dates, passwords, and even credit card information. The public announcement of these actions raised significant concerns among Sony customers and was arguably viewed as a violation of the implicit agreement to provide high-quality services.

It took Sony about one month to restore its system. Afterward, Sony offered its customers a welcome-back program that included upgrades and purchase credits. Sony also offered to enroll customers in identity theft protection programs at no cost to the customers. In a welcome-back video, Sony executive Kazuo Hirai offered his "sincere apologies for the inconvenience the service outage has caused." He went on to say

We know you've invested in Sony and the PlayStation network and Qriocity services, and we will do everything we can to regain your trust and confidence. We also realize that actions speak louder than words, and we're taking aggressive action to address the concerns that were raised by this incident.

Corporate violations of implicit contracts occur from time to time—sometimes inadvertently. In some cases, customer trust can be restored by appropriate managerial responses. Repeated violations, however, can destroy significant value.

Source: M. Williams (2011), "PlayStation Network Hack Timeline," *IDG News Service* (May 1).

Reputational Concerns

The answer to these questions is that reputational concerns act as a powerful force to motivate contract compliance. In particular, the market can impose substantial costs on institutions and individuals for unscrupulous behavior. Thus, market forces can provide powerful private incentives to act with integrity. (Chapter 22 contains an extended discussion on promoting ethical behavior within corporations.)

As an example, consider a firm that has a long-term contract to provide a metal part to a manufacturing firm each month at a price of $10,000. The cost of producing this product is $9,000, so the profit per unit is $1,000. It is possible for the supplier to produce a low-quality product for $2,000. However, it has agreed to provide a high-quality product. Suppose the quality of the part is known to the buyer only after the purchase; it would be possible for the supplier to make a profit of $8,000 by producing a low-quality part, yet claiming it to be high-quality. The buying firm, however, will detect the quality of the part after purchase and will cancel future purchases if it is cheated. The supplying firm thus faces a trade-off. It can gain an additional $7,000 in the short run by cheating. However, it loses a $1,000 per month future profit stream. The supplier has a strong incentive to be honest so long as the present value of the future profit stream is greater than the short-run gain from cheating.

Typically, the costs of cheating on quality are higher if the information about such activities is more rapidly and widely distributed to potential future customers. Within a market like the diamond trade in New York, misrepresenting quality to another merchant is quite rare. This market is dominated by a close-knit community of Hasidic Jews; information about dishonest behavior spreads rapidly throughout this market. In other broader markets, specialized services that monitor the market help ensure contract performance. *Consumer Reports* evaluates products from toasters to automobiles, the *Investment Dealer's Digest* reports on investment bankers, and *Business-Week* ranks MBA programs. By lowering the costs for potential customers to determine quality, these information sources increase the costs of cheating.

More generally, reputational concerns are more likely to be effective in promoting contract compliance when (1) the gains from cheating are smaller, (2) the likelihood of detecting cheating is higher, and (3) the expected sanctions imposed if cheating is detected are higher. (For instance, sanctions are likely to be higher if the relationship is anticipated to extend over a longer period.) When these conditions are not met, reputational concerns are less effective in motivating contract compliance. In many settings, reputational concerns are extraordinarily important in promoting cooperation and integrity. The ability to enter into self-enforcing agreements can reduce the costs of contracting within an organization materially: Fewer resources are used for negotiating and enforcing formal contracts.

Incentives to Economize on Contracting Costs

It is important to understand that everyone has incentives to resolve contracting problems in the least costly manner. By so doing, there are additional gains from trade to share among the parties. In the Good Tire example, if their incentive problems could be resolved costlessly, there would be an additional $900 of surplus to split between Good Tire and Brown & Brown. (If they didn't have to spend money on auditors and compliance, they could divide the resulting savings between themselves.)

It is in the self-interest of individuals to minimize total contracting costs in any relationship.[20] Incentives exist to negotiate contracts that provide monitoring and bonding activities to the point where their marginal cost equals the marginal gain from reducing the residual loss. This means that incentives exist within the contracting process to produce an efficient utilization of resources (at least from the standpoint of the contracting parties).

> **Basic Principle: Value Maximization**
> Incentive problems generate costs that reduce value. It is in the interests of all parties to a contract to develop efficient solutions to agency problems. More value is created, which can be shared among the contracting parties.

Viewing contracts as efficient responses to the particular contracting problem can be an extremely powerful tool in explaining observed organizational architectures. As a simple example, consider the difference between the way fruit pickers are paid and the way employees who assemble airplanes are paid. Agricultural workers usually are paid on a piecework basis: The more fruit they pick, the more pay they receive. Alternatively, employees who assemble airplanes often are paid a straight salary (the same salary is paid independent of output). What accounts for this difference in observed contracts? In general, output increases if people are paid on a piecework basis. A person will pick more pieces of fruit per hour if paid by the piece than by the hour. However, piecework payments generate their own set of incentive problems. These payments motivate people to focus more on output and less on quality. In fruit picking, a supervisor can monitor the quality of the output inexpensively

---

[20]Technical note: For this statement to be strictly true, production costs must be separable from agency costs and there must be no wealth effects. (The choices of the principal and agent are independent of their individual wealth levels.) When these conditions are violated, the individuals might not want to minimize total agency costs. Nonetheless, they still have strong incentives to consider these costs in designing contracts. For our purpose, it is reasonable and convenient to ignore these technical considerations.

ANALYZING MANAGERIAL DECISIONS: *eBay.com**

eBay operates the world's largest online auction. In early 2008, eBay operated in 39 counties with 276 million registered users worldwide. The total value of all successfully closed items in 2007 was $59 billion with an average of $2,039 worth of goods trading on the site every second. Sellers pay a small fee to eBay to list their items. They provide a description of the item, photographs, the minimum acceptable bid, accepted forms of payment, and other relevant information. Items can be sold at a fixed price or through an auction. In an auction, bidders submit electronic bids over the Internet. After the auction closes (auctions usually last several days), the high bidder receives an e-mail. The high bidder must contact the seller within three business days to claim the item and arrange payment and delivery. eBay provides other support services:

- *The Feedback Forum* is a place where eBay users leave comments about each other's buying and selling experiences. If you are a bidder, you can check the seller's Feedback Profile easily before you place a bid to learn about the other buyers' experience. If you're a seller, you can do the same thing to check out buyers. Each participant is given a Feedback Score based on the number of positive and negative ratings that they have received. Participants with sufficient positive ratings are flagged by colored stars. The highest rating is the "Red shooting star." eBay has created a set of policies to guard against "feedback manipulation" and "feedback abuse."

- eBay users are encouraged to settle transactions through *PayPal*. *PayPal* provides free insurance of up to $2,000 on some items to protect buyers in cases where they do not receive the item or it was less than expected.

- Participants sign user agreements that specify the trading rules and expectations. eBay's safety staff investigates alleged misuses at eBay such as fraud, trading offenses, and illegally listed items. Potential resolutions include such things as banning a person from future trading on eBay.

1. How does eBay create value?
2. What potential contracting problems exist on eBay?
3. How does eBay address these problems?
4. What are the contracting costs at eBay?
5. eBay claims that it has only a small problem with fraud and misuse of the system. Does this imply that it is overinvesting in addressing potential contracting problems? Underinvesting? Explain.

*To obtain more detailed information, go to www.ebay.com.

through direct inspection of the harvested fruit. In the case of airplanes, quality problems may not be detected until after the employee leaves the job (e.g., after the plane is delivered, put into service, and—in the most extreme case—crashes). In this situation, the contracting costs of piecework payments are larger than the benefits. We apply this type of logic throughout the remainder of this book to explain the design of organizations.

Summary

Treating a firm as if it were an individual decision maker who maximizes profits is a useful abstraction in some contexts. For example, this characterization has been used in previous chapters in analyzing output and pricing decisions. But to analyze organizational issues within the firm requires a richer definition. A particularly useful definition for our purposes is that the *firm is a focal point for a set of contracts.*

Since individuals are creative maximizers of their own well-being, there are likely to be incentive conflicts among the parties that contract with the firm. Examples include owner-manager, buyer-supplier, and free-rider conflicts. Contracts (explicit and implicit) specify a firm's *organizational architecture* (its decision right, performance evaluation, and reward systems). This architecture establishes a set of constraints and incentives that can reduce the costs of incentive conflicts. Contracts are unlikely to resolve incentive problems completely because they are costly to negotiate, administer, and enforce. *Asymmetric information* causes particularly important problems.

An *agency relationship* consists of an agreement under which one party, the *principal,* engages another party, the *agent,* to perform some service on behalf of the principal. Many agency relationships exist within firms. Agents do not act in the best interests of principals automatically—there are *incentive problems.*

Asymmetric information usually implies that incentive problems cannot be resolved costlessly by contracts. The principal usually can limit the divergence of interests by structuring the contract to establish appropriate incentives for the agent and by incurring *monitoring costs* aimed at limiting dysfunctional activities by the agent. Also, agents might incur *bonding costs* to help guarantee that they will not take certain actions or to ensure that the principal will be compensated if they do. Generally, it does not pay to resolve incentive conflicts completely. The dollar equivalent of the loss in the gains from trade that results due to the divergence of interests in the agency relationship is known as the *residual loss.* Total agency costs are the sum of the *out-of-pocket costs* (monitoring and bonding costs) and the opportunity cost of the residual loss.

Precontractual informational asymmetries can cause breakdowns in bargaining and *adverse selection.* Adverse selection refers to the tendency of individuals, with private information about something that affects a potential trading partner's costs or benefits, to make offers that are detrimental to the trading partner. Costs of adverse selection reduce the gains from trade and can cause market failures. Precontractual information problems can be mitigated by information collection, clever contract design, credible communication, and mechanisms such as warranties.

Many of the contracts within firms are *implicit contracts* rather than formal legal documents. Implicit contracts are difficult to enforce in a court of law and depend largely on the private incentives of individuals for enforcement. *Reputational concerns* can provide incentives to honor implicit contracts. These concerns are more likely to be effective when (1) the gains from cheating are smaller, (2) the likelihood of detecting cheating is higher, and (3) the expected sanctions imposed if cheating is detected are higher. It sometimes is possible to structure organizations in ways that increase the likelihood that reputational concerns will be more effective in encouraging individuals to behave with integrity.

Parties to a contract have incentives to resolve contracting problems in the least costly manner. By so doing, there are additional gains from trade to share among the parties. Viewing observed contracts as efficient responses to the particular contracting problem provides a powerful tool for explaining organizational architecture.

| Suggested Readings | O. Hart (1989), "An Economist's Perspective on the Theory of the Firm," *Columbia Law Review* 89, 1757–1774. |
| | M. Jensen and W. Meckling (1976), "Theory of the Firm: Managerial Behavior, Agency Costs and Ownership Structure," *Journal of Financial Economics* 3, 305–360. Pay particular attention to the first 11 pages. |

M. Jensen and C. Smith (1985), "Stockholder, Manager, and Creditor Interests: Applications of Agency Theory," in E. Altman and M. Subrahmanyam (Eds.), *Recent Advances in Corporate Finance* (Richard D. Irwin: Burr Ridge), 93–131.

J. McMillian (1992), *Games, Strategies, and Managers* (Oxford University Press: New York).

G. Miller (1992), *Managerial Dilemmas: The Political Economy of Hierarchy* (Cambridge University Press: Cambridge).

Self-Evaluation Problems

10–1. John owns a home construction company. His cost for building a new house is $300,000. Sue is a potential home buyer who would be willing to pay John up to $400,000 to construct a new house if she knew for certain that John would not cheat her (e.g., using below standard, less expensive building materials in constructing the house).

   a. Suppose that Sue does not buy the house because she decides there is no way to prevent John from cheating her. What are the *total agency costs?* Divide these costs into the *residual loss* and *out-of-pocket costs.*

   b. Suppose that Sue hires an engineer for a cost of $20,000 to monitor the construction process. Sue expects that the engineer's work will significantly decrease the likelihood that John will cheat on the contract. There, however, is still some chance that John will cheat. Because of this possibility, Sue values the house at $390,000 rather than $400,000. Given her $20,000 expenditure for the engineer, her maximum willingness to pay is $370,000. Suppose that Sue pays John $350,000 to construct the house. What are the total gains from trade and how are they split? What are the *total agency costs?*[21] Divide these costs into the *residual loss* and *out-of-pocket costs.*

   c. Suppose that an additional engineer could be hired at a cost of $20,000 that would reduce the probability of John's cheating to zero. Would it be in Sue and John's joint interest to hire the engineer? Explain.

   d. Why should Sue pay for the engineer? Isn't it John's responsibility to assure that he will comply with the contract?

10–2. Suppose that a health insurance company is considering offering insurance to a population consisting of healthy and unhealthy people. Healthy people are expected to have $1,000 per year in medical bills, while unhealthy people are expected to have bills of $5,000 per year. The company knows that the population consists of 25,000 healthy people and 25,000 unhealthy people. However, it cannot tell whether any given individual is healthy or unhealthy. Individuals know their own type and only purchase insurance if the premium is no more than $100 above their expected medical bills. The insurance must be priced at least $100 above expected per-person costs for the insurance company to cover its costs and to be profitable. In equilibrium, what price will the insurance charge in this market? Who will buy the insurance? Assume for this problem that there are no binding regulations that limit insurance prices or force people to purchase insurance.

Solutions to Self-Evaluation Problems

10–1. Postcontractual Information Problems and Agency Costs

   a. The potential gains from trade of $100,000 equal the difference between Sue's reservation price for the house and John's cost of building the house: $400,000 − $300,000 = $100,000. These gains from trade are lost when Sue doesn't transact because of the incentive problem. Therefore, the total agency costs are $100,000. There are no out-of-pocket expenses. The $100,000 is a residual loss.

---

[21]John's reduction in building costs if he cheats could produce a private benefit that should be included in the calculation of the gains from trade and agency costs. However, John is also likely to face costs if he cheats (e.g., lost reputation if he is caught) that would reduce the net benefits. For simplicity, assume that John's net benefit from cheating is zero after the hiring of the engineer (this would make him indifferent between cheating and not cheating). With this assumption, John's cost is $300,000 whether he cheats or not.

b. The total gains from trade are $65,000: $385,000 (Sue's valuation) − $20,000 (for the engineer) − $300,000 (John's costs) = $65,000. The total gains from trade of $65,000 are split as follows. Sue gets $15,000: $385,000 (her value for the house) − $20,000 (the cost of the engineer) − $350,000 (price of the house) = $15,000; John gets $50,000: $350,000 − $300,000 = $50,000. The total agency costs of $35,000 equal the difference between the potential gains from trade with zero contracting costs and the actual gains from trade given costly contracting: $100,000 (see part *a*) − $65,000 = $35,000. These costs are divided into out-of-pocket costs and the residual loss. The out-of-pocket costs are $20,000 for the engineer. The residual loss is the remaining $15,000: $35,000 (total agency costs) − $20,000 (out-of-pocket costs) = $15,000. This residual loss reflects the fact that due to the agency problem Sue gets a house that she values at $385,000 instead of $400,000.

c. It would not be in Sue and John's interest to hire another engineer. Hiring the additional engineer costs $20,000, while elimination of the remaining residual loss is worth only $15,000. Thus, the gains from trade would fall by $5,000 if they hired the extra engineer. [The gains would equal: $400,000 (Sue's value) − $300,000 (John's costs) − $40,000 (cost of the engineers) = $60,000, which is $5,000 lower than when only one engineer is hired.]

d. Paying for the engineer is a value-increasing expenditure that reduces total agency costs and increases the gains from trade. It is in the joint interests of John and Sue to hire the engineer since it increases their gains from trade. It is not important who writes the check to cover this expense. How the gains from trade are split is ultimately determined by the transaction price. For example, the same split would occur if John wrote the $20,000 check for the engineer, and Sue paid $370,000 for the house. [In some transactions, the gains from trade can depend on who writes the check, for example if one party can deduct the expense for tax purposes, while the other cannot.]

10–2. Precontract Information Problems: Adverse Selection

The equilibrium price is $5,100 and only unhealthy people will buy the insurance. The following explains why. If all 50,000 people bought the insurance, the company would expect to earn $100 per customer if it priced the insurance at $3,100. It would expect to lose $1,900 on each of the unhealthy people and make $2,100 on each of the healthy people. Given that there is a .5 probability that any given person is healthy, it would expect to make [(.5 × $2,100) − (.5 × $1,900)] = $100 per person (the necessary amount to stay in business). There, however, is *adverse selection* at the $3,100 price—people who know that they are healthy will not buy the insurance. Since only unhealthy people buy the insurance at $3,100, the company would expect to lose $1,900 per customer. The company, therefore, prices the insurance at $5,100 and only sells to people who know they are unhealthy. The company cannot charge more than $5,100 because no one will buy the insurance. If it charges less it will not make the necessary $100 per customer to stay in business. Potential gains from trade in selling insurance to healthy people are lost unless the company can devise a way to address the adverse selection problem.

Review Questions

10–1. What is a firm?

10–2. Give examples of incentive conflicts:
   a. Between shareholders and managers
   b. Between coworkers on teams

10–3. What is asymmetric information? How can it limit contracts from solving incentive conflicts?

10–4. Name the two parties involved in an agency relationship.

10–5. What potential problems exist in agency relationships?

10–6. Is it worthwhile for shareholders to seek to completely eliminate incentive problems with managers and directors through means such as monitoring? Why or why not?

10–7. What is adverse selection? Give an example.

10–8. How do reputational concerns aid in the enforcement of contracts?

10–9. Schmidt Brewing Company is family-owned and -operated. The family wants to raise some capital by selling 30 percent of the common stock to outside shareholders. The company has been profitable, and the family indicates that it expects to pay high dividends to shareholders. The family will maintain 70 percent ownership of the common stock and continue to manage the firm. The rights of shareholders are specified in the company's corporate charter. The charter specifies such items as voting rights (procedures and items subject to a vote), meeting requirements, board size, rights to cash flows, and so on. Once adopted, a charter can only be changed by a vote of the shareholders. What types of provisions in the corporate charter of Schmidt Brewing might motivate minority shareholders to pay higher prices for the stock? Explain.

10–10. Which of the following examples is an adverse-selection problem and which is an incentive problem? Explain why. In each case, give one method that the restaurant might use to reduce the problem.

    a. A restaurant decides to offer an all-you-can-eat buffet that is sold for a fixed price. The restaurant discovers that the customers for this buffet are not its usual clientele. Instead, the customers tend to have big appetites. The restaurant loses money on the buffet.

    b. A restaurant owner hires a manager who promises to work long hours. When the owner is out of town, the manager goes home early. This action results in lost profits for the firm.

10–11. In 1992, the state of California charged Sears Auto Centers with overcharging customers for unneeded or unperformed repairs. Sears agreed to a settlement that could cost as much as $20 million. Sears had compensated its salespeople with commissions based on total sales. Following the settlement, Sears dropped the commissions and went to a straight salary. Sears recently indicated that it is planning to reinstate commissions for salespeople in their Auto Centers. It even plans on paying commissions for selling customers brake jobs and wheel alignments. These two products were the core of the 1992 scandal. Sears says that it has taken steps to prevent a recurrence of past problems. In particular, the decision right to recommend repairs is granted to mechanics who are paid a straight salary. Sales consultants are paid commissions for selling repair services but are not authorized to recommend repairs. Under the old system that caused problems, these individuals diagnosed repair problems and sold the corresponding service to customers. Why do you think Sears wants to reinstall commissions for its salespeople? Do you think that the new safeguard that separates diagnosing problems from selling services will prevent a recurrence of past problems? Explain.

10–12. The Sonjan company currently purchases health insurance for all of its 1,000 employees. The company is considering adopting a flexible plan whereby employees can either have $2,000 in cash or purchase an insurance policy (which currently costs $1,000). Do you see any potential problems with the new plan? Explain.

chapter

11

Organizational Architecture

LEARNING OBJECTIVES

1. Describe the fundamental problem facing all organizations and how the architecture of markets differ from the architecture of firms.

2. List the three components of a firm's organizational architecture.

3. Explain how a firm's business environment and strategy help to determine its optimal organizational architecture.

4. Describe how the three components of an organization's architecture are interrelated and why it is important to design them in a balanced (complementary) fashion.

5. Describe the role of corporate culture and its connection to organizational architecture.

6. Understand why, how, and when firms change their organizational architecture.

Founded in 1919, Brabantia is one of Europe's largest manufacturers of household products such as ironing boards, waste bins, food storage canisters, kitchen tools, and mailboxes. Headquartered in the Netherlands with 1,000 employees and 2013 sales of about $150 million, the company specializes in steel and stainless steel utensils. Through the 1980s and 1990s Brabantia faced increased competition for its products. With the creation of a "single market" within the European Economic Union, other European companies entered Brabantia's local markets. As Europe's population growth slowed, the household utensil market became saturated. And large, mass-marketing retailers entered the European market driving out many of Brabantia's traditional outlets—small household specialty stores.[1]

Brabantia required new products and new channels of distribution. It had to become more efficient. It had high rates of rework and scrap, low levels of productivity, and high rates of employee absenteeism. The firm was organized quite centrally with traditional formal hierarchies, task specialization, and a functional structure. New products and programs were "top down" in nature and usually excluded input from lower-level operational staff. The firm assessed its performance based on cost, margins, and meeting output goals—not on measuring quality or customer satisfaction. Pay increases were based on seniority and companywide pay settlements.

[1]Source: "New Forms of Work Organization: Case Studies," European Commission, Directorate-General for Employment, Industrial Relations and Social Affairs, Unit V/D.3 (June 1998); and www.Brabantia.com.

To address its problems of increased competition, shrinking channels of distribution, low worker productivity, and a stale product line, Brabantia instituted a series of organizational changes that were designed to enhance performance. These changes involved three important aspects of the organization that we refer to as the firm's organizational architecture:[2]

- The assignment of decision rights within the firm
- The methods of rewarding individuals
- The structure of systems to evaluate the performance of both individuals and business units

Senior managers set the overall policies of the firm, including its organizational architecture. One change involved giving lower-level managers greater control over their work and substantial authority to make and implement decisions. Semiautonomous work teams were given considerable freedom in ordering raw materials, scheduling production, and recruiting new team members. All employees participated in writing a new mission statement that emphasized Brabantia's unique product designs and their usability. In other words, Brabantia decentralized the assignment of decision rights within the organization.

The company began to focus on innovation, new product development, rather than cost or output. It changed how employees were rewarded, placing greater emphasis on rewarding teams and individuals. It also restructured its information systems to monitor performance using a broader range of objectives, such as quality and customer satisfaction. Employees were trained to work in groups and to apply continuous improvement techniques with an emphasis on staff involvement. Formal policy statements were drafted to explain the new organizational architecture and mission statement to all employees.

The results have been impressive. The time to develop new products was reduced 20 percent. Quality and productivity have improved. Scrap and rework rates have fallen. And, employee satisfaction has improved.

This example of Brabantia illustrates that organizational architecture is an important determinant of the success or failure of firms. The purpose of this chapter is to introduce the concept of organizational architecture and to provide a broad overview of the factors that are likely to be important in designing the optimal architecture for a particular organization.

Understanding organizational architecture provides managers with powerful tools for affecting their firm's performance. As we shall see, managers must be careful and thoughtful in their use of these tools or the results can be counterproductive. This book presents material designed to help managers employ these tools more effectively.

We begin by discussing the fundamental problem facing firms and markets. We then examine how organizational architecture can help resolve this problem.[3]

---

[2]The importance of these three features of organizations has been recognized by a number of authors in economics and management. For instance, see M. Jensen and W. Meckling (1995), "Specific and General Knowledge, and Organizational Structure," *Journal of Applied Corporate Finance* 8:2, 4–18; P. Milgrom and J. Roberts (1992), *Economics, Organization & Management* (Prentice Hall: Englewood Cliffs); and D. Robey (1991), *Designing Organizations* (Richard D. Irwin: Burr Ridge).

[3]The first part of this chapter draws on M. Jensen and W. Meckling (1992), "Specific and General Knowledge, and Organizational Structure," *Journal of Applied Corporate Finance* 8:2, 4–18.

The Fundamental Problem

The primary goal of any economic organization is to produce the output customers want at the lowest possible cost. The challenge of discovering customer demands while reducing costs, both for economic systems and within individual firms, is complicated by the fact that important information for economic decision making generally is held by many different individuals. Furthermore, this information often is quite expensive to transfer (e.g., the information is *specific* as opposed to *general*). For example, a scientist is likely to know more about the potential of a specific research project than are executives higher in the firm. Similarly, individual machine operators normally know more about how to use their particular machines than do their supervisors. In both cases, communicating such information to headquarters for approval prior to acting on the information is likely to be cumbersome, resulting in many lost opportunities.

A second complication is that decision makers might not have appropriate incentives to make more effective decisions even if they have the relevant information. There are *incentive problems*. For example, a scientist might want to complete a research project out of scholarly interest, even if convinced the project is unprofitable. Similarly, machine operators might not want to use machines efficiently if this would mean additional work for them.

In sum, the principal challenge in designing firms (as well as entire economic systems) is to maximize the likelihood that decision makers have both the relevant information to make good decisions and the incentives to use the information productively.

There are many alternative ways of organizing economic activity to try to achieve these objectives. Economic transactions can occur within markets or firms. Firms can be organized as corporations, mutuals, partnerships, supplier cooperatives, employee-owned companies, or sole proprietorships. In each case, there are many different possible organizational architectures. All these alternatives involve costs as well as benefits. As we have discussed in previous chapters, individuals have incentives to select value-maximizing forms of organization. By maximizing the "size of the pie," there is more value to share among the parties to the transaction. To achieve this objective, it is important to have a detailed understanding of the architectures of both markets and firms.

Architecture of Markets

The price system helps resolve information and incentive problems in markets. In market economies, individuals have private property rights. If Jorge Ortega owns a building, he decides how it will be used. If Aldo Deng knows how to make better use of the building, Aldo can bid more for the building than it is worth to Jorge. Jorge can sell it and pocket the proceeds. Aldo has strong incentives to use the building productively because he bears the wealth effects.

Hence, the market provides an architecture that promotes efficient resource use. First, through market transactions, decision rights for resources are rearranged so that they tend to be held by individuals with the relevant specific knowledge for using those resources most productively. Individuals with the relevant specific knowledge will profit the most by owning the resources and thus are likely to be willing to pay a higher price to own them. Second, the market provides a mechanism for evaluating and rewarding the performance of resource owners: Owners bear the

ACADEMIC APPLICATIONS

One interesting feature of markets is how they often arise with limited human direction. As an example, economist R. A. Radford studied economic activity inside prisoner-of-war camps during World War II. In these camps, prisoners obtained rations from the Red Cross consisting of food, cigarettes, and other items. Of course, not all prisoners valued individual items the same. The English preferred drinking tea to coffee, whereas French prisoners preferred coffee to tea. Some prisoners smoked heavily, whereas others were nonsmokers. Potential gains from trade quickly motivated exchanges among prisoners. Before long, an organized market evolved. Cigarettes became the common currency. Prisoners quoted prices for goods in terms of the number of cigarettes. The price of individual items depended on supply and demand. For example, the price of chocolate would drop dramatically if a new Red Cross shipment increased supply substantially. The markets at the prisoner-of-war camps were quite active and emerged without a central planner saying "let's create a market." The welfare of the prisoners was significantly enhanced by the presence of these markets—although they benefited substantially more when they were liberated!

Source: R. Radford (1945), "The Economic Organization of a P.O.W. Camp," *Economica* 12, 189–201.

wealth effects of their actions. This mechanism generates important incentives to take efficient actions—actions for which benefits exceed costs. A valuable feature of the price system in a market economy is that this architecture is created spontaneously, requiring little conscious thought or human direction.

Architecture within Firms

Within firms, there are no automatic systems either for assigning decision rights to individuals with information or for motivating individuals to use information to promote a firm's objectives. Organizational architecture is created by executives through the implicit and explicit contracts that constitute the firm (see Chapter 10). For instance, decision rights are granted to employees through formal and informal job descriptions, whereas performance evaluations and rewards are specified in formal and informal compensation contracts. At Brabantia, both the old and new architectures were designed and implemented by senior management.

Decision Rights

Although transfer prices are used to allocate selected resources in some firms, most resources are allocated by administrative decisions.[4] For example, the CEO of a company typically transfers a manager from one division of the company to another by a simple command. Similarly, the utilization of a plant can be changed by administrative order. A critical responsibility of senior management is to decide how to assign decision rights among employees of the firm.[5] For instance, does the CEO make most major decisions, or are these decisions delegated to lower-level managers? Can machine operators deviate from procedures outlined in company manuals?

---

[4]In Chapter 17, we discuss the economics of transfer pricing.

[5]In small firms, senior management and owners often are the same. In large firms, owners (the shareholders) delegate most decision rights to the board of directors and the CEO. These parties are charged with developing the architecture for the firm. In this chapter, we do not distinguish between senior managers and owners. In subsequent chapters, we expand our analysis to discuss potential contracting problems between these two groups.

MANAGERIAL APPLICATIONS

Organizational Architecture at Century 21

Century 21 International is the largest residential real estate firm in the world. In 2014, Century 21's system consisted of 7,100 independently owned and operated offices in 75 countries with more than 102,000 sales professionals. Given the geographic and cultural diversity facing Century 21, it would not be productive for the U.S. headquarters to make all major decisions. Such centralized decision making would be especially problematic for the international operations, where laws and cultures can differ substantially from those in the United States. Rather Century 21's central management helps the international regions develop their offices. Each international office has a great deal of flexibility to design those practices and policies that best reflects their local housing market and real estate traditions.

Decentralized decision making requires a control system that promotes productive effort. At Century 21, most of the local operators are franchisees. Franchisees essentially are owners of their units and keep a large share of their units' profits. This ownership provides strong incentives to increase sales and value. Also, Century 21 reserves the right to terminate individual franchises that fail to maintain acceptable levels of service.

Source: www.century21.com

Controls

Through the delegation of decision rights, employees are granted authority over the use of company resources. Employees, however, are not owners: They cannot sell company property and pocket the proceeds. Therefore, employees have fewer incentives to worry about the efficient use of company resources than do owners. To help mitigate these incentive problems, managers must develop a *control system,* that is, managers must structure the other two basic pieces of the organization's architecture—the reward and performance-evaluation systems that help align the interests of the decision makers with those of the owners. As we discuss below, an optimal control system, consisting of the system of rewards and the system that evaluates performance, depends on how decision rights are partitioned in the firm, and vice versa.

Trade-Offs

Once the firm grows beyond a certain size, the CEO is unlikely to possess the relevant information for all major decisions. Consequently, the CEO faces three basic alternatives in designing organizational architecture. First, the CEO can make most major decisions, despite lacking relevant information. In this case, there are limited incentive problems and the development of a detailed control system is less critical.[6] However, lacking relevant information the CEO is likely to make suboptimal decisions. Second, the CEO can attempt to acquire the relevant information to make better decisions. This option can enhance decision making. Yet obtaining and processing the relevant information can be both costly and time-consuming. Third, the CEO can decentralize decision rights to individuals with better information. This choice assigns decision-making authority to employees with the relevant information. But delegating decision rights gives rise to increased incentive problems, which requires that control systems be developed. Another potential drawback of decentralization involves the costs of transferring information between the CEO and other decision makers in coordinating efforts across the organization.

[6]The manager still has a contracting problem in motivating lower-level employees to follow detailed instructions. However, this contracting problem is likely to be less severe than when the manager gives the lower-level employees greater discretion in making decisions.

Of course, CEOs can choose a mix of these basic alternatives. For example, executives generally choose to retain some decision rights while delegating others. The optimal choice, as we discuss later, depends primarily on the business environment and strategy of the firm. In some cases—especially in smaller firms operating within relatively stable industries—senior managers are likely to have most of the relevant information for decision making, and thus decision rights are more likely to be centralized at headquarters. In other cases—especially larger firms experiencing rapid change—senior managers and their corporate staff often will not be in the best position to make a broad array of decisions. In such cases, decision rights are more likely to be decentralized, with corresponding control systems adopted and implemented.

This discussion indicates that the CEO plays a major role in framing the basic architecture for the firm. Organizational decisions, however, are made by managers throughout the organization. For example, when the CEO delegates a set of decision rights to middle-level managers, these managers must decide which decisions to make themselves and which decisions will be delegated to lower-level managers. These lower-level managers then are faced with similar organizational questions. The overall architecture of a firm is determined through this process, ultimately involving employees throughout the organization.

Architectural Determinants

As suggested above, optimal architectures will differ across companies. Such structural differences are not random but vary in *systematic* ways with differences in certain underlying characteristics of the companies themselves. To illustrate the point, companies operating in the same industry tend to develop similar architectures. If an important aspect of an industry's environment changes, most companies in that industry will react by readjusting their decision rights and internal control systems.

In Figure 11.1, we summarize those factors which are likely to be most important in designing the optimal architecture for a given firm. At the top of the figure are three aspects of the firm's *external business environment: technology, markets,* and *regulation.* For any firm, these three factors—technologies that affect the production of or demand for its products, its methods of production, and its information systems; the structure of its markets (competitors, customers, and suppliers); and the regulatory constraints on its activities—are likely to have the greatest influence on its *strategy.* By *strategy,* we mean that broad set of issues discussed in Chapters 8 and 9, including the firm's primary goals—nonfinancial as well as financial; the firm's sources of comparative advantage; its choice of industry, products, and services; its target customers; and pricing policies.

Take the case of AT&T in the early 1980s, before it was separated into a long-distance carrier and regional operating companies called the Baby Bells. Regulation dictated many aspects of the firm's strategy—what services it could offer, what customers it could serve, and how much it could charge them. After the breakup of AT&T and the accompanying deregulation of the telecommunications industry, both the Baby Bells and the new AT&T were forced to devise new strategies to provide new products, serve new customer bases, and develop new pricing structures.

As depicted in Figure 11.1, the ultimate goals of the firm, as reflected in its strategy, in turn affect its optimal organizational architecture. As the celebrated architect Louis H. Sullivan—designer of the first skyscraper and founder of the American school of architecture—once observed, "Form ever follows function." Applying the

Figure 11.1 The Determinants of Strategy, Organizational Architecture, and Firm Value

Market conditions, technology, and government regulation are important determinants of strategy, which in turn helps determine organizational architecture. Two-way arrows are drawn to show important feedback effects. Both strategy and architecture affect the incentives and actions of employees within the firm and thus help determine the firm's value.

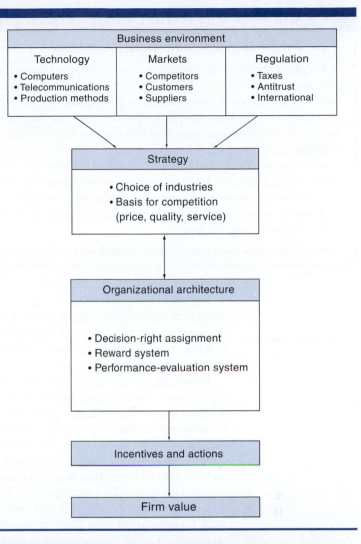

Business environment

Technology	Markets	Regulation
• Computers	• Competitors	• Taxes
• Telecommunications	• Customers	• Antitrust
• Production methods	• Suppliers	• International

Strategy

• Choice of industries
• Basis for competition (price, quality, service)

Organizational architecture

• Decision-right assignment
• Reward system
• Performance-evaluation system

Incentives and actions

Firm value

MANAGERIAL APPLICATIONS

Big-Bang Disrupters Nuke Corporate Strategies

With the plummeting cost of computing power coupled with the Internet's ability to make new products go viral, firms that were healthy and profitable one day, can be out of business the next because of a "Big-Bang Disrupter." Take the case of Sleep Health Centers, an operator of sleep disorders clinics where people stayed overnight to have their ailments diagnosed. In 2012, new cheap, wearable devices began appearing that allowed people to sleep at home while experts monitored their sleep remotely. Failing to devise a new strategy, Sleep Health Centers went out of business the next year. Other stories of big-bang disrupters exist. Apple's iTunes digital-music service adversely affected music companies. When the Google maps smartphone app, with turn-by-turn navigation, was launched, firms selling portable GPS navigation systems saw plummeting sales.

While Figure 11.1 depicts how changing technology, markets, and regulation affect a firm's strategy, it is a rare firm that can reinvent itself when "big-bang disrupters" hit. The evidence suggests that most firms are unable to find a new viable strategy and simply fail.

Source: The Economist (2014), "The Big Bang Theory," *The Economist* (January 11), 74.

MANAGERIAL APPLICATIONS

New Technology Provides Better Controls

A key part of the firm's organizational architecture involves controls—performance evaluation and rewards. All firms must protect their assets from loss—intentional and unintentional. Over 5 percent of all container movements worldwide develop transit problems. Twelve million cargo boxes enter the United States every year by ships, rail, and trucks. International freight companies must have controls over their shipping containers to avoid theft and misroutings, not to mention to prevent terrorists from using the boxes as a delivery system for explosives, chemicals, or nuclear bombs. The shipping industry is turning to "smart containers"—devices attached to shipping boxes that relay the container's current location, content, and condition via satellite or radio to both shipper and receiver. While equipping containers with such communication devices is not cheap—the cost per box ranges from $50 to $800 depending on functionality—the savings from just preventing shipping errors can be large. One shipper was informed that its container of citric acid was in Montreal (nowhere near its final destination in New Jersey) and had not moved in three days. The shipper called a broker and got the cargo on its way.

Source: D. Machalaba and A. Pasztor (2004), "Thinking Inside the Box," *The Wall Street Journal* (January 15), B1.

same principle within organizations, we see that significant changes in the business environment and hence in strategies typically call for major changes in decision-making authority, performance measures for evaluating employees, and incentive-compensation systems.

Returning to our telecommunications example, in the early 1980s a regulated AT&T faced little competition or pressure for technological innovation. It operated within a reasonably stable environment—one where it made sense for a huge formal bureaucracy to make the most important decisions from the top down. Since the breakup of the company, the telecommunications industry has experienced almost continuous upheaval, with deregulation, increased competition, and rapid technological change. In 1992, after a nearly decade-long series of incremental moves toward decentralization, AT&T established a large number of fairly autonomous profit centers run by managers on pay-for-performance plans tied to their units. In 1995, AT&T broke itself into three separate publicly traded companies, an equipment company—Lucent Technologies, a computer company, NCR, and a communications services company (which retained the AT&T name). The break up resulted in 40,000 layoffs and represented the largest voluntary breakup in the history of American business.[7] In 2005, one of the original Baby Bells, Southwestern Bell Corp, acquired AT&T Corp., creating the new AT&T.

Although in our discussion we have emphasized the effects of strategy on architecture, the effects are not all in one direction—note the two-headed arrow in Figure 11.1. Strategy also can be influenced by organizational architecture. A company might decide to enter a new market in part because its decision and control systems are especially well-suited for this new undertaking. For instance, before the 1980s, Atlanta, Georgia, was widely acknowledged as the banking center of the South. Yet in 2014, Charlotte, North Carolina, claims the title. Bank branching historically was regulated by the states. Georgia limited its banks' ability to branch, while North Carolina permitted statewide branching. As restrictions

[7]www.att.com/gen/investor-relations?pid=5711b

ANALYZING MANAGERIAL DECISIONS: *Tipping in Restaurants*

In most restaurants, waiters receive a large portion of their compensation through tips from customers. Generally, the size of the tip is decided by the customer. However, many restaurants require a 15 percent tip for parties of eight or more. Using the con- cepts from this chapter, discuss (a) why the practice of tipping has emerged as a major method of compensating the wait staff, (b) why the customer typically decides on the amount of the tip, and (c) why restaurants require tips from large parties.

on interstate banking fell in the 1980s, the North Carolina Banks—especially BB&T, NCNB (now Bank of America), First Union and Wachovia (who merged in 2001) exploited their experience in acquiring banks to create a statewide banking system to create regional and then national banks. These banks have been operating quite successfully, in part because their organizational architectures were better-suited to the new regulatory environment.

As another example of how changes in the environment can affect organizational architecture, consider the case of increased foreign competition in the 1980s and 1990s. For years, many large American companies (e.g., ITT, IBM, General Motors, Eastman Kodak, and Xerox) faced limited competition in their product markets. Many of these companies had substantial market power and had little external impetus to focus on rapid product development, high-quality production, or competitive pricing. Their organizations were highly bureaucratic, with quite centralized decision making and limited incentive compensation. Many of these firms experienced a dramatic increase in foreign competition over the past two decades—especially from the Japanese. This competition forced these large firms to rethink their basic strategies and increase their emphasis on quality, customer service, and competitive pricing. To accomplish these objectives, firms often had to change their organizational architectures. They frequently pushed decision rights lower in the organization, where specific knowledge about customer demands was located (recall the example of Brabantia). They also increased their use of incentive compensation and developed performance-evaluation systems that focused on quality and customer service. And in some cases like Kodak, the firm is unable to devise a viable strategy to address the foreign competition and new technologies; and eventually fail to survive.

In some ways, Figure 11.1 provides an overly simplified view of the determinants of strategy, architecture, and firm value. The figure admittedly ignores potentially important feedback effects among the environment, business strategy, and architecture. Consider, for example, how Microsoft invests resources to develop software that, in turn, alters the basic technology facing the firm. Large firms also often have political power that can be used to influence government regulation. Even though these types of feedback effects at times can be important, in most circumstances managers must take the business environment essentially as given. This environment, in turn, largely determines what the firm can expect to accomplish (its strategy) and its architecture. Figure 11.1 provides managers with a structured way of thinking about the factors that are likely to affect their firm's architecture. We use this structure throughout the book for analyzing organizational decisions.

Changing Architecture

Although changes in market conditions, technology, or government regulation can affect appropriate organizational design, organizational change is by no means a costless process. It is important to assess the costs as well as the benefits in evaluating the merits of an organizational restructuring. Organizational change should be undertaken only when the expected incremental benefits exceed the expected incremental costs.

First, there are direct costs. The new architecture has to be designed and communicated to employees throughout the company. Moreover, changes in architecture frequently require costly changes in the firm's accounting and information systems. Sometimes, what appears to be a straightforward change in the performance-evaluation system is a major and costly project for the firm's data processing and accounting departments. Literally hundreds of computer programs might have to be modified to alter the accounting and information systems.

Second, and perhaps more important, are indirect costs. Changes in architecture are likely to affect some employees positively—for example, by increasing their responsibility and possibilities for rewards—but others negatively. Thus, the attitudes toward change are likely to vary among employees. Dealing with the associated incentive problems of implementing change in a firm can be expensive (see Web Chapter 20, available via Connect). In addition, frequent changes in architecture can have undesirable incentive effects. Increasing the likelihood that workers will change assignments in the near future reduces their incentives to invest in learning current job assignments, devising more efficient production processes, and developing effective relations with coworkers. Frequent restructuring within a firm causes uncertainty about job assignments and will promote actions that focus more on short-run payoffs and less on long-run investments.

MANAGERIAL APPLICATIONS

Changing Organizational Architecture Requires Careful Analysis

At any point in time, a particular set of prominent management techniques is touted as the key to success. Popular techniques include "leadership by kindness and gentleness," reengineering, benchmarking, total quality management, worker empowerment, the learning organization, and skill-based pay. Most of these techniques involve fundamental changes in organizational architecture. For example, advocates of total quality management commonly recommend delegating decision rights to teams and not paying incentive compensation based on individual performance.

Adopting the most recent business trend or fad can get a firm in trouble unless the change is warranted by the actual circumstances facing the firm. Unfortunately, many firms appear to adopt changes without careful analysis of the relevant costs and benefits. One commentator argues, "There's an industry out there selling leadership 'secrets' to executives in American industry, and it seems to have an insatiable customer base" of insecure managers wanting to spout the latest buzzwords.*

Managers should not change their organization simply because it is the current fad. Certainly, some organizational changes can enhance value. However, managers should consider carefully whether the benefits of a change are larger than the costs, given their particular circumstances. (See Web Chapter 23, available via Connect, for a detailed analysis of management innovations.)

*B. Lutz (2012), "'Leadership By Kindness' and Other Dumb Management Fads," Forbes (May 12), www.forbes.com/sites/boblutz/2012/05/02/leadership-by-kindness-and-other-dumb-management-fads

Interdependencies and Complementarities within the Organization

It is important to understand that the components of organizational architecture are fundamentally interdependent. The appropriate control system depends on the allocation of decision rights, and vice versa. For example, if decision rights are decentralized, it is important to have a control system (performance measurement and rewards) that provides incentives for employees to make value-enhancing decisions. Reward and performance-evaluation systems have to be developed that compensate employees based on performance outcomes. Similarly, if a firm adopts a compensation plan to motivate employees, it is important to grant employees decision rights so that they can respond to these incentives. In this sense, the components of organizational architecture are like *three legs of a stool.* It is important that all three legs be designed so that the stool is balanced and functional. Changing one leg without careful attention to the other two is typically a mistake. For example, it is unlikely that Brabantia would have been as successful if managerial decision rights had been changed without accompanying changes in the firm's compensation plan.

Organizational architecture interacts with an array of other interrelated policies and systems within the firm. For example, incentive–compensation schemes for lower-level managers often are based on accounting performance for their particular business units. Changing business-unit structure and associated compensation plans therefore can require changes in the firm's accounting system. Similarly, it might be effective to pay the manager of a subsidiary based on the stock market performance of the subsidiary. But, for this policy to be implemented, shares in the subsidiary must be publicly traded. Thus, there can be interdependencies between the organizational architecture and the firm's financing policies. As another example, consider the design of the firm's organizational architecture and its computer/information systems. New computer programs provide expert systems that allow low-skilled workers to complete complicated tax returns, assess the qualifications of mortgage applicants, and perform other tasks that previously required extensive training and experience. These programs have allowed financial services companies to decentralize additional decision rights to lower-level employees. For example, lower-level employees in some financial institutions now have the rights to approve mortgage applications without supervisor approval if the computer program indicates that the applicant is qualified.

The three parts of the firm's Organizational Architecture in Figure 11.1 (decision-right assignment, the reward system, and the performance-evaluation system) along with other firm policies are not just interdependent, but should be chosen to complement the other parts and policies. Two or more organizational policies are said to be *complements* when doing more of one increases the returns from doing more of the

HISTORICAL APPLICATIONS

Changing Organizations Too Frequently: Not a New Phenomenon

We trained hard, but it seemed that every time we were beginning to form into teams we would be reorganized. I was to learn later in life that we tend to meet any new situation by reorganizing, and what a wonderful method it can be for creating the illusion of progress while producing confusion, inefficiency, and demoralization.

Petronius Arbiter, 210 BC.

others. When complementary policies are employed together the "whole is greater than the sum of the parts." A well-designed organization typically makes balanced use of a host of complementary policies (either high or low use of all of them).[8] For example, a firm that decentralizes decision rights will generally find it optimal to spend more resources on recruiting talented employees, training and development, performance measurement and incentive compensation. In contrast, a firm with highly centralized decision making will likely want to limit expenditures on all of these activities. The fact that many organizational policies are complements simplifies the organizational design problem to some extent. Rather than having to choosing many policies independently, managers can often limit their attention to a much smaller subset of "coherent systems," in which simultaneous high or low use is made of multiple policies. The optimal choice for any given firm depends on its business environment and strategy. In this book, we focus our attention on the three components of Organizational Architecture. However, good managers select other organizational policies (such as the employee recruitment process and training programs) to complement their firm's Organizational Architecture.

Corporate Culture

Corporate culture is one of the more frequently used terms in the literature on organizations. Corporate culture usually encompasses the ways work and authority are organized, the ways people are rewarded and controlled, as well as organizational features such as customs, taboos, company slogans, heroes, and social rituals. Managers are exhorted to develop high-powered, productive cultures. Yet, little concrete guidance is provided on how to accomplish this goal.

Our focus on organizational architecture is consistent with this concept of corporate culture. Indeed, our definition of organizational architecture corresponds to key aspects of what frequently is discussed as corporate culture. For example, the architecture specifies how authority (decision rights) is distributed among employees and how rewards are determined. An advantage of our approach is that it defines the key components of a firm's corporate culture and analyzes how managers might affect culture through identifiable actions.

As an example, recall our discussion of Merrill Lynch in Chapter 2. The old corporate culture at Merrill could be characterized as an environment where dishonest analysts regularly misled customers. After the scandal became public, Merrill had to find a way to change this corporate culture. Our approach provides direct guidance on how this change might be accomplished—in this case, by changing the compensation scheme.

Some dismiss the "softer" elements of corporate culture—for example, role models, company folklore, and rituals—as being unimportant. Rather, they stress formal architecture as being the primary, if not sole, determinant of a firm's value.[9] Economics, however, suggests at least two important roles for these elements of corporate culture: enhancing communication and helping to set employee expectations.

---

[8]J. Roberts (2004), *The Modern Firm: Organizational Design for Performance and Growth* (Oxford University Press: Oxford).

[9]For instance, managers who subscribe to the teachings of Frederick Taylor believe that the designs of work processes and incentive systems are the primary determinants of firm value. F. Taylor (1923), *The Principles of Scientific Management* (Harper & Row: New York).

MANAGERIAL APPLICATIONS

Netflix Corporate Culture Goes Viral

In 2009, Netflix released internally a 128-slide document titled "Reference Guide on our Freedom & Responsibility Culture." By 2014, it has been viewed by over 5 million on the Internet. Facebook chief operating officer Sheryl Sandberg says it "may well be the most important document ever to come out of the (Silicon) Valley."

The document starts by describing its culture as: "What gives Netflix the best chance of continuous success for many generations of technology and people?" It then goes on to list seven aspects of its culture: (1) "values are what we value," (2) high performance, (3) "freedom & responsibility," (4) "context, not control," (5) highly aligned, loosely coupled," (6) pay top of market, and (7) promotions & development. Each of these seven aspects is fully explained. For example, under "values are what we value" nine specific behaviors are described as valuable such as judgment, courage, and honesty. The slide deck then describes current Netflix policies that follow from each of the seven aspects. For example, under the second culture aspect, "high performance," Netflix managers are told to apply "The Keeper Test: Which of my people … would I fight hard to keep at Netflix? The other people should get a generous severance now, so we can open a slot to try to find a star for that role." Under the third culture aspect, "freedom & responsibility," two policies are described. The policy on employee reimbursement for travel and entertainment expense is "Act in Netflix's Best Interests." And, the policy on how many vacation days employees are allowed and tracking vacation days is: "There is no policy or tracking."

Netflix's corporate culture statement is one of the most elaborate and detailed, and illustrates how one company tries to communicate the desired behaviors and qualities it seeks in its employees.

Source: www.slideshare.net/reed2001/culture-1798664; and A. Shontell (2013), "Sheryl Sandberg: The Most Important Document Ever to Come Out of the Valley," *Business Insider* (February 4).

Corporate Culture and Communication

Most organizations do not write down all important features of their organizations in detailed procedures manuals. Rather, these features typically are communicated to employees in less formal yet frequently more effective ways. Aspects of the corporation such as slogans, role models, and social rituals can be methods of communicating organizational architecture to workers in a particularly memorable way. A slogan like *At Ford, Quality Is Job 1* emphasizes that workers are expected to focus on quality and customer service and that this focus will be rewarded by the company. Given this slogan and other reinforcing signals from top management, employees at Ford have a reasonably clear idea of how to respond to situations such as angry customers, even without formal policies to follow. But after 17 years, Ford dropped this slogan and adopted the new slogan in 1998 of "Better ideas. Driven by you." In 2014, Ford's slogan is "Go further." Besides slogans, social rituals, such as training sessions and company parties, can help disseminate information by increasing the interaction among employees who otherwise might not see each other on a frequent basis. Singling out role models or heroes for special awards is another way of communicating explicitly what the company values.

Less tangible features of organizations, such as rituals and role models, can be important in reinforcing and communicating organizational architecture. However, they also can increase the costs of changing architecture. Managers can change formal evaluation and compensation schemes and clearly communicate these changes to the relevant employees. But getting employees to change their heroes, customs, and social rituals can be more time-consuming and difficult. These features often are created through informal communication channels: They take time to dismantle as well as to create.

MANAGERIAL APPLICATIONS

Firms Use the Clout of Their Well-Connected Employees

A number of companies including Procter & Gamble Co. and Cisco Systems Inc. identify those among their employees who are particularly well-connected and trusted by their peers. These so-called "influencers" are then used to help develop new products, get other workers on board with big changes like mergers, or help disseminate information throughout the firm.

Often these influencers are identified by analyzing social media sites to see who has the most friends or the most connections. For example, Health Fitness Corp., a provider of corporate health services, mapped its social networks to identify employees who could help convince others of the importance of a major new technology platform. The company flew 30 influencers to its corporate offices to describe the project further and to build positive buzz among the other employees. The CEO of Health Fitness believes that the influencers helped in the transition to the new IT platform. The influencers also benefit with more money, possible promotions, and hobnobbing with top executives.

While the rise of social media and social networks can be used to identify influencers who can help improve communications throughout the firm, such programs also come with costs. If the firm rewards being an "influencer," employees will spend more time developing their networks, at the expense of doing other productive activities for the firm. Moreover, people can game the system to appear to be more "influential" than they really are.

Source: R. Feintzeig (2014), "Office 'Influencers' Are in High Demand," *The Wall Street Journal* (February 12), www.wsj.com/articles/SB10001424052702303874504579375313680290816

Corporate Culture and Employee Expectations

In the appendix to Chapter 9, we illustrated how the decisions of employees to exert effort and to cooperate with other employees can depend on their expectations about how other individuals will respond. In this example, employees work hard only if they think that other employees will work hard as well. Expectations of how other individuals will behave are shaped, in part, by the formal architecture of the firm. If Ehud Rabin observes that Colleen O'Shea is paid a commission on sales, it is reasonable for Ehud to forecast that Colleen will exert some effort in trying to increase sales. Expectations, however, also are affected by less formal aspects of corporate culture. For example, Microsoft has developed a reputation for hiring creative, hardworking individuals. If two Microsoft employees are placed together on a team, it is reasonable for each to expect that the other is clever and industrious.

This analysis suggests that it generally will be advantageous for managers to use both the formal architecture as well as the less formal aspects of corporate culture to foster expectations that promote productive choices by employees. For instance, suppose that employees are most likely to focus on quality if they think other employees have the same focus. A manager interested in increasing manufacturing quality thus might supplement changes in the formal evaluation and reward systems with slogans, executive speeches, employee relations campaigns, and clever use of the media, all aimed at creating a "quality-centered" culture.

A System of Complements

Features of organizations like rituals and role models can be effective in reinforcing and communicating the goals of the firm, and they possess the potential to produce influential aspects of a coherent architecture. Their effectiveness in specific cases has led some management gurus to claim that a productive corporate culture can be molded with no attention to formal evaluation and compensation schemes. Some people—for instance, quality expert W. Edwards Deming—argued that incentive pay

The Value of Corporate Culture

A study of S&P 500 companies found 85 percent of them have on their websites a section called "corporate culture" where they list those values that comprise their culture. Eighty percent of these websites list "innovation" followed by "integrity" or "respect" (70 percent). The researchers are unable to find any correlation between the frequency and prominence of these values to measures of short- and long-term performance.

The researchers then turn to survey data of employees of more than 1,000 U.S. firms that measure how cultural values are perceived by employees, including the level of integrity of management as perceived by the employees. Interestingly, the study documents that high levels of perceived integrity are positively correlated with higher productivity, profitability, and higher level of attractiveness to prospective job applicants.

The study suggests that firms with high-integrity managers perform better, but just listing "integrity" as part of the firm's corporate culture is "cheap talk."

Source: L. Guiso, P. Sapienza, and L. Zingales (2013), "The Value of Corporate Culture," *National Bureau of Economic Research* (October).

actually is detrimental to a productive organization. Our analysis suggests that it is a mistake to think of these hard and soft aspects of the organization as mutually exclusive or in competition with each other; both can play a valuable role in increasing firm value. The various elements of the organization are more likely to be *complements* than substitutes. In Chapter 20, we present a detailed discussion of Xerox's early

Scandal-Plagued European Banks Seek to Change Their Corporate Culture

A number of prominent U.K. banks have suffered a series of high-profile scandals involving circumventing regulatory rules, attempting to rig interbank lending rates (LIBOR), manipulating foreign exchange trading, and excessive compensation paid to senior managers. The media, politicians, and regulators blame the bankers for fostering a culture of excessive risk taking, greed, and bad behavior. To address these criticisms, some banks including Royal Bank of Scotland, HSBC U.K., Barclays, and Deutsche Bank (Germany) have attempted to change their corporate culture, often by hiring outside consultants. These consultants offer advice on ways to improve bankers' behavior at work.

Using their consultants, banks have tried various approaches to changing their corporate culture. To highlight the softer side of the banking industry Citigroup's London office began a choir that performed on television. Barclays changed its office notepads to now contain phrases such as "Respect," "Integrity" and "Stewardship." Deutsche Bank required 300 managing directors to attend time-consuming culture sessions at a research institute in Cologne, Germany. And to learn about managing in difficult environments Barclays sent top managers to an orphanage in Africa.

Some people believe banks can change their corporate culture. One U.K. lawmaker says, "there is a long, long way to go before we feel that the culture of banks has fundamentally changed." But another lawmaker argues that the various attempts to change culture are ineffective, "If [banks] think that is enough, then we are all screwed."

It is not clear whether these corporate culture change programs are designed as public relation ploys to pander to the public and appease lawmakers from writing tougher regulations, or if the banks believe that such programs really do work. The analysis in this chapter predicts that changing corporate culture will be very difficult and time-consuming. Firms attract and retain employees with personal characteristics, most valuable to the firm. Changing cultures often involves changing the characteristics of the firm's work force, often by gradually replacing the existing work force as they retire or quit with new employees with the now desired characteristics. And such a change will most likely be challenged by the existing employees with those characteristics that are now out of favor.

Source: M. Colchester (2014), "Scandal-Hit British Banks Turn to 'Weirdy Beardy'," *The Wall Street Journal* (March 26), www.wsj.com/articles/SB10001424052702304418404579463122893382480

efforts to increase product and service quality. Xerox CEO David Kearns initially focused on softer elements—slogans, speeches, and media campaigns—in his efforts to foster a quality culture within his organization. He soon realized that to be effective, he also had to change the company's formal evaluation and reward systems.

When Management Chooses an Inappropriate Architecture

Sometimes, managers are either unable or unwilling to design value-increasing architectures or strategies. Consider the management at RJR-Nabisco in the late 1980s, as highlighted in Chapter 10. In cases such as RJR-Nabisco, value can be created by replacing existing management with new managers who are willing and able to choose architectures and strategies that increase value.

Firing the Manager

In public corporations, the board of directors has the decision rights to hire, fire, and compensate senior managers. Evidence indicates that boards are most likely to fire managers when firm performance is poor (as measured by stock returns and accounting earnings).[10] Consider Eastman Kodak in 1993. The company was performing poorly, and senior managers acknowledged that a poorly designed architecture was among the company's most significant problems. These managers were unable to design a better one. The board of directors fired the CEO and hired a new one. The new CEO, George Fisher, rapidly changed both the architecture and the strategy of the company. The stock market greeted these actions with a substantial increase in the Kodak stock price. At the end of this chapter, we present a case study of this example.

Although firing the CEO is a relatively rare event, firings at other management levels are more common. When middle managers perform poorly by implementing ineffective strategies and inappropriate architectures for their business units, they can be fired or reassigned by senior managers. Middle managers, in turn, have decision rights to replace lower-level managers.

Market for Corporate Control

Another mechanism for replacing poor management is the market for corporate control—for example, tender offers and mergers. During the last few decades, the wealth of shareholders has increased by billions of dollars due to corporate takeovers. Typically, when a poorly performing company is acquired by another company, its management is replaced.[11] The architecture and strategy also are changed as a result. ITT's poor performance in 1988 motivated takeover speculation. Existing management took actions to increase the firm's value, and a takeover did not materialize. In contrast, the former management team at RJR-Nabisco did not make the necessary changes to increase its firm's value, and the company was acquired by Kohlberg, Kravis, Roberts & Company. KKR subsequently replaced the management team and implemented significant changes in RJR's architecture and strategy.

[10]J. Warner, R. Watts, and K. Wruck (1988), "Stock Prices and Top Management Changes," *Journal of Financial Economics* 20, 461–492; and M. Weisbach (1988), "Outside Directors and CEO Turnover," *Journal of Financial Economics* 20, 431–460. Similar evidence is observed in the nonprofit sector; see J. Brickley and L. van Horn (2002), "Incentives in Nonprofit Organizations: Evidence from Hospitals," *Journal of Law and Economics* 45, 227–249.

[11]For a summary of the evidence on corporate takeovers, see B. Eckbo (2010), *Modern Empirical Developments in Corporate Takeovers* (Elsevier/Academic Press: Amsterdam).

Product Market Competition

When all else fails, inefficient firms eventually go out of business. In Chapter 6, we discussed how competitive pressures tend to drive prices toward marginal cost. If a firm is inefficient and cannot cover its total costs at these prices, it eventually has to shut down. As discussed in Chapter 1, this competitive process resembles natural selection in biology—*the strong survive*. It is a process we refer to as economic Darwinism. Enron is a dramatic example of a firm that became insolvent due to the poor design of its architecture.

Managerial Implications

Organizational architecture provides a powerful framework for addressing management problems throughout the organization. In many cases, a problem can be traced directly to defects in organizational architecture (consider Enron and Merrill Lynch). By using this framework, managers can identify problems more quickly and craft solutions more effectively. In analyzing business problems and cases, students and managers often find it useful to refer to Figure 11.1 and ask themselves the following set of questions:

- Does the strategy fit the business environment (technology, market conditions, and regulation) and the capabilities of the firm?
- What are the key features of the current architecture?
- Does the current architecture fit the business environment and strategy? In particular, does the architecture link *specific knowledge* and decision rights in an effective manner and provide *incentives* to use information productively?

ACADEMIC APPLICATIONS

Marmots and Grizzly Bears

Business writers, consultants, and government regulators frequently claim that existing business practices are inefficient, and they propose changes that allegedly would improve productivity. The principle of economic Darwinism, however, suggests that many of these claims are likely to be misguided. In a competitive world, if organizations survive over the long run with a particular architecture, it is unlikely that there is some *obvious change* that could be implemented to increase profits. Sometimes the reasons for survival of a particular practice might not be clear to an outside observer. Existing practices, however, should not be deemed inefficient without careful analysis.

The interaction between marmots and grizzly bears serves to illustrate this point. Marmots are small groundhogs and are a principal food source for certain bears. Zoologists studying the ecology of marmots and bears observed bears digging and moving rocks in the autumn in search of marmots. They estimated that the calories expended searching for marmots exceeded the calories obtained from consuming marmots. Thus, searching for marmots appeared to be an inefficient use of the bear's limited resources. Given Darwin's theory of natural selection, bears searching for marmots should become extinct. A well-meaning consultant or government regulator, therefore, might recommend that bears quit searching for marmots.

Fossils of marmot bones near bear remains, however, suggest that bears have been searching for marmots for quite a long time. An explanation is that searching for marmots provides benefits to bears in addition to calories. For instance, bears sharpen their claws as a by-product of the digging involved in hunting for marmots. Sharp claws are useful in searching for food under the ice after winter's hibernation. Therefore, the benefit of sharpened claws and the calories derived from marmots offset the calories consumed gathering the marmots. The moral is that in biology or business, an outside observer should be cautious in concluding that long-standing practices are inefficient without careful study.

Source: J. McGee (1980), "Predatory Pricing Revisited," *Journal of Law & Economics* 23:2, 289–330.

- Are the three legs of the stool mutually consistent? Given the decision-right system, does the control system fit, and vice versa?
- If the answers to any of the previous questions suggest a problem, what changes in strategy and architecture should the firm consider?
- What problems will the firm face in implementing these changes?

Evaluating Management Advice

In a competitive marketplace, surviving firms tend to be those firms with the most productive strategies and architectures, given their business environments. This principle suggests that architectures are not random. There are sound economic explanations for the existing architectures within most industries. Consultants, however, frequently argue that long-standing practices obviously are inefficient and that companies would be better off by following their advice in changing the architecture. For example, many recent books on *empowerment* argue that most firms have made mistakes over a long time period in not delegating more decision rights to lower-level employees. Correspondingly, profits would be improved by further empowering workers. Although this advice clearly makes sense for some firms in some environments (especially if the environment recently has undergone some fundamental change that favors decentralization of decision rights), our analysis suggests that managers should be cautious in condemning prevailing organizational architecture without careful analysis. The discussion in the subsequent chapters provides important material to help conduct this analysis.

Benchmarking

Firms frequently *benchmark* other firms in an attempt to determine value-increasing policies. For example, a firm considering a change in its executive compensation plan is likely to collect information on the compensation plans of other similar firms.

MANAGERIAL APPLICATIONS

Benchmarking the Lincoln Electric Company

Lincoln Electric company has had a long history of delivering large profits. Often, this record is attributed to Lincoln's unique reward system, which places a heavy emphasis on incentive compensation (we describe this system in detail in Chapter 13). Managers from all over the world come to the Lincoln Electric headquarters at Cleveland, Ohio, to study the system. Our analysis suggests that these managers should consider Lincoln's business environment, strategy, and other elements of organizational architecture (for instance, its decision-right system) in their benchmarking. Lincoln's success should not be attributed to its reward system alone but to how well this feature fits with its environment and overall architecture.

Interestingly, Lincoln managers made the costly mistake of ignoring the complementary nature of these systems themselves. During the 1980s, the management at Lincoln decided to export its incentive system internationally through a series of mergers throughout Europe, Asia, and Latin America. Unfortunately, the system did not fit the business environments at many of their new locations. For instance, the influence of unions in Germany and labor laws in Venezuela made it impossible for Lincoln to implement its compensation system successfully. Lincoln ended up losing millions of dollars on these ventures. Lincoln might have avoided these mistakes if in its decision-making process it had applied carefully the framework discussed in this book.

This practice has obvious merit. Firms that survive in the marketplace tend to have strategies and architectures that fit their environment, and studying these firms has the potential to yield valuable insights. Our analysis has at least three implications for effective benchmarking. First, different architectures are appropriate for different environments. It is important to benchmark firms facing similar environments. Second, since it is unusual to find firms in identical environments, it is important to understand any differences in the environments of the benchmarked firms and to take these differences into account when analyzing the data on firms' policy choices. Third, it is important to view the architecture of other firms as a system of complements. Studying a single feature of another firm's architecture, without considering how it fits with other complementary elements of its architecture, can produce erroneous conclusions and lead to dysfunctional changes.

Summary

Organizational architecture includes three important components of organizational design that are major determinants of the success or failure of firms:

- The assignment of decision rights
- The methods of rewarding individuals
- The structure of systems to evaluate the performance of both individuals and business units

The fundamental problem facing both firms and economic systems involves trying to ensure that decision makers have the relevant information to make good decisions and that these decision makers have appropriate incentives to use their information productively. The price system provides an architecture that helps solve this problem in markets. Through market transactions, decision rights tend to be transferred to individuals with the relevant knowledge to make productive use of the resources. The market also provides a mechanism for evaluating and rewarding the performance of resource owners—owners bear the wealth effects of their actions. A valuable feature of markets is that this architecture is created spontaneously with little conscious thought or human direction.

Markets are not always the most efficient method for organizing economic activity—frequently, firms are more efficient. Within firms, there is no automatic system for either assigning decision rights to individuals with information or motivating individuals to use information to promote the firm's objectives. Organizational architecture has to be created. The appropriate architecture depends on the environment facing the firm. In some firms, senior management will have most of the relevant information for decision making, and relatively centralized decision making is more likely to be adopted. In firms where lower-level employees have the relevant information, decision rights are more likely to be decentralized. In this case, reward and performance-evaluation systems must be developed to control incentive problems and to promote better decision making.

Market conditions, technology, and government regulations interact to determine the firm's appropriate strategy and architecture. The strategy and architecture, in turn, are major determinants of the firm's value.

Changes in the external business environment can motivate changes in the firm's organizational architecture. Changing architecture, however, is costly. In addition to the direct costs of designing and implementing new procedures, there are potentially important indirect costs. Thus, changing architecture should be done only following careful analysis.

The components of organizational architecture are highly interdependent. They are like three legs of a stool. Changing one leg without careful attention to the others is usually a mistake. Organizational structure also is related to other policies and systems within a firm, including the accounting and information systems, marketing, and financial policy.

Corporate culture is a frequently used term. Corporate culture usually is meant to encompass the ways work and authority are organized and the ways people are rewarded and controlled, as well as organizational features such as customs, taboos, company slogans, heroes, and social rituals. Our focus on organizational architecture is consistent with this concept of corporate culture. Indeed, our definition of organizational architecture corresponds to key aspects of what is frequently defined as corporate culture. The advantage of our approach is that it defines the key components of corporate culture and analyzes how managers might affect culture through conscious action. It also helps explain why corporate cultures of firms vary systematically across industries—different environments motivate different architectures. Elements of corporate culture like customs, social rituals, folklore, and heroes perform at least two important roles: Enhancing communication and fostering more productive expectations among employees. These elements, however, are likely to be less effective unless they are reinforced by the formal architecture of the firm.

Sometimes, managers are unable or unwilling to adopt value-maximizing architectures or strategies. In such cases, value can be created through management replacement. Management replacement occurs through firings and corporate takeovers. If a firm remains inefficient, it eventually will go out of business in a competitive marketplace.

This chapter introduces the concept of organizational architecture and provides a broad overview of the factors that are likely to be important in determining the optimal architecture for a particular organization. The next six chapters contain a more in-depth discussion of each of the three components of organizational architecture: the assignment of decision rights, the reward system, and the performance-evaluation system.

Suggested Readings

M. Jensen (1983), "Organization Theory and Methodology," *The Accounting Review* 58, 319–339.

M. Jensen and W. Meckling (1995), "Specific and General Knowledge, and Organizational Structure," *Journal of Applied Corporate Finance* 8:2, 4–18.

D. Kreps (1990), "Corporate Culture and Economic Theory," in J. Alt and K. Shepsle (Eds.), *Perspectives on Positive Political Economy* (Cambridge University Press: Cambridge).

P. Milgrom and J. Roberts (1995), "Complementarities and Fit: Strategy, Structure and Organizational Change in Manufacturing," *Journal of Accounting and Economics* 19, 179–208. Focus particular attention on pages 191–208.

J. Roberts (2004) *The Modern Firm: Organizational Design for Performance and Growth* (Oxford University Press: Oxford).

Self-Evaluation Problems

11–1. Suppose that a manager decides that a company's decision making is too centralized. Will simply delegating more decisions to lower-level employees solve the problem? Explain.

11–2. Traditionally, many public utility companies (such as telephone and electric companies) have been highly regulated by the government. Thus, they have operated in stable environments, shielded from competition and rapid change. Recently, deregulation has substantially altered the environments of some of these companies. For the first time, they are being exposed to intense competition from other companies. Discuss how this change in the environment is likely to affect the optimal organizational architecture of utility companies.

Solutions to Self-Evaluation Problems

11-1. No. The other components of architecture (rewards and performance evaluation) probably also have to be changed to provide incentives to lower-level employees to make productive decisions.

11-2. Traditionally, public utilities have had relatively centralized decision making and have made limited use of incentive compensation (especially for lower-level managers and employees). Given the changes in the business environment, it is likely that local specific knowledge will become more important. For example, the tastes and preferences of customers can become more important to a company as it faces increased competition. Also, maintaining state of the art technology can become more important. These arguments suggest that deregulation might motivate a further decentralization of decision rights. Correspondingly, to make the three legs of the stool balance, one might expect increased use of incentive compensation. Empirical studies of deregulated industries tend to support these conjectures.

Review Questions

11-1. Describe the three aspects of organizational architecture.

11-2. What is a major difference between the architectures of markets and firms?

11-3. How might the softer elements of corporate culture help increase productivity in an organization? Give some examples of how managers might foster these elements to implement desired change in an organization.

11-4. Prominent management consultants sometimes argue that decision making in teams is usually more productive than decision making by individuals (important synergies arise when teams operate that are absent when individuals work by themselves). These consultants suggest that most companies have long failed to make proper use of teams. Their advice is that most firms should increase their use of teams significantly. Critique this advice.

11-5. Assume that some firms within the same industry are observed to be multidivisional, whereas others are functionally organized. Assume further that all firms are about the same size and have existed for a long period of time in their current organizational structures. Is this observation inconsistent with the "survival of the fittest" concept discussed in class? Explain.

11-6. Evaluate the following argument:

> *Management fads make no sense. One day it's TQM. The next, it is empowerment or business-process reengineering. There is no economic justification for these fads. Management are just like sheep following each other to the slaughter.*

11-7. Some of the electric generating plants of the Tennessee Valley Authority are powered by coal. Coal is purchased by a separate procurement division and is transferred to the plants for use. Plant managers often complain that the coal is below grade and causes problems with plant maintenance and efficiency. What do you think is causing this problem? What changes would you make to help correct this problem?

chapter 12

Decision Rights: The Level of Empowerment

LEARNING OBJECTIVES

1. Explain how jobs vary in their assignment of tasks and decision authority.
2. Describe the costs and benefits of centralization versus decentralization.
3. Describe the trade-offs between vertical and horizontal (lateral) decision-rights assignments.
4. Understand the costs and benefits of assigning decision rights to teams.
5. Compare the differences between decision management rights and decision control rights and explain how separating decision management from decision control mitigates agency problems.
6. Define influence costs and describe how they can affect the assignment of decision rights within a firm.

Honda Motor Company was founded in 1948 by Soichiro Honda.[1] Initially, decision making within the company was quite centralized. Mr. Honda made virtually all product and design decisions, whereas finance and marketing decisions were made by his partner, Takeo Fujisawa.

In 1973, Honda retired. Successors adopted a more decentralized decision system. Major decision-making authority was spread among nearly 30 senior executives, who spent much of their time gathered at conference tables hammering out policies in informal sessions called *waigaya*—a Honda word meaning "noisy-loud." Engineers in research and development had significant control of the design of new automobiles. Under this so-called Honda System, the company grew and prospered.

By the late 1980s Honda's growth had stalled and profits declined. Honda lost market share in the Japanese auto market, falling from third to fourth behind Mitsubishi, Nissan, and Toyota. Part of Honda's problem was that it failed to respond to changing tastes in the Japanese auto market. Many Japanese consumers wanted to purchase sporty cars with distinctive styling, yet Honda concentrated on producing four-door family sedans.

[1]Details of this example are from C. Chandler and P. Ingrassia (1991), "Just as U.S. Firms Try Japanese Management, Honda Is Centralizing," *The Wall Street Journal* (April 11), A1; M. Williams (1993), "Redesign of Honda's Management Faces First Test with Unveiling of New Accord," *The Wall Street Journal* (September 1), B1; E. Thornton, L. Armstrong, and D. Woodruff (1998), "Honda: A Heckuva Time to Switch Drivers," *BusinessWeek* (August 31), 42–44; and Y. Kageyama (2005), "Honda Profits Increase 27%," *Detnews.com* (April 27).

In April 1991, the new CEO, Nubuhiko Kawamoto, announced that he was changing the decision-making system at Honda by taking direct control of the company's automotive operations in Japan. He reasoned that the company had grown too large for group decision making. To quote Kawamoto,

> *We'd get the people from research, sales, and production together and everyone would say "not this" or "not that." We'd talk but there would be no agreement. Product planning would be on a tight schedule but we would have another discussion, another study and more preparation. Finally, the decision would come months later.*

The centralization of decision rights at Honda was seen as a cultural revolution. Even after Kawamoto obtained the retired Honda's support for this radical change, Honda employees resisted. Yet despite this resistance, the system was changed. In 1993, powerful "car czars" ran the development of new models, middle managers had clear job responsibilities, and according to some insiders, Kawamoto's power exceeded even that once held by Honda.

The first real test of the new management structure was the unveiling of the 1994 Accord in fall 1993. The vehicle was priced competitively and was widely acclaimed a success. The Accord was named one of the Top 10 Cars of 1994 by *Car and Driver* magazine and Import Car of the Year by *Motor Trend* magazine. In 2007 Honda, led by CEO Takeo Fukui, reported profits of $5 billion on revenues of $94 billion for the fiscal year ending in March 2007. The Accord is manufactured in 10 countries in Asia, North America, and Latin America as well as in Japan, and it is sold in approximately 140 countries.

Honda is just one of many firms that changed the assignment of decision rights within their organizations in the 1990s. In contrast to Honda, many firms decentralized decision rights—for example, through *empowering* employees. An example, again from the automobile industry, is Fiat. In 1992, Fiat announced that it was decentralizing certain decision rights, assigning them to the operating levels and reducing management positions. Other firms that decentralized decision rights in the 1990s include General Electric, Motorola, and United Technologies to name but a few. A common action has been to decentralize decision rights to teams of employees rather than to individuals. The financial press is replete with stories about how companies have improved profits, quality, and customer satisfaction through employee empowerment and other changes in their decision-making systems. Today we continue to observe successful firms that vary in their level of decentralization. Google is a prominent example of a successful firm with decentralized decision making in 2014. In contrast, prior to his death in 2011, Steve Jobs was critically involved in the development details of most of Apple Computer's highly successful new products.

These examples raise a number of important organizational questions:

- Can altering the assignment of decision rights really have an important impact on productivity and value?
- What factors affect the optimal allocation of decision rights within the firm?
- When is it optimal to delegate decision rights to a team of employees rather than to specific individuals?

The purpose of this chapter and the chapter that follows is to address these and related questions. This chapter focuses on a single decision right and asks where that right should be located within the firm. The next chapter considers multiple decision rights and examines how combinations of rights are bundled into jobs and subunits (e.g., divisions) of the firm.

This chapter begins by providing a detailed discussion of the problem of assigning tasks and decision rights within the firm. We then present a simple example that illustrates some of the important factors that determine the optimal assignment of a specific decision right—in this case, pricing a product. We use this example to discuss centralization versus decentralization, as well as the placement of a right among employees within the same hierarchical level. We also use this example as a springboard to discuss the trade-offs between assigning a decision right to an individual versus a team of individuals. Next, we consider the decision process in more detail and define the terms *decision management* and *decision control,* terms that are especially helpful in making the concept of empowerment more precise. Finally, we examine how the incentives of employees trying to influence decision makers can affect the optimal assignment of a decision right within the firm. The appendix to this chapter provides a more detailed analysis of some of the problems that can arise in team decision making.

Assigning Tasks and Decision Rights

Firms transform inputs into outputs, which are sold to customers. This *process* typically involves many *tasks.* For example, at Honda Motor Company, vehicles have to be designed, assembled, sold, and delivered. An important element of organizational architecture is partitioning of the totality of tasks within the organization into smaller blocks and assigning them to specific individuals and/or groups.

Through the process of designing the organization, specific *jobs* are created. For example, if a set of clerical tasks is bundled together and assigned to an individual, a secretarial job might be created. Jobs have at least two important dimensions: The *variety of tasks* that the employee is asked to complete and the *decision authority* to determine when and how best to complete those tasks.

Jobs vary substantially in terms of the variety of tasks and scope of decision authority. Figure 12.1 depicts four possibilities. Point 1 displays a combination of few tasks and limited decision authority. An example is an office receptionist who concentrates

---

Figure 12.1   Dimensions of Job Design

Two important dimensions of job design are the variety of tasks and scope of decision authority. This figure illustrates four possible combinations. Traditionally, many firms have created jobs like Point 1, which involve few tasks and limited decision authority. Lately, there has been a trend toward jobs like Point 4, which involve many tasks and broad decision authority. However, it is easy to give examples of jobs like Point 2, which involve many tasks and limited decision authority—for instance, certain clerical jobs. Similarly, it is easy to point to examples of jobs like Point 3, which involve few tasks and broad authority—for instance, certain sales jobs.

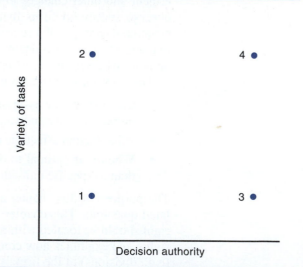

on a few tasks (answering the phone and taking messages) and has limited discretion as to what to do or how to do it. Point 2 shows a combination of many tasks and limited decision authority. For instance, clerical jobs typically involve numerous tasks (filing, word processing typing, answering the phone, and scheduling meetings, e.g.) but limited decision authority. Point 3 depicts a narrow set of tasks with broad decision authority. As an example, consider a sales representative who has broad decision rights concerning which customers to call, what sales pitch to make, what prices to charge, and so on. Yet the person concentrates on one principal task—selling products to customers. Recently, there has been a trend toward creating jobs like Point 4 that are less specialized and where employees have broader decision authority. Reasons for this trend will become evident as we proceed through the next two chapters.

As a manager moves up in the organization, these design issues consume larger amounts of the person's time. For example, the manager of a purchasing department plays an important role in defining the tasks each employee within the department performs. Unfortunately, the problem of partitioning tasks into jobs is extremely complex. It involves the assignment of literally thousands of tasks and decision rights. It also involves simultaneous consideration of other corporate policies such as performance-evaluation and compensation policy—the other two legs of the organizational architecture stool. Although current theory is not sufficiently well developed to provide a detailed solution to this general problem, through some relatively simple examples we can derive important insights. In this chapter, we present such an example to explore the issue of decision authority. The next chapter considers the problems of *bundling* tasks into jobs and jobs into subunits of the firm. Thus, this chapter concentrates on the horizontal axis in Figure 12.1 (decision authority), whereas the next chapter concentrates on the vertical axis (variety of tasks).

Our primary example in this chapter involves AutoMart, a firm selling automobiles in two cities. As depicted in Figure 12.2, the management of the firm consists

Figure 12.2   Organizational Structure of AutoMart Company

AutoMart markets automobiles in two cities. Roberto (Bob) Cruz is the CEO. The two local managers oversee the operations in the two cities. The one important decision right in this example is the pricing decision. The first question involves centralization versus decentralization. Should Bob make the pricing decisions or should they be decentralized to Colleen and Pekka? The second question involves horizontal placement of decentralized decision rights. If pricing decisions are decentralized, Bob could (1) grant each manager the pricing right for that manager's own location, (2) grant both decision rights to one manager who would make all pricing decisions, or (3) grant the decision rights for the two locations to both managers and ask them to work as a team.

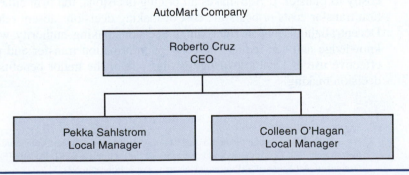

of Roberto (Bob) Cruz, the CEO, and two local managers, Pekka Sahlstrom and Colleen O'Hagan. The local managers oversee the operations in the two cities. We concentrate on one specific task/decision right, pricing. Assigning an individual the right to set prices at a local unit increases that person's decision authority. If Bob grants local managers the right to set prices, he reduces his decision authority and correspondingly increases the decision authority of the local managers. Initially, we assume that either Bob sets the prices at the local units or he grants the right to set prices to the local managers. In reality, Bob can grant the local managers some decision authority without giving them full pricing rights. For example, Bob might allow the managers to set prices within a given range. We consider these additional possibilities later in this chapter.

The issue of *centralization versus decentralization* focuses on which level of the firm's hierarchy to place the decision right. The firm is said to have centralized decision making if the right is assigned to Bob and decentralized decision making if the right is assigned to the local managers. A second issue is *choosing where within a given hierarchical level a decision should be made*. The decision authority of both local managers is increased if both are given decision rights for pricing. Alternatively, Bob might decide to increase the decision authority of only one of the local managers—for example, by letting Colleen make all pricing decisions. We begin by discussing centralization versus decentralization. We subsequently consider the lateral issue of where across a hierarchy to place the right.

Centralization versus Decentralization

Most of the analysis of assigning decision rights has focused on the question of whether to centralize or decentralize decision rights.[2] We employ AutoMart to illustrate the major implications of this analysis. The basic question is should Bob set the prices at the two locations or should the pricing decisions be decentralized to the local managers? The answer to this question depends on the benefits and costs of decentralized decision making (relative to centralized decision making).

Benefits of Decentralization

Effective Use of Local Knowledge
Local managers are likely to have important information about their local markets. For example, they are likely to have better information than Bob about the demands and price sensitivities of particular customers. They are also likely to know more about the quality and condition of their used cars. This information is potentially costly to transfer. If Bob makes all pricing decisions, the firm either incurs information transfer costs or bears the cost of making decisions absent relevant knowledge. Decentralizing decision rights links decision making authority with local specific knowledge and can reduce the costs of information transfer and processing. More effective use of local knowledge is thus one of the major benefits of decentralized decision making.

---

[2]For a technical discussion of these issues and a review of the associated literature, see P. Bolton and M. Dewatripont (2012), "Authority in Organizations," in R. Gibbons and J. Roberts (Eds.), *The Handbook Of Organizational Economics* (Princeton University Press, Princeton NJ), 342–372.

> ### MANAGERIAL APPLICATIONS
>
> ## How Much Decentralization at Google?
>
> This chapter implies that there is an important role for managers in organizations. Completely decentralized decision making would suffer from a wide range of incentive, coordination, and communication problems.
>
> Google is staffed with many very smart software engineers. Historically, people at the company were skeptical that managers added any value. Most of the software engineers wanted to spend their time on programming, not communicating with managers. In 2002, the founders of Google experimented with a completely flat organization with no managers. The experiment lasted but for a few months. Too much of the CEO's time was spent dealing with the many "nitty-gritty issues" that frequently arise with employees. The founders realized that managers contributed to the company in many ways, for example, in fostering coordination and communication among employees and in helping to assure proper incentive alignment.
>
> Google, however, remains a highly decentralized company. As of 2013, it has over 37,000 employees with only 5,000 managers, 1,000 directors, and 100 vice presidents. It is common to find engineering managers with as many as 30 direct reports. According to a Google engineer, this is done by design to prevent micromanaging: "There is only so much you can meddle when you have 30 people on a team, so you have to focus on creating the best environment for engineers to make things happen." Since the software engineers hold much of the specific knowledge, which Google has used to create value, it makes economic sense for them to have more decentralized decision rights.
>
> Source: D. Gavin (2013), "How Google Sold its Engineers on Management," *Harvard Business Review* (December).

Centralized decisions require local managers to seek permission to change prices. Local information has to be transferred to Bob or be ignored. Subsequently, Bob has to deliberate and convey his decisions back to local managers for implementation. This process takes time, and decision making is slower as a result. Such delays can lead to lost sales. Granting decision rights to the local managers promotes more rapid decision making and quicker responses to changing market conditions.[3]

Conservation of Management Time

If Bob makes local pricing decisions, substantial opportunity costs might be incurred: Using top-management time for pricing decisions means that time cannot be used for other decisions. Often, it is better to decentralize operating decisions to local managers and focus senior managers' attention on strategic decisions (e.g., which car lines to sell and how to promote them). As Alfred Sloan, former CEO of General Motors and an early proponent of decentralization, described,

> *My office force is small. That means we do not do much routine work with details. They never get up to us. I work fairly hard, but it is on the exceptions . . . not on routine or petty details.*[4]

Training and Motivation for Local Managers

It is important for firms to attract talented employees and to train them as eventual replacements for senior management. Decentralizing decision rights promotes both objectives. Granting responsibility helps attract and retain talented, ambitious local

---

[3]In the Honda example, decentralized decision making was slower than centralized decision making. However, in Honda's case, decision rights were decentralized to a team of employees rather than to an individual. Thus, the bottleneck was in the centralized coordination of the inputs from a number of team members. Later in this chapter we discuss how team decision making can be time-consuming.

[4]A. (Sloan (1924)). "The Most Important Thing I Ever Learned about Management," *System–the Magazine of Business* 44: p.137 (August).

ACADEMIC APPLICATIONS

Communication within Firms

To simplify the analysis, in this chapter we assume that one manager is better informed than the other and focus primarily on how to assign decision rights. But in general, managers can have incentives to acquire information and to intentionally distort their information before communicating it to other managers within the firm. An important line of research on the internal organization of firms examines the more general problem of communications within firms and the incentives to communicate honestly or to distort ones' information.

Crawford and Sobel describe how a better informed agent has an incentive to distort his private information, that is, communicated to the less informed principal who then uses the information to make a decision that affects each of their welfares. Their model shows that the agent's communication is inevitably distorted, and the agent introduces more noise when the principal's and agent's objectives are less congruent. The key insight from Crawford and Sobel is that communication from an agent to a principal invariably involves a loss of information, unless the agent's and principal's interests are perfectly aligned.

Crawford and Sobel only study the incentive of the agent to distort private information. Dessein extends their model by examining the relation between delegating decision rights to the agent and having the agent communicate his private information to the principal. Dessein shows that a principal decentralizes decision making to the better-informed agent rather than to communicate with this agent as long as the agent's and principal's interests are relatively aligned and the principal's uncertainty about the environment is not too great. In Dessein's model, a principal often delegates decision rights to avoid the inevitable noisy communication, and the resulting loss of information. The key insight provided by Dessein is to highlight the central trade-off between a loss of control under decentralization and a loss of information through communication.

Source: V. Crawford and J. Sobel (1982) "Strategic Information Transmission," *Econometrica* 50, 1431–1451; and W. Dessein (2002) "Authority and Communication in Organizations," *Review of Economic Studies* 69, 811–838. Also see, P. Bolton and M. Dewatripont (2013), "Authority in Organizations," in R. Gibbons and J. Roberts (Eds.), *The Handbook of Organizational Economics* (Princeton University Press, Princeton NJ), pp. 342–372.

managers who are likely to value this aspect of the job. It also provides experience in decision making that is important training for more senior positions. Finally, with the power to choose projects, lower-level managers can have stronger incentives to exert effort in finding, evaluating, and implementing new projects—decentralization increases the operating managers' level of commitment to their projects.[5]

Costs of Decentralization

Incentive Problems

Decentralizing decision rights marries authority with local specific knowledge. However, the local managers do not necessarily have strong incentives to act to maximize a firm's value. For example, the managers might sell cars to their friends at low prices or obtain kickbacks from customers in return for selling at low prices. Developing an effective control system to motivate desired actions is not always easy or inexpensive. Also, there is a residual loss because it generally does not pay to resolve incentive problems completely. Incentive problems usually are larger the lower in the organization decision rights are placed.[6]

[5]See P. Aghion and J. Tirole (1997) "Formal and Real Authority in Organizations," *Journal of Political Economy* 105, 1–29.

[6]There are incentive problems even with centralized decision making—the decision maker is concerned that employees might not follow orders. These incentive problems usually are less severe than the incentive problems from decentralized decision making.

MANAGERIAL APPLICATIONS

Decentralization Imposed Large Costs on General Motors

General Motors (GM), like most very large corporations, must decentralize the vast majority of the decision rights to lower-level managers. For example, take the decision that a lower-level GM manager made in 2004 when the ignition switch for the new Chevrolet Cobalt did not meet GM's original specification. This manager could have rejected the switch manufactured by an outside supplier, which would delay production and sales of Cobalts. Or, this manager could change the design specification so the faulty switch would pass. But accepting the lower quality switch could impair the safety and reliability of Cobalts. The decision was made to "accept" the switch. This decision turned out to be extremely costly.

If the driver bumped the key in the ignition or if the key chain was too heavy while the key was in the ignition, the switch could turnoff the engine even though the car was in motion. Numerous accidents and some fatalities occurred, leading to private law suits, regulatory investigations, and eventually U.S. Congressional hearings.

Lower-level GM managers decided against issuing a recall of vehicles, containing the faulty switch even though GM had evidence of crashes and fatalities starting in 2004. The newly appointed CEO of GM, Mary Barra did not learn of the faulty switch until January 2014. Not until February 2014 did GM officially recall vehicles containing the faulty switch. In April 2014, Barra was called before the U.S. Senate and House of Representatives for two days to answer blistering questions of why GM in the early 2000's allowed a part that did not meet GM's own technical specification to be installed, and whether GM tried to cover-up Cobalt's safety record.

The GM faulty ignition switch incident provides important lessons about the costs of decentralization. First, bad news is less likely to be communicated up the chain of command. Communicating bad news can delay projects that can hurt the bottom line. Lower-level managers, who often have the bad news and fear "shooting the messenger," are often reluctant to share it. Second, if good news is more likely communicated than bad news, senior managers can have an overly optimistic view of the entire firm. Senior managers require full information to make informed decisions, but what senior managers know depends on what gets communicated up the chain. And what gets communicated depends on the incentives that senior managers implicitly or explicitly create for lower-level managers to communicate.

Finally, the problem of inducing lower-level managers to disclose their private good and bad news is further complicated by the fact that this news often has implications about the sender's performance. For example, the manager of a project likely knows sooner than anyone else whether her project will succeed. She has incentive to delay releasing news that her project will fail in hopes of being able to turn it around. On the other hand, she has incentive to disclose favorable news that her project will succeed in hopes of getting additional resources to enhance the chance of project success. Professor Bengt Holmstrom at MIT describes this incentive problem as, "a CEO needs to trust the board enough to give directors information they ultimately could use to fire him."

Source: A. Auriemma (2014) "Chiefs at Big Firms Often the Last to Know," *The Wall Street Journal* (April 3), B1, and T. Basu (2014) "Timeline: A History Of GM's Ignition Switch Defect," (March 31), www.npr.org/2014/03/31/297158876/timeline-a-history-of-gms-ignition-switch-defect

Another incentive problem of decentralization occurs when a manager deliberately recruits weaker subordinates or refrains from developing employees under them.[7] Even though these behaviors reduce the performance of the manager's unit, they can enhance the manager's career because managers sometime view their subordinates as threatening. For example, suppose Bob, Mary's boss, has assigned the decision rights to Mary to hire her direct reports. Mary has an incentive to hire Phil, who is a weak employee relative to Mary. Bob may then view Mary as better suited for future job promotions than Phil. One way to counter this threat is by requiring communication about performance evaluations to pass through a "chain of command." Communication makes it easier to replace unproductive managers. But

[7] G. Friebel and M. Raith (2004), "Abuse of Authority and Hierarchical Communication," *Rand Journal of Economics* 35, 224–244.

MANAGERIAL APPLICATIONS

International Companies Blend Centralization and Decentralization

Large multinational companies must understand the specific customs and tastes of customers in their local markets. For example, P&G lost money in Europe when it tried to sell Secret solid stick and roll-on deodorant to a market accustomed to aerosols. Germans tend to shop at discounters more than their American counterparts. Toothpaste is sold in supermarkets and drugstores in the United States, but by law in some European countries toothpaste is only sold in drugstores.

Instead of standardizing their products across local markets, these large companies are adapting them to local tastes, customs, and laws. Instead of transferring the specialized knowledge of local tastes, customs, and laws to corporate headquarters, multinational firms hire local managers and decentralize decision rights to adapt the product to the local markets. Siemens, the large German electronics and engineering conglomerate, does 80 percent of its sales outside Germany. In most of these countries it employs local managers. But, decision rights over quality and values are retained at the corporate level. UBS of Switzerland, the banking and financial services firm, closely monitors its foreign operations, all of which carry the UBS name.

Source: C. Hymowitz (2003), "European Executives Give Some Advice on Crossing Borders," *The Wall Street Journal* (December 2), B1.

this increases the manager's propensity to hire less-competent workers. In some cases, it is best to limit communication.

Ideally, Bob would like to measure the effect of the local managers' decisions on the value of the firm. If Bob could, it would be relatively easy to use compensation schemes to motivate value-maximizing behavior. Unfortunately, identifying the effect of individual decisions on the value of the firm usually is impossible. Compensation schemes can be based on performance measures such as internal accounting numbers. For example, the local managers might be paid based on total profits for their units. However, as we will discuss in Chapters 14 through 17, developing effective compensation schemes and performance measures is difficult. The firm can use other mechanisms—for example, direct monitoring—to reduce incentive problems, but none of these techniques is costless and none will resolve these problems completely.

Coordination Costs and Failures

If the two local managers set prices independently, they might ignore important interaction effects. For instance, lowering the price in one city might divert sales from the other city, especially if they are nearby and share local media. It also might be wasteful for both managers to conduct the same type of market analysis to decide on their pricing policies if their markets are similar. For instance, most of the information might be obtained by conducting only one survey, or more precise estimates might be derived by pooling the data.

Less Effective Use of Central Information

Local managers do not necessarily have all the relevant information to make good pricing decisions. Bob might have important information about product costs, upcoming promotions, and new products from the automobile manufacturer. Bob also might have important knowledge and expertise for solving pricing problems. Often, central managers obtain important information from observing the effects of various policies implemented through time and across multiple locations. In contrast, local managers generally have more limited experience and obtain direct information from only one location. And if industry conditions are such that rapid decision making involving central information is important, the benefits of centralization of decision rights are even greater.

This discussion implies that an important role of central management in a decentralized decision system is to promote information flows and coordination among decision makers in the firm. These activities are likely to be costly. For instance, transferring information to local decision makers can be expensive. The value of coordination and central information will be lower when the product demands and costs for the local units are more independent (e.g., the locations are further apart) and more of the relevant knowledge for decisions is held by the local managers. The benefits and costs of decentralized decision making are summarized in the accompanying chart.

Forgone Scale Economies

Centralized decision making can sometimes be more cost effective than decentralized decision making due to scale economies. As an example, consider the decision rights to develop advertisements for a product that is marketed across several countries. These decision rights could be decentralized to the country level. Each country would employ staff to develop, test and produce advertising for the product. A company-wide advertising campaign, however, could be developed centrally with fewer staff and at lower cost.

Economies of scale are likely to be particularly relevant when local information is less important. In the preceding example, centralized decision making results in a coordinated ad campaign that is used across all countries, while decentralized decision making results in ads that are more effectively tailored to their local markets. Which option is better depends on the nature of the product and the characteristics of the local markets.

The Benefits and Costs of Decentralized Decision Making

Benefits	Costs
More effective use of local knowledge	Incentive problems
Conservation of senior management time	Coordination costs and failures
Training and motivation for local managers	Less effective use of central information
	Forgone scale economies

Illustrating the Trade-offs

To illustrate the basic trade-offs in this example, assume that the pricing decision can be decentralized to the local managers in varying degrees. We use D to represent the degree of decentralization of the pricing decision. When $D = 0$, all pricing decisions are made by Bob; as D increases, the local managers are granted more decision rights. For example, at a low level of D, the managers might have the authority to alter centrally determined prices within a 5 percent band. At a sufficiently high D, the local managers have full authority to set prices. For simplicity, assume that D is continuous. Also, suppose that the benefits of decentralization can be written as

$$\text{Benefits} = B \times D \tag{12.1}$$

where B is a positive constant. The benefits include better use of local knowledge, conservation of senior management time, and training/motivation for local managers.

There are, however, costs associated with decentralization. For instance, there are increased incentive problems, and the decisions of the local managers have to be

ACADEMIC APPLICATIONS

Theoretical Research in Economics of Decision Making Provides Useful Managerial Insights

In this chapter we summarize the major costs and benefits of decentralized decision making, as suggested by the ever-growing body of theoretical and empirical research on the internal organization of firms. This box summarizes several important papers that provide useful insights on how various factors stressed in this chapter are likely to affect the centralization–decentralization decision.

Consistent with the benefits and costs of decentralized decision making discussed in this chapter, Aghion and Tirole present a formal model that stresses the importance of information and incentives in driving the centralization–decentralization decision. In their model, there is a central manager (the principal/owner of the firm) and a local manager (the agent). The firm faces a menu of potential investment projects. Initially, neither manager can distinguish among the potential projects in terms of expected benefits. Both agree that without additional information, it is better not to invest in any of the potential projects. Either party can privately choose to exert costly effort and become fully informed about the projects, but the effort might fail. The preferences of the two managers, while not perfectly aligned (there is an agency conflict), are partially congruent. With full information about the benefits of each project, the managers would prefer different projects because of the "private benefits" they would receive. Each manager, however, benefits to some degree from the other manager's preferred project.

Initially, the central manager has the "formal authority" to make the decision, but this decision can be delegated to the local manager. The benefit of delegating the formal authority to the local manager (decentralizing the decision right) is that it provides greater incentives to the local manager to exert effort to become informed about the projects, since the local manager benefits by choosing the project preferred most by that manager. This choice also benefits the central manager to some degree. The cost to the central manager of delegating formal authority is that the central manager will not be able to choose her most preferred project, should she become fully informed by exerting effort. Having delegated formal authority, she has reduced incentives to exert effort in information acquisition. The central manager with formal authority will transfer "real authority" to the local manager to make the decision should the central manager's efforts in information acquisition fail. The local manager with real authority will only choose to invest in a project if he has successfully acquired the information. This investment benefits the central manager as well. The central manager's decision to retain or delegate formal authority (centralization vs. decentralization) depends on the congruence of the two managers' preferences (the incentive problem) and which manager has a relative advantage in information acquisition (as in our discussion of more effective use of local knowledge). The Aghion and Tirole analysis helps explain why some firms, such as British Petroleum and Johnson & Johnson, commit to lightly staff some of their corporate headquarter functions as a way to empower local managers. For example, EMC, which dominates the data-storage business with over $23 billion in revenue in 2013, is organized as "three federated businesses" with different names. The company explicitly gives local managers a "significant degree of local autonomy" to develop new ways to serve customers and to innovate. Their analysis also suggests a potential benefit of dispersed shareholders in large firms who delegate much of the formal authority for decision making to boards of directors and senior managers. The influential paper by Aghion and Tirole has motivated other economists to extend their line of inquiry.

Dessein and Santos study another aspect of decentralization—one which we have stressed in this chapter—coordination costs. Large firms employ many managers. Each specializes in certain tasks to increase her productivity. But such task specialization generates costs as the firm must communicate and coordinate the various tasks performed by its managers. In quickly changing environments, individual managers must redefine their tasks and then coordinate their new tasks with the other managers, but this increases communication costs. Under decentralization each manager is more specialized and hence more productive (as in our discussion of more effective use of local knowledge), but the firm incurs larger coordination and adaptation costs. Centralization allows better coordination and adaptation, but there are lower returns to specialization. Dessein and Santos' analysis suggests that firms facing volatile environments should centralize to lower coordination and adaptation costs. Their model helps explain why disaster relief is best accomplished by centralized organizations.

Source: P. Bolton and M. Dewatripont (2013), "Authority in Organizations," in R. Gibbons and J. Roberts (Eds.), *The Handbook of Organizational Economics* (Princeton University Press, Princeton NJ), 342–372; P. Aghion and J. Tirole (1997), "Formal and Real Authority in Organizations," *Journal of Political Economy* 105, 1–29; W. Dessein and T. Santos (2006), "Adaptive Organizations," *Journal of Political Economy* 114, 956–995; G. Friebel and M. Raith (2004), "Abuse of Authority and Hierarchical Communication," *Rand Journal of Economics* 35, 224–244.

Figure 12.3   **A Graphical Illustration of the Trade-offs between Centralization and Decentralization of Decision Making at AutoMart**

In this example, the local managers have important specific knowledge, that is, valuable for decision making, and timeliness of response is important. The benefits of decentralization are given by Benefits = *BD*, where *D* is the level of decentralization of pricing decisions and *B* is a positive constant. These benefits include better use of local knowledge, increased response times, conservation of the time of senior management, and training/motivation for local managers. The costs are given by Costs = $AD + CD^2$, where the first term, *AD*, represents the increased contracting costs from decentralization and the second term, CD^2, represents the increased coordination costs (*A* and *C* are positive constants). The optimal level of decentralization is $D^* = (B − A)/2C$. At this point, the marginal benefits and the marginal costs of decentralization are equal. (The slopes of the total benefit and cost curves are the same.)

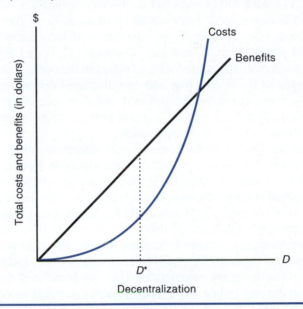

coordinated. Also, there are the increased costs of having to transfer central information to local decision makers. Assume the costs of decentralization are

$$\text{Costs} = (A \times D) + (C \times D^2) \tag{12.2}$$

where *A* and *C* are positive constants. The first term, *AD*, represents the contracting costs that arise from resolving the incentive problems of decentralization; the second term, *CD*, represents the coordination/central information costs. This formulation assumes that coordination/information costs increase at an increasing rate with decentralization.[8] For example, it becomes more and more difficult to coordinate decisions as decision rights become more decentralized.

The objective of the firm is to choose *D* to maximize the net benefits, where

$$\text{Net benefits} = \text{Benefits} − \text{Costs} = BD − AD − CD^2 \tag{12.3}$$

Figure 12.3 depicts the benefits and costs of decentralization. Net benefits are maximized where the vertical distance between the benefits and the costs is greatest. This condition occurs at

$$D^* = (B − A)/2C \tag{12.4}$$

[8]Coordination and central information costs do not have to be quadratic, and the other benefits and costs do not have to be linear. We use these functional forms to produce convenient solutions in our example, but the basic principles of our analysis do not depend on these simplifying assumptions.

As is standard in problems of this type, D^* is the level of decentralization at which the marginal benefits of decentralization equal the marginal costs.[9] At this point, the additional benefits from more decentralized decision making just offset the additional costs. (Note that at levels of decentralization below D^*, a small increase in decentralization would add more to benefits than to costs so net benefits would rise. Conversely, at levels above D^*, a small increase would add more to costs than to benefits so net benefits would fall. Thus, the maximum net benefit occurs where the slopes of the cost and benefit curves are equal.)

Over time, it is likely that the costs and benefits of decentralization will change. For example, the importance of local knowledge can change with changes in competition in the industry or shifts in consumer demand. Also, the costs of transferring information and controlling incentive problems can fall due to new technologies (e.g., consider cell phones and network computers). Changes in the benefits of decentralization can be represented by changes in B, the coefficient in the benefits equation. For example, if the importance of local knowledge increases with more global competition, B increases. Equation (12.4) and Figure 12.3 indicate that increases in B are associated with increases in the optimal amounts of decentralization. Changes in the contracting and coordination/information costs of decentralization can be represented by changes in A and C, respectively. Both Equation (12.4) and Figure 12.3 indicate that an increase in these costs is associated with a decrease in the optimal level of decentralization.

Our analysis of centralization versus decentralization can help us understand the changes in the assignment of decision rights at Honda in 1991. Recall that after Soichiro Honda retired in 1973, the relevant specific knowledge for decision making was spread among many executives, making the benefits of decentralization high. In the context of our example, Honda could be viewed during this period as operating with an appropriately high level of decentralization. By 1991, however, Honda had grown tremendously and consensus decision making no longer was effective. Also, Nubuhiko Kawamoto, the new CEO, had been a Honda engineer and had detailed specific knowledge about designing automobiles. Thus, the benefits of decentralization were smaller than in the past (when senior management possessed less of the relevant knowledge). In response to these changing conditions, Kawamoto decreased the level of decentralization. In the context of our example, there had been a reduction in the benefits of decentralization as well as an increase in the costs, resulting in a lower optimal level of decentralization.

Our graphical illustration simplifies the centralization/decentralization decision in many ways. For example, the analysis is much more complicated if the assignment of more than one decision right is considered. Also, the example takes the divisional structure of the firm as given (two operating divisions and a headquarters). More generally, the unit structure is determined along with the assignment of decision rights. (We discuss this issue in the next chapter.) It is particularly important to emphasize

---

[9]Technical note: The solution to this maximization process can be obtained through elementary calculus. Alternatively, Equation (12.3) is quadratic, and thus you can use the quadratic formula to solve for the roots of the equation. The two roots, 0 and $(B - A)/C$, are where net benefits equal 0. The parabola is at a maximum midway between the two roots: $(B - A)/2C$. Note that the optimal point D^* is where the vertical distance between the benefits and the costs is greatest. This point occurs where the slope of the benefit curve is equal to the slope of the cost curve. The slope of the benefit curve is the marginal benefit, whereas the slope of the cost curve is the marginal cost. Thus, the optimal point is where the marginal benefit of decentralization equals the marginal cost.

MANAGERIAL APPLICATIONS

Some Bureaucracy Can Be Good

One of the benefits of decentralization is effective use of local knowledge that speeds up decision making. Highly centralized companies have numerous layers of bureaucracy that make decision making slow. In highly competitive and dynamic markets such as high-tech firms, layers of bureaucracy can cause firms to miss windows of opportunities. For example, a Facebook company's motto is "Move Fast and Break Things." And when Larry Page took over as chief executive of Google, he felt it had become overly bureaucratic and he wanted to regain "the nimbleness and soul and passion and speed of a start-up." But layers of bureaucracy, such as centralized human resources departments, can cause delay and create inefficiency.

Decentralizing all decision making, including the human resource function, even in high-tech firms creates problems. For instance, assigning decision rights for personnel tasks to lower level managers can encourage these managers to hire and promote people just like them, a practice which can lead to discrimination law suits. Notably, GitHub, a web service for sharing and collaborating on software code, has been accused by a female engineer of fostering a culture of bullying and disrespect toward women. GitHub had decentralized many of the HR tasks to lower-level employees and there was little corporate oversight.

Moreover, Silicon-Valley start-up firms with centralized human resource departments appear to outperform firms using a decentralized model. One study of 200 of these firms found that nearly half of the companies decentralized traditional human resource tasks to lower-level employees, and only 6.6 percent had the type of formal HR departments typically found in other industries. However, those Silicon Valley start-ups with centralized HR departments were nearly 40 percent less likely to fail than start-ups that decentralized HR, and nearly 40 percent more likely to go public. This study suggests that there is an optimal amount of decentralization—complete decentralization of human resource tasks is unlikely to maximize firm value.

Source: D. Leonhardt (2014), "Yes, Silicon Valley, Sometimes You Need More Bureaucracy," *New York Times* (April 30), www.ny-times.com/2014/05/01/upshot/yes-silicon-valley-there-is-such-a-thing-as-not-enough-bureaucracy.html?_r=0

---

that when a firm changes its decision system, it typically is necessary to make corresponding changes in other organizational features, such as the performance-evaluation and reward systems. These aspects of organizational architecture are like three legs of a stool, and it is important to keep them in balance. It often is desirable to accompany decentralization with an increased emphasis on performance and incentive compensation to motivate the empowered decision makers. Our illustration is incomplete in that it does not incorporate simultaneous changes in these other organizational variables. Despite these limitations, the example highlights some of the important trade-offs in deciding on the degree of decentralization.

Management Implications

Our analysis indicates that decentralization involves both costs and benefits. These costs and benefits are likely to vary across firms and time. We now examine how the optimal level of decentralization is likely to vary across firms. We then discuss factors motivating recent trends toward decentralization within many firms.

Across Firms

We have discussed how the firm's business environment and strategy are major determinants of organizational architecture. We focused particular attention on three aspects of the environment: Technology, market conditions, and regulation. We expect that the net benefits of decentralization will be highest in rapidly evolving environments. Within unregulated industries where market conditions and production technologies frequently change, the timely use of local knowledge is likely to be particularly important. In more stable environments, companies can use centralized decision making and concentrate on gaining economies of scale through large-scale standardized production.

We expect that the benefits of decentralization are likely to increase as the firm enters more markets. If a firm offers a broad array of products, it is less likely that senior managers have the specific knowledge to select the most appropriate operating decisions across its various businesses. Although not always the case, decentralization frequently will be more important for firms following a strategy in which they develop differentiated products that command price premiums. Such a strategy requires effective use of information on customer demands and competitor offerings. Often, this information is held by people lower in the organization. With cost strategies that focus on low-cost production of standardized products, local knowledge normally is less important.

Another element of strategy is the degree of vertical integration; for instance, whether a manufacturing firm should make its own inputs or provide its own retail distribution and service network. In general, we expect that as the firm becomes larger, either through vertical integration or through geographic expansion, the appropriate level of decentralization will increase. As a firm's size increases, more decisions have to be made. Time and mental-processing constraints simply will preclude central managers from making all major decisions.

MANAGERIAL APPLICATIONS

Decentralization and the Global Supply Chain

As most toy sales are made during the Christmas holiday period, toy companies used to place their orders in January and February, blindly betting on demand. By December they would have shortages or stockpiles of duds. One notable underestimate involved Mighty Morphin Power Rangers in 1993. Demand was estimated to be 600,000, but they could have sold 12 million. New technology and global supply markets are changing the toy business.

New toys arrive in major retailers during the spring and summer. Toy companies download the daily sales of their toys at Walmart, Kmart, Toys "R" Us, and Target into computer models that update the projected Christmas demand forecast based on how the toys are selling during the spring and summer. One educational toy sold 360 units during its introductory weekend. Based on these numbers, the computer model doubled the toy's sales projections to 700,000 units. But the factory in China was only told to produce 350,000 units, and was given 12 months to produce them. To double output and do it in three months required more specialized tooling to produce all the plastic parts. Since the Chinese factory had designed the tools to make the parts, they had their design team reengineer the tools so that more parts could be made faster and with fewer defects, and the toys could be assembled faster. Because the Chinese factory had experience producing the toy, they knew how to improve the toy's design to reduce the defect rate from 5 percent to 0.3 percent.

The Chinese toy factory is a 14-acre integrated design and production facility that specializes in supply-chain efficiencies. Gaining access to real time sales data at the large retailers, toy companies are using this information to generate more accurate forecasts of final demand. The decision rights to change production schedules are decentralized lower in the toy companies. At the same time, the decision rights to change production designs are decentralized to companies that have the specialized knowledge of how to make the toys faster and better.

Source: G. Fowler and J. Pereira (2003), "Behind Hit Toy, A Race to Tap Seasonal Surge," *The Wall Street Journal* (December 18), A1, A12.

MANAGERIAL APPLICATIONS

Centralizing R&D to Boost Return on Investment

The large Swiss pharmaceutical company, Novartis, is seeing its profits erode. As its medicines lose patent protection, less-expensive generics enter the market, thereby allowing health care providers to choose lower-cost drugs. This is forcing Novartis to rethink its research-and-development strategies to channel resources to more-promising experimental drugs and avoid others that might be tempting but more difficult to deliver. First, Novartis took the risky step of raising its 2013 spending on in-house R&D by 5.6 percent to $9.85 billion. Second, it consolidated all of its R&D activities into four cities: Shanghai, Basel, Boston, and La Jolla, California. By centralizing R&D into these four locations, Novartis hopes to foster greater cooperation and interaction between researchers in different disciplines now at the same location and to tap the academic communities of the four cities. The Novartis CEO explains, "a larger group of people benefiting from the infrastructure that's been created at a research place is a better approach than having small groups with limited infrastructure spread around the world."

Source: M. Falconi (2014), "Novartis Chairman Stresses Need for R&D Investment, *The Wall Street Journal* (March 22), www.wsj.com/news/articles/SB10001424052702303380210457945309298573094

Centralized decision making has particular advantages when coordination of activities within the firm is important. For instance, hub-and-spoke airlines schedule flights from the spokes to arrive at roughly the same time at a central hub. Passengers connect to their next flights that leave later. Airlines using centralized scheduling are able to coordinate the flight schedules and arrange baggage connections at lower cost, offering greater convenience to customers, than if schedules were determined by multiple decentralized decision makers (e.g., the pilots).

Recent Trends

In contrast to Honda, the general trend over the last two decades has been toward greater decentralization. We have suggested that changes in organizational architecture are motivated by changes in the basic economic environment. We now examine those factors which have changed in the environment to promote decentralization.

Over the past two decades, global competition has increased tremendously within many industries. Consider, as examples, the automobile, cellular devices, and computer industries. This competition has placed pressures on firms to cut costs, produce higher-quality products, and meet the demands of customers in a more timely fashion. The information for improving quality, customer service, and efficiency often is located lower in the organization. Thus, these competitive pressures have increased the benefits of decentralization for many firms.[10]

Technology has motivated changes in the level of decentralization for two reasons. First, the rate of technological innovation has increased dramatically. Firms must either respond quickly to the resulting changes in market conditions and production technologies or lose profits. This innovation can prompt firms to

---

[10]Foreign competition also has reduced the power of labor unions to enforce inefficient work rules (e.g., contract restrictions limiting the tasks that specific employees can perform). When competition largely was restricted to domestic, heavily unionized firms, there was limited pressure to change work assignments and decision rights in American firms. Competition from more efficient foreign and nonunion competitors altered this environment.

MANAGERIAL APPLICATIONS

Decentralizing Decision Making to Computer Models

Many websites such as those for Amazon, Best Buy, United Airlines, Marriott, and Home Depot use dynamic pricing models to change the price of their goods or services frequently using complicated computer algorithms. For example, Amazon changed the price of a GE microwave oven nine times in one day, with the price fluctuating between $744.46 and $871.49. Best Buy's computer responded by lifting its online price on the oven to $899.99 from $809.99 after the Amazon prices rose, then lowering it again after Amazon dropped the price. These algorithms use data on consumer demand, competitors' prices, and even the time of day and weather conditions to update prices. Some Internet retailers try to maintain the lowest price, even by a penny, so their products are listed at the top of the search results when shoppers do price comparisons. Banks approve loans using computer models that incorporate up-to-date information on borrowers' payments on credit cards. These computer models are just one example of using computer models to make decisions that were once made by people.

Human decision making is limited by the quantity of data one person can assemble and process. Human decisions can be slow, biased, and unreliable. Computer models can process vast amounts of data, consistently, and quickly. They work 24/7, and do not require expensive control systems to resolve agency problems. Moreover, they can be programmed to learn from their mistakes. Chess-playing computer models can beat even the best grand masters. Computer models work best where the decision can be quantified, such as prices, there is an abundant amount of data, the decision must be made relatively frequently, and the underlying relations are stable.

But computer decision models can lead to problems. Amazon faced a fire storm after some customers who bought DVD movies began comparing notes online and learned they had been charged different prices for the same DVD. It turns out that Amazon had been conducting random pricing tests to determine the profit-maximizing price point that balanced profit margin and sales volume. The media picked up the story and Amazon ended up refunding 6,896 customers an average of $3.10 each, or a total of $21,377.60. Vast Internet databases allow pricing models to charge different prices based on individuals' billing information, purchasing history, zip codes, and other demographic data. Undoubtedly, this will create a demand for new websites that facilitate users fooling the models at other websites to "think" the consumer should be offered a lower price.

Sources: J. Angwin and D. Mattioli (2012), "Coming Soon: Toilet Paper Priced Like Airline Tickets," *The Wall Street Journal* (September 5), www.wsj.com/news/articles/SB1000087239639044 4914904577617333130724846; A. Nusca (2013), "The future of retail is dynamic pricing. So why can't we get it right?" *ZDNet* (October 2), www.zdnet.com/the-future-of-retail-is-dynamic-pricing-so-why-cant-we-get-it-right-7000021444/; and M. Martinez (2013), "Amazon Error May End 'Dynamic Pricing,'" (September 29), abcnews.go.com/Technology/story?id=119399.

decentralize decision rights when important aspects of the knowledge of new technologies are not held by the central corporate office. Second, new technologies have altered the costs of information transfer substantially (for instance, smart wireless devices). In some cases, these changes have worked to promote decentralization. For example, advanced telecommunications systems (satellites, Wi-Fi, and fiber optics) have reduced the costs and time of transferring central information to local decision makers to coordinate and enhance decentralized decisions. This technology has also made it less expensive to track the sales and production costs of individual products. This reduction in costs has increased the feasibility of developing more precise performance standards for local decision makers to use in incentive compensation plans.

In other cases, the effect has been in the opposite direction: Local information has become less expensive to transfer to central headquarters, thus favoring more centralized decision making. For example, supermarket electronic scan lines allow central tracking of inventory and can increase the benefits of centralized purchasing.

Many of the restocking decisions within Walmart now are handled by an automated system through which suppliers restock items at individual stores whenever the computer system indicates that inventories have fallen to a specified level. Managers at individual stores have few decision rights over inventory levels.

Technological advances also have allowed many firms to flatten their management structures. Traditionally, firms have relied on middle managers to transmit information and instructions from senior management to lower-level employees. Middle managers also have played an important role in coordinating and monitoring the actions of these lower-level employees. Cloud-based technology, by facilitating communication between senior management and lower-level employees, has reduced demands for middle managers. Technology also has motivated changes in the roles of middle managers. In many firms middle management's role has shifted from being a conduit in the information flow to one that more closely resembles the coach of a sports team—assembling the optimal set of players, helping them design winning strategies, providing motivation, and so on.

Lateral Decision-Right Assignment

Although discussion of decision rights often focuses on centralization versus decentralization, lateral issues also can be important. In our AutoMart example, if Bob decentralizes decision rights, he can

- Grant the two managers the pricing decisions for their own locations, or
- Grant both decision rights to one manager who makes all pricing decisions, or
- Grant the decision rights for pricing at the two locations to both managers and ask them to work as a team in deciding on the pricing policy.

As in the centralization versus decentralization problem, the relevant factors in making this choice include the distribution of knowledge and the costs of coordination and control. For example, granting decision rights to the managers separately takes greater advantage of local specific knowledge. But pricing at the two locations will not necessarily be well coordinated. Alternatively, granting all decision rights to one manager promotes coordinated decision making and takes advantage of any economies of scale in having one person make both decisions. But it comes at the potential expense of less effective utilization of the other manager's local knowledge. There also might be differences in contracting costs between these two alternatives. For example, it might be less expensive to monitor the decisions of one person than two. The value of the third option, granting decision rights to a team of managers, depends on a number of factors that we discuss in the next section. Which of the three options is best depends on the specific circumstances facing the firm. For instance, having the two managers make independent decisions is likely to dominate when the two markets are more independent and more of the relevant knowledge for pricing is at the individual unit level.

Questions relating to the lateral placement of decision rights frequently arise within organizations. For example, should personnel decisions be made within each individual division, or should these rights be granted to a separate human resources department? Should a divisional manager be in charge of R&D, or should this function be centralized elsewhere within the organization? Can the college or business operate its own career services center, or must it rely on centralized career services of the university?

Assigning Decision Rights to Teams

Our analysis of AutoMart suggests that a firm might want to assign a decision right to a team of employees rather than to one individual. In this discussion, we use the term *team* to refer broadly to the many different types of work groups that have decision-making authority (teams, committees, task forces, and so on); for our purposes, more refined definitions are unnecessary. Firms grant decision rights to teams of employees for at least three basic purposes: To manage activities, to make products, and to recommend actions. Teams that manage activities often are composed of individuals from different functional areas (e.g., marketing and finance). Teams that make products generally are located at the plant level. For instance, some firms have granted to teams of production employees the decision rights to set their own work schedules and assignments and to organize the basic production process. Both types of teams tend to be reasonably permanent. The assignment is to manage some particular business or process. Teams that recommend actions focus on specific projects and normally disband when the task is complete. We now discuss the benefits and costs of group decision making relative to assigning the decision right to a single individual.

Benefits of Team Decision Making

Improved Use of Dispersed Specific Knowledge

The relevant specific knowledge for decision making often is dispersed among many people within an organization. For instance, the relevant knowledge for designing new products often is held by a variety of employees, including scientists, engineers, and sales personnel. Through the use of teams, those individuals with specific knowledge are involved directly in the decision-making process. By definition, specific knowledge is expensive to assemble and transfer to a single decision maker. Also, it can be important for the individuals with the relevant knowledge to share information among themselves. By sharing information in a group setting, new ideas might be generated that would not occur in a sequence of bilateral communications between a central decision maker and each of the individuals. By sharing information, employees also become better informed for future decisions and actions. Granting decision rights to a team encourages the members to communicate and to brainstorm. Final decisions are made through consensus or some type of voting mechanism.

Employee Buy-In

Employees often are suspicious that management-initiated decisions benefit managers at the expense of other employees; managers frequently suggest that they grant

---

MANAGERIAL APPLICATIONS

Employing Teams to Assemble Knowledge

The board of directors at Home Properties (a real estate investment trust) decided to change the process by which it approves acquisitions that arise between regularly scheduled board meetings. Acquisitions valued below $70 million had been approved by use of a mail ballot. But board members became concerned that this process limited potentially valuable discussions among the members of the board. A property committee was established consisting of those outside board members with the most extensive real estate experience. All but the smallest acquisitions now are vetted by this group prior to presentation to the full board for approval by mail. (Larger acquisitions still must be approved at a formal board meeting.)

decision rights to groups of employees specifically to increase employee "buy-in." It is asserted that employees who take part in a decision process are more likely to support the final decision and be more active in its implementation. This occurs for at least three reasons: First, asymmetric information and uncertainty, in turn, prevent employees from knowing the full consequences of a decision. Second, a group of employees has less to fear if they make the decision themselves or if the decision is made by employees with similar interests (see also Web Chapter 20, available via Connect). Reduced concerns about the effects of the decision increase employee buy-in, even when the same decision might have been made by the central manager. Third, employees have stronger incentives to invest in implementing decisions that they recommend because their reputations depend on the ultimate outcomes of the decisions.

Costs of Team Decision Making

Collective-Action Problems

Collective decision making often is slower. Recall how senior executives at Honda Motor Company took months to reach a consensus on policy decisions. Also, group decisions are not always efficient or rational.[11] (Consider the old saying that a camel is a horse designed by a committee.) Group decision making also can be subject to manipulation and political influence. In the appendix to this chapter, we illustrate how the common decision rule of majority voting can be subject to manipulation; management implications of this analysis are highlighted.

Free-Rider Problems

Team members bear the full costs of their individual efforts but share the gains that accrue to the team. This arrangement encourages team members to free-ride on the efforts of others (see Chapter 10). As we discuss in subsequent chapters, free-rider problems can be reduced through appropriate performance-evaluation and reward schemes. However, these schemes are costly to design and administer.

Management Implications

When Will Team Decision Making Work Best?

Some managers and consultants suggest that team decision making is virtually always better than individual decision making.[12] Our discussion indicates that this suggestion is not correct. Team decision making is more likely to be productive in environments where the relevant specific knowledge for the decision is dispersed among individuals and where the costs of collective decision making and controlling free-rider problems are lower.

Team decision making is a common component of total quality management programs. Many firms have increased their use of team decision making in the last few years through the implementation of Total Quality Management or Six Sigma programs. Yet experience indicates that the *indiscriminate use* of teams in these programs can be counterproductive—in such cases, the costs exceed the benefits.

---

[11]K. Arrow (1963), *Social Choice and Individual Values* (John Wiley & Sons: New York).

[12]For example, http://humanresources.about.com/od/teambuildingfaqs/f/optimum-team-size.htm

Highly Decentralized Cargill Uses Teams at the Top

Cargill, a $140 billion global producer and marketer of food, agricultural, financial, and industrial products and services, employs 143,000 people in 67 countries. With over 70 decentralized business units, the CEO keeps his top team small. The senior governing body, the Cargill Leadership Team, consists of six people. This team allocates human and financial capital and sets the broad strategy, messaging, and tone. Below these six people is the Corporate Center, which includes CLT members and about 25 others who serve as functional and platform leaders, the latter monitor the 70 business units.

Cargill's Corporate Center is organized around 12 teams, such as the corporate food risk committee, the technology committee, the strategy and capital committee, and the Cargill brand reputation committee. These teams determine overall company policy and direction. The CEO states, "by keeping the CLT too small to conduct the day-to-day affairs of the company, it forces that accountability and ownership down the line. The role of the CLT is 'to put our noses in and keep our fingers out.' That's the right way to run a company this size."

Source: www.cargill.com; and G. Neilson and J. Wulf (2012), "How Many Direct Reports?" *Harvard Business Review* (April), Reprint R1204H.

Optimal Team Size

Increasing the size of the team enhances the knowledge base of the team. However, it also increases the incentives to free-ride, as well as other costs associated with collective decision making. For instance, as team size grows, it can become difficult to make decisions and work in a coordinated fashion. Team size is optimal at the point where the additional costs of adding a new member equal the incremental benefits. Consultants argue that virtually all effective teams have no more than 12 members and most were much smaller (ranging from 5 to 7).

ANALYZING MANAGERIAL DECISIONS: *Teams at Nucor versus Levi Strauss*

Nucor, the largest global steel joist and deck manufacturer and the biggest steel producer in the United States, had sales in 2013 of $19 billion. Under team-based production, each employee is assigned to a team, and each employee is evaluated and compensated based on the productivity of their team.

Nucor uses production teams of 12–20 people, and ties pay directly to the amount of quality steel produced each day. Its bonus system compensates teammates for improving the process including safely delivering quality product and operating more efficiently. Teammates receive an hourly rate or base salary for hours worked plus bonus and profit sharing. Bonuses are paid weekly based on each team's production. At the end of each year, employees receive profit sharing of 10 percent of company earnings. A typical Nucor steelworker can earn upwards of $90,000 per year. Nucor boasts of low employee turnover of 7 percent per year.

Levi Strauss adopted team-based production processes at its existing plants. Employees who had been previously paid on a piece-rate basis were put on a team-based process.

1. In general, what are the advantages and disadvantages of team-based processes?
2. Team-based production at the nucor is widely regarded as a success. By contrast, the Levi Strauss team-based initiative is widely regarded as a failure. Worker productivity has declined and employee morale is low. What factors caused the Nucor team-based production to be a success and the Levi Strauss experiment to be a failure? Why?

Source: M. Bolch (2007), "Rewarding the Team," *HR Magazine* (Febraury 2); and www.nucor.com

Decision Management and Control[13]

Thus far, our characterization of decision making has been rather simplified. In particular, we generally have assumed that an employee either has a decision right or does not. In reality, some aspects of a decision can be decentralized whereas others can be maintained at a higher level. For example, at AutoMart, the managers might be granted the right to set prices within some range but have to obtain approval from Bob for larger price changes. Thus, the decision authority of an employee can be increased (see Figure 12.1) without granting the employee all rights to a particular decision.

A useful characterization divides the decision-making process into four steps:

- **Initiation.** Generation of proposals for resource utilization and structuring of contracts
- **Ratification.** Choice of the decision initiatives to be implemented
- **Implementation.** Execution of ratified decisions
- **Monitoring.** Measurement of the performance of decision makers and implementation of rewards

> **Definition**
> **Decision management:** The initiation and implementation of decisions.
> **Decision control:** The ratification and monitoring of decisions.

Often, firms assign initiation and implementation rights to the same employees. Fama and Jensen refer to these functions as *decision management;* they use the term *decision control* to refer to the ratification and monitoring functions.

Employees normally do not bear the full wealth effects of their actions—there are incentive problems. Granting an employee decision management and decision control rights for the same decision typically will lead to dysfunctional behavior. In the case of AutoMart, if the local managers make pricing decisions and there is no monitoring or other control, the managers are more likely to use the decision rights for their own benefit. For instance, the managers might sell cars to family and friends below cost. Whenever decision makers are not owners, separating decision management and decision control limits conflicts of interest. Only when the decision maker also is the major residual claimant—the person with the legal rights to the profits of the enterprise once all the other claimants of the firm (e.g., bondholders and employees) are paid—does it make sense to combine decision management and control.

> **Basic Principle: Allocating Decision Rights**
> If decision makers do not bear the major wealth effects of their decisions, decision management and decision control will be held by separate decision makers.

Separation of Decision Management and Control

A prominent example of separating decision management and decision control is the presence of a board of directors at the top of all corporations. In large corporations, the residual claimants are shareholders. The management of the firm is largely the responsibility of the CEO, who typically owns less than 1 percent of the firm's stock. To mitigate potential incentive problems, shareholders grant major

---

[13]This section draws on E. Fama and M. Jensen (1983), "Separation of Ownership and Control," *Journal of Law & Economics* 26, 301–326.

decision-control rights to the board of directors. The board ratifies major decisions initiated by the CEO. The board also has monitoring authority and the rights to fire and compensate the CEO. However, since board members often are not major shareholders, there still is a role for other parties to "monitor the monitor." This role is performed by large blockholders (such as public pension funds) and takeover specialists. If board members do a poor job, they can be replaced through a proxy fight or corporate takeover.

The principle of separation of decision management and control helps explain the widespread use of hierarchies within organizations. In hierarchies, decision management is formally separate from decision control—that is, decisions of individuals are monitored and ratified by individuals who are above them in the hierarchy. The same employee might have both decision-control and decision-management functions. For example, divisional managers might have approval rights over certain initiatives of lower-level employees while at the same time have to request authorization for the division's capital expenditure plan. The important thing is that one employee not have both the decision management and decision control rights for the *same decision.* In smaller organizations, where one person (or a small number) has the relevant knowledge to make decisions, it is expensive to separate decision management from decision control. In this case, the two functions often are combined. In such cases the decision maker also tends to be the major residual claimant to avoid incentive problems. (For example, the company is organized as a sole proprietorship, partnership, or corporation where the managers own much of the stock.)

Although management and control rights for a decision often are granted to individuals at different levels in the organization, they sometimes are granted to separate individuals at the same level of the corporate hierarchy. For example, the quality of the output of a manufacturing division sometimes is monitored by a quality unit with equal status within the organization. Similarly, internal auditors often monitor units at the same hierarchical level.

Empowerment

The concepts of decision management and decision control also are useful in making the term *empowerment* more precise. Managers sometimes are unclear about what rights are being granted when they announce that they are empowering employees. This ambiguity can lead to disputes and conflicts between management and employees—for example, when management reverses the decisions of employees who thought they were empowered. The principle of separation of decision management and control suggests that empowerment should not mean that an employee has all rights to a particular decision. An empowered employee might have explicit rights to initiate and implement decisions; however, there is still an important role for managers to ratify and monitor decisions. Ratification does not necessarily mean that an employee must seek approval for every decision. In some cases, managers might want to preratify decisions within a particular range—*boundary setting.* For instance, we discussed how the managers at AutoMart might be given authority to set prices within some range. In any case, Bob would want to maintain monitoring rights over the decision. Often, conflicts over empowerment can be avoided by clearly delineating what rights actually are delegated to the employee.

MANAGERIAL APPLICATIONS

Failure to Separate Decision Management from Decision Control at JP Morgan—The Case of the London Whale

A fundamental principle in allocating decision rights is to separate Decision Management (initiation and implementation) from Decision Control (ratification and monitoring) unless the decision maker also owns the firm. Large financial institutions, including AIG, Merrill Lynch, and Société Générale, suffered substantial losses during the 2007–2008 financial crisis, arguably due in part to poor decision controls and monitoring of their traders. JP Morgan (JPM) emerged from this crisis with its reputation for strong risk management and controls largely intact. Its CEO, Jamie Dimon, was viewed as the "star" bank CEO in many circles.

In April 2012, the Wall Street Journal begin a series of articles on the "London Whale," whose huge trading losses significantly damaged JPM 's reputation for risk management. The London Whale was the name given to a JPM trader who had taken very large, risky positions in collateralized debt securities. As losses from his positions began to appear, JPM's Dimon characterized them as a "Tempest in a Teapot"—words he would quickly regret. On May 10th, JPM announced a loss of about $2 billion due to the Whale's trading (this loss later grew to over $4 billion). By then Dimon realized that the losses and damage to JPM's reputation were huge. He said the problem was the result of "the bank's own errors." In describing these errors he used strong words including, "flawed," "complex," "poorly reviewed," "poorly executed," "poorly monitored," and "self-inflicted."

In September 12, 2013, JPM announced a combination of actions that were directed toward further separating decision management and decision control for their trading activities. Among these, JPM budgeted an additional $4 billion and committed 5,000 extra employees to increase trading controls. JPM also granted greater authority to executives in charge of risk, legal, and compliance, which means they can no longer be overruled by business heads.

Source: M. Langley and D. Fitzpatrick (2013), "Embattled J.P. Morgan Bulks Up Oversight," *The Wall Street Journal* (September 13).

Decision-Right Assignment and Knowledge Creation

Much of our discussion thus far has focused on how to assign decision rights given the existing distribution of knowledge. As we have discussed, a potentially important benefit of decentralization is that it provides employees with the opportunity to act on their specific knowledge. However this is only part of the potential benefits of decentralization: An important facet of the optimal assignment of decision rights involves the firm's ability to create *new* knowledge. If the firm can identify employees who make particularly productive use of their specific knowledge and they can generalize from that experience to produce new methods or procedures that can be transferred to other employees, the productivity of a larger group within the firm can be increased.

We have discussed how value is created when wetware is converted into software. This process requires that employees be encouraged to experiment; successful experiments be identified; and reasons for their success be understood, codified, and implemented by others within the firm. Critical decision-control function for management within a decentralized organization is monitoring to identify superior performance. Therefore, one important function of the firm's performance-evaluation system is to identify excellence.

Note that this function does not have to be performed by managers at higher levels within the organization. For example, Home Properties is a real estate investment trust that owns and manages apartment communities. A critical responsibility

---

MANAGERIAL APPLICATIONS

Should CEO and Board Chair Be Separate?

Many commentators complain that boards of directors of U.S. companies fail to provide adequate discipline of senior managers. Of particular concern is the common practice of combining the titles of CEO and chair of the board. On the surface, this practice seems to violate the principle of separating decision management and decision control. Benjamin Rosen, chairman of Compaq Computer, voiced this concern succinctly:

> When the CEO is also Chairman, management has *de facto* control. Yet the board is supposed to be in charge of management. Checks and balances have been thrown to the wind.*

Large shareholder associations and pension funds in recent years have sponsored proposals at Sears, Roebuck and other large firms calling for separation of the titles. Government officials have considered regulations to force this change.

Contrary to the allegations of reformers, combining the CEO and chair titles does not necessarily violate the principle of separation of decision management and decision control. The extreme case of no separation exists only when the CEO is the board's sole member. Indeed, the boards of several large U.S. companies, including Dow, Ford, Mattel, Monsanto, Warnaco, and Xerox, have dismissed their CEOs/chair since 2000.

Estimates indicate that the titles are combined in over 80 percent of U.S. firms. In the vast majority of the remaining cases, the chair is the former CEO. Typically, when a new CEO is appointed, the old CEO/chair retains the position as board chair for a probationary period. With acceptable performance, the new CEO also receives the title of board chair and the old chair often retires. Proponents of regulations to force firms to appoint outsiders as chair essentially argue that almost all major firms in the United States are inefficiently organized. Although this assumption might be correct, reformers have presented no cogent argument for how such an important corporate control practice can be wealth-decreasing and still survive in the competitive marketplace for so long across so many companies.

While regulators have stopped short of a mandated board leadership structure, the Dodd-Frank Act of 2010 requires publicly traded companies to disclose whether and why they chose to combine or maintain separate positions for the CEO and Chairman. The SEC has mandated a similar disclosure requirement since December 2009.

*USA Today (April 22, 1993).

Source: J. Brickley, J. Coles, and G. Jarrell (1997), "Leadership Structure: Separating the CEO and Chairman of the Board," *Journal of Corporate Finance* 3, 189–220.

---

of the training department is to identify whether solutions to property management problems developed at one location can be applied to other properties. Training evaluates the knowledge generated in the wetware of individual employees and whether that wetware can be transformed into software that can be employed more widely within the organization. On the Home Properties organizational chart, training and property management are at similar levels; this responsibility to create software thus represents a lateral, rather than hierarchical, assignment of responsibility. Another frequently employed technique to identify more productive procedures is to form teams of employees. As Parsons notes, records from the productivity studies at Western Electric's Hawthorne plant indicate that the workers regularly experimented with different procedures for assembling switches, monitored their resulting productivity changes, and encouraged coworkers to adopt efficiency enhancing innovations (see Chapter 1). In this case, the responsibility was assigned to a team. Through such processes, the knowledge embedded in the wetware of individual employees is transformed into software that can be used more widely within the organization.

Influence Costs[14]

To this point, we have assumed that decision-making authority is granted either to an individual or to a team within the firm. Once the right is granted, the employee or team is involved actively in decision making (subject to ratification and monitoring from others). Sometimes, firms use bureaucratic rules that purposely limit active decision making. For example, airlines allocate routes to flight attendants based on seniority—there is no supervisor who decides who gets which route. Similarly, some firms base promotions solely on years worked with the firm. Some universities prohibit grade changes once the grade is recorded.

One potential benefit of limiting discretion in making decisions is that it reduces the resources consumed by individuals trying to influence decisions. Employees often are quite concerned about the personal effects of decisions made within the firm. For example, flight attendants care deeply about which routes they fly. Employees are not indifferent to which colleagues are laid off in an economic downturn. These concerns motivate politicking and other potentially nonproductive *influence activities*. For instance, employees might waste valuable time trying to influence decision makers. In vying for promotions, employees might take dysfunctional actions to make other employees look bad.

Not assigning the decision right to a specific individual lowers *influence costs*—there is no one to lobby. But such a policy can impose costs on an organization. Consider individuals who are competing for a promotion. These individuals have

---

HISTORICAL APPLICATIONS

Separate Decision Management and Control—Not a New Idea

The English merchant guilds were formed during the 12th century. These precursors to the modern corporation were chartered by the crown and given a monopoly to conduct trade within their own towns, usually in return for a payment to the crown. Each guild would specialize in a particular trade (carpenters, stone cutters, pewterers, etc.). The guilds held property and elected officials to manage the trade and property. Incorporation by the crown created a legal entity that could conduct business.

To protect the members of the guild from embezzlement and mismanagement by their elected officers, charters of the guilds contained provisions for election of auditors from the general membership to audit the financial records of the guild. For example, The Worshipful Company of Pewterers of the City of London was audited by its members. The Book of Ordinances of 1564 contains the following "order for ye audytors":

Also it is agreed that there shalbe foure Awdytours Chosen euery yeare to awdit the Craft accompte and they to parvese it and search it that it shall be perfect. And also to accompt it Correct it and allowe it So that they make an ende of the awdet therof between Mighelmas and Christmas yearely and if defaute made of ffenishings thereof before Christmas yearly euery one of the saide Awdytours shall paye to the Craft box vj s. viij d. pece.

Audits by members of the guild are early examples of separating decision management from control. The guild officers had decision management rights, but decision control rights in the form of annual monitoring of financial transactions were vested in member auditors.

Source: E. Boyd (1968), "History of Auditing," in R. Brown (Ed.), *History of Accounting and Accountants* (A.M. Kelley: New York), 79; and R. Watts and J. Zimmerman (1983), "Agency Problems, Auditing, and the Theory of the Firm: Some Evidence," *Journal of Law & Economics* 26, 613–633.

---

[14]This section draws on P. Milgrom (1988), "Employment Contracts, Influence Activities and Efficient Organization Design," *Journal of Political Economy* 96, 42–60.

ANALYZING MANAGERIAL DECISIONS: *Medford University*

Medford University is a research university with about 10,000 students. It has a good liberal arts undergraduate program, a top-rated medical school, and a fine law school. It employs about 12,000 people. A majority of these employees work at the university hospital. Lately, the university has faced significant financial pressures. It is in intense competition for quality students with other colleges. Recent financial donations have been small. The hospital is under intense pressure to reduce costs because of changing health care regulation and insurance coverage.

The university currently spends about $100 million annually on fringe benefits (health insurance, retirement plans, and so on). It also faces large future payments of promised medical benefits to current and future retirees. The president of the university, Hiromi Kobayashi, has appointed a task force to design a new fringe benefit package. The task force consists of faculty and staff from departments throughout the university. The task force has been asked to consider the university's tenuous financial condition. President Kobayashi wants to reduce expenditures on fringe benefits (while maintaining the quality of the faculty and staff). The president has appointed the chief administrator of the hospital as the chair of the task force. The president also has appointed one of her key

assistants, the vice provost, to serve as secretary of the task force (to take minutes and coordinate meeting schedules).

1. Why did President Kobayashi appoint a task force to consider the issue of fringe benefits? She could have asked the university's human resources department to design a plan.
2. Should the president anticipate that all members of the task force will strive to cut university expenses? What actions can the president take to increase the likelihood that the task force members have this objective as a major priority?
3. Why did the president appoint the administrator of the hospital as the chair of the task force? The chair, in turn, has delegated much of the work to subcommittees (a health insurance committee, a retirement committee, and so on). What advice would you offer the chair in appointing subcommittee chairs? Explain.
4. Does the president want to commit to accepting the committee report or does she want to reserve the right to make modifications? Explain.
5. Why did the president appoint a key assistant as secretary of the task force?

More complete answers to these questions can be developed by incorporating the material in the appendix to this chapter.

---

incentives to provide evidence to their supervisor that they are the most qualified for the promotion. This information often is useful in making better promotion decisions. However, this information comes at a cost: Employees spend time trying to convince their supervisor that they are the most qualified rather than focusing on other activities such as selling products. It makes sense to run a "horse race" so long as the incremental benefits from better information are greater than the incremental costs of the influence activity. But the race should be stopped at the point where the value of the additional information about individual qualifications is equal to the cost of the additional influencing activity.

In some cases, the firm's profits largely are unaffected by decisions that have an enormous impact on individual employee welfare. For example, United Airlines assigns flight attendants to routes using the following procedure: Once a month, the attendants request the routes they prefer, with conflicts resolved strictly on the basis of seniority. United's profits are virtually unaffected by which flight attendant gets the Hawaii route versus the Sioux Falls run. It is in such settings that bureaucratic rules for decision making are most likely. The firm benefits from a reduction in influence costs but is little affected by the particular outcome of the decision process. (There still is a potential cost to United; by not taking individual employees' preferences into account in making job assignments, the firm may have to pay higher wages to attract and retain.)

Summary

Firms transform inputs into outputs, which are sold to customers. An important element of organizations is partitioning the totality of *tasks* of the organization into smaller blocks and assigning them to individuals and/or groups within the firm. Through the design process, jobs are created. Jobs have at least two important dimensions: *variety of tasks* and *decision authority*. This chapter focuses on decision authority. The next chapter focuses on the bundling of tasks.

In *centralized decision systems,* most major decisions are made by individuals at the top of the organization. In *decentralized systems,* many decisions are made by lower-level employees. Decentralized decision making has both benefits and costs. Potential benefits include more effective use of local knowledge, conservation of senior management time, and training/motivation for lower-level managers. Potential costs include contracting and coordination costs and less effective use of central information. The optimal degree of decentralization depends on the incremental benefits and costs, which vary across firms and over time. There has been a recent trend toward greater decentralization, motivated in part by increased global competition and changes in technology.

Decision rights are not assigned just to a hierarchical level but to particular positions within the hierarchical level. Similar to the centralization versus decentralization problem, relevant factors in making this horizontal choice include the distribution of knowledge and the costs of coordination and control.

Sometimes, firms assign decision rights to *teams* of employees rather than to specific individuals. Firms assign decision rights to teams for at least three basic purposes: Managing activities, recommending actions, and making products. The use of team decision making sometimes can increase productivity; but this is not always the case. Team decision making is most likely to be productive when the relevant information is dispersed and the costs of collective decision making and controlling free-rider problems are low.

Decision management refers to the initiation and implementation of decisions, whereas *decision control* refers to the ratification and monitoring of decisions. When individuals do not bear the major wealth effects of their decisions, it generally is important to separate decision management from decision control. This principle helps explain the presence of *hierarchies* in most organizations. It also can help make the concept of empowerment more precise.

Sometimes, firms adopt rules that limit the discretion of decision makers; for example, airlines assign routes to flight attendants based on seniority. One benefit of limiting discretion is that it reduces incentives of individuals to engage in excessive *influencing activities*. Some influencing activity is valuable in that it produces information that improves decision making. Firms are, therefore, most likely to limit discretion when the firm's profits are not very sensitive to the decisions, yet the decisions are of considerable concern to employees.

Suggested Readings	P. Bolton and M Dewatripont (2013), "Authority in Organizations," The *Handbook of Organizational Economics*, R. Gibbons and J. Roberts eds, 342–372.
	E. Fama and M. Jensen (1983), "Separation of Ownership and Control," *Journal of Law & Economics* 26, 301–326.
	M. Jensen and W. Meckling (1995), "Specific and General Knowledge, and Organizational Structure," *Journal of Applied Corporate Finance* 8:2, 4–18.
	G. Miller (1993), *Managerial Dilemmas: The Political Economy of Hierarchy* (Cambridge University Press: Cambridge).

Self-Evaluation Problems

12–1. Joan Zimmerman owns a local CPA firm. The company employs 10 CPAs and some additional staff employees. Joan sets her own pay and makes most of the major decisions facing the firm. Joan often initiates new ideas and implements them. The company has no board of directors, and no one is responsible for monitoring Joan's actions. Does this organizational arrangement contradict the basic principle concerning the value of separating decision management and control? Explain.

12–2. Traditionally, lending decisions at financial institutions were made by people relatively high up in the organization. For instance, a senior loan officer might have to approve even a small loan. Recently, some financial institutions have decentralized this decision, sometimes to people without college degrees. Discuss why it might have historically made sense to centralize the lending decision. Discuss potential factors that might have motivated the decentralization of these rights in certain organizations.

Solutions to Self-Evaluation Problems

12–1. Separation of Decision Management and Decision Control

It is important to separate decision management and control when the decision maker is not the owner of the firm. Otherwise agency problems are likely to significantly reduce the value of the organization. In this example, Joan Zimmerman owns the company. Therefore, there is no agency problem between her and other owners. In this situation, combining decision management and control is ok.

12–2. Decentralization

Presumably the decision right was held high up in the organization because the relevant specific knowledge was located there. For example, the lending decision requires expert knowledge, credit histories, and so on, which might not have been available to lower-level workers.

- Technology—technology allows information on credit rules, credit reports, and the like, to be accessed by people lower in the organization. Also, expert systems allow the computer to do technical analysis previously performed by well-trained employees.

- Deregulation—increases competition and potentially increases the importance of speed and quality of customer service.

Review Questions

12–1. Discuss the costs and benefits of decentralized decision making relative to centralized decision making.

12–2. Mark Wilson, chief of personnel, has been instructed to increase the hiring of women at the Morton Cement Company. Mark will be evaluated by the company president Josh Cohen on his success or failure in meeting this goal. Mark does not evaluate the performance of any of the division chiefs, and each chief must approve all new division employees. Do you expect Mark to succeed in this endeavor? Why or why not? Explain your reasoning.

12–3. Define the terms *decision management* and *decision control*. Under what circumstances might it be optimal to make one individual responsible for both decision management and decision control? What do you expect the ownership of common stock to look like in such a firm? Explain.

12–4. Jan van der Schmidt was the founder of a successful chain of restaurants located throughout Europe. He died unexpectedly at the age of 55. Jan was sole owner of the company's common stock and was known for being quite authoritarian. He personally made most of the company's personnel decisions. He also made most of the decisions on menu selection, food suppliers, and advertising programs. Employees throughout the firm are paid fixed salaries and were closely monitored by van der Schmidt. Jan's son, Karl, spent much of his youth driving BMWs around Holland and Germany at high speeds. He spent little time working with his father in the restaurant business. Nonetheless, Karl is smart and just received his MBA degree from a leading business school. Karl has decided to follow his father as the chief operating officer of the restaurant chain. What advice about organizational architecture for the company would you offer Karl now that he has taken over?

12–5. Discuss the positive and negative effects of a university rule that would not allow professors to change a grade once recorded.

12–6. Many companies have been experimenting with organizing their manufacturing around teams of employees. The employees are given decision rights on such things as how to organize the work and employee schedules. Often the employees are paid based on team output. Sometimes, this organizational arrangement has worked well. In other cases, it has not. Discuss the conditions under which you think that this type of team organization is most likely to succeed.

12–7. A leading business school currently uses study teams in the MBA program. Each team has five members. Some of the work in the first year is assigned to study teams and graded on a group basis. Discuss the trade-offs involved with enlarging student study groups in the MBA program from five to six people.

12–8. It is frequently argued that for empowerment to work, managers must "let go of control" and learn to live with decisions that are made by their subordinates. Evaluate this argument.

12–9. It is sometimes argued that empowerment can be successful only if managers learn to live with decisions made by lower-level employees. Managers are to set clear boundaries within which employees can make decisions (e.g., allowing a salesperson to set prices between $15,000 and $20,000). Managers should never overturn a decision if it is within the boundaries. Rather, good decision making should be encouraged through proper incentives and training. Do you agree that for empowerment to work, managers should always set clear boundaries and live with decisions within these boundaries? Explain.

12–10. Several Fortune 100 companies have nominated members of the clergy to be members of their boards of directors. Discuss the advantages and disadvantages of such a proposal.

12–11. An organizational consultant evaluates your division. She indicates that she does not like the divisional manager's top-down management style. She recommends setting up a board that consists of the divisional manager and his top 10 department managers. The consultant suggests that all major policy decisions be made by the board by a majority-voting rule. She argues that this process will make for better use of information within the organization. She also argues that our political system is a democracy, which works well, and that the same concept could be applied beneficially within the corporation. Evaluate the recommendation.

12–12. The Colorado Symphony Orchestra (CSO) was formed after the Denver Symphony was no longer financially viable. CSO's corporate charter requires that it cannot have an operating deficit in any year. Revenues, donations, grants, and other income must equal or exceed operating expenses. CSO balances its budget each year by adjusting the musicians' salaries. For example, in 1999 the musicians were not paid for the last two weeks of the year.

CSO's board of directors and executive management committees are composed of one-third each of musicians, full-time CSO staff, and community supporters of the CSO.

In most organizations, it is unusual for labor to have representation on the board of directors and management committees. Explain why you would expect musicians to have seats on the CSO board and management committees.

12–13. Recently a number of companies have adopted what is known as *open-book management*. Under this concept lower-level employees are given training to help them understand the company's financial statements and how their individual actions affect financial performance. They are given access to information previously known only to more senior management. They are also given detailed revenue and cost data as it relates to their jobs. For instance, one company gave delivery drivers information about the maintenance costs of the company's vans, whereas a building company gave employees detailed cost information on such items as a spoiled batch of glue. Why do you think this management trend is occurring now, rather than say 20 years ago? Does this policy fit with other changes that are occurring in organizations? Explain. Do you think all companies should "open their books" to lower-level employees? Explain.

12–14. Encarta is a multimedia encyclopedia on CD-ROM, which Microsoft produced from 1993 to 2009. It had nine different editions. Examples include editions in British English, American, German, and Italian. The North American version alone had 40 million words and 45,000 articles. Microsoft delegated major editorial decisions to teams of local experts, mostly academics and specialists "who know their stuff." For example, a team of experts primarily from Italy was given editorial decisions for the Italian edition. Encyclopedia Britannica uses a different policy. Its central staff has decision rights to ensure a standard presentation is presented in all editions. Discuss the pluses and minuses of Microsoft's policy relative to Encylopedia Britannica's.

12–15. Blue Cross Blue Shield of Rochester is Rochester's largest health insurance provider. In exchange for the insurance premiums they pay, families insured by BCBS receive all their health care needs from a group of approximately 500 doctors approved by BCBS. (Families must choose their doctors from among these 500 doctors.)

When a patient insured by BCBS visits a doctor for a consultation, the patient pays a small copayment (usually $20). The doctor is reimbursed for the difference between the cost of the consultation and the copayment by RCIPA Corp. RCIPA Corp. is a firm owned by the 500 doctors who are BCBS-approved. At the beginning of each fiscal year, BCBS and RCIPA agree on a total dollar amount that BCBS will pay to RCIPA for medical services provided to patients covered by BCBS. BCBS further agrees that this dollar amount will not be adjusted for higher- or lower-than-expected medical care required by BCBS patients. RCIPA in turn pays member doctors, based on a fee schedule, for the medical services they provide to BCBS-insured patients. If, at the end of the year, there is any money left over, it is distributed to RCIPA members. If there is not enough money to pay for all the services provided by the member doctors, then the shortfall is allocated among the member doctors who must contribute cash to make up the shortfall.

Why do you think RCIPA serves as an intermediary between BCBS and the doctors who care for BCBS's clients? Why would BCBS risk paying "too much" for the medical care of their customers? Why would RCIPA and its members risk being "underpaid" for their services? Is one of the two parties forcing the other to agree to such an arrangement? If so, who is forcing whom? Why?

12-16. Studies of Information Technology (IT) services consistently show that IT services are organized differently in large versus small firms. Larger firms often locate independent IT centers throughout the firm (e.g., within each product division), where each center maintains its own decision rights. Smaller firms often have just one IT unit or center that serves all divisions. Provide a potential explanation for this observation.

In large firms, some business functions are consolidated centrally instead of being controlled by the various divisions of the company. One example is environmental compliance and control, which is a function responsible for complying with environmental regulations and managing the risk of impacts on the environment. Provide a potential explanation for this observation.

Some large firms are highly diversified and others are more focused. Holding firm size and the number of product divisions constant, which type of firm (diversified or focused) is more likely to have decentralized IT units? Explain.

12-17. By the year 2000, General Motors had decentralized primary decision rights for designing cars to vehicle line managers. In earlier years, General Motors had a centralized corporate design group. This group maintained key decision rights for the designs of all GM models. Discuss the trade-offs between these two organizational arrangements.

Appendix: Collective Decision Making[15]	Managers commonly delegate decisions to groups of employees through the use of teams, committees, and task forces. The presumption is that team members have important specific knowledge to make the decisions and that they are more likely to buy in to decisions when they participate in the decision-making process. Managers should realize that team members' interests are unlikely to be aligned either with each other or with the interests of the owners. Also, group decision processes sometimes can be manipulated by team members. It is critical to understand these potential problems with teams; they are the topic of this appendix.

The Example of Majority Voting

Suppose that Hassan Ragab, a senior executive, appoints a team of three managers to recommend a new marketing strategy. Patrick Stefan, Maria Lopez, and Sean Mac-Donald are from the finance, marketing, and sales departments, respectively. Hassan wants the three managers to recommend the strategy that would maximize the value of the firm. However, given their current compensation schemes and positions within the company, they are more closely aligned with the interests of their particular departments than with the firm as a whole. For instance, Sean is evaluated by the vice president of sales. Sean knows that his vice president will be unhappy with any recommendation that reduces the size or influence of the sales department. Sean thus has incentives to represent the vice president's views on the task force.

The managers are considering three options, labeled Plans A, B, and C. The top panel of Table 12.1 shows the preferences of the three managers. Each prefers a different plan. The managers decide to select a plan through a majority vote. When all three plans are considered together, each receives one vote and there is no winner. The managers, therefore, decide to conduct pairwise votes. The middle panel of Table 12.1 displays the outcomes of all possible pairwise votes. The bottom panel shows the ultimate outcomes from the three possible sequences of pairwise votes. Any one of the three plans can win, *depending on the order* in the election! This example suggests that agenda control can be critically important. If Maria has the right to select the order of voting (for instance, if she is appointed the team leader), she can manipulate the voting outcome in her favor.[16]

Majority voting is commonly used in group decision making—especially when the group is large. For instance, task forces of 20 or more people commonly vote on

---

[15]This appendix draws on K. Arrow (1963), *Social Choice and Individual Values* (John Wiley & Sons: New York). See also Chapter 19.

[16]Our example assumes that the managers vote their preferences in each round of the voting. Managers might choose to vote *strategically:* They might vote in a manner that is inconsistent with their preferences in the first round to achieve a preferred outcome in the final round of voting. (For example, some Republicans voted for Hillary Clinton in the 2008 Democrat primary in Texas, even though they planned to vote for John McCain in the general election. They reasoned that the longer Barack Obama had to campaign against Clinton, the more likely McCain would be successful in the general election.) Although strategic voting is a strong possibility in this setting, the basic point of our analysis remains: Managers can influence the outcome if they have agenda control. See Appendix Problem 2. Note also that majority voting does not always result in this type of order-dependence outcome. It depends on the preferences of the individual team members.

	Preferences		
	Most Favored	**Second Favored**	**Least Favored**
Pat	A	C	B
Maria	B	A	C
Sean	C	B	A
	Pairwise Votes		
	A versus B	**A versus C**	**B versus C**
Pat	A	A	C
Maria	B	A	B
Sean	B	C	C
Winner*	B	A	C
	Sequence of Pairwise Votes		
Round 1	**Round 2**		**Ultimate Winner**
A versus B	B† versus C		C
A versus C	A† versus B		B
B versus C	C† versus A		A

*Majority-voting rules.
†Winner of the first round.

Table 12.1   Majority Voting and Agenda Control

This table presents an example of how the outcome of a series of pairwise votes can depend on the order in which the votes are taken. The top section shows the preferences of the three managers who are voting on the proposals, A, B, and C. The middle section shows the outcomes of all possible pairwise votes. The example assumes that the managers vote their preferences in each election. A majority-voting rule is used. The bottom section displays the ultimate outcome of a sequence of pairwise votes (the winner of the first vote is run against the remaining proposal). Any outcome is possible, depending on the order of consideration. In contrast to this example, the order of consideration does not always matter in majority voting—it depends on the individual preferences of the voters.

issues. Sometimes, other voting rules are used. For instance, some groups require unanimity for passage (each person has a veto). Others require a supermajority (e.g., two-thirds of the votes). Small groups often do not vote on issues formally. Rather, they make decisions by consensus. Nonetheless, the basic points of our analysis continue to hold—the outcome need not be efficient, can be subject to manipulation, and can depend on the order in which proposals are considered. Indeed, Nobel prize–winner Kenneth Arrow has demonstrated that any collective decision-making mechanism, other than granting the decision right to an individual, is subject to the types of problems illustrated in this example (depending on the preferences of the individuals in the group).

The analysis in this appendix has several important implications for managers who delegate decisions to groups of employees:

- Managers should not presume that members of a team always will have the interests of the company as their primary objective—there are incentive problems. These problems must be considered in forming a team. Sometimes, people with important information should be excluded from a team if the contracting costs of including them on the team are substantial.

- Managers often can reduce the incentive problems on teams through incentive compensation plans. In our example, the existing compensation scheme motivated the managers to focus on their own departments rather than on the firm as a whole. Compensating the managers based on the firmwide valuation effects of the team's recommendation would alter these incentives. If all three managers were concerned about the overall value of the firm, there would be no problem.[17]

- Agenda control can be a powerful device in group decision making. Not only can the outcome be affected by the order of the voting (as in Table 12.1) but also it can be affected by the timing of the election. For instance, the vote might be set when it is known that a particular manager will be absent. Senior executives, therefore, have an interest in who is appointed to positions such as team leaders and committee chairs. In this example, the senior executive should favor a team leader who cares about firm-value maximization—agenda control would be used to benefit the overall firm.

Analyzing Managerial Decisions: Collective Decision Making

1. What factors should a manager consider when deciding on the composition of a team charged with making an important decision?

2. Suppose the managers in the example in this appendix do not necessarily vote according to their preferences in each round of the voting. Rather, they might vote for a less preferred option in the first round to obtain a preferred outcome in the final round. Suppose that Patrick has agenda control. How should he manipulate the agenda to achieve his preferred outcome?

---

[17]It is difficult to develop incentive schemes that completely resolve incentive problems within teams. As we discuss in the text, it is difficult to design schemes that hold individuals fully responsible for their own actions. Thus, there often are incentives to free-ride in teams. We discuss this issue in greater detail in subsequent chapters.

chapter

13

Decision Rights: Bundling Tasks into Jobs and Subunits

LEARNING OBJECTIVES

1. Describe the trade-offs between broad and specialized task assignments.
2. Describe the factors that cause firms to group jobs by function, products, and geography.
3. Explain how changes in the firm's business environment or strategy can affect subunit structure.
4. Identify matrix, mixed, and network organizations.
5. Discuss some recent trends in how firms assign decision rights.

Time Inc.—one of the largest branded media companies in the world and publisher of over 30 magazines including *Time, Sports Illustrated, People, Fortune, Golf,* and *Money*—announced plans to lay off 500 employees (about 6 percent of its staff) to simplify the operating structure of its magazines.[1] This reorganization eliminates the previous structure of Time's magazine group, which was organized into three units: Style and entertainment, sports and news, and lifestyle topics. Now all the magazines will be consolidated into a single group, and the various magazine editors will report to business managers at Time, instead of group editors. The proposal is designed to streamline the decision-making process and foster new products across its different magazine brands. Time justified the changes by arguing that the company must innovate to avoid further job cuts. Its CEO stated, "we need to dissolve the complex matrixed organization created several years ago, remove layers that slow us down, and free up investment dollars to deploy in growth areas."

New digital technologies rendered obsolete the old print-magazine model used by Time as well as most traditional publishers. In response, we observe firms changing their business strategies, which necessitates changing their organizational architectures. At Time, decision-right assignments were changed including how jobs are bundled into tasks. Instead of having separate managers for style and entertainment, sports and news, and lifestyle magazines, the individual magazine editors now report to just one of two central managers of Time Inc.

---

[1]Details of this example are from W. Launder (2014), "Time Inc. to Cut Jobs in Restructuring," *The Wall Street Journal* (February 4), www.wsj.com/news/articles/SB10001424052702304851104579362720955779980; and www.timeinc.com.

The results at Time Inc. suggest that the bundling of tasks into jobs and subunits can affect a firm's performance. This chapter examines these important managerial decisions. We begin by analyzing the problem of how to bundle tasks into jobs. We then consider the problem of combining jobs into subunits of the firm. We conclude the chapter by discussing recent trends in the assignment of decision authority and the bundling of tasks. The appendix to this chapter uses a simple game-theoretic example to illustrate some of the basic principles from this chapter.

Bundling Tasks into Jobs

In the previous chapter, we discussed how jobs have at least two important dimensions—breadth of decision authority and variety of tasks. We then analyzed the topic of decision authority in greater detail. We now focus on the second dimension, the bundling of tasks. The problem of how to bundle tasks obviously is quite complex; unfortunately, limited formal analysis of the topic exists. Nonetheless, the problem is economic in nature: Managers face a set of *economic trade-offs* when they bundle tasks. And fortunately, as in the case of decision authority, important insights into the nature of these trade-offs can be gained through analyzing simple examples.

Specialized versus Broad Task Assignment

FinWare Inc. is a distributor of financial software. Its customers include both individual consumers and businesses. Within FinWare, there are two primary activities or *functions,* selling software and after-sales service (helping customers install the software on their systems and managing its interface with other programs). Thus, as displayed in Figure 13.1, FinWare must perform four basic tasks—sales and service for each of its two customer groups. Of course, these four basic tasks could be subdivided into a much larger number of smaller tasks. To keep the analysis tractable, we ignore this finer partitioning and assume that the firm has but four tasks. Our analysis readily extends to more general cases.

FinWare operates at multiple locations throughout the country. At its planned new Greensboro office, each of the four tasks is expected to take four hours per day to complete. Thus, the firm must hire two full-time employees to staff this office. In structuring the two jobs, the most obvious alternatives are to have each employee specialize in

---

Figure 13.1   Tasks at FinWare

FinWare, Inc.

FinWare is a distributor of financial software. Its customers include individual consumers and businesses. Within FinWare, there are two primary activities or functions, selling software and after-sales service (helping customers install the software on their systems and interfacing it with other programs, for instance). As displayed in the figure, FinWare must perform four basic tasks in sales and service for each of the two customer groups.

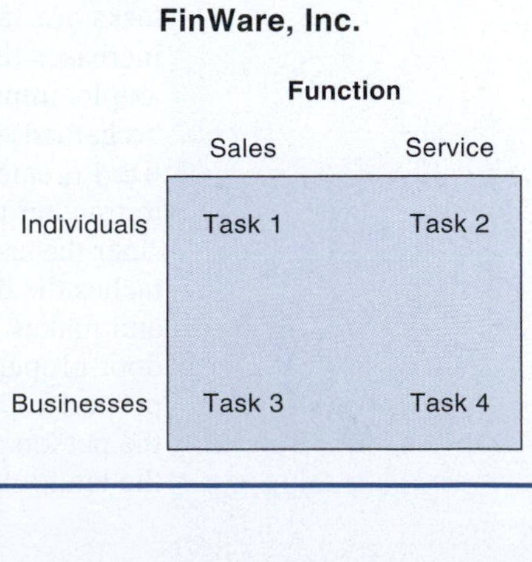

| | **Function** | |
	Sales	Service
Individuals	Task 1	Task 2
Businesses	Task 3	Task 4

Customer type

one function (either selling or service), that is, performed for both customer groups or have one employee provide both sales and service to individual consumers and the other employee perform both functions for business customers. We refer to the first alternative as *specialized task assignment* and the second as *broad task assignment*. We now examine the relative benefits and costs of these two groupings.

Benefits of Specialized Task Assignment

There are at least two important benefits that can arise from using specialized rather than broad task assignment:

- **Exploiting Comparative Advantage.** Specialized task assignment allows the firm to match people with jobs based on skills and training and correspondingly has employees concentrate on their particular specialties. For example, FinWare can hire salespeople to sell and technicians to provide service. The principle of comparative advantage suggests that this specialization often will produce higher output than having individuals perform a broad set of tasks—there are potential economies of scale in concentrating on a more focused set of tasks.

- **Lower Cross-Training Expenses.** With specialized task assignment, each employee is trained to complete one basic function. With broad task assignment, employees are trained to complete more than one function, which can be expensive. For instance, suppose at FinWare the service function requires a skilled technician with an advanced college degree, whereas the sales function requires an individual with only a high school diploma. Specialized task assignment allows FinWare to hire one person with an advanced degree and one person without an advanced degree. With broad task assignment, the level of education required is usually the highest level across the assigned tasks. Thus, broad task assignment requires FinWare to hire two people with advanced degrees and train them to perform both functions. Because it costs more for FinWare to hire a person with an advanced degree than a person with only a high school diploma, broad task assignment is more expensive than specialized task assignment.

Costs of Specialized Task Assignment

Specialized task assignment has advantages relative to broad task assignment, but it also has drawbacks. Some of the costs of specialized task assignment include

- **Forgone Complementarities across Tasks.** Sometimes, performing one task can lower the cost of having the same person perform another task. Two tasks are said to be "complements" when doing more of one activity either increases the benefits or reduces the costs of doing another activity. For example, important information about a customer's service requirements might be gained through the sales effort. This information is less likely to be utilized if sales and service are conducted by separate people: It can be costly to transfer the information to the other individual. As another example, consider the case of two employees on an automobile assembly line. The first attaches the door to the car frame; the second attaches the latching mechanism and makes sure the door latches to the frame. If the first does not align the door properly, the second will have more difficulty getting the door to latch properly. Combining both tasks into one job increases the care with which the person attaching the door checks for proper alignment prior to attaching the latch.

HISTORICAL APPLICATIONS

Adam Smith on the Economies of Specialization

With specialized task assignment, employees concentrate on performing a narrow set of tasks. Adam Smith, an important 18th-century economist and philosopher, was among the first to recognize the potential gains from this type of specialization. In his classic book, *The Wealth of Nations,* he argued how a number of specialized employees, each performing a single step in the manufacturing of pins, could produce far more output than the same number of generalists making whole pins. Smith presents the following description of a pin factory using specialized employees:

> One man draws the wire, another straightens it, a third cuts it, a fourth points it, a fifth grinds it at the top for receiving the head; to make the head requires two or three distinct operations; to put it on is a peculiar business, to whiten the pins is another; it is even a trade by itself to put them into the paper.

Smith argues that a small factory with 10 specialized employees could produce about 48,000 pins a day, while 10 employees working independently could not have produced 20 pins per day.

Source: A. Smith (1776), *The Wealth of Nations* (Modern Library: New York, 1937), 4.

- **Coordination Costs.** The activities of specialized employees have to be coordinated. For instance, FinWare would have to establish procedures for transferring sales orders to service technicians. Also, it might have to appoint a manager to handle exceptions to these procedures (for instance, before committing to the purchase of the software, a customer might demand authorization for specialized installation). Developing procedures and coordinating activities can be expensive.

- **Functional Myopia.** With specialized task assignment, employees tend to concentrate on their individual functions rather than on the overall process of providing good sales and service to customers. For example, a salesperson who is compensated primarily through commissions will have incentives to sell software to customers even if the sale imposes large service costs on the company, such as when the company's software is not well matched with the customer's existing computer system.

- **Reduced Flexibility.** Failure to cross-train employees has costs as well as benefits. For example, if only one person is trained to perform a particular function, what happens if the person is sick or on vacation? Also, having only one person trained to do a job in a firm can place the firm at a disadvantage when bargaining with the employee over salary and other benefits.[2] These problems are likely to be greatest in small companies, since large companies are more likely to have several people trained to perform any given task.

Incentive Issues

Our discussion of the costs and benefits of specialized versus broad task assignment has focused on informational and technological considerations. Incentive issues also can be important. From an incentive standpoint, sometimes it is better to have employees concentrate on a narrow set of tasks, while in other circumstances, a broad set of tasks is better.

---

[2]L. Stole and J. Zwiebel (1996), "Organizational Design and Technology Choice with Nonbinding Contracts," *American Economic Review* 86, 195–222.

Delta Airlines versus China Eastern Airlines: Broad versus Specialized Task Assignments

China Eastern Airlines, China's second largest carrier, has a call center in Shanghai with over 1,200 employees who only handle ticketing. If a customer calls for any other issue or complaint, the call is routed to other departments. This often results in long delays to resolve the issue, and ultimately to disgruntled passengers. The poor customer call service and other service-related problems (long baggage transfer times, long passenger connection times, and low-quality gates), provided by China Eastern and the other large Chinese carriers, have allowed other Asian carriers, mostly headquartered in South Korea, Hong Kong, and Japan, to capture a disproportionately high fraction of fliers between China and the United States. By some estimates these other Asian airlines are capturing additional revenues of about $250 million from the 3.8 million passengers flying between the United States and China.

Unlike China Eastern's call center, Delta Airlines' center handles a wide range of passenger problems from lost bags to missed connections, and ticketing problems. On average, Delta strives to resolve passenger complaints within 18 minutes. Delta call center agents sometime even write personal letters to complaining passengers.

China Eastern uses specialized task assignments where each call center agent is assigned a single type of problem, which causes its complaining passengers to be rerouted, frequently through several agents, until arriving at the one who can resolve the issue. Delta uses broad task assignments whereby each agent is trained to resolve a variety of problems, resulting in faster resolution times and happier customers.

Source: S. Carey (2014), "Delta, China Eastern Try to Solve Air Traffic Riddle," *The Wall Street Journal* (March 19), www.wsj.com/articles/SB10001424052702304732804579425363833070996

With broad task assignments, the firm is concerned not only with how hard employees work but also with how they allocate effort among the tasks.[3] For instance, senior managers at FinWare would be concerned with the way employees balance their efforts between sales and service. Designing an evaluation and compensation scheme that motivates an appropriate balance of effort is complicated by the fact that the effort exerted on some tasks often is more easily measured than for other tasks. At FinWare, the sales effort might be estimated easily by sales volume, while it might be quite difficult to measure the quality of after-sales service—for many producers there are no good direct indicators of service quality, and poor quality might reveal itself very slowly over time (primarily as customers fail to make repeat purchases). If FinWare pays a sales commission, employees will concentrate on sales at the expense of providing good after-sales service to customers: Selling increases their incomes, whereas providing better service has a small impact (it increases income through its effect on repeat purchases). FinWare can reduce this incentive to misallocate effort by not paying a sales commission. But this provides employees with relatively low incentives to exert effort on either task. One potential response to this problem is to use specialized task assignments. The salesperson could be provided high-powered incentives to concentrate on sales. The service person would not be evaluated on quantifiable output measures, but on more subjective measures, such as customer-satisfaction surveys. We discuss these issues in greater detail in Chapters 15 and 16, where we address how to measure performance.

---

[3]B. Holmstrom and P. Milgrom (1991), "Multitask Principal-Agent Analyses: Incentive Contract, Asset Ownership and Job Design," *Journal of Law Economics and Organization* 7, 24–52.

In some cases, producing output requires the coordinated execution of several separate tasks that individually are difficult to assess. Here, it can make sense to assign all the tasks to one individual who is accountable for the final product. For instance, in the example of attaching doors and latches to automobiles, assigning both tasks to one employee makes it easy to identify who is to blame if the door does not latch properly. Similarly, at FinWare the failure of a customer to make a repeat purchase might be due to either poor sales effort or poor service. Having one employee conduct both sales and service facilitates identification of the employee responsible for the unhappy customer.

Costs and Benefits of Specialized Task Assignment*

Benefits	Costs
Comparative advantage/economies of scale	Forgone complementarities across tasks
Lower cross-training expenses	Coordination costs
	Functional myopia
	Reduced flexibility

*Incentive issues can favor either specialized or broad task assignment, depending on the nature of the production technology and information flows.

Productive Bundling of Tasks

The choice between specialized and broad task assignments depends on the technological, informational, and incentive issues discussed above. One variable, that is, likely to be of particular importance in making this decision is the relative degree of complementarity among tasks within, versus across, functional areas. At FinWare, the magnitude of the benefits of specialized task assignment depends largely on how related the selling efforts are between the two customer groups. If there are only minor differences between selling to individuals and businesses, training employees to do one makes them well prepared to do the other. In contrast, if the selling tasks are quite different between individuals and businesses, little is gained by training one employee to perform the two selling tasks compared to training separate employees. As a consequence, any economies of scale that result from specializing in sales are likely to be small. Similarly, the costs of specialized task assignment at FinWare depend on the importance of complementarities across functional areas. When these complementarities are low (for instance, little valuable information is gained about service through the selling effort), little is lost by having employees concentrate on a single function. It also is relatively easy to coordinate the individual specialists through the use of routine procedures. Ultimately, the degree of complementarity among tasks depends on how specialized knowledge is created and the costs of transferring knowledge. It also depends on the technology used in the production process.

Our FinWare example is quite simplified, and in most settings, more complicated task divisions are feasible. For instance, the selling function might have two phases—initial contact and closing the deal. The initial contact requires less specialized product and service knowledge than closing the deal but is potentially more time-consuming. Here, it might be better for a salesperson to handle the initial contact and have a joint call by both the salesperson and service person to close the deal. As another example, at some locations, more complete specialization might be feasible. For instance, an employee at an office with a larger sales volume could concentrate solely on selling to individuals or to businesses. While our basic FinWare

ACADEMIC APPLICATIONS

Theoretical Research in Economics on Multitask Agency Problems Provides Useful Managerial Insights

In this chapter we summarize the major insights about task assignments, as suggested by the ever growing body of theoretical and empirical research on the internal organization of firms. This box summarizes several important theoretical papers that provide useful insights on how various factors stressed in this chapter are likely to affect the bundling of tasks.

Several influential papers in economics examine the general problem of motivating employees to work and providing incentives to allocate their attention among several different activities (or tasks). For example, a salesperson must allocate her effort between securing current sales from existing customers and cultivating future sales from new customers. How this salesperson allocates her effort to these two different tasks depends on the relative benefits she derives from the two tasks and by the technological complementarity or substitutability across tasks. The key theoretical insights are: Encouraging effort on one task often crowds out effort on the other task and when a single agent is given multiple tasks to perform, the incentive scheme must balance incentives across various tasks. These incentives depend on the ability of the principal to measure the agent's performance of the various tasks. Tasks that have similar degrees of measurability of whether the task was performed should be assigned to the same agent. Agents who are assigned tasks, that are easy to measures, can be given more powerful financial incentives. These economic models predict that the firm will assign tasks to agents that are all easy or hard to measure (with high-powered incentives provided only when precise measurement exists), or the firm will assign the various tasks to separate agents.

In the previous analysis, the two tasks do not conflict. Current sales and future sales both enhance firm's, value. Sometimes the two tasks do conflict, as in the case of launching a new product that cannibalizes the sales of the current product. If the same agent is tasked with selling both the current and the new product, the agent is likely to sabotage one product and focus on the other. To solve this problem, the job design should avoid these conflicts of interest by using a narrow task assignment. Each task should be assigned to managers specializing in that task. For example, assign the task of selling the current product to one manager and the task of selling the new product to a different manager. Then, rely on competition between the specialized managers to ensure overall balance.

Finally, multitask problems also arise when the labor market tries to infer the agent's talent from his output performance. In these models, the agent is paid a fixed wage and his incentive to work is solely his desire to convince the labor market that he has high talent, so he can secure future promotions. In this case, the agent's incentive to exert effort on one task depends on how the labor market infers the agent's talent based on his performance on that task. As the number of tasks the agent is assigned increases, it becomes more difficult for the market to infer his talent. By limiting the number of tasks assigned to the agent, the agent increases his total effort and the principal's total profit increases. The optimum task assignment is to have agents specialized in tasks that require similar talents, so as to enhance the labor market's ability to infer the agent's talent based on his overall performance.

Source: P. Bolton and M. Dewatripont (2013), "Authority in Organizations," in R. Gibbons and J. Roberts (Eds.), *The Handbook of Organizational Economics*, 342–372; and M. Dewatripont, I. Jewitt, and J. Tirole (2000), "Multitask Agency Problems: Focus and Task Clustering," *European Economic Review* 44, 869–877.

example abstracts from these more complicated considerations, it nonetheless isolates some of the key considerations in deciding on how to divide tasks into jobs.

Bundling of Jobs into Subunits

Our discussion of specialized versus broad task assignment highlights the economic trade-offs of bundling tasks into jobs. Managers are confronted with a similar set of trade-offs when they bundle jobs into subunits (e.g., departments, business units divisions, and subsidiaries).

Grouping people together within a subunit lowers the communication and coordination costs among the people *within the subunit*. For instance, they often report to the same manager, who facilitates information flows and coordination. Employees also are more likely to form closer working relationships if they share the same workspace—especially if they are evaluated and compensated on subunit performance. Managers, however, must devise methods of coordinating activities *across the subunits*. For instance, rules and procedures must be developed for coordinating activities among interdependent subunits, managers must be appointed and granted the authority to rule on exceptions to these procedures, and liaison staff and coordinating committees often must be appointed to address inter-unit issues. In summary, there is a trade-off between the benefits that come from grouping people together and the costs of coordinating their activities with those performed within other subunits. In addition, it is important to consider incentive issues: Some groupings make it easier to devise productive performance-evaluation and reward systems than other groupings (we elaborate on such incentive issues in Chapter 17 which discusses divisional performance evaluation).

In what follows, we begin by describing two standard methods of grouping jobs into subunits—by function and by product and/or geography. We then discuss the economic trade-offs between these two subunit designs. Following this discussion, we examine other methods that firms use to group jobs into subunits.

Grouping Jobs by Function

One common method of grouping jobs is by functional specialty (engineering, manufacturing, sales, finance, and so on). This organizational arrangement sometimes is referred to as the *unitary form (U form)* of organization because it places each primary function in one major subunit (rather than in multiple subunits). Figure 13.2 displays an organizational chart for FinWare under this type of functional grouping. Individual jobs are characterized by specialized task assignment. All the sales jobs in the organization are grouped together to form a sales department, and the service jobs are grouped together to form a service department. These departments are charged with managing their particular functions across the firm's entire product line. Senior management plays an important role in defining the architecture, coordinating activities across departments, making key operating decisions, and setting strategy. Rules and procedures are established for coordinating the activities across

Figure 13.2 FinWare as a Functional Organization

This figure displays an organizational chart for FinWare when jobs are grouped by functional specialty. These jobs are characterized by specialized task assignment. All the sales jobs in the organization are grouped together to form a sales department, and the service jobs are grouped together to form a service department. These departments are charged with managing their particular functions across the firm's entire product line. Senior management plays an important role in defining organizational architecture, coordinating activities across departments, and making key operating decisions.

the functions. For example, detailed procedures are established to transfer sales orders to the service department. Exceptions and special cases are handled by the senior management and/or coordinating committees (which often include senior division managers and corporate staff).

MANAGERIAL APPLICATIONS

Hertz Separates Equipment Rental Business from Car Rentals

Besides just renting cars, trucks, and vans, Hertz has a division that leases a variety of industrial and construction equipment such as aerial manlifts, air compressors, earthmoving equipment, power generators, forklifts, material handling machinery, pumps, and trucks and trailers as well as small tools such as chain saws, sanders, and welders. The Hertz Equipment Rental Division has 335 branches around the world, as well as numerous international franchisees. This division had revenues of over $1.5 billion in 2013. Worldwide car rentals in 2013 amounted to $8.7 billion.

In 2014, Hertz announced it was spinning off this division as a free-standing, publicly traded firm. Hertz stated it was doing this because "the separation will help each business to focus on its strategic and operational performance, ... create a stronger growth profile, and more competitive position for each company with enhanced management focus, resources, and processes that are more directly aligned with each business's unique strategic priorities and ... allow each business to attract and retain personnel by offering equity-linked compensation."

Although Hertz Equipment Rental already was organized as a separate "product line" from its car rental business, the spin off as a separate business allows the senior managers of the parent company to focus on its core business, which owns Hertz, Dollar, Thrifty and Firefly brands with nearly 12,000 corporate and franchisees in approximately 145 countries. The spin off also focuses the Hertz Equipment Rental managers squarely on increasing the value of their business, as they will be evaluated and rewarded on their share price.

Source: http://ir.hertz.com/2014-03-18-Hertz-Board-Approves-Separation-Of-Equipment-Rental-Business; and http://ir.hertz.com/company-overview.

Figure 13.3   FinWare as a Product and Geographic Organization

This figure shows how FinWare would look organized around product or geography. In the first case, the company is divided into a business products division and a consumer products division. Each of these divisions has its own sales and service departments that focus on the particular products of the division. (Often, jobs within the business units are grouped by functional area.) Organized geographically, the company is divided into a West Coast division and an East Coast division. In this case, the sales and service departments within each business unit serve both individual and business customers within their geographic areas.

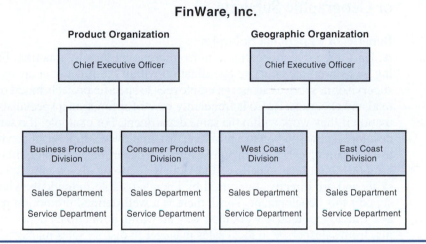

Grouping Jobs by Product or Geography

Another prominent subunit design is the *multidivisional form (M form)* of organization, which groups jobs into a collection of business units based on product or geographic area. Operating decisions such as product offerings and pricing are decentralized to the business-unit level. Senior management of the firm is responsible for major strategic decisions, including organizational architecture and the allocation of capital among the business units. Figure 13.3 shows how FinWare would look organized around product or geography. In the first case, the company

MANAGERIAL APPLICATIONS

Clorox CEO Surrounds Himself with Strong Functional Specialists

Don Knauss, CEO and Chairman of Clorox, gave three reasons for placing functional specialists on his senior management team. "First, I did it to get real-time feedback on strategy and operations and on the leaders from those functions who control most of the spending and people. Second, I wanted to force a more global view of the business. You're not just responsible for the United States—you're responsible for the company in total, and for driving capabilities, marketing, sales, R&D, and product supply globally. Third, it was to support their personal development. I think it forces people to be on their game a little more, too."

Source: G. Neilson and J. Wulf (2012), "How Many Direct Reports?" *Harvard Business Review* (April), Reprint R1204H.

is divided into a business products division and a consumer products division. Each of these divisions has its own sales and service departments that focus on the particular products of the division (often, jobs within the business units are grouped by functional area). Organized geographically, the company is divided into a West Coast division and an East Coast division. In this case, sales and service departments within each business unit serve both individual and business customers within their geographic areas.

Trade-offs between Functional and Product or Geographic Subunits

Benefits of Functional Subunits

At least three major benefits stem from grouping jobs by function. First, this grouping helps promote effective coordination within the functional areas. For instance, a supervisor in service can assign employees to specific projects based on current workload and expertise. It also is frequently easier for functional specialists to share information if they work within the same department. For example, if a service technician develops a new solution to a problem, that employee's supervisor can help promote its use by training other technicians within the department. Second, this grouping helps promote functional expertise. Individuals focus on developing specific functional skills and are directly supervised by knowledgeable individuals who can assist and support this development. Third, there is a well-defined promotion path for employees. Employees tend to work their way up within a functional department—for example, from salesperson to local sales manager to district sales manager. Having a well-defined promotion path can reduce employee uncertainty about career paths and thus can make it less expensive to attract and retain qualified employees (recall our discussion of risk aversion).

Functional grouping can often take advantage of economies of scale. For example, having a single firm-wide IT group responsible for the entire firm's e-mail system is likely to be cheaper than having each product or geographic subunit maintain its own e-mail system.

Problems with Functional Subunits

Although functional grouping has advantages, it also has disadvantages. First, there is the opportunity cost of using senior management's time coordinating functions and making operating decisions. This time might be focused more productively on activities such as strategic planning—deciding in which businesses the company should compete and how to be successful in those businesses. Second, there can be significant, time-consuming coordination problems across departments. At FinWare, when a sale is made by the sales department, the order has to be communicated to the service department, which in turn must schedule the required customer service. This process can cause lengthy delays in serving the customer. Moreover, important information can be lost in these transfers between departments. Third, employees sometimes concentrate on their functional specialties rather than on the process of satisfying customers. For instance, the sales department might focus on achieving department goals, even if that focus imposes costs on other departments in the firm. A salesperson might promise rapid installation to a customer even though the workload of the service department already is high.

MANAGERIAL APPLICATIONS

H-P Combines Two Operating Divisions

Faced with declining profits in its division that sells computer hardware to businesses that had 2003 sales of $21.1 billion but only $19 million in profits, H-P reorganized. In the $48 billion-a-year market for corporate computer services, H-P continued to lose market share. H-P competes aggressively between IBM's massive service offerings and Dell's low-cost hardware. H-P's services division that offers consulting solutions to businesses generated 2003 profits of $3.57 billion on $12.3 billion of revenues. To boost the performance of its computer hardware division, H-P combined the hardware and consulting services division to form the Technology Solutions Group responsible for computer servers, storage, services, and software. The new group is headed by Ann Livermore who previously headed the Services Group. Since customers are looking for a strategic relationship and a partner who can bring in the technology, H-P hardware sales are increasingly being driven by its consulting organization.

In April 2005, H-P replaced its CEO, Carly Fiorina, naming Mark Hurd CEO. H-P reported 2007 profits of $7.2 billion on revenues of $104.2 billion.

Source: D. Bank and G. McWilliams (2003), "H-P to Reorganize Operating Units; Latest Executive Shuffle Combines Two Divisions in Bid to Increase Growth," *The Wall Street Journal* (December 9), A3; hewlett-packard.com (2008).

Benefits of Product or Geographic Subunits

An advantage of the M form of organizing large corporations—especially within dynamic environments—is that decision rights for operations are assigned to individuals lower within the organization, where in many cases the relevant specific knowledge is located. For instance, the information required for the effective coordination of functions might depend more on local information that would be expensive to transfer to senior executives at headquarters. As we discussed in Chapter 12, decentralizing these decisions to the local managers of a geographic subunit helps ensure that this local information will be used effectively. Managers of business units are compensated based on the performance of their units; this provides incentives to use this specific knowledge more productively. Decentralizing decision rights to business-unit managers also frees senior management to concentrate on other, more strategic issues. The separation of the corporate office from operations focuses senior executives' attention on the overall performance of the corporation rather than on specific aspects of the functional components. A product or geographic focus promotes coordination among the functions that must be completed to produce and market a particular product or to serve a given geographic area.

Problems with Product or Geographic Subunits

Business-unit managers tend to focus on the performance of their own units. This focus is consistent with the maximization of a firm's value so long as product demands and costs are independent across business units. In this case, firm value is simply the sum of the values of the individual units. Frequently, there are important interdependencies or synergies among units that must be taken into account if a firm's value is to be maximized. For example, there is likely to be some overlap in customers, intermediate products often are transferred between subunits, and the units share common resources. If managers focus on their own units and do not consider these interdependencies, the overall value of the firm is reduced. For example, the West and East Coast divisions of FinWare might compete against each other for a national customer and reduce overall profits by selling products at a lower price than if they coordinated their marketing. This problem

MANAGERIAL APPLICATIONS

Citigroup Reorganizes to Control Conflicts

In 2002 Citibank was accused of having analysts mislead investors by distributing biased research to help land lucrative investment banking deals. Citibank was facing probes from the Securities and Exchange Commission, the New York attorney general, and Congress. Citigroup decided to reorganize, creating a new unit to separate analysts from investment bankers and thereby control potential conflicts of interest within their securities business. New York Attorney General Eliot Spitzer embraced the move as a productive initial step. "Anything that underscores the importance of insulating research from investment banking is positive," said attorney general spokesman Darren Dopp. "Actions like this could complement the broad industry reforms now being discussed."

Thus, although most decisions about how to group jobs into subunits focus on how to facilitate information flows and cooperation across employees, this case illustrates that there are special cases in which management wants to be able to convince customers and regulators that an inappropriate coordination of activities is not occurring, and the choice of job grouping can help in that process.

Source: T. Valdmanis (2002), "Citigroup Banks on Reform Plan," *USA Today* (October 31), 3B; and G. Stein (2002), "Citigroup Seeks to End Conflicts," *Bloomberg News* (October 31).

can be mitigated by forming *groups* of interrelated business units and basing a component of unit managers' compensation on overall group performance. However, as we discuss in the upcoming chapters, developing a compensation scheme that appropriately motivates unit managers is not easy. Splitting functional personnel among business units also forgoes potential economies that might result from combining similar specialists within one subunit.

Benefits and Costs of Functional Organization as Opposed to Product or Geographic Organization

Benefits	Costs
Improved coordination among functional specialists	Less effective use of local product or geographic information
Promotes functional expertise	Opportunity cost of senior management time
Provides a well-defined promotion path	Coordination problems among subunits
Captures economies of scale	Functional focus: It is difficult to design compensation plans that promote a focus on profits and customers

Where Functional Subunits Work Best

Functional grouping works best in small firms with homogeneous products and markets. In these firms, it is easier for senior managers to coordinate operating decisions across departments. For large firms with more diverse product offerings, senior executives are less likely to possess the relevant specific knowledge for making operational decisions for the company. In addition, the opportunity cost of having senior management concentrate on operating and coordination issues rather than on major strategic issues for the firm can be enormous.[4] In such cases, grouping by product or geography often will be the preferred alternative.

---

[4]O. Williamson (1975), *Markets and Hierarchies* (Free Press: New York).

Another variable, that is, likely to affect the desirability of functional subunits is the rate of technological change in the industry. Here, we consider technological change broadly to include new products, new production techniques, and organizational innovations. Functional subunits are more effective in environments with a more stable technology, since frequent communication across functional departments and specialists is less important and interactions can be handled through routine rules and procedures. In addition, senior management is likely to possess more of the relevant specific knowledge to coordinate functional areas.

In less stable environments, direct communication across functional areas is more important and new situations are more likely to arise that will challenge established coordination procedures. In turn, senior managers are less likely to have all the relevant specific knowledge to address these challenges. Rather, the specific knowledge is more likely to be spread across employees throughout the firm. For example, the frequent introduction of new products increases the benefits of communication among salespeople and design engineers about customer demands and preferences. Similarly, it is important for development and manufacturing personnel to share information when production techniques and technologies are changing more frequently.

Finally, in a rapidly changing environment, there is likely to be more uncertainty about the appropriate organizational architecture. With divisions organized around products or geography, different divisions can experiment with different architectures. For example, when Citibank began offering swaps, it opened trading desks in New York, Toronto, London, and Tokyo. The different operations competed not only with other financial institutions for business but also with each other. By encouraging experimentation with the architecture of these businesses, Citibank exploited the benefits of economic Darwinism within the firm. As experience mounted, the best procedures were made standard across the bank. Thus, when an environment is more dynamic, the desirability of a product or geographic organization increases.

Environment, Strategy, and Architecture

We have discussed how appropriate organizational architecture is influenced by the firm's business environment and strategy. Our discussion of the appropriate subunit configuration highlights this influence. Both environmental factors (such as the rate of technological change) and the firm's business strategy (whether the firm produces multiple products, chooses to operate in multiple locations, and so on) affect the desirability of functional versus product or geographic organization.

An important illustration of the influence of the environment and strategy on subunit design is the experience of large U.S. firms at the beginning of the 20th century. The first large firms in the United States were the railroad companies, which emerged around 1850.[5] These firms initially organized around basic functions such as finance, pricing, traffic, and maintenance. As the incidence of large firms increased in other industries in the late 1800s (such as steel, tobacco, oil, and meatpacking), most followed the lead of the railroads and organized around basic functions. As companies like Du Pont, General Motors, and General Electric continued to expand—both geographically and in the number of product lines—in the early 1900s, they began faring poorly in product markets where they faced smaller, more focused competitors. Their organizational architectures did not fit their changing

[5]A. Chandler, Jr. (1977), *The Visible Hand: The Managerial Revolution in American Business* (Belknap Press: Cambridge).

environments or strategies. In response, these companies began experimenting with different organizational forms. After significant experimentation, many large companies adopted the M form of organization. Economic historian Alfred Chandler concludes:[6]

> *The inherent weakness in the centralized, functionally departmentalized operating company . . . became critical only when the administrative load of the senior executives increased to such an extent that they were unable to handle their entrepreneurial responsibilities efficiently. This situation arose when the operations of the enterprise became too complex and the problems of coordination, appraisal, and policy formulation too intricate for a small number of top officers to handle both long-run, entrepreneurial, and short-run, operational administrative activities.*

Matrix Organizations

Some firms attempt to capture the benefits of both functional and product or geographic organization by using overlapping subunit structures.[7] These *matrix organizations* have functional departments such as finance, manufacturing, and development. But employees from these functional departments also are assigned to subunits organized around product, geography, or some special project. Matrix organizations are characterized by intersecting lines of authority—the term *matrix* refers to the intersecting lines resulting from such an organizational arrangement. Individuals report to both a functional manager and a product manager. Functional departments usually serve as the primary mechanism for personnel functions and professional development. The functional managers typically have the primary responsibility for performance reviews (since they have better technical knowledge for evaluating an employee's performance). Product or geographic unit managers provide input into these reviews. For example, in hospitals, nurses work with physicians and medical technicians in the delivery of health care in "product line" hospital units such as pediatrics or orthopedics. Much of the nurses' specific directions in caring for a particular patient comes from physicians. Yet in many hospitals, nurses are hired, supervised, and evaluated by other nurses who ultimately report to the director of nursing. Physicians are assigned only advisory authority in this process.

Matrix organization often is used in industries such as defense, construction, and management consulting. These industries are characterized by a sequence of new products or projects (e.g., building a new airplane or a new shopping mall). Individuals are assigned to work in teams on a particular project and when that project is completed, they are reassigned to new project teams. Given the nature of the projects in these industries, it is important for individuals across functional areas to communicate and to work together closely. For example, a successful airplane design must meet the demands of the customer; thus, there are benefits from the use of product-oriented teams. However, the plane must be aerodynamically sound. Thus, these projects also benefit from a high level of functional expertise, which is promoted by maintaining functional areas.

---

[6]A. Chandler, Jr. (1966), *Strategy and Structure* (Doubleday: Garden City), 382–383.

[7]For a more detailed discussion of matrix organizations, see W. Baber (1983), *Organizing for the Future* (The University of Alabama Press: Tuscaloosa).

Figure 13.4   FinWare as a Matrix Organization

This figure shows how FinWare might look organized as a matrix organization. The firm maintains functional divisions of sales and service. Individuals from these divisions simultaneously are assigned to either the business-products or consumer-products subunits (teams). These teams are indicated by the shaded rectangles. The functional managers focus on managing the particular function across both products, while the product managers focus on managing particular products across functions.

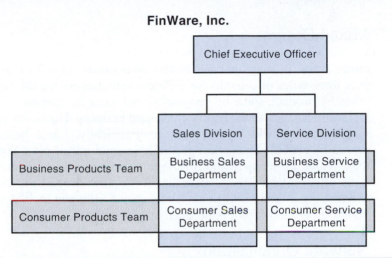

FinWare, Inc.

Figure 13.4 shows how FinWare might look if it were organized as a matrix organization. The firm maintains functional departments for sales and service. Employees from these departments are assigned simultaneously to either the business-product or consumer-product subunits (teams). Functional managers focus on managing their particular function across both products, whereas product managers focus on managing particular products across functions.

A potential advantage of a matrix organization, as opposed to a functional organization, is that employees are more likely to focus on the overall business process rather than on their own narrow functional specialty. However, in contrast to a pure product or geographic organization, functional supervision is maintained; there is a mechanism for helping ensure functional excellence and for providing clearer opportunities for advancement and development.

While matrix organizations look good on paper, in practice they often are difficult to implement. Potential problems with the matrix form of organization arise from the intersecting lines of authority. Employees who are assigned to product teams do not automatically have strong incentives to cooperate or be concerned about the success of the team. Rather, individuals might be more concerned about how their functional supervisors view their work, since functional supervisors are responsible for their primary performance reviews. Moreover, employees often see their roles as being representatives of their functional areas. Employees might be concerned excessively about how the decisions of a product team impact their particular area. These problems sometimes can be reduced by appropriate design of the performance-evaluation and reward systems. Individuals will be more concerned about the output of a product team if their compensation depends on team output. A related problem with matrix organizations is the potential for disputes between functional and product managers and the cost of resolving such disputes. Having both a functional and product manager also can increase influence costs—there are two supervisors to influence, not one. For instance, nurses might lobby with both their nursing supervisors as well as physicians to give them good performance reviews or specific assignments.

Finally, matrix organizations can have additional layers of managers that retard decision making. The reorganization by Time Inc. that begins this chapter involved eliminating its complex matrix organization to remove layers of managers to speed up decision making.

Mixed Designs

Often, firms use more than one method to organize subunits. Chase Manhattan Bank uses three types of subunits for different activities within the bank. Some are organized by product, some by geography, and some by customer. For example, Chase Delaware handles all the bank's credit card business. The business for individuals and middle-market firms is organized geographically. Large business customers are served by specific teams that generally operate out of New York City. Frequently, these teams are set up by industry. As another example, large multinational corporations often organize their international divisions around the matrix concept (with overlapping country and product managers), whereas their domestic subunits are organized around function, product, or geography.

Network Organizations

Firms (and groups of firms) have experimented with other methods of organizing subunits. One example is the network organization. *Network organizations* are divided into work groups based on function, geography, or some other dimension. The relationships among these work groups are determined by the demands of specific projects and work activities rather than by formal lines of authority. These relationships are fluid and frequently change with changes in the business environment.[8] The Japanese *keiretsu,* which is an affiliation of quasi-independent firms with ongoing, fluid relationships, is another example of a network organization. Networks can facilitate information flows and cooperative undertakings among work groups. However, their heavy reliance on implicit understandings and informal relationships also can lead to misunderstandings or opportunism.

Organizing within Subunits

We have examined the topic of partitioning the firm into major subunits. The same analysis applies to grouping jobs within subunits (e.g., departments). Grouping jobs into functional departments at a business-unit level is most likely to be effective when the unit is small and has a limited range of products. In contrast, in large business units with diverse product offerings, organizing by product or geography can be a more productive alternative. Product or geographic organization also is likely to be more effective in rapidly changing business environments, since senior management is less likely to have the relevant specific knowledge to make operating and coordination decisions.

[8]A. Bollingtoft, D. Hakonsson, J. Nielsen, C. Snow, and J. Ulhoi (2009) *New Approaches to Organization Design* (Springer: New York).

ANALYZING MANAGERIAL DECISIONS: *Jog PCS*

Jog PCS is a wireless telephone company. It sells cell phones to three customer groups: (1) business users, (2) high-volume individual users, and (3) low-volume individual users. Currently, the company is functionally organized. Primary functions include product development, marketing, sales, and customer service. The organizational chart is as follows:

1. The CEO, von Hugel, is considering reorganizing the company as a multidivisional firm organized around customer type. Draw the revised organizational chart.
2. Discuss the pros and cons of the proposed reorganization, relative to the current structure.

3. Jessica Wilde, vice president of product development, suggests that a matrix organization might be better. Draw the organization chart implied by her proposal.
4. Discuss the pros and cons of the matrix proposal relative to the multidivisional proposal.

Recent Trends in Assignments of Decision Rights

Traditionally, many firms have created jobs that specify limited decision authority and narrow task assignments. In turn, these jobs have tended to be grouped by functional specialty—either at the overall firm level or at the business-unit level. Starting in the 1990s, there was a significant shift toward granting employees broader decision authority and less specialized task assignments. Many companies also have shifted from functional subunits toward more product-oriented organizations. As we discuss below, these changes have been motivated by increased global competition and various technological changes.

To illustrate some of the factors that have motivated such organizational changes, we examine BankINC a hypothetical but representative financial institution engaged in lending to commercial clients. Figure 13.5 lists the basic functions that BankINC must perform to process a credit application. The credit of the applicant has to be checked; the deal must be priced (an interest rate must

Figure 13.5   Functions at BankINC

This figure lists the four basic functions that BankINC must perform in order to complete the process of transforming credit applications into formal credit offers.

BankINC Functions
- Credit checking
- Contract preparation
- Pricing
- Document preparation

MANAGERIAL APPLICATIONS

New Technology and Regulatory Changes Rejuvenates U.K. Auto Producers

In the 1990s Britain's auto industry faced extinction. It had high labor costs and unproductive factories building so-so vehicles. Starting in 1994, foreign-owned auto makers bought declining British brands such as Jaguar, Land Rover, Rolls Royce, and Mini. Germany's BMW spent over $1 billion automating the U.K. plant producing the Mini. Other foreign car companies have made substantial capital investments opening new or renovating existing plants, which are operating near full capacity.

Motivating these investments has been new government regulations in the United Kingdom that permit more flexible working conditions, which increase productivity. British workers are now more willing to adapt to a faster-paced, more highly automated manufacturing methods. For example, the Mini assembly center has an automated system that churns out 85 different types of five models; if options are included billions of permutations are possible. The Mini factory has a three-shift work schedule that allows for 22.5 hours of production a day, from a two-shift, 21-hour-a-day schedule.

Worker flexibility at the Mini plant is achieved by using a "working time account" model. This allows workers to accumulate extra working hours that they can then use during downtimes. Hourly pay remains the same, but production varies with demand. "This is impossible in the rest of Europe on any relevant scale because of local legislation that protects workers' rights and pay," said John Leech at KPMG.

BMW, which also manufactures Rolls Royce, uses "living" structures that "enable the BMW Group to react flexibly to customer demands and market requirements throughout the world. This includes flexible working time models and working time accounts as well as the capability to build additional numbers of certain models in other plants, if necessary."

These flexible working rules, coupled with lower payroll taxes, have made the U.K.'s labor costs much lower than in Western Europe. In 2011, U.K. auto workers earned an average of €25, an hour compared to €46 in Germany and €45 in France.

This example illustrates how local regulations that impede competition in one country create incentives for firms to move production to more "friendly" countries; at the same time we see that job tasks are redesigned to allow more flexible—and more efficient—production methods.

Source: M. Cauchi (2014), "Retooled Mini Plant Gears Up," *Wall Street Journal* (March 25), www.wsj.com/articles/ SB10001424052702303287804579446612901468536; and www.bmwgroup.com/e/0_0_www_bmwgroup_com/produktion/ produktionsnetzwerk/produktionsstandorte/standorte/index.html.

be chosen); formal contracts drafted; and final documents compiled and delivered to the applicant for execution.

Prior to the introduction of integrated IT systems for loan processing, BankINC used manual paper-based systems, and BankINC was organized around these four basic functions; it was divided into functional departments, including credit, pricing, contracts, and documents. Figure 13.6 shows an organizational chart for BankINC under this functional structure. Employees typically were assigned a specialized set of tasks within their functional areas and given limited decision authority on how to complete them. For example, a clerk in the credit department might have the simple task of logging applications using prescribed procedures. Coordination across functional departments was accomplished by senior management, often through formal rules and procedures. For example, BankINC had procedures for transferring credit applications among the various functional departments. Department heads served together on committees to assist in this coordination process. With this architecture, customers received relatively poor service. BankINC took about six days to process a credit application, and it was difficult to provide timely

Figure 13.6   BankINC with Functional Organization

Under a functional organization, the firm is divided into functional departments, including credit, contracts, pricing, and documents. Employees typically are assigned a specialized set of tasks within their functional areas.

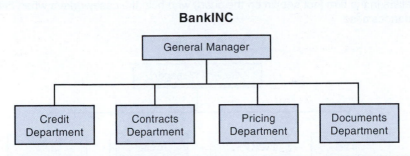

information to the customer about the status of an application. However, each application was subject to a careful credit check and each stage of the process was conducted by functional experts.

When government regulation of banking limited competition within BankINC's local market, few customers were lost due to delays in processing loan applications. Rather, BankINC could focus on careful and deliberate application procedures. However, banking deregulation allowed new commercial banks to enter BankINC's market and this increased pressure on BankINC to change its strategy to focus more on customer service and to shorten the time required to process a credit application. Otherwise, it faced a substantial decrease in business.

New information and computer technologies enabled BankINC to develop internal systems to support an organizational change. For instance, some of the necessary information for processing a credit application previously was stored in a manual filing system. Given this system, it made sense to assign certain tasks to individuals who had both familiarity with and proximity to this data. Computerizing this database allowed employees throughout the firm to access this information directly—a change that permitted the firm to reassign tasks more easily. Additionally, BankINC was able to develop computer programs to assist less skilled personnel in pricing loans. Such expert systems made functional expertise less important, thereby diminishing the importance of another of the advantages of their old organizational architecture.

Given these competitive pressures and new technologies, BankINC completely changed its assignment of decision rights. Under its new structure, pictured in - Figure 13.7, individual *caseworkers* have the primary decision rights and responsibility for completing all the steps required in the credit-granting process. Each financing request is assigned to one caseworker, who checks the applicant's credit, prices the deal, and draws the contracts. Employees have substantial decision authority in completing these tasks, and the functional subunits of the firm largely have been abandoned.[9] Performance-evaluation and reward systems

---

[9]Some functional specialists remained in the organization to help the caseworkers with difficult or unusual circumstances.

Figure 13.7 BankINC's Revised Organization

Under the revised structure, individual caseworkers have the primary decision rights and responsibility for completing all the steps in the credit-granting process. Each financing request is assigned to a caseworker, who checks the applicant's credit, prices the deal, completes the contracts, and so on. There are some functional specialists in the firm (not shown on the chart) who help the caseworkers when difficult or unusual circumstances arise.

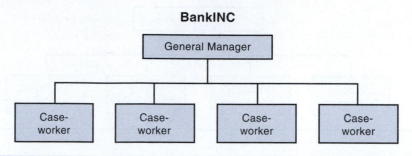

correspondingly were changed to focus more specifically on processing times and customer service. With this new organizational architecture, is able to process a credit application in about four hours. Customer satisfaction has increased as a result.

Today, many firms employ professional managers or hire consultants (often with Six Sigma Black Belt training) to analyze and redesign their internal business functions, thereby lowering costs and improving competitiveness. The success stories from these restructurings have led some management consultants to advocate widespread change for all firms throughout the world. The analysis in Chapters 12 and 13,

HISTORICAL APPLICATIONS

F.W. Taylor on Iron Workers

Frederick Winslow Taylor, an industrial engineer at the beginning of the 20th century, is known as the father of scientific management. His views were quite influential in affecting the assignment of decision rights in many firms. In particular, he argued that the attributes of lower-level employees dictated that they be granted limited decision authority and a narrow set of tasks. In his words,

> Now one of the very first requirements for a man who is fit to handle pig iron as a regular occupation is that he shall be so stupid and so phlegmatic that he more nearly resembles in his mental make-up the ox than any other type. The man who is mentally alert and intelligent is for this very reason entirely unsuited to what would, for him, be the grinding monotony or work of this character. Therefore the workman who is best suited to handling pig iron is unable to understand the real science of doing this class of work. He is so stupid that the word "percentage" has no meaning to him, and he must consequently be trained by a man more intelligent than himself into the habit of working in the accordance with the laws of this science before he can be successful.

Most modern managers reject this view of lower-level employees. The workforce of today is better educated than in Taylor's time, and modern production technologies often require less brawn but increased knowledge. Correspondingly, many managers have empowered lower-level employees by giving them broader decision authority and a less specialized set of tasks.

Source: F. Taylor (1923), *The Principles of Scientific Management* (Harper & Row: New York), 59.

MANAGERIAL APPLICATIONS

Flattened Firms Replace the Decentralized M Form

The decentralized M form of organization arose as firms diversified their businesses either by adding new products or moving into new geographic regions. Technology and new global markets motivated these strategic and organizational changes. Now, firms face vastly more complex and competitive environments. Markets demand shorter product life cycles that push firms to make faster decisions that are more responsive to customers. Advanced information technology improves access to data, facilitates coordination, and speeds communication within firms. These market and technology driven shocks have forced firms to adopt more focused, less diversified business strategies. New strategies require different organizational architectures: different ways of partitioning decision rights, different incentive schemes, and different human capital skills. To implement new business strategies, firms have modified their organizational architecture in ways that differ from the traditional, highly decentralized M-form organization.

Large firms are getting "flatter." They "delayered" by removing management levels and granting senior managers broader spans of control. Flattened firms frequently retain more decision rights at the top. For example, one layer that was removed is the position of Chief Operating Officer. Their CEOs also centralize more functions and have more functional managers reporting to the CEO, executives such as the Chief Financial Officer, Chief Human Resource Officer, Chief Quality Officer, Chief Information Officers, and so forth. While division managers in these flatter firms are now closer to the top and have more performance-based pay, in many cases their total compensation is less.

The flattened firm appears more centralized. But the simple terms of "centralization" or "decentralization" do not fully capture what is happening. Division managers make tactical decisions such as what products to offer and what prices to charge, whereas corporate headquarters retain decision rights over managing the corporate brand and implementing corporate-wide cost-cutting programs.

Source: J. Wulf (2012) "The Flattened Firm: Not as Advertised," *California Management Review* 55, 5–23.

---

however, indicates that a firm should not restructure without carefully considering whether a reassignment of decision rights is warranted given its particular business environment and strategy.

Although changes in technology and competition have changed the optimal assignment of decision rights within many firms, these shifts have not occurred in all industries. The benefits of narrow task assignment and functional specialization are still likely to be high for many firms in relatively stable industries. Consider, for example, a small coal-mining operation. Here, it is likely to continue to make sense to have some employees concentrate on mining the coal, while other employees sell it, and still other employees deliver it.

ANALYZING MANAGERIAL DECISIONS: *Bagby Copy Company*

Bagby Copy Company is a worldwide producer of copy machines. It manufactures 10 different copiers, ranging from low-end desktop copiers that sell for a few hundred dollars to high-volume document machines that retail for over $200,000.

Each copy machine requires a wiring bundle. Each bundle contains several hundred wires and connectors that provide circuits connecting the paper-flow units, scanner, and photoreceptor to the internal computer logic. The wire harness is plugged into various components during the assembly process. It is possible to assign each major task in this process to different employees. For example, a given employee might focus on one of the many connectors or on testing the completed wire harness. Alternatively, one individual might be assigned the task of producing and testing a completed harness.

In either case, there is a group of employees that is assigned individual tasks to produce a wire harness for a particular copier. In total, there are 10 subgroups of wire harness makers. One alternative is to place all 10 groups in one wire harness department. Another alternative is that each of these 10 subgroups can be assigned to and report to a manager responsible for a particular copier.

Bagby operates in five European countries. Currently, it has separate subunits in each country, where a country manager handles the manufacturing and marketing of all 10 copiers. The company is considering two alternatives. One would be to organize its foreign operations around products. In this case, there would be 10 international product managers with decision rights for managing the manufacturing and sale of a particular copier throughout Europe. The company also is considering a matrix organization, organized around product and country.

1. What are the trade-offs that Bagby faces in choosing between specialized and broad task assignment?
2. What are the trade-offs between these two methods of grouping wire harness makers into subgroups?
3. Which trade-offs does Bagby face in choosing among the country, product, and matrix forms of organizing its international operations?

Summary

The bundling of tasks into jobs and subunits of the firm is an important policy choice that can affect a firm's productivity dramatically. The primary purpose of this chapter is to examine this bundling decision.

We distinguish between two types of jobs: those with *specialized task assignment* and those with *broad task assignment*. With specialized task assignment, the employee is assigned a narrow set of tasks concentrated within one functional specialty—for example, sales. With broad task assignment, the employee is assigned a broader variety of tasks. The benefits of specialized task assignment relative to broad assignment include exploiting comparative advantage and lower cross-training expenses. The costs of specialized task assignment include forgone complementarities from not performing multiple functions, coordination costs, functional myopia, and reduced flexibility. Incentive issues might favor either specialized or broad task assignment, depending on the production technology and information flows. The appropriate bundling of tasks depends on the magnitude of the costs and benefits of each alternative. One variable, that is, likely to be of particular importance is the relative degree of complementarity among tasks within, versus across, functional areas. Specialized task assignment is favored when the complementarity of tasks within a functional area is relatively high.

Firms can group jobs into subunits based on functional specialty, geography, product, or some combination of the three. *Functional subunits* group all jobs performing the same function within one department (e.g., a sales department). Senior management plays a major role in coordinating these departments and in making operating decisions. Benefits of functional organization are the promotion of coordination and expertise within functional areas and provision of a well-defined promotion path for employees. Problems with functional organization include the high opportunity cost of employing senior management time to coordinate departments and make operating decisions, handoffs across departments that can take significant time, coordination failures across departments, and employees concentrating on their own functional specialties rather than on the customer. Functional subunits are likely to work best in smaller firms with a limited number of products operating in relatively stable environments.

Larger, more diverse firms often find it desirable to form subunits based on product or geography. In the *multidivisional (M form) firm,* operating decisions are decentralized to the business-unit level. Senior management of the firm is responsible for major strategic decisions, including finding the optimal organizational architecture and allocating capital among business units. A primary benefit of the M-form corporation is that decision rights for operations are assigned to individuals lower in the organization where relevant specific knowledge often is located. Managers of business units are compensated based on the performance of their units so as to provide incentives to use this specific knowledge productively. Decentralizing decision rights to business-unit managers also frees senior executives to concentrate on other issues. Problems with the M form of organization arise because business-unit managers often have incentives to take actions that increase the performance of their business units at the expense of other units within the firm. These problems can be controlled through careful design of business units and by basing a component of business-unit managers' compensation on *group performance*—where the group consists of profit centers with interrelated costs and demands. It is usually difficult, however, to control this problem completely. Multidivisional firms also forgo potential economies that might result from combining similar functional specialists within one unit.

Some firms maintain an overlapping structure of functional and product or geographic subunits. These *matrix organizations* have functional departments such as finance and marketing. Members of these departments are assigned to cross-functional product teams (subunits). Team members report to both a product manager and a functional supervisor. Generally, performance evaluation is conducted by the functional supervisor. Matrix organizations are common in project-oriented industries such as defense, construction, and consulting. They also are common in hospitals. An advantage of a matrix organization, in contrast to a pure functional organization, is that individuals are more likely to focus on the overall business process rather than just on their own narrow functional specialty. Potential advantages over a pure product organization are that the functional departments help ensure functional excellence and provide more clearly identified opportunities for advancement and development. Potential problems with the matrix organization arise from the intersecting lines of authority. An employee is likely to have loyalties divided between the goals of the project team and the goals of the functional department. This problem can be mitigated by appropriate design of the performance-evaluation and reward systems. However, as we shall see in subsequent chapters, accomplishing this objective can be difficult.

Firms often use more than one method for organizing subunits. They also use other less standard ways of organizing subunits. One example is a *network organization*.

Decisions on how to group jobs must be made at many levels in the organization. Our analysis of the costs and benefits of alternative groupings of jobs focuses on the overall firm level—how to form major subunits. This same basic analysis applies to the grouping of jobs at lower levels within the firm.

Historically, many firms have created jobs that are low in decision authority and narrow in task assignment. Recently, there has been a trend toward granting employees more decision authority and broader task assignments. Many companies also have shifted away from functional subunits toward more product-oriented organizations. These trends can be explained by specific technological changes and increases in global competition, along with accompanying changes in business strategies.

Suggested Readings

P. Bolton and M. Dewatripont (2013), "Authority in Organizations," in R. Gibbons and J. Roberts (Eds), *The Handbook of Organizational Economics* (Princeton University Press, Princeton NJ), 342–372.

A. Chandler, Jr. (1977), *The Visible Hand: The Managerial Revolution in American Business* (Belknap Press: Cambridge).

A. Chandler, Jr. (1966), *Strategy and Structure* (Doubleday: Garden City).

O. Williamson (1983), *Markets and Hierarchies* (Free Press: New York).

Self-Evaluation Problems

13–1. For many years, your firm has been protected by patents. Technological change and the introduction of new products have been slow. Soon, these conditions will change. Your patent protection is expiring, and the rate of technological change and innovation has increased substantially. Discuss how these changes are likely to affect your firm's optimal bundling of tasks into jobs and subunits.

13–2. In the early 1900s, General Motors had separate divisions that manufactured Buicks, Cadillacs, Chevrolets, Oaklands, and Oldsmobiles. Decision rights were highly decentralized, and there was little direction or coordination from the central corporate office. As a result, the divisions often failed to coordinate decisions on design standards, which prevented them from taking advantage of economies of scale in buying or making common components (e.g., spark plugs). Discuss potential organizational changes that GM might have adopted to reduce this coordination problem.

Solutions to Self-Evaluation Problems

13–1. Patent Expiration and Organization

With the old environment, technology was changing very slowly and there was limited competition in the product market. Such an environment is more likely to favor centralized decision making, specialized task assignment, individual decision making, and functional organization. Employees are better evaluated on their performance in narrowly defined tasks. With the new environment, technology is changing rapidly and product-market competition is more intense. In this environment, centralized decision making is less likely to work well because much of the relevant knowledge is located lower in the organization. Thus, decision rights are more likely to be more decentralized. Also, it is more important for employees to communicate horizontally (to address how to handle new situations, etc.). This will motivate less specialized task assignment, the use of teams, and a more process-based organization. The performance-evaluation and reward system will have to be changed in response to changes in decision rights; for example, teamwork and cooperation might be weighted more heavily.

13–2. Organization of GM

One possibility is to merge some of the units to form fewer divisions. Divisions producing similar products could be placed together. Another possibility is to keep the divisional structure but form larger groups of divisions. Some of the compensation of managers could be based on group performance. Another possibility is to take certain functions, such as purchasing, out of the divisions and place them in functional departments at the corporate level.

Review Questions

13–1. Discuss the costs and benefits of specialized task assignment relative to broad task assignment. What variables are likely to be particularly important in determining the optimal choice between these two alternatives?

13–2. Define the following: functional organizations, product organization, geographic organization, matrix organization, and network organization.

13–3. Discuss the circumstances under which you think functional organizations will work best.

13–4. Discuss the pluses and minuses of matrix organizations.

13–5. Why do you think many U.S. firms have reorganized their international divisions from a country focus to matrix organizations focusing on both country and product?

13–6. In the early 1990s, Chrysler Corporation placed nearly all decisions about the development of a new vehicle in the hands of a single, cross-functional product team. In contrast, General Motors used an approach that placed a stronger emphasis on functional specialties. Small teams were established that consisted of experts from the same functional field. Each team was charged with a particular assignment that related to its area of specialization. For example, one team might have had the primary responsibility for the design of the body of the vehicle, whereas another team might have been charged with developing the drive train. The teams worked simultaneously on their specific tasks. Some individuals on these teams also served on additional cross-functional teams that were charged with coordinating the development process across the functional areas. Discuss the relative advantages and disadvantages of these two approaches to product development.

13–7. Johnson & Johnson (J&J) is one of the largest medical products companies in the world. In 1994, it had 33 major lines of business, with 168 operating companies in 53 countries. Decision rights in J&J were quite decentralized. For instance, in 1993, the baby oil manager in Italy ran his own factory and got to decide such things as package size, pricing, and advertising. Similarly, other country managers had considerable discretionary authority for similar products sold in their countries. This type of decentralized decision making has served J&J well: Its returns to shareholders have been very good. Significant changes, however, are occurring in J&J's environment. In particular, trade barriers have been significantly reduced in Europe.

   a. Describe the advantages of J&J's decentralized decision making that have helped to explain the success of the company.

   b. What organizational changes do you think J&J should consider given the change in the environment? Explain. Draw a new organizational chart for J&J's international operations (based on your suggestions).

13–8. AutoMart Repair Shop is currently organized as follows: A repair manager meets with the customer to discuss the problems with the car. A repair order is completed. The mechanics specialize in particular types of repairs (e.g., air conditioning, body work, etc.). Typically, a car in the shop requires work by several specialists. The manager plans the sequence of service among the specialists. The car is then serviced by each of the necessary specialists in turn. Discuss how AutoMart Repair Shop might look if it reorganized around the process of fixing an automobile. Discuss the pluses and minuses of the current structure compared to the more product-oriented structure.

13–9. Many companies are making increased use of telecommuting, which consists of employees working out of their homes, linked to the central office by telephone, computer, and fax machine. Discuss the benefits and costs of telecommuting. What types of occupations are likely to be best suited for telecommuting? Explain why.

13–10. Evaluate the following statement: "It is usually best to organize as a matrix organization. Matrix organizations combine the best of both worlds, functional excellence and product focus."

13–11. Stable Inc. is in a relatively stable environment in terms of technology, competition, and regulation. Variance Inc. is in a relatively unstable environment with more frequent changes in technology, competition, and regulation. Both produce the same number of products. Which firm is more likely to be functionally organized? Explain why.

13–12. Professors Brickley and Smith are writing two chapters for a new book. Two primary tasks are involved. First, someone has to write each of the chapters. Second, someone has to copyedit the chapters. The second step involves making sure that the writing is good, that there are no typographical errors, etc. They are considering two alternative ways to organize the work. In one case, one of the professors would write both chapters, and the other professor would copyedit both chapters. In the other case, each professor would select one chapter and be responsible for all writing and copyediting. The two professors have equal abilities and knowledge. Discuss the trade-offs between these two methods of organizing the work. What factors do you think will be most important in deciding how to organize?

Appendix: Battle of the Functional Managers[10]

This appendix uses a simple game-theoretic example to illustrate some of the trade-offs that firms face in grouping jobs into subunits. Currently, the Quick Motorcycle Company is functionally organized. Two of its main departments are design and marketing. Pino Pentecoste is the manager of the design department, while Lan Nguyen manages marketing.

Pino has two options for designing a new product. One design focuses on speed, and the other design focuses on safety. Lan has two options for the corresponding marketing campaign. One option concentrates on magazine advertising and reaches older consumers, whereas the other option focuses on television and reaches younger audiences more effectively. Figure 13.8 displays the payoffs that Pino and Lan face for each combination of design and marketing programs (e.g., from their respective bonus plans or personal preferences). The payoffs indicate that coordinating the design and marketing is important. If Pino chooses design option 1, and Lan undertakes marketing plan 2, both Pino and Lan receive low payoffs ($100 each). A similar outcome exists if Pino chooses design option 2 and Lan chooses marketing plan 1. In this setting, two Nash equilibria are possible. One is design option 1 and marketing plan 1; the other is design option 2 and marketing plan 2. Pino and Lan have a conflict over which equilibrium each prefers. Pino receives a higher payoff in the first case, whereas Lan receives a higher payoff in the second case. Nonetheless, both Lan and Pino prefer either equilibrium to cases where they fail to coordinate.

Figure 13.8 Battle of the Functional Managers

Quick Motorcycle Company is functionally organized. Pino Pentecoste, the manager of the design department, selects from two designs for a new product. Lan Nguyen, the marketing manager, selects from two marketing plans. There are two Nash equilibria: Design option 1 and marketing plan 1; design option 2 and marketing plan 2. Both Pino and Lan prefer to coordinate their actions rather than not coordinate (and end up on the off diagonal). However, they disagree on the preferred equilibrium.

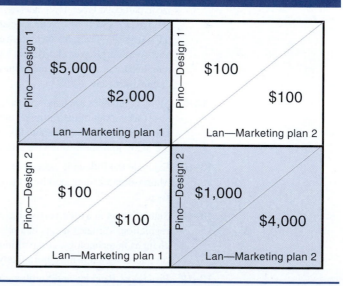

[10]This example is based on the "battle of the sexes" game. For example, see R. Gibbons (1992), *Game Theory for Applied Economists* (Princeton University Press: Princeton).

Suppose total firm profits are correlated with the combined payoffs for both Pino and Lan. In this case, the CEO of the firm prefers the combination of design option 1 and marketing plan 1. With complete information about the payoff structure, the CEO selects this option and then allows the design and marketing departments to focus on their specialties in implementing this program. This focus on specialization would allow each department to take advantage of its relative strengths. It also allows Pino and Lan to coordinate the new program with other design and marketing projects in their respective departments. Thus, this example illustrates that functional organization can work well if the CEO has the specific knowledge to coordinate the activities of the functional managers at low cost. This specific knowledge, in turn, is most likely to be held by the CEO in small firms within relatively stable environments.

In a rapidly changing environment it is unlikely that the CEO will know the payoffs facing the managers for each of the options (or even know all the available options). In this case, the CEO does not have the knowledge to order the profit-maximizing alternative. Both Pino and Lan prefer coordination to noncoordination. However, they do not agree on the preferred alternative. There is no guarantee that they will choose the value-maximizing equilibrium. Indeed, they might fail to reach either equilibrium. Pino and Lan have to make concurrent decisions.[11] In an attempt to achieve their preferred equilibrium, they might fail to coordinate and both will suffer. In any case, they will consume resources bargaining (battling) over which options to choose. In this environment, the CEO might want to reconfigure the subunits around products (the firm produces multiple products). The decisions on the design and marketing of each product would be made within one subunit. Profit-maximizing choices could be motivated through profit-based bonus plans. In choosing this organizational option, the CEO forgoes any efficiencies that come from combining a given functional activity (across all products) within one unit. If the benefits of functional grouping are high, rather than changing the subunit structure, the CEO might want to foster coordination through the formation of coordinating committees and changes in performance-evaluation and reward systems that promote value-maximizing choices.

---

[11]Both design and marketing require long lead times before a final product is brought to market. It obviously takes time to design and test a product. Similarly, in marketing, an advertising agency must be chosen, a marketing/advertising campaign must be developed, contracts with the media have to be negotiated, and so forth. In Lan's and Pino's case, both must commit to a specific option at about the same time.

Attracting and Retaining Qualified Employees

LEARNING OBJECTIVES

1. Describe how the firm's reward system is used to attract and retain qualified employees as well as to motivate them.
2. Explain how a competitive labor market sets the level of pay.
3. Define the term human capital and describe the difference between general and specific human capital.
4. Define compensating differentials.
5. Describe various ways firms learn if they have the wrong level of pay.
6. Describe the role of internal labor markets.
7. Define the term efficiency wage.
8. Understand how job seniority affects wages in internal labor markets.
9. Describe the key factors in choosing the mix between cash compensation and fringe benefits (the composition of the pay package).

S andler O'Neill, a small investment bank with 340 employees, has focused on small- and medium-sized commercial banks.[1] Sandler has underwritten their bank clients' stocks when they went public, made a market for these bank stocks, researched their stocks, traded their bonds, and helped them merge with and acquire other banks. At the end of 2000 it had over 1,000 clients, generated $100 million in revenues, and traded some $60 billion of bonds. Sandler was a good place to work. It was profitable. It paid its people well; like most investment banks, employees received large bonuses based on their productivity and overall firm profits. And it was a close-knit firm where people worked and played together.

One hundred and forty-eight of its 177 employees worked on the 104th floor of the second World Trade Center tower hit by terrorist attacks on September 11, 2001. Of the 83 Sandler employees in the WTC at the time, only 17 survived. Two of the three managing partners who ran the firm were killed. Forty percent of its employees died—all of its bond traders, 20 of the 24 people who worked on the equity desk, its entire syndication desk, and the three key people who ran its information and communications systems.

Besides losing its hardware (including its offices and the entire communications network that connected Sandler to Wall Street and made it possible to

[1]Details of this example are from K. Brooker (2002), "Starting Over," *Fortune* (January 21), 50–68; and D. Whitford (2011) "Sandler O'Neill's journey from Ground Zero" *Fortune* (September 5), http://management.fortune.cnn.com/2011/09/01/sandler-oneills-journey-from-ground-zero/.

execute trades) Sandler lost much of its wetware. The attack destroyed much of the company's knowledge—their contacts, the way they did business, their institutional memory. All written records of the phone numbers of every person Sandler's traders had done business with over the years were destroyed. Amazingly, an assistant who had answered the phones on the trading desk for years was able to reconstruct the list of names and numbers from memory.

Sandler O'Neill's very existence was threatened. They faced the daunting challenge of acquiring new office space and rebuilding its physical assets such as the information technology and communications systems. But it also had to replace its human assets, including all the associated wetware—it had to attract and retain a new set of employees. First, Sandler had to take full advantage of its surviving wetware. It promoted or transferred existing employees into critical positions. The week following the attacks the surviving partners appointed two partners to replace the managing partners who died. One bond salesman became a bond trader. The head of research took charge of the syndication desk. A 23-year-old assistant with less than a year's experience was the only person who understood the workings of a new Sandler proprietary financial model used to analyze banks. And this model was critical to a pending $700 million deal. The assistant assumed the job of his boss, who had been killed. Second, it hired new employees. Sandler was helped by the massive layoffs on Wall Street that occurred following September 11. Many people who had been out of Sandler's reach before 9/11 now were looking for a job. The surviving managing partner called friends at other investment banks who were laying off people and asked, "If there's someone good getting cut, let me know, but only if they're good. I can't waste my time on duds." It hired a 51-year-old retired Goldman Sachs vice president to work on the equity desk and to help recruit others for the equity desk. By mid-November the firm had recruited two dozen new people, including four bond traders, three investment bankers, and two researchers. Yet some surviving Sandler employees were so traumatized by the attack that even after months of counseling they could not return to work and some of those that did were unable to perform their previous duties. Some were let go with separation agreements and others reassigned.

Two months after the attack, Sandler O'Neill was profitable again. Falling interest rates caused small- and medium-size banks to sell more bonds; Sandler underwrote many of these deals. Sandler managed to finish every deal that was in the works before September 11. It paid its deceased employees' estates more compensation for 2001 than they had earned in their best year. More than 30 percent of Sandler's beginning 2001 capital was paid out to the victims' families. By 2007, Sandler O'Neill was one of the largest investment banks serving the banking and insurance industries with 262 employees.

Sandler O'Neill's survival following the catastrophic events of 9/11 represents an extraordinary example of a management problem faced by all firms—how to attract and retain qualified employees and how to motivate these employees to be more productive. All firms must offer a level of compensation that not only allows it to attract and retain employees but also is structured to provide incentives to these employees to increase the value of the firm.

This chapter concentrates on the first of these objectives—attraction and retention. We postpone a detailed discussion of incentive compensation until Chapter 15. Since the two topics are interrelated, we also discuss some incentive-related issues in this chapter. In particular, we examine how the level of pay can be used not only to attract and retain employees but also to motivate them.

MANAGERIAL APPLICATIONS

Supply and Demand for European Investment Bankers

Based on Deutsche Bank estimates, employment in European investment banks fell about 20 percent between 2010 and 2014. Moreover, pay of these investment bankers fell about 5 percent between 2013 and 2014. Driving these changes is stagnating revenues and profits caused by new regulations. U.S. regulators prohibit U.S. banks from trading securities for their own profit, which affects the U.S. banks' European operating units. Bank regulators in most countries require investment banks to hold more capital, which reduces their profitability. In fact, the 13 biggest investment banks' revenues have fallen 10 percent a year since 2009.

These changes illustrate the basic laws of supply and demand. Like most supply curves, the supply of bankers is upward sloping—as salaries increase the number of people wanting to be bankers increase. Like most demand curves, the demand for bankers slopes down. At a lower salary, the banks want more bankers. An investment bank's demand for bankers depends on the additional revenue the bank can generate by employing one more banker (what economists call the marginal revenue product). In other words, if the equilibrium salary plus benefits is $100,000, investment banks must generate additional revenue of $100,000 at the margin to justify hiring one more banker. Given the new regulations and the declining profit opportunities in Europe, the demand curve of European bankers has shifted to the left since 2009. Assuming there is no change in the supply curve of bankers, then both the equilibrium price of bankers and quantity of bankers decline.

Source: "The Law of Small(er) Numbers," *The Economist* (January 4), 55.

We begin by providing a more detailed discussion of the objectives of compensation contracting. We then present a benchmark economic model of employment and wages. Subsequently, we extend the basic model and examine the implications of investments in human capital, compensating differentials, costly information about market wage rates, internal labor markets, and the choice between salary and fringe benefits.

Contracting Objectives

It is in the joint interests of contracting parties to maximize the value created by their relationships. By exploiting fully the business opportunities the firm faces and maximizing value, the size of the overall "pie" is maximized; this permits all parties to be made better off. This general principle holds for labor contracts. By designing compensation contracts that maximize the value of employees' output net of costs, the firm's value is maximized and hence both the owners of the firm and their employees can be made better off.

Individuals will not participate in an employment relationship unless they expect to receive at least their opportunity cost. If they do not receive their *reservation utilities*—the level of satisfaction they could obtain in their next best alternative—they will quit and go to work for another firm (or withdraw from the labor force). Since individuals benefit from compensation, the level of compensation is a key factor in attracting and retaining qualified employees. Owners also must receive an adequate return on their investment, or they will close the business and reinvest elsewhere. In a competitive market, paying employees more than the competitive rate results in a cost disadvantage that in the long run could drive the company out of business. Owners thus have incentives to design compensation packages that allow them to attract and retain employees with the required skills at the lowest possible cost.

The Level of Pay

The Basic Competitive Model

In this section, we present a benchmark model of employment and compensation; it is patterned after the standard competitive model that we discussed in Chapter 6. This model is a useful starting point for analyzing issues related to the level of pay. Subsequently, we extend the analysis to consider other important issues.

Suppose the labor market is characterized by the following conditions:

- The labor market is *competitive*. Firms have no discretion over the wages they pay to employees; rather, wages are determined by supply and demand in the marketplace.
- Market wage rates are costlessly observable.
- Individuals are identical in their training and skills.
- All jobs are identical. They do not vary in their risk, location, level of intellectual challenge, travel opportunities, and so on.
- There are no long-term contracts. Rather, all labor is hired in the "spot" market for a single period.
- All compensation comes from monetary compensation. The firm provides no fringe benefits such as vacation pay or health insurance.

MANAGERIAL APPLICATIONS

High CEO Pay Reflects High Marginal Revenue Product

Goldman Sachs Group Inc. Chairman and Chief Executive Lloyd Blankfein's total pay package estimated at $23 million was the biggest for a major U.S. bank in 2013. While $23 million of compensation may seem high to many, it is only about one-tenth of 1 percent of Goldman's net income. Goldman Sachs stated Blankfein's compensation was, based in part on the company's record 2013, net income of $21.9 billion and a 14.2 percent return on common equity, and that it reflects "in part the recovery of some investment-banking businesses, the firm's ability to cut costs in a generally tough environment and its resolving some of the public-relations and legal headaches that followed the financial crisis."

Based on the analysis in this chapter, firms must pay wages to attract and retain employees and in equilibrium compensation levels reflect the marginal revenue product of the employee. CEOs make decisions about what deals to do, what markets to enter, what people to promote, and so forth. The impact of such decisions on firm value is especially high for the CEO of Goldman Sachs, one of the most prominent investment banks in the world. U.S. CEOs generally have more authority/responsibility than CEOs of other country's firms. Again, with more discretion/authority, the CEO's marginal revenue product is higher and the equilibrium level of pay should be higher as well.

Source: S. Raice and J. Stenberg (2014), "Goldman CEO's Pay Is Back on Top," *Wall Street Journal* (March 18), www.wsj.com/news/articles/SB10001424052702304017604579447631180090114.

Figure 14.1   How Firms Choose Employment and Wages: The Basic Competitive Model

In our basic model, firms have no discretion over the wages they pay to employees; rather, the wages are determined by supply and demand in the marketplace. As shown in the figure, individual firms continue to hire employees up to the point E^*, where the marginal revenue product equals the market-determined wage rate. Until this point, hiring additional employees produces more revenue for the firm than it costs to hire the employee. Past this point, the costs of hiring additional individuals are greater than the benefits.

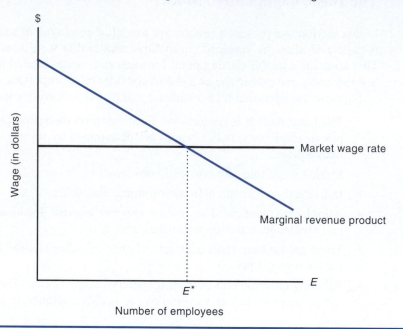

Figure 14.1 depicts the hiring decisions of individual firms within this simple market setting. Each firm continues to hire employees to the point where the marginal revenue product equals the market-determined wage rate. Before this point, hiring additional employees produces more revenue than it costs to hire the individuals. Past this point, the costs of hiring additional individuals are greater than their benefits. The hiring decisions of all firms in the market determine the demand curve for labor. The supply curve is determined by the decisions of individuals on whether to accept the given wage rate or stay out of the labor force. The market wage rate equates supply and demand.

The implications of this analysis are that if a firm pays too little (below the market wage rate), it will be unable to attract or retain qualified employees. On the other hand, a firm that pays too much will have long queues for job openings. However, the firm will incur higher costs and thus will report lower profits than firms that do not overpay. Given a competitive market for its products, it eventually will go out of business.

Human Capital[2]

In our benchmark model, all individuals are alike. Yet employees generally vary in their abilities, skills, and training. *Human capital* is a term that characterizes individuals as having a set of skills that they can rent to employers. The value of human

[2]This section draws on G. Becker (1983), *Human Capital* (University of Chicago Press: Chicago).

MANAGERIAL APPLICATIONS

CEO Pay Levels

A 2014 survey of CEO pay levels in the largest 50 U.S. public firms reports the median CEO pay was $9.8 million. Some CEOs such as John Chambers at Cisco were well above the median at $19.6 million. While these CEO pay levels might appear large, and are often trumpeted as being excessive by the media, a couple of points are worth noting. First, CEOs in U.S. firms exercise substantial discretion in making corporate decision making and the value implications of these decisions—the value of the marginal product—is enormous. In a competitive managerial labor market, their compensation should be set equal to their VMP. Second, much of what gets counted as CEO pay is not cash but rather restricted stock or option grants whose value depends on future firm performance. For example, a CEO might be granted 100,000 stock options with an exercise price of $12 per option that expire in three years (the exercise price is typically set equal to the stock price on the grant date). These options might have an estimated value of $4.50 each; hence $450,000 is reported as part of the CEO's pay. (Given some assumptions, this is an estimate of the current value of these options.) But they are not cash today; they are risky and only will have value if the firm's stock price rises above $12 over the next three years. Third, the $9.8 million median salary of CEOs in the largest 50 U.S. firms pales in comparison to the pay of top celebrities (Oprah Winfrey at $165 million, Steven Spielberg at $130 million, Howard Stern $105 million). The median pay of the top 50 CEOs ($9.8 million) is only about 10 percent of the median pay of the top 20 celebrities ($90 million).

Source: T. Francis and J. Lublin (2014), "CEO Pay Rising but Not for All," *Wall Street Journal* (March 26), www.wsj.com/news/articles/SB10001424052702304026304579448961007000986; and D. Pomerantz (2012), "Oprah Winfrey Tops Our List Of The Highest-Paid Celebrities," *Forbes* (August 27), www.forbes.com/sites/dorothypomerantz/2012/08/27/oprah-winfrey-tops-our-list-of-the-highest-paid-celebrities.

capital is determined by supply and demand in the marketplace. Individuals invest in their human capital through education and training, migration, and search for new jobs. The return on this investment consists of higher wage rates that come from having more valuable human capital—hence college graduates typically earn more than high school graduates.

It is useful to distinguish between *general* and *specific* human capital. General human capital consists of training and education, that is, valued equivalently by a broad array of different firms. Investments in general human capital include obtaining an MBA degree, mastering general principles of engineering, or becoming proficient in some new business software application. Specific human capital, on the other hand, is more valuable to the current employer than to alternative employers. Investments in specific capital include such things as learning the details of a particular firm's accounting system or product information. At Sandler O'Neill, specific capital

MANAGERIAL APPLICATIONS

U.S. Lags in Worker Human Capital Skills

A 2012 study of workforce skills of adults aged 16–65 ranked the United States 16th out of 23 industrialized countries. The survey judged four aspects of adult functional skills: Literacy, reading components, numerical calculations, and problem solving. These skills constitute the basic components of general human capital required for the workforce. And the problem is likely to get worse in the United States. Among adults aged 56–65, the United States was ranked above the average of the 23 countries surveyed; but among adults 16–24, Americans ranked below the average country.

Source: M. Goodman, R. Finnegan, L Mohadjer, T. Krenzke, and J. Hogan (2013), "Literacy, Numeracy, and Problem Solving in Technology-Rich Environments Among U.S. Adults," (NCES 2014-008). U.S. Department of Education, www.nces.ed.gov/pubs2014/2014008.pdf.

includes the proprietary financial model used to analyze banks and the relationships with and knowledge of their clients.

If we extend our benchmark model to allow for differences in training, firms would not invest in general training. The gains from general training go to the employees, not firms: If a firm is unwilling to pay the employee the market price for the new skills, the individual moves to another firm that is willing. Thus, employees pay for their own general training. Conversely, employees are unwilling to pay for specific training, since it does not increase their market values. Thus, in our benchmark model, firms must pay for specific training.

Compensating Differentials[3]

Our benchmark model ignores differences in working conditions across jobs. In reality, jobs vary in many dimensions, including quality of the work environment, geographic location, length of commute, exposure to danger, characteristics of coworkers, and the degree of monotony associated with the tasks. Facing equal salary levels across job offers, an individual will choose the job with the most desirable characteristics (such as low risk of injury and attractive location). To attract employees to less desirable jobs, firms must increase the level of pay.[4]

The *extra* wage that is paid to attract an individual to a less desirable job is called a *compensating wage differential.* For instance, an all-night restaurant probably has to pay more to attract a manager to work at night at a more dangerous location than it does to attract a manager to work during the day at a safer location.

The prediction that unpleasant jobs pay more than pleasant jobs *holds other factors constant.* Variation in job requirements for education, skills, and training also accounts for differences in pay. For example, an office job in a pleasant work environment might pay more than the relatively unpleasant job of garbage collector because the skills required for the office job are greater. However, garbage collectors will be paid more than similar unskilled labor engaged in more pleasant tasks.

Some of the most compelling evidence of compensating wage differentials is provided by studies that relate wages to the risk of fatal injury on the job.[5] Using data from around the world, wages were found to be positively associated with the risk of being killed on the job, holding other factors constant. The estimates of the magnitude of the compensating differential are relatively imprecise and vary across studies, but they indicate that employees receive between $20 and $300 more per year for

---

[3]In this section, we discuss the key points of the theory of compensating differentials as they relate to managerial decision making. For an expanded discussion of compensating differentials, see R. Ehrenberg and R. Smith (2015), *Modern Labor Economics: Theory and Public Policy,* 12th edition (Prentice Hall: Boston), Chapter 8.

[4]This prediction assumes that employees can obtain reasonably good information about important characteristics of the job either before or shortly after employment. This assumption is likely to be quite reasonable in many cases. For instance, applicants for a firefighter position in an arid location are likely to know that the job is hazardous. They also can observe the quality of the fire station and equipment. Applicants can collect additional information about the work environment from current or past employees which is often available on the Internet. Some argue that the level of scientific knowledge required to understand certain hazards is beyond that held by most employees or job applicants. Yet the recognition of basic correlations sometimes is sufficient. For instance, the expression "mad as a hatter" goes back to the nineteenth century—long before scientists understood the details of how the chemicals used to treat the pelts in hat making adversely affected brain function.

[5]For a more detailed summary of this empirical work, see Ehrenberg and Smith (2015), 268–269.

MANAGERIAL APPLICATIONS

Compensating Differentials on the "Slime Line"

At Taku Smokeries in Juneau, Alaska, gutting fish is cold, wet, smelly work done by humans, not machines, on the "slime line." Taku produces as much as 50,000 pounds of fish a day. The line consists of a dozen workers in orange rain gear, splattered with blood and fish guts. Using knives, spoons, and hoses they clean a flood of fish amidst constant noise and overpowering smell. But one of the workers, Bill Razpotnik, asserts he doesn't care. The $12 per hour salary plus time and a half for overtime allows him to feed his family of four. Razpotnik says, "What smell? It doesn't bother me, I've slimed several million fish and one fish is just another fish. Another day, another dead fish."

Source: E. Arnold (2002), "Dirty Work: Fish Processing," (August 22), www.npr.org/programs/morning/features/2002/aug/dirtywork/slimeline/index.html.

every 1 in 10,000 increase in the risk of being killed on the job. These estimates imply that a firm with 1,000 employees could reduce wage costs between $20,000 and $300,000 per year by increasing the level of safety enough to save one life every 10 years.

Compensating wage differentials have two important effects. First, all societies have unpleasant tasks that must be performed—for instance, most require morticians and garbage collectors. Compensating differentials attract people to these jobs and reward them for their efforts. Individuals who accept unpleasant tasks tend to be the ones who bear the lowest cost for performing them. For example, if a wage premium is offered for working in a noisy factory, the people most likely to apply are those least bothered by noise. Individuals who are particularly noise-averse would choose to work in a quiet environment at a lower wage. Second, compensating differentials cause employers who offer unpleasant work environments to have higher labor costs. Employers thus can reduce their labor costs by enhancing their work environments. This possibility implies that the firms providing better work environments will be those firms that can do so at low cost (since the marginal cost of providing a pleasant environment is low relative to the marginal benefit of reducing the penalty).

This discussion suggests that there is a job-matching process in labor markets where firms offer and individuals accept jobs in a manner that makes the most of

MANAGERIAL APPLICATIONS

Recruiting and Retaining Iraqi Soldiers

In December 2003, the U.S. army disclosed that about 300 of the 700 members of the newly formed Iraqi army had quit. Many of those leaving were married soldiers who were trying to support their families on a mere $60 per month. To recruit and retain an Iraqi army the U.S.-led coalition forces raised the pay of Iraqi soldiers. By June of 2005, a common Iraqi soldier's pay was up to $340 a month, and generals were paid $950 a month. With an Iraqi unemployment rate of 30 percent and with doctors in the best Baghdad hospitals earning $500 a month and most Iraqis earning $200 a month, the pay for Iraqi soldiers contained a significant compensating differential, in part to compensate Iraqi soldiers for the risk posed by the job.

By June 2005, the Iraqi army and paramilitary police numbered 169,000. The Iraqi army pay is so good, 7,000 men showed up at an army recruiting center one rainy day in November 2004 on the false rumors of a new enlistment call.

Source: (2003), "Coalition May Hike Iraqi Army Pay," (December 13), www.cnn.com/2003/WORLD/meast/12/13/sprj.irq.main/; and S. Tavernise and J. Burns (2005), "As Iraqi Army Trains, Word in the Field Is It May Take Years," *New York Times* (June 13).

their strengths and preferences. Organizations have incentives to reduce the risk of injury in order to reduce wage premiums. In turn, the people who take risky jobs are likely to be the most tolerant of risk—individuals *self-select* based on their risk preferences. For example, fishing companies often find it too expensive to reduce the risk of injury beyond some level, and thus they must offer wage premiums to crews of fishing boats. Individuals applying to work on these boats are likely to be among those most willing to place their lives at risk on the job. Because of this self-selection, the compensating differential is lower than if the firm attempted to hire a randomly selected person from the population. Firms that provide a safe environment at a low cost will offer low-risk jobs and lower wages; these positions will be filled by more risk-averse employees.

Costly Information about Market Wage Rates

In contrast to our benchmark model, compensation in many labor markets is not readily observable. Individuals vary in characteristics and generally are not perfect substitutes. Thus, observing the wage for one individual does not provide full information on what it would require to hire another. In addition, firms do not share complete information about their levels of compensation. The difficulty in observing the market price for labor means that it is not always easy to tell if a firm is underpaying or overpaying its employees.

Two important indicators of whether a firm is paying the market wage rate are the number of applications it receives for job openings and the quit rate among existing employees. If a firm is inundated by *qualified applicants* when it advertises a job opening and its quit rate is low, the firm probably is paying above the market wage rate.[6] In contrast, if the applicant rate is low and turnover is high, the firm probably is paying below the market.

In choosing the rate of pay, it is important to consider the trade-offs between incremental compensation and turnover costs. Turnover costs include the costs of recruiting employees, training expenses, and reduced productivity from employing inexperienced employees. In addition, if employees expect that they will work for the firm for only a short time, they are less likely to be concerned about how their actions affect the long-run cash flows of the firm. For instance, a salesperson might push to make a sale to collect a commission, knowing that the customer will be unhappy with the product and will reduce future purchases. Sometimes, employees who leave a firm take customers and trade secrets to competing firms. Nonetheless, turnover also has beneficial effects on the firm—for example, it adds "new blood" and fresh ideas to the organization.

Outside job offers made to existing employees also are indicative of market rates. Although these offers provide important information about the market value of existing employees, firms must be careful in deciding whether to match these offers. Failure to match can result in losing valued employees. But a policy of matching all outside offers encourages employees to invest in generating such offers. This activity might take time away from work and also might increase the likelihood that employees will receive offers that entice them to leave the firm.

---

[6]Paying above the market wage rate typically will place the firm at a competitive disadvantage. As we discuss next, however, there are several reasons why some value-maximizing firms might want to pay above the prevailing market wage rate.

Internal Labor Markets

While our benchmark model provides a reasonably good description of some labor markets, such as the market for unskilled agricultural workers, it does a poor job describing employment and wages in many other cases. In contrast to the model, many firms rarely reduce employee compensation and frequently invest in general training—such as paying tuition for an employee to obtain an MBA. Also, employees often invest their time and effort in developing firm-specific skills.

Many firms are better characterized as having *internal labor markets,* wherein outside hiring focuses primarily on filling entry-level jobs and most other jobs are filled from within the firm. Firms with internal labor markets establish *long-term relationships* with employees. The typical employee has been with his or her current employer for 4.6 years. But among older workers ages 55 to 64 the average tenure rises to 10.6 years. Women had stayed with their current employer 4.5 years. And, about 30 percent of men had 10 years or more of tenure with their current employer.[7]

Established career paths and the prospect for promotions play important roles in firms with internal labor markets. These firms interact with outside labor markets only on a limited basis. Rather than simply reflecting outside market conditions, the rates of pay (discussed in more detail later in this chapter) and job assignments in internal labor markets often are determined by administrative rules and implicit understandings. Firms can have more than one internal labor market. For example, the internal market for white-collar employees might have little interaction with the internal market for blue-collar employees. In addition, firms with internal labor markets typically offer some jobs that are well described by our basic model—for instance, certain low-skilled positions.

Agreements between employers and employees concerning compensation and responsibilities are contracts. Firms generally do not enter into formal written agreements (*explicit contracts*) with nonunion employees. Rather, most employees work under *implicit contracts*—a set of shared, informal understandings about how firms and employees will respond to contingencies.[8] Implicit contracts differ from explicit contracts in that they normally are unwritten and more difficult to enforce in a court of law. Firms and employees, however, often have strong economic incentives to honor implicit contracts to protect their reputations. A primary reason for the frequent use of implicit contracts is that it would be quite costly to detail all possible contingencies and associated responses in formal documents.

Reasons for Long-Term Employment Relationships

In Chapter 3, we discussed how all methods of organizing economic activity involve contracting costs. Firms have incentives to consider these costs and to organize economic exchanges in an efficient manner.[9] Spot-market exchange is not always the most efficient way to organize firm–employee relationships. There are at least three factors that help promote the widespread use of the long-term employment

---

[7]Bureau of Labor Statistics, "Employee Tenure Summary in 2014" U.S. Department of Labor (September 18, 2014) www.bls.gov/news.release/tenure.nr0.htm; and R. Hall (1982), "The Importance of Lifetime Jobs in the U.S. Economy," *American Economic Review* 72, 716–724.

[8]S. Rosen (1985), "Implicit Contracts," *Journal of Economic Literature* 23, 1144–1175.

[9]R. Coase (1988), *The Firm, the Market, and the Law* (University of Chicago Press: Chicago).

MANAGERIAL APPLICATIONS

Internal Labor Markets in Japan

Large companies in Japan used to make extensive use of internal labor markets. Many Japanese executives would spend their entire careers with the same firm. Senior executives virtually never moved from one major firm to another. Firms rarely went outside to hire for any position other than entry-level jobs. Turnover was extremely low. Pay was tied largely to seniority, and the differences in pay among employees were small relative to the differences in American companies.

Recently, poor performance has placed pressures on Japanese firms to reconsider their policies of lifetime employment guarantees. But by 2009 more than one third of Japan's labor force consisted of low-cost part-timers, contract workers, and temporary staff.

Source: R. Wartzman, "Japan: Rethinking Lifetime Employment" (September 04, 2009) Bloomberg Businessweek, www.business-week.com/managing/content/sep2009/ca2009094_141933.htm

---

relationships found in internal labor markets. These factors include specific human capital, employee motivation, and information about employee attributes.

Firm-Specific Human Capital

Long-term relationships provide stronger incentives for employers and employees to invest in specific training. If employers and employees expect that their relationships will be of short duration, limited incentives exist to make these investments. In contrast, long-term relationships allow firms and employees to capture the benefits of accumulated specific human capital.

Employee Motivation

The prospect of a long-term relationship with a firm provides powerful incentives for employees to work on behalf of their employers. Employees who consider shirking, stealing, or other dysfunctional activities must weigh their potential benefits of these actions against the costs of losing future benefits should they be caught and dismissed. Since there is more to lose in long-term relationships than in short-term relationships, the incentives both to engage in productive activities and to avoid dysfunctional activities are higher within long-term relationships.[10] Also, as we discuss below, long-term relationships increase the flexibility that a firm retains in designing compensation packages to motivate employee effort.

Learning Employee Attributes

Over time, managers receive much information about the skills, work habits, interests, and intelligence of individual employees. Employers then can use this information in matching employees and jobs within the firm. For example, firms with internal labor markets have fewer surprises in filling higher-level jobs than firms that rely on outside labor markets.

Costs of Internal Labor Markets

Not all firms have internal labor markets. Some firms rely heavily on outside markets to fill positions at all levels. The observation that some firms do not operate internal

---

[10]This statement assumes that an employee cannot costlessly replicate the same stream of benefits by changing to a new employer. For example, the new job might pay lower compensation, the individual might incur moving costs, there might be a period of unemployment, and so on.

labor markets suggests that the costs of these markets can be larger than their benefits. One potentially important problem with internal labor markets is the restricted competition for higher-level jobs within the organization. If a firm considers only internal candidates for higher-level jobs, it will not always hire the most qualified person—who may be from outside the firm. The likelihood of finding a desirable candidate in the outside labor market is highest when the job does not require specific training (since experience with the firm does not create an advantage in the job). Thus, firms are more likely to use internal labor markets where specific training is important. Indeed, firms in the steel, petroleum, and chemical industries, where complicated production technologies take significant time to learn, tend to rely on internal labor markets, whereas firms in the food services and hospitality industries do not. Firm-specific skills arguably are less important in garment and shoe manufacturing than in steel, petroleum, or chemicals.

Pay in Internal Labor Markets

Careers and Lifetime Pay

Employees who take jobs at firms with internal labor markets often expect that they will spend much of their *careers* at the same firm. Thus, in considering an entry-level job, prospective employees generally will focus on the entire stream of earnings over their anticipated career path. For example, an individual might accept a job at Firm A that pays less than another job offered at Firm B because the individual anticipates faster compensation growth at Firm A.

The fact that individuals tend to base employment decisions on career earnings gives firms with internal labor markets more flexibility over choosing the level and time profile of pay. In contrast to our basic model, firms do not need to pay the market wage rate (or equivalently, in equilibrium, the marginal revenue product) at each point in time. Rather, firms can vary compensation over a career path, as long as the overall value of the remaining stream is competitive at each point in time (valued as highly by employees as streams offered by competing firms in the labor market).

Economists have identified at least three ways that firms can use their flexibility in setting the level and time profile of pay to enhance employee motivation. These methods include the payment of efficiency wages, upward-sloping earnings profiles, and tying major pay increases to promotions. As we discuss below, however, influence costs can limit the extent to which firms exploit this potential flexibility.

Efficiency Wages

In many jobs, it is difficult to monitor employee actions. It also is difficult to devise incentive compensation schemes that motivate desired behavior. For example, manufacturing companies want production employees to work hard. In most cases, it is difficult to measure employee effort with much precision. In addition, the payment of piece rates or other output-based compensation can discourage employees from paying enough attention to quality.

One potential way of motivating employees in such cases is to pay compensation *above* the market rate. Paying a premium for employees obviously increases labor costs. However, it can have the desirable effect of motivating them not to shirk. Individuals who are paid a wage premium are likely to reduce their shirking because they understand that if they are caught and fired, they will have difficulty finding another job that offers such a premium. This effect will be greater for employees who have

MANAGERIAL APPLICATIONS

Lifetime Employment Collapses at Mitsubishi

During its peak, Mitsubishi employees were like lords of the universe. Hired from the top universities and treated as the elite, they had good jobs, security, and lifetime employment. But then the bubble burst. Using huge capital gains from real estate to make numerous bad investments in the 1980s created huge losses in the 1990s. Mitsubishi is actually a group of associated companies called a *keiretsu*. The main Mitsubishi companies (autos, banks, heavy industries) had a return on equity of 4 percent in contrast to the United States where anything less than 15 percent is considered poor. Now, recent hires quit and look for new jobs. There is no longer the same sense of security as before.

Source: J. Adams "The demise of 'lifetime employment' in Japan," Minnpost (May 5, 2009) 05/19/10, www.minnpost.com/global-post/2010/05/demise-lifetime-employment-japan.

longer time horizons with the firm, since they have more to lose. Economists refer to wage premiums of this type as *efficiency wages*. Efficiency wages also provide incentives for employees to stay with the firm. These incentives can be particularly important when the employee has specific human capital (the firm does not want to replace the employee with a person with less training and experience).[11]

ACADEMIC APPLICATIONS

Motivating Honesty in the Local Police Force

Economists Gary Becker and George Stigler were asked to consider ways of reducing corruption within the Chicago police force. The recommendation of these Nobel laureates was to pay the police more than the market wage rate. With sufficiently high premiums, the police would have incentives not to take bribes from criminals. For this condition to hold, the immediate gains from taking bribes must be offset by the expected loss in wage premiums given the possibility of being caught and fired. Thus, the required premium to prevent cheating depends on the size of the bribes and the likelihood of getting caught. Higher bribes and lower likelihood of getting caught translate into higher required premiums.

Paying wage premiums will entice a large number of people to apply for job openings. To reduce the surplus of applicants, Becker and Stigler suggested that the jobs be sold to officers. The price of jobs would reflect the expected premiums. Under this plan, the payment for a job can be considered as a bond posted by an officer not to cheat. If the officer is honest, the officer gets the bond back in the form of the premium wage. If the officer cheats and gets caught, the bond is forfeited.

The concept of buying jobs may seem unusual. However, this originally was the practice among yeoman warders—the beefeaters who guard the tower of London. And today many people essentially do this when they purchase the right to manage an outlet of a franchise company.

Source: G. Becker and G. Stigler (1974), "Law Enforcement, Malfeasance, and Compensation," *Journal of Legal Studies* 3, 1–18.

---

[11]For a more detailed analysis of efficiency wages, see G. Akerlof (1984), "Gift Exchange and Efficiency Wages: Four Views," *American Economic Review* 74, 78–83; C. Shapiro and J. Stiglitz (1984), "Equilibrium Unemployment as a Worker Discipline Device," *American Economic Review* 74, 433–444; and J. Yellen (1984), "Efficiency Wages Models and Unemployment," *American Economic Review* 74, 200–208. If all firms in an industry pay efficiency wages, there will be unemployment. (The supply of labor will exceed demand.) The threat of unemployment can provide incentives for employees not to shirk. Note that in our basic model, marginal revenue product and the wage rate are independent. The efficiency-wage concept, however, suggests that they can be related: Employees' marginal products can be affected by their wage rates due to incentive effects from potential dismissal for cause.

Figure 14.2 An Example of an Upward Sloping Earnings Profile

This figure displays both the marginal revenue product and compensation for a representative employee in a given firm. Within this particular firm, both marginal revenue product and compensation increase as the employee becomes more experienced. Compensation, however, increases at a faster rate. In the early years, the employee is paid below the marginal revenue product, whereas in later years the employee is paid more. The employee is underpaid in early years yet still is willing to work for the firm because of the expectation of being overpaid in subsequent years. Under this compensation plan, young employees have incentives to work hard to avoid both being fired and losing future wage premiums. Older employees, in turn, do not want to be dismissed because they receive more than they could earn at other firms.

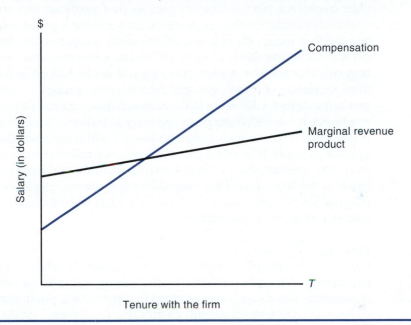

Job Seniority and Pay[12]

Compensation typically increases with seniority within the firm. Part of this increase is explained by increases in productivity that come from experience. In many firms, however, compensation increases faster than productivity as the employee ages. Firms frequently offer attractive retirement packages to encourage older employees to retire and (unless precluded by law) often have mandatory retirement. For example, the employee must retire at age 65.[13]

One explanation for these age-related policies is that they establish stronger incentives for employees to work in the best interests of the firm. To see how, consider the example depicted in Figure 14.2. This figure displays the growth patterns of the marginal revenue product and compensation for a representative employee within a particular firm. Both the marginal revenue product and compensation increase as the

---

[12]This section draws on E. Lazear (1979), "Why Is There Mandatory Retirement?" *Journal of Political Economy* 87, 1261–1284.

[13]Amendments made to the Age Discrimination Employment Act in 1978 and 1986 have precluded mandatory retirement for most workers in the United States.

employee becomes more experienced. (The analysis does not change if we allow for declines in productivity in later years.) Compensation, however, increases at a faster rate. In the early years, the employee is paid below the marginal revenue product, whereas in later years the employee is paid more. The employee is underpaid in early years but is willing to work for the firm because of the expectation of being overpaid in subsequent years. Under this compensation plan, younger employees have incentives to make firm-specific human capital investments and to work hard to avoid being fired and losing future wage premiums. Older employees do not want to get fired because they are being paid more than they could earn at other firms.

Firms that employ this type of compensation policy have short-run incentives to fire older employees, since older employees are paid more than they are worth. Unjustified dismissals of older employees, however, are not in the long-run interests of these firms because they reduce the incentive effects of the compensation plan: Younger employees will not believe that hard work will lead to wage premiums when they get older. To help convince younger workers that they will not be laid off in their later years, such firms frequently adopt job seniority rules whereby younger employees are dismissed first in the case of a downturn in the economy. Firms cannot pay premiums to all older employees for an indefinite period and stay in business. Thus, these firms will adopt policies that help ensure that older employees will retire when they reach a specified age. For example, if legally allowed a mandatory retirement age might be established where the present value of the underpayments in the early years offsets the overpayments in the later years. Thus, over their entire careers, employees are still paid their marginal revenue products (as in our basic model). Such a condition helps the firm survive in a competitive marketplace.

Promotions[14]

Firms are typically partitioned into hierarchical levels, where the jobs at a given level pay more than positions at lower levels. Employees move up this hierarchy through promotions. Since employees compete for promotions, promotions can be viewed as contests or tournaments among employees. Employees' productivity is higher as they try to win these contests.

Promotions obviously play an important role in providing incentives within many organizations.[15] One benefit of using a promotion-based incentive scheme is that it commits the firm to serious performance reviews of its employees. Promoting the wrong person to a job can impose material costs. Employers have incentives to conduct in-depth performance reviews to reduce the likelihood of making such mistakes. Another primary benefit is that promotion contests help filter out random shocks in evaluating performance. Typically, the employee with the best *relative performance* is chosen for promotion. Potential risk-sharing benefits come from using relative performance measures rather than absolute performance measures.[16] In particular, employees are less likely to be rewarded or penalized for factors beyond their control—common shocks that affect all the contestants in the promotion contest are filtered out of the decision.

---

[14]This section draws from the literature on tournament theory. See E. Lazear and S. Rosen (1981), "Rank Order Tournaments as Optimal Labor Contracts," *Journal of Political Economy* 89, 841–864.

[15]Promotions also play an important role in matching people with jobs based on skills and ability.

[16]Relative performance measures are based on how an employee performs compared to a peer group. Absolute performance measures compare the employee's performance to some predetermined standard.

MANAGERIAL APPLICATIONS

A Horse Race at General Electric

Sometimes, firms "run horse races" among internal candidates. Under this procedure, the candidates are notified that they are competing for a job with higher pay and prestige. The contest provides significant incentives for the candidates to perform since the prize for winning can be very large. General Electric ran such a horse race to fill the CEO position when Reginald Jones retired in 1981. The winner was Jack Welch. In 2000, Jeffrey Immelt won another leadership tournament and succeeded Welsh as GE CEO in 2001.

Source: R. Vancil (1987), *Passing the Baton* (Harvard Business School: Boston); and General Electric, "Notice of 2013 Annual Meeting and Proxy Statement" www.tscviewer.com/Ge/iversion/NoticeOf2013AnnualMeetingAndProxyStatement_i1.

Promotion-based systems can have several significant drawbacks.[17] First, judging people on relative performance can undermine employee cooperation, and employees might even sabotage the work of others. A survey of Australian companies finds that when promotion incentives are strong, workers are less likely to cooperate.[18] Second, promotions can be a rather crude tool for providing incentives. Promotions occur only at discrete intervals, and the employee is either promoted or not. Moreover, within smaller firms as well as for employees with specialized skills, promotion opportunities can be quite limited. Monetary incentives, such as bonus payments, are more flexible. Third, there can be serious conflicts between matching people for jobs and providing incentives. The so-called Peter principle argues that employees keep getting promoted until they reach jobs that they cannot handle. Fourth, employees do not always value promotions. For example, research scientists and professors often do not want administrative positions. Fifth, promotion contests can subject decision makers to significant influencing activities.[19]

Despite these drawbacks, promotions remain a useful method for motivating employees. For example, in one large firm there was little variation in pay based on performance for employees within the same job grade. Rather, most pay increases occurred when an employee was promoted to a higher job grade.[20] When pay increases are large for getting promoted, employees exert more effort. Professional golfers have lower scores and NASCAR racers drive faster when the prize money for winning the event is larger.[21] When more people compete for a promotion, the increase in pay for becoming CEO is larger.[22]

[17]G. Baker, K. Murphy, and M. Jensen (1988), "Compensation and Incentives: Practice and Theory," *Journal of Finance* 43, 593–616.

[18]R. Drago and G. Garvey (1998), "Incentives for Helping on the Job," *Journal of Labor Economics* 16, 1–25.

[19]Promotions are typically based on the subjective judgments of people rather than on objective output measures (such as pieces produced). As we discuss in more detail in Chapter 16, subjective performance evaluation can motivate nonproductive actions to influence the supervisor's rating.

[20]M. Gibbs and W. Hendricks (2004), "Do Formal Salary Systems Really Matter?" *Industrial & Labor Relations Review* 58:1, 71–93.

[21]R. Ehrenberg and M. Bognanno (1990), "The Incentive Effects of Tournaments Revisited: Evidence for the European PGA Tour," *Industrial Labor Relations Review* 43, 74–89; and B. Becker and M. Huselid (1992), "The Incentive Effects of Tournament Compensation Systems," *Administrative Science Quarterly* 37, 336–350.

[22]M. Conyon and S. Peck (2001), "Corporate Tournaments and Executive Compensation: Evidence from the UK," *Strategic Management Journal* 22, 805–815.

Influence Costs and Pay in Universities

The potential for influence activity is especially high in firms where employees have common knowledge about one another's pay. Our discussion suggests that these firms might limit the differences in pay to reduce influence costs. One study provides empirical evidence on this issue by examining compensation levels in academic departments at about 2,000 colleges. Common knowledge about pay is more likely in small departments, in departments where the members frequently interact on a social basis, and in public institutions (where public disclosure of pay often is required). Consistent with the influence-cost arguments, this study found that all three factors were associated with reductions in the dispersion of pay.

Source: J. Pfeffer and N. Langton (1988), "Wage Inequality and the Organization of Work: The Case of Academic Departments," *Administrative Sciences Quarterly* 33, 588–606.

Lately, the prospect for promotion in many firms has fallen due to an overall reduction in middle-management positions. This development reduces incentives for many employees, who think that the chances for promotion are low even if they do a good job. In response, many firms have tried to restore incentives by adopting more explicit pay-for-performance plans. One 1988 survey reports that 75 percent of employers in the United States have an incentive plan (such as profit- or gain-sharing plan) for rank-and-file employees.[23] The use of stock options to reward executives and employees increased steadily in North America in the late 1990s. According to a survey of *Fortune 200* companies, shares allocated for stock incentive plans more than doubled in the 1990s, amounting to 13 percent of all outstanding shares at the end of the decade. Two other surveys estimate that the value of stock options exercised by employees of large U.S. companies reached $100 billion in the year 2000, and that 19 percent of all employees were eligible for options in 1999, compared to 12 percent in 1998.[24]

Influence Costs

Teammates frequently compare compensation levels. Differences in pay among coworkers regularly prompt employees to seek explanations for compensation decisions. Employees also use information about the pay of other employees to lobby for pay increases. It frequently is conjectured that firms limit the differentials in pay to reduce this type of influence activity. Such a policy, however, comes at a cost; underperforming employees are likely to be paid too much, whereas more productive employees are likely to be undercompensated and leave the firm. Influence costs also help explain why many firms try to keep their compensation decisions confidential. In many cases, however, it is difficult to prevent teammates from sharing information on compensation.

Firms often expend substantial resources on evaluating and comparing jobs within the organization. One popular method is the Hay System.[25] Under this

---

[23]N. Perry (1988), "Here Come Richer, Riskier Pay Plans," *Fortune* (December 19), 50–58.

[24]E. Kupiec (2003), "Are Stock Options Good Business Options?" *Management* (May), www.managementmag .com.

[25]For a more detailed discussion, see G. Milkovich, J. Newman, and B. Gerhart (2014), *Compensation* 11th edition, (McGraw-Hill: New York).

system, each job within the organization is evaluated on factors such as required know-how, problem-solving skills, the number of people supervised, and accountability. Based on this evaluation, each job is assigned a total number of points and placed in a position within the firm's hierarchy. Jobs at a given level in the hierarchy have similar ranges in compensation. For example, jobs included in the same level might pay from $20,000 to $25,000, depending on experience and qualifications. Although salaries reflect external market rates to some extent, a major emphasis is placed on internal consistency among jobs (equal pay for equal work). Internal consistency appears to reduce employee complaints about compensation policies and helps protect the firm against liability in discrimination suits. However, if pay is related to the number of employees supervised, such a plan can lead to empire building by managers.

The Salary–Fringe Benefit Mix[26]

In our benchmark model, individuals receive their compensation in the form of cash payments. Most employees, however, receive a substantial amount of their compensation in the form of *fringe benefits*—compensation that is either in kind or deferred.

Examples of in-kind payments are health insurance and membership in a company recreation center, where the employee receives an insurance policy or a service rather than cash. Payments to pension plans and Social Security are examples of deferred compensation. For the typical American employee, about 75 percent of the total compensation package is pay for time worked, while about 25 percent is fringe benefits. Based on the cost to the employer, the most important fringe benefits are pensions and insurance, paid leave time (vacations and sick or other leave), and mandated contributions to Social Security and Workers' Compensation. Many employees also receive benefits such as company-paid education, dental care, discounted meals, and subsidized recreation programs. A survey of college grads found the following ranking as the most important job benefit: Medical insurance, pension benefits, annual salary raises, and dental and life insurance.[27]

Employee Preferences

Salary and fringe benefits typically are not perfect substitutes from an employee's viewpoint. One reason is taxes: Certain fringe benefits (such as health insurance) are not subject to income taxes when received by the employees. For example, an employee who wants to purchase an insurance policy that costs $5,000 would prefer that the firm provide the policy rather than $5,000 in cash. Since insurance premiums are not counted as taxable income, an employee in a 33.33 percent tax bracket would have to receive $7,500 in salary to purchase the policy. The employee also might want the firm to purchase fringe benefits because the benefits can be purchased by the firm at lower prices. For example, a firm might be able to provide group insurance at a lower cost per employee than if employees individually purchased the insurance. The potential cost advantage of employee group health and life insurance has two main

[26]This section draws on Ehrenberg and Smith (2015), Chapter 11.

[27]A. Karr (1998), "Special News Report about Life on the Job—and Trends Taking Shape There," *The Wall Street Journal* (May 5), A1.

Figure 14.3   Employee Preferences for Salary and Fringe Benefits

This figure displays an employee's preferences for salary and fringe benefits using indifference curves. The convexity of the curves implies that this employee is willing to substitute a relatively large amount of salary for additional fringe benefits when the employee receives few fringe benefits (possibly due to tax considerations). However, this willingness to substitute declines as the employee receives more fringe benefits (the employee wants cash for other purposes).

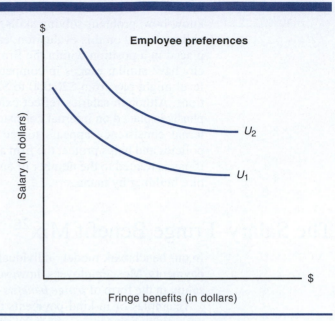

components: It reduces the adverse selection problems and lowers administrative and selling expenses. On the other hand, employees often prefer $5,000 in cash to $5,000 in fringe benefits, since the cash gives them more flexibility in selecting their purchases.[28]

In our initial discussion, we do not break fringe benefits into finer categories. Rather, we consider the choice between salary and overall fringe benefits. Later, we discuss the mix of fringe benefits. Figure 14.3 displays an employee's preferences for salary and fringe benefits using indifference curves. The convexity of the curves implies that this employee is willing to substitute a relatively large amount of salary for additional expenditures on fringe benefits when the employee is paid primarily cash (possibly due to tax considerations). However, this willingness to substitute

---

ANALYZING MANAGERIAL DECISIONS: *Structuring Cruise Line Compensation*

You work in the human resource office of a major cruise line that offers cruises in various locations around the world (the Caribbean, the Mediterranean, Asia, etc.). The CEO of your company has recently proposed that all employees in the corporate office (i.e., those employees who do not actually work on a ship) be offered free passage on your firm's cruises as a fringe benefit.

The CEO has asked for your thoughts on this proposal.

1. If this proposal is adopted, what will happen, if anything, to employee salaries? Why?
2. What are the advantages and disadvantages of this proposal? What factors should be considered when evaluating the proposal?

---

[28]D. Mayers and C. Smith (1981), "Contractual Provisions, Organizational Structure, and Conflict Control in Insurance Markets," *Journal of Business* 54, 407–434.

MANAGERIAL APPLICATIONS

Employee Preferences—Body Art

One out of seven Americans now sport tattoos, up from one out of a hundred in the 1970s. And it is not just blue-collar employees, Federal judges, lawyers, and business executives brandish various forms of body art—tattoos and body piercings. Corporate America has had to adapt in order to attract and retain a qualified workforce. While most employees choose tattoos that are not visible to coworkers or customers, several companies have adopted policies that generally allow visible discrete, non-offensive tattoos and body piercings that do not pose a safety risk. Tattoo policies vary across firms. Some managers believe that tattoos can distract coworkers and clients. Bank of America has no written rules prohibiting inked corporate employees. Some managers even see body art as a healthy way for employees to express their individuality, and that a no-tattoo policy might result in losing excellent candidates. Many medical facilities require a certain level of concealment during work hours to show professionalism as a way to gaining patients' trust. For example, the Cleveland Clinic's policy is: "Tattoos must be covered during working hours to ensure a consistent professional appearance while working."

One recent study reports that 31 percent of surveyed employers ranked "having a visible tattoo" as the top personal attribute that would cause them from promoting an employee. So, while firms are increasingly focused on diversity and inclusion, tattoo flaunting is probably best reserved for post-work hours.

Source: R. Hennessey (2013) "Tattoos No Longer A Kiss Of Death In The Workplace," *Forbes* (February 27), www.forbes.com/sites/rachelhennessey/2013/02/27/having-a-tattoo-and-a-job/.

---

declines as the employee receives more fringe benefits (the employee prefers cash for other purposes).

The employee, of course, would like to be on as high an indifference curve as possible. A firm, however, will be able to hire the individual so long as the compensation package meets the individual's reservation level of utility. If the compensation package provides this level of utility (or more), this person is at least as well off working at the firm as working for alternative employers or not working at all. For example, the reservation utility of the individual in Figure 14.3 might be depicted by the indifference curve labeled U_2. (Note that the reservation utility of the individual would increase if the compensation packages offered by other employers were increased so that other alternatives become more attractive.)

Employer Considerations

Initially, suppose that the firm's managers do not care whether they pay an employee cash or use the same amount of cash to provide fringe benefits. For instance, both expenditures might be deductible for corporate tax purposes, and so it costs the firm the same amount in either case. Figure 14.4 displays isocost curves for a representative firm under this assumption. Each curve is a straight line with a slope of -1; firm value is unaffected by the split between salary and fringe benefits. Along any isocost curve, expenditures to attract and retain employees are the same. The firm's value would be highest with the lowest isocost curve possible (since lower isocost curves imply lower employee expenses and higher profits).

The Salary–Fringe Benefit Choice

Suppose that all individuals the firm might hire have similar preferences for wages and fringe benefits. Figure 14.5 depicts an indifference curve for the reservation utility of a typical employee. The firm can hire this individual, using any

Figure 14.4 Employee Preferences for Paying Salary or Fringe Benefits

This figure displays isocost curves for a representative firm, under the assumption that the firm's value is unaffected by whether it pays the employee cash or uses the same amount of cash to provide fringe benefits. Each curve is a straight line with a slope of -1; firm value is unaffected by the split between paying a dollar for salary or a dollar for fringe benefits. Along any isocost curve, the labor expenses for the firm are the same. The firm's value is highest on the lowest isocost curve possible (since lower isocost curves mean lower labor expenses and higher profits).

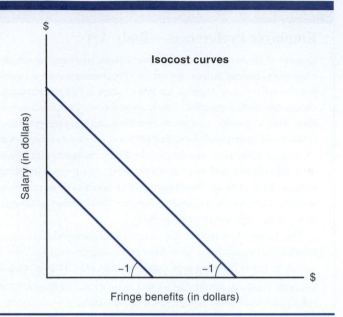

Figure 14.5 The Optimal Mix between Salary and Fringe Benefits

The figure pictures an indifference curve *U* for the reservation utility of a representative individual whom the firm is trying to hire. The firm can hire the individual using any compensation package along this curve. The figure also shows selected isocost curves for the firm. To maximize the firm's value, choose the compensation package that meets the reservation utility of the individual at the lowest cost. This optimal choice is *S**, *F**, where the indifference curve is tangent to the isocost curve. Management could choose other combinations along the indifference curve. However, these combinations are more expensive. Although the firm could offer combinations that are less expensive than *S**, *F**, these combinations would not meet the individual's reservation utility.

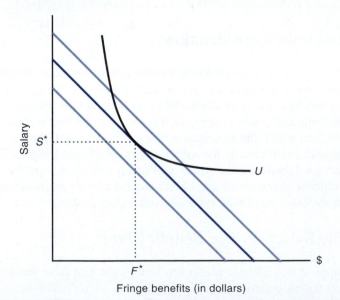

MANAGERIAL APPLICATIONS

Fringe Benefits and Overtime

In 2003 as companies emerged from the recession, many companies were reluctant to add new employees to meet their increased demand. Instead, companies began offering employees the opportunity to work overtime, for a higher wage per hour. A number of employees took advantage of this opportunity. Average weekly overtime rose from 4.3 hours in October to 4.4 hours in November. One worker with 10–15 hours of overtime a week commented, "I had some fantastic checks. It was nice, but you don't have a life." But other workers resisted and some even quit. Facing increased demand, why don't firms hire more employees who work a normal workweek at the regular wage rate? There are two major considerations: First, it is expensive to lay off workers and hence employers are reluctant to begin hiring until they are confident the observed increase in demand is not temporary. Second, fringe benefits generally do not increase with hours worked. For example, health insurance rates are determined by the number of employees, not the number of hours worked. Thus, the full cost of overtime can be less than the full cost of hiring additional workers.

Source: K. Maher (2003), "Overtime Increases as Employers Remain Cautious about Hiring," *The Wall Street Journal* (December 9), D6.

compensation package along this curve. The figure also shows selected isocost curves for the firm. Management's objective is to choose the compensation package that meets the reservation utility of the employee at the lowest cost. The optimal choice is S^*, F^*, where the indifference curve is tangent to the isocost curve. Management could choose other combinations along the indifference curve. However, these combinations are more expensive. Although management could offer combinations that are less expensive than S^*, F^*, these combinations would not meet the individual's reservation utility.

This analysis suggests that it is in management's interest to heed employee preferences about fringe benefits. If employees prefer that the company buy a dental policy rather than pay them the same amount in cash, the firm should offer the dental policy. Offering the dental policy makes the employees better off and the value of the firm no lower. Indeed, if the change would result in paying employees more than their reservation utilities, the firm can lower cash compensation further and share in these gains. (The firm might do this by giving lower raises in the subsequent years.) Designing more efficient contracts allows the firm to attract and retain employees at a lower cost.

We have assumed that the firm's value is unaffected by the split between paying a given amount of cash to employees and spending the same amount on fringe benefits. This assumption is likely to be valid in many cases, but there are at least two complicating factors. First, taxes at the firm level can be important. For example, the firm generally has to pay Social Security taxes on wages but not fringe benefits. This tax changes the slope of the firm's isocost curves. For example, assuming a Social Security tax rate of 6 percent, managers would be indifferent between paying $1.00 for salary or $1.06 for fringe benefits. The slope of the isocost curve is -0.943. As depicted in Figure 14.6, it is better to offer higher fringe benefits and lower salary than without the tax. Note that personal taxes are incorporated in the shape of employees' indifference curves, whereas the firm's taxes are incorporated in the slope of the firm's isocost curves. Thus, our analysis suggests that in designing compensation packages, management should consider the *total* tax bill for the employee and the firm.[29] Reducing the joint tax liabilities imposed on both the firm and its employees means that there is more money to split between the firm and its

[29]M. Scholes, M. Wolfson, M. Erickson, M.Hanlon, E. Maydew, and T. Shevlin (2015), *Taxes & Business Strategy*, 5th edition, (Prentice Hall: Boston).

Figure 14.6   Optimal Choice of Salary and Fringe Benefits with Payroll Taxes

This figure illustrates how payroll taxes can affect the optimal choice of salary and fringe benefits. In the first case, the firm does not pay payroll taxes (such as Social Security) on wages or fringe benefits. The optimal choice is S^*, F^*. In the second case, the firm pays payroll taxes on wages, but not fringe benefits. This tax flattens the isocost curves for the firm, and the optimal choice is S', F'. In the second case, the firm pays lower salaries and higher fringe benefits.

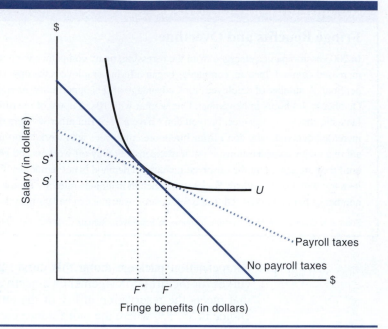

employees. It is generally inappropriate to focus only on the taxes of one party (e.g., the firm's taxes).

The second complication is that fringe benefits can affect employee behavior in ways that affect the firm's profits. For example, sick leave can motivate absenteeism. Similarly, liberal insurance coverage can reduce employee incentives to worry about prices for medical care. These types of incentive effects can affect the appropriate compensation package. For example, some firms have reduced insurance coverage to employees for the express purpose of providing employees with stronger incentives to negotiate with doctors over price. Presumably, employees do not like to bargain with doctors and must be offered higher wages both to offset this increased cost as well as

---

ANALYZING MANAGERIAL DECISIONS: *Paying for Fringe Benefits at Lincoln Electric*

The willingness of firms to listen to the preferences of employees suggests that employees pay for their own fringe benefits. For instance, most companies would be willing to pay higher salaries if employees did not want health insurance. Employees, therefore, face an opportunity cost of lost salary when they receive fringe benefits. Lincoln Electric, a manufacturing company in Cleveland, makes this trade-off quite clear to employees. Employees at Lincoln receive about half their compensation in the form of annual bonus payments. Fringe benefit costs are taken out of this bonus payment and are

shown on the employees' pay stubs. On several occasions, Lincoln employees have voted against dental plans because the majority of employees prefer cash.

Critically evaluate the following statement:

At Lincoln Electric, workers must pay for their own fringe benefits (e.g., health insurance). The payment for these benefits is taken out of the annual bonus checks. At other firms, the firm pays for fringe benefits. Therefore, the workers at Lincoln are worse off than at other firms.

to offset the reduced insurance coverage in the fringe benefit package. However, the cost to the firm will be reduced if the increase in wages is less than the reduction in insurance costs. These considerations can shift the slope of the isocost curves in either direction and thus can either increase or decrease the optimal amount of fringe benefits.

Using Fringe Benefits to Attract Particular Types of Employees

Employers often care about the personal characteristics of the individuals they hire. For example, firms facing higher costs of turnover might favor hiring people with families since they might be less likely to quit. Alternatively, firms with intense work environments, such as investment banks in New York City, might favor hiring single people because they are more likely to be willing to work longer hours. Firms are constrained in using salary offers to attract a particular type of labor force. For example, firms are likely to violate discrimination laws if they offer people with families more money than they offer single people. Firms, however, sometimes can use the mix between fringe benefits and salary to attract particular types of employees.[30] Figure 14.7

Figure 14.7 Using the Mix between Salary and Fringe Benefits to Attract Particular Types of Employees

The figure displays an isocost curve for the firm and indifference curves representing the reservation utilities of a person who is single and a person who has a family. In this example, people with families have a higher preference for fringe benefits (e.g., health insurance) than single people who prefer cash. If management wants to attract individuals with families, it will offer high fringe benefits and low wages ($\$_M$, F_M). In this case, only people with families will apply for the job. Single individuals will not apply because the package does not meet their reservation utilities. If, instead, management wants to hire single people, it will offer high salary and low fringe benefits ($\$_S$, F_S).

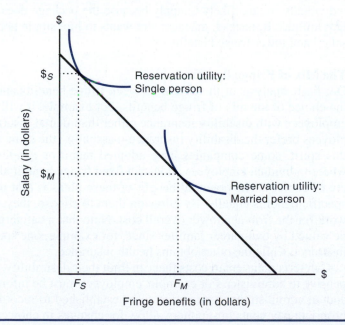

[30]Our objective in this section is to describe how firms use the salary and fringe benefit mix to attract particular types of individuals. We are not arguing that such a policy is ethical, just, or legal in all cases.

MANAGERIAL APPLICATIONS

Trend toward Temporary and Part-Time Workers

Part-time workers make up a growing portion of the workforce at United Parcel Service (UPS). If UPS has a peak load in the morning and another in the afternoon, hiring part-time employees offers UPS more flexibility than taking on more full-time employees. Many part-time employees like working a part-time schedule.

In contrast to part-time jobs, temporary jobs are full-time (40 hours per week) jobs, but not necessarily permanent. Many companies hire temps through employment agencies to fill in when permanent employees are on extended leave or if the job is temporary. These positions usually provide fewer fringe benefits. Microsoft and Time Warner have been in court over whether temps who have been in the position for several years are entitled to the same benefits as permanent employees. Who is the real employer—the employment agency or the company employing the "permatemps"? If it is the company, it owes the temp pension benefits. An IRS complaint against Microsoft claims that many of Microsoft's 6,000 temps are really common-law employees and entitled to company pension benefits. Following Microsoft's $97 million settlement in 2000, other firms such as Hewlett-Packard and Federal Express have been sued in "permatemp" litigation.

Source: R. Rosen, "America's Workers: Stressed Out, Overwhelmed, Totally Exhausted" *The Atlantic* (March 25, 2014) www.theatlantic.com/business/archive/2014/03/americas-workers-stressed-out-overwhelmed-totally-exhausted/284615/; A. Bernstein (1998), "When Is a Temp Not a Temp?" *BusinessWeek* (December 72), 67–72; and E. Frauenhein (2005), " Battles Wax and Wane in the 'Permatemp' Wars," *Workforce Management* (October 24).

depicts an example. The figure displays an isocost curve for the firm and indifference curves representing the reservation utilities of people who are single and people who have families. In this example, people with families have a higher preference for fringe benefits (e.g., health insurance) than single people. If management wants to attract individuals with families, it will offer higher fringe benefits and lower wages ($\$_M$, F_M). In this case, people with families are more likely to apply for the job. Single individuals are less likely to apply because the package does not meet their reservation utilities. If, instead, management wants to hire single people, it will offer higher salary and lower fringe benefits ($\$_S$, F_S).

The Mix of Fringe Benefits

Our basic analysis of the choice between fringe benefits and salary also applies to the choice of the mix of fringe benefits. For example, it will make sense to provide employees with disability insurance rather than dental insurance whenever the employees prefer the disability insurance—assuming the same cost to the company. In this spirit, some companies have adopted menu or *cafeteria-style* benefit plans, where individual employees allocate a fixed fringe benefit allowance among a variety of choices. The potential benefit of these plans is that not all employees value specific benefits equally. By allowing them to choose, they will be more willing to work for the firm at a lower overall cost. Note that a cafeteria plan is more likely to be valued by two-career families since, for example, one spouse can acquire dental insurance while the other obtains health insurance.

Cafeteria plans entail costs that can limit their desirability. First, they are more expensive to administer. For example, employees must be informed of all their options and an administrative system has to be established to record choices, make the appropriate payments to suppliers, allow for changes in choices, and complete the appropriate tax forms.

Second, cafeteria plans can generate adverse-selection problems that increase the cost of the benefits. Adverse selection is likely to be a particular problem with health,

ANALYZING MANAGERIAL DECISIONS: *Structuring Compensation Plans*

Parkleigh Pharmacy is a small department store in Rochester, NY, specializing in upscale, expensive personal accessories (e.g., sunglasses, beauty aids, leather goods) and home decorations (e.g., crystal, china, table lamps). Kaufmann's is a large department store chain, based in Pennsylvania, with several stores in the Rochester area. Kaufmann's carries a broader range of products and caters more to middle-income consumers.

Salespeople at Parkleigh are paid a straight hourly wage (i.e., no sales commissions). In addition, they are entitled to a 30 percent discount on anything they buy at the store. By contrast, salespeople at Kaufmann's are paid an hourly wage (lower than the hourly wage paid at Parkleigh) plus a commission of 5 percent on sales they make.

They receive no discount on products they buy at Kaufmann's.

1. Why do you think the compensation plans differ at the two firms? In particular, why do you think Kaufmann's pays commissions to salespeople, while Parkleigh does not? Why does Parkleigh offer employees discounts on purchases, while Kaufmann's does not?

2. Assume, for the moment, that neither store pays sales commissions. Parkleigh offers an hourly wage plus the employee discount. Kaufmann's offers only an hourly wage. Do you expect Kaufmann's hourly wage to be higher or lower than Parkleigh's? Why?

life, and disability insurance. Individuals know more about their likelihood of getting sick than an insurance company. This asymmetric information is less a problem if the insurance company provides the benefits to all employees as a group. When free to choose, the people who are most likely to buy insurance are those who find it a good deal at the quoted price. Thus, at any given price, the insurance company is likely to attract a clientele that causes it to lose money. To reduce the likelihood of losing money, the insurance company can do things like demand physical examinations and investigate past medical records before agreeing to insure an applicant. However, these actions increase the costs of supplying the coverage. To reduce the adverse-selection problem, companies often allow employees to opt out of health insurance only if they can document that their spouse has coverage at another firm. This policy limits the amount of discretion that employees have on whether to buy health insurance and helps ensure that the insurance company will have a reasonable cross section of health risks in the pool.

Summary

The previous two chapters discussed how firms assign decision rights. A second important component of organizational architecture is the reward system: Productive firms design compensation plans that *attract and retain* qualified employees and *motivate* them to exert effort and make decisions that exploit the business opportunities faced by the firm. This chapter examines how firms attract and retain qualified employees and how the level of pay can be used to motivate employees. The next chapter focuses on incentive compensation.

In our benchmark model of wages and employment—patterned after the standard competitive model—firms have no discretion over the wages paid to employees; rather, wages are determined by supply and demand in the marketplace. If a firm pays too little, it will have difficulty attracting employees to job openings and will experience high turnover. A firm that pays too much will have numerous job applicants and low turnover. In addition, the firm will have high costs and will compete poorly in the product market.

Human capital is a term that characterizes individuals as having a set of skills that can be "rented" to employers. We distinguish between *general* and *specific* human capital: General human capital consists of training and education, that is, equally useful to many different firms; specific human capital is more valuable to the current employer than to alternative employers. In our benchmark model, employees would be expected to pay for their own general training, and employers would pay for specific training.

Our benchmark model does not consider differences in working conditions across jobs. Yet actual jobs vary in many dimensions, such as geographic location and the level of danger. Holding other factors constant, unpleasant jobs must pay a *compensating differential* to attract employees. Compensating differentials attract employees to unpleasant tasks; they also provide employers with direct financial incentives to enhance the work environment whenever it is cost-effective.

In some settings, it can be difficult to tell whether a firm is paying the market wage rate to employees. Important indicators are the application and quit rates and the nature of outside job offers made to existing employees.

Our benchmark model provides a good description of some labor markets, such as the market for unskilled agricultural workers. It is less useful in describing employment and wages in many other cases. Many firms are better characterized as establishing *internal labor markets,* where outside hiring is done primarily for entry-level jobs; most other jobs are filled from within the firm. Internal labor markets are characterized by *long-term relationships* between the employee and the firm. Long-term relationships can be beneficial because they provide both employers and employees incentives to invest in specific training, offer incentives for employees to work to exploit the business opportunities facing the firm, and allow firms to take greater advantage of information about employee attributes. One cost of using internal labor markets is that it sometimes is undesirable to limit the search to the firm's current employees, especially when filling higher-level positions.

Employees accepting jobs with firms that employ internal labor markets evaluate *career earnings.* Thus, firms with internal labor markets have more flexibility in setting the level and career profile of pay. Firms can vary compensation over the career path, so long as the overall remaining stream of earnings is competitive at each point in time relative to the streams offered by other firms within the same labor market. Economists have identified at least three ways in which firms can use their flexibility in setting the level and sequencing of pay to enhance employee motivation. These methods include the payment of *efficiency wages, upward-sloping earnings profiles,* and the tying of major pay increases to *promotions.* However, influence costs can affect the desirability of exploiting this potential flexibility. Firms might reduce the dispersion of pay among coworkers to limit influence costs.

The typical American employee receives about 25 percent of total compensation in the form of *fringe benefits* such as vacation time, insurance coverage, and contributions to retirement plans. Salary and fringe benefits are not perfect substitutes for most employees. Tax benefits and the fact that the company often can purchase fringe benefits more cheaply favor fringe benefits. The desire for flexibility in making purchases can favor cash payments. Employers have incentives to heed the preferences of employees when it comes to the choice between salary and fringe benefits. By responding to their preferences, firms can design compensation packages that attract and retain qualified employees at the lowest cost. Firms sometimes can use the salary–fringe benefit mix to attract particular types of employees. For example, offering liberal insurance coverage is more likely to attract people with families than single individuals, who are more likely to prefer cash payments. Firms also have incentives to heed employee preferences when it comes to choosing the mix of fringe benefits. This incentive has motivated many firms to consider *cafeteria-style* benefits. Use of these plans is limited due to administrative costs and *adverse-selection problems.*

Suggested Readings	M. Aoki (1988), *Information, Incentives, and Bargaining in the Japanese Economy* (Cambridge University Press: Cambridge).
	G. Becker (1983), *Human Capital* (University of Chicago Press: Chicago).
	P. Doeringer and M. Piore (1971), *Internal Labor Markets and Manpower Analysis* (D. C. Heath: Lexington, MA).
	R. Ehrenberg and R. Smith (2015), *Modern Labor Economics: Theory and Public Policy,* 12th edition, (Prentice Hall: Boston), Chapters 8, 9, and 11.

Self-Evaluation Problems

14–1. When Ford purchased Volvo AB's car division in 1999, they had to decide what to do about the differences in the fringe benefits received by the employees. Although Ford plants have fitness centers, these centers do not have the amenities offered at the Volvo plants such as Olympic-size pools, badminton and tennis courts, tanning beds, and saunas. One reason for the high level of fringe benefits at Volvo is the extremely high tax rates in Sweden. Company-supplied services such as plush health facilities are not taxed by the government. However, Ford employees in the United States might be tempted to argue for "perk parity" especially during union contract negotiations.[31]

Suppose UAW negotiations argue for upgraded perquisites for Ford's U.S. employees to match those available in the Swedish plants Ford acquired from Volvo.
   a. Ford might achieve perk parity by upgrading U.S. facilities or by reducing Swedish facilities. What would be the implications of each policy?
   b. Ford might live with different levels of perks. What would be the implications?
   c. Suppose the difference in perks between U.S. and Swedish employees is reduced following the merger. What are the efficiency implications for the merger?

14–2. Consultants often spend much of their time away from home. Deloitte and Touche recently implemented a policy that curbs its consultants' travel time. Instead of spending five days a week at a client's office, consultants spend three nights and four days, fly home, and work a fifth day at their home cities. One observer argued that Deloitte and Touche is putting employee concerns ahead of good business. Deloitte and Touche should focus on company profits, not employee comfort. Do you agree that the firm is necessarily wasting company profits? Explain using concepts from class. In answering this question assume that employees would be more productive if they stayed at the client's office.

Solutions to Self-Evaluation Problems

14–1. Ford and Volvo Perk Parity
   a. If perks are increased by upgrading U.S. facilities (e.g., by adding saunas, etc.) costs will go up. Presumably, Ford was able to hire employees without the perks, and so there is no obvious offsetting benefit to Ford. Reducing the perks in Sweden will lower the pay of employees and make it more difficult to attract and retain employees (unless

---

[31]"Ford sells Volvo to Chinese carmaker Geely for $1.5 billion," *NY Daily News* (August 3, 2010), A. Latour (1999), "Detroit Meets a 'Worker Paradise,'" *The Wall Street Journal* (March 3), B1.

wages are increased). Presumably, the difference in perks between the two countries is driven in part by taxes. Higher taxes in Sweden imply that it is best for companies to pay higher fringe benefits/perks (which are not taxed) than is optimal in the United States. Even if Ford wants to increase pay for U.S. employees, increasing perks is likely to be an inefficient way to do so (they may cost Ford more than the value to the employees). The union understandably is focusing on the difference in perks, not the differences in salaries. International mergers involving companies with optimally different compensation packages often generate these types of internal conflicts.

b. Ford can expect ongoing debates with the labor union over the differences. Also it can make it more difficult for the company to transfer employees between the two countries because of the differences in the pay packages.

c. The result will be inefficient if Ford could design alternative pay package (such as those now in existence) that give the employees the same level of utility at a lower cost.

14–2. Corporate Travel Policy

Many employees do not like to be gone all week from their home (e.g., family concerns, etc.). Employers that demand this behavior will have to pay a compensating differential to attract and retain qualified employees. Reducing the time away from home reduces the compensating differential. The cost savings may be greater than the loss due to the drop in productivity. Thus, profits might increase from this change in policy.

Review Questions

14–1. Explain the following quotation: "My employer doesn't determine my salary; he determines where I work."

14–2. In the basic competitive model, why do employees pay for general training and firms pay for specific training?

14–3. Why do firms form internal labor markets?

14–4. Evaluate the following statement: "Firms are free to set salaries in any manner they want in an internal labor market."

14–5. Present an economic argument to explain why firms often have mandatory retirement (where allowed by law).

14–6. How do influence costs affect pay within internal labor markets?

14–7. The U.S. Congress has considered proposals that would limit the level of top executive pay to some multiple of the lowest-paid employee in the company (e.g., executive pay must be less than 10 times that of the lowest-paid employee). Do you think this type of proposal is a good idea? Explain what effect the proposal would have on the involved companies.

14–8. President Clinton proposed eliminating the tax deduction for all compensation over $1 million for CEOs unless the pay is tied to company performance. Proponents argue that this proposal will benefit shareholders. "Everyone knows that CEOs are overpaid and that their pay is not appropriately tied to performance. This legislation helps solve both problems." Present an argument against this proposal.

14–9. The Brown Tool Company is a multidivisional firm with offices throughout the country. The company sets the salaries of most of its positions at the central level. For example, secretaries are paid $8 per hour throughout the company. Discuss two important reasons why the firm might adopt such a policy. Discuss two important problems that the policy might cause.

14–10. A recent study concluded that many employees fake sickness to avoid going to work. The authors argue that through unwarranted sick leave, employees "steal" about $150 billion a year from firms. This amount is three times larger than the estimated loss from shoplifting. One proposal is for Congress to outlaw the granting of sick leave to employees. The argument is that companies would be much better off because they would not incur the giant losses associated with sick leave. Further, the costs of taking sick leave would be internalized with the employees. Comment on this proposal.

14–11. The University of Rochester used to pay all faculty a 10 percent bonus as a substitute for a retirement plan. Individuals could either place this money in a retirement fund or keep the cash. Placing money in the fund deferred taxes on the income until the point of withdrawal. Changes in the U.S. tax code forced the university to change this policy. In particular, employees cannot be given options of this type but must be either covered or not covered as a group. The university now has the following policy: All new faculty members without prior service at another university are given a 10 percent bonus in cash. This payment is treated as ordinary income for tax purposes. Most new faculty are young people fresh out of graduate school. All faculty members with more than two years of service must place the bonus in a retirement account. Taxes are deferred until withdrawal from the account. Explain why it might make economic sense for the university to have such a two-group plan, rather than treat all employees (old and new) the same.

14–12. The University of Medford pays the full tuition for the children of faculty members at any university in the world. Recently, this policy has received bad publicity. The argument has been made that people in other occupations have to pay the tuition costs for their children and so should college professors. According to this argument, it is not fair to have these relatively well-paid people get subsidized in this manner. The board of trustees of the University of Medford has been asked to reconsider this policy. Provide an economic argument to explain why the board of trustees might want to continue this policy.

14–13. Payments under some retirement plans are based on the average earnings in the last few years of employment. Discuss the potential incentive effects of this policy.

14–14. Companies can often gain if they listen to employees about what they prefer in the way of a fringe benefit package—a more preferred package serves to attract and retain employees at a lower cost. Nevertheless, many firms have shunned "menu plans" where each employee would be completely free to choose their own fringe benefit package. (For instance, those wanting health insurance could buy it through the company, whereas those who want some other benefit or cash would make different choices.) Why do you think many firms have avoided this type of menu plan?

14–15. The Good Beer Brewing Company currently purchases health insurance for its 10,000 employees. The company is considering a flexible plan where employees can have either $2,000 in cash or insurance coverage (the insurance costs $2,000). The company figures it will expend the same amount of money either way. However, employees will be better off because they can choose the option that is most preferred. Do you see any potential problems with this idea? Explain.

14–16. Public accounting firms have traditionally paid low starting salaries to new employees. Nevertheless, these firms have been able to hire and retain qualified employees (even though these employees could obtain higher salaries elsewhere). Is this observation inconsistent with economic theory? Explain.

14–17. People buying disability insurance on an individual basis are often required to take physical exams. Physical exams are typically not required when employees acquire disability insurance through a company-sponsored plan (which covers all employees in the firm). Provide an economic rationale for the different policies relating to physical exams.

14–18. Marks & Spencer is a large, established British retailer of apparel, housewares, and food products. The company has a large workforce. As part of the company's benefits package, employees receive a discount of 30 percent off all purchases of apparel.
   a. What are the advantages and disadvantages of offering a 30 percent discount off company merchandise?
   b. What are the advantages and disadvantages of offering a 30 percent discount off apparel, but not housewares and food products? Why do you think the company differentiates between apparel and other products?

14–19. A recent study found that CEOs in Europe are paid substantially less than CEOs in America, even after controlling for a firm's size and industry. Does this necessarily imply that American CEOs are overpaid? Explain.

14–20. Consider two states that are nearly identical in terms of such factors as income, climate, and population. There are public universities in both states. One state has a law which specifies that all professors of a given rank (assistant, associate, and full professor) have to be paid the same. Thus an assistant professor, whether in history or in law, has to be paid the same. Associate professors are paid more than assistant professors. However, all associate professors have to be paid the same. The same is true for full professors. The other state does not have such a law. In this state, law professors are paid substantially more than history professors within each rank. The laws in both states allow the universities to choose their own teaching loads for faculty. These loads can vary across faculty members.

    a. How do you expect the teaching loads to vary across the two states (you can focus on history and law departments)? Explain the economic reasoning behind your answer.

    b. Are either history or law professors in the state with the law necessarily better or worse off than their counterparts in the state without the law? Explain.

    c. Discuss how the residents of the state might be made worse off by such a law.

14–21. Some companies base promotions solely on seniority. Discuss the negative and positive aspects of such a policy.

14–22. Building on the discussion in Chapter 3 on minimum wage laws, how would you expect a large increase in the minimum wage to affect the pay package (mix between salary and benefits) offered by employers?

Incentive Compensation

LEARNING OBJECTIVES

1. Define the basic incentive problem.
2. Describe optimal risk sharing and how ownership mitigates the incentive problem.
3. List the important trade-offs in effective compensation plans.
4. Explain the basic principle-agent model and the associated list of factors that favor high incentive pay.
5. Define the informativeness principle.
6. Summarize the potential benefits and costs of group incentive compensation plans.
7. Discuss the multitask principal agent problem and its implications.
8. Identify the various forms of incentive pay.
9. Describe how incentive compensation can be used to cause employees to reveal their private information.
10. Discuss the controversy surrounding incentive pay.

In October 1988, DuPont's fibers division announced "one of the most ambitious pay-incentive programs in America."[1] Its plan covered nearly all of the division's 20,000 employees—both management and rank-and-file employees. Under the plan, a portion of employees' pay would be placed into an "at-risk pool." If the business exceeded its profit goals for the year, the employees would receive a multiple of the at-risk monies as a bonus. If not, the employees stood to lose the money in the pool. The intent was eventually to place as much as 6 percent of annual pay at risk. The plan initially was adopted for a three-year trial period. Many companies indicated that they were watching this experiment carefully to see what they could learn about incentive pay. "The attention that the American business community has given to the DuPont program is tremendous," said Robert C. Gore, a vice president at Towers Perrin Company—a major compensation consulting firm.

The largest of DuPont's chemical businesses, the fibers division comprises departments ranging from automobile seat covers to apparel. In 1990,

---

[1]Details of this example are from L. Hays (1988), "All Eyes on DuPont's Incentive Program," *The Wall Street Journal* (December 5), B1; and R. Koening (1990), "DuPont Plan Linking Pay to Fibers Profit Unravels," *The Wall Street Journal* (October 25), B1.

the division had to achieve a target of 4 percent real-earnings growth for its employees to recover their at-risk pay. But profits for the first nine months were off 26 percent, due largely to a poor economy and unexpectedly high input prices. Demand for the division's products had declined substantially due to weak housing and automobile markets, and oil prices had risen materially because of the Gulf War. By fall 1990, it was obvious that the employees were likely to lose all the monies placed in the bonus pool. Employee discontent was quite high: Employees were facing significant financial losses, largely due to factors beyond their control. In October 1990, DuPont precipitously canceled the incentive program with more than a full year left in the trial period. In the words of the fibers division chief, "I have to conclude it was an experiment that didn't work."

Given the widespread interest in this experiment, it is important to understand why the DuPont plan failed. Incentive pay, as some critics claim, simply might be a bad idea. If so, any firm adopting a large-scale incentive plan is making a mistake and should expect to experience a fate similar to DuPont's. Alternatively, the failure of this plan might be traced to basic design flaws that could have been avoided through more careful planning. In this chapter, we examine the economics of incentive compensation. Our analysis suggests that DuPont's failure was due largely to problems with the structure of its plan. Correspondingly, our analysis provides insights into how companies might design more effective compensation plans.

We begin this chapter by providing a more detailed discussion of incentive problems. We then examine how ownership can resolve some of these problems by providing strong incentives for individuals to take efficient actions. Next, we consider a critical limitation of ownership in controlling incentive problems—inefficient risk bearing. We then detail the implications of risk bearing for the design of compensation contracts. Next, we review some of the key insights about incentive compensation contained in the economics literature. We begin by discussing the standard principal-agent model. We then extend this basic analysis by considering the informativeness principle, group incentive pay, multitasking, alternative forms of incentive pay, and the role of incentive pay in the process of matching individuals with jobs. Toward the end of the chapter, we discuss the debate on whether incentive pay works, and we provide a case study on CEO compensation to allow the reader to apply some of the concepts we develop on compensation policy. In the appendix we examine multitasking problems in greater detail.

The Basic Incentive Problem

Incentive problems exist within firms because owners and employees have fundamentally different objectives. For example, the owners of an insurance company want its salespeople to sell insurance policies to customers, but salespeople might prefer to play golf. Similarly, stockholders of a research company want its scientists to develop marketable products, whereas scientists might prefer to work on more intellectually challenging but less marketable ideas. Presumably, employees at DuPont's fibers division have other interests than simply making and selling fibers products.

Consider the example of AssemCo, a small company that assembles components for several large electronics firms. As in most companies, there is a basic conflict between the aims of the owners and the aims of the employees. The owners would like employees to work diligently, but the employees would prefer longer coffee breaks and working at a more leisurely pace.

To add concreteness to our discussion, we focus on the problem of motivating a particular employee at AssemCo, Ian MacLeod. For simplicity, we focus on a given time period (e.g., motivating Ian over a single week). Ian's preferences with respect to income and work are portrayed by the following utility function:[2]

$$U = I - e^2 \qquad (15.1)$$

where I is his income for the period and e is the number of units of effort exerted (e.g., hours spent actually assembling components). This utility function, which measures utility in dollar equivalents, indicates that he is better off as his total income increases but becomes worse off as he exerts more effort on component assembly. As Ian exerts effort, he suffers decreased utility because he would rather engage in other activities. His reservation utility is equivalent to $1,000. AssemCo must meet this level of utility or Ian will not work for the firm.

As Ian exerts more effort, he assembles more units, and this benefits the firm. The benefits to AssemCo from his effort are

$$B = \$100e \qquad (15.2)$$

To begin with a simple case, suppose that his effort is costlessly observable and verifiable—hence, effort is contractible. In this case, the firm offers Ian a compensation contract that would pay him a sum of money if, and only if, he provides a specified level of effort, $\hat{e}$. He will accept this contract, so long as he is paid his reservation-utility. To meet this condition, the firm must pay him a wage of $1,000 + \hat{e}^2$. If he delivers that level of effort and is paid $1,000 + \hat{e}^2$, then his utility is $U = (\$1,000 + \hat{e}^2) - \hat{e}^2 = \$1,000$ and he receives his reservation utility. The profits to the firm π from his efforts are

$$\pi = \$100\hat{e} - (\$1,000 + \hat{e}^2) \qquad (15.3)$$

The firm then chooses the $\hat{e}$ that maximizes the firm's value.

Figure 15.1 provides a graphical illustration of this problem. The figure displays both the benefits to the firm ($100e$) and the costs ($1,000 + e^2$). Profits are the difference between the two. As the figure indicates, maximum profits occur at $e^* = 50$. At this effort level, Ian is paid $3,500 and the profits for AssemCo are $1,500. This outcome is the efficient bargaining solution. Ian is indifferent among the feasible effort choices—he is paid his reservation wage in all cases—and the firm's profits are maximized at 50. The firm could induce him to provide additional effort by paying him more. However, the additional costs to the firm would exceed the incremental benefits. At the optimal effort level of $e^* = 50$, the marginal costs of effort are equal to the marginal benefits; hence relevant benefits and costs to both parties are considered.[3]

Thus far, we have assumed that Ian's effort is costlessly observable. But this is rarely the case. Effort normally is observable neither by the firm nor by a court of law—effort is not contractible. In addition, the firm is unlikely to be able to tell whether Ian worked hard simply by observing his output. Sometimes, output is

---

[2]We chose this particular utility function (as well as the firm's benefit function, discussed below) to simplify the calculations. Our basic results, however, are quite general and are not specialized to this particular example.

[3]Technical note: Recall that the marginal benefit at a point is equal to the slope of the total benefit at that point. The same relation holds between marginal cost and total cost. Using elementary calculus, the slope of the total cost curve is $2e$, whereas the slope of the total benefit curve is 100. The optimal effort level is where they are equal or $2e = 100$; thus $e^* = 50$.

Figure 15.1   The Optimal Effort Choice at AssemCo

This figure pictures both the benefits and the costs to AssemCo from the efforts of a given employee, Ian MacLeod. Profits are the difference between the two. Maximum profits occur at $e^* = 50$. This example assumes that Ian will exert the agreed-upon effort as long as he is paid his reservation utility. To meet this constraint, the firm must pay a wage of $1,000 + e^2$. This payment meets Ian's reservation wage of $1,000 and reimburses him for his disutility of effort. Benefits to the firm are $100e$. At the optimal effort level, $e^* = 50$, $5,000 in gross benefits are generated. Ian is paid $3,500 and the firm's profits are $1,500. The firm could induce Ian to exert more effort by paying him more. However, the costs are larger than the benefits. The effort choice of 50 is efficient. Ian is indifferent among the possible choices (since he is paid his reservation utility in each case), and the profits for the firm are maximized at this level.

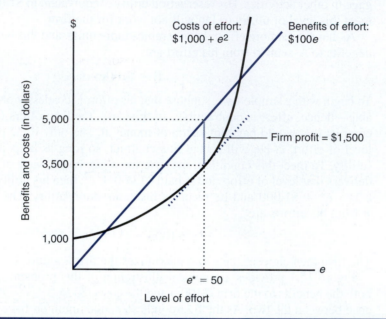

difficult to measure and is affected by factors beyond the employee's control.[4] In this case, there is a standard incentive problem. If Ian promises to provide 50 units of effort and is paid a fixed salary of $3,500, he has the incentive to renege on his promise and provide less effort. He gets paid anyway and benefits from exerting less effort. The firm might suspect that Ian did not work hard. However, it would not know for sure. In this case, a straight salary of $3,500 fails to provide Ian with appropriate incentives. Rather, AssemCo must devise some other type of contract that motivates him to provide additional effort.

This simple example illustrates three important points about incentive problems:

- If the interests of employees and employers were aligned perfectly, there would be no reason to worry about incentives. Incentive problems exist basically because of conflicts of interest between employers and employees.

---

[4]In our simplified example, the firm can infer e from observing Q, Ian's output. More generally, Q would be affected by factors that are beyond the control of the employee. For example, the following relation might hold: $Q = \$100e + \mu$, where μ is a random error. Random factors that might affect his output include the quality of raw materials and equipment failures. With the random error term, the firm cannot infer e simply from observing Q.

- Incentive conflicts do not cause problems when actions are contractible. Firms can identify the most efficient actions and pay employees only if those actions are taken. For instance, if the actions of employees at DuPont were costlessly observable, there would be no reason for the firm to adopt a profit-based plan for employees. Rather, the employees could be motivated appropriately by contracts based directly on their actions.

- In choosing the optimal action, there is a trade-off between the benefits of the action for the firm and the personal costs borne by the employees. In a competitive labor market, employees must be compensated for undertaking undesirable actions—there are compensating differentials. It normally is not sensible to have employees work as hard as physically possible.

Incentives from Ownership

In special cases, there is a simple way to resolve incentive problems, even when the actions of employees are unobservable. This solution is to sell each employee the rights to his or her total output. The incentive problem is caused by the fact that most of the costs of exerting effort are borne by employees, while much of the gains go to the owners. By selling employees their output, both the benefits and costs of exerting effort are internalized by employees and thus employees will make more productive choices. For instance, in our AssemCo example, the firm could sell Ian the rights to the value of his output ($100e) for a price of $1,500. AssemCo makes the same profits as when effort was costlessly observable. Ian's objective, in turn, is to maximize his personal utility given by

$$U = (\$100e - \$1,500) - e^2 \qquad (15.4)$$

where the first term represents the income from exerting effort (the value of the output minus the $1,500 payment to the company) and the second term represents the disutility of effort. Given this problem, Ian will choose to exert 50 units of effort and will have utility of $1,000.[5] This outcome is the same as in the perfect information case. It is achieved even though the employer cannot observe Ian's effort.

This discussion highlights the strong incentive effects that come from ownership. In practice, ownership often is used as an incentive mechanism. For example, a majority of the businesses in the United States are private. Moreover, the last 30 years have witnessed a large number of managerial buyouts of public firms and divisions of public firms, where the managers went from the status of employees to owners. Although some aspects of these buyouts might be controversial, the evidence indicates that the managers have operated the units more efficiently after they became owners.[6] Furthermore, about one-third of all retail sales in the United States are made through franchised outlets (including car dealers and gas stations). In franchising, the future profits of each unit are sold to franchisees, who as owners have strong incentives to maximize value.[7]

---

[5]Technical note: This solution can be found using elementary calculus (see footnote 3) or a graphical analysis, as in Figure 15.1. We present a more detailed analysis of the employee's effort choice later in this chapter.

[6]S. Kaplan (1989), "The Effects of Management Buyouts on Operating Performance and Value," *Journal of Financial Economics* 24, 217–254.

[7]J. Brickley and F. Dark (1987), "The Choice of Organizational Form: The Case of Franchising," *Journal of Financial Economics* 18, 401–420. In many franchise agreements, the central company receives an ongoing sales royalty from the franchisee. This royalty provides incentives to the central company to honor commitments on training and promoting the brand name. The franchisee's claim on future profits is typically limited to some time period—for example, 20 years. The contract often is renewable.

At least three important factors limit the use of ownership in resolving incentive problems:

- **Wealth Constraints.** Limited wealth can make the ownership solution infeasible. For instance, although senior managers at DuPont might have stronger incentives if they owned the company, few management groups have access to sufficient capital to finance this purchase.

- **Risk Aversion.** Typically, employees do not have full control over their outputs. Rather, output depends on random outside events in addition to employee efforts. For example, DuPont's profits are affected by changes in the oil, housing, and automobile markets. In making employees fully accountable for their actions, ownership also exposes them to random events that affect their output but are beyond their control. Given that employees do not like to bear risk, employee ownership entails a risk-bearing cost (see Chapter 2). As we discuss below, this cost must be considered in designing incentive contracts.

- **Team Production.** In most firms, there are production synergies; total output is greater than the sum of what each employee could produce individually. Identifying the separate contributions when there is this type of team production is problematic. Even if the firm were owned jointly by the employees, it would not solve this basic incentive problem—there still would be the free-rider problem discussed in Chapter 10.

Optimal Risk Sharing

To illustrate some of the basic principles of efficient risk sharing, consider an example, Abby Ross receives a monthly income from a trust fund. Depending on the performance of the fund, this income can be either $0 or $10,000, each with a probability of .5. Abby's expected income is $5,000.[8] However, the income stream is risky—half the time, Abby gets $0. Jess Rogers also has a trust fund with the same income possibilities. Half the time he gets $0; the other half, $10,000. The income flows for Abby and Jess are *independent*. (That is, regardless of the outcome for Abby, the probability is still .5 that Jess will get $0.)[9] The left column of Table 15.1 displays the joint distribution of outcomes for Abby and Jess.[10] The probability of each outcome is given in the middle column.

Assuming that Abby and Jess are *risk-averse* (holding expected income constant, the person prefers less dispersion in outcomes), they both can be made better off by agreeing to split their combined incomes. The possible payoffs for each individual are given in the right column of Table 15.1. The expected income per individual is still $5,000. By sharing the risks, however, the variability of their individual incomes has been reduced. The variability is reduced because the likelihood that both Jess and Abby will be lucky or unlucky is less than the likelihood that only one of them is

---

[8]The expected income is the *average* amount that Abby will receive in a month. It is calculated by adding together each possible income multiplied by the respective probability: ($10,000 × .5) + ($0 × .5) = $5,000.

[9]We assume that the flows are independent to simplify the calculations in the example. The basic insights of this analysis hold as long as the two flows are not perfectly positively correlated.

[10]A joint outcome ($X, $Y) refers to Abby receiving X dollars while Jess receives Y dollars. Since the events are independent, the probability of any joint outcome is the probability of the first event (that Abby receives $X) multiplied by the probability of the second event (that Jess receives $Y). For example, the probability that both will receive $0 is .5 × .5 = .25.

Joint Outcomes	Probability	Individual Payoffs from Splitting
($0;$0)	.25	$ 0
($0;$10,000)	.25	5,000
($10,000;$0)	.25	5,000
($10,000;$10,000)	.25	10,000
		E(Income) = $ 5,000

Table 15.1 Example of Risk Sharing

In this example, two people receive incomes from different trust funds. Each fund pays either $0 or $10,000, each with a probability of .5. The two funds have independent payoffs. The left column displays the possible joint payoff outcomes, and the middle column shows the probability of each outcome occurring. For instance, ($0;$0) is the outcome where both funds pay $0 for the period. The probability of this outcome is .25. The right column shows the individual incomes if the two people agree to split the payoffs from the two funds. Splitting the payoffs makes both better off, compared to relying solely on the payoffs from their individual funds. The expected income in either case is $5,000. However, risk is reduced by the pooling of the funds. For instance, each person has a .5 chance of receiving no income when keeping all the income from his or her own fund. The two people only have a .25 chance of receiving no income when they pool the funds.

lucky. For example, by sharing the risks, the probability of getting nothing is only .25, compared to .5 with no risk sharing. Being risk-averse, they prefer the less volatile income stream. (Ideally, they would like income streams that are certain.) It is this reduction in volatility from pooling risks that drives individuals to purchase insurance, as well as to invest in diversified portfolios—for example, mutual funds.

People often differ in their attitudes toward risk. Some people are more willing to tolerate large financial risks, whereas others are not. An efficient allocation of risk takes these differences in preference into account. For example, suppose that Jess is *risk-neutral,* whereas Abby is risk-averse. (A risk-neutral person cares only about the expected payoff and does not care about the dispersion in potential values around that expected value.) Jess will value each of the two random income flows at $5,000 (the expected value), whereas Abby will not. For example, Abby might be willing to accept a certain payment of $4,000 for her risky income flow. Here, there are gains from trade by having Jess buy Abby's income. A payment of $4,500 would split the potential gains of trade between the two parties. Each party would be better off by $500.

The common stock of large corporations typically is owned by many investors, each holding well-diversified portfolios. Because of this diversification, investors are less concerned about the fortunes of any one company. (Things that are specific to individual firms tend to average out over their entire portfolios; i.e., one firm is lucky, whereas another firm is unlucky.)[11] Employees, in contrast, receive large fractions of their incomes from their individual employers (each generally has but one job), and thus they care greatly about the fortunes of individual firms. This difference in outlook simply reflects the fact that employees of a firm have less effective methods to manage firm-specific risk than the firm's shareholders. (We are not saying that

[11]For example, H. Markowitz (1959), *Portfolio Selection* (John Wiley & Sons: New York); and W. Sharpe (1964), "Capital Asset Prices: A Theory of Market Equilibrium under Conditions of Risk," *Journal of Finance* 19, 179–211.

employees have different preferences than owners; rather, it is their ability to manage risk through well-diversified portfolios that makes shareholders in large corporations more willing to bear such risk.)

Assuming that the shareholders of the firm can manage firm-specific risks more effectively than employees, they will be willing to bear these risks at a lower price. Thus, it is better from a risk-sharing standpoint to pay employees fixed salaries and let the total risk of random income flows be borne by the shareholders. By paying fixed salaries, the firm avoids having to pay a compensating differential for risk bearing to attract and retain the desired workforce.

Effective Incentive Contracts

> **Basic Principle**
>
> Important trade-offs exist between incentives and risk sharing.

Our discussion to this point suggests that compensation contracts serve at least two important functions. First, they are used to motivate employees. Second, they are used to share risk more efficiently. Unfortunately, there is a trade-off between these two objectives. Efficient risk sharing suggests that it is better to pay employees fixed salaries, while incentive considerations suggest that it is better to tie pay to performance. An effective compensation contract strikes an appropriate balance between these two considerations.

- When the owners of a firm have a comparative advantage in bearing firm-specific risks, it is better from a *risk-sharing standpoint* to offer employees more fixed salaries and let more of the risk of random income flows be borne by owners (e.g., shareholders in large corporations).

- Fixed salaries do not provide strong incentives. Incentives are provided by basing pay on performance.

- The previous two points indicate that there is a trade-off between paying incentive compensation to increase effort and the associated costs of inefficient risk bearing. Often, an effective contract consists of a fixed salary and one or more variable components based on performance.

Economists have devoted substantial effort to studying how to design effective compensation contracts. In this section, we summarize some of the more important findings from this research. We begin with the most basic model in the economics literature, the standard principal-agent model. This model considers a contracting situation that closely resembles our example of Ian MacLeod of AssemCo. However, the model generalizes this example and focuses on choosing the optimal contract when the employer cannot observe the employee's effort. Following the introduction of the basic model, we extend the analysis by considering the informativeness principle, group incentive pay, multitasking, types of incentive pay, and the role of incentive pay in self-selection.

Principal-Agent Model

The Basic Model

Economic analysis of incentive compensation begins with the basic principal-agent model.[12] This model presents a relatively simple characterization of the contracting

---

[12]One of the first presentations of this model is B. Holmstrom (1979), "Moral Hazard and Observability," *Bell Journal of Economics* 10, 74–91.

process, illustrates the trade-offs between risk sharing and incentives, and provides a number of useful insights for designing more effective compensation plans. In this single-period model, there is an employer (the principal) who wants the employee (the agent) to work on the employer's behalf. The employer is risk-neutral, while the employee is risk-averse. The most basic analysis focuses on an individual employee. Concerns about teamwork do not arise within the basic model.

Consider the example of Erica Olsson of a biotech firm, DNAcorp. Erica's output Q is a function of her effort, plus some random effect, μ (with expected value 0 and variance, σ^2):

$$Q = \alpha e + \mu \tag{15.5}$$

where output is defined as the market value of her production. The model does not consider the possibility that Erica might manipulate the observed output level (e.g., by "cooking the books"). Both Erica and her supervisor, Jon Chang, can observe her output.

If Erica increases effort by one unit, output goes up by α dollars. Thus, α is Erica's marginal productivity—the higher the α, the higher her marginal productivity. The random effect μ reflects factors that can affect output but are beyond Erica's control (e.g., equipment failures). The higher σ^2, the more likely it is that the output will experience larger random shocks.

Optimal risk sharing suggests that there are benefits from having the owners of the DNAcorp bear the output risk and pay Erica a fixed salary. For example, Erica might agree to put forth effort level $\hat{e}$ and be paid a fixed salary W for this effort. The owners of DNAcorp receive the difference between the value of the output and W.

$$\text{Owners' profits} = (\alpha \hat{e} + \mu) - W \tag{15.6}$$

There is, however, an incentive problem with this arrangement if Erica's supervisor can observe neither her effort level nor μ, the random shock. Erica has the incentive to agree to $\hat{e}$ as an effort level but then to exert less effort. Jon will tend to observe lower output when she shirks. However, Erica always can claim that her low output was due to bad luck—that is, μ was negative.

Employee's Effort Problem

Incentives can be provided to Erica by basing part of her compensation on realized output. For example, consider Erica's incentives under the following contract:

$$\text{Compensation} = W_0 + \beta Q \tag{15.7}$$

where $0 \leq \beta \leq 1$. This contract pays Erica a fixed wage W_0, plus a proportion β of the output Q.[13] To illustrate Erica's effort choice, suppose $W_0 = \$1,000$, $\beta = .2$, $Q = \$100e + \mu$, and $C(e) = e^2$, where $C(e)$ is Erica's cost of effort in dollar equivalents. Given these values, the compensation contract is

$$\text{Compensation} = \$1,000 + .2(\$100e + \mu) \tag{15.8}$$

---

[13]For simplicity, we restrict our attention to linear compensation contracts. One justification for focusing on linear contracts is that in practice they are observed commonly. For instance, salespeople and real estate agents often are paid commissions, while factory employees frequently are paid piece rates. Linear contracts have the advantage of providing consistent incentives to the employee that do not depend on past output (the marginal payoff for increasing output by one unit is constant). In contrast, lump-sum bonuses that are paid once some threshold is reached lose their incentive effects once the target is met. For a technical justification for linear contracts, see B. Holmstrom and P. Milgrom (1987), "Aggregation and Linearity in the Provision of Intertemporal Incentives," *Econometrica* 55, 303–328.

Figure 15.2   The Employee's Effort Choice

This figure shows how the compensation and personal costs increase as the employee exerts more effort. The compensation function is $1,000 + $20e. The employee's cost function is e^2. The objective of the employee is to choose the effort level that maximizes the net benefits. This maximization occurs at $e^* = 10$. At this point, the marginal benefits of effort ($20) are equal to the marginal costs. The employee's expected compensation is $1,200.

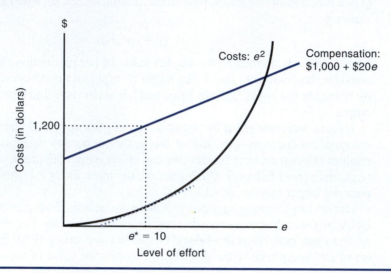

The benefit to Erica from exerting effort is that it increases compensation—each unit of effort increases her compensation by $20 (.2 × $100). Random shocks μ affect total compensation but do not affect the benefits of exerting effort. For any realization of μ, compensation is always $20 higher for every extra unit of effort provided. Thus, in choosing the optimal effort level, Erica can ignore μ. (It does not affect the costs or benefits of her effort.)[14] Erica's cost from exerting effort is e^2. Her objective is to choose the effort level that maximizes her net benefits.

Figure 15.2 depicts how Erica's compensation and personal costs increase as she exerts more effort. As shown in the figure, the optimal effort choice is 10. Note that this figure displays Erica's total costs and benefits. Her marginal benefits and marginal costs at any effort level are equal to the slopes of the total curves at that point. The difference between total costs and benefits is greatest when the slopes of the total curves are equal. Thus, at the optimal choice ($e^* = 10$), the marginal costs of effort are equal to the marginal benefits, and net benefits are maximized. If Erica exerts more than 10 units of effort, the extra income is insufficient to compensate her for the extra disutility she experiences from exerting more effort. When e is less than 10, Erica is made better off by exerting more effort, since the additional compensation is more than sufficient to cover the added costs of her additional effort.

---

[14]Technical note: Throughout our analysis, we assume that Erica's attitude toward risk does not change with her level of wealth. Relaxing this assumption means that she will consider an additional effect in choosing the effort level. In particular, the effort choice will affect her utility by altering the costs imposed on her from bearing risk. We ignore this potential effect because it complicates the analysis without providing substantially more insights.

Figure 15.3 How the Employee's Effort Choice Changes with Changes in the Fixed Wage and Incentive Coefficient

The initial contract is Compensation = $1,000 + .2($100e). The picture shows that increasing the fixed wage from $1,000 to $2,000 causes a parallel shift in the compensation function but does not alter the optimal effort choice (it stays at 10). Changing the incentive coefficient β from .2 to .3 changes the slope of the line and increases the optimal amount of effort to 15.

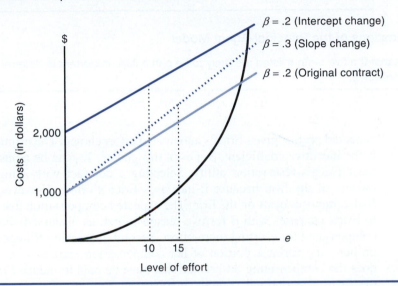

Figure 15.3 depicts how Erica's effort choice changes with changes in the fixed wage W_0 and the incentive coefficient β. Changing the fixed wage from $1,000 to $2,000 results in a parallel shift in compensation, but Erica still chooses $e^* = 10$.[15] The higher fixed wage *provides no incentives* for her to work harder since it does not affect the *marginal benefits* of effort. Marginal benefits are $20, regardless of the fixed wage. In contrast, when the incentive coefficient is increased, Erica selects a higher effort level. For instance, with $\beta = .3$, Erica selects 15 units of effort. In this case, marginal benefits increase to $30 and she exerts more effort.

The implications of this analysis should be contrasted with the common argument that well-paid employees work harder because they are happier on the job. In our analysis, higher pay does not provide incentives unless it is tied to good performance. It is important to note that our analysis focuses on a single time period. In a multi-period setting, a high level of pay can motivate employees if the *likelihood of being fired is contingent on performance*. (See the discussion in Chapter 14 on efficiency wages—in this case, the threat of dismissal effectively ties pay to performance.) But high pay and guaranteed tenure with the firm would provide no incentive effects.

The Optimal Contract

We have shown how Erica will choose effort under different compensation contracts. The firm's problem is to choose the specific compensation contract that maximizes

---

[15]We assume that the additional wage does not change Erica's trade-off between income and leisure.

Factors That Favor High Incentive Pay

---

1. The value of output is sensitive to the employee's effort.
2. The employee is not very risk-averse.
3. The level of risk, that is, beyond the employee's control is low.
4. The employee's response to increased incentives is high (the employee exerts substantially more effort).
5. The employee's output can be measured at low cost.

Table 15.2   Implications of the Principal-Agent Model

The model suggests that the five factors listed are likely to be particularly important in determining how strongly to base pay on performance.

---

expected profits, given Erica's anticipated effort choice. The primary choice variable is the incentive coefficient, β. Given this choice, W_0 can be adjusted up or down to meet Erica's reservation utility. Selecting a contract with a high β, benefits the owners of the firm because it increases Erica's effort. However, choosing a high β also imposes costs on the firm. The expected compensation that the firm must pay to Erica increases with β for two reasons. First, as discussed above, Erica must be compensated for exerting more effort. Second, increasing β imposes additional risk on her—the variable portion of her compensation increases. As risk increases, so does the compensating differential that must be paid to induce Erica to remain with the firm. The optimal contract involves an appropriate balancing of these costs and benefits.

Implications

Employees normally are offered an incentive contract that implies less effort than would be required if the employer could costlessly observe the effort choices. When effort is unobservable, the employer could elicit $\hat{e}$ by paying sufficiently high incentive pay. But with high incentive pay, the employee is forced to bear more risk. And we know that risk-averse employees must be compensated for bearing risk. In designing incentive contracts, the employer must balance the additional output from the higher effort that incentive contracts induce against the larger compensating differential for risk bearing. Hence, compensation contracts that have high levels of incentive pay to induce the agent to exert the effort level that maximizes firm value when effort is observable ($\hat{e}$) are likely undesirable after taking into consideration the additional risk premium required to compensate the employee for bearing so much risk.[16]

Our analysis suggests five factors that are likely to be important in selecting how strongly pay should be tied to performance. These factors are summarized in Table 15.2. The first factor is the sensitivity of the value of the output to additional effort from the employee. In our example, this factor is captured by α—Erica's marginal productivity. A high α implies that incentive pay (holding other factors

---

[16]The basic model assumes that the employer has the relevant knowledge to solve this problem, including knowledge of the production function, the employee's utility function, and the variance of the random error term. For a mathematical derivation of the results in this section, see Chapter 7 of P. Milgrom and J. Roberts (1992), *Economics, Organization, and Management* (Prentice Hall: Englewood Cliffs).

Using Incentive Pay

A study of 64,174 individual workers in 369 Finnish metal firms finds that piece-rate-based pay schemes are mostly used in small firms and in less complex tasks. Piece rates are usually adopted where the worker's output is easily observable, and hence where monitoring costs are low. The decision to adopt piece rates is also used to attract high-ability workers, and workers more willing to exert high effort. The study further reports that employees paid via piece rates earn much higher wages than the workers paid under fixed rates. Finally, when workers change from fixed-rate contracts to piece-rate contracts, they work for more hours.

Source: T. Pekkarineny and C. Riddell (2008), "The impact of piece rate contracts on wages and worker effort: Evidence from linked employer-employee data," *ILR Review* (April), 297–319.

constant) is effective because the benefits of motivating effort are high. A second factor is the risk aversion of the employee. Higher risk aversion implies a higher cost from inefficient risk bearing and thus reduces the use of incentive pay. The third factor is the level of risk, that is, beyond the employee's control (σ^2). When the level of risk is low, output is determined primarily by the employee's effort and it makes sense to pay higher levels of incentive compensation. But when this risk is high, incentive compensation imposes high costs for inefficient risk bearing. The fourth factor is how much additional effort the employee exerts as incentives are increased. If the employee is unresponsive to increased incentives, high incentive compensation imposes more risk on the employee while inducing little additional effort. Thus, there is less reason to provide high incentive pay. The responsiveness to incentive pay depends on the personal costs to the employee for exerting additional effort. For instance, changing the cost function in Figure 15.3 from e^2 to e^3 would make Erica less responsive to changes in incentives. With the original cost function, Erica increases effort by 5 units as β is increased from .2 to .3. But the increase is only .58 under the second cost function.[17] Finally, our analysis presumes that Erica's output can be observed costlessly. This is not always the case. The more expensive it is to measure her output, the less likely that she will be offered incentive pay. We discuss these measurement cost issues further in the next chapter.

DuPont Revisited

The principal-agent model suggests at least two problems with the DuPont plan. Both problems stem from using divisional profits as an output measure. First, under the plan, individuals bear the full costs of their own effort but realize only a small fraction of the output of their effort—it is shared with 19,999 other employees (β is quite small for individual employees). The limited incentives are due to the basic *free-rider problem* discussed in Chapter 10. We discuss this issue in greater detail later in this chapter under the topic of group incentives. The second problem is that divisional profits are affected by many random factors (σ^2 is high), as well as the effects of other employees throughout the division. Thus the compensation plan imposes substantial uncontrollable risk on the employees. DuPont would have provided more effective incentives if it had paid the employees based on disaggregated output measures over which they had greater control—in the limit, their own output.

---

[17]Technical note: It is the second derivative of the cost function, that is, important in determining the response rate: Larger second derivatives (or equivalently steeper marginal cost curves) translate into lower response rates.

Informativeness Principle[18]

Basic Principle:
Informativeness Principle

In designing compensation contracts, theory suggests that it is productive to include all performance indicators that provide additional information about the employee's effort (assuming the measures are available at low cost). Measuring the employee's effort with more precision reduces the costs of inefficient risk bearing and leads to a more efficient effort choice.

As we have seen, incentive problems exist because of imperfect information. If the actions of employees were observable at zero cost, it would be easy to write contracts to motivate appropriate behavior. It follows that the inefficiencies that result from incentive problems can be reduced by improvements in information. The standard principal-agent model assumes that there is only one indicator of an employee's effort, the employee's output. In many cases there are other sources of information that can be used to determine whether or not the employee worked hard. For instance, DuPont was able to tell that the decline in profits in 1990 was not due entirely to a lack of effort on the part of divisional employees by observing the increase in the price of oil and the performance of other companies as well as by gathering information such as government reports on general business conditions. Appropriate use of this type of information increases the precision by which employee effort is measured and, when included in the compensation contract (with the appropriate weights), reduces the costs of inefficient risk bearing. In theory, it is optimal to include all indicators that provide additional information about the employee's effort in the compensation contract—assuming the measures are available at low cost.[19] This basic idea is called the *informativeness principle*.

One important source of information about an employee's effort level is the output of coworkers performing similar tasks. For instance, if a salesperson's performance is poor in a given year, was the person unlucky or lazy? If average sales in the company declined substantially over the same time period, it is more likely that the employee was simply unlucky. If other salespeople had great years, the salesperson is more likely to have been lazy. The informativeness principle implies that information about other employees' sales should be included in the compensation contract as a benchmark—that is, the firm should employ a *relative performance contract*. Chapter 16 provides an extended discussion of relative performance evaluation and highlights several potential problems that can make relative performance evaluation undesirable.

The informativeness principle indicates that it typically is beneficial to include low-cost indicators in the compensation contract that improve the employee's performance measure. It also can be desirable for the firm to expend additional resources on developing even more precise measures of performance. Here, there is a trade-off between the costs of developing as well as implementing better performance measures and the benefits of improved effort motivation and more effective risk sharing.

The informativeness principle suggests that DuPont could have reduced the risk imposed on the employees by including other indicators in the contract. For instance, rather than use an absolute performance standard (such as 4 percent real earnings growth), the target could have been set relative to the growth of other firms in the

---

[18]Material in this section draws on B. Holmstrom (1982), "Moral Hazard in Teams," *Bell Journal of Economics* 13, 324–340.

[19]It is important to consider how simple or complex this relation is. To motivate employees, they have to understand the relation between their actions and their payoffs. If the plan gets so complicated that this link is broken, a simpler plan may be more effective.

ANALYZING MANAGERIAL DECISIONS: *Granting Stock Options*

Bobby's Burgers is a large restaurant chain with nearly 10,000 units worldwide. It is experiencing incentive problems among its outlet managers. The managers are not working very hard and are letting quality deteriorate at their units. CEO, Bobby Jones, is considering a stock plan where each unit manager would be given 500 shares of stock in Bobby's Burgers. He reasons that making the managers part owners of the company will motivate better service.

1. Critically evaluate the proposed stock plan.
2. Discuss other ways that Bobby Jones might motivate increased effort at the units.

same industry. This type of contract might have avoided some of the problems that the company faced in 1990, when employees were likely to lose money under the plan due to circumstances beyond their control.

The informativeness principle also suggests that DuPont could have reduced the uncontrollable risk imposed on its employees by adjusting earnings to reflect external changes in market conditions. For example, the company could have adjusted division profits for the change in oil prices from the first Gulf War. In fact, the firm might want to enter financial contracts (e.g., futures, forwards, swaps, or options) to transfer this risk from the fibers division to external markets to reduce the risk imposed on the division's employees and hence the required compensating differentials in their compensation packages.[20]

Group Incentive Pay

In the basic principal-agent model, employees are motivated by being paid based on their *own output*. Many firms, however, base incentive pay on *group performance*—DuPont is an example. In one study, 78 percent of responding companies offered nonexecutive employees performance-related pay in addition to base pay, and 28 percent of firms provided stock options to nonexecutives.[21] This group pay can take a variety of forms: Payoffs can be linked to the performance of the team, business unit, or the firm as a whole; and performance can be measured by stock prices, accounting earnings, or other more focused measures. (See Chapter 17 for a more extensive discussion of group performance measures.)

There are several reasons why firms might favor group incentive plans over individual plans:

- Individual performance generally is difficult to measure, while the performance of a group of employees often can be measured at reasonably low cost. For example, most firms' cost accounting systems measure the performance of business units for control purposes. Hence, at little additional cost these measures also can be used in administering compensation plans. However, further disaggregation—in the limit, providing a personalized measure of the performance of each employee—would be much more difficult and expensive.

---

[20]C. Smith (1995), "Corporate Risk Management: Theory and Practice," *Journal of Derivatives* 2, 21–30.

[21](2005), "Hewitt Study Shows Base Pay Increases Flat for 2006 With Variable Pay Plans Picking Up the Slack" *Business Wire* (August 31).

- Group pay encourages cooperation and teamwork, whereas some individual incentive plans (depending on design) motivate more self-centered actions.

- Group plans can motivate employees to monitor each other for poor performance. Mutual monitoring is beneficial because the specific knowledge about individual performance often is held by teammates.

- Group pay often is structured to help retain valued workers. Normally, it must be forfeited if the employee quits. Although employees must be compensated for this loss of flexibility, there can be important benefits of increased expected tenure; for example, it raises the expected payoffs of making certain firm-specific investments.

- Finally, if the demand for employees' labor services by competitors is positively correlated with their group's success, then using group incentive pay can help adjust compensation automatically to reflect changes in employees' opportunity costs. This can reduce contracting costs.[22]

Nonetheless, standard free-rider arguments provide a strong reason to question whether group plans provide effective incentives, particularly when the group is quite large. In DuPont's fibers division, with its 20,000 employees, contributions of individual employees have little discernible effect on the overall bottom line (profits are an incredibly noisy measure of any individual employee's output). Also individual employees receive only a small fraction of the value each creates (it is shared with 19,999 other divisional employees as well as senior DuPont executives and the owners of the firm). Thus, profit-sharing plans would appear to produce limited incentive effects. Yet this is not surprising. Should one really expect that paying a janitor on overall company performance would motivate that person to push the broom harder or to complain when other janitors shirk on their jobs?[23] These arguments suggest that large-group incentive plans (like DuPont's) impose risk on employees but produce limited benefits.

Although many economists find the free-rider arguments to be quite compelling, there are some offsetting considerations that potentially help explain the widespread popularity of group plans—despite the fact that free-riding is a problem. First, deferred compensation in the form of stock options or restricted stock makes it expensive for employees to leave and thus helps the firm retain employees. This will be especially effective when labor market conditions and stock prices are positively correlated. In this case, their plans index the employees' deferred compensation to their outside opportunities.[24] Second, it might be beneficial to increase the awareness of employees about the stock-price performance and profitability of the company. By focusing on these measures, employees learn how managerial and employee actions affect the bottom line. For instance, employees might be less likely to complain about a corporate restructuring when they see that it increases the firm's stock price. Indeed, it probably takes little stock ownership to motivate most employees to monitor the stock price on a frequent basis. Hence, these benefits can be obtained while shifting little risk to the employees. Third, employees might be less likely to take actions that harm other members of a group with whom they identify closely. Thus,

---

[22]P. Oyer (2004), "Why Do Firms Use Incentives That Have No Incentive Effects," *Journal of Finance* 59:4, 1619–1649.

[23]This example was suggested by K. J. Murphy.

[24]P. Oyer and S. Schaefer (2005), "Why Do Some Firms Give Options to All Employees? An Empirical Examination of Alternative Theories," *Journal of Financial Economics* 76, 49–133.

MANAGERIAL APPLICATIONS

Red Envelopes, Gold Stars, and Mugs

Many companies have formal recognition programs to praise employees who do an outstanding job on a special project or just to say thank you. Cheryl Quinn at Xerox received a red envelope with a $100 dinner certificate for providing some data for a senior manager's special project that was outside of Quinn's job description. Everyone in her department saw the red envelope being delivered to Quinn and knew it signified that she was being recognized for her performance. In fact there is a "recognition industry" that sells companies certificates, lapel pins, plaques, medallions, mugs, candles, key chains, and feel-good toys like the "Squeezable Praise" (a pocket-sized foam toy that says "way to glow"). Clearly, employees like praise and recognition. However, compensation consultants offer several warnings about such recognition programs. Don't hand out mugs to employees who have landed million-dollar contracts. It's demeaning. Don't pit employees against each other to see who can get the most recognition mugs. And most important, a plaque or certificate does not substitute for a good salary or benefits.

Source: R. Flanigan (2002), "Will Work for Praise," *Rochester Democrat and Chronicle* (November 4), E1.

when the group receives incentive pay, employees might not want to harm teammates by shirking on the job. In this case, attempting to avoid feelings like guilt or shame might motivate employees, even if they face limited direct financial consequences from shirking.[25] Fourth, paying employees on stock-price performance and profits sends signals to employees about what is valued within the company. These signals serve to reinforce a performance-based corporate culture. To be most effective, however, they must be complemented by other features of organizational architecture that provide more direct incentives.

Multitasking[26]

In the standard principal-agent model, effort is one-dimensional—the firm cares only about how hard the employee works. But most jobs involve a variety of tasks. For instance, employees on an assembly line can spend time increasing output, improving quality, performing preventative maintenance, or helping teammates. Similarly, professors at universities allocate their time among teaching, research, consulting, and administrative duties. Thus, managers usually have to be concerned not only with how hard employees work but also with how they allocate their time among assigned tasks; university officials are not indifferent to how professors allocate their time.

Motivating an employee to strike the appropriate balance among tasks is not easy. A complicating factor is that in some tasks, effort is more easily monitored and output more easily measured than in others. For instance, university officials can observe teaching ratings, whereas the quality of administrative service is harder to measure. Compensating employees based on what is measurable encourages them to exert effort on the compensated tasks but to shirk on the others. For example, paying professors based solely on teaching ratings would encourage effort on teaching at the expense of administrative service and research. Similarly, paying an assembler based on output would encourage the employee to produce more units but to ignore quality

[25]E. Kandel and E. Lazear (1992), "Peer Pressure and Partnership," *Journal of Political Economy* 100, 801–817.

[26]This section draws on B. Holmstrom and P. Milgrom (1991), "Multitask Principal-Agent Analysis: Incentive Contracts, Asset Ownership, and Job Design," *Journal of Law, Economics and Organization* 7, 24–52.

or helping teammates. These multitask considerations suggest that firms often might want to avoid paying employees based solely on measurable outputs. The appendix to this chapter provides a more detailed analysis of these considerations.

Given enough time, managers are likely to obtain information about the overall performance of employees. For example, deans have the opportunity to observe the service of professors on committees; they hear comments on faculty research from colleagues; they talk to students about teaching quality. Incentives can be provided to employees by basing promotions, terminations, and periodic pay adjustments on this type of information. Indeed, universities rely heavily on these mechanisms to motivate faculty. Evaluating this information usually requires *subjective judgments* on the part of managers. To provide proper incentives to employees, managers must develop reputations of being impartial and objective. To be most effective, firms must establish performance measures and rewards that motivate managers to develop these reputations. The next chapter provides an expanded discussion of subjective performance evaluation.

Forms of Incentive Pay

The term *incentive pay* frequently evokes images of piece rates, commissions, and cash bonus plans, where employees are paid based on measurable output. This image is not surprising given that more than a quarter of the employees in the U.S. manufacturing sector receive at least part of their income through such incentive plans. Our discussion in this chapter suggests that mechanisms like tying promotions and salary adjustments to performance also are forms of incentive pay. Broadly speaking, any compensation contract (explicit or implicit) that rewards employees for good performance or punishes employees for poor performance can be considered incentive pay. (Recall the Mary Kay Cosmetic Company's innovative use of incentives discussed in Chapter 11.) Under this definition, all the following are forms of incentive compensation:[27]

- Piece rates and commissions
- Bonuses for good performance
- Prizes for winning contests (e.g., vacations)
- Salary revisions based on performance
- Promotions and titles for good performance
- Preferred office assignments for good performance
- Stock ownership and profit-sharing plans
- Firings and other penalties for poor performance
- Deferred compensation and unvested pensions that are forfeited on dismissal

It is important to emphasize that rewards *do not have to be monetary*. Rewards can consist of anything that employees value. For example, managers in some organizations have little flexibility in what they pay employees. Nonetheless, incentives can be provided by rewarding more productive employees with desirable job assignments, better offices, preferred parking spaces, special honors, and trips to training sessions in attractive locations.

---

[27]G. Baker, M. Jensen, and K. Murphy (1988), "Compensation and Incentives: Practice versus Theory," *Journal of Finance* 43, 593–616.

Incentive Compensation and Information Revelation

The basic principal-agent model assumes that the employer and employee have the same information at the time of initial contract negotiations. In some contracting situations, precontractual information is asymmetric.[28] For example, prospective employees generally know more about their likelihood of quitting over the next year than the prospective employer. Similarly, sales representatives are more likely to know about the sales potential of their territories than are higher-level managers.

Sometimes it is possible for the firm to induce employees to reveal their private information by clever design of the compensation contract. Consider the example of Onex Copy Company. This company uses sales representatives throughout the country to sell copy machines to customers. Each salesperson is assigned a specific territory. Some territories have greater sales potential than others. For simplicity, suppose that there are only two types of territories, good and bad. Good territories have the potential to generate $2 million in sales, while bad territories have the potential to generate only $1 million in sales. The sales representatives know the quality of their own territories. Central managers have insufficient information to distinguish between good and bad territories.

The firm would like to use information about whether specific territories are good or bad to evaluate the performance of the sales representatives. The company also wants accurate forecasts to plan production cycles. The company simply could ask the sales representatives to state the quality of their territories. But the sales representatives with good territories are likely to be less than completely truthful: If the firm thinks that a good territory is bad, the representative will look better when sales are high. (Alternatively, the salesperson can generate the expected poor sales with only limited effort.)

In this example, the firm can induce the salesperson to tell the truth by offering the following menu of contracts. Sales representatives who state that their territories are good receive compensation contracts that pay 2.6 percent of sales. Sales representatives who state that their territories are bad receive a flat wage of $50,000. Given this choice, it is in the interests of all salespeople to tell the truth: Those with bad territories would prefer the $50,000 wage contract (2.6 percent of $1 million = $26,000), whereas those with good territories would prefer the contract that pays 2.6 percent of sales (for them, a $52,000 payout). The key to making the plan work is that the compensation for each type of employee is higher when the information is correctly reported than when it is not.

In this example, there are many potential compensation plans that would induce truth telling. The problem for the firm is to choose the most profitable contract. Onex is likely to want the compensation contract to provide strong performance incentives, as well as to induce truth telling. Thus, it might choose to pay commissions to both types of employees but structure different commission rates to induce truth telling.

---

[28]In Chapter 10, we divided asymmetric information into two categories—precontractual and postcontractual. Thus far, in this chapter, we have focused on postcontractual information problems (also called *moral-hazard* or agency problems). In this section, we discuss precontractual information problems (also called *adverse-selection* problems).

Selection Effects of Incentive Contracts

Chapter 14 described how firms can use compensation, and in particular the mix of fringe benefits and pay, to attract a particular type of employee. The example given was the use of health, life, and dental insurance plans, which are valued more highly by employees with families than by single employees. By offering a compensation package rich in such fringe benefits and slightly lower pay, more married employees will be attracted to the firm. This section describes a similar selection mechanism inherent in incentive compensation plans that can attract more productive workers to the firm.

The basic principal-agent model presented earlier in this chapter assumes that all agents are identical in terms of their marginal productivity [α in Equation (15.5)]. But employees generally have different marginal productivities. Firms that value more productive employees would like to attract these employees to their firms. Incentive contracts as in Equation (15.7) not only motivate employees like Erica to expend more effort, but also can help attract high α employees to work at the firm. To see this, assume that employees know their own marginal productivities (their α's), but the firm does not. For simplicity, further assume all employees have the same reservation utility, $1,100. While the firm does not know any single employee's α, the firm can set a W_0^* (fixed salary) and a β^* (piece rate) to ensure that workers who apply for the job and stay with the firm have a minimum marginal productivity of $\alpha > \alpha^*$. The resulting incentive contract, $W_0^* + \beta^* \times$ output, causes less productive employees ($\alpha < \alpha^*$) to leave the firm.

Recall that Erica has marginal productivity of $100 per unit of effort and disutility of effort, e^2. Given the expected compensation contract of $1,000 + .2 \times$ output, she chooses $e^* = 10$ (see Figure 15.2). With $e^* = 10$, Erica has expected compensation of $1,200 and expected utility of $1,100 ($1,200 − 10^2), which just equals her reservation utility. Suppose that Erica and Leo apply for this job. Leo, like Erica, also has reservation utility of $1,100, but Leo's marginal productivity is only $90 per unit

---

MANAGERIAL APPLICATIONS

Pros and Cons of Stock Options to Motivate Executives

Many firms, although not as many as in previous years, grant stock options to executives to help align the interests of managers and shareholders. In the 1970s and 1980s, some executives were accused of being more interested in empire-building to justify higher salaries and lavish expenses than in generating returns for shareholders. Granting options as part of their compensation packages gave managers stronger incentives to maximize the share price. However, options have prompted some executives to focus on the short-term performance of the shares rather than the long-term health of the business. Missing its quarterly earnings target can lower the firm's stock price and significantly reduce an executive's options pay off. Cutting back on research and development (R&D) expenses can raise short-run profits but adversely affect long-run firm value. In fact some executives reduce R&D and advertising right before these options vest and thus can be exercised. This boosts short-term profits to meet earnings targets and presumably reduces the likelihood of a stock price decline before the executive cashes out her stock options.

This article illustrates the dictum "there is no magic bullet." Although adding stock options to an executive's compensation package can control problems in some dimensions (options encourage executives to increase the share price and thus the value of their options), options also can generate perverse incentives in other dimensions.

Source: (2014), "Share Options: The law of unintended consequences," *The Economist* (February 8), www.economist.com/news/finance-and-economics/21595985-when-bosses-take-short-view-law-unintended-consequences.

of effort. Once Leo learns of the incentive contract, he is better off doing something else than working for this firm. Leo's expected compensation under the contract is $1,000 + .2 ($90e). Assuming Leo, like Erica, has the same cost of effort, e^2, he will choose to exert 9 units of effort and thus expects to earn $1,162, yielding expected utility of $1,081 ($1,162 − 9^2).[29] Leo's expected utility given the incentive contract is less than his reservation utility. Leo thus will elect to work elsewhere, whereas Erica elects to stay with the firm. By offering greater pay-for-performance incentive contracts, firms can attract a more productive workforce.

Lazear studied workers who install auto windshields at a particular firm that changed from fixed salaries to piece rates.[30] Productivity at this firm rose 35 percent while wages (salary plus incentive pay) increased 12 percent. One-third of the improved productivity arose because the less productive employees left the firm and were replaced by more talented employees. The Lazear study documents how incentive contracts can generate selection effects.

Does Incentive Pay Work?

Throughout this chapter, we have argued that compensation plans motivate employees. Although this argument is readily accepted by many people, it is not without controversy. Quality guru W. Edwards Deming went so far as to assert that "pay is not a motivator." In the same spirit, psychologist Alfie Kohn, in a controversial article on the merits of incentive pay, states, "Bribes in the workplace simply can't work."[31]

Critics of incentive pay generally rely on two basic arguments. The first is that money does not motivate employees. As support for this view, it is pointed out that employees usually rank money relatively low when it comes to factors that make a job attractive. Factors such as the nature of work and quality of colleagues appear more important. The second, more prominent criticism is that it is difficult (if not impossible) to design an effective incentive compensation plan. Support for this argument is provided by the many examples of flawed compensation plans that have produced unwanted behavior (e.g., the case of Merrill Lynch discussed in Chapter 2). Interestingly, these two lines of criticism are somewhat at odds with one another. If money did not motivate people, incentives plans would not produce the dysfunctional behavior that proponents of the second argument cite. In making a similar point, economist George Baker notes, "The problem is not that incentives can't work but that they work all too well."[32]

Certainly, it is easy to identify examples of compensation plans that have caused dysfunctional behavior among employees. We have done so throughout this book. Incentive plans also involve administrative costs, such as tracking output and explaining the system to employees. The important question is not whether incentive plans entail costs—they certainly do. Rather, is it possible to design incentive plans where the benefits exceed the costs? Examples like the Lincoln Electric Company (discussed in Chapter 16) suggest that the answer is yes. Also, applying Economic

---

[29]For the technically inclined, Leo will maximize his expected utility, $1,000 + .2($90e) − e^2. To find the level of effort (e^*) that maximizes his expected utility, take the derivative of this function and set it to zero: $18 − 2e^* = 0$. Or, $e^* = 9$.

[30]E. Lazear (2000), "Performance Pay and Productivity," *American Economic Review* 90:5, 1346–1361.

[31]A. Kohn (1993), "Why Incentive Plans Cannot Work," *Harvard Business Review* (September–October), 54–63.

[32]G. Baker (1993), "Rethinking Rewards," *Harvard Business Review* (November–December), 44–45.

ACADEMIC APPLICATIONS

The Power of Incentives—Evidence from Chinese Agriculture

One especially interesting piece of evidence on the effectiveness of incentive pay comes from one of the largest economic experiments in history—reforms in Chinese agriculture in the early 1980s. Between 1952 and 1978, the Maoist period, Chinese agriculture revolved around the commune system. Under this system, employees were divided into production teams. There were some attempts to tie pay to performance. However, these incentives were relatively weak, and there was a tendency to base pay on family size, independent of effort. From 1980 to 1984, under the rule of Deng Xiaoping, the commune system was gradually replaced by the "household-responsibility system." Under this system, each peasant family was given a long-term lease on a plot of land. The family had to deliver a quota of agricultural products to the government each year, but it could keep any production in excess of the quota. This additional output could be consumed by the family or sold to others.

Economic theory argues that the ownership of residual claims on output provides strong incentives. Thus, this theory predicts higher productivity under the household-responsibility system than the commune system. Empirical studies support this prediction. For instance, one study estimated that productivity in Chinese agriculture increased by nearly 50 percent over the period of the Dengist reforms.

Source: J. McMillan (1992), *Games, Strategies, and Managers* (Oxford University Press: New York), 96–98.

Darwinism (see Chapter 1), the fact that incentive plans—commissions, piece rates, bonus plans, and stock options—have survived so long in a competitive marketplace suggests that the net benefits of incentive pay often are positive.

The scientific evidence overwhelmingly supports the proposition that agents respond to incentives.[33] Prendergast describes a battery of tests from chicken farmers to professional athletes to CEOs that show incentives matter. But equally persuasive are studies of agents taking actions that benefit the agent at the cost of overall efficiency—agents gaming the system. But why is this surprising? The basic premise of agency theory is that employees act in their own self-interest. With incentive schemes, agents act to maximize their own self-interest, given the structure of the incentive contract; sometimes this involves gaming the system. And in poorly designed incentive schemes, actions that benefit the agent can reduce firm value. Incentive compensation schemes are more likely to be value enhancing if they are designed to limit the agent's gaming behavior. The evidence also points to significant selection effects from incentive contracts. More productive employees prefer higher pay-for-performance contracts because under these contracts more productive workers can earn more money.

When designing monetary incentives, one must also take account of the nonmonetary incentives, one needs to consider the implicit incentives (moral and social) that people already face. Take the example of Israeli day-care centers that began charging parents $3 every time they picked-up their children later than the specified time. The number of late pickups more than doubled.[34] The small monetary fine was not large enough to overcome the implicit incentives (the guilt of inconveniencing the day-care workers), and in fact, by paying the $3 fine now made it OK to be late. Most economists would agree that as the fine for being late increased to say $50, fewer late pickups would occur.

[33]This material draws heavily on C. Prendergast (1999), "The Provision of Incentives in Firms," *Journal of Economic Literature* (March), 7–63.

[34]http://freakonomics.com/2013/10/23/what-makes-people-do-what-they-do/

MANAGERIAL APPLICATIONS

Teachers Gaming Student Test Scores

To improve public education, a number of school districts reward educators with cash bonuses if their school's test scores rise. However, such systems have spawned cheating among teachers to boost their ratings. The Atlanta school district began paying teachers and principals bonuses if students' standardized tests scores improved, and they did. A State review into the improved test scores determined that some cheating occurred in more than half of Atlanta's elementary and middle schools starting in 2001 when standardized testing scores began. Thirty-five educators in the Atlanta school district, including principals, teachers, and testing coordinators were indicted by the local authorities for allegedly plotting to falsify students' standardized tests. Twenty-three have plead guilty. At least 178 teachers and principals, have said cheating may have been going on for years. Some administrators even held "erasing parties" to fix the tests. One principal even wore gloves when she altered students' tests to avoid leaving fingerprints. More than 80 educators confessed and many resigned.

Atlanta is not an isolated incident. Widespread teacher cheating has been uncovered in Kentucky in the late 1990s and in Philadelphia in 2014. These examples demonstrate that poorly designed incentive plans can induce dysfunctional behavior.

Source: K. Severson and A. Blinder (2014), "Test Scandal in Atlanta Brings More Guilty Pleas," *NY Times* (January 14), www.nytimes.com/2014/01/07/education/test-scandal-in-atlanta-brings-more-guilty-pleas.html?_r=0.

Although the evidence supports the view that incentives matter, for better or for worse, the evidence is mixed regarding other implications of the theory we described in this chapter. In particular, Table 15.2 predicts that when the level of risk, that is, beyond the employee's control is low, we should observe high levels of incentive pay, holding everything else constant (the sensitivity of output to employee effort, the employee's risk aversion, and so forth). Unfortunately, research has yet to document convincingly this simple proposition that greater environmental uncertainty causes less incentive pay to be used. A potential difficulty in examining this proposition involves issues we discussed in Chapter 12. If greater environmental uncertainty leads to more delegation of decision rights to the employee, then this greater delegation requires more (not less) incentive pay.[35]

Prendergast gives the example of a firm involved in two large construction projects: one in Canada, where there is little environmental uncertainty because it has a long track record of similar Canadian projects, and a new project in Armenia, where the firm has no experience and the economic environment is highly uncertain. The manager of the Canadian project receives a salary with a small bonus, whereas the Armenian project manager's pay is tied to project profitability. In Canada, the project manager is assigned few decision rights because central management knows what should be done and can directly monitor the Canadian project manager. But central management has little specialized knowledge of the Armenian project and must delegate more decision rights to the Armenian manager. It is more expensive for headquarters to monitor the Armenian manager than the Canadian manager. To motivate the Armenian manager to exercise these additional decision rights to maximize firm value, headquarters structures the Armenian manager's compensation plan to include more incentive pay. In this case, for risk-neutral managers, uncertainty and the amount of incentive pay are positively correlated. But, for risk-averse employees the correlation can be positive (if the delegation incentives

[35]C. Prendergast (2002), "The Tenuous Trade-off between Risk and Incentives," *Journal of Political Economy* (October), 1071–1102.

ANALYZING MANAGERIAL DECISIONS: *The Debate over CEO Compensation*

The most visible and highly paid person in most corporations is the chief executive officer (CEO). CEO compensation is particularly important to firms for three reasons. First, the compensation package is likely to be important in attracting and retaining good CEOs. Second, the form of the pay contract is likely to help determine whether the CEO focuses on value maximization or some other objective. Third, employees throughout the organization carefully follow their CEO's pay. Important morale problems can occur when employees think that the CEO is overpaid. For instance, employees complain bitterly when they are asked to take pay cuts because the company is in trouble, yet at the same time the CEO gets a big raise.

Controversy over CEO pay has increased substantially in recent years. One charge is that the *level* of CEO pay is too high. CEO pay is so huge that people don't believe they deserve it. It is easy to point to many CEOs who report compensation in the millions of dollars (reported compensation figures typically include salary and bonus payments, as well as the expected value of stock option and restricted stock grants). Consider the following two examples. Investors were outraged when the giant Swiss drug company Novartis gave its departing chairman, Daniel Vasella, $78 million as part of a non-compete contract, whereby Vasella would keep collecting his annual salary so long as he didn't go work for a competitor. After this turned into a giant PR disaster, Vasella and the board called the whole thing off. In 2009, Hewlett-Packard laid off 6,400 workers but paid its CEO Mark Hurd $24.2 million. In 1980, CEO compensation was 42 times that of the average worker. In 2013, it was 331 times.

The second major criticism of CEO pay concerns how CEOs are paid. Critics argue that CEOs are agents of stockholders and that CEO pay should be based heavily on stock-price performance. In some celebrated cases CEO pay appears disconnected to CEO performance. For example, the CEO of the health care provider *McKesson* not only earned $145 million in 2013 but also received an employment agreement containing an eye-popping $469 million severance payout should he be

terminated. The CEO of *General Growth Properties* received compensation of $66.7 million even though the firm spent most of 2010 in bankruptcy.

From 1980, the increasing use of stock options and restricted stock grants has boosted the sensitivity of the average CEO's wealth to firm performance. However, the absolute sensitivity of CEO wealth to performance remains small. Research indicates that for a $1,000 change in firm value, the wealth of the average CEO of a large public corporation changes by under $10 (depending on the year and estimation method). Some argue this relation (which is equivalent to the CEO owning less than 1 percent of the common stock) is too small and that most companies would be better off if they increased incentive pay for CEOs. Some support for this view seems to come from studies that document an increase in stock price when companies announce that they are increasing incentive pay for CEOs.

1. Do you think the fact that most American CEOs are paid so much more than rank-and-file employees suggests CEOs are overpaid? Explain.

2. Japanese CEOs generally receive much lower levels of compensation than CEOs in the United States. Does this imply that U.S. CEOs are overpaid?

3. Is it obvious that $10 per thousand is too low of an incentive pay for CEOs? Explain.

4. Does the observation that the stock price increases when firms increase incentive pay for CEOs suggest that most CEOs do not receive enough incentive compensation? Explain.

5. Are there any reasons why overpaying CEOs might be in the shareholders' interest (i.e., maximize shareholder value)?

SOURCE: M. Herper (2013), "Novartis' Exorbitant Pay Package For Former CEO Was More Ridiculous Than It Looked," *Forbes* (February 19); N. Hindman (2011), "The 10 Highest-Paid CEOs Who Laid Off The Most Workers," *Huffington Post* (September 1); www.aflcio.org/Corporate-Watch/Paywatch-2014; K. Murphy (2013), "Executive Compensation: Where We Are, and How We Got There," in G. Constantinides, M. Harris and R. Stulz (Eds.), *Handbook of the Economics of Finance* Vol 2, Part A, (Elsevier: Amsterdam), 211–356; A. Lomax (2011) "CEO Pay Defies the Laws of Gravity," *The Motley Fool* (December 16).

dominate the risk-aversion costs) or negative (if the risk-aversion costs dominate the delegation incentives).

While the empirical evidence does not support the simple proposition in Table 15.2 that risk and incentives should be negatively correlated, a potential problem is that the research has not held other things constant. For example, uncertainty affects both the risk imposed on the agent and also the delegation of decision rights. One of the benefits of decentralization is more effective use of local knowledge. In environments with greater uncertainty, local managers likely have better information than more senior managers. Thus, as described by Prendergast, one would expect more delegation of decision rights as uncertainty increases. This discussion again highlights the importance of Figure 11.1. The firm's organizational architecture varies depending on the strategies chosen. All three legs of the stool are designed to complement each other and to support the firm's strategy. Simple empirical tests that just examine one leg at a time (such as how compensation varies with risk) must control for how the other legs are also adjusted (such as how the assignment of decision rights varies with risk).

Summary

Incentive problems exist because of conflicts of interest between employers and employees. These problems are easily resolved when actions are costlessly observable. Firms can identify the most efficient actions by employees and pay employees only if these actions are taken. In most situations employee actions are not observable at low cost. Here, firms can motivate employees through incentive compensation.

In a competitive labor market, employees must be compensated for undertaking actions they find undesirable—there are compensating differentials. Thus, it is not sensible to have employees work as hard as possible. In eliciting particular actions, there is a trade-off between the benefits of the action for the firm and the personal costs to the employees.

Incentive problems arise because most of the costs of exerting effort are borne by employees, whereas most of the gains go to their employers. Sometimes, there is a simple way to resolve this incentive problem even when the actions of employees are unobservable. The solution is to sell each employee the rights to his or her total output. By selling employees their output, both the benefits and costs of exerting effort are internalized by employees and thus employees will make more productive choices. We observe this solution being approximated in private firms as well as in franchising. There are at least three important factors that limit the use of ownership in solving incentive problems: wealth constraints, team production, and costs of inefficient risk bearing.

Risk-averse individuals do not like to bear financial risks; they prefer income flows with less volatility. Risk-averse individuals can benefit from sharing risks because it lowers the volatility of the individual cash flows. People often vary in their attitudes toward risk. For instance, some people are more willing to tolerate financial risks than others. An efficient allocation of risk takes these differences in preferences into account. If one party is risk-neutral whereas another party is risk-averse, it is better to have the risk-neutral party bear all the risk and the other party to receive a fixed payment.

Stockholders of firms often hold diversified portfolios; this is a powerful method for managing firm-specific risks. Employees, in contrast, have much of their human capital invested in a single firm and hence have fewer opportunities to manage risk through diversification. Thus, from a risk-sharing standpoint, it is better to pay employees more through fixed salaries and to let the risk of random income flows be borne more by the shareholders. Yet fixed salaries provide limited incentives for employees to exert effort: *Therefore, there is a trade-off between optimal risk sharing and optimal incentives.*

Economic analysis of incentive compensation begins with the basic principal-agent model. This model presents a relatively simple characterization of the contracting process. However, it illustrates the trade-offs between risk sharing and incentives and provides a number of useful insights for designing better compensation plans. In particular, the model suggests that firms should pay more performance-based pay when (1) the sensitivity of the value of output to additional effort by the employee is higher, (2) the employee is less risk-averse, (3) the level of risk that is beyond the employee's control is lower, (4) the employee response to increased incentives in terms of exerting additional effort is more pronounced, and (5) employee output is more easily measured.

According to the *informativeness principle,* it is useful to include all indicators that provide additional information about employee effort into the compensation contract—provided that these indicators are available at low cost. Including these indicators in the contract reduces the randomness of payouts and thus the costs of inefficient risk bearing. One important source of information about an employee's effort is the output of coworkers performing similar tasks. The informativeness principle suggests that it is useful to employ *relative performance evaluation.* In Chapter 16, however, we discuss several factors that can limit the desirability of relative performance evaluations.

In the basic principal-agent model, employees are motivated by basing compensation on their own output. But many firms base incentive pay on *group performance.* Common reasons offered for group incentive pay are that group performance can be less expensive to monitor than individual performance, group performance emphasizes teamwork, and group plans motivate employees to monitor one another's performance. Standard free-rider arguments provide a strong reason to question whether group plans provide effective incentives—particularly when the group is large. At least three factors might help explain the widespread popularity of these plans, even though free-riding is a potential problem. First, it can be beneficial to increase employee awareness of stock-price performance and profitability (assuming employees can be motivated to monitor these measures by relatively modest plans that do not impose much risk on employees). Second, employees might feel guilty from shirking and imposing costs on teammates who are compensated on group performance. These feelings might motivate employees, even if the direct financial consequences are small. Third, paying employees on firm performance sends a strong signal to employees about what is valued within the company. To be most effective, however, these signals must be reinforced by other parts of the organizational architecture that provide more direct incentives.

Most jobs involve a variety of tasks. Motivating an employee to strike the appropriate balance among tasks is not easy. A complicating factor is that some tasks are more easily measured than others. Compensating the employee based on what is measurable will encourage the employee to exert more effort on the compensated tasks but shirk on other tasks. These *multitasking considerations* suggest that firms often want to avoid paying employees based solely on measurable outputs. Given enough time, managers are likely to obtain information about the overall performance of employees. Incentives can be provided by basing promotions, terminations, and periodic pay adjustments on this information. Often, this information is not easily quantifiable but is based on the subjective opinions of supervisors.

The term *incentive pay* conjures up images of piece rates, commissions, and cash bonus plans, where the employee is paid based on measurable output. Broadly speaking, however, any compensation contract (explicit or implicit) that rewards employees for good performance or punishes employees for poor performance can be considered incentive pay. *Rewards do not have to be monetary.* Rather, rewards consist of anything that employees value.

The basic principal-agent model assumes employers and employees have the same information at the time of initial contract negotiations. In many contracting situations precontractual information is asymmetric. Sometimes it is possible for the firm to induce employees to reveal their private information by clever design of the compensation contract. For such a plan to work, the payoffs to employees must be higher when they are honest than when they misrepresent information.

Throughout this chapter, we have argued that compensation plans motivate employees. Although this argument is accepted by many, it is not without controversy. Critics of incentive pay rely on two basic arguments. The first is that money does not motivate people. The second, more prominent criticism is that it is difficult (if not impossible) to design an effective incentive compensation plan. The first argument seems inconsistent with the many examples where monetary incentives have dramatically affected employee behavior. The second argument is correct: Developing an appropriate incentive plan rarely is easy. The important question is whether plans can be designed where the benefits exceed the costs. Examples such as Lincoln Electric suggest it can be done. Our intent is to provide insights into how managers might design value-maximizing contracts.

Suggested Readings

G. Baker, M. Jensen, and K. Murphy (1988), "Compensation and Incentives: Practice versus Theory," *Journal of Finance* 43, 593–616.

J. McMillan (1992), *Games, Strategies, and Managers* (Oxford University Press: New York), 91–129.

P. Milgrom and J. Roberts (1992), *Economics, Organization, and Management* (Prentice Hall: Englewood Cliffs), 206–247.

K. Murphy (2013), "Executive Compensation: Where We Are, and How We Got There," in G. Constantinides, M. Harris and R. Stulz (Eds.), *Handbook of the Economics of Finance* Vol 2, Part A, (Elsevier: Amsterdam) 211–356.

Self-Evaluation Problems

15–1. You work for a compensation consulting firm. You are designing a pay package for the CEO of a major corporation. The board has asked you to choose the parameters a, b, and c, in the following pay contract:

$$\text{Pay} = a + b[(\text{company stock return}) - c(\text{industry stock return})]$$

Discuss the key factors that will influence your recommendation for each of these three parameters.

15–2. You are a sales manager at the XYZ Corporation. You want to hire a new sales representative. You plan to make an offer to Sally Gomez. You can pay Sally a fixed salary of $20,000 per year or a 10 percent sales commission plus α (a fixed component in the compensation formula). She has a competing offer at another company for $20,000. You anticipate you can hire her if you meet the $20,000 fixed salary offer.

Sally's sales will be either high or low depending on whether she gets a corporate account. If she gets the account, sales will be $100,000. If she does not, sales will be $10,000. The probability of getting the account is .7. This probability is beyond Sally's control. Sally's utility function can be represented by

$$u(\text{compensation}) = (\text{compensation})^{1/2} \qquad (1)$$

She seeks to maximize *expected utility*. Expected utilities under the two plans are

$$\text{Fixed salary: } u = (20,000)^{1/2} \qquad (2)$$

$$\text{10 percent plan: } u = .7(\alpha + 10,000)^{1/2} + .3(\alpha + \$1,000)^{1/2} \qquad (3)$$

a. Sketch the graph of the function $u(x) = (x)^{1/2}$.

b. Is Sally's utility function convex or concave? Is she risk-loving or risk-averse?

c. What α makes Sally indifferent between the two plans?

d. As the sales manager, which plan do you select? Give an explanation that shows why this plan is optimal.

Solutions to Self-Evaluation Problems

15–1. Structuring Compensation

The optimal choice of c increases with the covariance of industry and company stock returns and decreases with the variance of industry stock returns. Industry stock returns are included in the pay package to produce a more informative measure of the ability/effort of the CEO. The information in these returns increases with the covariance between the two returns and decreases with the variance of industry returns.

The optimal choice of b depends on the trade-off between optimal risk sharing and incentives. It is optimal to choose a higher level of b when (1) the CEO's stock return is sensitive to his effort, (2) the CEO is not very risk-averse, (3) the level of risk that is beyond the CEO's control is low, and (4) the CEO's response to increased incentives is high (the CEO exerts a lot more effort).

The optimal choice of a depends on the "reservation utility" of the CEO (which in turn depends on his demand in the outside labor market). It must be chosen so that the overall pay package is sufficient to attract and retain the CEO.

15–2. Expected Utility and Structuring Compensation

a.

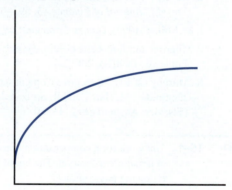

b. Concave, risk averse.

c. The $20,000 for certain gives a utility of about 141. You can answer this question by setting expected utility equal to 141 and solve by iteration (e.g., in Excel). The answer is around 13,000.

d. The fixed salary. Neither plan affects the effort of the employee. Thus the manager wants to choose the plan that allows him to hire Sally at the lowest expected compensation. Since she is risk-averse the fixed plan is better. You must pay expected compensation of $20,300 to hire Sally.

Review Questions

15–1. Evaluate the statement: "Investment banking is a demanding profession; investment banks want their employees to work as hard as possible."

15–2. Two employees are assigned to work overseas for a two-year period. One person sells his house in the United States, whereas the other leases it for two years to another family. Which house do you think will be in better condition after the two years? Explain.

15–3. Explain why an investor is usually better off if she holds a diversified portfolio rather than investing all her resources in the stock of one company.

15–4. Discuss trade-offs between efficient risk bearing and incentives in compensation plans.

15–5. Some companies reward salespeople based on their performance relative to other salespeople in the company. Why would a company want to do this?

15–6. Evaluate the statement: "Profit-sharing plans are good; they encourage teamwork."

15–7. Some school districts have compensated teachers based on the performance of students on standardized tests. Do you think this is a good idea? Explain.

15–8. Evaluate the following statement: "John is paid a straight salary with no bonus pay. Obviously, he has no incentives to do a good job."

15–9. Mrs. Fields' Cookie Company is a very successful company out of Salt Lake City, Utah. The company sells freshly baked cookies to customers in shopping malls. The company has expanded and opened outlets in other cities such as San Francisco. Debbie Fields has been on the cover of several business magazines. The articles stress that Mrs. Fields works very long hours and is often at the stores monitoring the quality of the product and making sure the cookies are produced with "tender loving care." The Fields have earned millions of dollars from this business. In 1986, they were planning to open new outlets throughout the country. They had a policy that they would not franchise units. To quote Mrs. Fields, "We do not want to turn into just another fast-food franchise company. Our success is based on high-quality products produced with great care and love. We do not want to lose this quality by expanding through franchises. Rather, we prefer to maintain ownership of all units to ensure continued good service and quality." Evaluate the Fields' franchising policy.

15–10. The Roman Empire taxed many faraway provinces. Rome would auction the rights to tax collection to the highest bidder. The winning bidder was given the right to set the tax rate for the province and the right to collect (and keep) the taxes. In turn, the winner would pay the bid amount to the Roman government. Assume (1) that the Roman Senate is interested in maximizing the present value of all future revenues to Rome from auctioning off the tax rights, and (2) that the auction for the rights to each province is conducted annually.

   a. Give two reasons why Rome would auction off the rights to tax collection rather than simply send a Roman soldier to collect the taxes.

   b. Discuss two problems this system might generate for the Senate.

15–11. There has been an increased emphasis on compensating employees through incentive pay. High incentive pay, however, is not likely to be productive in all settings. Discuss the factors that are likely to favor paying high incentive pay to employees.

15–12. In 1995, Philip Morris Company ratified a new labor pact that gave employees stock in lieu of pay increases. The agreement covered 7,800 employees, with each employee being given 94 shares (1994 value of about $60 per share). Employees cannot sell the stock for at least a year and forfeit the stock if they quit or are fired before the year expires. *BusinessWeek* argued that the "deal was good for Philip Morris" because the employees' base pay and fringe benefits did not rise. Also "current shareholders' shares won't be diluted, since employees probably will get less than 500,000 shares out of 850 million outstanding."[36] Discuss the pros and cons of this policy compared to a policy of simply giving a cash bonus to employees of a similar dollar value.

15–13. Two successful firms are observed with quite different compensation plans for their salespeople. One firm pays its salespeople on a commission basis, whereas the other firm pays its salespeople fixed salaries. Do you think that one of the two companies is making a mistake? Explain.

15–14. Susan Jones is a salesperson at Radex Co. Her utility function can be represented by $U = C^2$, where C is her compensation.

---

[36]A. Bernstein (1995), "At Philip Morris, Blue Chips for Blue Collars," *BusinessWeek* (March 27), 38.

a. The company is considering paying her a sales commission rather than a straight salary. The sales manager, however, is concerned that he will have to pay her a compensating differential for imposing risk on her, that is, beyond her control (sales at Radex are heavily dependent on macroeconomic factors and central company policies). Is the sales manager's concern about paying Susan higher compensation justified? Explain.

b. Is this example representative of the typical worker in most companies? Explain.

15–15. Top executives of European firms are typically paid substantially less than the top executives of American firms. They are also paid differently. For example, stock options are much more common among American than European executives. Do these differences imply (1) that American executives are overpaid, and (2) that the form of the compensation in either America or Europe is suboptimal? Explain.

15–16. Prior to 2004, American accounting rules did not require firms to expense stock options on their accounting statements. Thus, firms were able to grant executive stock options without impacting "bottom-line performance." Correspondingly, some people argued that the primary reason firms paid executives in the form of stock options was that they were free. Do you agree (1) that stock options were free, and (2) that this is the primary reason for paying executives in options? Explain.

15–17. How does the concept of a *risk premium* in incentive compensation relate to the concept of a *compensating differential* in compensation policy?

15–18. Consider two successful sales companies. One company pays its salespeople a high commission, whereas the other pays its salespeople a straight salary. Assume that both companies are paying their salespeople in an optimal manner. Explain potential differences in the firms that might help to explain the difference in pay policy.

15–19. Toledo Chicken is a large chicken processor that raises, processes, and packs both fresh and frozen chicken parts. The firm has five plants located around the United States. Factory employees have been paid a fixed salary, but recently Toledo switched to a piece-rate pay system. What affect, if any, might you expect this change in compensation system to have on Toledo's productivity and total wages paid to factory employees? And discuss what might be contributing to the change in productivity. In other words, what are the sources of the productivity change?

Appendix: Multitasking Theory[37]

This appendix provides a more detailed example of the multitask principal-agent model. It also uses this framework to analyze the corporate practice of *telecommuting*—employees working out of their homes and communicating with the central office via fax, computer, or telephone. This application illustrates how principal-agent theory can provide insights into specific managerial policy decisions.

Multitask Model

Adel el Gazzar is a production employee at the Bijar Dye Company. He works 10 hours per day. His job consists of two tasks, assembling parts and checking the quality of his output. He is paid a piece rate for each part that he assembles. He also receives a bonus, that is, based on the quality of his output. Denote t_1 and t_2 as the hours per day he devotes to producing output and checking quality, respectively. Adel's incentives are high enough so that he will not shirk: He works the full 10 hours. Therefore, $t_2 = (10 - t_1)$.

---

[37]This appendix requires elementary knowledge of calculus. This appendix draws on Milgrom and Holmstrom (1991).

Figure 15.4   Optimal Allocation of Effort

In this example, Adel must allocate his time between two activities, producing quantity and checking its quality. The number of hours devoted to quantity is t_1. Since he puts in 10-hour workdays, he devotes $t_2 = (10 - t_1^*)$ hours to quality. This figure illustrates the case where there is an interior optimum. At this optimum, the marginal benefit MB from allocating additional time to either activity is the same. Adel spends t_1^* hours on quantity and $(10 - t_1^*)$ hours on quality. But if the marginal benefits for quantity are higher than the marginal benefits from quality over the relevant range ($0 \le t_1 \le 10$), Adel allocates all his time to producing output—there is a corner solution.

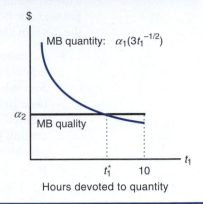

Suppose that Adel's compensation translates into the following relation between compensation and the time allocated to each activity:

$$\text{Compensation} = \alpha_1(6t_1^{1/2}) + \alpha_2 t_2 \tag{15.9}$$
$$= \alpha_1(6t_1^{1/2}) + \alpha_2(10 - t_1)$$

where the α's are the weights that the compensation plan places on quantity and quality (the *incentive coefficients*).[38] Adel's objective is to maximize his compensation. He chooses t_1 to meet the following first-order condition:

$$\alpha_1(3t_1^{-1/2}) = \alpha_2 \tag{15.10}$$

This condition has a straightforward interpretation. The left-hand term is the marginal benefit for allocating time to producing higher quantity, whereas the right-hand term is the marginal benefit for allocating time to producing higher quality. At an interior solution, these marginal returns must be equal. If the marginal benefits are not equal, Adel is better off devoting more time to the activity with the higher value and less time to the activity with the lower value. Figure 15.4 provides an illustration. When t_1 is small, the returns for devoting extra time to quantity are high relative to the returns from allocating time to quality. Here, it makes sense to increase the time devoted to quantity and correspondingly reduce the time spent on quality. As Adel continues to increase the amount of time he spends on quantity, the marginal benefit declines.[39] At the optimum t_1^*, the marginal returns are equal. Beyond t_1^*, the marginal returns from allocating time to quantity are less than for allocating time to quality.

If Adel's supervisor chooses α_1 and α_2 so that the marginal return for one of the activities is always higher over the relevant range, $0 \le t_1 \le 10$, Adel will devote all 10 hours to the activity with the higher marginal return (there is a corner solution).

Solving Equation (15.10) for t_1 yields

$$t_1 = 9(\alpha_1/\alpha_2)^2 \tag{15.11}$$

[38]The terms in this equation are chosen to simplify the calculations and yield reasonable values for the time allocated to the two activities. Our basic results, however, are quite general and are not specialized to this particular example.

[39]Technical note: For simplicity, we assume that time devoted to producing quantity is more strenuous than that devoted to quality. Thus, with more time devoted to quantity, he becomes tired and less productive. We have assumed that the marginal benefit from allocating time to quality is constant. This assumption is not necessary.

This equation shows that when $\alpha_1 = \alpha_2$, Adel will spend nine hours producing output and one hour checking its quality. Observing how t_1 and t_2 change with changes in the α's provides two important insights:

- A manager can motivate an employee to devote more time to a task in two ways: First, the manager can increase the incentive coefficient for that task. Second, the manager can reduce the incentive coefficient for the alternative task. In our example, Adel will devote more time to quantity if either α_1 is increased or α_2 is decreased. Increasing α_1 increases the direct return from investing in quantity, while decreasing α_2 reduces the opportunity cost (the compensation, i.e., lost from not investing in quality).

- If an incentive coefficient for a given task is sufficiently small, relative to the other incentive coefficient, an employee will devote no time to the task. In our example, if $(\alpha_1/\alpha_2)^2 > 1.12$, Adel will devote no time to quality ($1.12 \times 9 > 10$ hours). This result indicates that if a manager wants an employee to devote time to multiple tasks, the manager must be careful to provide balanced incentives. Setting too strong an incentive for one task can undermine effort on other tasks.

An Application: Telecommuting

Recently, there has been an increase in the use of telecommuting by large firms—working out of an office in the employee's own home. The asserted benefits of this practice are (1) companies can reduce office expense—it can be less expensive to reimburse an employee for a home office than to provide office space in an urban center, (2) employees avoid wasteful commutes to work, (3) firms can hire higher-quality employees at lower wages by offering them the flexibility to work out of their homes (for instance, employees can balance child care and career demands more easily), and (4) employees can be closer to customers (e.g., salespeople frequently have homes in their sales territories).

One potential drawback with telecommuting is the lost synergy that results from having employees work at separate locations. For instance, there is likely to be less information sharing, team production, and so on. While computer technologies (such as e-mail) reduce these concerns, they frequently are still important and limit the viability of telecommuting in many occupations. For instance, it would simply be infeasible for a dental assistant to telecommute. Another is the reduced ability to share specific equipment when individuals work from different locations. Our focus is on a third potential concern with telecommuting—the problem of motivating employees to exert effort on their jobs.

In analyzing telecommuting, it is useful to envision the employee being at home and choosing how to allocate time between two activities, home and work. The incentive coefficient for home activities (α_1) is the personal benefit the employee obtains from spending extra time playing with children, watching television, working in the garden, and so on. The incentive coefficient for working on company activities (α_2) depends on the compensation plan.

Viewed in this context, the multitask model has at least two important points relating to telecommuting. First, it usually is important to provide incentive compensation to telecommuters.[40] Without sufficient incentives, employees tend to shirk and devote too much of their time to home activities rather than work. Second,

---

[40]As discussed in the text, this incentive pay need not take the form of a commission or a piece rate. Rather, it can be a bonus plan, a promotion based on performance, and so on.

MANAGERIAL APPLICATIONS

Some Costs and Benefits of Telecommuting

Cisco Systems, the computer-networking company, claims that telecommuters improve their productivity 25 percent and save the company $1 million of overhead. Another company reported annual savings of $7,400 per telecommuting employee. The Federal Government has promoted telecommuting as a way to reduce energy consumption, traffic, and pollution. In 2004, Congress passed a bill that encouraged federal agencies to provide telecommuting options to all eligible employees. In 2007, over 110,000 federal employees were telecommuting. Many private companies have also begun using telecommuting. However, not all employers enthusiastically endorse telecommuting. One consultant estimates that 20 percent of the programs fail—causes include resistant managers, isolated employees, and insufficient opportunities for teamwork. Telecommuters have fewer opportunities to talk shop. Informal communications are reduced. Companies schedule meetings, informal lunches, and other social interactions that used to happen automatically. Other companies require telecommuters to spend at least a day or two at the office.

Source: A. Tergesen (1998), "Making Stay-at-Homes Feel Welcome," *BusinessWeek* (October 12), 155–156; and J. Greer, T. Buttross, G. Schmelzle (2002), "Using Telecommuting to Improve the Bottom Line," *Strategic Finance* (April), 46–50; and United States Office of Personnel Management (2007), "Status of Telework in the Federal Government."

---

the most viable jobs for telecommuting are those where output is easily measured, and thus incentive compensation can be used most readily. For instance, sales jobs often are good candidates for telecommuting, since incentives can be provided by sales commissions. (Synergies from having salespeople work out of a central location also are likely to be relatively low.) If it is difficult to measure employee output, it can be better to *require the employee to come to work* at a central location. This requirement has two effects. First, it is easier to monitor the employee's efforts. Second, it is equivalent to reducing the incentive coefficient on home activities to zero (the employee is unable to devote time to home activities and thus cannot gain from these activities). Since there are fewer activities that compete for their time, employees spend more time on work-related activities.

ANALYZING MANAGERIAL DECISIONS: *Insurance Distribution Systems*

Life insurance agents focus on selling policies. The company expects little follow-up in terms of providing ongoing customer service. In contrast, auto insurance agents often are expected to provide ongoing customer assistance after a policy is sold (answering questions about the policy, providing assistance in filing claims, and so on).

Some insurance companies use independent agents to sell their policies. These agents are paid solely on commission and are often allowed to sell the products of other companies (the agent presents the customer with a choice of plans across multiple companies). Other insurance companies hire their own agents. These employees are restricted from selling other companies' products and are sometimes paid a salary in addition to any commission they might receive.

1. Which type of insurance company, life or auto, is more likely to use the in-house agent? Explain. (Be sure to discuss why the in-house agent faces product restrictions and is not always paid on a pure commission basis.)

2. Some auto insurance companies separate the tasks of selling and customer service and assign them to different people. Why do you think they do this?

Individual Performance Evaluation

LEARNING OBJECTIVES

1. Describe how firms set performance benchmarks.
2. Define and apply the ratchet effect.
3. Explain why the amount spent on performance measure and the intensity of incentives in compensation plans tend to be positively correlated.
4. List examples of how employees can game performance measurement.
5. Define and apply the horizon problem.
6. Explain the benefits and costs of relative performance evaluation.
7. Discuss the advantages and disadvantages of subjective performance measures relative to objective measures.
8. Explain why some firms employ forced ratings systems and the kinds of problems that can arise with these systems.
9. Explain why many firms combine objective and subjective performance measures.
10. Describe key issues that arise in the evaluation of teams.

Lincoln Electric Company was founded in 1895 to manufacture electric motors and generators.[1] In the early part of the 20th century, the firm became the premier supplier of electric arc welding machines, welding disposables (electrodes), and cutting products. In 2007, Lincoln manufactured welding and cutting supplies and industrial electric motors in 30 plants across 18 countries. Prior to expanding manufacturing operations outside the United States in the 1980s, Lincoln Electric had an almost unbroken string of profitable years and often was cited as a model of productivity gains and cost savings.

Lincoln Electric's strategy involves building quality products at a cost lower than that of its competitors and passing these savings to customers by continuously lowering prices. Lincoln has been able to implement this strategy, in part, through an employee incentive system that fosters labor productivity increases arising from a pay-for-performance compensation plan. For production employees, wages are based entirely on piecework. In addition, they receive a year-end bonus which averages approximately 100 percent of regular compensation.

[1]Details of this example are from N. Fast and N. Berg (1975), "The Lincoln Electric Company," Harvard Business School Case 376–028; C. Bartlett (1998), "Lincoln Electric: Venturing Abroad," Harvard Business School Case 9-398–095; and Lincoln Electric's financial reports; and "Employees' Handbook" (2011)

A key element of Lincoln's organizational architecture, and the topic of this chapter, is its performance-evaluation system. There are two components of Lincoln's performance evaluation: Pieces produced and merit rating. The first component is an objective, readily quantifiable performance measure for each production employee—the number of good units produced. The employee's wage is equal to a piece rate times the number of good units produced. (Employees are not paid for defective units.) The piece rates—set by the time study department—allow employees producing at a standard rate to earn a wage comparable to those for similar jobs in the local labor market. However, by working hard—in some cases even through meal and coffee breaks—employees can double and sometimes triple their pay. Moreover, Lincoln's policies prohibit piece rate changes simply because an employee is making "too much" money. Finally, any employee who has been at Lincoln for at least two years is guaranteed employment for at least 75 percent of the standard 40-hour week.

The second component of Lincoln's evaluation system is the employee's merit rating. These ratings are used to determine the employee's share of the annual bonus pool. Although there is substantial annual variation, the size of the bonus pool averages about 30–40 percent of total wages and is typically about twice Lincoln's net income after taxes. Each employee's merit evaluation is based on employee dependability, quality, output, ideas, and cooperation—all of which are assessed primarily by the employee's immediate supervisor.

Lincoln was primarily a U.S. company until the mid-1980s, but a U.S. recession and competition from abroad led Lincoln to embark on a global expansion. It added manufacturing plants in 11 new countries, and attempted to export its unique management philosophy to these new plants. However, its efforts to replicate its highly productive system abroad failed. Lincoln took on large amounts of debt to finance its foreign expansion, mostly in Europe. In 1992, losses from the company's European operations were so steep that Lincoln was near default on its loans and was unable to pay its employees their year-end bonus. Several factors doomed Lincoln's interna-

MANAGERIAL APPLICATIONS

U.S. Health Care System Adopts Pay-for-Performance

The adoption of performance-based payment incentives is one of the most important changes in the U.S. health care system. Many large health insurers, including health maintenance organizations (HMOs), now employ pay-for-performance as a key mechanism to motivate their health care providers. Popular performance measures include rates of screening for various diseases (e.g., percent of diabetic patients undergoing annual testing) and immunization, patient satisfaction, and compliance rates for appropriate use of medications. One study examined 24 programs that varied in size from 50,000 to 11 million enrollees and covered hospitals, clinics, primary care physicians, and specialists such as cardiologists and general surgeons. It found that nearly all programs have increased the number of measures that factor into the calculation of performance bonuses. Payers have increased both the size of the financial incentives and the number of measures on which they are based. After adopting more pay-for-performance, some improvement was documented in various clinical areas such as diabetes care, cancer screening, and inpatient cardiac care. However, pay-for-performance still remains a small portion of total payments to providers.

Source: M. Rosenthal, B. Landon, K. Howitt, H. Song, and A. Epstein (2007), "Climbing Up the Pay-for-Performance Learning Curve: Where Are the Early Adopters Now?" *Health Affairs* (November/December), 1674–1683; and G. Young, D. Conrad, A. Fallat (2007), "Practical Issues in the Design and Implementation of Pay-for-Quality Programs," *Journal of Healthcare Management* (January/February), 10–20.

tional expansion including a recession in Europe, lack of familiarity with Europe's labor culture and regulation, and limited international expertise among its senior managers. Lincoln was forced to restructure its European operations. It wrote off most of its European facilities, increased U.S. production and sales, and hired top managers and nominated board members with substantial international experience. Finally, Lincoln managed to resume paying bonuses and to regain the trust of its employees.

Three important observations emerge from Lincoln Electric. First, the reward system uses as an input the output from the performance-evaluation system—the two systems are linked. Second, Lincoln Electric uses both quite objective and explicit (units produced) as well as subjective (dependability and cooperation) performance measures. Third, Lincoln managers failed to understand that all three components of the firm's organizational architecture must remain in balance. They naively believed that Lincoln's successful performance evaluation and reward systems could be exported to foreign countries. But European labor laws, labor unions, and culture are quite different than in the United States. An effective organizational architecture in the United States must fit within the constraints imposed by both the domestic legal system as well as U.S. culture. Simply exporting an organizational architecture without modification into a different legal and cultural environment is likely to fail.

Employee performance is evaluated for at least two reasons. First, performance evaluation provides employees with feedback on job achievement that provides important information on how they might improve performance. For instance, additional training in particular areas might be indicated. Second, performance evaluation is used in determining rewards and sanctions—wages, raises, bonuses, promotions, reassignments, and dismissals. These two purposes create somewhat different incentives. For example, if evaluations were used exclusively to provide feedback, employees would have fewer incentives to distort their evaluations to make themselves look better. But distortions to improve reported performance are more likely if employees are rewarded based on measured performance.

In this chapter, we focus primarily on the second reason for performance evaluation—as input for setting rewards and sanctions for employees. This chapter as well as the next describes the performance-evaluation system, the third leg of our three-legged stool that constitutes the firm's organizational architecture. Performance evaluation involves evaluating both individual employees and subunits of the firm. This chapter focuses on individual performance evaluation. The next chapter examines issues in evaluating subunits within the firm.

To organize our discussion of individual performance evaluation, we return to the basic principal-agent model presented in Chapter 15. In that model, the employee's output Q depends on effort e and a random component μ:

$$Q = \alpha e + \mu \tag{16.1}$$

where α is the employee's marginal productivity. For every unit of effort, α units of output are expected. In this model, e and μ are unobservable by management, but α is known by both management and the employee. If the employee is paid a fixed wage, independent of output Q, the employee has incentives to shirk because low Q can be blamed on negative μ, which is not observable. (Remember, effort is costly to the employee.) To limit such shirking, the firm bases employee compensation on output:

$$\text{Employee compensation} = W_0 + \beta Q \tag{16.2}$$

where β represents the sensitivity of pay to performance. Such compensation contracts create incentives for employees to reduce their shirking on effort. But these contracts also impose risk on employees because pay is now a function of μ, the random component in the production of output. Since the employee is risk-averse, the firm must compensate the employee for bearing this risk or else the employee will choose to work elsewhere. This additional compensation for bearing such risk is called a *compensating differential*. Thus, owners of firms must trade off the additional effort the employees will exert from more powerful incentives with the larger compensating differential to bear this risk.

In this basic principal-agent model, output is assumed contractible; Q is an *objective performance measure*. The employee and the firm can execute compensation contracts based on Q at relatively low cost. Hence, compensation and performance evaluation (two legs of the stool) are explicitly linked. The model implicitly includes the following assumptions:

- The principal knows the employee's production function ($Q = \alpha e + \mu$), but not the actual values for e and μ.
- The principal benefits from higher Q (output).
- Output can be observed at zero cost.
- There is only one quantitative measure of performance—output.
- The employee produces a single output.
- The employee cannot game the performance measure.
- The employee works independently; there is no team production.
- Any mutually beneficial contract is feasible; labor markets are unregulated.

Clearly in practice, managers must implement performance-evaluation systems in situations that do not conform to some or all of these assumptions. The remaining sections of this chapter describe various issues that arise when these assumptions are relaxed.

Setting Performance Benchmarks

Solving for the optimal β in Equation (16.2) requires management to know α in Equation (16.1). Since the employee's marginal productivity is not readily observable, management must estimate it. To illustrate the issues involved in estimating the employee's marginal productivity, consider the following simplified example. Conrad Mueller can assemble a particular model of welder at the following daily rate:

$$\text{Units assembled} = 5e_c + \mu_c \qquad (16.3)$$

where e_c is the number of hours of normal effort worked, and μ_c is a random error term. If Conrad worked 8 hours at a normal effort level, $e_c = 8$, then on average he would assemble 40 welders (5×8). On average, the error μ_c is zero. If Conrad worked 8 hours but at a faster, more strenuous pace ($e_c > 8$)—the equivalent of, say, 12 hours at a normal effort level ($e_c = 12$)—then 60 units per day would be assembled on average. If he slacked off and took numerous short breaks, e_c might only be 5, and 25 units on average would be assembled.

While the average error μ_c is zero, the number of units assembled is subject to potentially large shocks; this means that the variance of μ_c is not zero. For example, if Conrad were to receive low-quality parts or subassemblies, the number of units assembled would be down even if Conrad were to expend normal amounts of effort ($e_c = 8$) because more time would be required to fit together each slightly out-of-specification part. Or perhaps Conrad might be idled for a few minutes each hour waiting for parts delivery. In these cases, μ_c would be negative. Alternatively, he might get lucky and assemble more than $5e_c$ units because of an unusually well-produced set of parts, ample parts inventory, productive tools, or few distractions.

The assembly department in the preceding example might establish a benchmark of 40 welders assembled per employee per day. Production above 40 then would be considered good performance and less than 40 considered poor performance. The standard of 40 is absolute in the sense that it is fixed and known before the employee exerts effort. Management, however, might know neither the exact relation between effort and production (welders assembled = $5e + \mu$) nor that the average employee exerted 8 units of effort a day. Thus, the output of the average assembler must be estimated. There are at least two ways to do this: time and motion studies and historical production data analysis.

Time and Motion Studies

In time and motion studies, industrial engineers estimate how much time a particular task requires, with the goal of determining the most effective work method. Motion studies involve the systematic analysis of work methods, considering the raw materials, the design of the product, the process, the tools, and the activity at each step. Besides focusing on how long a particular activity should take, industrial engineers often are able to redesign the product or process to reduce the time required. Time studies employ a wide variety of techniques for determining the duration a particular activity requires under certain standard conditions. Work sampling (one type of time study) involves selecting a large number of observations taken at random intervals and observing how long employees take performing various components of the job. Time and motion studies often are expensive in terms of engineering time used in the studies. They usually must be redone whenever product design changes or new equipment is introduced. They also suffer from potential bias because of employees' incentives to establish lower quotas by underperforming during the study period.

Past Performance and the Ratchet Effect

Another common mechanism for setting performance goals uses historical data on past performance. Unfortunately, this method often leads to a perverse incentive called the *ratchet effect*.[2] The ratchet effect refers to basing next year's standard of performance on this year's actual performance. But performance targets usually are adjusted in only one direction: upward. A poor year usually causes subsequent years' targets to be reduced not at all, or to be reduced by very little. This "ratcheting up" of standards discourages employees from exceeding the quota substantially to avoid

---

[2]A. Leone and S. Rock (2002), "Empirical Tests of Budget Ratcheting and Its Effect on Managers' Discretionary Accrual Choices," *Journal of Accounting & Economics* 33, 43–67.

raising the standard for future periods by too much.[3] Many illustrations of dysfunctional behaviors induced by the ratchet effect exist:

- Companies often base a salesperson's bonus on meeting target sales where the target is based on last year's sales. If salespeople expect an unusually good year, they often will try to defer some sales into the next fiscal year. For instance, they might take the customer's order but delay processing it until the next fiscal year.

- In the old Soviet Union, central planners would set a plant's production quota based on past experience. Plant managers meeting their targets received various rewards, and those missing the target were punished. This created incentives for managers to exceed the quota just barely.

- In one automobile engine assembly plant, a labor productivity performance goal was mandated each year. Each department's target was based in part on last year's performance plus an increase. This created incentives for managers to defer making big productivity improvements in any one year, preferring instead to spread them over several years.[4]

Lincoln Electric avoids the dysfunctional problems of the ratchet effect by its policy that the piecework rate cannot be changed even if the employee is making too much money. Once a piecework rate is set by the time study department, it is never changed until production methods or processes are changed, or unless the employee challenges the rate and a new time study is conducted.

Another way to reduce problems caused by ratcheting up each year's performance targets is more frequent job rotation. If you know that next year someone else has to meet the sales figures you achieve this year, you will sell more now. However, job rotation can destroy job-specific human capital such as customer-specific relationships.

Measurement Costs

When it is costly to observe the employee's output, performance evaluation becomes much more complicated—and interesting. For example, your server at the restaurant might appear to have performed well. But you only begin to suspect that you were served caffeinated instead of decaffeinated coffee at 2 A.M. when you still cannot sleep. The quality of a patent attorney's work is not known until a challenge to the patent is filed. Measuring an elementary schoolteacher's output is complex. Relying on standardized test scores captures only a part of student learning. Or, a research scientist's output is difficult to quantify and observe. "Observability," "verifiability," and "contractibility" ultimately are questions of cost. Almost everything is observable—even effort—at some cost. For example, in jobs where physical effort is required, how hard an employee works might be measured by attaching heart-rate monitors or videotaping the person. But, such measurements frequently are quite costly.

---

[3]Some of the incentive not to exceed the target by a large amount is reduced if the employee's bonus is a function of the amount by which output exceeds the target. The actual dysfunctional incentives created by the ratchet effect depend on the precise form of the incentive compensation contract. For example, if past performance is used to set β in Equation (16.2), very different incentives are created than if past performance is used to set a target performance and a fixed bonus is paid so long as actual output exceeds this target.

[4]R. Kaplan and A. Hutton (1997), "Peoria Engine Plant (A)," Harvard Business School Case 9-193-082.

Measuring What Counts

Determining the weight of an orange may be a low cost, accurate operation. Yet what is weighed is seldom what is truly valued. The skin of the orange hides its pulp, making a direct measurement of the desired attributes costly. Thus the taste and amount of juice it contains are always a bit surprising.

Source: Y. Barzel (1982), "Measurement Cost and the Organization of Markets," *Journal of Law & Economics* XXV, 27–48.

Costs are incurred in generating performance measures. For example, accounting systems must be developed and maintained to keep track of sales, costs, quality, or divisional profits. Computer systems and software capable of producing detailed reports are more complicated. And if the measures are used for performance evaluation, additional management and clerical time must be spent ensuring the accuracy of the performance measures. High measurement costs can lower the net benefits of tying pay to performance.

In our simple principal-agent model, the employee's output is used in setting compensation. However, output depends on random factors. Even if output were costlessly observable, it still can be optimal to expend additional resources to measure the employee's effort level more precisely. To the extent the firm can reduce the employee's exposure to the variance of these random factors via more sophisticated performance measures, the lower the compensating differential the firm must pay the employee to bear this risk. The informativeness principle implies that whenever low-cost information is available that allows a more accurate assessment of the employee's effort, such information should be used in assessing performance. A value-maximizing firm will go to the point where the incremental cost of increasing the precision of its performance measurement (through more sophisticated accounting and information systems, for instance) equals the incremental benefits. These benefits include the reduction in the risk premium that must be paid to employees.

In general, the more incentive pay in the employee's compensation package, the more risk the employee bears and the more the firm should spend on measurement systems to quantify the impact of these random factors. Thus, the choice of the optimum β in Equation (16.2) and the choice of how much to spend measuring performance are jointly determined. These two legs of the stool are complements. Increasing the employee's incentive compensation β should be accompanied by increasing the precision with which effort is measured.[5]

In some cases, observing and measuring the employee's output becomes so expensive that the firm begins to look for alternative proxies that capture employee performance. For example, managers often are evaluated on the accounting profits of their divisions, even though the firm ultimately is interested in the total value created

---

[5]For a more formal treatment of this principle, see P. Milgrom and J. Roberts (1992), *Economics, Organizations, and Management* (Prentice Hall: Englewood Cliffs), 226. Firms sometimes can reduce the risk imposed on employees by basing pay on available *input-based measures*, such as hours worked, number of customers contacted, and new accounts created, than on output-based measures used in the basic model. Input-based measures, however, are generally less effective than output-based measures in encouraging employees to use their specific knowledge efficiently and thus are less desirable when local specific knowledge is important. See M. Raith (2008), "Specific Knowledge and Performance Measurement," *RAND Journal of Economics*, 39, 1059-1079.

MANAGERIAL APPLICATIONS

Technology to Reduce Measuring Costs of Individual Performance

Companies often use technology to evaluate individual performance. British Airways uses employee performance software to track how long their customer service representatives spend resolving customer complaints or issuing tickets. The software also tracks how many customers call back complaining about errors in their tickets or complaining that their previous complaint calls were not addressed satisfactorily, so ticket agents don't slough off in issuing the original ticket. Other software blocks employee nonbusiness chatting, surfing, shopping, and instant messaging. Firms use these systems to provide extra incentives to those employees whose digital records merit the pay. This is an example of how a reduction in the cost of measuring individual performance leads to a more precise estimate of employees' effort, thereby reducing the risk employees bear from random events (or errors) in measuring their performance, and thus increasing the proportion of incentive pay in their compensation package.

Source: M. Conlin (2002), "The Software Says You're Just Average," *BusinessWeek* (February 25), 126; and L. Kornblatt (2007), "Zihtec Introduces Innovative Software to Help Companies Control Online Productivity," *Business Wire* (April 16).

---

by its managers. This value includes not only short-term divisional profits (as measured by the accounting system) but future expected profits, as well as the effects of the manager's efforts on other divisions' profits. Similarly, schoolteachers often are evaluated on their students' performance on standardized tests, even though the school ultimately is interested in broader, harder-to-measure indicators of learning. Whether or not a particular proxy variable is good for purposes of performance evaluation depends on whether the employee's actions have similar effects on both the proxy variable and the underlying output variable.[6] For example, if paying a manager on divisional profits motivates more diligent effort as well as actions that increase underlying value, then divisional profits would be a useful performance measure. Alternatively, to the extent divisional profits motivate actions that do not enhance value (e.g., sacrificing substantial future profits to achieve only a modest increase in near-term profits), divisional profits are a poor performance measure. Ill-designed performance measures promote opportunism and gaming.

Opportunism

In our basic model, the agent is paid based on what the principal cares about—the employee's output, Q. As previously discussed, it may be feasible only to evaluate the agent on some alternative measure, which we label here as Y. Paying the agent on Y provides incentives to the agent to take actions to increase Y, which can be very different than the actions to increase Q—*you get what you pay for*. Imperfect performance measures often provide incentives to employees to behave opportunistically in ways that affect their performance evaluations. This section describes two examples of opportunistic behavior: Gaming and the horizon problem. Almost all performance measures suffer from these and other related problems (discussed later in this chapter). How heavily the firm should weight a performance measure, such as Y, depends on the magnitude of these problems compared to the increase in Q that the firm obtains in return.

---

[6] G. Baker (1992), "Incentive Contracts and Performance Measurement," *Journal of Political Economy* 100, 598–614.

MANAGERIAL APPLICATIONS

Gaming Objective Performance Measures

Dysfunctional behavior of mortgage originators appears to have been one cause of the financial crisis of 2007–2008. Specialists and brokers, who did not provide the funding directly, originated most mortgage loans in the United States. They sold the originated loans to other financial institutions and thus were rewarded based on the number and size of the originated loans. Under this system, originators can have limited incentives to insure that a loan is a good one, since the costs of default are largely borne by other parties. Some contracts between financial institutions and originators allow the mortgage to be "put" back to the originator if the homebuyer defaulted on the loan within some limited time period, for example, during the first year. Various mortgage originators gamed this provision prior to the crisis by promoting loans that offered below market interest rates for the first year ("teaser rates"). The low interest rate reduced the mortgage payment for the first year, limiting near-term defaults. The rate of defaults tended to be higher in year two and beyond when the interest rate was increased to actual market levels and the borrower could no longer afford to make the payments.

Source: M. Baily, R. Litan and M. Johnson (2008), "The Origins of the Financial Crisis," *Business and Public Policy at Brookings* (November).

Gaming

For simplicity, suppose that Q = action 1 + μ and Y = action 1 + action 2 + ϕ, where μ and ϕ are random shocks. While compensating an employee on Y can provide incentives for the employee to take action 1, it can also provide incentives for the employee to take action 2, even though it does not affect the firm's return, Q. This action is a pure social waste, and if the employee is paid a competitive wage (for attraction and retention) the cost is borne entirely by the firm. For example, suppose Q is a divisional manager's unobservable true contribution to firm value, while Y is the observed accounting earnings of the division. The manager's exertion of productive effort (action 1) contributes to both Q and Y, while engaging in questionable accounting choices (action 2) affects only Y. Evaluating the manager on divisional earnings can provide incentives to the manager to waste his time and other resources manipulating divisional accounting and place the firm at risk of possible regulatory actions. In a more extreme case, such as Q = action 1 + μ and Y = action 2 + μ, a contract based on Y will motivate no increases in Q. This is true even as in this example the two measures are perfectly correlated since they share a common noise term, μ. For instance, a police department might want a policeman to concentrate on arresting truly reckless drivers and having them convicted by a court of law (Q = the number of convicted truly reckless drivers), while the policeman is evaluated on the number of arrests and subsequent convictions of drivers who simply exceed the basic speed limit (Y). Whether a ticketed driver is convicted or not in all cases depends solely on which judge is randomly assigned to the case (some judges are more likely to convict than others). Here Q and Y would be highly correlated, but evaluating the policeman on Y would provide very limited incentives to concentrate on arresting truly reckless drivers. Arresting any driver who exeeds the speed limit increases his performance measure.

Recall the costs Merrill Lynch incurred when its analysts inappropriately recommended securities to its customers. Doing so increased the analysts' incomes but was extraordinarily damaging to Merrill. Other examples include the following: A salesperson offers customers discounts to shift sales from one evaluation period to another. An employee paid based on output reduces quality to increase output. A refuse hauler, compensated on the weight of trash delivered to the landfill, uses a fire hose to top off his load with water before weighing in at the truck scales. Finally, Lincoln

Electric installed counters to record the number of characters typed by their secretaries who were paid on this basis. But piecework for secretaries was abandoned when one secretary, who earned much more than the others, was found staying at her desk during lunch and coffee breaks depressing a repeating key on her keyboard, thus quite rapidly typing totally useless pages. Hence, seemingly objective measures of performance such as sales or output often create incentives for employees to take value-reducing actions (such as lowering product quality) if such actions increase their measured performance.

Performance evaluation almost always involves unintended consequences that often benefit the agent at the firm's expense. Jobs are complex and often involve several tasks, some of which are difficult to contract over. One particularly poignant example involves Ken O'Brien, the football quarterback who early in his career in the 1980s tended to throw interceptions. He was given a contract that penalized him for each interception. The unintended consequence was he frequently refused to throw the ball and ended up getting sacked or not throwing the ball when he should have.[7]

Horizon Problem

Objective output measures frequently focus on the near term because of the difficulty of objectively measuring consequences that might occur in the future. Short-run, objective performance measures can cause employees—especially those about to change jobs or leave the firm—to concentrate their efforts on producing results that will influence their appraisals favorably over their remaining horizon with the firm. For example, a 64-year-old salesperson, paid on commission and expecting to retire at age 65, has little incentive to work at developing long-term customer relationships.

Relative Performance Evaluation

Multiple employees performing similar tasks potentially can provide useful additional signals about the random errors affecting individual employees. For example, if in addition to Conrad, Dina van den Brink also assembles welders and her output is

$$\text{Units assembled by Dina} = 5e_d + \mu_d \qquad (16.4)$$

where e_d is the number of hours of normal effort worked by Dina, and μ_d is her random error term. In assembling welders, both Conrad and Dina expect that if they exert average effort of $e = 8$, each expects to produce 40 units. If Conrad's and Dina's error terms, μ_c and μ_d, are positively correlated because they depend on many of the same conditions (raw material quality and working conditions), then in evaluating Conrad's performance, management can look at Dina's output for information about uncontrollable factors affecting Conrad's production. If Dina were to have unusually low output, it is likely that there was some shock that would have lowered Conrad's output, as well.

More generally, suppose that in addition to Conrad and Dina, a number of other employees also assemble the same welders. The informativeness principle implies that an important source of information about an employee's effort is the output of coworkers performing similar tasks. Thus to reduce the risk of noncontrollable factors, management uses information about the average number of welders assembled

---

[7]C. Prendergast (1999), "The Provision of Incentives in Firms," *Journal of Economic Literature* (May), 21.

ACADEMIC APPLICATIONS

Relative Performance Evaluation for CEOs

CEO compensation (salary plus bonus) and turnover likelihoods depend on relative performance evaluation. Gibbons and Murphy examine 2,214 CEOs serving in 1,295 large, publicly traded U.S. corporations from 1974 to 1986. They find that CEOs' compensation is positively related to their own stock return performance and negatively related to the stock return in the market and industry. That is, compensation is higher when the CEO's own firm's stock return is higher and when the market or industry stock return is down. Finally, they study the likelihood that the CEO is replaced. Executive turnover is lower the larger the firm's own stock price return and the lower the industry return. If the industry is performing poorly, the CEO is more likely retained, holding everything else constant. However, CEOs also are compensated using awards of stock and options. The realized values of these awards are adjusted for overall market or industry performance only rarely. Thus, although some of the incentives of executives are based on relative performance, others are based on absolute performance. Another study of CEOs of large publicly traded firms from 1993 to 2003 also reports that CEOs' compensation is positively related to their own stock return performance and negatively related to a peer group's stock return. (Albuquerque uses industry and size to construct peer groups.)

Source: R. Gibbons and K. Murphy (1990), "Relative Performance Evaluation for Chief Executive Officers," *Industrial and Labor Relations Review* 43, 30S–51S; and A. Albuquerque (2005), "Who Are Your Peers?" doctoral thesis, University of Rochester.

by all these employees. Forty units per employee per day is the expected number of welders, given normal quality and no unusual events. Suppose the average number of welders across all the employees on a given day was 43. Then for this day, average $\mu = 3(43 - 40)$. And if Conrad produced 41 welders that day, his compensation would be adjusted by some part of his two-unit shortfall (41–43). Using the output of other employees to adjust the employee's output in the compensation contract is called *relative performance evaluation.* By filtering out common shocks from employee incentive pay, relative performance evaluation reduces the risk employees bear. This allows the firm to reduce the risk premium it must pay employees to bear this common risk, thereby reducing the firm's total labor costs. (The appendix to this chapter discusses methods to estimate the optimal adjustment.)

Within-Firm Performance

Using other employees' output within the same firm to estimate the average error is a useful method of reducing the risk employees bear from incentive compensation contracts if they all sell or manufacture the same products and face the same competitors and economywide factors. However, forming a reference group from employees inside the firm also can have drawbacks. Only in rare cases are employees' jobs identical. For instance, some salespeople have large established territories—others, small developing ones. Customer types can vary dramatically across sales territories.

If an internal reference group is formed and its group average is used to assess normal performance, the group has incentives to punish "rate busters"—extremely productive employees who raise the average. In a classic research study known as the Hawthorne experiments, employees were observed hitting colleagues who exceeded the commonly accepted output rate.[8] Thus, explicit employee collusion to hold down the benchmark can occur. Also, instances of sabotage are observed in relative performance evaluations. Instead of working diligently and increasing their own

[8]H. Parsons (1974), "What Happened at Hawthorne?" *Science* 183 (March 8), 927.

MANAGERIAL APPLICATIONS

Classic Example—Potential Costs of Relative Performance Evaluations

Individuals gaming performance-evaluation systems are not uncommon. Some people are willing to go to great lengths to sabotage others when their advancement is based on relative performance evaluations. For example, one reporter told of a friend who recently had been promoted at a large bank. When asked about it, the friend confessed that he had hacked into the bank's computer system and gained access to employees' messages as well as their calendars. "They would miss important meetings and be sent on wild-goose chases, only to look like complete buffoons when they showed up for appointments that were never made." By the time these poor fellows realized that their careers had been derailed, they were reporting to a new vice president.

Source: J. Dvorak (1988), "New Age of Villainy," *PC Magazine* (September 27).

performance, coworkers sabotage their peers within the reference group. Alternatively, employees might try to get themselves classified into a reference group that has weak performance so they will appear above average.

Relative performance evaluation also affects recruiting incentives. Employees often are involved in interviewing and selecting potential colleagues. If paid based on relative performance, such employees have the incentive to recommend hiring less competent new employees. This improves the relative performance of the current employees.

Across-Firm Performance

The Securities and Exchange Commission requires publicly traded firms when describing their executive compensation to select a benchmark reference group of other firms and report how their firm has performed relative to that benchmark. This is an example of selecting a reference group outside the firm. Some firms also employ external benchmarking to overcome the lack of an internal reference group or to avoid the pernicious actions of sabotage and collusion. Firms exchange information directly or do so through a trade association that aggregates information across several firms to mask individual firm data. Sometimes this information is obtained from compensation consultants that aggregate information across client firms. Thus, average performance in other firms is used as the reference group.

There are several disadvantages to external benchmarking. Use of this method often is precluded by a lack of data: Other firms view their performance data as proprietary and thus are unwilling to share it. Even if firms are willing to share data, for firms in the same industry such cooperation is potentially illegal under antitrust laws, and although job titles might be similar, the assignment of decision right can differ profoundly between firms. Moreover, employees in outside firms may not be subject to the same common shocks as the benchmarking firm's employees. Thus, external benchmarking might increase the risk to employees, rather than decrease it.

Subjective Performance Evaluation

Most jobs contain numerous dimensions. For example, baseball players have to field the ball, get hits (ranging from bunts to home runs), run the bases, and generally support the team. It is difficult to specify and measure all aspects of the job. If compensation is based on explicit measures that capture only some aspects, employees will deemphasize the unmeasured job attributes. For instance, if a veteran ballplayer is evaluated solely on his hitting, he has fewer incentives to spend time mentoring young ballplayers. Often, the firm augments its use of objective, explicit measures of output and uses more subjective yet comprehensive measures of performance. A key feature of subjective measures is that they cannot be verified by third parties.

Firms decentralize decision rights to individuals in the firm, in part to encourage them to participate in the conversion of wetware into software. Firms often use subjective performance evaluation to provide employees with greater incentives to take their skills and insights (wetware) and systematize them into valuable methods, formulas, or recipes (software). This software then can be leveraged throughout the organization. Many firms have formalized mechanisms to accomplish these goals, such as "Suggestion Boxes" to solicit ideas for improving organizational productivity.

Subjective performance reviews are conducted primarily because it is expensive to measure accurately all the dimensions of the employee's output that are valued by the firm. Subjective evaluations provide a more holistic view of an employee's performance because objective evaluations often exclude difficult-to-observe job tasks, or because the relative weights needed to aggregate objective evaluations change with current circumstances. In fact, it is rare for employees to be evaluated exclusively based on objective measures. Rather, their performance evaluations tend to include subjective elements. For example, most employees receive annual performance reviews from supervisors. These reviews often form the basis for setting salaries and promotions. Even when compensation is based entirely on objective measures (piece rates in agriculture), the firm reserves the right to fire employees for low-quality production, tardiness, inability to get along with coworkers, or other dysfunctional behavior. Lincoln Electric bases factory employees' wages entirely on piecework—an objective measure. But in addition to this objective measure, Lincoln also uses a subjective merit evaluation to set the employee bonus, which is approximately the same magnitude as wages.

We first describe an important reason firms use subjective performance measures—namely, assigning multiple tasks to employees. Then various subjective evaluation systems are described. Finally, problems with subjective evaluations are summarized.

Multitasking and Unbalanced Effort

Multiple tasks often are assigned to one employee because there are efficiency gains from bundling the tasks. For example, secretaries answer phones, word process, file, schedule appointments, and make travel plans. Or, an employee might be expected to sell products to existing customers, contact potential new customers, and fill out sales reports. These tasks all are complementary to selling the product.

Returning to the comparison of Q (what the firm actually cares about) and Y (the available performance measure), suppose that $Q =$ task 1 + task 2 + μ and $Y =$ task 1 + ϕ. In this case, a contract based on Y creates incentives to undertake the first task, but cannot create incentives to undertake task 2. If the firm wants the employee to devote effort to the second task, it must not use Y as its only measure of the employee's performance.[9]

[9]S. Datar, S. Kulp and R. Lambert (2001), "Balancing Performance Measures," *Journal of Accounting Research*, 39, 75–92; and G. Feltham and J. Xie (1994), "Performance Measure Congruity and Diversity in Multi-Task Principal/Agent Relationship," *Accounting Review* 69, 429–453.

MANAGERIAL APPLICATIONS

Self-Evaluation

Self-evaluation by the employee, that is, reviewed by the boss often forms a basis for compensation adjustments and promotions. In self-evaluations, employees enumerate accomplishments, discuss weaknesses, and point out strengths. One employee views the self-evaluation as a way to inform her boss about how she brings value to the company. Although she realizes that the self-evaluation is an opportunity to highlight her contributions to the company, she agonizes over the task. Ultimately there are only two major ways that you end up describing yourself: "(A) Self-flagellating lummox dumb enough to enumerate weaknesses that can be used against you at a later date. (B) Self-aggrandizing egomaniac who thinks no means yes, insults are a form of flattery—and you're pretty good looking to boot."

Self-evaluations can be unreliable and certainly are controversial tools. High self-esteem leads to grade inflation. Eighty-five percent of self-evaluators rate themselves in the top 25 percent. Females do not inflate as much as males. Overraters tend to make more money and get more promotions but have lower performance and shorter careers.

Source: J. Sandberg (2003), "Better than Great—And Other Tall Tales of Self-Evaluations," *The Wall Street Journal* (March 12).

Suppose, for example, that Conrad Mueller performs two tasks, assembling welders and training new employees to assemble welders. Some activities are more easily measured, such as counting the number of welders Conrad assembles; others, like training new assemblers, are more difficult to assess. If Conrad's evaluation is based primarily on the easily measured tasks (welders assembled), he has incentives to concentrate his efforts on these activities. Conrad will not allocate the optimal amount of time to the other unmeasured tasks. Remember: *You get what you pay for—and frequently, that is all you get.*

This multitasking problem can affect optimal job design. For example, a firm might want to have certain employees concentrate only on assembling welders when complementarities among tasks are low. These employees then could be evaluated on their output of assembled welders. Other employees would concentrate on training new assemblers and correspondingly be evaluated on their training. By separating the tasks, each employee can be given more focused incentives to perform their more limited range of tasks.

Subjective reviews evaluate an employee's performance on a more comprehensive basis. Aspects of the job that are measured less easily can be considered along with more easily measured activities. For example, the supervisor might consider the employee's efforts at being cooperative, being part of a team, being responsive to potential customers, or filling out reports accurately. Conrad's supervisor can observe how he instructs new hires, how patient he is, and how they ultimately perform as assemblers in assessing Conrad's performance as a trainer. Moreover, if Conrad games the performance measure—takes firm-value reducing actions that increase the objective performance measure—his supervisor (if aware of these dysfunctional actions) can penalize Conrad through his subjective performance evaluation.

Subjective Evaluation Methods

There are two widely used subjective performance-appraisal systems: Standard-rating-scale systems and goal-based systems. Goal-based systems tend to be more explicit and less subjective than standard-rating-scale systems.

Standard-Rating-Scale Systems

Standard rating scales require the evaluator to rank the employee on a number of different performance factors using, for example, a five-point scale: Far exceeds requirements, exceeds requirements, meets all requirements, partially meets requirements, does not meet requirements. The different performance factors judged vary across firms and positions within firms but often include the following:

- Achieves forecasts, budgets, objectives
- Organizes effective performance through oral and written communications
- Sets and attains high performance goals for self and group
- Updates knowledge of job-related skills
- Emphasizes teamwork among subordinates
- Identifies and resolves problems
- Evaluates subordinates objectively
- Ensures equal opportunities for all subordinates

After ranking the employee on each of these narrow criteria, the evaluator then assigns a rating for the overall job: Excellent, better than satisfactory, satisfactory, needs further improvement, and unsatisfactory. Most subjective performance appraisals contain a section where the supervisor provides detailed comments on the employee's strengths and weaknesses and offers specific recommendations for improvement and further development.

Goal-Based Systems

In a goal-based system, each employee is given a set of goals for the year. For example, goals might be "hold training sessions for all employees in the department by November 1," or "hire four additional qualified members of minority groups." These goals tend to be more objective and easier to measure than the more vague performance factors used in the standard rating scales such as "emphasizes teamwork." Nonetheless, these goals still are more subjective than standard piecework measures. At the end of the year, the supervisor writes a memo detailing the extent to which each goal has been met. An overall evaluation of the employee is based on the extent to which the goals are achieved.

MANAGERIAL APPLICATIONS

360-Degree Performance Reviews

Privately held W. L. Gore & Associates with sales of $2.3 billion in 2007 employs 8,000 employees and manufactures Gore-Tex waterproof fabric. Often ranked among the "100 Best Companies to Work for in America," all Gore employees are called associates. There are no "bosses," but each employee is assigned a "sponsor" who acts as a mentor. Gore has been using 360-degree evaluation as part of its performance feedback since 1958. Under this system, annual evaluations are gathered on all associates from the individual's peers, subordinates, and superiors. The evaluations are anonymous and rate employees on their contributions to the success of the business during the past year. All ratings on each employee receive equal weight. Compensation committees composed of sponsors with specialized knowledge of the area use the rankings to award pay increases or performance warnings.

A vice president of marketing at a large telecommunications company was told by her employees in a 360-degree review that "you are angry a lot." "That feedback was a life-altering experience for me," she reports.

Source: C. Hymowitz (2003), "Managers See Feedback from Their Staffers as the Most Valuable," *The Wall Street Journal* (November 11); J. Reingold (2007), "A Job That Lets You Pick Your Own Boss," http://money.cnn.com (October 8); and www.gore.com.

After evaluators have rated their employees using either a standard rating scale or a goal-based system, evaluators usually then review the evaluations with their supervisors. This helps ensure the accuracy of the review and promotes consistency of criteria across employees. After reviewing their evaluations, employees can respond to the evaluation in writing, including the expression of formal disagreement with any of the specifics in the appraisal. Finally, the evaluators and their supervisors review the feedback provided by the evaluators and the employees' responses.

In the majority of cases, the employee's immediate supervisor does the performance evaluation. In some cases, firms have experimented with peer evaluations—especially in situations where teams are important. The benefit of peer evaluations is that peers have information about typical performance in group assignments and the actual contribution of the individual to the team. Offsetting the better specific knowledge of peers is the added costs of training everyone in the team to do evaluations. Moreover, peer evaluation can increase the tensions within the team. For example, some team members might systematically lower everyone else's ratings to make themselves look better. Or, friends may be rated highly to increase their chance of being promoted to supervise their former colleagues. Finally, teammates might decide to collude to give everyone higher performance ratings.

Frequency of Evaluation

Most subjective performance evaluations are conducted yearly, primarily because most salary adjustments are made annually. The benefits of more frequent evaluations (say quarterly) unlikely offset the higher costs. However, there are some examples of more frequent review. For example, new hires typically receive more frequent evaluations; often a new employee is evaluated at the end of three months. During this probationary period, the firm must decide whether to keep the individual. Also during this period, frequent feedback helps the employee learn and improve performance. As another example, consultants are evaluated after each professional assignment by the partner-in-charge of the engagement. Especially where team composition changes from project to project, capturing performance-evaluation information on a timely basis is important. The person's performance is known, and there is no reason to wait until the end of the year. Moreover, the evaluation provides more timely information on which to base subsequent project assignments.

Problems with Subjective Performance Evaluations

There are several potential problems with subjective performance evaluation.

Shirking among Supervisors[10]

Disciplining employees and informing them of their shortcomings often are unpleasant tasks. Supervisors do not capture the full wealth effects of these actions. Hence, potential shirking among supervisors leads to the provision of inaccurate performance evaluations. The inaccuries can take several forms. Supervisors overstate the poor performers. That is, the supervisor is too lenient. A supervisor might be reluctant to give adverse ratings to avoid conflict with subordinates. A supervisor also might overrate poor employees' performance to promote their transfers to new

---

[10]C. Prendergast and R. Topel (1993), "Discretion and Bias in Performance Appraisals," *European Economic Review* (June), 355–365; C. Prendergast and R. Topel (1996), "Favoritism in Organizations," *Journal of Political Economy* 104 (October), 958–978.

positions in other parts of the firm. In other cases, supervisors compress ratings around some norm rather than distinguish good and poor performers. Or, a supervisor might rank employees based on personal likes and dislikes rather than on job performance. Bias adds noise to the performance-evaluation system; it typically reduces morale and consequently the employees' incentives to work diligently, thereby lowering overall firm performance.

Indirect empirical evidence suggests that managers tend to assign relatively uniform performance ratings to employees. In a study of 7,000 performance ratings of managers and professionals in two firms, the researchers report that 95 percent of all appraisals were in just two categories: Good and superior (outstanding).[11] A survey of employee attitudes at Merck & Co., a large U.S. pharmaceutical firm, reported the following attitudes:[12]

- Managers are afraid to give experienced people a 1, 2, or 3 rating. It's easier to give everyone a 4 and give new people a 3.

- Charlie's been in that job for 20 years. He hasn't done anything creative for the last 15 years. Do you think my manager would give him a 3 rating? No way! Then he'd have to spend 12 months listening to Charlie complain.

- What's the use of killing yourself? You still get the same rating as everyone else, and you still get the same 5 percent increase. It's demoralizing and demotivating.

This evidence suggests that low-rated, disgruntled employees can impose costs on supervisors. In response, supervisors have incentives to bias their evaluations. As a result, performance ratings are frequently inaccurate appraisals of the employee's true performance. Biased, inaccurate appraisals reduce the incentive of employees to improve their performance by working harder and can lead to the promotion of less qualified people. Here, the problem lies not in the evaluation system *per se,* but rather in the incentives for the evaluators.

At Lincoln Electric, supervisors have incentives to do a good job because they are evaluated and compensated on the job they do in evaluating lower-level employees. Also, employees can discuss their ratings with senior management. Problems of bias are likely to be lower if the supervisor is held accountable for the future performance of individuals who are promoted based on the supervisor's recommendation.

Forced Distributions

To overcome the tendency to rate all employees "above average," some firms impose a forced distribution where a fixed fraction of employees are assigned to each category (i.e., the supervisor must rank a certain percentage of the employees as poor). However, forced distributions may not reflect the true distribution of performance accurately in each work group. Forced ranking systems can cause problems, especially when the size of the group to be evaluated is small. For example, having to rank one of four employees as poor might force the supervisor to rate a good-performing employee as poor; inaccuracies from the forced distribution might be larger than those from a biased supervisor. Moreover, forced distributions do not necessarily reduce the costs imposed on the supervisor. Under a forced distribution,

[11]J. Medoff and K. Abraham (1980), "Experience, Performance, and Earnings," *Quarterly Journal of Economics* 95, 703–736.

[12]Quotes excerpted from a 1985 Merck report by K. Murphy (1992), "Performance Measurement and Appraisal: Motivating Managers to Identify and Reward Performance," in W. Bruns (Ed.), *Performance Measurement, Evaluation, and Incentives* (Harvard Business School: Boston), 37–62.

supervisors might assign ratings based on the potential costs employees will impose on them—not based on the employees' true performances.

Influence Costs

Influence costs include those nonproductive activities employees engage in to influence outcomes—in this case, politicking for higher ratings by their supervisor. One potential method of reducing these costs is to rotate supervisors or employees more frequently (getting on the good side of one supervisor is of limited benefit). Rotation of employees, however, can limit potential synergies and cost reductions that arise with repeated interaction between a given manager and employee. New supervisors have limited knowledge of employees' specialized skills. Also, more frequent rotation potentially increases total influence costs, since the employee has more lobbying opportunities.

ANALYZING MANAGERIAL DECISIONS: *Semco S.A.*

Semco S.A. in São Paulo, Brazil, has 500 employees and manufactures capital goods. The employees elect their managers and evaluate them every six months. Managers rated poorly are transferred or fired. There are 100 nonunion employees who set their own performance standards and arrange their own work schedules. Twice a year, the nonunion employees receive a market salary survey and are asked to set their own pay for the next six months. Employees setting their pay too low receive that amount, as do employees requesting too high a salary. If management decides after one year that the employees' salaries were above what they were worth to the company, these employees are fired. The 400 unionized employees' pay is set by union contract. Critically evaluate Semco's performance-evaluation system.

MANAGERIAL APPLICATIONS

Tips on Subjective Performance Reviews

Here are some tips for improving your next performance evaluation:

- Prepare a list of creative ways you are solving problems with limited resources. For example, to reduce travel costs you have been holding fewer, but more comprehensive, meetings.

- Show how your work bolsters the bottom line. For example, instead of requesting new computers because they are state-of-the-art, frame the request as the new computers will save 10 percent of operators' time.

- Focus on the future. Instead of dwelling on past failings, emphasize specific future plans, such as training programs to attend.

When appraising others:

- Give honest feedback. Don't rate problem employees as above average because of fear of confrontation. This merely prolongs and exacerbates the inevitable confrontation.

- Ask employees if they understand their current assignments, if they have any problems, or stresses.

- Focus on the future, upcoming goals, potential training opportunities, instead of dwelling on the past.

- Communicate the company's goals and shifting priorities via the performance review.

PPG Industries illustrates how one company implements many of the above suggestions. PPG uses "SMART goals" for employee objectives. SMART is an acronym for Specific, Measurable, Agreed-upon by employee and manager, Realistic, and Timebound. Instead of simply telling a sales manager to boost sales next year, a SMART goal would be: "Develop, by May 1, three new customers in the Eastern region with annual sales potential of $50,000."

Source: S. Scherreik (2001), "Your Performance Review: Make It Perform," *BusinessWeek* (December 17), 139–140.

Reneging

There is the potential that the firm will renege on promises to employees to reward good performance. For example, management might promise to give raises to those who perform well. Afterward, management might unjustifiably assert that work was poor and renege on the promised raise. It is less likely that an employee will be successful in a lawsuit involving subjective performance measurement than when the employee can document that a firm reneged on an explicit contract involving objective performance measures.

Managers in healthy firms generally have incentives to maintain good reputations for honoring implicit contracts. However, reneging on implicit contracts will appear most attractive to firms in financial difficulty (near bankruptcy). Reneging also can occur when a supervisor has a short horizon with the firm and is compensated on business-unit profits. (Unit profits might be increased in the short run by not granting raises to employees.) We discuss these issues further in Chapter 22.

Combining Objective and Subjective Performance Measures

Performance-evaluation systems generally fall on a continuum between the two extremes—objective and subjective evaluation systems. Objective measures consist of items like output and sales that can be quantified easily and thus explicitly measured. Objective measures can be used in formal contracts between the employee and the firm. Subjective measures consist of noncontractible judgments about employee performance (the year-end evaluation from a supervisor). Subjective measures are used in implicit contracts. Few job-performance measures are purely objective or purely subjective; most measures involve mixtures of both. In most cases, organizations that use objective measures also use subjective measures to evaluate the same employee (as does Lincoln Electric, e.g.). Investment bankers pay bonuses based on fees generated by the employee but also use subjective measures such as the "quality of the deals."

Both objective and subjective performance measures can be inaccurate measures of the employee's contribution to the firm's value. As the accuracy of either measure decreases, more weight will be placed on the other in determining performance (holding its accuracy constant). As the accuracy of each measure decreases, the risk the employee bears increases, as does the compensating differential the employee must be paid.[13]

Besides being inaccurate, both objective and subjective measures can induce various dysfunctional behaviors. We indicated earlier that objective measures can create incentives for gaming, that reduces the firm's value as in the case of the policy "churning" by an insurance agent (convincing a policyholder to use the accumulated cash value to purchase a new, larger policy). If supervisors shirk when writing subjective performance reviews, employees' incentives to work diligently are reduced. Also, employees will generate influence costs lobbying for higher subjective ratings. Finally, implicit contracts using subjective measures are more easily abrogated by the firm than formal contracts based on objective measures. Employees must trust that the firm will not renege on implicit contracts. An important constraint on the firm from reneging is its reputation. Thus, firms facing a greater likelihood of financial distress will find subjective evaluations more costly to use.

Because the costs and benefits of objective and subjective measures vary across jobs, in some situations primarily objective measures are observed, others are mixtures of both, and in other cases, primarily subjective performance measures are observed. Each firm will face specific costs and benefits of objective and subjective measures and will tailor its performance measures to its circumstances. Moreover, the costs and benefits are likely to vary over various divisions of the firm and jobs. However, employees performing similar tasks in similar industries tend to have similar performance-evaluation systems because the costs and benefits of alternative evaluation methods will be similar.

Both objective and subjective performance measures are costly. The larger these costs, the less firms tend to rely on performance evaluations for setting rewards and punishments. Paying employees straight salary and giving simple cost-of-living raises to all employees will lead to predictable shirking and other incentive problems. Yet these costs still can be lower than the costs of implementing a performance-based incentive plan.

Team Performance

Teams frequently are used at all levels of the organization. Teams are formed because they are more successful at assembling specialized knowledge for decision making than are alternative methods that might be used to pass the knowledge through the traditional hierarchy. For example, many companies often form new product development teams composed of people from engineering, marketing, manufacturing, finance, and distribution as a way to assemble the knowledge required to design, manufacture, and sell profitable products. As discussed below, teams also

[13]See C. Prendergast (1999), "The Provision of Incentives in Firms," *Journal of Economic Literature* 37 (March), 7–63, for a survey of the relevant papers.

MANAGERIAL APPLICATIONS

Increased Use of Quantifiable Performance Measures

A relatively large number of U.S. businesses overhauled their performance evaluation systems following the 2008–2009 recession in an attempt to better separate top performers from under achievers. One common change was to move from using a mix of objective and subjective performance measures to basing reviews only on quantifiable measures. According to Hewitt associates 10 percent of managers and 11 percent of other employees in U.S. companies were evaluated solely on quantifiable results in 2010, rather than on a combination of hard figures and softer behavioral characteristics. These estimates were up from 7 percent to 8 percent, five years earlier. The move toward quantifiable measures was motivated in part by commonly observed biases in subjective evaluations. One chief human resources officer noted that at his company the old, subjective evaluations had led to the corporate equivalent of grade inflation: "The chance of earning a good score was almost guaranteed."

While quantitative measures have certain advantages over subjective evaluations, they are also subject to gaming and can cause problems in multitask environments ("you get what you are paid for"). Therefore, it is not surprising that the vast majority of firms continue to use a mix of quantifiable and subjective measures in evaluating employees.

Source: J. Light (2010), "Performance Reviews by the Numbers," *The Wall Street Journal* (June 29).

---

can prove useful particularly when one employee's productivity affects the productivity of other employees. For instance, one complaint by employees at Lincoln Electric is that their pay suffers when employees ahead of them on an assembly line are unable to keep them supplied with work.

Team Production

To illustrate the performance measurement problems of teams, again consider welder assemblers Conrad Mueller and Dina van den Brink. To simplify the notation, assume they exert a common effort level e, whether in a team or not. If they work independently, their individual output is

$$\text{Individual output} = 5e + \mu \tag{16.5}$$

where e represents the individual effort of either Conrad or Dina and μ is a random error term with zero mean and positive variance. If Conrad and Dina work as a team, they produce

$$\text{Team output} = 4e^2 + \mu \tag{16.6}$$

For $e > 2.5$, the expected output working as a team is higher than the output of working independently:

$$\text{Expected team output} = 4e^2 > \text{Expected individual output} = 5e + 5e \tag{16.7}$$

As displayed in Figure 16.1, Conrad and Dina's team output always is larger than the sum of their individual outputs whenever they each exert 2.5 units of effort (they jointly exert 5 units of effort).

In this example, there are team-production effects: Output is potentially higher when Dina and Conrad work as a team. Team output can be larger because Dina and Conrad help each other. Large, awkward pieces can be attached in less than half the time by two people assisting each other than if they worked independently. In other cases, team output is larger than individuals working separately because the team is able to the different specialized knowledge of its members.

Figure 16.1   Comparing Individual and Team Outputs

When Conrad and Dina each exert at least 2.5 units of effort, their team output is greater than their outputs working independently.

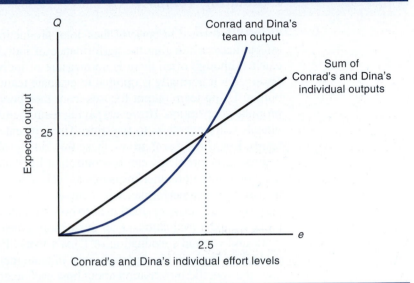

MANAGERIAL APPLICATIONS

Peer Pressure within Teams

Levi Strauss, maker of Levi jeans, installed multitask teams in its U.S. plants, replacing the old piecework system. Each team had 20–30 employees responsible for completing individual orders by assembling full pairs of pants, instead of each employee specializing as a zipper sewer or a belt-loop attacher. In essence, jobs were redesigned from being functional to being more multitask and process-oriented (recall Chapter 13's discussion). The much touted move was designed to empower workers, cut down on monotony, reduce stress, and increase productivity.

Employee incentive compensation was based on team output, which created free-rider problems, which in turn led to absenteeism and shirking, which caused tempers to flare. Supervisors on the plant floor spent more time intervening to prevent "big fights." One plant manager reported, "Peer pressure can be vicious and brutal." Before installing the multitask teams, each employee received two weeks of training in group dynamics and an additional one-day seminar in "let's-get-along sessions" with private consultants. These training sessions did not resolve the conflicts. In fact, productivity dropped and costs rose. The quantity of pants produced per hour worked fell in 1993 to 77 percent of preteam levels. At one plant, the cost of stitching a pair of Dockers went from $5 before teams to $7.50 with teams.

Then, Levi's share of the domestic men's denim-jeans market fell from 48 percent in 1990 to 26 percent in 1997. In 1997, Levi closed 11 U.S. plants and laid off 6,400 employees. While vowing to preserve the team strategy at its remaining U.S. plants, many of them unofficially went back to individual piecework. Robert Haas, Levi's CEO, admits, "teams created pressures and tensions and a lot of unhappiness, and some people would rather go back. Ours is a culture of experimentation and novelty, and we're not always successful." Between 1997 and 2004, Levi Strauss closed 45 plants and laid off 27,000 employees. In 2007 it operated five plants in Europe and Asia-Pacific and none in North America.

Source: R. Mitchell (1994), "Managing by Values," *BusinessWeek* (August 1), 50; R. King (1998), "Levi's Factory Workers Are Assigned to Teams and Morale Takes a Hit," *The Wall Street Journal* (May 20), A1; and Levi Strauss & Co., Form 10-K, Securities and Exchange Commission (February 12, 2008).

Evaluating Teams

Teams are formed because of their joint production effects.[14] These team production effects make evaluating the performance of individual team members quite complicated. Although often there is no measure of individual output—only team output is observed—it normally is optimal to evaluate team members, at least in part, on team output. Using team output focuses team members on a common objective and helps promote cooperation. However, paying team members on group output provides individuals with incentives to free-ride. These incentives are less pronounced in smaller teams. But as team size grows, these free-rider problems can become enormous.

Free-rider problems can be controlled by evaluating team members not only on team output but on other measures as well. For instance, the following factors might be used to assess performance by Conrad and Dina: the number of hours worked, a supervisor's subjective evaluation as to how hard they are working, the condition of their tools, and peer evaluations. Peer evaluations consist of Dina's evaluation of Conrad's work and Conrad's evaluation of Dina's work. Peer reviews often are important in evaluating the individual performance of team members because it is teammates who have the specific information about how each team member has performed.

Sometimes the costs of controlling free-rider problems within teams exceed the benefits that come from team production. In this case, it is better to work individually rather than as a team. For instance, if evaluating Dina and Conrad on team output provides low incentives to exert effort and the costs of monitoring individual performance of teammates (e.g., through supervisor or peer reviews) are high, the net value of their combined output might be higher with individual production and performance evaluation.

One of the key tasks for new teams is to develop the internal architecture for the team. Decision rights (task assignments) must be partitioned among the team members. Accordingly, members must decide how to evaluate the work efforts of team members. Finally, members must decide on the rewards and punishments for members of the group. Sometimes the rewards and punishments are social; for example, a shirking member may be ostracized.

ANALYZING MANAGERIAL DECISIONS: *Why Teams Fail*

Along with Mom and apple pie, teamwork has become a sacred cow to American businesses. Yet, one survey by Mercer Management found that only 13 percent of 179 teams received high ratings. "Somehow, we have to get past this idea that all we have to do is join hands and sing *Kum Ba Yah* and say, 'We've moved to teamwork.'" Many companies are narrowing the focus and time horizon of teams. A team manager at Texas Instruments counsels that not everyone has to be on a team and that only

5 percent of its workforce are on self-directed teams. Harvard Professor Amy Edmonson questions whether many firms "might be barking up the wrong tree" in stressing the use of teams: "I've begun to think that teams are not the solution to getting the work done." Discuss potential reasons why teams often fail to deliver the hoped for results.

SOURCE: E. Neuborne (1997), "Companies Save, But Workers Pay," *USA Today* (February 25), 1B; and M. Starvish (2012), "Why Leaders need to Rethink Teamwork," *Forbes.com* (December 28).

---

[14]A. Alchian and H. Demsetz (1972), "Production, Information Costs and Economic Organization," *American Economic Review* 62, 777–795.

As another example of evaluating team output, consider the case of student project teams in business school courses. Such projects build leadership skills and teach students how to work more effectively in teams. These projects also enhance learning by allowing students to share their understanding and by helping all students on the team to learn more than if they each did the project individually. Instructors assigning projects to study teams frequently give the same grade to all members of the team. Thus, the team is evaluated based on the team's joint output.

Rather than assign all the members of the team the same project grade, some instructors apportion the total project grade among the team members based on peer reviews where unequal grades for teammates are possible. Thus, although the overall project's grade might be a B+, some team members might receive an A− and others a B so long as the average across the team is a B+. Providing the team with the decision rights to evaluate one another reduces the free-rider problem and increases team production. But it can also reduce morale and lead to increased influence costs as team members lobby one another for better evaluations. Or, some team members might downgrade a team member unfairly to raise their own grades. These dysfunctional incentives are likely to be greater if the team is formed for a single project. As described in Chapter 10, free-rider problems are smaller if the team spans several courses and students have more incentives to invest in their reputations.

Government Regulation of Labor Markets

The basic principal-agent model assumes that both parties are free to arrive at any mutually agreeable contract and that labor markets are unregulated. However, government regulates labor markets and hence constrains the agreements employees and firms might otherwise reach. Since the 1960s, federal laws in the United States dealing with affirmative action and equal employment opportunity (EEO) have had a profound effect on both performance-evaluation systems and reward systems. Federal and state legislation and court actions have forced companies to document their compensation and promotion decisions to demonstrate that their actions are related to performance and are not influenced by the employee's race, religion, sex, age, or national origin.

Labor laws and court decisions have had a material impact on the performance-appraisal systems. In deciding cases involving alleged discriminatory employment practices, courts look more favorably at companies with the following characteristics:[15]

- The firm's job descriptions are clearly written and well defined.
- The appraisal system has clear criteria for evaluating performance such as written objective scales and dimensions.
- There are specific written instructions on how to complete the performance appraisal.
- Employees are provided feedback about their performance appraisal.
- Higher-level supervisors' evaluations are incorporated into the appraisal system.
- Individuals who receive similar evaluations in the firm are treated equally and consistently.

[15]Major federal legislation includes the Equal Pay Act of 1963, Title VII, and the Civil Rights Act of 1964. A. Barnes, T. Dworkin, and E. Richards (1994), *Law for Business* (Richard D. Irwin: Burr Ridge), Chapter 23; G. Milkovich and J. Newman (1993), *Compensation* (Richard D. Irwin: Burr Ridge), 316–318.

Although these characteristics appear sensible, even worthwhile for many firms, government regulation has negative side effects. The law does not permit companies and employees to "opt out" of these regulations. Even if these characteristics were appropriate and would be adopted voluntarily by the majority of firms, they are imposed on all firms and hence impose costs on that minority that would not have chosen them voluntarily.

The presence of potential legal scrutiny of the firm's performance-evaluation systems pushes these systems to become more formal, more objective, with less reliance on subjective appraisal. Every personnel action and appraisal must be documented. The firm's human resources department typically assumes the role of ensuring that the firm is complying with the labor laws.

The performance-appraisal system that meets these regulatory criteria would not necessarily maximize the firm's value absent the regulation. For example, many Japanese managers try "to make everybody feel that he is slated for the top position in the firm"[16] by delaying differentiating among cohorts and performance appraisals for 12–15 years after joining the firm. Such limitations on annual feedback to employees potentially would run afoul of affirmative-action laws in the United States and thus would be opposed strenuously by human resources departments at most large corporations. Hence, U.S. firms find it more difficult to use less formal, more subjective performance-evaluation systems than their foreign competitors, even though such systems might be value-enhancing for some firms if they could operate in a less regulated setting.

The U.S. tax code [Internal Revenue Code Section 162(m)(4)] limits the annual income tax deduction for compensation paid to high-ranking executives of publicly traded companies to $1 million. However, this $1 million income tax deduction limitation is waived if the amount of compensation over $1 million is "performance based." In order for the firm to be able to deduct executive compensation paid above $1 million as a tax expense, the compensation above $1 million should be tied to attaining one or more "performance goals." In order to qualify, the performance goals must be approved by the compensation committee of the board of directors. Also, the performance goals and the applicable corporate officers' compensation package must be disclosed to, and approved by, a majority of the shareholders. And, before any compensation is paid, the compensation committee of the board of directors must confirm that the performance goal has been met.

Government regulations, including tax laws, cause U.S. firms to spend more money than they would otherwise on appraisal systems that, to a court's satisfaction, document the firm's compliance with affirmative-action regulations. Thus, regulations likely cause some U.S. firms to adopt different performance-appraisal systems.

The United States is not the only country with government regulations governing their labor markets. For example, France has a complex set of rules regulating the circumstances companies must face before firing employees, how long French companies must wait before terminating various types of employees, severance payments that must be offered, and so forth. For example, French companies must prove that "permanent" employees are being terminated for "economic reasons," and engineers must be given three months' notice. French companies with 50 or more employees wishing to close a plant must provide the government with a "social plan" that places

---

[16]N. Hatvany and V. Pucik (1981), "Japanese Managerial Practices and Productivity," *Organizational Dynamics* 13, 4. Also, M. Aoki (1988), *Information, Incentives and Bargaining in the Japanese Economy* (Cambridge University Press: Cambridge).

a limit on the total number of layoffs and provides reemployment and/or retraining of terminated employees.[17] While such laws increase the costs of French employees, they also encourage firms to hire "temporary" workers who can be terminated more easily, to outsource jobs to other countries or to smaller French firms, and to substitute capital for labor.

The U.S. and French labor laws are other examples of how regulation affects the firm's optimal choice of organizational architecture. Web Chapter 21 (available via Connect), describes government regulation more generally and provides additional organizational architecture examples.

Summary	In the previous four chapters, we have examined the first two components of organizational architecture: the assignment of decision rights and the reward systems. In this chapter, we began to examine the third component: the performance-evaluation system.

Performance evaluation is conducted for both individuals within the firm and subunits of the firm: How did Taylor perform? How did Morgan's team perform? Such questions require individual and team performance evaluations. Also, Morgan and Taylor are in the automotive products division. How did this division perform? Answering this last question requires divisional performance measures. This chapter focuses on individual performance-evaluation systems; divisional performance evaluation is discussed in Chapter 17.

The simple principal-agent model in Chapter 15, suggests that part of the employee's compensation should be based on performance (output). But basing pay on output requires that output is observable at low cost and is difficult to manipulate by the firm or the employee. Among the costs of performance measures are the *compensating differentials* employees must be paid for bearing the additional risks of incentive pay. Moreover, the model assumes that the firm and employee are free to contract in an unregulated labor market. This chapter explores how individual performance evaluation is affected when these conditions are violated.

To set the optimum compensation package, management must know the employee's marginal productivity of effort. One way managers estimate these marginal productivities is to use time and motion studies or data on past performance. If past performance is used, dysfunctional incentives due to the *ratchet effect* can result; employees will limit output if they anticipate that the next period's target benchmark will be raised. To reduce the dysfunctional consequences of the ratchet effect, some firms set performance estimates at the beginning of the period and do not adjust them simply because employees are making high earnings.

In some cases, measuring output can be extremely costly. For example, accurately measuring the output of a teacher is likely to be quite costly. Firms will select performance evaluations based on the direct cost of the measure, the cost of employee opportunism induced by the performance measure, and the indirect cost incurred by imposing more risk on the employee.

Another assumption of the model is that the employee shirks only on effort. If output is not correlated perfectly with the firm's value, employees attempting to increase output might cause the value of the firm to decline. Such dysfunctional results can occur when employees game the system—as in the Prudential Insurance Company agents case of "churning" policies.

[17]F. Kramarz, and M. Michaud (2004), "The Shape of Hiring and Separation Costs," Forschungsinstitut zur Zukunft der Arbeit Institute for the Study of Labor, IZA Discussion Paper No. 1170 (June).

Often a manager has multiple signals available regarding the employee's output. The informativeness principle suggests that the manager should use all these signals (so long as they are available at low cost) because they allow the firm to reduce the risk the employee bears and hence lower the compensating differential the employee must be paid. The informativeness principle suggests that when several employees are performing similar tasks, their combined output provides information about common random shocks affecting all their outputs. Thus, the employee's compensation should be adjusted relative to peers. This is called *relative performance evaluation*. Relative performance evaluation requires the firm to establish a reference group of employees to use as a benchmark. But relative performance evaluations can lead employees to collude or sabotage coworkers to improve their evaluations. Moreover, establishing the appropriate reference group and measuring its performance is costly.

In some cases, the measurement costs or the costs from employees' dysfunctional attempts to maximize explicit performance measures become so great that alternative measures of performance are sought. *Subjective performance evaluations* are periodic reviews by supervisors that usually incorporate a comprehensive examination of all the employee's outputs. Subjective evaluations can be based on either standard rating scales for a number of different areas or goal-based systems. Standard rating scales have the appearance of objectivity but entail subjective judgments by the evaluator. Goal-based systems set performance targets at the beginning of the period that the evaluator uses at the end of the period to determine an overall, subjective evaluation.

Subjective performance measures also involve costs. It becomes easier for a manager or the firm to renege on the promise to reward good performance because it is harder to define "good." There is more latitude to exercise favoritism and introduce bias in subjective measures. Finally, subjective systems often generate greater influence costs as employees try to lobby for better ratings.

Subjective and objective performance evaluations usually complement each other. Subjective evaluations often are used to reduce the incentives of employees to engage in opportunistic behaviors that increase the costs of objective measures. For example, the Lincoln Electric secretary who typed meaningless characters during lunch could be penalized using a subjective system: The supervisor could dismiss the secretary or give the secretary a poor subjective evaluation.

Teams often are formed as a way to assemble knowledge held by individual team members. No one individual has all the knowledge necessary to perform the task. When employees work in teams, each individual's marginal contribution to the team's output depends on others' efforts. There are synergies or interdependencies among employees. Measuring individual output is difficult, and it is costly to disentangle individual shirking from others' effort. Evaluating teams of employees usually requires a measure of team performance while still recognizing individual contributions to the team. Individual performance (possibly measured using peer reviews) is rewarded to overcome free-rider problems. In some cases, each team member's bonus is based on individual performance, but the bonus is paid only if the entire team reaches its goals.

The principal-agent model assumes that the parties are free to contract, yet labor laws constrain their choices. The EEO laws in the United States have had a pronounced effect on performance-evaluation systems. For example, defending against affirmative-action lawsuits has encouraged firms to adopt more explicit, objective appraisal systems than they otherwise might have chosen voluntarily.

Suggested Readings

A. Alchian and H. Demsetz (1972), "Production, Information Costs and Economic Organization," *American Economic Review* 62, 777–795.

G. Baker, R. Gibbons, and K. Murphy (1994), "Subjective Performance Measures in Optimal Incentive Contracts," *Quarterly Journal of Economics* CIX, 1125–1156.

G. Baker, M. Jensen, and K. Murphy (1998), "Compensation and Incentives: Practice vs. Theory," *Journal of Finance* 63, 597–616.

Y. Barzel (1982), "Measurement Cost and the Organization of Markets," *Journal of Law & Economics* XXV, 27–48.

R. Gibbons and J. Roberts (2013), "Economic Theories of Incentives in Organizations," *The Handbook of Organizational Economics*, Edited by R. Gibbons and J. Roberts (Princeton University Press, Princeton NJ), 56–99.

E. Lazear and S. Rosen (1981), "Rank Order Tournaments as Optimal Labor Contracts," *Journal of Political Economy* 89, 841–864.

G. Milkovich and J. Newman (2007), *Compensation* (Irwin/McGraw-Hill: Burr Ridge).

C. Prendergast (1999), "The Provision of Incentives in Firms," *Journal of Economic Literature* 37 (March), 7–63.

Self-Evaluation Problems

16–1. Martina Genser sells copiers for Xerox. Her sales are a function of her effort e and can be expressed in the following manner:

$$\text{Sales} = 100e + \mu$$

where μ is a random error term with expected value of zero. Martina's personal cost of exerting effort is

$$C(e) = e^2$$

She is paid a straight salary plus a commission:

$$\text{Compensation} = \$1{,}000 + 0.10 \text{ sales}$$

Her personal objective is to maximize

$$U = E(\text{Compensation}) - C(e)$$

the difference between the expected value of her compensation and her cost of effort.

a. Find Martina's optimal effort level.

b. Now assume that Xerox compensates Martina based on her sales relative to the average sales for salespeople in the company. Assume that Martina's sales are not included in the calculation of this average and that she cannot affect the average sales through her effort. The expected value of average sales is 500. Her compensation is now

$$\text{Compensation} = \$1{,}000 + 0.10(\text{sales} - \text{average sales})$$

Calculate Martina's optimal effort level under this compensation plan.

c. Including average sales in the contract affects expected compensation. What adjustment must be made in the salary to keep expected compensation the same as before?

d. Does including average sales in the compensation contract affect the variance of Martina's compensation? Assume that her sales and average sales are positively correlated. Give a brief verbal explanation to support your answer.

16–2. The Quantum Division of Nextel Corp., based in San Jose, California, manufactures semiconductors that convert analog signals to digital signals. Lynn Kraft is the division manager. Her compensation consists of a base wage of $50,000 plus a bonus of 2 percent of division profits above $10 million. Last year's division profits were $12 million, and so Kraft received a bonus of $40,000.

This year two things happened that adversely affected division profits. First, the price of gold, a key ingredient in Quantum's chips, increased dramatically, causing the division's costs to be higher than expected. Second, an earthquake in the San Jose area caused Quantum's plant to be closed for six weeks and to require $1 million in repairs. Division profits for this year were $9 million.

Kraft believes her compensation plan should be adjusted for these events. She believes that, but for these events, division profits would have been $13 million for the year.

a. What issues should the CEO of Nextel consider when deciding whether to adjust Kraft's bonus plan?

b. Do you think the plan should be adjusted? Why?

Solutions to Self-Evaluation Problems

16–1. Xerox Salesforce Compensation

a. Her objective is to maximize $U = 1,000 + .10(\text{expected sales}) - e^2 = 1,000 + .10e - e^2$. The solution can be found by elementary calculus, graphically, or through iteration. The answer is $e^* = 5$.

b. The answer is still $e^* = 5$. The new term $(.10 + \text{average sales})$ is not affected by effort. The marginal benefits and costs of effort remain the same.

c. Expected compensation is reduced by 50 by including the term in the compensation contract. This can be offset by increasing the base salary to $1,050.

d. Yes. High (low) average sales are associated with high (low) μ/s. Appropriately weighted, including average sales in the contract reduces the variance of compensation by filtering out part of the random shock, μ.

16–2. Bonus Plan Adjustment

a. Making Kraft's compensation sensitive to such uncontrollable events increases the riskiness of her compensation. If Kraft is risk-averse, the firm will have to pay her a compensating differential for the compensation risk she is being required to bear. The firm must decide whether the (present value of the) compensating differential is greater or less than the increase in firm value as a result of making Kraft responsible for such events.

b. Why might it be value increasing for the firm to make Kraft accountable for such events. It is true that she cannot control those events. However, there are things she can do to minimize the consequences of the events. She can hedge against fluctuations in gold prices, and she can buy earthquake insurance. (It is not clear, however, that the cost of such hedging and insurance is greater than the benefits to the firm.) You will see more discussion of these issues in corporate finance. More importantly, Kraft can take actions after such events that reduce the costs to the firm. For example, after the earthquake, Kraft probably could have made a number of decisions that shortened the amount of time the plant was closed. If Kraft is not held accountable for the costs of the earthquake, then she has no incentive to take such cost-reducing (value-increasing) actions.

There is also the issue of influence costs. If the firm decides not to hold Kraft accountable for such events, then Kraft has incentives to argue that a lot of costs are associated with the events (i.e., more costs than actually were associated with the event). She will also argue that a lot of events were uncontrollable. Senior managers must therefore devote energy to determining which events were uncontrollable and which were not, and which costs were associated with the events and which were not. The firm does not incur these costs if they adopt the policy of making Kraft accountable for profits regardless of unforeseen events.

Review Questions

16–1. Discuss some of the costs and benefits of 360-degree evaluation systems.

16–2. In 360-degree performance review programs, personnel evaluations are collected anonymously from employees knowing the manager being evaluated (superiors, subordinates, and coworkers). These are tabulated and a consensus summary is provided to the manager.

Each manager being evaluated also does a self-evaluation, and this is used to benchmark how closely the manager and the coworkers' assessments match. About one-third of the managers match their coworkers, one-third have an inflated view, and one-third rate themselves lower. Those who overrate themselves tend to be judged "least effective" as perceived by their coemployees. However, these overraters are more common higher up in the organization.[18]

   a. What does the breakdown of three one-thirds indicate?

   b. Offer some plausible explanation of why overraters are higher up in the organization.

16–3. The following quote is based on statements made by quality expert W. Edwards Deming:

> *If by bad management the components of a company become competitive, the system is destroyed. . . . A common example lies in the practice of ranking people, divisions, teams, comparing them, with reward at the top and punishment at the bottom. Jobs and salaries are based on comparisons. Teams naturally become competitive; divisions become competitive. Each tries to outdo the other in some competitive measure. The result is higher costs, battle of market share. Everybody loses.*[19]

Do you agree with Deming that performance evaluations based on comparative rankings always reduce company value? Explain.

16–4. The U.S. Navy recently revamped its officer fitness report system.[20] Under the old system, officers were ranked into one of four categories, where 4.0 was the highest grade. This old system had been used for 20 years and grade inflation had become rampant. Eighty percent of all sailors routinely were ranked a perfect 4.0. One officer remarked, "Let's face it, 85 percent of the people are 4.0 and 80 percent [of those] have every mark in 4.0." A retired admiral commented, "The old system wasn't entirely broke, it was just deteriorating over time and became less and less useful."

The Navy decided to change the evaluation system because of the natural tendency for senior officers to promote their own subordinates over unknown sailors. Not everyone deserved a 4.0, but to get their own people promoted, senior officers had to play along because that's what everyone else was doing.

The new system requires each officer to be rated on a 1–5 scale in seven areas: professional expertise, leadership, support for equal opportunity programs, military bearing and appearance, teamwork, mission accomplishment, and interpersonal skills. The total points out of 35 possible are then used to provide an overall promotion recommendation:

- Clearly promote
- Must promote
- Promotable
- Progressing
- Don't promote

The number of ratings in the top two categories—"clearly promote" and "must promote"—will be severely restricted to at most 20 percent of the evaluations. If an officer is evaluating 10 junior officers, at the most only two can receive the top two ratings.

What are the expected consequences of this new system? What are the likely outcomes? What are the pros and cons of the new system?

16–5. Evaluate the following statement:

> *The overarching purpose of a measurement system should be to help a team, rather than senior managers, gauge its progress. A team's measurement system should primarily be a tool for telling the team when it must take corrective action.*[21]

---

[18]J. Lopez (1994), "A Better Way?" *The Wall Street Journal Supplement* (April 13), R6.

[19]R. Aguayo (1990), *Dr. Deming: The American Who Taught the Japanese about Quality* (Fireside Simon & Schuster: New York), vii–viii.

[20]E. Blazar (1995), "The New Standard of Excellence," *Navy Times* (March 20), 12–14.

[21]C. Meyer (1994), "How the Right Measures Help Teams Excel," *Harvard Business Review* (May–June), 96.

16–6. The Green Shoe Company is considering going to a piece-rate system, where manufacturing employees are paid based on their level of output. Discuss what factors the firm should consider in deciding whether this idea should be implemented. How should the initial piece rate be set? Under what circumstances should the company alter the piece rate once it is adopted?

16–7. Your company currently has a bonus plan for its sales managers. If annual sales for a manager's unit exceed $1 million, the manager receives a $10,000 bonus. In a typical year, about five of the 10 managers in the firm meet the target and receive the bonus. However, the number receiving the bonus varies from year to year due to the state of the economy, which in turn has an effect on sales. The company is considering replacing the bonus plan with a plan that rewards the top-five selling managers each year with a $10,000 bonus. Discuss the potential benefits and costs of the new plan relative to the old plan.

16–8. Communities are frequently concerned about whether police are vigilant in carrying out their responsibilities. Several communities have experimented with incentive compensation for police. In particular, some cities have paid members of the police force based on the number of arrests that they personally make. Discuss the likely effects of this compensation policy.

16–9. A consultant does not like the fact that you use subjective performance measures in your firm. He argues that they are arbitrary and should be replaced with objective measures. He stresses that objective measures provide a clear target for employees, but mentions none of the potential costs. What are the potential problems associated with using objective performance measures?

16–10. Some firms have recently adopted 360-degree performance evaluations. Under this evaluation system, the employee is evaluated not only by supervisors and peers but also by employees who report to the employee being evaluated. Discuss why a firm might want to adopt 360-degree reviews. What are the likely problems with this type of performance evaluation?

16–11. Evaluate the following quote:

> *Teams do not spring up by magic. Nor does personal chemistry matter as much as most people believe. Rather, we believe that . . . most people can significantly enhance team performance. And focusing on performance—not chemistry or togetherness or good communications or good feelings—shapes teams more than anything else.*[22]

16–12. A basic principle in accounting is that of "responsibility accounting." Under this principle, it is inappropriate to base performance evaluation on measures that are beyond the control of the employee. Do you think that you should ever include variables in a workers' compensation plan that are not under at least partial control of the employee? Explain.

16–13. Bob's Manufacturing Company has altered the determinants of pay raises for U.S. employees. Whereas in the past pay increases for managers, professionals, and hourly workers had been automatic, starting last year the company began determining the size of an annual bonus pool and then allocated lump-sum bonuses to employees on the basis of performance. Hourly workers were to be evaluated within their annual performance appraisals; professional-level employees would work with their supervisors to establish personal goals against which they would be measured.

    a. What problems do you foresee with the implementation of this arrangement? Be specific about who will be affected by the problems you've identified.

    b. What recommendations would you offer to top management at Bob's Manufacturing Company to preempt or minimize problems with the new reward system?

16–14. Agricultural workers are often paid piece rates. For example, pear pickers are paid a fixed amount for each box of pears they pick. Pear companies, however, pay tree thinners on an hourly basis. These thinners remove excess fruit from trees so that the remaining fruit can

[22]J. Katzenbach, and D. Smith (1993), *The Wisdom of Teams* (Harvard Business School: Boston), 61.

grow larger. (Each piece of fruit must be at least six inches apart on the tree.) Why do you think these companies pay thinners by the hour? Presumably, they would work harder if they were paid by the tree.

16–15. Evaluate the following statement:

> *I am a manager at a governmental agency. I have no control over compensation policy. All workers are paid the same salary, and I cannot fire them. Therefore, an understanding of the basic principles of organizational architecture will not help me be more effective in my job.*

16–16. The JAB Gold Mining Company observes that some firms pay their CEOs based on performance *relative* to the S&P 500. Most firms, however, have stock prices that are positively correlated with the S&P 500. JAB has a *negative beta*! (Its stock returns are negatively correlated with the index.) Does this mean that JAB would be wrong in paying its CEO based on performance relative to the S&P 500? Explain.

Appendix: Optimal Weights in a Relative Performance Contract[23]

In this chapter, we argued that it can be optimal to base an employee's pay on performance *relative* to some benchmark group such as employees within the same organization who perform similar tasks. The advantage of this type of system is that it filters out common shocks in the evaluation of employees and thus reduces the costs of inefficient risk bearing. In this appendix, we consider how a risk-neutral firm might optimally weight the performance of such a benchmark group in a compensation contract.

For simplicity, we restrict our attention to simple linear compensation contracts of the following form:

$$\text{Compensation} = W_0 + \beta(Q - \lambda \overline{Q}) \quad (16.8)$$

where W_0 and β are fixed parameters, Q is the employee's own output, and $\overline{Q}$ is the average output of the benchmark group (e.g., similar employees within the firm). W_0 is the employee's fixed wage under a relative performance contract. We are interested in how to choose the optimal λ. Note that if $\lambda = 0$, average output receives no weight and thus is left out of the contract. In contrast, if $\lambda = 1$, then compensation is based on a simple difference between own output and average output.

In the discussion that follows, we show that expected compensation can be held the same by simply adjusting W_0. Second, under certain assumptions, the employee's effort choice is independent of λ. Third, we show how to choose λ to minimize the risk the employee bears. Since expected compensation can be the same for any λ and if the effort choice isn't affected by λ, then the efficient contract is the one that minimizes the risk borne by the employee.

Expected Compensation

Rewriting Equation (16.8) yields

$$\text{Compensation} = W_0 + \beta Q - \beta \lambda \overline{Q} \quad (16.9)$$

Expected compensation in Equation (16.9) is $W_0 + \beta E(Q) - \beta \lambda E(\overline{Q})$ where $E(\cdot)$ denotes the expectation operator. Expected compensation can be held constant at any level of λ by adjusting W_0 by $+\beta \lambda E(Q)$.

---

[23]Technical note: This appendix requires elementary knowledge of statistics, decision theory, and calculus. Material in this appendix draws on the analysis in Milgrom and Roberts (1992), Chapter 10.

Effort Choice

Under certain assumptions, the employee's effort choice is independent of λ. In this case, the firm can choose λ without being concerned about how it might affect employee productivity. In particular, suppose that the employee's cost of exerting effort is given by the function $C(e)$, which expresses the disutility of effort in dollar equivalents. The employee's certainty equivalent can be approximated by the following formula:[24]

$$\text{Certainty equivalent} = E[W_0 + \beta E(Q - \lambda \overline{Q})] - 0.5rs^2 - C(e) \quad (16.10)$$

where r is the coefficient of absolute risk aversion, and s^2 is the variance of compensation. In this expression, the first term on the right-hand side represents expected compensation, the second term is the risk premium (employees discount the expected value because they are risk-averse), and the last term is the cost of effort. We make two additional assumptions: (1) the effort of the employee does not affect the average output of other employees of the benchmark group, and (2) r is a constant. Employees want to maximize their certainty equivalent with respect to the effort choice e—which is equivalent to maximizing their utility. Conceptually, the maximizing effort level is found by taking the partial derivative of the certainty equivalent with respect to effort e and setting it equal to zero. The first-order condition is therefore

$$\beta Q' = C'(e) \quad (16.11)$$

where Q' and $C'(e)$ are partial derivatives with respect to e. This expression indicates that the employee chooses the effort level that equates marginal benefits and marginal costs. The marginal benefit is the extra compensation that the employee receives from exerting more effort, and the marginal cost is the extra disutility that he experiences from working harder. Note that λ does not enter into this equation, since the average output of other employees does not depend on this employee's effort. Thus, in this case, the firm can choose any value for λ without affecting the employee's effort level.

Minimizing Employee Risk

Note from Equation (16.10) that the employee is made better off by reducing the variance of compensation (it lowers the discount for risk). The firm, on the other hand, is not harmed by this choice because the employee exerts the same effort level under any λ and W_0 can be adjusted to keep expected compensation the same. Indeed, the firm potentially can share in the gains from the risk reduction to the employee by paying a lower expected level of compensation—since the firm can meet the employee's reservation wage with a lower expected level of payout.

Basic statistics allows us to express the variance of compensation [Equation (16.8)] as

$$\text{Var(Compensation)} = \beta^2[\text{Var}(Q) + \lambda^2 \text{Var}(\overline{Q}) - 2\lambda \text{Cov}(Q, \overline{Q})] \quad (16.12)$$

---

[24]Technical note: A certainty equivalent is the amount of cash that employees would require with certainty to make them indifferent between this certain sum and the uncertain income stream. The approximation of the certainty equivalent in Equation (16.10) is a basic result from decision theory. It holds when the risk is small and the utility function is sufficiently smooth. J. Ingersoll (1987), *Theory of Financial Decision Making* (Rowman & Littlefield: Totowa), 38.

Figure 16.2 Choosing the Optimal Weight in a Relative Performance Contract

This figure reflects a simple linear contract of the form Compensation $= W_0 + \beta(Q - \lambda \overline{Q})$, where W_0 and β are fixed parameters, Q is the employee's own output, and $\overline{Q}$ is the average output of the benchmark group (e.g., similar employees in the firm). Pictured is the variance of compensation as a function of λ. Given the assumptions in the analysis, the optimal weight, $\lambda^* = \text{Cov}(Q, \overline{Q})/\text{Var}(\overline{Q})$. This is the value that minimizes the variance of compensation.

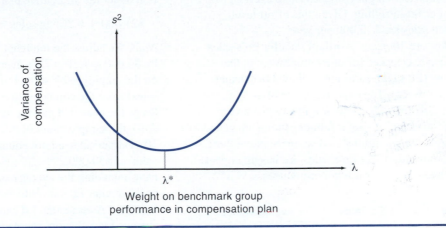

Weight on benchmark group
performance in compensation plan

Figure 16.2 shows a picture of this quadratic function. The optimal weight is λ^* at the bottom of the parabola. Using basic calculus, we can show that

$$\lambda^* = \text{Cov}(Q, \overline{Q})/\text{Var}(\overline{Q}) \tag{16.13}$$

Equation (16.13) has a quite intuitive interpretation. The numerator of the expression $\text{Cov}(Q, \overline{Q})$ is a measure of the association between this employee's own output and the average output of other employees. The higher this association, the more information average output contains about random shocks that affect the employee's output (the better is the "signal"). For example, if this covariance is zero, average output contains no information about these shocks and should not be included in the compensation contract. The denominator of the expression is the variance of average output. The higher this variance, the more noise there is in average output and the less information it contains about the employee's effort. The optimal weight λ^* can be estimated using a time series of observations on own output and average output.[25]

Firms sometimes base compensation on the simple difference between the employee's output and average output. This measure is equivalent to choosing $\lambda = 1$. Our analysis indicates that this choice is not always optimal and in some cases can be worse than excluding average output in the contract (e.g., when the covariance between the two variables is small). Indeed, the optimal weight could be negative if the two variables were negatively correlated.

[25]Technical note: Readers familiar with linear regression analysis should note that the right-hand side of Equation (16.13) is the formula for the slope coefficient in a simple linear regression, where the employee's output is the dependent variable and average output of other employees is the explanatory variable. Thus, this formula can be estimated through a simple regression.

ANALYZING MANAGERIAL DECISIONS: *Structuring Salesforce Compensation*

Assume that a salesperson, Edwynn Phillips, has the following annual compensation package:

$$C = \$15{,}000 + 0.2(\text{own sales})$$

This compensation plan induces Ed to exert a given level of effort in selling. Given this effort level, expected sales are $30,000 per year.

Below are 10 years' worth of data for Ed's sales and the average sales for other employees in the company (Ed's own sales are excluded in calculating this average). The expected value of average sales is also $30,000. However, in any given year, average sales might rise or fall, depending on general economic conditions, and so on. Some of these same conditions affect Ed's sales. Ed has no impact on the average sales for other employees.

Year	Ed's Sales	Average Sales
1	30,000	30,000
2	24,000	27,000
3	36,000	28,500
4	27,000	27,000
5	33,000	36,000
6	30,000	33,000
7	25,500	27,000
8	24,000	24,000
9	34,500	30,000
10	36,000	36,000

1. Based on the 10 years of data, calculate Ed's average annual pay and standard deviation under the existing compensation plan.
2. Calculate Ed's average pay and standard deviation under the alternative plan:

    $$\$21{,}000 + 0.2(\text{own sales} - \text{average sales})$$

    Note: We adjust the intercept of the pay plan by $6,000 to reflect Ed's average loss imposed on the employee by subtracting 0.2 (average sales) from the compensation. This adjustment keeps the expected pay the same as before. Also, the sample mean of average sales over a 10-year period need not equal the expected value of $30,000.
3. Does including the average sales in the pay package alter Ed's incentives to work hard? Explain. (Assume that Ed cannot affect the average by collusion, sabotage, etc.)
4. Is this pay plan superior to the original plan from a risk-sharing standpoint?
5. Devise an even better plan using the more general form:

    $$C = a + 0.2(\text{own sales} - \lambda \text{ average sales})$$

    (*Hint:* Remember to adjust the intercept to keep expected compensation the same.)
6. Calculate the average pay and standard deviation for this plan.

Divisional Performance Evaluation

LEARNING OBJECTIVES

1. Explain the differences between cost centers, expense centers, revenue centers, profit centers, and investment centers and when each is most appropriate.
2. Describe how return and assets and residual income provide different incentives for investment center managers.
3. Discuss the role of transfer pricing in firms.
4. Describe how the optimum transfer price changes between complete (perfect) information and asymmetric information.
5. Discuss common transfer-pricing methods and their trade-offs.
6. Explain how the internal accounting system is used to evaluate performance.
7. Discuss why internal accounting systems are more useful for managers exercising decision-control rights than for managers exercising decision-management rights.

Briggs & Stratton with 2013 sales of $1.9 billion is the world's largest producer of gasoline engines for outdoor power equipment.[1] B&S engines, primarily 3–25 horsepower, are purchased by original equipment manufacturers and incorporated into lawn and garden equipment such as mowers and garden tillers. In the 1980s, most of their manufacturing plants were unionized. Union work rules limited B&S's labor productivity, causing B&S's labor costs to exceed those of their competitors. To reduce their labor costs, B&S invested heavily in automation. While automation was consuming B&S's capital, competition (primarily from Japan) was reducing their profits. Moreover, a shift from independent dealers to mass merchandisers, such as Walmart, Kmart, and Home Depot, who insisted on price concessions from their suppliers, put further pressure on B&S's profit margins. In 1989, B&S reported a $20 million loss.

Their deteriorating financial situation coupled with a changing competitive landscape prompted B&S to reexamine their corporate strategy, to reorganize the firm, and to adopt new performance measurement and compensation schemes. B&S's traditional market had been high-volume basic small engines. The firm had ventured into the high-end market, only to lose money.

[1]Details of this example are from J. Stern and J. Shiely with I. Ross (2001), *The EVA Challenge: Implementing Value-Added Change in an Organization* (John Wiley & Sons, Inc, New York), 28–33. EVA is a registered trademark of Stern Stewart. www.briggsandstratton.com.

Briggs & Stratton refocused its strategy back to its core business to become the low-cost high-volume producer. To implement this strategy in the 1980s and to boost sales to the mass merchandisers, B&S had to economize on both capital and labor costs. This required a reassignment of decision rights. B&S had been functionally organized. This worked well when the engines were relatively simple and its environment was reasonably stable. But engines were becoming more complex and its operating environment more volatile. B&S reorganized around major products (the small-engine division for walk-behind mowers, large-engine division for ride-on mowers, aluminum castings division, and iron castings division). Decision rights were decentralized to product managers, who were held responsible for operating decisions and capital expenditures. Furthermore, to focus managers' attention on both operating and capital costs, the performance evaluation and reward systems were altered.

Briggs & Stratton changed the way performance was evaluated when it adopted Economic Value Added (EVA) in 1990. EVA is the after-tax operating profit of the division minus the total annual opportunity cost of the capital invested in the division. The total annual cost of capital is the product of the division's cost of capital times the amount of capital invested in the division. Thus, managers in the newly organized divisions became responsible for how much capital they were using. Moreover, they were given incentives to increase EVA (by increasing sales or by decreasing operating or capital costs) because 40 percent of their bonuses were based on corporate EVA, 40 percent on divisional EVA, and 20 percent on appraisal of personal performance by their superior.

These changes in organizational architecture—the new strategic focus, decentralization, and tying bonuses to EVA—had a dramatic effect. In 1989, before adopting EVA, B&S's EVA was negative $62 million. This means that its operating earnings fell short of covering its cost of capital by $62 million. By 1993, Briggs & Stratton showed a positive EVA, and it generated positive EVA from 1993 through 2000, including a record EVA of $50.9 million in 1999. The stock market recognized this performance and B&S's stock price rose from about $6 per share in the fall of 1990 to about $20 in 2000. Most of B&S's stock price increase occurred in the first four years after changing its strategy and organizational architecture. Between 1995 and 2005, B&S's stock price has tracked the broader market indexes, but since 2005 B&S's stock price has under performed the market. It is interesting to note that consistent with Figure 11.1, Briggs & Stratton adopted an integrated approach to organizational change, which involved matching a new strategy with a revised organizational architecture: decentralization of decision rights, EVA performance measure, and tying pay to EVA.

In Chapter 16, we described individual performance-evaluation systems. Our discussion is extended in this chapter to evaluating the performance of business units within the firm. Firms are organized in a variety of ways: By function, by product line, or by geography. Most organizations partition decision rights among subunits within the firm. Managers of these subunits are then rewarded based on the performance of their unit. In other words, the subunit's performance metric is used to measure and then reward that subunit's managers' performance. This chapter describes different ways organizations measure the performance of their various business units. The next section describes commonly used arrangements—cost centers, expense centers, revenue centers, profit centers, and investment centers. These subunits are assigned different sets of decision rights and accordingly use different performance-evaluation metrics—for instance, costs, revenues, profits, or EVA. Because business units within the organization interact with one another and often exchange goods or services among themselves, reported performance of each center involved in an exchange depends on the rules used to value the exchange. Performance evaluation of business units exchanging goods or services requires establishing an internal transfer price for these exchanges. The following section discusses these transfer-pricing issues. Finally, because most firms rely on their accounting systems to measure the performance of their business units, we discuss general issues involving use of the accounting system in measuring performance.

Measuring Divisional Performance[2]

All but the smallest organizations invariably are divided into subunits, each granted particular decision rights and then evaluated based on performance objectives for that subunit. Rewards typically are based on these performance evaluations. In effective organizations, performance-evaluation and reward systems are consistent with the decision rights granted the unit manager—the three legs of the stool are balanced. Chapter 13 described alternative organizational structures: U form, M form, and matrix organizations. In the U form, one unit might be responsible for manufacturing, another for R&D, another for marketing, and so forth. These basic building blocks of the organization are the work groups that define what each part of the firm does. Senior management attempts to evaluate the performance of these various subunits both for setting rewards for lower-level managers as well as for making business decisions—for instance, which businesses to expand.

Teams often are more productive than individuals working independently. The business units of the organization are, in effect, large production teams. For example, the maintenance department maintains facilities; the marketing group structures and implements marketing plans; research and development explores potential new products; support groups provide products and services to customers. Each unit generally can be characterized into one of five categories based on the decision rights it has been granted and the way its performance is evaluated: Cost centers, expense centers, revenue centers, profit centers, and investment centers. For instance, Briggs & Stratton changed from evaluating some of its divisions as cost or profit centers to evaluating them as investment centers.

Cost Centers

Cost centers are assigned the decision rights to produce a stipulated level of output; in achieving this objective, the unit's efficiency is measured and rewarded. Cost center managers are granted decision rights for determining the mix of inputs—labor, materials, and outside services—used to produce the output. Managers of cost centers are evaluated on their efficiency in applying these inputs to produce output. Since they are not responsible for selling their output, they are not judged on revenues or profits.

To evaluate the performance of a cost center, its output must be measurable. Moreover, because it retains the decision rights to specify the department's output or

---

[2]This section draws on M. Jensen and W. Meckling (1998), "Divisional Performance Measurement," in M. Jensen (Ed.), *Foundations of Organizational Strategy* (Harvard University Press: Cambridge), 345–361.

budget, central management must possess the requisite specialized knowledge. Manufacturing departments, like the welder assembly department at Lincoln Electric, normally are cost centers. The output of the welder assembly department is measured by counting the number of welders completed. Besides manufacturing settings, cost centers also are used in service organizations such as a railroad's railcar maintenance department (where output is measured as the number of railcars serviced), transaction processing by a bank (number of transactions processed), or food services in a hospital (number of meals served). In addition to measuring the quantity of output, its quality must be monitored effectively. If not, unit managers evaluated on costs have incentives to meet their targets by cutting quality. Thus, Lincoln Electric must have mechanisms to ensure that assembled welders meet quality standards, which requires that quality must be reasonably observable.

Various objectives are used for evaluating cost center performance. Two of the more widely used are

- Minimize costs for a given output.
- Maximize output for a given budget.

In order to maximize value, managers must select the optimal output Q^* and produce this output at minimum cost. Cost center managers focus primarily on the second of these activities—cost minimization. Their task is to choose the efficient input mix. For example, if Anthony Mancuso, the manager of the railcar maintenance department, is told to service 100 railcars per day, he is evaluated on meeting this production schedule and controlling the cost of servicing the railcars. The quantity decision tends to be made by central management. The first potential evaluation criterion focuses directly on cost minimization. Minimizing costs given a prespecified quantity (and quality) is consistent with value maximization, so long as the appropriate quantity, Q^*, is selected as the target output.

The second potential evaluation criterion, maximizing output for a specified budget, provides incentives equivalent to the first criterion, given that the specified budget is the minimal budget necessary for producing Q^*. For example, Tony might

MANAGERIAL APPLICATIONS

VA Administrators Game Their Performance Measures

The Secretary of the U.S. Department Veterans Affairs, General Eric Shinseki, was forced to resign following the disclosure of secret waiting lists at several V.A. hospitals serving former U.S. military personnel, many of whom were wounded in action. Administrators at veterans' hospitals were told to alter data to make patient-access numbers look good for their supervisors. These superiors did not want long reported wait times because their bonuses are tied directly to the waiting times of the veterans. Reporting long wait times produced unfavorable performance reviews, and hence a lower bonus. In one hospital, many veterans were not entered into the official electronic waiting list, thereby distorting actual delays in providing care. Another V.A. clinic changed its bonus system whereby 20 percent of physician performance pay would be paid only to doctors who limited patient follow-up visits to an average of two a year, as a way to reduce waiting times by persuading veterans to make fewer appointments.

This example illustrates (again) that pay for performance creates incentives to game the system. In other words, employees will attempt to game all performance measures, especially when they are used to determine rewards. The critical managerial question is: "By how much?"

Source: R. Oppel and A. Goodnough (2014), "Doctor Shortage Is Cited in Delays at V.A. Hospitals," *NY Times* (May 29).

Quantity	Price ($)	Revenue ($)	Total Cost ($)	Total Profits ($)	Average Cost ($)
1	35	35	78	−43	78.0
2	33	66	83	−17	41.5
3	31	93	90	3	30.0
4	29	116	99	17	24.8
5	27	135	110	25	22.0
6	25	150	123	27	20.5
7	23	161	138	23	19.7
8	21	168	155	13	19.4
9	19	171	174	−3	19.3
10	17	170	195	−25	19.5

Table 17.1   Example Demonstrating That Minimizing Average Cost Does Not Yield the Profit-Maximizing Level of Sales

Minimizing average unit cost is not the same as maximizing profits. Maximum profits occur where marginal costs and marginal revenues are equal, which need not be where average unit costs are lowest. In this simple example, profits are maximized by selling 6 units. However, minimum average cost occurs by producing 9 units.

be given a fixed budget ($27,500 per week) and evaluated based on the number of railcars serviced that meet quality specifications within his fixed budget. In either case, Tony has incentives to select the cost-minimizing input mix for producing Q^*.

For both objectives, the manager is constrained either by total output or by the budget. Effective implementation requires that central management choose either the value-maximizing output level or the appropriate budget for efficient production of this output level. Nonetheless under either cost center arrangement, Tony has incentives to reduce costs (or increase output) by lowering quality—hence, the quality of production in cost centers must be monitored.

Cost center managers sometimes are evaluated based on minimizing average cost. In this case, the manager has the incentive to choose the output at which average costs are minimized and to produce this output efficiently. It is important to understand that value maximization need not occur at the point where average costs are minimized. In general, minimizing average unit cost is not the same as maximizing value. For example, in Table 17.1, profits are maximized by selling 6 units; yet, average cost is minimized by producing 9 units. Maximum profits occur where marginal costs and marginal revenues are equal—this need not be where average unit costs are lowest. As another example, suppose a cost center has fixed costs in addition to constant marginal costs. Then average unit costs fall with increases in output. To illustrate, assume that total costs are

$$TC = \$6Q + \$300,000 \tag{17.1}$$

Fixed costs are $300,000, and marginal costs are a constant $6 per unit. Given the equation for total costs, average costs are derived by dividing both sides of the equation by Q to get

$$AC = \frac{TC}{Q} = \$6 + \frac{\$300,000}{Q} \tag{17.2}$$

With constant marginal cost, as quantity produced increases, AC falls. In this situation, a cost center manager who is evaluated based on average unit costs has incentives to increase output, even as inventories mount. Focusing on average costs can provide incentives for cost center managers to either overproduce or underproduce; it will depend on how the value-maximizing output level compares to the quantity where average costs are minimized.

Cost centers work most effectively when central managers have a good understanding of the business unit's cost structure, can determine the value-maximizing output level, can monitor quantity as well as quality, and can establish appropriate rewards; in addition, the cost center manager has specific knowledge of the optimal input mix.

Expense Centers

Cost centers are a common way of organizing manufacturing units. However, activities such as personnel, accounting, patenting, public relations, and research and development often are organized as expense centers. As in cost centers, expense center managers are given fixed budgets and asked to maximize service/output. The fundamental difference between expense centers and traditional cost centers is that output in expense centers is measured more subjectively than objectively. Thus, an expense center is basically a cost center that does not produce an easily measurable output.

The difficulty in observing the output of an expense center has several implications. As director of human resources, Salman Abassi is given a total budget and told to provide as much service as possible. Because the cost per unit of output is difficult to measure, the users of this expense center typically are not charged directly for the center's services.[3] Hence, his users tend to overconsume the services, and Salman regularly requests larger budgets. The central corporate budget-setting organization has difficulty determining the budget that maximizes the firm's value, again because output is not easily observed. Expense center managers frequently derive additional benefits from managing larger staffs (empire building), which reinforces the tendency of these centers to grow faster than the firm as a whole. If the central budget office tries to cut the human resource department's budget, Salman might threaten to reduce those services that are most highly valued by users to enlist their help lobbying against the proposed budget cuts. This behavior is yet another example of influence costs.

A number of devices are employed to control expense centers. One is to benchmark their budgets against those of comparable centers in similar-sized firms. Another is to reorganize the firm and place the expense center under the control of their largest user, who then not only has more specialized knowledge of the expense center's value but also has been delegated the decision rights to set the expense center's budget. Yet, this reorganized structure frequently supplies too little of the service to other units. If these other users are charged more than marginal cost, they demand too little of the services. Alternatively, without a charge-back system for the expense center's services, the controlling user might ration resources provided to other business units and again other users would receive too little of its services.

---

[3]In some cases, firms indirectly charge for these services through a cost allocation system. For example, human resources does not charge for services provided; rather, other business units are charged their pro-rata share of human resources costs based on head count.

HISTORICAL APPLICATIONS

Matching Decision Rights and Performance Metrics Not New

In 1922, James O. McKinsey, founder of the consulting firm McKinsey & Co., described the importance of matching the performance measure and decision rights assignment:

In the modern business organization, control is exercised through individuals who compose the organization. If control of expenses is to be affected through members of the organization, it is necessary that they be classified so as to show responsibility for each class. If responsibility is taken as the controlling factor in an expense classification, each department will be charged with those expenses over which the executive head of the department exercises control. In addition, it may be charged with some items of expense the amount of which is fixed or at least beyond the control of any officer.

To illustrate, the production department will be charged for the supplies used in production, for these supplies are under the control of the production manager, and in addition it will be charged with the depreciation on production equipment, the estimated amount of which is determined in most cases by others than the production manager.

Notice that McKinsey advocates matching the performance metric to the manager's responsibility (i.e., decision rights). He also argues in favor of charging not only expenses over which managers have direct control but also expenses they control indirectly, such as depreciation.

Source: J. McKinsey (1922), *Budgetary Control* (New York: Ronald Press), 281.

Revenue Centers

To organize the marketing activities of selling, distributing, and sometimes servicing finished products received from manufacturing, revenue centers are used. The idea behind a revenue center is to compensate the manager for selling a set of products. For example, a regional sales office might be evaluated as a revenue center. The regional sales manager, Eva Szabo, is given a budget for personnel and expenses and has decision rights as to how to deploy the budget to maximize revenue. Eva has limited discretion in setting the selling price; typically, she must keep the price within a prescribed range.

As with a cost center, various objectives can be used to evaluate revenue centers. One objective is to maximize revenue for a given price (or quantity) and budget for personnel and expenses. That is, the revenue center is told the price of each product it sells and is given a fixed operating budget. This objective is consistent with value maximization so long as central management chooses the correct price-budget combination for each product sold by the revenue center.

Delegating decision rights to Eva over product pricing or quantity and then evaluating her based on maximizing total revenue usually is inconsistent with value maximization. To maximize revenue, Eva goes to the point where marginal revenue equals zero—not to where it equals marginal cost. Since marginal cost usually is greater than zero, Eva's firm loses money on units sold at prices below marginal cost.

Revenue centers work best if sales managers have specialized knowledge of the demand curves of the customers within their sales district and understand how to sell products effectively while central managers understand aggregate market conditions—for instance, they need to be able to select the correct price-quantity combination as well as the optimal product mix (otherwise, salespeople might shift effort toward selling higher revenue-generating products rather than selling products that generate greater value).

Profit Centers

Profit centers often are composed of several cost, and possibly expense and revenue, centers. Profit center managers are given a fixed capital budget and allocated decision rights for input mix, product mix, and selling prices (or output quantities). Profit centers are most appropriate when the knowledge required to make the product mix, quantity, pricing, and quality decisions is specific to the division and this information is costly to transfer.

Profit centers usually are evaluated on the difference between actual and budgeted accounting profits for their division. Although measuring the profits of profit centers is seemingly straightforward, two complications often consume managers' attention: How to price transfers of goods and services between business units (transfer pricing) and which corporate overhead costs to allocate to specific business units. These are hotly debated topics within many firms. (We examine the transfer-pricing problem in the next section.)

When there are interdependencies among business units, motivating managers of individual profit centers to maximize the profits of their business units normally fails to maximize the value of the firm as a whole. For instance, individual units focusing on their own profits frequently ignore how their actions affect sales or costs of other units.[4] One division might free-ride on another division's quality reputation, thereby reaping short-run gains at the expense of the other division and the whole firm. For example, Chevrolet and Buick are two profit centers within General Motors. Suppose Chevrolet, in pursuit of higher profits, decides to raise its car quality. This might affect consumers' perceptions of the average quality of all General Motor cars—including Buick's perceived quality. An enhanced reputation for all General Motors cars helps Buick. But if Chevrolet receives no credit for additional Buick profits, it is likely to ignore this positive externality that it generates for Buick and will tend to underinvest in quality enhancements. To help managers internalize both positive and negative externalities that their actions impose on other profit centers, firms often base incentive compensation not just on the profits of the manager's own business unit but also on a group of related profit centers' profits and/or firmwide profits. Unless the group and/or the entire firm makes a certain profit target, no individual profit center manager receives a bonus. Managers at Briggs & Stratton had 40 percent of their bonus tied to corporate-wide EVA.

Investment Centers

Investment centers are similar to profit centers. However, they have additional decision rights for capital expenditures and are evaluated on measures such as return on investment. Investment centers are most appropriate where the manager of the unit has specific knowledge about investment opportunities as well as information relevant for making the unit's operating decisions.

Several profit centers often comprise investment centers. Investment centers have all the decision rights of cost and profit centers, as well as decision rights over the amount of capital to be invested. For example, suppose Lars Erikssen manages the

---

[4]Conceptually, other units could offer side payments to take these effects into account. However, in the presence of transaction costs, these offers are likely to be limited.

consumer electronics group of an electronics firm that is composed of three profit centers: The television division, the DVD division, and the stereo division. Lars has decision rights over the amount of capital invested in consumer electronics and is evaluated based on the return on the capital invested. There are two commonly used measures of performance for investment centers: Accounting return on investment and residual income (EVA).

Accounting Return on Assets

The most commonly used investment center performance measure is *return on assets* (ROA). ROA is the ratio of accounting net income generated by the investment center divided by total assets invested in the investment center. ROA has intuitive appeal because it can be compared to external market-based yields to provide a benchmark for a division's performance.[5] However, using ROA creates potential problems. ROA is not a measure of the division's economic rate of return because neither accounting income (the numerator) is a measure of economic profit nor assets (the denominator) is the market value of the division's assets. Economic profit is the change in value over the period. Accounting rules tend to be conservative: They dictate that accounting net income excludes some value increases and includes some value declines. For example, accounting net income excludes any appreciation in land value until the land is sold but recognizes permanent declines in market value even though the land has not been sold. Also, accounting depreciation, which is deducted from accounting profits, does not necessarily reflect the change in the economic value of the depreciable assets.

Lars has an incentive to reject profitable projects with ROAs below the mean ROA for the consumer electronics group because accepting these projects lowers the group's ROA. For example, suppose the group has an average ROA of 19 percent, 4 percent above its 15 percent cost of capital.[6] A new investment project that is 10 percent the size of the existing group total assets is available. Its ROA is 16 percent, which also is above its cost of capital of 15 percent; thus, taking this project would increase firm value. But if this project is accepted, the group's ROA falls to 18.7 percent (.90 × 19% + .10 × 16%). If his group is evaluated based on increasing ROA, Lars will reject the project, even though its returns exceed the opportunity cost of capital.

ROA can lead to accepting unprofitable projects, too. Gail Pratt runs a division that has a 15 percent cost of capital and an average ROA of 12 percent. A new project with an ROA of 14 percent is available. Even though it has a return below her division's cost of capital, Gail is tempted to accept the project because it raises her average ROA.

Riskier projects require a higher cost of capital to compensate investors for bearing additional risk. If managers are rewarded solely for increasing their ROA without being charged for any additional risk imposed on the firm, they have incentives to plunge the firm into risky projects. Finally, a manager near retirement who is evaluated based on ROA might take projects that boost ROA immediately, even if

---

[5]For firms with outstanding debt, it is important to add back interest expense to accounting income before comparing ROA to the firm's external market-based yields.

[6]Cost of capital is the rate of return the firm must pay the market to raise capital. If the firm can raise money at 15 percent and invest in projects earning 16 percent, the value of the firm increases.

they were expected to be unprofitable projects—this is just a specific case of the horizon problem.

Accounting Residual Income

To overcome some of the incentive deficiencies of ROA, such as divesting projects with ROAs above their cost of capital but below the division's average ROA, some firms use *residual income* to evaluate performance. Residual income measures business-unit performance by subtracting the opportunity cost of capital employed from the profits of the business unit. For example, suppose Amita Singal manages a division that has profits of $20 million (after tax but before interest expense) and total assets of $100 million. Furthermore, her division has a required cost of capital of 15 percent. Its ROA is 20 percent, which is in excess of its opportunity cost of capital (15 percent). Residual income is $5 million ($20M − 15% × $100M). Although divesting a project with an ROA of less than 20 percent but above 15 percent raises average ROA, it lowers residual income. Residual income also goes by other names such as "economic profits" and "Economic Value Added (EVA)."

Nonetheless, residual income has its own problems. Residual income is an absolute number; thus, larger divisions typically have larger residual incomes than smaller divisions. This makes relative performance-evaluation comparisons across investment centers of different sizes more difficult. To implement residual income requires that senior managers estimate the opportunity cost of capital for each division. In principle, each division will have a different required cost of capital to allow more precise performance evaluations by controlling for risk differences. However, these risk adjustments also potentially lead to greater influence costs as divisional managers lobby to lower their required capital costs.

Like ROA, residual income measures performance over a single year. It does not measure the impact of actions taken today on a firm's value in the future. For example, by cutting maintenance, current period residual income (and ROA) is increased, but future cash flow and hence the value of the firm might be jeopardized. Managers with short-term horizons will have incentives to avoid projects that have negative residual incomes in early years even if they are quite profitable in the long run. Thus, the use of residual income measures like EVA is not sufficient for making investment decisions.

Table 17.2 summarizes our discussion of the various types of subunits of the firm; it summarizes the measures used to evaluate performance for the different types of centers, the decision rights the various centers are granted, and circumstances under which particular centers are used most effectively. Notice that performance-evaluation measures and decision-right assignments are balanced: Decision rights assigned to the center and performance measures are matched. Note also the linkage between decision rights assigned to each center and the location of the specific knowledge. For example, if a center does not have knowledge of customer demand curves, it does not have decision rights for pricing and hence is evaluated as a cost center.

Although not explicit in Table 17.2, to ensure that our three-legged stool remains balanced, performance rewards must be tied to the performance evaluations. For example, besides introducing EVA in 1990, Briggs & Stratton also changed its management compensation plan. B&S managers were compensated based on both their division's EVA and firm EVA. Therefore, besides linking pay to the performance measure, EVA, B&S also changed its performance reward system.

Unit Type	Performance Measures	Decision Rights	Typically Used When
Cost center	Minimize total cost for a fixed output Maximize output for a fixed budget Minimize average cost	Input mix (labor, material, supplies)	Central manager can measure output, knows the cost functions, and can set the optimal quantity and appropriate rewards. Central manager can observe the quality of the cost center's output. Cost center manager has knowledge of the optimal input mix.
Expense center	Minimize total cost for a fixed level of services Maximize service for a fixed budget	Input mix (labor, material, supplies)	Output is difficult to observe and measure.
Revenue center	Maximize revenues for a given price (or quantity) and operating budget	Input mix (labor, material, supplies)	Central manager has the knowledge to select the optimal product mix. Central manager has the knowledge to select the correct price or quantity. Revenue center managers have knowledge of the demand curves of the customers in their sales districts.
Profit center	Actual profits Actual profits compared to budgeted profits	Input mix Product mix Selling prices (or output quantities)	Profit center manager has the knowledge to select the correct price/quantity. Profit center manager has the knowledge to select the optimal product mix.
Investment center	Return on investment Residual income EVA	Input mix Product mix Selling prices (or output quantities) Capital invested in center	Investment center manager has the knowledge to select the correct price/quantity. Investment center manager has the knowledge to select the optimal product mix. Investment center manager has knowledge about investment opportunities.

Table 17.2 Summary of Cost, Expense, Revenue, Profit, and Investment Centers

Performance measures and decision rights are balanced across the various subunits of the organization. Their use depends on the distribution of specific knowledge.

EVA Often Is Linked to a Change in the Compensation Plan

At the beginning of this chapter, Briggs & Stratton's use of economic value added was described as a performance measurement plan that is being widely heralded and adopted by such companies as AT&T, CSX, Coca-Cola, Equifax, and Quaker Oats. EVA is a variant of residual income. The formula for EVA is

$$\text{EVA} = \text{adjusted accounting earnings} - (\text{weighted average cost of capital} \times \text{total capital})$$

This is the same formula as residual income, but variables used in computing EVA are measured more carefully than historically has been done. Instead of using the same accounting procedures that are used in reporting to shareholders, different accounting procedures are used to arrive at "adjusted accounting earnings." For example, standard U.S. accounting rules require that the entire amount spent on research and development each year be deducted from earnings. This creates incentives for managers with a short time horizon to cut R&D spending. One adjustment to accounting earnings some EVA adopters make is to add back R&D spending and treat it as an asset to be amortized, usually over five years. Total capital, in the above formula, consists of all the firm's assets, including the amount invested in R&D and other adjustments made to earnings.

EVA uses a weighted average cost of capital, which reflects the cost of equity and debt. The cost of equity is the price appreciation and dividends the shareholders could have earned in a portfolio of companies of similar risk. This is the opportunity cost the shareholders bear by buying the company's stock. The cost of debt is the current market yield on debt of similar risk. The costs of debt and equity are weighted by the relative amounts of debt and equity. Suppose the cost of equity is 18 percent, the cost of debt is 10 percent, and the firm's capital structure is 40 percent debt and 60 percent equity. Then, the weighted average cost of capital is 14.8 percent ($0.60 \times 18\% + 0.40 \times 10\%$).*

EVA, like residual income, measures the total return after deducting the cost of all capital employed by the firm. It estimates the economic profits of the firm in the period (usually a year). Many of the firms adopting EVA to measure divisional performance did so as part of a corporate reorganization. Besides rewarding the CEO and other top managers based on EVA, many firms measure and then reward each of their divisional managers based on the division's EVA. Besides decentralizing decision rights and adopting EVA as the performance measure, firms also change the third leg of the three-legged stool, the reward system. Manager bonuses are based on EVA.

*EVA is calculated on an after-tax basis using adjusted accounting earnings before interest but net of income taxes. The weighted average cost of capital is computed as follows. The after-tax cost of debt is computed using 1 minus the marginal corporate tax rate times the market yield on debt of similar risk. For example, suppose the market yield on equivalent debt is 15 percent and the marginal corporate tax rate is 38 percent. The after-tax cost of debt is 9.3 percent [$15\% \times (1 - 0.38)$]. If the cost of equity is 20 percent and the proportions of debt and equity are the same, the after-tax weighted average cost of capital is 14.65 percent ($0.50 \times 9.3\% + 0.50 \times 20\%$).

Source: B. Stewart (2013), *Best-Practice EVA: The Definitive Guide to Measuring and Maximizing Shareholder Value* (John Wiley & Sons: Hoboken).

Boosting Return on Capital

Eaton, a maker of transmissions for large trucks, divided its different transmission components into three categories: Those for which other firms were more cost-effective because they had economies of scale, those for which Eaton was the most efficient producer or for which it had proprietary technology, and all other component parts of its transmissions. Eaton then outsourced the manufacturing of all component parts other than those for which it was the most efficient producer or for which it had proprietary technology. By doing this, Eaton significantly dropped the asset intensity of its business, thereby leading to better returns on capital.

Source: D. Katz (2010), "Lite Makes Right," *CFO* (November), 35–36.

Transfer Pricing[7]

As discussed earlier, firms organize into business units. Whenever business units transfer goods or services among themselves, measuring their performance requires that a *transfer price* be established for the goods and services exchanged. For example, recall that Briggs & Stratton reorganized and created several investment centers including the aluminum castings and small-engines divisions. Besides producing for and selling to outside customers, the aluminum castings division also sells intermediate products to other investment centers within B&S. In order to measure the performance of these investment centers, each of these internal transactions requires a transfer price. The purchasing division pays the transfer price; the producing division receives the transfer price.

Some executives do not view the transfer-pricing problem as important from the overall firm's perspective. They think that changing transfer-pricing methods merely shifts income among divisions and that, except for relative performance evaluation, little else is affected. But this is a mistake: *The choice of transfer-pricing method does not merely reallocate total company profits among business units, but affects the firm's total profits.* Think of the firm's total profit as a pie. Choice among transfer-pricing methods not only changes how the pie is divided among the business units, but also changes the size of the pie to be divided.

Managers make investment, purchasing, and production decisions based on the transfer prices they face. If from the firm's perspective these transfer prices do not reflect resource values accurately, the value of the firm will be reduced because managers will make inappropriate decisions. For example, if the opportunity cost to B&S of producing an aluminum casting is $20 but the transfer price is $30, the small-engines division will buy too few castings and firm value will be reduced. Purchasing division managers will have the incentive to shift away from the aluminum castings, perhaps outsourcing that purchase even though, in reality, outsourcing is more expensive. Also, because transfer prices affect managers' performance evaluations, incorrect transfer prices can result in inappropriate promotion and retention decisions.

Transfer prices are more prevalent in organizations than many managers realize. Firms often have extensive charge-back systems for internal service departments. Consider the charges that the advertising department receives from the maintenance department for janitorial service, as well as charges for telephones, security services, data processing, legal, or human resource services. Most firms charge inside users for these internally provided services. Such charge-back systems also exist in hospitals, universities, and other nonprofit organizations. These charge-back systems are internal transfer prices.

Because the use of transfer prices (including charge-back systems) is widespread and because transfer pricing affects performance evaluation and hence the rewards managers receive, fighting over the transfer price between divisions is virtually inevitable. Transfer pricing is a continuing source of tension within firms. Many managers in multidivisional firms are involved in a parade of transfer-pricing disputes over the course of their careers.

A potentially important factor in determining an optimal transfer price is taxes. If the producing and purchasing divisions are in different countries and subject to different tax rates, then taxes affect the opportunity cost of the product and thus the optimal

---

[7]This section draws on J. Brickley, C. Smith, and J. Zimmerman (1995), "Transfer Pricing and the Control of Internal Corporate Transactions," *Journal of Applied Corporate Finance* 8, 60–67.

MANAGERIAL APPLICATIONS

Transfer Pricing and Taxes

By some estimates, aggressive transfer pricing by U.S. companies cost the Federal treasury up to $60 billion per year. The Federal government closely monitors these firms' tax returns and often challenges what it deems to be improper transfer-pricing mechanisms. U.K.-based GlaxoSmithKline (GSK) agreed to settle its transfer-pricing dispute with the U.S. IRS by paying $3.1 billion. The government's original claim against GSK was for $11.5 billion for 16 years between 1989 and 2005. The dispute involved how GSK treated as part of the transfer price of making its popular ulcer drug Zantac the marketing expenses and R&D costs. In the United States, 30 percent of all corporate tax adjustments made each year involve transfer-pricing disputes.

Apple Inc. reduced its 2011 federal tax bill by billions of dollars. Apple conducts most of its research in the United States. Most of its key employees, long-lived assets, and retail stores are in the United States. But by employing legal transfer-pricing rules, Apple reports only 30 percent of its profits as being from the United States, which imposes one of the highest tax rates on corporate earnings (35 percent). However, some estimates place Apple's actual worldwide effective tax rate closer to 13 percent.

One pharmaceutical maker, Forest Laboratories, cut its tax bill by a third. Forest, headquartered in New York City, manufactures the drugs in Ireland, sells them primarily in the United States, and uses subsidiaries in the Netherlands and Bermuda to recognize the income tax. Setting high transfer prices between the United States and Ireland shifts the income first to Ireland. Then transfer prices shift the income from Ireland to the Netherlands and Bermuda, which have even lower tax rates than Ireland. By not returning the profits to the United States in the form of cash, Forest legally avoids most U.S. taxes on its income.

To attempt to streamline the transfer-pricing dispute-resolution process, the IRS instituted an Advanced Pricing Agreement (APA) Program. A taxpayer team and IRS team work together prospectively to develop the transfer-pricing method the taxpayer will use. As long as the taxpayer complies with the agreement, the IRS will not challenge subsequent years' transfer prices. The IRS had negotiated about 1,300 APAs by the end of 2013.

Source: IRS (2014), "Announcement and Report Concerning Advance Pricing Agreements (March 27); R. Fink (2004), "Haven or Hell," *CFO Magazine*, (March 1); M. Sullivan (2012), "Apple Reports High Rate but Saves Billions on Taxes," *Tax.com*, (February 13); A. Nevius (2010), "Advance Pricing Agreements for SMEs," *Journal of Accountancy*, (October), 86; and J. Drucker (2010), "Forest Laboratories' Globe-Trotting Profits," *Bloomberg Business Week*, (May 13).

transfer price. The producing division pays income taxes on the difference between its costs and what it receives for each unit, which is determined by the transfer price. In general, to minimize the sum of the two taxes, the firm should set the transfer price so as to allocate as much of the profit as possible to the division in the country with the lower tax rate.[8] To simplify the analysis, this section focuses on the organizational economics of transfer pricing and ignores these potentially important tax issues.

Economics of Transfer Pricing

The optimal transfer-pricing rule is quite simple to state: The optimal transfer price for a product or service is its opportunity cost—it is the value forgone by not using the product transferred in its next best alternative use. Unfortunately, as we will see, this rule, although simple to state, often is difficult to implement in practice.

---

[8]International tax treaties and local regulation constrain the transfer-pricing methods firms can use for tax purposes. See M. Scholes, M. Wolfson, M. Erickson, E. Maydew, and T. Shevlin (2009), *Taxes and Business Strategy: A Planning Approach*, 4th edition (Prentice Hall: Englewood Cliffs).

MANAGERIAL APPLICATIONS

Dual Transfer-Pricing Systems?

Some consultants advocate using two separate transfer-pricing systems, one aimed at satisfying tax reporting and another directed at internal decision making. Jay Tredwell, director of CEO Solutions for Answer*Think* Consulting Group, says, "Having a separate system can give senior managers a better view of . . . real profitability [as opposed to] their 'tax profitability.'" However, Michael Patton, a partner at Ernst and Young, counters,

> *An essential problem with separated reporting is that transfer prices already reflect the profitability of a division or project. If you are trying to make decisions about new activities or facilities, and trying to judge their returns on invested capital, you need good benchmarks to judge these by, and good transfer prices provide part of that. Basically, then the question is whether your current transfer prices reflect economic reality or not. If they do, there's little need for a new system. If not, the tax authorities may have a question or two for you on audit in a few years' time.*

Case Corp., a $6 billion farm and construction equipment maker, opposes separate transfer-pricing systems for statutory and internal reporting. They argue dual systems are costly. Case keeps all accounts around the world based on U.S. accounting practice and bases management results and compensation on actual transfer prices used by divisions for tax purposes.

Source: I. Springsteel (1999), "Separate but Unequal," *CFO* (August), 89–91; and C. Choe and C. Hyde (2007), "Multinational Transfer Pricing, Tax Arbitrage and the Arm's Length Principle," *Economic Record* (December), 398–404.

Transfer Pricing with Costless Information

To illustrate the concept of opportunity cost, we focus on two of a multinational firm's profit centers—U.S. manufacturing and European distribution. Senior management is considering making a product in the U.S. division and transferring it to its European division. Assume also that marginal cost of production is $3 per unit, and that the U.S. division has excess capacity. If the product is transferred to Europe, they can sell it and receive $5 for each unit, net of their own marginal cost. Also, everyone knows each division's cost and revenue data.

If the unit is not manufactured, the firm saves $3 in U.S. manufacturing costs but forgoes $5 in European revenue, hence reducing profit by $2. If the unit is manufactured and transferred, the firm forgoes $3 (marginal cost to produce) and receives $5, for a net receipt of $2. The better alternative is to manufacture and transfer the unit. The resources forgone by transferring it from the United States to Europe—and hence the opportunity cost of such a transfer—are $3 per unit, the same as U.S. manufacturing's marginal cost of production.

As this example is meant to suggest, the marginal cost of producing the unit often is its opportunity cost. But this is not always the case. Sometimes, the opportunity cost is the marginal revenue of selling the intermediate good externally. For example, suppose the U.S. division can produce one unit for $3, and can either transfer that unit to Europe or sell it for $6 in the United States, but, because of limited capacity, it cannot do both. In this case, by having the U.S. division transfer the unit to Europe, the firm forgoes selling the intermediate good in the U.S. market. And even though the marginal cost of producing the unit still is $3, the opportunity cost of making the transfer now is $6. Thus, it now is optimal to sell it externally rather than to transfer it to Europe.

More generally, the U.S. division will produce to the point where the marginal cost of the last unit equals the transfer price. Likewise, the European division will buy units from the U.S. division so long as their net receipts just cover the transfer price. When opportunity cost is used to set the transfer price and both divisions are maximizing their respective profits, total firm profits are maximized, assuming no other interdependencies between the divisions (we consider the case of dependencies among divisions later). Thus, in this simple example, the transfer price represents the marginal cost to the European division. If the transfer price is too high or too low relative to opportunity cost, Europe purchases either too few or too many units and the firm's profits thus are lower.

Transfer Pricing with Asymmetric Information

The preceding discussion assumes that everyone knows the U.S. division's marginal production cost, the intermediate product's external price, Europe's marginal revenue, and whether the U.S. division has excess capacity. Yet if all this knowledge were readily available, there would be no reason to decentralize decision making within the organization. Central management would have the knowledge to make the decision and could retain the decision rights or, if the decision rights were delegated, closely monitor the process at low cost. In reality, much of this information is not readily available to central management. Especially in large, multidivisional firms, such knowledge generally resides at lower levels within the firm. There, it is private knowledge, costly to either transfer or verify by senior management. In some circumstances, lower-level managers have incentives to distort the information they pass to senior managers. To illustrate these incentives, we consider a firm with market power.

Consider the situation where Hiroshi Komada, the manager of manufacturing, is the only person with detailed knowledge of his division's marginal costs, and assume that Hiroshi seeks to maximize the profits of his division. Even if distribution is allowed to purchase the product on the outside, if manufacturing has market power in setting the transfer price, it will attempt to set the price above marginal cost to increase its *measured* profits. When this happens, the firm manufactures and sells too few units of the product. This is another example of unexploited gains from trade from monopoly. The manufacturing division possesses what amounts to monopoly rights in information and hence behaves like a monopolist. Just as monopolists earn "monopoly profits" by raising prices and restricting output, manufacturing's higher profits lead to lower-than-optimal production levels and reduced total firm value.

As a simple illustration of this, consider a firm that produces one product and faces the following demand:

$$P = 110 - 5Q \qquad (17.3)$$

Assume that the product is produced at a constant marginal cost of $10. Profit maximization occurs by setting marginal revenue equal to marginal cost. At this condition, $Q^* = 10$ and $P^* = 60$. Firm profits are $500 ($60 \times 10 - 10×10). Figure 17.1 depicts this situation.

Assume that manufacturing produces the good at MC $= 10$ and transfers it to distribution at a transfer price, P_t. Suppose the only cost to the distribution division is the transfer price. (For simplicity, additional distribution costs equal zero.)

Distribution sells the product externally and thus the demand curve for its product is the firm's demand curve. How many units of the good will the manager of this unit want to buy at each possible transfer price? Note that distribution's marginal cost is the transfer price $MC_d = P_t$. Distribution maximizes division profit by setting $MC_d = MR_d$. Hence, in this case, the firm's marginal revenue curve represents distribution's demand for the good and thus is the derived demand curve facing manufacturing: $P_t = 110 - 10Q$ (the marginal revenue curve in Figure 17.1).

Next, assume that manufacturing sets the transfer price. It has monopoly power, and because of costly information, senior management cannot monitor the decision.

Figure 17.1 Profit-Maximizing Price

A firm faces the following demand curve: $P = 110 - 5Q$. The product is produced at a constant marginal cost of $10. Profit maximization occurs by setting marginal revenue equal to marginal cost. At this condition, $Q^* = 10$ and $P^* = 60$. Firm profits are $500 ($60 × 10 − $10 × 10).

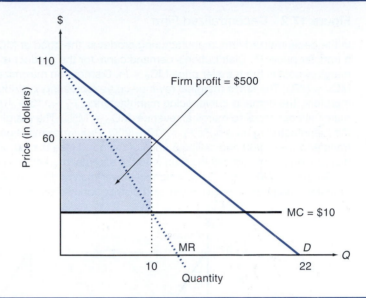

What price will manufacturing set and what quantity of the good will be produced? Hiroshi has one customer, the distribution division. To maximize his profits in manufacturing Hiroshi sets $MC_m = MR_m$. His marginal cost is $10. What is Hiroshi's marginal revenue? To answer that question we must look at his customer, the distribution division. Distribution has market power and faces the demand curve: $P = 110 - 5Q$. The distribution division's marginal cost is the transfer price: MC_d = transfer price. Distribution will take the transfer price and set it equal to its marginal revenue, in this case $MR_d = 110 - 10Q$. This marginal revenue curve for distribution displays how Hiroshi's customer (the distribution division) alters demand as Hiroshi varies the transfer price and hence his customer's marginal cost. For example, if Hiroshi sets the transfer price at $50, distribution will maximize its profits by setting $MC_d = MR_d$. Or,

---

ANALYZING MANAGERIAL DECISIONS: *The Copper Box Company*

You have been hired as a consultant to the CEO of the Copper Box Company. This company holds two patents, one for the technology for making the copper boxes and the other for a copper box design. The patent production technology belongs to the manufacturing division and the unique patented copper box design is sold by the distribution division. Distribution buys the boxes from manufacturing, and both divisions are run as profit centers. Manufacturing sells some of the copper boxes to outside firms, but outsiders cannot buy the patented copper boxes from manufacturing directly. These boxes are only available through the distribution

division. Further assume that manufacturing has enough capacity to sell both internally and externally. Thus, the opportunity cost of manufacturing's transfer is its marginal production cost.

The CEO of the Copper Box Company believes strongly in decentralization and the principle that the two division managers should be free to set the prices of their own products, including the right of manufacturing to set the price that distribution pays for the boxes produced by manufacturing. Write a memo to the CEO explaining why such a policy fails to maximize the value of the Copper Box Company.

Figure 17.2 Decentralized Firm

In the decentralized firm, manufacturing produces the good at MC = 10 and transfers it to distribution at a transfer price, P_t. Distribution's demand curve for the product is the firm's demand curve. Distribution's marginal cost is the transfer price $MC_d = P_t$. Distribution maximizes profit (for the unit) by setting $MC_d = MR_d$. The firm's marginal revenue curve represents distribution's demand for the good and is, therefore, the demand curve facing manufacturing: $P_t = 110 - 10Q$. The manager of manufacturing sets marginal cost equal to marginal revenue: $MC_m = MR_m$. The marginal cost = 10. The marginal revenue for the manufacturing division is $P_t = 110 - 20Q$. Profit maximization for manufacturing will involve setting the transfer price at $60 and selling 5 units of the good (see the left panel). Facing a transfer price of $60, distribution will in turn sell the 5 units to the external market at a price of $85 (right panel). Total firm profits are $375 (5 × $85 − 5 × $10), which are lower than at the firm profit-maximizing output of 10 units ($500). Manufacturing has profits of $250, and distribution has profits of $125.

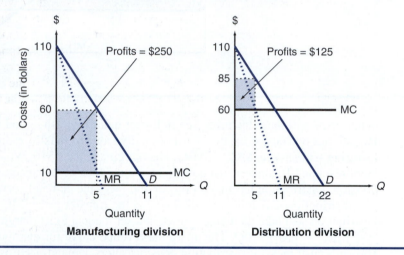

Manufacturing division	Distribution division

$50 = 110 − 10Q$. Solving for $Q^* = 6$ units. Therefore, if Hiroshi sets the transfer price at $50, distribution will buy 6 units. The important point to understand is that the demand curve Hiroshi faces is distribution's marginal revenue curve. The demand curve facing Hiroshi is not the firm's (or distribution's) demand curve but rather it is the firm's marginal revenue curve. Thus, manufacturing faces a *derived demand curve* equal to the marginal revenue curve for the firm: $P = 110 − 10Q$. Using this as his demand curve, Hiroshi's marginal revenue curve is $MR_m = 110 − 20Q$. To maximize his division's profits Hiroshi sets $MR_m = MC_m$. Or, $110 − 20Q = $10 and sells 5 units to distribution at a transfer price of $60 (transfer price $= P = 110 − 10 × 5$). (See the left panel in Figure 17.2.) Facing a transfer price of $60, distribution in turn will sell the 5 units to the external market at a price of $85 (right panel in Figure 17.2). Total firm profits are $375 (5 × $85 − 5 × $10), which are lower than at the firm's profit-maximizing output of 10 units—$500. Manufacturing reports profits of $250, and distribution books profits of $125. Both divisions are reporting profits, but total firm profits are lower in Figure 17.2 than in Figure 17.1.

The basic problem is that distribution, facing a transfer price of $60, overestimates the *opportunity cost* to the firm of producing extra units of the good (which is $10). Hence, from the firm's standpoint, distribution stops short of the optimal quantity to be sold to the external market. The transfer price that ensures firm profit maximization in this example is the marginal production cost of the unit. Note, however, that Hiroshi does not want to set $10 as the transfer price because manufacturing would report a lower profit—in this example, $0.

The earlier discussion thus illustrates the basic incentive problems associated with internal transfers when information is held privately by divisional managers. Opportunity cost is the transfer price that maximizes a firm's value. But because business-unit managers tend to have better knowledge of opportunity costs than senior management and because transfer prices frequently affect performance evaluation and managerial rewards, divisional managers have incentives to distort information to influence the transfer price.

Complicating matters further, getting the information necessary to calculate opportunity costs is especially difficult for senior management because opportunity costs depend on the firm's next best alternative use of the good or service. Central management is likely to know less about the next best use of a product, and about the resources used to make the product, than the manager of the division that produces it. Moreover, the next best alternative will change as the firm's business opportunities change. For example, sometimes the division has excess capacity and manufacturing can sell the good both internally and externally. At other times, manufacturing has only enough current capacity to produce for either the inside or outside user. This specialized knowledge of the alternatives is held primarily by the division managers.

Problems arise whether distribution or manufacturing has the decision rights to set the price of the goods or services transferred and the other division cannot purchase or sell outside. Manufacturing sets a price above opportunity cost to capture some monopoly profits, and distribution purchases fewer units than if the appropriate (lower) transfer price were set. But, if given the decision rights to determine the price, distribution would set a transfer price below the opportunity cost and manufacturing would supply too few units. Again, the number of units transferred is below the profit-maximizing level. If central management knew the opportunity cost, it would not have to decentralize decision making to the profit centers and could dictate both price and quantity decisions.

ANALYZING MANAGERIAL DECISIONS: *HiTek Bikes*

You work for HiTek Bikes that designs and manufactures a high performance road bike frame, the Dura Carbon Ace. The demand curve for this frame is given by $P = \$6,600 - 10Q$, where Q is the number of frames sold and P is the price. The total cost of production is $TC = Q^2$. Given this total cost curve, we know that marginal cost is $MC = 2Q$.

1. Verify numerically that when $TC = Q^2$ marginal cost is $MC = 2Q$.
2. What are the optimal output, price, and profits for the firm?
3. Now assume that the firm is divided into two profit centers. One division manufactures the product at a total cost of $TC = Q^2$ and then transfers it to a selling division that faces the firm's demand curve. The selling division has no other costs other than the transfer price for the product. Assume that the manufacturing division has the power to set the transfer price and that the selling division can only buy internally. The selling division, however, can select the quantity to purchase. What transfer price will the manufacturing unit select? What are the resulting profits of the two units?
4. From the firm's standpoint, what is the optimal transfer price?

The economics of transfer pricing is summarized well by the following quote:

The economist's first instinct is to set the transfer price equal to marginal cost. But it may be difficult to find out marginal cost. As a practical matter, marginal cost information is rarely known to anybody in the firm, because it depends on opportunity costs that vary with capacity use. And even if marginal cost information were available, there is no guarantee that it would be revealed in a truthful fashion for the purpose of determining an optimal transfer price.[9]

Common Transfer-Pricing Methods

The correct transfer price, then, is opportunity cost. But, determining opportunity costs is expensive—in part because the information necessary to calculate such costs resides with operating managers who have incentives to distort it. To address this problem, companies sometimes commission special studies of the firm's cost structure by outside experts. Such studies, however, are not only costly, but their findings become outdated whenever the firm's business opportunities or productive capacities change. If senior management simply vests the right to set the transfer price with either manufacturing or distribution, prices are likely to be set too high or too low, resulting in too few units transferred and the firm's value lower than it could be.

Because determining opportunity costs is itself an expensive undertaking, managers resort to various lower-cost approximations. There are at least four different methods for setting transfer prices that firms regularly use to approximate the opportunity cost of the units transferred: market price, marginal production cost, full cost, and negotiated pricing. As discussed below, each of these four methods is better than the others in some situations, but not in others. For example, if the divisions operate in different countries with different tax rates, then the choice of method will be driven in part by tax considerations. If manufacturing faces lower tax rates than distribution, full-cost prices will allocate more of the profit to the lower-taxed division than marginal-cost prices. In the remainder of this section we describe the various methods and set forth their advantages and disadvantages.

Market-Based Transfer Prices

The standard transfer-pricing rule offered by most textbooks is this: Given a competitive external market for the good, the product should be transferred at the external market price. If manufacturing cannot make a long-run profit at the external price, then the company is better off not producing internally and instead should purchase in the external market. If the purchasing division cannot make a long-run profit at the external price, then the company is better off not processing the intermediate product and instead should sell it in the external market.

The use of market-based transfer prices often is assumed to produce the correct make-versus-buy decisions. In many situations, however, market prices will not provide an accurate reflection of opportunity costs. If the firm and the market both are making the intermediate good, the fundamental question arises, *Can both survive in the long run?* If one can produce the good at a lower, long-run average cost than the other, the high-cost producer should not be producing the intermediate product.

[9]B. Holmstrom and J. Tirole (1991), "Transfer Pricing and Organizational Form," *Journal of Law, Economics, and Organizations* 7, 201–228.

Transactions generally take place inside rather than outside firms whenever the cost of repetitive internal contracting is cheaper than outsourcing.[10] For example, production of different kinds of goods tends to take place inside the same firm when there are important interdependencies or synergies among those products. And, of course, the more valuable such synergies, the more likely the firm will continue producing internally.[11]

As the synergies from internal production increase, the external market price becomes a less accurate reflection of the opportunity cost of internal production. For example, it is often the case either that an intermediate good is not being produced by other firms or that the good produced externally is not identical to the good produced internally. In one case, there is no market price; in the other, the market price often will be an unreliable guide to opportunity cost. And, even when there are virtually identical "cheaper" external products, producing internally still can make sense insofar as it provides greater quality control, more assurance of timeliness of supply, or better protection of proprietary information. When these factors are included in the analysis, the external market may no longer be "cheaper."

In such cases, use of the market price as the transfer price may understate the profitability of the product and its contribution to the value of the firm.[12] Suppose, for example, an intermediate product can be purchased (but not sold) externally for $3 per unit. Synergies such as high transaction costs of using the market make it effective to produce the item internally. Internal production avoids the costs of writing and enforcing contracts. Suppose there are $.50 worth of synergies, so that the correct transfer price is $2.50 in the sense that $2.50 is the opportunity cost to the firm. But, if the market price of $3.00 is used as the transfer price, distribution will purchase fewer units than if $2.50 were used, and the value of the firm will not be maximized.

Marginal-Cost Transfer Prices

If there is no external market for the intermediate good or if large synergies among business units cause the market price to be an inaccurate measure of opportunity cost, then marginal production cost may be the most effective alternative transfer price. As we saw earlier, marginal cost represents the value of the resources forgone to produce the last unit.

As with other transfer-pricing methods, there are problems with marginal production cost as a measure of opportunity cost. One is that manufacturing does not necessarily recover its fixed costs. If all manufacturing's output is transferred internally and

---

[10]Advantages to internal transactions include the elimination of credit risk, lower marketing costs, and learning from production. See Chapter 3 and R. Coase (1937), "The Nature of the Firm," *Economica* 4, 386–405. For a summary of the arguments for the types of costs that are lowered by firms, see R. Watts (1992), "Accounting Choice Theory and Market-Based Research in Accounting," *British Accounting Journal* 24, 242–246. These arguments include economies of scale in contracting, team production and monitoring, postcontractual opportunism, and knowledge costs. Chapter 19 discusses these topics.

[11]Interdependencies or synergies that cause production to occur inside the firm are classic economic externalities. If interdependencies in production or demand functions exist, the market price does not capture these interdependencies. The same occurs inside the firm and causes the external price to mismeasure the opportunity cost of one more unit being transferred.

[12]This point has been recognized by others. As one notes, "observed market prices cannot directly guide the owner of the input to perform in the same manner as if every activity he performs were measured and priced." In S. Cheung (1983), "The Contractual Nature of the Firm," *Journal of Law & Economics* 26 (April), 5.

marginal cost is below its average total cost, manufacturing's fixed costs are not recovered. Thus, manufacturing appears to be losing money.[13]

One variant of marginal-cost transfer pricing is to use a two-part price—to price all transfers at marginal cost while also charging distribution a fixed fee for these services. Distribution pays marginal cost for the additional units and buys the number of units that maximize the firm's profits. Unlike straight marginal-cost pricing, this variant allows manufacturing to cover its full cost and earn a profit. The fixed fee represents the rights by distribution to acquire the product at marginal cost, and it is set to cover manufacturing's fixed cost plus a return on equity.

Another problem with marginal-cost transfer pricing occurs in situations where the marginal cost per unit is not constant as volume changes. Suppose the marginal cost per unit increases as volume expands (say, a night shift is added with higher wages per hour). If marginal cost is greater than average cost and all users are charged the higher marginal cost, the total charged to all the users is greater than the total cost incurred by the firm. Users who did not expand their volume will still see their costs increase. In such cases, conflicts are likely within the firm over the appropriate measure of marginal cost and whether all users should pay the higher marginal cost or just those users who expanded output, thereby prompting the addition of the night shift.

A similar problem arises when manufacturing approaches capacity. To illustrate the problem, let's assume that manufacturing is considering a $2.5 million outlay to add more capacity. These capacity additions costs of $2.5 million are variable in the long run but become short-run fixed costs (depreciation and higher utilities and maintenance). Thus, conflicts arise between manufacturing and distribution as to whether these additional capacity costs should be included in the transfer price or not. Such conflicts are difficult to resolve because no indisputably objective method exists for calculating marginal costs. They are not reported in *The Wall Street Journal.* Instead, they have to be estimated, normally as "variable costs," from accounting records. Although many of the components of marginal cost are easily observed, such as the cost of direct labor and direct material, some components are quite difficult to estimate. For example, the additional costs imposed on the purchasing department when additional units are manufactured are not easily observed and hence difficult to estimate precisely.

Marginal-cost transfer pricing also creates incentives for manufacturing to distort marginal cost upward, perhaps by misstating some fixed costs as variable. For example, how much of the electricity bill is fixed and how much is variable? Since these classifications are to some extent arbitrary, resources are wasted as managers in manufacturing and distribution debate various costs and their allocations—and as senior managers are forced to spend time arbitrating such disputes.

Moreover, under marginal-cost transfer pricing, manufacturing can have an incentive to convert a dollar of fixed costs into more than a dollar of marginal costs—for example, by using higher-priced outsourcing of parts instead of cheaper internal manufacturing—even though this clearly reduces the value of the firm. For manufacturing, the use of outsourcing can remove the burden of any fixed costs while distribution, as well as the firm as a whole, bears the additional cost of such decisions.

---

[13]Of course, if central management knows the magnitude of the fixed costs, it can budget for this loss. But, once again, if central management knew the magnitude of the fixed costs, then it would know marginal cost, and thus there would be little reason to have a separate, decentralized business unit and transfer-pricing system in the first place.

Full-Cost Transfer Prices

Because of the information and incentive problems described earlier, simple, objective, hard-to-change transfer-pricing rules can lead to higher firm value than transfer-pricing rules that give one manager discretion over the transfer price. Objective transfer-pricing rules such as those based on full accounting cost often are adopted primarily to avoid unproductive disputes over measuring marginal costs. Since full cost is the sum of fixed and variable cost, full cost cannot be changed simply by reclassifying a fixed cost as a variable cost.

The problem, however, is that full-cost transfer pricing frequently overstates the opportunity cost to the firm of producing and transferring one more unit internally. And so distribution usually will buy too few units internally. Full cost also allows manufacturing to transfer any of its inefficiencies to distribution. Thus, manufacturing has less incentive to be efficient under a full-cost transfer-price rule.[14]

Despite all these problems, however, full-cost transfer pricing is quite common. In various surveys of corporate practice, full-cost transfer prices are used 40–50 percent of the time.[15] In most cases, moreover, the definition of *full cost* includes both direct materials and labor as well as a charge for overhead.

One reason for the popularity of full-cost transfer prices is their ability to deal with the problem of changes in capacity. As a plant begins to reach capacity, opportunity cost is likely to rise because of congestion and the cost of alternative uses of now-scarce capacity. Hence, opportunity cost is likely to be higher than direct materials and labor costs. In this case, full cost might be a closer approximation to opportunity cost than just the cost of materials and labor.

Perhaps the most important benefit of full-cost transfer pricing, however, is its simplicity and hence its low cost of implementation. Because of its simplicity and objectivity, full-cost transfer pricing reduces influence costs. That is, because operating managers have less ability to manipulate full-cost than marginal-cost calculations, senior management faces fewer calls to arbitrate disputes over calculating the transfer price. Nonetheless, managers should consider carefully whether full-cost pricing is appropriate for their particular situation. If the opportunity cost differs materially from full cost, the firm's forgone profits can be substantial.

Negotiated Transfer Prices

Transfer prices can be set by negotiation between manufacturing and distribution. This method can result in transfer prices that approximate opportunity cost because manufacturing will not agree to a price, that is, below its opportunity cost and distribution will not pay a price above what it can buy the product elsewhere.

With negotiated transfer prices, the two divisions have the incentive to set the number of units so as to maximize the combined profits of the two divisions. Once the value-maximizing number of units is established, the transfer price determines how the total profits are divided between the two divisions. In terms of Figure 17.1, if the two divisions negotiate over both price and quantity, they have the joint

---

[14]J. Zimmerman, (2014) *Accounting for Decision Making and Control,* 8th edition (McGraw-Hill Education: New York), Chapter 5.

[15]*Technical note:* To be sure, marginal-cost transfer prices also allow the selling division to export some of its inefficiencies to the purchasing division, but the problem is not as pronounced as under full cost. Nonetheless, the problem of exporting inefficiencies to the buying division through cost-based transfer prices is reduced if the purchasing division can purchase externally as well as from the selling division. This forces the selling division to remain competitive.

incentive to set $Q = 10$ because this maximizes the total profit to be split—$500. Yet if the two divisions just negotiate over price, there is no guarantee they will arrive at the transfer price that maximizes the firm's value.

While negotiation is a fairly common method, it too has drawbacks. It is time-consuming and can produce conflicts among divisions. Divisional performance measurement becomes sensitive to the relative negotiating skills of the two division managers. Moreover, if the two divisions negotiate a transfer price without at the same time agreeing on the quantity to be transferred at that price, there is no guarantee that they will arrive at the transfer price that maximizes the firm's value.

Reorganization: The Solution If All Else Fails

In some cases, transfer-pricing conflicts among profit centers can become sufficiently divisive to impose large costs on the firm. These costs take the form of both influence costs and the opportunity costs that arise when other than firm-value-maximizing transfer prices are chosen. Costly transfer-pricing disputes usually occur when the relative volume of transactions among divisions is large. In such cases, a small change in the transfer price can have a large effect on the division's reported profits. Hence, the potential for (and destructive effects of) opportunistic transfer-pricing actions by operating managers is substantial.

If transfer pricing becomes sufficiently dysfunctional, reorganize the firm. For example, senior management could combine two profit centers with a large volume of transfers into a single division. Alternatively, it might make more sense to convert manufacturing into a cost center rather than a profit center and compensate the operating head based on efficiency of production. Or, senior management might even organize both divisions as cost centers and keep the pricing and quantity decisions at a higher level within the firm.

Internal Accounting System and Performance Evaluation[16]

Accounting costs, revenues, profits, return on investment, and residual income usually are used as performance measures of cost, expense, revenue, profit, and investment centers. Accounting costs frequently are used as transfer prices. The accounting system is an important component of the firm's performance-evaluation system and thus is an integral part of the firm's control system—the performance-evaluation and reward systems. This section elaborates on accounting's role within the firm.

Uses of the Accounting System

Many people think of the firm's accounting system in terms of its external financial reports—balance sheets and income statements—to the shareholders, taxing authorities, regulators, and lenders. These external financial reports (both quarterly and annual) are an incredibly aggregated view of the enormous amount of data produced

---

[16]This section draws on analysis in Zimmerman (2014).

internally. Internally, managers rely on detailed operating reports of expenses, product costs, and customer account balances from the accounting system.

These internal reports are used by management for two general purposes: decision management and decision control. The decision-making process can be divided into decision management (initiation and implementation) and decision control (ratification and monitoring). Managers frequently have both decision-management and decision-control rights, but normally not for the same decisions. Senior managers in the firm tend to hold more decision-control rights, whereas decision-management rights tend to be delegated to managers lower in the firm. To exercise either decision-management or decision-control rights, managers require information. Some of that information is provided by the accounting system. Thus, although the accounting system is used for both decision management and decision control, its primary function within most firms is decision control.

Decision management requires estimates of future costs and benefits. Initiating an investment decision to build a new plant requires the manager to forecast future alternative uses of this plant; designing a marketing campaign requires judgments of likely future sales and competitors' responses. Managers frequently use accounting-based data as inputs to these decisions. Accounting numbers provide a starting point in forecasting future consequences of proposed actions. Most firms have accounting-based budget systems. Managers forecast costs and revenues for the next year in preparing their budgets. This process encourages managers to be forward-looking, to coordinate their operations with those managers most directly affected by their decisions and to share specialized knowledge of their markets and production technologies. Accounting-based budgets provide the framework for such coordination and knowledge sharing.

Although helpful for decision management, accounting systems generally are more useful for decision control (ratification and especially monitoring). In fact, this is the primary reason they evolved. Accounting systems are based on historical costs and historical revenues. Historical costs record what the firm paid for its current resource base and in this sense are backward-looking. Internal accounting systems protect against theft of company assets, fraud, and embezzlement. They also provide a scorecard to show how a business unit did historically by measuring costs, profits, or residual income. Monitoring is by definition a historical function, one well served by the accounting system. Since accounting systems are primarily used for decision control—to prevent malfeasance and to measure past performance—when it comes to providing managers with information for decision management, accounting systems often are found wanting.

Trade-offs between Decision Management and Decision Control

Considering how the accounting system is used for both decision management and decision control leads to a number of important insights. First, accounting measures, to the extent that they are used for monitoring purposes, are not under the complete control of the people being monitored—the operating managers.

Second, managers with decision-management rights tend to be dissatisfied with financial measures for making operating decisions. The data often are reported at such a high level of aggregation that it does not provide sufficient detail for the decision. In response, operating managers develop their own, often nonfinancial,

Massive Financial Fraud at Cendant

In the vast majority of cases, there are sufficient controls such as internal and external auditors to ensure that the firm's accounting reports accurately reflect the organization's financial performance. However, in rare situations, the managers have "cooked the books." Take the case of the bankrupt Adelphia Communications that agreed to pay more than $700 million to settle "one of the most extensive financial frauds ever to take place at a public company," according to the U.S. Securities and Exchange Commission (SEC). John Rigas founded Adelphia and grew it into the fifth largest cable TV provider in the United States. The SEC charged that Adelphia: (1) fraudulently excluded billions of dollars in liabilities from its consolidated financial statements by hiding them on the books of off-balance sheet affiliates; (2) falsified operations statistics and inflated earnings to meet Wall Street's expectations; and (3) concealed rampant self-dealing by the Rigas family, including the undisclosed use of corporate funds for Rigas family stock purchases and the acquisition of luxury condominiums in New York and elsewhere. The United States Attorney's Office also filed related criminal charges against several of the same defendants. In settling the case the Rigas family forfeited 95 percent of its assets–totaling more than $1.5 billion. After the Rigases left the management of Adelphia, the company claimed to be owed more than $3.2 billion from the Rigases, who "seemingly ran the company as if it were their own private cash machine." John Rigas and his son Timothy, the former chief financial officer, were convicted on 18 counts of securities fraud, bank fraud, and conspiracy. John Rigas at age 83 began serving a 15-year prison term, while his son, Timothy, was sentenced to 20 years in prison. In 2006 the majority of Adelphia's assets were acquired by Time Warner Cable and Comcast.

Source: D. Cook (2005), "Adelphia, Rigas Family Settle Fraud Case," CFO.com (April 26), www.cfo.com/article.cfm/3907889; Associated Press (2008), "Adelphia Communications founder, son lose final appeal on fraud convictions," (March 3); www.sec.gov/news/press/ 2002-110.htm.

information systems to provide more of the knowledge required for decision management. But at the same time, they rely on accounting-system output to monitor the managers who report to them.

Third, nonaccounting measures frequently are more timely than accounting measures. Not every decision requires ratification or monitoring. Decision monitoring can be based on aggregate data to average out random fluctuations. Instead of monitoring every machine setup, it usually is more effective to aggregate all setups occurring over the week or month and make sure the average setup cost is within acceptable levels.

One survey reports that managers rely on nonfinancial data (labor counts, units of output, units in inventory, units scrapped) to run their day-to-day operations. But when they are asked about their "most valuable report in general," they say it is the monthly income or expense statement because in part this is one of the measures used to judge their performance.[17]

In choosing among alternative accounting systems, managers often must make trade-offs between decision management and decision control. Consider the transfer-pricing decision. The transfer-pricing method that most accurately measures the opportunity cost to the firm of transferring one more unit inside the firm might not be the transfer-pricing method that gives internal managers the most effective incentives to maximize the firm's value. For example, if the transfer-pricing method that most accurately measures the opportunity cost of units transferred (decision management) also requires manufacturing to reveal privately held and hard-to-verify

[17]S. McKinnon and W. Bruns (1992), *The Information Mosaic* (Harvard Business School: Boston).

ANALYZING MANAGERIAL DECISIONS: *Celtex*

Celtex is a large, quite successful, decentralized specialty chemical producer organized into five independent investment centers. Each of the five investment centers is free to buy products either inside or outside the firm and is judged based on residual income. Most of each division's sales are to external customers. Celtex has the general reputation of being one of the top two or three companies in each of its markets.

Leopoldo Garcia, president of Synchem, Celtex's synthetic chemicals division, and Walid Murad, president of the consumer products division, are embroiled in a dispute. It all began two years ago when Wally asked Leo to modify a synthetic chemical for a new household cleaner. In return, Synchem would be reimbursed for out-of-pocket costs. After Synchem spent considerable time perfecting the chemical, Wally solicited competitive bids from Leo as well as several outside firms; he then awarded the contract to one of the outside firms, which was the low bidder. This annoyed Leo, who expected his bid to receive special consideration because he developed the new chemical at cost, yet the outside vendor took advantage of his division's R&D.

The current conflict has to do with Synchem's producing chemical Q47, a standard product, for consumer products. Because of an economic slowdown, all synthetic chemical producers have excess capacity. Synchem was asked to bid on supplying Q47 for consumer products. Consumer products is moving into a new, experimental product line and Q47 is one of the key ingredients. Although the magnitude of the order is small relative to Synchem's total business, the price of Q47 is quite important in determining the profitability of the experimental line. Leo bid $3.20 per gallon. Meas Chemicals, an outside firm, bid $3. This time, Wally is annoyed because he knows that Leo's bid

contains a substantial amount of fixed overhead and profit. Synchem buys the base raw material, Q4, from the organic chemicals division of Celtex for $1 per gallon. Organic chemical's out-of-pocket costs (i.e., variable costs) are 80 percent of the selling price. Synchem then further processes Q4 into Q47 and incurs additional variable costs of $1.75 per gallon. Allocated fixed overhead adds another $.30 per gallon.

Leo argues that he has $3.05 of cost in each gallon of Q47. If he turned around and sold the product for anything less than $3.20, he would be undermining his recent attempts to get his salespeople to stop cutting their bids and start quoting full-cost prices. Leo has been trying to enhance the quality of the business he is getting, and he fears that if he is forced to make Q47 for consumer products, all of his effort the last few months would be for naught. He argues, "I already gave away the store once to consumer products and I won't do it again." He questions, "How can senior managers expect me to return a positive residual income if I am forced to put in bids that don't recover full cost?"

Wally, in a chance meeting at the airport with Diana Philapados, senior vice president of Celtex, described the situation, and asked Philapados to intervene. Wally believed Leo was trying to get even after their earlier clash. Wally argued that the success of his new product venture depended on being able to secure a stable, high-quality source of supply of Q47 at low cost.

Diana has hired you as a consultant and has asked you to do the following:

1. Prepare a statement outlining the cash flows to Celtex of the two alternative sources of supply for Q47.
2. Offer advice regarding how Diana should handle the issues raised by Wally.

knowledge of costs, then manufacturing has substantial discretion over the transfer prices. If these prices are important in rewarding managers (decision control), manufacturing can distort the system to its benefit. Given the reward system, a transfer-pricing method, that is, less subject to managerial discretion might in the end be a more accurate measure of opportunity costs than one that requires managers to disclose private, hard-to-verify knowledge.

All accounting (as well as nonaccounting) performance measures are prone to managerial opportunism in the form of accounting manipulations and dysfunctional decisions. In other words, accounting numbers are prone to gaming. Managers can choose depreciation methods that reduce expenses and increase reported earnings (straight-line depreciation). These accounting choices artificially raise ROA. Investment center managers can increase ROA by rejecting (or divesting) profitable projects with ROAs below the average ROA of the division. Most accounting measures are short-term measures of performance. They all suffer from the horizon problem, whereby managers emphasize short-term performance at the expense of long-term returns. Therefore, any accounting-based performance-measurement system requires careful monitoring by senior managers to control dysfunctional behavior by lower-level managers.

In the United States, accounting methods are regulated and managers must choose accounting methods from *generally accepted accounting procedures* (GAAP). Yet managers still have considerable discretion. External, third-party auditors ensure the accuracy and consistency of the accounting reports. Most firms employ a single accounting system for multiple purposes: reporting to shareholders, taxes, internal decision management and control, and regulation.[18] Debt agreements, management compensation plans, and financial reports all use these accounting-based numbers. Using the same numbers for many purposes helps control the incentives to distort the numbers for any single purpose.

Finally, no performance-measurement and reward system works perfectly; no system eliminates all managerial decisions that will increase the manager's welfare at the expense of the firm's other claimholders. The key question is: Does the system outperform the next best alternative after all the costs and benefits are included? One should avoid the "nirvana fallacy," which suggests discarding a system because it fails to eliminate all managerial opportunism. The nirvana fallacy arises when one compares a real system to a hypothetical but unachievable "perfect" system.[19]

Summary

Decision rights are allocated to cost, expense, revenue, investment, and profit centers. These centers often are evaluated and rewarded based on accounting-based performance measures. Cost centers are delegated decision rights over how to produce the output, but not over price or quantity. Cost centers are evaluated on either minimizing total cost for a fixed output, or maximizing output for a fixed total cost. Expense centers such as the human resources department are like cost centers except that their output is not easily quantifiable. This difficulty in quantifying output means users often are not charged for the expense center's output; hence the demand for expense center services tends to grow faster than the firm's output.

Revenue centers also are similar to cost centers, with the difference that they are responsible for marketing the products. They have decision rights over how to sell or distribute the product, but not over the price-quantity decision. Revenue centers are evaluated on maximizing revenue for a given price or quantity and a fixed budget for operating expenses.

---

[18]Even though the firm has "one" accounting system, the accounting numbers often are adjusted for special purposes. For example, the system may use straight-line depreciation for shareholders but adjust these numbers to accelerated depreciation for taxes.

[19]H. Demsetz (1969), "Information and Efficiency: Another Viewpoint," *Journal of Law & Economics* XII, 1–22.

Profit centers have all the decision rights of cost centers plus product mix and pricing decisions. They do not have decision rights over the level of investment in their profit center. Profit centers are evaluated based on total profits. Finally, investment centers are like profit centers except that they also have decision rights over the amount of capital invested in their division. Evaluating performance of investment centers involves adjusting profits for the amount of capital invested. Two commonly used investment center measures are return on assets and residual income (or EVA). Both measures create incentives for managers to eliminate assets that are not covering their opportunity cost of capital. However, ROA gives incentives to eliminate profitable projects with returns below the average ROA for the division. Residual income avoids this incentive problem, but as a performance measure it makes comparing divisions of different sizes more difficult.

Large companies, particularly those operating across multiple lines of business, typically are organized into multiple business units or divisions. Such an organizational architecture is intended to furnish senior managers with information about the profitability or efficiency of different businesses and to provide accountability and incentives for the operating managers charged with running those businesses.

Nonetheless, when there are significant interdependencies among different business units, often involving internal transfers, motivating individual profit centers to maximize their own profits generally will not maximize profits for the firm as a whole. Individual units focusing on their own profits often will ignore how their actions affect the sales and costs of other units.

One valuable role of a transfer-pricing method, then, is to lead managers to allocate resources internally in ways that take account of such interdependencies among divisions. But transfer pricing is a quite complicated undertaking. The likelihood of getting the wrong answer is high, and the consequences of so doing—primarily in the form of poor pricing and output decisions—can be substantial. Transfer prices not only change how total profits are divided among business units but affect total firm profits.

The opportunity cost of a transferred resource is the correct transfer price. But accurate information about opportunity cost usually is known only by local divisional managers. If either the buying or selling division can set the transfer price unilaterally, it has incentives to behave opportunistically. The selling division will set too high a price trying to capture monopoly profits, and too few units will be transferred. If the buying division is allowed to set the transfer price, a price below the true opportunity cost is likely to be chosen; in this case, too few units will be produced and transferred.

Because accurate information about opportunity costs is quite expensive to obtain (or at least to verify), managers generally rely on approximations such as market values, marginal costs, full costs, or negotiated prices. Each of these approximations works better than others in certain circumstances. Market-based transfer prices are most useful when competitive external markets exist. But if an external market is employed, why is the firm producing the good or service? If there are important synergies favoring internal production, the external market price is unlikely to capture them. For example, if there are transaction costs of using the market, such as writing and enforcing contracts, then the transfer price is the market price less these transaction costs. Marginal cost is another popular transfer-pricing method. But marginal cost is expensive to estimate and can generate influence costs as managers debate whether certain expenditures are "marginal" or not. Full-cost transfer prices are objective, simple-to-compute transfer prices. They also are used widely in practice. However, full-cost transfer prices likely suffer from setting the transfer price above opportunity cost. Negotiated transfer prices, although time-consuming to establish, give both parties to the contract the incentive first to negotiate the quantity that maximizes the firm's profits and then negotiate the transfer price that determines how the total profits will be divided.

No matter what transfer-pricing method is used, it normally is important to permit both buying and selling divisions access to the external market. In this case, the external market acts as a check on opportunistic managerial behavior. But again, if the external market is employed regularly, one must examine whether the firm should be producing the intermediate product at all.

Finally, most divisional performance-evaluation systems rely on internally generated accounting-based numbers. These accounting-based performance metrics are for decision control (decision ratification and decision monitoring). Besides exercising decision-control rights, employees also exercise decision-management rights (decision initiation and implementation). Exercising decision-management rights requires information; often managers turn to their accounting systems for this information. But the accounting systems of most firms are designed for decision control—not necessarily for decision management. This leads to a trade-off between these two uses and to the general conclusion that most managers find their accounting systems wanting when it comes to providing information for decision management.

Suggested Readings

R. Eccles (1985), *The Transfer Pricing Problem: A Theory for Practice* (Lexington Books: Lexington).

J. Gould (1964), "Internal Pricing in Firms When There Are Costs of Using an Outside Market," *Journal of Business* 37, 61–67.

J. Hirshleifer (1964), "Internal Pricing and Decentralized Decisions," in C. Bonini, P. Jaediecke, and R. Wagner (Eds.), *Management Controls: New Directions in Basic Research* (McGraw-Hill: New York).

B. Holmstrom and J. Tirole (1991), "Transfer Pricing and Organizational Form," *Journal of Law, Economics, and Organizations* 7, 201–228.

D. Solomons (1985), *Divisional Performance: Measurement and Control,* 2nd edition (Richard D. Irwin: Burr Ridge, IL).

B. Stewart (1991), *The Quest for Value* (Harper Business: New York).

J. Zimmerman (2014), *Accounting for Decision Making and Control,* 8th edition (McGraw-Hill Education: New York).

Self-Evaluation Problems

17–1. Chips Computer Company assembles personal computers and sells them in the retail marketplace. The company is organized into two profit centers: the assembly division and the distribution division. The demand curve facing the company (and the distribution division) is $P = 3,000 - 10Q$. The marginal cost for assembly (which includes purchasing the parts) is constant at $500. The distribution division faces constant marginal distribution costs of $50 per unit.

   a. What is the profit-maximizing retail price and output for the firm as a whole?

   b. If the assembly division has monopoly power to set the transfer price, what transfer price will it select (assuming it knows all the information above)? Calculate the profits for the two divisions in this case.

17–2. Scoff Division of World-Wide Paint is currently losing money, and senior management is considering selling or closing Scoff. Scoff's only product, an intermediate chemical called Binder, is used principally by the latex division of the firm. If Scoff is sold, the latex division can purchase ample quantities of Binder in the market at sufficiently high-quality levels to meet its requirements. World-Wide requires all of its divisions to supply product to other World-Wide divisions before servicing the external market.

Scoff Division Profit/Loss Last Quarter (in thousands of dollars)

Scoff's statement of operations for the latest quarter is as follows:

Revenue:		
Inside	$200	
Outside	75	$275
Operating expenses:		
Variable costs	$260	
Fixed costs	15	
Allocated corporate overhead	40	315
Net income (loss) before taxes		$(40)

Notes:
1. World-Wide Paint has the policy of transferring all products internally at variable cost. In Scoff's case, variable cost is 80 percent of the market price.
2. All of Scoff's fixed costs are avoidable cash flows if Scoff is closed or sold.
3. Ten percent of the allocated corporate overhead is caused by the presence of Scoff and will be avoided if Scoff is closed or sold.

Calculate the annual net cash flows to World-Wide Paint of closing or selling Scoff.

Solutions to Self-Evaluation Problems

17–1. Chips Computer Transfer Prices

a. The profit-maximizing retail price and quantity are found as follows:

$$P = 3,000 - 10Q$$
$$MR = 3,000 - 20Q$$
$$MC = 500 + 50 = 550$$

Profit maximization:

$$3,000 - 20Q = 550$$
$$2,450 = 20Q$$
$$Q = 122.5$$
$$P = \$1,775 \text{ (from the demand curve)}$$

b. Assembly Division has monopoly power:
Distribution Division's demand:

$$P_T + 50 = 3,000 - 20Q$$
$$P_T = 2,950 - 20Q$$

Assembly Division maximizes profits by selecting:

$$2,950 - 40Q = 500$$
$$2,450 = 40Q$$
$$Q = 61.25$$
$$P_T = \$1,725$$

Profits for Distribution:

$$[\$2,387.5 \text{ (retail price)} \times 61.25] - [61.25 (1,725 + 50)] - \$37,516$$

Profits for Assembly Division:

$$61.25 (1,725 - 500) = \$75,031$$

17–2. Division Closing at World-Wide Paint

The key to this problem is recognizing that the transfer price is quite favorable to the latex division and is causing Scoff to appear unprofitable. If Scoff is closed or sold, the latex division will have to pay the market price for Binder, which is higher than the current transfer price. Also, not all of the corporate overhead is saved by closing or selling Scoff.

Selling or closing Scoff changes the potential synergies within the firm. Can World-Wide Paint maintain the same quality/delivery times on Binder? One question to raise is what these are worth. Having to analyze these "intangibles" will only be necessary if an outside offer is larger than the value of the cash flows forgone from selling Scoff. The table below indicates that Scoff is generating positive cash flow to World-Wide despite the operating losses reported.

Quarterly Net Cash Flows to World-Wide Paint from Closing Scoff Division Last Quarter Ending ($ thousands)

Operating expenses saved:		
Variable costs	$260	
Fixed costs	15	
Allocated corporate overhead	4	
Scoff's operating expenses avoided		$279
Revenues forgone:		
Outside		(75)
Market purchases by latex division of Binder ($200 ÷ 80%)		(250)
Decline in quarterly cash flows		($46)
× 4 quarters per year		× 4
Annual decline in World-Wide cash flows		($184)

Review Questions

17–1. Auto-fit is a multidivisional firm that produces auto parts. It has the capacity for annual production of 100 units of a particular part. The marginal cost of producing each unit is $10. These units can be sold internally either to other divisions or to external customers. The external market price is $20. The allocated share of corporate overhead for each part produced is $5. Total corporate overhead expenditures do not vary with the production of the part. How many units of the part should the company produce? What is the theoretically correct transfer price (should the company decide to transfer the part internally)? Explain.

17–2. High Tech, Inc., has strong patent protection on a particular type of computer chip. High Tech uses the chip for the internal production of PCs. It also sells the chip to other manufacturers on the open market. Does High Tech necessarily want to charge the same price to both external and internal customers? Explain.

17–3. A firm has a demand curve: $P = 50 - Q$. Its total costs are

$$TC = 110 + Q + 3Q^2$$

Prepare a table that computes the profit-maximizing quantity. What quantity minimizes average cost? (*Hint:* Prepare a table similar to Table 17.1 for $Q = 1, 2, \ldots 10$.)

17–4. The Xtrac Computer Company is organized into regional sales offices and a manufacturing division. The sales offices forecast sales for the upcoming year in their territories. These figures are then used to set the manufacturing schedules for the year. Prices of the computers are determined by corporate headquarters, and the salespeople are paid a fixed wage and a commission on sales. The regional sales offices are evaluated as revenue centers. The regional sales manager is paid a small wage (about 30 percent of total pay) and a commission on all sales in her territory (about 70 percent of total pay) that exceeds the budget.

Xtrac has a notoriously bad track record for forecasting computer sales. Its budgets always underforecast sales, and then, during the year, manufacturing scrambles to produce more units, authorizes labor overtime, and buys parts on rush orders. This drives up manufacturing costs. At first, management thought the underforecasting problem was due to high unexpected growth in the computer industry. But Xtrac even underforecasts sales when the economy is slow and the industry growth is below its long-run average.

a. What is the likely reason Xtrac persistently underforecasts sales?

b. What are some likely explanations for the reason in part (a)?

c. Propose three likely solutions and critically evaluate each of them.

17–5. Suppose a firm has two different accounting systems. For example, suppose it uses EVA to measure and reward management performance. To calculate EVA, annual spending on research and development is recorded as an asset and then depreciated in calculating earnings. In reporting earnings to shareholders, R&D spending in any given year is expensed against earnings.

Describe some of the likely consequences that can arise if the firm tries to maintain two different accounting systems.

17–6. An organizational consultant does not like the way your company compensates profit center managers (currently a large part of their pay is based on the center's profits). He argues that you should compensate the managers based on whether or not they made "reasonable decisions" and not based on the outcome of the decisions, which is partly beyond the control of the managers. The consultant argues that the managers will then have incentives to make good decisions but will not be subject to undue levels of risk. Evaluate this argument.

17–7. Below is a suggestion from a leading economics text on how to set optimal transfer prices. In this context, both the manufacturing and distribution divisions are profit centers. Do you think it would work? Explain.

> *The manufacturing division could be supplied data on the net marginal revenue curve for the distribution division and told to use this as its relevant marginal revenue curve in determining the quantity it should supply. By choosing the output where marginal revenue equals marginal cost, firm profits are maximized. The transfer price should be the marginal cost at this output level.*

17–8. Xerdak Inc. has a corporate jet, which it uses to fly managers from Rochester to Chicago. The associated costs (monthly) of maintaining and flying the jet are as follows:

Pilot:	$10,000
Depreciation:	10,000
Overhead:	10,000

In addition, each round trip to Chicago costs $10,000 in fuel. Commercial airlines (e.g., United) charge $600 for a round trip to Chicago. Managers consider the commercial service and the company service to be identical. The company plane flies a maximum of 20 times each month and has 50 seats. There are always more managers wanting to fly on the plane than there are seats. The company wants to buy some more planes. Unfortunately, they are back-ordered, and so the company will not be able to obtain additional capacity in the near future. According to economic theory, what is the optimal transfer price for a round trip to Chicago? Explain why.

17–9. Geriatrics Inc. has a patent on a new type of hospital bed. The marginal cost of producing each bed is $400. The company has significant production capacity. Geriatrics sells the beds to customers on the open market and also uses them internally throughout its nursing home chain. The external demand for the product is given by $P = 5,000 - Q$. Assuming that Geriatrics wants to profit-maximize, what is the optimal external market price? What is the optimal internal transfer price?

17–10. Biotech Inc. is a new company that invests in technologies relating to the use of plants in drugs. The stock market perceives that the company has the potential to generate large profits once it develops a line of products. To date, however, the company has not reported positive profits and does not anticipate doing so over the next five years or more. The owners of Biotech are particularly concerned about the investment choices of the managers. They are concerned that the managers do not have the right incentives to choose value-maximizing investments. They are considering adopting an EVA evaluation and compensation plan for the managers. Do you think this is a good idea? Explain.

17–11. Speed Company sells printers. It is divided into a manufacturing unit and a sales unit. The marginal cost of producing a printer is $200. External demand is given by $P = 1,000 - 0.01Q$. Selling and distribution costs total $150 per unit.
   a. What is the profit-maximizing retail price and quantity? What are firm profits?
   b. Suppose the manufacturing unit has monopoly power to set the transfer price and knows all the information in this problem. What transfer price will it charge? What are the resulting retail price, quantity, and firm profits?

17–12. Do you agree with the following statement? Explain.

> *Obviously the correct transfer price is the opportunity cost of the resource. Any firm that uses full cost (which includes an allocation of corporate overhead) is doing it wrong.*

17–13. You are the owner and CEO of a large divisionalized firm, with operations in a number of diverse industries. Reporting to you are a number of division managers. Division managers have considerable decision-making responsibility with respect to the day-to-day operations of their divisions, but you must approve any capital investments above $100,000 before they are made.
   a. As owner, what type of capital investments would you like your division managers to be proposing to you?
   b. Is there a potential agency problem between you, as owner, and your division managers with respect to capital investments? What is the nature of that problem? Why is it a problem?
   c. How might you attempt to solve that agency problem?
   d. Do you think you can solve the problem entirely? Why or why not?

17–14. The Jameson Company has recently formed a subsidiary, Bright Ideas, to manufacture and sell household appliances.
   a. What is the difference between an investment center and a profit center?
   b. What factors should Jameson consider in deciding whether to evaluate Bright Ideas as a profit or investment center?

CAPSTONE CASE STUDY ON ORGANIZATIONAL ARCHITECTURE

Arthur Andersen LLP[1]

Introduction and Overview

It is difficult to find an example of a more spectacular business failure than the collapse of Arthur Andersen in 2002. Within a few years, Andersen moved from one of the largest professional service organizations in the world to extinction. The impact of the firm's failure on its employees, customers, investors, and the general public is hard to overstate. Its once proud reputation had been reduced to shambles. Even the President of the United States joked:

> *We just received a message from Saddam Hussein. The good news is that he's willing to have his nuclear, biological, and chemical weapons counted. The bad news is he wants Arthur Andersen to do it.*[2]

The dramatic demise of Andersen (along with the failures of companies such as Enron and Global Crossing) has raised concerns among managers throughout the world. They want to understand what caused the collapse of the company so that they can take actions to avoid similar fates.

Over the years, Andersen's business environment and strategy changed in material ways. Their management responded by making associated changes in their organizational architecture (decision right, performance evaluation, and reward systems). Chapters 11–17 of this book have argued that ill designed organizational architectures can result in poor performance and even company failure. An important question is whether Andersen's failure can be traced to inappropriate organizational choices. An even more critical question is whether other managers can learn from Andersen's mistakes. We believe that the answer to both questions is yes.

Our case study begins by summarizing the history and events that led to the collapse at Arthur Andersen. This discussion is followed by a series of questions that ask the reader to analyze the demise of Andersen in the context of the framework introduced in this book. Our purpose is not to present all the relevant analysis ourselves. Rather it is to provide readers with the opportunity for an integrated analysis and capstone discussion of an important business problem that relies on material drawn from across Chapters 11–17 of this book. It also provides a forum for

---

[1]This case study is based on public news accounts, company documents, and press releases. Among the most important sources are K. Brown and I. J. Dugan (2002), "Sad Account: Andersen's Fall from Grace Is a Tale of Greed and Miscues," *The Wall Street Journal,* (June 7); and a series of articles from the *Chicago Tribune* published in September 2002.

[2]Joke made by President George W. Bush at a dinner talk in January 2002 as quoted in the *MBA Jungle,* December 2002–January 2003, 70.

discussing the root causes of the business scandals that rocked the international business community.

Arthur Andersen: The Early Years

A 28-year-old Northwestern accounting professor named Arthur Andersen started his own business in 1914. Andersen's strategy was to offer high-quality accounting services to clients—promoting integrity and sound audit opinions over higher short-run profits. Soon after Andersen formed the firm, the president of a local railroad demanded that he approve a transaction that would have lowered his company's expenses and increased its reported earnings. Andersen, who was not sure he could even meet his firm's payroll, told the president that there was "not enough money in the city of Chicago" to make him do it. The president promptly severed his relationship with Andersen. However, Andersen soon was vindicated when the railroad filed for bankruptcy a few months later.

In the 1930s, the federal government adopted new laws to require public companies to submit their financial statements to an independent auditor every year. These regulatory changes, along with Andersen's reputation, helped the firm to grow. During these formative years, the organization continued to promote its "four cornerstones" of good service, quality audits, well-managed staff, and profits for the firm. Quality audits were valued more than higher short-run firm profits. Leonard Spacek, who succeeded Andersen as managing partner in 1947, produced more company folklore when he accused powerful Bethlehem Steel of overstating its profits in 1964 by more than 60 percent. He also led a crusade to motivate the Securities and Exchange Commission to crack down on companies that cooked their books. The yellowing press clippings of his bold efforts were still on display at the company's main training center near Chicago in 2002.

Between 1914 and the late 1980s, "tradition was everywhere" at Arthur Andersen. The firm installed heavy wooden doors at the entrance of all its offices. Andersen employees were known to be "one of a kind"—clean-cut, straightlaced, and dressed in pinstripes. Employees were taught to recite the partnership's motto, "Think straight, talk straight." Auditors were rewarded and promoted for making sound audit decisions. Top management assigned significant decision rights to the central office's Professional Standards Group. This group, which consisted of internal experts, monitored audits and issued opinions on how specific types of transactions should be handled. The objective was to promote consistent and well-reasoned opinions throughout the firm.

Andersen's insistence on quality and high standards enhanced its reputation and promoted consistent growth. Auditors in the firm did not become wealthy in these formative years. However, Andersen partners were well respected within their local communities and earned enough to purchase comfortable houses, nice cars, and memberships at local country clubs. In the late 1960s, a mid-level partner at Arthur Andersen made about $30,000—or $213,000 in 2014 dollars.

Andersen Enters the Consulting Business

In 1950, an Andersen engineer named Joseph Glickauf demonstrated that computers could be used to automate bookkeeping. This event led to monumental changes in the partnership. In addition to its basic auditing function, Andersen also could help clients automate their accounting systems. The firm launched its new computer consulting business in 1954 when it began providing services to General Electric's state-of-the-art appliance factory near Louisville, Kentucky. Andersen soon developed the largest technology practice of any accounting firm.

During the 1950s and 1960s, the consulting business grew but remained a relatively minor activity compared to Andersen's auditing business. During the 1970s, Andersen's consulting business exploded as the demands for information technology increased. By 1979, 42 percent of Andersen's $645 million in worldwide fees came from consulting and tax work, as opposed to auditing and accounting. Consulting became the leading contributor to Andersen's revenues and bottom line in the mid-1980s.

Family Feud

As Andersen's consulting business continued to grow, tensions within the firm mounted. The consultants, who were contributing more to profits than the auditors, felt that they were subsidizing the audit partners. Consultants began to realize that they were underpaid relative to their market opportunities. Auditing partners resented the fact that the consultants wanted a higher share of the profits. The auditing partners, who controlled the managing board, made few concessions to the consulting partners. In response, a number of the top consultants left Andersen for other firms or to start their own consulting businesses.

Because of mounting tension, the firm separated its consulting and auditing businesses in 1989 by forming a new Geneva-based holding company, Andersen Worldwide (AW). Under the AW umbrella were two subsidiaries, Andersen Consulting (AC) and Arthur Andersen (AA). AC was to focus on providing consulting services to large corporations (primarily in the areas of computer systems integration and business strategy). AA, in turn, would focus primarily on audit and tax engagements. However, AA was allowed to provide consulting services to smaller companies (annual revenues of less than $175 million). The more profitable business was to share part of its profits with the other unit. Compensation no longer had to be the same across consulting and auditing partners. Each unit had significant decision rights over its own business.

Strategic and Organizational Changes at Andersen

The implications for the auditing partners were grim. The traditional accounting business was growing quite slowly due to increased competition and the large number of mergers in the 1990s; auditing quickly was becoming a low margin activity. Despite the long hours, accountants' salaries began lagging behind those of other professionals, such as lawyers and investment bankers. AA accountants particularly resented being eclipsed by their consulting counterparts at AC.

The auditors decided to "fight back." As top partner (at the time) Richard Measelle said, "it was a matter of pride." AA adopted a new strategy that focused on generating new business and cutting costs. AA began evaluating its partners on how much new business they brought to the firm. Superb auditors "who could not get a lick of business" were secure in their jobs in the 1970s, but not in the 1990s. According to Measelle, partners began to feel that "the number one thing was to make your numbers and to make money."

To reduce costs, AA began requiring partners to retire at age 56, enforcing a policy that had long been overlooked. The increased emphasis on revenue growth and expense reduction led to substantially higher revenues and profits per partner. As the twentieth century drew to a close, the average AA partner made around $600,000. However, these new policies also led to less experienced auditors and fewer partners overseeing audits.

A new breed of partner rose to the top within this new environment. One prominent example was Steve Samek, who was in charge of the Boston Chicken audit. Top partners gave Samek high praise for "turning a $50,000 audit fee at Boston Chicken into a $3 million full-service engagement." Samek, however, allowed the chain to keep details of losses at its struggling franchises off its own financial statements as it moved toward an initial public offering. The overstated financial statements helped make the IPO a "rousing success." Boston Chicken's subsequent collapse and bankruptcy led to legal actions against AA for helping to create a "facade of corporate solvency." In 2002, AA agreed to settle these suits by paying $10 million. Samek, however, had left the Boston Chicken account in 1993 to move on to bigger and more important assignments.

Robert Allgyer was known within AA as the "the Rainmaker" due to his success at cross-selling services to audit clients. One of his biggest "successes" was Waste Management, which paid $17.8 million in nonaudit fees to AA between 1991 and 1997, compared to $7.5 million in audit fees. At the same time, Allgyer was signing off on inaccurate financial statements. Among other things, the company wasn't properly writing off the value of its assets such as garbage trucks as they aged. As a result, profits were substantially overstated. In 1998, AA agreed to pay $75 million to settle shareholder suits over its auditing of Waste Management.

Boston Chicken and Waste Management were not the only problems to arise at AA over this period. In 2001, AA agreed to pay $110 million to settle shareholder suits arising from its audits of Sunbeam Corporation. These suits also arose over AA's attestation of financial statements that were alleged to be overly positive.

Continued Changes as AA Moves into the Twenty-First Century

AC partners complained that AA's consulting with large companies violated their internal agreement to separate the two businesses—indeed, AC and AA competed for some of the same consulting engagements. In 1997, AC partners voted unanimously to split off entirely and filed a formal arbitration claim with the International Chamber of Commerce. Eventually AC was allowed to separate and form a new independent company, Accenture. AA partners suffered a significant financial setback when the arbitrator ruled that AA would not receive a $14 billion payment it had expected from AC upon separation.

In 1998, Samek became the managing partner at Arthur Andersen. Among his initial moves was to formulate a new strategy that included advice on how partners should *empathize* with clients. Samek surprised many of the auditing partners when he announced his new "2X" performance evaluation system. Partners were expected to bring in two times their revenues in work outside their area of practice. If an auditor brought the firm $2 million a year in auditing fees, he was expected to bring in an additional $4 million in fees from nonaudit services, such as tax advice and technology services. Partners who achieved this standard were rewarded, while others were penalized and in some cases dismissed from the company.

In addition to changing Andersen's organizational architecture, Samek tried to change the softer elements of the firm's corporate culture. For example, the dress code was relaxed, the wooden doors at Andersen's office entrances were removed, and the firm adopted a new corporate logo, the rising sun.

Soon Andersen partners began offering a new service to clients. Rather than just handling the once-a-year audit of the public books, the firm offered to take over the entire internal bookkeeping function for their clients and provide internal audit services. Critics, such as Arthur Levitt (chairman of the SEC at the time), voiced concerns that this practice at least would impair the perceived quality of audits. Accounting firms engaged in this practice would essentially be checking their own work. In 2000, the SEC proposed new regulations that would limit the consulting work at accounting firms. In testimony before the Senate Banking Committee in July 2000, Samek called the SEC proposal "fatally flawed." He argued that the proposal was being made "just as we need to take an even more active role in making needed changes in the measurement and reporting system in support of better information for decision making by corporations, investors, and government." Intense lobbying by the "Big Five" accounting firms defeated the SEC proposal.

Enron

Arthur Andersen began auditing Enron's books in 1986. By early 2001, Enron had grown into what was widely considered the "premier energy company" involved in wholesale energy trading and marketing, gas transmission, and electric utilities. Its market value of its equity in early 2001 was approximately $75 billion.

In the mid-1990s, Andersen hired Enron's entire team of 40 internal auditors. It added its own people and opened an office in Enron's Houston headquarters. With more than 150 people on site, Andersen staff attended Enron meetings and provided input into new businesses and other strategic issues. While the revenues from Enron represented a small fraction of Andersen's overall revenues, they were a large fraction of the Houston office's revenue and much of the livelihood of the firm's lead auditor in Houston, David Duncan.

In an attempt to speed up decision making and give local offices more power, Andersen's once-powerful Professional Standards Group was moved out of the Chicago headquarters and dispersed to local offices. Carl Bass was the PSG member at the Houston office. In 1999, he told Duncan that Enron should take a $30 million to $50 million accounting charge related to a specific transaction. Four months later, Andersen's management removed Bass from his oversight role at Enron in response to complaints by Enron's chief accounting officer, who wanted him off the audit. As one former staffer observed, "There were so many people in the Houston office with their fingers in the Enron pie. If they had somebody who said we can't sign this audit, that person would be fired."[3] This suggests that Andersen's auditors were aware of the accounting problems at Enron but chose to ignore them.

As 2001 drew to a close, Enron announced that it would take a $544 million after-tax charge against earnings related to its LJM2 Co-investment partnership. It also indicated that it would restate its financial statements for 1997–2001 because of accounting errors related to it partnerships. The company filed for bankruptcy on December 2, 2001—at that time the biggest bankruptcy filing in U.S. history. Numerous scandals relating to excessive compensation and perquisites for top

[3]N. Byrnes, "Accounting in Crisis," *BusinessWeek,* January 28, 2002.

executives, accounting fraud, and negligence on the part of Enron's board quickly followed. Enron's stock price fell from around $90 per share a year earlier to near zero by the end of 2001. Widespread concern among investors, regulators, and the public arose worldwide. Conflicts of interest apparently had motivated Andersen to sign off on what it knew were questionable accounting practices at Enron.

The Demise of a Once Great Company

Arthur Andersen was subsequently charged with obstructing justice due to the shredding of documents and other evidence related to the case. Many outside observers concluded that Andersen staffers had shredded the documents to hide their own roles in producing fraudulent accounting statements. On January 24, 2002, Andersen issued the following press release:

> *While Andersen acknowledges the serious nature of actions and errors made by several of its Enron engagement employees, it also asks that all concerned be mindful that Andersen is 85,000 honorable, hardworking professionals worldwide—including 28,000 individuals and their families in the United States.*

Andersen placed most of the blame on David Duncan, who they claimed had violated the firm's ethical standards. Andersen quickly fired him.

Arthur Andersen ultimately was found guilty on a felony charge that it had obstructed the SEC's investigation of Enron when it shredded important documents and was prohibited from auditing publicly traded companies. The firm discontinued its auditing practice in August 2002. Andersen's reputation as an independent auditor was destroyed as the facts of its involvement with Enron's questionable accounting practices came to light. As early as January 2002, after Andersen announced it had shredded Enron documents, but before the federal government issued criminal indictments for obstructing justice, Andersen clients began switching independent auditors. In fact, prior to August 2002, the date when Andersen was barred from auditing public companies because of its conviction for obstructing justice, 690 of its 2,300 public companies had already dropped Andersen as their independent public accountant. To many observers, Andersen's guilty verdict and eventual liquidation was a sad end for an organization that had once been the largest personal services firm in the world.

As a postscript, the U.S. Supreme Court in May 2005 unanimously overturned Andersen's guilty verdict in the Enron document shredding case and remanded the case back to a lower court for retrial.[4] Yet, by this time Andersen no longer existed as a public accounting firm; 28,000 Andersen employees lost their jobs when Andersen was indicted in June 2002. The federal government has not refiled the original obstruction of justice charges against Andersen.

Questions

1. Discuss the environmental, strategic, and organizational changes that occurred over the life of Andersen in the context of Figure 11.1.

2. Evaluate Andersen's claim that their problems on the Enron audit were due to a few "bad partners" in the organization. If you disagree with this claim, discuss what you think were the root causes of the problem.

[4]B. Mears, "Andersen Conviction Overturned," *Money.cnn.com*, May 31, 2005.

3. Suppose you were Andersen's managing partner in the early 1990s. Would you have done anything differently than the actual management (assuming you knew only what they did at the time)? Explain.

4. Discuss the relation between what happened at Andersen and multitask principle agent theory.

5. Discuss the relation between the "hard" and "soft" elements of a firm's corporate culture in the context of this case.

6. Do you think that the problems at Andersen were unique to them or did they exist at the other big accounting firms? Suppose you were the top partner at one of the other major accounting firms at that time of Andersen's demise. What actions, if any, would you take in response? Explain.

7. In 2000, the SEC proposed new regulations that would limit consulting work by accounting firms. This proposal was not passed by Congress. Do you think that the legislators were trying to act in the public interest when they failed to pass this proposal? Explain.

8. The American Institute of Certified Public Accountants is the primary professional association for certified public accountants. It has developed a *Code of Professional Conduct* that sets the standards of conduct for CPAs. People can file complaints about the ethical conduct of a CPA with the AICPA, which can levy sanctions and other penalties against its members. Do you think that the unethical conduct at Andersen (and possibly other accounting firms) was the fault of the AICPA for not setting and enforcing higher ethical standards among its members? Explain.

9. The Sarbanes–Oxley Act of 2002 established a new five-person board to oversee financial accounting in publicly traded corporations. The board is appointed by the Securities and Exchange Commission. Prior to the creation of this board the industry relied primarily on self-regulation through the American Institute of Certified Public Accountants. Do you think the establishment of the new oversight board was a good idea or should the profession have continued to be self-regulated?

chapter 18

Corporate Governance

LEARNING OBJECTIVES

1. Distinguish between closely held and publicly traded corporations.
2. Describe the ownership patterns of large publicly traded corporations in the United States.
3. List the three key objectives of corporate governance.
4. Discuss the implications of the separation of ownership and control in large corporations.
5. Discuss the benefits that have contributed to the survival of the corporate form of organization.
6. Define corporate governance as the firm's high level Organizational Architecture
7. Describe the decision authority and incentives of shareholders, boards of directors, and top management of large corporations.
8. Describe the role of public accounting firms and other "external" monitors in corporate governance.
9. Discuss key issues in international corporate governance.
10. Explain how market forces contribute to corporate governance.

Bernard "Bernie" Ebbers had worked as a bouncer, milkman, high school basketball coach, and hotel operator. He met with business partners at a coffee shop in Hattiesburg, Mississippi, in 1983 to sketch out an idea for a long-distance telephone company on the back of a napkin. This legendary meeting resulted in the formation of a company named LDDS (Long Distance Discount Service). The company purchased long-distance phone services from AT&T using volume discounts and resold the services to small businesses. Effectively, it took advantage of ATT's price discrimination strategy. LDDS grew very rapidly through acquisitions and mergers, changing its name to WorldCom in 1995. Its $40 billion acquisition of MCI in 1998 was, at the time, the largest merger in history. By 2000, WorldCom had become a global communications company with $39 billion in annual revenues.

WorldCom was one of the "darlings of Wall Street" during the 1990s with its stock reaching a high of $64.51 in June 1999. CEO Bernie Ebbers owned 27 million shares valued at $1.2 billion in May 2000. His 500,000-acre ranch in British Columbia was the largest working ranch in Canada. Ebbers—with his cowboy boots, colorful background, beard, and informal style—was a folk hero who epitomized the "American Dream."

WorldCom's growth stalled when the Department of Justice blocked its $129 billion acquisition of Sprint in July 2000. The stock price fell precipitously from that point and by January 2002 was below $10 per share. Ebbers resigned as CEO in April 2002. In June 2002, WorldCom announced that it had understated line costs in past accounting statements by over $3.85 billion. Expenditures that should have been recorded as expenses according to Generally Accepted Accounting Principles (GAAP) had been recorded as assets. The company filed for bankruptcy in July 2002—the largest filing in history. The bankruptcy was followed by an announcement that WorldCom's income had been overstated between 1999 and 2002 by an additional $3.8 billion.

The U.S. Department of Justice charged the top officers of WorldCom with fraud. The chief financial officer and several other managers pleaded guilty and agreed to testify against Ebbers. Ebbers was convicted on nine counts of fraud in 2005 and sentenced to 25 years in jail. Members of the board of directors settled shareholder lawsuits by agreeing to pay over $20 million out of their own pockets. Stock analysts who had touted the stock encountered heavy criticism and legal problems, as did the auditor, Arthur Andersen. "Star" telecom analyst Jack Grubman, who covered WorldCom for Salomon Smith Barney, agreed to pay millions of dollars and accept a permanent bar from the securities industry to settle legal charges. Major investment and commercial banks, such as Citigroup, JPMorgan Chase, ABN Amro (Holland), Tokyo Mitsubishi (Japan), Goldman Sachs, and UBS (Switzerland), settled lawsuits by agreeing to pay billions of dollars to WorldCom investors for their alleged part in facilitating the fraud.

The collapse of WorldCom, along with other governance scandals (such as Enron, Tyco, Adelphia, and Global Crossing), led many to question whether the U.S. corporate governance system is fatally flawed. In response, Congress passed the Sarbanes-Oxley Act of 2002—the most important corporate disclosure and governance legislation since the 1930s. Subsequent business scandals at international companies, such as Parmalat (Italy), Royal Ahold (Netherlands), Shell (Netherlands/UK), and SK Global (South Korea), highlighted that corporate governance is a global issue.

Corporate governance is the popular term for describing the organizational architecture at the top of the firm. Top-level incentives and the partitioning of decision rights among shareholders, the board of directors, top management, and outside monitors (such as independent auditors and banks) are critically important issues in publicly traded corporations. Corporate governance is a topic that requires volumes to cover in depth. This chapter presents a broad overview of corporate governance utilizing the organizational architecture framework developed in previous chapters. Our objectives are for the reader to obtain a general understanding of the key issues in corporate governance and insights into how to design more effective governance systems. The chapter also offers insights into the causes and implications of contemporary governance scandals and the effects of the Sarbanes-Oxley Act of 2002.

The remainder of this chapter is organized as follows. The first section describes the basic attributes and governance concerns of publicly traded corporations. The second section provides an overview of the U.S. corporate governance system (top-level organizational architecture)—focusing specific attention on the decision authority and incentives of shareholders, the board of directors, top management, and outside monitors (such as the independent auditors). The remaining sections examine governance from an international perspective, the role of market forces in the governance process, the Sarbanes-Oxley Act of 2002, and corporate governance from a historical perspective. The chapter concludes with a summary. The Web Appendix to this chapter (available via McGraw-Hill *Connect*) presents an economic analysis of the more fundamental choice of organizing as a corporation versus other legal alternatives.

Publicly Traded Corporations

Important examples of alternative legal forms of organization include corporations, individual proprietorships, partnerships, and nonprofit organizations. Corporations are the most important form of organization in terms of employment and sales. The 1997 Economic Census reports that corporations were responsible for 91 percent of the total sales in the United States and 89 percent of the total employment. Much of this activity occurred in large publicly traded corporations, such as General Electric and Walmart.

This chapter focuses on governance in large publicly traded corporations. The Web Appendix to this chapter (available via McGraw-Hill *Connect*) discusses the important economic factors that drive the choice among the broader set of organizational alternatives, such as profit versus nonprofit status, single proprietorships, and public versus private corporations.

Corporate Form of Organization

Corporations are formed by filing the appropriate paperwork with and paying fees to officials in the state of incorporation. Corporations have the legal standing of an individual (distinct from its shareholders) and can enter into contracts and participate in lawsuits. Corporations have the right to issue stock and to exist indefinitely. State laws require corporations to have a board of directors that is assigned the primary decision control rights for the firm. Shareholders have the rights to vote on certain "fundamental" issues and in the election of the board.[1] In the United States, boards have a fiduciary responsibility to represent the interests of the corporation and its shareholders. Corporations are free to select their boards and governance procedures (for instance, voting rules) within the legal boundaries. Shareholders have limited liability (only their initial capital contribution is subject to risk and they usually are not legally responsible for the debts of the corporation).

Some corporations are *closely held,* while others are *publicly traded.* Closely held corporations are characterized by stock that is not freely traded and often held by only a few shareholders (often within the same family). While many closely held corporations are small, some are very large. In 2004, the three largest were Cargill, Koch Industries, and Mars with annual sales of $66.7 billion, $60 billion, and $19.1 billion, respectively. Publicly traded corporations are characterized by stock that is sold to and traded among the general public. Examples include Walmart, General Electric, Coca Cola, Microsoft, Daimler Benz (German), Royal Dutch/Shell Group (UK), and Toyota Motor (Japan). (See the Web appendix to this chapter for an analysis of the trade-offs between closely held and publicly traded firms).

---

[1] *Common stock* holders own title to the residual profits of the firm. While most stock in the United States is common stock, some firms also issue *preferred stock*. The dividends paid on preferred stock are fixed and "guaranteed." Our discussion focuses on common stockholders.

Stock Exchanges

Publicly traded companies often are listed on organized stock exchanges. The largest exchange in the world is the New York Stock Exchange (NYSE), which provides an extremely active and liquid market for trading shares. In 2005, there were nearly 2,800 companies listed on the NYSE with an aggregate market value of over $20 trillion.[2] Prominent international stock exchanges include the Tokyo Stock Exchange, London Stock Exchange, and Euronext with combined domestic equity capitalization at year-end 2004 of nearly $9 trillion.[3] In 2005, 54 regulated exchanges from around the world were members of the World Federation of Stock Exchanges (a trade association jointly accounting for over 97 percent of the world stock market capitalization).

Stock Ownership Patterns

Institutional stock ownership (e.g., by mutual funds) increased dramatically in the United States during the second half of the twentieth century. In 1950, individual households owned over 90 percent of the publicly traded stock in the United States, while pension funds and other institutional investors owned only about 7 percent. By 2000, institutional investors owned over 50 percent of the stock—mutual funds owned an estimated $3.6 trillion of stock, followed by private pension funds, state and local pension funds, and life insurance companies with $2.5 trillion, $2.0 trillion, and $1.0 trillion, respectively.

While the typical large firm has thousands of "small" shareholders, many have *blockholders* that own a nontrivial fraction of the shares. Studies document that the top five shareholders in the typical publicly traded U.S. corporation own about 25 percent of the shares, while the top 20 shareholders own over 35 percent.[4] For descriptive purposes, we define a *widely held corporation* as one in which no one owner controls more than 10 percent of the shares. In 1995, 80 percent of the 20 largest firms and 50 percent of the "medium-sized" firms in the United States were widely held. In most of the remaining firms the dominant blockholder controlled less than 20 percent of the shares.[5]

The frequency of widely held corporations is lower in many other countries. Examples based on the largest 20 firms in the country in 1995 include Japan (50 percent), Switzerland (50 percent), Germany (35 percent), France (30 percent), Italy (15 percent), New Zealand (5 percent), Singapore (5 percent), Mexico (0 percent), and Portugal (0 percent). Similar cross-country patterns hold for medium-sized firms. Block ownership by families, the state, and banks is more prominent in other countries than in the United States. The relatively high frequency of widely held corporations in the United States is partially explained by the country's well-developed stock markets and legal system that help to protect the interests of small shareholders. Also, regulation historically restricted bank stock ownership in the United States. As discussed later in this chapter, differences in stock ownership across countries give rise to somewhat different types of governance problems.

---

[2]Data are from the NYSE Web site (www.nyse.com) and the NASDAQ Web site (www.nasdaq.com).

[3]Data are from the Annual Report of the World Federation of Stock Exchanges, May 9, 2005.

[4]See H. Demsetz and K. Lehn (1985), "The Structure of Corporate Ownership: Causes and Consequences," *Journal of Political Economy* 93, 1155–1177.

[5]See R. La Porta, F. Lopez-de-Silanes, and A. Shliefer (1999), "Corporate Ownership Around the World," *Journal of Finance* 54, 471–515.

Governance Objectives

As stated earlier, *corporate governance* is the popular term, which is used to describe organizational architecture at the top of a corporation. Corporate governance focuses on the allocation of decision rights among the shareholders, board of directors, top managers, and various external monitors (e.g., independent auditors, stock exchanges, governmental regulators, and financial analysts) and the associated incentives of these parties. Corporate governance also encompasses the type and frequency of information corporations must disclose to various constituents. Alternative governance systems often are evaluated based on three key objectives that relate to value creation and the survival of corporations:

1. The motivation of value-maximizing decisions.
2. The protection of assets from unauthorized acquisition, use, or disposition.
3. The production of proper financial statements that meet the legal requirements.

Separation of Ownership and Control

Incentive Issues

We have discussed how alienable private property rights, along with free markets, promote the collocation of decision rights and knowledge and provide incentives for productive actions. The analysis considered the case where asset ownership and decision-making authority are held by the same person. If Bob Hayek owns a farm, he has incentives to grow the most valuable crops since he bears the negative wealth effects of growing something else. If Alice Coase knows how to use the land more productively, there are likely to be gains from trade if Bob sells the land to Alice.

Much of the stock of large publicly traded corporations is held by diversified investors who take little interest in the governance of individual firms. Operational control of large corporations is delegated to professional managers and overseen by a board of directors who have limited financial interests in the firm. Thus, in contrast to the analysis in Chapter 3, there is *separation of ownership and control*. This separation implies that corporate decision makers have weaker incentives to use assets productively than in small businesses where ownership and control are held by the same person. Managers also have weaker incentives than owners to transfer control of the corporation to more informed management teams. (Chapter 10 provides a more detailed discussion of incentive conflicts that arise in corporations between the shareholders and managers, as well as among other contracting parties in the firm.)

Concerns about the separation of ownership and control have led some scholars to question the social and productive efficiency of the corporate form of organization. For example, legal scholars Adolf Berle and Gardiner Means, in their influential 1933 book *The Modern Corporation and Private Property,* argue that widely held corporations will be run inefficiently by professional managers.[6] More recently Michael Jensen argued that the public corporation was being "eclipsed" by more efficient forms of organization that have concentrated managerial stock ownership.[7] The

---

[6]A. Berle, Jr. and G. Means (1933), *The Modern Corporation and Private Property* (MacMillan: New York), 8–9.

[7]M. Jensen (1989), "Eclipse of the Public Corporation," *Harvard Business Review* (September), 61–74.

2001–2002 governance scandals generated public concerns about whether managers run corporations primarily for their own benefit (e.g., to receive "excess" compensation and perquisites). WorldCom and other prominent firms had failed to meet all three objectives of corporate governance (motivation of value-maximizing decisions, protection of assets, and production of proper financial statements).

Survival of Corporations

In spite of these concerns, large publicly traded corporations have accounted for most of the free worlds' industrial output for decades. The principle of *Economic Darwinism* implies that publicly traded corporations have economic advantages in many business settings. Otherwise publicly traded corporations would have been replaced by more efficient organizational alternatives through the competitive process.

Critics have been particularly vocal about the governance of U.S. firms as evidenced by widespread criticisms of executive compensation and perquisites. Given the intensity of this criticism, one would think that the U.S. stock market must have performed very poorly. This, however, has not been the case.[8] Over the past 80 years U.S. stocks experienced average annual returns of about 10 percent. While U.S. stocks fell dramatically between 2001 and 2003 in the wake of the dot-com–telecom bust and corporate scandals, they experienced relatively high returns between 2003 and 2005. While stock returns are determined by many factors besides corporate governance, the data suggest that corporate governance has not placed U.S. companies at a significant competitive disadvantage.

Economic Darwinism implies that international governance systems will tend to converge with increased global competition if some governance features are inherently superior to others. As discussed below, there has been some international movement toward the U.S. corporate governance system.

Benefits of Publicly Traded Corporations

Since the separation of ownership and control generates costs relative to combined ownership and control there must be offsetting benefits to explain the existence of large corporations. Firms often can reduce the costs of raising equity capital by selling stock to diversified investors in public capital markets. Risk-averse individuals must be compensated for bearing risk to entice them to invest in a firm. Investors demand compensation only for a portion of the total risk associated with a given corporation's cash flows, since some of the risk is eliminated by holding the investment in a diversified portfolio. Raising capital from diversified investors is particularly important for large firms that require significant funds to finance investment, and is the primary reason why most large firms are organized as publicly traded corporations. For example, Google and UPS recently went public raising billions of dollars of equity capital. Public corporations also benefit from not having to restrict the supply of top managers to people who are rich enough to buy large firms.

The widespread existence of corporations suggests that the net benefits of the corporate form of organization must be positive in many environments. This

---

[8]See B. Holmstrom and S. Kaplan (2003), "The State of U.S. Corporate Governance: What's Right and What's Wrong?" *Journal of Applied Corporate Finance* 15 (3), 8–20.

ACADEMIC APPLICATIONS

Adam Smith—Right about Markets; Wrong about Firms

Adam Smith (1723–1790) was a famous Scottish philosopher and economist. His influential book *The Wealth of Nations* (1776) presented the economic underpinnings of free markets and played a huge role in popularizing laissez-faire economic policies. Smith understood that publicly traded corporations (known as joint stock companies in this day) had an advantage in raising capital. In *The Wealth of Nations* he wrote:

> *This total exemption from trouble and from risk, beyond a limited sum, encourages many people to become adventurers in joint stock companies, who would, upon no account, hazard their fortunes in any private copartnery. Such companies, therefore, commonly draw to themselves much greater stocks than any private copartnery can boast of. The trading stock of the South Sea Company, at one time, amounted to upwards of thirty-three millions eight hundred thousand pounds. The divided capital of the Bank of England amounts, at present, to ten millions seven hundred and eighty thousand pounds.*

Nevertheless, Smith argued that agency problems would destroy joint stock companies (unless they were assisted by the government).

> *The directors of such companies, however, being the managers rather of other people's money than of their own, it cannot well be expected that they should watch over it with the same anxious vigilance with which the partners in a private copartnery frequently watch over their own. Like the stewards of a rich man, they are apt to consider attention to small matters as not for their master's honour, and very easily give themselves a dispensation from having it. Negligence and profusion, therefore, must always prevail, more or less, in the management of the affairs of such a company. It is upon this account that joint stock companies for foreign trade have seldom been able to maintain the competition against private adventurers.*

Smith failed to foresee how a well-designed organizational architecture can help to control agency problems in the publicly traded corporation. He would not have been surprised by WorldCom, Parmalat, or other corporate scandals. He would have been surprised that these types of scandals are the exception, rather than the rule.

Source: A. Smith (1776), *An Inquiry into the Nature and Causes of the Wealth of Nations,* Goldsmiths'-Kress Library of Economic Literature, no. 11392.

observation implies that it is possible to design cost-effective governance systems (top-level architectures) to address the incentive problems that arise from the separation of ownership and control. Since surviving organizational architectures are optimal in a *relative* versus an *absolute* sense—that is, they are the best among the competition—there is always the possibility that governance might be improved through time as value-enhancing innovations are discovered and implemented.

Top-Level Architecture in U.S. Corporations

In contrast to popular perception, the organizational architecture of the typical corporation in the United States does not give absolute authority to professional managers. Rather, decision rights are divided among shareholders, the board of directors, top management, and external monitors (e.g., the independent auditors and lenders) in a manner that attempts to separate *decision control* (ratification and monitoring of a decision) from *decision management* (initiation and implementation of a decision). This separation is critical when, as in the publicly traded corporation, decision makers do not bear the full wealth effect of their actions. Consistent with Chapters 15–17, corporations also attempt to foster productive decisions among top-level decision makers through performance-based compensation and other incentive and control mechanisms.

ANALYZING MANAGERIAL DECISIONS: *CEO Pay in Public and Private Firms*

Numerous firms including Hertz, Bausch & Lomb, HCA, Clear Channel, and J. Crew have exited the public capital market via going-private transactions. In these deals a private equity firm such as Kohlberg Kravis Roberts & Co. (KKR) or The Carlyle Group puts up a modest amount of the equity (usually from large private investors and institutions) and borrows the rest from banks. These funds then buy out the public shareholders; the new owner is the private equity firm who either retains the current managers or replaces them. For example, KKR bought VNU, a $4.3 billion media company, and hired David Calhoun, who had been running General Electric's (GE) $47 billion aircraft unit. Mr. Calhoun's pay package at VNU was worth more than $100 million, many times more than his GE compensation.

Or, consider the case of Millard Drexler who was hired to turn around J. Crew after a successful 16-year career at running Gap. His annual J. Crew salary was $200,000 and no bonus. He also was granted millions of shares of stock, which at the time were not being traded. After J. Crew again became a public company, Mr. Drexler's ownership in J. Crew was worth over $300 million. In fact, it is often the case that executives earn more money running privately held firms than public companies, and they do not have to deal with unruly shareholders claiming they are overpaid.

1. Explain why executives might be paid more to run private companies than these same companies would have paid their executives when they were public.
2. What might these employment packages have to say about the argument that public company executives are overpaid?

SOURCE: A. Sorkin and E. Dash (2007), "Private Firms Lure C.E.O.s with Top Pay," *The New York Times* (January 8).

This section begins with a discussion of the sources of decision authority at the top of the corporation. Subsequently, we present a more detailed examination of the decision-making authority and incentives of shareholders, the board of directors, top management, and outside monitors.

Sources of Decision Rights

Top-level authority in corporations is divided among shareholders, the board of directors, and top management. Other groups that can have roles in the decision-making process include bondholders, preferred stockholders, lenders, independent auditors, and stock/credit analysts. The allocation of decision rights at the top of the firm is determined by law/regulation and voluntary choices, such as signing an agreement that grants specific decision rights to the contracting parties. This section provides a brief discussion of these "sources" of top-level decision rights.

Incorporation occurs at the state, not the federal, level in the United States. Examples of state laws that affect the partitioning of decision rights include requirements relating to the size of the board of directors and restrictions on shareholder voting. For instance, some states allow firms to use cumulative voting in the election of directors, while other states do not. (Cumulative voting allows a large minority shareholder to elect some directors even if their election is opposed by the majority of shareholders.)

The allocation of decision rights also is affected by federal laws and regulations. For example, the Securities Exchange Commission (SEC), which regulates the U.S.

securities industry, recently debated new rules that would give large shareholders limited rights to nominate board members through the normal proxy process. Nominations currently are made by the existing board of directors (unless there is a proxy fight). The Sarbanes-Oxley Act of 2002 affects decision rights, for example, by restricting corporate interactions with public accounting firms. It also assigns responsibility to the chief executive officer and the chief financial officer to certify the corporation's financial statements and the effectiveness of internal controls over the financial reports. Criminal penalties exist for violations of the law.

Laws are interpreted through court decisions, which also can have important effects on the assignment of corporate decision rights. For example, Delaware courts (where many firms are incorporated) have established legal precedents that generally emphasize directors' fiduciary responsibilities to stockholders in takeover contests (as opposed to the interests of other parties, such as employees).

International corporations are affected by the laws and regulations in their own countries. For instance, supervisory boards in German corporations must contain employee representatives.

The firm can be viewed as a focal point for a set of contracts (see Chapter 10). The firm is always one party to the many contracts that make up the firm. Examples include employee contracts, supplier agreements, loans, bonds, and stocks. Contracts frequently contain provisions that assign specific decision rights to the contracting parties. The contractual rights of shareholders are largely specified in the corporate charter and bylaws. For example, when allowed by law, some corporations adopt charter or bylaw provisions that require a supermajority of shareholder votes (more than 50 percent) to approve a merger, while other firms require only a simple majority. The charter and bylaws specify such things as board size, shareholder meeting procedures, and quorum requirements, as well as the general responsibilities of the board, its committees, and top management. Contracts with preferred stockholders can include provisions that allow the affected security holders to participate in the election of directors when preferred stock dividends are in arrears.

When a corporation lists its stock on an exchange it agrees to comply with the rules of the exchange. Stock exchanges often require member firms to have specific governance provisions. In the aftermath of WorldCom and other corporate scandals, the NYSE began requiring member firms to have a board of directors consisting of a majority of "independent" directors. Member firms are also required to have independent audit, governance, and compensation committees (consisting entirely of independent directors). Similar rules were adopted by NASDAQ. Foreign exchanges also often have governance requirements. For example, the Italian stock exchange adopted a "code of conduct" in 1999 in an attempt to improve corporate governance among Italian firms. Most stock exchanges also require minimum disclosure rules for financial information; such disclosures presumably allow external shareholders to better monitor management.

Shareholders

Decision Authority of Shareholders

While shareholders traditionally are viewed as the ultimate owners of the corporation, they have only limited powers to participate in the management of the company. Shareholders have the right to vote in the election of directors, but the board has primary authority for managing the firm. Shareholders also often vote to ratify the independent auditors and on "fundamental" issues, such as changes in the articles of incorporation (part of their contract with the corporation) and significant proposals that are not in the regular course of business (e.g., large mergers, the issuance of additional shares, equity-based compensation plans, and the dissolution of the corporation).

Prior to shareholder meetings, managers furnish shareholders with proxy statements that contain information, much of which is specified by the SEC. Managers (with board approval) make recommendations on voting issues and ask for the shareholders' proxies to vote their shares. In most elections, management obtains enough votes to pass their proposals and elect their recommended slate of candidates for the board. On rare occasions, a dissident shareholder who is unhappy with the current management's performance will wage a "proxy contest" and solicit votes to elect board members that are not supported by management. Academic research suggests that this proxy process imposes constraints on management that help to increase share value.[9] For example, share prices increase significantly around proxy contests; subsequent to proxy fights firms often make operational changes or are taken over, even if the dissidents fail to elect their proposed board members. Sometimes management will make operational changes to avoid a proxy fight.

While each shareholder normally has one vote for each share held, this is not always the case. Some firms have dual-class voting shares, where one class of stock has the primary claim to the residual profits and few voting rights, while the other class has a smaller claim to the residual profits but retains more of the voting rights. Jointly locating voting control and residual-claim rights usually is optimal since it gives those with ultimate control the incentives to maximize value and facilitates the efficient transfer of control among the shareholders.[10] Nonetheless, it sometimes can be efficient to issue shares with limited voting rights. One example arises when the private benefits of control (frequently nonpecuniary) are sufficiently large to offset the agency costs associated with separating control and residual-claim rights. For example, a founder who values control might issue shares with limited voting rights, even if shares with full voting rights would command a higher price.[11] Increased voting control also can provide management with incentives to invest in organizational-specific human capital.[12]

While shareholders of U.S. firms have ratification rights for major proposals initiated by the board, they do not have significant authority to initiate corporate actions. Shareholders can make recommendations to the board, for example, on executive compensation and corporate governance. However, U.S. boards have no legal obligation to adopt these proposals even if they receive substantial support in shareholder voting. For example, from 1997 through 2003 there were at least 131 shareholder resolutions to do away with staggered boards that passed by a

[9]For a summary of the academic literature on this topic, see J. F. Weston, M. L. Mitchell, and J. H. Mulherin (2004), *Takeovers, Restructuring and Corporate Governance,* 4th edition (Prentice Hall: Upper Saddle River).

[10]See S. Grossman and O. Hart (1988), "One Share- One Vote and the Market for Corporate Control," *Journal of Financial Economics* 20, 175–202; and M. Harris and A. Raviv (1988), "Corporate Governance: Voting Rights and Majority Rules," *Journal of Financial Economics* 20, 203–235.

[11]Evidence suggests that the typical limited voting right stock sells at a discount of over 5 percent relative to its superior voting right counterpart. Thus if a founder decides to go public with a limited voting rights stock issue, he might expect to sell it at a discount relative to what he would receive for a full voting right stock issue of similar size. See R. Lease, J. McConnell, and W. Mikkelson (1983), "The Market Value of Control in Publicly traded Corporations," *Journal of Financial Economics* 11, 439–471.

[12]For example, see R. Stulz (1988), "Managerial Control of Voting Rights: Financing Policies and the Market for Corporate Control," *Journal of Financial Economics* 20, 25–54.

ANALYZING MANAGERIAL DECISIONS: *Sotheby's Holdings—The Sting of the "Killer B" Stocks*

Christie's International PLC and Sotheby's Holdings are the two largest fine arts auction houses in the world. In January 2000, the announcement that Christie's had agreed to cooperate with the U.S. Justice Department in its investigation of price fixing sent Sotheby's stock down $3.50 per share (or 15 percent) to $20.50. In return for amnesty, Christie's admitted that it had conspired with Sotheby's to fix auction commissions. Price fixing is illegal under American and European antitrust laws. Ultimately, lawsuits were settled for hundreds of millions of dollars and Sotheby's chairman, Alfred Taubman, was sentenced to a jail term and a $7.5 million fine.

Prior to the price-fixing scandal, Sotheby's had two classes of common stock. Each of the 42,269,201 Class A shares was entitled to one vote, while each of the 16,585,650 Class B shares was entitled to 10 votes. Taubman, who owned much of the Class B stock (known as "killer B's"), controlled the company with 62.5 percent of the voting rights but had only 23 percent of the cash-flow rights. Baron Capital Group (headed by Ron Baron) in contrast was entitled to 40 percent of the cash flows, but had only 11 percent of the voting rights.

Prior to the scandal becoming public, Ron Baron indicated that he had significant faith in Taubman's leadership and was not concerned about Taubman's control through his ownership of the "killer B" stock. After the scandal became public and the stock price fell, significant conflict arose between Baron and Taubman. Baron wanted Taubman and his son to leave the company. Baron feared that Taubman's incentives were no longer aligned with the company and its shareholders, and that he might use company funds in an unreasonable legal settlement to protect himself from prosecution. The Taubmans refused to give up control, and Baron did not have enough votes to force them to leave. In a screaming match with Baron, son Robert Taubman announced that his family had no intention of giving up control of their company.

Ultimately the conflict was resolved. However, this example illustrates the conflicts that can arise when there is a separation of ownership and control rights. The Taubmans would have been forced to give up control of the company more quickly if, as in the typical company, their claim for 23 percent of the cash flows was associated with 23 percent of the voting rights. (Note that this conflict does not imply that it necessarily was suboptimal for Sotheby's to issue dual-class shares when they originally were sold. But it does illustrate vividly some of the costs associated with dual-class shares that can arise after the fact.)

The governance structure at Sotheby's appeared to give Taubman absolute control. Nevertheless the company was able to resolve the antitrust problem relatively quickly without significant opportunism by Taubman. Ultimately, this resolution helped to limit the losses to minority shareholders.

What forces and incentive mechanisms helped this settlement come to pass?

SOURCE: S. Tully (2000), "Sotheby's: A House Divided," *Fortune* (December 18), 264–273.

---

majority vote in U.S. corporations.[13] As of fall 2004, 69 percent of the companies had not implemented the proposal. Shareholders in the United Kingdom have more legal authority than in the United States. For example, U.K. shareholders can propose changes to the articles of incorporation and any corporate decision. The board must adopt a shareholder proposal if it receives more than 75 percent of the votes cast

---

[13]The data are from L. Bebchuk (2005), "The Case for Increasing Shareholder Power," *Harvard Law Review* 188, 854. The terms *staggered board* and *classified board* are synonymous. An example of such a board is as follows. The company has nine directors who are divided into three classes. Board members serve three-year terms. In any given year, only one class comes up for election. Opponents of classified boards argue that they harm shareholders because they increase the time it takes to accomplish hostile takeovers (a majority of the board does not come up for election in a given year). Others argue that staggered boards are good since they help to assure that there are always experienced people on the board.

MANAGERIAL APPLICATIONS

Charles Schwab Corporation Refuses to Include Shareholder Proposal in Proxy Statement

The corporate bylaws or charter often give shareholders the right to vote on the ratification of auditors. Shareholders, however, do not have this right in all firms.

On November 23, 2004, the Sheet Metal Worker's National Pension Fund requested that the Charles Schwab Corporation place the following shareholder proposal in their 2005 proxy statement:

Resolved: That the shareholders of Charles Schwab (the "Company") request that the Board of Directors and its Audit Committee adopt a policy that the selection of the Company's independent auditor be submitted to the Company's shareholders for their ratification at the Company's annual meeting.

Corporate legal counsel advised that Schwab did not have to comply with this request. The SEC rule on shareholder proposals allows companies to exclude a proposal by a stockholder if it "deals with a matter relating to the company's ordinary business operations." The SEC had affirmed in several previous cases that proposals relating to the selection of auditors could be excluded on this criterion. According to Schwab's legal counsel:

The responsibility for selecting the independent auditors rests with the Company's Audit Committee of the Board of Directors. The Company is incorporated under the laws of the State of Delaware. Section 141(a) of the Delaware General Corporation Law (the "DGCL") provides that the "business and affairs of every corporation organized under this chapter shall be managed by or under the direction of a board of directors, except as may be otherwise provided in this chapter or in its certificate of incorporation."

On February 23, 2005, the SEC's Office of Chief Counsel Division of Corporation Finance wrote the corporation a letter. The letter affirmed that Schwab's legal counsel had "some basis" for the view that the company could exclude the proposal. The SEC staff stated that they would "not recommend enforcement action to the Commission if Charles Schwab omits the proposal from its proxy materials in reliance on rule 14a-8(i)(7)."

This example highlights that while shareholders might be viewed as the ultimate owners of the corporation, they have only limited powers to participate in the management of the company. Primary authority for managing the company is delegated by the shareholders to the board of directors.

Source: SEC and corporate documents provided by Robert Oppenheimer, Esq.

at the meeting. Some commentators argue that shareholders should be given additional legal authority in the United States.[14] Others argue that most shareholders do not have detailed specific knowledge about the firms in their portfolios. Many also lack incentives to be involved in the governance process. Therefore, it is potentially more efficient to have shareholders delegate primary decision-making authority to an elected board of directors who can become appropriately informed on specific issues at lower cost.[15] Giving additional rights to shareholders could complicate the proxy process and allow special interest groups to impose costs on the firm and its shareholders. In the aftermath of the Enron and WorldCom scandals, debate continues among the SEC and other interested parties about whether laws and regulations should be changed to give shareholders more decision rights. While corporations have some ability to amend their own charters and bylaws to increase shareholder rights, they face some legal constraints under existing laws and regulations.[16]

[14]See L. Bebchuk (2005), "The Case for Increasing Shareholder Power," *Harvard Law Review* 188, 833–914; and L. Bebchuck and J. Fried (2004), *Pay without Performance: The Unfulfilled Promise of Executive Compensation* (Harvard University Press: Cambridge).

[15]See F. Easterbrook and D. Fischel (1991), *The Economic Structure of Corporate Law* (Harvard University Press: Cambridge), 87–88.

[16]See L. Bebchuk (2005), "The Case for Increasing Shareholder Power," *Harvard Law Review* 118, 888–891.

Common law countries such as the United States and the United Kingdom tend to provide stronger legal protection to shareholders than French civil law countries, such as France, Italy, Indonesia, and Brazil.[17] Common law countries also tend to have more active securities markets, less corrupt governments, more efficient courts, and better financial disclosure than many other countries. Research suggests that sound legal and financial markets have helped the United States and certain other common law countries to achieve high economic growth rates.[18] An important counterexample is China that has grown rapidly despite its poor legal and financial systems.[19] In China, reputation and relationships among the contracting parties appear to substitute for more formal legal protections. Understanding the links among shareholder protection, financial markets, and growth continues to be an active area of academic research.

Shareholder Incentives

Shareholders can be divided into three basic types: Small shareholders, institutional investors, and large blockholders. All shareholders benefit from increases in share value. However, they vary in their incentives to participate in the governance process and in countervailing incentives that can motivate actions that are inconsistent with maximizing the value of the shares.

Small shareholders do not have incentives to take an active role in the governance process (unless they get consumption value from the activity). If Maria Cruz owns 100 shares of stock in a large company, she is unlikely to have the power to influence the direction of the corporation or its management. Even if she could take actions that increase share price, most of the gains would go to other shareholders. While it is in the collective interests for small shareholders to be involved in the governance process, from Maria's viewpoint it is rational to free ride on the efforts of others. Consistent with this argument, small shareholders vote less frequently in corporate elections than blockholders.

Institutional investors (e.g., pension funds, insurance companies, actively managed mutual funds, index funds, and trusts) hold the majority of shares of large U.S. corporations. Institutional investors tend to be more informed about governance issues than most small shareholders and are more likely to vote their shares due to legal obligations and other concerns. Yet, institutional investors have been criticized for not taking a more active role in corporate governance. Critics correctly argue that institutional investors that fear loss of other business with the company (such as insurance companies) have incentives not to challenge management actions.[20] The

---

[17]Legal traditions vary around the world. There are two broad classifications: Civil law and common law. Legislation is the primary source of law in civil law countries, while the primary sources of law in common law countries are legal precedents set by the courts. Civil law countries are frequently divided into three groups: French, German, and Scandinavian. Dutch civil law is not easily placed in one of the three categories. The Russian civil code is based partly on a translation of the Dutch code. There is some ambiguity in classifying specific country legal systems. For example, the legal systems in Portugal and Italy evolved from both French and German influence. The major legal traditions were developed in Europe and spread throughout the world through colonization. The legal systems in Japan, China, and South Korea were most influenced by German civil law. Research indicates that French civil law countries tend to be the weakest in terms of shareholder protections, efficient/fair court systems, and corporate disclosure.

[18]Surveying the large body of research on this topic is beyond the scope of this book. A good starting point is the work of Rafael La Porta, Florencio Lopez-de-Silanes, Andrei Shleifer, and Robert W. Vishny.

[19]See F. Allen, J. Qian, and M. Qian (2005), "Law, Finance, and Economic Growth in China," *Journal of Financial Economics* 77, 57–116.

[20]See J. Brickley, R. Lease, and C. Smith (1988), "Ownership Structure and Voting on Antitakeover Amendments," *Journal of Financial Economics* 20, 267–291, for evidence that other business interests affect the voting behavior of institutional investors.

ANALYZING MANAGERIAL DECISIONS: *Stock Market Reactions to 13D Filings*

An investor must file a 13D form upon accumulation of 5 percent of the stock of a publicly traded company. Typically the stock market reacts quite favorably to these announcements. But outside block ownership has both costs and benefits.

1. Provide a brief description of these costs and benefits.
2. Does the evidence on the stock market reactions to 13D filings suggest that the benefits of outside block ownership are typically larger than the costs? Explain.

most active institutions have been public pension funds (for instance, TIAA-CREF, Hermes, and CalPERS), which are relatively insensitive to management pressures. There is some evidence that institutional investors have become more active in the governance process in the post-WorldCom environment (e.g., in challenging executive compensation and the accounting for options).

Blockholders have stronger incentives to participate in the governance process than small shareholders since they internalize more of the benefits and have more power to effect corporate behavior. Small shareholders benefit when blockholders take actions to increase share value. Blockholder and small shareholder interests can conflict when the blockholder is able to extract "private benefits" from the firm. For example, Joaquin Rodriquez, CEO of the Green Food Company, might use his 20 percent ownership to block an outside takeover so that he can continue to obtain excess compensation and perquisites. Empirical research suggests that managerial stock ownership might have both positive and negative effects on share value depending on the level of ownership. Negative effects (if they exist) appear most likely in intermediate ranges of ownership (e.g., when the managers own between 5 and 20 percent of the stock).[21] It is within this range that managers are most likely to have both the ability and incentive to "entrench" themselves against value-increasing takeovers. They do not have the power at lower levels of ownership; they do not have the incentives at higher levels of ownership (since they bear much of the negative wealth effect).

Board of Directors

Authority of the Board

While the board of directors has primary legal authority for managing the firm, the typical board delegates much of this authority to professional managers. Consistent with the organizational architecture framework, the board's primary function is top-level decision control—general oversight of the corporation and ratification of important decisions. It is not to micromanage the firm. Among the board's most important charges are to monitor, compensate, and when necessary replace the CEO. Significant strategic and investment decisions generally have to be authorized by specific board resolutions. For example, large firms have capital expenditure

---

[21]R. Morck, A. Shleifer, and R. Vishny (1988), "Management Ownership and Market Valuation: An Empirical Analysis," *Journal of Financial Economics* 20, 293–315.

approval processes that require board votes for large projects. Board members also provide input and advice to managers on business decisions based on their own past experiences and expertise.

In the United States, board members have a fiduciary responsibility to represent the interests of the corporation and its shareholders. Specific fiduciary duties include good faith, reasonable care, and loyalty (avoiding self-serving actions against the interests of the corporation). Board members are given broad legal protection under the *business judgment rule*. Board members generally avoid legal liability even for disastrous business outcomes if they take reasonable care to make business decisions that they believe are in the best interests of the corporation. This legal precedent avoids placing judges and/or juries in the position to have to "second guess" business decisions after the fact. Corporations also provide insurance coverage to directors to protect them against lawsuits. It would be difficult to attract qualified board members without this coverage. The multimillion dollar legal settlements by directors at WorldCom and Enron announced in 2005 are among the first major out-of-pocket settlements made by U.S. directors.

The typical corporate board in the United States has about 12 members; over half of these members are *outside directors* (not existing managers or their family members). However, there is substantial variation in board size and composition across firms. For example, boards ranged in size from 4 to 33 among *Fortune 1000* firms in 1999. The CEO almost always is on the board and in about 80 percent of U.S. firms serves as the chairman of the board. The typical board has one or two other top managers (e.g., the president, chief operating officer, and or chief financial officer). The typical board meets seven to eight times per year in regular session, along with any special meetings.

Efficiency dictates that much of the work of the board be conducted by committees. Committee reports and recommendations are discussed at the full board meeting where voting takes place. Most firms have audit, compensation, nominating, and executive (empowered to make various decisions between board meetings) committees. Other committees, such as a finance committee, are found in many firms.

The audit committee has top-level responsibility for monitoring the firm's financial reporting, ethics, and control systems. WorldCom and other accounting scandals have highlighted the importance of this committee. The Sarbanes-Oxley Act of 2002 requires that independent auditors report critical accounting issues and disputes between the independent accountant and management to the audit committee. It also places composition and procedural requirements on audit committees. Many firms have increased the compensation of the chair of the audit committee due to the increased workload in the Sarbanes-Oxley environment.

Some researchers argue that firm value decreases systematically with the size of the board.[22] They view small boards as superior because they are potentially less political and have fewer free-rider problems and coordination costs than large boards. The current business and regulatory environment, however, places a practical lower-bound on board size. NYSE firms must have independent audit, nominating, and compensation committees. Thus, they must have at least six outside directors on the board if the committees are to have four members and no one individual is to serve on more than two committees. In addition, the typical firm is likely to want to place outside directors on the executive and other committees.

---

[22]See D. Yermack (1996), "Higher Market Valuation for Companies with a Small Board of Directors," *Journal of Financial Economics* 40, 185–211.

Our organizational architecture framework suggests that the optimal size, composition, committee structure, and processes of the board are likely to vary with the firm's environment and strategy. For example, a firm in the defense industry might create a committee focusing on government relations, while a firm in the retail sector would not. The differences in committee structure could generate differences in both the optimal size and composition of the board. Consistent with this view, board composition, structure, and processes vary significantly across firms and through time—no one design is optimal for all firms. A good starting point for analyzing board design is to benchmark firms with similar environments and strategies.

According to some commentators, good board members act as skeptics who carefully scrutinize and question the managers' actions and proposals. Independence and separation between the board and management is stressed. It is important to recognize, however, that well-functioning boards do more than simply monitor managers. Board members can also be among the CEO's most trusted colleagues and advisors. They have specific knowledge about the firm and often have experiences and skills that complement the CEO. While it is important for board members to take their monitoring and oversight roles seriously, it is likely to be undesirable for the board and the CEO to have an adversarial relationship. Conversely, a harmonious relationship between a CEO and board does not imply that the board is failing in its decision control function.

Board Member Incentives

Outside directors typically own limited amounts of stock in the firm. For example, one study found that half of the directors in their sample owned less than .005 percent of their firm's common stock.[23] Primary incentives to focus on the corporation and its shareholders are likely to come from reputational concerns. Academic studies indicate that board members are less likely to be retained and are offered fewer board positions at other firms when their firms experience poor financial performance.[24] The 2001–2002 business scandals and associated media, legal, and regulatory responses have generated increased concerns among existing and potential board members about reputation and legal liability. On the positive side, these concerns motivate board members to take their responsibilities seriously. On the negative side, they can result in too much caution and impede the corporate decision-making process. They also reduce the supply of qualified individuals who are willing to serve on corporate boards. As the editor of *Chief Executive* magazine observed following the out-of-pocket settlements at WorldCom, some prospective directors are "leaving the playing field . . . they do not want to take the personal risk."[25] The average outside director receives over $115,000 in annual compensation. Typically, part of this compensation comes in the form of equity (or options), which helps to align the interests of the board and shareholders.

Critics argue that the financial and reputational incentives of board members are small relative to the incentives to capitulate to top management. Board members frequently depend on top management to maintain their board seats (even if they are formally nominated by an "independent" committee). Board members can also have incentives to support management to foster business contacts or simply out of

---

[23]J. Core, W. Guay, and D. Larcker (1999), "Corporate Governance, Chief Executive Officer Compensation, and Firm Performance," *Journal of Financial Economics* 51, 371–406.

[24]For example, see S. Gilson (1990), "Bankruptcy, Boards, Banks, and Blockholders," *Journal of Financial Economics* 27, 355–387; S. Kaplan and D. Reishus (1990), "Outside Directorships and Corporate Performance," *Journal of Financial Economics* 27, 389–410.

[25]W. HOLSTEIN, "The Big Chill in the Board Room" (2005), *New York Times* (May 22).

MANAGERIAL APPLICATIONS

Hewlett-Packard Fires Its Chairman/CEO

On September 4, 2001, Hewlett-Packard (HP) announced that it intended to merge with Compaq Computers through a $25 billion acquisition. While HP's CEO Carly Fiorina touted the synergistic potential of the merger, the stock market greeted the announcement with considerable skepticism—the stock fell about $5 per share (20 percent decline) at the announcement.

The proposed merger required majority approval in a vote by shareholders. HP's largest shareholder, the Packard family's charitable foundation, announced that it was going to vote against the proposed merger. Major institutional investors decided to side with Fiorina and support the deal. The proposed merger passed by a very close vote. Walter Hewlett, son of one of the founders, filed suit to block the merger. In April 2002, the Delaware Court allowed the merger to proceed.

The controversy placed significant pressure on Fiorina to perform. The benefits of the merger did not materialize as HP's stock price languished over the next few years. The HP board fired Fiorina on February 9, 2005. HP's stock price increased $1.39 per share to $21.53 on the day of the firing. Some observers argued that the board should never have supported Fiorina in the first place, and that it bore part of the blame for the company's problems. Nevertheless, the board action indicates that it was not completely "captured by the CEO." Ultimately, Fiorina was held accountable when the firm failed to perform.

---

friendship. According to this view, boards are largely "captured" by top management subject to legal and reputational constraints that limit egregious actions that harm the corporation and its shareholders.

CEO turnover provides evidence on the degree of independence of boards. While the probability of a CEO firing is relatively low, there are prominent examples of boards that have fired powerful top executives. A well-publicized example from 2005 is Hewlett-Packard's firing of Chairman/CEO Carly Fiorina (see the related box for more detail). Research documents that the likelihood of removing a manager with poor stock-price performance increases with the percentage of outside directors on the board.[26] There is also evidence that outside directors help to align board and shareholder interests in mergers and the adoption of takeover defenses.[27] While this evidence suggests that boards are not completely captured by top management, the degree of independence remains a debated issue. Our view is that public and regulatory reactions to WorldCom and other corporate scandals have increased the independence of corporate boards.

Top Management

Top Management Authority

The chief executive officer (CEO) is the top executive officer of the corporation. While CEOs are arguably the single most important person in most corporations,

---

[26]See M. Weisbach (1988), "Outside Directors and CEO Turnover," *Journal of Financial Economics* 20, 431–460.

[27]See J. Brickley, J. Coles, and R. Terry (1994), "Outside Directors and the Adoption of Poison Pills," *Journal of Financial Economics* 35, 371–390; and J. Byrd and K. Hickman (1992), "Do Outside Directors Monitor Managers? Evidence from Tender Offer Bids," *Journal of Financial Economics* 32, 195–207. See B. Hermalin and M. Weisbach (2003), "Board of Directors as an Endogenously Determined Institution: A Survey of the Economic Literature," *Economic Policy Review,* Federal Reserve Bank of NY (April), 7–26, for a more detailed discussion of the empirical and theoretical research on boards.

they are hired by and report to the board of directors. Ultimately the CEO's decision authority flows from the board.

The CEO does not have the relevant knowledge or time to make all (or even most) of the decisions within a large and complex organization. One individual cannot be expected to be a fully informed expert in all facets of a complex organization (including operational strategies, finance, accounting, corporate law, internal controls, marketing, pricing, manufacturing, research and development, and so on). Limits on managerial knowledge and time explain why most large and complex firms decentralize decision making to varying degrees. Evidence indicates that top managers delegate more decision rights as the size and complexity of the firm increase.[28]

The typical CEO's knowledge, experience, and position are most likely to add value in focusing on broader corporate-level questions, such as: How does the proposal fit with the firm's corporate strategy? How does the proposal relate to other business activities within the firm? Does the proposal affect the firm's ability to undertake future initiatives? Law professor, Robert W. Hamilton, summarizes this principle:[29]

> *In practice, the CEO, as the head of a large bureaucratic organization, cannot hope to run details of the business operations. To be effective, he must delegate authority over day-to-day operations, including personnel, financing, advertising, and production. The CEO should concentrate on the broadest issues relating to the business.*

While many decision rights are delegated to lower-level managers, certain decisions and activities are performed by the CEO (or other senior executives). For example, top-level executives generally have responsibilities for shaping the company's strategic vision and direction, establishing the overall organizational architecture, recruiting and retaining key managers, succession planning, and serving as the primary external spokesperson for the organization.

Large firms often use a "team" of executives to perform the top management functions. Many assignments of decision rights at the top of the organization are possible. The optimal design is likely to depend on the company's environment and strategy, as well as on the specific abilities, specialized knowledge, and talents of the managers. One relatively common design is to divide the top executive duties between a CEO and a chief operating officer (COO).[30] In this configuration, the CEO often focuses on external activities, such as investor relations, the media, regulators, and customers, while the COO concentrates on managing internal operations. As described below, often the COO is in line to become the next CEO.

Complex finance, accounting, and legal issues often arise in CEO decision making. While some CEOs have finance, accounting, or legal training, many do not. It would be rare for a CEO to have technical expertise in all three areas. The typical CEO relies on a group of internal and external experts for advice and consultation on such issues. The typical group of experts includes the chief financial officer (CFO), other finance managers, the controller (chief accounting officer), internal legal staff, an independent accounting firm, tax advisors, external law firms, investment and

---

[28]For example, see M. Colombo and M. Delmastro (2004), "Delegation of Authority in Business Organizations: An Empirical Test," *Journal of Industrial Economics* 52, 53–80; and A. Christie, M. Joye, and R. Watts (2003), "Decentralization of the Firm: Theory and Evidence," *Journal of Corporate Finance* 9, 3–36.

[29]R. Hamilton (2000), *Law of Corporations (in a Nutshell)* (West Group: Saint Paul), 391.

[30]The second in command may hold other titles, such as "President" or "President/COO."

commercial bankers, and members of the board of directors with the appropriate expertise (particularly members of the audit committee).

The CFO is among the most important positions in the corporation. As described by the Department of Labor:

> *Chief financial officers direct the organization's financial goals, objectives, and budgets. They oversee the investment of funds and manage associated risks, supervise cash management activities, execute capital-raising strategies to support a firm's expansion, and deal with mergers and acquisitions.*[31]

The CFO often supervises other senior financial managers such as the controller, treasurer, and risk managers. The role of a CFO in the typical corporation has evolved from a narrow focus on finance and financial reporting to include broader management responsibilities.

WorldCom and other scandals highlight the importance of properly monitoring the CFO. The CFO played a prominent role in many of these scandals, and several CFOs either pleaded guilty or were found guilty of fraud and other charges (e.g., at Enron, WorldCom, and Tyco). Large firms often have internal auditors that monitor the internal controls and transactions within the firm. One of their roles is to limit fraud. The accounting fraud at WorldCom was initially detected by the head of internal audit, Cynthia Cooper. Cooper reported directly to CFO Scott Sullivan, who eventually pleaded guilty to fraud charges. While Sullivan had ordered Cooper to focus on other activities, she persisted in detecting the improper accounting, ultimately bringing it to the audit committee's attention. Investigations initiated by the audit committee revealed that her concerns were valid. The WorldCom example highlights how important it is for internal auditors to have a close relationship with the board's audit committee. While internal auditors might report to the CFO, they often report directly to the audit committee. The absence of an independent relationship between internal audit and the audit committee at WorldCom increased the personal risk that Cooper faced in pursuing the investigation over her boss's direct orders.

While corporations can exist indefinitely, the current management will eventually leave the firm. Top management succession is an important process that should be carefully planned by both the CEO and the board. While the board has ultimate responsibility for CEO succession, CEOs often participate in the development and implementation of the succession process and in grooming their replacements.

The COO (or whatever title is second in command) is often the "heir apparent." Conditional on good individual and firm performance, the COO is likely to succeed the current CEO. Often there is a transition period where the retiring CEO stays on for a year or so as the chairman of the board after the COO assumes the CEO title. The new CEO then becomes the chairman and CEO, while the retired CEO either leaves the board or stays on as an "ordinary" director. This common succession pattern is called *passing the baton*.[32] Some large firms, such as General Electric, employ a *horse race* where several top executives compete for the top spot until one is chosen as the new CEO. While horse races can generate productive performance incentives among the candidates, such contests also reduce the incentives for cooperation. Thus, a horse race is most effective when there are multiple qualified internal candidates for the job, and close cooperation among the candidates is not of critical importance to the organization. (Chapter 14 describes horse races and other tournament-type schemes as incentive processes.)

---

[31]Bureau of Labor Statistics, U.S. Department of Labor, *Occupational Outlook Handbook*, 2004–2005 Edition, Top Executives, www.bls.gov/oco/ocos012.htm.

[32]See R. Vancil (1987), *Passing the Baton* (Harvard Business School Press: Boston).

Top Management Incentives

Performance-based compensation can help align executive and shareholder interests. The analysis in Chapter 15 predicts that firms will pay top managers substantial performance-based compensation, and that managers will receive higher incentive pay in firms where they are more likely to have an important impact on value. The data are generally consistent with these predictions. While the typical CEO of an S&P 500 company received over $6 million in pay in 2004, only about 20 percent of the total pay was straight salary. The remainder consisted of performance-based bonuses, stock options, and other types of performance-based pay. Current U.S. tax laws do not allow corporations to deduct executive compensation in excess of $1 million unless it is performance-based. Top management also owns a reasonable fraction of the typical company's shares. Research has documented that the mean and median percentages of managerial equity ownership among exchange-listed firms in the United States increased from 12.9 percent and 6.5 percent, respectively, in 1935 to 21.1 percent and 14.4 percent in 1995.[33] The largest firms (those with market values in the top 10 percent of sales) had mean and median managerial ownership of 5.4 percent and 1.5 percent in 1995. Researchers have also found that executives tend to receive a higher fraction of their compensation as performance-based pay when they are more likely to have an important effect on the firm (e.g., in high-growth firms).[34]

Lucian Bebchuk and Jesse Fried argue the typical CEO receives rents (pay in excess of the competitive labor market benchmark) and less incentive-based pay than predicted by standard economic analysis (as summarized in Chapter 15).[35] According to their *managerial power* theory, (1) the typical corporate board is captured by managers; (2) some firms have better governance and less managerial capture than others; (3) managers want high pay that is guaranteed (not performance-based); (4) "public outrage" places constraints on the excessive pay that can be taken by the managers; and (5) competition in product, labor, and takeover markets helps to limit executive pay and promote optimal contracts but does not work perfectly. Their analysis produces three testable hypotheses. First, the level of CEO compensation is expected to be lower in firms with better governance. Second, top managers are expected to receive more incentive-based compensation in firms with better governance. Third, firms are expected to "camouflage" compensation by paying managers in ways that avoid stark disclosure (e.g., through certain retirement compensation schemes).

The existing empirical evidence is generally consistent with the managerial power hypotheses. For example, CEOs tend to be paid more and have less incentive pay in firms with large boards, less independent boards, and less concentrated ownership. The research, however, is plagued by various statistical problems that are difficult to address with the available data.[36] They also are subject to alternative interpretations.

---

[33]See C. Holderness, R. Kroszner, and D. Sheehan (1999), "Were the Good Old Days That Good? Changes in Managerial Stock Ownership since the Great Depression," *Journal of Finance* 54, 435–469.

[34]See J. Gaver and K. Gaver (1993), "Additional Evidence on the Association between the Investment Opportunity Set and Corporate Financing, Dividend and Compensation Policies," *Journal of Accounting and Economics* 16, 125–160; and C. Smith and R. Watts (1992), "The Investment Opportunity Set and Corporate Financing, Dividend, and Compensation Policies," *Journal of Financial Economics* 32, 263–292.

[35]L. Bebchuck and J. Fried (2004), *Pay without Performance: The Unfulfilled Promise of Executive Compensation* (Harvard University Press: Cambridge).

[36]Observed correlations between compensation and various board characteristics can be driven by omitted variables that drive both compensation and board characteristics. For example, B. Hermalin and M. Weisbach (1998), "Endogenously Chosen Boards of Directors and Their Monitoring of the CEO," *American Economic Review* 88, 96–118, presents a model where CEO talent simultaneously drives executive compensation and board independence. Sorting out cause and effect is difficult given existing data and theory.

Some academics, in fact, argue that it can be optimal to pay a CEO "excessively" since it provides strong incentives to lower-level managers who want the job.[37] While there are some obvious abuses in executive compensation, it is a debatable issue whether the average CEO is paid excessively or inefficiently. In any case, the agency problems have not been so large as to prevent publicly traded corporations from being the dominant form of organization in the economy.

In contrast to the incentive alignment argument, some critics argue that equity-based compensation (most specifically, stock options) actually increases the agency conflicts between managers and shareholders. These critics point out that the fraudulent accounting at companies such as WorldCom was motivated in part by the top managers' desire to maintain temporarily high stock prices while they exercised their stock options. However, problems caused by poorly designed incentive plans do not imply that all incentive plans are bad and even well-designed incentive systems are subject to a certain amount of "gaming." The incentives for fraudulent accounting would have been lower at the scandal-plagued companies had top managers not been in the position to exercise their options (i.e., if the options had longer vesting periods). The scandals do suggest that the design of executive compensation plans could be improved in some firms. They do not imply that equity-based compensation is always an inappropriate way to motivate managers.

External Monitors

External parties (sometimes called "watchdogs" or "gatekeepers") also monitor corporate decisions. This section provides a brief discussion of some of the most important external monitors: public accounting firms, stock market analysts, commercial banks, credit rating agencies, attorneys, and regulatory authorities (Securities Exchange Commission [SEC] and state attorneys general). Many of these external monitors experienced criticism and litigation following the 2001–2002 business scandals.

All publicly traded companies are audited annually by independent accounting firms.[38] Independent audits are a "bonding" mechanism that fosters increased investor confidence in the firm's financial disclosures and thus demand for the firm's securities. The board and top management also rely on accountants for assessing the validity of internal accounting reports that are used in decision making and control. For example, independent auditors help to assure that divisional managers are not reporting fraudulent accounting information to top management and the board. Corporate scandals, such as WorldCom, generated concern about whether auditors are sufficiently independent from the firms that they audit. Arthur Andersen was essentially destroyed as a company following the Enron scandal. In response to these concerns, major provisions in the Sarbanes-Oxley Act of 2002 are directed at increasing the independence of public accounting firms. For example, the law limits public accounting firms from providing certain consulting services to their audit clients, and

---

[37]See E. Lazear and S. Rosen (1981), "Rank Order Tournaments as Optimal Labor Contracts," *Journal of Political Economy* 89, 841–864; and S. Rosen (1982), "Authority, Control, and the Distribution of Earnings," *Bell Journal of Economics* 13, 311–323.

[38]The term *independent accounting firms* is standard usage. It denotes an accounting firm that is separate from the firm being audited. As we discuss, there is debate as to whether independent auditors are sufficiently independent from the firms they audit (e.g., due to other business relationships). Another term, that is, used to describe independent auditors is *external auditors*.

MANAGERIAL APPLICATIONS

Commercial Banks and Prepay Transactions

Commercial banks were sued and heavily criticized for their participation in billions of dollars worth of prepay transactions with Enron and other firms. While prepays are legitimate transactions in some settings, they appear to have been used by some firms simply to produce inappropriately favorable positive accounting statements.

The following is a simplified description of the questionable transactions between major banks (such as Chase and Citicorp) and Enron. In the typical example, a new company was formed to engage in a transaction with the bank. The bank agreed to accept the future delivery of some commodity, such as oil, from the new company. The bank, in turn, "prepaid" for the delivery by providing cash to the new company. The new company would then enter into a contract with Enron under which (1) Enron agreed to deliver the commodity to the new company in the future, and (2) the company prepaid for the delivery by giving the cash it had received from the bank to Enron. At this point, the new company had completely offsetting transactions. It had no cash and offsetting contracts for the receipt and delivery of the commodity. To complete the cycle, Enron would enter into a forward contract with the bank agreeing to accept future delivery of the commodity from the bank. In contrast to the other contracts, however, Enron did not prepay the bank for the delivery. Rather, it promised to pay at the time of delivery. The net result of the transactions was that all three parties had offsetting positions with respect to the commodity. Enron, however, had the bank's cash and a promise to pay the cash back (with implied interest) on the specified delivery date of the commodity.

The net result of the prepay transaction is identical to a loan. Enron obtained cash from the bank at time 0 and agreed to pay it back with interest at time 1. The complicated prepay transaction, however, was not accounted for as ordinary debt. Also, the cash was reported as cash flow from operations. These prepay transactions enhanced the appearance of Enron's financial statements compared to the standard accounting for bank loans. Accountants who subsequently reviewed these transactions concluded that the accounting was improper. Lawsuits asserted that the banks had engaged in the transactions knowing that they were designed to produce misleading accounting statements and had no legitimate business purpose. Many of the banks and investment banks that helped design and execute these complicated transactions made large payments to the plaintiffs to settle the lawsuits.

---

created the Public Company Accounting Oversight Board to monitor the auditing activities of public accounting firms.

Researchers argue that commercial banks provide important monitoring of corporate decisions.[39] Commercial banks are likely to be well informed about a firm from depository and lending relationships. Banks have financial and reputational incentives to monitor their loan customers' business decisions. Depending on the bank's organizational architecture, however, bank employees can have incentives to take inappropriate actions to foster business relationships with large corporate customers. Large commercial banks were subject to substantial criticism and litigation following the 2001–2002 business scandals. Commercial and investment banks from around the world agreed to pay billions of dollars to settle litigation relating to Enron and WorldCom. Investors claimed that the banks had knowingly helped craft and finance transactions that served no other purpose than misleading investors by producing misleading accounting statements.

Investors frequently rely on stock market analysts in making investment decisions. Stock analysts often work for investment banking firms, such as Merrill Lynch, that derive revenue from corporations through such activities as underwriting securities and work on mergers. Investment banking firms allegedly risk losing

---

[39]For example, see D. Diamond (1984), "Financial Intermediation and Delegated Monitoring," *Review of Economic Studies* 51, 393–414.

HISTORICAL APPLICATIONS

Elihu Root's Timeless Advice on Attorney Conduct

Scholars widely regard Elihu Root (1845–1937) as among the most important and distinguished public servants in American history. Root was a prominent attorney who served as both Secretary of State and Secretary of War under President Theodore Roosevelt. He also was a U.S. senator from New York and won the Nobel Peace Prize in 1912 for his many efforts on behalf of increasing international understanding.

Theodore Roosevelt who served as America's 26th president (1901–1909) was a very strong-willed and intimidating person. Root was among the few people that Roosevelt could always count on for a candid opinion. In Root's words, "about half the practice of a decent lawyer is telling his clients that they are damned fools and should stop."

The SEC named attorneys as respondents or defendants in more than 30 enforcement actions in 2003 and 2004. A common charge was that the attorney had failed to give candid legal advice to the board or the audit committee about an illegal accounting transaction. In reflecting on these charges, the SEC's director of enforcement stated:

> *Many of those we charged could have avoided problems if they had heeded Elihu Root's advice. We have many examples of lawyers who twisted themselves into pretzels to accommodate the wishes of company management, and failed in their responsibility to insist that the company comply with the law.*

Source: S. M. Cutler, Director of the Division of Enforcement of the SEC (2004), "The Themes of Sarbanes-Oxley as Reflected in the Commission's Enforcement Program," speech, UCLA School of Law, September 20.

significant investment banking fees if their analysts produce reports that are critical of the company, thereby upsetting management. Investigations by the New York Attorney General produced colorful examples where analysts promoted a stock strongly to the public, while privately acknowledging that the company was in serious trouble. Major investment banks agreed to large payments and structural changes to settle and prevent potential litigation. Several Merrill Lynch executives were sentenced to jail for helping Enron enhance its financial statements through the improper sale of floating power plants in Nigeria. While management pressures have motivated some analysts to be overly optimistic, research indicates that reputational concerns help to limit analyst optimism.[40] The Sarbanes-Oxley Act of 2002 contains provisions that are directed at reducing the pressure that investment banks place on research analysts to produce positive reports.

S&P, Moody, and Fitch rate the corporate debt of large companies for default risk. Special regulatory status allows these rating agencies to obtain information from companies that are not provided to other outsiders. Rating agencies were criticized for not being more active in detecting or preventing the 2001–2002 corporate scandals. Critics stressed the potential conflict of interest that arises from the fact that companies pay the rating agencies to rate their debt issues. This conflict, however, is arguably small since corporate debt issuers have little choice in using the major rating agencies. Also, no one corporate client is responsible for a large share of the rating companies' revenues.

Firms frequently obtain advice from outside law firms on corporate disclosures and transactions. Some law firms obtain a substantial portion of their revenues from large corporate clients. Law firms were criticized in the 2001–2002 corporate scandals for not bringing specific concerns about management, transactions, and disclosures to the attention of the board. The Sarbanes-Oxley Act of 2002 contains provisions pertaining to attorneys. For example, it requires the SEC to set minimum standards for professional conduct for attorneys practicing before it.

[40]A. Leone and J. Wu (2007), "What Does It Take to Become a Superstar? Evidence from Institutional Rankings of Financial Analysts," working paper, University of Rochester, Rochester, NY.

A cornerstone for monitoring by outsiders, including shareholders, is the timely and accurate disclosure of corporate financial information. The Securities Acts of 1933 and 1934 were primarily targeted at improving corporate disclosures. One of the SECs principle functions is to help assure that investors receive material information for making investment decisions. The SEC also investigates companies for possible violations of securities laws. As a governmental agency with limited staff, the SEC is not intended to have primary responsibility for assuring proper financial statements among the roughly 13,000 publicly traded corporations. For example, the SEC, which has been in existence since 1934, did not initially detect the 2001–2002 scandals, including those at Enron, WorldCom, and Tyco. Ultimate responsibility falls on corporate managers who are monitored by independent auditors and other private-sector entities. State attorneys general also monitor corporations (incorporation occurs under state law). The New York Attorney General has been particularly active in investigating companies following the 2001–2002 business scandals.

International Corporate Governance

Germany and Japan frequently are cited for corporate governance that differs from that in the United States. In contrast to the United States, German and Japanese corporations are not directed primarily at maximizing shareholder wealth. Rather, their traditional focus has been on a broader set of stakeholders including employees, banks, affiliated companies, the broader community, and shareholders. Both of these countries historically have had weaker shareholder protection laws than in the United States.

Japanese corporations generally have somewhat larger boards than found in U.S. companies. Historically these boards have been comprised of managers, former employees, managers of affiliated companies, and bank managers. Few, if any, of these boards have had independent directors. Banks have taken an active role in governance—especially when firms are in financial distress. Another common characteristic of traditional Japanese firms is extensive reciprocal holdings of common stock among affiliated corporations. Because of regulation and the distribution of stock ownership, hostile takeovers have been rare in Japan.

German companies have a two-tier board system. The supervisory board consists of large shareholders (including banks, corporations, and insurance companies) and employee representatives. Employee representatives have 50 percent of the board seats. The supervisory board selects a management board that has primary operational authority. Similar to Japan, reciprocal holdings of the voting stock of affiliated companies are common; banks have taken an active role in governance; hostile takeovers are rare.

Top-level executives receive incentive-based compensation throughout the world. According to Towers Perrin's 2003–2004 survey of worldwide compensation, the typical U.S. CEO received 63 percent of compensation in the form of variable pay.[41] The average German and Japanese CEO received 51 percent and 19 percent, respectively. U.S. CEOs had the highest percentage of variable-based pay among the 26 countries that were surveyed; the second highest was Singapore (59 percent). CEOs in New Zealand and China (Shanghai) had the smallest percentages (15 percent and 18 percent, respectively). According to Towers Perrin, the dominant form of equity-based compensation is stock options. Of the countries surveyed, France

[41]www.towersperrin.com/hrservices/webcache/towers/United_States/publications/Reports/2003_04_Worldwide_Remuneration/WWTR_2003_English.pdf

led with 90 percent of companies reporting the use of stock options, followed by Belgium, Canada, and the United States (85 percent). Companies in China, represented by Hong Kong and Shanghai, reported usage levels of 55 percent and 35 percent, respectively. While China trailed most large industrial nations, it ranked ahead of regional competitor India, at 20 percent. Towers Perrin reports that there has been a relative increase in the use of restricted stock awards in the United States and several other countries due to changes in accounting rules relating to the expensing of options and public concerns about option plans. The average CEO in the United States receives significantly higher total compensation than in other countries.

The most common incentive conflict in the United States is between outsider shareholders and the board/managers who own limited amounts of stock in the firm. Conflicts between controlling inside shareholders and outside shareholders are frequently observed in other countries where the stock is less widely held. The Italian company Parmalat provides an important example of this type of conflict. Parmalat was founded by Calisto Tanzi in the early 1960s. By 2002 it had become a publicly traded corporation with reported global sales of over 7.5 billion euros. Nevertheless, the Tanzi family maintained voting control of Parmalat's stock, and five Tanzi family members served on the company's seven-member board. In December 2003, Parmalat revealed that it had overstated assets by billions of dollars through fictitious accounts. Tanzi admitted to "siphoning off 500 million euros" from the company. Expropriations of corporate assets by other Tanzi family members were documented. The SEC called Parmalat "one of the largest and most brazen corporate financial frauds in history;" and it was dubbed by the media the "European Enron."[42] Outside shareholders who had little control over the firm's activities essentially lost their entire investments when the fraud was revealed.

The relatively strong performance of U.S. companies during the 1990s motivated many foreign countries and companies to adopt "investor reforms" based on the U.S. model. Japanese regulations were changed to allow executive stock options, and Japanese companies have begun adding outside directors to company boards. Other examples include Brazil, India, Kyrgyz Republic, Malaysia, South Africa, Thailand, and various western European countries. Many of these proshareholder governance changes were motivated by hopes of enticing foreign investors who are reluctant to invest in countries and/or companies with weak shareholder protections. A recent survey of institutional investors by McKinsey and Company indicates that institutional investors consider governance issues as important as financial analysis in deciding on whether or not to invest in a given company. Movement toward the U.S. model has not stopped due to the governance scandals of 2001 and 2002.

The increased emphasis on shareholder wealth in other countries is evidenced in the turnover of CEOs. Historically U.S. CEOs faced a higher risk of performance-based turnover than CEOs in most other countries. This was not the case in 2004. CEO turnover reached historic highs in 2004 in Europe and various Asian/Pacific countries.[43] Much of this turnover was performance related. For example, CEO turnover increased to 17.5 percent per year in Europe from 11 percent in 2003; turnover was even smaller in earlier years. Close to 45 percent of the 2004 turnovers in Europe were classified as performance-related.

---

[42]Parmalat has also been compared to the U.S. scandal at Adelphia where members of the founding family were accused (and in some cases convicted) of various charges relating to fraud and theft from the firm.

[43]Data are from an annual survey of CEO turnover conducted by Booz Allen Hamilton. See www.boozallen.de/content/downloads/ceo_succession_2004.pdf

---

MANAGERIAL APPLICATIONS

Hermes' Focus on Corporate Governance in Japan

Hermes Pension Management Limited is a large British institutional investor. In 2000 it announced it had appointed a resident Japanese corporate governance advisor to assist with the development of its international governance programs.

The new position was staffed by Mr. Ariyosh Okumura, formerly chief executive of IBJ Asset Management. His first tasks were to supervise a Japanese translation of Hermes' International Governance Practices and to explain these governance principles to the 450 Japanese public companies in which Hermes has shareholdings. Hermes also planned to hold private meetings with as many companies as possible to discuss their governance practices.

Hermes has been among the most active of European institutional investors in the corporate governance process. It has formed joint agreements with major U.S. pension funds to collaborate on governance issues both in the United States and internationally.

This example illustrates the active role that some institutional investors (especially public pension funds) play in the corporate governance process.

Source: Hermes (2000), company press release (March 28).

U.S. corporate governance is sometimes criticized for being overly focused on shareholders. After all, aren't employees and other corporate stakeholders important? These critics fail to recognize that shareholder value is not maximized by mistreating employees, cheating customers, or destroying local communities. If a company is successful in making profits over the long run many stakeholders benefit. The company survives; workers are employed; communities receive tax revenues; customers obtain products that they value. Companies that continually fail to make profits eventually go out of business, and many stakeholders suffer. By focusing on shareholder value (the residual cash flows) managers have incentives to search for new revenue-producing opportunities and for less costly production methods. Ultimately this activity leads to more efficient use of the limited resources in the economy and higher standards of living.

When companies are growing and profitable, shareholder and employee interests largely coincide. Focusing on the interests of multiple stakeholders causes few problems under these conditions. A prominent case where stakeholder interests diverge is when firms need to downsize or move employment "offshore" to remain competitive. Under these conditions, if a firm fails to reduce domestic employment shareholders suffer, and ultimately the firm will go out of business. Nevertheless, employees who expect to lose their jobs would be better off if the firm did not downsize (even if it causes the firm to suffer financially and eventually to go out of business). The U.S. governance model provides managers with clear guidance in this situation—reduce domestic employment since it increases shareholder value. Governance models that focus on multiple stakeholders do not provide clear guidance on how managers should weigh the interests of the competing stakeholders. While competitive pressures may ultimately force companies with stakeholder objectives to make employment adjustments, the adjustments are likely to be delayed and more expensive than under the U.S. model. Global competition placed extreme pressure on German manufacturing companies during the 1990s to reduce employment at domestic plants and to increase employment at foreign subsidiaries that paid substantially lower wages. German companies adjusted, but only after significant public controversy and costly negotiations with trade unions. As an example,

---

MANAGERIAL APPLICATIONS

Sony Corporation (Japan) Increases Outside Directors

The Japanese economy entered a period of sustained decline in the 1990s, following its meteoric rise in the 1980s. During the 1990s, the Japanese stock market declined by 50 percent, while the U.S. stock market soared. Many features of the traditional Japanese corporation could not be maintained in this new environment. For example, many Japanese companies had to renege on implicit lifetime employment contracts. They also were motivated to make changes in their governance systems to promote foreign investment.

Sony Corporation issued a press release in January 2003 announcing "reforms" in its management structure that were being made "to strengthen the distinction between oversight and business operation roles." The following changes were among those listed in their press release:

Composition of Board of Directors: The Board of Directors will have between 10 and 20 directors. Regulations governing the qualifications for director-candidates will be established in order to eliminate conflicts of interest and ensure independence. The intention is to increase the number of outside directors from the present level of three.

Chairman of the Board: Separation between Chairman of the Board and Representative Corporate Executive Officer will be regulated.

Composition of Committees:

Nomination Committee: The Nomination Committee will be composed of five or more directors and the majority will be outside directors. However there will be at least two internal directors.

Compensation Committee: The Compensation Committee will be composed of three or more directors and the majority will be outside directors. However there will be at least one internal director. The CEO and COO will not be chosen for this Committee.

Audit Committee: The Audit Committee will be composed of three or more directors and the majority will be outside directors. There will be at least one full-time member. All members of the Audit Committee will not have business operation responsibilities and will satisfy the independence requirements of U.S. corporate reform legislation. In principle, Audit Committee members will not become Nomination Committee or Compensation Committee members.

Source: Sony Group (2003), company press release, "Reforming the Sony Group Management Structure to Strengthen Corporate Governance," (January 28).

Siemens increased employment outside Germany by 40 percent to 162,000 between 1985 and 1995, while reducing German employment by 12 percent (156,000 to 141,000).[44] Making these changes required Siemens to deal with resistance from employee representatives on the board, trade unions, and the media. Japanese companies faced similar problems in adjusting to economic shocks in the 1990s.

Market Forces

Corporate boards and managers face important constraints imposed by external control mechanisms. In this section, we briefly discuss three important external control mechanisms: the market for corporate control, the managerial labor market, and product market competition.

Market for Corporate Control

One of the most important external control mechanisms is the market for corporate control. If a management team fails to maximize the value of the firm, it can prompt

---

[44]D. Audretsch and M. Fritsch (2003), "Linking of Entrepreneurship to Growth: The Case of West Germany," *Industry and Innovation* 10(1), 65–73.

ACADEMIC APPLICATIONS

Postretirement Incentives of CEOs

Career concerns potentially mitigate agency problems between managers and shareholders. Such concerns arise from both the external labor market, which provides managers with outside opportunities, and the internal labor market, which determines how quickly and on what terms a manager is promoted through the hierarchy in his or her own organization. Managers realize that if they perform poorly, these labor markets will downgrade the assessments of their abilities and demand for the managers will decline.

It regularly has been argued that career concerns became negligible during the last years of active employment. Evidence suggests, however, that CEOs face career concerns even in this later period of employment. Retired CEOs frequently hold multiple board seats that give them both pecuniary and nonpecuniary benefits. Both the likelihood of CEOs serving on their own boards two years after departure as well as the likelihood of serving as outside directors on other boards are positively and strongly related to the financial performance of their firms in their final years of active employment. Assuming the typical CEO values these positions, the effect of performance on postretirement opportunities provides incentives to CEOs in their final years of active employment.

Source: J. Brickley, J. Linck, and J. Coles (1999), "What Happens to CEOs After They Retire? New Evidence on Career Concerns, Horizon Problems, and CEO Incentives," *Journal of Financial Economics* 52, 344–377.

a hostile takeover offer from a competing management team who thinks they can do a better job. The United States, with a relatively protakeover regulatory environment, has had a particularly active takeover market. For example, between 1993 and 1999 the value of corporate mergers represented 8.4 percent of the gross domestic product (GDP).[45] The market for corporate control, while important in many countries, is less active where there are greater legal restrictions on takeovers.

In order for market forces to perform their control functions, a certain level of information must be provided to these markets. For example, the market for corporate control must be able to identify firms that are not maximizing shareholder value. Again, we see the often overlooked, but vitally important, roles of financial disclosure in corporate governance.

Managerial Labor Market

Another important external control mechanism is the managerial labor market.[46] Reputation is important in determining the professional opportunities that an individual receives. Managers who perform poorly at one company are less likely to be offered management positions or board seats at other companies.

Product Market

Inefficient firms have higher costs than more efficient firms and eventually fail in a competitive marketplace. Thus, the product market is another external mechanism that limits managerial agency problems.[47] Global Crossing, WorldCom, and other

[45]See J. Weston, J. Siu, and B. Johnson (2001), *Takeovers, Restructuring and Corporate Governance,* 3rd edition (Prentice Hall: Upper Saddle River).

[46]See E. Fama (1980), "Agency Problems and the Theory of the Firm," *Journal of Political Economy* 88, 288–307.

[47]See A. Alchian (1950), "Uncertainty, Evolution and Economic Theory," *Journal of Political Economy* 58, 211–221; and O. Hart (1983), "The Market Mechanism as an Incentive Scheme," *Bell Journal of Economics* 14, 366–382.

companies involved in recent scandals ultimately filed bankruptcy petitions when their revenues were unable to cover their costs. Managers have both financial and reputational incentives to avoid bankruptcy.

Sarbanes-Oxley Act of 2002

Congress was under substantial pressure to take action after the business scandals that emerged in late 2001 through the middle of 2002. It responded in July 2002 by passing the Sarbanes-Oxley Act of 2002 (SOX). SOX has a wide range of provisions and touches on many of the issues that arose during the business scandals, including internal monitoring, public auditing, activities of external monitors, executive loans, and disclosure.[48]

SOX establishes the Public Companies Accounting Oversight Board (PCAOB) to oversee public accountants' audits of publicly traded corporations. The PCAOB is appointed by the Securities and Exchange Commission ("after consultation with" the Chairman of the Federal Reserve Board and the Secretary of the Treasury). The Act contains various rules and regulations that affect public accounting firms, the boards and management of public companies, and other monitors such as research analysts. The Act prohibits various transactions between companies and their management (such as personal loans to executives). It requires CEOs and CFOs to certify the accuracy of their financial statements, and establishes civil and criminal penalties for violations of the Act.

MANAGERIAL APPLICATIONS

WorldCom—An Important Lesson in Ethics for All Employees

The Sarbanes-Oxley Act of 2002 focuses much of its attention on top-level executives. The example of Betty Vinson at WorldCom, however, emphasizes that lower-level employees also have legal and ethical responsibilities.

Betty Vinson was a midlevel manager who made fraudulent entries in the accounting system at WorldCom. She pleaded guilty to fraud in 2002 and cooperated with the government in its case against Bernard Ebbers. Following Ebber's conviction, she was sentenced to five months in prison on August 5, 2005.

Vinson testified that she was pressured by the CFO to make the false accounting entries. The CFO had told her that Ebbers did not want to lower Wall Street expectations. She was assured by the CFO that "all was well." She stated, "I felt like if I didn't make the entries, I wouldn't be working there." Asked how she chose which accounts to alter, Vinson testified, "I just really pulled some out of the air. I used some spreadsheets."

While Vinson acknowledged her guilt, she had hoped to avoid prison time because she had cooperated with the government. U.S. District Judge Barbara Jones was sympathetic, but nevertheless held Vinson responsible. Jones concluded, "Ms. Vinson was among the least culpable members of the conspiracy at WorldCom. Still, had Ms. Vinson refused to do what she was asked, it's possible this conspiracy might have been nipped in the bud."

Corporate fraud often requires the assistance of multiple individuals. Lower-level employees may feel pressured to comply with a superior's request to engage in an illegal action. The lesson from WorldCom and other recent scandals is that employees should not expect to escape criminal or civil liability simply because they "were following orders." Employees are legally and ethically responsible for their own actions, whether or not they are ordered to do something by their boss.

Source: M. Graybow (2005), "Former WorldCom Accountant Sentenced," Reuters (August 5).

---

[48]See www.aicpa.org/info/sarbanes_oxley_summary.htm for a detailed summary of the law.

MANAGERIAL APPLICATIONS

The Economic Costs of Sarbanes-Oxley (SOX)

To gauge the total economic costs associated with SOX, one study examines broad movements in the stock market surrounding key events leading to the passage of Sarbanes-Oxley. On the assumption that the market incorporates into stock prices in a timely and unbiased fashion the release of new information about future discounted cash flows, the study indicates the cumulative abnormal return of the market index stemming from the legislative events leading to the passage of SOX is about $1.4 trillion. This amount represents the decline in the market value of publicly traded equities in the United States on those days that SOX moved through the legislative process.

The largest SOX-related stock market decline occurred when President Bush, in a speech on July 9, 2002, signaled a change of attitude in Washington stating the federal government had to get tough on corporate crime. The passage of SOX-type laws that were considered inconceivable before the speech became imminent after President Bush expressed his agreement with Senate Democrats on the goals of reforms. The market realized a significant negative abnormal return (-2.28 percent) on the day of his speech. Furthermore, firms with more complex business lines and more extensive foreign operations experienced a larger decline in their market returns on account of SOX, a further indication of the economic effect on business. In addition, the cumulative abnormal market returns associated with the announcement that some firms would obtain an extension on when they had to comply with SOX experienced higher positive abnormal market returns than firms that were subject to early compliance.

The study also examined other news events occurring during the SOX deliberations that potentially might confound significantly abnormal negative stock returns attributable to SOX. Although there were other government rulemaking activities, accounting scandals, and economic reports that became public during the SOX deliberations, an examination of the exact timing of these news releases indicates that they are unlikely to account for the huge negative market return over the key SOX-related legislative events.

The study's author offers a caveat on the $11.4 trillion estimate of the economic costs of SOX. This figure incorporates not just the economic costs of SOX, but any additional concerns the market has that SOX also might signal a change in the behavior of lawmakers toward tighter anti-business government controls.

Source: I. Zhang (2007), "Economic Consequences of the Sarbanes-Oxley Act of 2002," *Journal of Accounting and Economics* 44, 74–115.

Section 404 has proven to be the most controversial and costly provision in SOX. Section 404 requires companies to report annually on the internal controls over their financial statements. Independent auditors are to attest to and report on managements' assessment of the firm's internal controls over the financial reports. Complying with this provision has turned out to be a massive undertaking. Industry estimates put the national cost of just complying with Section 404 of SOX at $35 billion.[49]

The relative costs and benefits of alternative organizational forms can change due to changes in the business environment and/or strategy of the firm. SOX represents a significant change in the business environment. The new demands on corporate boards and the limitations on management contracts and corporate actions increase the costs of organizing as a public corporation substantially. While many large firms have no feasible alternative to organizing as publicly traded corporations, some smaller firms have chosen to "go private" and convert to closely held companies. Other firms have delayed going public. Moreover, it is likely that the availability of financing for start-up firms will decline since venture capitalists will require a higher threshold of success to help assure that they can liquidate their investment by taking the start-up public. Some foreign companies have decided to quit being listed on U.S. exchanges. SOX might also encourage mergers if there are scale economies in

[49]See T. Bisoux (2005), "The Sarbanes-Oxley Effect," *BizEd* (July/August), 24–29.

complying with the Act. While the overall merits of the Act can be debated, one potentially unanticipated consequence is its effect on organizational choice.

Various researchers have tried to estimate the realized costs and benefits of SOX. While the evidence is controversial, it generally supports the notion that the costs have been significant, while the benefits have been elusive.[50] Concerns about compliance costs have motivated the SEC to take various actions, such as delaying Section 404 application for small and foreign firms.

Corporate Governance: An Historical Perspective

The 2001–2002 spate of scandals produced worldwide concern about corporate governance and whether it was fatally flawed in most, if not all, publicly traded corporations. These concerns contributed to the 23 percent decline in the S&P 500 stock market index that occurred in 2002. Nevertheless, the dominance of publicly traded corporations has continued, and the stock market has rebounded. The S&P 500 increased nearly 40 percent between the end of 2002 and August 2005 despite a surge in oil prices and worldwide concerns about war and terrorism.

The ongoing strength of the stock market is not surprising when viewed in an historical perspective. Throughout history, as business environments have changed (markets, regulation, and technology) new control problems have developed that have resulted in business scandals. This process has not resulted in the demise of the public corporation. Rather, corporate governance has evolved, and business has progressed.

Consider the profound changes that occurred in the economy in the early 1900s. After World War I, the U.S. economy grew rapidly under President Coolidge's probusiness policies. From 1923 to 1929 the quantity of manufactured goods almost doubled. Automobile sales grew from 1.5 million in 1921 to 4.5 million in 1929. The stock market soared. During this time period the publicly traded corporation asserted itself as the dominant form of organization in the industrial sector. On "Black Tuesday" (October 19, 1929), the stock market crashed and the Great Depression followed. During the 1920s, the Dow Jones Industrial Average (major stock market index) nearly quadrupled reaching a historic high of 381.17 on September 3, 1929; by June 1932 it had fallen to 41.22 (losing almost 90 percent of its value).

Subsequent investigations alleged accounting "scams," illegal trading, conflicts of interests, and other major problems with corporate governance. These allegations, however, resulted in private sector and governmental changes in corporate governance—not the demise of the publicly traded corporation. No governance system works perfectly, and other business scandals occurred over time. In 1938, McKesson and Robbins executives embezzled more than $18 million and hid the theft by creating a fake division representing one-fifth of the company's assets. The auditor, Price Waterhouse, missed the fraud. Large scandals arose in the 1960s and 1970s at Mates Fund and Equity Funding. Despite the occurrence of these and other scandals, public corporations continued to survive, and governance systems have continued to evolve. The Dow Jones on December 1, 2005, was around 10,900 compared to its 1920s high of 381.

The second half of the twentieth century witnessed profound economic change with the development of the "information age" and the globalization of markets. Public corporations were confronted with new control problems, which put stress on existing control systems. As Federal Reserve Chairman Alan Greenspan remarked in July 2002,

---

[50]See L. Ribstein (2005), "Sarbanes-Oxley After Three Years," Illinois Law and Economics, working paper, #LE05-016 for a review and discussion of this research.

Tyco International—Corporate Governance Failure or Success?

Tyco International Ltd. is a diversified manufacturing and services company that was embroiled in a large corporate governance scandal. Problems initially surfaced in December 1999 when Tyco disclosed that the SEC was conducting an informal inquiry of the company. In June 2000, Tyco announced it was amending its reported earnings for 1999 and the first quarter of 2000. During the first five months of 2002, Tyco's stock price fell from $56 to less than $10 per share. CEO Dennis Kozlowski abruptly resigned on June 3, 2002. On September 13, 2002, Kozlowski and the former CFO were indicted for theft, fraud, and violation of securities laws. The indictment charged that they had used Tyco as a "personal piggy bank" to purchase millions of dollars worth of residences, yachts, artwork, personal investments, and even $17,000 umbrella stands. The indictment charged that the total illegal enrichment was around $600 million. The former CEO and CFO were subsequently found guilty in court.

Tyco hired Ed Been from Motorola as its new CEO in July 2002. Been's top priority was to improve Tyco's corporate governance and to restore confidence in the company. He encouraged more internal policing by installing an ombudsman at Tyco and giving workers an ethics guide called "Doing the Right Thing." He replaced all of Tyco's top executives, two of its five division presidents, and asked the former board to resign. He moved Tyco's operating headquarters from New York City to a more modest office park in West Windsor, N.J. In the three years since Been was hired, Tyco's stock price tripled, substantially outperforming the S&P 500.

Tyco has been cited as a major corporate governance failure—yet one more example of fatally flawed governance in U.S. corporations. From a longer-term perspective, Tyco could be characterized as a governance success. While the company and its shareholders suffered when the scandal surfaced, the guilty parties were ultimately sent to jail and the governance problems corrected. Three years later the company was "back on track" and performing well. Consistent with the principle of Economic Darwinism, Tyco had to respond to external pressures and change its organizational architecture to survive.

"the avenues to express greed have grown enormously." CFO Andrew Fastow used complex derivatives to commit fraud at Enron; a financial "tool" that did not even exist 20 years earlier. Fraud had been easier to detect and monitor in the "simple world" of stocks and bonds.

Increased complexity in the world implies that managers should carefully evaluate the control issues when contemplating expansions into new activities and markets. Strategic decisions that might look good from a pure business standpoint can prove unwise when one considers the governance costs. Consider Royal Ahold's corporate strategy in 2000 and 2001 to expand its grocery store business around the world through multiple acquisitions. The company, which is headquartered in the Netherlands, acquired at least 13 new companies in the United States, Scandinavia, Spain, Argentina, and the Netherlands during this two-year period alone. The rapid expansion produced control problems that the company was not prepared to confront, and an accounting scandal surfaced in 2003. Foreign subsidiaries had produced massively fraudulent accounting statements, apparently orchestrated by divisional managers who wanted to earn higher accounting-based bonuses. Following the scandal, Royal Ahold retreated from its rapid merger strategy, sold off various "noncore" assets, and strengthened internal controls at both the corporate and divisional levels.

The debate on how to improve corporate governance continues in the aftermath of the recent corporate scandals. This debate is useful since it could lead to new insights into how to improve corporate governance. It is important to recognize, however, that corporate governance is not as flawed as some critics contend. In contrast to popular characterizations, top executives are not given absolute authority to run corporations as personal fiefdoms. Consistent with the organizational architecture framework, the U.S. governance model attempts to separate decision management from decision control and to provide incentives to corporate decision makers to take productive actions. From time to time, business scandals emerge. However, this will occur under any feasible governance system, especially in times of rapid change. Designing governance systems that eliminate all agency conflicts is usually too costly. It is probably efficient for some scandals to occur. As SOX illustrates, new regulation entails both costs and benefits, as do privately initiated changes in governance at the firm level. While improvements in governance are conceptually possible, it is critical to consider both the costs and benefits when evaluating governance changes at either the firm or regulatory level.

Summary

Corporations have the legal standing of an individual (distinct from its shareholders) and can enter into contracts and participate in lawsuits. Shareholders have limited liability (only their initial capital contribution is subject to risk). Some corporations are *closely held,* while others are *publicly traded.* Publicly traded companies are often listed on organized stock exchanges. The largest exchange in the world is the New York Stock Exchange (NYSE), which provides an extremely active and liquid market for trading shares.

Institutional investors (e.g., mutual and pension funds) now own about 50 percent of the stock of publicly traded corporations. While the typical large firm has thousands of "small" shareholders, many have *blockholders* that own a nontrivial fraction of the shares. The relatively high frequency of widely held corporations in the United States is partially explained by the country's well-developed stock markets and legal system that help to protect the interests of small shareholders.

Corporate governance is the popular term used to describe organizational architecture at the top of a corporation. Alternative governance systems are often evaluated based on three key objectives that relate to value creation and survival of corporations: (1) the motivation of value-maximizing decisions; (2) the protection of assets from unauthorized acquisition, use, or disposition; and (3) the production of proper financial statements that meet the legal requirements.

Operational control of large corporations is delegated to professional managers who are overseen by a board of directors who have limited financial interests in the firm. Concerns about *separation of ownership and control* have led some scholars to question the social and productive efficiency of the corporate form of organization. Nevertheless, large publicly traded corporations have accounted for most of the free world's industrial output for decades. Raising capital from diversified investors is particularly important for large firms that require significant funds to finance investment, and is the primary reason why most large firms are organized as publicly traded corporations. Public corporations also benefit from not having to restrict the supply of top managers to people who are rich enough to buy large firms.

Separation of *decision control* and *decision management* is critical when, as in the case of publicly traded companies, decision makers do not bear the full wealth effect of their actions. Top-level authority in corporations is divided among shareholders, the board of directors, and top management. Other groups that can have roles in the decision-making process include the bondholders, preferred stock stockholders, lenders, independent auditors, and stock/credit analysts. The allocation of decision rights at the top of the firm is determined by law/regulation and voluntary choices, such as signing an agreement that grants specific decision rights to the contracting parties.

While shareholders are traditionally viewed as the ultimate owners of the corporation they have only limited powers to participate in the management of the company. Controversy exists as to whether shareholders should be given additional decision rights in the United States. Shareholders can be divided into three basic types: Small shareholders, institutional investors, and large blockholders. All shareholders benefit from increases in share price. However, they vary in their incentives to participate in the governance process and in terms of countervailing incentives that can motivate actions that are inconsistent with maximizing the value of the shares.

While the board of directors has primary legal authority for managing the firm, the typical board delegates much of this authority to professional managers. The board's primary function is top-level decision control—general oversight of the corporation and ratification of important decisions. Board composition, structure, and processes vary significantly across firms and through time—there is no one design that is optimal for all firms. Debate exists over whether the typical board is "captured by managers." Prominent examples exist where boards have fired powerful chairmen/CEOs.

The *chief executive officer* (CEO) is the top executive officer of the corporation. The CEO does not have the relevant knowledge or time to make all (or even most) of the decisions within a large and complex organization. Many decisions are delegated to lower-level employees. *Succession planning* is an important task performed by the board and top management.

Top managers from throughout the world receive a reasonable fraction of their pay in the form of *performance-based compensation*. Nevertheless, debate continues on whether the typical firm uses optimal incentive plans and whether the typical CEO receives more than a competitive wage.

Prominent external monitors include public accounting firms, stock market analysts, commercial banks, credit rating agencies, attorneys, and regulatory authorities [Securities Exchange Commission (SEC) and state attorneys general]. Many of these external monitors experienced criticism, litigation, and increased regulation following the recent business scandals.

German and Japanese governance systems are not directed at maximizing shareholder wealth. Rather their traditional focus has been on a broader set of *stakeholders* including employees, banks, affiliated companies, the broader community, and shareholders. The relatively strong performance of U.S. companies during the 1990s motivated many foreign countries and companies to adopt "investor reforms" based on the U.S. model. One problem with governance systems that focus on multiple stakeholders is that they do not provide clear guidance to managers when the interests of stakeholders conflict.

Corporate boards and managers face important constraints imposed by external control mechanisms. Three of the most important external control mechanisms are the market for corporate control, the managerial labor market, and product market competition. Corporate disclosures of financial information allow these external mechanisms to help control corporate insiders.

Congress responded to a flurry of business scandals by passing the *Sarbanes-Oxley Act of 2002 (SOX)*. SOX has a wide range of provisions and touches on many of the issues that arose during the business scandals, including internal monitoring, public auditing, activities by external monitors, executive loans, and disclosure. The new demands on corporate boards and the limitations on management contracts and corporate actions increase the costs of organizing as a public corporation substantially. While many large firms have no feasible alternative to organizing as publicly traded corporations, some smaller firms have chosen to "go private" and convert to closely held companies. Others have delayed going public. While the evidence is controversial, it generally supports the notion that the costs of SOX have been significant, while the benefits have been elusive.

The debate on how to improve corporate governance continues in the aftermath of the 2001–2002 corporate scandals. This debate is useful since it could lead to new insights into how to improve corporate governance. Nevertheless, it is important to recognize that corporate governance is not as flawed as some critics contend. While improvements in governance are conceptually possible, it is critical to consider both the costs and benefits when evaluating governance changes at either the firm or regulatory level.

Suggested Reading	D. Chew Jr. and S. Gillan, Eds. (2005), *Corporate Governance at the Crossroads, A Book of Readings* (McGraw-Hill Education: New York).

Self-Evaluation Problems

18–1. Your boss notes that "small shareholders typically free ride on the voting process, while traditionally most institutional investors have not been active in the governance process. Thus, management often appears to control the proxy solicitation process. Moreover, their proposals almost always pass." Based on these observations she has concluded that shareholder voting is a "useless process." She asks your opinion.

18–2. Cisco shareholders recently voted down a shareholder proposal that asked Cisco's management to pay out its large cash reserves to shareholders in the form of dividends (Cisco currently has significant short-term assets, including cash and investment securities). The sponsor of the proposal argued that it is the shareholders' money and that it should be distributed to them. The vote was nearly 10 to 1 against the proposal.

    a. Does the outcome of this vote imply that the voting process is controlled by managers and that shareholders do not have a voice in the company? Explain.

    b. The proponent of the proposal also asserts that management's reluctance to pay dividends is related to the way they are compensated. Explain why this argument might be true.

Solutions to Self-Evaluation Problems

18–1. Shareholder Voting

No. While corporate voting is perfunctory in routine cases, it has been actively used in certain cases to force change in an organization. For example, dissident shareholders can engage in a proxy contest to elect nonmanagement supported board members. When these contests are successful there is often a subsequent merger or restructuring that benefits shareholders. Even if proxy contests don't occur on a routine basis, the threat of a proxy contest can help to discipline managers (recall the example of Chrysler Motors). The empirical evidence suggests that proxy contests are an important governance mechanism that increases shareholder value. Concentrated owners have incentives to take an active role in the voting process. Recall the example of HP.

18–2. Cisco Shareholder Proposal

    a. This outcome does not necessarily imply that the process is controlled by managers. It could be in the interests of shareholders for the company to maintain the cash reserves. For example, Cisco might have potential investment options and the shareholders might want the company to hold onto the cash to finance these options. Just because one shareholder wants higher dividends does not make it value maximizing to increase the payouts.

b. Executive stock options are not usually dividend protected—the exercise price is not adjusted for decreases in stock price that are due to dividend payments. Thus, an important variable in valuing these options is the company's dividend yield. Higher dividends result in lower option prices. Cisco executives receive a substantial part of their compensation through stock options. Thus, they can have an incentive not to pay out dividends (to maintain the value of these options).

Review Questions

18–1. What is a corporation? Describe the major characteristics of a large publicly traded corporation.

18–2. What incentive conflicts exist in corporations?

18–3. What mechanisms are used to address the incentive conflicts in corporations?

18–4. What costs do incentive conflicts in corporations generate?

18–5. Is it optimal to completely eliminate incentive conflicts in corporations through extensive monitoring and bonding activities? For example, is the optimal amount of corporate fraud zero?

18–6. Do recent corporate scandals suggest that there are serious governance problems in most large corporations?

18–7. What are the three key objectives of corporate governance?

18–8. What is the "business judgment rule"? Discuss the economic logic for this legal precedent.

18–9. What are the major costs and benefits of organizing as a publicly traded corporation?

18–10. What are the primary sources of decision rights at the top of publicly traded corporations? Discuss the allocation of decision rights at the top of the typical U.S. corporation.

18–11. Why is it important to separate decision management and control in publicly traded corporations? Discuss how a well-designed governance system achieves this objective.

18–12. Are the stock exchanges' new rules relating to corporate boards of directors the answer to existing governance concerns in the United States?

18–13. What characteristics do you think are important in evaluating the quality of a corporate board?

18–14. What incentives, if any, do board members and management have to work in the interests of shareholders and the corporation?

18–15. Discuss how "market forces" help to reinforce internal governance systems.

18–16. What is the Sarbanes-Oxley Act of 2002 (SOX)? List its major provisions. Discuss the costs and benefits of the SOX and evidence on whether the net benefits have been positive or negative.

18–17. What external parties monitor managers? Assess how these parties performed their roles in the 1990s. Discuss the current pressures on these parties.

18–18. Compare and contrast the key features of the traditional corporate governance systems found in the United States, Japan, and Germany.

18–19. Briefly discuss the effects and motives for recent changes and trends in corporate governance in Europe and Japan.

18–20. What role does the SEC play in corporate governance in the United States?

18–21. What does it mean to "overpay" a CEO? Do you think that some CEOs are overpaid? What about the "typical" CEO?

18–22. Are stock options to blame for the earnings management scandals?

18–23. Have institutional investors been very active in the corporate governance process over the past 20 years? Which institutional investors have been the most active? Why?

18–24. What changes have been taking place in shareholder activism since the recent business scandals?

18–25. Have shareholder proposals been an important governance mechanism over the past 20 years? Do you see any changes occurring in today's environment?

18–26. What is meant by cumulative voting, classified board, and voting by proxy?

18–27. What are the benefits and costs of corporate voting over the Internet? Do you think this type of voting will increase in the future?

18–28. What is a proxy fight? What potential effects do proxy fights have on managerial incentives?

18–29. Discuss why CEO succession planning is an important activity for the board of directors.

18–30. Describe the "passing the baton" approach to CEO succession. What other methods are used?

18–31. Is the likelihood of CEO turnover related to firm performance? Give several examples to support your position.

18–32. (Extended activity) Go to the SEC EDGAR Web site (www.sec.gov/cgi-bin/srch-edgar). Search for the recent SEC filings of a publicly traded company (such as Walmart Stores Inc.). Review the firm's most recent proxy statement (form DEF 14 A). Summarize and evaluate the firms' board of directors (composition, committee structure, etc.) and executive compensation policies.

18–33. Suppose you were to estimate a statistical model explaining the relation between the degree of ownership concentration and the following variables: (1) the degree of regulation in the industry, (2) firm size, and (3) stock price volatility. Predict the signs on each of these variables and explain the logic for your predictions.

Web Appendix: Choosing among the Legal Forms of Organization

The Appendix to Chapter 18, "Choosing among the Legal Forms of Organization," can be found via McGraw-Hill *Connect*®. For more information, refer to the Preface.

chapter 19

Vertical Integration and Outsourcing

LEARNING OBJECTIVES

1. Identify what the vertical chain of production is for a particular industry.

2. Discuss the benefits of purchasing inputs and downstream services in competitive markets.

3. Explain how contracting costs, market power, taxes/regulation, and other considerations can motivate firms to acquire inputs and downstream services through nonmarket transactions.

4. Describe the major factors that determine whether it is better for a firm to vertically integrate or to obtain inputs and downstream services from other firms through long-term contracts.

5. Define the term firm-specific assets and explain why they can cause problems in contracting with outside suppliers and distributors.

6. List and explain the major determinants of the optimal contract length.

7. Discuss how free rider problems can arise when contracting with multiple independent distributors and how various contract provisions can be used to reduce these problems.

8. Explain the double-markup problem and how various contract provisions can be used to address it.

9. Describe the underlying factors that have motivated the observed trends in outsourcing over the past few decades.

In 1983, Apple Computer executives bragged that the Macintosh was a "machine that is made in America."[1] A few years later while he was managing NeXT Computer, Steve Jobs asserted, "I am as proud of our factory as I am the computer." As late as 2002, top Apple executives would drive about two hours to visit the company's iMac plant in Elk Grove, California. Today in 2014, Apple does almost no manufacturing or assembly "in house." Rather it *outsources* the manufacturing and assembly of its millions of iPhones, iPad's, and computers to outside and mostly foreign companies. Many of these outside companies provide services to other companies, some of which compete with Apple. For example, Foxconn—the large Taiwanese multinational that assembles iPhones—manufactures products

[1] Sources for the motivating examples in this section include, C. Duhigg and K. Bradsher (2012), "How the U.S. Lost out on iPhone Work," *New York Times* (January 21); and Special Report: Outsourcing and Offshoring (2013) "Here, There and Everywhere," *The Economist* (January 19), 4.

for other tech firms, such as Blackberry, Kindle, PlayStation 4 and Xbox One. The typical U.S. manufacturer across all industries now outsources between 70 and 80 percent of its finished product. "Crucial semiconductors" inside the iPhone 4 and 4S are manufactured in Austin, Texas in a factory owned by one of Apple's primary competitors, Samsung of South Korea. Outsourcing is not limited to manufacturing. Companies spend billions of dollars annually to acquire a wide range of services and products from other companies, including data processing, catering, copying, call centers, advertising, bookkeeping/payroll, transportation, security, janitorial services, refuse collection, and software testing.

While companies outsource many activities, they perform others in-house using their own employees and assets. For example, Apple owns a large chain of retail stores staffed by company employees, and its U.S. employees perform most of the company's product and software development, as well as design and marketing functions. Apple recently built a $500 million data center in North Carolina.

Firms change their outsourcing decisions over time. Prominent U.S. companies, such as Google, General Electric, Caterpillar, and Ford Motor Company, recently have "re-shored" various activities that they previously had outsourced to foreign suppliers by bringing production back to America. In December 2013, Apple said that it would start making a line of its Mac Computers in America. Some of these companies are bringing activities back in-house; in other cases they are outsourcing them to outside companies operating in the United States. Lenovo, which by some measures is now the biggest PC-maker in the world, recently opened a plant in Whitsett, North Carolina. Lenovo is a highly successful Chinese technology company, which bought IBM's ThinkPad PC business in 2005.

Outsourcing involves a fundamental change in organizational architecture. First, it reassigns decision rights relating to certain assets and employees from one firm to another. For example, Foxconn owns the dozens of facilities in Asia, Eastern Europe, Mexico, and Brazil that assemble an estimated 40 percent of the world's consumer electronics for customers such as Amazon, Dell, Hewlett Packard, Motorola, Nintendo, Samsung, and Sony. Foxconn retains all of the decision rights at these plants that are not specified in their contracts with other companies or by law. Second, compensation and performance-evaluation systems generally change with outsourcing. The Foxconn factory in China, which assembles iPhones, employs around 230,000 people. In comparison to Apple employees in the United States, Foxconn expects its employees to work longer hours each week. While compensation is much lower in China, employees live in company provided barracks and over the past few years have been paid about $17 a day. Some pay raises have been conditional on the employee passing a three-month performance evaluation.

This discussion of outsourcing raises a number of important questions:

- What are the costs and benefits in choosing between the alternative architectures that are implied by within-firm production versus outsourcing?

- What activities are most likely to be outsourced? Why are functions such as manufacturing, data processing, catering, copying, and trucking among the more frequently outsourced services? Why does Apple maintain ownership of assets that are used on-site by some of their outsourcing partners?

- When a company outsources, what are the determinants of the specific contract provisions? Why might a company negotiate a 10-year contract instead of a 1-year contract? Why do some firms grant distributors exclusive rights to particular territories?

- What has motivated the trend in increased outsourcing over the past few decades and why have some major companies recently brought various functions back to the United States?

We begin by discussing the process of producing and marketing products. We then discuss trade-offs among alternative ways of organizing the steps in this process (market transactions, long-term contracts, and vertical integration), the appropriate length of a contract, contracting with independent distributors, and reasons for the recent increases in outsourcing. In the appendix to this chapter, we provide a more detailed example that highlights some of the trade-offs between company ownership and outsourcing.

Vertical Chain of Production

Consumer goods are produced through a series of steps described by the *vertical chain of production*.[2] Figure 19.1 depicts this vertical chain for personal computers. At the top of the chain are the raw materials such as chemicals, metals, and rubber that are used as inputs to produce PCs. These inputs are transported to processors that make the intermediate products used in the final construction of PCs (for instance, plastics manufacturers, chip makers, and operating software producers). The intermediate goods are transported to companies that assemble them into PCs. Finally, the

Figure 19.1   The Vertical Chain of Production for Personal Computers

At the top of the chain are the raw materials, such as chemicals, metals, and rubber, that are used as inputs to produce PCs. These inputs are transported to intermediate-goods processors. These processors (for instance, plastics manufacturers, chip makers, and operating software producers) make the intermediate products used in the final construction of the PCs. These intermediate goods must be transported to the companies that assemble them into the final consumer products. These products then are transported to retail stores, which sell them to consumers. Each step of the vertical chain is supported by administrative services such as accounting, finance, and marketing.

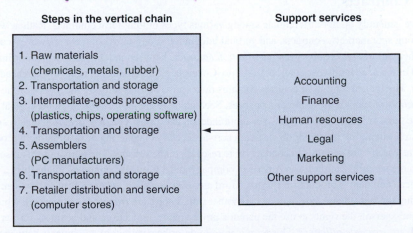

[2]D. Besanko, D. Dranove, and M. Shanley (1995), *The Economics of Strategy* (John Wiley & Sons: New York), 71.

PCs are transported to retail stores, which sell them to consumers and provide after-sales servicing. Each step of this vertical chain is supported by administrative services such as accounting, finance, and marketing. Firms can locate at different positions along the vertical chain. Intel is an intermediate-goods processor that manufactures computer chips; Dell Computers sells PCs and concentrates on final assembly and distribution. Firms also can specialize in providing support services (for instance, shipping and accounting firms).

When a firm participates in more than one successive stage in the vertical chain, it is said to be *vertically integrated.* Firms vary dramatically in their degree of vertical integration. Dell Computers leases much of its manufacturing space and makes virtually none of its component parts. It does not make or even stock the many software products that it sells. IBM historically has been much more vertically integrated, producing many of its component parts and much of its software in-house. IBM also maintains its own sales force for mainframe computers.

Firms change their degree of integration over time. An organization that begins to produce its own inputs is engaging in *backward,* or *upstream,* integration, whereas an organization that begins to market its own goods or to conduct additional finishing work is engaging in *forward,* or *downstream,* integration. Lincoln Electric integrated backward when it began manufacturing certain inputs for its welding machines that previously were supplied by outside companies. Apple integrated forward when it opened Apple stores to sell its desktops, laptops, and iPods.

The term *outsourcing* frequently is used to describe a movement away from vertical integration—moving an activity outside the firm that formerly was done within the firm. An example of this usage is "Manulife outsourced its computer operations to IBM in 2011 in a seven-year $665 million deal." The term *outsourcing* also is used to describe an ongoing arrangement whereby a firm obtains a part or service from an external firm. An example of this usage is "Reebok always has outsourced most of its footwear production to foreign companies."

MANAGERIAL APPLICATIONS

Long-Term Contracts

In this chapter, we generally do not differentiate among various types of long-term contracts. Rather, we focus on how firms choose among spot markets, contracts, and vertical integration. Long-term contracts, however, can take a variety of forms. First, there are *standard supply and distribution contracts* between independent firms. For instance, in 2014 EMCOR entered into a new, multiyear contract to supply Coverglass Interconnected Cells to Lockheed Martin for its satellite program. The typical long-term contract contains many provisions specifying the nature of the service and the duties and obligations of each of the contracting parties. Second, there are *joint ventures.* In the typical joint venture, a new firm is formed that is jointly owned by two or more independent firms. The new firm might be responsible for conducting research, supplying inputs, or downstream activities such as marketing or distributing a product. Drug companies form research joint ventures to conduct basic research on new drugs. The output of this research is shared by the partners in the venture. Similarly, an American company and a European company might form a joint venture to market the American company's products in Europe. Third are *lease contracts,* where a firm acquires an asset such as a machine or building through a lease agreement with another firm. Fourth are *franchise agreements,* which grant an independent businessperson the rights to use the parent's proven name, reputation, and business format in a given market area. Fifth are *strategic alliances.* This term is used to describe a variety of agreements between independent firms to cooperate in the development and/or marketing of products. For instance, an airline company and a car rental company might agree to promote each other's products and to participate in joint promotional activities.

Figure 19.2 Outsourcing: Choosing along a Continuum

It often is useful to think of the outsourcing decision as a choice along a continuum of possibilities. At one extreme, a product or service can be purchased from any one of a large number of potential suppliers in the spot market. At the other extreme, the company can produce the product or service internally within a division of the vertically integrated firm. Between these extremes are various long-term contracts. Contracts take a variety of forms, including standard supply and distribution contracts, joint ventures, lease contracts, franchise agreements, and strategic alliances.

Spot markets   Long-term contracts   Vertical integration

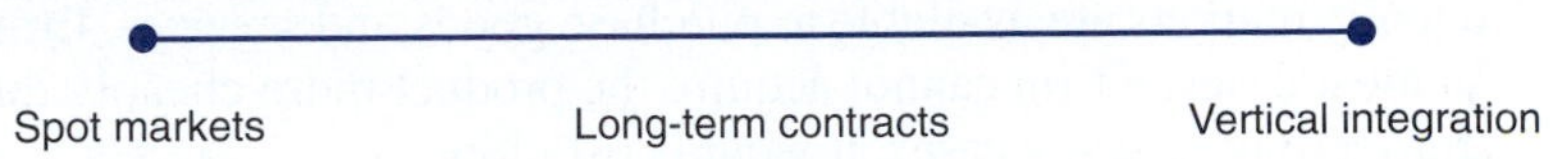

Often it is useful to think of the outsourcing decision as a choice along a continuum of possibilities. As depicted in Figure 19.2, at one extreme, the part or service is purchased from any one of a large number of potential suppliers in the *spot market* (where the exchange is made immediately at the current market price with no long-term commitment between the buyer and the seller). At the other extreme, a company vertically integrates and produces the part or service internally.[3] Between these extremes are long-term contracts between independent or quasi-independent firms. Long-term contracts take many forms, including long-term supply and distribution contracts, franchise agreements, leasing contracts, joint ventures, and strategic alliances. Many of the recent outsourcing decisions move the firm from vertical integration to long-term contracting (Manulife and IBM for various computer services, DuPont and Lanier for copying services). We begin our analysis of outsourcing by considering some of the advantages of acquiring parts and services in spot markets. We use the term *market transactions* to refer to sales and purchases in the spot market; we use the term *nonmarket transactions* to refer either to vertical integration or to long-term contracts.

MANAGERIAL APPLICATIONS

Vertical Outsourcing by Taiwan Semiconductor

For years electronic companies like Motorola produced most of their chips to "in-house" to control quality and design. By 2002 Motorola had outsourced a substantial fraction of the chips it used. In that year, Taiwan Semiconductor Manufacturing Co. (TSMC) and Motorola announced an expanded outsourcing program wherein TSMC would double its chip manufacturing capacity by 2006. In the late 1990s, TSMC obtained most of its revenues from chip manufacturing. Since then TSMC has vertically integrated additional design and manufacturing services to get customers to outsource both these functions. In 2013, TSMC recorded $20 billion in sales compared to only $1.5 billion in 1999. Its outsourcing customers include one of the world's leading semiconductor and system companies (e.g., Advanced Micro Devices), as well as integrated devices manufacturers, such as Texas Instruments.

Source: J. Moore (1999), "TSMC's Chip Business Booms as More Companies Outsource," *BusinessWeek* (June 21), 128; Motorola.com (June 26, 2002); and TSMC (2014), SEC *Form 20-F* (April 14).

---

[3]See Chapter 17 for a discussion of how firms organize internal production into divisions and the corresponding transfer-pricing issues.

Benefits of Buying in Competitive Markets

Figure 19.3 presents the standard diagram of a competitive equilibrium. The figure illustrates that competitive markets result in efficient production: Production occurs at the lowest possible average cost per unit. Price equals average cost, implying that buyers acquire the product at cost (which of course includes a normal rate of return on investment).[4] Over time, suppliers adopt technological advances that lower the costs of production and/or enhance the quality of the product. Lower costs are passed to buyers in the form of lower prices. This analysis suggests that when competitive outside markets are available to purchase goods and services, firms should use them. In most cases, a firm cannot acquire the product more cheaply through a nonmarket transaction; in many cases, it would cost more.

One common concern with internal production is generating sufficient volume to take advantage of scale economies in production. In Figure 19.3, the minimum point on the average cost curve is at a volume of Q^* units. Individual firms in the marketplace produce this volume. If a firm requires less than Q^* units and produces only that amount internally, it will incur higher average costs. The firm could produce Q^* and sell the surplus in the open market. However, this choice requires the firm to

---

Figure 19.3   Competitive Equilibrium

This figure illustrates that competitive markets result in efficient production. The right panel displays the supply-and-demand curves for the industry. Their intersection determines the market price. The left panel pictures the output decision of the marginal firm in the industry. Production occurs at the lowest-possible long-run average cost (LRAC). Buyers acquire the product at cost (P^* = LRAC = LRMC, where LRMC = long-run marginal cost). The analysis suggests that when competitive outside markets for inputs are available, firms should use them. In most cases, the firm cannot produce more cheaply itself, and in many cases it will cost more.

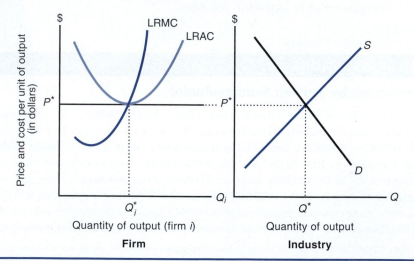

---

[4]Recall that if price is above long-run average cost, firms are making economic profits and new firms enter the industry. The increase in supply drives down the price. Alternatively, if price is below long-run average cost, firms are losing money and exit occurs.

enter a new market—one that is not its primary line of business. Diversifying into unrelated fields can reduce value. Empirical studies suggest that diversified firms frequently perform poorly relative to firms that are more focused.[5]

Another concern with nonmarket procurement is the cost of motivating efficient production. Divisions within large firms can be inefficient, yet continue to survive, so long as they are subsidized by more profitable units within the firm. Firms must adopt costly incentive and control systems to motivate internal managers to engage in efficient production. Similarly, parties to a long-term supply contract must be motivated to carry out their parts of the agreement. Independent firms, on the other hand, face more direct market pressures. If they are inefficient in their main line of business, they lose money and eventually are forced to liquidate.

Due to such concerns, most firms use markets to acquire many, if not most, of their inputs. Few companies produce their own trucks, fuel, copy machines, pencils, staples, telephones, office furniture, or bathroom fixtures. Most of these products are acquired through market transactions. Also, firms generally rely on external markets for many of their downstream activities, such as product distribution. For instance, Procter & Gamble sells many of its products, such as soap and toothpaste, through independent grocery stores and drugstores. The key point is that well-functioning markets provide powerful incentives for efficient production and low prices. It is value-maximizing to acquire many goods and services through market transactions.

Reasons for Nonmarket Transactions

Our analysis might appear to argue against nonmarket transactions: Firms should concentrate on a particular stage of the production/distribution process and acquire other inputs and services using market transactions with outside suppliers and distributors. There are, however, at least three potentially important reasons why firms use nonmarket transactions to acquire inputs and downstream services: contracting costs, market power, and taxes/regulation.

Contracting Costs

We have discussed the architecture of markets. We argued that markets effectively link specific knowledge and decision rights; moreover, they provide incentives for decision makers to use this information effectively. We posed the question: *Why aren't all economic transactions conducted through markets?* Ronald Coase provided the basic answer to this question by arguing that market transactions are not costless.[6] For instance, they involve the costs of searching for trading partners and negotiating relevant prices. Parties to a transaction have incentives to use other mechanisms, such as internal production, when the transaction can be accomplished at a lower cost. At least four factors can make the costs of nonmarket transactions

---

[5]P. Berger and E. Ofek (1995), "Diversification's Effect on Firm Value," *Journal of Financial Economics* 37, 39–65; R. Comment (1995), "Corporate Focus and Stock Returns," *Journal of Financial Economics* 37, 67–87; and K. John and E. Ofek (1995), "Asset Sales and Increase in Focus," *Journal of Financial Economics* 37, 105–126.

[6]For a collection of Coase's 1991 Nobel-Prize winning work on this topic, see R. Coase (1988), *The Firm, the Market, and the Law* (University of Chicago Press: Chicago).

MANAGERIAL APPLICATIONS

Made in the USA

Companies sometimes label their products "Made in the USA." This statement apparently appeals to the sentiment among some consumers that Americans should purchase only American-made products to protect domestic jobs. The claim also helps companies gain contracts from the U.S. government. The common practice of acquiring many inputs from outside suppliers, however, makes it difficult to define what really is made in the USA. For example, today an "American" car sold in Chicago could have rolled off an assembly line in Tennessee with parts made in dozens of different countries.

The Federal Trade Commission (FTC) is charged with policing firms for false or misleading claims about the country of origin. Defining the country of origin, however, is very difficult in practice and that is why it takes the FTC 40 pages to try to explain the rules. According to the FTC, a California radio manufacturer can claim its product was made in America even though it has a plastic case made from imported oil. Similarly, so can a computer maker in Texas, that is, building a PC from American made parts that include a disk drive with a case made from steel imported from overseas. However, a wrench produced in Ohio with steel imported from Korea, cannot be labeled as made in America because the steel represents a "significant cost" of production. The rules are somewhat ambiguous to say the least. The FTC typically warns a first-time offender that it believes is making a misleading claim. If the company "breaks the rules again" is likely be hit with a large fine for each infraction.

Source: J. Schoen (2010), "Made in America' rules are complex, confusing," *NBCNEWS.com* (March 15).

---

lower than the costs of market exchanges. These factors include *firm-specific assets*, *costs of measuring quality*, *externalities,* and *coordination problems*.

Firm-Specific Assets[7]

Production typically requires investment in assets. As examples, IBM requires mainframe computers to provide computer services to other companies and suppliers require machines to make parts. Sometimes these assets can be transferred easily among alternative uses. Mainframe computers are general-purpose machines that can be used to serve a variety of companies. Other assets are significantly more valuable in their current use than in their next best alternative. For example, the Alaska Pipeline is materially more valuable for transporting oil than for any other conceivable use. If IBM writes a specialized computer program to run a given company's payroll, the program is more valuable for that firm's payroll than for some other firm's payroll (which might offer different fringe benefits, for instance). Although the program could be adapted for use by other firms, changing the program is costly. Assets that are substantially more valuable in their current use than in their next best alternative use are referred to as *firm-specific assets*. Asset specificity is most likely to occur in four particular instances.[8]

- **Site Specificity.** The asset is located in a particular area that makes it useful only to a small number of buyers or suppliers, and it cannot be moved easily. An example is the Alaska Pipeline, which can be used only by oil producers on Alaska's north slope.

- **Physical-Asset Specificity.** Product design makes the asset especially useful only to a small number of buyers. An example is a specialized machine tool that is used to make parts for one particular model of automobile.

---

[7]This section draws on B. Klein, R. Crawford, and A. Alchian (1978), "Vertical Integration, Appropriable Rents, and the Competitive Contracting Process," *Journal of Law & Economics* 24, 297–326.

[8]O. Williamson (1985), *The Economic Institutions of Capitalism* (Free Press: New York).

- **Human-Asset Specificity.** The transaction requires specialized knowledge on the part of the parties to the transaction. An example is the knowledge that IBM employees must acquire about another company's unique processes in order to provide computer services to the company.

- **Dedicated Assets.** The expansion in facilities is necessitated only by the requirements of a few buyers. An example is a chip producer who adds extra capacity to serve one particular computer company.

If a supplier invests in a specific asset to serve a particular customer, that supplier places itself in a tenuous position for future negotiations. For example, consider a supplier who invests $50,000 for a machine tool (such as a metal punch-press die) to produce a particular part. The part is used only by one manufacturer, and the die has no other uses or salvage value—it is extremely firm-specific. The variable cost of production is $1 per unit and the useful life of the die is 50,000 units. The supplier must be able to sell the parts for at least $2 per unit to break even. The buyer, however, is in a strong position to argue for a price concession after the investment in the die is made. At this point, the investment is a *sunk cost,* and the supplier will continue to operate as long as it can cover its variable costs of $1 per unit. Thus, the buyer potentially can force the supplier to accept a price as low as $1, even though the supplier loses its initial investment. Anticipating this *holdup problem,* the supplier will not invest in the machine tool in the first place unless it receives some effective guarantee that the buyer will continue to pay at least $2 per unit and will buy 50,000 units.

Buyers face potential holdup problems as well if they purchase key inputs from a single supplier that has invested in the relevant firm-specific assets. For instance, a specialized chip supplier might demand a large price increase when it knows that a computer company has a large backlog of orders and that it has no alternative sources of supply.

These potential holdup problems can be controlled by vertical integration. If the buying firm invests in the machine and produces the part internally, it does not have to worry about subsequent renegotiations with its supplier over prices. An alternative to integration would be for the buyer and supplier to enter into a long-term supply contract. The buyer might agree to purchase 50,000 units from the supplier over the next five years at a cost of $2.10 per unit. Contracts are not costless to write or to enforce, and so the preferred alternative depends on the relative costs of vertical integration versus contracting. This trade-off is considered in greater detail below.

Measuring Quality

It is difficult to monitor the quality of some inputs and services. The buyer might not be able to learn that a part is defective until long after purchase. In such cases sellers can have the incentive to cheat buying firms: Once a price is set, a supplier can increase its profits by supplying a lower-quality, lower-cost product. Buyers sometimes can avoid these problems by transacting with companies that have established reputations for quality and/or can offer credible warranties for their products. Otherwise, buyers either should negotiate a long-term supply contract that provides appropriate incentives for quality production or should produce such products in-house. Internal production and long-term contracts are especially useful when maintaining the quality of the part is critical for the overall success of the product. These nonmarket forms of organization do not necessarily change the distribution of information among the parties. However, they allow the company to develop contractual incentives that motivate quality production.

Controlling Externalities

Firms often invest in developing reputations and customer loyalty. This investment can increase the demand for a company's products. However, firms can have problems motivating independently owned distributors to invest sufficient resources to maintain a brand name—there is a free-rider problem. Independent retailers in a distribution system have incentives to shirk on advertising and depend on the efforts of other units in the system to attract customers. These retailers also might want to cut costs by hiring less skilled, lower-priced labor. A given owner of a retail unit receives all the benefits from reducing the unit's labor costs but bears only part of the costs from providing poor service to customers: Any decline in future sales is likely to be shared with other units. The incentives to free-ride are particularly large when the retailer deals with customers who are not likely to make repeat purchases at the particular unit.

This free-rider problem can be controlled either through vertical integration, where managers of stores are compensated in ways that discourage free-riding, or through long-term contracts with terms that motivate increased sales efforts. We provide a more detailed discussion of such distribution contracts later in this chapter.

Extensive Coordination

Some activities require extensive coordination. For example, railroads rely on extensive feeder traffic for their routes. In principle, it would be possible to use the price system for each link within this network. Rail companies could pay one another to use their lines, with prices adjusting to changes in supply and demand. But such a system would be complicated and expensive to operate. An alternative is for the railroad companies in the network to merge and to manage the various coordination problems internally. Railroad companies were among the first large firms in the United States. These large firms were motivated, at least in part, by the benefits of using internal managers, rather than market transactions, to coordinate rail activity.[9]

A related reason for vertical integration is to coordinate pricing and service decisions among retail units. The pricing decisions of individual retailers can have effects on other units in the system—they produce a kind of externality. For instance, it might be optimal from a companywide standpoint to set prices where some units sustain losses. (When McDonald's stays open, customers are less likely to try Burger King.) Independent retailers cannot be expected to set optimal systemwide prices since they care only about the profits from their own units. In principle, the central company could set the retail prices; but antitrust law limits this solution. The company can coordinate prices if it owns its retail outlets.

Market Power

A firm with market power might use vertical integration to increase profits in several different ways. The following example illustrates one of these methods—using vertical integration to price-discriminate.[10] Consider a firm, DrugCo, that has a patent on a particular chemical compound used as an input in the production of two different pharmaceutical products. One of the products is a pain reliever that competes with many other pain relievers. The other helps cure a particular type of

---

[9]A. Chandler (1977), *The Visible Hand—The Managerial Revolution in American Business* (Belknap Press: Cambridge). Also, D. Carlton and M. Klamer (1983), "The Need for Coordination among Firms with Special Reference to Network Industries," *University of Chicago Law Review* 50, 446–465.

[10]For additional methods, see Carlton and Perloff (1990), Chapter 6.

cancer and faces no close substitutes. The industry demand for the two retail products (pain reliever and cancer drug) is given by

$$\text{Pain relief:} \qquad P = 100 - 5Q \qquad (19.1)$$
$$\text{Cancer drug:} \qquad P = 200 - 10Q \qquad (19.2)$$

The marginal cost to DrugCo for producing the chemical compound is $10 per gram. For simplicity, suppose that a drug manufacturer can take the chemical compound and transform it into 1 gram of either retail product (pain reliever or cancer drug) at zero marginal cost incurring no additional distribution or marketing costs. Many manufacturers can produce and distribute the retail drugs. Competition among these retail manufacturers will drive the retail prices of the pain reliever and cancer drug down to the retail manufacturers' marginal costs, which in this example is the wholesale price of DrugCo's chemical compound. Thus, the demand curves facing DrugCo at the wholesale level are the same as the retail demand curves given in Equations (19.1) and (19.2).

To maximize total profits, DrugCo would like to set marginal revenue equal to marginal cost in each market. As shown in Figure 19.4, the optimal price to charge retail drug manufacturers who produce the pain reliever is $55. The optimal price for those who produce the cancer drug is $105.[11] Since both retail markets are competitive and

Figure 19.4   Using Vertical Integration to Price-Discriminate

DrugCo has a patent on a chemical compound used as an input in the production of two different pharmaceutical products: a pain reliever that competes with many other products and a cancer drug. The marginal cost to DrugCo for producing the chemical compound is $10 per gram. The industry-level demand curves for the two products are the same demand curves facing DrugCo for the chemical compound. The optimal price to charge manufacturers who produce the pain reliever is $55. The optimal price for those who produce the cancer drug is $105. However, if DrugCo tries to sell to some companies at $55 and others at $105, potential arbitrage is available. One way to price-discriminate effectively is for DrugCo to integrate forward into the retail market for pain relievers. It would sell the pain reliever to consumers at $55 and the chemical compound to the manufacturers of the cancer drug at $105.

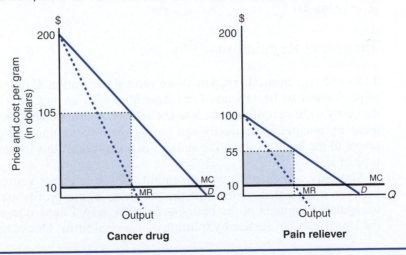

Cancer drug   Pain reliever

[11]Recall from Chapter 7 that these prices are easily found by setting the marginal revenue in each market (implied by the two demand curves) equal to the marginal cost of $10.

MANAGERIAL APPLICATIONS

Price Discrimination and Antitrust Law

Firms that integrate vertically to engage in price discrimination sometimes can be held accountable under antitrust law. Alcoa had market power in the production of virgin aluminum ingots, an intermediate good. It integrated into the lower-priced markets (e.g., rolled sheet) and "squeezed" competitors in these markets. The judge who wrote the opinion in the antitrust case proposed a "transfer-price test" to assess whether a firm is engaged in a price squeeze. The test considers whether the integrated firm could sell the final output profitably at prevailing prices, assuming it had to pay the same price for the input as it charges downstream competitors. The court determined Alcoa could not. (Note that in our example from the previous section, DrugCo would operate at a loss if it paid $105 for the input and sold the pain reliever to consumers at $55.)

Source: *United States v. Aluminum Company of America* (1945), 148 F. 2d, 416.

---

there are no other costs, the price to consumers in the two markets would be $55 and $105. However, if DrugCo tries to sell to some manufacturers at $55 and other manufacturers at $105, potential *arbitrage* is available: Manufacturers who buy at $55 can resell the chemical compound to other manufacturers at less than $105 and make a profit. They will undercut any attempt by DrugCo to sell to manufacturers at $105.

One way that DrugCo can prevent such arbitrage is to integrate forward and manufacture the pain reliever. The company would price the pain reliever at $55 in the retail market and sell the base drug at $105 in the wholesale market. Arbitrage is no longer possible (assuming that the pain reliever cannot be transformed back into the chemical compound at low cost). Integrating forward into the retail market for the cancer drug will not solve the problem. If DrugCo tries to price the cancer drug at $105 and sell the chemical compound at a wholesale price of $55, other retail manufacturers would begin to produce and market the cancer drug (after buying the chemical compound at $55) and assuming DrugCo does not have a patent for the process of producing the cancer drug. DrugCo would not be able to maintain a price of $105. It must integrate forward into the lower-priced (more *elastic*) pain-reliever market.

Taxes and Regulation

Taxes and regulation also can motivate vertical integration. If the profits of one stage of production are heavily taxed and those of another are not, total taxes might be reduced by shifting profits to the low-tax activity. A firm potentially can capture these gains by integrating vertically and having the low-tax unit charge higher transfer prices to the high-tax unit. Tax authorities are aware of this incentive and limit this type of activity.[12]

Similarly, a regulated company might want to integrate vertically to shift profits from a regulated segment of the business, where profits are restricted, to an unregulated segment of the business. In 1984, AT&T settled an antitrust suit with the Department of Justice by splitting into several firms. One of the concerns of the

---

[12]M. Scholes, M. Wolfson, M. Erickson, E. Maydew, and M. Hanlon (2011), *Taxes and Business Strategy: A Planning Approach,* 4th Edition (Prentice Hall: Englewood Cliffs), Chapters 10–11.

Justice Department was that it was difficult to monitor cost-shifting among AT&T's regulated businesses (e.g., telephone service) and other less regulated businesses (for instance, telephone equipment). The breakup of AT&T reduced these concerns.[13]

Other Considerations

Another potential motive for nonmarket procurement is to ensure the supply of an important input. In contrast to the standard economic model, shortages sometimes occur in actual markets. For example, theaters do not always raise ticket prices for popular movies. Rather, tickets are allocated on a first-come, first-served basis when demand exceeds theater capacity for a performance. Similarly, companies sometimes face rationing or short supply of particular inputs. Companies might integrate vertically or enter long-term contracts to increase the reliability of receiving an input.

Firms also use nonmarket procurement to avoid sharing proprietary information with other firms. For instance, a firm might be reluctant to provide an independent supplier with detailed information about its production processes because it fears that the supplier might share the information with other firms. Normally, it is easier to control the leakage of sensitive information when dealing with internal employees or long-term suppliers.

Another common explanation for nonmarket transactions relies on technological factors. For example, some people explain the common ownership of steel milling and steel production by the close technological links of the two processes. But this argument is flawed. Although it is true that there are benefits from having these operations at one location, technology does not dictate ownership. In principle, a steel mill could buy hot steel ingots from other companies located in the same building. The reasons it does not are due not to technological factors, but rather result from contracting problems: Independent companies do not want to expose themselves to potential holdup problems that arise from such firm-specific investments.

Vertical Integration versus Long-Term Contracts[14]

We have discussed reasons why a firm might acquire a good or service through a nonmarket transaction. We now consider the trade-offs between the two general types of nonmarket transactions, vertical integration and long-term contracts. We examine these trade-offs using the example of AutoCorp, a producer of new automobiles. AutoCorp is considering whether to produce its own auto bodies or to obtain them from an independent supplier through a long-term contract. In either case, a new auto body plant must be constructed. There will be ongoing production, maintenance, and capital-replacement costs. AutoCorp wants to choose the organizational arrangement that maximizes value.

---

[13]D. Carlton and J. Perloff (1990), *Modern Industrial Organization* (HarperCollins: New York).

[14]This section draws on Williamson (1985). Important references on this topic include Klein, Crawford, and Alchian (1978); S. Grossman and O. Hart (1986), "The Costs and Benefits of Ownership: A Theory of Vertical and Lateral Integration," *Journal of Political Economy* 94, 691–719; and O. Hart (1995), *Firms, Contracts, and Financial Structure* (Oxford Press: Oxford).

Incomplete Contracting

If contracts were costless to plan, negotiate, write, and enforce, it would not matter if AutoCorp made its own auto bodies or bought them from an outside supplier. In either case, a *complete contract* would be negotiated, one that specified exactly what was expected of each party under all possible future contingencies. Severe penalties would ensure compliance. The actions of each party would be chosen to maximize value (the level of investment, ongoing expenditures, production quantities, designs, and so on). With vertical integration, the contracts would be between the firm and employees, whereas a long-term supply contract would be between two independent firms.

Contracting, however, can be expensive. First, it is difficult to foresee and plan for all possible contingencies. AutoCorp surely will want to make future changes in the design of its auto bodies if customer tastes change or if a competitor develops a superior body design. However, AutoCorp's managers are unlikely to know the appropriate response until the new situation actually confronts them. Second, it is expensive to negotiate contracts. Self-interested parties often find it difficult to agree on contracts—consider the record of strikes by professional athletes. Third, it is costly to enforce contracts. Contracting costs necessitate *incomplete contracts:* Many contingencies will be omitted and thus left open for future negotiation. For example, some IBM outsourcing contracts state that IBM must maintain a state-of-the-art data center. The exact technology, software, and communications system are rarely specified. When contractual disputes arise, the contracting parties are likely to incur legal expenses and spend valuable time either preparing for court or renegotiating contracts.

The prospect of future negotiations can motivate suboptimal investment. Parties to the contract realize that part of the gains from their investments (in capital or effort) are likely to go to other parties: They are not protected by a complete contract. For example, as we discuss below, a supplier will be reluctant to invest effort or capital to reduce production costs if the buyer is likely to capture most of the gains by renegotiating a lower purchase price for the input.

Ownership and Investment Incentives

The owner has the right to determine the *residual use* of an asset—any use that does not conflict with prior contract, custom, or law. Residual rights give an individual increased ability to capture the gains from an investment and can affect investment incentives. For instance, house owners have the residual rights with respect to their properties. As long as their actions are consistent with the law and existing contracts (e.g., zoning requirements and restrictive covenants in the deed), they are free to sell or rent their houses. The ability of owners to capture the gains from investing in house repairs through higher selling prices makes it more likely that owners will take better care of houses than renters. Renters are reluctant to invest in repairs if much of the gains goes to owners.[15]

---

[15]C. Smith and L. Wakeman (1985), "Determinants of Corporate Leasing Policy," *Journal of Finance* 40, 896–908.

MANAGERIAL APPLICATIONS

Renting and Asset Abuse

Renters do not bear the total costs from abusing an asset, since it is owned by the rental company; thus, rental assets frequently are abused. "In one case, a fellow rented a sports car with 12 miles on it. He took out the high-powered engine and installed it in a 'stock car,' to run a high-speed 500-mile race. After crossing the finish line, he reinstalled the engine in the rental car and returned it. The rental company could not successfully prosecute because it failed to establish the number of miles that had been put on the engine. The rental car still showed low mileage, and the rental fee to the customer/car racer was only $24." More recently, there have been a growing number of videos posted on YouTube documenting extreme car rental abuse. Various companies now offer car rental companies GPS services that help to track and report on unwanted driving styles, including certain types of abuse that previously were difficult to detect.

Source: D. McIntyre (1988), "Rent a Reck," *Financial World* (September 20), 72; GPS Systems (2014), "Top 5 Car Rental Abuse Videos," gpssystems.net.

Vertical integration and long-term contracts differ in their assignment of ownership rights. Vertical integration keeps the ownership rights for the relevant assets within one firm, whereas long-term contracting apportions them between firms. As we discuss below, the optimal choice between vertical integration and long-term contracts depends, at least in part, on which ownership structure motivates the most productive investment decisions.

Specific Assets and Vertical Integration

Specific assets can cause substantial investment distortions among independent contractors. Consider the investment incentives of BodyWorks, a potential supplier to AutoCorp. BodyWorks would have to construct a plant next to one of AutoCorp's major production facilities. Transportation costs and special designs make this plant quite specific: It is of much less value to other car companies that are farther away and use different body designs. Asset specificity places BodyWorks in a tenuous position. Without the guarantee of a complete contract, BodyWorks will be concerned that AutoCorp will try to lower the price for auto bodies once the investment is made (recall from Chapter 5 that BodyWorks has incentives to operate as long as price is greater than *average variable cost*). AutoCorp might claim that BodyWorks is supplying low-quality products and demand a price concession. Given litigation costs, BodyWorks might be forced to accept the lower price. This concern reduces BodyWorks' incentives to invest in the plant. Similarly, AutoCorp might be reluctant to tailor-make their cars to fit BodyWorks products because it fears that BodyWorks will be opportunistic and increase the price for its auto bodies. In this example, investment incentives can be improved through vertical integration. If AutoCorp constructs its own auto body plant (or buys BodyWorks), it is in a position to capture the gains from its investment. It does not have to worry that some outside firm will try to extract part of the returns by demanding a different price for auto bodies. Other contracting costs might decline as well, since the companies do not have to negotiate a complicated legal contract.

Looking at the history of the U.S. auto industry suggests that this is, in fact, what happened. Originally, an automobile manufacturer would sell their customer an engine and transmission mounted on a frame with tires and wheels. The customer would then take the automobile to a coach-works company to build the body and seats. General Motors (GM) decided it would be more efficient if the engine, frame, and body were designed and produced jointly. GM acquired Fisher, a prominent coach-works manufacturer, and made it the Fisher Auto Body Division of GM.

These arguments help explain why vertical integration can be preferred to long-term contracting. Why is this not always the case? What limits the entire economy from being served by one gigantic firm that produces everything? The answer lies again in investment incentives. Consider AutoCorp's purchase of lightbulbs from LightCo. Since lightbulbs are not a specialized product, the purchasing arrangement harms neither LightCo's nor AutoCorp's investment incentives. LightCo is willing to make investments that reduce the costs of making lightbulbs because it benefits from these investments. If AutoCorp tries to capture some of the benefits from LightCo's investment by offering a lower price for lightbulbs, LightCo simply will sell the bulbs to another customer. If LightCo tries to raise the price of its bulbs to extract profits from AutoCorp, it simply will buy bulbs from one of LightCo's rivals, such as Philips Electronics or General Electric. In contrast, if AutoCorp purchases LightCo and operates it as an internal division, investment incentives might be distorted. As divisional managers, LightCo's management might face reduced incentives to invest in innovative activities, since part of the credit for value-enhancing ideas will go to AutoCorp's senior management. In addition, LightCo's management might invest in unproductive activities, such as trying to *influence* senior management's decisions (salaries, allocating capital to the divisions, and so on).[16]

These arguments suggest that *the likelihood of vertical integration increases with the specificity of the asset*. With less specialized assets, market transactions or long-term contracts are more likely to produce efficient investment incentives. This proposition is one of the most important ideas in the economic literature on organizations. Empirical tests support its validity. As an example, J. Stuckey examined aluminum refineries that are located near bauxite mines.[17] Not only are the refineries specific to particular mines owing to transportation costs, but the refineries also invest in specialized equipment. Stuckey found that in virtually all cases, there is vertical integration.

Research indicates that specific assets are especially likely to motivate integration in *uncertain environments*. In uncertain environments, the contracting problems with specific assets are particularly severe: It is nearly impossible to specify what actions each party should perform under all future contingencies. In more stable environments, the range of possible circumstances to cover is more limited and relatively complete contracts that mitigate relevant holdup problems can be negotiated at lower cost.

The arguments in this section are summarized in Figure 19.5. When asset specificity is low, it is generally best to rely on market exchange, regardless of the level of uncertainty. As the degree of asset specificity increases, the desirability of nonmarket

---

[16]P. Milgrom and J. Roberts (1994), "Bargaining Costs, Influence Costs, and the Organization of Economic Activity," in J. Alt and K. Shepsle (Eds.), *Perspectives on Positive Political Economy* (Cambridge University Press: Cambridge), 57–89.

[17]J. Stuckey (1983), *Vertical Integration and Joint Ventures in the Aluminum Industry* (Harvard University Press: Cambridge). See also E. Anderson (1985), "The Salesperson as Outside Agent or Employee: A Transaction Cost Analysis," *Marketing Science* 4, 234–254; E. Anderson and D. Schmittlein (1984), "Integration of the Sales Force: An Empirical Examination," *Rand Journal of Economics* 15, 385–395; and W. Kim, D. Mayers, and C. Smith (1996), "On the Choice of Insurance Distribution Systems," *Journal of Risk and Insurance* 63, 207–227.

Figure 19.5   Asset Specificity, Uncertainty, and the Procurement Decision

When asset specificity is low, it generally is optimal to use simple market transactions for procurement. As the degree of asset specificity increases, nonmarket transactions (contracts and vertical integration) become more desirable. When uncertainty is low, relatively complete contracts can be written. Thus, contracts can be used to resolve incentive conflicts motivated by firm-specific assets. As uncertainty increases, contracting becomes more expensive. Vertical integration of firm-specific assets becomes more likely as uncertainty increases.

<table>
<tr><th rowspan="2"></th><th colspan="3">Uncertainty</th></tr>
<tr><th>Low</th><th>Medium</th><th>High</th></tr>
<tr><th>Low</th><td>Market transaction</td><td>Market transaction</td><td>Market transaction</td></tr>
<tr><th>Medium</th><td>Contract</td><td>Contract or vertical integration</td><td>Contract or vertical integration</td></tr>
<tr><th>High</th><td>Contract</td><td>Contract or vertical integration</td><td>Vertical integration</td></tr>
</table>

(Row labels Low, Medium, High are grouped under the vertical axis label "Asset Specificity".)

transactions increases. Uncertainty increases the desirability of vertically integrating firm-specific assets; when asset specificity and uncertainty are both high, vertical integration is likely to be the preferred alternative.

This analysis of firm-specific assets helps explain why catering, trucking, copying, and mainframe computing are among the more frequently outsourced services. These activities are sufficiently specialized that spot-market transactions are not viable. Nonetheless, these activities involve assets that are not highly firm-specific. Food-service equipment, trucks, copy machines, and computers can be used by many different companies; therefore, the potential for holdup actions is relatively low. Furthermore, for activities like copying, it is easy to write a relatively complete contract (uncertainty is reasonably low). There also are potential benefits from using independent firms that specialize in large-volume production. Moreover, the transactions are quite *repetitive;* thus, it makes sense to contract with a single supplier on a long-term basis. (The supplier makes customer-specific investments in learning how to serve the customer; hence, it is expensive to change suppliers.) These factors imply that it often is optimal to contract for these services.

One advantage of having IBM provide computer services to Manulife is that IBM provides similar services to other companies. This higher volume can lower the cost for Manulife. The costs of training technical specialists can be spread across more users; software can be written, that is, used by more than one company. Also, IBM is able to attract higher-quality computer specialists than can Manulife, since IBM's scale of operation provides a much richer set of future career opportunities. Conceptually, Manulife could capture some of these gains by purchasing IBM and operating the two companies as one large enterprise. However, the costs of managing such a large, diverse enterprise likely would outweigh the benefits.

ACADEMIC APPLICATIONS

Vertical Integration in the Aerospace Industry

Scott Masten was among the first to provide empirical evidence on the determinants of vertical integration by studying the make-versus-buy policies of a major aerospace contractor. The firm made many products for the U.S. government. The company had to choose between making each product or subcontracting it to another firm for production. Economic theory suggests that internal production is more likely when the assets are specific and the uncertainties in contracting are large.

Masten used two measures of asset specificity for each product. The first measured design (physical-asset) specificity, whereas the second measured site specificity. He also measured the complexity of the product design, which was intended to proxy for uncertainties in contracting. Consistent with the theory, he found that products which were more design specific and quite complex were more likely to be produced internally. When the product was both design specific and complex, there was a 92 percent probability of internal production. If the product was design specific but not complex, the probability of internal production was 31 percent. The probability of internal production was only 2 percent when the product was neither design specific nor complex. For this particular company, site specificity was unimportant.

In the years since Masten's study, a large number of researchers have provided evidence from other industries that support Masten's initial findings and related predictions that derived from Oliver Williamson's "Transaction-Cost Theory." A detailed review of these studies concludes: "The weight of the evidence is overwhelming. Indeed, virtually all predictions from transaction-cost analysis appear to be borne out by the data."

Source: S. Masten (1984), "The Organization of Production: Evidence from the Aerospace Industry," *Journal of Law & Economics* 27, 403–417; and F. LaFontaine and M. Slade (2007), "Vertical Integration and Firm Boundaries: The Evidence," *Journal of Economic Literature* 45(September), 631–687.

Asset Ownership[18]

We have concentrated on potential holdup problems that occur after the initial investment. Our major point is that these problems can be reduced through vertical integration. However, common ownership can be achieved in our example either if AutoCorp owns BodyWorks or if BodyWorks owns AutoCorp. Which alternative, if either, is best? Considering ongoing specific investment provides a partial answer to this question. In their ongoing interaction, companies like AutoCorp and BodyWorks generally benefit from specific investments, which are difficult to observe or use as the basis for contracts. For example, the management of BodyWorks might invest in learning about AutoCorp's future design plans so that it can plan more effectively for potential changes. This planning might increase the speed at which new models could be developed and thus improve overall corporate performance. Similarly, AutoCorp might invest in learning more about BodyWorks' production processes to develop lower-cost body designs. Investments of this type are hard to observe and depend on the managers' incentives to make them. These incentives, in turn, can depend on ownership structure.

If AutoCorp buys BodyWorks it will structure BodyWorks as a division of the firm. The management of BodyWorks will be evaluated primarily on divisional performance and will have relatively low incentives to invest in activities that primarily

[18]This section draws on Grossman and Hart (1986).

benefit other divisions (although they may have limited incentives to do so through stock ownership and profit-sharing plans). Thus they will invest little in learning about AutoCorp's design plans if the benefits go primarily to AutoCorp. Yet AutoCorp's management, being at the top of the corporation, will be evaluated on overall corporate performance. They will have incentives to invest in all activities that benefit the overall corporation. Thus they will work to invest in lowering BodyWorks' costs if it increases the overall value of the firm. In contrast, if BodyWorks owns AutoCorp the reverse situation holds. BodyWorks' management has incentives to invest in activities that increase total firm value, whereas AutoCorp's management will focus primarily on divisional performance. Which ownership structure is best depends on whose investments are most important. Typically it is better for the party whose investments have the bigger impact on the value of the firm to be the owner. If both parties' investments are important, it can be best to maintain separate ownership and use contracts. This idea is explored in more detail in the appendix.

Other Reasons

Unions are another factor that can affect the choice between vertical integration and contracting. For instance, some of the major airlines have threatened labor unions that they will outsource their kitchen operations to other companies to avoid paying union wages. The major automobile companies have made similar statements with respect to the manufacturing of component parts. Some firms are reluctant to integrate into a unionized activity because they fear that the move might motivate their employees to organize.

Controlling sensitive, proprietary information can affect decisions of outsourcing versus vertical integration. Along these lines, Prahalad and Hamel argue that it often is unwise for a company to outsource its "core competencies" (those capabilities which are fundamental to a firm's performance and strategy). Rather, according to this argument, firms should keep core competencies within the firm to enhance their development and to prevent other firms from developing similar capabilities (see Chapter 8).[19]

The financial press often argues that obtaining inputs through contracts with other firms "frees companies to use scarce capital for other purposes." This claim is questionable given access to well-developed capital markets. Having another firm produce a product does not reduce investment; it simply shifts the capital expenditures to another firm. Buyers still pay for this investment through the price of the product. The important question is whether more value is created by producing the product internally or externally. If internal production is more valuable, the firm can raise money in the capital market for financing the relevant assets: Capital is not "scarce" for good projects. If external production is more valuable, funds must be raised by the supplier.[20]

---

[19]C. Prahalad and G. Hamel (1990), "The Core Competence of the Corporation," *Harvard Business Review* 68 (May–June), 79–91.

[20]One situation where this argument might make sense could involve an international business transaction between a firm from an industrialized country and a firm from a developing economy. For example, Boeing might offer to lease airplanes to a Chinese airline—thus bundling its product with a financing package—because Boeing has more effective access to global capital markets than does its customer.

Vertical Integration to Avoid Contracting with Competitors

Prior to 1975, virtually all community banks obtained products and services (such as loan participations and check clearing) through correspondent relationships with large regional and/or money-center banks. During the last quarter of the 20th century, some small community banks reduced their traditional reliance on correspondent banks for upstream products and services by joining bankers' banks—a form of business cooperative and a move from outsourcing to a type of vertical integration.

Explanations for vertical integration have traditionally focused on firm-specific investment, market power, and government regulation. However, formation of bankers' banks is difficult to explain in terms of these standard vertical-integration motives. Research suggests that bankers' banks are a response to technological change and deregulation that results in increased costs faced by community banks in dealing with correspondent banks as both suppliers and potential competitors. For instance, loan participations require sharing proprietary information about major loan customers, something a community bank would not want to provide to a potential competitor.

When United Banker's Bank (UBB) formed in 1975 its founding community-based banks faced serious threats such as new laws that made it easier for large system-wide competitors to invade their local markets, thereby competing for their customers. The UBB founders believed they were doing business with the enemy. In fact, UBB's founding vision was to "Level the competitive playing field with systems banks by providing community banks with a full range of innovative correspondent services secure in the knowledge that nobody would ever come after their customers."

Source: J. Brickley, J. Linck and C. Smith (2012), "The Economic Determinants of Vertical Organization: Evidence from Bankers' Banks." *Journal of Financial Economics* 105(1), 113–130.

Some U.S. firms also claim that they outsource manufacturing to companies in China and other foreign countries because "that is where the sales are." While this can explain why a firm would locate its manufacturing in a foreign country, it does not explain why the firm would choose to outsource the activity. For example, Japanese automobile companies manufacture cars in the United States in plants that they own. Presumably the choice between ownership and outsourcing in a foreign country depends on other factors, such as the political risk of expropriation of assets.

Continuum of Choice

Although we have discussed long-term contracting versus vertical integration as a choice between two policies, it is important to keep in mind that the outsourcing decision falls on a continuum. For example, sometimes it is desirable for a firm to maintain ownership of a firm-specific asset and contract with another firm to operate it. Apple does this with some of its outside suppliers. This ownership pattern reduces potential holdup problems because if there is a contract dispute, the owner can take the asset and simply contract with an alternative firm to provide the service (neither side faces large losses). This ownership pattern is most viable if the asset can be moved at low cost and the value of the asset is relatively insensitive to asset maintenance or abuse. Alternatively, the owner must be able to provide the service operator with sufficient incentives to maintain and not to abuse the asset.

A related example is companies choosing to contract with IBM for providing operating software and hardware but to maintain responsibility for applications

ANALYZING MANAGERIAL DECISIONS: *BioChem Pricing Policy*

BioChem has a patent on a chemical product, that is, used as a key input in producing farm and home agricultural fertilizer. Currently, BioChem produces the product and sells it to companies who manufacture the final products for the farm and home users. BioChem faces the following demand curves from the farm and home market segments:

$$\text{Farm:} \quad P = 300 - 10Q$$
$$\text{Home:} \quad P = 100 - 5Q$$

BioChem can produce the product at a constant marginal cost of $1.

1. Calculate the optimal prices that BioChem would like to charge in each market segment to maximize profits.
2. Discuss how vertical integration might be used to accomplish this pricing policy. Be sure to indicate the market into which BioChem should vertically integrate (assume they can integrate only into one). Explain why you chose this market.

software. Development of applications software is likely to be more specific to a given company than developing of operating software that can be used for many different applications and firms. IBM, therefore, has greater incentives to focus on developing operating software. The location of specific knowledge reinforces these incentives: A company knows more about its specific applications, and IBM knows more about general computing. The observed organizational arrangement reflects these incentive and information effects.

Contract Duration

A major advantage of long-term contracts over short-term contracts is that they increase the incentives of the contracting parties to make firm-specific investments. For example, IBM would have limited incentives to invest in learning Manulife's special computing demands if it anticipated only a short-term relationship between the two companies.[21] On the other hand, it is costly to write and litigate long-term contracts in uncertain environments, where it is difficult to plan for potential changes in technology, input prices, product demands, and the like. Thus, firms might be expected to enter long-term contracts when the desired investment is relatively firm-specific and where the environment is relatively stable. Alternatively, if the firm faces a highly uncertain environment and large investments in firm-specific assets,

---

[21]Long-term contracts provide the greatest incentives when they have uncertain expiration dates (the parties expect the contracts might be renewed). There are strong incentives to cheat in the last period when a contract has a known ending date, since maintaining the reputation as a good partner has no benefit (ignoring third-party effects). The parties, knowing that they will not cooperate in the last period, have incentives to cheat in the next-to-last period. (There are no reputational concerns since they know that the other party will not cooperate in the last period.) The incentives to cheat in the next-to-last period affect the incentives in the previous period, and so on. In this case, the contract can unravel, so that the parties have the incentive to cheat in the first period. L. Telser (1980), "A Theory of Self-Enforcing Agreements," *Journal of Business* 53, 27–44.

ACADEMIC APPLICATIONS

Economic Determinants of Contact Duration

Many contracts, including most commercial, labor, and real estate agreements, contain explicit expiration dates. Typically, the terms of an agreement (e.g., the rent in a lease contract) are not renegotiated until the contract expires, barring some event such as default. Major changes in contracts typically are renegotiated only when the agreements are renewed.

Economic models suggest that recontracting costs, relationship-specific investment, and environmental uncertainty are important determinants of contract duration. The potential benefits of longer-term contracts are lower recontracting costs (since recontracting occurs less frequently) and reduced "hold-up" of relationship-specific investment. Thus contract length is expected to increase with recontracting costs and specific investment. The potential costs of longer-term contracts arise from rigidities that limit the parties' abilities to respond to environmental changes (assuming that it is more expensive to renegotiate an agreement prior to expiration). Since these costs are likely to increase with environmental uncertainty, most models predict that contract length will decrease with uncertainty.

A study based on a large sample of franchise contracts provides evidence that supports these hypotheses. The authors find that the term of the contract systematically increases with the franchisee's physical and human capital investments, measures of recontracting costs, and the franchisor's experience in franchising (which presumably is negatively related to uncertainty about optimal contract provisions). These results are consistent with the basic argument that the optimal contract duration involves a trade-off between protecting the parties against potential hold-up of relationship-specific investment and reducing the flexibility that the parties have to respond to environmental changes.

Source: J. Brickley, S. Misra and L. Van Horn (2006), Contract Duration: "Evidence from Franchise Contracts," *Journal of Law and Economics* 49 (April), 173–196.

vertical integration is more likely to be the preferred alternative. Finally, if the investment in firm-specific assets is relatively low or if the lives of the assets are relatively short, the firm can more easily enter into short-term contracts with suppliers or rely on spot market transactions.

Contracting with Distributors

Although our examples have focused on supply contracts, the same analysis applies to distribution contracts. As assets become more specific, vertical integration becomes more desirable. Yet a number of other interesting issues arise in distribution contracts. We now examine these issues.

Free-Rider Problems

Earlier in this chapter, we noted the incentives of independent distributors to free-ride on the reputation of a brand name and how these incentives can motivate suboptimal sales efforts—for example, insufficient expenditures on advertising and other inputs. One method of reducing this problem is vertical integration.[22] The other method is to

---

[22]H. Marvel (1982), "Exclusive Dealing," *Journal of Law & Economics* 25, 1–25.

MANAGERIAL APPLICATIONS

Outsourcing Gone Bad

Not all outsourcing ventures work—some end in divorce. A dramatic example is the $4 billion deal between the U. S. Navy and EDS to manage voice, video, networking training and desktops for 350,000 Navy and Marine Corp users. One year later EDS wrote off close to $350 million due to its inability to come even close to fulfilling its obligations. EDS had obtained the contract in 2003 after beating out competitors, such as IBM and Accenture. The reasons behind the failure are complex. One of the major problems was that EDS, perhaps anxious to win the prize, did not realize until it was too late that the Navy and Marine Corps had tens of thousands of legacy and customer applications for which it was expected to either integrate or rip and replace. An EDS spokesman indicated that the company's goal was to get the number of legacy apps down to a "mere" 10,000–12,000. This example illustrates how lack of specific knowledge about the other firm's situation at the time of initial contract can lead to subsequent problems and divorce.

There are many other "horror stories" about firms that have outsourced functions unsuccessfully "offshore." These stories range from conflicts of interest (such as service providers getting kickbacks from landlords on the leased space) to projects being torn apart by huge turnover rates. As one outsourcing consultant notes, "you end up with project teams that are hugely inconsistent. You might have a good team in place, but a month later, three-quarters of the team has transitioned."

Even well thought out ventures have some probability of failure. However, these examples suggest that managers on both sides of the contract should be careful to analyze costs, benefits, and risks before entering an outsourcing venture.

Source: E. Schwartz (2008), "Painful Lessons from IT Outsourcing gone Bad," *InfoWorld* (August 25).

---

use contracts with specific provisions to control free-rider problems. Two contract terms that specifically address this concern are advertising provisions and exclusive territories.

Advertising Provisions

Firms use several related methods to increase advertising at the local level. First, a company can charge its retail units an advertising fee and have the central company retain the responsibility for advertising. For instance, most franchise contracts require that, in addition to the base royalty payment, individual units pay a percentage of sales to the central company to provide advertising. One potential problem with this approach is that the local unit, not the central company, might have the

---

MANAGERIAL APPLICATIONS

Conflicts over Advertising Provisions

Meineke Discount Muffler Shops were initially ordered to pay $600 million to its franchisees by a federal district court in North Carolina. Franchisees started noticing that the franchiser had been reducing advertising. Newspaper ads were waning, and TV spots were appearing after midnight. It appeared that instead of the contractually specified 2 percent, Meineke was pocketing $17 million, or 15 percent of the communal ad funds. The judge said the franchiser had a fiduciary duty to ensure that the franchisees' funds were properly managed. The case was subsequently reviewed by an appeals court. Meineke owners almost settled the case for around $100 million before the appellate court's decision came through. Lucky for them, they did not. The appeals court ruled in their favor concluding that there was no legal basis for imposing liability on the company and the case was dismissed.

Source: A. Lorenz (2009), *GKN: The Making of Business, 1759–2009* (John Wiley and Sons: West Sussex).

specific knowledge relevant for effective local advertising. A second alternative that addresses this concern is for the central company to share in the local advertising costs; for example, it might pay half of any advertising expenditures. The decisions on local advertising are made by the local managers, but by reducing the effective cost of advertising, they encourage the local unit managers to advertise more extensively. A third alternative is to require distributors to contribute to regional advertising funds. The distributors have the primary decision rights to decide how to spend the monies in the funds.

Exclusive Territories

One of the most common methods to control free-riding is to grant individual distributors exclusive rights to operate in a given market area. For example, an AutoCorp dealership might have a contract that prevents the company from opening another dealership within 30 miles. By giving distributors exclusive rights for specific market areas, there are fewer incentives to free-ride, since the distributors internalize more of the benefits from their sales efforts and fewer benefits go to other units not owned by the given distributor. Exclusive territories also can create extra profits for local distributors. These profits can provide additional incentives not to free-ride: If the manufacturer catches the distributor free-riding and terminates the contract, future profits are lost.[23]

Double Markups

Granting distributors market power within specific areas reduces free-rider problems, but it can create another problem—*double markups*. Since both the manufacturer and the distributor face downward-sloping demand curves, each has the incentive to mark up the product's price above marginal cost. Unchecked, this results in the customer's facing two markups rather than one. Hence, both the quantity of the product demanded and the combined profits for the manufacturer and distributor are less than they would be if this incentive were controlled. The following is a numerical example illustrating this problem, as well as the contract terms that might be used to control it.

Example

Suppose that AutoCorp faces the following demand for its Rhino automobiles in the Medford, Oregon, market area:

$$P = 55,000 - 100Q \qquad (19.3)$$

AutoCorp can produce Rhinos at a constant marginal cost of \$5,000. To simplify the computations, assume that there are no fixed costs in producing or selling cars. To maximize profits, AutoCorp must select the quantity and price where marginal revenue equals marginal cost. As depicted in Figure 19.6, the optimal quantity and price are $Q^* = 250$ and $P^* = \$30,000$. The firm's profits are \$6.25 million.

Now suppose that AutoCorp sells its vehicles through SUVmart, an independent distributor that has the exclusive right to sell Rhinos in the Medford market area. Under the contract, AutoCorp sets the wholesale price, while SUVmart selects the

---

[23]B. Klein and K. Murphy (1988), "Vertical Restraints as Contract Enforcement Mechanisms," *Journal of Law & Economics* 31, 265–297; and J. Brickley (1999), "Incentive Conflicts and Contractual Restraints: Evidence from Franchising," *Journal of Law and Economics* 42, 745–774.

Figure 19.6 Optimal Output in an Example of the Double Markup Problem

AutoCorp can produce automobiles at a constant marginal cost of $5,000. To maximize profits, AutoCorp must select the quantity and price where marginal revenue equals marginal cost. The optimal quantity and price are $Q^* = 250$ and $P_w^* = \$30,000$. Firm profits are $6.25 million (assuming no fixed costs).

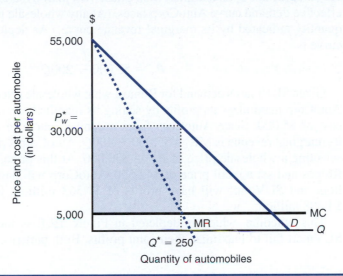

Quantity of automobiles

---

quantity to purchase and the retail price. For simplicity, suppose that the only marginal cost facing SUVmart for Rhinos is the price charged by AutoCorp. (There are no variable distribution costs.) The owners of SUVmart care only about their own profits, and the managers of AutoCorp care only about AutoCorp's profits. The problem facing AutoCorp is to choose the wholesale price, P_w, that maximizes its profits.

ACADEMIC APPLICATIONS

Company Ownership versus Franchising

We have discussed how a central company can reduce the incentives of an independent distributor to free-ride on the brand name through contracts with terms that motivate increased sales efforts. When the free-rider problem is severe, it can be less expensive simply to own the distribution units centrally. Managers of a company-owned unit have fewer incentives than an independent distributor to free-ride on the reputation, since they do not get to keep the profits from the unit—the reduction in costs (e.g., from decreased advertising) flow through to the central company, not the managers.

Most franchise companies do not franchise all their retail outlets. The typical company franchises about 80 percent of the units and owns the other 20 percent. Our argument suggests that central companies are most likely to own the units that receive a significant amount of business from customers who are unlikely to make repeat purchases at the particular units (the incentives to free-ride in this case are large). On average, fast-food restaurants are more likely to serve transient customers than auto-service companies. (Customers tend to use the same unit repeatedly for oil changes and tune-ups.) Consistent with the theory, the typical restaurant franchise company owns about 30 percent of its units, and the typical auto service franchise company owns about 13 percent of its units.

Source: J. Brickley and F. Dark (1987), "The Choice of Organizational Form: The Case of Franchising," *Journal of Financial Economics* 18, 401; and R. Blair and F. Lafontaine (2014), *The Economics of Franchising* (Amazon Kindle Edition).

To solve this problem, AutoCorp's management would like to know the quantity that SUVmart would purchase at each feasible wholesale price. AutoCorp can infer this demand curve by analyzing the problem from the perspective of SUVmart. SUVmart faces the retail demand curve for autos given in Equation (19.3). SUVmart maximizes its profits by setting its marginal revenue, implied by this retail demand curve, equal to P_w, its marginal cost. Thus, SUVmart's marginal revenue curve is the effective demand curve AutoCorp faces. (At any wholesale price, SUVmart buys the quantity indicated by its marginal revenue curve.) As depicted in Figure 19.6, this curve is

$$P_w = 55,000 - 200Q \qquad (19.4)$$

Given SUVmart's demand for Rhinos, what wholesale price will AutoCorp choose? AutoCorp maximizes its profits by setting its marginal revenue equal to its marginal cost of $5,000. Since AutoCorp faces a demand curve of $P_w = 55,000 - 200Q$, its marginal revenue is MR $= 55,000 - 400Q$. AutoCorp's profits are maximized by selecting a wholesale price of $P_w^* = \$30,000$. At this price, SUVmart will buy 125 Rhinos and set a retail price of $42,500. AutoCorp will have profits of $3.125 million, and SUVmart will have profits of $1.563 million, for combined profits of $4.688 million.

This outcome, which is depicted in Figure 19.7, is inefficient. AutoCorp and SUVmart fail to maximize their joint profits. Both parties could be made better off

---

Figure 19.7 Example of Double Markups

AutoCorp sets the wholesale price for its automobiles, while SUVmart selects the quantity to purchase and the retail price. SUVmart maximizes profits by setting the wholesale price equal to its marginal revenue. Thus, SUVmart's marginal revenue curve is AutoCorp's demand curve. AutoCorp maximizes profit by setting its marginal cost of $5,000 equal to its marginal revenue. AutoCorp selects a wholesale price P_w^* of $30,000, a $25,000 markup above its marginal cost, whereas SUVmart selects a retail price P_r^* of $42,500, a $12,500 markup above its marginal cost. SUVmart sells 125 cars at this price. The combined profits are $4.688 million. The two companies could earn combined profits of $6.25 million if they cooperate and sell 250 automobiles to consumers at a price of $30,000.

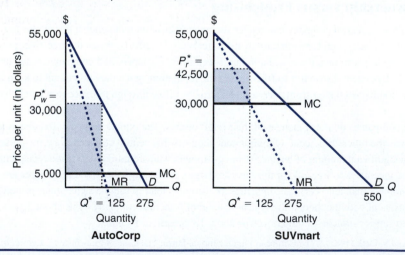

by coordinating their prices and volume choices—we already have shown that they could earn up to $6.25 million (vs. $4.688 million). In addition, with the double markups, consumers pay $42,500 for 125 Rhinos rather than $30,000 for 250.

This problem does not automatically disappear if AutoCorp merges with SUVmart. We saw in Chapter 17 that exactly the same problem can arise within firms, when products are sold between two profit centers using internal transfer prices. As we discussed, the transfer-pricing problem can be reduced by appropriate organizational design. Our current focus is to look at how this problem might be reduced between two independent firms through specific contractual terms.

Two-Part Pricing

SUVmart will purchase 250 Rhinos if AutoCorp sets a wholesale price of $5,000. This quantity maximizes the joint profits of the two firms and results in a retail price of $30,000. The entire profits, however, go to SUVmart, since AutoCorp is selling the automobiles at cost. One solution is for AutoCorp to charge SUVmart an up-front franchise fee—thereby extracting its share of the profits through this fee—and then to sell automobiles to SUVmart at $5,000 each. Since SUVmart's purchasing decision is based on marginal cost, not total cost, it still will purchase 250 automobiles and set a retail price of $30,000. If AutoCorp charges SUVmart an up-front fee of $3.125 million for the exclusive rights to the Medford market area, the combined profits of $6.25 million are split evenly between the two companies. Once the fee is collected, AutoCorp might try to increase the wholesale price of the automobiles to increase its profits. Thus, for such a solution to work, AutoCorp must be able to commit credibly to sell automobiles to SUVmart at marginal cost.

Quotas

An alternative method for maximizing the combined profits is for the two companies to agree on a minimum purchase requirement. SUVmart could agree to purchase at least 250 automobiles at a prespecified wholesale price (above $5,000). Given the details in this example, SUVmart will purchase exactly 250 automobiles and sell them at $30,000 to retail customers. The level of the prespecified wholesale price determines the split of the profits between the two companies. A wholesale price of $17,500 splits the profits evenly (each company nets $12,500). AutoCorp must be able to commit credibly to the wholesale price, and SUVmart must purchase the agreed-upon quota.

Regulatory Issues

Some regulators and scholars are suspicious of contract terms such as exclusive territories that potentially limit competition. Nonetheless, most nonprice contract terms are not *per se* illegal (always illegal) under federal antitrust law. They are judged on a *rule of reason,* where the court attempts to consider the benefits of the terms (such as increased sales efforts) against potential anticompetitive effects. In some states, automobile dealers and franchisees have successfully lobbied their legislators to limit the control that central companies impose—for example, in setting quotas and terminating contracts. In addition, federal law restricts central companies from

ANALYZING MANAGERIAL DECISIONS: *Oil Industry Distribution Systems*

Major oil companies use a dual distribution system for gasoline. Some stations are *direct-serve*, where the oil company delivers gasoline to the station. Other stations are served by distributors. Distributors are independent businesspeople who buy gas from the oil company and sell it to stations. Distributors also own their own stations. The land, tanks, and equipment at the direct-serve stations are owned by the oil company and leased to the dealer (franchisee). The dealer buys gas from the oil company and pays rent for the land. The dealer keeps the profits from the station over the life of the lease. (Some direct-serve stations are centrally owned by the oil company. At these locations, the oil company hires a manager to operate the station.) At direct-serve stations, the oil company is responsible for environmental cleanup, local advertising, monitoring of the station (to protect the brand name), and so on. The distributors are responsible for these activities at the stations they serve. Typically the oil company sells gas to distributors at about 7 cents less per gallon than it sells gas to dealers at its direct-serve stations.

1. Oil companies do not allow dealers (franchisees) to buy gas from distributors. Dealers must buy gas from the central oil company. Dealers often complain that this is unfair. The practice has been the subject of antitrust lawsuits. Oil company executives argue that this policy is important because it limits *free-riding* on the part of the distributors. Explain the executives' arguments in more detail.
2. Suppose the courts ruled that the oil companies must allow the dealers to buy gas from distributors. What effects do you think such a ruling would have on the operational policies of the oil companies?
3. Some direct-serve gasoline stations provide repair services, and others concentrate almost exclusively on self-service gasoline sales. Which type of station is more likely owned by the central oil company and which type is more likely to be franchised? Explain.
4. Typically the stations served (and owned) by distributors are located in rural areas, whereas the direct-serve stations are located in urban areas. Give two economic reasons to explain why you might expect such a pattern.

directly controlling the pricing by distributors at the retail level. A detailed treatment of these regulatory issues is beyond the scope of this book.[24] Suffice it to say that it usually is important for firms to engage expert legal counsel to advise in designing supply and distribution contracts.

Trends in Outsourcing

Major companies make much greater use of outsourcing today than they did in the 1980s. At least four factors have contributed to this change. First, new flexible production technologies allow suppliers to adapt more easily to customer demands. Thus, in some cases, assets are becoming less firm-specific—a technological innovation that favors contracting over vertical integration. Second, improvements in information and communications technology make it easier to identify potential partners and to communicate with them after an agreement is reached. Electronic data interchange allows firms to connect their computers to each other. These computers can automatically

[24]For a more detailed treatment of these issues, see R. Posner (1976), *Antitrust Law* (University of Chicago Press: Chicago); and D. Carlton and J. Perloff (1990), *Modern Industrial Organization* (HarperCollins: New York).

MANAGERIAL APPLICATIONS

The Politics of International Outsourcing

In 2001, Daimler Chrysler decided to overhaul its computing systems by inviting IBM, EDS, and other U.S. giants to bid on the job. It awarded the task to the Indian firm Infosys Technologies, Ltd. Infosys's cost was 25 percent lower. Since then, other Indian and Chinese software companies have been undercutting Western adversaries by as much as 70 percent. In 2000, 125 of the top 500 U.S. firms outsourced software projects to Indian firms. By 2003, 285 of these firms have Indian software and technology suppliers, including Boeing, Cisco, and Lehman Brothers. To compete with the lower labor costs in Asia, India, and Eastern Europe, large U.S. technology firms like IBM, Accenture, Dell, and Hewlett-Packard have either acquired Indian companies or are opening Indian offices. In 2003, IBM and Accenture each hired between 4,000 and 5,000 employees in India.

And it is not just software jobs that are moving overseas. Call centers, architectural services, medical transcription, and other service jobs are moving offshore. Goldman Sachs estimated that between 2001 and 2003, 200,000 service jobs had been outsourced overseas to U.S. affiliates. Worried about its image of stealing U.S. jobs and the possibility of U.S. government legislation that might stem the outsourcing of U.S. jobs to India, the Indian government engaged several large Washington-based lobbying firms to design an "educational" campaign extolling the benefits of closer U.S. ties with India. One lobbying firm was paid $600,000 in 2003 to advise India and to lobby Congress to prevent antioutsourcing legislation.

International outsourcing became a major issue in the 2004 U.S. presidential campaign. Presidential candidate Senator John Kerry charged President Bush with wanting "to export more of our jobs overseas." Gregory Mankiw, President Bush's chief economic advisor, claimed that sending U.S. service jobs abroad "is probably a plus for the economy in the long run" because foreign workers can do the jobs more cheaply, thereby reducing costs for U.S. consumers and companies.

Source: M. Kripalani and S. Hamm (2004), "Scrambling to Stem India's Onslaught," *BusinessWeek* (January 26), 81; M. Schroeder (2003), "India Aims to Calm U.S. Outsourcing Fears," *The Wall Street Journal* (November 13); and B. Davis (2004), "Some Democratic Economists Echo Mankiw on Outsourcing," *The Wall Street Journal* (February 12), A4.

order inventory directly from a supplier with little human intervention. Third, there has been a dramatic increase in worldwide competition. This competition has placed greater pressure on firms to reduce costs and increase efficiency. Some scholars argue that many American firms were "flush with cash" in the 1960s and 1970s and were more likely to waste this cash through such actions as engaging in too much integration.[25] Some recent outsourcing decisions thus might be corrections for poor investment decisions of the past. Fourth, during the early 1990s, there was a worldwide recession, which caused excess capacity in many industries. In this environment, firms often could obtain large discounts from external vendors. (This effect should be more cyclical than permanent.)

Many recent outsourcing decisions do not move firms from internal production to the other end of the spectrum (spot market transactions). Rather, the movement has been to an intermediate arrangement—long-term contracting. Many firms also have moved away from acquiring inputs in the spot market. To improve quality and lower unit costs, firms such as General Motors and Xerox have cut their number of suppliers dramatically and correspondingly have increased the number of long-term partnerships with independent firms. Thus, those trends can be viewed as movements from each end of the spectrum toward the middle.

---

[25]M. Jensen (1986), "Agency Costs of Free Cash Flow, Corporate Finance and Takeovers," *American Economic Review* 76, 323–329.

ANALYZING MANAGERIAL DECISIONS: *AutoCorp*

AutoCorp produces automobiles. It has asked the Amalgamated Fabric Company to consider a proposal to become a supplier of automobile seats. Under the proposal, Amalgamated Fabric would construct a $20 million plant near one of Auto-Corp's production facilities. AutoCorp would purchase 100,000 car seats per year at a price of $280 per seat for 15 years—the useful life of the plant. (The actual proposal contains an adjustment for inflation. Ignore this complication in the analysis.)

Amalgamated Fabric's financial analysts have examined the proposal. It appears to be a profitable opportunity. The amortized cost of the plant is $2.6 million per year (at a discount rate of 10 percent). The annual costs are $25.4 million per year. Therefore, the average total cost is $280 per seat—ATC = ($25.4 million + $2.6 million)/ 100,000 = $280. The financial analysts have examined AutoCorp's financial outlook. Although it has not been highly profitable in all years, there is essentially no probability of bankruptcy over the next 15 years. Since the proposed price covers the cost, the financial analysts think that the proposal should be accepted. (It breaks even with a fair rate of return on invested capital of 10 percent.)

You have been asked to analyze the contract proposal. You have seen the financial analysis and think the cost estimates are reasonable. You are aware that, due to its location, the proposed plant has no alternative use other than supplying seats to AutoCorp. The salvage value of the plant, in the event of liquidation, is $2 million.

1. One concern you have is that AutoCorp might try to lower the effective purchase price of the seats after the plant is built (by reneging on the contract or demanding higher-quality seats for the same price). Once the plant is built, how much can the purchase price fall before Amalgamated Fabric liquidates the plant?

2. What factors would you consider to decide whether opportunistic behavior by AutoCorp is a likely possibility?

3. Does AutoCorp have to worry about any opportunistic actions by Amalgamated Fabric?

4. What factors might make it difficult to write a contract that would limit opportunistic behavior by both companies?

5. What are the costs and benefits of AutoCorp vertically integrating and supplying its own automobile seats?

6. What are the costs and benefits of having AutoCorp construct the plant and letting Amalgamated Fabric operate it on a contractual basis?

Technological changes, such as just-in-time production methods, electronic data interchanges, and total quality manufacturing, require close links between manufacturers, suppliers, and distributors. Rather than inspecting parts and materials from numerous suppliers on delivery, a few suppliers are selected and their production processes are certified as meeting high-quality standards. Thus, although the various activities in the manufacturing/distribution process are conducted by different firms, it is important that these firms remain closely linked. In such cases, these factors make spot market transactions undesirable.

Recently, however, some companies have moved some activities that were outsourced internationally back into the United States.[26] For example, well-known companies such as Google, General Electric, Caterpillar, and Ford Motor Company have brought some of their production and other functions back to America with some of it being done "in-house." In 2013, Apple announced it would start making a line of

[26]See Special Report: Outsourcing and offshoring (2013) "Here, there and everywhere," *The Economist* (January 19).

its Mac computers in America. The most important reason for this reversal is that global labor "arbitrage" is being eliminated through competition in international labor markets. ("Law of One Price" at work). Wages in China and India have been increasing at rates between 10 and 20 percent per year over the past decade; while wages in America and Europe have been stagnate. Continued low wages in Vietnam, Eastern Europe, Indonesia, and the Philippines have attracted some new outsourcing ventures, but they do not have China's scale, efficiency or supply chains. Also the cost of shipping heavy goods halfway around the world by sea has increased significantly making foreign production of goods ultimately sold in the United States less attractive. U.S. companies also have become increasingly concerned about the threat of losing intellectual property and with the risk that remote supply chains will be disrupted by war or other violence.

Summary

When a firm participates in more than one successive stage of the production or distribution of a product or service, it is said to be *vertically integrated.* Firms change their degree of integration over time. An organization that begins to produce its own inputs is engaging in *backward* or *upstream* integration, whereas an organization that begins to market its own goods or to conduct additional finishing work is engaging in *forward* or *downstream* integration. The term *outsourcing* frequently is used to describe a movement away from vertical integration—moving an activity outside the firm that formerly was done within the firm. The term *outsourcing* also is used to describe an ongoing arrangement where a firm obtains a part or service from an external firm. It is useful to think of the outsourcing decision as a choice along a continuum of possibilities, ranging from spot market transactions to vertical integration with an array of long-term contracts in-between.

Well-functioning markets provide powerful incentives for efficient production and low prices; thus, firms acquire many goods and services through market transactions. Economists have identified at least three primary reasons why a firm might want to engage in nonmarket procurement: *Contracting costs, market power,* and *taxes/regulation.* Four factors can make the contracting costs of nonmarket procurement lower than the costs of market exchange. These factors include firm-specific assets, costs of measuring quality, externalities, and coordination problems.

Firm-specific assets are assets that are substantially more valuable in their current use than in their next best alternative use. Investment in firm-specific assets can cause enormous problems between suppliers and buyers and is a primary reason for nonmarket transactions. Once the investment in firm-specific assets is made, there is a *sunk cost*—the supplier has incentives to continue the relationship as long as the variable costs are covered—even if total costs are not. This incentive subjects the supplier to a potential *holdup problem.* The buyer also can be held up by the supplier. One way of reducing these problems is to integrate vertically. The other method is to negotiate a detailed contract that spells out the rights and responsibilities of each party.

Due to contracting costs, most contracts are *incomplete:* Many contingencies are unspecified and subject to future negotiation. The prospect of future negotiations can motivate suboptimal investment in both capital and effort. Parties to the contract realize that part of the gains from their investments are likely to go to other parties: They are not protected by a complete contract.

The owner has the right to determine the *residual use* of an asset—any use that does not conflict with prior contract, custom, or law. Residual rights give an individual increased ability to capture the gains from an investment and thus can provide investment incentives. Vertical integration and long-term contracts differ in their assignment of ownership rights. Vertical integration keeps the ownership rights for the relevant assets within one firm, whereas long-term contracting apportions them between firms. The choice between vertical integration and long-term contracts depends, at least in part, on which ownership structure creates more productive investment decisions.

A primary prediction of the economics literature is that as an asset becomes more firm-specific, the firm is more likely to choose vertical integration over long-term contracting. The analysis suggests that firms will enter long-term contracts when the desired investment is relatively firm-specific and where the environment is relatively stable and predictable (in stable environments, the range of possible circumstances to cover is more limited and negotiating more complete contracts is less costly). Conversely, if the firm faces a more uncertain environment and large investments in firm-specific assets, vertical integration is more likely to be the preferred alternative. Finally, if the investment in firm-specific assets is relatively low (the assets are unspecialized) or the lives of the assets relatively short, the firm can either enter into short-term contracts with suppliers or rely on spot market transactions.

Independent distributors can have incentives to *free-ride* on a brand name. One method to reduce this problem is vertical integration. Another method is to use contracts with specific provisions that control free-rider problems. Two types of contract terms that specifically address this concern are *advertising provisions* and *exclusive territories*. Exclusive territories help internalize free-rider problems, but they create another problem—*double markups*. This problem (which is analogous to the transfer-pricing problem examined in Chapter 17) can be reduced through *two-part pricing* or *quotas*.

At least four factors have contributed to the observed trends in outsourcing that have occurred over the last few decades increased worldwide competition, the development of less firm-specific production technologies, improvements in information and communication technologies, and excess capacity from a worldwide recession. The trend, however, is not from vertical integration to spot market transactions. It is a movement from both ends of the spectrum toward an intermediate solution of some form of long-term contracting. Technological changes, such as just-in-time production methods, electronic data interchanges, and total quality management, require closer links between manufacturers, suppliers, and distributors. These changes reduce the desirability of spot market transactions in many cases. More recently, increases in the wage rates in China and India, along with increased transportation costs and concerns about international violence, have motivated some large U.S. companies to move some internally outsourced activities back to the United States.

Suggested Readings

D. Carlton and J. Perloff (1999), *Modern Industrial Organization,* 3rd edition (HarperCollins: New York), Chapter 16.

O. Hart (1995), *Firms, Contracts, and Financial Structure* (Oxford Press: Oxford).

B. Holmstrom and J. Robert (1998). "The Boundaries of the Firm Revisited," *Journal of Economic Perspectives* 12(4): 73–94.

B. Klein, R. Crawford, and A. Alchian (1978), "Vertical Integration, Appropriable Rents, and the Competitive Contracting Process," *Journal of Law & Economics* 24, 297–326.

F. LaFontaine and M. Slade (2007), "Vertical Integration and Firm Boundaries: The Evidence," *Journal of Economic Literature* 45, 629–685.

P. Rubin (1990), *Managing Business Transactions* (Free Press: New York).

M. Whinston (2003), "On the Transaction Cost Determinants of Vertical Integration," *Journal of Law, Economics, and Organization* 19(1): 1–23

O. Williamson (1985), *The Economic Institutions of Capitalism* (Free Press: New York).

Self-Evaluation Problems

19–1. Assume that Ford Motor Company can produce an automobile at a constant marginal cost of \$4,000. The demand for the car in the Rochester area is $P = 60,000 - 100Q$.
   a. What is the profit-maximizing price and quantity? What are the profits from this activity?
   b. Now suppose that Ford sells its cars through an independent distributor, Rochester Autos, which has the exclusive right to sell new Fords in the Rochester area. Under the contract, Ford sets the wholesale price, and Rochester Motors selects the quantity to purchase and the retail price. The only cost facing Rochester Motors is the wholesale price of the car. Ford and Rochester Autos both strive to maximize their own profits. What are (1) the wholesale price, (2) the retail price, (3) the quantity sold, and (4) the combined profits of Ford and Rochester Autos?
   c. Describe how Ford might use a two-part pricing scheme to eliminate this successive monopoly problem with Rochester Motors. (No calculations are necessary.)

19–2. In explaining a decision to purchase an independent R&D laboratory, an executive of the acquiring company said,

> *We felt we had to purchase the company to give us patent rights on any important discoveries. Without these rights, we would have few incentives to invest in the marketing and distribution systems that are necessary to support the discoveries.*

Evaluate this logic.

Solutions to Self-Evaluation Problems

19–1. Ford Motor Distribution
   a.
$$\text{MR} = \text{MC}$$
$$60,000 - 200Q = 4,000$$
$$Q^* = 280$$
$$P^* = 60,000 - 100 \times 280 = \$32,000$$
$$\text{Profits} = (32,000 - 4,000) \times 280 = \$7,840,000$$

   b. Ford's demand curve is Rochester Auto's marginal revenue curve. Thus it will set:
$$60,000 - 400Q = 4,000$$

It will sell 140 autos to Rochester Autos at a wholesale price of \$32,000. The retail price will be \$46,000. Combined profits will be \$5,880,000 (\$3,920,000 + \$1,960,000).
   c. Ford could charge an up-front licensing fee to Rochester Autos to transfer profits from Rochester Autos to Ford. Ford would then sell the cars to Rochester Autos at marginal cost (\$4,000). Ford would sell 280 automobiles to customers at a retail price of \$32,000. Joint profits would be maximized.

19–2. R&D Lab Purchase

This quote only considers half of the contracting problem. Ownership by the acquiring company might increase the investment incentives of that company; however, it can decrease the investment incentives of the managers at the R&D laboratory (because they are less likely to capture the gains from the investment). The optimal ownership pattern depends, in part, on whose investment incentives are more important.

19–1. Discuss the pros and cons of the policy described in the following quote from *Fortune*[27]:

> *According to the new thinking, any kind of work to which a company can't bring a special set of skills should be spun off, outsourced or eliminated. Thus AT&T, GE, IBM, and Shell Oil are in the process of spinning off legal, public relations, billing, payroll, and other services. What's left, whether it's a $100 million corporation or a $100 billion corporation, is the ideal size. . . . For example, if marketing is a competitive advantage in an industry, then it should build up its marketing muscle and employ outside suppliers and service firms to do everything else.*

19–2. The Black Diamond Company mines coal. It would like to build a processing plant right next to its major mine. The location of this mine is relatively remote and is not near other coal mines. Tax considerations, as well as government regulations, dictate that the processing plant be owned and operated by some independent company (other than Black Diamond). Your company, the Greg Norman Coal Company, is considering building and operating the plant for Black Diamond on a contract basis. Your job is to negotiate the contract with Black Diamond. Discuss the terms that you will try to get Black Diamond to agree to in the contract. Explain why these terms are important to you.

19–3. Evaluate the following quote:

> *The major advantage to outsourcing is that it reduces a company's capital costs, freeing the company to use scarce capital for other purposes.*

19–4. In explaining the recent acquisition of a supplier, an executive made the following argument: "We purchased the supplier so that we could keep the profit rather than pay it to some other firm." Evaluate this argument.

19–5. Cable television companies lay cables to individual households in the communities they serve to carry the television signal. How specific is this investment? What kind of arrangements would you expect the cable companies to make with local communities about the pricing and taxation of cable services? Explain.

19–6. The Hidden Fence Company sells invisible electric fences to contain dogs within yards. For a half-acre lot, the cost is $2,000 for the system and installation. The market for invisible dog fencing is competitive: Several companies sell similar products at about the same price. In each case, the dog wears a battery-powered collar. The collar give the dog a shock if it gets near the boundary of the property. Hidden Fence uses a specially designed collar that uses batteries made specifically for Hidden Fence by the Battery-O-Vac Company. The batteries last for three months and cost $25 apiece. Hidden Fence has a patent on these batteries, and there are no alternative sources of supply. Other fence companies produce products that use generic batteries. Currently, the battery costs of these other systems are the same as for Hidden Fence.

   a. Suppose that you purchase the system from Hidden Fence. After you purchase the system, how much will Hidden Fence be able to raise the price of its batteries before you discontinue use of the system and buy a different system from another company? (Suppose that you do want to maintain an invisible fence.) For this question, assume a 10 percent annual discount rate, no inflation, and an infinite life for the invisible fence, yourself, and the patent for the batteries.

   b. As the manager of Hidden Fence Company, what might you do to convince a worried prospective customer that opportunistic behavior with respect to battery prices is not a likely occurrence?

19–7. Advanced Interconnect Manufacturing Inc. (AIM) is an independent company. It was previously owned by one of its major customers before being purchased by five managers (with the help of outside investors). AIM assembles wire harnesses for use in machines such as copiers and x-ray machines. The vice president of the company claims that the

---

[27]B. Dumaine and J. Labate (1992), "Is Big Still Good?" *Fortune* (April 20), 50.

company is more efficient because "as an independent company, AIM doesn't have to share any of its major customer's corporate overhead." As he notes, the company's CEO doesn't get paid by us."

a. Evaluate the vice president's explanation for the increased efficiency of AIM since the ownership was changed.

b. Give an alternative explanation for the increased efficiency.

19–8. Jimmy's Stereo Company manufactures stereo equipment. Its business strategy is to provide retail customers with high-quality equipment, along with good service and warranty protection. It currently distributes its products through licensed dealers who have exclusive territories. Discuss (1) why Jimmy's might offer its distributors exclusive territories, (2) the potential problems that this policy might create in terms of retail pricing, and (3) potential policies that Jimmy's might use to address this pricing problem.

19–9. BQT Manufacturing produces electric lamps. To produce these lamps, BQT must either make or acquire bases for the lamps. Currently, the company outsources the production of the bases for their lamps to the ACE Lamp Company. BQT maintains ownership of the machinery, that is, used to produce the bases. ACE uses BQT's machines at plants owned by ACE.

a. Why do you think BQT is subcontracting the production of the bases?

b. Why do you think BQT maintains ownership of the production equipment?

c. What problems might be caused by BQT's maintaining ownership of the production equipment?

d. What might BQT do to reduce the magnitude of these problems?

19–10. Most of the McDonald's restaurants in the Rochester area are owned by one individual. Discuss why this ownership pattern makes economic sense.

19–11. You are at a cocktail party, where you meet the CEO of a pharmaceutical company who has been thinking recently about her overseas distributors who have exclusive sales territories. She can't quite figure out what is troubling her, but she is dissatisfied with these distributors. You describe the "double markup" problem. The CEO's eyes light up. "You are exactly right," she says. "The distributors are setting prices for our product that are too high." A year passes. You meet the CEO at another party. She heads straight for you and says,

> *You were wrong. There was no double markup problem. After our talk a year ago, I terminated the contracts with all our overseas distributors. I sent our own people overseas to set up in-house distributors. To motivate the region managers I tied a big part of their compensation to the profitability of their regions. I was sure I would see a big change, but overseas prices are just about the same as they were when we used exclusive distributors. I guess prices weren't that bad with the distributors.*

Do you think the CEO's conclusions are correct? Why or why not?

19–12. The Boswell Medical Center is the only hospital in a rural community. It requires significant janitorial services to clean its buildings and equipment. It also requires a relatively large lab for conducting tests of various types (e.g., MRIs, blood tests, and ultrasound tests). Do you think that Boswell is more likely to outsource its janitorial services or lab work? Explain.

19–13. The Hanson Clinic is a well-regarded medical center located in a semirural area in the Midwest. One of its specialty areas is treating rare forms of cancer. To support this activity Hanson wants to construct a new lab. The lab will require very specialized equipment, a specially designed building, and a skilled staff. The estimated cost of the equipment and building is $50 million.

The clinic is considering three possible organizational arrangements. The first is vertical integration. The second is outsourcing (where another company constructs the building, purchases the equipment, and provides contractual services to the clinic). The third is for the clinic to purchase the equipment and building, and lease them to an independent operator (who would provide contractual services to the clinic).

Discuss the pluses and minuses of each of the three alternative structures. What factors do you think are most important in making this choice?

19–14. Koji Incorporated produces high-end cameras. Its typical camera comes with an array of options. The company has a good brand name.
- **a.** Koji distributes its cameras through independent dealers who are given exclusive distribution rights for their respective market areas. Discuss why it might make economic sense for Koji to grant its distributors exclusive territories.
- **b.** Since Koji adopted this distribution system, it has experienced a double markup problem. What is a double markup problem?
- **c.** Discuss how Koji might use a two-part pricing scheme to reduce the double markup problem. (Be sure to specify what the two-part pricing scheme would entail.)
- **d.** Describe one other method that Koji might use to address the double markup problem.

Appendix: Ownership Rights and Investment Incentives[28]

This appendix provides a more detailed example of how ownership rights can affect investment incentives (in this case, investments in effort). Through this example, some of the important trade-offs between vertical integration and long-term contracts become more evident.

Basic Problem

The AGT Company manufactures computer modems. The company is owned by Valentina Vezzali. The Custom Circuit Company makes circuit boards for AGT. AGT is Custom's only customer, and Custom is AGT's sole supplier of circuit boards. The boards are tailor-made for AGT and cannot be used by other manufacturers (the boards are firm-specific). Custom Circuit is owned by Phillipe Daurelle.

AGT might want to make future design changes in its circuit boards. For simplicity, suppose that the future benefit of a design change to AGT can take only two values, 20 or 40, whereas the costs to Custom of making the change can be either 10 or 30. The likelihood of a high benefit and a low cost is influenced by both Tina's and Phil's efforts. Let x equal the probability that the benefit is 40. Tina can affect this probability through her efforts—in fact, we assume that Tina's efforts completely determine x. For instance, by working with customers, she can determine the best design change to make. She also can spend time marketing the revised product. These types of activities increase the probability that the benefits from the design change will be large. However, the personal cost to Tina of exerting effort is $10x^2$. As an example, if Tina exerts enough effort so that x is 0.5, she incurs a personal cost of $10(0.5)^2 = 2.5$. Similarly, Phil's actions completely determine y, the probability that the cost equals 10, at a personal cost of $10y^2$. For instance, Phil can exert effort on developing more cost-effective ways to manufacture the new circuit boards.

Neither Tina's nor Phil's effort choices are observable by the other party. Tina does not know y and Phil does not know x. Although both Tina and Phil ultimately can observe the realized costs and benefits of the design change, they cannot be verified by a third party. Thus, neither effort, costs, nor benefits are contractible; it is not possible to provide either party with incentives through a contract tied to realized costs or benefits of the design change.

---

[28]This appendix uses elementary probability theory and calculus. This section draws on B. Holmstrom and J. Tirole (1989), "Theory of the Firm," in R. Schmalensee (Ed.), *Handbook of Industrial Organization,* Vol. 1 (North Holland: Amsterdam), 69–72.

Ideal Effort Choices

Value is created by a design change whenever the benefits of the change exceed the costs. The only time that the design change does not create value is when the benefits are 20 and the costs are 30. Both Tina and Phil are risk-neutral. It is in their joint interests to choose effort levels that maximize expected surplus. By maximizing the size of the pie, there is more value to share and both parties can be made better off. Ideally, the joint expected surplus S_J for the two companies is

$$S_J = (40 - 10)xy + (40 - 30)x(1 - y) + (20 - 10)(1 - x)y - 10x^2 - 10y^2 \quad (19.5)$$
$$= 30xy + 10x(1 - y) + 10(1 - x)y - 10x^2 - 10y^2$$
$$= 10xy + 10x + 10y - 10x^2 - 10y^2$$

This equation is maximized by choosing effort levels of $y = x = 1$.[29] The joint expected surplus net of effort costs is 10.

Actual Effort Choices under the Contract

The specific contract between AGT and Custom requires that a design change be approved by both companies. Since Tina and Phil have equal bargaining power, they anticipate splitting the surplus, that is, available from any future design change. For instance, if the benefits are 40 and the costs are 10, the total surplus is 30. A price for the circuit boards of 25 splits the gains: Tina gains $40 - 25 = 15$ and Phil gains $25 - 10 = 15$.

Tina and Phil *choose their effort levels privately* (the effort choices cannot be observed by the other person). Each person chooses an effort level that maximizes his or her own surplus, given the anticipated effort choice of the other party. As we shall see, both parties choose effort levels below the values that maximize the joint surplus. The low effort choices result from the standard free-rider problem. Tina and Phil bear the total costs of their personal efforts but receive only half the benefits. Consider Tina's problem. Her expected surplus S_T is

$$S_T = .5(40 - 10)x\bar{y} + .5(40 - 30)x(1 - \bar{y}) + .5(20 - 10)(1 - x)\bar{y} - 10x^2 \quad (19.6)$$
$$= 15x\bar{y} + 5x(1 - \bar{y}) + 5(1 - x)\bar{y} = 10x^2$$
$$= 5x\bar{y} + 5x + 5 - 10x^2$$

where $\bar{y}$ is the effort level that she expects Phil to exert.[30] Taking the partial derivative with respect to x and setting it equal to zero,

$$\partial S_T/\partial x = 5\bar{y} + 5 - 20x = 0 \quad (19.7)$$

Phil's first-order condition is, similarly,

$$\partial S_P/\partial y = 5\bar{x} + 5 - 20y = 0 \quad (19.8)$$

In a Nash equilibrium, both Phil's and Tina's first-order condition will be met and the effort choices will be $x = 1/3$ and $y = 1/3$ (at these values, neither party has the

---

[29]Technical note: The first three terms in Equation (19.5) are the three possible outcomes of positive surplus multiplied by the probability of the outcome. The last two terms are the effort costs. Note: If the benefits are 20 and the costs are 30, the design change is not implemented; the term $(0)(1 - x)(1 - y)$ drops out of Equation (19.5). The first-order conditions are $10 + 10y - 20x = 0$ and $10 + 10x - 20y = 0$. The solution is $x = y = 1$.

[30]She bears the full cost of her effort, $10x^2$, but receives only half the benefits.

incentive to alter his or her choice). The total surplus, net of effort costs, is 5.6 [substitute $y = x = 1/3$ into Equation (19.5)].

Vertical Integration

One way to change effort incentives is for the two firms to integrate vertically, either by having AGT buy Custom or by having Custom buy AGT. Consider the case where Tina purchases Custom from Phil and hires him as an employee to manage AGT's "Custom Circuit Division." Ownership gives Tina the decision rights to implement the design change without Phil's approval (she has the *residual use rights*). Since Phil has no bargaining power, all the surplus goes to Tina. Phil has no incentives to exert effort on increasing the likelihood of a low production cost: He bears all the costs for his personal effort and reaps none of the benefits. (Recall that we have ruled out incentive contracts tied to realized costs or benefits of design changes.) Given $y = 0$, the cost of implementing the design change is 30 for certain. Tina's benefits from investing are

$$(40 - 30)x - 10x^2 \qquad (19.9)$$

Tina will choose $x = 1/2$. The total surplus, net of investment costs, is 2.5.[31] The case where Custom buys AGT is symmetrical, Phil invests $y = 1/2$, and total net surplus is 2.5.[32] Clearly, vertical integration is not superior to a long-term contract.

Optimal Organizational Choice

When Tina and Phil negotiate the sale of either company, they can share the expected surplus in any manner by negotiating the appropriate purchase price. They have incentives to choose the ownership structure that maximizes the expected net surplus. Given the numbers in this example, they will choose not to combine the two companies. Separate ownership creates more value than integration.

This example illustrates that ownership structure can matter because it affects investment incentives (in this case, investments in effort). Ownership gives individuals increased power to capture the fruits of their efforts (see Chapter 10) and thus can provide important incentives. In this example, separate ownership is better than integration because both parties' investments are important. It is better to provide moderate incentives to both Phil and Tina than strong incentives to only one party. It is easy to envision cases where integration will be the preferred alternative. For instance, suppose that Tina can exert effort to affect the benefits of the design change, but Phil has little control over the costs. Here, it would make sense for AGT to own Custom. This ownership structure provides strong incentives for Tina to exert effort and weak incentives for Phil. These incentives are optimal, since only Tina's effort matters. Conversely, it makes sense for Custom to own AGT when Phil's effort is substantially more important than Tina's.

In this example, we have ruled out the possibility that effort can be motivated by incentive compensation (making payments based on the realized costs and benefits). We made this extreme assumption specifically to isolate the important incentive effects of ownership. More generally, owners can motivate internal

---

[31]Tina's first-order condition is $10 - 20x = 0$. The solution is $x = 1/2$. The total surplus is found by substituting $x = 1/2$ and $y = 0$ into Equation (19.6).

[32]This symmetry is a result of the cost and benefit functions in our example. More generally, it can matter who buys whom.

ANALYZING MANAGERIAL DECISIONS: *Insurance Industry Distribution Systems*

Insurance companies contract with independent agents to sell policies and provide ongoing services to customers. Ongoing client services tend to be more important in auto insurance companies than life insurance companies. In some insurance companies, the agents "own" the client list. If they stop representing the firm, they can take the clients with them to a new company. In other cases, the insurance company owns the list. The agent is not allowed to take clients to another company. (There is a formal contract with this provision.) Do you think life insurance companies or auto insurance companies are more likely to employ independent agents who own their client lists? Explain.

employees through incentive compensation. For instance, if AGT purchased Custom, Tina might be able to pay Phil in a manner that would encourage him to exert some effort to reduce costs. Similarly, in the separate ownership case, AGT and Custom might be able to include incentive clauses in the contract that would encourage investment (for instance, Custom might receive extra revenue from AGT if it can produce the new design at low cost). As we discussed in Chapters 15 through 17, incentive schemes and performance evaluation are not costless activities. In a more detailed analysis, AGT and Custom would have to compare the value that could be created using an optimal supply contract without integration to the value that could be created using optimal incentive compensation contracts under integration. The basic point of our analysis continues to hold—*ownership structure matters because it can affect investment incentives.*

Leadership: Motivating Change within Organizations

LEARNING OBJECTIVES

1. Define leadership and list two important characteristics of good leadership.
2. Discuss the obstacles to having business plans adopted and implemented.
3. Describe how changing the firm's organizational architecture can help motivate changes within the firm.
4. Discuss the trade-offs associated with maintaining flexibility in the proposal stage versus the implementation stage of a business plan.
5. Explain how a manager can market a business plan within the firm.
6. Define organizational power; give specific examples.
7. Explain how symbols can be used to shape employee expectations of appropriate behavior.

This chapter can be found via Create or McGraw-Hill *Connect*®. For more information, refer to the Preface.

Understanding the Business Environment: The Economics of Regulation

LEARNING OBJECTIVES

1. Discuss the importance of the regulatory environment to corporate managers.
2. Describe the role of government intervention in the marketplace in defining and enforcing property rights, in dealing with potential market failures, and in the redistribution of wealth.
3. Illustrate a basic explanation of the economic theory of regulation and the market for regulation.
4. Explain how regulation can be used to promote market power by restricting entry by potential competitors.
5. Discuss business participation in the political process.

In May 1998, the U.S. Justice Department charged Microsoft Corp. with crushing competition and stifling innovation in the software industry.[1] Even though the lawsuit had been rumored widely, Microsoft shares still fell 3.8 percent upon filing the legal action. Nineteen states ranging from California to New York joined the suit. This litigation alleged that Microsoft's long-standing practice of adding features to its Windows operating system without a separate charge amounts to predatory pricing: It drives out existing competitors and dissuades other firms from entering the software market. In particular, Microsoft was accused of damaging rivals Netscape and Sun Microsystems.

The federal government contended that Microsoft has used its Windows, which was installed on 90 percent of new machines, to pressure personal computer makers to favor Microsoft's browser over Netscape's. Offered as evidence were records of a meeting between Microsoft and Netscape executives in June 1995 where Microsoft allegedly proposed dividing the browser market between the two companies. At the trial in October 1998, Microsoft argued that it was "set up" by Netscape. According to Microsoft, Netscape used the June 1995 meeting to create a record that could be passed to the Justice Department to further its case against Microsoft.

[1] J. Wilke (1998), "U.S. Sues Microsoft on Antitrust Grounds," *The Wall Street Journal* (May 19), A3; "Microsoft Says It Was 'Set Up,'" *Democrat and Chronicle* (October 27, 1998), D12; D. Bank (1998), "Is Microsoft a New Public Utility?" *The Wall Street Journal* (May 19), B1; and M. France, P. Burrows, L. Himelstein, and M. Moeller (1999), "The Microsoft Ruling," *BusinessWeek* (November 22), 38–41.

The government's case was based on the assumption that the PC operating system is an "essential facility." So many people rely on their Windows-based computers that software "competitors now need the hand of government to give them a place on the PC screen." Microsoft had acquired a virtual monopoly in the market for PC operating systems—but by itself, that was not illegal. The government also had to show that the company used predatory practices to restrain trade. For example, the government made much of a quote from a Microsoft vice president who stated that it was "necessary to fundamentally blunt [Sun Microsystems'] Java to protect our core Windows assets." But Microsoft Chairman Bill Gates scoffed at the idea that such statements indicate illegal actions. "It's no surprise to me that there are quotes from inside Microsoft that say, 'Let's compete, let's do a better product.'" Microsoft defended its actions by arguing that consumers have not been harmed and that "this suit is about Microsoft's right to innovate."

One remedy the government considered would be to prohibit Microsoft from dictating what Internet content appears on the Windows desktop. For example, users seeking travel reservations on the Web were routed to Microsoft's Expedia site. Such routing was unfair, claimed Terrell Jones, president of Sabre Interactive, which operated the competing travel-arrangement site, Travelocity. Jones claimed that Microsoft denied him a favored position on desktops.

On November 5, 1999, U.S. District Judge Thomas P. Jackson concluded that Microsoft routinely used its monopoly power to crush competitors. Judge Jackson's fact findings were so critical of Microsoft that the breakup of Microsoft became a real possibility. After two year of appeals, legal maneuvering, and a new president in the White House, on November 2, 2002, U.S. District Court Judge Colleen Kollar-Kotelly accepted a settlement between Microsoft and the Justice Department. The agreement prevents Microsoft from participating in exclusive deals that could hurt competitors, allows manufacturers and customers to remove icons for some Microsoft features, and requires Microsoft to release certain types of sensitive technology to its rivals so software developers can write programs for Windows that work as well as Microsoft products do. Microsoft settled several state lawsuits that alleged the agreement with the Justice Department was insufficient to protect Microsoft's competitors. In 2003 Microsoft agreed to pay California up to $1.1 billion to settle that suit.

Importance of Regulation to Managers

Recall Figure 11.1, which provides a flowchart of the framework underlying this book. In that figure the external business environment—technology, markets, and regulation—drives the firm's choice of business strategy and in turn the firm's organizational architecture. Numerous examples have been provided throughout the book regarding how the three legs of the organizational architecture stool can become unbalanced when the firm's business environment and its strategy change. In Chapter 8 we discussed how a firm might develop a business strategy that both creates consumer value and allows the firm to capture that value.

In the federal and state lawsuit against Microsoft, government regulators argued that they were trying to protect consumers by fostering competition. Yet government regulation often limits entry into industries. For instance, electric utilities explicitly were granted effective monopolies to supply electricity to customers within specific geographic regions. New entrants were prohibited from building generating plants or selling electricity at lower prices. As states now deregulate power production, new companies are competing for customers. This has lowered prices and created new businesses ranging from consulting firms who advise large power customers about ways of exploiting the new competitive environment to power brokers who buy electric power from new power plant operators and resell it to large consumers of electricity. Thus, these regulatory changes have altered firms' strategies as well as their organizational architectures.

Government regulation takes a variety of forms: The Microsoft lawsuit is only one example of the government regulating business conduct. The following is but a partial list of the many ways regulation affects business:

- The U.S. government has enacted an array of antitrust legislation that makes illegal such practices as collusive pricing that restrict trade.

- The Environmental Protection Agency (EPA) was established in 1970 to limit pollution of air and water by controlling the disposal of solid waste, pesticides, radiation, and toxic substances.

- All companies with publicly traded stock must follow the Securities and Exchange Commission regulations; for instance, financial disclosure regulation requires that these companies file audited financial statements with the SEC—statements that are prepared in accordance with Generally Accepted Accounting Principles.

- Intellectual property laws, price and entry restrictions, labor laws, occupational safety regulations, import and export laws, and immigration acts both protect and constrain commercial activities.

- Some regulations focus on specific industries; for example, financial services (banks, savings and loans, credit unions, mutual funds, investment banks, and insurance companies), energy (electric utilities, gas pipelines, coal, and oil), and transportation (airlines, railroad, and trucking).

- Federal corporate tax rates of roughly 33 percent imply that all firms in effect have a partner who is entitled to almost one-third of the firm's profits.

This chapter discusses various roles of government including its role in regulating business, how the market for regulation works, and how successful managers manage the regulatory process.

MANAGERIAL APPLICATIONS

Europe Relaxes Its Labor Laws

Europe has rather strict worker protection laws that regulate the days people work, their vacations, layoffs, and other aspects of the employment relationship. One manager said, "we can divorce from our husbands and wives, but we can't divorce from our employees." These laws have made it quite expensive to dismiss employees when business slowed. This has caused companies to be extremely cautious in expanding within Europe during upturns, preferring to expand production in less regulated countries, often in Asia. The result has been slow job growth in Europe. But since the mid-1990s, with the support of politicians, companies are increasingly getting around these restrictive labor laws by hiring temporary employees—many of the most restrictive laws apply only to permanent employees.

Most European countries now have adopted laws legalizing temporary employee agencies, such as Manpower. These temp companies provide employers more flexibility to dismiss "long-term temporary help." And the countries that have relaxed their labor laws the most have enjoyed the greatest job growth.

Source: H. Cooper and T. Kamm (1998), "Much of Europe Eases Its Rigid Labor Laws, and Temps Proliferate," *The Wall Street Journal* (June 4), A1.

Economic Motives for Government Intervention

Governments perform various functions; they provide a system of laws and legal institutions that define and enforce property rights, and they address market failures. Markets are said to fail whenever a competitive, unfettered market does not generate an efficient resource allocation for those within the economy. Later we examine a number of reasons for such market failures: Externalities, public goods, monopolies, and information asymmetries. To finance these potentially beneficial government functions of enforcing property rights and resolving market failures, revenues must be raised—usually through taxes. However, governments also use taxes as well as other means to redistribute resources in ways that impose costs on society. We now discuss each of these aspects of government intervention.

Defining and Enforcing Property Rights

When engaging in trade, each party to the transaction generally expects that its rights in the contract will be enforced. If Mark Danchak promises to deliver 200 spring suits to Melanie Caoile's store next February in return for $20,000 today and $80,000 in April, Mel expects that Mark will deliver the clothing that she ordered and Mark expects that he will receive the $80,000. If the suits do not arrive and she has no legal recourse, her future willingness to buy clothing from his factory is reduced. Similarly, if Mel does not pay the $80,000 she promised and Mark has no legal recourse, his willingness to sell Mel clothing in the future is reduced.

The government creates legal institutions, such as courts, that enforce property rights. To enforce its rulings, the court has access to police powers of the state. If Mark breaches the contract that states he will deliver 200 suits, the court can force him to make restitution. If Mel does not pay, the court has the power to force compliance.

By enforcing contracts between private parties and adjudicating disputes, the government reduces transaction costs. With lower transaction costs, there are greater gains from trade, more transactions, more consumer and producer surplus,[2] and greater wealth. If Mel could obtain comparable suits from an extremely reputable supplier (one with no risk of default) for $102,000 and she expects to incur more than $2,000 in costs of litigating the transaction with Mark, she will not buy his suits. But if she believes the government will enforce the contract at a cost to her of less than $10 per suit, then she will buy the 200 suits and will have consumer surplus of as much as $2,000. If the government can enforce this contract for less than $2,000, then it's efficient for the government to perform this role (even ignoring any producer surplus).

A system of well-enforced, stable property rights increases incentives for people to make investments. Knowing that Mark can sell his output incurring low transaction costs supports his incentives to build a suit factory. Not only will more customers be willing to buy Mark's products because their transaction costs will be lower, but also his transaction costs will be lower. The government enforces property rights in other ways as well; for instance, Mark expects that the state will provide protection against someone stealing his goods prior to their delivery.

---

[2]Chapter 7 defined consumer surplus as the difference between what the consumer is willing to pay and what is actually paid for a product. Analogously defined, producer surplus is the difference between the price the producer receives for the product and the cost of producing it.

MANAGERIAL APPLICATIONS

War and Hunger

Wars, such as those in Africa, Kosovo, Chechnya, Afghanistan, and Iraq, regularly produce widespread hunger among the population. During wars, the power of the central government to enforce property rights and contracts is reduced dramatically. Without protection from the government supporting their ability to reap the rewards of a harvest, farmers are reluctant to plant crops. Especially near contested areas, farmers fear that their land might turn into a battlefield or that any crops they grow might be seized by one of the combatants. Agricultural output is slashed due to the reduced incentives to plant because the farmers' ability to capture the fruits of their investments is diminished. Besides the obvious reason that wars create hunger by consuming real resources (labor and property), wars also create hunger by reducing incentives to invest in agriculture.

Most governments enforce patents, copyrights, and trademarks. By granting inventors patents (which protect the inventor from others copying their inventions for a stipulated time period), inventors and investors devote more resources to inventive activities. Developing countries without strong patent and trademark protection often have difficulty attracting investment because people fear that their investments will be expropriated.

The transaction costs of writing and enforcing contracts are higher in countries with poorly enforced property rights. For instance in the former Soviet Union, large firms employ their own security forces for protection. Workers frequently are paid in cash because the banking system is unreliable. Delivering the payroll to remote sites requires expensive security measures. All these transaction costs reduce gains from trade, lower the volume of transactions, limit investment incentives, and reduce wealth.[3]

In developed countries, relatively few commercial transactions are litigated. The threat of litigation as well as concerns about one's reputation—especially in repeated business dealings—cause most businesspeople to honor contracts voluntarily.[4] Nonetheless, commercial litigation is a growing problem in the United States. Between 1971 and 1991 more than 4 million federal lawsuits were filed, with almost 2.5 million involving at least one business entity. Moreover, this litigation is quite expensive. Combined wealth losses by firms have been estimated to be 1 percent of their equity value or about $21 million per lawsuit.[5] Lawsuits also increase operating costs. For instance, experts argue that one reason health care costs in the United States are so high is that doctors practice defensive medicine—for example, by ordering extra tests to bolster their legal defense in the event that they are sued. Similarly, to limit their liability, few public swimming pools have diving boards. Excessive litigation limits consumers' choices and thus their welfare.

On the one hand, the legal system can promote efficiency by lowering transaction costs by making property rights more secure; on the other, the legal system can raise costs by creating incentives to litigate frivolous suits. A jury ordered McDonald's to pay $2.7 million to Stella Liebeck, a drive-through customer who burned herself with hot coffee after placing the cup between her legs to remove the top and add cream:

[3]A. Grief and E. Kandel (1995), "Contract Enforcement Institutions: Historical Perspective and Current Status in Russia," in E. Lazear (Ed.), *Economic Transition in Eastern Europe and Russia: Realities of Reform* (Hoover Press: Stanford).

[4]In Chapter 22, we discuss these issues in greater detail.

[5]S. Bhagat, J. Brickley, and J. Coles (1994), "The Costs of Inefficient Bargaining and Financial Distress," *Journal of Financial Economics* 35 (April), 221–247.

MANAGERIAL APPLICATIONS

Multinational Counterfeiting

Counterfeit products used to be mostly pirated music CD-ROMs, cheap Rolex watches, and software. Today, virtually all branded products compete with their counterfeit twin. In 2004 Brazilian police seized more than $1 million worth of bogus Hewlett-Packard inkjet cartridges. The Chinese confiscated everything from counterfeit Buick windshields to phony Viagra. Guam Secret Service uncovered bogus North Korean–made pharmaceuticals, cigarettes, and $100 bills. General Motors is suing a Chinese carmaker for ripping off its Chevrolet Spark minicar. In 2003 Pfizer recalled some 16.5 million tablets of its cholesterol-lowering drug Lipitor after discovering they were fakes. The list goes on and on. U.S. customs seizures of counterfeit goods have risen from under $50 million in 2000 to $140 million in 2004, and experts estimate that less than 5 percent of total counterfeits entering the United States are intercepted.

Many counterfeiters are multinationals—diversifying their sourcing and manufacturing across borders. Investors often include Middle East middlemen, local entrepreneurs, and even organized crime. The counterfeiters range from fly-by-night operators to legitimate companies. Some are licensed producers of brand-name goods that produce an extra, unauthorized batch. Others are former licensees who kept the designs or are generic manufacturers who moonlight as makers of fakes. Five factories in China are licensed to make Yamaha motorcycles, but 50 plants have produced bikes labeled "Yamaha."

China, which produces nearly two-thirds of all pirated goods, is key to any solution. Chinese factories quickly copy new products. "If you can make it, they can fake it," says David Fernyhough, director of brand protection at investigation firm Hill & Associates Ltd. in Hong Kong. But getting Chinese cooperation is tough. Chinese authorities have ignored the problem because the victims were usually foreign brand owners. One pirate of fake windshields for General Motors, DaimlerChrysler, and Mitsubishi Motors was fined just $97,000 and given a suspended sentence. China gets tough on counterfeiters when Chinese are at risk. After 15 infants died from phony milk powder, the counterfeiter was sentenced to eight years in prison. However, mounting international pressure is forcing China to toughen its legal sanctions. Yet the big problem is too many counterfeiters have ties to local Chinese officials, and counterfeit operations provide a major source of local employment.

Source: F. Balfour (2005), "Fakes!" *BusinessWeek* (February 7), 54–63.

She claimed the coffee was just too hot. The U.S. securities acts potentially lower transaction costs in security markets by regulating brokers and requiring publicly traded firms to make timely operating information disclosures. However, these acts also allow investor lawsuits if the firm makes what turn out to be false disclosures. The out-of-pocket cost to plaintiffs of filing such a lawsuit is under $200, whereas the average settlement is $7 million. Such a disparity encourages frivolous suits. (In some countries, the incentive to file frivolous suits is reduced by making the losing party responsible for part of their opponent's legal expenses.)

Redressing Market Failures

Chapter 3 describes how a well-functioning market provides an efficient allocation of resources without shortages or surpluses. But unregulated markets do not always function well. Externalities, public goods, monopolies, and informational failures can produce "market failures" that limit the efficient allocation of resources. In these cases, some economists argue that an appropriate role of government is to enter and regulate the market to redress the failure. Yet, even after accepting the fact that such market failures exist, two questions still must be addressed before one should conclude that government regulation will help. First, can government resolve the problem at a cost lower than that of the inefficiency caused by the market failure? Government intervention is

---

MANAGERIAL APPLICATIONS

Alternative Dispute Resolution

To reduce the high cost of commercial litigation, many companies are turning to alternative dispute resolution (ADR) mechanisms: Arbitration and mediation. Many commercial contracts now contain provisions binding the parties to use ADR instead of litigation. Professional ADR firms providing such services streamline the dispute process by avoiding lengthy court delays and more costly legal procedures.

---

not free. Regulators must be hired and their regulations enforced. These actions consume real resources. To increase welfare, these total resources must be lower than the cost of the market failures eliminated. Second, will the regulators act in the public interest to resolve the market failure and not in their self-interest? Later in this chapter we examine this second question.

Externalities

Government regulation can reduce market failures caused by externalities. Chapter 3 describes externalities as the costs or benefits created by the actions of one party imposed on involuntary participants where the consequences of these actions are not regulated by the system of prices. Air pollution is an example of an externality. When you buy and consume gasoline, the purchase price compensates everyone in the supply chain from landowners to oil explorers, drillers, refiners, and gas station owners for providing that gallon. But the people who breathe the carbon monoxide produced when you use that gasoline are not compensated. The Coase Theorem states that resource allocations remain efficient, even in the presence of externalities, as long as property rights are clearly assigned and the transaction costs of enforcing and exchanging them are sufficiently low. Hence, government can reduce market

---

MANAGERIAL APPLICATIONS

Frivolous Lawsuits

In June 1994 Orange County, a California municipality, which defaulted on its debt payment because of losses from trading interest-rate derivatives, received $400 million from Merrill Lynch in an out-of-court settlement. Merrill Lynch was the investment bank that sold the derivatives to Orange County. The litigation alleged that Merrill should have known that the county officials were trading inappropriately and, if so, it should have refused to do business with the county. Merrill argued that county officials were sophisticated, acting in full public view. The precise duty a seller of financial products owes to its customers is frustratingly vague, in part because this kind of case tends to be settled out of court and thus no legal precedent is established. "There is nothing to stop a loss-making client's imagination from running wild over the settlement that threats might achieve." Without a resolution of these legal uncertainties, bankers simply cannot know their clients "too well."

Orange County is an extreme example of the hindsight often employed by courts. As long as Orange County was not losing money on its derivatives, there was no lawsuit. Courts enter and undo deals that go sour. Thus lawsuits are like embedded options. If the product or service works, there's no legal action. If the product or service fails, a lawsuit results. Anticipating such lawsuits the seller of the product or service must price the option at the time of sale, so the buyer must pay for this option. The market for the product or service collapses if the seller and buyer cannot agree on a price for the product/service including the embedded option.

Source: "Orange County Seller Beware," *The Economist* (June 6, 1998), 75.

Direct and Indirect Costs of the Food and Drug Administration

"The FDA ensures that the food we eat is safe and wholesome, that the cosmetics we use won't harm us, and that medicines, medical devices . . . are safe and effective." To accomplish its mandate, the FDA has 9,000 employees and a 1999 budget of over $1 billion. Yet, the cost of protecting consumers from unsafe drugs includes more than just the FDA's $1 billion budget. Following FDA-mandated procedures, it can take 15 years to approve a new drug; in the meantime, people who could have been helped are not. And despite all its efforts, the FDA process is not foolproof. Many new drugs are pulled from the market because of some unforeseen problem. Duract was yanked after four patients died and eight needed liver transplants. Pretrial tests cannot include all the possible drug interactions from other medications. And doctors often prescribe drugs for conditions other than those for which the drugs were approved.

This example illustrates that regulation generates both direct costs and indirect costs. The indirect costs are opportunity costs—drug therapies denied to potential patients because of delays in the approval process.

Sources: www.fda.gov/opacom/faqs/genfaqs.html; and A. Barrett (1998), "The Big Hole in the Drug Safety Net," *BusinessWeek* (July 6), 37.

failures caused by externalities by defining property rights or by reducing the transaction costs of enforcing property rights.[6]

Consider the example of the federal government's creating a market in pollution rights. In 1995, it set a cap on the number of tons of sulfur dioxide allowed into the air.[7] Each year thereafter, the cap declines. The government issued to the 110 dirtiest power plants tradable certificates that matched their share of the cap. If companies cut their emissions below their caps, they could sell the excess to other companies that hadn't made the necessary cuts. Companies can save certificates from year to year, but federal clean-air standards still limit pollution. Sulfur dioxide certificate trading amounted to about $3 billion in 2003.[8] One company had to reduce emissions by 30,000 tons. It removed 20,000 tons cheaply by switching to low-sulfur coal. The remaining 10,000 tons could be removed only by spending $130 million on scrubbing equipment. Instead, it bought certificates for the remaining 10,000 tons, saving the company $100 million. This program, which reduced emissions 30 percent nationwide, is an example of the government's reducing an externality using market-based mechanisms by defining and enforcing tradable property rights in pollutants.

The market for pollution rights works because firms whose costs to reduce pollution are lower than the market price of the rights can sell their rights to firms that face higher costs of pollution abatement. Thus, society achieves the greatest reduction in pollution for the smallest aggregate cost. Moreover, there are an indefinite set of sulfur dioxide producers whose sulfur dioxide production is already monitored; thus, the costs of enforcing these contracts are reasonably small.

---

[6]Note that some regulations establish and enforce property rights, but effectively make them nonmarketable (inalienable). For example, the Occupational Safety and Health Administration is charged with enforcing workplace safety regulations that specify an employee's right to work in an environment that satisfies certain conditions. Employees cannot waive these rights. Thus, even though an employee might be willing to bear a risk for additional compensation that was lower than the cost of reducing the risk, such an employment agreement is not allowed, and potential gains from trade are unexploited.

[7]J. Fialka (1997), "Breathing Easy," *The Wall Street Journal* (October 3), A1; J. Fialka (1998), "EPA Plans Emission-Trading Program to Reduce Nitrogen-Oxide Pollution," *The Wall Street Journal* (April 30), B11.

[8]www.epa.gov/airmarkets/trading.

Public Goods

Public goods are those commodities whose consumption by one person does not diminish the amount available to others. Moreover, purchasers of a public good cannot exclude nonpurchasers. A classic example of a public good is national defense; defending you against foreign attack does not necessarily reduce the amount of protection available to others. Moreover, it is difficult to exclude your neighbors from national defense if they don't pay their share. A lighthouse guiding ships at sea is a public good; one ship's use of the lighthouse does not diminish another's use of the lighthouse, and it is difficult to exclude nonpurchasers. An apple is a private good: Your consumption of an apple precludes others' consumption of that apple. It often is difficult for a market to determine the appropriate quantity and price of a public good because free-riders are not excluded easily.

Total welfare would be maximized if quantity produced were set where the public good's marginal cost equaled the sum of each consumer's marginal value. For example, suppose a firm is considering launching a new satellite that will broadcast 500 channels. Aggregate welfare increases so long as the satellite's cost is less than the sum of what each user would be willing to pay. Suppose there are 1 million potential users—half willing to pay $100 each ($50 million) and the other half willing to pay only $10 each ($5 million). If the cost of the satellite is less than $55 million, it is efficient to launch. But a competitive market might not reach this outcome if satellite transmissions are a public good. If the company tries to charge consumers for receiving the signals, all users might claim they only value the signal at $10, so the firm would collect only $10 million. Each user might try to *free-ride*. (Recall the incentive conflicts from free-riders involving joint ownership of assets described in Chapter 10.) Aware of this free-rider problem, the satellite firm will launch the satellite only if its cost is lower than $10 million. The problem is how to identify and charge the users who value the service at $100—a price above $10.

One solution to this free-rider problem is for the government to launch the satellite and pay for it with a tax. This is the basic rationale for using general taxes as the mechanism to finance such government-supplied public goods as defense, police, and fire services. Note that this rationale presumes that the government somehow can estimate the consumers' level of demand accurately. Yet, the government is not immune to particular groups of consumers' overstating their valuation in order to ensure that their desired project is completed. Moreover, the government will be lobbied by satellite makers and others who will profit from this endeavor should the project be undertaken.

Besides having the government provide the public good, another possibility exists: Convert the public good into a private good and exclude those potential customers with low valuations. For example, the company might scramble the satellite signals; those wishing to purchase the signal would have to rent a decoding box for something less than $100. Now, if the satellite costs plus the cost of the scrambling and decoding equipment is less than $50 million, a private firm will provide the service. But in this case, the potential gains from trade between the firm and the 500,000 customers who value the service at only $10 are lost.

Monopoly

Chapter 6 describes how monopolies create resource misallocations. A monopolist sets prices above the competitive price (long-run marginal production cost) and output below the competitive output level. Some customers are willing to pay more than marginal cost, yet do not receive the product. Thus, not all gains from trade are exhausted. One potentially beneficial role of government is to limit the amount by

---

Interstate Commerce Commission

During the 1880s, midwestern farmers complained bitterly that rail rates were unfair; the sum of the costs to ship goods from Chicago to Cleveland, Cleveland to Buffalo, and Buffalo to New York City was substantially greater than the cost of shipping from Chicago to New York—the sum of the short-haul rates exceeded the long-haul rates. At this time, railroads competed on long hauls but not on short hauls because there was usually just one railroad serving adjacent cities such as Chicago and Cleveland, but several railroads serving more distant cities such as Chicago and New York. (You could ship from Chicago to New York through Pittsburgh as well as Buffalo.) The federal government created the ICC to regulate railroad freight rates. To ensure that the commissioners understood the industry they were to oversee, railroad executives were appointed to the commission. The ICC "fixed" the rate disparities by raising the long-haul rates and prohibiting price competition. When the trucking industry began competing with railroads for short hauls (competition that would have eliminated the initial problem if the industry had been left unregulated), the ICC expanded its scope to regulate the interstate trucking industry as well. Regulation raised interstate trucking rates where trucks had been taking short-haul business from the railroads. The ICC provides an example of how regulators can be "captured" by the industry they are regulating and end up protecting producers rather than consumers.

---

which the monopolist's price exceeds marginal cost, and thus realizing more of the potential gains from trade. For example, state and federal regulators retain the authority to set or approve public utilities' prices. However, performing this role well requires the regulator to know the utility's true cost function.

In the United States, antitrust laws dating back to the 1890 Sherman Act give the federal government the power to limit the ability of these monopolies to set prices above competitive levels. The U.S. Justice Department and the Federal Trade Commission have broad powers to ensure the effectiveness of the market and protect competition by overseeing pricing practices, approving mergers, scrutinizing advertising, and regulating other business practices.

In determining whether a monopoly exists, the government must show that the alleged defendant has substantial market power to set prices above the competitive level. In most antitrust cases, the definition of the relevant market becomes a central focus of the lawsuit. In the Microsoft case the government argued that the relevant market that Microsoft controlled involves operating systems, and Microsoft has 90 percent of that market. Microsoft contends that the relevant market is for browsers and that in that market Microsoft's Explorer does not have a dominant position.

Moreover, for this regulation to improve the overall resource allocation, regulators must operate in the public's interest and not be "captured" by the utility or some other party. For example, some politicians think that Internet users should pay a tax to subsidize low-income individuals' access to the Internet. These politicians argue that the poor deserve the same Internet access as the wealthy and that an Internet tax is a good way to achieve such an important social end. While this goal might be laudatory, such taxes are inefficient: They discourage Internet use whenever the tax exceeds the user's marginal benefits. Moreover, some low-income individuals value receiving other goods and services more than they value a connection to the Internet.

It is somewhat ironic, given this array of efficiency issues raised by firms with market power, that many of the monopolized industries were created by various government acts. For example, public utilities (such as electric companies, cable TV, or telephone companies) often are granted exclusive operating franchises to provide services within a specific geographic region.

MANAGERIAL APPLICATIONS

Cost of Regulation—Proprietary Information

IRS officials now release portions of the "advance pricing" agreements they make with businesses. Through these APAs, companies agree in advance with the IRS on how to set transfer prices for internal transactions among units. Although the IRS says it removes sensitive details (taxpayer's identity, trade secrets, and other confidential information), some tax specialists worry. "Companies really bare their souls in filing for APAs," says Timothy McCormally of Tax Executives Institute. He says companies may skip the program rather than risk disclosure.

This is an example of the opportunity costs imposed by regulation. A firm can reduce expected legal costs by negotiating an APA with the IRS. However, filing an APA can expose the firm to considerable risk by having some of its most sensitive cost information outside its control in the hands of a government regulatory agency.

Source: "Tax Report," *The Wall Street Journal* (February 3, 1999), A1.

Finally, some advocates of additional regulation implicitly presume that the government can act with almost surgical precision, identifying and stopping inappropriate activities while leaving appropriate activities unaffected. Yet it is difficult to implement regulation perfectly. Even well-meaning regulators make mistakes. Recognizing that regulatory sanctions might be imposed on managers who are not behaving illegally (or inappropriately), these managers quite rationally might modify their actions to reduce the likelihood that sanctions will be imposed. And such modified actions reduce the firm's value to the extent that they are costly—perhaps because managers are diverted from actions that would have increased value.

Informational Failures

Chapter 10 describes how adverse selection can lead to market failures. Adverse selection refers to the situation in which an individual with private information that affects a potential trading partner's benefits makes an offer, that is, detrimental to the trading partner. The classic example is the "lemons" problem—sellers of used cars generally know more about their mechanical condition than buyers.[9] Thus, at any given price, sellers are more likely to offer "lemons" than high-quality cars. Suppose the average resale price of one-year-old Ford Broncos is $20,000. Used-car buyers do not expect vehicles offered will be in perfect mechanical condition. The $20,000 price thus reflects buyers' forecasts of mechanical problems for one-year-old Broncos offered in the used-car market. For instance, Lena Cardone is the owner of a one-year-old Bronco with no mechanical problems. But if she cannot credibly convince a potential buyer that her Bronco has no problems and that she has another reason for selling, she must sell her Bronco for $20,000. Knowing that it is worth more than $20,000, Lena might prefer to keep it—some economists argue that a market failure results.[10] Some state

[9] G. Akerlof (1970), "The Market for 'Lemons': Quality Uncertainty and the Market Mechanism," *Quarterly Journal of Economics* 84, 488–500.

[10] We believe that this argument requires care. It is true that if information were costless, unexploited gains from trade would exist. But information is a good, one that is expensive to produce and transfer. Given the distribution of information and technology for producing and transferring information, the allocation of resources is efficient. We see little difference in arguing that "compared to a world where information costs are lower, the current allocation of resources is inefficient" and that "compared to a world where the cost of steel is lower, resources are misallocated." Ultimately, efficiency must be judged given the costs implied by available technology—not against a benchmark of zero costs. This is another example of the Nirvana fallacy discussed in Chapter 17.

governments have tried to limit this market failure by passing a "lemon law," which requires used-car dealers to fix mechanical defects in used cars up to 30 days after the sale. (Note that although this law might raise retail prices of used cars by increasing the demand by buyers, it will not raise the wholesale price to sellers.)

The U.S. securities laws attempted to overcome alleged market failures that were blamed for the 1929 market crash. Here the information asymmetry involved investors and corporate executives. Advocates for the securities acts claimed that investors were fooled into buying overvalued securities because unscrupulous executives did not disclose information about companies honestly. Of course investors have incentives to anticipate such behavior and only offer prices that reflect expected quality.[11] The U.S. securities acts require such disclosures to reduce the asymmetry, thereby increasing the demand for securities.

Again, these laws are not costless. Regulators must be hired, and firms must expend real resources publishing financial results. Some of the mandated disclosures might involve proprietary information, that is, more valuable to competitors in crafting effective corporate strategies than to potential investors. And knowing that the information cannot be kept confidential, managers might be less likely to invest in its production. Moreover, external auditors must be hired to attest to the accuracy of the disclosures. Note that private solutions might be less costly than government regulation. Investors discount the price of securities unless the company makes credible disclosures. Thus, firms face private incentives to provide information for investors. Similarly, used-car buyers can hire auto inspectors or used-car sellers can certify that their preowned cars do not have mechanical defects and voluntarily provide warranties. Car buyers will pay more for used cars with warranties. In these cases, the contracting parties have incentives to overcome potential information asymmetries.

Redistributing Wealth

So far we have discussed two potentially beneficial roles of government: enforcing contracts to facilitate trade and eliminating market failures. In both roles the invisible hand of the free market can be improved (at least in principle) by government intervention. However, details of the implementation of policies to address these problems create opportunities for self-interested individuals to use this intervention as an opportunity to enrich themselves. For example, national defense clearly is a valuable service provided by the government—one that addresses a potential market failure. But if an influential legislator can ensure that a defense contract is granted to a favored firm on lucrative terms, a large transfer of wealth results. Moreover, government must finance this intervention. It generally does so by levying taxes, but governments also raise revenue through user fees for toll roads, tariffs on imports, and licensing and registration fees. In financing government intervention, there are additional opportunities to engineer wealth transfers. Throughout this book we employ the standard assumption that individuals operate in their own self-interest. This assumption also is useful in explaining how individuals behave when working for the government or interacting within the political process. For example, auditors have an incentive to lobby

---

[11]Moreover, for the price to be too high, it is not enough that some investors are misled (or even that the average investor is unsophisticated and is misled); the marginal investor must be misled to affect prices. The marginal investor—that investor who is just on the fence between buying and not buying, so that small differences in price or information may change the decision to buy—is likely to be knowledgeable.

Figure 21.1   Wealth Transfers via Government Quotas on the Number of Taxis

S and *D* are the supply and demand curves for taxicab rides. Absent government intervention, the price is *P** and *Q** is the equilibrium number of cab rides. If the government restricts the number of cabs and thus cab rides to *Q′*, the price of a ride increases to *P′*. Consumer surplus falls by the shaded area. Industry profit is the area *π*. Those cab owners expecting to survive should be willing to spend up to *π*, lobbying government to restrict the number of taxis.

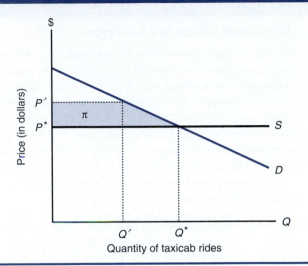

for securities laws that increase the total demand for audited financial statements, especially if they can restrict entry into the auditing profession.

As an example of government effecting wealth transfers, consider taxi licensing that restricts the number of cabs. Figure 21.1 depicts the supply and demand curves for taxi rides in a perfectly competitive, unregulated market. Each cab owner charges price *P** equal to average (and marginal) cost and hence (assuming identical suppliers) makes no economic profit. Absent government intervention, the price of a cab ride is *P** and the number of cab rides is *Q**. Suppose the government—in the name of protecting the public from low-quality cabs—restricts the number of taxis and thus the number of cab rides to *Q′*. To operate a cab, the driver must display a taxi medallion, which are limited in number. The price of a taxi ride rises to *P′*, and the marginal cost per ride is *P**. Consumer surplus falls by the shaded area. Profit per ride is *P′* − *P**, and total industry profit is the rectangular area *π*. There are fewer taxi owners, but those expecting to be in business are willing to spend up to *π* lobbying the government to restrict the number of cabs. In the extreme case, this entire profit stream will be expended on lobbyists and political campaign contributions.[12]

Consumers should be willing to spend their forgone consumer surplus (the shaded area) lobbying to prevent restricting the number of cabs. Yet because of free-rider problems, it is difficult to raise this amount for an effective lobbying campaign. So long as the cab owners are easier to organize—there are fewer of them and their wealth implications are more concentrated—taxi regulation can be passed despite the fact that the forgone consumer surplus for the riders exceeds the surplus gained by the owners. The lobbying expenditures by the surviving cab owners and consumers yield no productive benefits to society. If the number of taxis is limited to, say, *Q′*, there is a wealth transfer from cab riders to taxi owners, lobbyists, politicians, and regulators. This example illustrates how government regulation can transfer wealth among various parties. The example also indicates that both consumers and producers have incentives to lobby.

---

[12]Note that profit *π* is a flow. Thus, the taxi owners should be willing to spend up to the present value of the incremental profit stream on lobbying activities.

MANAGERIAL APPLICATIONS

Regulated Limos in Las Vegas

The Nevada State Transportation Services Authority (TSA) requires all limousine operators to have a certificate of public convenience and necessity. One would-be limo owner describes the system like this: "The TSA regulatory system is designed to protect large companies and to prevent entrepreneurs like me from competing." To get a limo certificate, applicants must show that "the granting of the certificate will not unreasonably and adversely affect other carriers operating in the territory." Existing certified limo companies can pose questions and raise objections that the applicant must answer. One applicant filed 1,000 pages of information ranging from maintenance records to customer lists and spent over $15,000 on the process. His application was denied. In 20 years, only three new certificates have been granted. The area's two largest firms (with 170 limos between them) have lodged objections to all new applicants.

The existing limo firms thus have used the TSA system to help limit entry, reduce competition, and maintain high prices for limo services.

Source: R. Fitzgerald (1999), "Mugged by the Law," *Readers Digest* (January), 98–103.

Other examples of wealth transfers exist. Taxes are among the most obvious. Import quotas and tariffs transfer wealth from domestic consumers to domestic producers. Import quotas also help foreign producers act as a cartel. Licensing of doctors, dentists, and lawyers restricts entry into these professions and transfers wealth from the consumers of these services to the incumbent members of the professions. Although zoning restrictions can address externalities, thereby raising land values, they also transfer wealth. These wealth transfers generally are from the initial landowners whose property is restricted to those landowners whose land has no restrictions (or land where the restrictions are not expected to be binding). Subsequent owners of the restricted-use land buy the land at lower prices that reflect the value of the restrictions. Government farm supports, which pay farmers not to grow certain crops, transfer wealth from consumers to the producers when the subsidy is created. (Again, subsequent purchasers of the farm land pay a higher price for the land as long as the subsidy is linked to the land.) Student financial aid, government support of university research, welfare, and Small Business Administration loans with below-market interest rates all involve wealth transfers.

Managers interested in understanding how government regulation affects the value of their firms must understand the inherent "market" for government regulation. There is both a demand for and a supply of government regulation. If they ignore this market, managers place themselves and their firms at risk. Most organizations find themselves at times lobbying for or against various proposed regulations at the local, state, federal, and even international levels. For example, General Motors argues for lower property assessments and local property taxes, fewer state environmental regulations, increased federal defense department procurement of its products, and more aggressive intervention by international trade organizations to help it gain better access to foreign consumer markets. In the next section we present an economic theory of this market for government regulation.

Economic Theory of Regulation

Before presenting the theory of how the market for regulation works, we begin by first describing the underlying principles (demand, supply, self-interested politicians, and coalition formation).

Special Interests and the Microsoft Antitrust Suit

Only 19 of the 50 states joined the federal government suit alleging Microsoft violated the antitrust laws. It is interesting to look at which states participated in the suit and the special interests located in the state. Microsoft's major competitors, Sun Microsystems and Netscape, are California-based companies; Novell is located within Utah. Both California and Utah joined the suit. Washington, home of Microsoft, is not participating, neither is Texas. Texas computer makers Dell, Compaq, and Tandy—who bundle Microsoft Windows into their machines—oppose the suit. It appears as though politicians and regulators in the various states represent the interests of the computer firms in their states when it comes to joining the federal government suit against Microsoft.

Source: C. Georges (1998), "Politics Play a Role in States' Status in Microsoft Suit," *The Wall Street Journal* (May 28), A24.

Demand for Regulation: Special Interests

Special interest groups are composed of self-interested individuals who, because of their current circumstances, stand to benefit from a proposed government legislation. The special interest group might be bicycle riders seeking a bike lane; they might be landowners, construction companies, and labor unions seeking a new federal highway project in their area; they might be milk farmers, organized labor, or the Sierra Club sponsoring legislation that furthers their causes. In most cases the demanded legislation comes at the expense of some other group that either will pay for the legislation or will have their rights restricted by the legislation. The special interest group backing legislation to raise the sales tax collections to pay for a new sports stadium might consist of football fans, construction companies, skilled trades people, hotel and bar owners in the area, and sports reporters working for the local media. A new stadium would make each of these individuals better off. People who are not sports fans are made worse off by the higher sales taxes. For most proposed government action, two special interest groups can be identified—those made better off and those made worse off.

Supply of Regulation: Politicians

Politicians, including members of the legislative and executive branches of government, are the primary market participants who supply the regulations. They act as brokers among special interest groups favoring and opposing regulations. But more than just brokering these transactions, they often are active entrepreneurs in

Political Support

U.S. Senator Trent Lott collected $850,000 from 144 individuals for his and other Republican representatives' campaigns. *The Wall Street Journal* contacted these individuals and reported that "four out of five donors to the Lott [Political Action Committee] had identifiable stakes in specific programs and policies pending before government. One shipping executive said, 'I gave because I have an interest in how he votes on maritime issues. It's self-interest.'"

Source: G. Hitt and P. Kuntz (1998), "The Money Trail," *The Wall Street Journal* (May 28), A1.

MANAGERIAL APPLICATIONS

Regulators Exhibit Self-Interest in Microsoft Antitrust Suit

The states' suit against Microsoft is brought by the attorneys general (AGs) in each state. AGs are either elected or appointed public officials. According to *The Wall Street Journal*,

> [A] number of the AGs (the letters sometimes are said to stand for "aspiring governors") involved in the suit are seeking higher office. [The Microsoft suit is] the type of case attorneys general dream about, regardless of how deeply it affects—or fails to directly affect—their states' consumers or businesses. It's a case filled with legal twists and turns, and high publicity. "We look forward to taking on big players," says West Virginia Deputy Attorney General Jill Miles.

Thus, regulators (or at least attorneys general) are more than just passive representatives of their constituents' interests. Rather, they also have their own interests, which often include election to higher public offices.

Source: C. Georges (1998), "Politics Play a Role in States' Status in Microsoft Suit," *The Wall Street Journal* (May 28), A24.

---

proposing regulations and then helping mobilize special interest groups. Politicians must get elected and reelected. They do this by promising to pass (or defeat) legislation that helps (or harms) their constituents. This frequently involves proposing new legislation.

Economists assume that consumers, business owners, and managers are self-interested (Chapters 2 and 10); politicians are similarly motivated. Just because politicians claim that they are public-spirited does not make it so. As in private organizations, agency problems exist within the government. Politicians' activities are difficult to monitor. Simply promising to help deliver a particular regulation does not mean a politician will exert substantial effort to do so. It is difficult for voters to observe the level of effort exerted: Although politicians' voting records are observable, their behind-the-scenes actions generally are not.

This view of public officials as self-interested individuals seeking to enrich themselves by supplying legislation that benefits some group is based on numerous, carefully executed studies of public choice.[13] Our purpose here is to summarize the major managerially relevant insights from that research.

Incentives to Free-Ride and Form Coalitions

The market for government regulation is a competition among those special interest groups supporting and opposing the regulation. The political power of a coalition depends on both its size and how well it is organized to deliver votes and political contributions relative to its opposition. For instance, opinion polls typically show that the majority of Americans favor stricter gun control. Yet the relatively small, but quite well-organized and well-financed, National Rifle Association regularly defeats most proposed firearm regulation. Although most Americans favor additional firearm regulation, they do not feel strongly enough to take the time and expend the resources to organize an effective coalition. They rationally choose to stay on the sidelines. This example illustrates several important points. Forming a politically effective special interest group is costly. Its members must be kept informed of pending legislation. They must be willing to write letters to politicians, to make campaign contributions, and ultimately to vote for those who support their position. Whether for emotional or financial reasons, people must feel strongly enough about the cause

---

[13]For a review of the material, see R. McCormick (1993), *Managerial Economics* (Prentice Hall: Englewood Cliffs), Chapter 15.

MANAGERIAL APPLICATIONS

Washington Lobbyists

Harold Ickes, former White House deputy chief of staff to President Clinton, has become a lobbyist charging clients anywhere from $10,000 to $20,000 a month. His clients include the American Federation of Teachers, the New York City Council, Greater New York Hospital Association, and the Commonwealth of Puerto Rico. One client, the Coalition for Asbestos Resolution, wants protection from huge worker-health claims. Another, American Crop Protection Association that represents pesticide makers, worries that a new pesticide law passed in 1996 is so broad that the EPA is going to run wild.

Ickes says, "I know a lot of people [in Washington] and how the place works. Business operates on paranoia. This fear leads to a thirst for information—and with my contacts, I can supply it."

Source: L. Walczak (1998), "Got a Problem? Dr. Ickes Is In," *BusinessWeek* (July 13), 106.

to overcome their incentives to free-ride on the actions of others. Organizing an effective coalition involves many of the same organizational architecture issues described throughout this book—namely, creating incentives and monitoring devices to generate participation in the process.

For a coalition to be effective, the benefits of the government regulation each party in the coalition expects to receive must exceed the costs they bear in forming the coalition and lobbying. Consider a government import quota on foreign cars that raises the price of domestic cars $100. If consumers keep their cars an average of five years, they could save about $20 per year by effectively opposing such quotas. Yet these diffuse costs are generally too small to justify incurring the costs of forming a broad coalition, becoming informed of pending legislation, and acting on this information. Thus, most consumers rationally choose to remain uninformed. However, a $100 price hike on each car amounts to hundreds of millions of dollars for each domestic car company. These concentrated benefits are more than sufficient to justify the costs of forming and maintaining their coalition.

Market for Regulation[14]

To illustrate the market for regulation, consider an industry represented by the demand curve in the left panel of Figure 21.2. Marginal cost is constant at MC. If the industry is competitive and unregulated, the market price is $P_c = $ MC. But if all the firms in the industry could collude and behave as a single monopolist, the price would be P_m—the monopoly price would be set where marginal cost and marginal revenue are equal. The right-hand panel of Figure 21.2 represents industry profit as a function of price.[15] Maximum profit π_m occurs when the price is set at the monopoly price P_m (assuming no price discrimination among customers). If the price is P_0, nothing is sold and hence (with no fixed costs) profit is zero. Profit also is zero when the price is at the competitive level, P_c.

---

[14]This section draws on G. Stigler (1987), *Theory of Price,* fourth edition (Macmillan Publishing Company, New York), Chapter 20.

[15]Although we usually think of profit as a function of price, we plot price as the vertical axis to comparisons across the graphs easier.

Figure 21.2 Industry Profits in Competitive and Monopolized Markets

The left panel graphs industry demand and marginal cost. The unregulated competitive price is P_c and the monopoly price is P_m. The right panel represents industry profit as a function of price. Maximum profit π_m occurs when the price is set at the monopoly price P_m.

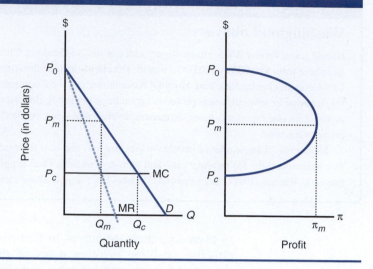

In Figure 21.3 suppose an industry regulator, Ann Melville, is interested in maximizing political support from her constituents—owners of the firms in the industry and the consumers of the industry's output. Regulation gives her the right to set the price in this industry and thus to determine industry profits. Owners want high profits; consumers want low prices.

Figure 21.3 displays two curves that represent those combinations of prices and profits that yield equal political support in terms of campaign contributions and votes.[16] For example, Ann is indifferent between setting price at P_x and profit at π_x and setting price at P_y and profit at π_y. Both combinations yield equivalent political support. At P_x and π_x she gets more support from consumers but less from producers.

Figure 21.3 Political Support Functions

A PS curve graphs combinations of profit and price levels that produce equivalent political support from industry and consumers. Thus, the regulator is indifferent between setting price at P_x and profit at π_x and setting price at P_y and profit at π_y—both combinations yield equivalent levels of political support. However, the regulator prefers to be on PS$_2$ than on PS$_1$.

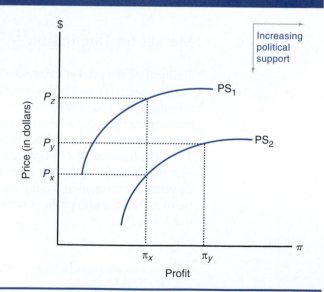

---

[16]Note that these curves are similar in concept to indifference curves in Chapter 2 and isoquants in Chapter 5.

MANAGERIAL APPLICATIONS

Cost of Protection: Automobile Import Restrictions

In the 1980s, the U.S. and Japanese governments agreed on a "voluntary restriction" on Japanese cars imported into the United States to protect American auto jobs. By limiting the number of cars imported, the price of Japanese cars rose about $1,000, the price of European cars rose about $2,000, and the price of U.S. cars rose about $500. By one estimate, the cost of saving one U.S. automotive job via this voluntary import restriction approached $200,000. Thus, U.S. consumers paid about $200,000 per American auto job saved.

Source: E. Dinopoulos and M. Kreinin (1988), "Effects of the U.S.–Japan Auto VER on European Prices and on U.S. Welfare," *Review of Economics and Statistics* 70, 484–491.

At P_y and π_y she gets less consumer support but more producer support. Ann prefers to be on political support curves that are lower and to the right—for instance, she prefers PS_2 to PS_1. On PS_2, consumers have lower prices (and hence Ann gets more consumer support) for a given level of profit. For example, hold industry profits constant at π_x; if Ann is on PS_2, consumers face a lower price P_x than if Ann is on PS_1 and consumers face a higher price P_z—Ann thus receives less consumer support. These political-support functions have positive slope. Higher prices reduce consumer support that can be offset only with higher support from industry via higher profits. These curves are concave because at low prices, small price changes are little noticed by consumers. But at higher prices, they garner greater notice, thereby requiring larger industry profits to offset them. For example, when gasoline prices increased dramatically in 2005 following Hurricane Katrina's production disruptions, politicians appeared on television supporting consumers and promising to investigate the high prices.

Although Ann prefers to be on a political support function as far to the right as possible, the actual political support function she can achieve depends on the trade-off between profits and prices as determined by specific conditions in the industry. Figure 21.4 combines the analysis in the earlier two figures. Given the profit-price profile in Figure 21.2, Ann is able to achieve political support PS_2. Here she will set

Figure 21.4   Equilibrium Regulated Price

The regulator sets the regulated price P_r^* to be less than the monopoly price P_m, but more than the zero-profit competitive price P_c. At higher prices, the regulator loses more support from consumers than is gained from industry. At lower prices, the regulator loses more industry support than is gained from consumers.

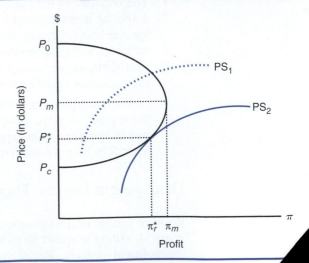

MANAGERIAL APPLICATIONS

Brazil Deregulates Airfares

"For decades, Brazil's airlines competed only in the corridors of [the capital] Brasilia, where politicians dispensed favors in return for free airline tickets and other goodies." Airfares between Rio de Janeiro and São Paulo averaged $500 (round trip). Deregulation has sparked intense competition. Fares on this route have fallen to about $200, and Brazil's largest airlines are currently complaining that they are losing money. This is an example of how regulators can choose between prices and industry profits.

Source: P. Fritsch (1998), "Brazilian Carriers Plunge into First Fare War as Deregulation Ignites Ferocious Competition," *The Wall Street Journal* (May 12), A15.

---

the regulated price at P_r^*. Industry profits are π_r^*, which is less than maximum profits of π_m. Ann favors a price between the monopoly and competitive prices. If she sets a higher price to generate more support from the industry, she loses support from consumers and finds herself on a lower political support curve. If she sets a lower price to garner more consumer support, she loses so much industry support that again she finds herself with lower overall political support.

Several important insights arise from this analysis:

- Regulators do not always behave in obviously consistent ways. They might reduce monopoly prices but seek to form cartels in competitive industries where they can raise prices. Although appearing inconsistent, both types of regulation move price away from favoring entirely either consumers or producers.

- If consumers are unorganized, they offer regulators little political support relative to an organized industry group. In the case of completely unorganized and ill-informed consumers, the political support function in Figure 21.4 becomes vertical (at least over the relevant range) and the regulator maximizes support by setting the monopoly price. Conversely, if consumers are well organized but industry owners are disorganized and offer no political support, the regulator faces a horizontal support function and will set the price at the competitive, zero-profit level.

- The outcome of the political process depends on the relative political support a special interest group can achieve. The more organized and the larger the special interest group, the more political support it can offer. Executives attempt to make the political support function steeper by increasing political contributions, organizing their employees to vote for the candidate, and reducing consumer opposition through a public relations campaign.

- Government programs tend to benefit small groups (aerospace contractors) at the expense of large groups (taxpayers). Holding constant the total amount of wealth transferred, the larger the losing group, the smaller the average loss per loser. Similarly, the smaller the winning group, the larger the benefits per winner.

Deadweight Losses, Transaction Costs, and Wealth Transfers

Because special interest groups can enrich themselves at the expense of others, each group is willing to spend up to the amount they are expected to win or lose providing political support. Recall from Figure 21.1—where government restricts the

Conservative Choices of Accounting Methods

Large, highly visible firms like IBM, General Motors, and Microsoft tend to use more conservative accounting procedures than smaller, less visible firms. For example, large firms are more likely to use depreciation methods that write assets off faster, thereby lowering reported earnings. This evidence is consistent with these firms' seeking to reduce their political exposure by reporting lower accounting earnings. Since large accounting profits are often viewed as measures of monopoly profits and hence attract more media attention, managers of firms subjected to these charges attempt to blunt them by choosing income-decreasing accounting methods. This can reduce the amount of political opposition these firms face.

Source: R. Watts and J. Zimmerman (1986), *Positive Accounting Theory* (Prentice Hall: Upper Saddle River).

supply of taxis, thereby driving up the cost of cab rides—that the lost consumer surplus (the shaded area) is a deadweight loss to society. The surviving cab owners are making a profit because now price is above their cost. But to limit the number of cabs, a government taxi licensing office must be created to issue permits. Police and courts must incur costs as they attempt to catch and punish unauthorized cab drivers. In addition to these costs, each side will incur costs of organizing, lobbying, and providing political support for the politician. Minimizing these costs and deadweight losses is in both the winners' and losers' interests. Thus, government policies that generate smaller reductions in economic efficiency are more likely to be adopted because the losers are harmed less and will oppose the regulations with less zeal, and winners will lobby harder since they have more to share.

Managerial Implications

Having laid out the essential features of the market for regulation, in this section we describe the important managerial implications such as entry restrictions, forming coalitions, and business participation in the political process.

Restricting Entry and Limiting Substitutes

In Chapter 8 we describe how firms develop strategies that both create value and capture value. Recall that it is not enough to build a better mousetrap; you must prevent others from copying your ideas and entering the market. We discussed patents, copy-

Why Do Ships Register in Liberia?

Taking a cruise from Miami to the Caribbean? Why is the ship registered in Liberia? In fact most cruise lines register their ships in Liberia. The answer is simple. If the ship is registered in the United States, it must be owned and crewed by Americans, making it subject to U.S. labor laws, including the minimum wage. Liberia does not have such labor laws and hence registering the ship in Liberia exempts it from U.S. laws, saving the ship's owner a boatload of costs. This is an example of how companies seek creative ways to reduce the costs of costly regulation.

Source: R. Tucker (2001), "Why Do Ships Register in Liberia?" *Fortune* (June 11), 42.

> ### MANAGERIAL APPLICATIONS
>
> ## Restricting Entry into European Retailing
>
> "The fight against outlet malls will continue. If we allow one, the dam will break, and we'll be swamped," stated the director of the German Retailers' Association. U.S. and U.K. retailers are trying to enter European markets. To keep them out, shops cannot stay open evenings and Sundays. Mall developers must contend with high wage rates, restrictive zoning laws, and high property taxes. Public officials battle developers over signage and government permits. In Austria, the chamber of commerce is lobbying hard to keep out foreign competitors. One retailer says, "Low prices will be our downfall." Thus, to limit the competition they face (especially from foreign firms), European retailers use a wide variety of government regulations to restrict entry.
>
> Source: E. Beck (1997), "Outlet Malls Make Headway in Europe Despite Opposition by Local Retailers," *The Wall Street Journal* (September 17), A17.

rights, and trademarks as means to protect intellectual property. Now we examine how government regulations might be used to create additional barriers to entry.

The most direct way to restrict competition is a government regulation limiting entry. For example, labor union laws that prevent unionized firms from hiring nonunion employees raise wages in these firms. Immigration laws limit the numbers of foreign workers allowed into the country to protect the domestic labor force. It is illegal for private delivery services to deliver mail to a customer's mailbox. Professions like law, medicine, accounting, and dentistry limit competition by setting professional licensing standards such as passing exams and requiring work-related experience. Public utilities such as telephone, gas, electric, and cable television companies have been granted exclusive franchises within specific geographic areas.

A less direct method of limiting competition is a government regulation that imposes a cost on certain competitors and potential entrants. For example, consider health codes that require restaurants to meet various regulations concerning the preparation and storage of food. Although such health codes increase all restaurants' costs, they increase street vendors' costs proportionately more than those of full-service restaurants. Thus, health codes restrict the number and types of street vendors and hence potential competition from new entrants. Or, recall Netscape's involvement in the federal government's antitrust suit against Microsoft. Microsoft argues that it was "set up" by Netscape in a June 1995 meeting where Netscape allegedly created a record that Microsoft proposed splitting the browser market with Netscape. Documents referring to this meeting were a key argument in the government's case. In its settlement agreement with the Justice Department Microsoft agreed to disclose various technical data on software currently being developed so that other companies can write programs for Windows that compete with Microsoft products. This remedy reduces Microsoft's competitive position and makes Netscape more competitive.

To illustrate how government regulation can change the relative competitiveness of firms, consider the market for rugs.[17] Suppose there are two ways to produce the same rug. Labor-intensive firms employ 10 workers an hour at $15 per hour and use 30 pounds of wool at $5 per pound. It takes 1 hour to produce a rug at a total cost of $300 (10 × $15 + 30 × $5). Material-intensive firms also produce 1 rug per hour, also at a cost of $300, but they use 5 workers at $15 per hour and 45 pounds of wool at $5 per pound. Material-intensive firms cannot switch to become labor-intensive firms, and

---

[17]This example is based on R. McCormick (1993), Chapter 15.

Figure 21.5 Imposing a Payroll Tax Allows Low-Labor Firms to Earn Profits

Two hundred labor-intensive and 200 material-intensive firms are selling 400 rugs at $300 each. Imposing a payroll tax shifts the supply curve for all firms, but it shifts more for labor-intensive firms. The equilibrium price rises by $10, and the quantity falls to 250. One hundred and fifty labor-intensive firms exit the industry and each material-intensive firm earns economic profits of $5 per rug—so long as they can prevent new material-intensive firms from entering.

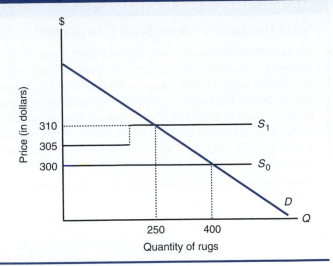

vice versa; moreover, firm sizes are fixed. The rug market is competitive and each rug sells for $300. There are only 200 labor-intensive firms and only 200 material-intensive firms. Total quantity produced and sold is 400 rugs per hour. In Figure 21.5 the market demand curve and the original supply curve intersect at a quantity of 400 rugs and a price of $300. Neither type of firm makes abnormal profits.

Now the material-intensive firms are able to get a $1 per employee per hour payroll tax implemented by the government. All firms are required to pay this tax. The total cost of a labor-intensive firm rises to $310 ($10 \times \$16 + 30 \times \$5$). The total cost of a material-intensive firm rises to $305 ($5 \times \$16 + 45 \times \$5$). The price of rugs rises to $310 because the demand curve intersects the new supply curve at a price of $310. The material-intensive firms are making abnormal profits of $5 per rug. The remaining labor-intensive firms are breaking even. But only 250 rugs per hour are produced. The result is that 150 labor-intensive firms go out of business. The 200 material-intensive firms continue to make abnormal profits of $5 per rug so long as they can prevent new material-intensive firms from entering.

This example illustrates an important managerial implication. A firm might rationally support government regulations that impose costs on itself, as long as competing firms incur higher costs. This drives the high-cost firms from the industry and allows remaining firms to earn economic profits because the marginal firm (or the next firm to enter) is a high-cost firm. Managers often support these regulations by arguing that they are in the public interest. For example, managers might argue the payroll tax is used to support social programs such as employee health benefits.

Other examples illustrate the pervasiveness of cost-increasing regulations that restrict entry. General Motors lobbied for stringent miles-per-gallon standards in the early 1980s. Burlington Industries supported Occupational Safety and Health Administration cotton dust standards for textile manufacturers. These standards imposed relatively higher costs on smaller plants, thereby allowing the larger plants to generate economic rents. Truckers support train safety regulation. Local merchants want tougher building codes. In the 1800s, English steam-powered mill owners argued for rules limiting child labor in factories. (This case is like that in Figure 21.5 where a payroll tax is imposed; it favors capital-intensive firms—steam-powered mills—at

Steel Producers versus Steel Consumers

In March 2002, the United States imposed a tariff on imported steel that increased the cost by as much as 30 percent. American automakers and other steel-consuming industries complained that the tariffs have increased their costs, cut their profits, delayed expansions, and caused them to lay off employees. However, since the tariffs, the U.S. steel industry has invested more than $3 billion in streamlining their operations. On December 3, 2003, President Bush rescinded the steel tariff. This is an example of how one industry—steel—used federal regulations to reduce competition and impose costs on other domestic parties—steel consumers.

Source: E. Becker (2003), "U.S. Tariffs on Steel Are Illegal, World Trade Organization Says," *New York Times* (November 11), A1; and J. Curl and J. Sparshott (2003), "Bush Rescinds Steel Tariffs," *Washington Times* (December 5), Washingtontimes.com.

the expense of other labor-intensive firms.) Finally, large accounting firms supported regulations that required all CPAs to have extensive periodic peer review evaluations. These requirements impose relatively higher costs on smaller CPA firms, forcing them out of markets (such as those for publicly traded client firms) where large CPA firms dominate.

Forming Coalitions

The economic theory of regulation emphasizes the critical importance of coalition formation. Winning coalitions supply more political support to politicians (votes and campaign contributions) than losing coalitions. One way to increase political support is to expand the number of people supporting the regulation. This process sometimes produces unusual alliances. For instance, in the South during the early 1900s, illegal liquor producers (bootleggers) wanted to reduce competition from legal distillers. Bootleggers supported a coalition of church members who wanted to ban the sale of all alcohol. Responding to this lobbying, a number of counties in southern states became "dry" by passing legislation prohibiting the sale of alcoholic beverages. Since the bootleggers had been operating illegally for years and avoiding prosecution from federal alcohol tax collectors, continuing to operate their underground businesses posed relatively few new problems. This is a classic case of "politics make strange bedfellows" and has been called the "Bootleggers and Baptists Phenomenon."[18]

We often observe a special interest group that lobbies to restrict entry because it furthers its economic interest (bootleggers) joining forces with a special interest group that lobbies to correct a social ailment (Southern Baptists). Another example is western coal producers supporting environmental groups who lobby for tighter air-quality emission standards that make burning high-sulfur eastern coal more expensive than their low-sulfur coal. Winning coalitions frequently contain industry groups, "public interest" groups, and regulators to produce a strong political force pitted against consumers and rival companies. For example, aerospace contractors to the space program form coalitions with science "buffs" to lobby Congress for more space funding.

[18]McCormick (1993), 649.

Forming political coalitions is similar to forming coalitions within the firm to advocate new proposals. Members of a political coalition are usually risk-averse, and so new government regulations that are uncertain are more likely to be opposed. Ways of increasing the coalition's support of a proposed regulation is to reduce the uncertainty in the regulation, emphasize a crisis, and organize a logroll.

On Business Participation in the Political Process

Some will question whether a firm should be an active participant in the political process. Certainly our analysis suggests that collectively, we would be better off if we could limit the government's ability to pass regulation that restricts competition. In such a case, consumer prices would be lower and the deadweight costs and transaction costs associated with both lobbying for government regulations and enforcing the regulations would be saved.

Yet in evaluating company participation, we believe several points are important to consider. First, managers have a fiduciary responsibility to maximize the value of

---

ANALYZING MANAGERIAL DECISIONS: *Effect of the Microsoft Case on Other Computer Firms*

One might expect that the government's antitrust actions against Microsoft would have affected the values of other computer firms. In particular, direct competitors such as Netscape and Sun should be made better off, whereas firms selling complementary products such as Dell and Compaq would be made worse off. A study of the stock price movements of 159 computer-related firms surrounding major news announcements of antitrust actions against Microsoft from March 1991 to December 1997 yields some interesting findings. These 159 computer firms (excluding Microsoft) had a total stock market value of $754 billion in December 1997. This group experienced an aggregate drop in stock value of $35 billion on the three days surrounding the 29 news announcements that increased the antitrust enforcement against Microsoft. Conversely, when antitrust news favorable to Microsoft was announced, these firms' value increased $70 billion. Negative (positive) movements of Microsoft stock at the time of antitrust enforcement actions coincide with negative (positive) returns for the industry. Notice that the 159 computer firms include those firms supposedly wanting the

government antitrust suit to succeed. Surprisingly, there is no evidence that individual firms such as Netscape, Sun, Novell, or Apple realized higher stock returns when antitrust actions were taken against Microsoft. Repeated antitrust actions against Microsoft have not increased the expected earnings of other computer firms. "Surprisingly, government action against Microsoft appears to inflict capital losses on the computer sector as a whole. . . . Withdrawals from policy enforcement have been accompanied by positive shareholder returns throughout the computer sector."

Sun, Netscape, and Apple have encouraged the government to pursue its antitrust suit against Microsoft; California, where these firms are headquartered, has joined the suit; yet Bittlingmayer and Hazlett (2000) *JFE* find no evidence that these firms realize higher stock returns when antitrust actions are taken against Microsoft. How might you explain these facts?

Source: G. Bittlingmayer and T. Hazlett (2000), "DOS *Kapital*: Has Antitrust Action against Microsoft Created Value in the Computer Industry?" *Journal of Financial Economics* 55, 329–359.

ANALYZING MANAGERIAL DECISIONS: *World Motors*

World Motors (WM) is a large U.S. automobile manufacturing company. Eighty percent of its plants and sales are in the United States. WM is considering whether it should hire lobbyists to try to influence a variety of pending legislation. There are bills in Congress proposing to tighten automobile emission standards as part of the clean air laws, laws restricting union activity, increasing worker safety rules, reducing the miles-per-gallon standards on automobiles, and imposing import quotas. WM supports legislation that increases its firm's value. Each piece of pending legislation is evaluated using this criteria. The following briefly describes each piece of pending legislation.

Emission Standards   Tighter emission standards increase the cost of cars because they require more expensive emission-control devices such as more precise fuel injection systems and catalytic converters. One of WM's major competitors has a patent on a proprietary fuel emission system that allows cars equipped with its technology to meet the tighter emission standards. WM's competitor can install this proprietary technology on its cars cheaper than WM can install its device required to meet the higher emission standards.

Labor Union Laws   Labor laws increase the bargaining power of unions and thus their ability to extract higher pay or benefit concessions or provide lower amounts of work. The pending legislation proposes rules that make it harder for a local union to call a labor strike.

Worker Safety Rules   The Occupational Safety and Health Administration (OSHA) is proposing that plants making metal castings (such as automobile engine blocks) be equipped with air ventilation systems that replace the air in the plant more frequently than the current air-quality standard requires. Most of WM's engines are cast off shore, whereas most of its competitors cast their engine blocks in the United States.

Miles-per-Gallon Standards   To conserve gasoline, the federal government has mandated that automobiles produced by each company must comply with a minimum miles-per-gallon standard. These standards are met by producing lighter cars with more efficient fuel systems. New rules requiring tighter, more fuel-efficient vehicles are being proposed. The mix of WM's produced vehicles is very similar to those of its major competitors in terms of car sizes and their fuel efficiency. No auto company has any proprietary technology to improve fuel system efficiency.

Import Quotas   Citing the unfavorable trade deficit, the U.S. government is considering regulations limiting the number of foreign cars imported into the United States.

1. For each piece of proposed legislation, should WM support or oppose it?
2. Which pieces of legislation do you expect WM's local labor unions to oppose or support?

their firm—not to maximize social welfare. Regulation can have a material impact on a firm's value. Second, companies did not create this system that allows these welfare-reducing regulations to be adopted—politicians did. Unfortunately, eliminating this wasteful activity seems unlikely. Far too much wealth is at stake. Too many vested interest groups (including politicians, regulators, lobbyists, and lawyers) exist to expect that these very same people will adopt new laws reducing the demand for their services. Third, even if a firm decides not to pursue political activities designed to produce wealth transfers, it almost certainly will be confronted with trying to prevent regulation aimed at reducing its value. As Pericles (430 BC) noted, "Just because you do not take an interest in politics doesn't mean that politics won't take an interest in you." Managers who avoid participation in the political process that would benefit their firms reduce shareholder wealth. This places their companies' continued existence at risk and calls into question their fiduciary responsibility to shareholders.

Finally, it is important to evaluate carefully the strategic aspects of participation in the political process. Managers must consider carefully how government regulators and other affected parties will react to the manager's lobbying activities. For example, managers must decide whether it is better to be a "first mover" or "second mover" in lobbying. Managers must ensure that their lobbying is "credible" in the sense that rivals change their beliefs because the manager has sufficient commitment to the strategy. And, managers must consider how their lobbying on the current government regulation will affect repeated interactions in the future. Government regulation is another example of where game theory can help managers better understand and plan their actions.

Summary	This chapter presented a framework for understanding how government regulation affects a firm's strategy and hence the value of a firm. Chapter 8 and Figure 11.1 emphasize that government regulation is a key environmental factor affecting a firm's value. From changing the extent and nature of the competitiveness of markets, to regulating labor and capital markets, to taxation, governments touch virtually all aspects of organizations. In this chapter we discuss the managerial importance of government regulation and the benefits and costs of this regulation, and present an economic theory of regulation. This theory helps managers to understand better how various regulations come about and how to participate in the markets for regulation more effectively.

Governments provide a system of laws and legal institutions that facilitate production and exchange; they also address various market failures. Legal institutions which define and enforce property rights lower transaction costs, thereby increasing both producer and consumer surplus. For example, the patent process increases the amount invested in research and development and ultimately the value of goods and services flowing from this R&D. Governments also seek to redress market failures such as externalities (air pollution), public goods (national defense), monopolies (antitrust laws), and informational failures (lemon laws).

It is important to realize that it is costly to enforce property rights and to resolve these market failures. To finance these beneficial functions, governments must raise revenues, usually through taxes. In the process of performing these functions and raising the revenues to finance them, governments also can redistribute wealth, which imposes costs on society. Government agencies, courts, and legislative processes must be financed out of taxes and fees. And besides the direct costs of operating governments, there are potential indirect costs imposed on society associated with the wealth transfers that undoubtedly arise from most government actions. These wealth transfers are not merely zero sum games, in the sense that what one group receives another loses. Rather, there are transaction costs and deadweight losses (reduced consumer and producer surplus). In the process of transferring some of the pie from Peter to Paula, the pie is smaller because knowing that he might lose some of the pie to Paula, Peter has *less* incentive to make the pie as big as possible. Income taxes are another example. Paying, say, 30 percent of my income to the government in the form of income taxes causes me to engage in less work[19] and consume more leisure.

The economic theory of regulation is based on those who demand regulation (special interests) and those who supply it (politicians). Special interest groups who are

---

[19]Suppose I am paid $20 per hour, H, and my utility function for work is $20H(1 - t) - 0.5H^2$. I have disutility of work, that is quadratic. The tax rate on income is t. Taking the first derivative with respect to H and setting it equal to zero yields $H^* = 20 - 20t$. If $t = 0$, I work 20 hours. If $t = 50$ percent, I work only 10 hours.

made better off by the regulation will lobby in its favor, whereas those harmed will lobby against it. Politicians are made better off by brokering these transactions. They generate political support in the form of campaign contributions and votes from the various coalitions formed to support or oppose the regulation. The size and political power of a coalition depend on both how well it is organized to deliver votes and political contributions as well as how poorly organized its opposition is. People must feel strongly enough about the cause for either emotional or financial reasons to overcome their incentives to free-ride on the actions of others. If consumers are unorganized, they offer regulators little political support relative to an organized industry group. The outcome of the political process depends on the relative political support a special interest group can achieve. The more organized and the larger the special interest group, the more political support it can offer the regulator.

This theory of regulation has several important managerial implications. To develop strategies that both create value and capture value—it is not enough to build a better mousetrap—you must limit entry by competitors. The most direct way to limit competition is a government regulation limiting entry (for instance, zoning laws or taxi medallions). A less direct method for limiting competition is a government regulation that imposes a cost on certain competitors and potential entrants (for instance, health codes, worker safety standards, and pollution emission laws).

Another implication of the economic theory of regulation emphasizes the importance of coalition formation. Effective coalitions supply political support to politicians (votes and campaign contributions). One way to increase political support is to expand the number of people supporting the regulation. Coalitions are like other types of organizations—they have organizational architectures. To make coalitions more effective within the political process, the coalition should be structured using the concepts of organizational architecture presented throughout this book. In particular, incentives to participate and performance measures can be used to reduce free-rider problems within the coalition.

Finally, regulation can have a material impact on a firm's value. Managers must decide whether or how to participate in the market for regulation. Remaining neutral does not guarantee that your firm's value is unaffected. Managers who avoid participating place their company's continued existence at risk and call into question their fiduciary responsibility to shareholders.

Self-Evaluation Problems

21–1. Proposed legislation would required 48-hour notification to all neighbors (within 150 feet of your property) for all pesticide applications that may be made to your property by trained, professional applicators. This legislation is labeled "environmentally friendly." Analyze the impact to the environment. (Note that pesticides come in varying strengths with more toxic products having a longer residual impact and thus requiring less frequent application.)

21–2. California (and other states) has passed laws that restrict the exercise of termination provisions in franchise agreements. Your boss says that he thinks this is a good idea—firms have an incentive to terminate profitable franchises and replace them with company-owned outlets. He asks what you think.

Solutions to Self-Evaluation Problems

21–1. Pesticide Application Notification and the Environment

By raising the cost of a pesticide application, firms will be less likely to apply less toxic products on an as needed basis, and more likely to use more toxic products on a "calendar spray" basis. Pest management techniques that require monitoring and treating only when and where needed (techniques generally hailed as environmentally friendly) will become more expensive relative to traditional methods of blanket treating properties.

21–2. Franchise Termination Legislation

Both contracting parties voluntarily included termination agreements in franchise contracts, presumably because they increased the value of the contract, net of the costs of the clause. Franchisees pay less for franchises with these clauses because there is a chance they would be terminated. Franchisers presumably were willing to receive less from the franchisee when these clauses were included because it gave the franchiser flexibility to change the ownership structure of the stores if future conditions warrant such changes. If both parties to the contract are intelligent, rational parties, they "priced" such termination clauses in the contract. Such clauses on net created value. The government passing laws restricting such voluntary agreements reduces the value of new franchises. They result in wealth transfers from the franchiser, who paid for these termination provisions in terms of lower franchise fees, to the franchisee.

Review Questions

21–1. "When I bought this land, it was zoned only for farming. But the longer I live here, the more I resent the wealth transfer I'm paying to other landowners without such restrictions." Comment.

21–2. Adam Smith often is quoted as saying, "People of the same trade seldom meet together, even for merriment and diversion, but the conversation ends in a conspiracy against the public or in some contrivance to raise prices." If Smith is right, does this justify a role for government?

21–3. At a city council meeting, the Taxi Cab Owners Association argued for a fare increase. They note that the market price to buy or rent taxi medallions has been rising, and with these higher costs, profitability is reduced. Evaluate this argument.

21–4. In 1997 Canadian 2 × 4 lumber studs with two holes drilled in them (so that electricians could run wires) were categorized by customs agents as Category #4418 and free of any tariffs. If they had been categorized as #4407, they would have fallen under a quota system whereby only the first 14.7 billion board-feet of lumber Canada imports to the United States are duty free. The next 650 million are subject to a $50 export fee per 1,000 board-feet, and beyond that, a $100 fee. Roughly 15 billion board-feet of lumber is imported to the United States each year from Canada. If the Canadian 2 × 4 studs with holes are classified as #4407, this adds about $3,000 to the cost of a new home. Discuss the expected lobbying behavior of lawmakers from timber producing states (Montana and Alabama), the National Association of Homebuilders, and U.S. lumber companies (for instance, Georgia Pacific).

21–5. What would be the impact of raising the federal minimum wage?

21–6. What are the benefits and costs of government regulation of air quality within cotton mills—for instance, specifying maximum levels of cotton dust (prolonged exposure leads to "white lung" disease)?

21–7. What are the benefits of government regulation of air pollution from automobiles? What are the costs of this regulation?

21–8. Various politicians have proposed an Internet tax. One proposal would be to tax both outgoing e-mail and every Web page downloaded. What groups are likely to support such a tax and what groups would oppose it?

21–9. Dubliners often complain that there are too few pubs in their city. At night pubs can be quite crowded and prospective customers often are turned away. Some Dubliners blame this pub "shortage" on the English who originally enacted laws restricting pubs centuries ago when they ruled Ireland. Is it appropriate to blame the English? Explain.

21–10. Passing through Louisiana you notice billboards proclaiming "Louisiana's shame—the only state that does not license chiropractors." Who do you expect finances these billboards? If licensing were adopted, who would be affected and how?

Ethics and Organizational Architecture*

LEARNING OBJECTIVES

1. Describe how corporate ethics and organizational architecture are linked.

2. Explain how, although it is over 2,500 years old, there is no universally accepted theosophical consensus as to which behaviors are ethical.

3. Explain how monopolies and externalities provide a role for regulation—in these cases, private contracts and markets may lead to resource misallocation.

4. Understand how economists view social responsibility.

5. Describe how obtaining a diversity of input, legal standards, and business norms help shape corporate policy choices.

6. Understand how market mechanisms like repeat sales, warranties, third-party monitors, disclosure, and ownership structure can encourage ethical behavior.

7. Discuss how the adoption of a code of ethics can increase firm value.

I n December 1990, the head of Salomon Brothers' government-bond trading desk, Paul W. Mozer, submitted bids for 35 percent of a 4-year Treasury note auction. He also submitted another $1 billion bid under the name of Warburg Asset Management—a Salomon Brothers customer—but without the customer's knowledge or consent. The two bids, which represented 46 percent of the issue, violated the Treasury's auction rules that limited the amount sold to any single bidder to 35 percent of the issue.[1] Mozer repeated this tactic at Treasury note auctions in February and April.

In April, Mozer became concerned that the Treasury was about to uncover his illicit bidding tactics. He admitted his unauthorized bidding in the February auction at a meeting with Salomon Chairman John Gutfreund, President Thomas Strauss, Vice Chairman John Meriwether, and General Counsel Donald Feuerstein. They apparently accepted his confession to a one-time, not-to-be-repeated mistake and no immediate action was taken.

*Portions of this chapter were published in C. Smith (1992), "Economics and Ethics: The Case of Salomon Brothers," *Journal of Applied Corporate Finance* 5:2, 23–28; and J. Brickley, C. Smith, and J. Zimmerman (1994), "Ethics, Incentives, and Organizational Design," *Journal of Applied Corporate Finance* 7:2, 20–30.

[1] In auctioning Treasury bonds, the U.S. Treasury awarded bonds first to the highest bidder at their quoted prices, then they moved to the next-highest bidder. This process continued until the issue was exhausted. If the Treasury received multiple bids at the price that exhausted the issue, it allocated bonds in proportion to the bid size. But Treasury auction rules limited the amount of an issue sold to any single bidder to no more than 35 percent of the issue.

In May, he again employed this bidding tactic in another Treasury note auction. In June, the Securities and Exchange Commission and the Justice Department issued subpoenas to Salomon and some of its clients for records involving bond auctions. Salomon then initiated a review of its government-bond operations and in August disclosed its unauthorized bids over the period between December and May.

By May 1992, the government had imposed a number of penalties on Salomon Brothers. The Treasury barred Salomon from bidding in government securities auctions for customer accounts. While allowing Salomon to retain its designation as a primary dealer, the Federal Reserve Bank of New York suspended its authority to trade with the bank for two months. The firm agreed to pay $122 million to the Treasury for violating securities laws and $68 million for claims made by the Justice Department. It established a $100 million restitution fund for payments of private damage claims that might result from approximately 50 civil lawsuits that the firm still faced stemming from the scandal. Monies in this fund not paid to the plaintiffs reverted to the Treasury, not Salomon.

Although these legal and regulatory penalties were substantial, they represent but a fraction of the total costs borne by the firm. In the week that the information about the unauthorized bids was released, Salomon Brothers' stock price dropped by one-third. This $1.5 billion fall in market value suggests that the market expected Salomon to bear significant costs as a result of these actions. Further, the drop seems too large to reflect simply fines and other expected legal and regulatory sanctions. In addition to the penalties and decline in the market value of Salomon's stock, all of the senior officers who knew of the illicit bids, but failed to act swiftly, were forced to leave the firm—and none of these individuals has since worked in a major securities firm. Salomon was acquired by the Travelers Insurance Company in 1997 and, after Travelers merged with Citibank, became part of Citigroup. In 2002, Citigroup announced a major restructuring and would reduce the use of the Salomon name substantially. The case of Salomon Brothers illustrates that market forces can impose material sanctions on parties engaged in unethical behavior.

Over the past decade, much public attention has been devoted to the issues of business ethics and corporate social responsibility. Politicians and social critics have deplored materialism; the media have treated the public to sensational accounts of corporate scandal; and business schools across the country offer courses in ethics.

In recent years, many U.S. corporations have responded by issuing formal codes of conduct, appointing ethics officers, and offering employee training programs in ethics. Such codes and programs cover a wide range of behavior, but most emphasize the following:

- Compliance with laws and statutory regulations
- Honesty and integrity in dealings with customers and other employees
- Avoidance of conflicts of interest with the company

Although few would quarrel with such aims, equally few proponents of such corporate initiatives have bothered to ask questions like the following: Are such codes and programs likely to be effective in deterring unethical behavior by corporate managers and employees? And, more pointedly, is the behavior enjoined by such codes consistent with the normal incentives of employees or managers, *given the current organizational architecture* of the firm?

MANAGERIAL APPLICATIONS

Monitoring Employee Ethics

Monitoring employee actions—including those with important ethical aspects—is a critical part of the organization's performance evaluation and control system. For example, the Transportation Security Administration launched a crackdown on theft over the past two years. The TSA has been sending "bait bags" through airport screening containing iPads, watches, and jewelry to entice dishonest agents. The program appears to be working; last year 56 screeners were fired for theft and turned over to the police. This year, there have been 22 firings. Moreover, the number of complaints filed against the TSA for handling property fell by 13 percent compared to the same period the year before. Catching and dismissing dishonest agents who are caught has a direct impact on employee theft. But the more important implication is likely to come from deterring theft by communicating the program's existence and results.

Source: S. McCartney (2014) "New Tactics in the Fight Against Stolen Luggage," *The Wall Street Journal* (August 14).

Although it is recognized rarely in most public discussions of the subject, corporate ethics and organizational architecture are closely related. To increase the likelihood that individuals will behave ethically in their roles as managers and employees, corporate performance-evaluation systems, reward systems, and assignments of decision rights can be designed to encourage such behavior.

In this chapter, we present five basic arguments:

First, the term *ethics* is elusive. It has many different meanings, and these meanings vary across cultures and over time. The term *business ethics* has been used to mean everything from corporate social responsibility to maximizing shareholder value.

Second, if the corporation is to survive in a competitive environment, it must maximize its value to its owners (primarily the stockholders). Taking care of other corporate stakeholders such as employees and local communities is important, but such care can be taken too far. If the firm reduces the owners' value, this care can imperil corporate survival.

Third, a company's reputation for ethical behavior, including its integrity in dealing with noninvestor stakeholders, is part of its brand-name capital; as such, this component of the firm's value is reflected in the value of its securities. By the same token, individuals' human capital—which determines their future earnings prospects—is based in no small part on their reputation for ethical behavior. In this sense, private markets provide important incentives for ethical behavior by imposing substantial costs on institutions and individuals that depart from accepted ethical standards. The Salomon Brothers trading scandal illustrates that the magnitude of these costs can be enormous.

Fourth, considerable emphasis in corporate ethics programs is on what we would argue are misplaced efforts to change employees' preferences by attempting to persuade them to put the interests of the organization or its customers ahead of their own. Instead our approach, accepts people's preferences and assumes they will follow their perceived self-interest. We focus on structuring the organization in ways that better align incentives of managers and employees with the corporate aim of maximizing value.

Fifth, even if ethical guidelines and training programs are unlikely to alter fundamental preferences, they nonetheless have the potential to add value by more explicitly communicating the firm's expectations to its employees. However, to be most effective, such guidelines must be reinforced by formal aspects of the firm's organizational architecture.

GM's Recall

In 2001, GM engineers detected that the ignition switch used on their compact cars was faulty. An inquiry was opened and a solution was offered. But apparently no action was taken until GM issued a recall in February 2014. By then, the faulty switches had been installed in over 1 million cars. Moreover, these faulty switches have been linked to 12 deaths. After the recall, GM CEO Mary Barra apologized for the delay, offered condolences to family members who lost loved ones, initiated an internal probe by the Jenner & Block law firm, and appointed Jeff Boyer to the new position of vice president of global vehicle safety. She charged him with handling all safety-related issues. Clarence Ditlow, head of the Center for Auto Safety, said Ms. Barra's appointment of a safety czar is a "big step in the right direction . . . the jury is still out on whether there is going to be long-term change."

Source: J. Bennett (2014) "General Motors Recalls 1.7 Million More Vehicles," *The Wall Street Journal* (March 17); and J. Bennett (2014) "GM CEO Apologizes for Recall Delay, Vows Changes," *The Wall Street Journal* (March 18).

Ethics and Choices

People make choices. A cornerstone of this book is that individuals make choices to maximize their expected utility. Individuals have preferences over just about everything and choose how much to spend on food, transportation, housing, charitable contributions, and other purchases. People choose how to allot their time between work, leisure, and charitable activities as well as how to allocate their time among alternative leisure activities—for example, watching television, playing golf, or attending a symphony concert. Economics is the study of how people make choices; it is basically a descriptive study seeking to explain people's observed decisions. In this book, our analysis has been descriptive, not normative. We have avoided suggesting what decisions people *should* make; we have not suggested that people *should* spend more time fund-raising for their local charities and less time watching television. We have argued that given people's preferences, they will tend to select those activities that maximize their perceived well-being.

This chapter is also about choices—in particular, choices among actions that are perceived to have ethical implications. Much of the study of ethics specifically focuses on how people should make choices: It is the study of those behaviors people should pursue. In large part, ethics is normative, not descriptive. When philosophers speak of ethics, they are dealing with the millennia-old discipline that seeks to identify those behaviors which are right or wrong, good or bad, virtue or vice. Moral philosophers have been debating ethics since ancient times, and all religions involve statements of which behaviors are ethical and which are unethical. All major religions—Buddhism, Christianity, Confucianism, Hinduism, Islam, and Judaism—espouse the Golden Rule: "Do unto others as you would have them do unto you."[2] Western religions are based on the Ten Commandments, a code of ethical behavior.

Behaviors such as lying, cheating, stealing, and killing are almost universally viewed as wrong—except under mitigating circumstances (murder in self-defense is usually justifiable, for instance). However, certain behaviors viewed as wrong by some are viewed by others as right. For example, some people view abortion as wrong, whereas others view denying women the right to choose as wrong. Similar conflicts exist regarding birth control and a person's right to die. In these cases, there

[2]W. Shaw (1991), *Business Ethics* (Wadsworth Publishing: Belmont), 12.

MANAGERIAL APPLICATIONS

Martha Stewart Loses $275 Million Attempting to Save $80,000

On December 26, 2001, Martha Stewart sold 3,928 shares of biotech firm ImClone for about $60 a share, the day before ImClone disclosed to the stock market that the FDA had rejected its cancer drug application. Federal authorities claim that Martha Stewart had been tipped off by her friend, Samuel Waksal, CEO of ImClone, of the FDA decision and that Stewart had illegally traded on inside information. Stewart denies the allegations. Martha Stewart's investment in ImClone on December 26 was worth about $240,000. In a little over a week, ImClone fell $20 a share. Had Martha Stewart waited a week to sell her ImClone stock, she would have lost about $80,000. By selling on December 26, 2001, she saved about $80,000. But, at what cost? If Stewart knew she was trading on inside information, then she was putting her reputation and the reputation of her firm, Martha Stewart Living, at substantial risk.

Stewart owned about 31 million shares of the publicly traded stock in Martha Stewart Living, where she is CEO. She has over 90 percent of the voting rights in the company. In June 2002 stories broke in the press that Stewart and Waksal of ImClone had ties and that Waksal was being investigated for insider trading of ImClone stock. Over the next two months securities regulators began investigating Stewart for possible insider-trading violations. A shareholder in Martha Stewart Living sued Stewart claiming she had a duty to investors to "maintain her good name and reputation and to avoid situations that could negatively impact her name and reputation." Shares in Martha Stewart Living fell from about $17 per share at the beginning of June 2002 to about $8 a share in August, after the shareholder suit was filed and Congress held public hearings where Stewart denied any wrongdoing. The 47 percent decline in Martha Stewart Living compares to about a 10 percent decline in the market over the same period. This $9 per share fall wiped out about $280 million of Martha Stewart's wealth. And this does not count any likely lawsuit settlements or legal fees she will pay.

Ethics is about choices. If Martha Stewart had any hint from Samuel Waksal that she was receiving insider information about Waksal's ImClone before she sold her stock, she should not have sold the stock. Trying to save some or all of her $240,000 investment in ImClone affected Stewart's reputation and a large portion of her 90 percent ownership of Martha Stewart Living. Ms. Stewart appears to have made a bad decision on December 26, if she did in fact trade based on a phone call from Sam Waksal. In 2003, Stewart was convicted of obstruction of justice and securities fraud and served five months in jail, five months of house arrest, and two years' probation.

Source: http://money.cnn.com/2002/08/05/news/companies/martha_lawsuit/index.htm; http://money.cnn.com/2002/10/21/news/martha/; Dow Jones News Service (2002), "Martha Stewart Down 12% on Concerns about Ex-Imclone CEO" (June 12); Martha Stewart Living Omnimedia, Inc., Schedule 14A, Proxy Statement (April 3, 2002); http://biography.yourdictionary.com/articles/why-did-martha-stewart-go-to-jail.html.

simply is no universally accepted code of ethics on which one can rely to assess right and wrong.

Business ethics seeks to proscribe those behaviors in which businesses should not engage. Such actions range from the giving or taking of gifts, bribing government officials, misrepresenting data, discriminatory hiring practices, and boycotting third parties. For example, some deemed it unethical for a company to do business in South Africa while that country practiced apartheid.

Business ethics and organizational architecture are interdependent. Organizational architecture, we have argued throughout this book, establishes incentives and thus affects the decisions managers and employees undertake. If it is important for businesspeople to behave ethically in their roles as managers and employees, it is important that the organization be structured to foster ethical behavior. In examining these issues, we first focus on external ethics policies controlling interaction between the firm and parties like customers, investors, and the local community. We then turn to internal ethics policies that deal with employees and managers.

Corporate Mission: Ethics and Policy Setting

What is the mission of the corporation, and does it involve ethics? Most people have a pretty good idea about what they mean when they describe an individual as "ethical." Most of us feel an emotional allegiance to the Golden Rule that urges us to treat others as we would have them treat us, and we value qualities such as honesty, integrity, fairness, and commitment to the task at hand. But what does it mean for a corporation to behave ethically? First, we have to understand what the term *ethical* means and then how it relates to the firm's mission.

Ethics

Ethics is a branch of philosophy. Western ethical philosophy can be traced back at least 2,500 years to Socrates, Plato, and Aristotle. These ancient Greeks searched for a generally understood set of principles of human conduct. Their treatises revolve around the terms *happiness* and *virtue*. Writing in the thirteenth century, St. Thomas Aquinas "argues that the first principle of thought about conduct is that good is to be done and pursued and evil avoided."[3]

There are numerous ethical theories, ranging from egoism (an act is correct if and only if it promotes the individual's long-term interests)[4] to utilitarianism (behaviors should "produce the greatest possible balance of good over bad for everyone affected by our action").[5] Kantian ethics judges the nature of the act, not the outcome; Kant argued that only good deeds matter.[6] Adam Smith argued that through the invisible hand of market competition driven by self-interested traders, resources are directed to their most productive use and societal wealth is maximized. Ethical relativism holds "that moral principles cannot be valid for everybody; and . . . that people ought to follow the conventions of their own group."[7]

Even a cursory review of the major ethical philosophies yields two immediate observations. First, ethics is an enormous subject area that has engaged some of history's best minds. Second, despite considerable effort, there is no universally accepted philosophical consensus across time and societies as to which behaviors are ethical and which are not.

Furthermore, when it comes to defining the ethics of organizations like public corporations that encompass large groups of people, there is bound to be confusion. A corporation, after all, is simply a collection of individuals—or, more precisely, a set of contracts that bind together individuals with different, often conflicting, interests (see Chapter 10). In this sense, organizations themselves do not behave ethically or unethically—only individuals do. And if managers and employees are not pursuing their own interests, then whose interests are they serving? Their bosses'? The shareholders'? The board's? And what if there are major conflicts among these various interests?

---

[3]J. Haldane (1991), "Medieval and Renaissance Ethics," in P. Singer (Ed.), *A Companion to Ethics* (Basil Blackwell: Oxford), 135.

[4]K. Baier (1991), "Egoism," in P. Singer (Ed.), *A Companion to Ethics* (Basil Blackwell: Cambridge), 197.

[5]W. Shaw (1991), *Business Ethics,* 49.

[6]W. Shaw (1991), 74.

[7]R. Brandt (1970), "Ethical Relativism," in T. Donaldson and P. Werhane (Eds.), *Ethical Issues in Business: A Philosophical Approach* (Prentice Hall: Englewood Cliffs), 78.

Value Maximization

Economic Darwinism

Maximizing the firm's value is the mission most economists ascribe to managers. By maximizing the size of the pie, each party contracting with the firm can receive a larger slice—including shareholders, bondholders, managers, employees, customers, suppliers, charities, and local cultural institutions. If the firm faces competition for both inputs and outputs, the prices the firm pays for its inputs and receives for its outputs will be driven to competitive levels, and the firm will not receive any abnormal profits. Economic Darwinism and survival were discussed in Chapter 1. Long-run survival in a competitive environment dictates that firms seek to produce products of a specified quality at the lowest possible cost. In the absence of barriers to entry, firms that survive in the long run are those that deliver products consumers want at the lowest cost. This means that managers must adopt policies that maximize the value of the firm—or, what amounts to the same thing, the net present value of future cash flows distributable to the firm's investors. If managers follow other policies that raise their costs, value-maximizing competitors enter, supply products at lower costs, and sell them at lower prices. Eventually, firms that deviate materially from value maximization will fail.

Role for Regulation

There are two important cases where value maximization leads to predictable resource misallocation. First, if the firm has monopoly power, it will reduce output and set price above long-run marginal cost. Second, if there are externalities—if firms' actions impose costs or benefits on uninvolved third parties—the firm has incentives to produce too much or too little of an item. For example,

---

· MANAGERIAL APPLICATIONS

The Tragedy of the Space Commons

In November 2013, the 1.2 ton GOCE satellite, launched by the European Space Agency to study the earth's gravitational field, reentered the earth's atmosphere, burned up, and scattered debris across the southern Atlantic Ocean. From the more than 7,000 spacecraft that have been launched since 1957, NASA estimates that there are over 20,000 pieces of space junk larger than a grapefruit and 500,000 larger than a dust speck. This might not sound like a big deal until you realize that each piece travels at 17,000 miles per hour. The damage that can be caused at these speeds was dramatized in the 2013 movie, *Gravity*. Although there are technical challenges to getting this mess cleaned up, organizing such an effort faces a major challenge, what economists call the tragedy of the commons. Individuals acting rationally and independently can deplete shared resources like fishing zones to the detriment of the larger population. Since no one owns the ocean, you can get "overfishing"; each boat captures the benefit of catching additional fish while all the fishing boats share the costs associated with depleting the stock of fish. Similarly, here the ultimate problem is that no one "owns" outer space and hence the incentives to use it carefully and keep it "clean" are reduced. If the United States were to underwrite the costs of such a cleanup project, it would have to share the benefits with the rest of the world. It is like the litter problem faced by most local parks; visitors frequently do not dispose of trash as carefully as they would in their own homes. But litter is rarely observed at Disney World. Since the Walt Disney Company owns this property, they hire an army of maintenance workers to keep their park virtually spotless.

Source: G. Hardin (1968) "The Tragedy of the Commons," *Science* 162, 1243–1248; and B. Bremner and P. Robinson (2014) "Cleaning Up the Final Frontier," *Bloomberg Businessweek* (January 16).

because no one has readily enforceable property rights to clean air, factories may produce too much air pollution. In both cases, one potential limiting factor in these problems is government regulation. Thus, if appropriate regulation constrains any resource misallocation from monopolies or externalities, firms can focus on value maximization within the bounds of the regulation.[8]

Compensating Differentials

Maximizing a firm's value requires managers to assess all costs and benefits of proposed actions accurately. Suppose George Wilson, manager of DisposeCo, is considering entering the business of the disposal of hazardous wastes. Employees exposed to such hazards usually demand a compensating wage differential to offset the higher risks of illness from such work (see Chapter 14). Therefore, when evaluating whether to enter this business, George must include these compensating differentials in his estimated costs.

Pharmacies are facing a difficult situation regarding their pharmacists who are refusing to fill contraception and morning-after prescriptions because dispensing the medications violates their moral or religious beliefs. Pharmacists across the country face dismissal or other disciplinary action when refusing to dispense certain medications. Walgreens, the nation's largest pharmacy, put four Illinois pharmacists on unpaid leave, stating they violated state law requiring pharmacists to sell medications approved by the U.S. Food and Drug Administration. Some pharmacies are allowing pharmacists who object to filling certain prescriptions to pass them to other pharmacists willing to dispense the pills.[9] But this increases costs—either two pharmacists must be on duty all the time, or the consumer must wait to get the prescription (or go to another pharmacy). Pharmacies may have to pay higher wages to attract pharmacists willing to fill contraception and morning-after prescriptions. (Of course, this compensating differential is reduced by pharmacists who are pro choice and endorse family planning.) In such cases, the costs of business decisions that some view as unethical are higher because of these higher compensating differentials, employee disciplinary actions and turnover, and potentially adverse publicity associated with such decisions.

MANAGERIAL APPLICATIONS

Coca-Cola's View of Corporate Responsibility

In the 1996 Coca-Cola annual report, CEO Roberto Goizueta wrote, "Governments are created to help meet civic needs. Philanthropies are created to meet social needs. And companies are created to meet economic needs." In 1997 four Atlanta-based philanthropies donated $220 million to local causes. These four foundations held Coke stock valued at $7.6 billion.

Source: A. Ehrbar (1998), *EVA The Real Key to Creating Wealth* (John Wiley & Sons, Inc.: New York), 18–19.

---

[8]There are a number of issues implied by this brief discussion. In general, within the government, individuals are not always acting to maximize social welfare. Thus, even if appropriate regulation could reduce these problems in principle, there is no assurance that regulations are adopted to do so. See Chapter 21 and G. Stigler (1971), "The Theory of Economic Regulation," *Bell Journal of Economics* 2, 3–21.

[9]R. Stein (2005), "Pharmacists' Rights at Front of New Debate," *Washington Post* (March 28), A1; and J. Suhr (2005), "Discipline of Pharmacists Spark Complaint," The Associated Press (December 8).

MANAGERIAL APPLICATIONS

Taxes and Corporate Philanthropy

One potential benefit to the owners of a firm from having the corporation donate to charities is a reduction in taxes paid to the government. Assume that both the corporate and personal tax rate is 50 percent.[*] Suppose a corporation has profits of $5,000 before taxes and distributes all its after-tax profits to the shareholders as dividends. The firm has four equal shareholders who collectively wish to contribute $1,000 to a particular charity. If the firm makes the contribution, it is deductible from corporate income before taxes. Thus, the corporation has $4,000 of taxable income ($5,000 − $1,000), of which $2,000 is paid in taxes and $2,000 is paid to the owners who pay personal taxes on the dividends they receive. After personal taxes, each shareholder has $250 ($2,000 ÷ 4 × 50%).

Now suppose the shareholders donate $250 each to the charity and the corporation makes no contribution. The firm has pretax profits of $5,000, pays taxes of $2,500 (50% of $5,000), and distributes $2,500 to shareholders. Each shareholder receives $625 ($2,500 ÷ 4) before personal taxes, makes the contribution ($250), and has taxable income of $375 ($625 − $250). Each pays taxes of $187.50 and has after taxes $187.50 ($625 − $250 − $187.50). By having the firm make the charitable contribution, each shareholder has $62.50 ($250 − $187.50) more than when the shareholder makes the charitable contribution. When the firm makes the contribution, the gift shields $1,000 from corporate taxation.

These tax reduction gains for corporate philanthropy are most compelling when all the shareholders agree on the amount and nature of the donations. Gifts to charities not valued by some shareholders reduce these shareholders' welfare. Unfortunately, corporate stakeholders are unlikely to agree about which charities should receive corporate donations and how much each should receive. Customers, employees, or independent sales agents objecting to the firm's choice of charities may take their business or services elsewhere. Moreover, corporate managers do not have an obvious comparative advantage in choosing which charities to support. If it is time-consuming for managers to sort through charitable requests and make the selections, this is time that could have been spent on other activities that more predictably increase the firm's value. Thus, even with the tax advantage of corporate philanthropy, shareholders are not necessarily better off by having the firm make charitable donations instead of doing it themselves.

[*] The Bush-era tax revisions lowered the tax rate on qualifying dividends to 15 percent. Although this adjustment makes the calculations more complicated the basic result is unaffected.

Corporate Social Responsibility

One source of confusion about the corporate mission is the concept of "corporate social responsibility," which often is used interchangeably with corporate ethics. In 1969, Ralph Nader along with several other lawyers launched their Project on Corporate Responsibility with the following statement:[10]

> Today we announce an effort to develop a new kind of citizenship around an old kind of private government—the large corporation. It is an effort which rises from the shared concern of many citizens over the role of the corporation in American society and the uses of its complex powers. It is an effort which is dedicated toward developing a new constituency for the corporation that will harness these powers for the fulfillment of a broader spectrum of democratic values.

As Nader's statement suggests, the goal of some advocates of corporate social responsibility is nothing less than to change the objective function of the corporation. In

[10]J. Collins (1979), "Case Study—Campaign to Make General Motors Responsible," in T. Donaldson and P. Werhane (Eds.), *Ethical Issues in Business* (Prentice-Hall: Englewood Cliffs), 90.

Nader's view, the corporation should be transformed from a means of maximizing investor wealth into a vehicle for using private wealth to redress social ills. The corporate social responsibility movement seeks to make management responsible for upholding "a broader spectrum of democratic values." Corporate support for such values could take the form of philanthropic activities, the provision of subsidized goods and services to certain segments of the community, or the use of corporate resources on public projects such as education, environmental improvement, and crime prevention. If all firms in the marketplace face the same social requirements, then the survival of any given firm is less of an issue. However, if some firms are exempted from redressing social ills, others' survival in a competitive environment is more in doubt.[11]

Economists' View of Social Responsibility

The conflict between Nader's and economists' views of the corporation is perhaps not as pronounced as it might appear. Corporations intent on maximizing firm value generally find it in their interest to devote substantial resources to noninvestor stakeholders such as employees, customers, suppliers, and local communities. For example, a company with a large plant in an inner city might decide that investing corporate resources and personnel to improve area schools leads to better-trained job applicants, more productive employees, and lower-cost products. Giving money to the local university might benefit the firm by improving its R&D, increasing its access to top graduates, or enhancing cultural and educational opportunities for its employees. Improving the environment lowers the company's legal exposure to damage claims and also might reduce its wage bill to the extent that a cleaner local environment lowers the cost of attracting and retaining employees.

Maximizing firm value means allocating corporate resources to all groups or interests that affect the value of the firm—but only to the point where the incremental benefits from such expenditures at least equal their additional costs. Thus, value maximization might require expending the firm's resources on members of an important corporate constituency to improve the terms on which it contracts with the company, to maintain the firm's reputation, or to reduce the threat of restrictive regulation.

ANALYZING MANAGERIAL DECISIONS: *Wilmorite Mall Development*

Wilmorite Corporation owned a large tract of land and proposed erecting a large, modern enclosed shopping mall south of town. The mall was opposed by an environmental group that argued that the land had areas with standing water that waterfowl used in their spring and fall migrations. The challenges resulted in a substantial delay in the development of the land; more extensive environmental impact statements had to be prepared and plans had to be redrawn.

1. Was this development ethical?
2. The largest contributor to the environmental group happened to own Southtown Mall, an older strip mall across the road from the proposed new mall. Was his contribution to the environmental group ethical?

---

[11]M. Jensen and W. Meckling (1978), "Can the Corporation Survive?" *Financial Analysts Journal* 34, 31–37.

Milton Friedman's View of Corporate Social Responsibility

What does it mean to say that the corporate executive has a "social responsibility" in his capacity as businessman? If this statement is not pure rhetoric, it must mean that he is to act in some way that is not in the interest of his employers. For example . . . that he is to make expenditures on reducing pollution beyond the amount that is in the best interests of the corporation or that is required by law in order to contribute to the social objective of improving the environment . . .

[The problem in this case is that] the corporate executive would be spending someone else's money for a general social interest . . . [when] the stockholders or the customers or the employees could separately spend their own money on the particular action if they wished to do so.

Source: M. Friedman (1970), "The Social Responsibility of Business Is to Increase Its Profits," *New York Times Magazine* (September 13).

Many managers are inclined to endorse Nobel Laureate Milton Friedman's prescription that the social mission of the corporation is "to make as much money for its owners as possible while conforming to the basic rules of society." As we have noted, some companies will find it in their shareholders' interest to "invest" in social causes of various kinds, but corporate investments that systematically fail to provide adequate long-term returns to private investors are wealth transfers that end up reducing social as well as private wealth.

Absent tax benefits, it usually is more efficient for the corporation to focus on creating wealth and to let its shareholders, employees, and customers choose the beneficiaries of their charitable contributions. By maximizing their shareholders' (or owners') wealth, corporations effectively enlarge the pool of individual (noncorporate) resources available for charity.[12]

Do's and Don'ts of Corporate Giving

Philanthropic spending by U.S. corporations in 2001 was estimated to be $9 billion or 1.3 percent of pretax profits. Nell Minow, at a corporate governance research group, argues, "Corporate charitable contributions should be seen as part of the company's marketing strategy. If they promote the company's products or brand identity, then it's fine. If the money goes to the ballet so the CEO's wife can be on the ballet board, or to the local university whose president happens to be the chair of the company board's compensation committee, not fine." An increasing number of corporate charitable gifts are coming under public scrutiny. Perhaps the most spectacular case involved Tyco International and its former chairman, Dennis Kozlowski, who was indicted for federal racketeering, fraud, tax evasion, grand larceny, and misuse of company funds. Tyco contends that a $2.5 million fund at Middlebury College was endowed with its money but named for Kozlowski. But other situations are attracting attention. Part of Jacques Nasser's retirement package as CEO of Ford Motor included a commitment by Ford to endow a scholarship at the educational institution of Mr. Nasser's choice.

Deborah Patterson, president of the Monsanto Fund, offers the advice that firms establish clear parameters for their corporate giving including categories of gifts and the focus of their giving such as education, environment, medical research, and so forth. The CEO can propose a gift, but if it doesn't fall into the preestablished parameters, then the gift is denied. Moreover, CEOs should make it very clear whether the gift is from them personally or from the corporation. For example, Dick Jenerette was insistent that his giving was not confused with Equitable Insurance's, when he was CEO at Equitable.

Source: S. Strom (2002), "In Charity, Where Does a C.E.O. End and a Company Start?" *New York Times* (September 22), B1–B12.

[12]J. Brickley (1988), "Managerial Goals and the Court System: Some Economic Insights," *Canada–United States Law Journal* 13, 79.

People who advocate ever-larger corporate contributions to charities and social causes such as retraining displaced workers and environmental cleanup (without consideration of their own long-run profitability) are effectively calling for higher implicit taxes on corporations. If all companies are so taxed, the taxes are borne ultimately by shareholders in the form of lower returns to capital, by employees in the form of lower wages, and by customers in the form of higher prices. Thus, ironically, potential social consequences of such an increase in corporate social responsibility include lower rates of economic growth, lower corporate values, lower employment, and reduced charitable donations (if reductions in donations by individuals more than offset the increases in corporate giving).

Corporate Policy Setting

Once a corporation has determined its mission, implementing the mission requires a set of operating policies. Again, ethical issues arise. It is futile to think that one can reduce excruciatingly difficult corporate policy issues to simple, universally applauded policy decisions. Consider questions like

- Should we use laboratory animals for product testing?
- Should we market infant formula in Central Africa?

MANAGERIAL APPLICATIONS

Drugmakers Help People—and Themselves

Developing new prescription drugs is a quite costly proposition. It takes years to develop and test drugs before they are approved, and many compounds must be examined to yield one federally approved medicine. Some drugs targeted at esoteric diseases have limited markets. So to recoup their investment, drug companies must charge very high prices. For example, in 2003 the U.S. Food and Drug Administration approved a drug for a rare genetic disease, MPS-VI, that costs patients $300,000 a year. To cope with higher prescription drug costs, patients must pay higher insurance premiums and co-pays (a fraction of the prescription's cost). But some patients cannot afford their premiums and co-pays that can amount in some cases to several thousand dollars a week. Instead of losing these sales, the drug companies are making donations to charities that then give money to patients to pay their premiums and to make their co-pays. Drug company money allows patients to keep their insurance, and keeps the insurance companies paying for the high-priced medicines.

"It's a win-win situation," says Dana Kuhn, president of Patient Services, a charity that solicits donations from drugmakers. "Patients are helped and companies are helped. They make a small contribution to help the patient and get much more money back when the insurer pays for the drug." In 2004 Patient Services raised $22 million, $17 million from 12 drug companies, and helped 20,000 patients. Genzyme, which makes the drug Fabrazme, donated money to Patient Services to cover the $5,400 per patient co-pay for Fabrazme. And this $5,400 donation brings in $185,000 per patient per year for Genzyme. In 2005 Patient Services raised $30 million. And Patient Services is just one such charity that collects donations from drug companies to help patients.

Besides making donations to charities to help keep patients insured, drugmakers also donate high-priced drugs to uninsured patients. These programs allow pharmaceutical companies to charge high prices to invest in R&D, to recover their enormous costs, and to provide a return to their shareholders—and helps patients make their insurance payments and get their medicine. In effect, these corporate charity programs allow drug companies to engage in more effective price discrimination (see Chapter 7). The drugmakers effectively charge different consumers different prices, based on their income and willingness to pay.

Source: G. Anand (2005), "Drugmakers Help People—and Themselves," *The Wall Street Journal* (December 1), A1.

- Should we do business with a company that employs child labor in its Asian textile factory?
- Should we adopt different procedures for handling and disposing of hazardous wastes in Latin American plants than we use in the United States?
- Should we pay "fees" to expedite paperwork for export permits to an African market?
- Should we tow our obsolete North Sea oil rig to deep water and sink it?

Because there is no widely embraced definition of ethical behavior, these problems require careful analysis in establishing appropriate corporate policy. In particular, managers should be careful to collect data for estimating the total cost and benefits of alternative actions, including costs of adverse publicity, tarnished reputation, and lost customers. Although we cannot solve the above problems, we can suggest steps to help craft an appropriate policy.

Diversity of Input

In questions with potentially contentious ethical implications, it is particularly important to obtain input from a broad cross section of potentially affected stakeholders in the firm. Here, diversity in perspective can be especially valuable in identifying potentially sensitive areas that require additional analysis prior to setting policy. Diversity in backgrounds can help the management team better assess the potential total costs of alternative policies.

Legal Standards

It is important to understand the legal consequences of potential policy choices. The first, most obvious, question is—*Is it legal?* Yet this knowledge alone is generally far from sufficient to frame policy. For example, after the United States bombed Libya in 1986, some U.S. banks faced a dilemma: The U.S. Federal Reserve and the State Department required that Libyan funds in U.S. banks be frozen. But the Central Bank of Greece simultaneously announced that under Greek law, any Libyan funds on deposit in Greece must be available on demand.

MANAGERIAL APPLICATIONS

Happier Animals Help Corporate Profits

Edmond Pajor, an animal behavior and welfare professor at Purdue University, gives pigs a choice. The pigs can use their snouts either to get into a pen where they can socialize with other pigs, or they can stay in their own pens and eat alone. "We want to know: How important is social contact and space? What do they like and need?" Professor Pajor's research and other's like it are being financed by the big food companies like MacDonald's, Burger King, KFC, and Wendy's because the research helps these companies devise new standards aimed at ensuring more humane treatment of animals destined for their customers. Todd Duvick, a food analyst at Bank of America Securities says, "The whole drumbeat in the U.S. for the last century has been to reduce the cost of food. Now people are paying attention to things like how food is produced and how animals are treated."

By sponsoring research directed at more humane treatment of animals that ultimately end up in their kitchens, the large food companies are hoping to increase the demand for their products. This is an example of corporate philanthropy that increases their bottom line.

Source: D. Barboza (2003), "Animal Welfare's Unexpected Allies," *New York Times* (June 25), A1.

ACADEMIC APPLICATIONS

Food Fraud

Nobel-prize winner Gary Becker examined the economics of crime. He argued that the incidence of crime in general and fraud in particular would increase (1) the greater the benefits of fraud, (2) the lower the probability of the fraud being detected, and (3) the smaller the expected consequences of being caught. Food fraud in Great Britain appears to fit this model quite well. For example, British inspectors found 22 tons of long-grain rice being sold as pricier Basmati. Trading Standards officers seized nearly 2,500 jars of sugar syrup labeled as honey. This type of crime appears to be growing. In 2007, the British Food Standards Agency established a food fraud database. From 49 reports in 2007, reports grew to 1,528 in 2013. Europol thinks that some crooks who once focused on drugs have switched to food. Although the use of drugs apparently is falling in the United Kingdom, everyone consumes food. Moreover, few resources are being devoted to detecting such fraud. And if caught, penalties for food fraud are substantially lower than for smuggling drugs or guns.

Source: Anon (2014), "A la Cartel," *The Economist* (March 15), 55.

If Libya had funds on deposit in Citibank's Athens branch and requested the funds, the bank would have to choose between violating U.S. law or Greek law. Or, consider potential consequences of hiring child labor in a textile mill in Pakistan, even if it is legal there; some customers might object because the practice would be illegal in the United States or Europe.

Moreover, illegality may not be the determining factor. For example, it is doubtful that Federal Express would adopt a policy of firing a driver who violates the law by receiving a parking ticket. Hence, it is important to understand what sanctions might be imposed if a law is violated.

Finally, laws are not constant over time. For instance, although the 1995 Congress rolled back certain environmental regulations, some firms appear reluctant to take advantage of the entire range of newly allowed activities. They appear to be concerned that if the political pendulum swings back, they might face some future liability.

Business Norms

In the business community, there are expectations in transactions that do not have the force of law but nonetheless represent expected behavior. These norms are rarely written down; knowledge of them accumulates primarily with experience. These issues can be especially important when entering a new market. For instance, when Lincoln Electric decided to expand into Japan, it encountered unexpected difficulties in selling its products. Lincoln's managers had failed to appreciate the strong preference accorded long-standing business partners by Japanese companies.

In special cases, these norms are codified. Adopting procedures developed by an external group to handle sensitive issues can be quite useful. For example, standards for using laboratory animals in product testing are established by the U.S. Department of Agriculture, the National Institutes of Health, and the Public Health Service. Most organizations that undertake animal research adhere to these standards. Nongovernmental groups also participate in this process. For instance, firms in the motion picture industry frequently voluntarily adopt standards developed by the American Society for the Prevention of Cruelty to Animals. By stating that you adhere to the ASPCA code, a film company may be able to deflect much criticism.

Press Standard

Another useful device managers use in determining the ethical issues in setting corporate policies involves assessing the public's likely reaction. Examples of companies withdrawing support for Planned Parenthood due to protests and boycotts from "Right to Life" groups illustrate the often important interaction among ethics, public relations, and the media. Ethics consultants regularly counsel corporate managers to apply the press standard to help determine which behaviors are ethical. This criteria suggests that to judge whether an action is ethical, you should ask yourself whether you would be comfortable reading about your decision on the front page of the newspaper or seeing it reported on television.[13] Suggesting that a decision is a good idea but only if it is kept confidential is quite likely to be a mistake. Remember, the business press is quite sophisticated. Counting on a questionable decision being overlooked or ignored might be characterized better as wishful thinking than thoughtful analysis. Therefore, when considering a difficult ethical decision, try writing a press release. If you are unwilling to distribute the release, then the decision is unlikely to be appropriate.

Using publication of your behavior as an ethical benchmark for judging a decision highlights the linkage between ethical behavior and reputation. Below, we discuss market forces that create incentives for people and firms to behave ethically. The argument is that unethical behavior adversely affects reputation, and one way to assess a decision's reputational effects is to ask how it would read in *The Wall Street Journal* or the *Financial Times*.

Mechanisms for Encouraging Ethical Behavior

Ethical lapses frequently are manifestations of conflicts of interest—incentive problems. As stated earlier, in most market exchanges, parties to the contracts have incentives to devise mechanisms to reduce contracting costs, thereby raising the prices

---

[13]Thomas Jefferson offered similar advice in a letter to Peter Carr: "Whenever you are to do a thing, though it can never be known but to yourself, ask yourself how you would act were all the world looking at you, and act accordingly." T. Jefferson (1785), in N. Beilson (Ed.), *Thomas Jefferson: His Life and Words* (1986) (Peter Pauper Press: White Plains), 47.

MANAGERIAL APPLICATIONS

Signaling Quality by External Monitoring—Rice Aircraft

In 1991, Rice Aircraft Company became the first company in its industry to earn ISO 9002 accreditation, an international standard for quality management. This was a significant, highly visible signal of change within the firm. For in August 1989, Bruce J. Rice, CEO of Rice Aircraft, had pled guilty to fraud and was sentenced to four years in prison. The Defense Department forbade its contractors to do business with the company for five years, and annual sales fell from $15 million to $5 million. At this point, Paula DeLong Rice, Rice's wife, took over and set out to save the company by visibly and radically transforming it. She implemented a total quality initiative and provided classes in statistical process control, time management, and communications for all the company's employees.

Paula DeLong Rice's strategy appears to have been quite effective. Profit margins increased from 12 percent in 1992 to 27 percent in 1993 without benefit of price increases, order cycle time was reduced by 50 percent, and on-time deliveries increased 98 percent. Paula DeLong Rice, moreover, is now in great demand as a speaker on managing for quality.

Source: T. Pare (1994), "Rebuilding a Lost Reputation," *Fortune* (May 20), 176.

---

they receive for their products or services. For example, when taking their firms public for the first time, founders of companies normally retain large positions in the stock and voluntarily impose restrictions on their own future stock sales to help ensure that their interests are consistent with those of their new investors. Such arrangements effectively raise the price investors are willing to pay.

Likewise, external public auditors voluntarily prohibit themselves from owning stock in the companies they audit. By not owning any stock, auditors do not gain by withholding unfavorable financial information. This increases their independence from their clients, raises the value of the audit, and hence increases the price firms are willing to pay for it.

As we noted earlier, because reputational capital is an important determinant of future earnings, market forces provide incentives for firms and individuals to behave ethically. But the effectiveness of market forces in controlling conflicts of interest and enforcing contracts varies among different kinds of transactions. Among the most important characteristics of such transactions are the difficulty of ascertaining product quality prior to purchase and the likelihood that the transaction will be repeated.

Take the case of a buyer purchasing a product. For products whose quality can be determined at low cost prior to purchase, markets readily solve this problem. If buyers can monitor quality cheaply, they will do so. For example, a buyer negotiating a purchase of gold for Tiffany & Co. can confidently and cheaply ascertain its quality by assay.

For some products, quality is virtually impossible to determine prior to purchase. For example, you can know the quality of an airplane ticket only after the plane has landed, it is parked at the gate, you have deplaned, and retrieved your luggage. Although sellers have incentives to cheat on quality when quality is expensive to measure, rational sellers will provide products of lower-than-promised quality only if the expected gains exceed the expected costs.

Repeat Sales

One important constraint on such cheating is the potential for future sales.[14] Moreover, corporations with established market positions and valuable brand names face higher costs of cheating and hence are less likely to cheat than start-up firms. The

---

[14]L. Telser (1980), "A Theory of Self-Enforcing Agreements," *Journal of Business* 53, 27–44.

ACADEMIC APPLICATIONS

Evidence on the Penalty from Fraud

Researchers have examined the stock market's reaction to announcements of fraud charges against corporations. They specifically focus on cases where the damaged party does business with the accused firm—thus, they focus on frauds alleged against customers, suppliers, employees, and investors (but not damages to third parties such as in pollution dumping). The evidence suggests that in the days around the first announcement in *The Wall Street Journal,* the average fall in the firm's stock price is 1.58 percent. Thus, press reports of alleged fraud are associated with statistically significant and economically material losses in value. Moreover, these losses were much too large to be explained by legal costs and fines.

Source: J. Karpoff and J. Lott (1993), "The Reputational Penalty Firms Bear from Committing Criminal Fraud," *Journal of Law & Economics* XXXVI, 757–802.

costs of cheating on quality also are higher if the information about such activities is more rapidly and widely distributed to potential future customers. For example, in markets like the diamond trade in New York, which is dominated by a close-knit community of Hasidic Jews, cheating on quality is extremely rare.[15]

Warranties

Seller-provided product warranties are another mechanism to reduce the likelihood of cheating. Since sellers bear higher warranty costs if they cheat on quality, they have less incentive to cheat. Seller warranties will be most prevalent when product failures result from factors that are under the firm's control (such as manufacturing tolerances). In this case, warranties directly impose the cost of failure on the parties who have the most control over product quality or failure. However, when failures are due primarily to factors that are under the customers' control (such as the way the product is used or maintained), the moral-hazard problem will be greater and warranties are less frequently employed as a quality-assurance mechanism.

Third-Party Monitors

In some markets, specialized information services monitor the market, certify quality, and help ensure contract performance. For example, *Consumer Reports* evaluates products from toasters to automobiles, the *Investment Dealer Digest* details activities of investment bankers, and A.M. Best Company rates financial conditions of insurance companies. These third-party information sources lower the costs for potential customers to determine quality and so increase the expected costs of cheating.

In credit markets, specialized credit information services like Moody's and Dun & Bradstreet perform both a monitoring and an information dissemination function. The existence of such intermediaries provides an opportunity for the firm to guarantee quality. For this reason, corporate issuers pay Moody's to have their debt rated over the life of the bond issue. By issuing rated public debt, a firm lowers the cost to other potential corporate claimholders (including potential customers) of ascertaining the firm's financial condition.[16]

---

[15]Other examples of ethnic communities, like the Chinese in Singapore, support the view that choosing trading partners from within one's own ethnic community economizes on the costs of contracting. J. Landa (1981), "A Theory of the Ethnically Homogeneous Middlemen Group: An Institutional Alternative to Contract Law," *Journal of Legal Studies* 10, 349–362.

[16]L. Wakeman (1983), "The Real Function of Bond Rating Agencies," *Chase Financial Quarterly* 1, 18–26.

Disclosure

The required level of disclosure in markets can also be important in determining quality. For example, a study of two wholesale used-car markets with different levels of required disclosure found higher prices in the market with more required disclosure.[17] The ability to "precommit" to disclose information reduces the potential information disparity between buyer and seller thereby reducing the discount buyers apply to their demand prices. Also, eBay.com, the online auction website, encourages participants to write messages about their experiences with their partner in the transaction. This provides future participants with more information about the performance of a potential trader (the accuracy of product descriptions, the timeliness of shipping) and thus enables them to have more confidence in their transactions. Moreover, by creating this feedback mechanism, eBay provides sellers with a means of developing a reputation. This improves the performance of auction participants.

Ownership Structure

Incentives to provide high-quality products vary across ownership structures. Take the case of franchise companies such as fast-food and lawn-care firms. Such companies typically franchise some units rather than own all their stores in order to take advantage of the incentive benefits of decentralized ownership while retaining scale economies in advertising and brand-name promotion.

Yet outlets that have little repeat business create a special problem. The franchise owners of these stores have an incentive to cheat on quality because they can benefit from a steady stream of one-time sales while reducing the reputation of the entire organization; this is another example of the standard free-rider problem. At these locations, the central company is more likely to own the unit than to franchise it, in part because a salaried manager has fewer incentives to cheat on quality.[18]

Companies with large amounts of debt in their capital structure can face a significant probability of financial distress. Such firms are more likely to cheat on

---

MANAGERIAL APPLICATIONS

Alibaba Expels Resellers

Alibaba Group Holding, the Chinese e-commerce company, is removing some listings from its online shopping sites to attract more luxury brands. For example, Burberry PLC had been worried about discount Burberry products—some of which are fake—on Alibaba's online marketplaces. These sites accounted for 80 percent of China's estimated $300 billion in online shopping in 2013. But Burberry had authorized none of these vendors to sell its products. Burberry was told that Alibaba would do its best to get those products off its sites if it would open its own shop on Alibaba's online mall. It opened a store on Alibaba's Tmall in April 2014. Alibaba's offer to crack down on "gray-market" goods for brands that opened Tmall stores provides a powerful incentive for brands to join the site. Their intervention can be quite effective. For example, nearly four dozen Tmall shops sold Estée Lauder beauty products earlier in 2014. But around the time it opened its Tmall store in May, all third-party products had vanished.

Source: K. Chu and J. Chiu (2014), "To Woo Lux Brands, Alibaba Purges Resellers," *The Wall Street Journal* (August 11).

---

[17]H. Grieve (1984), "Quality Certification in a 'Lemons' Market: An Empirical Test of Certification in Wholesale Used-Car Auctions," working paper, University of Rochester.

[18]One study finds that franchise companies in lines of business with more repeat sales at individual units (e.g., lawn-care and beauty shops) are likely to franchise a higher percentage of total units than franchise lines with less repeat business (such as motels, car rental agencies, and restaurants). J. Brickley and F. Dark (1987), "The Choice of Organizational Form: The Case of Franchising," *Journal of Financial Economics* 18, 401–420.

quality than financially healthy firms because repeat sales are less likely. Therefore, some firms "bond" product quality by adopting conservative financial policies. Since financial distress is more costly for firms that market products where quality is difficult to ascertain, such firms have incentives to adopt financing policies that lead to a lower probability of financial distress—policies such as lower leverage, fewer leases, and more hedging.

Contracting Costs: Ethics and Policy Implementation

In our examples of Enron (Chapter 1), Merrill Lynch (Chapter 2), and Salomon Brothers (Chapter 22), none of these firms had formal corporate strategies of engaging in unethical behavior. Rather, their ethical problems arose from ineffectively controlling the behavior of individuals granted particular decision rights within the firm. They are examples of incentive problems within firms. Chapter 10 described the general incentive problem as the difficulty in making corporate managers and employees perform in ways consistent with the aims of the firm's owners. In addressing these internal ethical issues, this section makes two key points: First, the incentive problem of shirking or of opportunistic actions by an employee often is labeled an ethical lapse; and second, if all employees reduced their opportunistic actions (behaved more ethically), contracting costs would be lower.

To review the incentive problems that can arise with performance evaluation and monitoring, take the simple case of Alice Brown's hiring Olaf Kolzig to paint her house. Especially in performing tasks that are hard to monitor by inspection after the job is completed, such as surface preparation (sanding, scraping, and priming), Olaf has incentives to shirk—or, at least, to do a job that may not be as thorough as Alice might like. Of course, Olaf also will be prompted by other considerations to do a good job. It may be a matter of private conscience; that is, Olaf's sense of self-worth might be tied up with the quality of the workmanship, and violating such a self-imposed standard would impose major "costs" in the form of a tarnished self-image. Or Olaf might be constrained by the desire to maintain his commercial reputation (and, though it might take some time for a poor job of surface preparation to show its effects, quality eventually will reveal itself). As we noted earlier in this chapter, reputation is an important contributor to the capitalized value of one's expected future earnings.

But because the prompting of conscience and the desire to maintain a reputation are neither universal nor constant, it's impossible for Alice to know the extent to which Olaf is bound by such considerations. Alice faces an information problem: When hiring Olaf, she does not know the kind of surface preparation she will get, nor will she be capable of ascertaining that until well after the job is done and the bill is paid.

To reduce her vulnerability in such circumstances of informational asymmetry, Alice likely will ask for a list of references (if Olaf has not already provided one). Such references should give Alice a better basis for assessing Olaf's time horizon and the importance he attaches to reputation. Olaf also might offer, or Alice might insist on, a one-or-more-year warranty on the job. (As discussed above, such common practices as the use of warranties, third-party references, and credit checks can play an important role in reducing contracting costs in the business world.)

But despite such assurances, some uncertainties about Olaf's level of performance remain. For example, will he be around to make good on the warranty if the paint peels in a year? Perhaps Olaf has heavy debts and is about to declare personal

A CEO's View of Verbal Contracts

Most of our products were custom-made. Customers called in their orders over the phone. The orders . . . generally required delivery of goods within one or two days. It meant we would usually begin production before receiving a confirming purchase order. (This was before faxes.) The customer's word alone was enough. In my 20-year stint as CEO, not once did a customer go back on it. Unusual? Not at all. Without such trust, business couldn't be conducted. Similar transactions happen every day. . . . [W]e learned there are two ways to go: An eye for an eye, or do unto others what you would have them do unto you. In business, the latter philosophy is far more common, simply because it makes things work better.

Source: H. Aaron (1994), "The Myth of the Heartless Businessman," *The Wall Street Journal* (February 7), A14.

bankruptcy. Or perhaps the job he does for Alice will be Olaf's last before he embarks on a new career painting and family portraits.

As a consequence of the possibility of shirking and her own remaining uncertainty, Alice effectively reduces the price she is willing to pay. Or, to state the converse of this proposition, if there were some means for Olaf to provide Alice with complete assurance about his level of commitment, Alice would be willing to pay a higher price for the job.

Three points emerge from this simple example. First, let's assume Alice were able to design a perfect contract; for the sake of argument, let's say that Alice had a camera which enabled her to observe Olaf's activity at random intervals (and Olaf knew she had it) and that Alice were able to structure a pay schedule based on the observed effort. Even if she were able to devise such a monitoring and reward system, it would clearly not pay her to do so. The cost to Alice of writing, of administering, and, most important, of monitoring compliance with such a contract would be substantial—perhaps even greater than the value of the painting job itself. Thus, as this simple illustration is meant to point out, in most cases it does not pay to attempt to eliminate all possible shirking; because of the costs of writing and monitoring compliance with contracts, it is efficient to leave some slack in the system. The *optimal* amount of shirking or opportunistic behavior by an agent is not zero.

Second, the *expected* level of opportunism or shirking—which, again, is greater than zero—is priced in the contract. Thus, the principals do not bear the full costs of opportunistic actions by their agents. Typically, at least some of these costs are shifted back to agents in the form of lower prices for their services or products.

Third, higher ethical standards among agents, whether corporate employees or participants in market exchanges, would lead (over time) to a reduction in the level of *expected* opportunistic behavior and hence a reduction in contracting costs. As a result, there would be more transactions (including more jobs created) and higher prices paid to agents by principals (including higher corporate wages). This would occur not only because of a reduction in the amount of shirking but also because the costs of writing and monitoring contracts would fall. Both principals and agents would be better off. Economist Jack Hirshleifer makes this last point: "Altruism economizes on the costs of policing and enforcing contracts."[19] In discussing economic development, one writer lists low business ethics as an important factor impeding growth. During the late nineteenth century, such practices as confidence men

[19]J. Hirshleifer (1977), "Economics from a Biological Viewpoint," *Journal of Law and Economics* 20, 28.

selling shares, bankruptcy with concealed assets, and squandering capital increased the difficulty of raising capital to finance new ventures such as the construction of the railroads.[20]

The retired CEO's story in the accompanying box illustrates an important point about the economic consequences of ethics: Ethical standards within an organization—or within an economy—affect the resources devoted to ensuring contract compliance and, hence, help determine overall productivity. If everyone voluntarily were to reduce opportunistic behavior (such as withholding important information about product quality), then resources devoted to monitoring and enforcing exchanges could be used in other, more productive pursuits.[21]

Codes of Ethics

We view important aspects of the corporate ethics problem primarily as problems of controlling incentive problems. And generalizing from the above discussion, there are several potential ways to control them. One way to control incentive problems would be to get corporate managers and employees to voluntarily adopt higher, more stringent ethical standards. A second is to use contracts that better align the interests of managers and employees with those of shareholders. Examples of such contracts in corporations are executive or employee stock options, bonus plans, and profit-sharing arrangements (see Chapter 15). (Such contracts also will act to reinforce voluntary codes.) Both more cost-effective incentive contracts and higher ethical standards can be expected to lead to lower contracting costs, greater corporate efficiency, higher corporate values, and greater social welfare.

As mentioned earlier, many companies and most professions have written codes of conduct, and some companies also have educational programs dealing with ethics for their employees. Such codes and programs regularly emphasize the following:[22]

- Employees must obey the laws and observe statutory regulations.
- Customer relations in terms of the reputation and integrity of the company are of great importance.
- Employees must support the company's policies when interacting with customers.
- Conflicts of interest between the company and the employee must be avoided.
- Confidential information gained in the course of business must not be used improperly.
- It is improper to conceal dishonesty or to protect others in their dishonesty.
- Advice to customers should be restricted to facts about which the employee is confident.

Why have corporations adopted such codes? The most cynical view is that a corporate code of ethics is nothing more than a document that helps the firm defend itself against allegations of illegal behavior. Sentencing guidelines issued by the U.S. Sentencing Commission in November 1991 strongly encourage corporations to establish and communicate compliance standards and procedures for employees and

---

[20]T. Cochran (1964), *The Inner Revolution* (Harper & Row: New York).

[21]E. Noreen (1988), "The Economics of Ethics: A New Perspective on Agency Theory," *Accounting, Organizations and Society* 13, 359–369.

[22]These codes are not unique to the United States. For example, similar codes are observed in Australian firms. B. Kaye (1992), "Codes of Ethics in Australian Business," *Journal of Business Ethics* 11, 857.

other agents through training programs and publications. For example, when an individual is found guilty of wrongdoing, the organization also might be vulnerable to federal sanctions such as fines. These penalties can be reduced by more than 50 percent simply by demonstrating that the organization has a compliance program that meets the Sentencing Commission's standards.[23] A compliance program consists at least of a code of ethics and a training program. These federal sentencing guidelines thus have blurred the line between legal and ethical issues.

But corporate ethical codes, as we just have argued, also have the potential to perform the economically valuable function of reducing the costs of monitoring and enforcing contracts. To the extent that they reduce managerial and employee opportunism, better ethical standards enhance the organization's reputation and hence increase shareholders' wealth.

The critical questions, however, are these: *Are ethical codes effective in deterring unethical behavior? And if they are, how and why are they effective?*

Altering Preferences

There are two basic ways to view the function of corporate codes of conduct in reducing opportunistic behavior. One way is by appealing directly to employees' consciences, attempting to instill in them loyalty to the organization and its goals. An economist might describe this as an attempt to alter people's "preferences."

Now, there is undoubtedly some value to this approach. As we noted earlier, personal codes of conduct and the guilt one suffers in violating such codes undeniably are constraints on many people's behavior. Individuals' utility functions contain many nonpecuniary factors, including conscience and guilt. As the following statement by Nobel Laureate Kenneth Arrow suggests, subjective concepts like ethics and morality surely are consistent with the economist's notion of rational self-interest:

> *Certainly one way of looking at ethics and morality . . . is that these principles are agreements, conscious or, in many cases, unconscious, to supply mutual benefits. . . . Societies in their evolution have developed implicit agreements to certain kinds of regard for others, agreements which are essential to the survival of the society or at least contribute greatly to the efficiency of its working. . . . The fact [that] we cannot mediate all our responsibilities to others through prices . . . makes it essential in the running of society that we have what might be called "conscience," a feeling of responsibility for the effects of one's actions on others.*[24]

The problem in applying this logic to corporate management, however, is that such "agreements to supply mutual benefits to others" are likely to be too amorphous to serve as a practical guide to individual behavior in large public companies with diffuse stock ownership. If employees are understandably unmoved by serving an anonymous group of "wealthy" shareholders, then who precisely are "the others" whose interests their morality is intended to serve? And what should employees do in those cases, noted earlier, where there appear to be (at least short-run) conflicts between the interests of the corporation's shareholders and those of its noninvestor constituencies? After all, as we have seen earlier, the effective management of scarce resources often means saying no to the requests or desires of some employees, customers, and local communities. Moreover, the entire situation is complicated by the fact

[23]N. Gilbert (1994), "1-800-ETHICS," *Financial World* (August 16), 20–25.
[24]K. Arrow (1974), *Limits of Organization* (W.W. Norton: New York), 26–27.

that the fundamental goal of the corporation—making money for its owners—is viewed as immoral or unethical by many advocates of corporate ethics.

Given this confusion about, and even conflict between, some professed ethical objectives and the goal of the corporation, we are skeptical about organizational attempts to instill conscience or a sense of guilt in their employees—that is, to alter employees' preferences. To the extent that these corporate ethics programs are aimed at trying to bring about material changes in employees' preferences, we are skeptical that they will succeed.

Consider the transfer-pricing problem faced by corporations with multiple divisions that buy and sell to one another. In Chapter 17, the firm value-maximizing solution to this problem was described as setting the transfer price to the buyer at the seller's opportunity cost of producing one more unit. But let's assume (as tends to be the case) that managers of the selling division have better information about their costs than the purchasing division's managers.

In such a situation, to the extent that a manager's compensation is based on divisional profits, the selling division's managers have the incentive to set the transfer price substantially above opportunity cost. In such a case, managers' pursuit of their own division's profits and their own business will come at the expense of total firmwide profits (because the managers of the buying division will purchase fewer than the optimal number of units).

Now, if adoption of a code of ethics somehow were to succeed in inducing divisional managers to reveal their private information about costs, units within the firm would be transferred at opportunity cost, and the firm's profits would be increased. But as long as division managers are being *paid* based on the profits of their own divisions, they are unlikely to reveal their actual costs.

Most economists generally assume that individuals' preferences are given and for the most part are difficult to alter. We thus suggest that managers, rather than attempting to alter preferences, should design the firm's architecture to motivate their employees' to take certain actions. For example, in the above case, senior management might attempt to find a means of giving the divisional managers some stake in the profitability of the division to which they "sell" the product. A common, though only partly effective, solution to this problem is to give divisional managers stock options with payoffs tied to the overall value of the company in addition to bonuses for divisional performance.

Education

Even if corporate codes of ethics are unlikely to either change preferences or eradicate self-interest, such codes still can play a potentially important role in modifying behavior. Up to this point, we have assumed that corporate managers and employees know the "right thing" to do to promote the interests of the organization. But this assumption does not always hold. In many cases, managers' and employees' uncertainty about ethical standards—or how to live up to them in practice—may well be a greater corporate problem than their failure to work hard or to act in accordance with standards that are well established and clearly defined.

We earlier described the confusion about the corporate mission stemming from the aims and actions of the social responsibility movement. Another potential source of confusion resides in the variability of ethical standards. What might have been acceptable behavior 10 or 20 years ago may not be so today. Social changes such as those brought about by movements as disparate as civil rights and women's

MANAGERIAL APPLICATIONS

The Appearance of Impropriety at Citibank, Argentina

A newspaper article reported that H. Richard Handley, the president of Citibank Argentina, had sold portions of Citibank's Argentine assets to some of his friends at "what now look like bargain prices." Citicorp spokesmen dismissed that talk as "Monday morning quarterbacking," pointing out that, at the time of the first sales, there was an equal chance that the value of Argentine investments would rise or fall thereafter.

It is not important whether the terms of this particular set of transactions were appropriate or not; they may well have been deals that furthered important business interests of Citicorp in Argentina. What this case highlights, however, are the costs associated with the *potential* for self-dealing by corporate managers and the importance of stating and enforcing policies for business dealings on less than an arm's length basis. The structure of this deal has forced Citibank to defend its actions to employees, investors, and regulators.

Source: *Miami Herald* (April 24, 1994).

rights, on the one hand, and corporate restructuring, on the other, clearly have altered conceptions of socially accepted behavior. Moreover, the progressive globalization of product markets and a more diverse workforce are increasingly forcing corporate employees to recognize and adapt to differences in national or regional cultural expectations.

Given this large and, in some ways, growing uncertainty about what constitutes ethical behavior within large organizations, corporate codes of ethics and training programs potentially play an important educational role by communicating corporate expectations to employees effectively and by demonstrating to them how certain kinds of behavior reduce the value of the firm. For example, misrepresentations of products and services to customers for short-term gain can be shown to reduce the value of the firm by hurting its reputation and thus lowering its brandname capital. Moreover, in the process of globalizing and thus dealing with customers worldwide, companies might be forced to respond to the increasing cultural differences—or absence of shared expectations—among their managers and employees by providing more explicit communication of standards and expectations.

Besides issuing a clear set of rules governing employee relations with consumers, corporations also are likely to benefit from communicating guidelines for dealings among managers and employees within the firm. For example, many companies develop their executives by rotating them through a series of jobs. The resulting management turnover can undermine informal agreements among managers and employees. Explicit, corporatewide communication of expectations can reduce uncertainty about enforcing unwritten agreements and thereby increase internal efficiency.

Virtually all professions—medicine, law, accounting—have professional ethics codes. Prospective candidates must pass entry exams that test their understanding of these codes. Most professional codes contain detailed descriptions of behaviors that reduce the value of the profession's services. For example, professional accountants are prohibited by their code of ethics from serving on the board of directors of their client firms. Such memberships reduce the appearance of independence of the auditor when rendering an opinion on the client's financial statements. If one accountant is caught not disclosing a known financial fraud,

ANALYZING MANAGERIAL DECISIONS: *The Tylenol Tragedy and J&J's* Credo

Johnson & Johnson sells a diverse array of products, including baby care, first aid and surgical products, prescription drugs, and industrial products. It operates in a decentralized fashion through 190 companies in 175 countries. Each business unit has its own focused mission. Some units employ thousands of people, and others, as few as six. Each business unit is organized around a given market and a given set of customers. In 1943, General Robert Wood Johnson, who led J&J in its metamorphosis from a small family-owned business to a worldwide enterprise, articulated the company's basic philosophy in the J&J *credo*. It has the following basic elements:

- Our first responsibility is to our customers—doctors, nurses, patients, and mothers—to supply high-quality services and products at reasonable prices.

- We are responsible to our employees to respect their dignity and job security in a safe working environment; compensation must be fair and adequate.

- We are responsible to our communities to support education, good works, and charities and bear our fair share of taxes.

- Our final responsibility is to our stockholders. To provide a sound profit, we must make investments in R&D, new products, and facilities. When we operate according to these principles, the stockholders should realize a fair return.

One manager described how the *credo* affects J&J managers:

All of our management is geared to profit on a day-to-day basis. That's part of the business of being in business. But too often, in this and other businesses, people are inclined to think, "We'd better do this because if we don't, it's going to show up on the figures over the short term." The credo allows them to say, "Wait a minute. I don't have to do that. The management has told me that they're really interested in the long term, and they're interested in me operating under this set of principles. So I won't."

In 1982, J&J was stunned when seven people died in the Chicago area after taking Tylenol capsules that had been adulterated with cyanide. Tylenol (capsules and tablets), manufactured by McNeil Consumer Products division, was one of J&J's most profitable businesses and accounted for 8 percent of J&J's sales. Subsequent investigation determined that tampering with the capsules occurred outside of J&J's facilities. McNeil's operating managers took immediate action, withdrawing all Tylenol capsules from the United States and replacing them with tablets (not involved in the tampering). They stopped producing Tylenol capsules and began redesigning the packaging to make the capsules tamperproof. This redesign process took several months. J&J's profits fell by over $100 million and its stock dropped from over $46 at the time of the announcement of the first death to below $39.

Press coverage of the unfolding tragedy was extensive. In an interview, a McNeil executive was asked whether employees would receive any remuneration during the time it would take to redesign the packaging and reconfigure the production line. Rather than simply state that no decision had been made, he made the commitment that no employees involved in producing Tylenol would be laid off over this period. Similarly, a reporter probing the costs of this packaging redesign asked an executive how much this would increase Tylenol's price. Although the issue had not been discussed, he announced that the product price would not be increased.

1. Explain how the *credo* helped guide the managers in the McNeil division.
2. Most discussions of J&J's handling of this tragedy have been laudatory, yet J&J's stock price fell by more than $7. Does this mean that the stock market thinks J&J's managers reacted poorly?
3. Analyze the decision not to raise Tylenol prices.
4. Discuss the advantages and disadvantages of listing shareholders as fourth priority in J&J's *credo,* especially in light of the Tylenol tragedy.

5. Suppose the packaging redesign and retooling required a longer time period, extensive cost, and that all Tylenol products were affected—not just capsules. Might McNeil managers have taken a different set of actions and how might the *credo* have guided these decisions?

6. Despite the above indications of a strong ethical culture within the company, a number of civil and criminal actions have been instituted against J&J. In November 2013, a massive $2.2 billion settlement was made to resolve claims resulting from the promotion of unapproved or off-label uses for three drugs and alleged kickbacks to physicians and a nursing home pharmacy distributor.

 a. Discuss the impact of this settlement on J&Js market value.

 b. These drugs were produced and distributed by Janssen Pharmaceuticals, a J&J subsidiary. Discuss the potential implications of having the drugs labelled as produced and distributed by a business unit within J&J versus by Janssen, a subsidiary of J&J, versus Janssen with no mention of J&J.

this reduces the value of other accountants' audit opinions. Thus, professions, like firms, have incentives to monitor their members for ethical breaches. However, the accounting profession's ethics code did not prevent the failure of Arthur Andersen arising from its involvement with Enron (see the Andersen case in Chapter 18). Moreover, Andersen's collapse and the public outcry cast a pall over the accounting profession, which led to increased government regulation of the profession.

Corporate Culture

More generally, codes of conduct and training programs in ethics have the potential to contribute to the building and maintaining of a value-based corporate culture. Like corporate ethics, *corporate culture* is an ill-defined term, but it generally encompasses such factors as the ways in which work and authority are organized within a company as well as organizational features such as customs, taboos, company slogans, heroes, and social rituals. For example, a slogan like that of Federal Express—"When it absolutely positively has to be there overnight"—helps communicate the message that employees are expected to focus on meeting delivery schedules and that this focus will be recognized and rewarded by the organization. Singling out role models or heroes for special awards is another way of communicating the values of the company. Similarly, social rituals such as training sessions and company parties can help disseminate information by increasing interaction among employees and encouraging discussion of ethical standards. Indeed, the *process* by which a code of ethics is produced and the training programs through which these standards are communicated are potentially as important as the code itself in developing and maintaining the desired corporate culture.

Nonetheless, to create the value-based or consumer-focused organization that many companies seek to become, these less tangible aspects of corporate culture must be reinforced by more tangible actions. That is, the more formal organizational systems that partition decision rights and evaluate and reward performance, as well as sanctions for unethical behavior, all must be internally consistent and designed to encourage firm value-increasing behavior.

Summary

Business ethics is the study of those behaviors that businesspeople should or should not follow. This book is also about business behaviors, in particular, about how firms are organized to motivate and control the behavior of self-interested employees to maximize a firm's value. The focus of this book has been primarily descriptive. Assuming that people are motivated by self-interest, how are they expected to behave under alternative organizational architectures? Ethics is primarily normative: It is about how people should behave. Managers often endorse the ethical philosophy espoused by Adam Smith. In Smith's view, through private ownership of property, self-interest, and competition, a society's resources are put to the best use and produce the highest quantity and quality of goods and services at the lowest prices—value maximization.

Value maximization requires that all costs and benefits be considered. If a particular business decision conflicts with an employee's or customer's own personal belief, that person is worse off. If enough people are affected, costs are imposed on the firm through compensating wage differentials, higher turnover, and forgone sales.

Moral philosophers and all religions have debated ethics since ancient times and yet we still do not have a universally accepted code of ethics. Witness the current debates over abortion or the use of animals for product testing. There is considerable confusion about the meaning of corporate ethics. It appears unlikely that a universally accepted code of business conduct will emerge. The corporate social responsibility movement has focused less on raising corporate ethical standards than on transferring shareholders' wealth to other parties such as customers, employees, local communities, charities, or cultural institutions. Although other corporate stakeholders are important, if the corporation is to survive, it must maximize its value to its owners—a goal that in turn promotes efficient use of scarce resources.

Many of the issues raised in this chapter are recurring themes in the popular press and are likely to continue to be in the future. You may be called on to resolve a sexual harassment case, an environmental issue, or a product recall dispute. There is no doubt that at least once during your career you will be faced with a key decision that some will label a major ethical dilemma. This chapter seeks to demonstrate that the same basic framework we presented in the earlier chapters can provide guidance for understanding issues involving ethics.

A number of important managerial implications are raised by the discussion in this chapter.

First, behaviors that others classify as unethical impose real costs on the firm by lowering the firm's brand-name capital, especially when they are reported in the media. These costs from reduced reputation include forgone sales or higher costs because parties outside the firm are less willing to contract with the firm. Many ethical problems are similar to other incentive problems discussed throughout the text, and much of the same analysis of incentive problems can be used to analyze ethical problems.

Second, ethics has many different meanings, ranging from making firms socially responsible (transferring wealth from the firm to other parties) to trying to make employees less self-interested. Another use of ethics means informing employees that certain behaviors impose large reputational costs on the firm, and hence the firm will impose sanctions on employees found engaging in such actions.

Third, mechanisms arise to constrain unethical behavior. Like contracting costs, costs of unethical behavior create incentives to minimize these costs. Managers should understand these mechanisms to ascertain under what conditions unethical behavior is most likely. For example, extra care should be exerted when structuring deals with firms in financial distress.

Fourth, decisions that have major ethical dimensions almost invariably involve potential adverse publicity and a decline in the firm's brand-name capital. How the firm responds to the press affects how the public perceives the issue. In dealing with the media, the following application of our framework usually is helpful:

- News reporters are pursuing their own self-interest—not yours. They are trying to maximize their value, which usually means increasing their audience in order to sell more newspapers or TV and radio advertising. Reporters know more about their job than you do.

- Having access to the media is valuable. Developing brand-name capital is quite costly to do through advertising. Use your access to the media to present the firm's position in a credible, honest way. Lying or misrepresenting the facts to the media is likely to backfire because reporters have the incentive and skills to uncover these misrepresentations—again, because such uncovered lies make juicy stories.

Fifth, ethics programs occasionally are used to try to alter people's preferences. Senior managers concerned about the ethical conduct of their employees would do better to spend less time searching, like Diogenes, for "an honest man." Rather, they should pay more attention to the incentives created by the firm's organizational architecture (the three-legged stool). It is unlikely that Merrill Lynch would have faced widely reported consumer indignation and legal sanctions from inappropriate securities recommendations had it anticipated the (quite predictable) incentives its compensation plan would give its employees. Incentives work. If the compensation plan pays employees for unethical behavior, then unethical behavior is exactly what the company will get. Our approach suggests recognizing the potential incentive problems and then redesigning organizational architecture—not people's preferences. Managers must structure their subordinates' incentives to ensure that they do not reduce the total value of the firm.

Sixth, ethical guidelines can highlight behaviors that increase, as well as behaviors that reduce, a firm's value. Codes of conduct, rather than trying to change employees' preferences, can communicate to employees those value-reducing actions that will not be tolerated and would lead to sanctions imposed on the employee, in addition to those value-increasing actions that are encouraged and would be rewarded.

Suggested Readings

T. Cochran (1964), *The Inner Revolution* (Harper & Row: New York).

T. Donaldson and P. Werhane (Eds.) (1999), *Ethical Issues in Business: A Philosophical Approach,* 6th edition (Prentice Hall: Englewood Cliffs).

M. Jensen and W. Meckling (1978), "Can the Corporation Survive?" *Financial Analysts Journal* 34, 31–37.

L. Nash (1991), "Ethics without the Sermon," *Harvard Business Review* (November–December).

L. Newton and M. Ford (1998), *Taking Sides: Clashing Views on Controversial Issues in Business Ethics,* 5th edition (Dushkin/McGraw-Hill: Guilford).

E. Noreen (1988), "The Economics of Ethics: A New Perspective on Agency Theory," *Accounting, Organizations and Society* 13, 359–369.

W. Shaw (1999), *Business Ethics,* 3rd edition (Wadsworth Publishing: Belmont).

W. Shaw and V. Barry (2000), *Moral Issues in Business,* 8th edition (Wadsworth Publishing: Belmont).

C. Smith (1992), "Economics and Ethics: The Case of Salomon Brothers," *Journal of Applied Corporate Finance* 5:2, 23–28.

B. Toffler (1986), *Tough Choices: Managers Talk Ethics* (John Wiley & Sons: New York).

Self-Evaluation Problems

22–1. Seventh Generation of Colchester, Vermont, manufactures and markets "environmentally friendly" household products—vegetable-based, chlorine-free laundry products and nontoxic cleaners. Seventh Generation used to sell its products through natural-food outlets and direct mail catalogs. In 1992, the CEO of Seventh Generation, Jeffrey Hollander, concluded that to continue to grow, his company had to appeal to a broader range of customers. The only way to do this was to lower his prices. He concluded, "The research that says people will pay more for socially responsible goods simply isn't true."

Hollander reformulated his products and compromised on environmental purity. Environmentally harmful phosphates and chlorines were still excluded, but cheaper petroleum-based cleaning agents were substituted. These changes allowed a dish detergent's price to be lowered from $3.50 to $2.50. While margins are lower, sales are up 20 percent. Also, the new formulas work better.

Seventh Generation is criticized by some of its old customers for paying less attention to core customers and substituting profits for idealism. Hollander says to his critics, "They not only have greater access to our products, but also can get them cheaper."

a. Do you agree with Hollander that people aren't willing to pay more for socially responsible goods? Explain why or why not.

b. Is Seventh Generation behaving ethically by substituting petroleum-based cleaners into its products?

c. What additional information would you request to help Seventh Generation address its ethical questions?

Solutions to Self-Evaluation Problems

22–1. Seventh Generation and Product Formulation

a. Many consumers are not willing to pay more for environmentally safe products because of the free-rider problem. Individuals pay the full cost of the more expensive environmentally safe product but receive only a fraction of the benefits. Government laws dictating product content supposedly control the externality of products polluting the environment. If some people want even lower levels of pollution, they can pay for this by buying more expensive products. They "consume" the safer product's environment benefits by knowing they are using environmentally friendly products. But they are not able to capture all the benefits.

b. Whether Mr. Hollander is behaving ethically depends on the definition of ethics employed. In Adam Smith's view, the legal pursuit of profits drive resources to their most efficient use. Hence, given that perspective, Seventh Generation is behaving ethically. If on the other hand, Seventh Generation developed a reputation for complete product purity and is not informing its customers of the shift, then it is deceiving them. (*Note: We do not believe that there is a single right answer to this question, rather; we find this question useful to motivate an open discussion of the range of opinions on these issues.*)

c. You would like to know what the marginal costs and marginal benefits of this decision are. That should depend on factors like:
- increase in quantity sold from the reduction in price (elasticity);
- reduction in demand from changing inputs, holding prices fixed (the shift in demand);

- reduction in demand for other of the firm's products because of this change in policy;
- cost reduction from substitution of inputs; and
- potential cost reduction from similar substitutions in the firm's other products.

Review Questions	

22–1. Ben and Jerry's Homemade Inc. has received much favorable press for its Rainforest Crunch ice cream. It uses official rain forest nuts and berries and all natural ingredients; it also sends a percentage of profits to charities. However, another flavor, Cherry Garcia, contains sulfur dioxide preservatives, and other flavors use margarine, not butter. What are the problems a firm faces if it is "politically correct" in some products but not others?

22–2. The Body Shop has been widely noted for its ethical stands in its business: natural cosmetics, "Products for People Tested by People," and First World wages for Third World products. Recently, Jon Entine published an analysis of the Body Shop in *Business Ethics,* alleging false advertising and other ethical lapses. Would you expect such charges to have more or less of an impact on a company like the Body Shop that touted its business ethics than if the same charges were leveled against a competitor who made fewer claims?

22–3. The Body Shop started its business by developing an extensive network of franchisees. Recently, franchisees have complained about the company's competing with their franchises through direct catalog sales and over the Internet. How does an expansion of Internet and direct catalog selling affect the Body Shop?

22–4. Eastman Kodak charged that the Fuji Corporation of Japan was illegally dumping film in U.S. markets. It asked the U.S. government to investigate and impose sanctions on Fuji for its unfair practices. But the world film market is dominated by Kodak and Fuji. If the government agrees to sanction Fuji, Kodak will obtain significant market power in the U.S. film market. Is it ethical for Kodak to attempt to use the government to undermine its competitor?

Organizational Architecture and the Process of Management Innovation

LEARNING OBJECTIVES

1. Explain why management innovation is a popular topic.
2. Discuss the demand for management innovation.
3. Discuss why management innovations often fail.
4. Identify the costs of changes associated with management innovations.
5. Explain the importance of sequencing organizational changes.

This chapter can be found via Create or McGraw-Hill *Connect*®. For more information, refer to the Preface.

Index

Page numbers followed by n indicate material found in notes.